The Sociology of Health and Illness

CRITICAL PERSPECTIVES

Fifth Edition

● ● ● ● ● ●

Edited by

Peter Conrad
Brandeis University

St. Martin's Press
New York

Editor-in-chief: Steve Debow
Manager, Publishing services: Emily Berleth
Publishing services associate: Meryl Gross
Project management: Richard Steins
Production supervisor: Joe Ford
Cover design: Patricia McFadden

Library of Congress Catalog Card Number: 95-73192

Manufactured in the United States of America.

1 0 9 8 7
f e d c b a

For information, write:
St. Martin's Press, Inc.
175 Fifth Avenue
New York, NY 10010

ISBN: 0-312-11229-7

Acknowledgments

John B. McKinlay and Sonja M. McKinlay, "Medical Measures and the Decline of Mortality." Under the title "The Questionable Contribution of Medical Measures to the Decline of Mortality in the United States in the Twentieth Century," this article originally appeared in *Milbank Memorial Fund Quarterly/Health and Sociology,* Summer 1977, pp. 405–428. Reprinted by permission of the Milbank Memorial Fund and John B. McKinlay.

S. Leonard Syme and Lisa F. Berkman, "Social Class, Susceptibility, and Sickness." Reprinted by permission for *The American Journal of Epidemiology,* vol. 104, pp. 1–8, 1976.

Colin McCord and Harold P. Freeman, "Excess Mortality in Harlem." Reprinted with permission of the *New England Journal of Medicine* Vol. 322, 25: 173–177, 1990. Copyright 1990. Massachusetts Medical Society. All rights reserved.

Ingrid Waldron, "What Do We Know about Causes of Sex Differences in Mortality?" Reprinted with permission of the United Nations. Source: *Population Bulletin of the United Nations,* No. 18 (Sales number 85. XIII. 6).

Acknowledgments and copyrights are continued at the back of the book on pages 534–536, which constitute an extension of the copyright page. It is a violation of the law to reproduce these selections by any means whatsoever without the written permission of the copyright holder.

Contents

• • • • • •

v

Preface

. . . . . .

In the past three decades, medical sociology has grown from a rather esoteric subspecialty to a major area of scholarly activity and student interest. In 1979, when I conceived *The Sociology of Health and Illness* with Rochelle Kern, there were few good teaching sources available and none from a critical perspective. This book was born out of our frustrations teaching with available materials—we would have to photocopy dozens of articles for class use—and our vision of what teaching the sociology of health and illness with a critical bent might be like. We were (and remain) committed to drawing on diverse sources: Articles are primarily by sociologists, but also by public health specialists, health activists, feminists, and social critics. A criterion in choosing selections is that they be interesting, readable, and make important sociological and conceptual points about health and health care. For each section we provide substantive introductions that contextualize the issues at hand and highlight each selection's main points.

There are few areas in society changing as rapidly as the health care system. Health costs have risen more rapidly than virtually any other part of society, new treatments and technologies continually become available, more people have become "uninsured," professional power has declined as corporate power has increased, and pressures remain on the health system to change in ways not always in the patients' interests. While health and medical care just doesn't stand still for our sociological study, it is possible to examine them as the health system is being transformed.

As we now present the fifth edition, sixteen years after the first edition was published (1981), the continuities and changes in sociology of health and illness are reflected in the book. Only twelve of the articles from the original edition are still here; the other thirty-four were added in subsequent editions as older selections were dropped. When we produced the first edition, issues like environmental disease, HIV-AIDS, neonatal infant care, wellness programs, rationing, genetics, and managed care had not yet moved to the fore, but they are now included in this edition.

Even since the fourth edition of the book significant changes have occurred in health care in the United States. The most obvious of these was the failure of the Clinton administration's attempt at health reform. Less conspicuous to the public is the emerging dominance of "managed care" as a method of organizing health care delivery. But persistent problems with health and health care abound: from the uninsured to the overtreated; from the promise of technology to the failure of cost controls; and from the conundrums of HIV and cancer to the impact of genetics. I continue to believe that a critical and conceptual sociological orientation is necessary to understand the problems in our health care system. The purpose here is to better understand the issues underlying our health care crisis and to promote more informed discussion on the continuing changes in the health system.

The fifth edition of *The Sociology of Health and Illness: Critical Perspectives* maintains the overall thematic framework of previous editions and incorporates eight new selections. This includes an entirely revamped section on "Financing Medical Care," including more developed discussions of the history and contemporary social impacts on medical reforms. In addition, new articles are included on the stigma of AIDS, the shifting power in the medical system, social impacts of the new genetics, and continuity and change in the British National Health Service.

Acknowledgments

I would like to thank Rochelle Kern for her contributions to four editions of *The Sociology of Health and Illness*. I am grateful to the many adopters who were kind enough to share their reactions to previous editions and whose comments helped to strengthen this fifth edition. I only wish there was space to include every good suggestion. Libby Bradshaw and the late Irving Kenneth Zola provided helpful comments on some of the changes in this edition. Stimulating conversations with Susan Bell, Phil Brown, Donald Light, Deborah Stone, and Stefan Timmermans, among others, helped clarify some issues in our changing health scene. Jean Elson Poznik deserves special acknowledgment. Her sharp insights and excellent management of the many tasks involved in revising this book improved this revision. Finally, thanks to my longtime contact Emily Berleth and the rest of the staff at St. Martin's Press for their care and attention in publishing this book.

Peter Conrad

General Introduction

· · · · · ·

Three major themes underlie the organization of this book: that the conception of medical sociology must be broadened to encompass a sociology of health and illness; that medical care in the United States is presently in crisis; and that the solution of that crisis requires that our health care and medical systems be reexamined from a critical perspective.

Toward a Sociology of Health and Illness

The increase in medical sociology courses and the number of medical sociological journals now extant are but two indicators of rapid development in this field.[1] The knowledge base of medical sociology expanded apace so that this discipline moved in less than two decades from an esoteric subspecialty taught in a few graduate departments to a central concern of sociologists and sociology students. The causes of this growth are too many and too complex to be within the scope of this book. However, a few of the major factors underlying this development are noted below.

The rise of chronic illness as a central medical and social problem has led physicians, health planners, and public health officials to look to sociology for help in understanding and dealing with this major health concern. In addition, increased government involvement in medical care has created research opportunities and funding for sociologists to study the organization and delivery of medical care. Sociologists have also become increasingly involved in medical education, as evidenced by the large number of sociologists currently on medical school faculties. Further, since the 1960s the social and political struggles over health and medical care have become major social issues, thus drawing additional researchers and students to the field. Indeed, some sociologists have come to see the organization of medicine and the way medical services are delivered as social problems in themselves. In recent years, sociologists have been deeply involved in research on how to prevent HIV-AIDS and best stem the AIDS epidemic.

Traditionally, the sociological study of illness and medicine has been called simply medical sociology. Straus (1957) differentiated between sociology "of" medicine and sociology "in" medicine. Sociology *of* medicine focuses on the study of medicine to illuminate some *sociological concern* (e.g., patient-practitioner relationships, the role of professions in society). Sociology *in* medicine, on the other hand, focuses primarily on *medical problems* (e.g., the sociological causes of disease and illness, reasons for delay in seeking medical

1

aid, patient compliance or noncompliance with medical regimens). As one might expect, the dichotomy between these two approaches is more distinct conceptually than in actual sociological practice. Be that as it may, sociologists who have concentrated on a sociology of medicine have tended to focus on the profession of medicine and on doctors and to slight the social basis of health and illness. Today, for example, our understanding of the sociology of medical practice and the organization of medicine is much further developed than our understanding of the relationship between social structure and health and illness.

One purpose of this book is to help redress this imbalance. In it, we shift from a focus on the physician and the physician's work to a more general concern with how health and illness are dealt with in our society. This broadened conceptualization of the relationship between sociology and medicine encourages us to examine problems such as the social causation of illness, the economic basis of medical services, and the influence of medical industries, and to direct our primary attention to the social production of disease and illness and the social organization of the medical care system.

Both disease and medical care are related to the structure of society. The social organization of society influences to a significant degree the type and distribution of disease. It also shapes the organized response to disease and illness—the medical care system. To analyze either disease or medical care without investigating its connection with social structure and social interaction is to miss what is unique about the sociology of health and illness. To make the connection between social structure and health, we must investigate how social factors such as the political economy, the corporate structure, the distribution of resources, and the uses of political, economic, and social power influence health and illness and society's response to health and illness. To make the connection between social interaction and health we need to examine people's experiences, face-to-face relationships, cultural variations within society, and in general how society constructs "reality." Social structure and interaction are, of course, interrelated, and making this linkage clear is a central task of sociology. Both health and the medical system should be analyzed as integral parts of society. In short, instead of a "medical sociology," in this book we posit and profess a *sociology of health and illness*.[2]

The Crisis in American Health Care

It should be noted at the outset that, by any standard, the American medical system and the American medical profession are among the best in the world. Our society invests a great amount of its social and economic resources in medical care; has some of the world's finest physicians, hospitals, and medical schools; is no longer plagued by most deadly infectious diseases; and is in the forefront in developing medical and technological advances for the treatment of disease and illness.

This said, however, it must also be noted that American health care is in a state of crisis. At least that is the judgment not of a small group of social and political critics, but of concerned social scientists, thoughtful political leaders, leaders of labor and industry, and members of the medical profession itself. But although there is general agreement that a health-care crisis exists, there is, as one would expect, considerable disagreement as to what caused this crisis and how to deal with it.

What major elements and manifestations of this crisis are reflected in the concerns expressed by the contributors to this volume?

Medical costs have risen exponentially; in four decades the amount Americans spent annually on medical care increased from 4 percent to nearly 14 percent of the nation's gross national product. In 1994, the total cost was over $940 billion. Indeed, medical costs have become the leading cause of personal bankruptcy in the United States.

Access to medical care has become a serious problem. An estimated 37 million people have no health insurance and perhaps another 40 million are underinsured, so that they do not have adequate financial access to health care when they are sick. American health care suffers from "the inverse coverage law": the more people need insurance coverage, the less they are likely to get it (Light, 1992).

Increasing specialization of doctors has made *primary-care* medicine scarce. Fewer than one out of four doctors can be defined as primary-care physicians (general and family practitioners, and some pediatricians, internists, and obstetrician-gynecologists). In many rural and inner-city areas, the only primary care available is in hospital emergency rooms, where waits are long, treatment is often impersonal, continuity of care is minimal, and the cost of service delivery is very high.

Although the quality of health and medical care is difficult to measure, a few standard measures are helpful. *Life expectancy,* the number of years a person can be expected to live, is at least a crude measure of a nation's health. According to United Nations data, the U.S. ranks twenty-fourth among nations in life expectancy for males and twentieth for females. *Infant mortality,* generally taken to mean infant death in the first year, is one of our best indicators of health and medical care, particularly prenatal care. The U.S. ranks eighteenth in infant mortality, behind such countries as Sweden, Finland, Canada, Japan, and the United Kingdom (United Nations Demographic Yearbook, 1990).

Our medical system is organized to deliver "medical care" (actually, "sick care") rather than "health care." Medical care is that part of the system "which deals with individuals who are sick or who think they may be sick." Health care is that part of the system "which deals with the promotion and protection of health, including environmental protection, the protection of the individual in the workplace, the prevention of accidents, [and] the provision of pure food and water. . . ." (Sidel and Sidel, 1983: xxi–xxii).

Very few of our resources are invested in "health care"—that is, in *prevention* of disease and illness. Yet, with the decrease in infectious disease and the subsequent increase in chronic disease, prevention is becoming ever more important to our nation's overall health and would probably prove more cost-effective than "medical care" (Department of Health and Human Services, 1991).

There is little *public accountability* in medicine. Innovations such as Health Systems Agencies, regional organizations designed to coordinate medical services (now defunct), and Peer Review Organizations, boards mandated to review the quality of (mostly) hospital care, had limited success in their efforts to control the quality and cost of medical care. (The incredible rise in the number of malpractice suits may be seen as an indication not of increasing poor medical practice but of the fact that such suits are about the only form of medical accountability presently available to the consumer.) Numerous other attempts to control medical costs—in the form of Health Maintenance Organizations (HMOs), Diagnostic Related Groups (DRGs) and "managed care"—have also largely failed. The lastest attempt, "managed care," is changing how medicine is delivered. But it is not yet clear if it controls costs, and it is most unlikely to increase public accountability.

Another element of our crisis in health care is the *"medicalization"* of society. Many, perhaps far too many, of our social problems (e.g., alcoholism, drug addiction, and child abuse) and of life's normal, natural, and generally nonpathological events (e.g., birth, death, and sexuality) have come to be seen as "medical problems." It is by no means clear that such matters constitute appropriate medical problems per se. Indeed, there is evidence that the medicalization of social problems and life's natural events has itself become a social problem (Zola, 1972; Conrad, 1992).

Many other important elements and manifestations of our crisis in health care are described in the works contained in this volume, including the uneven distribution of disease and health care, the role of the physical environment in disease and illness, the monopolistic history of the medical profession, the role of government in financing health care, inequalities in medical care, the challenge of self-help groups, and possibilities of health care reform. The particularities of America's health crisis aside, most contributors to this volume reflect the growing conviction that the social organization of medicine in the United States has been central to perpetuating that crisis.

Critical Perspectives on Health and Illness

The third major theme of this book is the need to examine the relationship between our society's organization and institutions and its medical care system from a "critical perspective." What do we mean by a critical perspective?

A critical perspective is one that does not consider the present fundamental organization of medicine as sacred and inviolable. Nor does it assume that some other particular organization would necessarily be a panacea for all our health-care problems. A critical perspective accepts no "truth" or "fact" merely because it has hitherto been accepted as such. It examines what is, not as something given or static, but as something out of which change and growth can emerge. In contrast, any theoretical framework that claims to have all the answers to understanding health and illness is not a critical perspective. The social aspects of health and illness are too complex for a monolithic approach.

Further, a critical perspective assumes that a sociology of health and illness entails societal and personal values, and that these values must be considered and made explicit if illness and health-care problems are to be satisfactorily dealt with. Since any critical perspective is informed by values and assumptions, we would like to make ours explicit: (1) The problems and inequalities of health and medical care are connected to the particular historically located social arrangements and the cultural values of any society. (2) Health care should be oriented toward the prevention of disease and illness. (3) The priorities of any medical system should be based on the needs of the consumers and not the providers. A direct corollary of this is that the socially based inequalities of health and medical care must be eliminated. (4) Ultimately, society itself must change for health and medical care to improve.

While economic concerns dominated the health policy debate in the 1980s, the development of critical perspectives on health and illness are central to the reform of health care in the 1990s (Mechanic, 1993). Bringing such critical perspectives to bear on the sociology of health and illness has thus informed the selection of readings contained in this volume. It has also informed editorial comments that introduce and bind together the book's various parts and subparts. Explicitly and implicitly, the goal of this work is to generate awareness that informed social change is a prerequisite for the elimination of socially based inequalities in health and medical care.

NOTES

1. Until 1960 only one journal, *Milbank Memorial Fund Quarterly* (now called *Health and Society*), was more or less devoted to medical sociological writings, although many articles on medicine and illness were published in other sociological journals. Today four more journals focus specifically on sociological work on health, illness, and medicine: *The Journal of Health and Social Behavior; Social Science and Medicine; International Journal of Health Services; Sociology of Health and Illness.* So do the annual volumes *Research in the Sociology of Health Care* and *Advances in Medical Sociology.* Such medical journals as *Medical Care* and *American Journal of Public Health* frequently publish medical sociological articles, as do various psychiatric journals.

2. Inasmuch as we define the sociology of health and illness in such a broad manner, it is not possible to cover adequately all the topics it encompasses in one volume. Although we attempt to touch on most important sociological aspects of health and illness, space limitations preclude presenting all potential topics. For instance, we do not include sections on professional socialization, the social organization of hospitals, and the utilization of services. Discussions of these are easily available in standard medical sociology textbooks. We have made a specific decision not to include materials on mental health and illness. While mental and physical health are not as separate as was once thought, the sociology of mental health comprises a separate literature and raises some different issues from the ones developed here.

REFERENCES

Conrad, Peter. 1992. "Medicalization and social control." Annual Review of Sociology. 18:209–232.

Light, Donald W. 1992. "The practice and ethics of risk-rated health insurance." Journal of American Medical Association. 267:2503–2508.

Mechanic, David. 1993. "Social research in health and the American sociopolitical context: The changing fortunes of medical sociology." Social Science and Medicine. 36:95–102.

Sidel, Victor W., and Ruth Sidel. 1983. A Healthy State. rev. ed. New York: Pantheon Books.

Straus, Robert. 1957. "The nature and status of medical sociology." American Sociological Review. 22 (April): 200–204.

U.S. Department of Health and Human Services. 1991. Healthy People 2000. Washington, D.C.: U.S. Government Printing Office.

Zola, Irving Kenneth. 1972. "Medicine as an institution of social control." Sociological Review. 20:487–504.

The Social Production of Disease and Illness

· · · · · ·

Part One of this book is divided into five sections. While the overriding theme is "the social production of disease and the meaning of illness," each section develops a particular aspect of the sociology of disease production. For the purposes of this book, we define *disease* as the biophysiological phenomena that manifest themselves as changes in and malfunctions of the human body. *Illness,* on the other hand, is the experience of being sick or diseased. Accordingly, we can see disease as a physiological state and illness as a social psychological state presumably caused by the disease. Thus pathologists and public health doctors deal with disease, patients experience illness, and ideally clinical physicians treat both (cf. Cassell, 1979). Furthermore, such a distinction is useful for dealing with the possibility of people feeling ill in the absence of disease or being "diseased" without experiencing illness. Obviously, disease and illness are related, but separating them as concepts allows us to explore the objective level of disease and the subjective level of illness. The first three sections of Part One focus primarily on disease; the last two focus on illness.

All the selections in Part One consider how disease and illness are socially produced. The so-called *medical model* focuses on organic pathology in individual patients, rarely taking societal factors into account. Clinical medicine locates disease as a problem in the individual body, but although this is clearly important and useful, it provides an incomplete and sometimes distorted picture. In the face of increased concern about chronic disease and its prevention (U.S. HHS, 1991), the selections suggest that a shift in focus from the internal environment of individuals to the interaction between external environments in which people live and the internal environment of the human body will yield new insights into disease causation and prevention.

The Social Nature of Disease

· · · · · ·

When we look historically at the extent and patterns of disease in Western society, we see enormous changes. In the early nineteenth century the infant mortality rate was very high, life expectancy was short (approximately forty years), and life-threatening epidemics were common. Infectious diseases, especially those of childhood, were often fatal. Even at the beginning of the twentieth century the United States' annual death rate was 28 per 1000 population compared with 9 per 1000 today, and the cause of death was usually pneumonia, influenza, tuberculosis, typhoid fever, or one of the various forms of dysentery (Cassell, 1979: 72). But patterns of *morbidity* (disease rate) and *mortality* (death rate) have changed. Today we have "conquered" most infectious diseases; they are no longer feared and few people die from them. Chronic diseases such as heart disease, cancer, and stroke are now the major causes of death in the United States (see Figure 1-3).

Medicine usually receives credit for the great victory over infectious diseases. After all, certain scientific discoveries (e.g., germ theory) and medical interventions (e.g., vaccinations and drugs) developed and used to combat infectious diseases must have been responsible for reducing deaths from those diseases, or so the logic goes. While this view may seem reasonable from a not too careful reading of medical history, it is contradicted by some important social scientific work.

René Dubos (1959) was one of the first to argue that social changes in the environment rather than medical interventions led to the reduction of mortality by infectious diseases. He viewed the nineteenth-century Sanitary Movement's campaign for clean water, air, and proper sewage disposal as a particularly significant "public health" measure. Thomas McKeown (1971) showed that biomedical interventions were not the cause of the decline in mortality in England and Wales in the nineteenth century. This viewpoint, or the "limitations of modern medicine" argument (Powles, 1973), is now well known in public health circles. The argument is essentially a simple one: Discoveries and interventions by *clinical medicine* were not the cause of the decline of mortality for various populations. Rather, it seems that social and environmental factors such as (1) sanitation, (2) improved housing and nutrition, and (3) a general rise in the standard of living were the most significant contributors. This does not mean that clinical medicine did not reduce some people's sufferings or prevent or cure diseases in others; we know it did. But social factors appear much more important than medical interventions in the "conquest" of infectious disease.

In the keynote selection in this book, John B. McKinlay and Sonja M. McKinlay assess "Medical Measures and the Decline of Mortality." They offer empirical evidence to support the limitations of medicine argument and point to the social nature of disease. We must note that mortality rates, the data on which they base their analysis, only crudely measure "cure" and don't measure "care" at all. But it is important to understand that much of what is attributed to "medical intervention" seems not to be the result of clinical medicine per se (cf. Levine et al., 1983).

The limitations of medicine argument underlines the need for a broader, more comprehensive perspective on understanding disease and its treatment (see also Tesh, 1988), a perspective that focuses on the significance of social structure and change in disease causation and prevention.

REFERENCES

Cassell, Eric J. 1979. The Healer's Art. New York: Penguin Books.

Dubos, René. 1959. Mirage of Health. New York: Harper and Row.

Levine, Sol, Jacob J. Feldman, and Jack Elinson. 1983. "Does medical care do any good?" Pp. 394–404 in David Mechanic (ed.), Handbook of Health, Health Care, and the Health Professions. New York: Free Press.

McKeown, Thomas. 1971. "A historical appraisal of the medical task." Pp. 29–55 in G. McLachlan and T. McKeown (eds.), Medical History and Medical Care: A Symposium of Perspectives. New York: Oxford University Press.

Powles, John. 1973. "On the limitations of modern medicine." Science, Medicine and Man. 1: 1–30.

Tesh, Sylvia Noble. 1988. Hidden Arguments: Political Ideology and Disease Prevention. New Brunswick, N.J.: Rutgers University Press.

U.S. Department of Health and Human Services. 1991. Healthy People 2000: National Health Promotion and Disease Prevention Objectives. Washington, D.C.: U.S. Government Printing Office.

1

Medical Measures and the Decline of Mortality

• • • • • •

John B. McKinlay and Sonja M. McKinlay

... by the time laboratory medicine came effectively into the picture the job had been carried far toward completion by the humanitarians and social reformers of the nineteenth century. Their doctrine that nature is holy and healthful was scientifically naive but proved highly effective in dealing with the most important health problems of their age. When the tide is receding from the beach it is easy to have the illusion that one can empty the ocean by removing water with a pail.
R. Dubos, Mirage of Health, *New York: Perennial Library, 1959, p. 23*

Introducing a Medical Heresy
....

The modern "heresy" that medical care (as it is traditionally conceived) is generally unrelated to improvements in the health of populations (as distinct from individuals) is still dismissed as unthinkable in much the same way as the so-called heresies of former times. And this is despite a long history of support in popular and scientific writings as well as from able minds in a variety of disciplines. History is replete with examples of how, understandably enough, self-interested individuals and groups denounced popular customs and beliefs which appeared to threaten their own domains of practice, thereby rendering them heresies (for example, physicians' denunciation of midwives as witches, during the Middle Ages). We also know that vast institutional resources have often been deployed to neutralize challenges to the assumptions upon which everyday organizational activities were founded and legitimated (for example, the Spanish Inquisition). And since it is usually difficult for organizations themselves to directly combat threatening "heresies," we

often find otherwise credible practitioners, perhaps unwittingly, serving the interests of organizations in this capacity. These historical responses may find a modern parallel in the way everyday practitioners of medicine, on their own altruistic or "scientific" grounds and still perhaps unwittingly, serve present-day institutions (hospital complexes, university medical centers, pharmaceutical houses, and insurance companies) by spearheading an assault on a most fundamental challenging heresy of our time: *that the introduction of specific medical measures and/or the expansion of medical services are generally not responsible for most of the modern decline in mortality.*

In different historical epochs and cultures, there appear to be characteristic ways of explaining the arrival and departure of natural vicissitudes. For salvation from some plague, it may be that the gods were appeased, good works rewarded, or some imbalance in nature corrected. And there always seems to be some person or group (witch doctors, priests, medicine men) able to persuade others, sometimes on the basis of acceptable evidence for most people at that time, that they have *the* explanation for the phenomenon in question and may even claim responsibility for it. They also seem to benefit most from common acceptance of the explanations they offer. It is not uncommon today for biotechnological knowledge and specific medical interventions to be invoked as *the major reason* for most of the modern (twentieth century) decline in mortality.[1] Responsibility for this decline is often claimed by, or ascribed to, the present-day major beneficiaries of this prevailing explanation. But

10

both in terms of the history of knowledge and on the basis of data presented in this paper, one can reasonably wonder whether the supposedly more sophisticated explanations proffered in our own time (while seemingly distinguishable from those accepted in the past) are really all that different from those of other cultures and earlier times, or any more reliable. Is medicine, the physician, or the medical profession any more entitled to claim responsibility for the decline in mortality that obviously has occurred in this century than, say, some folk hero or aristocracy of priests sometime in the past?

Aims

Our general intention in this paper is to sustain the ongoing debate on the questionable contribution of specific medical measures and/or the expansion of medical services to the observable decline in mortality in the twentieth century. More specifically, the following three tasks are addressed: (a) selected studies are reviewed which illustrate that, far from being idiosyncratic and/or heretical, the issue addressed in this paper has a long history, is the subject of considerable attention elsewhere, attracts able minds from a variety of disciplines, and remains a timely issue for concern and research; (b) age- and sex-adjusted mortality rates (standardized to the population of 1900) for the United States, 1900–1973, are presented and then considered in relation to a number of specific and supposedly effective medical interventions (both chemotherapeutic and prophylactic). So far as we know, this is the first time such data have been employed for this particular purpose in the United States, although reference will be made to a similar study for England and Wales; and (c) some policy implications are outlined.

Background to the Issue

The beginning of the serious debate on the questionable contribution of medical measures is commonly associated with the appearance, in Britain, of Talbot Griffith's (1967) *Population Problems in the Age of Malthus*. After examining certain medical activities associated with the eighteenth century—particularly the growth of hospital, dispensary, and midwifery services, additions to knowledge of physiology and anatomy, and the introduction of smallpox inoculation— Griffith concluded that they made important contributions to the observable decline in mortality at that time. Since then, in Britain and more recently in the United States, this debate has continued, regularly engaging scholars from economic history, demography, epidemiology, statistics, and other disciplines. Habakkuk (1953), an economic historian, was probably the first to seriously challenge the prevailing view that the modern increase in population was due to a fall in the death rate attributable to medical interventions. His view was that this rise in population resulted from an increase in the birth rate, which, in turn, was associated with social, economic, and industrial changes in the eighteenth century.

McKeown, without doubt, has pursued the argument more consistently and with greater effect than any other researcher, and the reader is referred to his recent work for more detailed background information. Employing the data and techniques of historical demography, McKeown (a physician by training) has provided a detailed and convincing analysis of the major reasons for the decline of mortality in England and Wales during the eighteenth, nineteenth, and twentieth centuries (McKeown et al., 1955, 1962, 1975). For the eighteenth century, he concludes that the decline was largely attributable to improvements in the environment. His findings for the nineteenth century are summarized as follows:

> . . . the decline of mortality in the second half of the nineteenth century was due wholly to a reduction of deaths from infectious diseases; there was no evidence of a decline in other causes of death. Examination of the diseases which contributed to the decline suggested that the main influences were: (a) rising standards of living, of which the most significant feature was a better diet; (b) improvements in hygiene; and (c) a favorable trend in the relationship between some micro-organisms and the human host. *Therapy made no contributions, and the effect of immunization was restricted to smallpox which accounted for only about one-twentieth of the reduction of the death rate.* (Emphasis added. McKeown et al., 1975, p. 391)

While McKeown's interpretation is based on the experience of England and Wales, he has examined its credibility in the light of the very different circumstances which existed in four other European countries: Sweden, France, Ireland, and Hungary (McKeown et al., 1972). His interpretation appears to withstand this cross-examination. As for the twentieth century (1901–1971 is the period actually considered), McKeown argues that about three-quarters of the decline was associated with control of infectious diseases and the remainder with conditions not attributable to microorganisms. He distinguishes the infections according to their modes of transmission (air-, water- or food-borne) and isolates three types of influences which figure during the period considered: medical measures (specific therapies and immunization), reduced exposure to infection, and improved nutrition. His conclusion is that:

> The main influences on the decline in mortality were improved nutrition on air-borne infections, reduced exposure (from better hygiene) on water- and food-borne diseases and, less certainly, immunization and therapy on the large number of conditions included in the miscellaneous group. Since these three classes were responsible respectively for nearly half, one-sixth, and one-tenth of the fall in the death rate, it is probable that the advancement in nutrition was the major influence. (McKeown et al., 1975, p. 422)

More than twenty years of research by McKeown and his colleagues recently culminated in two books—*The Modern Rise of Population* (1976a) and *The Role of Medicine: Dream, Mirage or Nemesis* (1976b)—in which he draws together his many excellent contributions. That the thesis he advances remains highly newsworthy is evidenced by recent editorial reaction in *The Times* of London (1977).

No one in the United States has pursued this thesis with the rigor and consistency which characterize the work by McKeown and his colleagues in Britain. Around 1930, there were several limited discussions of the questionable effect of medical measures on selected infectious diseases like diphtheria (Lee, 1931; Wilson and Miles, 1946; Bolduan, 1930) and pneumonia (Pfizer and Co., 1953). In a presidential address to the American Association of Immunologists in

1954 (frequently referred to by McKeown), Magill (1955) marshalled an assortment of data then available—some from England and Wales—to cast doubt on the plausibility of existing accounts of the decline in mortality for several conditions. Probably the most influential work in the United States is that of Dubos who, principally in *Mirage of Health* (1959), *Man Adapting* (1965), and *Man, Medicine and Environment* (1968), focused on the nonmedical reasons for changes in the health of overall populations. In another presidential address, this time to the Infectious Diseases Society of America, Kass (1971), again employing data from England and Wales, argued that most of the decline in mortality for most infectious conditions occurred prior to the discovery of either "the cause" of the disease or some purported "treatment" for it. Before the same society and largely on the basis of clinical experience with infectious diseases and data from a single state (Massachusetts), Weinstein (1974), while conceding there are some effective treatments which seem to yield a favorable outcome (e.g., for poliomyelitis, tuberculosis, and possibly smallpox), argued that despite the presence of supposedly effective treatments some conditions may have increased (e.g., subacute bacterial endocarditis, streptococcal pharyngitis, pneumococcal pneumonia, gonorrhea, and syphilis) and also that mortality for yet other conditions shows improvement in the absence of any treatment (e.g., chickenpox). With the appearance of his book, *Who Shall Live?* (1974), Fuchs, a health economist, contributed to the resurgence of interest in the relative contribution of medical care to the modern decline in mortality in the United States. He believes there has been an unprecedented improvement in health in the United States since about the middle of the eighteenth century, associated primarily with a rise in real income. While agreeing with much of Fuchs' thesis, we will present evidence which seriously questions his belief that "beginning in the mid '30s, major therapeutic discoveries made significant contributions independently of the rise in real income."

Although neither representative nor exhaustive, this brief and selective background should serve to introduce the analysis which follows. Our intention is to highlight the following: (a) the debate over the questionable contribution of medical measures to the modern decline of mortality has a long history and remains topical; (b) although sometimes popularly associated with dilettantes such as Ivan Illich (1976), the debate continues to preoccupy able scholars from a variety of disciplines and remains a matter of concern to the most learned societies; (c) although of emerging interest in the United States, the issue is already a matter of concern and considerable research elsewhere; (d) to the extent that the subject has been pursued in the United States, there has been a restrictive tendency to focus on a few selected diseases, or to employ only statewide data, or to apply evidence from England and Wales directly to the United States situation.

How Reliable Are Mortality Statistics?

We have argued elsewhere that mortality statistics are inadequate and can be misleading as indicators of a nation's overall health status (McKinlay and McKinlay, forthcoming). Unfortunately, these are the only types of data which are readily accessible for the examination of time trends, simply because comparable morbidity and disability data have not been available. Apart from this overriding problem, several additional caveats in the use of mortality statistics are: (a) difficulties introduced by changes in the registration area in the United States in the early twentieth century; (b) that often no single disease, but a complex of conditions, may be responsible for death (Krueger, 1966); (c) that studies reveal considerable inaccuracies in recording the cause of death (Moriyama et al., 1958); (d) that there are changes over time in what it is fashionable to diagnose (for example, ischaemic heart disease and cerebrovascular disease); (e) that changes in disease classifications (Dunn and Shackley, 1945) make it difficult to compare some conditions over time and between countries (Reid and Rose, 1964); (f) that some conditions result in immediate death while others have an extended period of latency; and (g) that many conditions are severely debilitating and consume vast medical resources but are now generally non-fatal (e.g., arthritis and diabetes). Other obvious limitations could be added to this list.

However, it would be foolhardy indeed to dismiss all studies based on mortality measures simply because they are possibly beset *with known limitations*. Such data are preferable to those the limitations of which are either unknown or, if known, cannot be estimated. Because of an overawareness of potential inaccuracies, there is a timorous tendency to disregard or devalue studies based on mortality evidence, even though there are innumerable examples of their fruitful use as a basis for planning and informed social action (Alderson, 1976). Sir Austin Bradford Hill (1955) considers one of the most important features of Snow's work on cholera to be his adept use of mortality statistics. A more recent notable example is the study by Inman and Adelstein (1969) of the circumstantial link between the excessive absorption of bronchodilators from pressurized aerosols and the epidemic rise in asthma mortality in children aged ten to fourteen years. Moreover, there is evidence that some of the known inaccuracies of mortality data tend to cancel each other out.[2] Consequently, while mortality statistics may be unreliable for use in individual cases, when pooled for a country and employed in population studies, they can reveal important trends and generate fruitful hypotheses. They have already resulted in informed social action (for example, the use of geographical distributions of mortality in the field of environmental pollution).

Whatever limitations and risks may be associated with the use of mortality statistics, they obviously apply equally to all studies which employ them—both those which attribute the decline in mortality to medical measures and those which argue the converse, or something else entirely. And, if such data constitute acceptable evidence in support of the presence of medicine, then it is not unreasonable, or illogical, to employ them in support of some opposing position. One difficulty is that, depending on the nature of the results, double standards of rigor seem to operate in the evaluation of different studies. Not surprisingly, those which challenge prevailing myths or beliefs are subject to the most stringent methodological and statistical scrutiny, while supportive studies, which frequently employ the flimsiest impressionistic data and inappropriate techniques of analysis, receive general and uncritical acceptance. Even if

Figure 1-1. *The Trend in Mortality for Males and Females Separately (Using Age-adjusted Rates) for the United States, 1900–1973**

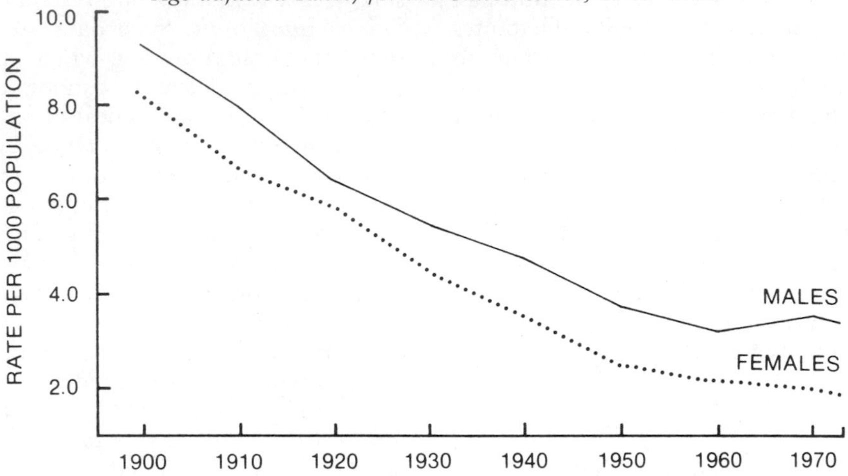

*For these and all other age- and sex-adjusted rates in this paper, the standard population is that of 1900.

all possible "ideal" data were available (which they never will be) and if, after appropriate analysis, they happened to support the viewpoint of this paper, we are doubtful that medicine's protagonists would find our thesis any more acceptable.

The Modern Decline in Mortality

Despite the fact that mortality rates for certain conditions, for selected age and sex categories, continue to fluctuate, or even increase (U.S. Dept. HEW, 1964; Moriyama and Gustavus, 1972; Lilienfeld, 1976), there can be little doubt that a marked decline in overall mortality for the United States has occurred since about 1900 (the earliest point for which reliable national data are available).

Just how dramatic this decline has been in the United States is illustrated in Fig. 1-1 which shows age-adjusted mortality rates for males and females separately.[3] Both sexes experienced a marked decline in mortality since 1900. The female decline began to level off by about 1950, while 1960 witnessed the beginning of a slight increase for males. Figure 1-1 also reveals a slight but increasing divergence between male and female mortality since about 1920.

Figure 1-2 depicts the decline in the overall age-and sex-adjusted rate since the beginning of this century. Between 1900 and 1973, there was a 69.2 percent decrease in overall mortality. The average annual rate of decline from 1900 until 1950 was .22 per 1,000, after which it became an almost negligible decline of .04 per 1,000 annually. Of the total fall in the standardized death rate between 1900 and 1973, 92.3 percent occurred prior to 1950. Figure 1-2 also plots the decline in the standardized death rate *after* the total number of deaths in each age and sex category has been reduced by the number of deaths attributed to the eleven major infectious conditions (typhoid, smallpox, scarlet fever, measles, whooping cough, diphtheria, influenza, tuberculosis, pneumonia, diseases of the digestive system, and poliomyelitis). It should be noted that, although this latter rate also shows a decline (at least until 1960), its slope is much more shallow than that for the overall standardized death rate. A major part of the decline in deaths from these causes since about 1900 may be attributed to the virtual disappearance of these infectious diseases.

An absurdity is reflected in the third broken line in Fig. 1-2 which also plots the increase in the proportion of Gross National Product expended annually for medical care. *It is evident that the*

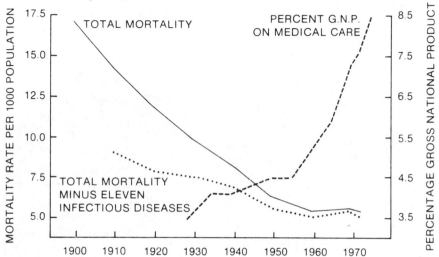

Figure 1-2. *Age- and Sex-adjusted Mortality Rates for the United States, 1900–1973, Including and Excluding Eleven Major Infectious Diseases, Contrasted with the Proportion of the Gross National Product Expended on Medical Care*

beginning of the precipitate and still unrestrained rise in medical care expenditures began when nearly all (92 percent) of the modern decline in mortality this century had already occurred.[4]

Figure 1-3 illustrates how the proportion of deaths contributed by the infectious and chronic conditions has changed in the United States since the beginning of the twentieth century. In 1900, about 40 percent of all deaths were accounted for by eleven major infectious diseases, 16 percent by three chronic conditions, 4 percent by accidents, and the remainder (37 percent) by all other causes. By 1973, only 6 percent of all deaths were due to these eleven infectious diseases, 58 percent to the same three chronic conditions, 9 percent to accidents, and 27 percent were contributed by other causes.[5]

Now to what phenomenon, or combination of events can we attribute this modern decline in overall mortality? Who (if anyone), or what group, can claim to have been instrumental in effecting this reduction? Can anything be gleaned from an analysis of mortality experience to date that will inform health care policy for the future?

It should be reiterated that a major concern of this paper is to determine the effect, if any, of specific medical measures (both chemotherapeu-tic and prophylactic) on the decline of mortality. It is clear from Figs. 1-2 and 1-3 that most of the observable decline is due to the rapid disappear-ance of some of the major infectious diseases. Since this is where most of the decline has occurred, it is logical to focus a study of the effect of medical measures on this category of condi-tions. Moreover, for these eleven conditions, there exist clearly identifiable medical interven-tions to which the decline in mortality has been popularly ascribed. No analogous interventions exist for the major chronic diseases such as heart disease, cancer, and stroke. Therefore, even where a decline in mortality from these chronic conditions may have occurred, this cannot be ascribed to any specific measure.

The Effect of Medical Measures on Ten Infectious Diseases Which Have Declined

Table 1-1 summarizes data on the effect of major medical interventions (both chemotherapeutic and prophylactic) on the decline in the age- and sex-adjusted death rates in the United States, 1900–1973, for ten of the eleven major infec-tious diseases listed above. Together, these dis-

Figure 1-3. *Pictorial Representation of the Changing Contribution of Chronic and Infectious Conditions to Total Mortality (Age- and Sex- adjusted), in the United States, 1900–1973*

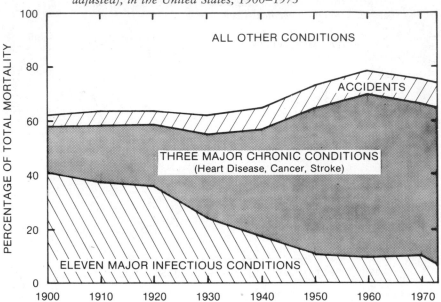

eases accounted for approximately 30 percent of all deaths at the turn of the century and nearly 40 percent of the total decline in the mortality rate since then. The ten diseases were selected on the following criteria: (a) some decline in the death rate had occurred in the period 1900–1973; (b) significant decline in the death rate is commonly attributed to some specific medical measure for the disease; and (c) adequate data for the disease over the period 1900–1973 are available. The diseases of the digestive system were omitted primarily because of lack of clarity in diagnosis of specific diseases such as gastritis and enteritis.

Some additional points of explanation should be noted in relation to Table 1-1. First, the year of medical intervention coincides (as nearly as can be determined) with the first year of widespread or commercial use of the appropriate drug or vaccine.[6] This date does *not* necessarily coincide with the date the measure was either first discovered, or subject to clinical trial. Second, the decline in the death rate for smallpox was calculated using the death rate for 1902 as being the earliest year for which this statistic is readily available (U.S. Bureau of the Census,

1906). For the same reasons, the decline in the death rate from poliomyelitis was calculated from 1910. Third, the table shows the contribution of the decline in each disease to the total decline in mortality over the period 1900–1973 (column b). The overall decline during this period was 12.14 per 1,000 population (17.54 in 1900 to 5.39 in 1973). Fourth, in order to place the experience for each disease in some perspective, Table 1-1 also shows the contribution of the relative fall in mortality after the intervention to the overall fall in mortality since 1900 (column e). In other words, the figures in this last column represent the percentage of the total fall in mortality contributed by each disease after the date of medical intervention.

It is clear from column b that only reductions in mortality from tuberculosis and pneumonia contributed substantially to the decline in total mortality between 1900 and 1973 (16.5 percent and 11.7 percent, respectively). The remaining eight conditions *together* accounted for less than 12 percent of the total decline over this period. Disregarding smallpox (for which the only effective measure had been introduced about 1800),

Table 1-1. The Contribution of Medical Measures (Both Chemotherapeutic and Prophylactic) to the Fall in the Age- and Sex-adjusted Death Rates (S.D.R.) of Ten Common Infectious Diseases, and to the Overall Decline in the S.D.R., for the United States, 1900–1973

Disease	Fall in S.D.R. per 1,000 Population, 1900–1973 (a)	Fall in S.D.R. as % of the Total Fall in S.D.R. $(b) = \frac{(a)}{12.14} \times 100\%$	Year of Medical Intervention (Either Chemotherapy or Prophylaxis)	Fall in S.D.R. per 1,000 Population After Year of Intervention (c)	Fall in S.D.R. After Intervention as % of Total Fall for the Disease $(d) = \frac{(c)}{(a)}$	Fall in S.D.R. After Intervention as % of Total Fall in S.D.R. for All Causes $(e) = \frac{(b)(c)}{(a)}\%$
Tuberculosis	2.00	16.48	Izoniazid/ Streptomycin, 1950	0.17	8.36	1.38
Scarlet Fever	0.10	0.84	Penicillin, 1946	0.00	1.75	0.01
Influenza	0.22	1.78	Vaccine, 1943	0.05	25.33	0.45
Pneumonia	1.42	11.74	Sulphonamide, 1935	0.24	17.19	2.02
Diphtheria	0.43	3.57	Toxoid, 1930	0.06	13.49	0.48
Whooping Cough	0.12	1.00	Vaccine, 1930	0.06	51.00	0.51
Measles	0.12	1.04	Vaccine, 1963	0.00	1.38	0.01
Smallpox	0.02	0.16	Vaccine, 1800	0.02	100.00	0.16
Typhoid	0.36	2.95	Chloramphenicol, 1948	0.00	0.29	0.01
Poliomyelitis	0.03	0.23	Vaccine, Salk/ Sabin, 1955	0.01	25.87	0.06

Table 1-2. Pair-wise Correlation Matrix for 44 Countries, between Four Measures of Health Status and Three Measures of Medical Care Input

Variable		Matrix of Coefficients							
1.	Infant Mortality Rate (1972)								
2.	Crude Mortality Rate (1970–1972)	−0.14							
3.(a)	Life Expectancy (Males) at 25 years	−0.14	−0.12						
3.(b)	Life Expectancy (Females) at 25 years	−0.12	0.04	0.75					
4.(a)	Life Expectancy (Males) at 55 Years	−0.01	0.10	0.74	0.93				
4.(b)	Life Expectancy (Females) at 55 Years	−0.13	0.01	0.75	0.98	0.95			
5.	Population per Hospital Bed (1971–1973)	0.64	−0.30	0.05	−0.02	0.17	0.0		
6.	Population per Physician (1971–1973)	0.36	−0.30	0.11	0.04	0.16	0.07	0.70	
7.	Per Capita Gross National Product: In $U.S. Equivalent (1972)	−0.66	0.26	0.16	0.18	0.07	0.22	−0.56	−0.46
	Variable (by number)	1	2	3a	3b	4a	4b	5	6

SOURCES: 1. *United Nations Demographic Yearbook: 1974,* New York, United Nations Publications, 1975. (For the Crude and Infant Mortality Rates). 2. *World Health Statistics Annual: 1972,* Vol. 1, Geneva, World Health Organization, 1975, pp. 780–783. (For the Life Expectancy Figures). 3. *United Nations Statistical Yearbook, 1973 and 1975.* New York, United Nations Publications, 25th and 27th issues, 1974 and 1976. (For the Population Bed/Physician Ratios). 4. *The World Bank Atlas.* Washington, D.C., World Bank, 1975. (For the Per Capita Gross National Product).

only influenza, whooping cough, and poliomyelitis show what could be considered substantial declines of 25 percent or more after the date of medical intervention. However, even under the somewhat unrealistic assumption of a constant (linear) rate of decline in the mortality rates, only whooping cough and poliomyelitis even approach the percentage which would have been expected. The remaining six conditions (tuberculosis, scarlet fever, pneumonia, diphtheria, measles, and typhoid) showed negligible declines in their mortality rates subsequent to the date of medical intervention. The seemingly quite large percentages for pneumonia and diphtheria (17.2 and 13.5, respectively) must of course be viewed in the context of relatively early interventions—1935 and 1930.

In order to examine more closely the relation of mortality trends for these diseases to the medical interventions, graphs are presented for each disease in Fig. 1-4. Clearly, for tuberculo-

sis, typhoid, measles, and scarlet fever, the medical measures considered were introduced at the point when the death rate for each of these diseases was already negligible. Any change in the rates of decline which may have occurred subsequent to the interventions could only be minute. Of the remaining five diseases (excluding smallpox with its negligible contribution), it is only for poliomyelitis that the medical measure appears to have produced any noticeable change in the trends. Given peaks in the death rate for 1930, 1950 (and possibly for 1910), a comparable peak could have been expected in 1970. Instead, the death rate dropped to the point of disappearance after 1950 and has remained negligible. The four other diseases (pneumonia, influenza, whooping cough, and diphtheria) exhibit relatively smooth mortality trends which are unaffected by the medical measures, even though these were introduced

Figure 1-4. *The Fall in the Standardized Death Rate (per 1,000 Population) for Nine Common Infectious Diseases in Relation to Specific Medical Measures, for the United States, 1900–1973*

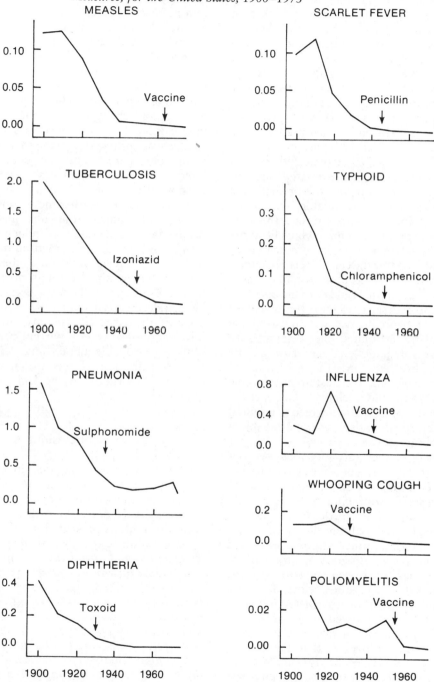

relatively early, when the death rates were still notable.

It may be useful at this point to briefly consider the common and dubious practice of projecting estimated mortality trends (Witte and Axnick, 1975). In order to show the beneficial (or even detrimental) effect of some medical measure, a line, estimated on a set of points observed prior to the introduction of the measure, is projected over the period subsequent to the point of intervention. Any resulting discrepancy between the projected line and the observed trend is then used as some kind of "evidence" of an effective or beneficial intervention. According to statistical theory on least squares estimation, an estimated line can serve as a useful predictor, but the prediction is only valid, and its error calculable, within the range of the points used to estimate the line. Moreover, those predicted values which lie at the extremes of the range are subject to much larger errors than those nearer the center. It is, therefore, probable that, even if the projected line was a reasonable estimate of the trend after the intervention (which, of course, it is not), the divergent observed trend is probably well within reasonable error limits of the estimated line (assuming the error could be calculated), as the error will be relatively large. In other words, this technique is of dubious value as no valid conclusions are possible from its application, and a relatively large prediction error cannot be estimated, which is required in order to objectively judge the extent of divergence of an observed trend.

With regard to the ten infectious diseases considered in this paper, when lines were fitted to the nine or ten points available over the entire period (1900–1973), four exhibited a reasonably good fit to a straight line (scarlet fever, measles, whooping cough, and poliomyelitis), while another four (typhoid, diphtheria, tuberculosis, and pneumonia) showed a very good quadratic fit (to a curved line). Of the remaining two diseases, smallpox showed a negligible decline, as it was already a minor cause of death in 1900 (only 0.1 percent), and influenza showed a poor fit because of the extremely high death rate in 1920. From Fig. 1-4 it is clear, however, that the rate of decline slowed in more recent years for most of the diseases considered—a trend which could be anticipated as rates approach zero.[7]

Now it is possible to argue that, given the few data points available, the fit is somewhat crude and may be insensitive to any changes subsequent to a point of intervention. However, this can be countered with the observation that, given the relatively low death rates for these diseases, any change would have to be extremely marked in order to be detected in the overall mortality experience. Certainly, from the evidence considered here, only poliomyelitis appears to have had a noticeably changed death rate subsequent to intervention. Even if it were assumed that this change was entirely due to the vaccines, then only about one percent of the decline following interventions for the diseases considered here (column d of Table 1-1) could be attributed to medical measures. Rather more conservatively, if we attribute some of the subsequent fall in the death rates for pneumonia, influenza, whooping cough, and diphtheria to medical measures, then perhaps 3.5 percent of the fall in the overall death rate can be explained through medical intervention in the major infectious diseases considered here. Indeed, given that it is precisely for these diseases that medicine claims most success in lowering mortality, 3.5 percent probably represents a reasonable upper-limit estimate of the total contribution of medical measures to the decline in mortality in the United States since 1900.

Conclusions

Without claiming they are definitive findings, and eschewing pretentions to an analysis as sophisticated as McKeown's for England and Wales, one can reasonably draw the following conclusions from the analysis presented in this paper:

In general, medical measures (both chemotherapeutic and prophylactic) appear to have contributed little to the overall decline in mortality in the United States since about 1900— having in many instances been introduced several decades after a marked decline had already set in and having no detectable influence in most instances. More specifically, with reference to those five conditions (influenza, pneumonia, diphtheria, whooping cough, and poliomyelitis) for which the decline in mortality appears sub-

stantial after the point of intervention—and on the unlikely assumption that all of this decline is attributable to the intervention—it is estimated that at most 3.5 percent of the total decline in mortality since 1900 could be ascribed to medical measures introduced for the diseases considered here.

These conclusions, in support of the thesis introduced earlier, suggest issues of the most strategic significance for researchers and health care legislators. Profound policy implications follow from either a confirmation or a rejection of the thesis. If one subscribes to the view that we are slowly but surely eliminating one disease after another because of medical interventions, then there may be little commitment to social change and even resistance to some reordering of priorities in medical expenditures. If a disease X is disappearing primarily because of the presence of a particular intervention or service Y, then clearly Y should be left intact, or, more preferably, be expanded. Its demonstrable contribution justifies its presence. But, if it can be shown convincingly, and on commonly accepted grounds, that the major part of the decline in mortality is unrelated to medical care activites, then some commitment to social change and a reordering of priorities may ensue. For, if the disappearance of X is largely unrelated to the presence of Y, or even occurs in the absence of Y, then clearly the expansion and even the continuance of Y can be reasonably questioned. Its demonstrable ineffectiveness justifies some reappraisal of its significance and the wisdom of expanding it in its existing form.

In this paper we have attempted to dispel the myth that medical measures and the presence of medical services were primarily responsible for the modern decline of mortality. The question now remains: if they were not primarily responsible for it, then how is it to be explained? An adequate answer to this further question would require a more substantial research effort than that reported here, but is likely to be along the lines suggested by McKeown which were referred to early in this paper. Hopefully, this paper will serve as a catalyst for such research, incorporating adequate data and appropriate methods of analysis, in an effort to arrive at a more viable alternative explanation.

NOTES

1. It is obviously important to distinguish between (a) advances in knowledge of the cause and natural course of some condition and (b) improvements in our ability to effectively treat some condition (that is, to alter its natural course). In many instances these two areas are disjoint and appear at different stages of development. There are, on the one hand, disease processes about which considerable knowledge has been accrued, yet this has not resulted (nor necessarily will) in the development of effective treatments. On the other hand, there are conditions for which demonstrably effective treatments have been devised in the absence of knowledge of the disease process and/or its causes.

2. Barker and Rose cite one study which compared the ante-mortem and autopsy diagnoses in 9,501 deaths which occurred in 75 different hospitals. Despite lack of a concurrence on *individual* cases, the *overall* frequency was very similar in diagnoses obtained on either an ante-mortem or post-mortem basis. As an example they note that clinical diagnoses of carcinoma of the rectum were confirmed at autopsy in only 67 percent of cases, but the incorrect clinical diagnoses were balanced by an almost identical number of lesions diagnosed for the first time at autopsy (Barker and Rose, 1976).

3. All age and sex adjustments were made by the "direct" method using the population of 1900 as the standard. For further information on this method of adjustment, see Hill (1971) and Shryock et al. (1971).

4. Rutstein (1967), although fervently espousing the traditional view that medical advances have been largely responsible for the decline in mortality, discussed this disjunction and termed it "The Paradox of Modern Medicine." More recently, and from a perspective that is generally consistent with that advanced here, Powles (1973) noted the same phenomenon in England and Wales.

5. Deaths in the category of chronic respiratory diseases (chronic bronchitis, asthma, emphysema, and other chronic obstructive lung diseases) could not be included in the group of chronic conditions because of insurmountable difficulties inherent in the many changes in disease classification and in the tabulation of statistics.

6. In determining the dates of intervention we relied upon: (a) standard epidemiology and public health texts; (b) the recollections of authorities in the field of infectious diseases; and (c) recent publications on the same subject.

7. For this reason, a negative exponential model is sometimes used to fit a curved line to such data. This was not presented here as the number of points available was small and the difference between a simple quadratic and negative exponential fit was not, upon investigation, able to be detected.

REFERENCES

Alderson, M. 1976. *An Introduction to Epidemiology.* London: Macmillan Press. pp. 7–27.

Barker, D.J.P., and Rose, G. 1976. *Epidemiology in Medical Practice.* London: Churchill Livingstone, p. 6.

Bolduan, C.F. 1930. *How to Protect Children From Diphtheria.* New York: N.Y.C. Health Department.

Dubos, R. 1959. *Mirage of Health.* New York: Harper and Row.

Dubos, R. 1965. *Man Adapting.* New Haven, Connecticut: Yale University Press.

Dubos, R. 1968. *Man, Medicine and Environment.* London: Pall Mall Press.

Dunn, H.L., and Shackley, W. 1945. *Comparison of cause of death assignments by the 1929 and 1938 revisions of the International List: Deaths in the United States, 1940 Vital Statistics—Special Reports 19:153–277, 1944,* Washington, D.C.: U.S. Department of Commerce, Bureau of the Census.

Fuchs, V.R. 1974. *Who Shall Live?* New York: Basic Books, p. 54.

Griffith, T. 1967. *Population Problems in the Age of Malthus.* 2nd ed. London: Frank Cass.

Habakkuk, H.J. 1953. English Population in the Eighteenth Century. *Economic History Review,* 6.

Hill, A.B. 1971. *Principles of Medical Statistics.* 9th ed. London: Oxford University Press.

Hill, A.B. 1955. Snow—An Appreciation. *Proceedings of the Royal Society of Medicine* 48:1008–1012.

Illich, I. 1976. *Medical Nemesis.* New York: Pantheon Books.

Inman, W.H.W., and Adelstein, A.M. 1969. Rise and fall of asthma mortality in England and Wales, in relation to use of pressurized aerosols. *Lancet* 2:278–285.

Kass, E.H. 1971. Infectious diseases and social change. *The Journal of Infectious Diseases* 123 (1): 110–114.

Krueger, D.E. 1966. New enumerators for old denominators—multiple causes of death. In *Epidemiologial Approaches to the Study of Cancer and Other Chronic Diseases,* edited by W. Haenszel. National Cancer Printing Office, pp. 431–443.

Lee, W.W. 1931. Diphtheria Immunization in Philadelphia and New York City. *Journal of Preventive Medicine* (Baltimore) 5:211–220.

Lilienfeld, A.M. 1976. *Foundations of Epidemiology.* New York: Oxford University Press. pp. 51–111.

McKeown, T. 1976a. *The Modern Rise of Population.* London: Edward Arnold.

McKeown, T. 1976b. *The Role of Medicine: Dream, Mirage or Nemesis.* London: Nuffield Provincial Hospitals Trust.

McKeown, T.; Brown, R.G.; and Record, R.G. 1972. An interpretation of the modern rise of population in Europe. *Population Studies* 26:345–382.

McKeown, T., and Record, R.G. 1955. Medical evidence related to English population changes in the eighteenth century. *Population Studies* 9:119–141.

McKeown, T., and Record, R.G. 1962. Reasons for the decline in mortality in England and Wales during the nineteenth century. *Population Studies* 16:94–122.

McKeown, T.; Record, R.G.; and Turner, R.D. 1975. An interpretation of the decline of mortality in England and Wales during the twentieth century, *Population Studies* 29:391–422.

McKinlay, J.B., and McKinlay, S.M. *A refutation of the thesis that the health of the nation is improving.* Forthcoming.

Magill, T.P. 1955. The immunologist and the evil spirits. *Journal of Immunology* 74:1–8.

Moriyama, I.M.; Baum, W.S.; Haenszel, W.M.; and Mattison, B.F. 1958. Inquiry into diagnostic evidence supporting medical certifications of death. *American Journal of Public Health* 48:1376–1387.

Moriyama, I.M., and Gustavus, S.O. 1972. *Cohort Mortality and Survivorship: United States Death—Registration States, 1900–1968.* National Center for Health Statistics, Series 3, No. 16. Washington, D.C.: U.S. Government Printing Office.

Pfizer, C. and Company. 1953. *The Pneumonias, Management with Antibiotic Therapy.* Brooklyn.

Powles, J. 1973. On the limitations of modern medicine. *Science, Medicine and Man.* 1:2–3.

Reid, O.D., and Rose, G.A. 1964. Assessing the comparability of mortality statistics. *British Medical Journal* 2:1437–1439.

Rutstein, D. 1967. *The Coming Revolution in Medicine.* Cambridge, Massachusettes: MIT Press.

Shryock, H., et al. 1971. *The Methods and Materials of Demography.* Washington, D.C.: U.S. Government Printing Office.

The Times (London). 1977. The Doctors Dilemma: How to Cure Society of a Life Style That Makes People Sick. Friday, January 21.

U.S. Bureau of the Census. 1906. *Mortality Statistics 1900–1904.* Washington, D.C.: Government Printing Office.

U.S. Department of Health, Education and Welfare. 1964. *The Change in Mortality Trend in the United*

States. National Center for Health Statistics, Series 3, No. 1. Washington, D.C.: U.S. Government Printing Office.

Weinstein, L. 1974. Infectious Disease: Retrospect and Reminiscence. *The Journal of Infectious Diseases.* 129 (4):480–492.

Wilson, G.S., and Miles, A.A. 1946. In Topley and Wilson's *Principles of Bacteriology and Immunity.* Baltimore: Williams and Wilkins.

Witte, J.J., and Axnick, N.W. 1975. The benefits from ten years of measles immunization in the United States. *Public Health Reports* 90 (3):205–207.

This paper reports part of a larger research project supported by a grant from the Milbank Memorial Fund (to Boston University) and the Carnegie Foundation (to the Radcliffe Institute). The authors would like to thank John Stoeckle, M.D. (Massachusetts General Hospital) and Louis Weinstein, M.D. (Peter Bent Brigham Hospital) for helpful discussions during earlier stages of the research.

Who Gets Sick? The Unequal Social Distribution of Disease

Disease is not distributed evenly throughout the population. Certain groups of people get sick more often, and some populations die prematurely at higher rates than others. The study of what groups of people get sick with what disease is called *epidemiology* and has been defined by one expert as "the study of the distributions and determinants of states of health in human populations" (Susser, 1973: 1). By studying populations rather than individuals, epidemiologists seek to identify characteristics of groups of people or their environments that make them more or less vulnerable to disease (*morbidity*) or death (*mortality*).

A growing body of research has found significant associations between a range of social and cultural factors and the risk for disease and death. The term *social epidemiology* has been adopted by some researchers to emphasize the importance of social variables in the patterning of disease. By focusing on the connections between social processes and the risk for disease, the study of social epidemiology provides the social scientist with an important opportunity to understand more fully the relationship between society and the individual. Among the historical predecessors of today's social epidemiology was the emergence in the nineteenth century of "social medicine" with a number of important studies in Western Europe. In England, Edwin Chadwick studied the death rates of populations and identified relationships between disease and social problems—most notably poverty—thus laying an important foundation for the developing Public Health Movement (Chadwick, 1842, in Susser, 1973). Another early investigator in social medicine was Rudolf Virchow, who was asked by the Prussian government to study the causes of a terrible typhus epidemic. His pioneering research identified connections between disease and a number of social factors, including the economy, conditions of work, and the organization of agriculture (Virchow, 1868, 1879, in Waitzkin, 1978).

The readings in this section examine selected associations between the distribution of disease and social variables, including social class, race, gender, and lifestyle. These studies highlight the relevance of a social epidemiological perspective and point to several promising directions for future research.

In the United States, one of the most striking and consistent patterns in the distribution of disease is its relationship to poverty. By and large, death and disease rates vary inversely with social class; that is, the poorer the population, the higher the risk for sickness and death (Kitagawa and Hauser, 1973; Najman, 1993). While it has been known for well over a century that poor people suffer from more disease than others, just how poverty influences health is not yet well understood. And the situation is not getting better. Despite an overall decline in death rates in the United States, the poor are still dying at higher rates than those with higher incomes, and the disparity between socioeconomic groups has actually increased (Pappas, Queen, Hadden, and Fisher, 1993). Some have suggested that the unequal distribution of income in a society, rather than only poverty, has a negative impact on health (Wilkinson, 1994). Other recent evidence notes that there is a continuous impact of social class on health (Adler, Boyce, Chesney, et al., 1994); that is, the health effects of socioeconomic status extend to all classes along a gradient from the lower to higher classes, although with more negative impacts in the lower classes. While the research is becoming more sophisticated and subtle, the evidence of the impact of social class on health remains stronger than ever. In "Social Class, Susceptibility, and Sickness," S. Leonard Syme and Lisa F. Berkman explore the relationship between social class and sickness, reviewing the evidence of the influence of stress, living conditions, nutrition, and medical services on the patterns of death and disease among the poor. They focus on how the living conditions of the lower class may compromise "disease defense systems" and engender greater vulnerability to disease.

In American society, race and class are highly associated in that a disproportionate number of African Americans and other minorities are living in poverty. In general, African Americans have higher morbidity and mortality rates than do whites and a shorter life expectancy (69.6 compared with 76.6 in 1992). Although the infant mortality (death before the age of one) rate in the U.S. has declined dramatically in this century, it remains twice as high among African Americans than whites. *The Report of the Secretary's Task Force on Black and Minority Health* stated that minorities had 60,000 "excess" deaths annually (U.S. Department of Health and Human Services, 1986). There is some evidence that middle-class African Americans and whites have rather similar mortality rates (Schoendorf et al., 1992), but that blacks living in poverty have much worse health outcomes. In "Excess Mortality in Harlem," Colin McCord and Harold P. Freeman show how the intertwining of race and social class can have a devastating impact on health. Harlem, an area of New York City, is 96% black with 40% of its residents living below the poverty line. The mortality rate in Harlem, adjusted for age, was the highest in New York City—more than double that of whites and 50% higher than the national average among African Americans. Although Harlem is located in the midst of a modern, sophisticated, and wealthy city, the death rates for its inhabitants between the ages of 5 and 65 were worse than their peers' in Bangladesh, one of the poorest countries in the world. The logical conclusion to be drawn from this fact is that social conditions and the state of health of the population in certain impoverished inner-city areas engender health outcomes equivalent to those encountered in the third world.

Another interesting and consistent pattern is the difference between the distribution of disease and death in men and women. Women have higher illness rates than men, while men have higher death rates. (Such comparisons rely on "age-adjusted" samples in order to eliminate the effects of age on gender differences.) There is a great deal of disagreement about the explanation for these patterns, including debates over whether women actually do get sick more often than men or whether they are more likely to report symptoms or seek medical care (e.g., Muller, 1991; Verbrugge, 1979; Gove and Hughes, 1979). The growing feminist scholarship on women's health and the more recent epidemiological interest in studying patterns of physical disease in female populations have begun to clarify the debate. It now appears that women *do* in fact have higher rates of sickness than men *and* that they are more likely than men to report symptoms and use medical services (e.g., Nathanson, 1980; Wingard, 1982).

Ingrid Waldron examines these findings in "What Do We Know about the Causes of Sex Differences in Mortality?" It has long been recognized that in American society women live longer than men; currently, women live seven years longer. Because life expectancy varies significantly from society to society and is thus not given in nature, the excess mortality and decreased life expectancy of men require explanation. Waldron locates a number of causes in sex role differences, especially in terms of life habits (e.g., cigarette smoking) and risk-taking behavior. The results of these cultural factors suggest that the social gender structure is significant in the production of disease and disability. Waldron raises the question of whether the continuing changes in women's social roles will lead to a decrease in the ratio of male to female deaths. Some evidence suggests that in part the historical health "advantage" of women seems to be disappearing (Verbrugge, 1982).

It is important to note that *intergender* differences (that is, differences between male and female populations) may mask significant *intragender* patterns (that is, patterns among men or among women). In fact, there is evidence that the distribution of disease and death within male and female populations is patterned by other social factors, and importantly, that these patterns differ for men and women. Social class, race, age, marital status, presence and number of children in the home, and employment outside the home have all been found to be associated with rates of disease within male and female populations, accounting for at least some of the differences between the sexes (e.g., Nathanson, 1980; Haynes and Feinleib, 1980; Wingard, 1982).

In the fascinating selection "A Tale of Two States," Victor R. Fuchs compares the health of the populations of two neighboring states: Nevada and Utah. While similar in many ways, these populations have very different patterns of death. Fuchs argues that the explanation for this difference is to be found in the lifestyles of each of the populations and that these lifestyle differences are the result of the cultural environments, values, and norms of each of the populations.

The findings of these authors and the developing social epidemiology to which they contribute challenge the traditional medical model by seeing social factors as part of the process of disease production. While not dismissing the possibility that some biological processes contribute to the risk for disease among some groups, the bulk of the evidence supports a view that much of the epidemiological significance of race, gender, and age results from the social and cultural consequences of being, for example, a black, a woman, or an elderly person.

The importance of social processes in disease production is also supported by the consistent findings of the significance of social networks such as community and family ties and stress. Included in the definition of *stress* are the chronic stresses of jobs, family obligations, and economic pressures, and the stress produced by the relatively rare "stressful life events" (Dohrenwend and Dohrenwend, 1981; Kessler and Workman, 1989). These stressful events are the more dramatic and unusual occurrences, such as divorce, job loss, or the birth of a child, that produce major changes in people's lives. These researchers have found a consistent connection between these events and the individual's vulnerability to disease. Social networks and stress have been found to be associated with the development of physical diseases (e.g., coronary heart disease, hypertension) as well as psychological disorders (e.g., depression) (see for example, Berkman and Syme, 1979; Wheatley, 1981; Dohrenwend and Dohrenwend, 1981).

Clearly, there is a need for a new and broader conceptualization of disease production than the traditional medical model can provide. Attention must shift from the individual to the social and physical environments in which people live and work. The development of an adequate model of disease production must draw on the conceptual and research contributions of several disciplines not only to identify the social production of diseases, but to elaborate this process and provide important information on which to base effective primary intervention and prevention strategies.

REFERENCES

Adler, Nancy E., Thomas Boyce, Margaret A. Chesney, Sheldon Cohen, Susan Folkman, Robert L. Kahn, and Leonard Syme. 1994. "Socioeconomic status and health: The challenge of the gradient." American Psychologist. 49:15–24.

Berkman, Lisa F., and S. L. Syme. 1979. "Social networks, host resistance, and mortality: A nine-year follow-up study of Alameda County residents." American Journal of Epidemiology. 109:(July) 186–204

Chadwick, Edwin. 1842. Report on the Sanitary Condition of the Labouring Population of Great Britain. Reprinted 1965. Edinburgh: Edinburgh University Press.

Dohrenwend, Barbara S., and Bruce P. Dohrenwend, eds. 1981. Stressful Life Events and Their Contexts. New York: Prodist.

Gove, Walter, and Michael Hughes. 1979. "Possible causes of the apparent sex differences in physical health: An empirical investigation." American Sociological Review. 44:126–146.

Haynes, Suzanne, and M. Feinleib. 1980. "Women, work and coronary heart disease: Prospective findings from the Framingham Heart Study." American Journal of Public Health. 70, 2 (February): 133–141.

Kessler, Ronald C., and Camille B. Workman. 1989. "Social and psychological factors in health and illness." Pp. 69–86 in Howard Freeman and Sol Levine (eds.), Handbook of Medical Sociology. Englewood Cliffs, N.J.: Prentice-Hall.

Kitagawa, Evelyn M. and P.M. Hauser. 1973. Differential Mortality in the United States: A Study in Socioeconomic Epidemiology. Cambridge, MA: Harvard University Press.

Muller, Charlotte. 1991. Health Care and Gender. New York: Russell Sage.

Najman, Jake M. 1993. "Health and poverty: Past, present and prospects for the future." Social Science and Medicine. 36:157–166.

Nathanson, Constance. 1980. "Social roles and health status among women: The significance of employment." Social Science and Medicine. 14A: 463–471.

Pappas, Gregory, Susan Queen, Wilbur Hadden, and Gail Fisher. 1993. "The increasing disparity in mortality between socioeconomic groups in the United States, 1960 and 1986." New England Journal of Medicine. 329:103–09.

Schoendorf, Kenneth C., Carol J.R. Hogue, Joel Kleinman, and Diane Rowley. 1992. "Mortality among infants of black as compared with white college-educated parents." New England Journal of Medicine. 326:1522–1526.

Susser, Mervyn. 1973. Causal Thinking in the Health Sciences, Concepts and Strategies in Epidemiology. New York: Oxford University Press.

United States Department of Health and Human Services. 1986. Report of the Secretary's Task Force on Black and Minority Health. Washington, D.C.: U.S. Government Printing Office.

Verbrugge, Lois. 1979. "Marital status and health." Journal of Marriage and Family. (May): 267–285.

Verbrugge, Lois. 1982. "Sex differentials in health." U.S. Public Health Reports. 97,5 (Sept–October): 417–437.

Virchow, Rudolf. 1958. Disease, Life and Man. Tr. Lelland J. Rather. Stanford: Stanford University Press.

Waitzkin, Howard. 1978. "A Marxist view of medical care." Annals of Internal Medicine. 89:264–278.

Wheatley, David, ed. 1981. Stress and the Heart. 2nd ed. New York: Raven Press.

Wilkinson, Richard G. 1994. "The epidemiological transition: From material scarcity to social disadvantage." Daedalus. 123:61–78.

Wingard, Deborah. 1982. "The sex differential in mortality rates." American Journal of Epidemiology. 115 (2): 105–216.

2

Social Class, Susceptibility, and Sickness

■ ■ ■ ■ ■ ■

S. Leonard Syme and Lisa F. Berkman

Social class gradients of mortality and life expectancy have been observed for centuries, and a vast body of evidence has shown consistently that those in the lower classes have higher mortality, morbidity, and disability rates. While these patterns have been observed repeatedly, the explanations offered to account for them show no such consistency. The most frequent explanations have included poor housing, crowding, racial factors, low income, poor education and unemployment, all of which have been said to result in such outcomes as poor nutrition, poor medical care (either through non-availability or non-utilization of resources), strenuous conditions of employment in non-hygienic settings, and increased exposure to noxious agents. While these explanations account for some of the observed relationships, we have found them inadequate to explain the very large number of diseases associated with socioeconomic status. It seemed useful, therefore, to reexamine these associations in search of a more satisfactory hypothesis.

Obviously, this is an important issue. It is clear that new approaches must be explored emphasizing the primary prevention of disease in addition to those approaches that merely focus on treatment of the sick (1). It is clear also that such preventive approaches must involve community and environmental interventions rather than one-to-one preventive encounters (2). Therefore, we must understand more precisely those features of the environment that are etiologically related to disease so that interventions at this level can be more intelligently planned.

Of all the disease outcomes considered, it is evident that low socioeconomic status is most strikingly associated with high rates of infectious and parasitic diseases (3–7) as well as with higher infant mortality rates (8,9). However, in our review we found higher rates among lower class groups of a very much wider range of diseases and conditions for which obvious explanations were not as easily forthcoming. In a comprehensive review of over 30 studies, Antonovsky (10) concluded that those in the lower classes invariably have lower life expectancy and higher death rates from all causes of death, and that this higher rate has been observed since the 12th century when data on this question were first organized. While differences in infectious disease and infant mortality rates probably accounted for much of this difference between the classes in earlier years, current differences must primarily be attributable to mortality from non-infectious disease.

Kitagawa and Hauser (11) recently completed a massive nationwide study of mortality in the United States. Among men and women in the 25-64–year age group, mortality rates varied dramatically by level of education, income, and occupation, considered together or separately. For example . . . white males at low education levels had age-adjusted mortality rates 64 per cent higher than men in higher education categories. For white women, those in lower education groups had an age-adjusted mortality rate 105 per cent higher. For non-white males, the differential was 31 per cent and, for non-white females, it was 70 per cent. These mortality differentials also were reflected in substantial differences in life expectancy, and . . . for most specific causes of death. . . . White males in the lowest education groups have higher age-adjusted mortality rates for every cause of death for which data are available. For white females, those in the lowest education group have an excess mortality rate for all causes except cancer of the breast and motor vehicle accidents.

These gradients of mortality among the social classes have been observed over the world by many investigators (12–18) and have not changed materially since 1900 (except that non-whites, especially higher status non-whites, have experienced a relatively more favorable improvement). This consistent finding in time and space is all the more remarkable since the concept of "social class" has been defined and measured in so many different ways by these investigators. That the same findings have been obtained in spite of such methodological differences lends strength to the validity of the observations; it suggests also that the concept is an imprecise term encompassing diverse elements of varying etiologic significance.

In addition to data on mortality, higher rates of morbidity also have been observed for a vast array of conditions among those in lower class groups (19–28). This is an important observation since it indicates that excess mortality rates among lower status groups are not merely attributable to a higher case fatality death rate in those groups but are accompanied also by a higher prevalence of morbidity. Of special interest in this regard are data on the various mental illnesses, a major cause of morbidity. As shown by many investigators (29–35), those in lower as compared to higher socioeconomic groups have higher rates of schizophrenia, are more depressed, more unhappy, more worried, more anxious, and are less hopeful about the future.

In summary, persons in lower class groups have higher morbidity and mortality rates of almost every disease or illness, and these differentials have not diminished over time. While particular hypotheses may be offered to explain the gradient for one or another of these specific diseases, the fact that so many diseases exhibit the same gradient leads to speculation that a more general explanation may be more appropriate than a series of disease-specific explanations.

In a study reported elsewhere (36), it was noted that although blacks had higher rates of hypertension than whites, blacks in the lower classes had higher rates of hypertension than blacks in the upper classes. An identical social class gradient for hypertension was noted among whites in the sample. In that report, it was concluded that hypertension was associated more with social class than with racial factors, and it was suggested that the greater prevalence of obesity in the lower class might be a possible explanation. The present review makes that earlier suggestion far less attractive since so many diseases and conditions appear to be of higher prevalence in the lower class groups. It seems clear that we must frame hypotheses of sufficient generality to account for this phenomenon.

One hypothesis that has been suggested is that persons in the lower classes either have less access to medical care resources or, if care is available, that they do not benefit from that availability. This possibility should be explored in more detail, but current evidence available does not suggest that differences in medical care resources will entirely explain social class gradients in disease. The hypertension project summarized above was conducted at the Kaiser Permanente facility in Oakland, California, which is a prepaid health plan with medical facilities freely available to all study subjects. The data in this study showed that persons in lower status groups had utilized medical resources more frequently than those in higher status categories (37). To study the influence of medical care in explaining these differences in blood pressure levels, all persons in the Kaiser study who had ever been clinically diagnosed as hypertensive, or who had ever taken medicine for high blood pressure, were removed from consideration. Differences in blood pressure level between those in the highest and lowest social classes were diminished when hypertensives were removed from analysis, but those in the lowest class still had higher (normal) pressures. Thus, while differences in medical care may have accounted for some of the variation observed among the social class groups, substantial differences in blood pressures among these groups nevertheless remained. Similar findings have been reported from studies at the Health Insurance Plan of New York (38).

Lipworth and colleagues (39) also examined this issue in a study of cancer survival rates among various income groups in Boston. In that study, low-income persons had substantially less favorable one and three-year survival rates following treatment at identical tumor clinics and hospitals; these differences were not accounted for by differences in stage of cancer at diagnosis, by the age of patients, or by the specific kind of treatment patients received. It was concluded that patients from lower income areas simply did not fare as well following treatment for cancer. While it is still possible that lower class patients received less adequate medical care, the differences observed in survival rates did not seem attributable to the more obvious variations in quality of treatment. Other studies support this general conclusion but not enough data are available to assess clearly the role of medical care in explaining social class gradients in morbidity and mortality; it would seem, however, that the medical care hypothesis does not account for a major portion of these gradients.

Another possible explanation offered to explain these consistent differences is that persons in lower socioeconomic groups live in a more toxic, hazardous and non-hygienic environment resulting in a broad array of disease consequences. That these environments exert an influence on disease outcome is supported by research on crowding and rheumatic fever (5), poverty areas and health (40), and on air pollution and respiratory illnesses (41). While lower class groups certainly are exposed to a more physically noxious environment, physical factors alone are frequently unable to explain observed relationships between socioeconomic status and disease outcome. One example of this is provided by the report of Guerrin and Borgatta (16) showing that the proportion of people who are illiterate in a census tract is a more important indicator of tuberculosis occurrence than are either economic or racial variables. Similarly, the work of Booth (42) suggests that perceived crowding which is not highly correlated with objective measures of crowding may have adverse effects on individuals.

There can be little doubt that the highest morbidity and mortality rates observed in the lower social classes are in part due to inadequate medical care services as well as to the impact of a toxic and hazardous physical environment. There can be little doubt, also, that these factors do not entirely explain the discrepancy in rates between the classes. Thus, while enormous improvements have been made in environmental quality and in medical care, the mortality rate gap between the classes has not diminished. It is true that mortality rates have been declining over the years, and it is probably true also that this benefit is attributable in large part to the enormous improvements that have been made in food and water purity, in sanitary engineering, in literacy and health education, and in medical and surgical knowledge. It is important to recognize, however, that these reductions in mortality rates have not eliminated the gap between the highest and the lowest social class groups; this gap remains very substantial and has apparently stabilized during the last 40 years. Thus, while improvements in the environment and in medical care clearly have been of value, other factors must be identified to account for this continuing differential in mortality rate and life expectancy.

The identification of these new factors might profitably be guided by the repeated observation of social class gradients in a wide range of disease distributions. That so many different kinds of diseases are more frequent in lower class groupings directs attention to generalized susceptibility to disease and to generalized compromises of disease defense systems. Thus, if something about life in the lower social classes increases vulnerability to illness in general, it would not be surprising to observe an increased prevalence of many different types of diseases and conditions among people in the lower classes.

While laboratory experiments on both humans and animals have established that certain "stressful events" have physiologic consequences, very little is known about the nature of these "stressful events" in non-laboratory settings. Thus, while we may conclude that "something" about the lower class environment is stressful, we know much less about what specifically constitutes that stress. Rather than attempting to identify *specific* risk factors for *specific* diseases in investigating this question, it may be more meaningful to identify those factors that affect *general* susceptibility to disease. The specification of such factors should rest on the identification of variables having a wide range of disease outcomes. One such risk factor may be life change associated with social and cultural mobility. Those experiencing this type of mobility have been observed to have higher rates of diseases and conditions such as coronary heart disease (43–46), lung cancer (47), difficulties of pregnancy (48, 49), sarcoidosis (50), and depression (30). Another risk factor may be certain life events; those experiencing what are commonly called stressful life events have been shown to have higher rates of a wide variety of diseases and conditions (51–57).

Generalized susceptibility to disease may be influenced not only by the impact of various forms of life change and life stress, but also by differences in the way people cope with such stress. Coping, in this sense, refers not to specific types of psychological responses but to the more generalized ways in which people deal with problems in their everyday life. It is evident that such coping styles are likely to be products of environmental situations and not independent of such factors. Several coping responses that have a wide range of disease outcomes have been described. Cigarette smoking is one such coping response that has been associated with virtually all causes of morbidity and mortality (58); obesity may be another coping style associated with a higher rate of many diseases and conditions (59,60); pattern A behavior is an example of a third coping response that has been shown to have relatively broad disease consequences (61). There is some evidence that persons in the lower classes experience more life changes (62) and that they tend to be more obese and to smoke more cigarettes (63,64).

To explain the differential in morbidity and mortality rates among the social classes, it is important to identify additional factors that affect susceptibility and have diverse disease consequences; it is also important to determine which of these factors are more prevalent in the lower classes. Thus, our understanding would be enhanced if it could be shown not only that those in the lower classes live in a more toxic physical environment with inadequate medical care, but also that they live in a social and psychological environment that increases their vulnerability to a whole series of diseases and conditions.

In this paper, we have emphasized the variegated disease consequences of low socioeconomic status. Any proposed explanations of this phenomenon should be capable of accounting for this general outcome. The proposal offered here is that those in the lower classes consistently have higher rates of disease in part due to compromised disease defenses and increased general susceptibility. To explore this proposal further, systematic research is needed on four major problems:

(1) The more precise identification and description of subgroups within the lower socioeconomic classes that have either markedly higher or lower rates of disease: Included in what is commonly called the "lower class" are semi-skilled working men with stable work and family situations, unemployed men with and without families, the rural and urban poor, hard core unemployed persons, and so on. The different disease experiences of these heterogeneous subgroups would permit a more precise understanding of the processes involved in disease etiology and would permit a more precise definition of social class groupings.

(2) The disentanglement of socio-environmental from physical-environmental variables: It is important to know whether high rates of illness and discontent in a poverty area, for example, are due to the poor physical circumstances of life in such an area, to the social consequences of life in such an area, or to the personal characteristics of individuals who come to live in the area.

(3) The clarification of "causes" and "effects": The implication in this paper has been that the lower class environment "leads to" poor health. Certainly, the reverse situation is equally likely. Many measures of social class position may be influenced by the experience of ill health itself. Further research is needed to clarify the relative importance of the "downward drift" hypothesis. One way of approaching such study is to use measures of class position that are relatively unaffected by illness experience. An example of one such measure is "educational achievement" as used by Kitagawa and Hauser (11). In this study, educational level was assumed to be relatively stable after age 20 and was felt to be a measure relatively unaffected by subsequent illness experience.

(4) The more comprehensive description of those psycho-social variables that may compromise bodily defense to disease and increase susceptibility to illness: The possible importance of life events, life changes, and various coping

behavior has been suggested but systematic research needs to be done to provide a more complete view of the factors involved in this process. Of particular interest would be research on the ways in which social and familial support networks (48,55) mediate between the impact of life events and stresses and disease outcomes.

The research that is needed should not be limited to the study of the specific risk factors as these affect specific diseases. Instead, the major focus of this research should be on those general features of lower class living environments that compromise bodily defense and thereby affect health and well-being in general. This research should go beyond the superficial description of demographic variables associated with illness and should attempt the identification of specific etiologic factors capable of accounting for the observed morbidity and mortality differences between the social classes.

The gap in mortality and life expectancy between the social classes has stabilized and may be increasing; the identification of those factors that render people vulnerable to disease will hopefully provide a basis for developing more meaningful prevention programs aimed toward narrowing the gap.

REFERENCES

1. Winkelstein W Jr, French FE: The role of ecology in the design of a health care system. Calif Med 113:7–12, 1970.
2. Marmot M, Winkelstein W Jr: Epidemiologic observations on intervention trials for prevention of coronary heart disease. Am J Epidemiol 101:177–181, 1975.
3. Tuberculosis and Socioeconomic Status. Stat Bull, January 1970.
4. Terris M: Relation of economic status to tuberculosis mortality by age and sex. Am J Public Health 38:1061–1071, 1948
5. Gordis L, Lilienfeld A, Rodriguez R: Studies in the epidemiology and preventability of rheumatic fever. II. Socioeconomic factors and the incidence of acute attacks. J Chronic Dis 21:655–666, 1969.
6. Influenza and Pneumonia Mortality in the U.S., Canada and Western Europe. Stat Bull, April 1972.
7. Court SDM: Epidemiology and natural history of respiratory infections in children. J Clin Pathol 21:31, 1968.
8. Chase HC (ed): A study of risks, medical care and infant mortality. Am J Public Health 63: supplement, 1973.
9. Lerner M: Social differences in physical health. In: Poverty and Health. Edited by J Kozsa, A Antonovsky, IK Zola. Cambridge, Harvard University Press, 1969, pp 69–112.
10. Antonovsky A: Social class, life expectancy and overall mortality. Milbank Mem Fund Q 45:31–73, 1967.
11. Kitagawa EM, Hauser PM: Differential Mortality in the United States. Cambridge, Harvard University Press, 1973.
12. Nagi MH, Stockwell EG: Socioeconomic differentials in mortality by cause of death. Health Serv Rep 88:449–465, 1973.
13. Ellis JM: Socio-economic differentials in mortality from chronic disease. In: Patients, Physicians and Illness. Edited by EG Jaco. Glencoe, Ill, The Free Press, 1958, pp 30–37.
14. Yeracaris J: Differential mortality, general and cause-specific in Buffalo, 1939–1941. J Am Stat Assoc 50:1235–1247, 1955.
15. Brown SM, Selvin S, Winkelstein W Jr: The association of economic status with the occurrence of lung cancer. Cancer 36:1903–1911, 1975.
16. Guerrin RF, Borgatta EF: Socio-economic and demographic correlates of tuberculosis incidence. Milbank Mem Fund Q 43:269–290, 1965.
17. Graham S: Socio-economic status, illness, and the use of medical services. Milbank Mem Fund Q 35:58–66, 1957.
18. Cohart EM: Socioeconomic distribution of stomach cancer in New Haven. Cancer 7:455–461, 1954.
19. Socioeconomic Differentials in Mortality. Stat Bull, June 1972.
20. Hart JT: Too little and too late. Data on occupational mortality, 1959–1963. Lancet 1:192–193, 1972.
21. Wan T: Social differentials in selected work-limiting chronic conditions. J Chronic Dis 25:365–374, 1972.
22. Hochstim JR, Athanasopoulos DA, Larkins JH: Poverty area under the microscope. Am J Public Health 58:1815–1827, 1968.
23. Burnight RG: Chronic morbidity and socioeconomic characteristics of older urban males. Milbank Mem Fund Q 43:311–322, 1965.
24. Elder R, Acheson RM: New Haven survey of joint diseases. XIV. Social class and behavior in response to symptoms of osteoarthritis. Milbank Mem Fund Q 48:499–502, 1970.
25. Cobb S: The epidemiology of rheumatoid disease. In: The Frequency of Rheumatoid Disease. Edited

by S Cobb. Cambridge, Harvard University Free Press, 1971, pp 42–62.

26. Graham S: Social factors in the relation to chronic illness. *In:* Handbook of Medical Sociology. Edited by HE Freeman, S Levine, LG Reeder. Englewood Cliffs, NJ, Prentice-Hall Inc, 1963, pp 65–98.

27. Wan T: Status stress and morbidity: A sociological investigation of selected categories of working-limiting conditions. J Chronic Dis 24:453–468, 1971.

28. Selected Health Characteristics by Occupation, U.S. July 1961–June 1963. National Health Center for Health Statistics, Series 10 21:1–16, 1965.

29. Abramson JH: Emotional disorder, status inconsistency and migration. Milbank Mem Fund Q 44:23–48, 1966.

30. Schwab JJ, Holzer CE III, Warheit GJ: Depression scores by race, sex, age, family income, education and socioeconomic status. (Personal communication, 1974).

31. Srole L, Langner T, Michael S, et al: Mental Health in the Metropolis: the Midtown Study. New York, McGraw-Hill, 1962.

32. Jackson EF: Status consistency and symptoms of stress. Am Sociol Rev 27:469–480, 1962.

33. Hollingshead AB, Redlich FC: Social Class and Mental Illness. New York, John Wiley and Sons Inc. 1958.

34. Gurin G, Veroff J, Feld S: Americans View Their Mental Health. New York, Basic Books Inc. 1960.

35. Langner TS: Psychophysiological symptoms and the status of women in two Mexican communities. *In:* Approaches to Cross-cultural Psychiatry. Edited by AH Leighton, JM Murphy. Ithaca, Cornell University Press, 1965. pp 360–392.

36. Syme SL, Oakes T, Friedman G, et al: Social class and racial differences in blood pressure. Am J Public Health 64:619–620, 1974.

37. Oakes TW, Syme SL: Social factors in newly discovered elevated blood pressure. J Health Soc Behav 14:198–204, 1973.

38. Fink R, Shapiro S, Hyman MD, et al: Health status of poverty and non-poverty groups in multiphasic health testing. Presented at the Annual Meeting of the American Public Health Association, November 1972.

39. Lipworth L, Abelin T, Connelly RR: Socioeconomic factors in the prognosis of cancer patients. J Chronic Dis 23:105–116, 1970.

40. Hochstim JR: Health and ways of living. *In:* Social Surveys. The Commmunity as an Epidemiological Laboratory. Edited by I Kessler, M Levine. Baltimore, Johns Hopkins Press, 1970, pp 149–176.

41. Winkelstein W Jr, Kantor S, Davis EW, et al: The relationship of air pollution and economic status to total mortality and selected respiratory system mortality in men. I. Suspended particulates. Arch Environ Health 14:162–171, 1967.

42. Booth A: Preliminary Report: Urban Crowding Project. Canada, Ministry of State for Urban Affairs, August 1974 (mimeographed).

43. Syme SL, Hyman MM, Enterline PE: Some social and cultural factors associated with the occurrence of coronary heart disease. J Chronic Dis 17:277–289, 1964.

44. Tyroler HA, Cassel J: Health consequences of cultural change. II. The effect of urbanization on coronary heart mortality in rural residents. J Chronic Dis 17:167–177, 1964.

45. Nesser WB, Tyroler HA, Cassel JC: Social disorganization and stroke mortality in the black populations of North Carolina. Am J Epidemiol 93:166–175, 1971.

46. Shekelle RB, Osterfeld AM, Paul O: Social status and incidence of coronary heart disease. J Chronic Dis 22:381–394, 1969.

47. Haenszel W, Loveland DB, Sirken N: Lung-cancer mortality as related to residence and smoking histories. I. White males. J Natl Cancer Inst 28:947–1001, 1962.

48. Nuckolls KB, Cassel J, Kaplan BH: Psychosocial assets, life crisis, and the prognosis of pregnancy. Am J Epidemiol 95:431–441, 1972.

49. Gorusch RL, Key MK: Abnormalities of pregnancy as a function of anxiety and life stress. Psychosom Med 36:352–362, 1974.

50. Terris M, Chaves AD: An epidemiologic study of sarcoidosis. Am Rev Respir Dis 94:50–55, 1966.

51. Rahe RH, Gunderson EKE, Arthur RJ: Demographic and psychosocial factors in acute illness reporting. J Chronic Dis 23:245–255, 1970.

52. Wyler AR, Masuda M, Holmes TH: Magnitude of life events and seriousness of illness. Psychosom Med 33:115–122, 1971.

53. Rahe RH, Rubin RT, Gunderson EKE, et al: Psychological correlates of serum cholesterol in man: A longitudinal study. Psychosom Med 33:399–410, 1971.

54. Spilken AZ, Jacobs MA: Prediction of illness behavior from measures of life crisis, manifest distress and maladaptive coping. Psychosom Med 33:251–264, 1971.

55. Jacobs MA, Spilken AZ, Martin MA, et al: Life stress and respiratory illness. Psychosom Med 32:233–242, 1970.

56. Kasl SV, Cobb S: Blood pressure changes in men undergoing job loss; A preliminary report. Psychosom Med 32:19–38, 1970.

57. Hinkle LE, Wolff HG: Ecological investigations of the relationship between illness, life experiences,

and the social environment. Ann Intern Med 49:1373–1388, 1958.

58. US Dept of Health, Education, and Welfare: The Health Consequences of Smoking. National Communicable Disease Center, Publication No 74-8704, 1974.

59. US Public Health Service, Division of Chronic Diseases: Obesity and Health. A Source Book of Current Information for Professional Health Personnel. Publication No 1485. Washington DC, US GPO, 1966.

60. Build and Blood Pressure Study. Chicago, Society of Actuaries, Vol I and II, 1959.

61. Rosenman RH, Brand RH, Jenkins CD, et al: Coronary heart disease in the Western collaborative group study: Final follow-up experience of 8½ years. (Manuscript).

62. Dohrenwend BS (ed): Stressful Life Events: Their Nature and Effects. New York, Wiley-Interscience, 1974.

63. US Dept of Health, Education, and Welfare: Adult Use of Tobacco 1970, Publication No HSM-73-8727, 1973.

64. Khosla T, Lowe CR: Obesity and smoking habits by social class. J Prev Soc Med 26:249–256, 1972.

3

Excess Mortality in Harlem

▪ ▪ ▪ ▪ ▪

Colin McCord and Harold P. Freeman

Mortality rates for white and nonwhite Americans have fallen steadily and in parallel since 1930 (Fig. 3-1). Lower rates for nonwhites have been associated with an improved living standard, better education, and better access to health care.[1,2] These improvements, however, have not been evenly distributed. Most health indicators, including mortality rates, are worse in the impoverished areas of this country.[3–9] It is not widely recognized just how much certain inner-city areas lag behind the rest of the United States. We used census data and data from the Bureau of Health Statistics and Analysis of the New York City Health Department to estimate the amount, distribution, and causes of excess mortality in the New York City community of Harlem.

The Community

Harlem is a neighborhood in upper Manhattan just north of Central Park. Its population is 96 percent black and has been predominantly black since before World War I. It was the center of the Harlem Renaissance of black culture in the 1920s, and it continues to be a cultural center for black Americans. The median family income in Harlem, according to the 1980 census, was $6,497, as compared with $16,818 in all New York City, $21,023 in the United States, and $12,674 among all blacks in the United States. The families of 40.8 percent of the people of Harlem had incomes below the government-defined poverty line in 1980. The total population of Harlem fell from 233,000 in 1960 to 121,905 in 1980. In the same 20-year period the death rate from homicide rose from 25.3 to 90.8 per 100,000.

The neighborhood is not economically homogeneous. There is a middle-to-upper-class community of about 25,000 people living in new, private apartment complexes or houses, a less affluent group of 25,000 living in public housing projects, and a third group of about 75,000 who live in substandard housing. Most of the population loss has been in the group living in substandard housing, much of it abandoned or partially occupied buildings.

The pattern of medical care in Harlem is similar to that reported for other poor and black communities.[10,11] As compared with the per capita averages for New York City, the rate of hospital admission is 26 percent higher, the use of emergency rooms is 73 percent higher, the use of hospital outpatient departments is 134 percent higher, and the number of primary care physicians per 1000 people is 74 percent lower.[12]

Methods

Age-adjusted death rates for whites and non-whites were taken from *Vital Statistics of the United States, 1980.*[13] Age-adjusted rates for nonwhites rather than blacks were used in Figure 3-1 because the deaths of blacks were not reported separately before 1970. Age-adjusted mortality rates for blacks in the United States have been slightly higher in recent years than those for all nonwhites (8.4 per 1000 for blacks and 7.7 per 1000 for all nonwhites in 1980). The age-adjusted mortality rates for Harlem in 1960, 1970, and 1980, as well as certain disease-specific death rates, were calculated from data supplied by the New York City Health Department. The U.S. population in 1940 was used as the reference for all the age-adjusted rates in Figure 3-1.

Tapes were provided by the New York City Health Department containing everything but personal identifying information from all death certificates in 1979, 1980, and 1981. Deaths were recorded by age, sex, underlying cause, health-center district, and health area. The Central Harlem Health Center District corresponds to the usual definition of the Harlem community. For our analysis, we calculated age-, sex-, and cause-specific death rates for Harlem using the recorded deaths for 1979, 1980, and 1981 and population data from the 1980 census. New York City determines the underlying cause of death by the methods proposed by the National Center for Health Statistics.[14] We used the diagnostic categories of the ninth revision of the

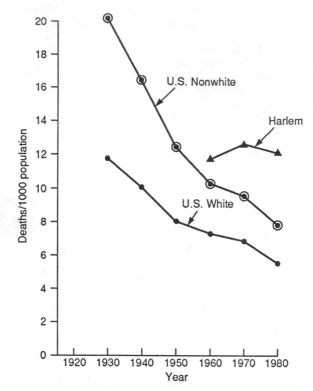

Figure 3-1. *Age-Adjusted Death Rates in Harlem (1960–1980) and the United States (1930–1980)*

International Classification of Diseases.[15] They were generally but not always grouped in the way that the New York City Bureau of Health Statistics and Analysis groups diagnoses in its annual reports of vital statistics according to health areas and health-center districts. For example, "cardiovascular disease" refers to diagnostic categories 390 through 448 in the *International Classification of Diseases,* and "ill defined" refers to categories 780 through 789.

The reference death rates we used to calculate the standardized mortality ratios (SMRs) are those of the white population of the United States, as published in *Vital Statistics of the United States, 1980.*[13] To calculate the SMRs, the total number of observed deaths in 1979, 1980, and 1981 for each age group, sex, and cause was divided by the expected number of deaths, based on the population of each sex and

Figure 3-2. *Survival to the Age of 65 in Harlem, Bangladesh, and among U.S. Whites in 1980*

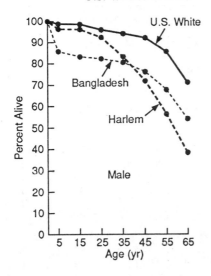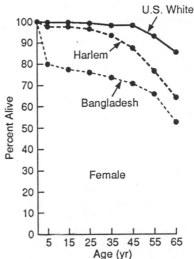

age group and the reference death rate. Using the same methods, we calculated the SMR for deaths under the age of 65 for each health area in the city with a population of more than 3000. New York City has 353 health areas, with an average population of 21,000. Only 11 have a population of less than 3000.

The survival curves in Figure 3-2 were constructed with the use of life tables. The tables for Bangladesh were from a report of the Matlab study area of the International Center for Diarrheal Disease Research,[9] modified from 5-year to 10-year age intervals. Life tables for Harlem were calculated with the same formulas and for the same 10-year intervals. Life tables for the United States are from *Vital Statistics of the United States, 1980.*[13]

Results

Since 1950, when the New York City Health Department began to keep death records according to health-center district, Central Harlem has consistently had the highest infant mortality rate and one of the highest crude death rates in the city. In 1970 and 1980, age-adjusted mortality rates for Harlem residents were the highest in New York City, much worse than the rates for

nonwhites in the United States as a whole, and they had changed little since 1960 (Fig. 3-1). This lack of improvement in the age-adjusted death rate reflected worsening mortality rates for persons between the ages of 15 and 65 that more than offset the drop in mortality among infants and young children (Fig. 3-3).

Figure 3-2 shows the survival curves for male and female residents of Harlem, as compared with those for whites in the United States and those for the residents of an area in rural Bangladesh. Bangladesh is categorized by the World Bank as one of the lowest-income countries in the world. The Matlab demographic-study area is thought to have somewhat lower death rates than Bangladesh as a whole, but the rates are typical for the region. Life expectancy at birth in Matlab was 56.5 years in 1980, as compared with an estimated 49 years for Bangladesh and 57 years for India in 1986.[9,16] For men, the rate of survival beyond the age of 40 is lower in Harlem than Bangladesh. For women, overall survival to the age of 65 is somewhat better in Harlem, but only because the death rate among girls under 5 is very high in Bangladesh.

The SMRs for Harlem (Table 3-1) were high for those of all ages below 75, but they were particularly high for those between 25 and 64 years old and for children under 4. In the three

Figure 3-3. *Age-Specific Death Rates in Harlem from 1960 to 1980**

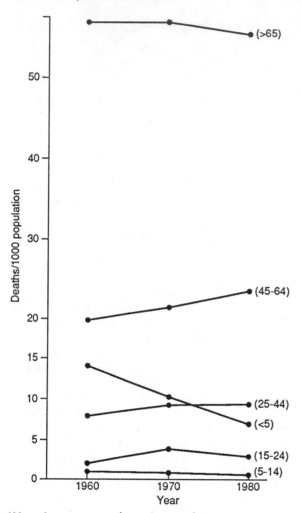

Note: Age groups are shown in parentheses.

Table 3-1. Standardized Mortality Ratios for Harlem, 1979 to 1981*

Age (Yr)	Observed Deaths (No.)	Standardized Mortality Ratio	Annual Excess Deaths†
Male			
0–4	81	2.45	462
5–14	10	1.10	4
15–24	105	2.28	214
25–34	248	5.77	911
35–44	347	5.98	1401
45–54	521	3.28	1824
55–64	783	2.10	2026
65–74	727	1.23	945
≧75	747	1.001	14
Total	3569	1.72	878
Total <65	2095	2.91	948
Female			
0–4	57	2.19	291
5–14	9	1.80	17
15–24	32	1.88	48
25–34	98	6.13	330
35–44	148	4.63	510
45–54	303	3.40	927
55–64	508	2.09	973
65–74	699	1.47	968
≧75	992	0.96	−315
Total	2846	1.47	449
Total <65	1155	2.70	445

*Reference death rates are those for U.S. whites in 1980.
†Per 100,000 population in each age group.

years 1979 to 1981, there were 6415 deaths in Harlem. If the death rate among U.S. whites had applied to this community, there would have been 3994 deaths. Eighty-seven percent of the 2421 excess deaths were of persons under 65.

Table 3-2 compares the numbers of observed and expected deaths among persons under 65, according to the chief underlying causes. A large proportion of the observed excess was directly due to violence and substance abuse, but these causes did not account for most of the excess.

Cirrhosis, homicide, accidents, drug dependency, and alcohol use were considered the most important underlying causes of death in 35 percent of all deaths among people under 65, and in 45 percent of the excess deaths.

For people between the ages of 65 and 74 the SMRs in Harlem were much lower than those for people younger than 65. For residents of Harlem 75 years old or older, overall death rates were essentially the same as those for U.S. whites (Table 3-1). Disease-specific SMRs for people over the age of 65 were below those of younger age groups in almost every category. In several categories (notably cardiovascular disease in Harlem residents 75 or older), they were lower than in whites. This may represent the survival of the fittest in this area of excess mortality.

To estimate the number of people in New York

Table 3-2. Causes of Excess Mortality in Harlem, 1979 to 1981*

Cause	Observed Deaths (No.)	Standard-ized Mortality Ratio	Annual Excess Deaths per 100,000	% of Excess Deaths
Cardiovascu-lar disease	880	2.23	157.5	23.5
Cirrhosis	410	10.49	120.4	17.9
Homicide	332	14.24	100.2	14.9
Neoplasm	604	1.77	84.9	12.6
Drug dependency	153	283.1	49.5	7.4
Diabetes	94	5.43	24.9	3.7
Alcohol use	73	11.33	21.6	3.2
Pneumonia and influenza	78	5.07	20.3	3.0
Disorders in newborns	64	7.24	17.9	2.7
Infection	65	5.60	17.3	2.6
Accident	155	1.17	7.2	1.1
Ill defined	44	2.07	7.4	1.1
Renal	26	4.54	6.6	0.9
Chronic ob-structive pulmonary disease	35	1.29	2.6	0.4
Congenital anomalies	23	1.21	1.3	0.2
Suicide	33	0.81	−2.5	—
All other	181	3.13	40.0	6.0
All causes	3250	2.75	671.2	100.0

*The calculations are based on the deaths of all persons—male and female—under the age of 65. The reference death rates are those for U.S. whites in 1980.

City whose mortality rates were similar to those of people in Harlem, SMRs for persons under the age of 65 were calculated for each of New York's 342 health areas with populations over 3000. There were 54 areas with SMRs of 2.0 or higher for persons under the age of 65. This means that these 54 health areas had at least twice the expected number of deaths (Fig. 3-4). The total population of these high-risk areas was 650,000. In 53 of them more than half the population was black or Hispanic. There was much more variation in the SMRs of the health areas predomi-nantly inhabited by members of minority groups than in the areas that were less than half nonwhite (Fig. 3-4). White areas were relatively narrowly clustered around a mean SMR of 0.97. The SMRs for predominantly black or Hispanic health areas ranged from 0.59 to 3.95, with a mean of 1.77. The SMRs for the 10 health areas in Harlem ranged from 2.16 to 3.95.

It is believed that recent U.S. censuses have undercounted blacks and other minority groups, particularly young men. This would lead to an increase in the age-specific mortality rates used to calculate life tables and SMRs. The Bureau of the Census has estimated the scale of undercounting in various ways—the highest figure is 19 percent for black men in the 25-to-34-year-old group.[17] Because the absolute amount of the observed excess mortality in Harlem is so great, recalcula-tion has little effect on the data presented here, but for the calculations required for Figure 3-3 and Tables 3-1 and 3-2 we increased the 1980 census population in each sex and age group by an amount conforming to the largest Census Bureau estimate of the undercounting. This produced a slight increase in the percentage shown to be still living at the age of 65 in Figure 3-2 and a slight reduction in the SMRs in Tables 3-1 and 3-2. (With this correction the SMR for male residents under the age of 65 was 2.91 rather than 3.15.)

Discussion

An improvement in child mortality in Harlem between 1960 and 1980 was accompanied by rising mortality rates for persons between the ages of 25 and 65. There was therefore no improvement in overall age-adjusted mortality. Death rates for those between the ages of 5 and 65 were worse in Harlem than in Bangladesh.

We have not attempted to calculate SMRs since 1981, because the 1980 census is the most recent reliable estimate of the population of New York City, but all available evidence indicates that there has been very little change since then. The total number of deaths in Harlem from 1985 through 1987 was 1.6 percent higher than from 1979 through 1981. According to the New York City Planning Department, the decline in Har-

Figure 3-4. *Standardized Mortality Ratios for Persons under 65 in 342 Health Areas in New York City, 1979 to 1981**

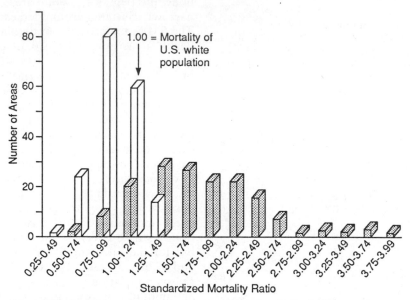

*Note: The shaded bars denote communities more than half of whose residents are nonwhite, and the open bars communities that are half or more white. Bars to the right of the arrow represent communities in which the mortality of persons under the age of 65 was higher than that of U.S. whites.

lem's population stopped in 1980 and the total population has been growing at the rate of 1 percent per year since then.[18] If this estimate is accepted, there has been a slight drop in the crude death rate for Harlem since 1980, but not large enough to affect any of our conclusions. Since 1980 the number of deaths of persons 25 to 44 years of age has increased considerably (31 percent), and the acquired immunodeficiency syndrome (AIDS) has become the most common cause of death in this age group in Harlem and in all New York City. The number of deaths from AIDS is expected to continue to rise.

The situation in Harlem is extreme, but it is not an isolated phenomenon. We identified 54 health areas (of 353) in New York City, with a total population of 650,000, in which there were more than twice as many deaths among people under the age of 65 as would be expected if the death rates of U.S. whites applied. All but one of these health areas have populations more than half composed of minority members. These are

areas that were left behind when the minority population of the city as a whole experienced the same improvement in life expectancy that was seen in the rest of the United States.[19] Similar pockets of high mortality have been described in other U.S. cities.[3,20] Jenkins et al. calculated SMRs for all deaths in Roxbury and adjacent areas of Boston that were almost as high in 1972–1973 as those reported here.[20] This area of highest mortality in Boston was the area with the highest proportion of minority groups.

It will be useful to know more about the circumstances surrounding premature deaths in high-risk communities to determine the relative importance of contributing factors such as poverty, inadequate housing, psychological stress, substance abuse, malnutrition, and inadequate access to medical care. But action to correct the appalling health conditions reflected in these statistics need not wait for more research. The essential first steps are to identify these pockets of high mortality and to recognize the urgent severity of the problem. Widespread poverty and inadequate housing are obvious in Harlem and demand a direct attack wherever they are present. The most important health investigations will be those designed to evaluate the effectiveness of measures to prevent and treat the causes of death already identified. The SMR for persons under 65 years of age may be a useful tool both to identify the high-mortality areas and to monitor the effect of measures to reduce mortality. This ratio is simpler to calculate than the years of productive life lost,[6] and the information obtained is similar.

Those responsible for implementing health programs must face the reality of high death rates in Harlem and the enormous burden of disease that requires treatment in the existing facilities. The health care system is overloaded with such treatment and is poorly structured to support preventive measures, detect disease early, and care for adults with chronic problems. At the same time, the population at highest risk has limited contact with the health care system except in emergencies. Brudny and Dobkyn reported that 83 percent of 181 patients discharged from Harlem Hospital with tuberculosis in 1988 were lost to follow-up and did not continue treatment.[21] New approaches must be developed to take preventive and therapeutic measures out of the hospitals, clinics, and emergency rooms and deliver them to the population at highest risk.

Intensive educational campaigns to improve nutrition and reduce the use of alcohol, drugs, and tobacco are needed and should be directed at children and adolescents, since habits are formed early and the death rates begin to rise immediately after adolescence. Education will have little effect unless it is combined with access to adequate incomes, useful employment, and decent housing for these children and their parents. Education can help in controlling epidemic drug use and associated crime only if it is combined with effective and coordinated police and public action. AIDS in Harlem is largely related to intravenous drug use and is not likely to be controlled until drugs are controlled, but effective education about this disease is also urgently needed.

Knowledge of the history of previous efforts to improve health in Harlem does not lead to optimism about the future. The Harlem Health Task Force was formed in 1976 because Harlem and the Carter administration recognized that death rates were high. An improved system of clinics, more drug-treatment centers, and active community-outreach programs were recommended. The recommendations have been implemented to varying degrees, but funding has been limited. The preventive and curative health care system is essentially unchanged today. Drug use has increased, and the proportion of the population receiving public assistance has increased. There has been no decrease in the death rates.

In 1977 Jenkins et al. pointed out that the number of excess deaths recorded each year in the areas of worst health in Boston was considerably larger than the number of deaths in places that the U.S. government had designated as natural-disaster areas. They suggested that these zones of excess mortality be declared disaster areas and that measures be implemented on this basis.[20] No such action was taken then or is planned now. If the high-mortality zones of New York City were designated a disaster area today, 650,000 people would be living in it. A major political and financial commitment will be needed to eradicate the root causes of this high mortality: vicious poverty and inadequate access to the basic health care that is the right of all Americans.

NOTE

We are indebted to Meril Silverstein, Chih Hwa, John Ross, and Elmer Struerning for advice and assistance. The authors alone are responsible for the calculations and conclusions.

REFERENCES

1. Manton KG, Patrick CH, Johnson KW. Health differentials between blacks and whites: recent trends in mortality and morbidity. Milbank Q 1987; 65:Suppl 1:125–99.
2. Davis K, Lillie-Blanton M, Lyons B, Mullan F, Powe N, Rowland D. Health care for black Americans: the public sector role. Milbank Q 1987; 65:Suppl 1:213–47.
3. Kitagawa EM, Hauser PM. Differential mortality in the United States: a study in socioeconomic epidemiology. Cambridge, Mass.: Harvard University Press, 1973.

4. Woolhandler S, Himmelstein DU, Silber R, Bader M, Harnly M, Jones A. Medical care and mortality: racial differences in preventable deaths. Int J Health Serv 1985; 15:1–22.

5. Savage D, Lindenbaum J, Van Ryzin J, Struerning E, Garrett TJ. Race, poverty, and survival in multiple myeloma. Cancer 1984; 54:3085–94.

6. Black/white comparisons of premature mortality for public health program planning—District of Columbia. MMWR 1989; 38:33–7.

7. Freeman HP, Wasfie TJ. Cancer of the breast in poor black women. Cancer 1989; 63:2562–9.

8. Cancer in the economically disadvantaged: a special report prepared by the subcommittee on cancer in the economically disadvantaged. New York: American Cancer Society, 1986.

9. Demographic surveillance system—Matlab. Vital events and migration tables, 1980. Scientific report no. 58. Dhaka, Bangladesh: International Centre for Diarrheal Disease Research, 1982.

10. Davis K, Schoen C. Health and the war on poverty: a ten-year appraisal. Washington, D.C.: Brookings Institution, 1978.

11. Blendon RJ, Aiken LH, Freeman HE, Corey CR. Access to medical care for black and white Americans: a matter of continuing concern. JAMA 1989; 261:278–81.

12. Community health atlas of New York. New York: United Hospital Fund, 1986.

13. Vital statistics of the United States 1980. Hyattsville, Md.: National Center for Health Statistics, 1985. (DHHS publication no. (PHS) 85-1101.)

14. Vital statistics: instructions for classifying the underlying cause of death, 1980. Hyattsville, Md.: National Center for Health Statistics, 1980.

15. The international classification of diseases. 9th revision, clinical modification: ICD-9-CM, 2nd ed. Washington, D.C.: Department of Health and Human Services, 1980. (DHHS publication no. (PHS) 80-1260.)

16. The state of the world's children 1988 (UNICEF). New York: Oxford University Press, 1988.

17. Fay RE, Passel JS, Robinson JG. Coverage of population in the 1980 census. Washington, D.C.: Bureau of the Census, 1988. (Publication no. PHC 80-E4.)

18. Community district needs, 1989. New York: Department of City Planning, 1987. (DCP publication no. 87-10.)

19. Summary of vital statistics, 1986. New York: Bureau of Health Statistics and Analysis, 1986.

20. Jenkins CD, Tuthill RW, Tannenbaum SI, Kirby CR. Zones of excess mortality in Massachusetts. N Engl J Med 1977; 296:1354–6.

21. Brudny K, Dobkyn J. Poor compliance is the major obstacle in controlling the HIV-associated tuberculosis outbreak. Presented at the Fifth International Conference on Acquired Immune Deficiency Syndrome, Montreal, June 8, 1989.

4

What Do We Know about Causes of Sex Differences in Mortality? A Review of the Literature

▪ ▪ ▪ ▪ ▪ ▪

Ingrid Waldron

Women live longer than men in all contemporary economically developed countries. For example, in the United States in 1986, female life expectancy was seven years longer than male life expectancy. Females' greater life expectancy reflects lower mortality for females than for males at all ages. Females' greater longevity has substantial social implications. For example, in the United States there are almost twice as many women as men over the age of 75, and women are substantially more likely than men to be widowed.

Sex differences in life expectancy have varied historically and cross-culturally. In general, females' longevity advantage was much smaller in the early twentieth century, and females' longevity advantage continues to be small in most contemporary developing countries. Indeed, in some contemporary developing countries, males have a greater life expectancy than females. For example, in India in 1970–72, male life expectancy was almost three years longer than female life expectancy.

What causes are responsible for these varying sex differences in longevity and mortality? This question is addressed in the paper that follows. The evidence presented indicates that sex differences in mortality are influenced by a wide variety of environmental and genetic factors. Sex differences in behavior have been one major cause of sex differences in mortality, and cultural influences on behavior have been a major cause of historical and cross-cultural variation in sex differences in mortality.

Introduction

The present paper reviews current evidence concerning the causes of sex differences in mortality. One useful approach to the topic has been to identify major causes of death that contribute to sex differences in total mortality and then to identify factors that contribute to sex differences for those causes of death. Results of that approach are summarized in the first section of the present review. The second section ... discusses several general issues and hypotheses concerning the causes of sex differences in mortality, together with relevant evidence.

The evidence to be presented shows that a wide variety of factors influence sex differences in mortality. Genetic factors of relevance include effects of inherent sex differences in reproductive anatomy and physiology, effects of

sex hormones, and effects of X-chromosome linked genes. Environmental factors of importance include cultural influences on sex differences in risky behavior, such as cigarette smoking, and cultural influences that determine sex differences in access to resources, such as nutrition and health care. Additional environmental factors of importance include technological and economic changes that have decreased or increased mortality risks to which either males or females are particularly vulnerable. Those varied factors have interacting effects on sex differences in mortality and the importance of any given factor varies considerably in different situations. . . .

Causes of Sex Differences for Major Causes of Death

The present section reviews factors that influence sex differences in mortality for infectious and parasitic diseases, accidents and other violence, ischemic heart disease, and malignant neoplasms. The contribution of each of those categories to sex differences in total mortality varies depending on age and historical and cultural conditions, but each is of major importance in some cases.

Infectious and Parasitic Diseases

Males tend to have higher death rates than females for infectious and parasitic diseases, particularly for ages above 30 (see [Figure 4-1]; see also Holzer and Mijakowska, 1983; Preston, 1976; United Nations 1982). For the age range 1–30, reversals of that sex difference, with higher infectious and parasitic disease death rates for females, have been fairly common. . . .

Males' generally greater susceptibility to infectious disease mortality may be due in part to genetic factors (Waldron, 1983a). . . .

An environmental factor that appears to influence sex differences in infectious disease mortality in some cases is differential access to nutrition and health care. For example, in parts of South Asia and Algeria and according to some historical data from Europe, girls have had higher death

Figure 4-1. *Sex Mortality Ratios by Age for Total Mortality and Several Major Causes of Death, Selected Developed and Developing Countries*

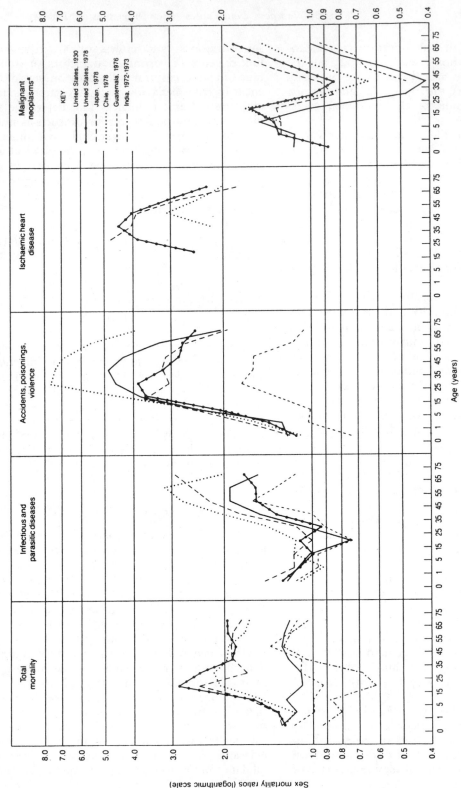

SOURCES: Graphs adapted from Ingrid Waldron, "Sex differences in human mortality: the role of genetic factors", *Social Science and Medicine*, vol. 17, No. 6 (1983); based on data from World Health Organization, *World Health Statistics Annual: Vital Statistics and Causes of Death*, for 1977, 1980 and 1981 (Geneva); National Academy of Sciences, National Research Council, Committee on Population and Demography, Panel on India, *Vital Rates in India, 1961–1981*, Report No. 24 (Washington, D.C., National Academy Press, 1984); Samuel H. Preston, Nathan Keyfitz, and Robert Schoen, *Causes of Death: Life Tables for National Populations* (Seminar Press, New York, 1972).

NOTE: Sex mortality ratios are the ratios of male-to-female death rates. Age groups with less than 100 deaths for a particular cause in a particular country have been excluded. For India, reliable death rates by cause of death were not available, so data are given only for total mortality.

[a]Data for the United States for 1920 include benign neoplasms and those of unspecified nature.

rates for infectious diseases than boys, and that appears to have been due in large part to less adequate nutrition and health care for girls than for boys (Chen and others, 1981; D'Souza and Chen, 1980; Johansson 1980; Miller, 1981; Tabutin, 1978; Vallin, 1983). . . .

In summary, sex differences in infectious disease mortality are influenced by cultural factors, such as differential access of males and females to food and medical care, and probably also by genetic factors, such as X-linked differences in levels of one major type of immunoglobulin.

Fatal Accidents and Other Violent Deaths

Death rates for accidents and other violent causes have been higher for males than for females in almost all available historical and international data, although the magnitude of the male excess has varied considerably (see the figure; Lopez and Ruzicka, 1983; Preston, 1976). Analyses of data for the United States of America and other Western countries have shown that a variety of sex differences in behavior contributes to men's higher mortality due to accidents and other violence.

In the United States, men drive more than women and men have more fatal accidents per mile driven, and both factors appear to contribute to men's higher death rates for motor vehicle accidents (Veevers, 1982; Waldron, 1976, 1982a). Men's higher rates of fatal accidents per mile driven suggest that they drive less safely, and that has been confirmed by observational studies showing that men tend to drive faster and less cautiously than women and men more often violate traffic regulations.

For accidents other than motor vehicle accidents, a major cause of men's higher rates (at least in the United States) is accidents on the job (Waldron, 1976, 1980, 1982a). Men have more work accidents than women because more men are employed and because the jobs men hold are more physically hazardous on the average. United States data also indicate that males have much higher rates than females for accidental drownings and fatal gun accidents.

Men's greater use of guns appears to contribute to their higher suicide rates (Waldron, 1976). In suicidal behavior, men more often use guns and women more often use drugs. Since guns are more lethal than drugs, that contributes to men's higher suicide rates and women's higher rates of non-fatal suicide attempts. However, sex differences in suicide methods are not the only factor that contributes to sex differences in suicide rates, since men have higher suicide rates for each method and, also, men have higher suicide rates even in a population where males and females used similar suicide methods (Alexander and others, 1982; Waldron, 1976). One factor that may be important is that women may more often use a suicide attempt as a desperate, last-ditch plea for help, while men, who feel more pressure to be strong, may be less willing to plead for help and more likely to carry a suicidal act through to a fatal conclusion (Waldron, 1976).

Heavier alcohol consumption among men is another cause of their higher rates of fatal accidents and other violent deaths (Ferrence, 1980; Hetzel, 1983; Waldron, 1976, 1982). In Western countries, male drivers are considerably more likely than female drivers to have high blood-alcohol levels, and drunken drivers are responsible for roughly one quarter to one half of fatal auto accidents, including those in which the driver him- or herself is killed. (Men's heavier consumption of alcohol is also the major cause of men's higher rates of cirrhosis of the liver, at least in Western countries.)

Much of the behavior that contributes to men's higher rates of fatal accidents and other violent deaths has been more socially accepted or expected of males than of females. Use of guns, drinking alcohol, taking risks physically and working at sometimes hazardous jobs have all been more expected of males than of females in Western societies as well as in many nonWestern societies (Waldron, 1976, 1982a). Even in infancy sex differences in relevant types of behavior are expected and encouraged. For example, experiments have shown that babies presented as boys were encouraged to be more physically active than the same babies presented as girls (Honig, 1983). Differential socialization of boys and girls is widespread cross-culturally, and those cultural influences appear to be an important reason for the sex differences in behavior that contribute to males' higher rates of fatal accidents and other violent deaths (Waldron, 1976, 1983a).

Another hypothesis is that male sex hormones may predispose males to higher levels of physical activity and physical aggressiveness (Hines, 1982; Schiavi and others, 1984; Waldron, 1983a). Although some of the available evidence supports that hypothesis, inconsistent results and methodological problems prevent any definite conclusions. A related hypothesis has been that the Y chromosome contributes to increased aggression. That hypothesis has been tested in studies that have compared males who have the normal XY genotype with males who have either XYY or XXY genotypes. Findings from those studies do not support the hypothesis that an extra Y chromosome specifically contributes to greater aggressiveness, but rather suggest that defects resulting from an extra chromosome may contribute to deviance.

The observation that mortality due to accidents and other violent causes is higher for males in almost all available data, together with the observation that related sex differences in behavior are very widespread cross-culturally, has suggested that there may be a genetic basis for those sex differences in behavior. However, it is possible that the contribution of genetic factors is a rather indirect one—namely, that inherent sex differences in reproductive function have influenced the cultural evolution of sex roles, including sex differences in risk-taking behavior (Waldron, 1983a). Specifically, it appears that because only women can bear and nurse children, women have been assigned the primary responsibility for the care of babies and young children in all or almost all cultures. Probably as a consequence, dangerous tasks and other tasks that are incompatible with child care have been assigned primarily to men. Related to those widespread differences in adult sex roles, there are differences in the socialization of boys and girls which are widespread cross-culturally and which prepare boys to participate in the more hazardous activities typically associated with the male role. Thus, inherent sex differences in reproductive function appear to have influenced the cultural evolution of sex roles, and the cultural environment in turn fosters behaviors, in males which contribute to their higher rates of fatal accidents and other violent deaths.

Ischemic Heart Disease

Death rates for ischemic heart disease (previously called coronary heart disease) have consistently been higher for men than for women in almost all available international and historical mortality data (see [Figure 4-1]; Johansson and others, 1983; Lopez 1983). Because ischemic heart disease is such a major cause of death in Western countries, the substantial male excess for ischemic heart disease is, on the average, responsible for about one third of the sex difference in adult mortality. However, the magnitude of the sex difference for ischemic heart disease has varied considerably in different regions, historical periods and ethnic groups.

One major reason why death rates for ischemic heart disease are higher for men than for women is that more men than women smoke cigarettes and, among smokers, men generally have more hazardous smoking habits than women (United States Department of Health and Human Services, 1980; Waldron, 1983a). . . . The importance of the sex differences in cigarette-smoking habits is indicated by the observation that sex differences in ischemic heart disease mortality are considerably lower among non-smokers than among the general population (Waldron, 1976, 1982a). Data for the United States suggest that, depending on the age range, approximately one-quarter to three-fifths of the sex difference in ischemic heart disease mortality may be related to cigarette smoking.

Sex differences in cigarette smoking habits are very widespread cross-culturally. Surveys have shown that more men than women smoke cigarettes in Western and Eastern Europe, the United States, Australia, New Zealand, Jerusalem, Latin America, the Far East, South Asia, and the Pacific Islands (Anon., 1982; Benjamin, 1982; Finau and others, 1982; Joly, 1975; LeMeitour-Kaplan, 1977; Miller and Ashcroft, 1971; Pool, 1983; United States Department of Health and Human Services, 1980; Waldron, 1983a). A greater prevalence of cigarette smoking among men has been observed in both urban and rural areas. A few exceptions to the pattern have been observed, for teenagers in the United States and Western Europe in recent years and among the Maoris in New Zealand. Nevertheless, it is clear that a greater prevalence of cigarette smoking among men has been widespread cross-culturally and historically. . . .

One important reason for the sex differences in cigarette-smoking habits has been greater social pressure against cigarette smoking by women (Waldron, 1983a). Social pressures against cigarette smoking by women have been reported for areas as diverse as the United States during the early twentieth century and Sri Lanka and several Pacific islands in recent decades. Social pressures against cigarette smoking by women have varied in intensity, and that appears to be a major reason for the considerable variation in the magnitude of sex differences in cigarette smoking in different regions and different historical periods. . . .

Although sex differences in cigarette smoking are a major cause of men's higher rates of ischemic heart disease mortality, other factors must also contribute. Even among non-smokers men have substantially higher rates of ischemic heart disease mortality than women (Doll and others, 1980; Shurtleff, 1974; Waldron, 1976). An additional behavioral factor that may contribute to sex differences in risk of ischemic heart disease is the higher prevalence of hostility and mistrust of others among males than among females (Matthews and others, 1992). In addition, biological differences between the sexes contribute to men's higher ischemic heart disease mortality.

Current evidence indicates that female sex hormones reduce women's risk of ischemic heart disease, in part by reducing LDL cholesterol, a major contributor to ischemic heart disease risk (Kalin and Zumoff, 1990; Waldron, 1995). In contrast, male sex hormones appear to reduce levels of the protective HDL cholesterol, and this may also contribute to the sex difference in ischemic heart disease risk (Bagatell and others, 1992; Waldron, 1995). Sex differences in the distribution of body fat appear to be another important cause of sex differences in ischemic heart disease mortality (Larsson and others, 1992; Waldron, 1995). Men tend to accumulate fat in the upper body (especially the abdomen), whereas women tend to accumulate fat in the lower body (buttocks and thighs). Abdominal body fat has more harmful effects on body physiology than lower body fat, and it appears

that men's greater abdominal body fat may be a major cause of their higher ischemic heart disease mortality. Other biological differences between the sexes, such as men's higher levels of stored iron, may also contribute to men's higher ischemic heart disease mortality (Waldron, 1995).

In conclusion, multiple behavioral and biological factors interact to produce the observed sex differences in ischemic heart disease mortality. Current evidence indicates that men's higher ischemic heart disease mortality is due in large part to men's higher rates of smoking, men's greater abdominal body fat, and protective effects of female sex hormones.

Malignant Neoplasms

Mortality due to malignant neoplasms or cancer is higher for males than for females over most of the age span in many countries (see the figure; United Nations, 1982; Waldron, 1983a). . . . It should be noted that malignant neoplasms constitute a variety of diseases with disparate causes, and thus both the pattern and causes of sex differences vary for different types of malignant neoplasms.

A major cause of men's higher cancer mortality has been the sex differences in cigarette smoking habits described in the previous section. Two studies in the United States have found that for adults who had never smoked regularly there was little or no sex difference in cancer mortality (Enstrom and Godley, 1980; Hammond and Seidman, 1980). In national mortality statistics for the United States, if cancers known to be related to cigarette smoking are excluded, sex differences in cancer mortality are very small (Waldron, 1982a). Lung cancer alone is responsible for approximately three-quarters of men's excess cancer mortality in developed countries, and sex differences in cigarette-smoking habits are the major cause of men's higher lung cancer mortality (Lopez, 1983; Waldron, 1976). (Sex differences in cigarette-smoking habits are also a major cause of men's higher mortality for other diseases of the respiratory system, such as emphysema and bronchitis (Preston, 1970; Waldron, 1976).)

Occupational exposures also contribute to men's higher cancer mortality, including men's higher lung-cancer mortality (Waldron, 1980,

1982a; Walker and others 1983). For example, in the United States many more men than women have been exposed to asbestos occupationally, and it has been estimated that those occupational exposures to asbestos may contribute to one-tenth or more of men's lung-cancer deaths. Men are exposed more than women to a variety of additional occupational carcinogens that have been linked to lung cancer, bladder cancer and a number of other types of cancer. . . .

In addition to those behavioral factors, sex differences in reproductive anatomy and the effects of sex hormones influence the sex differences in cancer mortality (Waldron, 1976, 1983a). . . . Women have a much higher risk of breast cancer than men, and that reflects inherent sex differences in anatomy and physiology. . . .

In summary, sex differences in cancer mortality are influenced by multiple behavioral, anatomical and physiological differences between the sexes. Sex differences in cigarette smoking, as well as in occupational exposures and alcohol consumption, are important factors contributing to higher cancer mortality for men. Sex differences in reproductive anatomy and effects of sex hormones contribute to higher cancer mortality for women, particularly for breast cancer. It appears that in many cases the balance of those multiple effects results in higher cancer mortality for males, but in other cases the balance of effects results in higher cancer mortality for females. . . .

General Issues and Hypotheses

Sex Differences in Illness Incidence and Prognosis

In analyzing the causes of sex differences in mortality, one important question is the extent to which those differences are due to sex differences in incidence of disease (i.e., the probability of developing a disease) or sex differences in prognosis (i.e., the probability of surviving once a person has developed a disease). Considerable data are available concerning that question for various types of cancer and ischemic heart disease in the more developed countries.

For most types of cancer, sex differences in incidence are the primary determinant of sex differences in mortality (Waldron, 1983b). In general, sex differences in prognosis are smaller and less consistent than sex differences in incidence, and sex differences in prognosis appear to make little or no contribution to sex differences in mortality for most types of cancer. Factors such as sex differences in cigarette smoking, alcohol consumption and occupational exposures make substantial contributions to sex differences in cancer incidence, but those factors appear to make much smaller contributions to sex differences in prognosis. One major reason is that prognosis is assessed only for individuals who have already developed a disease and sex differences in behavioral risk factors tend to be much smaller for those who have developed a disease than for the general population.

It has been hypothesized that women may be inclined to notice symptoms earlier and to seek medical care earlier than men, and a shorter lagtime in obtaining medical care might contribute to a better prognosis for women. However, available evidence indicates that men and women do not differ in the lagtime between first noticing symptoms and seeking medical care for various types of cancer (Marshall and others, 1982; Waldron, 1983b). Furthermore, in most cases there do not appear to be sex differences in the stage of cancer at first diagnosis. The apparent absence of sex differences in seeking medical care for cancer is congruent with the absence of consistent or substantial sex differences in prognosis for most types of cancer.

Similar results have been found for those forms of ischemic heart disease than can be diagnosed on the basis of relatively objective criteria (Johansson and others, 1984; Martin and others, 1983; Waldron, 1983b). The incidence of sudden coronary death and myocardial infarction is substantially higher for men than for women, and men have more atherosclerosis of the coronary arteries. In contrast, sex differences in prognosis are generally small and inconsistent in different studies of patients with myocardial infarction or substantial atherosclerosis of the coronary arteries. The lagtime between onset of symptoms of an acute episode of ischemic heart disease and obtaining medical care is at least as long for women as for men. Also, the proportion of myocardial infarctions that have not been recognized and have not been treated medically is as high for women as for men. Thus, it appears that women are not more likely than men to seek prompt medical care, and that is compatible with the absence of any consistent female advantage in prognosis for those forms of ischemic heart disease. . . .

In conclusion, for most types of cancer and ischemic heart disease, sex differences in incidence are the primary determinants of sex differences in mortality. Sex differences in prognosis are smaller and make little or no contribution to the sex differences in mortality. A major reason why sex differences in prognosis are generally smaller than sex differences in incidence is that sex differences in risk factors are generally smaller for those who have already developed a disease (for whom prognosis is assessed) than for the general population (for whom incidence is assessed). Also, current research has found little or no sex difference in seeking prompt medical care for those diseases, so it appears that there is little or no contribution of differential use of medical care to sex differences in prognosis. . . .

Risk-Taking and Preventive Behavior

It has been proposed that in Western countries males are more likely than females to take risks that may injure their health, and females are more likely than males to engage in preventive behaviors designed to preserve and improve their health (Nathanson, 1977; Waldron, 1976). The evidence summarized below indicates that in Western countries males do engage in more risk-taking behaviors of certain types, particularly behaviors that involve physical daring or illegal behavior. However, for other types of risky behavior and for preventive behavior sex differences are variable.

In the United States males engage in more physically risky recreational activities and that is one factor contributing to their higher accident rates (Waldron, 1983b). Men also tend to drive faster and less cautiously than women and men more often drive while under the influence of alcohol, and such risky behavior contributes to men's higher rates of fatal motor vehicle acci-

dents. Evidence of greater risk-taking by men is also provided by the pattern of sex differences in the use of psychoactive substances (Nathanson, 1977; Waldron, 1976, 1983b). More men than women use illegal psychoactive substances and drink alcohol heavily, both of which carry substantial health risks. In contrast, women are more likely than men to use medically prescribed psychotropic drugs.

Cigarette smoking is another type of hazardous substance use which has been more common among men than among women in many different parts of the world, and among smokers men have more risky smoking habits than women. However, recent trends in cigarette smoking suggest that sex differences in the propensity to take risks are not the primary determinant of sex differences in cigarette smoking. Sex differences in cigarette smoking have decreased during the recent period in Western countries at the same time as the dangers of cigarette smoking have become more evident and more widely publicized (LeMeitour-Kaplan, 1977; United States Department of Health and Human Services, 1980; Waldron, 1983b). It appears that the major determinant of sex differences in cigarette smoking has been the changing patterns of social acceptability of cigarette smoking for women, and those patterns appear to have varied independently of knowledge of the health risks involved.

With respect to preventive behavior, sex differences are quite variable depending on the type of behavior and the culture considered. In the United States and Canada women make more use of some types of preventive medical care (Kohn and White, 1976; Nathanson, 1977; Verbrugge, 1982). However, in some European countries more men than women had been immunized within the previous twelve months or had had a physical examination for reasons other than illness, injury or pregnancy. As discussed in the section above, women are not more likely than men to seek early medical care for symptoms of various types of cancer or acute ischemic heart disease. However, in Western countries women do make more frequent visits to physicians than men, and that may result in more effective control of some life-threatening conditions such as hypertension (Apostolides and others, 1980; Verbrugge, 1982; Waldron, 1982a, 1983b).

For other types of preventive behavior, sex differences are also inconsistent (Waldron, 1983b). For example, no consistent sex differences have been found in the use of seat belts. Data for the United States indicate that women more often than men take vitamins, but men get as much (or more) vigorous exercise as women. Thus, the available evidence does not support a general pattern of a greater propensity for males to take risks and for females to engage in preventive behavior. Rather there are varied sex differences in risk-taking and preventive behavior, and those reflect multiple cultural influences on sex differences in specific types of behavior. In addition, there may be an inherent tendency for males to be more active physically which may contribute to the observed patterns.

Sex Roles

There appear to be a number of important links between traditional sex roles and sex differences in mortality. Most of them have been discussed above, but it is useful to summarize briefly the most important points.

One important link between traditional sex roles and sex differences in mortality is the effects of employment on health. More men than women are employed and men's jobs tend to be more hazardous than women's jobs (data for the United States in Waldron, 1976, 1980, 1982a). Men's greater exposure to occupational carcinogens contributes to their higher rates of lung cancer and bladder cancer. Accidents on the job are an important cause of men's higher accident rates. It appears likely that sex differences in exposure to accidents on the job were particularly important in the early twentieth century when jobs were probably more hazardous and accidents and other violence were responsible for about half of the sex difference in life expectancy in the United States (Retherford, 1975).

Recently there has been considerable interest in the question of whether the increased employment of women in Western countries will lead to increased mortality for women. Current evidence for the United States suggests that, on the average, women's jobs are less hazardous than men's jobs and consequently employment has had less harmful effects on women's health than on men's health. Longitudinal data for a United States sample indicate that, on the average, employment had neither harmful nor beneficial effects on the general health of married, middle-aged women (Waldron and others, 1982). . . .

Genetic and Environmental Influences on Sex Differences in Mortality

Evidence presented in previous sections indicates a number of genetic factors that influence sex differences in mortality. Inherent sex differences in reproductive anatomy and physiology are responsible for women's higher rates of maternal mortality and breast cancer. Effects of endogenous sex hormones may reduce women's risk of ischemic heart disease. Effects of X chromosome-linked genes may contribute to greater resistance to infectious diseases for females. In addition, males are more vulnerable to X-linked recessive disorders, although that appears to make only a minor contribution to male excess mortality (Waldron, 1976, 1983a).

Evidence presented in previous sections also indicates several environmental factors that influence sex differences in mortality. For example, cultural influences on sex differences in cigarette smoking and alcohol consumption make a major contribution to excess male mortality in more developed countries. Culturally influenced behavior has also resulted in less adequate nutrition and health care for females in some cases that in turn has contributed to excess female mortality.

Culturally influenced behavioral effects can reinforce or counteract inherent sex differences in risk. For example, in many countries sex differences in cigarette smoking have reinforced the apparent protective effects of endogenous female sex hormones with respect to ischemic heart disease. In contrast, in some regions greater access of males to food and health care appears to have counteracted any inherent disadvantage males may have with respect to resistance to infectious diseases.

Another type of interaction between environmental and genetic factors is that environmental factors influence the levels of mortality for causes of death with an inherent sex bias. One example is that improved health care has contributed to a decline in maternal mortality and that has been one factor responsible for the growing mortality advantage for females relative to males at young adult ages. . . .

This example illustrates the important point that the impact of a given genetic factor on sex differences in mortality varies considerably depending on environmental conditions. Thus it can be seen that any estimate of the relative contributions of genetic and environmental factors to sex differences in mortality will apply only for the specific conditions studied and cannot be extrapolated to other conditions.

Numerous additional methodological difficulties have been encountered in attempts to estimate the relative contributions of genetic and environmental factors to sex differences in mortality (Waldron, 1983a). For example, Madigan (1957) attempted to estimate the contribution of genetic factors by studying a group for whom he argued there was little sex difference in environment or social roles—namely, Roman Catholic brothers and sisters engaged in educational work. However, a variety of evidence indicates that there may have been important environmental differences—for example, a more widespread prohibition of smoking for the sisters. Consequently the study does not provide an adequate basis for estimating the relative contributions of genetic and environmental factors to sex differences in mortality (Waldron, 1983a).

Another line of argument has been that the "universality" of male excess mortality among humans, non-human primates and other animals indicates that male excess mortality is due primarily to a fundamental biological difference between the sexes (Mitchell, 1979). Several lines of evidence argue against that hypothesis. A male mortality disadvantage is by no means universal, since excess female mortality has frequently been observed for humans and for many non-human animals (Lopez and Ruzicka, 1983). Also, the history of human sex differences in mortality suggests a lack of continuity between any male mortality disadvantage observed for non-human primates and the male mortality disadvantage for contemporary humans. Data for Europe indicate that from the Paleolithic through the Middle Ages, women generally had higher mortality than men and

only in more recent times has it become common for men to have higher mortality than women (Waldron, 1983a). Thus, it appears unlikely that there is any direct link between any general biological disadvantage for males that may be observed in other animals and the contemporary male mortality disadvantage observed for humans. Indeed, the rather rapid historical variations in sex differences in mortality indicate the importance of environmental influences on sex differences in mortality.

In conclusion, there is clear evidence that a variety of genetic and environmental factors influence sex differences in mortality, and that there are important interactions between those genetic and environmental factors. Due to methodological problems, it has not been possible to make quantitative estimates of the relative importance of genetic and environmental factors in determining sex differences in mortality. . . .

Conclusion

The evidence presented demonstrates that a considerable variety of environmental and genetic factors influence sex differences in mortality, and the relative importance of particular factors varies greatly in different situations. For example, cultural influences on behavior appear to make a major contribution to sex differences in mortality in most circumstances, but the specific cultural influences of importance vary in different countries and different historical periods. In industrial societies, the most important cultural influences have been social pressures that have encouraged men more than women to smoke cigarettes, to drink heavily, to work in hazardous occupations and to engage in certain other risky behavior. In some preindustrial societies, it appears that cultural practices that result in less adequate nutrition and health care for females have been a major factor contributing to higher mortality for girls and young women than for boys and young men.

The relative importance of specific genetic factors also varies depending on the situation. Under conditions of inadequate health care and nutrition, women's inherent vulnerability to maternal mortality can make a substantial contribution to excess female mortality at reproductive ages. In industrial societies maternal mortality is relatively unimportant, and the most important genetic contribution may be a protective effect of women's endogenous sex hormones, which may reduce women's risk of ischemic heart disease.

Historical trends and cross-cultural variations in sex differences in mortality have been linked to a variety of environmental causes. For example, the increasing male mortality disadvantage in industrial countries in the twentieth century was due in large part to the widespread introduction of cigarettes, which, in combination with greater social acceptance of men's smoking, contributed to increasing ischemic heart disease and lung cancer mortality for males. In addition, improvements in the quality of medical care and general standard of living contributed to decreases in mortality for several causes of death with a female excess and increases in the relative importance of other causes of death with a male excess. Other causes of historical trends and cross-cultural variation in sex differences in mortality include variation in the extent and impact of discrimination against females and variation in social norms concerning acceptable or desirable male and female behavior (for example, varying social acceptance of women's smoking).[1]

In light of the diversity and complexity demonstrated by current evidence, it is necessary to reject or to qualify several generalizations that have been proposed previously. For example, earlier claims of a universal male mortality excess are countered by the evidence that excess female mortality has been common for children and young adults in less developed countries. Similarly, although historical trends in sex differentials in mortality often show an increasing male mortality disadvantage, in some cases trends toward a decreasing male mortality disadvantage or the emergence of a female mortality disadvantage have been observed. Thus, analyses of the causes of sex differences in mortality and the causes of trends in sex differences in mortality must take those more complex patterns into account.

Several hypotheses concerning the causes of sex differences in mortality in Western countries should also be modified on the basis of current evidence. For example, it has been hypothesized that there is a general tendency for men to take more health risks and for women to engage in more preventive behavior. That generalization may be valid for risk-taking that involves physical daring or illegal behavior, but for other types of risk-taking and for preventive behavior, patterns of sex differences are inconsistent. Another hypothesis has been that in Western countries women use medical care more than men and that may contribute to women's greater longevity. However, for most types of cancer and ischemic heart disease, women delay as long as men in seeking medical care, and there is little or no sex difference in prognosis. That suggests that for those major causes of sex differences in mortality, sex differences in use of curative medicine are small and make a negligible contribution to males' mortality disadvantage. Thus, there is a need to clarify the specific ways in which females' greater use of medical care may contribute to their greater longevity. . . .

This review of the causes of sex differences in mortality has illustrated several important general principles. Mortality is influenced by a wide variety of environmental and genetic factors. One important environmental factor is culture, which influences both the physical resources available and the adoption of behaviors that increase or decrease mortality risk. Of particular importance for understanding sex differences in mortality is the observation that social roles, such as sex roles, influence the adoption of behaviors which, in turn, have substantial effects on mortality risk.

Given the importance of sex roles and associated behaviors, it is of interest to address the question: Will current trends toward more similar roles for women and men result in smaller sex differences in mortality in the future? The answer to this question is unclear. On the one hand, current evidence suggests that employment is not harmful to women's health, on the average. On the other hand, smoking clearly is harmful to health, and the increasing similarity of women's and men's smoking habits has contributed to a recent decrease in females' longevity advantage. In the United States in the last decade, the female longevity advantage has decreased from 7.8 to

7.0 years. Thus, current evidence indicates that if more females adopt the risky behaviors that previously were more widespread among males, then sex differences in mortality will decrease in the future.

NOTE

1. A more complete discussion of the patterns and causes of historical and cross-cultural variation in sex differences in mortality is presented in the original paper.

REFERENCES

Alexander, Greg R. and others (1982), "South Carolina's suicide mortality in the 1970s," *Public Health Reports*, vol. 97, No. 5 (1982). pp. 476–482.

Anon. (1982), "Smoking and health in Asia," *WHO Chronicle*, vol. 36, No. 4, pp. 156–159.

Apostolides, Aristide Y. and others (1980), "Impact of hypertension information on high blood pressure control between 1973 and 1978," *Hypertension*, vol. 2 (1980), pp. 708–713.

Bagatell, Carrie J. and others (1992), "Physiologic testosterone levels in normal men suppress high-density lipoprotein cholesterol levels," *Annals of Internal Medicine*, vol. 116, pp. 967–973.

Benjamin, Bernard (1982), "Smoking and mortality," in Samuel H. Preston, ed., *Biological and Social Aspects of Mortality and the Length of Life* (Liège, Ordina Editions, 1982), pp. 433–445.

Chen, Lincoln C., Emdadul Huq and Stan D'Souza (1981), "Sex bias in the family allocation of food and health care in rural Bangladesh," *Population and Development Review*, vol. 7, No. 1 (March 1981), pp. 55–70.

Doll, Richard and others (1980), "Mortality in relation to smoking," *British Medical Journal*, vol. 280 (5 April 1980), pp. 967–971.

D'Souza, Stan and Lincoln C. Chen (1980), "Sex differentials in mortality in rural Bangladesh," *Population and Development Review*, vol. 6, No. 2 (June 1980), pp. 257–270.

Enstrom, James E. and Frank H. Godley (1980), "Cancer mortality among a representative sample of nonsmokers in the United States during 1966–1968," *Journal of the National Cancer Institute*, vol. 65, No. 5 (November 1980), pp. 1,175–1,183.

Ferrence, Roberta G. (1980), "Sex differences in the prevalence of problem drinking," *Research Advances in Alcohol and Drug Problems*, vol. 5 (1980), pp. 69–124.

Finau, Sitaleki A., John M. Stanhope and Ian A. M.

Prior (1982), "Kava, alcohol and tobacco consumption among Tongans with urbanization," *Social Science and Medicine*, vol. 16 (1982), pp. 35–41.

Hammond, E. Cuyler and Herbert Seidman (1980), "Smoking and cancer in the United States," *Preventive Medicine*, vol. 9 (1980), pp. 169–173.

Hetzel, Basil S. (1983), "Life style factors in sex differentials in mortality in developed countries," in Alan D. Lopez and Lado T. Ruzicka, eds., *op. cit.*, pp. 247–277.

Hines, Melissa (1982), "Prenatal gonadal hormones and sex differences in human behaviour," *Psychological Bulletin*, vol. 92, No. 1 (1982), pp. 56–80.

Holzer, Jerzy Z. and Jadwiga Mijakowska (1983), "Differential mortality of the sexes in the Socialist societies of Eastern Europe," in Alan D. Lopez and Lado T. Ruzicka, *op. cit.*, pp. 121–139.

Honig, Alice Sterling (1983), "Sex role socialization in early childhood," *Young Children* (September 1983), pp. 57–70.

Johansson, Saga, Anders Vedin and Claes Wilhelmsson (1983), "Myocardial infarction in women," *Epidemiologic Reviews*, vol. 5 (1983), pp. 67–95.

—— and others (1984), "Sex differences in preinfarction characteristics and long-term survival among patients with myocardial infarction," *American Journal of Epidemiology*, vol. 119, No. 4 (1984), pp. 610–623.

Johansson, Sheila Ryan (1980), "Sex and death in Victorian England," in M. Vicinus, ed., *A Widening Sphere: Changing Roles of Victorian Women* (Bloomington, Indiana University Press, 1980), pp. 163–181.

Joly, Daniel J. (1975), "Cigarette smoking in Latin America: a survey of eight cities," *Bulletin of the Pan American Health Organization*, vol. 9, No. 4 (1975), pp. 329–344.

Kalin, Marcia F. and Barnett Zumoff (1990), "Sex hormones and coronary disease," *Steroids*, vol. 55, pp. 331–352.

Kohn, R. and K. White, eds. (1976), *Health Care—An International Study: Report of the World Health Organization/International Collaborative Study of Medical Care Utilization* (London, Oxford University Press, 1976).

Larsson, Bo and others (1992), "Is abdominal body fat distribution a major explanation for the sex difference in the incidence of myocardial infarction?" *American Journal of Epidemiology*, vol. 135, pp. 266–273.

LeMeitour-Kaplan, Annette (1977), "Situational analysis: profile of women's smoking habits in continental Western Europe," in J. Steinfeld and others, eds., *Proceedings of the Third World Conference on Smoking and Health-II* (Washington, D.C., United

States Department of Health, Education and Welfare, 1977), pp. 309–327.

Lopez, Alan D. (1983), "The sex mortality differential in developed countries," in Alan D. Lopez and Lado T. Ruzicka, eds., *op. cit.,* pp. 53–120.

—— and Lado T. Ruzicka, eds. (1983), *Sex Differentials in Mortality* (Canberra, Australian National University, Demography Department, 1983).

Madigan, Francis C. (1957), "Are sex mortality differentials biologically caused?" *Milbank Memorial Fund Quarterly,* vol. 35 (1957), pp. 202–223.

Marshall, James R., David I. Gregorio and Debra Walsh (1982), "Sex differences in illness behavior: care seeking among cancer patients," *Journal of Health and Social Behavior,* vol. 23 (1982), pp. 197–204.

Martin, Craig A. and others (1983), "Long-term prognosis after recovery from myocardial infarction," *Circulation,* vol. 68, No. 5 (November 1983), pp. 961–969.

Matthews, Karen A. and others (1992), "Influence of age, sex, and family on Type A and hostile attitudes and behaviors," *Health Psychology,* vol. 11, pp. 317–323.

Miller, Barbara D. (1981), *The Endangered Sex: Neglect of Female Children in Rural North India* (Ithaca, New York, Cornell University Press, 1981).

Miller, G. J. and M. T. Ashcroft (1971), "A community survey of respiratory diseases among East Indian and African adults in Guyana," *Thorax,* vol. 26 (1971), pp. 331–338.

Mitchell, G. (1979), *Behavioral Sex Differences in Nonhuman Primates* (New York, Van Nostrand Reinhold, 1979).

Nathanson, Constance A. (1977), "Sex roles as variables in preventive health behavior," *Journal of Community Health,* vol. 3, No. 2 (1977), pp. 142–155.

Pool, Ian (1983), "Changing patterns of sex differentials in survival: an examination of data for Maoris and Non-Maoris in New Zealand," in Alan D. Lopez and Lado T. Ruzicka, eds., *op. cit.,* pp. 193–219.

Preston, Samuel H. (1970), *Older Male Mortality and Cigarette Smoking* (Berkeley, California, Institute of International Studies, 1970). (Reprinted in 1976 by Greenwood Press, Westport, Connecticut.)

—— (1976), *Mortality Patterns in National Populations* (New York Academic Press, 1976).

Retherford, R. D. (1975), *The Changing Sex Differential in Mortality,* Studies in Population and Urban Demography No. 1. (Westport, Connecticut, Greenwood Press, 1975).

Schiavi, Raul C. and others (1984), "Sex chromosome anomalies, hormones and aggressivity," *Archives of General Psychiatry,* vol. 41, No. 1 (January 1984), pp. 93–99.

Shurtleff, D. (1974), "Some characteristics related to the incidence of cardiovascular disease and death: Framingham Study, 18–year follow up," in W. B. Kannel and T. Gordon, eds., *The Framingham Study,* Section 30 (Washington, D.C., United States Department of Health, Education and Welfare, 1974).

Tabutin, Dominique (1978), "La surmortalité féminine en Europe avant 1940," *Population,* No. 1 (1978), pp. 121–148.

United Nations, Department of International Economic and Social Affairs (1982), *Levels and Trends of Mortality since 1950* (United Nations publication, Sales No. E.81.XIII.3).

United States Department of Health and Human Services (1980), *The Health Consequences of Smoking for Women, A Report of the Surgeon General* (Washington, D.C., United States Government Printing Office, 1980).

Vallin, Jacques (1983), "Sex patterns of mortality," in Alan D. Lopez and Lado T. Ruzicka, eds., *op. cit.,* pp. 443–476.

Veevers, Jean (1982), "Women in the driver's seat: trends in sex differences in driving and death," *Population Research and Policy Review,* vol. 1, No. 2 (May 1982), pp. 171–182.

Verbrugge, Lois (1982), "Sex differentials in health," *Public Health Reports,* vol. 97, No. 5 (1982), pp. 417–437.

Waldron, Ingrid (1976), "Why do women live longer than men?" *Social Science and Medicine,* vol. 10 (1976), pp. 349–362.

—— (1980), "Employment and women's health," *International Journal of Health Services,* vol. 10, No. 3 (1980), pp. 435–454.

—— (1982a), "An analysis of causes of sex differences in mortality and morbidity," in Walter R. Gove and G. R. Carpenter, eds., *The Fundamental Connection between Nature and Nurture* (Lexington, Massachusetts, Lexington Books, 1982), pp. 69–116.

—— (1983a), "Sex differences in human mortality: the role of genetic factors," *Social Science and Medicine,* vol. 17, No. 6 (1983), pp. 321–333.

—— (1983b), "Sex differences in illness incidence, prognosis and mortality: issues and evidence," *Social Science and Medicine,* vol. 17, No. 16 (1983), pp. 1107–1123.

—— and others (1982), "Reciprocal effects of health and labor force participation among women: evidence from two longitudinal studies," *Journal of Occupational Medicine,* vol. 24, No. 2 (February 1982), pp. 126–132.

—— (1993), "Contributions of biological and behavioural factors to changing sex differences in ischemic heart disease mortality," in Alan Lopez and others, eds., *Adult Mortality in Developed Countries: From Description to Explanation* (New York, Oxford University Press, 1982), pp. 161–178.

Walker, Alexander M. and others (1983), "Projections of asbestos-related disease 1980–2009," *Journal of Occupational Medicine,* vol. 25, No. 5 (May 1983), pp. 409–425.

World Health Organization (1980 and 1981), *World Health Statistics Annual,* Vol. I, *Vital Statistics and Causes of Death* (Geneva, 1980 and 1981).

5

A Tale of Two States

▪ ▪ ▪ ▪ ▪ ▪

Victor R. Fuchs

In the western United States there are two contiguous states that enjoy about the same levels of income and medical care and are alike in many other respects, but their levels of health differ enormously. The inhabitants of Utah are among the healthiest individuals in the United States, while the residents of Nevada are at the opposite end of the spectrum. Comparing death rates of white residents in the two states, for example, we find that infant mortality is about 40 percent higher in Nevada. And lest the reader think that the higher rate in Nevada is attributable to the "sinful" atmosphere of Reno and Las Vegas, we should note that infant mortality in the rest of the state is almost exactly the same as it is in these two cities. Rather . . . infant death rates depend critically upon the physical and emotional condition of the mother.

The excess mortality in Nevada drops appreciably for children because, as shall be argued below, differences in life-style account for differences in death rates, and these do not fully emerge until the adult years. As [Table 5–1] indicates, the differential for adult men and women is in the range of 40 to 50 percent until old age, at which point the differential naturally decreases.

The two states are very much alike with respect to income, schooling, degree of urbanization, climate, and many other variables that are frequently thought to be the cause of variations in mortality. (In fact, average family income is actually higher in Nevada than in Utah.) The numbers of physicians and of hospital beds per capita are also similar in the two states.

What, then, explains these huge differences in death rates? The answer almost surely lies in the different life-styles of the residents of the two states. Utah is inhabited primarily by Mormons, whose influence is strong throughout the state. Devout Mormons do not use tobacco or alcohol and in general lead stable, quiet lives. Nevada, on the other hand, is a state with high rates of cigarette and alcohol consumption and very high

Table 5-1. **Excess of Death Rates in Nevada Compared with Utah, Average for 1959–61 and 1966–68**

Age group	Males	Females
< 1	42%	35%
1–19	16%	26%
20–29	44%	42%
30–39	37%	42%
40–49	54%	69%
50–59	38%	28%
60–69	26%	17%
70–79	20%	6%

indexes of marital and geographical instability. The contrast with Utah in these respects is extraordinary.

In 1970, 63 percent of Utah's residents 20 years of age and over had been born in the state; in Nevada the comparable figure was only 10 percent; for persons 35–64 the figures were 64 percent in Utah and 8 percent in Nevada. Not only were more than nine out of ten Nevadans of middle age born elsewhere, but more than 60 percent were not even born in the West.

The contrast in stability is also evident in the response to the 1970 census question about changes in residence. In Nevada only 36 percent of persons 5 years of age and over were then living in the same residence as they had been in 1965; in Utah the comparable figure was 54 percent.

The differences in marital status between the two states are also significant in view of the association between marital status and mortality discussed in the previous section. More than 20 percent of Nevada's males aged 35–64 are single, widowed, divorced, or not living with their spouses. Of those who are married with spouse present, more than one-third had been previously widowed or divorced. In Utah the comparable figures are only half as large.

The impact of alcohol and tobacco can be readily seen in [Table 5–2 in] the comparison of death rates from cirrhosis of the liver and malignant neoplasms of the respiratory system. For both sexes the excess of death rates from these causes in Nevada is very large.

The populations of these two states are, to a considerable extent, self-selected extremes from the continuum of life-styles found in the United States. Nevadans, as has been shown, are pre-

Table 5-2. Excess of Death Rates in Nevada Compared with Utah for Cirrhosis of the Liver and Malignant Neoplasms of the Respiratory System, Average for 1966–68

Age	Males	Females
30–39	590%	443%
40–49	111%	296%
50–59	206%	205%
60–69	117%	227%

dominantly recent immigrants from other areas, many of whom were attracted by the state's permissive mores. The inhabitants of Utah, on the other hand, are evidently willing to remain in a more restricted society. Persons born in Utah who do not find these restrictions acceptable tend to move out of the state.

Summary

This dramatic illustration of large health differentials that are unrelated to income or availability of medical care helps to highlight the [following] themes . . .

1. From the middle of the eighteenth century to the middle of the twentieth century rising incomes resulted in unprecedented improvements in health in the United States and other developing countries.
2. During most of this period medical care (as distinct from public health measures) played an insignificant role in health, but, beginning in the mid-1930s, major therapeutic discoveries made significant contributions independently of the rise in real income.
3. As a result of the changing nature of health problems, rising income is no longer significantly associated with better health, except in the case of infant mortality (primarily post-neonatal mortality)—and even here the relationship is weaker than it used to be.
4. As a result of the wide diffusion of effective medical care, its marginal contribution to health is again small (over the observed range of variation). There is no reason to believe that the major health problems of the average American would be significantly alleviated by increases in the number of hospitals or physicians. This conclusion might be altered, however, as the result of new scientific discoveries. Alternatively, the *marginal* contribution of medical care might become even smaller as a result of such advances.
5. The greatest current potential for improving the health of the American people is to be found in what they do and don't do to and for themselves. Individual decisions about diet, exercise, and smoking are of critical importance, and collective decisions affecting pollution and other aspects of the environment are also relevant.

These conclusions notwithstanding, the demand for medical care is very great and growing rapidly. As René Dubos has acutely observed, "To ward off disease or recover health, men as a rule find it easier to depend on the healers than to attempt the more difficult task of living wisely."[1]

NOTE

1. René Dubos, *The Mirage of Health* (New York: Harper, 1959), p. 110.

Our Sickening Social and Physical Environments

• • • • • •

Over the past two decades, there has been an increase in public awareness and concern about health dangers in the social and physical environments in which we live and work. (See for example, Chavkin, 1984; Coye, 1984; Tesh, 1988.) Workers' struggles for occupational health and safety have resulted in changes not only in the physical and social organization of work, but in popular and scientific ideas about the nature and effect of work on ill health. A growing number of communities, including Love Canal and Three Mile Island, have had to face the physical and psychological consequences— sometimes occurring decades after initial exposure—of toxic and radioactive industrial wastes that have been dumped into water, land, and air supplies. Often, victims of such human-made disasters have become embroiled in prolonged legal and political conflicts over claims for medical and economic assistance (Kliman, Kern, and Kliman, 1982).

There is also growing evidence that the stresses and demands (e.g., situations that make us anxious, angry, or frustrated) of our social environments—both at work and at home—are also factors in disease production (Page and O'Brien, 1973; House, 1981; Levy, 1994). Stress has been found to contribute to the development of a number of chronic diseases, including coronary heart disease, hypertension, and cancer; a number of acute diseases (for example, infections); and a range of psychological disorders (for example, minor and major depression, onset of psychotic episodes) (Kessler and Workman, 1989).

Today's major diseases are often slow-developing, chronic, and incurable disorders. This section explores the relation of chronic diseases to the social and physical environments in which they develop.

In the previous section, we explored the relationship between society and the distribution of disease and death. We saw that in American society diseases are patterned by sociocultural factors, including social class, gender, race, and lifestyle. Here we continue to search for an understanding of the interface between diseases and society by examining the sociological contexts of three serious health disorders in the United States: coronary heart disease, black lung disease, and leukemia.

Social scientists have little difficulty analyzing the social nature of such problems as homicide, suicide, and automobile accidents. Only rarely, however, have they applied sociological perspectives to understanding the causes and prevention of diseases such as cancer or hypertension. The selections in this section share the theme that at least some of these chronic diseases have developed as a result of modern industrialization, and so are deeply connected to the organization and characteristics of social life.

According to the U.S. Department of Health and Human Services, approximately 33 percent of all deaths in 1992 were caused by diseases of the heart and circulatory system (coronary heart disease, hypertension, and stroke), and an additional 24 percent of deaths in 1992 were the result of some form of cancer (National Center for Health Statistics, 1994). These data give us a general picture of the significant impact of chronic disease on our population's health. Chronic diseases generally develop and persist over a long period of time. Their signs often go unnoticed or unidentified until they cause serious damage to the victim's body, and they usually have complex rather than simple or single causes. Medical treatment generally aims to alleviate symptoms, prevent or slow down further organic damage, or minimize physical discomfort, primarily through treatments with medications or surgery. Treatment rather than prevention is the dominant medical approach to these diseases.

Although *prevention* of chronic diseases seems to be the most logical, safe, and perhaps the most moral approach, few financial resources have been devoted in the United States to the elimination of the physical and social causes of chronic health disorders. (To the contrary, the federal government continues to subsidize the tobacco industry in the United States despite the surgeon general's warning that cigarette smoking is the leading cause of death from lung cancer and a major risk factor for other diseases.) The growing recognition of the environmental component in many chronic diseases has led some critics to question the priorities of our current medical care system, as well as the limits of its approach to the treatment, let alone prevention, of these disorders.

For example, Samuel Epstein has argued that the "epidemic" of cancer in the United States is both a medical and social issue, involving as it does a range of political and economic factors including the use of chemicals in manufacturing to increase profits, the economic and political pressures on industry scientists, and the relatively low priority given to cancer prevention research (Epstein, 1979; Patterson, 1989). If many cancers are environmentally produced—and the federal government has estimated that as many as 90 percent may be so—why has medical research and treatment focused on cure rather than prevention (Muir and Sasco, 1991)?

In "Black Lung: The Social Production of Disease," Barbara Ellen Smith describes the controversy that has surrounded the identification of black lung disease as an occupational health hazard among coal miners. Like victims of environmental dumping, workers in sickening occupational environments are frequently faced with political and legal resistance to their claims for medical or economic assistance. The resulting politicization of health hazards and illness has often drawn physicians into struggles in which their expert testimony has been used by industry and government to deny the legitimacy of victims' claims about unsafe living or working conditions. By examining the emergence of black lung disease historically, Smith argues that scientific knowledge about the disease, as well as governmental and industrial policies for protecting and compensating workers, are all products of social and economic changes.

Over the last decade toxic waste has become one of the major environmental issues facing our society. How do we dispose of dangerous materials produced as a by-product of our industrial society? What consequences do these toxic materials have for people's health and welfare? Polluting industries rarely point to the dangers of toxic waste; rather, most problems have been uncovered by community action or government intervention. In the second selection, "Popular Epidemiology: Community Response to Toxic Waste–Induced Disease," Phil Brown presents the case of the leukemia cluster in Woburn, Massachusetts. Brown shows how community initiative—

what he calls "popular epidemiology"—with the aid of scientists uncovered the link between the corporate dumping of toxic wastes, the pollution of the drinking water, and the increase in childhood leukemia. He presents popular epidemiology as one strategy people can use to struggle against forces that create dangerous and sickening environments.

Public health analysts have long known that the physical environment can produce disease, but in recent years evidence has accumulated that the social environment may also produce ill health. For example, studies have shown that the social organization of the work environment (House and Cottington, 1984), social stress (Kasl, 1984) and social support (Cohen and Syme, 1985) can affect health status and outcome. Among the most intriguing work in this area are the studies that show the importance of social relationships to health. There is continuing evidence that individuals with few social relationships are at increased risk for disease (morbidity) and death (mortality). In "Social Relationships and Health," James S. House, Karl R. Landis, and Debra Umberson review the existing research and conclude that a significant causal relationship exists between social relationships and health. They contend the evidence is as strong as that for cigarette smoking and health in 1964, when the surgeon general issued the first report on the dangers of smoking, although the specificity of the associations is not yet as well-known. While we don't really know how social relationships affect health, it is increasingly clear that these factors need to be considered seriously in terms of etiology and prevention. This awareness is especially important because evidence exists that the quantity and quality of social relationships in our society may be declining.

The final selection, "Social Class and Cardiovascular Disease" by Michael Marmot and Tores Theorell, argues that the social organization of the work environment is a significant factor in coronary heart disease. The authors show how the psychosocial environment—especially work stress, "decision latitude," and boring or monotonous work—may affect risk factors and lead to higher rates of coronary heart disease mortality. Using evidence from several industrialized countries, they show how psychosocial working conditions make lower-class workers particularly susceptible to heart disease. This line of research is encouraging in that it allows us to consider how to alter the social organization of work to make it a more health-inducing environment (see also Syme 1986).

REFERENCES

Chavkin, Wendy, ed. 1984. Double Exposure, Women's Health Hazards on the Job and at Home. New York: Monthly Review Press.

Cohen, Sheldon, and S. Leonard Syme. 1985. Social Support and Health. New York: Academic Press.

Coye, Molly Joel, Mark Douglas Smith, and Anthony Mazzochi. 1984. "Occupational health and safety." In Victor W. Sidel and Ruth Sidel, Reforming Medicine, Lessons of the Last Quarter Century. New York: Pantheon.

Epstein, Samuel. 1979. The Politics of Cancer. New York: Anchor/Doubleday.

House, James. 1981. Work Stress and Social Support. Reading, MA: Addison-Wesley.

House, James S., and Eric M. Cottington. 1984. "Health and the workplace." In David Mechanic and Linda H. Aiken (eds.) Applications of Social Science to Clinical Medicine and Health Policy. New Brunswick, NJ: Rutgers University Press.

Kasl, Stanislav. 1984. "Stress and health." Annual Review of Public Health. 5: 319–341.

Kessler, Ronald C., and Cammile B. Wortman. 1989. "Social and psychological factors in health and illness." Pp. 69–86 in Howard Freeman and Sol Levine (eds.), Handbook of Medical Sociology. Englewood Cliffs, NJ: Prentice-Hall.

Kliman, Jodie, Rochelle Kern, and Ann Kliman. 1982. "Natural and human-made disasters: Some therapeutic and epidemiological implications for crisis intervention." In Uri Rueveni, Ross V. Speck, and Joan L. Speck (eds.). Therapeutic Intervention, Healing Strategies for Human Systems. New York: Human Sciences Press.

Levy, Barry (ed.). 1994. Occupational Health: Recognizing and Preventing Work-Related Disease. New York: Little, Brown.

Muir, C. S., and A. J. Sasco. 1991. "Prospects for cancer control in the 1990s." Annual Review of Public Health. 11:143–64.

National Center for Health Statistics. 1994. Health, United States, 1994. Washington, DC: U.S. Government Printing Office.

Page, Joseph, and M. O'Brien. 1973. Bitter Wages. New York: Grossman.

Patterson, James. 1989. The Dread Disease: Cancer and American Culture. Cambridge: Harvard University Press.

Syme, S. Leonard. 1986. "Strategies for health promotion." Preventive Medicine. 15: 492–507.

Tesh, Sylvia. 1988. Hidden Arguments: Political Ideology and Disease Prevention. New Brunswick, NJ: Rutgers University Press.

6

Black Lung: The Social Production of Disease

■ ■ ■ ■ ■ ■

Barbara Ellen Smith

The recognition that certain forms of ill health are socially produced and therefore possibly preventable is one of the most important sources of progressive political vitality in the United States today. During the past decade, sporadic protest has erupted over hazardous situations in isolated workplaces and communities, from the controversy over toxic waste disposal in the Love Canal area to the protest against use of dioxin-contaminated herbicides in the Pacific Northwest. In some instances, more prolonged and widespread struggles have developed, such as the movement for black lung compensation and the current mobilization against nuclear power. These phenomena are admittedly quite diverse in their social bases, ideologies, and political goals. However, to varying degrees, all have involved the politicization of health hazards and illness, and thereby have drawn into the arena of political controversy one of the most elite professional domains in the United States—scientific medicine.

These controversies characteristically have originated in the bitter suspicions of lay people who fear that certain of their health problems are caused by industrial practices and products, but who have no scientifically credible proof to substantiate their concern. In some cases, scientists have scornfully dismissed as "housewife data" lay efforts to document these health problems (1). Indeed, health advocates' demands for compensatory or preventive action have often encountered their most formidable ideological opposition from the ranks of the medical establishment, who come armed with the seemingly unassailable authority of "science" and characteristically argue that no action is justified until further evidence is collected. Especially in contexts like that of the petrochemical industry, where workers and sometimes residential communities are exposed to manifold hazards about which little is known and whose effects may not be manifested for decades, health advocates can be forced into a no-win situation: they must prove their case with data that do not exist, using a model of disease causation that is ill suited to multiple and/or synergistic hazards, and which a growing chorus of critics argue is structurally incapable of explaining the major health problems of our place and time, such as heart disease and stress (2).

This article examines one health struggle, the black lung movement, during which the scientific authority of the medical establishment was itself questioned in the course of an intense political controversy over the definition of disease. The movement arose in southern West Virginia in 1968 and had as its initial goal the extension of workers' compensation coverage to victims of "black lung," a generic term for the ensemble of respiratory diseases that miners contract in the workplace. To elucidate the medical politics of this struggle, this article looks at three aspects of the history of black lung. The first section explores the major changes in medical perceptions of black lung and presents evidence suggesting that these shifting perceptions have been occasioned by social and economic factors ordinarily considered extrinsic to science. This section also points out the ideological and political functions of the medical definitions of this disease. The second part focuses on the history of black lung itself and argues that the respiratory disease burden is intimately related to the political economy of the workplace, the site of disease production. The final section describes the recent battle over black lung compensation, focusing on the strikingly different definitions of disease that miners and the medical establishment elaborated.

Medical Constructions of Black Lung

The history of science is popularly conceived as a continuum of concepts and paradigms evolving through time toward an ever more comprehensive and accurate understanding of a "given" external reality. However, there is a growing tradition of literature that challenges this positivist approach by classifying the scientific knowledge of any society as part of its historically specific belief systems, and viewing scientific concepts as both a consequence of and an influence upon the overall structure of social relations. Efforts to pursue this approach with regard to medical science have been especially fruitful and abundant. Scholarship has focused primarily on the ways in which medical practice has tended to reflect and uphold socially structured inequality (especially that based on class, sex, and race). Some analysts have also begun to investigate the exceedingly complex correspondence between the structures, forces, and dynamics that medical knowledge invests in the human body and the dynamics of social relations in the "body politic."(3)

The case of black lung provides an exceptionally clear example of the ways in which factors external to science have shaped and changed medical knowledge. In the United States, medical perceptions of black lung fall into three periods, bounded by major shifts in the political economy of the coal industry. Observations of miners' unusual respiratory disease burden and speculation as to its workplace origins characterized the first medical construction of black lung. This viewpoint originated in the anthracite coalfields of Pennsylvania during a period when medical knowledge and practice, health care delivery arrangements, and industrial relations between miners and operators were all in a state of flux. A completely different concept of black lung emerged in a later period from the expanding bituminous coalfields, where tight corporate con-

trol over the health care system, a stark class structure, and other factors were relevant to the medical outlook. A third concept of black lung developed gradually after World War II in the context of a highly unionized, increasingly capital-intensive industry with a union-controlled health plan for miners and their families.

The first written documents concerning miners' unusual respiratory trouble originated from the anthracite region of eastern Pennsylvania; here was located the first large-scale coal mining operations in the United States, dominated by the affiliates of nine railroads. During the 1860s and 1870s, a few physicians acquainted with this region began to publish articles remarking on miners' respiratory difficulties and speculating that they were related to the inhalation of dusts and gases in the workplace. These articles are remarkable for their detailed accounts of unhealthy working conditions and their inclusion of statements by miners themselves on their workplace health (4).

This period prior to the hegemony of scientific medicine was characterized by a relative eclecticism and fluidity in medical knowledge, practice, and health care delivery arrangements. Some medical historians argue that the uncertain financial, professional, and social status of physicians lent more equality and negotiability to the doctor-patient relationship than is customary today (5). In the anthracite coalfields, miners were beginning to finance their health and welfare needs through mutual benefit associations that gave financial assistance in cases of sickness, disability and death (6). This brief period of relative fluidity in the health care system was soon eclipsed, however, by the simultaneous eradication of the benefit associations and the growth of the company doctor system. The most significant episode in this process was the strike of 1874–1875, which led to the famous Molly Maguire murder trials and resulted in the disintegration of the major anthracite trade union, the Miners' and Laborers' Benevolent Association. The powerful Philadelphia and Reading Railroad, whose affiliate Coal and Iron Company was the largest anthracite coal producer, subsequently attempted to replace the union's health and welfare functions with a Beneficial Fund financed by miners and controlled by the company. During the last two decades of the nineteenth century, as mining corporations gradually extended their control over health care delivery through the company doctor system, physicians in the anthracite fields grew silent on the subject of miners' occupational lung disease. The anthracite industry subsequently entered a period of decline from which it never recovered; the center of U.S. coal production shifted to the bituminous fields, where physicians elaborated a completely different concept of black lung.

The bituminous industry of southern Appalachia achieved national economic importance around the turn of the century and by the end of World War I was rapidly becoming the heart of U.S. coal production. In the coal camps of this rural and mountainous region, physicians did not simply ignore the existence of black lung, as many have suggested; rather, they viewed miners' diseased state as normal and nondisabling, and therefore unworthy of scientific investigation. The sources of this perception may be found partly in the political economy of the coal industry, which left a peculiarly repressive stamp on the structure of health care delivery in Appalachia (7).

In the southern bituminous industry, coal operators initially assumed a direct role in establishing, maintaining, and controlling many social and political institutions, such as the public schools, churches, and the police. Their activities derived in part from practical necessity: companies often had to import much of their labor force into this sparsely populated area, and in order to keep these workers had to provide housing, food, and a minimum of public services. However, the operators' role was neither benign nor merely practical. The profits to be made from housing, food, and to a lesser extent medical care were often quite significant to companies attempting to survive in the highly competitive, unstable business environment of bituminous coal. Moreover, totalitarian control of coal communities, including issuance of a separate currency (scrip), domination of the police, and even control of the physical access to the towns, enabled these companies to forestall what they perceived as one of the most pernicious threats to their economic status—unionization.

Health care did not escape the logic of this competitive environment and direct domination of the work force. The company doctor was the only source of medical care in almost all rural Appalachian coal camps. Under this system, the coal company controlled the employment of a doctor, but miners were required as a condition of employment to pay for his services. The company doctors' accountability to the coal operators is one of the most obvious and fundamental reasons for the medical concepts of miners' occupational health developed during this period. Work-related accidents and later diseases spelled economic liability for the coal operators under the workers' compensation system. Any agitation for preventive action would have represented an even greater nuisance. There was instead a uniform tendency to ascribe accidents and diseases to the fault of the miner—his carelessness and personal habits, such as alcoholism. Thus, one physician in 1919, after reciting a litany of occupational safety and health hazards, including dust, gob piles, electricity, poisonous gases, and contaminated water supplies, managed to conclude: "Housing conditions, and hurtful forms of recreation, especially alcoholism, undoubtedly cause the major amount of sickness. The mine itself is not an unhealthful place to work." (8)

The medical ideology surrounding black lung was more complex than this outright denial of occupational causation. Physicians dubbed the widespread breathlessness, expectoration of sputum, and prolonged coughing fits "miners' asthma." These symptoms of lung disease were *constituted as a norm;* as such, they were to be expected and by definition were nondisabling. For example, in 1935, one physician in Pennsylvania wrote (9):

> As far as most of the men in this region are concerned, so called "miners' asthma" is considered an *ordinary* condition that needs cause no worry and therefore the profession has not troubled itself about its finer pathological and associated clinical manifestations (emphasis added).

A miner who complained of disability due to respiratory trouble was diagnosed as a case of "malingering," "compensationitis," or "fear of the mines." The social control aspects of this ideology are obvious: if disease was natural, inevitable, and nondisabling, then prevention was unnecessary. Moreover, exhibiting disability from a respiratory disease was a medically stigmatized sign of psychological weakness or duplicity (10).

Although the company doctor system provides one explanation for this medical concept, it may also be related to class interactions in the coalfields and to some of the basic precepts of scientific medicine. It may be speculated that the company doctor's social as well as medical perspective on the coal miner and his family was influenced by the relative status of each within the coal camp environment (11). The mono-economy of the Appalachian coalfields produced a rather simple and vivid class structure, in which physicians, lawyers, and a few other professionals formed an island in a working-class sea. On the one hand, the superiority of the doctors' status relative to the working class was everywhere apparent in their standard of living, language, etc. On the other hand, these physicians were in a distinctly inferior position by the standards of the medical profession as a whole, and moreover were denied numerous amenities available in more cosmopolitan surroundings. Their degraded social and physical environment was embodied in and no doubt in many cases attributed to coal miners themselves—their ramshackle houses, coarse language, "lack of culture," and so on. What was "normal" for miners, including even a chronic respiratory condition, was by no means normal for the company doctor (12).

The outlook of scientific medicine, which around the turn of the century was gaining hegemony over other forms of medical theory and practice, is also relevant to the company doctors' conceptualization of black lung. With the rise of scientific medicine, production of medical knowledge gradually became the province of research scientists, divorced from the human patient by their location in the laboratory. Building on the precepts of cell theory and the discovery of bacteria, their efforts focused on the isolation of specific aberrations in cell function, and their correlation with discrete disease agents. The "germ theory" of disease causation, which essentially holds that each disease is caused by a specific bacterium or agent, became the basis of scientific medicine. This theory confounded the microscopic *agent* of disease with the *cause* of disease; it thus implicitly denied a role to social and economic factors in disease causation and displaced the social medicine of an earlier period.

At the level of medical practice, diagnosis became a process of identifying separate disease entities, with confirmation of the diagnosis sought in the laboratory; the patient's own testimony as to his/her condition was relegated to a decidedly secondary status. Indeed, scientific medicine involved what Jewson (5) termed the "disappearance of the sick-man" from the medical world view. The patient increasingly appeared almost incidentally as the medium for disease, eclipsed by the focus on identifying discrete pathologies. In the absence of a verifiable clinical entity, the patient was by definition (health is the absence of disease) pronounced healthy. His/her protestations of feeling ill became a matter for the psychiatrist (13).

These features of the scientific medical outlook dovetailed with previously mentioned factors to produce the company doctors' conceptualization of black lung. To the extent that any company doctor seriously attempted to diagnose a miner's respiratory condition, the effort was informed by the search for previously established clinical entities, especially silicosis and tuberculosis. Up until very recently, silica was considered the only dust seriously harmful to the respiratory system. Moreover, silicosis possesses characteristics that scientific medicine is most conducive to recognizing as a legitimate clinical entity: it is associated with one specific agent; it produces gross pathological change in lung tissue, apparent upon autopsy; and it reveals itself relatively clearly in a characteristic pattern on an X-ray. Most coal miners were not exposed to silica in significant quantity, and their X-rays did not exhibit the classic silicotic pattern. To the extent that their X-rays revealed the pathological changes now associated with coal workers' pneumoconiosis, these too were considered normal—for coal miners (14). Moreover, as a group, miners seemed to experience a low mortality rate from tuberculosis, considered the prime public health problem of this period. Hence developed the perversely ironic "coal dust is good for you" theory: "It is in the highest degree possible that coal-dust possesses the property of hindering the development of tuberculosis, and of arresting its progress." (15)

The company doctor system did not go unchallenged by coal miners; unrest over its compulsory character occasionally led to strikes and generated the demand for a health care plan organized on the opposite basis—union control and industry financing. Following a protracted strike and federalization of the mines in 1946, miners finally won a contract establishing such a system, the Welfare and Retirement Fund. Financed by a royalty assessed on each ton of mined coal, the Fund provided pensions, hospitalization, and medical care for miners and their families. Although officially directed by a tripartite board composed of representatives from industry, the union, and the public, in reality the Fund was controlled by the United Mine Workers. At the time of its creation, progressives in the health care field almost unanimously viewed the Fund as an innovative leap forward in health care delivery. Contradictions embedded in coal's postwar industrial relations subsequently compromised this vision and constricted the Fund's activities. Nevertheless, in its first decade and heyday, the Fund transformed the structure and quality of health care in the Appalachian coalfields (16).

The establishment of the Fund made possible the beginning of a third period in the medical conceptualization of miners' respiratory disease. Progressive physicians, many organized in prepaid group practice financed through the Fund, undertook clinical research on the respiratory problems of their coal miner patients. The Fund also employed in its central office a physician whose primary responsibility was to educate the medical profession about coal miners' dust disease. These physicians were largely responsible for the trickle of literature on coal workers' pneumoconiosis that began to appear in U.S. medical journals during the early 1950s; of the articles they did not write, most depended on data from Fund-affiliated hospitals and clinics. All argued essentially that "authoritative opinion to the contrary notwithstanding," coal miners suffer from a "disabling, progressive, killing disease which is related to exposure to coal dust." (17)

Despite these efforts, medical recognition of coal workers' pneumoconiosis did not evolve in an orderly, linear fashion, advanced by the inquiring gaze of these scientists. They remained a minority within the medical establishment, and coal miners in most states continued to be denied workers' compensation for occupational lung disease. The recognition that black lung was rampant among U.S. coal miners did not evolve of its own accord within the boundaries of medical science. It was forced on the medical community by the decidedly political intervention of miners themselves.

Black Lung and the Transformation of the Workplace

Since the changing medical concepts of black lung reveal more about the development of the coal industry and health care delivery systems than the nature and extent of respiratory disease among coal miners, observers may well wonder what the history of black lung actually entails. It is extremely difficult to reconstruct satisfactorily. Epidemiological data on miners' lung disease are simply nonexistent, except for the very recent period. The early commentaries cited previously suggest that pervasive respiratory problems accompanied the growth of the anthracite and bituminous coal industries, a conclusion corroborated by nonmedical sources (18); however, acceptance of "miners' asthma" and a dearth of medical literature swiftly followed. Between 1918 and 1940, a few scattered studies, primarily by the U.S. Public Health Service, uncovered "extraordinary" excess mortality from influenza and pneumonia among anthracite and bituminous coal miners; their susceptibility was likely due to the work-related destruction of their respiratory systems. However, all U.S. Public Health Service research on miners' occupational respiratory disease focused on silicosis; the resulting data were mixed, but the invariable conclusion was that bituminous miners were not exposed to silica in significant quantity and were not seriously disabled by work-related lung disease (19).

Although the lack of statistics precludes documentation of the extent of black lung, it is possible to trace the changing causes of disease by analyzing the site of disease production—the workplace. By "workplace" is meant not only the physical characteristics of the site of coal production but also the social relations that shape and are part of the workplace. The interaction between miners and operators under historically given circumstances has shaped the timing and character of technological innovation, the nature of the work process, the pace of work, and other factors relevant to the production of occupational disease. The history of black lung is thus internally related to the history of the workplace, as a physical site and a social relationship.

This history may be divided into two major periods, distinguished by their different technologies, work organizations, industrial relations, and sources of respiratory disease: handloading and mechanized mining. During the initial handloading era, which persisted until the 1930s, of utmost importance to the production of coal and disease was the highly competitive and labor-intensive character of the industry. Fragmented into thousands of competing companies, bituminous coal suffered from chronic bouts of overproduction, excess capacity, low profit margins, and fluctuating prices. Because labor represented approximately 70 percent of the cost of production, a prime tactic in the competitive struggle was to cut the cost of labor, principally by lowering the piece rate. In addition, the craft nature of the labor process rendered companies relatively powerless to control productivity and output, except by manipulating the miners' wages (20).

These economic dynamics had important implications for the workplace as a site of disease production. The instability of the industry frequently resulted in irregular work and a lowering of the piece rate, both of which forced miners to work faster and/or longer hours in an attempt to maintain their standard of living. The impact on health and safety conditions was almost invariably negative, as miners necessarily reduced nonproductive, safety-oriented tasks, such as roof timbering, to a minimum (21). Working longer hours in mines where "towards quitting time [the air] becomes so foul that the miners'

lamps will no longer burn" (22) no doubt increased the respiratory disease risk. Moreover, a financially mandated speedup encouraged miners to re-enter their work areas as soon as possible after blasting the coal loose from the face, an operation that generated clouds of dust and powder smoke (23).

Respiratory hazards often were especially grave in non-gassy mines, where ventilation tended to be poorest. The prospect of losing their entire capital investment in one explosion encouraged mine owners to install better ventilation systems in mines where methane gas was liberated; the non-gassy mines, however, tended to "kill the men by inches." (4, p. 244) Writing around the turn of the century, one mine inspector described in detail the ventilation problem and its implications for miners' health (22, pp. 449–450):

... adequate ventilation is not applied in such [non-gassy] mines, because they can be wrought without going to the expense of providing costly and elaborate furnaces or fans, air-courses, stoppings, and brattice. From four to six cents a ton are thus saved in mining the coal that should be applied in ventilating, but saved at the expense of the workmen's health.... Constant labor in a badly-aired mine breaks down the constitution and clouds the intellect. The lungs become clogged up from inhaling coal dust, and from breathing noxious air; the body and limbs become stiff and sore, the mind loses the power of vigorous thought. After six years' labor in a badly ventilated mine—that is, a mine where a man with a good constitution may from habit be able to work every day for several years—the lungs begin to change to a bluish color. After twelve years they are black, and after twenty years they are densely black, not a vestige of natural color remaining, and are little better than carbon itself. The miner dies at thirty-five of coal-miners' consumption.

During the 1930s, the introduction of mechanical loading equipment dramatically altered the workplace, while the organizing successes of the United Mine Workers transformed relations between miners and operators. Although mechanical cutting devices were introduced into underground coal mines as early as 1876, their adoption was gradual and associated with only a partial reorganization of the craft work process.

The classic changes produced by mechanization and Taylorization, such as elevated productivity, loss of job control, de-skilling, and an increased division of labor, appeared slowly in bituminous coal during the first three decades of the twentieth century. However, the widespread introduction of loading machines in the 1930s broke the craft organization of work once and for all. More technological innovation swiftly followed, with the introduction of continuous mining technology after World War II. This technology did not increase the already specialized division of labor as much as it replaced several tasks (and miners) with one central production worker—the continuous miner operator.

Virtually all sources agree that the mechanization of underground mining greatly increased dust levels and magnified the existing problems with respiratory disease (24). Miners were quick to rename the Joy loaders "man killers" and to protest the unemployment, physical hardships placed on older miners, and health and safety problems that attended their introduction. For example, at the 1934 UMWA convention, miners debated at length a resolution demanding the removal of these machines from the mines; the few delegates who spoke against it were nearly shouted down by the tumultuous convention. One miner argued (25, p. 192):

> I heard one of the brothers say that they don't hire miners over forty years of age in their locality. I want to tell you brothers that there is no miner that can work in the mines under those conveyors [loading machines] and reach the age of forty. Those conveyors are man killers and I believe this convention should do its utmost to find some way whereby those conveyors will be abolished. . . . The young men after they work in the mine six or eight hours daily become sick, either getting asthma or some other sickness due to the dust of the conveyors and they can no longer perform their duty.

Another miner, during debate over continuous mining machinery at a UMWA convention 22 years later, echoed those comments (26):

> . . . [T]hey are putting coal moles [continuous miners] in our mines, and I hope they don't put them in anybody else's mines. We had one man die from the effects of that procedure. We had to give them a 15-minute shift. We have had any number who have had to get off because of health. It seems that someone forgot the miners who have [to operate] the moles. . . . He stands up there and inhales the fumes and the oil and the steam that is created by the heat from the mole. He doesn't get sufficient oxygen. . . .

It would be mistaken to conclude that because mechanization was associated with increased dust levels, machines themselves were the cause of this problem. Here again, the economic and political circumstances of technological innovation were critical in determining its impact on the workplace. The large coal operators introduced continuous mining technology in the midst of a desperate competitive struggle with oil and natural gas, which by the 1950s had usurped coal's traditional markets in home heating and the railroads. By making coal a capital-intensive industry and vastly increasing labor productivity, the large operators hoped to force the small, labor-intensive producers into bankruptcy and win a respectable share of the growing utility market. Of crucial importance to the pace, nature, and success of this mechanization strategy was the role of the union. Headed by the authoritarian but charismatic John L. Lewis, the United Mine Workers not only accepted but aggressively promoted mechanization, believing that it would lead to institutional security, high wages, and economic prosperity (27). Although there was widespread rank-and-file discontent with mechanization, the very process replaced labor with machinery, rendering miners redundant and their protest ineffective. Despite scattered strikes and other expressions of unrest, miners were unable to modify the policy of their union or exert significant control over the impacts of mechanization on their workplace and communities.

The result was not simply increased respirable dust in the workplace, but social and economic disaster in the coalfields. In the space of 20 years, between 1950 and 1969, the work force shrank by 70 percent. For the unemployed, the monoeconomy of the Appalachian coalfields left no alternative but migration. Coal-dependent communities became ghost towns, as some counties lost half their population in the space of 10 years. Those who managed to keep their jobs in large mines confronted increased dust, noise, high-voltage electricity, and other hazards. Supervision intensified, as the operators attempted to recoup their investments in machinery by pushing productivity higher and higher (28).

The black lung controversy that erupted in 1968 was very much a product of and a challenge to this history. The movement represented an effort by miners and their families to reclaim the political and economic potency denied them for almost 20 years. Black lung disease in a sense became a metaphor for the exploitative social relations that had always characterized the coalfields, but worsened during two decades of high unemployment, social dislocation, and rank-and-file weakness vis-à-vis the coal industry. The goal of black lung compensation represented, in part, a demand for retribution from the industry for the devastating human effects of its economic transformation.

The Battle Is Joined

By 1968, when the black lung movement arose, the union's overt cooperation with the large operators had outworn its usefulness to the industry and outlived its tolerability for the rank and file. The major producers had thoroughly mechanized their mines, reduced intraindustry competition from small companies, and held their own against external competition from alternative fuels. Capital was flowing into the industry not only through the enormously increased productivity of its workers, which tripled between 1950 and 1969, but also in the form of investment by the oil industry. Electric utilities seemed to offer unlimited market potential. Threatening the rosy forecasts, however, were an increasingly rambunctious work force and a projected manpower shortage. An enormous turnover was beginning in the work force, as the miners who managed to keep their jobs during postwar mechanization were now retiring en masse, replaced by young workers with no necessary allegiance to the UMWA leadership. The economic prosperity rankled workers already beginning to question the sluggish collective bargaining

advances of their union leaders and made strikes a more potent weapon (29).

The first unmistakable evidence that rank-and-file rebellion was afoot erupted in the winter of 1968–1969 with the birth of the black lung movement. Originating in southern West Virginia, the movement was based in the older generation of workers who were leaving the mines. They faced retirement with a sparse pension of $100 per month (if they could meet the Fund's increasingly arbitrary and strict eligibility requirements), without the traditional cushion of the extended family and without compensation for the respiratory disease from which so many suffered (30). Discontent focused on the demand that the West Virginia legislature pass a bill recognizing black lung as a compensable disease under the state's workers' compensation statutes. Opposing the movement were the combined forces of the coal industry and the medical establishment. A member of the latter insisted, "There is no epidemic of devastating, killing and disabling man-made plague among coal workers." (31) Another argued, "The control of coal dust is not the answer to the disabling respiratory disease of our coal miners." (32)

Exasperated by strident opposition and legislative inaction, miners began to quit work in February 1969 in a strike that eventually brought out 40,000 workers and shut off coal production throughout the state. Their solidarity and economic muscle forced a black lung compensation bill through the legislature; although less liberal than what miners had hoped for, they declared a victory and returned to work after the governor signed the bill into law.

This was the most dramatic and widely reported phase of the black lung movement, but it marked only the beginning. Coupled with the death of 78 miners in the violent Farmington mine explosion in November 1968, the black lung movement generated a national political debate over health and safety conditions in U.S. coal mines. In December 1969, the Congress passed a Coal Mine Health and Safety Act, which detailed to an unprecedented degree mandatory work practices throughout the industry and offered compensation to miners disabled by black lung and the widows of miners who died from the disease. Large coal companies vigorously opposed certain, but not all of the act's provisions. Most notably, they fought the extremely strict respirable dust standard of 3.0 mg/m³, scheduled to drop to 2.0 mg/m³ after three years; this was designed to prevent black lung. The compensation program, by contrast, was to their liking: not only did it seem to promise that the turmoil over black lung would dissolve, the program also relieved them of liability for compensation by financing benefits with general tax revenues from the U.S. Treasury.

Ironically, passage of the act ensured that the issue of black lung compensation would not die but remain the focus of a continuing movement. In 1970, the Social Security Administration began administering the claims process for compensation benefits; within the program's first week of operation, 18,000 claims poured into agency offices (33). By the fall of the same year, letters of denial began to flow back into the coalfields. The bitterness and confusion that ensued derived partly from a pattern that repeated itself throughout thousands of these rural communities: several disabled miners and widows received black lung benefits, but their brothers or uncles or neighbors down the road were denied, even though by all appearances they were equally or even more disabled by lung disease. In other words, the criteria by which the Social Security Administration judged claimants' eligibility appeared completely arbitrary and violated local perceptions of who was disabled by black lung. Thus miners and their families pitted themselves against Social Security and the medical establishment in a bitter struggle over who would control the definition of disease and disability.

The Social Security Administration initially based its eligibility criteria on the orthodox medical conception of black lung, a view that reflects the rigidity and narrowness of the germ theory. According to this perspective, black lung is limited exclusively to one clinical entity—coal workers' pneumoconiosis (CWP); this is the only lung disease considered occupational in origin and therefore compensable. The agent (and cause) of CWP is, by definition (pneumoconiosis means "dust-containing lung"), the inhalation of respirable coal mine dust, which produces certain pathological changes in one organ (the lungs) and

which are revealed in a characteristic pattern on an X-ray. The disease process is linear and quantitative; the stage of CWP is determined by the number and size of opacities on the lung field, as revealed through an X-ray. The first stages of disease, categorized as "simple" pneumoconiosis, are considered compatible with health, whereas advanced or "complicated" pneumoconiosis is severely disabling and sometimes fatal (34).

This conception of black lung has highly significant political and ideological functions. Most important, it minimizes and depoliticizes the problem. If the *cause* of CWP is respirable dust, then prevention is a technical matter of controlling this inanimate object, rather than a political question involving the relations of power in the workplace. Moreover, most surveys find a 3 percent prevalence of complicated CWP; if this is the only stage of disease considered disabling, then a relatively small number of coal miners are functionally impaired by occupational lung disease and deserve compensation. Respiratory disability in miners with simple CWP is attributed to nonoccupational factors, above all the victims themselves and their cigarette smoking. Obviously, this entire train of thought functions to shift medical and political emphasis away from the workplace as a source of disease and onto the worker (35).

The entire diagnostic and claims procedure also functioned to individualize what miners and other activists considered a collective problem. On a practical level, the dominant medical concept of black lung meant that claimants with evidence of complicated CWP, even if they experienced little disability, automatically received compensation; some with lesser stages who met a complex combination of other criteria also received benefits. But thousands of miners and the widows of miners, who by all appearances were equally or more disabled by respiratory disease, were denied compensation.

In the course of their movement to achieve more liberal eligibility criteria, miners and other activists implicitly elaborated a completely different understanding of black lung and its causes. Their view was not articulated by a single spokesperson or written down in a single position paper; it was woven into the culture and ideology of the movement, and in almost all respects ran counter to the dominant medical view of black lung. Indeed, the very act of insisting collectively on the reality of their own disease experience was in itself a challenge to scientific medicine, insofar as the latter tends to individualize health problems and denigrate the patients' perceptions of their own condition.

It should be stressed that the movement's ideology did not involve a wholesale rejection of science and was not based on fundamentalist religion or other anti-scientific sensibilities. Indeed, some activists made skillful use of the scientific arguments of a few physicians who, because of their research findings, lent support to the black lung cause (36). Overall, the movement's ideology was based in the collective experience of its participants. Their skepticism toward the medical establishment had historical roots in the company doctor system, which for many activists was a bitter and living memory. Their view of black lung itself was based in their own holistic experience of disease—its physical as well as psychological, social, and economic aspects. And their understanding of the causes of black lung derived from their experiences with the coal industry, as workers, as widows of men killed by the mines, and as residents of coal towns where "there are no neutrals" (37)—even scientists.

For movement participants, the medical definition of black lung as a single clinical entity principally affecting one organ of the body had little meaning, because black lung meant a transformation in their whole way of life. As one 56-year-old miner, disabled by black lung since the age of 48, described (38):

> Black lung is a cruel disease, a humiliating disease. It's when you can't do what you like to do; that's humiliating. I had to lay down my hammer and saw, and those were the things I got the most pleasure out of. The next thing I liked to do was work in my garden; now my garden's the biggest weed patch in Logan County. There were times in 1971 when I was still working that it was difficult for me to get to the bedroom when I was feeling bad. Now, of course, that's humiliating.

Many miners' analysis of the agents and causes of black lung also contrasted with the orthodox medical view. They argued that many features of the workplace had damaged their lungs, such as working in water over their ankles or breathing the fumes from cable fires. Moreover, they asserted that although respirable dust was the agent of CWP, the cause of the whole disease experience ultimately was economic:

> Where do we get the black lung from? The coal companies! They've had plenty of time to lessen the dust so nobody would get it. It's not an elaborate thing to keep it down: spray water. They just don't put enough of it on there. They don't want to maintain enough in materials and water to do that. . . . (39)
>
> Should we all die a terrible death to keep those companies going? (40)

Thus, miners developed a belief that they were *collectively entitled* to compensation, not at all because of individualized medical diagnoses of CWP but because of the common health-destroying experience that defined them as a group: work in the mines. Implicit in this view was the idea that black lung is a destructive process that begins when a miner starts work, not something that acquires legitimacy only when a radiologist can find it on an X-ray.

A disabled coal miner reported (41):

> I worked in the cleaning plant, an outside job. I had four conveyors to bring to the storage bin. I had, I'd say, 16 holes in this galvanized pipe, two rows, that's 32 holes in all, little tiny holes, to keep down the dust. I stood many a time across from that conveyor and somebody'd be on the other side, and all you could see was their cap lamp. And that's in the cleaning plant; that's outside! That's not even at the face.
>
> In the Black Lung Association, we're asking due compensation for a man who had to work in the environment he worked in. Not that a man can't choose where he works. But he's due more than just a day's wages. He and his family ought to be compensated for the environment he worked in.

These beliefs found expression in a multitude of political demands concerning the black lung compensation program, eventually and most clearly in the demand for automatic compensation after a specified number of years' work in the mines. Federal legislation to effect this change went down to defeat in 1976. However, medical and legal eligibility requirements for compensation were so liberalized by amendments passed in 1972 and 1978 that most miners and the widows of miners who worked a substantial period of time in the mines are now receiving black lung benefits (42).

The black lung movement has been rightly criticized for its lack of a preventive focus. Despite the clear and widely held perception that the coal companies were to blame for black lung, activists never directed their struggle at the heart of the problem, prevention in the workplace. This was partly due to the initial, erroneous view that the cost of state compensation (financed by industry) would force the companies to improve health conditions in the mines. A lasting and effective prevention campaign would have required a tighter alliance between working miners, disabled miners, and widows; a much firmer conviction that black lung is not inevitable; and, at least eventually, a political vision of how miners might improve their occupational health by asserting greater control over the workplace.

However, the black lung movement suggests that even within the confines of an after-the-fact struggle for compensation, important and intensely political issues may be at stake. This article has explored the history of black lung on many levels—as a medical construct, a product of the workplace, a disease experience, and a political battle. The evidence presented suggests that miners' experientially based view of black lung and challenge to the medical establishment have historical justification. Medical science's understanding of black lung has not derived from observation unencumbered by a social and economic context, but has been profoundly shaped by that context; as a result, it has performed crucial political and ideological functions. In one era, it served to "normalize" and thereby mask the existence of disease altogether; in the more recent period, it has tended to minimize and individualize the problem.

By contrast, black lung activists succeeded in challenging the scientific medical establishment by insisting on the validity of their own definition of disease. They viewed black lung as an experience affecting the whole person in all aspects of life. Rather than focusing on a causal relationship between one discrete agent and one disease, they looked at the workplace as a total environment where the miner confronts an array of respiratory hazards. Finally, activists defined black lung as a collective problem whose ultimate cause was economic. In its entirety, the history of black lung suggests that a similar task of redefinition awaits other health advocates if they wish to challenge effectively the social production of disease.

NOTE

Acknowledgments—This article was written under a research fellowship at the International Institute for Comparative Social Research in Berlin, West Germany. I wish to thank the Institute and its staff for their financial support, friendship, and intellectual stimulation. Conversations and correspondence with Norm Diamond, Gerd Göckenjan, and Meredeth Turshen were also an invaluable part of the process that led to this article.

REFERENCES

1. NOVA. A plague on our children. WGBH Educational Foundation, Boston, 1979, film transcript, p. 35.
2. For a clear presentation of the overall argument, see Doyal, L. (with Pennell, I.). *The Political Economy of Health*, Pluto Press, London, 1979. See also Turshen, M. The political ecology of disease. *Review of Radical Political Economics* 9(1): 45–60, 1977. See also Eyer, J. Hypertension as a disease of modern society. *Int J. Health Serv.* 5(4): 539–558, 1975.
3. Many analysts have pointed out this relationship on a theoretical level, but only a few have attempted to apply it in concrete investigation. See the discussion concerning the relationship between capitalist work relations and technology and the scientific model of brain function (as factory manager, telephone exchange, and, today, computer) in Rose, A. *The Conscious Brain.* Alfred A. Knopf, New York, 1974. For a more general discussion, see Figlio, K. The historiography of scientific medicine: An invitation to the human sciences. *Comparative Studies in Society and History* 19: 262–286, 1977. See also Foucault, M. *The Birth of the Clinic.* Vintage Books, New York, 1975.
4. The most comprehensive discussion I found was Sheafer, H. C. Hygiene of coal-mines. In *A Treatise on Hygiene and Public Health*, edited by A. H. Buck, vol. 2, pp. 229–250. William Wood and Company, New York, 1879. Sheafer wrote: "Any one who has seen a load of coal shot from a cart, or has watched the thick clouds of dust

which sometimes envelop the huge coal-breakers of the anthracite region so completely as almost to hide them from sight, can form an idea of the injurious effect upon the health of constant working in such an atmosphere. The wonder is not that men die of clogged-up lungs, but that they manage to exist so long in an atmosphere which seems to contain at least fifty per cent of solid matter" (p. 245). See also Carpenter, J. T. Report of the Schuylkill County Medical Society. *Transactions of the Medical Society of Pennsylvania,* fifth series, part 2, pp. 488–491, 1869.

5. Figlio (3). Jewson, N. D. The disappearance of the sick-man from medical cosmology, 1770–1870. *Sociology* 10(2): 225–244, 1976.

6. On early financing of medical care in the coalfields, see Ginger, R. Company-sponsored welfare plans in the anthracite industry before 1900. *Bulletin of the Business Historical Society* 27(2): 112–120, 1953. See also Falk, L. A. Coal miners' prepaid medical care in the United States—and some British relationships, 1792–1964. *Med. Care* 4(1): 37–42, 1966.

7. A comprehensive survey of health care under the company doctor system was extracted from the U.S. government by the United Mine Workers of America during temporary federalization of the mines in 1946. The result was the so-called Boone report. U.S. Department of the Interior, Coal Mines Administration. *A Medical Survey of the Bituminous-Coal Industry.* Government Printing Office, Washington, D.C., 1947.

8. Hayhurst, E. R. The health hazards and mortality statistics of soft coal mining in Illinois and Ohio. *J. Ind. Hygiene* 1(7): 360, 1919.

9. Rebhorn, E. H. Anthraco silicosis. *Med. Soc. Reporter* 29(5): 15, Scranton, Pennsylvania, 1935.

10. Those who persisted in their complaints of breathlessness were eventually referred to psychiatrists, according to the testimony of miners and their families during interviews with the author. The argument that miners' symptoms of lung disease were psychological in origin may be found in Ross, W. D., et al. Emotional aspects of respiratory disorders among coal miners. *J.A.M.A.* 156(5): 484–487, 1954.

11. My thoughts on this relationship were stimulated and clarified by Figlio, K. Chlorosis and chronic disease in 19th century Britain: The social constitution of somatic illness in a capitalist society. *Int. J. Health Serv.* 8(4): 589–617, 1978.

12. This view persists today. Abundant examples may be found, especially in journalistic and sociological literature on Appalachia. Miners are alternatively romanticized and reviled; in either case, they are "a breed apart."

13. See Brown, E. R. *Rockefeller Medicine Men.* University of California Press, Berkeley, 1979. On the germ theory and its implications for the doctor-patient relationship, see Jewson (5), Figlio (3), and Berliner, H. S., and Salmon J. W. The holistic health movement and scientific medicine: The naked and the dead. *Socialist Review* 9(1): 31–52, 1979.

14. "One radiologist in southern West Virginia says until five years ago he regularly encountered chest X-rays from physicians that showed massive lung lesions labeled 'normal miner's chest.' " Aronson, B. Black lung: Tragedy of Appalachia. *New South* 26(4): 54, 1971.

15. Meiklejohn, A. History of lung disease of coal miners in Great Britain: Part II, 1875–1920. *Br. J. Ind. Med.* 9(2): 94, 1952. This view apparently originated in Britain and was picked up by physicians in the United States.

16. See Seltzer, C. Health care by the ton. *Health PAC Bulletin* 79: 1–8, 25–33, 1977.

17. Martin, J. E., Jr. Coal miners' pneumoconiosis. *Am. J. Public Health* 44(5): 581, 1954. See also Hunter, M. B., and Levine, M. D. Clinical study of pneumoconiosis of coal workers in Ohio river valley. *J.A.M.A.* 163(1): 1–4, 1957. See also the numerous articles by Lorin Kerr in this period, especially Coal workers' pneumoconiosis. *Ind. Med. Surg.* 25(8): 355–362, 1956.

18. Nonmedical literature from all over the world suggests that coal miners have long experienced black lung. Friedrich Engels discusses miners' "black spittle" disease in *The Condition of the Working Class in England.* Alden Press, Oxford, 1971. Emile Zola's character Bonnemort in the novel *Germinal* is clearly a victim of black lung. And John Spargo, a progressive era reformer intent on the prohibition of child labor, discusses the respiratory problems of the anthracite breaker boys in *The Bitter Cry of the Children.* Macmillan Company, New York, 1906, p. 164.

19. U.S. Public Health Service. The health of workers in dusty trades, Part III. Public Health Bulletin Number 208, Government Printing Office, Washington, D.C., 1933; U.S. Public Health Service. Anthraco-silicosis among hard coal miners. Public Health Bulletin Number 221, Government Printing Office, Washington, D.C., 1936; U.S. Public Health Service and Utah State Board of Health. The working environment and the health of workers in bituminous coal mines, non-ferrous metal mines, and non-ferrous metal smelters in Utah, 1940.

20. A lucid discussion of the labor process in this per-

iod may be found in Dix, K. *Work Relations in the Coal Industry: The Hand-Loading Era, 1880–1930.* Institute for Labor Studies, West Virginia University, Morgantown, West Virginia, 1977. On the economics of the industry, see Suffern, A. E. *The Coal Miners' Struggle for Industrial Status.* Macmillan Company, New York, 1926. See also Hamilton, W. H., and Wright, H. R. *The Case of Bituminous Coal.* Macmillan Company, New York, 1925.

21. One study actually found an inverse statistical relationship between employment levels and the rate of fatal accidents. See the discussion in Dix (20), pp. 101–104.

22. Roy, A. *History of Coal Miners of the U.S.* J. L. Trauger Printing Company, Columbus, Ohio, 1907, p. 119.

23. In some cases, state law or local practice dictated that coal be shot down at the end of the day, allowing the atmosphere to clear overnight. However, this was not uniform practice throughout the industry.

24. Physicians, miners, and government officials seem to agree on this point; representatives from industry in some cases demur. There is also disagreement about the magnitude of any increase in respiratory disease. See *Papers and Proceedings of the National Conference on Medicine and the Federal Coal Mine Health and Safety Act of 1969.* Washington, D.C., 1970. Debate on these questions also runs through the many volumes of testimony on the 1969 act. See U.S. Senate, Committee on Labor and Public Welfare, Subcommittee on Labor, *Coal Mine Health and Safety.* Hearings, 91st Congress, 1st Session, Government Printing Office, Washington, D.C., 1969.

25. United Mine Workers of America. *Proceedings of the 33rd Consecutive Constitutional Convention.* United Mine Workers of America, Indianapolis, Indiana, 1934, vol. 1.

26. United Mine Workers of America. *Proceedings of the 42nd Consecutive Constitutional Convention.* United Mine Workers of America, Washington, D.C., 1956, see pp. 306–331.

27. Lewis clearly articulated this position in his book, *The Miners' Fight for American Standards.* Bell Publishing Company, Indianapolis, Indiana, 1925.

28. This paragraph compresses an enormous social and economic transformation into a few sentences. For a detailed description of the changed industrial relations in this period, see Seltzer, C. The United Mine Workers of America and the coal operators: The political economy of coal in Appalachia, 1950–1973. Ph.D. dissertation, Columbia University, 1977.

29. See David, J. P. Earnings, health, safety, and welfare of bituminous coal miners since the encouragement of mechanization by the United Mine Workers of America. Ph.D. dissertation, West Virginia University, 1972. David demonstrates how miners fell behind workers in certain other unionized industries during this period.

30. In 1969, the U.S. Surgeon General estimated that 100,000 coal miners were afflicted with CWP. A study of 9,076 miners, conducted between 1969 and 1972, found a 31.4 percent prevalence of the disease among bituminous miners; among those who had worked 30 to 39 years in the mines, prevalence rose to over 50 percent. See Morgan, W.K.C., et al. The prevalence of coal workers' pneumoconiosis in U.S. coal miners. *Arch. Environ. Health* 27: 222, 1973. Current prevalence in the work force runs around 15 percent. These data are all on CWP. Black lung, i.e. the whole disease experience that miners consider occupational in origin, is not considered a legitimate concept by scientific medicine, and its prevalence is unknown. In scientific medical terms, black lung includes CWP, bronchitis, emphysema, and possibly other unrecognized disease processes. The prevalence of this ensemble of diseases is of course higher than that of CWP alone.

31. Dr. Rowland Burns, as quoted in the Charleston (West Virginia) *Daily Mail,* January 15, 1969.

32. Dr. William Anderson, as quoted in the Charleston (West Virginia) *Gazette,* April 16, 1969.

33. U.S. House, Committee on Education and Labor. *Black Lung Benefits Program.* First Annual Report. Government Printing Office, Washington, D.C., 1971.

34. The views of W.K.C. Morgan and his associates represent the dominant position of the medical establishment on CWP. See Morgan, W.K.C. Respiratory disease in coal miners. *Am. Rev. Resp. Dis.* 113: 531–559, 1976.

35. For example: "The presence of severe shortness of breath in a coal miner with simple CWP is virtually always related to a nonoccupationally related disease, such as chronic bronchitis or emphysema, rather than to coal mining. . . . Smoking is by far the most important factor in producing respiratory symptoms and a decrease in ventilatory function." Morgan (34), pp. 540–541.

36. Several physicians took the side of miners in the black lung controversy, arguing that the degree of respiratory disability does not correlate with X-ray stages of CWP and that disability in miners with simple CWP is often occupationally related. Some explained this phenomenon by hypothesizing that the disease process is pulmonary vascular

in nature, i.e. it affects the small vessels of the lungs, impairing their ability to exchange gases with the bloodstream. See Hyatt, R. E., Kistin, A. D., and Mahan, T. K. Respiratory disease in southern West Virginia coal miners. *Am. Rev. Resp. Dis.* 89(3): 387–401, 1964. See also Rasmussen, D. L., et al. Respiratory impairment in southern West Virginia coal miners. *Am. Rev. Resp. Dis.* 98(10): 658–667, 1968.

37. This is a line from a famous song by Florence Reese, "Which Side Are You On?", inspired by the mine wars in Harlan County, Kentucky, during the 1930s.

38. Author's interview with disabled coal miner, Logan County, West Virginia, September 6, 1978.

39. Author's interview with disabled coal miner, Raleigh County, West Virginia, September 19, 1978.

40. Author's interview with working coal miner, Raleigh County, West Virginia, August 24, 1978.

41. Author's interview with disabled coal miner, Raleigh County, West Virginia, September 19, 1978.

42. By 1978, approved claims exceeded 420,000, and amendments enacted in that year are pushing the total even higher. This does not mean, however, that eligibility requirements will not be tightened in the future. Indeed, the current trend is to do so. See General Accounting Office. *Legislation Allows Black Lung Benefits To Be Awarded without Adequate Evidence of Disability*. Report to the Congress. Government Printing Office, Washington, D.C., 1980.

7

Popular Epidemiology: Community Response to Toxic Waste–Induced Disease

▪ ▪ ▪ ▪ ▪ ▪

Phil Brown

Residents of Woburn, Massachusetts, were startled several years ago to learn that their children were contracting leukemia at exceedingly high rates. By their own efforts, the affected families confirmed the existence of a leukemia cluster and demonstrated that it was traceable to industrial waste carcinogens that leached into their drinking water supply. These families put into process a long train of action which led to a civil suit against corporate giants W. R. Grace and Beatrice Foods, which opened in Boston in March 1986. On 28 July 1986, a federal district court jury found that Grace had negligently dumped chemicals on its property; Beatrice Foods was absolved. The case then proceeded to a second stage in which the plantiffs would have to prove

that the chemicals had actually caused leukemia. As this part of the case was under way, the judge decided that the jury had not understood the hydrogeological data that were crucial to the suit, and on 17 September he ordered the case to be retried. Because of this decision, an out-of-court settlement with Grace was reached on 22 September 1986.[1] The Woburn families filed an appeal against Beatrice in May 1987 on the grounds that the judge was wrong to exclude evidence and effects of pre-1968 dumping from the case.

This case has received much national attention and has a number of important effects. It has focused public attention on corporate responsibility for toxic wastes and their resultant health effects. For some time now, civic activists have organized opposition to environmental contamination, and the Woburn situation provides a valuable case study which can help to understand, forecast, and perhaps even to catalyze similar efforts in the future. It has also demonstrated that the health effects of toxic wastes are not restricted to physical disease but also include emotional problems. The Woburn plaintiffs were one of the first groups of toxic waste plaintiffs to introduce such evidence in court. These data can expand our knowledge of the effects of toxic wastes as well as our understanding of the psychological effects of disasters and trauma.

Woburn also offers a valuable example of lay communication of risk to scientific experts and government officials. Citizens in other locations and situations have previously attempted to convey risks to appropriate parties. In Woburn and other recent cases, however, a more concerted effort was made, which involved varying degrees of investigation into disease patterns and their potential or likely causes. I term this type of activity *popular epidemiology.*

Popular epidemiology is defined as the process by which laypersons gather statistics and other information and also direct and marshall the knowledge and resources of experts in order to understand the epidemiology of disease. Popular epidemiology is not merely a matter of public participation in what we traditionally conceive of as epidemiology. Lilienfeld defines epidemiology as "the study of the distribution of a disease or a physiological condition in human populations and of the factors that influence this distribution." These data are used to explain the etiology of the condition and to provide preventive, public health, and clinical practices to deal with the condition.[2] Popular epidemiology includes more elements than the above definition in that it emphasizes basic social structural factors, involves social movements, and challenges certain basic assumptions of traditional epidemiology. Nevertheless I find it appropriate to retain the word "epidemiology" in the concept of popular epidemiology because the *starting point* is the search for rates and causes of disease.

In order to develop the concept of popular epidemiology, I will first provide a brief capsule of the Woburn events. Following that, I will show commonalities between Woburn and other communities in popular epidemiological investigation. Finally, I will expand on the original definition of popular epidemiology by examining in detail five components of that concept.

Brief History of the Woburn Leukemia Cluster

In May 1979 builders found 184 55-gallon drums in a vacant lot along the Aberjona River. They called the police, who then called the state Department of Environmental Quality Engineering (DEQE). Water samples from wells G and H showed large concentrations of organic compounds that were known carcinogens in laboratory animals. Of particular concern were trichloroethylene (TCE) and tetrachloroethylene (PCE). The EPA's risk level for TCE is 27 parts per billion (ppb), and well G had ten times that concentration. The state ordered that both wells be closed due to their TCE and PCE levels.[3]

But town and state officials had prior knowledge of problems in the Woburn water. Frequent complaints about dishwasher discoloration, bad odor, and bad taste had led to a 1978 study by private consultants. They used an umbrella screen for organic compounds and reported a carbon-chloroform extract (CCE) concentration of 2.79 mg/L, while stating that the level should not exceed 0.1 mg/L. This Dufresne-Henry report led Woburn officials to ask the state Department of Public Health (DPH) to allow the town to change its chlorination method, because they assumed that chlorine was interacting with minerals. The DPH allowed this change and in the same letter told the officials not to rely on wells G and H because of high concentrations of salt and minerals. The DPH did not mention another important piece of information it possessed: In 1975 a DEQE engineer, who had been applying a more exact screening test to all wells in the state, found wells G and H to have higher concentrations of organic compounds than nearby wells. In retrospect, he stated that the level seemed high, but "at the time I was doing research only on the method and nobody knew how serious water contamination problems could be." Thus, before the discovery of the visible toxic wastes, both local and state officials had some knowledge of problems in Woburn water and specifically in the two wells in question.[4]

The first popular epidemiological efforts also predated the 1979 well closings. Anne Anderson, whose son, Jimmy, had been diagnosed with acute lymphocytic leukemia in 1972, had gathered information about other cases by word of mouth and by chance meetings with other victims at stores and at the hospital where Jimmy was being treated. She began to theorize that the growing number of leukemia cases may have been caused by something carried in the water. She asked state officials to test the water but was told that this could not be done on an individual's initiative. Anderson's husband did not support her in this effort but rather asked the family pastor to help her get her mind off what he felt to be an erroneous idea. This development led to one of the key elements of the Woburn story, since Reverend Bruce Young became a major actor in the community's efforts.[5]

Another fortuitous circumstance occurred in June 1979, just weeks after the state ordered the wells shut down. A DEQE engineer, on his way to work, drove past the nearby Industri-Plex construction site and thought that there might be violations of the Wetlands Act. Upon investigation, EPA scientists found dangerous levels of lead, arsenic, and chromium, yet they told neither the town officials nor the public. Only in September did a Woburn newspaper break the news. At this point, Reverend Young began to agree with Anne Anderson's conclusions about the water supply, and so he placed an ad in the Woburn paper, asking people who knew of childhood leukemia cases to respond. He prepared a map and a questionnaire, in consultation with Dr. Truman, the physician treating Jimmy Anderson. Several days later, Anderson and Young plotted the cases. There were 12, with 6 of them closely grouped. The data convinced Truman, who called the Centers for Disease Control (CDC). The activists spread the word through the press and succeeded in persuading the City Council on 19 December 1979 to request the CDC to investigate. In January 1980 Young, Anderson, and 20 other people formed For a Safe Environment (FACE) to generate public concern about the leukemia cluster.[6]

Five days after the City Council request to the CDC, the Massachusetts DPH issued a report that contradicted the Young-Anderson map model of the leukemia cluster. According to the DPH, there were 18 cases, when 10.9 were expected, but the difference was not so great for a ten-year period. Further, the DPH argued that a cluster pattern was not present. Despite this blow, the activists were buoyed by growing public awareness of the environmental hazard and by popular epidemiological efforts in other places. In June 1980, Anderson and Young were asked by Senator Edward Kennedy to testify at hearings on the Superfund. Young told the hearing:

> For seven years we were told that the burden of proof was upon us as independent citizens to gather the statistics. . . . All our work was done independent of the Commonwealth of Massachusetts. They offered no support, and were in fact one of our adversaries in this battle to prove that we had a problem.[7]

On 23 May 1980 the CDC and the National Institute for Occupational Safety and Health (NIOSH) sent John Cutler to lead a team affiliated with the Massachusetts DPH to study the Woburn case. This report, released on 23 January 1981, five days after the death of Jimmy Anderson, stated that there were 12 cases of childhood leukemia in East Woburn, when 5.3 were expected. The incidence of kidney cancer was also elevated. The discussion of the data was, however, inconclusive, since the case-control method failed to find characteristics that differentiated victims from nonvictims. Further, a lack of environmental data for earlier periods was an obstacle to linking disease with the water supply.[8]

The conjuncture of Jimmy Anderson's death and the report's failure to confirm the water-leukemia hypothesis led the families and friends of the victims, along with their local allies, to question the nature of the scientific study. As DiPerna puts it, a layperson's approach to epidemiological science evolved.[9] The Woburn residents were helped in this direction when Larry Brown from the Harvard School of Public Health (SPH) invited Anderson and Young to present the Woburn data to a SPH seminar. Marvin Zelen, an SPH biostatistician present at the seminar, became interested. At this time, clusters of cancer and other diseases were being investigated around the United States, although the CDC did not inform Woburn residents of this heightened public and scientific interest in cluster studies. Moreover, the DPH issued a follow-up report in November 1981 which stated that the number of childhood leukemia deaths began to rise in the 1959–1963 period, before the wells were drilled. Assuming an average latency period of 2–5 years, the DPH report agreed that deaths should not have started to increase until 1969–1973, when in fact the rate was lower than expected.[10]

In order to elicit more conclusive data, Zelen and his colleague, Steven Lagakos, undertook a more detailed study of health status in Woburn, focusing on birth defects and reproductive disorders, since these were widely considered to be environmentally related. The biostatisticians and the FACE activists teamed up in what was to become a major epidemiological study and a prototype of a popular epidemiological alliance between citizen activists and sympathetic scientists. FACE coordinated 301 Woburn volunteers who administered a telephone survey from April to September in 1982, which was designed to reach 70% of the city's population who had phones.[11]

At the same time, the state DEQE conducted a hydrogeology study which found that the bedrock in the affected area of Woburn sloped in a southwest direction and was shaped like a bowl, with wells G and H in the deepest part. The agency's March 1982 report addressed the location of the contamination: the source was not the Industri-Plex site as had been believed, but rather W.R. Grace's Cryovac Division and Beatrice Foods' Riley tannery. This major information led eight families of leukemia victims to file a $400 million suit in May 1982 against those corporations for poor waste disposal practices, which led to groundwater contamination and hence to fatal disease.[12] A smaller company, Unifirst, was also sued but quickly settled before trial.[13]

The Harvard School of Public Health/FACE Study

Sources of data included information on 20 cases of childhood leukemia (ages 19 and under) which were diagnosed between 1964 and 1983, the DEQE water model of regional and temporal distribution of water from wells G and H, and the health survey. The survey gathered data on adverse pregnancy outcomes and childhood disorders from 5,010 interviews, covering 57% of Woburn residences with telephones. The researchers trained 235 volunteers to conduct the health survey, taking precautions to avoid bias.[14]

On 8 February 1984, the Harvard SPH data were made public. Childhood leukemia was found to be significantly associated with exposure to water from wells G and H, both on a cumulative basis and on a none-versus-some exposure basis. Children with leukemia received an average of 21.2% of their yearly water supply from the wells, compared to 9.5% for children without leukemia. The data do not, however, explain all 11 excess cases; the cumulative method explains 4 excess cases and the none-versus-some metric explains 6 cases.

Controlling for important risk factors in pregnancy, the investigators found the access to contaminated water was not associated with spontaneous abortions, low birth weight, perinatal deaths before 1970, or with musculoskeletal, cardiovascular, or "other" birth anomalies. Water exposure was associated with perinatal deaths since 1970, eye/ear anomalies, and CNS/chromosomal/oral cleft anomalies. With regard to childhood disorders, water exposure was associated with only two of nine categories of disease: kidney/urinary tract and lung/respiratory. There was no association with allergies, anemia, diabetes, heart/blood pressure, learning disability, neurologic/sensory, or "other" disorders.[15] If only the *in-utero* cases are studied, the results are even stronger in terms of the positive associations.[16]

The researchers conducted extensive analyses to demonstrate that the data were not biased. They compared baseline rates of adverse health effects for West Woburn (never exposed to wells G and H water) and East Woburn (at a period prior to the opening of the wells): no differences were found. They examined transiency rates to test whether they were related to exposure and found them to be alike in both sectors. Various tests also ruled out a number of biases potentially attributable to the volunteer interviewers.[17]

The report was greeted with criticism from

many circles: the CDC, the American Cancer Society, the EPA, and even the Harvard SPH Department of Epidemiology. These criticisms demonstrate both legitimate concerns and clear examples of elitism and opposition to community involvement in scientific work. One of the legitimate concerns was the grouping of diseases into categories, despite their different etiologies. Similarly, the biostatisticians were criticized for grouping diverse birth defects under the broad heading of "environmentally associated disease."[18] The researchers argue, however, that they grouped defects because there could never be sufficient numbers of each of the numerous defects. Further, they claim that their grouping was based on the literature on chemical causes of birth defects. In fact, if the grouping was incorrect, they note that they would not have found positive results.[19] Some critics questioned whether the water model was precise enough, and whether it was independently verified.[20] Actually, the DEQE officials failed to release the water data in a timely fashion, making it impossible to obtain other validation. A more detailed model is now available, although it has been consistently hard to get funds to conduct new analyses.[21] Critics have also noted that there were increasing numbers of cases even after the wells were shut down, and that these new cases were more likely to be in West Woburn than in East Woburn. If wells G and H were the culprit, such critics ask, is it possible that there could be yet another cluster *independent* of the one studied?[22] In fact, given the chemical soup in Woburn, it is indeed plausible that this could be the case. Excavations at the Industri-Plex site produced buried animal hides and chemical wastes. A nearby abandoned lagoon was full of lead, arsenic, and other metals. A sampling from 61 test wells in East Woburn turned up 48 toxic substances on the EPA priority list as well as raised levels of 22 metals.[23]

The criticisms of most interest here are those that argue against the basic concept of public participation in science. Critics held that the study was biased precisely because volunteers conducted the health survey and because the study was based on a political goal. These arguments will be addressed below, as I develop the five elements of popular epidemiology. First, though, we will take a look at commonalities

between several communities that engaged in forms of popular epidemiology.

Elements of Popular Epidemiology

Commonalities in Popular Epidemiology

Couto studied Yellow Creek, Kentucky, where residents identified problems of creek pollution caused by untreated residential and commercial sewage. Comparing this and other locations, Couto develops a model which is a valuable starting place on which I shall expand. Couto identifies three sets of actors. The *community at risk* is the community and people at risk of environment hazards. The *community of consequence calculation* includes the public and private officials who allocate resources related to environmental health risks. The *community of probability calculation* consists of epidemiologists and allied scientists.[24]

The community at risk is where popular epidemiological action begins. In Yellow Creek the shared evidence of obvious pollution was from fish kills, disappearances of small animals, and corrosion of screens and other materials. This "street-wise or creek-side environmental monitoring" precedes awareness of health risks.[25] My interviews with Woburn residents show the same phenomenon: People noticed the water stains on dishwashers and the bad odor long before they were aware of any adverse health effects. Love Canal residents remembered years of bad odors, rocks that exploded when dropped or thrown, sludge leakage into basements, chemical residues on the ground after rainfall, and children's foot irritations after playing in fields where toxic wastes were dumped.[26] Residents of South Brunswick, New Jersey, noticed foul tasting water and saw barrels marked "toxic chemicals" dumped, bulldozed, and ruptured.[27]

The next stage in Couto's model is *common sense epidemiology*, where people intuit that a higher than expected incidence of disease is attributable to pollution.[28] As a result of such judgments, people organize and approach public officials. Another avenue, not mentioned by Couto, is taking the issue to court, for blame, redress, organizing, and legitimation. When citizens organize publicly, they first encounter the community of consequence calculation, a community that usually resists them by denying the problem or its seriousness, and even by blaming the problem on the lifestyle and habits of the people at risk.[29] This is in part due to "environmental blackmail," whereby officials fear that plants will close and jobs and taxes will be lost.

The initial shock at the existence of the toxic substances gives way to anger at the public and private officials who do little or nothing about the problem.[30] This reaction is found in residents' attitudes toward corporate and governmental officials in Woburn and in numerous other sites.[31] . . .

We can now build on Couto's work to generate a broader model of popular epidemiology. Although my examples often involve toxic waste–induced disease, the concept of popular epidemiology clearly extends into other areas.

Popular Participation and the Myth of Value-Neutrality

Popular epidemiology opposes the widely held belief that epidemiology is a value-neutral scientific enterprise which can be conducted in a sociopolitical vacuum. Directly related to this assumption is the belief that epidemiological work should not be conducted only by experts. Those who criticized volunteer bias and political goals in the Woburn study posited a value-free science of epidemiology in which knowledge, theories, techniques, and actual and potential applications are devoid of self-interest or bias. The possibility of volunteer bias is a real concern, of course, but in the Woburn case the care with which the biostatisticians controlled for bias is noteworthy.

Beyond the methodological and statistical controls for bias are a number of other important issues. Science is limited in its practice by factors such as financial and personnel resources. Without popular participation, it would often be impossible to carry out much of the research needed to document health hazards. Science is also limited in its conceptualization of what are problems and how they should be studied and addressed. Without popular involvement there

might be no professional impetus to target the appropriate questions. These aspects of popular involvement are very evident in the history of the women's health movement,[32] the occupational health and safety movement,[33] and the environmental health movement.[34] These movements have been major forces in advancing the public's health and safety by pointing to problems that were otherwise not identified, by showing how to approach such problems, by organizing to abolish the conditions giving rise to them, and by educating citizens, public agencies, health care providers, officials, and institutions. Without such popular participation, how would we have known of such hazards and diseases as DES, Agent Orange, pesticides, unnecessary hysterectomies, sterilization abuse, black lung, brown lung, and asbestos? Couto's discussion of the "politics of epidemiology" argues that the scientific assumptions of traditional epidemiology are not completely suited to environmental hazards. Epidemiologists prefer false negatives to false positives—i.e., they would prefer to claim (falsely) no association between variables when there is one than to claim an association when there is none. Epidemiologists require evidence to achieve scientific statements of probability, but this need exceeds the evidence required to state that something should be done to eliminate or minimize a health threat.[35] In this view,

> The degree of risk to human health does not need to be at statistically significant levels to require political action. The degree of risk does have to be such that a reasonable person would avoid it. Consequently, the important political test is not the findings of epidemiologists in the probability off nonrandomness of an incidence of illness but the likelihood that a reasonable person, including members of the community of calculation, would take up residence with the community at risk and drink and bathe in water from the Yellow Creek area or buy a house along Love Canal.[36]

Indeed, these are the kinds of questions presented to public health officials, researchers, and government members in every setting where there is dispute between the citizen and official perceptions. These questions bring out the metaphors and symbols employed by lay citizens in risk communication, and they stand in contrast to scientific, corporate, and governmental metaphors and symbols.

Popular epidemiology obviously challenges some fundamental epidemiological preconceptions of a "pure" study and its appropriate techniques, such as the nomenclature of disease classifications and the belief that community volunteers automatically introduce bias.[37] Such disputes are not settled primarily within the scientific community. Professional antagonism to popular participation in scientific endeavors is common. Medical sociology has long been aware that such antagonism only occasionally revolves around questions of scientific fact; it usually stems from professional dominance, institutional dominance, and political-economic factors. Professional dominance in science plays an important role here. Professionals generally do not want to let lay publics take on the work that they control as professionals, a particularly ironic situation in the case of epidemiology since the original "shoeleather" epidemiological work that founded the field is quite similar to popular epidemiological efforts. The Woburn residents' efforts are in fact reminiscent of John Snow's classic study of cholera in London in 1854. The scientific paternalism that holds that lay people cannot involve themselves in scientific decisionmaking is a perspective quite familiar to analysts of health care, and which has been widely discredited in recent years.

Further, environmental health groups challenge the canons of value-neutrality and statistical reasoning, thus undermining the core foundations of professional belief systems. By putting forth their own political goals, they may challenge scientists to acknowledge that they have their own political agendas, even if covert, unconscious, or unrecognized. Corporate legal defenses may not be in collusion with professional dominance, but there is an affinity between the two in the courtroom. Corporate attorneys make much of the challenge that citizen activists are untrained individuals who are incapable of making valid judgments regarding pollution.[38] This affinity is due to the fact that popular participation threatens not only the professional-lay division of knowledge and power but also the social structures and relations that give rise to environmental hazards.

The Activist Nature of Popular Epidemiology

Popular epidemiology is by nature activist, since the lay public is doing work that should be done by corporations, experts, and officials. Popular epidemiology may involve citizen-propelled investigation of naturally occurring diseases for which no firm is responsible. With regard to the recognition of and action around Lyme Disease in Connecticut, where a tick-borne disease was the issue, citizen activists became involved because they considered health officials to be dragging their heels in the matter. Despite such examples, however, popular epidemiology is particularly powerful when the issue is environmental pollution, occupational disease, or drug side effects. In those cases, persons and organizations are seen to be acting against the public health, often in light of clear knowledge about the dangers. The process of popular epidemiological investigation is therefore an activist one, in which epidemiological findings are immediately employed to alleviate suffering and causes of suffering.

Environmental health activists are by definition acting to correct problems that are not corrected by the established corporate, political, and scientific communities. Logically, the first step in protecting people from the hazards of toxic chemicals is appropriate corporate action, relating to the judicious use and safe disposal of toxic chemicals. It is well known that manufacturers are often lax in this sphere and frequently violate known laws and safe practices.

Given this situation, and given the fact that many corporations purchase land and factories about which they know nothing concerning their past use of toxic chemicals, public agencies present the next line of defense. These agencies include local boards of health, local water boards, state boards of health, state environmental agencies, and the federal EPA. Lay people often begin at the public agency level rather than the corporate level. As the case studies of Woburn, Yellow Creek, South Brunswick, Love Canal, and many other sites indicate, officials are often skeptical or even hostile to citizen requests and inputs.

Even when public agencies are willing to carry out studies, they often demand a different level of proof than community residents want. Further, agencies tend to undertake "pure" epidemiological research without reference to practical solutions to the problem. Moreover, even if they want to, many public bodies have no legal or effective power to compel cleanups, and they rarely can provide restitution to victims. Popular epidemiology emphasizes the practical nature of environmental health issues, and its practitioners are therefore impatient with the caution with which public agencies approach such problems. As with so many other areas of public policies, the fragmentation of agencies and authority contributes to this problem. Community activists cannot understand why more immediate action cannot be taken, particularly when they are apt to define the situation as more of a crisis than do the officials. . . .

Conclusion

By examining examples of popular epidemiology and by constructing a theoretical framework for it, we have shown it to be a highly politicized form of action. Popular epidemiology is also a form of risk communication by lay persons to professional and official audiences, and as such it demonstrates that risk communication is indeed an exercise of political power. In a growing number of instances, organized communities have been able to successfully communicate risk in such a way as to win political, economic, and cultural battles.

Yet there are some structural problems associated with such victories. Experts and officials may demand increasingly higher levels of proof, requiring field studies that are prohibitive in terms of time, skills, and resources. Concerted political action may win a case but not necessarily build up scientific credibility or precedence. People may fear such a result and begin to tailor their efforts toward convincing experts and officials, thus possibly diminishing the impact of their efforts on their communities.

Solutions to these structural problems are not simple; community residents will have to find ways to work on several fronts simultaneously, and we should not assume that the task is theirs alone. Academics and health and public health professionals can play an important role in informing their colleagues and government officials that there are new ways to understand risk. The public as a whole needs to work toward more stringent and actively enforced environmental legislation and regulation as well as greater social control over corporations.

We are only in the earliest stages of understanding the phenomenon of popular epidemiology. Most research has been on empirical studies of individual cases, with a few preliminary stabs at theoretical and analytical linkages. The existing and future successes of popular epidemiological endeavors can potentially play a major role in reformulating the way that lay people, scientists, and public agencies view public health problems. This is an exciting possibility and one with which by definition we can all be involved.

Acknowledgments—This research was supported in part by funds from the Wayland Collegium, Brown University. This paper is a revised version of a presentation to the Boston Area Medical Sociologists meeting, 6 April 1987, where participants offered important feedback. Many of the ideas here have developed during a year-long faculty seminar at Brown University, where I have benefited from interacting with Anne Fausto-Sterling, John Ladd, Talbot Page, and Harold Ward. Other ideas and data have come from my collaboration with Edwin J. Mikkelsen on a book about Woburn. Dorothy Nelkin and Alonzo Plough provided valuable comments on the manuscript.

NOTES

1. Jerry Ackerman and Diego Ribadeneira, "12 Families, Grace Settle Woburn Toxic Case," *Boston Globe*, 23 September 1986; William F. Doherty, "Jury: Firm Fouled Wells in Woburn," *Boston Globe*, 29 July 1986.
2. Abraham Lilienfeld, *Foundations of Epidemiology* [New York: Oxford, 1976], p. 4.
3. Paula DiPerna, *Cluster Mystery: Epidemic and the Children of Woburn, Mass.* (St. Louis: Mosby, 1985), pp. 106–108.
4. *Ibid.,* p. 75–82.
5. *Ibid.,* pp. 53–70.
6. *Ibid.,* pp. 111–155.
7. *Ibid.,* p. 161.
8. *Ibid.,* pp. 164–173.
9. *Ibid.,* p. 175.
10. *Ibid.,* pp. 176–199.
11. *Ibid.,* pp. 200–211.

12. *Ibid.*, pp. 209–215.
13. Jan Schlictmann, interview, 12 May 1987.
14. Steven W. Lagakos, Barbara J. Wessen, and Marvin Zelen, "An Analysis of Contaminated Well Water and Health Effects in Woburn, Massachusetts," *Journal of the American Statistical Association.* Volume 81, Number 395 (1984): 583–596.
15. *Ibid.*
16. Steven Lagakos, interview, 6 April 1987.
17. *Ibid.*
18. DiPerma, *op. cit.,* pp. 168–169.
19. Marvin Zelen, interview, 1 July 1987.
20. DiPerna, *op. cit.,* pp. 251–273.
21. Zelen, *op. cit.*
22. Allan Morrison lecture, Brown University, Department of Community Health, 25 February 1987.
23. Lagakos *et al., op. cit.*
24. Richard A. Couto, "Failing Health and New Prescriptions: Community-Based Approaches to Environmental Risks," in Carole E. Hill, ed., *Current Health Policy Issues and Alternatives: An Applied Social Science Perspective* (Athens: University of Georgia Press, 1986).
25. *Ibid.*
26. Adeline Gordon Levine, *Love Canal: Science,* *Politics, and People* (Lexington, Mass.: Heath, 1982), pp. 14–15.
27. Celene Krauss, "Grass-Root Protests and Toxic Wastes: Developing a Critical Political View." Paper presented at a 1986 meeting of the American Sociological Association.
28. Couto, *op. cit.*
29. *Ibid.*
30. *Ibid.*
31. Nicholas Freudenberg, *Not in Our Backyards: Community Action for Health and the Environment* (New York: Monthly Review, 1984).
32. Helen Rodriguez-Trias, "The Women's Health Movement: Women Take Power," in Victor Sidel and Ruth Sidel, eds., *Reforming Medicine: Lessons of the Last Quarter Century* (New York: Pantheon, 1984), pp. 107–126.
33. Daniel Berman, "Why Work Kills: A Brief History of Occupational Health and Safety in the United States," *International Journal of Health Services.* Volume 7, Number 1 (1977): 63–87.
34. Freudenberg, *Not in Our Backyards, op. cit.*
35. Couto, *op cit.*
36. *Ibid.*
37. DiPerna, *op. cit.,* p. 379.
38. Krauss, *op. cit.*

8

Social Relationships and Health

▪ ▪ ▪ ▪ ▪ ▪

James S. House, Karl R. Landis, and Debra Umberson

. . . my father told me of a careful observer, who certainly had heart-disease and died from it, and who positively stated that his pulse was habitually irregular to an extreme degree; yet to his great disappointment it invariably became regular as soon as my father entered the room.—Charles Darwin (1)

Scientists have long noted an association between social relationships and health. More socially isolated or less socially integrated individuals are less healthy, psychologically and physically, and more likely to die. The first major work of empirical sociology found that less socially integrated people were more likely to commit suicide than the most integrated (2). In subsequent epidemiologic research age-adjusted mortality rates from all causes of death are consistently higher among the unmarried than the married (3–5). Unmarried and more socially isolated people have also manifested higher rates of tuberculosis (6), accidents (7), and psychiatric disorders such as schizophrenia (8, 9). And as the above quote from Darwin suggests, clinicians have also observed potentially health-enhancing qualities of social relationships and contacts.

The causal interpretation and explanation of these associations has, however, been less clear. Does a lack of social relationships cause people to become ill or die? Or are unhealthy people less likely to establish and maintain social relationships? Or is there some other factor, such as a misanthropic personality, which predisposes people both to have a lower quantity or quality of social relationships and to become ill or die?

Such questions have been largely unanswerable before the last decade for two reasons. First, there was little theoretical basis for causal explanation. Durkheim (2) proposed a theory of how social relationships affected suicide, but this theory did not generalize to morbidity and mortality from other causes. Second, evidence of the association between social relationships and health, especially in general human populations, was almost entirely retrospective or cross-sectional before the late 1970s. Retrospective studies from death certificates or hospital records ascertained the nature of people's social relationships after they had become ill or died, and cross-sectional surveys of general populations determined whether people who reported ill health also reported a lower quality or quantity of relationships. Such studies used statistical control of potential confounding variables to rule out third factors that might produce the association between social relationships and health, but could do this only partially. They could not determine whether poor social relationships preceded or followed ill health.

In this article, we review recent developments that have altered this state of affairs dramatically: (i) emergence of theoretical models for a causal effect of social relationships on health in humans and animals; (ii) cumulation of empirical evidence that social relationships are a consequential predictor of mortality in human populations; and (iii) increasing evidence for the causal impact of social relationships on psychological and physiological functioning in quasi-experimental and experimental studies of humans and animals. These developments suggest that social relationships, or the relative lack thereof, constitute a

major risk factor for health—rivaling the effects of well-established health risk factors such as cigarette smoking, blood pressure, blood lipids, obesity, and physical activity. Indeed, the theory and evidence on social relationships and health increasingly approximate that available at the time of the U.S. Surgeon General's 1964 report on smoking and health (10), with similar implications for future research and public policy.

The Emergence of "Social Support" Theory and Research

The study of social relationships and health was revitalized in the middle 1970s by the emergence of a seemingly new field of scientific research on "social support." This concept was first used in the mental health literature (11, 12), and was linked to physical health in separate seminal articles by physician-epidemiologists Cassel (13) and Cobb (14). These articles grew out of a rapidly developing literature on stress and psychosocial factors in the etiology of health and illness (15). Chronic diseases have increasingly replaced acute infectious diseases as the major causes of disability and death, at least in industrialized countries. Consequently, theories of disease etiology have shifted from ones in which a single factor (usually a microbe) caused a single disease, to ones in which multiple behavioral and environmental as well as biologic and genetic factors combine, often over extended periods, to produce any single disease, with a given factor often playing an etiologic role in multiple diseases.

Cassel (13) and Cobb (14) reviewed more than 30 human and animal studies that found social relationships protective of health. Recognizing that any one study was open to alternative interpretations, they argued that the variety of study designs (ranging from retrospective to experimental), of life stages studied (from birth to death), and of health outcomes involved (including low birth weight, complications of pregnancy, self-reported symptoms, blood pressure, arthritis, tuberculosis, depression, alcoholism, and mortality) suggested a robust, putatively causal, association. Cassel and Cobb indicated that social relationships might promote health in several ways, but emphasized the role of social relationships in moderating or buffering potentially deleterious health effects of psychosocial stress or other health hazards. This idea of "social support," or something that maintains or sustains the organism by promoting adaptive behavior or neuroendocrine responses in the face of stress or other health hazards, provided a general, albeit simple, theory of how and why social relationships should causally affect health (16).

Publications on "social support" increased almost geometrically from 1976 to 1981. By the late 1970s, however, serious questions emerged about the empirical evidence cited by Cassel and Cobb and the evidence generated in subsequent research. Concerns were expressed about causal priorities between social support and health (since the great majority of studies remained cross-sectional or retrospective and based on self-reported data), about whether social relationships and supports buffered the impact of stress on health or had more direct effects, and about how consequential the effects of social relationships on health really were (17–19). These concerns have been addressed by a continuing cumulation of two types of empirical data: (i) a new series of prospective mortality studies in human populations and (ii) a broadening base of laboratory and field experimental studies of animals and humans.

Prospective Mortality Studies of Human Populations
....

Just as concerns began to surface about the nature and strength of the impact of social relationships on health, data from long-term, prospective studies of community populations provided compelling evidence that lack of social relationships constitutes a major risk factor for mortality. Berkman and Syme (20) analyzed a probability sample of 4775 adults in Alameda County, California, who were between 30 and 69 in 1965 when they completed a survey that assessed the presence or extent of four types of social ties—marriage, contacts with extended family and friends, church membership, and other formal and informal group affiliations. Each type of social relationship predicted mortal-

ity through the succeeding 9 years. A combined "social network" index remained a significant predictor of mortality (with a relative risk ratio for mortality of about 2.0, indicating that persons low on the index were twice as likely to die as persons high on the index) in multivariate analyses that controlled for self-reports in 1965 of physical health, socioeconomic status, smoking, alcohol consumption, physical activity, obesity, race, life satisfaction, and use of preventive health services. Such adjustment or control for baseline health and other risk factors provides a conservative estimate of the predictive power of social relationships, since some of their impact may be mediated through effects on these risk factors.

The major limitation of the Berkman and Syme study was the lack of other than self-reported data on health at baseline. Thus, House et al. (21) sought to replicate and extend the Alameda County results in a study of 2754 adults between 35 and 69 at their initial interview and physical examinations in 1967 through 1969 by the Tecumseh (Michigan) Community Health Study. Composite indices of social relationships and activities (as well as a number of the individual components) were inversely associated with mortality during the succeeding 10- to 12-year follow-up period, with relative risks of 2.0 to 3.0 for men and 1.5 to 2.0 for women, after adjustment for the effects of age and a wide range of biomedically assessed (blood pressure, cholesterol, respiratory function, and electrocardiograms) as well as self-reported risk factors of mortality. Analyzing data on 2059 adults in the Evans County (Georgia) Cardiovascular Epidemiologic Study, Schoenback et al. (22) also found that a social network index similar to that of Berkman and Syme (20) predicted mortality for an 11- to 13-year follow-up period, after adjustment for age and baseline measures of biomedical as well as self-reported risk factors of mortality. The Evans County associations were somewhat weaker than those in Tecumseh and Alameda County, and as in Tecumseh were stronger for males than females.

Studies in Sweden and Finland have described similar results. Tibblin, Welin, and associates (23, 24) studied two cohorts of men born in 1913 and 1923, respectively, and living in 1973 in

Gothenberg, Sweden's second largest city. After adjustments for age, baseline levels of systolic blood pressure, serum cholesterol, smoking habits, and perceived health status, mortality in both cohorts through 1982 was inversely related to the number of persons in the household and the men's level of social and outside home activities in 1973. Orth-Gomer et al. (25) analyzed the mortality experience through 1981 of a random sample of 17,433 Swedish adults aged 29 to 74 at the time of their 1976 or 1977 baseline interviews. Frequency of contact with family, friends, neighbors, and co-workers in 1976–77 was predictive of mortality through 1981, after adjustment for age, sex, education, employment status, immigrant status, physical exercise, and self-reports of chronic conditions. The effects were stronger among males than among females, and were somewhat nonlinear, with the greatest increase in mortality risk occurring in the most socially isolated third of the sample. In a prospective study of 13,301 adults in predominantly rural eastern Finland, Kaplan et al. (26) found a measure of "social connections" similar to those used in Alameda County, Tecumseh, and Evans County to be a significant predictor of male mortality from all causes during 5 years, again after adjustments for other biomedical and self-reported risk factors. Female mortality showed similar, but weaker and statistically nonsignificant, effects.

These studies manifest a consistent pattern of results, as shown in Figs. 8-1 and 8-2, which show age-adjusted mortality rates plotted for the five prospective studies from which we could extract parallel data. The report of the sixth study (25) is consistent with these trends. The relative risks (RR) in Figs. 8-1 and 8-2 are higher than those reported above because they are only adjusted for age. The levels of mortality in Figs. 8-1 and 8-2 vary greatly across studies depending on the follow-up period and composition of the population by age, race, and ethnicity, and geographic locale, but the patterns of prospective association between social integration (that is, the number and frequency of social relationships and contacts) and mortality are remarkably similar, with some variations by race, sex, and geographic locale.

Only the Evans County study reported data for blacks. The predictive association of social integration with mortality among Evans County black males is weaker than among white males in Evans County or elsewhere (Fig. 8-1), and the relative risk ratio for black females in Evans County, although greater than for Evans County white females, is smaller than the risk ratios for white females in all other studies (Fig. 8-2). More research on blacks and other minority populations is necessary to determine whether these differences are more generally characteristic of blacks compared to whites.

Modest differences emerge by sex and rural as opposed to urban locale. Results for men and women are strong, linear, and similar in the urban populations of Alameda County (that is, Oakland and environs) and Gothenberg, Sweden (only men were studied in Gothenberg). In the predominantly small-town and rural populations of Tecumseh, Evans County, and eastern Finland, however, two notable deviations from the urban results appear: (i) female risk ratios are consistently weaker than those for men in the same rural populations (Figs. 8-1 and 8-2), and (ii) the results for men in more rural populations, although rivaling those in urban populations in terms of risk ratios, assume a distinctly nonlinear, or threshold, form. That is, in Tecumseh, Evans County, and eastern Finland, mortality is clearly elevated among the most socially isolated, but declines only modesty, if at all, between moderate and high levels of social integration.

Explanation of these sex and urban-rural variations awaits research on broader regional or national populations in which the same measures are applied to males and females across the full rural-urban continuum. The current results may have both substantive and methodological explanations. Most of the studies reviewed here, as well as others (27–29), suggest that being married is more beneficial to health, and becoming widowed more deterimental, for men than for women. Women, however, seem to benefit as much or more than men from relationships with friends and relatives, which tend to run along same-sex lines (20, 30). On balance, men may benefit more from social relationships than women, especially in cross-gender relationships.

Figure 8-1. *Level of Social Integration and Age-Adjusted Mortality for Males in Five Prospective Studies**

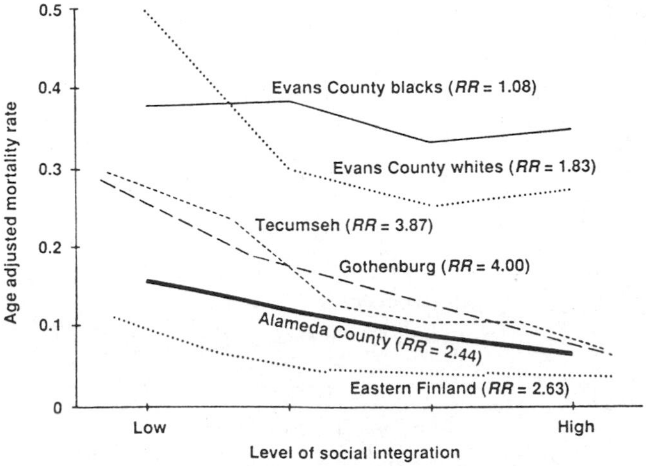

Note: RR, the relative risk ratio of mortality at the lowest versus highest level of social integration.

Small communities may also provide a broader context of social integration and support that benefits most people, except for a relatively small group of socially isolated males.

These results may, however, have methodological rather than substantive explanations. Measures of social relationships or integration used in the existing prospective studies may be less valid or have less variance in rural and small town environments, and for women, thus muting their relationship with mortality. For example, the data for women in Fig. 8-2 are similar to the data on men if we assume that women have higher quality relationships and hence that their true level of social integration is moderate even at low levels of quantity. The social context of small communities may similarly provide a moderate level of social integration for everyone except quite isolated males. Thus measures of frequency of social contact may be poorer indices of social integration for women and more rural populations than for men and urban dwellers.

Variations in the results in Figs. 8-1 and 8-2 should not, however, detract from the remarkable consistency of the overall finding that social relationships do predict mortality for men and women in a wide range of populations, even after adjustment for biomedical risk factors for mortality. Additional prospective studies have shown that social relationships are similarly predictive of all-cause and cardiovascular mortality in studies of people who are elderly (*31–33*) or have serious illnesses (*34, 35*).

Experimental and Quasi-experimental Research

The prospective mortality data are made more compelling by their congruence with growing evidence from experimental and clinical research on animals and humans that variations in exposure to social contacts produce psychological or physiological effects that could, if prolonged, produce serious morbidity and even mortality. Cassel (*13*) reviewed evidence that the presence of a familiar member of the same species could buffer the impact of experimentally induced stress on ulcers, hypertension, and neurosis in rats, mice, and goats, respectively; and the presence of familiar others has also been shown to reduce

Figure 8-2. *Level of Social Integration and Age-Adjusted Mortality for Females in Five Prospective Studies**

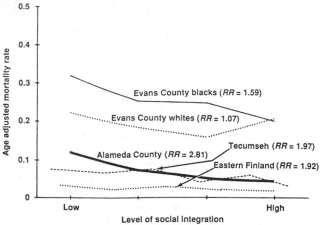

Note: RR, *the relative risk ratio of mortality at the lowest versus highest level of social integration.*

anxiety and physiological arousal (specifically secretion of free fatty acids) in humans in potentially stressful laboratory situations (*36, 37*). Clinical and laboratory data indicate that the presence of or physical contact with another person can modulate human cardiovascular activity and reactivity in general, and in stressful contexts such as intensive care units (*38,* pp. 122–141). Research also points to the operation of such processes across species. Affectionate petting by humans, or even their mere presence, can reduce the cardiovascular sequelae of stressful situations among dogs, cats, horses, and rabbits (*38,* pp. 163–180). Nerem *et al.* (*39*) found that human handling also reduced the arteriosclerotic impact of a high fat diet in rabbits. Recent interest in the potential health benefits of pets for humans, especially the isolated aged, is based on similar notions, although the evidence for such efforts is only suggestive (*40*).

Bovard (*41*) has proposed a psychophysiologic theory to explain how social relationships and contacts can promote health and protect against disease. He reviews a wide range of human and animal studies suggesting that social relationships and contacts, mediated through the amygdala, activate the anterior hypothalamic zone (stimulating release of hu-

man growth hormone) and inhibit the posterior hypothalamic zone (and hence secretion of adrenocorticotropic hormone, cortisol, catecholamines, and associated sympathetic autonomic activity). These mechanisms are consistent with the impact of social relationships on mortality from a wide range of causes and with studies of the adverse effects of lack of adequate social relationships on the development of human and animal infants (*42*). This theory is also consistent with sociobiological processes which, due to the survival benefit of social relationships and collective activity, would promote genetic selection of organisms who find social contact and relatedness rewarding and the lack of such contact and relatedness aversive (*43*).

The epidemiologic evidence linking social relationships and supports to morbidity in humans is limited and not fully consistent. For example, although laboratory studies show short-term effects of social relationships on cardiovascular functioning that would, over time, produce cardiovascular disease, and prospective studies show impacts of social relationships on mortality from cardiovascular disease, the link between social relationships and the incidence of cardiovascular morbidity has yet to be firmly demonstrated (*19, 44*). Overall, however, the theory and evidence for the impact of social relationships on health are building steadily (*45, 46*).

Social Relationships as a Risk Factor for Health: Research and Policy Issues

The theory and data reviewed above meet reasonable criteria for considering social relationships a cause or risk factor of mortality, and probably morbidity, from a wide range of diseases (*10; 46; 47*, pp. 289–321). These criteria include strength and consistency of statistical associations across a wide range of studies, temporal ordering of prediction from cause to effect, a gradient of response (which may in this case be nonlinear), experimental data on animals and humans consistent with nonexperimental human data, and a plausible theory (*41*) of biopsychosocial mechanisms explaining the observed associations.

The evidence on social relationships is probably stronger, especially in terms of prospective studies, than the evidence which led to the certification of the Type A behavior pattern as a risk factor for coronary heart disease (*48*). The evidence regarding social relationships and health increasingly approximates the evidence in the 1964 Surgeon General's report (*10*) that established cigarette smoking as a cause or risk factor for mortality and morbidity from a range of diseases. The age-adjusted relative risk ratios shown in Fig. 8-1 and 8-2 are stronger than the relative risks for all cause mortality reported for cigarette smoking (*10*). There is, however, less specificity in the associations of social relationships with mortality than has been observed for smoking, which is strongly linked to cancers of the lung and respiratory tract (with age-adjusted risk ratios between 3.0 and 11.0). Better theory and data are needed on the links between social relationships and major specific causes of morbidity and mortality.

Although a lack of social relationships has been established as a risk factor for mortality, and probably morbidity, three areas need further investigation: (i) mechanisms and processes linking social relationships to health, (ii) determinants of levels of "exposure" to social relationships, and (iii) the means to lower the prevalence of relative social isolation in the population or to lessen its deleterious effects on health.

Mechanisms and Processes Linking Social Relationships to Health

Although grounded in the literature on social relationships and health, investigators on social support in the last decade leaped almost immediately to the interpretation that what was consequential for health about social relationships was their supportive quality, especially their capacity to buffer or moderate the deleterious effects of stress or other health hazards (*13, 14*). Many recent studies have reported either a general positive association between social support and health or a buffering effect in the presence of stress (*49*), but these studies are problematic because the designs are largely cross-sectional or retrospective and the data usually self-reported. The most compelling evidence of the causal significance of social relationships on health has come from the experimental studies of animals and humans an the prospective mortality studies reviewed above—studies in which the measures of social relationships are merely the presence or absence of familiar other organisms, or relative frequency of contact with them, and which often do not distinguish between buffering and main effects. Thus, social relationships appear to have generally beneficial effects on health, not solely or even primarily attributable to their buffering effects, and there may be aspects of social relationships other than their supportive quality that account for these effects.

We now need a broader theory of the biopsychosocial mechanisms and processes linking social relationships to health than can be provided by extant concepts or theories of social support. That broader theory must do several things. First, it must clearly distinguish between (i) the existence or quantity of social relationships, (ii) their formal structure (such as their density or reciprocity), and (iii) the actual content of these relationships such as social support. Only by testing the effects on health of these different aspects of social relationships in the same study can we understand what it is about social relationships that is consequential for health.

Second, we need better understanding of the social, psychological, and biological processes that link the existence, quantity, structure, or content of social relationships to health. Social support—whether in the form of practical help, emotional sustenance, or provision of information—is only one of the social processes involved here. Not only may social relationships affect health because they are or are not supportive, they may also regulate or control human thought, feeling and behavior in ways that promote health, as in Durkheim's (2) theory relating social integration to suicide. Current views based on this perspective suggest that social relationships affect health either by fostering a sense of meaning or coherence that promotes health (50) or by facilitating health-promoting behaviors such as proper sleep, diet, or exercise, appropriate use of alcohol, cigarettes, and drugs, adherence to medical regimens, or seeking appropriate medical care (51). The negative or conflictive aspects of social relationships need also to be considered, since they may be detrimental to the maintenance of health and of social relationship (52).

We must further understand the psychological and biological processes or mechanisms linking social relationships to health, either as extensions of the social processes just discussed [for example, processes of cognitive appraisal and coping (53)] or as independent mechanisms. In the latter regard, psychological and sociobiological theories suggest that the mere presence of, or sense of relatedness with, another organism may have relatively direct motivational, emotional, or neuroendocrine effects that promote health either directly or in the face of stress or other health hazards but that operate independently of cognitive appraisal or behavioral coping and adaptation (38, pp. 87–180; 42, 43, 54).

Determinants of Social Relationships: Scientific and Policy Issues

Although social relationships have been extensively studied during the past decade as independent, intervening, and moderating variables affecting stress or health or the relations between them, almost no attention has been paid to social relationships as dependent variables. The determinants of social relationships, as well as their consequences, are crucial to the theoretical and causal status of social relationships in relation to

health. If exogenous biological, psychological, or social variables determine both health and the nature of social relationships, then the observed association of social relationships to health may be totally or partially spurious. More practically, Cassel (13), Cobb (14), and others became interested in social support as a means of improving health. This, in turn, requires understanding of the broader social, as well as psychological or biological, structures and processes that determine the quantity and quality of social relationships and support in society.

It is clear that biology and personality must and do affect both people's health and the quantity and quality of their social relationships. Research has established that such factors do not, however, explain away the experimental, cross-sectional, and prospective evidence linking social relationships to health (55). In none of the prospective studies have controls for biological or health variables been able to explain away the predictive association between social relationships and mortality. Efforts to explain away the association of social relationships and supports with health by controls for personality variables have similarly failed (56, 57). Social relationships have a predictive, arguably causal, association with health in their own right.

The extent and quality of social relationships experienced by individuals is also a function of broader social forces. Whether people are employed, married, attend church, belong to organizations, or have frequent contact with friends and relatives, and the nature and quality of those relationships, are all determined in part by their positions in a larger social structure that is stratified by age, race, sex, and socioeconomic status and is organized in terms of residential communities, work organizations, and larger political and economic structures. Older people, blacks, and the poor are generally less socially integrated (58), and differences in social relationships by sex and place of residence have been discussed in relation to Figs. 8-1 and 8-2. Changing patterns of fertility, mortality, and migration in society affect opportunities for work, marriage, living and working in different settings, and having relationships with friends and relatives, and can even affect the nature and quality of these relations (59). These demographic patterns are themselves subject to influence by both planned and unplanned economic and political change, which can also affect individuals' social relationships more directly—witness the massive increase in divorce during the last few decades in response to the women's movement, growth in women's labor force participation, and changing divorce law (60, 61).

In contrast with the 1950s, adults in the United States in the 1970s were less likely to be married, more likely to be living alone, less likely to belong to voluntary organizations, and less likely to visit informally with others (62). Changes in marital and childbearing patterns and in the age structure of our society will produce in the 21st century a steady increase of the number of older people who lack spouses or children—the people to whom older people most often turn for relatedness and support (59). Thus, just as we discover the importance of social relationships for health, and see an increasing need for them, their prevalence and availability may be declining. Changes in other risk factors (for example, the decline of smoking) and improvements in medical technology are still producing overall improvements on health and longevity, but the improvements might be even greater if the quantity and quality of social relationships were also improving.

REFERENCES AND NOTES

1. C. Darwin, *Expression of the Emotions in Man and Animals* (Univ. of Chicago Press, Chicago, 1965 [1872]).
2. E. Durkheim, *Suicide* (Free Press, New York, 1951 [1897]).
3. A. S. Kraus and A. N. Lilienfeld, *J. Chronic Dis.* 10, 207 (1959).
4. H. Carter and P. C. Glick, *Marriage and Divorce: A Social and Economic Study* (Harvard Univ. Press, Cambridge, MA, 1970).
5. E. M. Kitigawa and P. M. Hauser, *Differential Mortality in the United States: A Study in Socio-Economic Epidemiology* (Harvard Univ. Press, Cambridge, MA, 1973).
6. T. H. Holmes, in *Personality, Stress and Tuberculosis,* P. J. Sparer, Ed. (International Univ. Press, New York, 1956).
7. W. A. Tillman and G. E. Hobbs, *Am. J. Psychiatr.* 106, 321 (1949).
8. R. E. L. Faris, *Am. J. Sociol.* 39, 155 (1934).

9. M. L. Kohn and J. A. Clausen, *Am. Sociol. Rev.* 20, 268 (1955).
10. U.S. Surgeon General's Advisory Committee on Smoking and Health, *Smoking and Health* (U.S. Public Health Service, Washington, DC, 1964).
11. G. Caplan, *Support Systems and Community Mental Health* (Behavioral Publications, New York, 1974).
12. President's Commission on Mental Health, *Report to the President* (Government Printing Office, Washington, DC, 1978), vols. 1 to 5.
13. J. Cassel, *Am. J. Epidemiol.* 104, 107 (1976).
14. S. Cobb, *Psychosomatic Med.* 38, 300 (1976).
15. J. Cassel, in *Social Stress,* S. Levine and N. A. Scotch, Eds. (Aldine, Chicago, 1970), pp. 189–209.
16. J. S. House, *Work Stress and Social Support* (Addison-Wesley, Reading, MA, 1981).
17. K. Heller, in *Maximizing Treatment Gains: Transfer Enhancement in Psychotherapy,* A. P. Goldstein and F. H. Kanter, Eds. (Academic Press, New York, 1979), pp. 353–382.
18. P. A. Thoits, *J. Health Soc. Behav.* 23, 145 (1982).
19. D. Reed *et al., Am. J. Epidemiol.* 117, 384 (1983).
20. L. F. Berkman and S. L. Syme, *ibid.* 109, 186 (1979).
21. J. S. House, C. Robbins, H. M. Metzner, *ibid.* 116, 123 (1982).
22. V. J. Schoenbach *et al., ibid.* 123, 577 (1986).
23. G. Tibblin *et al.,* in *Social Support: Health and Disease,* S. O. Isacsson and L. Janzon, Eds. (Almqvist & Wiksell, Stockholm, 1986), pp. 11–19.
24. L. Welin *et al., Lancet* i, 915 (1985).
25. K. Orth-Gomer and J. Johnson, *J. Chron. Dis.* 40, 949 (1987).
26. G. A. Kaplan *et al., Am. J. Epidemiol.,* in press.
27. M. Stroebe and W. Stroebe, *Psychol. Bull.* 93, 279 (1983).
28. W. R. Gove, *Soc. Forces* 51, 34 (1972).
29. K. J. Helsing and M. Szklo, *Am. J. Epidemiol.* 114, 41 (1981).
30. L. Wheeler, H. Reis, J. Nezlek, *J. Pers. Soc. Psychol.* 45, 943 (1983).
31. D. Blazer, *Am. J. Epidemiol.* 115, 684 (1982).
32. D. M. Zuckerman, S. V. Kasl, A. M. Ostfeld, *ibid.* 119, 410 (1984).
33. T. E. Seeman *et al., ibid.* 126, 714 (1987).
34. W. E. Ruberman *et al., N. Eng. J. Med.* 311, 552 (1984).
35. K. Orth-Gomer *et al.,* in *Social Support: Health and Disease,* S. O. Isacsson and L. Janzon, Eds. (Almqvist & Wiksell, Stockholm, 1986), pp. 21–31.

36. L. S. Wrightsman, Jr., *J. Abnorm. Soc. Psychol.* **61** 216 (1960).

37. K. W. Back and M. D. Bogdonoff, *Behav. Sci.* **12**, 384 (1967).

38. J. J. Lynch, *The Broken Heart* (Basic Books, New York, 1979).

39. R. M. Nerem, M. J. Levesque, J. F. Cornhill, *Science* **208**, 1475 (1980).

40. J. Goldmeier, *Gerontologist* **26**, 203 (1986).

41. E. W. Bovard, in *Perspectives on Behavioral Medicine*, R. B. Williams (Academic Press, New York, 1985), vol. 2.

42. J. Bowlby, in *Loneliness: The Experience of Emotional and Social Isolation*, R. S. Weiss, Ed. (MIT Press, Cambridge, MA, 1973).

43. S. P. Mendoza, in *Social Cohesion: Essays Toward a Sociophysiological Perspective*, P. R. Barchas and S. P. Mendoza, Eds. (Greenwood Press, Westport, CT, 1984).

44. S. Cohen, *Health Psychol.* **7**, 269 (1988).

45. L. F. Berkman, in *Social Support and Health*, S. Cohen and S. L. Syme, Eds. (Academic Press, New York, 1985), pp. 241–262.

46. W. E. Broadhead *et al.*, *Am. J. Epidemiol.* **117**, 521 (1983).

47. A. M. Lilienfeld and D. E. Lilienfeld, *Foundations of Epidemiology* (Oxford Univ. Press, New York, 1980).

48. National Heart, Lung and Blood Institute, *Circulations* **63**, 1199 (1982).

49. S. Cohen and S. L. Syme, *Social Support and Health* (Academic Press, New York, 1985).

50. A. Antonovsky, *Health, Stress and Coping* (Jossey-Bass, San Francisco, 1979).

51. D. Umberson, *J. Health Soc. Behav.* **28**, 306 (1987).

52. K. Rook, *J. Pers. Soc. Psychol.* **46**, 1097 (1984).

53. R. S. Lazarus and S. Folkman, *Stress, Appraisal, and Coping* (Springer, New York, 1984).

54. R. B. Zajonc, *Science* **149**, 269 (1965).

55. J. S. House, D. Umberson, K. Landis, *Annu. Rev. Sociol.*, in press.

56. S. Cohen, D. R. Sherrod, M. S. Clark, *J. Pers. Soc. Psychol.* **50**, 963 (1986).

57. R. Schultz and S. Decker, *ibid.* **48**, 1162 (1985).

58. J. S. House, *Socio Forum* **2**, 135 (1987).

59. S. C. Watkins, J. A. Menken, J. Bongaarts, *Am. Sociol. Rev.* **52**, 346 (1987).

60. A. Cherlin, *Marriage, Divorce, Remarriage* (Harvard Univ. Press, Cambridge, MA, 1981).

61. L. J. Weitzman, *The Divorce Revolution* (Free Press, New York, 1985).

62. J. Veroff, E. Douvan, R. A. Kulka, *The Inner American: A Self-Portrait from 1957 to 1976* (Basic Books, New York, 1981).

63. Supported by a John Simon Guggenheim Memorial Foundation Fellowship and NIA grant 1-PO1-AG05561 (to J.S.H.), NIMH training grant 5-T32-MH16806-06 traineeship (to K.R.L.), NIMH training grant 5-T32-MH16806-05 and NIA 1-F32-AG05440-01 postdoctoral fellowships (to D.U.). We are indebted to D. Buss, P. Converse, G. Duncan, R. Kahn, R. Kessler, H. Schuman, L. Syme, and R. Zajonc for comments on previous drafts, to many other colleagues who have contributed to this field, and to M. Klatt for preparing the manuscript.

9

Social Class and Cardiovascular Disease: The Contribution of Work

······

Michael Marmot and Tores Theorell

Introduction

One of the dominant features of the epidemiology of cardiovascular diseases is their relation to social class. One of the dominant themes of recent research on psychosocial factors and cardiovascular disease is the importance of working life. In this contribution we attempt to put these together; first by reviewing the evidence and implications of the social class distribution of cardiovascular disease; second by placing the findings on work characteristics and cardiovascular diseases in the context of other psychosocial factors and other biomedical risk factors for cardiovascular disease. We then consider the extent to which the psychosocial characteristics of lower status jobs might account for the higher rates of cardiovascular disease of people of lower social status. We conclude with a justification of our focus on work in terms of both research and public health action.

To anticipate: our conclusion gives a rationale for singling out work characteristics from the other features that characterize the differences between social classes in modern industrialized societies. Our focus is not, however, to "explain away" social class differences in disease occurrence. We do not seek to show that social class differences in disease can be accounted for by differences in the characteristics of individuals. Much of the work on psychosocial factors has attempted to accord these factors the status of another individual risk factor, analogous to plasma cholesterol, smoking, or blood pressure level. This is not our intention. We acknowledge that it is of interest to know if people who are hostile or display type A behavior or lack a hardy personality are at increased risk of coronary heart disease (CHD). If this were the case, these could be considered individual risk factors. This fits into a clinical approach to disease—find individuals and treat them. It lacks a social/causal perspective. Why are individuals hostile, type A, or nonhardy? Our concern is with the links between social position and disease occurrence. To concentrate only on individual characteristics ignores the powerful social influences that are reflected in social class differences in disease rates.

It is not our intention to discuss all of the literature linking social class to cardiovascular disease but to articulate a specific research program that has examined this subject over the last decade. This program has been built up in an international collaborative effort based upon epidemiological population registers and psychophysiological stress research in Sweden, sociological expertise in the United States and West Germany, and medical epidemiological research traditions in Great Britain.

Persistence over Time and Place

In British national data, social class has traditionally been based on occupation using the Registrar-General's classification into classes from I (professional) to V (unskilled manual). In Figures 9-1 and 9-2, classes are grouped into nonmanual and

Figure 9-1. *Standardized Mortality Ratios in Men Aged 20–64 for Death due to All Causes, Lung Cancer, Coronary Heart Disease (CHD) and Cerebrovascular Disease (Cerebro VD) in Great Britain, 1970–72 and 1979–83, for Manual (o–o) and Nonmanual (●–●) Groups*

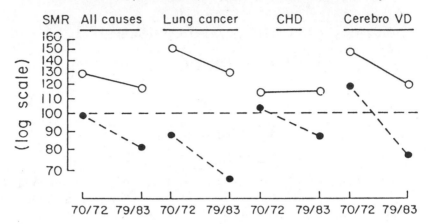

manual since this diminishes the possible effects of changes over time in classification (1). The data come from successive Registrar-General's reports, 1970–72 and 1979–83, or mortality according to occupation around the 1971 and 1981 censuses. All-cause mortality has declined, over the decade, in men and women and in manual and nonmanual classes, but the gap between manual and nonmanual that existed in 1970–72 has increased. For CHD there has actually been an increase in mortality for manual and a decline in mortality for nonmanual groups. Tracing mortality further back to the 1930s confirms the impression that, although mortality rates have declined, the relative disadvantage of lower social classes has increased (2).

Great Britain is not alone in having such social class differences. It is true in Scandinavia (3), other Western European countries (4), North America (5), and Japan (6). Data are not readily available on social class and cardiovascular disease in developing countries. That the picture may be different is shown by the experience of immigrants to England and Wales (7) (Figure 9-3). Among immigrants from European countries, the familiar inverse association is seen: lower class–higher mortality; but there is no association among immigrants from the Indian subcontinent, and higher mortality in nonmanual classes among immigrants from the Caribbean.

Pathways Linking Social Class to Cardiovascular Disease

In the Whitehall study of British Civil Servants, we have had the opportunity to investigate the links between social position and disease rates. As indicated in Figure 9-4, there is a steep inverse association between grade (level) of employment and mortality from CHD and a range of other causes (8). This gradient is steeper than that seen nationally when mortality is compared across the Register-General's social classes. The Whitehall gradient has therefore been dismissed as somehow atypical (9). It is instructive to ask what "atypical" might mean. The Whitehall population consisted of all office-based civil servants, overwhelmingly of one ethnic group, with one employer, in one geographical district, in stable employment, not exposed to the physical environmental hazards of factory and outdoor work. Why then should the gradient in mortality between administrators and clerks be so large?

It is this type of question that we will discuss in the remainder of this article. It may be the very homogeneity of the civil service that allows the social gradients to emerge so starkly. Administrative grade civil servants are likely to have more in common with each other than do the diversity of occupations that make up social class I in the country as a whole. They are largely university-educated (a

Figure 9-2. *Standardized Mortality Ratios in Married Women Aged 20–54, Classified by Husband's Occupation, for Death Due to All Causes, Lung Cancer, Coronary Heart Disease (CHD), and Cerebrovascular Disease (Cerebro VD) in Great Britain, 1970–72 and 1979–83, for Manual (o–o) and Nonmanual (●–●) Groups**

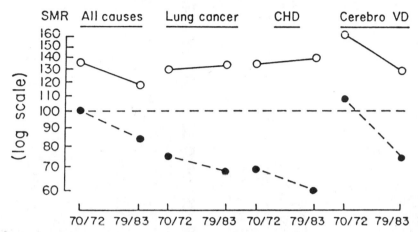

Note: For each cause the SMR in 1979–81 is 100.

high proportion of them have studied at the most prestigious British universities at Oxford and Cambridge) in stable, highly responsible, well-paid, and relatively fulfilling jobs. Before the explosion of high-paying jobs in the City of London (the financial sector), the administrative grades of the civil service were seen as a highly favored option by the elite of the country's graduates.

The clerical grades of the civil service differ sharply from this, but there is likely to be greater homogeneity within the clerical grades than within social class III nonmanual in the country as a whole. This homogeneity within and heterogeneity between grades makes the civil service population appropriate for the investigation of social class differences.

There are clear differences between the grades in risk-related behaviors and biological risk factors (Table 9-1). These "explain" a part, but not the large part, of the social gradient in cardiovascular and other diseases (8). Here we must clarify what we mean by "explain." It is incomplete to state that differences in the prevalence of smoking are partly the reason for the social differences in the rate of occurrence of CHD, lung cancer, or chronic obstructive air-

ways disease. We must ask why there are social class differences in smoking. Thus two types of questions emerge—why are there social class differences in risk-related behaviors and biological risk factors such as blood pressure, and what may account for the link between social position and disease that acts independently of these risk factors?

To what extent might the link between social position and disease be a result of the influence of psychosocial factors? The social classification is based on occupation. Does this suggest that circumstances at work, as discussed in one of the sections below, might be responsible? Or should we be inquiring after other social differences among people in these occupations?

Interpretation of Social Class Differences

Social class is a complex concept. It arose in Marxist analysis (10) which pointed out that owners of financial resources had the power of buying work and that they tended to buy it at the least expensive price. This would, of course, mean that there was always a risk of unreasonable exploitation of workers whenever they had

Figure 9-3. *All-cause Mortality in England and Wales, 1970–72, by Country of Birth (Ireland, Indian Subcontinent, Caribbean Community, and All Countries) and Registrar-General's Social Class; Standardized Mortality Ratios (SMRs) for Men Aged 20–69*

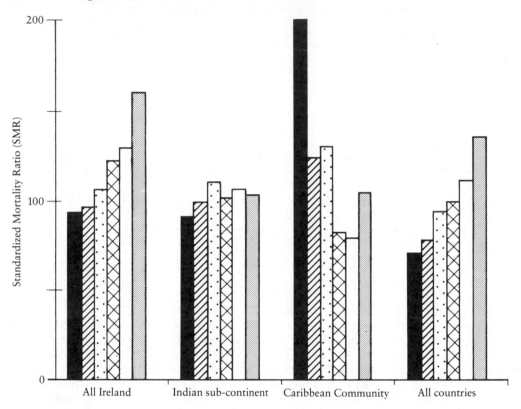

too little to say in the beginning process. When industrial development expanded, the situation of workers became influenced increasingly by the process of selling their labor power. For instance, workers often lived in special areas built for them and shops grew up to serve this special market. Thus, the effect of the industrial process was not limited to work but extended to the whole of life. Our concept of social class must evolve, but it is still likely to be associated not only with work situations—which is the basis of social class allocation—but also with living conditions, upbringing of children, eating habits, leisure activities, etc. Therefore, it is difficult to separate the effects of work conditions from effects of other conditions of life in epidemiological analysis. It is also obvious that there may be strong intergen-

erational effects of social class; i.e., the children are strongly influenced by their parents with regard to dietary habits, physical activity, and many psychological reaction patterns. For instance, a father coming home from a boring job that gives him no pride and provides no possibilities to learn new things—a situation that could be assumed to be more common in lower social classes than in higher ones—may release his feelings of frustration and tension at home, with his children as spectators. Therefore, social class should preferably not be studied as a one-generational phenomenon.

There has been much criticism of the Registrar-General's classification based on occupation. It has been suggested that occupations were ranked by standard mortality ratios and social classes

Figure 9-4. *Percentage of Men Dying in 10 Years from All Causes, from Coronary Heart Disease (CHD), and Non-CHD, by Grade in the British Civil Service (Age-adjusted Figures)*

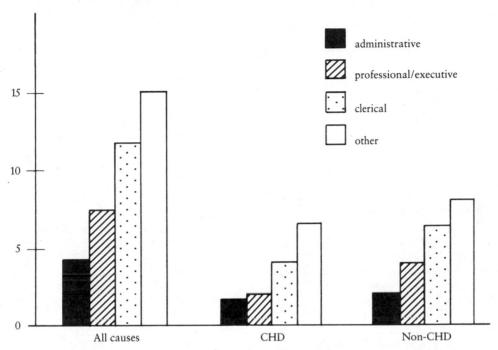

artificially constructed to fit the data (11) and that social class has outlasted its usefulness.

However valid these criticisms, the striking consistence of the inverse association between social class and cardiovascular disease in industrialized countries suggests that social class continues to be worthy of attention. The countries listed in which social class differences have been reported vary in culture and their position along various spectra: capitalist/socialist, more/less egalitarian, oriental/Western. Yet all show a similar social class–CHD pattern. What can account for this consistency in different countries and historical periods? It may, of course, reflect material conditions of life. Housing, nutrition, child care facilities, physical working conditions, and possibilities for recreation are all likely to follow people of higher socioeconomic status in different countries and at different times. The undoubted importance of inequalities in material conditions in generating social inequalities in health was emphasized by the Black Report in the United Kingdom (12).

Regrettably, material poverty is still in evidence in wealthy countries. This is unlikely, however, to be the complete explanation. It is arguable that the decline in mortality in England and Wales, for example, is the result of improvement in material conditions. Yet at the same time, the relative difference in mortality between social classes has increased. This might reflect increased relative differences in material conditions, but clearly in the lower grades of the civil service we are not dealing with poverty in any absolute sense. Compared with social classes IV and V in the 1930s, 40s, and 50s, a clerical officer is not poor. What may be at issue is inequality. Certainly a civil service executive officer is not poor but he has a higher mortality risk than an administrator although a lower risk than a clerical officer.

Syme (13) suggests that, above a threshold of poverty, position on the social hierarchy per se

Table 9-1. Major Risk Factors in Different Grades: Age-adjusted Means and Percentage Showing Increased Value

Variable	Grade			
	Administrative	*Professional/ Executive*	*Clerical*	*Other*
Systolic blood pressure				
Mean (SEM) (mm Hg)	133.7(0.67)	136.0(0.19)	136.8(0.42)	137.9(0.64)
Percentage ≥ 160 mm Hg	10.7	12.2	13.8	16.5
Plasma cholesterol				
Mean (SEM) (mmol/liter)	5.20(0.04)	5.13(0.01)	5.08(0.03)	4.96(0.04)
Percentage ≥ 6.72 mmol/liter	12.6	10.2	10.5	7.8
Smoking (%)				
Smokers	28.8	37.3	53.0	60.9
Never smoked	33.0	23.2	17.0	14.8
Ex-smokers	38.1	39.6	29.9	24.3
Body mass index (weight/height)				
Mean (SEM) (kg/M^2)	24.5(0.09)	24.8(0.03)	24.6(0.07)	25.0(0.10)
Percentage ≥ 28 kg/m^2	9.9	11.8	13.8	17.4
Leisure, physical activity				
Percentage inactive	26.3	29.5	43.0	56.0
Height				
Mean (SEM) (cm)	178.5(0.20)	176.3(0.05)	174.0(0.13)	173.2(0.23)
Percentage > 183 cm (6 ft)	21.1	12.8	7.6	8.7
Family history				
1st-degree relatives with heart-disease (%)	21	16	10	7

may be a more important determinant of health and disease than material conditions. We must then ask what is it about position in the social hierarchy that is important? One clear possibility is psychosocial conditions. These are considered in the next section, which tries to bring the psychosocial work conditions into a social class perspective.

Psychosocial Work Conditions in Relation to Coronary Heart Disease

Initially, when psychosocial factors were explored in relation to CHD, the common wisdom was that demands and psychological "load" would be the main problem. The assumption was that "stress" would increase with increasing demands, and consequently stress diseases would be more common in more demanding occupations. Most researchers seemed to assume that the most de-

manding occupations were upper-class occupations (14). Thus, great confusion arose when epidemiological studies of occupations started to show that cardiovascular mortality, presumably "stress dependent," is lower in upper-class occupations than in other occupations (15–16).

In more recent stress research, it has been considered necessary to relate psychological demands in the work situation to the resources that are available to the worker. This relates to our discussion concerning social class, since most kinds of resources are more readily available in the upper classes than in the lower classes. The resources may determine whether the worker will be able to cope effectively with the demands made upon him or her (17). We will confine this analysis to psychological resources, following the hypothesis introduced by Syme (13) that in the present period of history in the Western countries, psychological conditions may be more important than material ones to health. Research on psychological resources at work has a long tradition. At present, three basic psychological dimensions describing resources at work summarize the literature, namely, skill discretion (use of skills and development of new skills), authority over decisions, and social support. Each one of these dimensions has several synonyms, but it would reach far beyond the limits of this review to describe them in detail.

One concept that has been extensively studied in this research and has a close relationship to social class is "decision latitude," which was introduced by Karasek. The first measure of decision latitude was constructed on the basis of the American Quality of Employment Surveys (18). A series of factor analyses were performed which indicated that decision latitude had two components: "skill discretion" and "authority over decisions." These closely related statistically, and in most studies the two dimensions have been added to one another. It could be assumed, on theoretical grounds, that skill discretion may be a more basic dimension than authority over decisions. When workers have the possibility to learn new skills they can also master unpredicted future situations in a much better way, and since they feel more secure in their role they may be ready and able to make more and more decisions on their own, which, of course, means increasing decision latitude. Fellow workers and supervisors will also know that such workers can make more decisions and will therefore allow them to do so. Almost by definition, both skill discretion and authority over decisions decrease with descending social class.

Social support at work has been illuminated by several research groups, which have shown that different aspects of support are central to health (19). A good support may mean emotional support as well as feedback from superiors and fellow workers. Most studies of social support at work indicate that low social class is associated with poor social support at work (20). Thus, those who work in low status jobs are likely to be on the low end of all three basic dimensions of psychological resources. The obvious question will then be whether part of the association between social class and cardiovascular disease may be due to this unequal distribution of psy-

chological resources at work. Karasek (21), Karasek and associates (22), and Johnson (17) have developed theoretical models for analyzing the possible joint effects of demands, lack of decision latitude, and lack of social support at work on the pathogenesis of CHD. Several epidemiological studies, cross-sectional as well as prospective, have tested these models (23–26). Such studies have been performed by means of two different methods:

1. *Individual-based* in which subjects have described their own psychological work situation. These descriptions have subsequently been related to the prevalence or incidence of cardiovascular disease or cardiovascular risk factors in the same individuals. The psychological dimensions have been constructed by means of factor analyses in the United States (21)—demands and decision latitude—and in Sweden—demands, decision latitude (17, 25), and social support (17).
2. *Group-based* ("aggregated") in which representative samples of the working population have been interviewed. On the basis of response distributions in each occupation, all occupations were characterized with regard to demands and decision latitude. In the analysis of health outcome, all workers in an occupation were assumed to have the same work conditions. In the U.S. version of this classification (18, 27), it is possible to adjust the individual's occupational scores with regard to age, race, and education. Men and women were analyzed separately. The occupation classification score was treated like a cardiovascular risk factor. In a simplified Swedish classification system, occupations were classified with regard to each one of a number of single questions regarding "monotony," "rush," etc. on the basis of the Swedish Survey of Living Conditions (23). In a later version adjustment was made for the individual's age (24).

The estimates of associations given by these two methods—individual-based and group-based—are complementary. The individual method may be vulnerable to personality traits; for instance, a "hostile" person may be more likely to describe the social support as poor and habitually denying subjects may underreport all psychosocial problems. The group-based method, on the other hand, is less vulnerable to these "subjective" measurement problems but may provide crude estimates and require large samples.

The individual method was used in a follow-up study of working men in Sweden (25). This showed that working men who described their job as demanding and reported a low level of decision latitude were more likely than others to develop cardiovascular symptoms and to die cardiovascular deaths during follow-up. Another study using similar questionnaires (28) showed that men who had developed a myocardial infarction before age 45 and who were interviewed within three months after the disease onset regarding their pre-infarction job situation described less skill discretion than men without myocardial infarction. This held true even when the relevant biomedical factors, as well as education and type A behavior, had been taken into account. In multivariate analysis, job monotony was a significant discriminator between "cases" (myocardial infarction men) and "controls" (noninfarction men). Hahn (29) has made an individual prospective study of male Finnish industry workers. This study showed a clear-cut association in the predicted direction between high work demands and a low decision latitude at work on the one hand and elevated risk of developing angina pectoris or myocardial infarction during follow-up. Another individual-based study was made on the Framingham cohort (26). This study showed results in the predicted direction both for women and for men, although the results were statistically significant only for the female participants—the more demands and the less decision latitude, the more angina pectoris and myocardial infarction during follow-up. Both these latter studies showed that the association persisted even after adjustment for biomedical risk factors.

Group-based analyses of myocardial infarction prevalence in U.S. working men (18) showed that the prevalence was higher in high demand/low decision latitude occupations than in other occupations, even when biomedical factors and education had been taken into account. Two Swedish prospective group-based studies have shown that occupations with a high frequency of monotony and nonlearning have a higher myocardial infarction incidence than other occupations, particularly when the "rush" is reported to be common. These findings were true even when a number of socioeconomic factors had been taken into account.

Table 9-2. Mortality from Coronary Heart Disease, Expressed as Standardized Mortality Ratio (SMR) in Men Aged 15–64, by Occupation, in England and Wales; Occupations Are Classified According to the Swedish System of Work Characteristics[a]

Job Characteristic	SMR	SMR Adjusted for Social Class
Monotomy		
Yes	113	104
No	102	102
Possibility of learning new things		
"Poor"	114	106
"Good"	98	98
Hectic work		
Yes	104	102
No	112	104

[a]Some occupations were excluded because the Swedish and British occupational codes differed.

Table 9-2 shows an analysis based upon three digit occupation titles of all working men and married women classified according to their husband's job in the British Census in 1971 and the corresponding information at the time of death for all working men and married women who died in Great Britain during the years 1970 to 1972. Since there is no British occupation classification system, both the simplified Swedish (23) and the U.S. system (27) were tested. The findings were quite similar. Men working in occupations classified as "nonlearning" or "monotonous" were more likely to die from cardiovascular disease than other men. In this study, it did not make any difference whether workers commonly reported "hectic work" or not. Adjusting for social class decreased the magnitude of the association but the relationship was still clear. For women classified according to their husband's occupation, similar findings were made, but in this case controlling for social class made the association disappear completely. Thus, there is substantial evidence that a low level of decision latitude—in particular the skill discretion component—is associated with increased cardiovascular disease risk.

An analysis of all components (demands–lack of control; demands–lack of support; lack of control—lack of support; demands—lack of support—lack of control) performed by Johnson (17) showed that all three psychological main dimensions, as well as interactions between them, add to the cardiovascular health predictions. Thus, it is likely that psychological work conditions constitute an important part of the association between social class and cardiovascular disease risk. The multivariate analyses taking social class indicators into account show that there is a partial but not complete overlapping between social class and psychological work conditions. Furthermore, the observation has been made that the psychosocial work descriptions have stronger predictive power in lower social classes than in upper ones.

Psychosocial Factors at Work and Cardiovascular Risk Factors

The psychological work environment may relate to cardiovascular illness in two different ways. Either it may influence known cardiovascular risk factors such as blood lipids, blood pressure, smoking habits, and leisure time physical activity, or it may have more direct effects via known physiological stress mechanisms. Smoking habits and blood pressure have been shown to have important relationships with the psychosocial work environment. Research regarding blood lipoproteins has produced more ambiguous results so far. However, according to Siegrist and associates (30), blue-collar workers working under psychosocially stressful conditions have adversely affected lipoproteins. A few examples will be described that relate to this discussion.

Pieper and co-workers (31) have recently examined four U.S. data bases: the Health Examination Survey, the Health and Nutrition Examination Survey, the Exercise Heart Study, and the Western Collaborative Group Study. These examinations of large groups of American men were linked to a U.S. occupation descriptive system based upon the American Quality of Employment Surveys. Occupation title was available in the data base, and this job title was then tied to the occupation descriptive system assuming, for instance, that bakers in general have similar conditions. For each individual, data on

biomedical risk factors were available. In three of the data bases there was a significant association between a low level of decision latitude (so-called "strain") in an occupation and average systolic blood pressure at rest in the same occupation. For diastolic blood pressure the associations were less convincing. In each data base there was a significant inverse association between decision latitude and smoking habits—the lower the decision latitude in an occupation, the higher the proportion of smokers. For serum cholesterol no clear pattern was observed.

A study of 28-year-old men in Sweden showed that young men working in "nonlearning occupations" were more likely to have high levels of plasma adrenaline at rest and high systolic blood pressure at rest than others (32). A high plasma adrenaline at rest was associated not only with a job classified as boring but also with a poor social network in general. In the same analysis, the other biomedical factor of great importance to elevated systolic blood pressure at rest—overweight—was significantly associated with "lack of employment security," a dimension constructed on the basis of factor analysis. Lack of employment security is also more common in lower social classes than in others.

Variations in Blood Pressure (as an Indicator of Arousal) in Relation to Psychosocial Work Conditions

There have also been studies of longitudinal blood pressure changes that are relevant to the discussion on psychosocial work environment, its association with social class, and its effect on cardiovascular health. In the study of young Swedish men mentioned above, those who had a high blood pressure at the age of 18 (and had thus shown a tendency to react with blood pressure elevation) and who were now working in occupations characterized as "strain" occupations (such as waiter and driver) were more likely to have a marked systolic blood pressure elevation at work than others (33). Furthermore, in a recent study, men and women in different occupations were followed four times during a year. When self-perceived demands rose in relation to self-reported decision latitude, average systolic blood pressure during work hours was rising. This occurred particularly among subjects with a positive family history of hypertension and in low decision latitude jobs (baggage handlers and waiters) (34). In a recent study, fully automated 24-hour recordings of blood pressure were made in widely different occupations in New York. The results showed that occupations with a low decision latitude had a much higher proportion of hypertensive men than other occupations (35).

Psychosocial Conditions at Work and at Home in Relation to Blood Pressure Variations

In a study of civil servants in Great Britain, participants were instructed to measure their own blood pressure at work and at home. The findings were related both to social grade and to job conditions. Both systolic and diastolic blood pressure at work increased with increasing "job stress"—a score that was combined, after factor analysis, from dimensions describing "lack of skill utilization" (which relates to the long-term development of decision latitude discussed above), "tension," and "lack of clarity" in tasks. Thus, men with a combination of these three factors had higher blood pressure than others. For each one of the job stress factors there was a rising systolic and diastolic blood pressure with rising level of stress, but the combinations of factors was particularly damaging. The rise in blood pressure from the lowest to the highest job stress score was much larger among low-grade men than among upper-grade men—a finding that supports the epidemiological cardiovascular illness finding described above. Blood pressure at home, on the other hand, was not related to job stress level. The interesting observation was made that men in upper and lower grades had the same average blood pressure levels in the clinic and at work but marked differences in blood pressure at home; upper-grade men had much lower systolic and diastolic blood pressure at home than had low-grade men. All the blood pressure levels in the study of civil servants had been adjusted for age, reported alcohol consumption, body mass index, serum high density lipoprotein level, and hemoglobin (5) (Figure 9-5). These findings indicate that different social domains may affect different physiological reactions; the work conditions are

likely to affect the physiological states during working hours—exactly as we would expect.

Although several studies point to an association between psychosocial job factors and the "accepted" cardiovascular risk factors, this does not mean that all of the association between psychosocial job factors and heart disease is due to these associations. The previously mentioned study of men who had suffered a myocardial infarction before the age of 45 in Stockholm showed that in multivariate analysis, "lack of variety at work" explained as much of the (retrospectively recorded) early myocardial infarction risk as family history of early coronary heart disease and almost as much as excessive tobacco smoking habits. Lipoprotein patterns explained more of the total risk than the other recorded factors. Several factors that were more common among the patients than in a healthy matched group of men did not appear to be significant in the multivariate analysis, such as type A behavior pattern, disturbed carbohydrate metabolism, and level of education (28). Other biomedical mechanisms have been proposed to be of importance in this association. For instance, in a study of civil servants, Marmot (36) showed that men who reported a low level of decision latitude were likely to have high fibrinogen levels in the blood. Since fibrinogen is important in coagulation and coagulation is important in atherosclerosis, increased production or lack of breakdown of fibrinogen may be a mechanism of importance.

Studies of occupation and smoking (31, 37) have indicated that occupations characterized in national surveys as low on decision latitude have a higher proportion of cigarette smokers than other occupations. The explanation of such findings may simply be that boredom and lack of skill discretion may make the workers feel that they need to smoke in order to stay awake. Another mechanism that may be operating is that smoking may have a social role. In some occupations, in particular the "caring" occupations, taking a pause with smoking colleagues may be one way of releasing tension.

Our review of the cardiovascular risk factors shows that psychosocial work conditions may indeed influence the risk factors directly. Thus, it is likely that psychosocial work conditions are

Figure 9-5. *Blood Pressure (BP) in Male British Civil Servants Recorded at Work and at Home According to Grade of Employment, Adjusting for Age, Body Mass Index (BMI), Hemoglobin (Hb), and High Density Lipoproteins (HDL)*

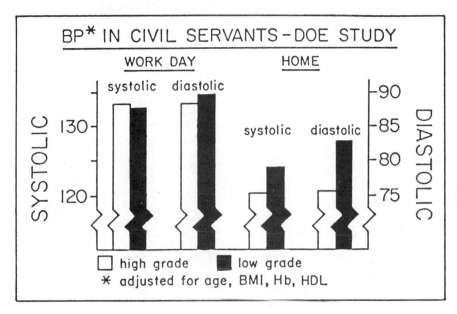

an important link between social class and heart disease.

The Contribution of Working Conditions to Social Inequalities in Cardiovascular Disease

In cardiovascular epidemiology, there has been a tendency to pose questions that take the form: how much of the variance in disease occurrence can be attributed to a given set of risk factors? For example, it is commonly asserted that about half the international variation in rates of occurrence of CHD can be explained on the basis of the main coronary factors: serum cholesterol, blood pressure, and smoking. This approach has value in focusing attention on what is known and what is not. It has two limitations in addressing the topic of this section: measurement problems and failure to proceed in the light of a causal model.

Parametric statistical techniques, such as analysis of covariance, are used because they are convenient in sorting through intercorrelated variables. We should be wary, however, of the precise quantitative measures they give us. Assuming that a relationship exists, the strength of the association between social class and CHD will depend on both the validity and the precision of the social class measurement. As long as uncertainty exists as to the concept and definition of social class, we shall be uncertain if we have a valid measure. An observed association with disease may therefore yield a spuriously low (or high) quantitative estimate. Whatever the validity of the measure (systematic error), the less precise it is (more random error) the weaker will be the apparent association. Hence the difficulty in attempting to quantify the degree to which work characteristics could account for social class differences. We have imprecision on measures of both social class and work characteristics. If, for example, the measure of smoking is more precise, other things being equal, it will appear to have a stronger association with disease. Hence the difficulty in deciding the relative importance of different factors.

Quite apart from measurement difficulties, to

ask whether smoking or blood pressure rather than work characteristics "explain" social class differences in CHD may be the wrong way to pose the question. Similarly, it may be inappropriate to ask whether work characteristics are related to disease risk, independent of social class. An appropriate causal model is needed. As indicated in the previous sections, social position (social class) may be related to cardiovascular disease risk through the association with behaviors such as smoking or diet, or physiological factors such as blood pressure. If this is the case, we could not conclude, comfortably, that these risk factors account for social class differences, but ask why there is the link between social position and risk.

Psychosocial characteristics such as working conditions may be in part responsible for the higher cardiovascular risk in lower social classes, because they may influence established risk factors or act via other, neuroendocrinal pathways. To control statistically for social class in an analysis of the relation between working conditions and disease may, therefore, be to control out the variation of interest. The causal model might be, in turn: social class → low skill utilization at work → smoking and physiological changes in homeostasis such as blood pressure and endocrine secretions → cardiovascular disease.

Given the imprecise nature of the social class concept, and the large variety of ways by which people in the lower social strata differ from those in the higher, why have we focused on working conditions? Among the answers we might give is the possibility of translating research findings into social change. One response to evidence of persisting social inequalities in health and disease is that little can be done about it without fundamental political change. As Bertil Gardell showed, working conditions *can* be influenced. Research findings on the health consequences of certain types of work have the potential to influence decisions on the design of work. It therefore represents one possible way of breaking the nexus between low social position and higher disease risk.

REFERENCES

1. Marmot, M. G., and McDowell, M. E. Mortality decline and widening social inequalities. *Lancet* 2: 274–276, 1986.

2. Pamuk, E. R. Social class inequality in mortality from 1921 to 1972 in England and Wales. *Population Studies* 39: 17–31, 1985.

3. Valkonen, T. Social inequality in the face of death. *Central Statistical Office of Finland*, pp. 201–261. Helsinki, 1987.

4. Derriennic, F., Ducimetiere, P., and Kritsikis, S. Cardiac mortality among working middleaged Frenchmen according to their socio-economic class and geographic region. *Rev. Epidemiol. Sante Publ.* 25: 131–146, 1977.

5. Buring, J. E., et al. Occupation and risk of death from coronary heart disease. *JAMA* 258(6): 791–793, 1987.

6. Kagamimori, S. Occupational life tables for cerebrovascular disease and ischaemic heart disease in Japan compared with England and Wales. *Jpn. Circ. J.* 45: 195–201, 1981.

7. Marmot, M. G., Adelstein, A. M., and Bulusu, L. Immigrant mortality in England and Wales 1970–78. OPCS *Studies of Medical and Population Subjects,* No. 47. Her Majesty's Stationary Office, London, 1984.

8. Marmot, M. G., Shipley, M. G., and Rose, G. Inequalities in death—specific explanations of a general pattern? *Lancet* 1: 1003–1006, 1984.

9. Pocock, S. J., et al. Social class differences in ischaemic disease in British men. *Lancet* 1: 197–201, 1987.

10. Marx, K. *Capital,* Vol. I. International Publishers, New York, 1967.

11. Jones, I. G., and Cameron, D. Social class analysis—an embarrassment to epidemiology. *Community Med.* 6: 37–46, 1984.

12. Department of Health and Social Security. Inequalities in Health: Report of a Research Working Group. DHSS, London, 1980.

13. Syme, S. L. Strategies for health promotion. *Prev. Med.* 15:492–507, 1986.

14. Kasl, S. V. The challenge of studying the disease effects of stressful work conditions (editorial). *Am. J. Public Health* 71(7): 682–684, 1981.

15. Antonowsky, A. Social class and the major cardiovascular diseases. *J. Chronic Dis.* 21: 65–106, 1968.

16. Lehman, E. W. Social class and coronary heart disease: A sociological assessment of the medical literature. *J. Chronic Dis.* 20: 381–391, 1967.

17. Johnson, J. V. The Impact of Workplace Social Job Demands and Work Control upon Cardiovascular Disease in Sweden. Department of Psychology, Report No. 1, University of Stockholm, 1986.

18. Karasek, R. A., et al. Job characteristics in relation to the prevalence of myocardial infarction in the

U.S. HES and HANES. *Am. J. Public Health,* in press, 1988.

19. Johnson, J. V., and Hall, E. M. Social support in the work environment and cardiovascular disease. In *Social Support and Cardiovascular Disease,* edited by S. Shumaker and S. Czajkowski. Plenum Publishing Corporation, New York, in press, 1988.

20. Orth-Gomer, K., Unden, A. L., and Edwards, M. E. Social isolation and mortality in ischemic heart disease: A ten year follow-up study of 150 middle aged men. *Soc. Sci. Med.,* in press, 1988.

21. Karasek, R. A. Job demands, job decision latitude and mental strain: Implications for job redesign. *Administrative Sci. Q.* 24: 285–308, 1979.

22. Krasek, R. A., Russell, R., and Theorell, T. Physiology of stress and regeneration in job related cardiovascular illness. *J. Hum. Stress* 3: 29–42, 1982.

23. Alfredsson, L., Karasek, R. A., and Theorell, T. Myocardial infarction risk and psychosocial work environment: An analysis of the male Swedish working force. *Soc. Sci. Med.* 16: 463–467, 1982.

24. Alfredsson, L., Spetz, C. L., and Theorell, T. Type of occupation and near-future hospitalization for myocardial infarction and some other diagnoses. *Int. J. Epidemiol.* 14: 378, 1985.

25. Karasek, R. A., et al. Job decision latitude, job demands and cardiovascular disease: A prospective study of Swedish men. *Am. J. Public Health* 71: 694–705, 1981.

26. La Croix, A. Z. Occupational Exposure to High Demand/Low Control Work and Coronary Heart Disease Incidence in the Framingham Cohort. Dissertation, University of North Carolina, Chapel Hill, 1984.

27. Schwartz, J. E., Pieper, C., and Karasek, R. A. Job characteristics linkage procedure. *Am J. Public Health,* in press, 1988.

28. Theorell, T., et al. Psychosocial work conditions before myocardial infarction in young men. *Int. J. Cardiol.* 15:33–46, 1987.

29. Hahn, M. Psychosocial Work Conditions and Risk of Coronary Heart Disease. Academic thesis, Department of Sociology, University of California at Berkeley, 1986.

30. Siegrist, J., et al. Atherogenic risk in men suffering from occupational stress. *Atherosclerosis* 69: 211–218, 1986.

31. Pieper, C., Schwartz, J. E., and Karasek, R. A. Cardiovascular risk factors and occupational characteristics in the HANES and HES. In preparation, 1988.

32. Knox, S., et al. The relation of social support and working environment to medical variables associated with elevated blood pressure in young males: A structural model. *Soc. Sci. Med.* 21: 525–531, 1985.

33. Theorell, T., et al. Blood pressure variations during a working day at age 28: Effects of different types of work and blood pressure level at age 18. *J. Hum. Stress* 11: 36–41, 1985.

34. Theorell, T., et al. Changes in job strain in relation to changes in physiological state—a longitudinal study. *Scand. J. Work Environ. Health,* in press, 1988.

35. Schnall, P., Karasek, R. A., and Pickering, T. G. Blood pressure and psychosocial job characteristics in American men. In preparation, 1988.

36. Marmot, M. Does stress cause heart attacks? *Postgrad. Med. J.* 62: 683–686, 1986.

37. Alfredsson, L. Myocardial Infarction and Environment: Use of Registers in Epidemiology. Academic thesis from Department of Social Medicine, Karolinska Institute and National Institute for Psychosocial Factors and Health, Stockholm, Sweden, 1983.

The Social and Cultural Meanings of Illness

■ ■ ■ ■ ■ ■

Analysts in recent years have often drawn the distinction between disease and illness. Put simply, disease is the biophysiological phenomenon that affects the body, while illness is a social phenomenon that accompanies or surrounds the disease. The shape of illness is not necessarily determined by the disease. What an illness is involves the interaction of the disease, sick individuals, and society. To examine illness, we must focus on the subjective worlds of meaning and experience. In the next section, we explore this area when we look at "The Experience of Illness." Here, rather than focusing on individual experience, we investigate the social images and moral meanings that are attributed to illnesses.

In this perspective, we view illness as a social construction. While most illnesses are assumed to have a biophysiological basis (i.e., an underlying disease), this is not a necessary condition for something to be defined as an illness. As Joseph Gusfield (1967) notes, "Illness is a social designation, by no means given by the nature of medical fact." Thus, we can conceivably have illnesses without diseases or illnesses whose meaning is completely independent from the actual biomedical entity. In examining the social meaning of illness, we focus on the role of social and cultural values that shape the perception of a disease or malady. Illness can reflect cultural assumptions and biases about a particular group or groups of people, or it can become a cultural metaphor for extant societal problems.

Illnesses may reflect deeply rooted cultural values and assumptions. This is perhaps particularly evident in the medical definition and treatment of women and women's maladies. During the nineteenth century, organized medicine achieved a strong dominance over the treatment of women and proceeded to promulgate erroneous and damaging conceptualizations of women as sickly, irrational creatures at the mercy of their reproductive organs (Barker-Benfield, 1976; Wertz and Wertz, 1989). Throughout history we can find similar examples of medical and "scientific" explanations of women's health and illnesses that reflect the dominant conceptions of women in society. For example, a century ago common medical knowledge was replete with assumptions about the "fragile" nature of upper-class women, a nature first believed to be dominated by reproductive organs and later by psychological processes innate in women (Ehrenreich and English, 1978). Assumptions about women's nature frequently set cultural limits on what women could do. In the late nineteenth century physicians opposed granting women the right to vote on the grounds that concern about such matters would strain their "fragile" brains and cause their ovaries to shrink! The creation of the "cult of invalidism" among upper-class women in the nineteenth century—at the same time working-class women were considered capable of working long, hard hours in sweatshops and factories—can be interpreted as physicians acting as agents of social control. In this case, the physicians' use of definitions of health and illness kept women of both classes

106

"in their place," both overtly and subtly, through a socialization process in which many women came to accept being sickly as their proper role and in which many more unquestioningly accepted the physicians' claim to "expertise" in treating women's health and sexual problems. While physicians did not invent sexism, they reflected common sexist attitudes which they then reinforced in their definition and treatment of women.

While the grossest biases about women and their bodies have diminished, the effects of gender bias on the meanings of illness are now subtler and more complex. Since the 1930s, a significant number of women's problems—childbirth, birth control, abortion, menopause, and premenstrual syndrome—have become "medicalized" (see "The Medicalization of American Society" in Part Three). While the consequences of medicalization are probably mixed (Riessman, 1983), various feminist analysts see it as an extension of medicine's control over women (see, for example, Boston Women's Health Book Collective, 1985). Looking at one example, premenstrual syndrome (PMS), we see that medicalization can legitimate the real discomforts of many women who had long been told their premenstrual pain was "all in their head." On the other hand, one consequence of the adoption of PMS as a medical syndrome is the legitimation of the view that all women are potentially physically and emotionally handicapped each month by menstruation and thus not fully capable of responsibility. Wide adoption of PMS as a syndrome could undercut some important gains of the contemporary women's movement.

The current treatment of menopause provides another example of the changing medical meanings of women's disorders. Several analysts (Kaufert, 1982; McCrea, 1983; Bell, 1987) have described how menopause, a natural life event for women, became defined as a "deficiency disease" in the 1960s when medical therapy became readily available to treat it. The treatment, estrogen replacement therapy, promised women they could stay "feminine forever" and preserve their "youth and beauty." Feminists argued that menopause is part of the normal aging process and thus not an illness. They also argued that the treatment is usually unnecessary and, since estrogen has been linked to cancer, always dangerous. Recently, studies have suggested that both the meanings and experience of menopause may be culturally bound. In Japan, for example, cessation of menstruation is not given much importance and is seen as a natural part of aging, not a disease-like condition. Even the experience is different: Japanese women report few "hot flashes" but rather typically suffer from stiff shoulders (Lock, 1993). PMS and menopause provide contemporary examples of how cultural assumptions of gender can be reflected in the medical definitions of disorder, which affect the medical treatment of women.

The meaning attributed to medical problems often reflects the attitudes of a given culture. In this section's first selection, "Anorexia Nervosa in Context," Joan Jacobs Brumberg examines the cultural bases of the current epidemic of anorexia among young, middle-class women in American society. While this disorder may have biological and psychological components, Brumberg describes how it also reflects changing social expectations and roles of women in American society. Feminists have often pointed out how anorexia relates to the great preoccupation with women's weight and body image and the middle-class values placed on control and self-presentation (see Bardo, 1993).

While recognizing that the cultural explanation has some limitations, Brumberg provocatively depicts anorexia as an "addiction to starvation" and a "secular form of perfection," a disorder that reflects the strains and ambiguities of changing gender roles in our society.

All illnesses are not created and treated equally. Certain illnesses may engender social meanings that affect our perception and treatment of those who suffer the illness. One important example of this is "stigmatized illness" (Gussow and Tracy, 1968). Certain illnesses, including leprosy, epilepsy, sexually transmitted diseases, and AIDS, have acquired moral meanings that are inherent in the very construction of the illness's image and thus affect our perception of the illness and our reaction to those who have it. These illnesses carry considerable potential to stigmatize individuals, adding social suffering to physical difficulties. Frequently, as much energy must be invested in managing the stigma as the disorder itself (e.g., Schneider and Conrad, 1983).

The social meaning can shape the social response to illness. Illness can become imbued with a moral opprobrium that makes its sufferers outcasts. For example, Cotton Mather, the celebrated eighteenth-century New England Puritan minister, declared that syphilis was a punishment "which the Just judgment of God has reserved for our later ages" (cited in Sontag, 1988:92). The social definition of epilepsy fostered myths (e.g., epilepsy was inherited or it caused crime) that further stigmatized the disorder (Schneider and Conrad, 1983). Finally, the negative image of venereal diseases was a significant factor in the limited funds allocated for dealing with these illnesses (Brandt, 1985).

AIDS, perhaps more than any other example in the twentieth century, highlights the significance that social meaning has on the social response to illness. A fear virtually unprecedented in contemporary society led to an overreaction to the disease sometimes bordering on hysteria (Conrad, 1986). When AIDS was first discovered, it was thought to be a "gay disease" and thus was stigmatized and its research underfunded (Altman, 1986; Perrow and Guillén, 1990). Although we have learned a great deal about AIDS in recent years, the image of AIDS remains fundamentally shaped by the stigma attached to it and the fear of contagion (Nelkin et al., 1991; Rushing, 1995). In the second selection, "An Epidemic of Stigma: Public Reaction to AIDS," Gregory M. Herek and Eric K. Glunt examine AIDS-related stigma in terms of its societal and individual sources and its impact on people with the illness. The characterization of AIDS as an incurable, contagious, and deadly disease linked to previously stigmatized groups, especially homosexuals and IV drug users, created a particularly negative image of the disease and shaped the social response to it. While the relative proportions of HIV infection and AIDS have shifted some in the past decade—we see an increasing incidence among minorities, women, and heterosexuals—the stigmatized meanings of AIDS are still pervasive (Herek and Capitanio, 1993) and continue to shape our responses to the epidemic and affect all those who have the disease. The authors' suggestions for how to eradicate AIDS-related stigma, essentially by changing the social meanings of the illness, remain unfulfilled and a social challenge to us all.

To understand the effects of disease in society, it is also necessary to understand the impact of illness. For it is in the social world of illness that the sick and the well must face one another and come to terms.

REFERENCES

Altman, Dennis. 1986. AIDS in the Mind of America. New York: Anchor/Doubleday.

Bardo, Susan. 1993. Unbearable Weight: Feminism, Western Culture and the Body. Berkeley: University of California Press.

Barker-Benfield, G.J. 1976. The Horrors of the Half-Known Life. New York: Harper and Row.

Bell, Susan E. 1987. "Premenstrual syndrome and the medicalization of menopause: A sociological perspective." Pp. 151–73 in Benson E. Ginsburg and Bonnie Frank Carter (eds.), Premenstrual Syndrome: Ethical and Legal Implications in a Biomedical Perspective. New York: Plenum.

Boston Women's Health Book Collective. 1985. The New Our Bodies, Ourselves. New York: Simon and Schuster.

Brandt, Allen M. 1985. No Magic Bullet. New York: Oxford University Press.

Conrad, Peter. 1986. "The social meaning of AIDS." Social Policy. (Summer): 51–56.

Ehrenreich, Barbara, and Deirdre English. 1978. On Her Own. New York: Doubleday.

Gusfield, Joseph R. 1967. "Moral passage: The symbolic process in the public designations of deviance." Social Problems 15:175–88.

Gussow, Zachary, and George Tracy. 1968. "Status, ideology, and adaptation to stigmatized illness: A study of leprosy." Human Organization. 27: 316–25.

Herek, Gregory M., and John P. Capitanio. 1993. "Public reactions of AIDS in the United States: A second decade of stigma." American Journal of Public Health. 83: 574–77.

Kaufert, Patricia A. 1982. "Myth and the menopause." Sociology of Health and Illness. 4: 141–66.

Lock, Margaret. 1993. Encounters with Aging: Mythologies of Menopause in Japan and North America. Berkeley: University of California Press.

McCrea, Frances. 1983. "The politics of menopause: The 'discovery' of a deficiency disease." Social Problems. 31:111–123.

Nelkin, Dorothy, David P. Willis, and Scott Parris. 1991. A Disease of Society: Cultural and Social Responses to AIDS. New York: Cambridge University Press.

Perrow, Charles, and Mauro F. Guillén. 1990. The AIDS Disaster. New Haven: Yale University Press.

Riessman, Catherine K. 1983. "Women and medicalization." Social Policy. 14: 3–18.

Rushing, William. 1995. The AIDS Epidemic: Social Dimensions of an Infectious Disease. Boulder, CO: Westview Press.

Schneider, Joseph W., and Peter Conrad. 1983. Having Epilepsy: The Experience and Control of Illness. Philadelphia: Temple University Press.

Sontag, Susan. 1988. Illness and Its Metaphors. New York: Farrar, Straus and Giroux.

Wertz, Richard, and Dorothy Wertz. 1989. Lying-In: A History of Childbirth in America. New Haven. Yale University Press.

10

Anorexia Nervosa in Context*

. . . . . .

Joan Jacobs Brumberg

The American public discovered anorexia nervosa only recently. Although the disease was known to physicians as early as the 1870s, the general public knew virtually nothing about it until the 1970s, when the popular press began to feature stories about young women who refused to eat despite available and plentiful food. In 1974, the "starving disease" made its first appearance as an independent subject heading in the *Readers' Guide to Periodical Literature,* a standard library reference tool that also provides a useful index to contemporary social issues. By 1984, the disease had become so commonplace that "Saturday Night Live" featured jokes about the "anorexic cookbook," and a comedian in the Borscht Belt drew laughs with a reference to a new disease, "anorexia ponderosa." In *Down and Out in Beverly Hills,* 1986 film audiences tittered at the predictable presence of an anorexic daughter in a lush suburban setting. Today nearly everyone understands flip remarks such as "You look anorexic." Anorexia nervosa has become common parlance, used as hyperbole by those outside the medical profession (particularly women) to comment on one another's bodies.

Our national education on the subject of anorexia nervosa can be traced to a variety of published popular sources in the decade of the 1970s. An early article in *Science Digest* reported on a "strange disease" in adolescent girls characterized by a "morbid aversion" to eating. Despite

a new permissiveness in many areas of social behavior, parents in the 1960s were counseled against taking adolescent food refusal lightly or allowing it to continue. In 1970, at the outset of a decade of national education about anorexia nervosa, the press warned American parents to seek professional medical intervention as soon as possible, because there was "no safe leeway for home-style cure attempts."[1]

Newspapers as diverse as the *New York Times* and the *Weekly World News* pursued the subject in their own inimitable ways. The *Times's* first discussion of the disease was a synthetic overview of state-of-the-art medical treatment, defined as New York City and Philadelphia clinical practice. The *World News,* a tabloid equivalent of the *National Enquirer* and the *Star,* ran a provocative banner headline—"The Bizarre Starving Disease"—and featured a horrifying picture of a 55-pound woman in shorts and a halter. While the *Times* reported a fatality rate of 5 to 15 percent, the *World News* claimed 30 to 50 percent.[2] From whatever newspaper one draws information, anorexia nervosa has been taught to a variety of people from different class and educational backgrounds since the 1970s.

The disease has always had particular salience for women and girls. Not surprisingly, the three magazines that generated the largest volume of national coverage on anorexia nervosa—*People, Mademoiselle,* and *Seventeen*—all cater to the primary constituency for the disease: adolescent and young adult women. Another important source of information about anorexia nervosa suggests that the disease has a specific class constituency. Alumnae magazines from the elite eastern women's colleges took up the cause of the disease by alerting former students to the problem of anorexia nervosa on campus. Alumnae coverage provided information on what the typical anorectic was like: intelligent, attractive, polite, demanding on herself. In effect, she was the mirror image of much of their own student body.[3]

All of the women's magazines wrote about the disease with a common sense of urgency. Without being entirely certain of the data, they spoke of "epidemics," proclaiming that there were somewhere between one hundred thousand and one million Americans with anorexia nervosa. In addition, they reported that between 5 percent and 15 percent of anorectics in psychiatric treatment died, giving it one of the highest fatality rates of any psychiatric diagnosis. Although the notion of adolescent death through compulsive starvation seemed silly to some, anorexia nervosa was becoming a growing subject of concern among mothers in private discussions and among psychiatrists in clinical practice.

In 1978, after nearly three decades of clinical experience treating eating disorders, psychiatrist Hilde Bruch (1904–1984) published a book on anorexia nervosa for lay audiences. *The Golden Cage,* based on seventy case histories, was a popular success. Bruch began by saying: "New diseases are rare, and a disease that selectively befalls the young, rich, and beautiful is practically unheard of. But such a disease is affecting the daughters of well-to-do, educated, and successful families." She explained that "for the last fifteen or twenty years anorexia nervosa [has been] occurring at a rapidly increasing rate. Formerly it was exceedingly rare." As a practicing psychiatrist in Houston, Bruch observed that most of her colleagues "recognized the name as something they had heard about in medical school, but they never saw a case in real life." By the time her book was published, Bruch claimed that anorexia nervosa was "so common" that it was a "real problem in high schools and colleges."[4] Bruch's extensive knowledge of the condition, combined with her sense of urgency about the disease, contributed to the growing cultural perception of an epidemic. In effect, anorexia nervosa was the disease of the 1970s, to

be obscured only by AIDS and the accompanying specter of contagion and pollution that absorbs public attention at this moment.

The Question of Epidemiology

Is an epidemic of anorexia nervosa in progress? When did the numbers of anorectics really begin to accelerate?

An increase in the number of cases of anorexia nervosa appears to have started about twenty years ago. During the Great Depression and World War II, in times of scarcity, voluntary food refusal had little efficacy as an emotional strategy and anorexic girls were a relative rarity in American clinical practice. A comment by Mara Selvini-Palazzoli, an Italian pioneer in the psychiatric study of anorexia nervosa, confirmed the relationship between anorexia nervosa and post-World War II affluence: "During the whole period of World War II in Italy (1939–1945) there were dire food restrictions and no patients at all were hospitalized at the Clinic for anorexia [nervosa]." After the war, however, "concurrent with the explosion of the Italian economic miracle and the advent of the affluent society," Selvini-Palazzoli did see hospitalizations for anorexia nervosa.[5]

By the 1960s wartime experiences of rationing, famine, and concentration camps were fading from memory. In the postwar culture of affluence many aspects of personal behavior were transformed: sexuality, relations between the generations, forms of family life, gender roles, clothing, even styles of food and eating. . . . From a psychiatrist's perspective, the postwar years brought an increasing number of adolescent female patients who used appetite and eating as emotional instruments much as they had in early childhood. In the 1960s Bruch published extensively on the subject of anorexia nervosa, and her work was a bellwether that marked the beginning of a rise in the number of diagnosed cases, a rise that became even more precipitous in the next two decades.[6]

The dimensions of the recent increase are hard to ascertain, however, because of problems in collecting and interpreting data as well as lack of standardization in diagnostic criteria. Not all patients with anorexia nervosa have exactly the same symptoms in the same degree or intensity. Not all cases present exactly the same symptoms as those elaborated in the American Psychiatric Association's *Diagnostic and Statistical Manual*, the standard reference guide to modern psychiatric disorders. The DSM-III criteria are the following: refusal to maintain normal body weight; loss of more than 25 percent of original body weight; disturbance of body image; intense fear of becoming fat; and no known medical illness leading to weight loss.[7] Yet some clinicians differentiate between primary and secondary anorexia, some favor a less stringent weight criterion, and some include hyperactivity and amenorrhea as symptom criteria.[8] There is also the matter of how anorexia nervosa is related to bulimia, the binge-purge syndrome. Until 1980, when it was listed in DSM-III as a separate diagnostic entity, bulimia (from the Greek meaning ox hunger) was only a symptom, not an independent disease. But in 1985, in DSM-III-R, bulimia obtained independent disease status; according to the newest categorization, anorexia nervosa and bulimia are separate but related disorders. In the diagnosis of anorexia nervosa, there is increasing support for subtyping anorexic patients into those who are pure dieters ("restrictive anorectics") and those who incorporate binging and purging ("bulimic anorectics" and/or "bulimarexics").[9] Who gets counted (and who does not) is never entirely clear or consistent, so that diagnostic imprecision makes the numbers difficult to assess.

Despite these problems, the evidence does suggest that we have experienced an absolute increase in the amount of anorexia nervosa over the past two decades. For example, twenty years ago the University of Wisconsin Hospital typically admitted one anorectic a year; in 1982 over seventy cases were admitted to the same institution. A retrospective review of incidence rates in Monroe County, New York, revealed that the number of cases of anorexia nervosa doubled between 1960 and 1976.[10]

In terms of the general population, however, anorexia nervosa is still a relatively infrequent disease: the annual incidence of the disorder has never been estimated at more than 1.6 per 100,000 population.[11] Still, among adolescent girls and young women there is an increasing and disturbing amount of anorexia nervosa and bulimia; by a number of different estimates, as many as 5 to 10 percent are affected. On some college campuses estimates run as high as 20 percent.[12]

Two critical demographic facts about the contemporary population of anorectics are relevant to the question of an "epidemic." Ninety to 95 percent of anorectics are young and female, and they are disproportionately white and from middle-class and upper-class families. Anorexia nervosa can exist in males but with a quite different clinical picture. The rare anorexic male exhibits a greater degree of psychopathology, tends to be massively obese before becoming emaciated, and has a poorer treatment prognosis. Moreover, the male anorexic is less likely to be affluent.[13] Anorexia nervosa is not a problem among contemporary American blacks or Chicanos; neither was it a conspicuous problem among first-generation and second-generation ethnic immigrants such as Eastern European Jews.[14] As these groups move up the social ladder, however, their vulnerability to the disorder increases. In fact, the so-called epidemic seems to be consistently restrained by age and gender but promoted by social mobility.

In a similar vein, the "contagion" is also confined to the United States and Western Europe, Japan, and other areas experiencing rapid Westernization. A description of anorexia nervosa compiled by a Russian psychiatrist in 1971 was basically a report of clinical cases drawn from outside his country. Physicians looking for anorexia nervosa in developing nations or countries of the Third World have been unsuccessful in finding it, a fact which has led to its classification as a "culture-bound syndrome."[15] In other words, the anorexic population has a highly specific social address.

In the United States, as well as in Western Europe, the growth of anorexia nervosa is due in part to heightened awareness and reporting on the part of families and doctors. Rising numbers of anorectics do reflect "diagnostic drift"—that is, the greater likelihood that a clinician who sees a very thin adolescent female with erratic eating habits and a preoccupation with weight will describe and label that patient as a case of anorexia nervosa, rather than citing some other mental disorder where lack of appetite is a secondary feature (such as depression or schizophrenia).[16] Simple anorexia—meaning lack of appetite—is a secondary symptom in many medical and psychiatric disorders ranging from the serious to the inconsequential. For some girls an episode of anorexia is mild and transitory; others, perhaps as many as 19 percent of the diagnosed cases, die from it.[17] In the 1980s there may well be a medical tendency to place temporary and chronic anorexias under one diagnostic rubric precisely because of our familiarity with the disease. Most thoughtful clinicians agree that anorectics are not necessarily a homogeneous group and that more attention should be paid to defining and specifying their psychological and physiological characteristics.

This situation reflects a basic medical reality—that there are fashions in diagnosis. In 1984 Dr. Irving Farber, a practitioner in Jamaica, New York, wrote to his state medical journal about the overdiagnosis of anorexia nervosa: "In my experience, a significant number of girls and young women who have been diagnosed by professionals, and [girls] themselves, are not suffering from this disorder." A group of physicians from the Department of Pediatrics, Long Island Jewish-Hillside Medical Center, responded that Farber's point was "well-taken," although they disagreed with his analysis of a specific case.[18]

The statistical increase in the number of anorexics over the past two decades can be explained also by the amount of media attention paid to the disorder. Anorexia nervosa has become *au courant,* an "in" disease among affluent adolescent and young adult women, a phenomenon that confirms long-standing beliefs about the susceptibility of girls to peer influence. One prominent psychologist specializing in treatment of the disorder estimates that 30 percent of all current cases are what Bruch once called "me too" anorectics. Bruch herself wrote: "The illness used to be the accomplishment of an isolated girl who felt she had found her own way to salvation. Now it is more a group reaction."[19] This mimetic or copycat phenomenon is hard to assess statistically and only adds confusion to an already complex problem in psychiatric epidemiology. In sum: although the total number of actual anorectics is hard to assess and probably not enormous, incidence of the disorder is higher today than at any other time since the discovery of the disease over a century ago. In addition, among the constituency most vulnerable to the disease, bourgeois adolescent and young adult women, there is the perception of an epidemic—a perception fueled in part by messages coming from American popular culture.

The Influence of Popular Culture

In a society committed to hearing nearly everyone's story, the anorectic has come "out of the closet" like so many others—homosexuals, adopted people, substance abusers, molested children, born-again Christians and Jews. To be sure, the genre of disclosure has different ideological sources and purposes. Yet the current interest in experience and our self-confessional tendencies have generated a plethora of writing about anorexia nervosa, ranging from self-help books to autobiographical accounts to adolescent fiction. This concern for personal testimony and authenticity is revealed in the fact that the American Anorexia and Bulimia Association (AA/BA), founded in 1978, maintains a daily hot line across the country that provides telephone access to a recovered anorectic.

The disclosure in January 1983 that thirty-two-year-old popular singer Karen Carpenter had died of heart failure associated with low serum potassium—a consequence of prolonged starvation—fueled interest in the disease. Carpenter's tragic death confirmed the fact that anorexia nervosa could be fatal rather than just annoying. The news media emphasized that the best and most expensive medical treatment on both coasts had been ineffective against the disease. Although Carpenter's anorexia was described as a psychiatric disorder generated by her own insecurities and personality, she was also called a "victim" of anorexia nervosa, as if the disease were totally involuntary, or even contagious.[20] Carpenter's death focused national attention on the life-and-death drama of anorexia nervosa.

In the 1980s one can experience anorexia nervosa vicariously through films as well as books.

Two made-for-television movies about anorexia nervosa have been shown in prime time on the major networks. The first, *The Best Little Girl in the World* (1981), had a screenplay by New York psychologist Steven Levenkron and was promoted with an advertisement that said simply, "A Drama of Anorexia Nervosa." The adviser assumed that the disease was familiar and that its characteristic tensions and struggles generated audience involvement. At least one episode of "Fame," a program that portrays life at a select New York City high school for the performing arts, revolved around anorexia nervosa in a young student and its impact on her teachers and peers. In Marge Piercy's 1984 novel, *Fly Away Home,* the central character is a middle-aged, middle-class divorcée who is both a successful Boston cookbook author and the mother of an anorexic daughter.

Two other popular sources of information about anorexia nervosa are important for understanding the process of learning about the disease: fiction designed specifically for the adolescent market, and autobiographical accounts by sufferers. As a genre, anorexia stories are intended to provide adolescent girls with both a dramatic warning and a source of real information. The books are notable for their graphic descriptions of the anorectic's food preoccupations (for instance, never allowing oneself to eat more than three curds of cottage cheese at one sitting) and for their endorsement of medical and psychiatric intervention. In fact, the novel is used primarily as a device for getting adolescents to understand that professional intervention is imperative.[21]

In the typical anorexia story, psychiatrists and psychologists are portrayed as benign and compassionate figures whose only offense is that they ask a lot of questions. There is no real presentation of the classic battle for control that absorbs so much time and energy in psychotherapeutic treatment of the disorder. Nor is there any mention that patients with anorexia nervosa generate great anger, stress, and helplessness in the medical personnel who treat them. Clinicians report that anorectics have resorted to all of the following kinds of deceptions: drinking enormous amounts of water before being weighed; using terrycloth towels as napkins to absorb foods and food supplements; recalibrating scales; and inserting weights in the rectum and vagina. Consequently, anorectics are not popular patients, a fact confirmed by the comment of a New York physician: "Referral of an eating disorders patient to a colleague is not usually considered a friendly act."[22]

These stories are nearly formulaic: they emphasize family tensions and the adolescent girl's confused desire for autonomy and control, but they do not advance any particular interpretation of the cause or etiology of the disease. The plot almost always involves an attractive (usually 5 feet 5 inches), intelligent high school girl from a successful dual-career family. The mother is apt to be a fashion designer, artist, actress, or writer; the father is a professional or self-made man. In two of the novels the central characters say that they want to go to Radcliffe.

Naturally enough, the protagonist becomes interested in reducing her weight. Like virtually all American girls, she wishes to be slim because in American society slim is definitely a good thing for a female to be. Francesca, the principal character of *The Best Little Girl in the World,* cuts out pictures of models and orders them by thinness. Her goal is to be thinner than her thinnest picture. In each of the anorexia stories, for a number of different reasons all of which have to do with the difficulties of adolescence, ordinary dieting becomes transformed into a pattern of bizarre food and eating behavior that dominates the life of the central character. Some girls eat only one food, such as celery, yogurt, or dry crackers; others steal from the refrigerator at night and refuse to be seen eating. In one novel the parents are persuaded by their daughter to allow her to take supper alone in her room so that she can do homework at the same time. The mother acquiesces only to discover that for over a year her daughter has been throwing her dinner out the window of their Central Park West apartment.

In all of the fiction, girlhood anorexia curtails friendships and makes both parents extraordinarily tense, unhappy, and solicitous. Because the main characters are depicted as still in high school and living at home, mothers are central to the story. The fictive anorectic both dislikes and loves her mother and feels perpetually guilty about hurting and deceiving her. Mothers, not fathers, are the usual source of referral to professional help, a fact that is reflected in the real world composition of many anorexia nervosa support groups. Mothers of anorectics commonly join such groups to share their experiences; the AA/BA was founded by a mother for precisely that purpose.

Even though all of the novels move the story to the critical point of therapeutic intervention, few provide any valid information about the physical and emotional discomfort that lies ahead. In *Second Star to the Right* Leslie, age fifteen, is hospitalized in a behavior-modification program on a ward of anorectics where she is required to consume five glasses of liquid food per day or else she will be fed involuntarily. Her visits with parents and friends, as well as her television watching, are controlled and allocated on the basis of her weight. Yet the story stops short of describing the realities of forced feeding. By the end of the book Leslie wants to get well but has made little physical progress. Most of the fiction for teenagers finesses the difficult, lengthy, and often unpleasant recovery period. With only one exception, none of the fictional anorectics die.

Personal testimonials provide another compelling perspective on anorexia nervosa. Between 1980 and 1985 a number of autobiographical accounts achieved wide readership: in particular, novelist Sheila MacLeod's detailed account of her anorexic girlhood in Britain and Cherry Boone O'Neill's intimate story of her anorexia, marriage, and dedication to the evangelical Christian faith.[23] Unlike the fiction, which protects its youthful readers from the harsh realities of the recovery process, these are testimonies to extraordinary and protracted personal suffering. Few details are spared. Boone, for example, describes an incident in which her eating behavior became so bizarre that she stole slimy scraps from a dog's dish.

In the effort to educate and raise public awareness about particular diseases, some contemporary celebrities have been forthcoming about their personal health histories. Rock Hudson's 1985 deathbed revelation that he had AIDS was a powerful and poignant example; Mary Tyler Moore, a lifelong diabetic, openly identifies herself with that disease. For the purposes of our

story, Jane Fonda's 1983 disclosure that she suffered from bulimia was a critical public event. Fonda's revelation that she binged and purged throughout her years at Vassar College and during her early film career had the effect of imprinting bulimia and anorexia nervosa on the national consciousness.[24] Since then, many autobiographical narratives from contemporary bulimic women have surfaced. These are among the most disturbing and unhappy documents generated by women in our time. They describe obsessive thinking about food and its acquisition; stealing food; secret, ritualistic eating; and compulsive vomiting, often with orgiastic overtones.[25] Compared to the restrictive anorectic who typically limits herself to between 200 and 400 calories a day, the bulimic may ingest as much as 8,000 calories at one sitting. The public discovery of bulimia in the early 1980s meant that anorexia nervosa no longer stood alone as the solitary example of aberrant female appetite. Rather, it was the jagged, most visible tip of the iceberg of eating disorders.

. . . The cultural explanation of anorexia nervosa is popular and widely promoted. It postulates that anorexia nervosa is generated by a powerful cultural imperative that makes slimness the chief attribute of female beauty. In casual conversation we hear this idea expressed all the time: anorexia is caused by the incessant drumbeat of modern dieting, by the erotic veneration of sylphlike women such as Twiggy, and by the demands of a fashion ethic that stresses youth and androgyny rather than the contours of an adult female body. The common wisdom reflects the realities of women's lives in the twentieth century. In this respect the cultural model, more than any other, acknowledges and begins to explain why eating disorders are essentially a female problem.

Important psychological studies by Susan and Orlando Wooley, Judith Rodin, and others confirm that weight is woman's "normative obsession."[26] In response to the question, "How old were you when you first weighed more than you wanted?" American women report a preoccupation with overweight that begins before puberty and intensifies in adolescence and young adulthood. Eighty percent of girls in the fourth grade in San Francisco are dieting, according to researchers at the University of California. At three private girls' schools in Washington, D.C., 53 percent of the students said they were unhappy with their bodies by age thirteen; among those eighteen or older, 78 percent were dissatisfied. In the same vein, a 1984 *Glamour* magazine survey of thirty-three thousand women between the ages of eighteen and thirty-five demonstrated that 75 percent believed they were fat, although only 25 percent were actually overweight. Of those judged underweight by standardized measures, 45 percent still thought they were too fat. Clinicians often refer to people with weight preoccupations of this sort as "obesophobic."[27]

The women in the *Glamour* survey confirm that female self-esteem and happiness are tied to weight, particularly in the adolescent and young adult years. When asked to choose among potential sources of happiness, the *Glamour* respondents chose weight loss over success at work or in interpersonal relations. The extent to which "feeling fat" negatively influences female psychological adjustment and behavior is only beginning to be explored. A 1984 study, for example, demonstrates that many college-age women make weight a central feature of their cognitive schema. These women consistently evaluate other women, themselves, and their own achievements in terms of weight. A 1986 study revealed that "feeling fat" was significantly related to emotional stress and other external stimuli. Obviously, being and feeling thin is an extremely desirable condition in this culture, whereas feeling fat is not: "I become afraid of getting fat, of gaining weight. [There is] something dangerous about becoming a fat American."[28]

All indications are that being thin is particularly important to women in the upper classes. (This social fact is reflected in the widely quoted dictum, attributed to the Duchess of Windsor, "A woman can never be too rich or too thin.") A study by Stanford University psychologist Sanford M. Dornbusch revealed a positive correlation between gender, social class, and desire to be thin. Controlling for the actual level of fatness, Dornbusch's data, based on a nationwide sample of more than seventy-five hundred male and female high school students, showed that adolescent females in higher social classes wanted to be

thinner more often than those in the lower classes. (Not surprisingly, most obese women come from the working class and the poor.) By contrast, the relationship between social class and the desire to be thin was minimal in males. Because body preference differs among girls according to social class, those from middle-class and upper-class families are the most likely to be dissatisfied and troubled by the normal development associated with sexual maturation.[29]

According to the cultural model, these class-specific ideas about body preference pervade the larger society and do enormous harm. The modern visual media (television, films, video, magazines, and particularly advertising) fuel the preoccupation with female thinness and serve as the primary stimulus for anorexia nervosa. Female socialization, in the hands of the modern media, emphasizes external qualities ("good looks") above all else. As a consequence, we see few women of real girth on television or in the movies who also have vigor, intelligence, or sex appeal. Young girls, fed on this ideological pablum, learn to be decorative, passive, powerless, and ambivalent about being female. Herein lies the cause of anorexia nervosa, according to the cultural model.

The most outspoken and influential proponents of this model of the etiology of anorexia nervosa are feminists, often therapists, concerned with the spectrum of eating disorders that ranges from overeating to noneating. In the work of Kim Chernin, Marcia Millman, Susie Ohrbach, and Marlene Boskin-White and William C. White, the obese, the anorectic, and the bulimic all receive sympathetic treatment.[30] The tendency of these authors is to avoid casting the behavior as pathological. Instead, they seek to demonstrate that these disorders are an inevitable consequence of a misogynistic society that demeans women by devaluing female experience and women's values; by objectifying their bodies; and by discrediting vast areas of women's past and present achievements. Both overeating and non-eating are a "protest against the way in which women are regarded in our society as objects of adornment and pleasure."[31] A strain of Socialist feminism, popular in women's studies scholarship, also marks these and related critiques. To wit, our society's exaltation of thin, weak women expresses the inner logic of capitalism and patriarchy, both characterized by the sexual division of labor and female subordination. In response to these brutal economic and cultural imperatives, women turn to an excessive concern with food as a way of filling their emptiness and dealing with their fear and self-hate.

Following the organizational models of the contemporary feminist movement (that is, collective consciousness raising and networking), advocates of the cultural model suggest that above and beyond psychotherapy women with eating disorders should (1) talk with other women who are similarly afflicted and (2) organize to educate the public about their problem. The AA/BA, for example, sponsors such groups in a number of different metropolitan areas. Many former anorectics and bulimics attribute their recovery to the experience of listening and sharing with others. Group therapy and peer support groups for anorectics and bulimics are common. In May 1986 in New York City, Susie Ohrbach, a leader in the feminist therapy community, organized a Speak-Out against eating disorders, an event that sought to bring the experience and pain of eating disorders to a larger audience through the presentation of personal statements and testimonials. In its most simplistic form, the cultural model suggests that merely by speaking up about sexism and subordination, women with eating disorders can cure themselves and society.

The popular feminist reading of anorexia nervosa has much to commend it. First and foremost, this interpretation underscores the fact that a total reliance on medical models is inadequate. Because of feminist sensitivity to the interrelationship of culture, gender, and food, the impact and meaning of weight obsession in women's lives is now a serious area of theory and research in the academic disciplines and in the mental health professions. Before Chernin, Ohrbach, and Millman, women's dieting and weight concerns were trivialized or interpreted as masking a strictly individual psychological problem without consideration of the ways in which culture stimulated, exacerbated, and gave shape to a pattern of problematic behaviors.[32]

This contemporary feminist analysis has a literary analogue in the writing of academic feminist critics on nineteenth-century women, medicine, and madness. Their interpretation is rooted in the study of nineteenth-century medical texts and the male physician's view, in that era, of the female body. The analysis is confined to examination of the discourses and representations that evolved in the discussion of women and their diseases in nineteenth century Britain and the United States.[33] In this mode of analysis the primary focus is on epistemology, or how we conceptualize mental disorder. Following Michel Foucault, these scholars argue that women's bodies are a locus of social control; that in the nineteenth century male-dominated medicine created nosologies that marked women as deviant; and that "female diseases" are socially constructed states that symbolize both the hegemony of scientific medicine and Victorian social constraints on women.[34] In conditions such as anorexia nervosa, where there are no discernible lumps, lesions, or germs, there are those who question whether there is a disease at all. The problematic behavior, in this case refusal of food, is interpreted strictly as a form of symbolic interaction. Thus, anorexia nervosa is painted as a young woman's protest against the patriarchy— that is, as a form of feminist politics.

The strength of this analysis is that it identifies a troubling, if not misogynistic, set of ideas about women's bodies and minds that was part of the intellectual world of Victorian medical men and, inevitably, shaped some part of their clinical practice. While I respect the contribution of feminist literary critics to our understanding of the discourse that surrounded medical treatment in the nineteenth century, I am disquieted by the tendency to equate all female mental disorders with political protest. Certainly we need to acknowledge the relationship between sex-role constraints and problematic behavior in women, but the madhouse is a somewhat troubling site for establishing a female pantheon. To put it another way: as a feminist, I believe that the anorectic deserves our sympathy but not necessarily our veneration.

Feminist insistence on thinking about anorexia nervosa as cultural protest leads to an interpretation of the disorder that overemphasizes the level of conscious control at the same time that it presents women and girls as hapless victims of an all-powerful medical profession. Anyone who has worked with anorectics or read the clinical literature understands that food refusal becomes increasingly involuntary as the physiological process of emaciation unfolds. In full-blown cases of anorexia nervosa, the patient cannot eat even when she wants to. The cultural model denies the biomedical component of this destructive illness by obscuring the helplessness and desperation of those who suffer from it. After years of treatment a disheartened anorexic student wrote to me: "I too hope more than one could ever express that one day I will be well and my future will be bright and fulfilling. The frustration and fear I feel now is tremendous, as each day is a struggle for survival." This is hardly the voice of social protest.[35]

The romanticization of anorexia nervosa (and female mental disorders in general) can lead to some unwise and counterproductive therapeutic strategies. For example, in 1978 when Susie Ohrbach declared fat a "feminist issue," some took her to mean that feminists should allow themselves to get fat, thereby repudiating both patriarchal and capitalist imperatives. More recently, as the number of anorectics and bulimics has grown, some writers, in a well-intentioned but desperate attempt to dignify these all-too-frequent disorders, have tried to transform anorexia nervosa into the contemporary moral equivalent of the hunger strikes associated with early-twentieth-century English suffragists such as Emmeline and Sylvia Pankhurst.[36]

In the *Wisconsin Law Review* (1984) Roberta Dresser, an attorney and professor of law, argued that all medical and parental orders for renourishment of anorectics should be opposed on civil libertarian grounds. Dresser's intention, to make the case for minimizing state intrusion in personal medical decisions, was altogether admirable, but her understanding of anorexia nervosa was naive (in terms of both the psychology and the physiology of the disorder) and insensitive (in terms of historical precedents). Dresser based her argument on the idea, drawn from literary analysis, that "socio-cultural explanations of anorexia nervosa challenge the notion that the condition is a mental illness attributable to sources within the individual."[37] She posited that anorectics and early-twentieth-century hunger strikes were essentially the same and that an-

orexia nervosa is a freely chosen method of communicating and asserting power—in essence, an exercise of free will. (Dresser did not consider that anorectics may become physically unable to eat and that at some point the behavior may become involuntary.)

Although some earnestly believe that anorexia nervosa is a conscious and/or symbolic act against sexism that follows in a direct line from early-twentieth-century feminism, it is difficult from a historical perspective to see the analogy between the articulate and life-affirming political strategies of the Pankhursts and the silent, formulaic behavior of the modern Karen Carpenters.[38] The suffragists had a specific political goal to achieve, at which point food refusal ended. In contrast, the anorectic pursues thinness unrelentingly (in the same way that a paranoid schizophrenic attempts to elude imagined enemies), but she has no plan for resumption of eating. If the anorectic's food refusal is political in any way, it is a severely limited and infantile form of politics, directed primarily at parents (and self) and without any sense of allegiance to a larger collectivity. Anorectics, not known for their sisterhood, are notoriously preoccupied with the self. The effort to transform them into heroic freedom fighters is a sad commentary on how desperate people are to find in the cultural model some kind of explanatory framework, or comfort, that dignifies this confusing and complex disorder.

Finally, there is a strain of cultural analysis that implicates recent social change in the etiology of anorexia nervosa, particularly increased educational, occupational, and sexual options for women. In *The Golden Cage* Hilde Bruch suggested such a connection. In 1978 she wrote: "Growing girls can experience . . . liberation as a demand and feel that they have to do something outstanding. Many of my patients have expressed the feeling that they are overwhelmed by the vast number of potential opportunities available to them . . . and [that] they had been afraid of not choosing correctly."[39] Yet, as a sophisticated clinician, Bruch did not blame social change or feminism for anorexia nervosa. She understood that confusion about choices was only a partial explanation, for most young women handled the same array of new options with enthusiasm and optimism and did not develop the disease. Some antifeminists will still insist, however, that feminism is to blame for the upsurge in eating disorders. This interpretation usually asserts, incorrectly, that anorexia emerged for the first time in the late 1960s and 1970s, at the same time as the modern women's movement. To the conservative mind, anorexia nervosa might go away if feminism went away, allowing a return to traditional gender roles and expectations. The mistaken assumption is that anorexia nervosa did not exist in past time, when women's options were more limited.

In sum, the explanatory power of the existing cultural models is limited because of two naive suppositions: (1) that anorexia nervosa is a new phenomenon created by the pressures and circumstances of contemporary life and (2) that the disease is either imposed on young women (as victims) or freely chosen (as social protest) without involving any biological or psychological contribution. Ultimately, the current cultural models fail to explain why so many individuals *do not* develop the disease even though they have been exposed to the same cultural environment. This is where individual psychology as well as familial factors must come into play. Certainly, culture alone does not cause anorexia nervosa.

In order to understand anorexia nervosa, we must think about disease as an interactive and evolving process. I find the model of "addiction to starvation" particularly compelling because when we think about anorexia nervosa in this way, there is room for incorporating biological, psychological, and cultural components. Let me demonstrate. An individual may begin to restrict her food because of aesthetic and social reasons related to gender, class, age, and sense of style. This constitutes the initial "recruitment" stage. Many of her friends may also be doing the same thing, because in the environment in which they live being a fat female is a social and emotional liability. Being thin is of critical importance to the young woman's sense of herself. Contemporary culture clearly makes a contribution to the genesis of anorexia nervosa.

An individual's dieting moves across the spectrum from the normal to the obsessional because of other factors, namely emotional and personality issues, and personal physiology and body chemistry. If refusing food serves a young woman's emotional needs (for instance, as a symbolic statement about herself, as a bid for attention, as a way of forestalling adult sexuality, as a means of hurting her parents or separating from them, as a form of defiance), she may continue to do so because it seems like an efficacious strategy. It becomes more and more difficult to back off and change direction if the denial and control involved bring her emotional satisfaction. In some families the symptom (not eating) and the girl's emaciated appearance are overlooked or denied longer than in other families, thereby creating a situation that may actually contribute to the making of the disorder.

After weeks or months of starvation the young woman's mind and body become acclimated to both the feeling of hunger and nutritional deprivation. This constitutes a second stage of the disorder. There is evidence to suggest that hunger pangs eventually decrease rather than intensify and that the body actually gets used to a state of semistarvation, that is, to a negative energy balance. At some unidentified point in time, in certain girls, starvation may actually become satisfying or tension relieving—a state analogous perhaps to the well-known "runner's high."[40] Certain individuals, then, may make the move from chronic dieting to dependence on starvation because of a physiological substrate as well as emotional and family stresses. This is where biochemical explanations (such as elevated cortisol levels in the blood or some other neuroendocrine abnormality) come into play. The fact that many anorectics seem unable to eat (or develop withdrawal symptoms when they begin to eat regularly) suggests that something biological as well as psychological is going on.

Obviously, only a small proportion of those who diet strenuously become addicted to it, presumably because the majority of young women have neither a psychic nor a biological need for starvation. For most, even normal dieting, for short periods, is an unpleasant necessity that brings more frustration than it does satisfaction (hence the current rash of popular women's cartoons about eating as a form of forbidden pleasure and self-expression, and dieting as a futile endeavor).[41] Yet in alcohol and drug dependence and in anorexia nervosa, there appears to be a correlation between the level of exposure and the prevalence of a dependence. Simply put, when and where people become obesophobic and dieting becomes pervasive, we can expect to see an escalating number of individuals with anorexia nervosa and other eating disorders.[42] Thus, we have returned full circle to the cultural context and its power to shape human behavior.

For this study the critical implication of the dependency-addiction model is that anorexia nervosa can be conceptually divided into two stages. The first involves sociocultural context, or "recruitment" to fasting behavior; the second incorporates the subsequent "career" as an anorexic and includes physiological and psychological changes that condition the individual to exist in a starvation state.[43] The second stage is obviously the concern of medicine and mental health professionals because it is relatively formulaic and historically invariant. Stage one involves the historian, whose task it is to trace the forces and events that have led young women to this relatively stereotypical behavior pattern.

History is obviously important in understanding how and why we are where we are today vis-à-vis the increasing incidence of the disorder. A historical perspective also contributes to the debate over the etiology of anorexia nervosa by supplying an interpretation that actually reconciles different theoretical models. Despite the emphasis here on culture, my interpretation does not disallow the possibility of a biomedical component in anorexia nervosa. In fact, when we take the long history of female fasters into account, it becomes apparent that there are certain historical moments and cultural settings when a biological substratum could be activated by potent social and cultural forces. In other words, patterns of culture constitute the kind of environmental pressure that interacts with physiological and psychological variables.

. . . My assertion that the post-1960 epidemic of anorexia nervosa can be related to recent social change in the realm of food and sexuality is not an argument for turning back the clock. As a feminist, I have no particular nostalgia for what is deceptively called a "simpler" past. Moreover, historical investigation demonstrates that anorexia nervosa was latent in the economic and emotional milieu of the bourgeois family as early as the 1850s. It makes little sense to think a cure will be achieved by putting women back in the kitchen, reinstituting sit-down meals on the nation's campuses, or limiting personal and professional choices to what they were in the Victorian era. On the basis of the best current research on anorexia nervosa, we must conclude that the disease develops as a result of the intersection of external and internal forces in the life of an individual. External forces such as those described here do not, by themselves, generate psychopathologies, but they do give them shape and influence their frequency.

In the confusion of this transitional moment, when a new future is being tentatively charted for women but gender roles and sexuality are still constrained by tradition, young women on the brink of adulthood are feeling the pain of social change most acutely.[44] They look about for direction, but find little in the way of useful experiential guides. What parts of women's tradition do they want to carry into the future? What parts should be left behind? These are difficult personal and political decisions, and most young women are being asked to make them without benefit of substantive education in the history and experience of their sex. In effect, our young women are being challenged and their expectations raised without a simultaneous level of support for either their specific aspirations or for female creativity in general.

Sadly, the cult of diet and exercise is the closest thing our secular society offers women in terms of a coherent philosophy of the self.[45] This being the case, anorexia nervosa is not a quirk and the symptom choice is not surprising. When personal and social difficulties arise, a substantial number of our young women become preoccupied with their bodies and control of appetite. Of all the messages they hear, the imperative to be beautiful and good, by being thin, is still the strongest and most familiar. Moreover, they are caught, often at a very early age, in a deceptive cognitive trap that has them believing that body weight is entirely subject to their conscious control. Despite feminist influences on the career aspirations of the present college-age generation, little has transpired to dilute the basic strength of this powerful cultural prescription that plays on both individualism and conformity. The unfortunate truth is that even when she wants more than beauty and understands its limitations as a life goal, the bourgeois woman still expends an enormous amount of psychic energy on appetite control as well as on other aspects of presentation of the physical self.

And what of the future? I believe that we have not yet seen the crest of the late-twentieth-century wave of eating disorders. Although historians need to be cautious about prognostication, a few final observations seem in order.

In affluent societies the human appetite is unequivocally misused in the service of a multitude of nonnutritional needs. As a result, both anorexia nervosa and obesity are characteristic of modern life and will continue to remain so.

We can expect to see the evolution of a more elaborate medical classification scheme for eating disorders, and greater attention to distinguishing one syndrome from another. Modern medicine is built on this kind of refinement. There is also the possibility that, as eating behavior is subjected to closer scrutiny by doctors and other health professionals, more eating disorders will be identified. The new syndromes will probably be described in terms that suggest a biomedical (rather than biosocial) etiology. Some clinics specializing in weight and appetite control already advertise a specific treatment for "carbohydrate addiction."

Although eating disorders certainly deserve medical attention, an exclusive concentration on biomedical etiology obscures the ways in which social and cultural factors were implicated in the emergence of these disorders in the past century and in their proliferation today. As we approach the twenty-first century, it will surely become apparent that the postindustrial societies (the United States, Canada, Western Europe, Australia, and Japan) generate many people, not just adolescents, whose appetites are out of kilter. In effect, capitalism seems to generate a peculiar set of human difficulties that might well be characterized as consumption disorders rather than strictly eating disorders.

As Western values and life-styles are disseminated throughout the world and, in the wake of that process, traditional eating patterns disappear, anorexia nervosa will probably spread.

Where food is abundant and certain sociocultural influences predominate, there will be some women whose search for perfection becomes misguided, translating into a self-destructive pathology such as anorexia nervosa. Our historical experience suggests that a society marching in a particular direction generates psychopathologies that are themselves symptomatic of the culture.

Finally, we can expect to see eating disorders continue, if not increase, among young women in those postindustrial societies where adolescents tend to be under stress. For both young men and young women, vast technological and cultural changes have made the transition to adulthood particularly difficult by transforming the nature of the family and community and rendering the future unpredictable. According to psychologist Urie Bronfenbrenner and others, American adolescents are in the worst trouble: we have the highest incidence of alcohol and drug abuse among adolescents of any country in the world; we also have the highest rate of teenage pregnancy of any industrialized nation; and we appear to have the most anorexia nervosa.[46]

Although the sexually active adolescent mother and the sexually inactive adolescent anorectic may seem to be light-years apart, they are linked by a common, though unarticulated, understanding. For adolescent women the body is still the most powerful paradigm regardless of social class. Unfortunately, a sizable number of our young women—poor and privileged alike—regard their body as the best vehicle for making a statement about their identity and personal dreams. This is what unprotected sexual intercourse and prolonged starvation have in common. Taken together, our unenviable preeminence in these two domains suggests the enormous difficulty involved in making the transition to adult womanhood in a society where women are still evaluated primarily in terms of the body rather than the mind.

Although the disorder we have examined here is part of a general pattern of adolescent discomfort in the West, anorexia nervosa ultimately expresses the predicament of a very distinct group, one that suffers from the painful ambiguities of being young and female in an affluent society set adrift by social change. Intelligent, anxious for personal achievement, and determined to maintain control in a world where things as basic as food and sex are increasingly out of control, the contemporary anorectic unrelentingly pursues thinness—a secular form of perfection. In a society where consumption and identity are pervasively linked, she makes nonconsumption the perverse centerpiece of her identity. In a sad and desperate way, today's fasting girls epitomize the curious psychic burdens of the dutiful daughters of a people of plenty.

NOTES

Footnotes have been abridged, condensed, and renumbered for this volume. For complete notes, see original book.

1. Carol Amen, "Dieting to Death," *Science Digest* 67 (May 1970), 27–31. A shorter version of this article appeared earlier in *Family Weekly*.
2. Sam Blum, "Children Who Starve Themselves," *New York Times Magazine* (November 10, 1974), 63–79; C. Michael Brady, "The Dieting Disease," *Weekly World News* 4 (March 22, 1983), 23. The *Star* of March 23, 1983, proposed that Britain's Diana, Princess of Wales, and her sister, Lady Sarah McCorquodale, are both anorectics. The *National Enquirer* has speculated that Michael Jackson is anorexic.
3. Between March 1974 and February 1984 the *Reader's Guide* lists almost fifty articles on anorexia nervosa.
4. Hilde Bruch, *The Golden Cage: The Enigma of Anorexia Nervosa* (Cambridge, Mass., 1978), pp. vii–viii.
5. Mara Selvini-Palazzoli, "Anorexia Nervosa: A Syndrome of the Affluent Society," translated from the Italian by V.F. Di Nicola, *Transcultural Psychiatric Research Review* 22: 3 (1985), 199.
6. Hilde Bruch, "Perceptual and Conceptual Disturbances in Anorexia Nervosa," *Psychosomatic Medicine* 24: 2 (1962), 187–194.
7. American Psychiatric Association, *Diagnostic and Statistical Manual of Mental Disorders* 69 (3rd ed., Washington, D.C., 1980; 3rd ed., rev., Washington, D.C., 1987).
8. On weight criteria see N. Rollins and E. Piazza, "Diagnosis of Anorexia Nervosa: A Critical Reappraisal," *Journal of the American Academy of Child Psychiatry* 17 (1978), 126–137. On amenorrhea see Katherine Halmi and J. R. Falk, "Behavioral and Dietary Discriminators of Menstrual Function in Anorexia Nervosa," in *Anorexia Nervosa: Recent Developments in Research,* ed.

P. L. Darby et al. (New York, 1983), 323–329. On hyperactivity see L. Kron et al., "Hyperactivity in Anorexia Nervosa: A Fundamental Clinical Feature," *Comparative Psychiatry* 19 (1978), 433–440.
9. In bulimia (without anorexia nervosa) weight loss may be substantial, but the weight does not fall below a minimal normal weight.
10. William J. Swift, "The Long Term Outcome of Early Onset of Anorexia Nervosa: A Critical Review," *Journal of the American Academy of Child Psychiatry* 21 (January 1982), 38–46; D. J. Jones et al., 'Epidemiology of Anorexia Nervosa in Monroe County, New York: 1960–1976," *Psychosomatic Medicine* 42 (1980), 551–558. See also M. Duddle, "An Increase in Anorexia Nervosa in a University Population," *British Journal of Psychiatry* 123 (1973), 711–712; A. H. Crisp, R. L. Palmer, and R. S. Kalucy, "How Common Is Anorexia Nervosa? A Prevalence Study," ibid. 128 (1976), 549–554.
11. R. E. Kendell et al., "The Epidemiology of Anorexia Nervosa," *Psychological Medicine* 3 (1973), 200–203.
12. Herzog and Copeland, "Eating Disorders," p. 295; Jane Y. Yu, "Eating Disorders," *Vital Signs* (September 1986), Cornell University Health Services, p. 2.
13. Paul E. Garfinkel and David M. Garner, *Anorexia Nervosa: A Multidimensional Perspective* (New York, 1982), pp. 103, 190; Gloria R. Leon and Stephen Finn, "Sex Role Stereotypes and the Development of Eating Disorders," in *Sex Roles and Psychopathology,* ed. C. S. Wilson (New York, 1984), pp. 317–337; A. H. Crisp et al., "The Long Term Prognosis in Anorexia Nervosa: Some Factors Predictive of Outcome," in *Anorexia Nervosa,* ed. R. A. Vigersky (New York, 1977), pp. 55–65. The fact that anorexia nervosa only rarely exists in males supports the idea that cultural factors play a role in producing the disorder.
14. There are some reports of anorexia nervosa among blacks: see A. J. Pumariega, P. Edwards, and L. B. Mitchell, "Anorexia Nervosa in Black Adolescents," *Journal of the American Academy of Child Psychiatry* 23 (1984), 111–114; T. Silber, "Anorexia Nervosa in Black Adolescents," *Journal of the National Medical Association* 76 (1984), 29–32; George Hsu, "Are Eating Disorders More Common in Blacks?" *International Journal of Eating Disorders* 6 (January 1987), 113–124.
15. See Hiroyuki Suematsu et al., "Statistical Studies on the Prognosis of Anorexia Nervosa," *Japanese Journal of Psychosomatic Medicine* 23 (1983),

23–30. In general, physicians have looked unsuccessfully for anorexia nervosa in other cultures. See Raymond Prince, "The Concepts of Culture Bound Syndromes: Anorexia Nervosa and Brain-Fag," *Social Science Medicine* 21: 2 (1985), 197–203; Pow Meng Yap, "The Culture Bound Reactive Syndromes," in *Mental Health Research in Asia and the Pacific,* ed. William Caudill and Tsung-yi Lin (Honolulu, 1969), pp. 33–53; Satish Varma, "Anorexia Nervosa in Developing Countries," *Transcultural Psychiatric Research Review* 16 (April 1979), 114–115; R. Prince, "Is Anorexia Nervosa a Culture Bound Syndrome?" ibid. 20: 1 (1983), 299–300.

16. There have been a number of attempts to place anorexia nervosa within other established psychiatric categories. See for example G. Nicolle, "Prepsychotic Anorexia," *Lancet* 2 (1938), 1173–74; D. P. Cantwell et al., "Anorexia Nervosa: An Affective Disorder?" *Archives of General Psychiatry* 34 (1977), 1087–93; H. D. Palmer and M. S. Jones, "Anorexia Nervosa as a Manifestation of Compulsive Neurosis," *Archives of Neurology and Psychiatry* 41 (1939), 856. More recently, the focus has been on the behavioral signs and symptoms, and on biological similarities to depressive disorder.

17. Katherine A. Halmi, G. Broadland, and C. A. Rigas, "A Follow Up Study of 79 Patients with Anorexia Nervosa: An Evaluation of Prognostic Factors and Diagnostic Criteria," in *Life History Research in Psychopathology,* ed. R. D. Wirt, G. Winokur, and M. Roff, vol. 4 (Minneapolis, 1975).

18. *New York State Journal of Medicine* 84 (May 1984), 228. On the overdiagnosis of bulimia see George Groh, "You've Come a Long Way, Bulimia," *M.D., Medical Newsmagazine* 28 (February 1984), 48–57.

19. Quote from Steven Levenkron in the newsletter of AA/BA, based on Bruch, *The Golden Cage,* p. xii.

20. See the coverage of Karen Carpenter's death in *People Weekly* (February 21 and November 21, 1983; May 31, 1985). In the earliest accounts, low serum potassium was reported to have caused an irregularity in Carpenter's heartbeat. By 1985, the reports were that Carpenter had died of "cardiotoxicity" brought on by the chemical emetine. The suggestion is that Carpenter was abusing a powerful over-the-counter drug, Ipecac, used to induce vomiting in case of poison.

21. Some examples of novels about anorexia nervosa are Deborah Hautzig, *Second Star to the Right* (New York, 1981); Steven Levenkron, *The Best Little Girl in the World* (New York, 1978); Rebecca Joseph, *Early Disorder* (New York, 1980); Ivy Ruckman, *The Hunger Scream* (New York, 1983); Margaret Willey, *The Bigger Book of Lydia* (New York, 1983); John Sours, *Starving to Death in a Sea of Objects* (New York, 1980); Emily Hudlow, *Alabaster Chambers* (New York, 1979); Isaacsen-Bright, *Mirrors Never Lie* (Worthington, Ohio, 1982).

22. See Andrew W. Brotman, Theodore A. Stern, and David B. Herzog, "Emotional Reactions of House Officers to Patients with Anorexia Nervosa, Diabetes and Obesity," *International Journal of Eating Disorders* (Summer 1983), 71–77, and, for the comment of John Schowalter, *AA/BA Newsletter* 8 (September–November 1985), 6.

23. For personal testimonials see Sheila MacLeod, *The Art of Starvation: A Story of Anorexia and Survival* (New York, 1983); Cherry Boone O'Neill, *Starving for Attention* (New York, 1983); Aimee Liu, *Solitaire* (New York, 1979); Sandra Heater, *Am I Still Visible? A Woman's Triumph over Anorexia Nervosa* (Whitehall, Va., 1983); Camie Ford and Sunny Hale, *Two Too Thin: Two Women Who Triumphed over Anorexia Nervosa* (Orleans, Mass., 1983). The last-named work shares with O'Neill's book an evangelical Christian emphasis.

24. Fonda's experience with bulimia, although the author never used the clinical term, was described by Thomas Kiernan in *June: An Intimate Biography of Jane Fonda* (New York, 1973), p. 67.

25. See for example Lisa Messinger, *Biting the Hand that Feeds Me: Days of Binging, Purging and Recovery* (Moonachie, N.J., 1985); Jackie Barrile, *Confessions of a Closet Eater* (Wheaton, Ill., 1983).

26. Judith Rodin, Lisa Silberstein, and Ruth Streigel-Moore, "Women and Weight: A Normative Discontent," in *1984 Nebraska Symposium on Motivation,* ed. Theodore B. Sonderegger (Lincoln, 1985); April E. Fallon and Paul Rozin, "Sex Differences in Perceptions of Desirable Body Shape," *Journal of Abnormal Psychology* 94 (1985), 102–105.

27. See *Time* (January 20, 1986), 54, and *Los Angeles Times,* February 15 and March 29, 1984, for a report on the work of anthropologist Margaret MacKenzie. For a report of the *Glamour* survey see *Palm Beach Post,* December 26, 1985.

28. These studies are summarized in Ruth Streigel-Moore, Gail McAvay, and Judith Rodin, "Psychological and Behavioral Correlates of Feeling Fat in Women," *International Journal of Eating Disorders* 5: 5 (1986), 935–947; quoted in Ana-Maria Rizzuto, Ross K. Peterson, and Marilyn Reed, "The Pathological Sense of Self in Anorexia

Nervosa," *Psychiatric Clinics of North America* 4 (December 1981), 38.

29. Sanford M. Dornbusch et al., "Sexual Maturation, Social Class, and the Desire to Be Thin among Adolescent Females," *Journal of Developmental and Behavioral Pediatrics* 5 (December 1984), 308–314.

30. Susie Ohrbach, *Fat Is a Feminist Issue: The Anti-Diet Guide to Permanent Weight Loss* (New York, 1978); idem, *Hunger Strike: The Anorectic's Struggle as a Metaphor for Our Age* (New York, 1986); Kim Chernin, *The Obsession: Reflections on the Tyranny of Slenderness* (New York, 1981); idem, *The Hungry Self;* Marcia Millman, *Such a Pretty Face: Being Fat in America* (New York, 1980); Marlene Boskin-White and William C. White, *Bulimarexia: The Binge Purge Cycle* (New York, 1983).

31. Ohrbach, *Hunger Strike*, p. 63.

32. Feminist analysis has begun to suggest that the medical models for understanding obesity are inadequate and that rigid appetite control and body-image preoccupations have negative developmental consequences for many women. See for example, Barbara Edelstein, *The Woman Doctor's Diet for Women* (Englewood Cliffs, N.J., 1977); C. P. Herman and J. Polivy, "Anxiety, Restraint, and Eating Behavior," *Journal of Abnormal Psychology* 84 (December 1975), 666–672.

33. For examples see Sandra Gilbert and Susan Gubar, *The Madwoman in the Attic* (New Haven, 1979); Elaine Showalter, *The Female Malady: Women, Madness and English Culture, 1830–1980* (New York, 1985).

34. See Bryan Turner, *The Body and Society: Explorations in Social Theory* (Oxford, 1984).

35. Personal communication to the author, April 1987.

36. Ohrbach's *Hunger Strike* (1986) implies in its title that anorexia nervosa is a form of political protest.

37. Dresser, "Feeding the Hunger Artists," p. 338.

38. Showalter, *The Female Malady,* p. 162, writes of the suffragists in 1912, "The hunger strikes of militant women prisoners brilliantly put the symptomatology of anorexia nervosa to work in the service of a feminist cause."

39. Bruch, *The Golden Cage,* p. ix.

40. J. Blumenthal, "Is Running an Analogue of Anorexia Nervosa? An Empirical Study of Obligatory Running and Anorexia Nervosa," *Journal of the American Medical Association* 252 (1984), 520–523.

41. I refer here to cartoons by Sylvia (Nicole Hollander), Cathy (Cathy Guisewaite), and Linda Barry.

42. Ruth Striegel-Moore, Lisa R. Silberstein, and Judith Rodin, "Toward an Understanding of Risk Factors in Bulimia," *American Psychologist* 41 (March 1986), 256–258, make a similar argument.

43. The distinction between recruitment and career evolved in conversations with Dr. William Bennett, whose command of the medical literature (and sensitivity to historical concerns) improved my understanding of the relationship between etiology and symptoms.

44. In *Theories of Adolescence* (New York, 1962) R. E. Muuss wrote, "Societies in a period of rapid transition create a particularly difficult adolescent period; the adolescent has not only the society's problem to adjust to but his [or her] own as well" (p. 164). See also Paul B. Baltes, Hayne W. Reese, and Lewis P. Lipsitt, "Life Span Developmental Psychology," *Annual Review of Psychology* 31 (1980), 76–79; J. R. Nesselroade and Paul B. Baltes, "Adolescent Personality Development and Historical Change: 1970–1972," *Monographs of Society for Research in Child Development* 39 (May 1974), ser. 154.

45. My view of this issue complements ideas presented in Robert Bellah et al., *Habits of the Heart: Individualism and Commitment in American Life* (New York, 1986).

46. These data are synthesized in Urie Bronfenbrenner, "Alienation and the Four Worlds of Childhood," *Phi Delta Kappan* (February 1986), 434.

11

An Epidemic of Stigma:
Public Reaction to AIDS

■ ■ ■ ■ ■ ■

Gregory M. Herek and Eric K. Glunt

A Massachusetts teacher was ordered to take a medical leave and then to resign when rumors circulated that he was being treated for AIDS. After demonstrating to school officials that his medical problems were associated with a blood disorder not related to AIDS, he was allowed to return to teaching. Threatening phone calls and harassment continued, however, and he felt compelled to take a leave of absence (Shipp, 1986).

In White Plains, New York, a mail carrier refused to deliver mail to an AIDS task force office for two weeks because he feared catching the disease ("Mail Service Ordered to AIDS Center," 1987).

In Arcadia, Florida, three brothers tested positive for human immunodeficiency virus (HIV). After word spread of their infection, their barber refused to cut the boys' hair, and the family's minister suggested that they stay away from Sunday church services. Eventually, the family's house was burned down (Robinson, 1987).

In the *American Spectator*, Christopher Monckton (1987) wrote: "Every member of the population should be blood tested every month to detect the presence of antibodies against [AIDS], and those found to be infected with the virus, even if only as carriers, should be isolated compulsorily, immediately, and permanently" (p. 30).

In 1987, 1,042 incidents of harassment against gay people were reported to the National Gay and Lesbian Task Force (NGLTF) that involved references to AIDS; two thirds of the local groups who reported incidents to NGLTF expressed the belief that fear and hatred associated with AIDS have fostered antigay violence (NGLTF, 1988).

In a 1986 Op/Ed piece in the *New York Times*, William F. Buckley, Jr., proposed that "everyone detected with AIDS should be tattooed in the upper forearm, to protect common-needle users, and on the buttocks, to prevent the victimization of other homosexuals" (p. A27).

Understanding the AIDS epidemic in the United States requires understanding the phenomenon of widespread, intensely negative reactions to HIV-infected persons. These negative reactions have shaped the behavior of infected individuals and have limited the effectiveness of prevention efforts.

Persons infected with HIV must bear the burden of societal hostility at a time when they are most in need of social support. Attempts to avoid such hostility may compromise individuals' health: Fear of being harassed, of facing job discrimination, and of losing insurance coverage, for example, deters individuals from being tested for HIV infection and seeking early treatment for symptoms.

At a societal level, the opprobrium attached to AIDS directly interferes with research and public health efforts to monitor the epidemic by, for instance, discouraging physicians from reporting cases (King, 1986). Further, prevention efforts are hampered by social disapproval of behaviors that can transmit AIDS. The Centers for Disease Control, for example, withheld funding for educational programs that included explicit instructions for engaging in safe sex behavior (Panem, 1987), and the U.S. Senate has twice endorsed an amendment by Jesse Helms (R–NC) that would prohibit federal funds for AIDS education materials that "promote or encourage, directly or indirectly, homosexual activities" ("Limit Voted on AIDS Funds," 1987). By constricting the scope

125

of risk-reduction education, such actions contribute to the epidemic's spread.

In the present article, we refer to these and similar phenomena as *AIDS-related stigma*. Under this rubric, we include all stigma directed at persons perceived to be infected with HIV, regardless of whether they actually are infected and of whether they manifest symptoms of AIDS. . . . We purposely avoid using terms that imply individual pathology, such as "AIDS phobia" or "AIDS hysteria." Instead, we base our analysis on the assumption that AIDS-related stigma is a socially constructed reaction to a lethal illness that has been most prevalent among groups that already were targets of prejudice.

A stigma is a mark of shame or discredit. The focus of social psychological research on stigma is not on the mark itself, however, so much as on the social relationships in which a particular mark is defined as shameful or discrediting (Goffman, 1963). In line with this approach we are concerned here with the social psychological processes through which people are discredited when they are perceived to be infected with HIV. We will briefly examine individual attitudes and behaviors that express fear or hostility toward persons with AIDS, as well as institutional policies that impose hardships on particular individuals or groups without slowing the spread of AIDS. We also will offer suggestions for combating stigma at both the individual and institutional levels.

Sources of Stigma

AIDS is now perceived as a lethal disease that can be transmitted by specific behaviors and is most prevalent among gay men and users of intravenous drugs. This definition of the syndrome results in a dual stigma: first, from identification of AIDS as a serious illness; second, from the identification of AIDS with persons and groups already stigmatized prior to the epidemic (Des Jarlais, Friedman, & Hopkins, 1985; Herek, 1984).

Illness and Stigma

As an illness, AIDS manifests the characteristics of stigma described by Jones et al. (1984). First, it

is an incurable and progressive condition and, because it is transmissible, people infected with HIV are often perceived as placing others at risk; survey data show that almost all Americans have heard of AIDS and that most know it is transmitted through blood and sexual contact (Singer, Rogers, & Corcoran, 1987). Second, people with HIV infection often are blamed for causing their condition through riskful behavior; approximately half of Americans agree that "most people with AIDS have only themselves to blame" (Gallup poll, July 10, 1987)[1] and that "in general, it's people's own fault if they get AIDS" (Gallup poll, October 23, 1987). Finally, in face-to-face encounters, the symptoms of AIDS-related illnesses are frequently visible to others, often disfiguring, and likely to disrupt an individual's social interactions.

Like other life-threatening illnesses, AIDS confronts even the noninfected with the reality of death, provoking what Schutz (1962) described as the "fundamental anxiety." When people interact with a person with AIDS, hear AIDS discussed, or simply read about it in a newspaper, they are reminded of their own mortality; their day-to-day sense of reality is challenged in a profoundly disturbing way. According to Schutz, the pragmatic objective of daily life (the "natural attitude") is to construct experiences that avoid this fundamental anxiety. AIDS-related stigmatization represents such a construction: Healthy individuals distance themselves from death by defining the illness as an affliction of others. Early news reports about AIDS "risk groups," for example, permitted most Americans (those who were not gay men, intravenous (IV) drug users, Haitians, or hemophiliacs) to see themselves as removed from the epidemic and protected from it.

With some serious illnesses, such attempts to maintain the natural attitude lead to attributions of individual character flaws to diseased persons. Cancer patients, for example, are portrayed as repressing emotions or lacking the will to be well (Sontag, 1977). Although considerable victim-blaming on the basis of individual characteristics has also occurred with AIDS, blaming the social groups to which most Americans with AIDS belong has been much more common. We turn now to this second source of AIDS-related stigma.

AIDS and Preexisting Stigma

Because of the characteristics it displays as an illness, AIDS probably would have been stigmatized to some extent regardless of whom it infected. Through an accident of history, however, AIDS in the United States has been largely a disease of already stigmatized groups. Most adults diagnosed with AIDS in this country are men who were infected through homosexual behavior (63%). The second most common route of HIV transmission in the United States has been through sharing intravenous needles for illegal drug use (19%). Another 7% of cases fit both categories. Additionally, Blacks and Hispanics are disproportionately represented in all transmission categories except hemophilia (Centers for Disease Control, 1988).

In short, the American epidemic of AIDS has been socially defined as a disease of marginalized groups, especially gay men. Consequently, the stigma attached to AIDS as an illness is layered upon preexisting stigma. The result is that as public perceptions of AIDS become inextricably tied to perceptions of the groups among which it is prevalent, the stigma of disease and death become attached to the groups themselves. AIDS has become a symbol: Reactions to AIDS are reactions to gay men, drug users, racial minorities, or outsiders in general.

This linkage of AIDS with stigmatized groups has been an integral part of the history of the epidemic. A name initially proposed for the syndrome was Gay-Related Immune Deficiency (GRID) (Shilts, 1987a), and press coverage has referred to AIDS as the "gay plague" (VerMeulen, 1982). Indeed, little press coverage of AIDS occurred until 1983, when it was discovered that individuals outside of the "risk groups" of homosexual and bisexual men and IV drug users could be infected (Baker, 1986; Panem, 1987). Shilts (1987a) pointed out that the *New York Times* published only six stories about AIDS during 1981 and 1982, none of them on the front page. In contrast, the *Times* printed 54 stories in 1982 about the discovery of poisoned Tylenol capsules in Chicago in October of that year; four of those stories were on the front page. Seven people died from poisoned Tylenol; of the 634 Americans who had been diagnosed with AIDS by October 5, 1982, 260 had died. Shilts argued that the epidemic was virtually ignored by the nongay media because it was merely a "story of dead and dying homosexuals" (p. 191).

AIDS-related stigma interacts with preexisting stigma in complex ways. If a diagnosis of AIDS . . . reveals a man's previously hidden homosexuality, for example, a double stigma immediately results. Using Goffman's (1963) terminology, being identified as a person with AIDS transforms a man from discreditable (secretly gay) to discredited (publicly gay). Such marking of individuals as outsiders (because they are gay or because they have AIDS) can increase a community's solidarity by clearly demarcating its boundaries (Durkheim, 1895/1982). The frequent use of the phrase "the general public" as a counterpart to "risk groups" conveys this distinction between in-group and out-group; gay men, IV drug users, and their sexual partners are not part of "the general public." Similarly, persons who did not contract AIDS through homosexual behavior or drug use have often been categorized as "innocent victims" (Albert, 1986). For example, a *Newsweek* caption early in the epidemic described a teenage hemophiliac and an infant with AIDS as "the most blameless victims" ("The Social Fallout From an Epidemic," 1985). The opposite, of course, is a "blameable victim," that is, one who was infected with HIV during stigmatized behavior.

Because of its prevalence among already stigmatized groups, AIDS can easily be exploited for ideological and political purposes. A Houston mayoral candidate (and former mayor), for example, publicly joked that his solution to the city's AIDS problem would be to "shoot the queers" (Shilts, 1987b). Such political uses of AIDS, in turn, heighten the stigma associated with the disease and the groups most affected by it.

The definition of AIDS as an ideological and political issue is exemplified in the following comments by Republican columnist Patrick Buchanan (1987):

> There is one, only one, cause of the AIDS crisis—the willful refusal of homosexuals to cease indulging in the immoral, unnatural, unsanitary, unhealthy, and suicidal practice of anal intercourse, which is the primary means by which the AIDS virus is being

spread through the "gay" community, and thence, into the needles of IV drug abusers [and to others] (p. 23).

Buchanan further suggested that the

Democratic Party should be dragged into the court of public opinion as an unindicted coconspirator in America's AIDS epidemic [for] seeking to amend state and federal civil rights laws to make sodomy a protected civil right, to put homosexual behavior, the sexual practice by which AIDS is spread, on the same moral plane with being female or being black (p. 23).

In his attempt to link AIDS with the opposition political party and with homosexual behavior exclusively, Buchanan not only made illness a politicized issue, he also ignored the worldwide epidemic. AIDS is overwhelmingly an epidemic of heterosexual transmission (Institute of Medicine, 1986).

The federal government's initial slow response to AIDS can be understood in part as a response to this politicization of stigma. Although other organizational variables also were important (Panem, 1987), antigay sentiment appears to have played an important role in the Reagan administration's failure to confront the epidemic (Shilts, 1987a).

Other groups have responded to AIDS on the basis of its association with stigmatized sexuality. The Catholic Church, for example, argued against civil rights protection for gay people in a statement that was widely interpreted as referring to AIDS: "Even when the practice of homosexuality may seriously threaten the lives and well-being of a large number of people, its advocates remain undeterred and refuse to consider the magnitude of the risks involved" (Congregation for the Doctrine of the Faith, 1986, p. 8). AIDS was equated with homosexual behavior and was used to justify antigay discrimination and hostility.

We have cited examples of AIDS-related stigma occurring at the level of groups and institutions. The construction of AIDS at this level helps to shape individual beliefs, attitudes, and behaviors related to the epidemic.

The Social Psychology of AIDS-Related Stigma

We have mentioned some of the social psychological processes related to stigma (e.g., Goffman, 1963; Shultz, 1962). In this section we will explore these processes more extensively, with special attention to insights contributed by psychologists.

AIDS as Illness: Stigma, Anxiety, and Decision Making

AIDS evokes anxiety because of its association with death. Research on risk assessment (e.g., Slovic, 1987) further illustrates the characteristics of AIDS that evoke anxiety: It is a new illness that is uniformly fatal; it is caused by an unseen infectious agent that can remain latent in the body for an unknown period of time; the epidemic is perceived as both out of control and potentially catastrophic. Because of these characteristics, individual judgments and decisions associated with AIDS are often made under conditions of anxiety and are thus likely to be defective.

Anxiety evoked by AIDS, for example, may lead people to believe that not enough time remains to weigh carefully the strengths and weaknesses of various alternative solutions to an AIDS-related problem (e.g., whether to vote for a political candidate who advocates mandatory HIV testing, how to respond to a coworker with AIDS, whether to send one's child to a school where an HIV-infected child is enrolled). This belief is likely to foster a hypervigilant style of decision making in which the easiest or most readily available perceived solution is embraced precipitously without considering its consequences (Janis & Mann, 1977).

Because HIV is transmissible, for example, an individual might equate AIDS with other, previously encountered transmissible diseases, such as influenza. The consequence could be an overestimation of the danger of transmitting AIDS through media other than semen and blood. Those displaying this hypervigilant style of decision making might, then, endorse a policy of quarantine for persons infected with HIV. Because of the felt need to decide quickly, the individual would be unlikely to consider carefully the serious flaws (e.g., public health and civil liberties) of a quarantine policy. He or she may misuse cognitive heuristics, such as the representativeness heuristic, which involves assessing an event's probability by the ease with which various instances of it can be brought to mind (Tversky & Kahneman, 1974).

Even when public officials attempt to allay fears and counteract this process, their pronouncements on AIDS may be greeted with skepticism. This disbelief is fueled in part by another inappropriate use of the representativeness heuristic: Prominent examples of public officials' dishonesty in other situations (e.g., Watergate, Three Mile Island) can be easily recalled (see Morin, 1984); the fact that these earlier situations are not directly comparable to the AIDS epidemic is not recognized.

Public misunderstanding of scientists' use of probabilistic statements in describing the risks posed by AIDS further exacerbates the problem. A scientist, for example, might accurately say that the risk of HIV transmission through saliva is theoretically possible but extremely unlikely; as a person trained to know that the null hypothesis cannot be proved, however, the scientist will refrain from saying that such transmission is impossible. Lay people may misinterpret this phrasing, however, to mean that such transmission is possible or somewhat likely and may adopt a heuristic of "better safe than sorry" or "you can't be too careful" to guide their behavior.

AIDS and Stigmatized Minorities

As noted earlier, AIDS-related stigma is complicated by the epidemic's association with already marginalized groups. Consequently, most individuals do not respond to AIDS simply as a lethal and transmissible disease. Rather, they respond to it as a lethal and transmissible disease of gay men and other minorities. AIDS thus provides many people with a metaphor for prejudice—a convenient hook on which to hang their hostility toward out-groups. Approximately one fourth of the respondents to the *Los Angeles Times* polls, for example, consistently have agreed that "AIDS is a punishment God has given homosexuals for

the way they live" (28% on December 5, 1985; 24% on July 9, 1986; and 27% on July 24, 1987). Several researchers have found that respondents who express negative attitudes toward gay people are more likely than others to be poorly informed about AIDS and are more likely to stigmatize people with AIDS (Gabay & Morrison, 1985; Herek, in press; Lennon & McDevitt, 1987; O'Donnell et al., 1987). These data suggest that understanding the social psychological processes underlying AIDS-related stigma will require examination of the dynamics of antigay attitudes.

The first author's research, for example, has demonstrated the utility of a functional approach to heterosexuals' attitudes toward lesbians and gay men (Herek, 1984, 1986, 1987). Within this perspective, attitudes are understood according to the psychological needs they meet. Antigay attitudes appear to fit into two broad functional categories. First, antigay attitudes can help a heterosexual person to fit experiences (past or anticipated) with lesbians and gay men into existing cognitive categories, thereby guiding future behavior with the goal of maximizing benefits to oneself. Second, expressing antigay attitudes can help an individual to increase self-esteem, reduce anxiety, or secure social support.

The psychological functions served by attitudes concerning AIDS may be closely related to those served by attitudes toward gay people. For example, people with AIDS may be assigned to a cognitive category already existing for gay people; the affect resulting from negative experiences with gay people may be transferred to people with AIDS. Negative stereotypes of gay people (e.g., as preying on young people) may be imputed to people with AIDS as well. Alternatively, a fundamentalist Christian might condemn homosexuality as a way of affirming her or his sense of self as a good Christian and thereby increasing self-esteem. AIDS might be interpreted as God's punishment for homosexuality, and expressing a similar condemnation for people with AIDS might bolster self-esteem. Or a person whose hostility toward gay people is based on unresolved intraspychic conflicts may experience similar anxieties associated with AIDS; because AIDS links homosexuality with death, it may offer a focus for anxieties associated with both.

Strategies for Eradicating
AIDS-Related Stigma
....

We have pointed to both individual and societal levels of AIDS-related stigma. Because of the dialectical relation between cultural ideologies and individual attitudes, any attempt to eradicate AIDS-related stigma must target both levels. AIDS-education programs must be designed not only to impart information to individuals but also to reduce the stigma attached to AIDS. Public policy not only must respond to the technical issues of treatment and prevention but also must help to establish clear social norms of respect and compassion for HIV-infected persons.

Changing Individual Attitudes

To the extent that individuals respond to AIDS primarily as a threat to personal well-being (their own or that of their loved ones), they will be most influenced by educational programs that clearly present factual information about AIDS in a context that reduces anxiety (e.g., by reassuring the audience that sufficient time is available to make careful decisions) while explicitly countering the misuse of cognitive heuristics.

Individuals whose responses to AIDS result primarily from its associations with stigmatized minorities, in contrast, are unlikely to be affected by educational campaigns that provide only facts about AIDS. Educational programs for them must also address the preexisting stigma. For example, an individual who advocates quarantine for persons with AIDS because of an underlying hostility toward gay men is not likely to be influenced by factual discussions about the ineffectiveness of quarantine; the individual's antigay prejudice also must be confronted.

Stigma and Public Policy

Eliminating AIDS-related stigma requires government action in at least three areas. First, an individual's HIV status must remain confidential; given the inevitably damaging effects of being identified as HIV-infected (Batchelor, 1987), stiff penalties should be attached to unauthorized disclosure of this information. Second, discrimination on the basis of HIV status should be prohibited; as noted by Admiral James D. Watkins, chair of the Presidential Commission on the Human Immunodeficiency Virus Epidemic, the fear of discrimination "will limit the public's willingness to comply with the collection of epidemiological data and other public health strategies, will undermine our efforts to contain the HIV epidemic, and will leave HIV infected individuals isolated and alone" ("Excerpts From Report," 1988, p. A16). Third, public education efforts must directly confront AIDS-related stigma. This means providing clear and explicit information about how AIDS is and is not transmitted to reduce fears of contact with HIV-infected persons, as well as to educate the public about safer personal practices.

Confronting stigma also means that AIDS-education programs must be designed to reduce the antigay prejudice that is so closely linked to AIDS-related stigma. Public policy that perpetuates antigay prejudice must be viewed as a major obstacle to stopping the epidemic. State sodomy statutes, for example, create the untenable situation in which safe-sex educational programs necessarily encourage criminal conduct; such laws should be overturned as part of an effective response to AIDS. The lack of legal sanctions against antigay discrimination in housing, employment, and services means that most HIV-infected individuals in the United States must legitimately fear discrimination based on presumptions about their sexual orientation even if AIDS-related discrimination is illegal; laws should be enacted prohibiting discrimination based on sexual orientation.

Although we have focused on the connection between AIDS-related stigma and antigay prejudice, other types of prejudice that fuel AIDS-related stigma should not be ignored. The stigmatization of IV drug users, for example, often leads to the assumption that behavior change is impossible in this group and consequently that AIDS-prevention efforts would be wasted. Increased street demand for sterile needles, however, indicates an awareness among drug users of how AIDS is transmitted and a desire to reduce personal risk (De Jarlais et al., 1985). Public policy must encourage innovative approaches to AIDS education among drug users, while also expanding the availability of drug-treatment programs to assist users in overcoming their drug dependency.

As already noted, Blacks and Hispanics are overrepresented among people with AIDS in most categories of transmission. Because of preexisting racism, both individual and institutional, White policymakers have remained ignorant of the special needs of minority communities. Although increasing numbers of public officials, researchers, and educators realize that the content of risk-reduction programs must be tailored to the target communities, they often do not know how to accomplish this objective. Two issues of stigma thus must be confronted: (a) the stigma attached to AIDS, homosexual behavior, and intravenous drug use within minority communities, and (b) stigmatization of the minority communities by the prevailing White culture. . . .

AIDS-related stigma is a problem for all of society. It imposes severe hardships on the people who are its targets, and it ultimately interferes with treating and preventing HIV infection. By attacking AIDS-related stigma, we create a social climate conducive to a rational, effective, and compassionate response to this epidemic.

NOTES

1. Unless otherwise indicated, data from public opinion polls were obtained through the Roper Center, University of Connecticut at Storrs. We thank Professor Bliss Siman of Baruch College, City University of New York, for her assistance in securing these data.

REFERENCES

Albert, E. (1986). Illness and deviance: The response of the press to AIDS. In D. A. Feldman & T. M. Johnson (Eds.), *The social dimension of AIDS* (pp. 163–178). New York: Praeger.

Baker, A. J. (1986). The portrayal of AIDS in the media: An analysis of articles in *The New York Times*. In D. A. Feldman & T. M. Johnson (Eds.), *The social dimension of AIDS* (pp. 179–194). New York: Praeger.

Batchelor, W. F. (1987). Real fears, false hopes: The human costs of AIDS antibody testing. *AIDS & Public Policy Journal* 2(4), 25–30.

Buchanan, P. J. (1987, December 2). AIDS and moral bankruptcy. *New York Post*, p. 23.

Buckley, W. F., Jr. (1986, March 18). Crucial steps in combating the AIDS epidemic: Identify all the carriers. *New York Times*, p. A27.

Centers for Disease Control. (1988, June 6). *AIDS Weekly Surveillance Report*. Atlanta: Author.

Congregation for the Doctrine of the Faith. (1986). *Letter to the bishops of the Catholic Church on the pastoral care of homosexual persons*. Vatican City: Author.

Des Jarlais, D. C., Friedman, S. R., & Hopkins, W. (1985). Risk reduction for the acquired immunodeficiency syndrome among intravenous drug users. *Annals of Internal Medicine, 103,* 755–759.

Durkheim, E. (1982). *The rules of sociological method* (S. Lukes, Ed., & W. D. Halls, Trans.). New York: Free Press. (Original work published 1895).

Excerpts from report by AIDS panel chairman. (1988, June 3). *New York Times*, p. A16.

Gabay, E. D., & Morrison, A. (1985, August). *AIDS-phobia, homophobia, and locus of control*. Paper presented at the annual meeting of the American Psychological Association, Los Angeles.

Goffman, E. (1963). *Stigma: Notes on the management of spoiled identity*. Englewood Cliffs, NJ: Prentice-Hall.

Herek, G. M. (1984). Beyond "homophobia": A social psychological perspective on attitudes toward lesbians and gay men. *Journal of Homosexuality, 10*(1), 1–21.

Herek, G. M. (1986). The instrumentality of attitudes: Toward a neofunctional theory. *Journal of Social Issues, 42*(2), 99–114.

Herek, G. M. (1987). Can functions be measured? A new perspective on the functional approach to attitudes. *Social Psychology Quarterly, 50*(4), 285–303.

Herek, G. M. (in press). Heterosexuals' attitudes toward lesbians and gay men: Correlates and gender differences. *Journal of Sex Research*.

Institute of Medicine. (1986). *Confronting AIDS: Directions for public health, health care and research*. Washington, DC: National Academy Press.

Janis, I. L., & Mann, L. (1977). *Decision making: A psychological analysis of conflict, choice, and commitment*. New York: Free Press.

Jones, E. E., Farina, A., Hastorf, A. H., Markus, H., Miller, D. T., & Scott, R. A. (1984). *Social stigma: The psychology of marked relationships*. New York: W. H. Freeman.

King, W. (1986, May 27). Doctors cite stigma of AIDS in declining to report cases. *New York Times*, p. A1.

Lennon, R., & McDevitt, T. (1987, August). *Predictors of AIDS-phobic responses*. Paper presented at the annual meeting of the American Psychological Association, New York.

Limit voted on AIDS funds. (1987, October 15). *New York Times*, p. B12.

Mail service ordered to AIDS center. (1987, April 7). *New York Times*, p. B7.

Monckton, C. (1987, January). AIDS: A British view. *American Spectator*, pp. 29–32.

Morin, S. F. (1984). AIDS in one city: An interview with Mervyn Silverman. *American Psychologist, 39,* 1294–1296.

National Gay and Lesbian Task Force. (1988). *Anti-gay violence, victimization, and defamation in 1987.* Washington, DC: Author.

O'Donnell, L., O'Donnell, C. R., Pleck, J. H., Snarey, J., Snarey, R., & Richard, M. (1987). Psychosocial responses of hospital workers to acquired immunodeficiency syndrome. *Journal of Applied Social Psychology, 17*(3), 269–285.

Panem, S. (1987). *The AIDS bureaucracy.* Cambridge, MA: Harvard University Press.

Robinson, J. (1987, September 12). Senators told of family's plight with AIDS. *Boston Globe,* p. 1.

Schutz, A. (1962). Multiple realities. In M. Natanson (Ed.), *Collected papers, Vol. I. The problem of social reality* (pp. 207–259). The Hague: Nijhoff.

Shilts, R. (1987a). *And the band played on: Politics, people, and the AIDS epidemic.* New York: St. Martin's Press.

Shilts, R. (1987b, July 30). In Houston, "AIDS is spelled G-A-Y." *San Francisco Chronicle*, pp. 1, 4.

Shipp, E. R. (1986, February 17). Physical suffering is not the only pain that AIDS can inflict. *New York Times,* p. A8.

Singer, E., Rogers, T. F., & Corcoran, M. (1987). The polls, a report: AIDS. *Public Opinion Quarterly, 51,* 580–595.

Slovic, P. (1987). Perception of risk. *Science, 236,* 280–285.

The social fallout from an epidemic. (1985, August 12). *Newsweek,* pp. 28–29.

Sontag, S. (1977). *Illness as metaphor.* New York: Farrar, Straus, & Giroux.

Tversky, A., & Kahneman, D. (1974). Judgement under uncertainty: Heuristics and biases. *Science, 185,* 1124–1130.

VerMeulen, M. (1982, May 31). The gay plague. *New York Magazine.*

The Experience of Illness
• • • • • •

Disease not only involves the body. It also affects people's social relationships, self-image, and behavior. The social psychological aspects of illness are related in part to the biophysiological manifestations of disease, but are also independent of them. The very act of defining something as an illness has consequences that are independent of any effects of biophysiology.

> When a veterinarian diagnoses a cow's condition as an illness, he does not merely by diagnosis change the cow's behavior; to the cow, illness [disease] remains an experienced biophysiological state, no more. But when a physician diagnoses a human's condition as an illness, he changes the man's behavior by diagnosis: a social state is added to a biophysiological state by assigning the meaning of illness to disease (Freidson, 1970: 223).

Much of the sociological study of illness has centered on the *sick* role and *illness behavior*. Talcott Parsons (1951) argued that in order to prevent the potentially disruptive consequences of illness on a group or society, there exists a set of shared cultural rules (norms) called the "sick role." The sick role legitimates the deviations caused by illness and channels the sick into the reintegrating physician-patient relationship. According to Parsons, the sick role has four components: (1) the sick person is exempted from normal social responsibilities, at least to the extent it is necessary to get well; (2) the individual is not held responsible for his or her condition and cannot be expected to recover by an act of will; (3) the person must recognize that being ill is undesirable and must want to recover; and (4) the sick person is obligated to seek and cooperate with "expert" advice, generally that of a physician. Sick people are not blamed for their illness but must work toward recovery. There have been numerous critiques and modifications of the concept of the sick role, such as its inapplicability to chronic illness and disability, but it remains a central sociological way of seeing illness experience (Segall, 1976).

Illness behavior is essentially how people act when they develop symptoms of disease. As one sociologist notes, it includes "the way in which given symptoms may be differentially perceived, evaluated, and acted (or not acted) upon by different kinds of persons . . . whether by reason of early experience with illness, differential training in respect to symptoms, or whatever" (Mechanic, 1962). Reaction to symptoms, use of social networks in locating help, and compliance with medical advice are some of the activities characterized as illness behavior.

Illness behavior and the sick role, as well as the related concept of *illness career* (Suchman, 1965), are all more or less based on a perspective that all (proper) roads lead to medical care. They tend to create a "doctor-centered" picture by making the receipt of medical care the centerpiece of sociological attention. Such concepts are essentially "outsider" perspectives on the experience of illness. While these viewpoints may be useful in their own right, none of them has as a central concern the actual subjective experience of illness.

They don't analyze illness from the sufferer's (or patient's) viewpoint. A few sociologists (e.g., Strauss and Glaser, 1975; Schneider and Conrad, 1983; Charmaz, 1991) have attempted to develop more subjective "insider" accounts of what it is like to be sick. These accounts focus more on individuals' perceptions of illness, interactions with others, the effects of illness on identity, and people's strategies for managing illness symptoms than do the abstract notions of illness, careers, or sick roles. Recent reports from studies of epilepsy, multiple sclerosis, diabetes, arthritis, and end-stage renal disease demonstrate an increasing sociological interest in examining the subjective aspects of illness (see Roth and Conrad, 1987; Anderson and Bury, 1988).

The two selections in this section present different faces of the experience of illness. How people manage the uncertainties that accompany illness has been a longstanding sociological concern (Davis, 1960; Conrad, 1987). In the first selection, "Uncertainty and the Lives of Persons with AIDS," Rose Weitz examines how the uncertainties of diagnosis, prognosis, meaning, and social response affect persons with AIDS. She shows how the uncertainties change over time and suggests that persons with AIDS attempt to gain some control over their lives through learning about their illness and planning their own deaths. It is clear from this selection and others (e.g., Comaroff and McGuire, 1981) that managing uncertainty is a key issue in the experience of illness.

The second reading, "The Meanings of Medications: Another Look at Compliance" by Peter Conrad, examines the important issue of how people manage their medication regimens. As part of a study of the experience of epilepsy, Conrad found that a large portion of his respondents did not take their medications as prescribed. From a medical point of view these patients would be depicted as "noncompliant"; i.e., they do not follow doctors' orders. However, from the perspective of people with epilepsy the situation looks quite different. Conrad identifies the meanings of medications in people's everyday lives, and suggests that from this perspective it makes more sense to conceptualize these patients' behavior as self-regulation than as noncompliance. By focusing on the experience of illness we can reframe our understanding of behavior and see what may be deemed a "problem" in a different light.

Issues such as uncertainty and managing medication regimens are crucial aspects of the illness experience and are independent of both the disease itself and the sick role. When we understand and treat illness as a subjective as well as objective experience, we no longer treat patients as diseases but as people who are sick. This is an important dimension of human health care.

REFERENCES

Anderson, Robert, and Michael Bury (eds.). 1988. Living with Chronic Illness: The Experience of Patients and Their Families. London: Unwin Hyman.

Charmaz, Kathy. 1991. Good Days, Bad Days: The Self in Chronic Illness and Time. New Brunswick: Rutgers University Press.

Comaroff, Jean, and Peter McGuire. 1981. "Ambiguity and the search for meaning: Childhood leukemia in the modern clinical context." Social Science and Medicine 15B: 115–23.

Conrad, Peter. 1987. "The experience of illness: recent and new directions." In Julius Roth and Peter Conrad (eds.), The Experience and Management of Chronic Illness (Research in the Sociology of Health Care, Volume 6). Greenwich, CT: JAI Press.

Davis, Fred. 1960. "Uncertainty in medical prognosis: clinical and functional." American Journal of Sociology 66: 41–47.

Freidson, Eliot. 1970. Profession of Medicine. New York: Dodd, Mead.

Mechanic, David. 1962. "The concept of illness behavior." Journal of Chronic Diseases. 15: 189–94.

Parsons, Talcott. 1951. The Social System. New York: Free Press.

Roth, Julius, and Peter Conrad. 1987. The Experience and Management of Chronic Illness (Research in the Sociology of Health Care, Volume 6). Greenwich, CT: JAI Press.

Schneider, Joseph W., and Peter Conrad. 1983. Having Epilepsy: The Experience and Control of Illness. Philadelphia: Temple University Press.

Segall, Alexander. 1976. "The sick role concept: Understanding illness behavior." Journal of Health and Social Behavior. 17 (June): 163–70.

Strauss, Anselm, and Barney Glaser, 1975. Chronic Illness and the Quality of Life. St. Louis: C. V. Mosby.

Suchman, Edward. 1965. "Stages of illness and medical care." Journal of Health and Social Behavior. 6: 114–28.

12

Uncertainty and the Lives of Persons
with AIDS

. . . . . .

Rose Weitz

This article explores how gay and bisexual men who have Acquired Immune Deficiency Syndrome (AIDS) are affected by and manage uncertainty.

Uncertainty exists whenever people lack a cognitive framework for understanding their situations and thus feel that they cannot predict the outcome of their behavior. At least as far back as Malinowski (1948, originally 1926), researchers have recognized that few people handle uncertainty well and that people therefore generally seek ways to reduce or, if that is not possible, to cope with uncertainty. Researchers have identified means of developing with uncertainty as disparate as developing magical or religious rituals (Felson and Gmelch, 1979) and rigorously gathering scientific information about the consequences of various possible actions (Janis and Mann, 1977). Most recently, scholarly interest in uncertainty has produced a vast amount of literature on how persons perceive and respond to the risks of natural and man-made technological disasters (e.g., Douglas and Wildavsky, 1982; National Research Council, 1982; Slovic, Fischhoff, and Lichtenstein, 1977).

Medical sociologists have long recognized that uncertainty is a central problem for all chronically and terminally ill persons (Conrad 1987, p. 7–9; Glaser and Strauss, 1968), and a major source of stress in their lives (Mishel 1984; Mishel *et al.*, 1984; Molleman *et al.*, 1984). The nature of that uncertainty and the coping strategies available to ill persons differ in one significant way from that experienced by persons facing most other life crises. In the latter case, individuals generally face uncertainty about which of the choices open to them will result in the best outcomes. In contrast, the choices available to ill persons may improve their emotional health or slow the progress of their disease, but cannot significantly alter eventual outcomes. For ill persons, therefore, uncertainty centers not so much on what they should do as on what will happen to them despite their actions, when it will happen, and why.

Despite these differences, in the broadest terms both groups cope in similar ways. Although the models of coping developed by researchers in psychology, sociology, anthropology, business, and risk assessment are not easily compared or integrated, most models suggest two basic ways people cope with uncertainty: through vigilance and avoidance.

Vigilance occurs when people attempt to reduce uncertainty by seeking knowledge and acting on that knowledge. For example, people who wonder if they should buy flood insurance can study the evidence so they can make the best decision. Ill persons can also respond to their situations with vigilance; those whose physicians prove unable to diagnose their problems, for example, can research possible diagnoses themselves (Schneider and Conrad, 1983; Stewart and Sullivan, 1982). Once their illnesses are identified, they can reduce uncertainty about why disease has struck them and about what they can expect in the future by searching for similarities between their cases and those of fellow sufferers

(Comaroff and Maguire, 1981; Cowie, 1976; Roth, 1963; Schneider and Conrad, 1983; Wiener, 1975).

Avoidance occurs when people cope with uncertainty by protecting themselves against unpleasant knowledge. For example, some individuals respond to fears of flooding by skipping over any newspaper articles on the topic. Similarly, many ill persons deal with uncertainty about what their initial symptoms signify by attributing those symptoms to less serious ailments or to preexisting illnesses and by avoiding any contact with physicians (Cowie, 1976; Schneider and Conrad, 1983). Even after they seek medical care, they may prefer not to know their diagnoses or prognoses and may listen only to persons who support their optimistic definitions of their situations (McIntosh, 1976; Comaroff and Maguire, 1981).

These two antithetical strategies are linked by a common goal: the construction of normative frameworks that enable individuals to explain their situations to themselves. These frameworks give people the sense that they understand what has happened and will happen to them. By making the world seem predictable, these frameworks help individuals to choose (albeit sometimes from among limited options) how they will live their lives. Thus even when normative frameworks are factually inaccurate, and when the resulting actions seem short-sighted or self-destructive, I would hypothesize that these frameworks reduce the stresses of uncertainty by enabling people to feel at least minimally in control of their lives. I will suggest in this paper that in the final analysis, it is this sense of control that enables people to tolerate uncertainty.

This paper describes how uncertainty affects persons with AIDS (or PWAs, as they call themselves), and how they cope with that uncertainty. Few published research studies have analyzed the experiences of PWAs, and none has looked specifically at the issue of uncertainty. Instead, the social science literature on AIDS largely consists of quantitative studies regarding why people do or do not change their sexual behavior to protect themselves against infection (reviewed in Becker and Joseph, 1988).

Because most medical authorities believe that AIDS eventually kills all its victims, it may seem that uncertainty is not an issue for PWAs. As this paper will show, however, uncertainty affects PWAs in several ways.[1] Even before health problems appear, persons who are at risk of getting AIDS most wonder if they will get the disease. Once symptoms start, PWAs experience uncertainty about how to interpret and respond to those symptoms. After they receive their diagnoses, PWAs must question why this calamity has fallen on them. Because AIDS causes unpredictable flare-ups and remissions, PWAs face uncertainty each morning about how ill they will be that day. As their illness progresses, they also experience anxiety about whether they will be able to live with dignity even though they are ill and about whether AIDS eventually will kill them. Finally, those who conclude that death is inevitable must cope with their doubts about whether they will be allowed to die with dignity.[2] This paper will describe how PWAs seek control over these uncertainties and how their illness impairs their ability to do so.

Methods and Sample

Between July 1986 and March 1987, I interviewed twenty-five Arizona residents who had either AIDS or AIDS-Related Complex (ARC). Four to six months after the initial interviews, I re-interviewed thirteen respondents. (Two respondents declined to participate in the follow-up interviews, two moved without leaving an address, and eight died or suffered brain damage in the interim). Two of the twenty-five respondents were heterosexual women who had used intravenous drugs. The rest were men, all of whom described themselves as gay or bisexual (although none mentioned any recent relationships with women). Three of these men also had used drugs. The data presented in this paper come from the twenty-three initial and eleven follow-up interviews with gay and bisexual men, except where otherwise noted.

At the time the study began, the Arizona Department of Health Services had confirmed 110 reports of AIDS cases. State officials believed approximately forty of these cases were still living, as well as an unknown number of ARC cases. Because AIDS is still rare in Arizona, the situation of PWAs there is very different from their situation in places like New York or California, where most previous research on PWAs has taken place. Research conducted in Arizona, unlike that conducted to date, can help us understand what it is like to have AIDS in an area which lacks a politically powerful gay community and in which AIDS is just beginning to have an impact. This study can therefore help us predict what the lives of PWAs will be like in the future, as the disease spreads from the current center of infection to more conservative and typical areas of the country.

Most respondents learned of this study through letters mailed to them by the Arizona AIDS Project (N = 15) or Tucson AIDS Project (N = 4), two non-profit groups that offer emotional and financial support to PWAs. To increase sample size and diversity, I posted signs in gay bars, ran announcements in gay newspapers and the mainstream press, and announced the study in AIDS political-action groups. I also asked several physicians and AIDS support group counselors to inform their clients of the study. Finally, I asked my respondents to give my name to any other PWAs they knew. No names were given to me by any source. Instead, PWAs were invited to contact me if they wanted to participate.

The sample is comparable to the state population in terms of religion and is comparable to the population of reported Arizona AIDS cases in terms of sex, geographical location (overwhelmingly urban), and mode of transmission (Arizona Dept. of Health Services, February 2, 1987). Because participating in the interviews required both mental competence and some physical stamina, the sample undoubtedly underrepresents the more seriously ill PWAs. It also underrepresents persons with Kaposi's Sarcoma (8 percent of the sample but 21 percent of reported cases), perhaps because these individuals do not want a stranger to see their disfigurement. In addition, the sample underrepresents nonwhites (100 percent of the sample but 87 percent of reported cases), who typically are less integrated into the AIDS support networks and therefore were less likely to have heard of the study. Finally, the sample overrepresents persons in their thirties (60 percent of the sample but 42 percent of reported cases) and underrepresents older persons.

For this analysis, I have combined persons with AIDS and persons with ARC because I could not reasonably separate the two according to either medical diagnoses or self-diagnosis. Although the prognosis for persons with AIDS is grimmer than that for persons with ARC, some persons with AIDS survive longer and with less disability than some persons with ARC. Moreover, some individuals are told by their physicians that they have ARC when they clearly have AIDS and some are told they have AIDS when they apparently have ARC. Some believe that the two diseases are essentially identical and some believe that they are very different. Finally, some persons vacillate in their statements about which disease they have and the prognosis for that disease.

The data for this paper were obtained through semi-structured interviews. I entered each interview with a preset list of questions, but I also probed into any areas that emerged as potentially significant during the course of the interview. Initial interviews ranged from two to five hours in length and averaged about three hours, while follow-up interviews were considerably shorter. All interviews were audiotaped and transcribed and took place at respondents' homes unless they preferred another location (usually my home). I attempted to ask all questions and respond to all answers in an unbiased and nonjudgmental manner, whether my respondent was describing sadomasochistic homosexual behaviors or fundamentalist Christian theology. I believe I was successful in that no respondents acted in a hostile way, broke off the interviews (except from physical exhaustion), or in any other way suggested that they felt uncomfortable discussing these issues with me.

Following the suggestions of Glaser and Strauss (1967), I analyzed the data using categories that emerged from the respondents' descriptions of their situations. After each interview, I revised the interview schedule to focus it more closely on these emerging themes. I used subsequent interviews to hone my understanding of these themes. When collapsed and reorganized, these themes formed the structure of this paper. This form of data analysis is particularly appropriate for helping to understand how PWAs perceive and manage their situations.

Findings
·················

"Will I Get AIDS?"

Fear of contracting AIDS permeates the lives of many gay and bisexual men. Several respondents, in fact, had simply assumed that they were infected, long before they were diagnosed. The rest, though, had lived through long months of anxiety about whether they would become ill, for although they could change their behavior to protect themselves against future infection, they could not stop the disease's development if they had already been infected.

Unable to control their health prospects, these men coped with uncertainty about whether they would get AIDS by finding ways to at least *feel* in control of their lives. They did this by developing theories which explained why, despite their behaviors, they were not really at risk. These theories typically suggested that AIDS attacks only physically weak, promiscuous persons, who choose their parameters unwisely. In addition, these theories emphasized that AIDS only occurs elsewhere. For example, one Phoenix resident explained that he and his friends had not used safe sex because they had convinced themselves that "there's only nine people in Arizona who had it and four of them are dead and two of them live in Tucson. So what are your chances? Even though we knew about it and we knew how awful it was, it was like, no, that's something that happens someplace else, not in Phoenix."

As more cases of AIDS appeared, however, these theories provided less comfort (especially for the nine respondents who had seen friends or lovers die). As a result, most found themselves alternately denying and brooding on the risks they had taken—emotionally unable to accept the fact that they might die from a dread disease yet intellectually unable to reject the possibility. One man, for example, shifted in a matter of moments from describing how his fear of contracting AIDS had kept him awake nights to describing how he "thought it would never happen to me."

Beginning in about June 1985, Arizonans could eliminate some uncertainty by having their blood tested to see if they had been exposed to the AIDS virus. The test could significantly reduce uncertainty for those who tested negative. For those who tested positive, however, the test merely traded one form of uncertainty for another, because it could not tell whether they would develop AIDS. Moreover, a positive test result could significantly increase stigma and anxiety (Beeson, Zones and Nye, 1986; Moulton, 1985). As a result, all but two of the men decided that they would feel more in control of their destinies by refusing to obtain such ambiguous knowledge. As one said, "I figured if I was tested and tested positive, I'd worry myself into coming down with it, . . . so I decided against it. . . . If I came down with it, I came down with it, and I'd have to worry about it then."

"What Do My Symptoms Mean?"

People who have been infected with AIDS may remain asymptomatic and therefore ignorant that they are infected for several years. Once symptoms start to appear, however, they must decide what those symptoms mean and how or if they should react.

Because symptoms generally build gradually, PWAs at first can accommodate the difficulties they cause. As a result, they, like persons who develop other chronic illnesses (Bury, 1982, p. 170; Cowie, 1976, p. 88; Schneider and Conrad, 1983; Stewart and Sullivan, 1982), initially may explain their symptoms using preexisting cognitive frameworks that minimize the symptoms' importance. Several men, for example, blamed their night sweats and exhaustion on the Arizona heat. Others confused the symptoms of AIDS with the side effects of drug use, for both can cause weight loss, sweating, and diarrhea. Although these theories eventually proved wrong, in the interim they allowed the men to feel that they understood their situations and thus reduced stress.

While in some cases, the men minimized their symptoms out of ignorance, in other cases the men appeared to have consciously or unconsciously chosen to downplay their symptoms because they preferred uncertainty to the certainty of an AIDS diagnosis. One individual, for example, explained that he did not go to a physician despite a variety of symptoms because "I didn't want to find out I had AIDS. Even though I kind of figured I did, I didn't want to know. I wanted to live a normal life for as long as I could." By so doing, he was able to assert control over his emotional wellbeing despite his lack of control over his physical wellbeing.

Those who for whatever reason minimize their symptoms may defer seeing a physician for some time. As the disease progresses, however, they eventually find that they can neither control their bodies nor maintain their everyday living patterns. Once this point is reached, PWAs can no longer maintain their cognitive frameworks and are motivated to seek diagnosis and treatment.

As they soon discover, however, seeing a physician will not necessarily end their uncertainty. Many physicians simply lack the knowledge needed to diagnose AIDS (Lewis, Freeman, and Corey, 1987). Others may not consider diagnoses of AIDS unless they know their clients are at risk, even if their clients' symptoms fit the classic patterns for AIDS. Yet clients may not disclose that they are at risk for fear of the social consequences.

Even if physicians have the intellectual knowledge to diagnose AIDS, they may lack the emotional ability to do so. Several respondents complained that physicians neither tested them for, nor diagnosed them with, AIDS, even though the clients had multiple, classic symptoms, stated that they were gay, and requested AIDS testing. For example, one man described how his physician refused his several requests for AIDS testing, even though the physician knew he was gay and knew something was wrong with his immune system:

> I was concerned. The symptoms were there, and I was not getting any better, not feeling any better, still getting weaker and weaker, losing more weight, "Look, I've been reading more articles about AIDS." And he said, "Oh, people are just panic stricken. You don't have AIDS. I'm not doing a test on you."

Stories such as this one suggest that even in obvious cases some physicians consciously or unconsciously avoid diagnosing AIDS.

For all these reasons, then, PWAs may not receive accurate diagnoses until several months after they seek care. Initially, some of my respondents accepted or even welcomed the alternative diagnoses that their physicians proposed. When symptoms continued, however, these men found themselves in what Stewart and Sullivan (1982, p. 1402) have described (with regard to multiple sclerosis) as "an ambiguous and uncertain limbo," in which they suffered anxieties about the meaning of their symptoms and could not function normally, but lacked social support for adopting the sick role (cf. Bury, 1982, p. 172; Schneider and Conrad, 1983; Stewart and Sullivan, 1982; Waddell, 1982). Consequently, they could not maintain these definitions indefinitely. To cope with this situation, some went from doctor to doctor to obtain a diagnosis. Others researched their symptoms, diagnosed themselves, and then pressed their physicians to test them for AIDS. Only then did their uncertainty about the nature of their illnesses end.

"Why Have I Become Ill?"

Diagnosis with AIDS ends individuals' uncertainty about what is wrong with them. It raises new questions, however, about why this terrible thing has happened to them. Only by answering these questions can PWAs make their illness comprehensible.

Despite the price exacted by AIDS, two of my subjects developed positive explanations for their illnesses. One, a fundamentalist Christian, felt that having AIDS had allowed him to share his religious faith with others. He had accepted several invitations to speak about having AIDS at schools and churches, and had used these opportunities to share his belief "that you can be a homosexual and still go to heaven." Another, whose disastrous choice of lovers had left him suicidal on several occasions, considered his diagnosis literally an "answer to a prayer" because it provided the extra incentive he needed to avoid any further romantic entanglements.

The rest, however, had no such comforting explanations. Their search for meaning was a painful one, set as it was in the context of popular belief that AIDS is punishment for sin.

At least on the surface, the majority rejected the idea that AIDS was divine punishment. Instead, they argued that AIDS results from the same biological forces that cause other illnesses. Consequently, they dismissed the idea that they or anyone else deserved AIDS.

Nobody deserves it. I have friends that say, "Well, hey, if we weren't gay, we wouldn't get this disease." That's bullshit. I mean, I don't want to hear that from anybody. Because no germ has mercy on anybody, no matter who they are—gay, straight, babies, adults.

Yet other statements by some of these same men suggested that at a less conscious level they did feel they were to blame for their illnesses (Moulton, 1985). For example, one man denied that he deserved AIDS yet later suggested that AIDS might have been God's way of punishing him for being gay or "for not being a good person. . . . I should have helped people more, or not have yelled at somebody, or been better to my dad even though we have never gotten along. . . . Maybe if I had tried to get along better with him, maybe this wouldn't be happening."

Others maintained that they did not deserve AIDS, but used language which suggested considerable ambivalence. Several, for example, attributed their illness not to their "nonmonogamy" or "multiple sexual partners" but rather to their "promiscuity." One said he got AIDS "probably because I was a royal whore for about four years." Their use of such morally loaded terms suggests that they were not just describing their behavior objectively but rather were condemning it on moral grounds. Thus it seems that they believed emotionally, if not intellectually, that they deserved punishment, although perhaps less severe punishment than AIDS.

Still other respondents had no doubts that they deserved AIDS. Some felt that they deserved AIDS simply because of their lack of forethought in engaging in high-risk behaviors. For example, one stated, "I knew better. I mean, it's like, you deserve it. You knew what was going on and yet you slipped and this is the consequence." Others explicitly stated that they deserved AIDS as punishment for their immoral activities. In these cases, diagnosis with AIDS seemed to unleash pre-existing guilt that these men had felt about being gay or bisexual (or, in one case, about using drugs). Such guilt seemed particularly prevalent among the nine respondents from fundamentalist Christian or Mormon families, more than half of whom expressed regret about being gay and two-thirds of whom

at least partially believed that they deserved AIDS. For example, one fundamentalist Christian who had engaged in homosexual behavior for several years said, "I reaped what I sowed: I sowed sin, I reaped death. I believe, biblically, I received AIDS as a result of my sexual sin practices."

Regardless of how an individual explained why he got AIDS, simply having an explanation made it easier to tolerate having the illness. For this reason, the persons who showed the most distress were those who believed that others deserved to get AIDS but that they themselves did not. Consequently, they raged at the unfairness of their situations.

> I get real angry. I don't know how to explain why I got it and somebody else didn't because I don't consider myself that I was that promiscuous. When I go out I see other guys out in the bars and they're hopping around, two and three guys a night basically, and it's like why aren't they getting it? Why is it me?

Similarly, some persons who believed they were born gay considered it unfair that their innate orientation put them at risk for AIDS. They had to cope not only with the physical trauma of illness but also with the emotional trauma of losing their faith that this is a just world.

"Will I Be Able to Function Tomorrow?"

Like many chronic illnesses, AIDS causes unpredictable flare-ups and remissions. As a result, PWAs can never know from one day to the next how sick they will be.

> Probably the hardest thing is not knowing when you're well what's going to happen tomorrow because when you're well all you're thinking about is, "What am I going to get? What's the next infection I'm going to have to put up with?" Of course, when you're sick it's like, "Well, I hope they can make me well. I wonder if they can or not."

Because PWAs can become incapacitated without warning, they expose themselves to possible disappointment whenever they make long- or even short-range plans. One man, for example, said that he feared going "for a little trip tomorrow even though I am capable of doing that, but I may have diarrhea and who wants to be driving down the highway with shit in your pants?" He and others like him accepted that they had lost control over their physical health. As one man said, "AIDS has become my life. I live for AIDS. I don't live for me anymore, I live for AIDS. I'm at its beck and call and I'll do what it tells me when it tells me." Such individuals choose never to make plans as a way to protect themselves against disappointment (Charmaz, 1983). By thus acknowledging their lack of control over their physical health they could assert control over their emotional health.

Although avoiding plans protects PWAs against disappointment, it increases their frustration. As one man explained, "I may have a day where I feel great, where I have plenty of energy and everything is fine, and then you have nothing going, you're just sitting in the house rotting. So that is really frustrating." Consequently, PWAs must walk a tightrope—making the plans needed to lead a meaningful life without setting themselves up for disappointment when those plans collapse. For this reason, several respondents compared themselves to recovering alcoholics, who must learn to live "one day at a time."

"Will I Be Able to Live with Dignity?"

AIDS takes its toll on the human body in myriad ways. Some of these ways leave individuals with little dignity during either their living or their dying. Consequently, PWAs face tremendous uncertainty about the nature of their remaining days.

Fear of death is minimal compared with fear of what their lives may become. As a man who had already suffered one agonizingly debilitating episode said, "Death doesn't bother me. Being ill as I was terrifies me." In particular, PWAs fear that they will be among the 70 percent who suffer neurological impairment or the 10 percent who become disfigured by the lesions of Kaposi's Sarcoma. In addition, they especially fear esoteric illnesses whose effects they cannot predict.

I'm not [as] afraid of getting infections from people as I am from inanimate objects, like fruits and moldy tile. . . . I know what a cold is like. . . . [It's]

something that I have experienced. I've never experienced a mold infection.

PWAs have little control over whether they will develop such infections. To cope with the uncertainty that this lack of control creates, some PWAs endeavor to develop a realistic picture of what they can expect in the future. To learn about the consequences and treatments of various infections (as well as to obtain emotional support), PWAs may attend support groups offered by community organizations. Others research their illnesses on their own, in some cases developing extensive libraries on AIDS. The knowledge that they gain allows them to feel that they can respond appropriately should some problem arise, and thus can exert some control over their situations.

Conversely, other PWAs cope with anxiety about what their lives will be like by endeavoring to maintain unrealistic images of their futures. For example, one man had not joined an AIDS support group because he did not "want to see what other people look like." This sentiment was especially common among the healthier respondents, who feared that gaining knowledge would lead to depression and that choosing to maintain ignorance was therefore the most sensible approach.

"Will I Be Able to Beat AIDS?"

All PWAs must grapple with questions about the likelihood of an early death. These questions seem less answerable to those who initially receive diagnoses of ARC. Faced with conflicting, probable estimates of when and whether they will get AIDS, persons with ARC experience enormous stress. One person, whose diagnosis changed from ARC to AIDS between the initial and follow-up interviews, said:

The worst feeling was when I was ARC, waiting for a bomb to explode. Not knowing when or if ever it would do it. There was always that tentative in my life that it may or may not—beware! Now that the diagnosis has come, it's like "Okay. I can relax now. The worst is over."

Even persons diagnosed with AIDS, however, may continue to wonder whether God or medicine will cure them. To cope with this uncertainty and to gain a sense of control over their lives, the group I studied searched for and adopted any courses of action that might preserve or improve their health. A few relied primarily on prayer. The rest ate more balanced meals; took vitamins, limited use of caffeine, tobacco, and illegal drugs, and exercised if possible. They tried to limit their exposure to germs by, for example, avoiding animals and swimming pools and scanning public buses for passengers who looked unhealthy before choosing a seat. And they sought any potential treatments, including experimental, illegal, or toxic ones, which might increase their chances for survival.

Faced with the prospects of an early death, some PWAs are willing to go to extraordinary lengths to obtain any promising treatments. The drug most in demand by my respondents was azidothymidine (AZT). AZT is now available by prescription (although at a cost of about $12,000 per year). During most of the study period, however, PWAs could get AZT legally only if they were among the few chosen to participate in pharmaceutical experiments. The rest had to rely on various subterfuges to obtain it. Some convinced their physicians to diagnose them inaccurately so they would meet the experimenters' criteria. Some received AZT from physicians who continued collecting pills from the researchers for clients who had died. Others obtained unused pills from friends who were research subjects. These friends gave away pills that they had been instructed by the experimenters to destroy when they either had forgotten to take their pills on schedule or had skipped them because of problems with side effects. Friends could also obtain an extra set of pills to give away by registering as research subjects under two names with two physicians.

Finally, PWAs also tried to increase their chances for survival and their sense of control over their lives by maintaining a positive attitude. As one man explained, "the main killer with having AIDS is that mental psyche, because your mind controls your body. . . . There are so many people that can't get past that 'I'm sick and going to die.' And therefore, they don't even start—they die." He and others like him simply refused to believe that they would die or to make plans

for their deaths. One man, for example, said that he had not written a will because of "that whole will to live bit. Once I get that done, that means one less thing I have to do. As long as I don't have it done, it seems like, well, I can't die yet." He went on to explain his belief in the importance of

being active about this disease, whether it involves drinking a certain kind of tea or standing on your head twice a day or doing something, something that gives the patient a feeling of control over his own life that if you do these things, this might help you a little bit. . . . It's a sense of being in control, of being actively involved in your own health, which in itself produces health.

"Will I Be Able to Die with Dignity?"

Despite the lengths to which PWAs will go to survive, their biggest fear is not death but being kept alive against their will and beyond the point of meaningful life. As one said, "I'm not afraid to die. I can truthfully say I'm not. I'm a Christian, I'm saved, and I'm going to heaven. It's getting from here to there that worries me. That's the rough spot."

To alleviate uncertainty and maintain a sense of control over the nature of their dying, several respondents had made plans to commit suicide should that seem warranted. As one explained, "If I'm going to die, I would rather it be my business. I guess it's a lack of control. I want to reassert as much control as I can." Others had decided to let the disease take its natural course. They had signed living wills to prohibit physicians from keeping them alive through extraordinary means and had decided to stop taking their medications once life no longer seemed worthwhile. One man, who had thrown away all his medications without informing his physician, explained, "I don't want to die, but I don't have a choice. I have to—period. I mean, no question. So if I have to die, why not tackle the chore and get it over with?"

Learning to Live with AIDS

By the time of the follow-up interviews (four to six months after the initial interviews), AIDS had become far more comprehensible to my respondents. The men now had cognitive frameworks which enabled them to understand the changes in their bodies.

> I remember, a little over a year ago when I was first told what I had, it was very frightening. . . . You didn't know what the future held. A lot of that has been, at least, resolved. I don't worry about it so much, as I did in that respect. It's still not something I want, but I guess you learn to live with it a little better. Then, when you get a case of pneumonia you know what it is, and you don't really think anything of it, other than the fact, that well, "we know what's caused this."

Not only had uncertainty been reduced but it also had become an accepted part of life. Stress had decreased because the men had learned both to assert control over some aspects of their lives and to accept that they could not control other aspects. For example, one man, comparing his feelings at the initial and follow-up interviews, said, "All I think I've done is adjust to it. I'm not so afraid. I guess I have realized that there's nothing that I can do about it."

While most still hoped for a cure, their frenetic search for one had abated.

> At first, I got on the bandwagon of vitamins and getting nutrition and proper meals and eating my spinach and everything. One day I finally said, "What for? It's not going to save me." I don't know of anybody that has not died from AIDS just because they ate spinach.

Those who accepted that death was inevitable now focused on living for the present—doing whatever they could to give pleasure to themselves and their loved ones. By so doing, they could feel that they at least partially controlled their present circumstances, even if they could not control their futures.

Discussion

Previous studies have shown that uncertainty is a central concern for all seriously ill persons. This study demonstrates that uncertainty has an even greater impact on PWAs than on those who suffer from most other illnesses. First, PWAs are more likely than most to know prior to diagnosis that they are at risk. As a result, they experience difficulties that other ill persons do not, for uncertainty and anxiety often sap their emotional energy and physical resources months or even years before they become ill. Second, PWAs are more likely to feel guilt about the behaviors that caused their illness and, consequently, to believe that they deserve their illness. Moreover, PWAs are far more likely to find that their friends, families, and the general public also believe that PWAs caused and deserve their own illness. As a result, these others often reinforce the guilt that PWAs feel. Third, PWAs are more likely to face difficulties in obtaining an accurate diagnosis. Like other illnesses, AIDS can be difficult to diagnose because it is rare and causes multiple symptoms. These problems are exacerbated, however, because physicians often deliberately (although at times unconsciously) avoid questions or actions that would lead to diagnosis. Fourth, PWAs face greater uncertainty than other ill persons in predicting how their illness will affect their lives because AIDS causes more extensive and less predictable physical and mental damage than most other illnesses. Finally, because AIDS is such a new disease, PWAs are more likely to lack answers to their questions about treatment and prognosis. Moreover, because what physicians know about AIDS is rapidly developing and constantly changing, PWAs often are reluctant to trust the answers they do receive.

Uncertainty can be even more troublesome for PWAs who (unlike those described in this paper) are not gay men. Other PWAs face additional problems in obtaining diagnoses because they may not know they are at risk. Some women, for example do not know that their male partners are bisexual. And some bisexual men (as well as many heterosexuals, including those who use drugs) may believe that only gays are at risk. Moreover, their physicians may be less alert for and knowledgeable about AIDS than the physicians of gay men, who in many instances specialize in gay health care.

Following diagnosis, PWAs who are not gay and who cannot argue that god-given biological needs forced them to put themselves at risk for AIDS may experience more guilt and loss of self-esteem. (In fact, all three gay drug users in the sample exhibited more guilt about their drug use than about their sexuality.) Nongay PWAs (especially women) also experience more difficulty in predicting their futures because so many studies have only looked at how AIDS affects the health of gay men. Moreover, they are far less likely to have networks of fellow suffers to turn to for advice and information. Some live on the margins of society and lack either access to or knowledge of community resources. Others are either unwilling to accept help from groups dominated by gay men because of their own homophobia or unable to get help because their problems are too different from those of gay men. Finally, other PWAs may suffer greater uncertainty about whether they might transmit AIDS to others. While many gay men function in social circles where everyone is presumed to be at risk, other PWAs may feel overwhelmed by the belief that they are the sole potential source of infection for their loved ones.

Despite all the difficulties PWAs face because of uncertainty, however, they are not completely helpless against it. Rather, as this paper has described, PWAs find ways to reduce or, if necessary, to live with uncertainty.

These data on how PWAs cope with uncertainty have significant implications for the study of uncertainty in general, as they highlight the role that control plays in making uncertainty tolerable. Previous research on uncertainty had hinted at how loss of control might make uncertainty stressful, while studies on helplessness had demonstrated that loss of control causes stress and depression (Lazarus, 1966; Peterson and Seligman, 1984). This study further specifies the links between uncertainty, loss of control, and stress. As this paper has shown, individuals can cope with uncertainty by developing normative frameworks that make their situations comprehensible. These frameworks, combined with other tactics (such as, in the case of PWAs, deciding not to make plans) help individuals to gain control or, at least the sense of control, over their lives. Thus, in some situations they enable people to reduce uncertainty while in other situations, where uncertainty is either unavoidable or preferable to certainty, they enable them to reduce the stresses of living with uncertainty.

Policy Implications

Given that achieving a sense of control is the key to coping with the uncertainty of having AIDS, health care workers who treat PWAs must become aware both of how uncertainty affects their clients and of how they can help their clients to feel in control. Paradoxically, in some cases, this will mean learning to recognize when patients would prefer to maintain uncertainty rather than learning the truth about their situation. In most cases, however, this will mean involving patients in their own care—making sure that they understand what is happening to them and feel that decisions (including ones about when to terminate care)—are left to them. Physicians must learn that PWAs may feel more in control of their destinies if they are able to take some action, including actions that may appear useless or even harmful to physicians. Thus, physicians must learn to provide information about—if not help in obtaining—all possible options. Moreover, they must learn that their patients may adopt alternative therapies against their advice. This being the case, physicians need to understand that both trust and medical effectiveness will suffer unless they learn how to encourage their patients to feel that they can safely and honestly discuss any alternatives they are using.

Finally, physicians must recognize that PWAs have a strong need to find a logical explanation for their illness. Physicians must learn how their own language of "risk behaviors" reinforces patients' feelings of responsibility and guilt, and thus can increase PWAs' emotional difficulties. Physicians must learn to ascertain whether PWAs are blaming themselves and to intervene—or at least to refer for counseling—in such instances. In sum, physicians must learn to treat the whole person with AIDS and not just the diseased body.

NOTES

This research was made possible by a grant from the Arizona Disease Control Research Commission and by a small grant from Arizona State University College of Liberal Arts and Sciences. The comments of Peter Conrad, Rochelle Kern, Karolynn Siegel, and the anonymous reviews were much appreciated, as was the research assistance of Kathleen Abbott, Melissa Bolyard, and Shirley Philip.

1. Although uncertainty about contagion is a major cause of social rejection, this paper does not address how uncertainty affects the social relationships of PWAs. I have chosen to address this subject in a separate paper both because of its complexity and because stigma rather than uncertainty seems the more crucial factor affecting PWAs' social lives.

2. It should be noted that these various aspects of uncertainty need not be sequential. For example, individuals may question whether they will be well enough to work tomorrow even before obtaining names for their illnesses.

REFERENCES

Arizona Department of Health Services. Feb. 2, 1987. *Definitive and Presumptive AIDS Cases in Arizona and AIDS-Related Complex (ARC): Surveillance Report for Arizona.*

Becker, Marshall H., and Jill G. Joseph. 1988. "AIDS and behavioral change to reduce risk: A review." *American Journal of Public Health* 78:394–410.

Beeson, Diane, Jane S. Zones, and John Nye. 1986. "The Social Consequences of AIDS Antibody Testing: Coping with Stigma." Paper presented at the 1986 Annual Meeting of the Society for the Study of Social Problems, New York.

Bury, Michael. 1982. "Chronic illness as biographical disruption." *Sociology of Health and Illness* 4:167–82.

Charmaz, Kathy. 1983. "Loss of Self: A fundamental form of suffering in the chronically ill." *Sociology of Health and Illness* 5:168–195.

Comaroff, Jean, and Peter Maguire. 1981. "Ambiguity and the search for meaning: Childhood leukaemia in the modern clinical context." *Social Science and Medicine* 15B:115–23.

Conrad, Peter. 1987. "The experience of illness: Recent and new directions." *Research in the Sociology of Health Care* 6:1–31.

Cowie, Bill. 1976. "The cardiac patient's perception of his heart attack." *Social Science and Medicine* 10:87–96.

Douglas, Mary, and Aaron Wildavsky. 1982. *Risk and Culture.* Berkeley: University of California Press.

Felson, Richard B., and George Gmelch. 1979. "Uncertainty and the use of magic." *Current Anthropology* 20:587–9.

Glaser, Barney G., and Anselm L. Strauss. 1967. *The Discovery of Grounded theory: Strategies for Qualitative Research.* New York: Aldine.

Glaser, Barney G., and Anselm L. Strauss. 1968. *Time for Dying.* Chicago: Aldine.

Janis, Irving L., and Leon Mann. 1977. *Decision Making: A Psychological Analysis of Conflict, Choice, and Commitment.* New York: Free Press.

Lazarus, Richard S. 1966. *Psychological Stress and the Coping Process.* New York: McGraw-Hill.

Lewis, Charles E., Howard E. Freeman, and Christopher R. Corey. 1987. "AIDS-related competence of California's primary care physicians." *American Journal of Public Health* 77:795–800.

Malinowski, Bronislaw. 1984. *Magic, Science, and Religion and Other Essays.* Boston: Beacon.

McIntosh, Jim. 1976. "Patients' awareness and desire for information about diagnosed but undisclosed malignant disease." *Lancet* 2:300–03.

Mishel, Merle H. 1984. "Perceived uncertainty and stress in illness." *Research in Nursing and Health* 7:163–71.

Mishel, Merle H., Thelma Hostetter, Barbara King, and Vivian Graham. 1984. "Predictors of psychosocial adjustment in patients newly diagnosed with gynecological cancer." *Cancer Nursing* 7:291–9.

Molleman, Eric, Pieter J. Krabbendam, Albertus A. Annyas, Heimen S. Koops, Dirk T. Sleijfer, and Albert Vermey. 1984. "The significance of the doctor-patient relationship in coping with cancer." *Social Science and Medicine* 18:475–80.

Moulton, J. M. 1985. *Adjustment to a Diagnosis of AIDS or ARC in Gay Men.* Ph.D. dissertation, California School of Professional Psychology, Berkeley.

National Research Council, Committee on Risk and Decision Making. 1982. *Risk and Decision Making.* Washington, D.C.: National Academy Press.

Peterson, Christopher, and Martin E.P. Seligman. 1984. "Causal explanations as a risk factor for depression: Theory and evidence." *Psychological Review* 91:347–74.

Roth, Julius A. 1963. *Timetables.* Indianapolis: Bobbs-Merrill.

Schneider, Joseph W., and Peter Conrad. 1983. *Having Epilepsy: The Experience and Control of Illness.* Philadelphia: Temple University Press.

Slovic, P., B. Fischhoff and S. Lichtenstein. 1977. "Behavioral decision theory." *Annual Review of Psychology* 28:1–39.

Stewart, David C., and Thomas J. Sullivan. 1982. "Illness behavior and the sick role in chronic disease: The case of multiple sclerosis." *Social Science and Medicine* 16:1397–1404.

Wiener, Carolyn L. 1975. "The burden of rheumatoid arthritis." Pp. 1–88 in *Chronic Illness and the Quality of Life,* edited by Anselm L. Strauss. St. Louis: C.V. Mosby Co.

13

The Meaning of Medications:
Another Look at Compliance

■ ■ ■ ■ ■ ■

Peter Conrad

Compliance with medical regimens, especially drug regimens, has become a topic of central interest for both medical and social scientific research. By compliance we mean "the extent to which a person's behavior (in terms of taking medications, following diets, or executing lifestyle changes) coincides with medical or health advice" [1]. It is noncompliance that has engendered the most concern and attention. Most theories locate the sources of noncompliance in the doctor–patient interaction, patient knowledge or beliefs about treatment and, to a lesser extent, the nature of the regimen or illness.

This paper offers an alternative perspective on noncompliance with drug regimens, one situated in the patient's experience of illness. Most studies of noncompliance assume the centrality of patient–practitioner interaction for compliance. Using data from a study of experience of epilepsy, I argue that from a patient-centered perspective the meanings of medication in people's everyday lives are more salient than doctor–patient interaction for understanding why people alter their prescribed medical regimens. The issue is more one of self-regulation than compliance. After reviewing briefly various perspectives on compliance and presenting a synopsis of our method and sample, I develop the concept of medication practice to aid in understanding patients' experiences with medication regimens. This perspective enables us to analyze "noncompliance" among our sample of people with epilepsy in a different light than the usual medically-centered approach allows.

Perspectives on Compliance

Most studies show that at least one-third of patients are noncompliant with drug regimens; i.e., they do not take medications as prescribed or in their correct doses or sequences [2–4]. A recent review of methodologically rigorous studies suggests that compliance rates with medications over a large period tend to converge at approximately 50% [5].

Literally hundreds of studies have been conducted on compliance. Extensive summaries and compilations of this burgeoning literature are available [1, 6, 7]. In this section I will note some of the more general findings and briefly summarize the major explanatory perspectives. Studies have found, for example, that noncompliance tends to be higher under certain conditions: when medical regimens are more complex [8]; with asymptomatic or psychiatric disorders [9]; when treatment periods last for longer periods of time [5]; and when there are several troublesome drug side effects [4]. Interestingly, there seems to be little consistent relationship between noncompliance and such factors as social class, age, sex, education and marital status [8].

Two dominant social scientific perspectives have emerged that attempt to explain variations in compliance and noncompliance. One locates the source of the problem in doctor–patient interaction or communication while the other postulates that patients' health beliefs are central to understanding noncompliant behavior. These perspectives each are multicausal and in some ways are compatible.

There have been a series of diverse studies suggesting that noncompliance is a result of some problem in doctor–patient interaction (see [10]). Researchers have found higher compliance rates are associated with physicians giving explicit and appropriate instructions, more and clearer information, and more and better feedback [2, 10]. Other researchers note that noncompliance is higher when patients' expectations are not met or their physicians are not behaving in a friendly manner [12, 13]. Hulka *et al.* [3], Davis [2] and others suggest that the physician and his or her style of communicating may affect patient compliance. In short, these studies find the source of noncompliance in doctor–patient communication and suggest that compliance rates can be improved by making some changes in clinician–patient interaction.

The importance of patient beliefs for compliant behavior is highlighted by the "health-belief model." The health-belief model is a social psychological perspective first developed to explain preventative health behavior. It has been adapted by Becker [14–16] to explain compliance. This perspective is a "value-expecting model in which behavior is controlled by rational decisions taken in the light of a set of subjective probabilities" [17]. The health-belief model suggests that patients are more likely to comply with doctors orders when they feel susceptibility to illness, believe the illness to have potential serious consequences for health or daily functioning, and do not anticipate major obstacles, such as side effects or cost. Becker [15] found general support for a relationship between compliance and patients' beliefs about susceptibility, severity, benefits and costs.

Both perspectives have accumulated some supporting evidence, but make certain problematic assumptions about the nature and source of compliant behavior. The whole notion of "compliance" suggests a medically-centered orientation; how and why people follow or deviate from doctors orders. It is a concept developed from the doctor's perspective and conceived to solve the provider defined problem of "noncompliance." The assumption is the doctor gives the orders; patients are expected to comply. It is based on a consensual model of doctor–patient relations, aligning with

Parsons' [18] perspective, where noncompliance is deemed a form of deviance in need of explanation. Compliance/noncompliance studies generally assume a moral stance that not following medical regimens is deviant. While this perspective is reasonable from the physicians' viewpoint, when social scientists adopt this perspective they implicitly reinforce the medically-centered perspective.

Some assumptions of each perspective are also problematic. The doctor–patient interaction perspective points to flaws in doctor–patient communication as the source of noncompliance. It is assumed that the doctor is very significant for compliance and the research proceeds from there. Although the health belief model takes the patient's perspective into account, it assumes that patients act from a rational calculus based on health-related beliefs. This perspective assumes that health-related beliefs are the most significant aspects of subjective experience and that compliance is a rational decision based on these beliefs. In an attempt to create a succinct and straightforward model, it ignores other aspects of experience that may affect how illness and treatment are managed.

There is an alternative, less-developed perspective that is rarely mentioned in studies of compliance. This patient-centered perspective sees patients as active agents in their treatment rather than as "passive and obedient recipients of medical instructions" [19]. Stimson [19] argues that to understand noncompliance it is important to account for several factors that are often ignored in compliance studies. Patients have their own ideas about taking medication—which only in part come from doctors—that affect their use of medications. People evaluate both doctors' actions and the prescribed drugs in comparison to what they themselves know about illness and medication. In a study of arthritis patients Arluke [20] found that patients evaluate also the therapeutic efficacy of drugs against the achievement of specific outcomes. Medicines are judged ineffective when a salient outcome is not achieved, usually in terms of the patient's expected time frames. The patient's decision to stop taking medications is a rational-empirical method of testing their views of drug efficacy. Another study found some patients augmented or diminished their treatment regimens as an attempt to assert control on the doctor–patient relationship [21]. Hayes-Bautista [21] notes, "The need to modify treatment arises when it appears the original treatment is somehow not totally appropriate" and contends noncompliance may be a form of patient bargaining with doctors. Others [22] have noted that noncompliance may be the result of particular medical regimens that are not compatible with contexts of people's lives.

These studies suggest that the issue of noncompliance appears very different from a patient-centered perspective than a medically-centered one. Most are critical of traditional compliance studies, although still connecting compliance with doctor–patient interactions [19,21] or with direct evaluation of the drug itself [19, 20]. Most sufferers of illness, especially chronic illness, spend a small fraction of their lives in the "patient role" so it is by no means certain that the doctor–patient relationship is the only or even most significant factor in their decisions about drug-taking. A broader perspective suggests that sufferers of illness need to manage their daily existence of which medical regimens are only a part (cf. [23]). Such a perspective proposes that we examine the meaning of medications as they are manifested in people's everyday lives.

This paper is an attempt to further develop a patient- or sufferer-centered perspective on adhering to medical regimens. We did not set out to study compliance *per se*; rather this paper reflects themes that emerged from our larger study of people's experiences of epilepsy [24]. We examine what prescribed medications mean to the people with epilepsy we interviewed; and how these meanings are reflected in their use.

Method and Sample

The larger research project from which these data are drawn endeavors to present and analyze an "insider's" view of what it is like to have epilepsy in our society. To accomplish this we interviewed 80 people about their life experiences with epilepsy. Interviews were conducted over a three-year period and respondents were selected on the basis of availability and willingness to participate. We used a snowball sampling technique, relying on advertisements in local newspapers,

invitation letters passed anonymously by common acquaintances, and names obtained from local social agencies, self-help groups and health workers. No pretense to statistical representativeness is intended or sought. Our intention was to develop a sample from which theoretical insight would emerge and a conceptual understanding of epilepsy could be gained (see [25]).

We used an interview guide consisting of 50 open-ended questions and interviewed most of our respondents in their homes. The interviews lasted 1–3 hours and were tape-recorded. The recordings were transcribed and yielded over 2000-single-spaced typed pages of verbatim data.

Our sample ranged in age from 14 to 54 years (average age 28) and included 44 women and 36 men. Most respondents came from a metropolitan area in the midwest; a small number from a major city on the east coast. Our sample could be described as largely lower-middle class in terms of education and income. None of our respondents were or had been institutionalized for epilepsy; none were interviewed in hospitals, clinics or physicians' offices. In short, our sample and study were independent of medical and institutionalized settings. More detail about the method and sample is available elsewhere [24].

Epilepsy, Medication and Self-regulation

The common medical response to a diagnosis of epilepsy is to prescribe various medications to control seizures. Given the range of types of epilepsy and the variety of physiological reactions to these medications, patients often see doctors as having a difficult time getting their medication "right." There are starts and stops and changes, depending on the degree of seizure control and the drug's side effects. More often than not, patients are stabilized on a medication or combination at a given dosage or regimen. Continuing or altering medications is the primary if not sole medical management strategy for epilepsy.

Medications are important to people with epilepsy. They "control" seizures. Most take this medication several times daily. It becomes a routine part of their everyday lives. Although all of our respondents were taking or had taken these drugs, their responses to them varied. The effectiveness of these drugs in controlling seizures is a matter of degree. For some, seizures are stopped completely; they take pills regularly and have no seizures. For most, seizure frequency and duration are decreased significantly, although not reduced to zero. For a very few of our respondents, medications seem to have little impact; seizures continue unabated.

Nearly all our respondents said medications have helped them control seizures at one time or another. At the same time, however, many people changed their dose and regimen from those medically prescribed. Some stopped altogether. If medications were seen as so helpful, why were nearly half of our respondents "noncompliant" with their doctors' orders?

Most people with illnesses, even chronic illnesses such as epilepsy, spend only a tiny fraction of their lives in the "patient role." Compliance assumes that the doctor–patient relationship is pivotal for subsequent action, which may be the case. Consistent with our perspective, we conceptualize the issue as one of developing a *medication practice*. Medication practice offers a patient-centered perspective of how people manage their medications, focusing on the meaning and use of medications. In this light we can see the doctor's medication orders as the "prescribed medication practice" (e.g., take a 20 mg pill four times a day). Patients interpret the doctor's prescribed regimen and create a medication practice that may vary decidedly from the prescribed practice. Rather than assume the patient will follow prescribed medical rules, this perspective allows us to explore the kinds of practices patients create.[1] Put another way, it sees patients as active agents rather than passive recipients of doctors' orders.

Although many people failed to conform to their prescribed medication regimen, they did not define this conduct primarily as noncompliance with doctors' orders. The more we examined the data, the clearer it was that from the patient's perspective, doctors had very little impact on people's decisions to alter their medications. It was, rather, much more a question of regulation of control. To examine this more closely we developed criteria for what we could call self-regulation. Many of our respondents occasionally missed taking their medicine, but otherwise were regular in their medication practice. One had to do more than "miss" medications now and again (even a few times a week) to be deemed self-regulating. A person had to (1) reduce or raise the daily dose of prescribed drugs for several weeks or more or (2) skip or take extra doses regularly under specific circumstances (e.g., when drinking, staying up late or under "stress") or (3) stop taking the drugs completely for three consecutive days or longer. These criteria are arbitrary, but they allow us to estimate the extent of self-regulation. Using this definition, 34 of our 80 respondents (42%) self-regulated their medication.[2]

To understand the meaning and management of medications we need to look at those who follow a prescribed medications practice as well as those who create their own variations. While we note that 42% of our respondents are at variance with medical expectations, this number is more suggestive than definitive. Self-regulators are not a discrete and separate group. About half the self-regulators could be defined as regular in their practice, whatever it might be. They may have stopped for a week once or twice, or take extra medication only under "stressful" circumstances; otherwise, they are regular in their practice. On the other hand, perhaps a quarter of those following the prescribed medical practice say they have seriously considered changing or stopping their medications. It is likely there is an overlap between self-regulating and medical-regulating groups. While one needs to appreciate and examine the whole range of medication practice, the self-regulators provide a unique resource for analysis. They articulate views that are probably shared in varying degree by all people with epilepsy and provide an unusual insight into the meaning of medication and medication practice. We first describe how people account for following a prescribed medication practice; we then examine explanations offered for altering prescribed regimens and establishing their own practices. A final section outlines how the meaning of medications constructs and reflects the experience of epilepsy.

A Ticket to Normality

The availability of effective seizure control medications early in this century is a milestone in the treatment of epilepsy (Phenobarbital was introduced in 1912; Dilantin in 1938). These drugs also literally changed the experience of having epilepsy. To the extent the medications controlled seizures, people with epilepsy suffered fewer convulsive disruptions in their lives and were more able to achieve conventional social roles. To the extent doctors believed medications effective, they developed greater optimism about their ability to treat epileptic patients. To the degree the public recognized epilepsy as a "treatable" disorder, epileptics were no longer segregated in colonies and less subject to restrictive laws regarding marriage, procreation and work [24]. It is not surprising that people with epilepsy regard medications as a "ticket" to normality. The drugs did not, speaking strictly, affect anything but seizures. It was the social response to medications that brought about these changes. As one woman said: "I'm glad we've got [the medications] . . . you know, in the past people didn't and they were looked upon as lepers."

For most people with epilepsy, taking medicine becomes one of those routines of everyday life we engage in to avoid unwanted circumstances or improve our health. Respondents compared it to taking vitamins, birth control pills or teeth brushing. It becomes almost habitual, something done regularly with little reflection. One young working man said: "Well, at first I didn't like it, [but] it doesn't bother me anymore. Just like getting up in the morning and brushing your teeth. It's just something you do."

But seizure control medications differ from "normal pills" like vitamins or contraceptives. They are prescribed for a medical disorder and are seen both by the individual and others, as indicators or evidence of having epilepsy. One young man as a child did not know he had epilepsy "short of taking [his] medication." He said of this connection between epilepsy and medication: "I do, so therefore I have." Medications represent epilepsy: Dilantin or Phenobarbital are quickly recognized by medical people and often by others as epilepsy medications.

Medications can also indicate the degree of one's disorder. Most of our respondents do not know any others with epilepsy; thus they examine changes in their own epilepsy biographies as grounds for conclusions about their condition. Seizure activity is one such sign; the amount of medications "necessary" is another. A decrease or increase in seizures is taken to mean that epilepsy is getting better or worse. So it is with medications. While the two may be related—especially because the common medical response to more seizures is increased medication—they may also operate independently. If the doctor reduces the dose or strength of medication, or vice versa, the patient may interpret this as a sign of improvement or worsening. Similarly, if a person reduces his or her own dose, being able to "get along" on this lowered amount of medication is taken as evidence of "getting better." Since for a large portion of people with epilepsy seizures are considered to be well-controlled, medications become the only readily available measure of the "progress" of the disorder.

Taking Medications

We tried to suspend the medical assumption that people take medications simply because they are prescribed, or because they are supposed to control seizures, to examine our respondents' accounts of what they did and why.

The reason people gave most often for taking medication is *instrumental*: to control seizures, or more generally, to reduce the likelihood of body malfunction. Our respondents often drew a parallel to the reason people with diabetes take insulin. As one woman said, "If it does the trick, I'd rather take them [medications] than not." Or, as a man who would "absolutely not" miss his medications explained, "I don't want to have seizures" (although he continued to have 3 or 4 a month). Those who deal with their medication on instrumental grounds see it simply as a fact of life, as something to be done to avoid body malfunction and social and personal disruption.

While controlling body malfunction is always an underlying reason for taking medications, psychological grounds may be equally compelling. Many people said that medication *reduces worry,* independent of its actually decreasing seizures. These drugs can make people feel secure, so they don't have to think about the probability of seizures. A 20 year-old woman remarked: "My pills keep me from getting hysterical." A woman who has taken seizure control medication for 15 years describes this "psychological" function of medication: "I don't know what it does, but I suppose I'm psychologically dependent on it. In other words, if I take my medication, I feel better." Some people actually report "feeling better"—clearer, more alert and energetic—when they do not take these drugs, but because they begin to worry if they miss, they take them regularly anyhow.

The most important reason for taking medication, however, is to insure "normality." People said specifically that they take medications to be more "normal": The meaning here is normal in the sense of "leading a normal life." In the words of a middle-aged public relations executive who said he does not restrict his life because of epilepsy: "Except I always take my medication. I don't know why. I figure if I took them, then I could do anything I wanted to do." People believed taking medicine reduces the risk of having a seizure in the presence of others, which might be embarrassing or frightening. As a young woman explained:

> I feel if it's going to help, that's what I want because you know you feel uncomfortable enough anyway that you don't want anything like [a seizure] to happen around other people; so if it's going to help, I'll take it.

This is not to say people with epilepsy like to take medications. Quite the contrary. Many respondents who follow their medically prescribed medication practice openly say they "hate" taking medications and hope someday to be "off' the drugs. Part of this distaste is related to the dependence people come to feel. Some used the metaphor of being an addict: "I'm a real drug addict"; "I was an addict before it was fashionable"; "I'm like an alcoholic without a drink; I *have* to have them [pills]"; and "I really don't want to be hooked for the rest of my life." Even while loathing the pills or the "addiction"

people may be quite disciplined about taking these drugs.

The drugs used to control seizures are not, of course, foolproof. Some people continue to have seizures quite regularly while others suffer only occasional episodes. Such limited effectiveness does not necessarily lead these people to reject medication as a strategy. They continue, with frustration, to express "hope" that "they [doctors] will get it [the medication] right." For some, then, medications are but a limited ticket to normality.

Self-regulation: Grounds for Changing Medication Practice

For most people there is not a one-to-one correspondence between taking or missing medications and seizure activity. People who take medications regularly may still have seizures, and some people who discontinue their medications may be seizure-free for months or longer. Medical experts say a patient may well miss a whole day's medication yet still have enough of the drug in the bloodstream to prevent a seizure for this period.

In this section we focus on those who deviate from the prescribed medication practice and variously regulate their own medication. On the whole, members of this subgroup are slightly younger than the rest of the sample (average age 25 vs 32) and somewhat more likely to be female (59–43%), but otherwise are not remarkably different from our respondents who follow the prescribed medication practice. Self-regulation for most of our respondents consists of reducing the dose, stopping for a time, or regularly skipping or taking extra doses of medication depending on various circumstances.

Reducing the dose (including total termination) is the most common form of self-regulation. In this context, two points are worth restating. First, doctors typically alter doses of medication in times of increased seizure activity or troublesome drug "side effects." It is difficult to strike the optimum level of medication. To people with epilepsy, it seems that doctors engage in a certain amount of trial and error behavior. Second, and more important, medications are defined, both by doctors and patients, as an indicator of the degree of disorder. If seizure activity is not "controlled" or increases, patients see that doctors respond by raising (or changing) medications. The more medicine prescribed means epilepsy is getting worse; the less means it is getting better. What doctors do does not necessarily explain what patients do, but it may well be an example our respondents use in their own management strategies. The most common rationales for altering a medication practice are drug related: the medication is perceived as ineffective or the so-called side effects become too troublesome.

The efficacy of a drug is a complex issue. Here our concern is merely with perceived efficacy. When a medication is no longer seen as efficacious it is likely to be stopped. Many people continue to have seizures even when they follow the prescribed medication practice. If medication seemed to make no difference, our respondents were more likely to consider changing their medication practice. One woman who stopped taking medications for a couple of months said, "It seemed like [I had] the same number of seizures without it." Most people who stop taking their medicine altogether eventually resume a medication practice of some sort. A woman college instructor said, "When I was taking Dilantin, I stopped a number of times because it never seemed to *do* anything."

The most common drug-related rationale for reducing dose is troublesome "side effects." People with epilepsy attribute a variety of side effects to seizure control medications. One category of effects includes swollen and bleeding gums, oily or yellow skin, pimples, sore throat and a rash. Another category includes slowed mental functioning, drowsiness, slurred speech, dullness, impaired memory, loss of balance and partial impotence.[3] The first category, which we can call body side effects, were virtually never given as an account for self-regulation. Only those side effects that impaired social skills, those in the second category, were given as reasons for altering doctors' medication orders.

Social side effects impinge on social interaction. People believed they felt and acted differently. A self-regulating woman described how she feels when she takes her medication:

I can feel that I become much more even. I feel like I flatten out a little bit. I don't like that feeling. . . . It's just a feeling of dullness, which I don't like, almost a feeling that you're on the edge of laziness.

If people saw their medication practice as hindering the ability to participate in routine social affairs, they were likely to change it. Our respondents gave many examples such as a college student who claimed the medication slowed him down and wondered if it were affecting his memory, a young newspaper reporter who reduced his medication because it was putting him to sleep at work; or the social worker who felt she "sounds smarter" and more articulate when "off medications."

Drug side effects, even those that impair social skills, are not sufficient in themselves to explain the level of self-regulation we found. Self-regulation was considerably more than a reaction to annoying and uncomfortable side effects. It was an active and intentional endeavor.

Social Meanings of Regulating Medication Practice

Variations in medication practice by and large seem to depend on what medication and self-regulation mean to our respondents. Troublesome relationships with physicians, including the perception that they have provided inadequate medical information [14], may be a foundation on which alternative strategies and practices are built. Our respondents, however, did not cite such grounds for altering their doctors' orders. People vary their medication practice on grounds connected to managing their everyday lives. If we examine the social meanings of medications from our respondents' perspective, self-regulation turns on four grounds: testing; control of dependence; destigmatization; and practical practice. While individual respondents may cite one or more of these as grounds for altering medication practice, they are probably best understood as strategies common among those who self regulate.

Testing

Once people with epilepsy begin taking seizure-control medications, given there are no special problems and no seizures, doctors were reported to seldom change the medical regimen. People are likely to stay on medications indefinitely. But how can one know that a period without seizures is a result of medication or spontaneous remission of the disorder? How long can one go without medication? How "bad" is this case of epilepsy? How can one know if epilepsy is "getting better" while still taking medication? Usually after a period without or with only a few seizures, many reduced or stopped their medicine altogether to test for themselves whether or not epilspsy was "still there."

People can take themselves off medications as an experiment, to see "if anything will happen." One woman recalled:

> I was having one to two seizures a year on phenobarb . . . so I decided not to take it and to see what would happen . . . so I stopped it and I watched and it seemed that I had the same amount of seizures with it as without it . . . for three years.

She told her physician, who was skeptical but "allowed" her this control of her medication practice. A man who had taken medication three times a day for 16 years felt intuitively that he could stop his medications:

> Something kept telling me I didn't have to take [medication] anymore, a feeling or somethin'. It took me quite a while to work up the nerve to stop takin' the pills. And one day I said, "One way to find out . . ."

After suffering what he called drug withdrawal effects, he had no seizures for 6 years. Others tested to see how long they can go without medication and seizures.

Testing does not always turn out successfully. A public service agency executive tried twice to stop taking medications when he thought he had "kicked" epilepsy. After two failures, he concluded that stopping medications "just doesn't work." But others continue to test, hoping for some change in their condition. One middle-aged housewife said:

> When I was young I would try not to take it . . . I'd take 'em for a while and think, "Well, I don't need it anymore," and I would not take it for, deliberately,

just to see if I could do without. And then [in a few days] I'd start takin' it again because I'd start passin' out . . . I will still try that now, when my husband is out of town . . . I just think, maybe I'm still gonna grow out of it or something.

Testing by reducing or stopping medication is only one way to evaluate how one's disorder is progressing. Even respondents who follow the prescribed medication regimen often wonder "just what would happen" if they stopped.

Controlling Dependence

People with epilepsy struggle continually against becoming too dependent on family, friends, doctors or medications. They do, of course, depend on medications for control of seizures. The medications do not necessarily eliminate seizures and many of our respondents resented their dependence on them. Another paradox is that although medications can increase self reliance by reducing seizures, taking medications can be *experienced* as a threat to self-reliance. Medications seem almost to become symbolic of the dependence created by having epilepsy.

There is a widespread belief in our society that drugs create dependence and that being on chemical substances is not a good thing. Somehow, whatever the goal is, it is thought to be better if we can get there without drugs. Our respondents reflected these ideas in their comments.

A college junior explained: "I don't like it at all. I don't like chemicals in my body. It's sort of like a dependency only that I have to take it because my body forced me to . . ." A political organizer who says medications reduce his seizures commented: "I've never enjoyed having to depend on anything . . . drugs in particular." A nurse summed up the situation: "The *drugs* were really a kind of dependence." Having to take medication relinquished some degree of control of one's life. A woman said:

> I don't like to have to *take* anything. It was, like, at one time birth control pills, but I don't like to take anything *everyday*. It's just like, y'know, controlling me, or something.

The feeling of being controlled need not be substantiated in fact for people to act upon it. If people *feel* dependent on and controlled by medication, it is not surprising that they seek to avoid these drugs. A high school junior, who once took medicine because he feared having a seizure in the street, commented:

> And I'd always heard medicine helps and I just kept taking it and finally I just got so I didn't depend on the medicine no more, I could just fight it off myself and I just stopped taking it in.

After stopping for a month he forgot about his medications completely.

Feelings of dependence are one reason people gave for regulating medicine. For a year, one young social worker took medication when she felt it was necessary; otherwise, she tried not to use it. When we asked her why, she responded, "I regulate my own drug . . . mostly because it's really important for me not to be dependent." She occasionally had seizures and continued to alter her medication to try to "get it right":

> I started having [seizures] every once in a while. And I thought wow, the bad thing is that I just haven't regulated it right and I just need to up it a little bit and then, you know, if I do it just right, I won't have epilepsy anymore.

This woman and others saw medications as a powerful resource in their struggle to gain control over epilepsy. Although she no longer thinks she can rid herself of epilepsy, this woman still regulates her medication.

In this context, people with epilepsy manipulate their sense of dependence on medications by changing medication practice. But there is a more subtle level of dependence that encourages such changes. Some reported they regulated their medication intake in direct response to interventions of others, especially family members. It was as if others *wanted* them to be more dependent by coaxing or reminding them to take their medications regularly. Many responded to this encouraged greater dependence by creating their own medication practice.

A housewife who said she continues regularly to have petit mal seizures and tremors along with an occasional grand mal seizure, remarked:

> Oh, like most things, when someone tells me I have to do something, I basically resent it. . . . If it's my

option and I choose to do it, I'll probably do it more often than not. But if you tell me I have to, I'll bend it around and do it my own way, which is basically what I have done.

Regardless of whether one feels dependent on the drug or dependent because of others' interventions around drug taking, changing a prescribed medication practice as well as continuing self-regulation serve as a form of *taking control* of one's epilepsy.

Destigmatization

Epilepsy is a stigmatized illness. Sufferers attempt to control information about the disorder to manage this threat [38]. There are no visible stigmata that make a person with epilepsy obviously different from other people, but a number of aspects of having epilepsy can compromise attempts at information control. The four signs that our respondents most frequently mentioned as threatening information control were seizures in the presence of others, job or insurance applications, lack of a driver's license and taking medications. People may try to avoid seizures in public, lie or hedge on their applications, develop accounts for not having a driver's license, or take their medicine in private in order to minimize the stigma potential of epilepsy.

Medication usually must be taken three or four times daily, so at least one dose must be taken away from home. People attempt to be private about taking their medications and/or develop "normal" pill accounts ("it's to help my digestion"). One woman's mother told her to take medications regularly, as she would for any other sickness:

> When I was younger it didn't bother me too bad. But as I got older, it would tend to bother me some. Whether it was, y'know, maybe somebody seeing me or somethin', I don't know. But it did.

Most people develop skills to minimize potential stigmatization from taking pills in public.

On occasion, stopping medications is an attempt to vacate the stigmatized status of epileptic. One respondent wrote us a letter describing how she tried to get her mother to accept her by not taking her medications. She wrote:

This is going to sound real dumb, but I can't help it. My mother never accepted me when I was little because I was "different." I stopped taking my medication in an attempt to be normal and accepted by her. Now that I know I need medication it's like I'm completely giving up trying to be "normal" so mom won't be ashamed of me. I'm going to accept the fact that I'm "different" and I don't really care if mom gives a damn or not.

Taking medications in effect acknowledges this "differentness."

It is, of course, more difficult to hide the meaning of medications from one's self. Taking medication is a constant reminder of having epilepsy. For some it is as if the medication itself represents the stigma of epilepsy. The young social worker quoted above felt if she could stop taking her medications she would no longer be an epileptic. A young working woman summed up succinctly why avoiding medications would be avoiding stigma: "Well, at least I would not be . . . generalized and classified in a group as being an epileptic."

Practical Practice

Self-regulators spoke often of how they changed the dose or regimen of medication in an effort to reduce the risk of having a seizure, particularly during "high stress" situations. Several respondents who were students said they take extra medications during exam periods or when they stay up late studying. A law student who had not taken his medication for 6 months took some before his law school exams: "I think it increases the chances [seizures] won't happen." A woman who often participated in horse shows said she "usually didn't pay attention" to her medication in practice but takes extra when she doesn't get the six to eight hours sleep she requires: "I'll wake up and take two capsules instead of one . . . and I'll generally take it like when we're going to horse shows. I'll take it pretty consistently." Such uses of medication are common ways of trying to forestall "possible trouble."

People with epilepsy changed their medication practice for practical ends in two other kinds of circumstances. Several reported they took extra medication if they felt a "tightening" or felt a seizure coming on. Many people also said they

did not take medications if they were going to drink alcohol. They believed that medication (especially Phenobarbital) and alcohol do not mix well.

In short, people change their medication practice to suit their perceptions of social environment. Some reduce medication to avoid potential problems from mixing alcohol and drugs. Others reduce it to remain "clear-headed" and "alert" during "important" performances (something of a "Catch-22" situation). Most, however, adjust their medications practically in an effort to reduce the risk of seizures.

Conclusion: Asserting Control

Regulating medication represents an attempt to assert some degree of control that appears at times to be completely beyond control. Loss of control is a significant concern for people with epilepsy. While medical treatment can increase both the sense and the fact of control over epilepsy, and information control can limit stigmatization, the regulation of medications is one way people with epilepsy struggle to gain some personal control over their condition.

Medication practice can be modified on several different grounds. Side effects that make managing everyday social interaction difficult can lead to the reduction or termination of medication. People will change their medication practice, including stopping altogether, in order to "test" for the existence or "progress" of the disorder. Medication may be altered to control the perceived level of dependence, either on the drugs themselves or on those who "push" them to adhere to a particular medication practice. Since the medication can represent the stigma potential of epilepsy, both literally and symbolically, altering medication practice can be a form of destigmatization. And finally, many people modify their medication practice in anticipation of specific social circumstances, usually to reduce the risk of seizures.

It is difficult to judge how generalizable these findings are to other illnesses. Clearly, people develop medication practices whenever they must take medications regularly. This is probably most true for long-term chronic illness where medication becomes a central part of everyday life, such as diabetes, rheumatoid arthritis, hypertension and asthma. The degree and amount of self-regulation may differ among illnesses—likely to be related to symptomatology, effectiveness of medications and potential of stigma—but I suspect most of the meanings of medications described here would be present among sufferers of any illness that people must continually manage.

In sum, we found that a large proportion of the people with epilepsy we interviewed said they themselves regulate their medication. Medically-centered compliance research presents a skewed and even distorted view of how and why patients manage medication. From the perspective of the person with epilepsy, the issue is more clearly one of responding to the meaning of medications in everyday life than "compliance" with physicians' orders and medical regimens. Framing the problem as self-regulation rather than compliance allows us to see modifying medication practice as a vehicle for asserting some control over epilepsy. One consequence of such a reframing would be to reexamine the value of achieving "compliant" behavior and to rethink what strategies might be appropriate for achieving greater adherence to prescribed medication regimens.

ACKNOWLEDGMENT

My thanks and appreciation to Joseph W. Schneider, my co-investigator in the epilepsy research, for his insightful comments on an earlier version of this paper. This research was supported in part by grants from the Drake University Research Council, the Epilepsy Foundation of America and the National Institute of Mental Health (MH 30818-01).

NOTES

1. Two previous studies of epilepsy which examine the patients' perspective provide parallel evidence for the significance of developing such an approach in the study of "noncompliance" (see [26] and [27]).
2. Reports in the medical literature indicate that noncompliance with epilepsy regimens is considered a serious problem [28–32]. One study reports that 40% of patients missed the prescribed medication dose often enough to affect their blood-level medication concentrations [33]; an important review article estimates noncompliance with epilepsy drug regimens between 30 and 40%, with a range from 20 to 75% [34]. Another study suggests that noncompliant patients generally had longer duration of the disorder, more complicated regimens and more medication changes [35]. Attempts to increase epilepsy medication compliance include improving doctor–patient communication, incorporating patients more in treatment programs, increasing patient knowledge and simplifying drug regimens. Since noncompliance with anti-convulsant medication regimens is deemed the most frequent reason why patients suffer recurrent seizures [30], some researchers suggest, "If the patient understands the risks of stopping medication, he *will not stop*" [36]. Yet there also have been reports of active noncompliance with epilepsy medications [37]. In sum, epilepsy noncompliance studies are both typical of and reflect upon most other compliance research. In this sense, epilepsy is a good example for developing an alternative approach to understanding how people manage their medications.
3. These are reported side effects. They may or may not be drug related, but our respondents attribute them to the medication.

REFERENCES

1. Haynes R. B., Taylor D. W. and Sackett D. L. (Eds) *Compliance in Health Care*. Johns Hopkins University Press, Baltimore, 1979.
2. Davis M. Variations in patients' compliance with doctor's advice: an empirical analysis of patterns of communication. *Am. J. Publ. Hlth* 58, 272, 1968.
3. Hulka B. S., Kupper L. L., Cassel J. LC. and Barbineau R. A. Practice characteristics and quality of primary medical care: the doctor–patient relationship. *Med Care* 13, 808–820, 1975.
4. Christenson D. B. Drug-taking compliance: a review and synthesis. *Hlth. Serv. Res.* 6, 171–187, 1978.
5. Sackett D. L. and Snow J. C. The magnitude of compliance and non-compliance. In *Compliance in Health Care* (Edited by Haynes R. B. *et al.*), pp. 11–22. Johns Hopkins University Press, Baltimore, 1979.
6. Sackett D. L. and Haynes R. B. (Eds.) *Compliance with Therapeutic Regimens*. Johns Hopkins University Press, Baltimore, 1976.
7. DiMatteo M. R. and DiNicola D. D. *Achieving Patient Compliance*. Pergamon Press, New York, 1982.
8. Hingson R., Scotch N. A., Sorenson J. and Swazey

J. P. *In Sickness and in Health: Social Dimensions of Medical Care.* C. V. Mosby, St. Louis, 1981.

9. Haynes R. B. Determinants of compliance: the disease and the mechanics of treatment. In *Compliance in Health Care* (Edited by Haynes R. B. *et al.*), pp. 49–62. Johns Hopkins University Press, Baltimore, 1979.
10. Garrity T. F. Medical compliance and the clinician–patient relationship: a review. *Soc. Sci. Med.* **15E,** 215–222, 1981.
11. Svarstad B. L. Physician–patient communication and patient conformity with medical advice. In *Growth of Bureaucratic Medicine* (Edited by Mechanic D.), pp. 220–238. Wiley, New York, 1976.
12. Francis V., Korsch B. and Morris M. Gaps in doctor–patient communication: patients' response to medical advice. *New Engl. J. Med.* **280,** 535, 1969.
13. Korsch B., Gozzi E. and Francis V. Gaps in doctor–patient communication I. Doctor–patient interaction and patient satisfaction. *Pediatrics* **42,** 885, 1968.
14. Becker M. H. and Maiman L. A. Sociobehavioral determinants of compliance with health and medical care recommendations. *Med Care* **13,** 10–24.
15. Becker M. H. Sociobehavioral determinants of compliance. In *Compliance With Therapeutic Regimens* (Edited by Sackett D. L. and Haynes R. B.), pp. 40–50. Johns Hopkins University Press, Baltimore, 1976.
16. Becker M. H., Maiman L. A., Kirscht J. P., Haefner D. L., Drachman R. H. and Taylor D. W. Patient perceptions and compliance: recent studies of the health belief model. In *Compliance in Health Care* (Edited by Haynes, R. B. *et al.*), pp. 79–109. Johns Hopkins University Press, Baltimore, 1979.
17. Berkanovic E. The health belief model and voluntary health behavior. Paper presented to Conference on Critical issues in Health Delivery Systems, Chicago, 1977.
18. Parsons T. *The Social System.* Free Press, Glencoe, 1951.
19. Stimson G. V. Obeying doctor's orders: a view from the other side. *Soc. Sci. Med.* **8,** 97–104, 1974.
20. Arluke A. Judging drugs: patients' conceptions of therapeutic efficacy in the treatment of arthritis. *Hum. Org.* **39,** 84–88, 1980.
21. Hayes-Battista D. E. Modifying the treatment: patient compliance, patient control and medical care. *Soc. Sci. Med.* **10,** 233–238, 1976.
22. Zola I. K. Structural constraints in the doctor–patient relationship: the case of non-compliance.

In *The Relevance of Social Science for Medicine* (Edited by Eisenberg L. and Kleinman A.), pp. 241–252. Reidel, Dordrecht, 1981.
23. Strauss A. and Glaser B. *Chronic Illness and the Quality of Life,* pp. 21–32. C. V. Mosby, St. Louis, 1975.
24. Schneider J. and Conrad P. *Having Epilepsy: The Experience and Control of Illness.* Temple University Press, Philadelphia, 1983.
25. Glaser B. and Strauss A. *The Discovery of Grounded Theory.* Aldine, Chicago, 1967.
26. West P. The physician and the management of childhood epilepsy. In *Studies in Everyday Medicine* (Edited by Wadsworth M. and Robinson D.), pp. 13–31. Martin Robinson, London, 1976.
27. Trostle J. *et al.* The logic of non-compliance: management of epilepsy from a patient's point of view. *Cult. Med. Psychiat.* **7,** 35–56, 1983.
28. Lund M., Jurgensen R. S. and Kuhl V. Serum diphenylhydantoin in ambulant patients with epilepsy. *Epilepsia* **5,** 51–58, 1964.
29. Lund M. Failure to observe dosage instructions in patients with epilepsy. *Acta neurol. scand.* **49,** 295–306, 1975.
30. Reynolds E. H. Drug treatment of epilepsy. *Lancet* **II,** 721–725, 1978.
31. Browne T. R. and Cramer I. A. Antiepileptic drug serum concentration determinations. In *Epilepsy: Diagnosis and Management* (Edited by Browne T. R. and Feldman R. G.). Little, Brown, Boston, 1982.
32. Pryse-Phillips W., Jardine F. and Bursey F. Compliance with drug therapy by epileptic patients. *Epilepsia* **23,** 269–274, 1982.
33. Eisler J. and Mattson R. H. Compliance with anticonvulsant drug therapy. *Epilepsia* **16,** 203, 1975.
34. The Commission for the Control of Epilepsy and Its Consequences. The literature on patient compliance and implications for cost-effective patient education programs with epilepsy. In *Plan for Nationwide Action on Epilepsy,* Vol. II, Part 1, pp. 391–415. U.S. Government Printing Office, Washington, DC, 1977.
35. Bryant S. G. and Ereshfsky L. Determinants of compliance in epileptic conditions. *Drug Intel. Clin. Pharmac.* **15,** 572–577, 1981.
36. Norman S. E. and Browne T. K. Seizure disorders. *Am. J. Nurs.* **81,** 893, 1981.
37. Desei B. T., Reily T. L., Porter R. J. and Penry J. K. Active non-compliance as a cause of uncontrolled seizures. *Epilepsia* **19,** 447–452, 1978.
38. Schneider J. and Conrad P. In the closet with illness: epilepsy, stigma potential and information control. *Soc. Probl.* **28,** 32–44, 1980.

The Social Organization of Medical Care

· · · · · ·

In Part Two, we turn from the production of disease and illness to the social organizations created to treat it. Here we begin to examine the institutional aspects of health and illness—the medical care system. We look at the social organization of medical care historically, structurally, and, finally, interactionally. We seek to understand how this complex system operates and how its particular characteristics have contributed to the current health care crisis.

Creating and Maintaining the Dominance of Medicine

· · · · · ·

Physicians have a professional monopoly on medical practice in the United States. They have an exclusive state-supported right, manifested in the "licensing" of physicians, to medical practice. With their licenses, physicians can legally do what no one else can, including cutting into the human body and prescribing drugs.

Until the latter part of the nineteenth century, various groups and individuals (e.g., homeopaths, midwives, botanical doctors) competed for the "medical turf." By the second decade of this century, virtually only M.D. physicians had the legal right to practice medicine in this country. One might suggest that physicians achieved their exclusive rights to the nation's medical territory because of their superior scientific and clinical achievements, a line of reasoning which suggests that physicians demonstrated superior healing and curative skills, and the government therefore supported their rights against less effective healers and quacks. But this seems not to have been the case. As we noted earlier, most of the improvement in the health status of the population resulted from social changes, including better nutrition, sanitation, and a rising standard of living rather than from the interventions of clinical medicine. Medical techniques were in fact rather limited, often even dangerous, until the early twentieth century. As L. J. Henderson observed, "somewhere between 1910 and 1912 in this country, a random patient, with a random disease, consulting a doctor chosen at random, had, for the first time in the history of mankind, a better than fifty-fifty chance of profiting from the encounter" (Blumgart, 1964).

The success of the American Medical Association (AMA) in consolidating its power was central to securing a monopoly for M.D. physicians. In recent years the AMA has lost some power to the "corporate rationalizers" in medicine (e.g., health insurance industry, hospital organizations, HMOs [Alford, 1972]). While physicians still maintain a monopoly over medical practice, the "corporatization" of medicine has sharply reduced their control over medical organizations (see also selections 21 and 22 by Relman and by Waitzkin). By virtue of their monopoly over medical practice, physicians have exerted an enormous influence over the entire field of medicine, including the right to define what constitutes disease and how to treat it. Friedson's (1970a: 251) observation is still valid: "The medical profession has first claim to jurisdiction over the label illness and *always* to how it can be attached, irrespective of its capacity to deal with it effectively."

Physicians also gained "professional dominance" over the organization of medical services in the United States (Friedson, 1970b). This monopoly gave the medical profession functional autonomy and a structural insulation from outside evaluations of medical practice. In addition, professional dominance includes not only the exclusive right to treat disease but also the right to limit and evaluate the performance of most other medical care workers. Finally, the particular vision of medicine that became institutionalized included a "clinical mentality" (Friedson, 1970a) that focused on medical responsibility to *individual* patients rather than to the community or public.

Physicians' professional dominance has been challenged in the past two decades. The rise of corporate and bureaucratic medicine, the emphasis on cost containment by third-party payers, the complexity of medical technology, and the dramatic increase in malpractice suits have left the medical profession feeling besieged (Stoeckle, 1988). There is evidence that professional sovereignty is declining and commercial interest in the health sector is increasing. One analyst has suggested that this is partly due to the actual "surplus" of doctors in this country and the increasing power of "third parties" in financing medicine (Starr, 1982). A lively debate exists over whether professional dominance has waned to the point that physicians are relegated to the position of other workers, a kind of professional "proletariat" (McKinlay and Arches, 1985), or whether professional dominance itself begot the changes that are challenging medical sovereignty (Light and Levine, 1989). In the changing medical environment, professional dominance is clearly changing and is reshaping the influence and authority over medical care.

In the first selection, "Professionalization, Monopoly, and the Structure of Medical Practice," Peter Conrad and Joseph W. Schneider present a brief review of the historical development of this medical monopoly. They examine the case of abortion in the nineteenth century to highlight how specific medical interests were served by a physician-led crusade against abortion. By successfully outlawing abortion and institutionalizing their own professional ethics, "regular" physicians were able to eliminate effectively some of their competitors and secure greater control of the medical market.

Richard W. Wertz and Dorothy C. Wertz expanded on this theme of monopolization and professional dominance in "Notes on the Decline of Midwives and the Rise of Medical Obstetricians." They investigate the medicalization of childbirth historically and the subsequent decline of midwifery in this country. Female midwifery, which continues to be practiced in most industrialized and developing countries, was virtually eliminated in the United States. Wertz and Wertz show that it was not merely professional imperialism that led to the exclusion of midwives (although this played an important role), but also a subtle and profound sexism within and outside the medical profession. They postulate that the physicians' monopolization of childbirth resulted from a combination of a change in middle-class women's views of birthing, physicians' economic interests, and the development of sexist notions that suggested that women weren't suitable for attending births. Physicians became increasingly interventionist in their childbirth practice partly due to their training (they felt they had to "do" something) but also due to their desire to use instruments "to establish a superior status" and treat childbirth as an illness rather than a natural event. In recent years we have seen the reemergence of nurse midwives, but their work is usually limited to hospitals under medical dominance (Rothman, 1982). Also, there are presently a small number of "lay" midwives whose practice is confined to limited and sometimes illegal situations outside of medical control (See Sullivan and Weitz, 1988). See selection 29 by Barbara Katz Rothman for a description of how modern midwives' clinical perspectives were transformed through their experiences attending homebirths.

In the third selection, "Corporatization and the Social Transformation of Doctoring," John B. McKinlay and John D. Stoeckle examine how the changes in the health care system are affecting the position of the medical profession and the everyday work of doctoring. They argue that these changes have undermined professional dominance and dramatically shifted the control of medicine. While their hypothesis of "proletarianization" may be controversial, there is no doubt that corporatization and bureaucratization of medicine has reduced the medical profession's power.

Donald W. Light, in the final selection, "Countervailing Power," posits a changing balance of power among professions and related social institutions. "The notion of countervailing powers locates professions within a field of institutional and cultural forces in which one party may gain dominance by subordinating the needs of significant other parties, who, in time, mobilize to counter this dominance" (Hafferty and Light, 1995: 135). In American society, professional medicine historically dominated health care, but we now see "buyers" (e.g., corporations who pay for employees' medical insurance, along with other consumers); "providers" (e.g., physicians, hospitals, HMOs, nursing homes, and other medical care providers); and "payers" (e.g., insurance companies and governments) all vying for power and influence over medical care. This changes the nature of professional power and dominance. Light points out that as medical care evolves more into a buyer-driven system, fundamental tenets of professionalism—including physicians' autonomy over their work and their monopoly over knowledge—are thrown into question. As the twentieth century closes, physicians certainly maintain aspects of their dominance and sovereignty, but it is clearly a situation undergoing dynamic changes.

REFERENCES

Alford, Robert. 1972. "The political economy of health care: Dynamics without change." Politics and Society. 2:127–164.

Blumgart, H. L. 1964. "Caring for the patient." New England Journal of Medicine. 270:449–56.

Friedson, Eliot. 1970a. Profession of Medicine. New York: Dodd, Mead.

———. 1970b. Professional Dominance. Chicago: Aldine.

Hafferty, Fredric W., and Donald W. Light. 1995. "Professional dynamics and the changing nature of medical work." Journal of Health and Social Behavior. Extra issue: 132–153.

Light, Donald, and Sol Levine. 1988. "The changing character of the medical profession." Milbank Quarterly. 66 (Suppl. 2): 1–23.

McKinlay, John B. and Joan Arches. 1985. "Toward the proletarianization of physicians." International Journal of Health Services. 15: 161–95.

Rothman, Barbara Katz. 1982. In Labor. New York: Norton.

Starr, Paul. 1982. The Social Transformation of American Medicine. New York: Basic Books.

Stoeckle, John D. 1988. "Reflections on modern doctoring." Milbank Quarterly. 66 (Suppl. 2): 76–91.

Sullivan, Deborah A., and Rose Weitz. 1988. Labor Pains: Modern Midwives and Home Birth. New Haven, CT: Yale University Press.

14

Professionalization, Monopoly, and the Structure of Medical Practice

• • • • • •

Peter Conrad and Joseph W. Schneider

. . . Medicine has not always been the powerful, prestigious, successful, lucrative, and dominant profession we know today. The status of the medical profession is a product of medical politicking as well as therapeutic expertise. This discussion presents a brief overview of the development of the medical profession and its rise to dominance.

Emergence of the Medical Profession: Up to 1850
·················

In ancient societies, disease was given supernatural explanations, and "medicine" was the province of priests or shamans. It was in classical Greece that medicine began to emerge as a separate occupation and develop its own theories, distinct from philosophy or theology. Hippocrates, the great Greek physician who refused to accept supernatural explanations or treatments for disease, developed a theory of the "natural" causes of disease and systematized all available medical knowledge. He laid a basis for the development of medicine as a separate body of knowledge. Early Christianity depicted sickness as punishment for sin, engendering new theological explanations and treatments. Christ and his disciples believed in the supernatural causes and cures of disease. This view became institutionalized in the Middle Ages, when the Church dogma dominated theories and practice of medicine and priests were physicians. The Renaissance in Europe brought a renewed interest in ancient Greek medical knowledge. This

marked the beginning of a drift toward natural explanations of disease and the emergence of medicine as an occupation separate from the Church (Cartwright, 1977).

But European medicine developed slowly. The "humoral theory" of disease developed by Hippocrates dominated medical theory and practice until well into the 19th century. Medical diagnosis was impressionistic and often inaccurate, depicting conditions in such general terms as "fevers" and "fluxes." In the 17th century, physicians relied mainly on three techniques to determine the nature of illness: what the patient said about symptoms; the physician's own observations of signs of illness and the patient's appearance and behavior; and more rarely, a manual examination of the body (Reiser, 1978, p. 1). Medicine was by no means scientific, and "medical thought involved unverified doctrines and resulting controversies" (Shryock, 1960, p. 52). Medical practice was a "bedside medicine" that was patient oriented and did not distinguish the illness from the "sick man" (Jewson, 1976). It was not until Thomas Sydenham's astute observations in the late 17th century that physicians could begin to distinguish between the patient and the disease. Physicians possessed few treatments that worked regularly, and many of their treatments actually worsened the sufferer's condition. Medicine in colonial America inherited this European stock of medical knowledge.

Colonial American medicine was less developed than its European counterpart. There were no medical schools and few physicians, and because of the vast frontier and sparse population, much medical care was in effect self-help. Most American physicians were educated and trained by apprenticeship; few were university trained. With the exception of surgeons, most were undifferentiated practitioners. Medical practices were limited. Prior to the revolution, physicians did not commonly attend births; midwives, who were not seen as part of the medical establishment, routinely attended birthings (Wertz and Wertz, 1977). William Rothstein (1972) notes that "American colonial medical practice, like European practice of the period, was characterized by the lack of any substantial body of usable scientific knowledge" (p. 27). Physicians, both educated and otherwise, tended to treat their patients pragmatically, for medical theory had little to offer. Most colonial physicians practiced medicine only part-time, earning their livelihoods as clergymen, teachers, farmers, or in other occupations. Only in the early 19th century did medicine become a full-time vocation (Rothstein, 1972).

The first half of the 19th century saw important changes in the organization of the medical profession. About 1800, "regular," or educated, physicians convinced state legislatures to pass laws limiting the practice of medicine to practitioners of a certain training and class (prior to this nearly anyone could claim the title "doctor" and practice medicine). These state licensing laws were not particularly effective, largely because of the colonial tradition of medical self-help. They were repealed in most states during the Jacksonian period (1828–1836) because they were thought to be elitist, and the temper of the times called for a more "democratic" medicine.

The repeal of the licensing laws and the fact that most "regular" (i.e., regularly educated) physicians shared and used "a distinctive set of medically invalid therapies, known as 'heroic' therapy," created fertile conditions for the emergence of *medical sects* in the first half of the 19th century (Rothstein, 1972, p. 21). Physicians of the time practiced a "heroic" and invasive form of medicine consisting primarily of such treatments as bloodletting, vomiting, blistering, and purging. This highly interventionist, and sometimes dangerous, form of medicine engendered considerable public opposition and resistance. In this context a number of medical sects emerged, the most important of which were the homeo-

pathic and botanical physicians. These "irregular" medical practitioners practiced less invasive, less dangerous forms of medicine. They each developed a considerable following, since their therapies were probably no less effective than those of regulars practicing heroic medicine. The regulars attempted to exclude them from practice; so the various sects set up their own medical schools and professional societies. This sectarian medicine created a highly *competitive* situation for the regulars (Rothstein, 1972). Medical sectarianism, heroic therapies, and ineffective treatment contributed to the low status and lack of prestige of early 19th-century medicine. At this time, medicine was neither a prestigious occupation nor an important economic activity in American society (Starr, 1977).

The regular physicians were concerned about this situation. Large numbers of regularly trained physicians sought to earn a livelihood by practicing medicine (Rothstein, 1972, p. 3). They were troubled by the poor image of medicine and lack of standards in medical training and practice. No doubt they were also concerned about the competition of the irregular sectarian physicians. A group of regular physicians founded the American Medical Association (AMA) in 1847 "to promote the science and art of medicine and the betterment of public health" (quoted in Coe, 1978, p. 204). The AMA also was to set and enforce standards and ethics of "regular" medical practice and strive for exclusive professional and economic rights to the medical turf.

The AMA was the crux of the regulars' attempt to "professionalize" medicine. As Magali Sarfatti Larson (1977) points out, professions organize to create and control *markets*. Organized professions attempt to regulate and limit the competition, usually by controlling professional education and by limiting licensing. Professionalization is, in this view, "the process by which producers of special services sought to constitute *and control* the market for their expertise" (Larson, 1977, p. xvi). The regular physicians and the AMA set out to consolidate and control the market for medical services. As we shall see in the next two sections, the regulars were successful in professionalization, eliminating competition and creating a medical monopoly.

Crusading, Deviance, and Medical Monopoly: The Case of Abortion

The medical profession after the middle of the 19th century was frequently involved in various activities that could be termed social reform. Some of these reforms were directly related to health and illness and medical work; others were peripheral to the manifest medical calling of preventing illness and healing the sick. In these reform movements, physicians became medical crusaders, attempting to influence public morality and behavior. This medical crusading often led physicians squarely into the moral sphere, making them advocates for moral positions that had only peripheral relations to medical practice. Not infrequently these reformers sought to change people's values or to impose a set of particular values on others. . . . We now examine one of the more revealing examples of medical crusading: the criminalization of abortion in American society.[1]

Most people are under the impression that abortion was always defined as deviant and illegal in America prior to the Supreme Court's landmark decision in 1973. This, however, is not the case. American abortion policy, and the attendant defining of abortion as deviant, were specific products of medical crusading. Prior to the Civil War, abortion was a common and largely legal medical procedure performed by various types of physicians and midwives. A pregnancy was not considered confirmed until the occurrence of a phenomenon called "quickening," the first perception of fetal movement. Common law did not recognize the fetus before quickening in criminal cases, and an unquickened fetus was deemed to have no living soul. Thus most people did not consider termination of pregnancy before quickening to be an especially serious matter, much less murder. Abortion before quickening created no moral or medical problems. Public opinion was indifferent, and for the time it was probably a relatively safe medical procedure. Thus, for all intents and purposes, American women were free to terminate their pregnancies before quickening in the early 19th century. Moreover, it was a procedure relatively free of the moral stigma that was attached to abortion in this century.

After 1840 abortion came increasingly into public view. Abortion clinics were vigorously and openly advertised in newspapers and magazines. The advertisements offered euphemistically couched services for "women's complaints," "menstrual blockage," and "obstructed menses." Most contemporary observers suggested that more and more women were using these services. Prior to 1840 most abortions were performed on the unmarried and desperate of the "poor and unfortunate classes." However, beginning about this time, significantly increasing numbers of middle- and upper-class white, Protestant, native-born women began to use these services. It is likely they either wished to delay childbearing or thought they already had all the children they wanted (Mohr, 1978, pp. 46–47). By 1870 approximately one abortion was performed for every five live births (Mohr, 1978, pp. 79–80).

Beginning in the 1850s, a number of physicians, especially moral crusader Dr. Horatio Robinson Storer, began writing in medical and popular journals and lobbying in state legislatures about the danger and immorality of abortion. They opposed abortion before and after quickening and under Dr. Storer's leadership organized an aggressive national campaign. In 1859 these crusaders convinced the AMA to pass a resolution condemning abortion. Some newspapers, particularly *The New York Times,* joined the antiabortion crusade. Feminists supported the crusade, since they saw abortion as a threat to women's health and part of the oppression of women. Religious leaders, however, by and large avoided the issue of abortion; either they didn't consider it in their province or found it too sticky an issue to discuss. It was the physicians who were the guiding force in the antiabortion crusade. They were instrumental in convincing legislatures to pass state laws, especially between 1866 and 1877, that made abortion a criminal offense.

Why did physicians take the lead in the antiabortion crusade and work so directly to have abortion defined as deviant and illegal? Undoubtedly they believed in the moral "rightness" of their cause. But social historian James Mohr (1978) presents two more subtle and important reasons for the physicians' antiabortion crusading. First, concern was growing among medical people and even among some legislators about the significant drop in birthrates. Many claimed that abortion among married women of the "better classes" was a major contributor to the declining birthrate. These middle- and upper-class men (the physicians and legislators) were aware of the waves of immigrants arriving with large families and were anxious about the decline in production of native American babies. They were deeply afraid they were being betrayed by their own women (Mohr, 1978, p. 169). Implicitly the antiabortion stance was classist and racist; the anxiety was simply that there would not be enough strong, native-born, Protestant stock to save America. This was a persuasive argument in convincing legislators of the need of antiabortion laws.

The second and more direct reason spurring the physicians in the antiabortion crusade was to aid their own nascent professionalization and create a monopoly for regular physicians. . . . The regulars had formed the AMA in 1847 to promote scientific and ethical medicine and combat what they saw as medical quackery. There were, however, no licensing laws to speak of, and many claimed the title "doctor" (e.g., homeopaths, botanical doctors, eclectic physicians). The regular physicians adopted the Hippocratic oath and code of ethics as their standard. Among other things, this oath forbids abortion. Regulars usually did not perform abortions; however, many practitioners of medical sects performed abortions regularly, and some had lucrative practices. Thus for the regular AMA physicians the limitation of abortion became one way of asserting their own professional domination over other medical practitioners. In their crusading these physicians had translated the social goals of cultural and professional dominance into moral and medical language. They lobbied long and hard to convince legislators of the danger and immorality of abortion. By passage of laws making abortion criminal any time during gestation, regular physicians were able to legislate their code of ethics and get the state to employ sanctions against their competitors. This limited these competitors' markets and was a major step toward the regulars' achieving a monopolization of medical practice.

In a relatively short period the antiabortion crusade succeeded in passing legislation that made abortion criminal in every state. A by-product of this was a shift in American public opinion from an indifference to and tolerance of abortion to a hardening of attitudes against what had until then been a fairly common practice. The irony was that abortion as a medical procedure probably was safer at the turn of the 20th century than a century before, but it was defined and seen as more dangerous. By 1900 abortion was not only illegal but deviant and immoral. The physicians' moral crusade had successfully defined abortion as a deviant activity. This definition remained largely unchanged until the 1973 Supreme Court decision, which essentially returned the abortion situation to its pre-1850 condition. . . .

Growth of Medical Expertise and Professional Dominance

Although the general public's dissatisfaction with heroic medicine remained, the image of medicine and what it could accomplish was improving by the middle of the 19th century. There had been a considerable reduction in the incidence and mortality of certain dread diseases. The plague and leprosy had nearly disappeared. Smallpox, malaria, and cholera were less devastating than ever before. These improvements in health engendered optimism and increased people's faith in medical practice. Yet these dramatic "conquests of disease" were by and large *not* the result of new medical knowledge or improved clinical medical practice. Rather, they resulted from changes in social conditions: a rising standard of living, better nutrition and housing, and public health innovations like sanitation. With the lone exception of vaccination for smallpox, the decline of these diseases had nearly nothing to do with clinical medicine (Dubos, 1959; McKeown, 1971). But despite lack of effective treatments, medicine was the beneficiary of much popular credit for improved health.

The regular physicians' image was improved well before they demonstrated any unique effectiveness of practice. The AMA's attacks on irregular medical practice continued. In the 1870s the regulars convinced legislatures to outlaw abortion and in some states to restore licensing laws to restrict medical practice. The AMA was becoming an increasingly powerful and authoritative voice representing regular medical practice.

But the last three decades of the century saw significant "breakthroughs" in medical knowledge and treatment. The scientific medicine of the regular physicians was making new medical advances. Anesthesia and antisepsis made possible great strides in surgical medicine and improvements in hospital care. The bacteriological research of Koch and Pasteur developed the "germ theory of disease," which had important applications in medical practice. It was the accomplishments of surgery and bacteriology that put medicine on a scientific basis (Freidson, 1970a, p. 16). The rise of scientific medicine marked a death knell for medical sectarianism (e.g., the homeopathic physicians eventually joined the regulars). The new laboratory sciences provided a way of testing the theories and practices of various sects, which ultimately led to a single model of medical practice. The well-organized regulars were able to legitimate their form of medical practice and support it with "scientific" evidence.

With the emergence of scientific medicine, a unified paradigm, or model, of medical practice developed. It was based, most fundamentally, on viewing the body as a machine (e.g., organ malfunctioning) and on the germ theory of disease (Kelman, 1977). The "doctrine of specific etiology" became predominant: each disease was caused by a specific germ or agent. Medicine focused solely on the internal environment (the body), largely ignoring the external environment (society) (Dubos, 1959). This paradigm proved fruitful in ensuing years. It is the essence of the "medical model." . . .

The development of scientific medicine accorded regular medicine a convincing advantage in medical practice. It set the stage for the achievement of a medical monopoly by the AMA regulars. As Larson (1977) notes, "Once scientific medicine offered sufficient guarantees of its superior effectiveness in dealing with disease, the state willingly contributed to the creation of a monopoly by means of registration and licensing" (p. 23). The new licensing laws created regular medicine as a *legally enforced monopoly of*

practice (Freidson, 1970b, p. 83). They virtually eliminated medical competition.

The medical monopoly was enhanced further by the Flexner Report on medical education in 1910. Under the auspices of the Carnegie Foundation, medical educator Abraham Flexner visited nearly all 160 existing medical schools in the United States. He found the level of medical education poor and recommended the closing of most schools. Flexner urged stricter state laws, rigid standards for medical education, and more rigorous examinations for certification to practice. The enactment of Flexner's recommendations effectively made all nonscientific types of medicine illegal. It created a near total AMA monopoly of medical education in America.

In securing a monopoly, the AMA regulars achieved a unique professional state. Medicine not only monopolized the market for medical services and the training of physicians, it developed an unparalleled "professional dominance." The medical profession was *functionally autonomous* (Freidson, 1970b). Physicians were insulated from external evaluation and were by and large free to regulate their own performance. Medicine could define its own territory and set its own standards. Thus, Eliot Freidson (1970b) notes, "while the profession may not everywhere be free to control the *terms* of its work, it is free to control the *content* of its work" (p. 84).

The domain of medicine has expanded in the past century. This is due partially to the prestige medicine has accrued and its place as the steward of the "sacred" value of life. Medicine has sometimes been called on to repeat its "miracles" and successful treatments on problems that are not biomedical in nature. Yet in other instances the expansion is due to explicit medical crusading or entrepreneurship. This expansion of medicine, especially into the realm of social problems and human behavior, frequently has taken medicine beyond its proven technical competence (Freidson, 1970b). . . .

The organization of medicine has also expanded and become more complex in this century. In the next section we briefly describe the structure of medical practice in the United States.

Structure of Medical Practice
·················

Before we leave our discussion of the medical profession, it is worthwhile to outline some general features of the structure of medical practice that have contributed to the expansion of medical jurisdiction.

The medical sector of society has grown enormously in the 20th century. It has become the second largest industry in America. There are about 350,000 physicians and over 5 million people employed in the medical field. The "medical industries," including the pharmaceutical, medical technology, and health insurance industries, are among the most profitable in our economy. Yearly drug sales alone are over $4.5 billion. There are more than 7000 hospitals in the United States with 1.5 million beds and 33 million inpatient and 200 million outpatient visits a year (McKinlay, 1976).

The organization of medical practice has changed. Whereas the single physician in "solo practice" was typical in 1900, today physicians are engaged increasingly in large corporate practices or employed by hospitals or other bureaucratic organizations. Medicine in modern society is becoming bureaucratized (Mechanic, 1976). The power in medicine has become diffused, especially since World War II, from the AMA, which represented the individual physician, to include the organizations that represent bureaucratic medicine: the health insurance industry, the medical schools, and the American Hospital Association (Ehrenreich and Ehrenreich, 1970). Using Robert Alford's (1972) conceptualizations, corporate rationalizers have taken much of the power in medicine from the professional monopolists.

Medicine has become both more specialized and more dependent on technology. In 1929 only 25 percent of American physicians were fulltime specialists; by 1969 the proportion had grown to 75 percent (Reiser, 1978). Great advances were made in medicine, and many were directly related to technology: miracle medicines like penicillin, a myriad of psychoactive drugs, heart and brain surgery, the electrocardiograph, CAT scanners, fetal monitors, kidney dialysis machines, artifical organs, and transplant surgery, to name but a few. The hospital has become the primary medical workshop, a center for technological medicine.

Medicine has made a significant economic expansion. In 1940, medicine claimed about 4 percent of the American gross national product (GNP); today it claims about 9 percent, which amounts to more than $150 billion. The causes for this growth are too complex to describe here, but a few factors should be noted. American medicine has always operated on a "fee-for-service" basis, that is, each service rendered is charged and paid for separately. Simply put, in a capitalist medical system, the more services provided, the more fees collected. This not only creates an incentive to provide more services but also to expand these medical services to new markets. The fee-for-service system may encourage unnecessary medical care. There is some evidence, for example, that American medicine performs a considerable amount of "excess" surgery (McCleery and Keelty, 1971); this may also be true for other services. Medicine is one of the few occupations that can create its own demand. Patients may come to physicians, but physicians tell them what procedures they need. The availability of medical technique may also create a demand for itself.

The method by which medical care is paid for has changed greatly in the past half-century. In 1920 nearly all health care was paid for directly by the patient-consumer. Since the 1930s an increasing amount of medical care has been paid for through "third-party" payments, mainly through health insurance and the government. About 75 percent of the American population is covered by some form of medical insurance (often only for hospital care). Since 1966 the government has been involved directly in financing medical care through Medicare and Medicaid. The availability of a large amount of federal money, with nearly no cost controls or regulation of medical practice, has been a major factor fueling our current medical "cost crisis." But the ascendancy of third-party payments has affected the expansion of medicine in another way: more and more human problems become defined as "medical problems" (sickness) because that is the only way insurance programs will "cover" the costs of services. . . .

In sum, the regular physicians developed control of medical practice and a professional dominance with nearly total functional autonomy. Through professionalization and persuasion concerning the superiority of their form of medicine, the medical profession (represented by the AMA) achieved a legally supported monopoly of practice. In short, it cornered the medical market. The medical profession has succeeded in both therapeutic and economic expansion. It has won the almost exclusive right to reign over the kingdom of health and illness, no matter where it may extend.

NOTE

1. We rely on James C. Mohr's (1978) fine historical account of the origins and evolution of American abortion policy for data and much of the interpretation in this section.

REFERENCES

Alford, R. The political economy of health care: dynamics without change. *Politics and Society* 1972 2 (2), 127–64.

Cartwright, F. F. *A Social History of Medicine.* New York: Longman, 1977.

Coe, R. *The Sociology of Medicine.* Second edition. New York: McGraw-Hill, 1978.

Dubos, R. *Mirage of Health.* New York: Harper and Row, 1959.

Ehrenreich, B., and Ehrenreich, J. *The American Health Empire.* New York: Random House, 1970.

Freidson, E. *Profession of Medicine.* New York: Dodd, Mead, 1970a.

Freidson, E. *Professional Dominance.* Chicago: Aldine, 1970b.

Jewson, N. D. The disappearance of the sick-man from medical cosmology, 1770–1870. *Sociology,* 1976, 10, 225–44.

Kelman, S. The social nature of the definition of health. In V. Navarro, *Health and Medical Care in the U.S.* Farmingdale, N.Y.: Baywood, 1977.

Larson, M. S. *The Rise of Professionalism.* Berkeley: California, 1977.

McCleery, R. S., and Keelty, L. T. *One Life-One Physician: An Inquiry into the Medical Profession's Performance in Self-regulation.* Washington, D.C.: Public Affairs Press, 1971.

McKeown, T. A historical appraisal of the medical task. In G. McLachlan and T. McKeown (eds.), *Medical History and Medical Care: A Symposium of Perspectives.* New York: Oxford, 1971.

McKinlay, J. B. The changing political and economic context of the physician-patient encounter. In E. B. Gallagher (ed.), *The Doctor-Patient Relationship in the Changing Health Scene.* Washington, D.C.: U.S. Government Printing Office, 1976.

Mechanic, D. *The Growth of Bureaucratic Medicine.* New York: Wiley, 1976.

Mohr, J. C. *Abortion in America.* New York: Oxford, 1978.

Reiser, S. J. *Medicine and the Reign of Technology.* New York: Cambridge, 1978.

Rothstein, W. G. *American Physicians in the Nineteenth Century: From Sects to Science.* Baltimore: Johns Hopkins, 1972.

Shryock, R. H. *Medicine and Society in America: 1660–1860.* Ithaca, N.Y.: Cornell, 1960.

Starr, P. Medicine, economy and society in nineteenth-century America. *Journal of Social History,* 1977, 10, 588–607.

Wertz, R., and Wertz, D. *Lying-In: A History of Childbirth in America.* New York: Free Press, 1977.

15

Notes on the Decline of Midwives
and the Rise of Medical Obstetricians

• • • • •

Richard W. Wertz and Dorothy C. Wertz

. . . The Americans who were studying medicine in Great Britain [in the late eighteenth century] discovered that men could bring the benefits of the new midwifery to birth and thereby gain income and status. In regard to the unresolved question of what medical arts were appropriate, the Americans took the view of the English physicians, who instructed them that nature was usually adequate and intervention often dangerous. From that perspective they developed a model of the new midwifery suitable for the American situation.

From 1750 to approximately 1810 American doctors conceived of the new midwifery as an enterprise to be shared between themselves and trained midwives. Since doctors during most of that period were few in number, their plan was reasonable and humanitarian and also reflected their belief that, in most cases, natural processes were adequate and the need for skilled intervention limited, though important. Doctors therefore envisaged an arrangement whereby trained midwives would attend normal deliveries and doctors would be called to difficult ones. To implement this plan, Dr. Valentine Seaman established a short course for midwives in the New York (City) Almshouse in 1799, and Dr. William Shippen began a course on anatomy and midwifery, including clinical observation of birth, in Philadelphia. Few women came as students, however, but men did, so the doctors trained the men to be man-midwives, perhaps believing, as Smellie had contended, that the sex of the practitioner was less important than the command of new knowledge and skill.[1]

As late as 1817, Dr. Thomas Ewell of Washington, D.C., a regular physician, proposed to establish a school for midwives, connected with a hospital, similar to the schools that had existed for centuries in the great cities of Europe. Ewell sought federal funding for his enterprise, but it was not forthcoming, and the school was never founded. Herein lay a fundamental difference between European and American development of the midwife. European governments provided financial support for medical education, including the training of midwives. The U.S. government provided no support for medical education in the nineteenth century, and not enough of the women who might have aspired to become midwives could afford the fees to support a school. Those who founded schools turned instead to the potentially lucrative business of training the many men who sought to become doctors.[2]

Doctors also sought to increase the supply of doctors educated in America in the new midwifery and thus saw to it that from the outset of American medical schools midwifery became a specialty field, one all doctors could practice.

The plans of doctors for a shared enterprise with women never developed in America. Doctors were unable to attract women for training, perhaps because women were uninterested in studying what they thought they already knew and, moreover, studying it under the tutelage of men. The restraints of traditional modesty and the tradition of female sufficiency for the management of birth were apparently stronger than the appeal of a rationalized system for a more scientific and, presumably, safer midwifery system.

Not only could doctors not attract women for training in the new science and arts, but they could not even organize midwives already in practice. These women had never been organized among themselves. They thought of themselves as being loyal not primarily to an abstract medical science but to local groups of women and their needs. They reflected the tradition of local self-held empiricism that continued to be very strong in America. Americans had never had a medical profession or medical institutions, so they must have found it hard to understand why the European-trained doctors wished to organize a shared, though hierarchical, midwifery enterprise. How hard it was would be shown later, when doctors sought to organize themselves around the new science of midwifery, in which they had some institutional training. Their practice of midwifery would be governed less by science and professional behavior than by empirical practice and economic opportunity.

In the years after 1810, in fact, the practice of midwifery in American towns took on the same unregulated, open-market character it had in England. Both men and women of various degrees of experience and training competed to attend births. Some trained midwives from England immigrated to America, where they advertised their ability in local newspapers.[3] But these women confronted doctors trained abroad or in the new American medical schools. They also confronted medical empirics who presented themselves as "intrepid" man-midwives after having imbibed the instrumental philosophy from Smellie's books. American women therefore confronted a wide array of talents and skills for aiding their deliveries.

Childbirth in America would not have any neat logic during the nineteenth century, but one feature that distinguished it from childbirth abroad was the gradual disappearance of women from the practice of midwifery. There were many reasons for that unusual development. Most obvious was the severe competition that the new educated doctors and empirics brought to the event of birth, an event that often served as entrance for the medical person to a sustained practice. In addition, doctors lost their allegiance to a conservative view of the science and arts of midwifery under the exigencies of practice; they

came to adopt a view endorsing more extensive interventions in birth and less reliance upon the adequacy of nature. This view led to the conviction that a certain mastery was needed, which women were assumed to be unable to achieve.

Women ceased to be midwives also because of a change in the cultural attitudes about the proper place and activity for women in society. It came to be regarded as unthinkable to confront women with the facts of medicine or to mix men and women in training, even for such an event as birth. As a still largely unscientific enterprise, medicine took on the cultural attributes necessary for it to survive, and the Victorian culture found certain roles unsuitable for women. Midwives also disappeared because they had not been organized and had never developed any leadership. Medicine in America may have had minimal scientific authority, but it was beginning to develop social and professional organization and leadership; unorganized midwives were an easy competitive target for medicine. Finally, midwives lost out to doctors and empirics because of the changing tastes among middle- and upper-class women; for these women, the new midwifery came to have the promise of more safety and even more respectability.[4]

Midwives therefore largely ceased to attend the middle classes in America during the nineteenth century. Except among ethnic immigrants, among poor, isolated whites, and among blacks, there is little significant evidence of midwifery. This is not to say that there were no such women or that in instances on the frontier or even in cities when doctors were unavailable women did not undertake to attend other women. But educated doctors and empirics penetrated American settlements quickly and extensively, eager to gain patients and always ready to attend birth. The very dynamics of American mobility contributed to the break-up of those communities that had sustained the midwives' practices.

Because of continued ethnic immigration, however, by 1900 in many urban areas half of the women were still being delivered by immigrant midwives. The fact that ethnic groups existed largely outside the development of American medicine during the nineteenth century would pose a serious problem in the twentieth century.

Native-born educated women sought to become doctors, not midwives, during the nineteenth century. They did not want to play a role in birth that was regarded as inferior and largely nonmedical—the midwife's role—but wished to assume the same medical role allowed to men.

It is important to emphasize, however, that the disappearance of midwives at middle- and upper-class births was not the result of a conspiracy between male doctors and husbands. The choice of medical attendants was the responsibility of women, upon whom devolved the care of their families' health. Women were free to choose whom they wished. A few did seek out unorthodox practitioners, although most did not. But as the number of midwives diminished, women of course found fewer respectable, trained women of their own class whom they might choose to help in their deliveries.

In order to understand the new midwifery [i.e. medical obstetrics], it is necessary to consider who doctors were and how they entered the medical profession. The doctors who assumed control over middle-class births in America were very differently educated and organized from their counterparts in France or England. The fact that their profession remained loosely organized and ill-defined throughout most of the nineteenth century helps to explain their desire to exclude women from midwifery, for often women were the only category of people that they could effectively exclude. Doctors with some formal education had always faced competition from the medical empirics—men, women, and even freed slaves—who declared themselves able to treat all manner of illnesses and often publicly advertised their successes. These empirics, called quacks by the orthodox educated doctors, offered herbal remedies or psychological comfort to patients. Orthodox physicians objected that the empirics prescribed on an individual, trial-and-error basis without reference to any academic theories about the origins and treatment of disease. Usually the educated physician also treated his patients empirically, for medical theory had little to offer that was practically superior to empiricism until the development of bacteriology in the 1870s. Before then there was no convincing, authoritative, scientific nucleus for medicine, and doctors often had difficulty translating what knowledge they

did have into practical treatment. The fundamental objection of regular doctors was to competition from uneducated practitioners. Most regular doctors also practiced largely ineffective therapies, but they were convinced that their therapies were better than those of the empirics because they were educated men. The uneducated empirics enjoyed considerable popular support during the first half of the nineteenth century because their therapies were as often successful as the therapies of the regulars, and sometimes less strenuous. Like the empirics, educated doctors treated patients rather than diseases and looked for different symptoms in different social classes. Because a doctor's reputation stemmed from the social standing of his patients, there was considerable competition for the patronage of the more respectable families.

The educated, or "regular," doctors around 1800 were of the upper and middle classes, as were the state legislators. The doctors convinced the legislators that medicine, like other gentlemen's professions, should be restricted to those who held diplomas or who had apprenticed with practitioners of the appropriate social class and training. State licensure laws were passed, in response to the Federalist belief that social deference was due to professional men. The early laws were ineffectual because they did not take into account the popular tradition of self-help. People continued to patronize empirics. During the Jacksonian Era even the nonenforced licensing laws were repealed by most states as elitist; popular belief held that the practice of medicine should be "democratic" and open to all, or at least to all men.[5]

In the absence of legal control, several varieties of "doctors" practiced in the nineteenth century. In addition to the empirics and the "regular" doctors there were the sectarians, who included the Thomsonian Botanists, the Homeopaths, the Eclectics, and a number of minor sects of which the most important for obstectrics were the Hydrotherapists.

The regular doctors can be roughly divided into two groups: the elite, who had attended the better medical schools and who wrote the textbooks urging "conservative" practice in midwifery; and the great number of poorly educated men who had spent a few months at a proprietary medical school from which they were graduated with no practical or clinical knowledge. (Proprietary medical schools were profit-making schools owned by several local doctors who also taught there. Usually such schools had no equipment or resources for teaching.) In the eighteenth century the elite had had to travel to London, or more often Edinburgh, for training. In 1765, however, the Medical College of Philadelphia was founded, followed by King's College (later Columbia) Medical School in 1767 and Harvard in 1782. Obstetrics, or "midwifery," as it was then called, was the first medical specialty in those schools, preceding even surgery, for it was assumed that midwifery was the keystone to medical practice, something that every student would do after graduation as part of his practice. Every medical school founded thereafter had a special "Professor of Midwifery." Among the first such professors were Drs. William Shippen at Philadelphia, Samuel Bard at King's College, and Walter Channing at Harvard. In the better schools early medical courses lasted two years; in the latter half of the nineteenth century some schools began to increase this to three, but many two-year medical graduates were still practicing in 1900.

A prestigious medical education did not guarantee that a new graduate was prepared to deal with patients. Dr. James Marion Sims, a famous nineteenth-century surgeon, stated that his education at Philadelphia's Jefferson Medical College, considered one of the best in the country in 1835, left him fitted for nothing and without the slightest notion of how to treat his first cases.[6] In 1850 a graduate of the University of Buffalo described his total ignorance on approaching his first obstetrical case:

> I was left alone with a poor Irish woman and one crony, to deliver her child ... and I thought it necessary to call before me every circumstance I had learned from books—I must examine, and I did—But whether it was head or breech, hand or foot, man or monkey, that was defended from my uninstructed finger by the distended membranes, I was as uncomfortably ignorant, with all my learning, as the foetus itself that was making all this fuss.[7]

Fortunately the baby arrived naturally, the doctor was given great praise for his part in the event, and he wrote that he was glad "to have escaped the commission of murder."

If graduates of the better medical schools made such complaints, those who attended the smaller schools could only have been more ignorant. In 1818 Dr. John Stearns, President of the New York Medical Society, complained, "With a few honorable exceptions in each city, the practitioners are ignorant, degraded, and contemptible."[8] The American Medical Association later estimated that between 1765 and 1905 more than eight hundred medical schools were founded, most of them proprietary, money-making schools, and many were short-lived. In 1905 some 160 were still in operation. Neither the profession nor the states effectively regulated those schools until the appearance of the Flexner Report, a professional self-study published in 1910. The report led to tougher state laws and the setting of standards for medical education. Throughout much of the nineteenth century a doctor could obtain a diploma and begin practice with as little as four months' attendance at a school that might have no laboratories, no dissections, and no clinical training. Not only was it easy to become a doctor, but the profession, with the exception of the elite who attended elite patients, had low standing in the eyes of most people.[9] ...

... Nineteenth-century women could choose among a variety of therapies and practitioners. Their choice was usually dictated by social class. An upper-class woman in an Eastern city would see either an elite regular physician or a homeopath; if she were daring, she might visit a hydropathic establishment. A poor woman in the Midwest might turn to an empiric, a poorly-educated regular doctor, or a Thomsonian botanist. This variety of choice distressed regular doctors, who were fighting for professional and economic exclusivity. As long as doctors were organized only on a local basis, it was impossible to exclude irregulars from practice or even to set enforceable standards for regular practice. The American Medical Association was founded in 1848 for those purposes. Not until the end of the century, however, was organized medicine able to re-establish licensing laws. The effort succeeded only because the regulars finally accepted the homeopaths, who were of the same social class, in order to form a sufficient majority to convince state legislators that licensing was desirable.

Having finally won control of the market, doctors were able to turn to self-regulation, an ideal adopted by the American Medical Association in 1860 but not put into effective practice until after 1900. Although there had been progress in medical science and in the education of the elite and the specialists during the nineteenth century, the average doctor was still woefully undereducated. The Flexner Report in 1910 revealed that 90 percent of doctors were then without a college education and that most had attended substandard medical schools.[10] Only after its publication did the profession impose educational requirements on the bulk of medical practitioners and take steps to accredit medical schools and close down diploma mills. Until then the average doctor had little sense of what his limits were or to whom he was responsible, for there was often no defined community of professionals and usually no community of patients.

Because of the ill-defined nature of the medical profession in the nineteenth century and the poor quality of medical education, doctors' insistence on the exclusion of women as economically dangerous competitors is quite understandable. As a group, nineteenth-century doctors were not affluent, and even their staunchest critics admitted that they could have made more money in business. Midwifery itself paid less than other types of practice, for many doctors spent long hours in attending laboring women and later had trouble collecting their fees. Yet midwifery was a guaranteed income, even if small, and it opened the way to family practice and sometimes to consultations involving many doctors and shared fees. The family and female friends who had seen a doctor "perform" successfully were likely to call him again. Doctors worried that, if midwives were allowed to deliver the upper classes, women would turn to them for treatment of other illnesses and male doctors would lose half their clientele. As a prominent Boston doctor wrote in 1820, "If female midwifery is again introduced among the rich and influential, it will become fashionable and it will be considered indelicate to employ a physician."[11] Doctors had to eliminate midwives in order to protect the gateway to their whole practice.

They had to mount an attack on midwives, because midwives had their defenders, who argued that women were safer and more modest than the new man-midwives. For example, the *Virginia Gazette* in 1772 carried a "LETTER on the present State of MIDWIFERY," emphasizing the old idea that "Labour is Nature's Work" and needs no more art than women's experience teaches, and that it was safer when women alone attended births.

> It is a notorious fact that more Children have been lost since Women were so scandalously indecent as to employ Men than for Ages before that Practice became so general. . . . [Women midwives] never dream of having recourse to Force; the barbarous, bloody Crochet, never stained their Hands with Murder. . . . A long unimpassioned Practice, early commenced, and calmly pursued is absolutely requisite to give Men by Art, what Women attain by Nature.

The writer concluded with the statement that men-midwives also took liberties with pregnant and laboring women that were "sufficient to taint the Purity, and sully the Chastity, of any Woman breathing." The final flourish, "True Modesty is incompatible with the Idea of employing a MAN-MIDWIFE," would echo for decades, causing great distress for female patients with male attendants. Defenders of midwives made similar statements throughout the first half of the nineteenth century. Most were sectarian doctors or laymen with an interest in women's modesty.[12] No midwives came forward to defend themselves in print.

The doctors' answer to midwives' defenders was expressed not in terms of pecuniary motives but in terms of safety and the proper place of women. After 1800 doctors' writings implied that women who presumed to supervise births had overreached their proper position in life. One of the earliest American birth manuals, the *Married Lady's Companion and Poor Man's Friend* (1808), denounced the ignorance of midwives and urged them to "submit to their station."[13]

Two new convictions about women were at the heart of the doctors' opposition to midwives: that women were unsafe to attend deliveries and that no "true" woman would want to gain the knowledge and skills necessary to do so. An anonymous pamphlet, published in 1820 in Boston, set forth these convictions along with other reasons for excluding midwives from practice. The author, thought to have been either Dr. Walter Channing or Dr. Henry Ware, another leading obstetrician, granted that women had more "passive fortitude" than men in enduring and witnessing suffering but asserted that women lacked the power to act that was essential to being a birth attendant:

> They have not that power of action, or that active power of mind, which is essential to the practice of a surgeon. They have less power of restraining and governing the natural tendencies to sympathy and are more disposed to yield to the expressions of acute sensibility . . . where they become the principal agents, the feelings of sympathy are too powerful for the cool exercise of judgment.[14]

The author believed only men capable of the attitude of detached concern needed to concentrate on the techniques required in birth. It is not surprising to find the author stressing the importance of interventions, but his undervaluing of sympathy, which in most normal deliveries was the only symptomatic treatment necessary, is rather startling. Clearly, he hoped to exaggerate the need for coolness in order to discountenance the belief of many women and doctors that midwives could safely attend normal deliveries.

The author possibly had something more delicate in mind that he found hard to express. He perhaps meant to imply that women were unsuited because there were certain times when they were "disposed to yield to the expressions of acute sensibility." Doctors quite commonly believed that during menstruation women's limited bodily energy was diverted from the brain, rendering them, as doctors phrased it, idiotic. In later years another Boston doctor, Horatio Storer, explained why he thought women unfit to become surgeons. He granted that exceptional women had the necessary courage, tact, ability, money, education, and patience for the career but argued that, because the "periodical infirmity of their sex . . . in every case . . . unfits them for any responsible effort of mind," he had to oppose them. During their "condition," he said, "neither life nor limb submitted to them would be as safe as at other times," for the condition was a "temporary insanity," a time when women were "more prone than men to commit any unusual or outrageous act."[15]

The author of the anonymous pamphlet declared that a female would find herself at times (i.e., during menstruation) totally unable to manage birth emergencies, such as hemorrhages, convulsions, manual extraction of the placenta, or inversion of the womb, when the newly delivered organ externally turned itself inside out and extruded from the body, sometimes hanging to the knees. In fact, an English midwife, Sarah Stone, had described in 1737 how she personally had handled each of these emergencies successfully. But the author's readers did not know that, and the author himself could have dismissed Stone's skill as fortuitous, exercised in times of mental clarity.[16]

The anonymous author was also convinced that no woman could be trained in the knowledge and skill of midwifery without losing her standing as a lady. In the dissecting room and in the hospital a woman would forfeit her "delicate feelings" and "refined sensibility"; she would see things that would taint her moral character. Such a woman would "unsex" herself, by which the doctors meant not only that she would lose her standing as a "lady" but also, literally, that she would be subject to physical exertions and nervous excitements that would damage her female organs irreparably and prevent her from fulfilling her social role as wife and mother.[17]. . .

. . . The exclusion of women from obstetrical cooperation with men had important effects upon the "new practice" that was to become the dominant tradition in American medical schools. American obstetric education differed significantly from training given in France, where the principal maternity hospitals trained doctors clinically alongside student midwives. Often the hospital's midwives, who supervised all normal births, trained the doctors in normal deliveries. French doctors never lost touch with the conservative tradition that said "Dame Nature is the best midwife." In America, where midwives were not trained at all and medical education was sexually segregated, medicine turned away from the conservative tradition and became more interventionist.

Around 1810 the new midwifery in America appears to have entered a new phase, one that shaped its character and problems throughout the century. Doctors continued to regard birth as a fundamentally natural process, usually sufficient by itself to effect delivery without artful assistance, and understandable mechanistically. But this view conflicted with the exigencies of their medical practice, which called upon them to demonstrate skills. Gradually, more births seemed to require aid.

Young doctors rarely had any clinical training in what the theory of birth meant in practice. Many arrived at birth with only lectures and book learning to guide them. If they (and the laboring patient) were fortunate, they had an older, experienced doctor or attending woman to explain what was natural and what was not. Many young men were less lucky and were embarrassed, confused, and frightened by the appearances of labor and birth. Lacking clinical training, each had to develop his own sense of what each birth required, if anything, in the way of artful assistance; each had to learn the consequence of misdirected aids.[18]

If the doctor was in a hurry to reach another patient, he might be tempted to hasten the process along by using instruments or other expedients. If the laboring woman or her female attendants urged him to assist labor, he might feel compelled to use his tools and skills even though he knew that nature was adequate but slow. He had to use his arts because he was expected to "perform." Walter Channing, Professor of Midwifery at Harvard Medical School in the early nineteenth century, remarked about the doctor, in the context of discussing a case in which forceps were used unnecessarily, that he "must do something. He cannot remain a spectator merely, where there are too many witnesses and where interest in what is going on is too deep to allow of his inaction." Channing was saying that, even though well-educated physicians recognized that natural processes were sufficient and that instruments could be dangerous, in their practice they also had to appear to *do* something for their patient's symptoms, whether that entailed giving a drug to alleviate pain or shortening labor by using the forceps. The doctor could not appear to be indifferent or inattentive or useless. He had to establish his identity by doing something, preferably something to make the patient feel better. And if witnesses were present there was perhaps even more reason to "perform." Channing concluded: "Let him be collected and calm, and he will probably do little he will afterwards look upon and regret."[19]

If educated physicians found it difficult in practice to appeal before their patients to the reliability of nature and the dangers of instruments, one can imagine what less confident and less competent doctors did with instruments in order to appear useful. A number of horror stories from the early decades of the century have been retailed by men and women who believed that doctors used their instruments unfairly and incompetently to drive midwives from practice.[20] Whatever the truth may be about the harm done, it is easy to believe that instruments were used regularly by doctors to establish their superior status.

If doctors believed that they had to perform in order to appear useful and to win approval, it is very likely that women, on the other hand, began to expect that more might go wrong with birth processes than they had previously believed. In the context of social childbirth, which . . . meant that women friends and kin were present at delivery, the appearance of forceps in one birth established the possibility of their being used in subsequent births. In short, women may have come to anticipate difficult births whether or not doctors urged that possibility as a means of selling themselves. Having seen the "best," perhaps each woman wanted the "best" for her delivery, whether she needed it or not.

Strange as it may sound, women may in fact have been choosing male attendants because they wanted a guaranteed performance, in the sense of both guaranteed safety and guaranteed fashionableness. Choosing the best medical care is itself a kind of fashion. But in addition women may have wanted a guaranteed audience, the male attendant, for quite specific purposes; namely, they may have wanted a representative male to see their pain and suffering in order that their femininity might be established and their pain verified before men. Women, then, could have had a range of important reasons for choosing male doctors to perform: for themselves, safety;

for the company of women, fashion; for the world of men, femininity.

So a curious inconsistency arose between the principle of noninterference in nature and the exigencies of professional practice. Teachers of midwifery continued to stress the adequacy of nature and the danger of instruments. Samuel Bard, Dean of King's College Medical School, wrote a text on midwifery in 1807 in which he refused even to discuss forceps because he believed that interventions by unskilled men, usually inspired by Smellie's writings, were more dangerous than the most desperate case left to nature. Bard's successors made the same points in the 1830s and 1840s. Dr. Chandler Gilman, Professor of Obstetrics at the College of Physicians and Surgeons in New York from 1841 to 1865, taught his students that "Dame Nature is the best midwife in the world. . . . Meddlesome midwifery is fraught with evil. . . . The less done generally the better, Non-interference is the cornerstone of midwifery."[21] This instruction often went unheeded, however, because young doctors often resorted to instruments in haste or in confusion, or because they were poorly trained and unsupervised in practice, but also, as we have indicated, because physicians, whatever their state of knowledge, were expected to do something.

What they could do—the number of techniques to aid and control natural processes—gradually increased. In 1808, for example, Dr. John Stearns of upper New York State learned from an immigrant German midwife of a new means to effect the mechanics of birth. This was ergot, a powerful natural drug that stimulates uterine muscles when given orally. Ergot is a fungus that grows on rye and other stored grains. It causes powerful and unremitting contractions. Stearns stressed its value in saving the doctor's time and in relieving the distress and agony of long labor. Ergot also quickens the expulsion of the placenta and stems hemorrhage by compelling the uterus to contract. Stearns claimed that ergot had no ill effects but warned that it should be given only after the fetus was positioned for easy delivery, for it induced an incessant action that left no time to turn a child in the birth canal or uterus.

There was in fact no antidote to ergot's rapid and uncontrollable effects until anesthesia became available in later decades. So if the fetus did not move as expected, the drug could cause the uterus to mold itself around the child, rupturing the uterus and killing the child. Ergot, like most new medical arts for birth, was a mix of danger and benefit. Critics of meddlesome doctors said that they often used it simply to save time. However true that was, ergot certainly fitted the mechanistic view of birth, posed a dilemma to doctors about wise use, and enlarged the doctors' range of arts for controlling birth. Doctors eventually determined that using ergot to induce labor without an antidote was too dangerous and limited its use to expelling the placenta or stopping hemorrhage.[22]

Despite the theory of the naturalness of birth and the danger of intervention, the movement in midwifery was in the opposite direction, to less reliance on nature and more reliance on artful intervention. The shift appeared during the 1820s in discussions as to what doctors should call themselves when they practiced the new midwifery. "Male-midwife," "midman," "man-midwife," "physician man-midwife," and even "androboethogynist" were terms too clumsy, too reminiscent of the female title, or too unreflective of the new science and skill. "Accoucheur" sounded better but was French. The doctors of course ignored Elizabeth Nihell's earlier, acid suggestion that they call themselves "pudendists" after the area of the body that so interested them. Then an English doctor suggested in 1828 that "obstetrician" was as appropriate a term as any. Coming from the Latin meaning "to stand before," it had the advantage of sounding like other honorable professions, such as "electrician" or "geometrician," in which men variously understood and dominated nature.[23]

The renaming of the practice of midwifery symbolized doctors' new sense of themselves as professional actors. In fact, the movement toward greater dominance over birth's natural processes cannot be understood unless midwifery is seen in the context of general medical practice. In that perspective, several relations between midwifery and general practice become clearly important. In the first place, midwifery continued during the first half of the nineteenth century to be one of the few areas of general practice where doctors had a scientific understanding and useful medical arts. That meant that practicing midwifery was central to doctors' attempts to build a practice, earn fees, and achieve some status, for birth was one physical condition they were confident they knew how to treat. And they were successful in the great majority of cases because birth itself was usually successful. Treating birth was without the risk of treating many other conditions, but doctors got the credit nonetheless.

In the second place, however, birth was simply one condition among many that doctors treated, and the therapeutic approach they took to other conditions tended to spill over into their treatment of birth. For most physical conditions of illness doctors did not know what processes of nature were at work. They tended therefore to treat the patient and the patient's symptoms rather than the processes of disease, which they did not see and were usually not looking for. By treating his or her symptoms the doctors did something for the patient and thereby gained approbation. The doctors' status came from pleasing the patients rather than from curing diseases. That was a risky endeavor, for sometimes patients judged the treatment offered to relieve symptoms to be worthless or even more disabling than the symptoms themselves. But patients expected doctors to do something for them, an expectation that carried into birth also. So neither doctors nor patients were inclined to allow the natural processes of birth to suffice.

There is no need to try to explain this contradiction by saying that doctors were ignorant, greedy, clumsy, hasty, or salacious in using medical arts unnecessarily (although some may have been), for the contradiction reflects primarily the kind of therapy that was dominant in prescientific medicine.

The relations between midwifery and general medical practice become clearer if one considers what doctors did when they confronted a birth that did not conform to their understanding of birth's natural processes. Their mechanistic view could not explain such symptoms as convulsions or high fevers, occasionally associated with birth. Yet doctors did not walk away from such conditions as being mysterious or untreatable, for they were committed to the mastery of birth. Rather, they treated the strange symptoms with general therapies just as they might treat regular symptoms of birth with medical arts such as forceps and ergot.

Bloodletting was a popular therapy for many symptoms, and doctors often applied it to births that seemed unusual to them. If a pregnant woman seemed to be florid or perspiring, the doctor might place her in a chair, open a vein in her arm, and allow her to bleed until she fainted. Some doctors bled women to unconsciousness to counter delivery pains. A doctor in 1851 opened the temporal arteries of a woman who was having convulsions during birth, "determined to bleed her until the convulsion ceased or as long as the blood would flow." He found it impossible to catch the blood thrown about during her convulsions, but the woman eventually completed her delivery successfully and survived. Bloodletting was also initiated when a woman developed high fever after delivery. Salmon P. Chase, Lincoln's Secretary of the Treasury and later Chief Justice, told in his diary how a group of doctors took 50 ounces of blood from his wife to relieve her fever. The doctors gave careful attention to the strength and frequency of her pulse, debating and deliberating upon the meaning of the symptom, until finally Mrs. Chase died.[24]

For localized pain, doctors applied leeches to draw out blood from the affected region. A distended abdomen after delivery might merit the application of twelve leeches; a headache, six on the temple; vaginal pain also merited several.[25]

Another popular therapy was calomel, a chloride of mercury that irritated the intestine and purged it. A woman suffering puerperal fever might be given extended doses to reduce swelling by purging her bodily contents. If the calomel acted too violently, the doctors could retard it by administering opium. Doctors often gave emetics to induce vomiting when expectant women had convulsions, for they speculated that emetics might be specifics for hysteria or other nervous diseases causing convulsions.

An expectant or laboring woman showing unusual symptoms might be subjected to a battery of such agents as doctors sought to restore her symptoms to a normal balance. In a famous case in Boston in 1833 a woman had convulsions a month before her expected delivery. The doctors bled her of 8 ounces and gave her a purgative. The next day she again had convulsions, and they took 22 ounces of blood. After 90 minutes she had a headache, and the doctors took 18 more ounces of blood, gave emetics to cause vomiting, and put ice on her head and mustard plasters on her feet. Nearly four hours later she had another convulsion, and they took 12 ounces, and soon after, 6 more. By then she had lapsed into a deep coma, so the doctors doused her with cold water but could not revive her. Soon her cervix began to dilate, so the doctors gave ergot to induce labor. Shortly before delivery she convulsed again, and they applied ice and mustard plasters again and also gave a vomiting agent and calomel to purge her bowels. In six hours she delivered a stillborn child. After two days she regained consciousness and recovered. The doctors considered this a conservative treatment, even though they had removed two-fifths of her blood in a two-day period, for they had not artificially dilated her womb or used instruments to expedite delivery.[26]

Symptomatic treatment was intended not simply to make the patient feel better—often the treatment was quite violent, or "heroic"—but to restore some balance of healthy appearances. Nor were the therapies given to ailing women more intrusive or different from therapies given to suffering men. The therapies were not, in most instances, forced upon the patients without their foreknowledge or consent. People were often eager to be made healthy and willing to endure strenuous therapies to this end. Doctors did believe, however, that some groups of people were more susceptible to illness than others and that different groups also required, or deserved, different treatments.

These views reflected in large part the doctors' awareness of cultural classifications of people; in other words, the culture's position on the relative social worth of different social classes influenced doctors' views about whose health was likely to be endangered, how their endangered health affected the whole society, and what treatments, if any, were suitable. For birth this meant, for example, that doctors believed it more important for them to attend the delivery of children by middle- and upper-class women than the delivery of children by the poor. It meant that doctors expected "fashionable" women to suffer more

difficult deliveries because their tight clothing, rich diet and lack of exercise were unhealthy and because they were believed to be more susceptible to nervous strain. It also meant that doctors thought it fitting for unmarried and otherwise disreputable mothers not to receive charitable care along with other poor but respectable women.

There is abundant evidence that doctors came to believe in time that middle- and upper-class women typically had more difficult deliveries than, for example, farm women. One cannot find an objective measure of the accuracy of their perception, nor, unfortunately and more to the point, can one find whether their perception that some women were having more difficult deliveries led doctors consistently to use more intervention in attending them than in attending poorer women with normal deliveries. Doctors' perception of the relative difficulty of deliveries was part of their tendency to associate different kinds of sickness with different social classes. They expected to find the symptoms of certain illnesses in certain groups of people, and therefore looked for those particular symptoms or conditions. In the nineteenth century upper-class urban women were generally expected to be sensitive and delicate, while farm women were expected to be robust. Some doctors even believed that the evolutionary result of education was to produce smaller pelves in women and larger heads in babies, leading to more difficult births among civilized women. There is no evidence that these beliefs were medically accurate. Whether a doctor considered a patient "sick" or "healthy" depended in part upon class-related standards of health and illness rather than on objective scientific standards of sickness.

Treatment probably varied according to the doctor's perception of a woman's class and individual character. At some times and places the treatment given probably reflected the patient's class as much as her symptoms. Thus some doctors may have withheld the use of instruments from their upper-class patients in the belief that they were too fragile to undergo instrumental delivery. The same doctors may have used instruments needlessly on poor patients, who were considered healthy enough to stand anything, in order to save the doctor's time and permit him to rush off to the bedside of a wealthier patient. On the other hand, some doctors may have used instruments on the upper-class women in order to shorten labor, believing that they could not endure prolonged pain or were too weak to bring forth children unassisted, and also in order to justify higher fees. The same doctors may have withheld forceps from poor, women whom they considered healthy enough to stand several days of labor. Unfortunately, there is no way of knowing exactly how treatments differed according to class, for very few doctors kept records of their private patients. The records now extant are for the small number of people, perhaps 5 percent of the population, who were treated in hospitals in the nineteenth century. Only poor women, most unmarried, delivered in hospitals, so the records do not cover a cross-section of classes. These hospital records do indicate a large number of instrumental deliveries and sometimes give the reasons as the patient's own "laziness" or "stupidity" in being unable to finish a birth. It is likely that doctors' expectations of lower-class performance are reflected here. Hospital records also reflect the use of poor patients for training or experimentation, another reason for a high incidence of instrumental deliveries.

The fact that doctors' tendency to classify patients according to susceptibility did not lead to consistent differences in treatment is an important indication that they were not merely slavish adherents to a mechanistic view of nature or to cultural and class interests. Doctors were still treating individual women, not machines and not social types. The possibility of stereotypical classification and treatment, however, remained a lively threat to more subtle discernments of individual symptoms and to truly artful applications of treatment in birth.

At the same time, it was possible that patients would find even unbiased treatments offensively painful, ineffective, and expensive, or would doubt that the doctor had a scientific reason for giving them. Such persons could seek other treatments, often administered by laypeople or by themselves. Yet those treatments, including treatments for birth, were also directed toward symptoms. At a time when diseases were unrecognized and their causes unknown, the test of

therapy was the patient's whole response, not the curing of disease. So patients who resented treatments as painful, ineffective, or officious rejected the doctor and the treatments. A woman who gave birth in Ohio in 1846 recalled that the doctor bled her and then gave her ergot even though the birth was proceeding, in her view, quite normally. She thought he was simply drunk and in a hurry and angrily judged him a "bad man."[27]

The takeover of birth by male doctors in America was an unusual phenomenon in comparison to France and England, where traditional midwifery continued as a much more significant part of birth. Practice developed differently in America because the society itself expanded more rapidly and the medical profession grew more quickly to doctor in ever new communities. American mobility left fewer stable communities than in France or England, and thus networks of women to support midwives were more often broken. The standards of the American medical profession were not so high or so strictly enforced as standards in other countries, and thus there were both more "educated" doctors and more self-proclaimed doctors in America to compete with midwives. So American midwives disappeared from view because they had less support from the stable communities of women and more competition from male doctors.

The exclusion of women from midwifery and obstetrics had profound effects upon practice. Most obviously, it gave obstetrics a sexist bias; maleness became a necessary attribute of safety, and femaleness became a condition in need of male medical control. Within this skewed view of ability and need, doctors found it nearly impossible to gain an objective view of what nature could do and what art should do, for one was identified with being a woman and the other with being a man.

The bias identified functions, attributes, and prerogatives, which unfortunately could become compulsions, so that doctors as men may have often felt that they had to impose their form upon the processes of nature in birth. Obstetrics acquired a basic distortion in its orientation toward nature, a confusion of the need to be masterful and even male with the need for intervention.

Samuel Bard, one of the few doctors to oppose the trend, remarked that the young doctor, too often lacking the ability to discriminate about natural processes, often became alarmed for his patient's safety and his own reputation, leading him to seek a speedy instrumental delivery for both. A tragedy could follow, compounded because the doctor might not even recognize that he had erred and might not, therefore, learn to correct his practice. But doctors may also have found the "indications" for intervention in their professional work—to hurry, to impress, to win approval, and to show why men rather than women should attend births.

The thrust for male control of birth probably expressed psychosexual needs of men, although there is no basis for discussing this historically. The doctor appears to history more as a ritualistic figure, a representative man, identifying and enforcing sexual roles in critical life experiences. He also provided, as a representative scientist, important rationalizations for these roles, particularly why women should be content to be wives and mothers, and, as a representative of dominant cultural morality, determined the classifications of women who deserved various kinds of treatment. Thus the doctor could bring to the event of birth many prerogatives that had little to do with aiding natural processes, but which he believed were essential to a healthy and safe birth.

Expectant and laboring women lost a great deal from the exclusion of educated female birth attendants, although, of course, they would not have chosen men if they had not believed men had more to offer, at least in the beginning decades of the century. Eventually there were only men to choose. Although no doubt doctors were often sympathetic, they could never have the same point of view as a woman who had herself borne a child and who might be more patient and discerning about birth processes. And female attendants would not, of course, have laid on the male prerogatives of physical and moral control of birth. . . .

REFERENCES

1. Valentine Seaman, *The Midwives' Monitor and Mother's Mirror* (New York, 1800); Lewis Scheffey, "The Early History and the Transition Period of Obstetrics and Gynecology in Philadelphia," *Annals of Medical History*, Third Series, 2 (May, 1940), 215–224.
2. John B. Blake, "Women and Medicine in Ante-Bellum America," *Bulletin of the History of Medicine* 34, No. 2 (March-April 1965): 108–109; see also Dr. Thomas Ewell, *Letters to Ladies* (Philadelphia, 1817) pp. 21–31.
3. Julia C. Spruill, *Women's Life and Work in the Southern Colonies* (New York: Norton, 1972), pp. 272–274; Jane Bauer Donegan, "Midwifery in America, 1760–1860: A Study in Medicine and Morality." Unpublished Ph.D. dissertation, Syracuse University, 1972, pp. 50–52.
4. Alice Morse Earle (ed.), *Diary of Anna Green Winslow, a Boston Schoolgirl of 1771* (Detroit: Singing Tree Press, 1970), p. 12 and n. 24.
5. William G. Rothstein, *American Physicians in the Nineteenth Century: From Sects to Science* (Baltimore: Johns Hopkins Press, 1970), pp. 47–49.
6. J. Marion Sims, *The Story of My Life* (New York, 1888), pp. 138–146.
7. *Buffalo Medical Journal* 6 (September, 1850): 250–251.
8. John Stearns, "Presidential Address," *Transactions of the New York State Medical Society* 1:139.
9. Sims, *Story of My Life*, pp. 115–116.
10. Abraham Flexner, *Medical Education in the United States and Canada: A Report to the Carnegie Foundation for the Advancement of Teaching* (New York, 1910).
11. Anonymous, *Remarks on the Employment of Females as Practitioners in Midwifery*, 1820, pp. 4–6. See also Samuel Gregory, *Man-Midwifery Exposed and Corrected* (Boston, 1848) pp. 13, 49; Donegan, "Midwifery in America," pp. 73–74, 240; Thomas Hersey, *The Midwife's Practical Directory; or, Woman's Confidential Friend* (Baltimore, 1836), p. 221; Charles Rosenberg, "The Practice of Medicine in New York a Century Ago," *Bulletin of the History of Medicine* 41 (1967):223–253.
12. Spruill, *Women's Life and Work*, p. 275; Gregory, *Man-Midwifery Exposed*, pp. 13, 28, 36.
13. Samuel K. Jennings, *The Married Lady's Companion and Poor Man's Friend* (New York, 1808), p. 105.
14. Anonymous, *Remarks*, p. 12.
15. Horatio Storer, M.D., *Criminal Abortion* (Boston, 1868), pp. 100–101n.
16. Sarah Stone, *A Complete Practice of Midwifery* (London, 1737).
17. Anonymous, *Remarks*, p. 7.
18. Harold Speert, M.D., *The Sloane Hospital Chroni-*

cle (Philadelphia: Davis, 1963), pp. 17–19; Donegan, "Midwifery in America," p. 218.

19. Walter Channing, M.D., *A Treatise on Etherization in Childbirth, Illustrated by 581 Cases* (Boston, 1848), p. 229.

20. Gregory, *Man-Midwifery Exposed,* pp. 13, 28, 36; Hersey, *Midwife's Practical Directory,* p. 220; Wooster Beach, *An Improved System of Midwifery Adapted to the Reformed Practice of Medicine . . .* (New York, 1851), p. 115.

21. Speert, *Sloane Hospital Chronicle,* pp. 31–33, 77–78.

22. Palmer Findlay, *Priests of Lucina: The Story of Obstetrics* (Boston, 1939), pp. 220–221.

23. Elizabeth Nihell, *A Treatise on Art of Midwifery: Setting Forth Various Abuses Therein, Especially as to the Practice with Instruments* (London, 1760), p. 325; Nicholson J. Eastmen and Louis M. Hellman, *Williams Obstetrics,* 13th Ed. (New York: Appleton-Century-Crofts, 1966), p. 1.

24. Rothstein, *American Physicians,* pp. 47–49.

25. *Loc. cit.*

26. Frederick C. Irving, *Safe Deliverance* (Boston, 1942), pp. 221–225.

27. Harriet Connor Brown, *Grandmother Brown's Hundred Years, 1827–1927* (Boston, 1929), p. 93.

16

Corporatization and the Social Transformation of Doctoring

▪ ▪ ▪ ▪ ▪ ▪

John B. McKinlay and John D. Stoeckle

We are witnessing a transformation of the health care systems of developed countries that is without parallel in modern times (1, 2). This dramatic change has implications for patients and, without exception, affects the entire division of labor in health care. What are some of these changes and how are they manifesting themselves with respect to doctoring?

The Changes

Over the last few years especially, many multinational corporations, with highly diverse activities, have become involved in all facets of the generally profitable business of medical care, from medical manufacturing and the ownership of treatment institutions to the financing and purchase of services in preferred provider organizations and health maintenance organizations (HMOs) (3, 4). Conglomerates such as General Electric, AT&T, and IBM, among many others, now have large medical manufacturing enterprises within their corporate divisions. Aerospace companies are involved in everything from computerized medical information systems to life support systems. Even tobacco companies and transportation enterprises have moved into the medical arena. In addition to this industrial or manufacturing capital, even larger financial capital institutions (e.g., commerical banks, life insurance companies, mutual and pension funds, and diversified financial organizations) are also stepping up their involvement in medical care and experiencing phenomenal success (5, 6).

Besides corporate investments in health care,

corporate mergers of treatment organizations and industrial corporations are also taking place. Privately owned hospital chains, controlled by larger corporations, evidence continuing rapid growth. Much of this growth comes from buying up local, municipal, and voluntary community hospitals, many of which were "going under" as a result of cutbacks in government programs and regulations on hospital use and payment. By 1990, about 30 percent of general hospital beds will be managed by investor hospital chains (5, 7–9). Because the purpose of an investor-owned organization is to make money, there is understandable concern over the willingness of such organizations to provide care to the 35 million people who lack adequate insurance coverage and who are not eligible for public programs (10–15).

Responses

Regulations

Confronted with an ever deepening fiscal crisis, the state continues to cast around for regulatory solutions—one of the latest of which is diagnosis related groups (DRGs) for Medicare patients, which reimburse hospitals by diagnosis and with rates determined by government. If the actual cost of treatment is less than the allowable payment, then the hospital makes a profit; if treatment costs are more, then the hospital faces a loss, even bankruptcy, especially since an average of 40 percent of hospital revenues come from Medicare patients. This probably ineffective measure follows many well-documented policy failures (e.g., Professional Standards Review Organizations), and its consequences for the health professions are profound. These regulatory efforts, corporate mergers, investor-owned hospital chains, federally mandated cost-containment measures, among many other changes, are transforming the shape, content, and even the moral basis of health care (16–19). How are these institutional changes affecting the everyday work of the doctor?

New Management

By all accounts, hospitals are being managed by a new breed of physician administrators (20–22),

whom Alford aptly terms "corporate rationalizers" (23). While some have medical qualifications, most are trained in the field of hospital administration, which emphasizes, among other things, rationalization, productivity, and cost efficiency. Doctors used to occupy a privileged position at the top of the medical hierarchy. Displaced by administrators, doctors have slipped down to the position of middle management where their prerogatives are also challenged or encroached upon by other health workers. Clearly, managerial imperatives often compete or conflict with physicians' usual mode of practice. Increasingly, it seems, administrators, while permitting medical staff to retain ever narrower control of technical aspects of care, are organizing the necessary coordination for collaborative work, the work schedules of staff, the recruitment of patients to the practice, and the contacts with third-party purchasers, and are determining the fiscal rewards.

Some argue that many administrators are medically qualified, and thus act so as to protect the traditional professional prerogatives. This view confuses the usual distinction between status and role. As many hospital and HMO doctors will attest, a physician who is a full-time administrator is understandably concerned to protect the bottom line, not the prerogatives of the profession. When these interests diverge, as they increasingly must, it becomes clear where the physician/administrator's divided loyalty really resides. One recent survey of doctors shows that a majority do not believe that their medical directors represent the interests of the medical staff. As a result, the American Medical Association (AMA) has concluded that "as hospital employees . . . medical directors may align their loyalty more with hospitals than with medical staff interests" (24). To counteract these trends, it has been seriously suggested that "physicians should be trained in organization theory . . . to act as liaisons among all those with an interest in medicine, including patients, health care providers, insurers, politicians, economists, and administrators."

Specialization-Deskilling

Specialization in medicine, while deepening knowledge in a particular area, is also circumscribing the work that doctors may legitimately perform. Specialization can, with task delegation, reduce the hospital's dependence on its highly trained medical staff. Other health workers (e.g., physicians' assistants and nurse practitioners) with less training, more narrowly skilled, and obviously cheaper can be hired. Doctors, while believing that specialization is invariably a good thing, are being "deskilled"—a term employed by Braverman (25) to describe the transfer of skills from highly trained personnel to more narrowly qualified specialists. Many new health occupations (physicians' assistants, nurse practitioners, certified nurses) have emerged over the last several decades to assume some of the work that doctors used to perform. Not only is work deskilled but it is increasingly conducted without M.D.s' control as other professional groups and workers seek their own autonomy. These processes receive support from administrators constantly searching for cheaper labor, quite apart from the controlled trials revealing that "allied health professionals" can, in many circumstances, do the same work just as effectively and efficiently for those patients who must use them. Preference for the term "allied health professional" rather than "physician extender" or "physician assistant" reflects the promotion of this occupational division of labor.

Just over a decade ago, Victor Fuchs (26) viewed the physician as "captain of the team." Around that time, doctors (usually male) were the unquestioned masters and other health workers (usually female), especially nurses, worked "under the doctor" to carry out his orders. That subordination is disappearing. Nowadays, physicians are required to work alongside other professionals on the "health care team." The ideology of *team work* is a leveler in the hierarchical division of health care labor. Other health workers—for example, physiotherapists, pharmacists, medical social workers, inhalation therapists, podiatrists, and even nurses in general—may have more knowledge of specific fields than physicians, who are increasingly required to defer to other workers, now providing some of the technical and humane tasks of doctoring. While some M.D.s continue to resist these trends, and have publicly complained about "the progressive exclusion of doctors from nursing affairs" (27–29), still others

have accommodated to the changing scene captured in the title of a recent article: "At This Hospital, 'The Captain of the Ship' is Dead" (27).

Commentators have identified the "gatekeeping" function performed by doctors (to determine and legitimate access to generally scarce resources, e.g., certain medications and highly specialized personnel) as a special characteristic that distinguishes them from other health workers and reinforces their central position in the division of labor. But even this gatekeeping function appears to be changing. For example, in some 21 states, nurses are now able to prescribe a wide range of medications. Despite opposition from doctors, pharmacists in Florida may now prescribe drugs for many minor ailments (30). Physician organization and resistance have been unable to curtail the introduction and growth of midwifery in some areas of the country.

Specialization has also weakened the political position of doctors because they now tend to affiliate only with disparate professional societies relevant to their own field of practice, rather than the generic and increasingly distant AMA. AMA membership continues to decline annually, and there are estimates that less than half of all doctors now belong. Fragmentation of the profession through subspecialty societies severely curtails the influence of the AMA in representing all the profession. One recalls the power of the AMA only a decade ago when it successfully delayed and then shaped Medicare and Medicaid legislation. In contrast, the AMA is now losing significant battles in the courts over issues that affect the position and status of doctors. Antitrust rulings (permitting doctors to advertise) and decisions prohibiting any charges over and above the federally determined DRG rates are major examples. In Chicago in 1987, a federal judge issued an injunction ordering the AMA to immediately end its professional boycott of chiropractors on the grounds that it violated the Sherman Act with "systematic, long-term wrongdoing and the longer-term intent to destroy a licensed profession" (31). Responding to recent proposals to introduce a flat, all-inclusive payment for doctors' services associated with each type of hospital case, Dr. Coury (Chairman of the AMA's Board of Trustees) claims that doctors are becoming "indentured servants of the government" (32).

Doctor Oversupply

The growing oversupply of doctors in developed countries reinforces these trends in medical work and professional power by intensifying intraprofessional competition and devaluing their position in the job market. During the 1970s, the supply of physicians increased 36 percent, while the population grew only 8 percent. Medical schools in the United States continue to pump 17,000 physicians into the system annually. One report projected an oversupply of 70,000 physicians in the United States by 1990 and an excess of 150,000 by the year 2000. The ratio of doctors to general population is expected to reach 1 to 300 by 1990 (33, 34). This level of intensity, obviously much higher in the northeast and on the west coast, renders fee-for-service solo practice economically less feasible. Again, the changes occurring are captured in the title of a recent article: "Doctor, the Patient Will See You Now" (33). There are reliable reports that doctors are unemployed in a number of countries and increasingly underemployed in quite a few others (34). Doctors have apparently received unemployment payments in Scandanavian countries, Canada, and Australia. Official recognition of physician oversupply exists in Belgium, which is restricting specialty training, and the Netherlands, which is reducing both medical school intake and specialty training (35).

The oversupply of doctors is thought to be a major reason for the recent shift to a salaried medical staff, which has been so dramatic as to be termed "the salary revolution" (36). There are estimates that over one half of all U.S. doctors are now in salaried arrangements, either part- or full-time (36). It is projected that by the year 2000, the proportion of doctors in solo or independent fee-for-service practice will have declined to about one quarter (36–41). Young medical graduates are especially affected by the trends described and are often prepared to accept a limited job (and role) for a guaranteed fixed income (without heavy initial investment in setting up a practice and obtaining liability protection from astronomical malpractice insur-

ance premiums) with the promise of certain perks (regular hours, paid vacation, retirement plan, etc.). The division of labor in health care is increasingly stratified by age and gender, with female and younger doctors disproportionately in salaried positions. Forty-seven percent of physicians under 36 years of age were salaried in 1985, while only 19.4 percent of their colleagues over 55 were employees. The percentage increase for this youngest category of physicians between 1983 and 1985 was significantly larger than for the other age groups, increasing 5.3 percentage points. Female physicians were nearly twice as likely to be employees as their male colleagues. Only 23.5 percent of male physicians were salaried in 1985 versus 45.5 percent of females. Again, the percentage increase for female employee physicians was larger than for males over the period 1983–85. While self-employed physicians consistently earned nearly $38,000 more per year than salaried physicians ($118,600 versus $80,400, respectively, for 1985), self-employed doctors worked an average of one and a half weeks more in 1985 (47.4 weeks versus 45.9), spent an average of six hours more per week on patient care activities (52.6 hours per week versus 46.6), and saw an average of 19 more patients per week (122.6 visits per week versus 103.9) (42). One survey of over 200 hospitals found that the trend to a salaried medical staff was most marked in areas with high ratios of doctors to population. Physician oversupply and the associated economic vulnerability may force doctors to accept lower incomes and the increasingly alienating work conditions practicing in HMOs, clinics, and hospitals of "today's corporate health factories," just as 19th century craftsmen accepted the factory floor forced on them by their move to the industrial plant (43).

Anecdotal reports from older doctors indicate that medicine today is not like "the good old days" (44). The malpractice crisis, DRGs, the likelihood of fixed fees, and shrinking incomes (projected at a 30 percent decline over the next decade) all combine to remove whatever "fun" there was in medical practice. Some wonder aloud whether they would choose medicine if, with the benefit of hindsight, they had to do it all over again. While doctors used to want their children to follow in their footsteps, many report that they would not recommend medicine today. Recent graduates have doubts of other kinds. They fear that their debts will force them into specialities on the basis of anticipated earnings rather than intrinsic interest (46). College advisors may dissuade the highly talented students they counsel from choosing medicine because its job market looks so bleak. The number of medical school applicants dropped 4.8 percent in 1986 and is expected to decline 9 percent more in 1987, according to the AMA and the Association of American Medical Colleges. First-time enrollments in medical schools in 1986 were down for the fifth straight year. Although it is difficult to identify a single factor responsible for these declines, it appears that they are due to students' fear of a glutted market, concern over an average debt of $33,499 (a 117.2 percent increase since 1980), alarm over soaring malpractice insurance rates, and a perception that the practice of medicine is becoming less individualistic, with more government regulation and more doctors working in "managed care" systems that have corporate-like structures (47). These professional concerns are expressed in the urban academic medical centers (where physicians with international reputations presumably enjoy a privileged status) as well as in local community hospitals throughout the country.

Unionization—A Harbinger of a Trend?

There are reports from across the United States that physicians are rebelling against the continuing challenges to their authority and attempts to cut their incomes by HMOs and other corporate-like means of organizing profitable production of medical care (34, 48, 49). One recent manifestation of doctors' frustration with the profound changes already described is increased interest in unionization. Several unions have been or are being formed in different areas of the country to represent doctors working as full-time employees of state and local government and in HMOs. The largest is the Union of American Physicians and Dentists, based in Oakland, California, with a membership of around 43,000 in 17 states. Some unions (e.g., the Group Health Association in Washington, D.C.) have even staged strikes. The HMOs' organizational structure and that of other similar prepaid health care plans appears to generate disgruntlement among their salaried physician employees who were socialized to expect considerably more status and professional autonomy than the HMOs permit. There are now 625 of these medical factories in the United States serving some 25.8 million individuals, up from 260 with 9.1 million subscribers in 1980. Legal obstacles to physician unionization are presented by anti-trust laws, which prohibit independent businesspersons, including doctors in private practice, from organizing to fix prices. Recognizing this, the Minnesota Medical Society recently passed a resolution asking the AMA to seek government permission to form a union. National attention has recently focused on a struggle in Minneapolis where salaried physician employees of the Physician's Health Plan of Minnesota (the largest HMO in the state) are organizing to unionize (50). According to Dr. Paul Ellwood (a leading health services researcher who first coined the term "health maintenance organization"), the Minneapolis dispute portends "a critical turning point. . . . There are very few places where it's gone as far as it has here, but it's moving in that general direction everywhere" (50).

For understandable reasons, many physicians and the lay public recoil at the thought of and disparage unionized doctors. Only a decade ago unionization among physicians was unthinkable, a movement commonly considered to be working class. Aaron Nathensen, an ophthalmologist with the Minneapolis Physician's Health Plan, expresses a widely held view as follows: "When I entered the practice 15 years ago, unionization was thought of as totally unprofessional, unmedical and unAmerican. But there's a growing feeling that we're losing control—losing control of patients, losing control of the health industry" (50).

Theories of Change

Some of the forces transforming medical care and the work of doctors have been described. How does one *explain* what is occurring? *Why* is it happening?

Probably the best account of the stage-by-stage

transformation of the labor process under capitalism is provided by Karl Marx. Although not concerned with health care (51), his thesis is applicable. During the precapitalist period, small-scale independent craftsmen (solo practitioners) operated domestic workshops, sold their products on the free market, and controlled the production of goods. Over time, capitalists steered many of these skilled workers into their factories (hospitals) where they were able to continue traditional crafts semi-autonomously in exchange for wages. Eventually, the owners of production (investors) began to rationalize the production process in their factories by encouraging specialization, allocating certain tasks to cheaper workers, and enlisting managers to coordinate the increasingly complex division of labor that developed. Rationalization was completed during the final stage when production was largely performed by engineering systems and machines, with the assistance of unskilled human machine-minders (52). The worker's autonomy and control over work and the workplace diminished, while the rate of exploitation increased with each successive stage in the transformation of production.

Weber's (53) account of the same process (bureaucratization) is strikingly similar. According to Weber, bureaucracy is characterized by the following: (a) a hierarchical organization; (b) a strict chain of command from top to bottom; (c) an elaborate division of labor; (d) assigning specialized tasks to qualified individuals; (e) detailed rules and regulations governing work; (f) hiring personnel based on competence, specialized training, and qualifications (as opposed to family ties, political power, or tradition); and (g) expectations of a life-time career from officials (54). He described how workers were increasingly "separated from ownership of the means of production or administration." Bureaucratic workers became specialists performing circumscribed duties within a hierarchical structure subject to the authority of superiors and to established rules and procedures. According to Weber, bureaucratic employees are "subject to strict and systematic discipline and control in the conduct of the office" they occupy. For Weber, the bureaucratic form of work was present not only in the area of manufacturing but also in churches, schools,

and government organizations. It is noteworthy that he also included hospitals: "this type of bureaucracy is found in private clinics, as well as in endowed hospitals or the hospitals maintained by religious orders." While Weber viewed bureaucracy as the most rational and efficient mode of organizing work, he also saw the accompanying degradation of working life as inevitable (27, 54).

It is argued that the process outlined by Marx and Weber with respect to a different group of workers, during a different historical era, is directly applicable to the changing situation of doctors today, now that the "industrial revolution has finally caught up with medicine" (George Rosen). Whereas, generally speaking, most other workers have been quickly and easily corporatized, physicians have been able to postpone or minimize this process in their own case. Now, primarily as a result of the bureaucratization that has been forced on medical practice, physicians are being severely reduced in function and their formerly self-interested activities subordinated to the requirements of the highly profitable production of medical care.

While Marx offers a most complete and theoretically well-grounded explanation of the social transformation of work (including doctoring), other commentators have described threats to professional autonomy. C. Wright Mills (55) warned of a "managerial demiurge" suffusing all the professions, including doctoring. In 1951, he wrote (55, p. 112):

Most professionals are now salaried employees; much professional work has become divided and standardized and fitted into the new hierarchical organizations of educated skill and service; intensive and narrow specialization has replaced self cultivation and wide knowledge; assistants and subprofessionals perform routine, although often intricate, tasks, while successful professional men become more and more the managerial type. So decisive have such shifts been, in some areas, that it is as if rationality itself had been expropriated from the individual and been located as a new form of brain power in the ingenuous bureaucracy itself.

Describing "The Physicians' Changing Hospital Role" over 20 years ago, Wilson (56) saw the growth of specialization in medicine producing diminished perceptions of doctors' expertise and a routinization of charisma. This theme was developed by Myerhoff and Larson (57) when they argued that doctors were losing their charisma and becoming culture heroes: a major difference between the charismatic and culture hero is that the former is a force for social change, while the latter is the embodiment of tradition. The culture hero appears to serve as an agent of social control (58).

During the 1970s, Haug (59, 60) detected a trend toward deprofessionalization that had its origin in the changing relations between professionals and consumers. The unquestioned trust that a client has in a professional is often thought to distinguish professionals from other "ordinary" workers. According to Hughes (61), relations with professionals are embodied in the motto *credat emptor,* "let the taker believe in us," rather than *caveat emptor,* "let the buyer beware," which exists in most other areas of commerce. According to Haug (59, 60), consumers' questioning trust in professionals is diminishing as the knowledge gap between the medical profession and the consumer diminishes. She regarded the modern consumer as better educated and more likely to comprehend medical subjects, which results in a narrowing of the knowledge gap. She also viewed the computerization of knowledge as making it more accessible to all. New specialized occupations have arisen around new bodies of knowledge and skill that physicians themselves are, understandably, no longer competent to employ. These and related trends have, in Haug's view, deprofessionalized medicine, a consequence of which is reduction of physicians to mere specialists dependent on rational, well-informed consumers who approach their service with the same skepticism (caveat emptor) that they bring to other commodity purchases. As a result of deprofessionalization, the doctor's work is becoming just another health occupation.

Margarli Larson (62) provides a penetrating systematic description of the progressive loss of autonomy and control over work among professionals. She distinguishes three areas in which the loss of autonomy (or the alienation) is occurring: economic, organizational, and technical. According to her formulation, doctors experience *economic* alienation when they become salaried employees of hospitals or when, in common with most other workers, they must place hospital interests above their own. *Organizational* alienation occurs when cost-conscious hospital administrators, or managers, create systems and procedures to increase doctors' productivity and efficiency, and coordinate their work with others in the division of medical labor. *Technical* alienation refers to the process of curtailing or removing the actual decisions involved in diagnosing and treating patients. From what has been described above, it appears that doctors are experiencing loss of autonomy in all three of these dimensions, albeit at different rates depending on where they work and what specialty they practice.

Is the Profession Still Dominant?

During the late 1960s, Freidson developed a view of professionalism (articulated in two influential books published in 1970: *Profession of Medicine* and *Professional Dominance*) which asserted that the medical profession (doctors) dominated other health care occupations in the division of labor. Nearly two decades after his original work and while conceding profound organizational changes and a transitional status (63, 64), he still views the medical profession as (64, p. 13):

> Dominant in a division of labor in which other occupations were obligated to work under the supervision of physicians and take orders from [them], with its exclusive license to practice medicine, prescribe controlled drugs, admit patients to hospitals, and perform other critical gatekeeping functions, the medical profession is portrayed as having a monopoly over the provision of health services.

Attention is focused here on Freidson's view of professional dominance solely because it remains the dominant view of professionalism. However, it is increasingly subject to challenge (1, 48, 52, 62, 65, 66). In one of his more recent contributions (64), Freidson tests the accuracy of alternative explanations of the changing position of doctors (especially deprofessionalization and proletarianization) against the "standard" of his own view of professional dominance.

While perhaps an adequate description of the situation of doctors back in the 1960s, much water has passed under the bridge since that time. Indeed, Freidson seems to overlook the period that has elapsed since his original important contributions. Defending his position in 1985 (64), he refers to the position that he "asserted not long ago" (in 1970). A great deal of change has occurred over the intervening 15 years however, some of which has been described above. There is nothing wrong with modifying, refining, or evolving a position on the basis of intervening change or new data and experience (67).

Quite apart from the fact that it is now necessarily somewhat dated, Freidson's description and approach has additional limitations.

1. Grounded in the social constructionist perspective (68), it *raises more questions than it is able to answer*. Its ability to accommodate the macrostructural changes that have occurred in health care has been described elsewhere (48).
2. The professional dominance perspective is a *description of an earlier state of affairs*—a snapshot of the position of doctors back in the 1960s—*not an explanation or theory* that sustains close scrutiny today. Practicing physicians familiar with Freidson's work view it as a fairly accurate account of an earlier and much preferred golden age (69). Freidson bases his work in the past (the 1960s) and attempts to explain the present. The thesis of corporatization, or proletarianization, looks toward the future and argues, on the basis of what is presently occurring and has already occurred in other sectors of the economy, that this is also likely to happen to doctors in the future.
3. Freidson (64, 70) bemoans the absence of evidence to support the rival theories of deprofessionalization and proletarianization. One should note that apart from the observational work reported in 1975 in *Doctoring Together*, Freidson has *never gathered or reported primary data to support his own viewpoint* (only secondary sources are used). Moreover, it is extraordinarily difficult to obtain information from, say, the AMA, or to gain access to medical institutions. The evidence for professional dominance is no stronger, or weaker, than that used to advance the rival theories of deprofessionalization and proletarianization. The point is that we are all groping under the same light, which is often kept deliberately dim. Moreover, it is very difficult, if not inappropriate, to apply traditional positivistic techniques to the study of change of the order captured by the notion of proletarianization. Imagine asking yeoman farmers and artisans in Elizabethan England, through questionnaires and interviews, if they appreciated the long-term consequences of the enclosure movement! Quite the same limitation is present in the modern study of the historically changing relation of doctors to the means of medical care production.
4. Freidson (64) has often depicted competing theorists as political visionaries, their work being "too grand and sweeping to have much more than a rhetorical and possibly political value"; "proletarianization is not a concept as much as a slogan"; and "it would be a mistake to regard such literature [proletarianization] as evidence of actual change instead of desire for change" (64). One should note that concern over the changing situation of doctors and the worrisome direction of health care is also coming from some of the most conservative circles—from Harry Schwarz, in the *New York Times* (30), who writes that "MD's are getting a raw deal," to Arnold Relman, editor of the *New England Journal of Medicine* (18), who warns of the danger of the medical-industrial complex, a work that bears a resemblance to earlier work on the medical-industrial complex in *Monthly Review* in 1978 (71).

Toward Proletarianization

The healthy debate over the changing position of doctors within the rapidly changing health care system is likely to continue for some time. Along with others in Britain (72, 73), Australia (74), Canada (52, 64, 72, 75, 76), Scandinavia (77), and the United States (24, 33, 43, 66, 76), we have elaborated one viewpoint (proletarianization), and have presented as much data as can be easily mustered. Although Freidson views it as "equivocation," several clarifying caveats have been deliberately introduced in an attempt to minimize misunderstandings associated with the notion of proletarianization. The theory of proletarianization seeks to explain *the process by which an occupational category is divested of control over certain prerogatives relating to the location, content, and essentiality of its task activities, thereby subordinating it to the broader requirements of production under advanced capitalism.* That is admittedly and necessarily a general definition. However, in order to provide operational specificity, and to facilitate the collec-

Table 16-1. Some Differences between the Working Conditions of Doctors in the United States around 1900 and Today

Key Prerogatives of an Occupational Group	Physicians in Small-scale, Fee-for-Service Practice (1900)	Physicians in Bureaucratic Practice Today (1988)
1. Criteria for entrance	Almost exclusively upper- and middle-class white male students.	Medical schools forced to recruit proportion of minorities and women.
2. Content of training	Largely dictated by the AMA through local medical societies.	Federal government and other "outside" interests affect the content and scope of curriculum through training programs, student loans, etc.
3. Autonomy over the terms and content of work	Work typically more generalized and controlled by the individual practitioner himself.	Work typically segmentalized and directed by administrators in accordance with organizational constraints (profit).
4. The object of labor	Patients usually regarded as the physician's "own patients."	Patients are technically clients, or members of the organization, whom physicians share with other specialists.
5. The tools of labor	Equipment typically owned or leased by the practitioner, and employees are hired by the practitioner.	Technology typically owned by the employing organization and operated by other bureaucratic employees.
6. The means of labor	The physical plant is typically owned or rented and operated by physicians themselves.	The physical plant typically owned by and operated in the interests of the organization (profit).
7. Remuneration for labor	The hours worked, the level of utilization, and the fees charged are pretty much determined by the individual practitioner.	Work schedule and salary level determined by organization. Sometimes limitations on "outside practice."

tion of the evidence that everyone desires, seven specific professional prerogatives, that are lost or curtailed through the process of proletarianization, are identified as follows (34):

1. *The criteria for entrance* (e.g., the credentialing system and membership requirements);
2. *The content of training* (e.g., the scope and content of the medical curriculum);
3. *Autonomy regarding the terms and content of work* (e.g., the ways in which what must be done is accomplished);
4. *The objects of labor* (e.g., commodities produced or the clients served);
5. *The tools of labor* (e.g., machinery, biotechnology, chemical apparatus);
6. *The means of labor* (e.g., hospital buildings, clinic facilities, laboratory services); and
7. *The amount and rate of remuneration for labor* (e.g., wage and salary levels, fee schedules).

Which of these prerogatives is lost, or curtailed, through proletarianization, is associated with the relative power of any occupation and is a function of the degree of unity or cohesiveness within an occupational group, the stage of production associated with the sector in which the occupation is located, and the extent to which the tasks of the occupation can be technologized.

These important prerogatives are listed in Table 16-1, and the situation in the United States of small-scale fee-for-service doctors in the past (say, around the turn of the 20th century) is contrasted to the situation of bureaucratically employed doctors today. Every single prerogative listed has changed, many changes occurring over the last decade. The net effect of the erosion of these prerogatives is the reduction of the members of a professional group to some common level in the service of the broader interests of capital accumulation. One of the difficulties for the proponents of proletarianization is that the process is very difficult to recognize. Indeed, it is occurring at such a level and so slowly in some cases that it may only be amenable to historical analysis some time in the future. It would be a mistake to view this as a "cop-out."

For doctors who are increasingly subject to this process, it is masked both by their false consciousness concerning the significance of their everyday activities and by an elitist conception of their role, so that even if the process is recognized, doctors are quite reluctant to admit it.

While experiencing, on a daily basis, what has been described above, many physicians do not comprehend the historical magnitude of the process we have been describing. To capture the level of our analysis of what is occurring, it may be useful to draw a parallel with early industrial developments in cottage industry–based Elizabethan England or, closer to home, changes in American agriculture, in both of which situations industrialization and corporatization slowly shunted aside small-scale production, eroding the market situation of independent workers. A major effect of the enclosure movement in England was to slowly drive many small growers and grazers off the land into the cities where factories were developing and where they would become wage earners. These factories, in turn, eventually penetrated the countryside, destroying the yeoman-based agriculture and cottage industry in much the same way that large-scale agricultural interests in the United States have been squeezing out small farmers.

It is thus our argument that the industrial revolution has fully caught up with medicine. We are beginning to see the same phenomena in this sphere of work. From the preceding description, it is clear that we view the theory of proletarianization as a useful explanation of a process under development, *not* a state that has been or is just about to be achieved. The process described will most likely continue for a considerable period of time. An earlier article, on the social transformation of doctoring, was entitled, "Towards the Proletarianization of Physicians," not "The Proletarianized Physician" (34). The term "proletarianization" denotes a *process*. Use of the preposition "towards" was intended to

indicate that the process is still continuing. Roemer (78) has recently offered a critique of the notion of proletarianization. He raises serious points and no doubt the thesis could benefit from some fine tuning (79). No one can have the final word on this subject, especially when we are attempting to explain a trend of which we are in the midst. Only time will tell who is most correct in assessing the historical trends discussed. Perhaps this work should be put aside until the turn of the century. If what occurs in the next 18 years is anything like the dramatic transformation we have witnessed over the last 18 years (since 1970), doctoring will bear little resemblance to that which is being discussed today.

REFERENCES

1. Starr, P. *The Social Transformation of American Medicine.* Basic Books, New York, 1982.
2. Light, D. W. Corporate medicine for profit. *Sci. Am.* 255: 38–54, 1986.
3. McKinlay, J. B. (ed.). *Issues in The Political Economy of Health Care.* Tavistock, London, 1984.
4. Institute of Medicine. *For-Profit Enterprise in Health Care.* National Academy Press, Washington, D.C., 1986.
5. Salmon, J. W. Organizing medical care for profit. In *Issues in the Political Economy of Health Care,* edited by J. B. McKinlay, pp. 143–186. Tavistock, New York, 1984.
6. Navarro, V. *Crisis, Health, and Medicine.* Tavistock, London, 1986.
7. Salmon, J. W. Profit and health care: Trends in corporatization and proprietization. *Int. J. Health Serv.* 15(3): 395–418, 1985.
8. Kennedy, L. The proprietarization of voluntary hospitals. *Bull. N.Y. Acad. Med.* 61: 81–89, 1985.
9. Eisenberg, C. It is still a privilege to be a doctor. *N. Engl. J. Med.* 314: 1114, 1986.
10. Robert Wood Johnson Foundation. *Updated Report on Access to Health Care for the American People.* Princeton, N.J., 1983.
11. U.S. Bureau of the Census. Economic characteristics of households in the United States: Fourth quarter 1983. In *Current Population Reports,* pp. 70–84. Government Printing Office, Washington, D.C., 1985.
12. Farley, P. J. Who are the underinsured? *Milbank Mem. Fund Q.* 63: 476–503, 1985.
13. Iglehart, J. K. Medical care of the poor—a growing problem. *N. Engl. J. Med.* 313: 59–63, 1985.

14. Sloan, F. A., Valvona, J., and Mullner, R. Identifying the issues: A statistical profile. In *Uncompensated Hospital Care: Rights and Responsibilities,* edited by F. A. Sloan, J. F. Blumstein, and J. M. Perrins, pp. 16–53. Johns Hopkins University Press, Baltimore, 1986.

15. Himmelstein, D. U., et al. Patient transfers: Medical practice as social triage. *Am. J. Public Health* 74: 494–496, 1984.

16. Daniels, N. Why saying no to patients in the United States is so hard. *N. Engl. J. Med.* 314: 1380–1383, 1986.

17. Cunningham, R. M., Jr. Entrepreneurialism in medicine. *N. Engl. J. Med.* 309: 1313–1314, 1983.

18. Relman, A. S. The new medical industrial complex. *N. Engl. J. Med.* 303: 963–970, 1980.

19. Relman, A. S. The future of medical practice. *Health Affairs* 2: 5–19, 1983.

20. Eisenberg, L., and Virchow, R. L. K. Where are you now that we need you? *Am. J. Med.* 77: 524–532, 1984.

21. Freedman, S. A. Megacorporate health care: A choice for the future. *N. Engl. J. Med.* 312: 579–582, 1985.

22. Himmelstein, D. U., and Woolhandler, S. Cost without benefit: Administrative waste in U.S. health care. *N. Engl. J. Med.* 314: 441–445, 1986.

23. Alford, R. *Health Care Politics: Ideological and Interest Group Barriers to Reform.* University of Chicago Press, Chicago, 1975.

24. American Medical Association. Effects of competition in medicine. *JAMA* 249: 1864–1868, 1983.

25. Braverman, H. *Labor and Monopoly Capital.* Monthly Review Press, New York, 1974.

26. Fuchs, V. *Who Shall Live?* Basic Books, New York, 1975.

27. Blackwood, S. A. At this hospital "the captain of the ship" is dead. *RN* 42: 77–80, 1979.

28. Garvey, J. L., and Rottet, S. Expanding the hospital nursing role: An administrative account. *J. Nurs. Admin.* 12: 30–34, 1982.

29. Alspach, J., et al. Joint physician-nurse committee ensures safe transfer of tasks. *Hospitals* 56: 54–55, 1982.

30. Florida says pharmacists may prescribe drugs. *New York Times,* April 12, 1986.

31. AMA ordered to end chiropractic boycott. *Boston Globe,* August 29, 1987.

32. Plan would alter doctors' payment under medicare. *New York Times,* November 14, 1984.

33. Friedman, E. Doctor, the patient will see you now. *Hospitals* 55: 117–118, 1981.

34. McKinlay, J. B., and Arches, J. Towards the proletarianization of physicians. *Int. J. Health Serv.* 15(2): 161–195, 1985.

35. Berube, B. Italian health care: Who's minding the clinic? *Can. Med. Assoc. J.* 130: 1625–1627, 1984.

36. Anderson, A. *Health Care in the 1990's: Trends and Strategies.* American College of Hospital Administrators, Chicago, 1987.

37. Freshnock, L. J. *Physician and Public Attitudes on Health Care Issues.* AMA, Chicago, 1984.

38. Glandon, G. L., and Werner, J. L. Physicians' practice experience during the decade of the 1970's. *JAMA* 244: 2514–2518, 1980.

39. Taylor, H. *Medical Practice in the 1990's: Physicians Look at Their Changing Profession.* H. J. Kaiser Family Foundation, Menlo Park, Cal., 1981.

40. Iglehart, J. K. The future supply of physicians. *N. Engl. J. Med.* 314: 850–854, 1986.

41. Schroeder, S. A. Western European responses to physician oversupply. *JAMA* 252: 373–384, 1984.

42. American Medical Association. *Socioeconomic Monitoring System Survey.* Center for Health Policy Research, AMA, Chicago, 1986.

43. Berrien, R. What future for primary care private practice? *N. Engl. J. Med.* 316: 334–337, 1987.

44. Friedman, E. Declaration of interdependence. *Hospitals* 57: 73–80, 1983.

45. Freidson, E. Review essay: Health factories, the new industrial sociology. *Social Problems* 14(4): 493–500, 1967.

46. McCarty, D. J. Why are today's medical students choosing high-technology specialties over internal medicine? *N. Engl. J. Med.* 317: 567–568, 1987.

47. *New York Times,* August 30, 1987.

48. McKinlay, J. B. The business of good doctoring or doctoring as good business: Reflections on Freidson's view of the medical game. *Int. J. Health Serv.* 8(3): 459–488, 1977.

49. Marcus, S. Unions for physicians. *N. Engl. J. Med.* 311: 1508–1511, 1984.

50. Doctor's dilemma: Unionizing. *New York Times,* July 13, 1987.

51. Marx, K. *Capital,* Vol. I. Random House, New York, 1977.

52. Wahn, M. The Decline of Medical Dominance in Hospitals. Unpublished manuscript, University of Manitoba, Winn., 1985.

53. Weber, M. *Economy and Society,* Bedminster Press, New York, 1968.

54. Gerth, H., and Mills, W. C. *From Max Weber.* Oxford University Press, New York, 1968.

55. Mills, C. W. *White Collar.* Oxford University Press, New York, 1953.

56. Wilson, R. The physician's changing hospital role. In *Medical Care,* edited by W. R. Scott and E. H.

Volkart, pp. 408–420. Wiley and Sons, New York, 1966.

57. Myerhoff, B. G., and Larson, W. R. The doctor as cultural hero: The routinization of charisma. *Hum. Organization* 17, 1958.

58. Zola, I. K. Medicine as an institution of social control. *Sociol. Rev.* 20(4): 487–504, 1972.

59. Haug, M. Deprofessionalization: An alternate hypothesis for the future. In *Professionalization and Social Change,* edited by P. Halmos, pp. 195–211. Sociological Review Monographs, Vol. 20, Keele, 1973.

60. Haug, M. The erosion of professional authority: A cross-cultural inquiry in the case of the physician. *Milbank Mem. Fund Q.* 54: 83–106, 1976.

61. Hughes, E. C. *The Sociological Eye.* Aldine, New York, 1971.

62. Larson, M. S. Proletarianization and educated labor. *Theory and Society* 9: 131–175, 1980.

63. Freidson, E. The medical profession in transition. In *Applications of Social Science to Clinical Medicine,* edited by L. H. Aiken and D. Mechanic, pp. 63–79. Rutgers University Press, New Brunswick, N.J., 1986.

64. Freidson, E. The reorganization of the medical profession. *Med. Care Rev.* 42: 11–33, 1985.

65. Coburn, D., Torrance, G. M., and Kaufert, J. M. Medical dominance in Canada in historical perspective: The rise and fall of medicine? *Int. J. Health Serv.* 13: 407–432, 1983.

66. Oppenheimer, M. The proletarianization of the professional. In *Professionalization and Social Change,* edited by P. J. Halmos, pp. 213–227. Sociological Review Monographs, Vol. 20, Keele, 1973.

67. McKinlay, J. B. On the professional regulation of change. In *Professionalization and Social Change,* edited by P. J. Halmos, pp. 61–84. Sociological Review Monographs, Vol. 20, Keele, 1973.

68. Bucher, R., and Stelling, J. Characteristics of professional organizations. *J. Health Soc. Behav.* 10: 3–15, 1969.

69. Burnham, J. C. American medicine's golden age: What happened to it? *Science* 215: 1474–1479, 1982.

70. Freidson, E. The future of professionalization. In *Health and the Division of Labour,* edited by M. Stacey et al., pp. 144–160, Croom Helm, London, 1977.

71. McKinlay, J. B. On the medical-industrial complex. *Monthly Rev.* 30(75), 1978.

72. Armstrong, D. The decline of medical hegemony: A review of government reports during the NHS. *Soc. Sci. Med.* 10: 157–163, 1976.

73. Parry, N., and Parry, J. Professionals and unionism: Aspects of class conflict in the National Health Service. *Sociol. Rev.* 25: 823–841, 1977.

74. Willis, E. *Medical Dominance: The Division of Labor in Australian Health Care.* Allen and Unwin, Sydney, Australia, 1983.

75. Esland, G. Professionalism. In *The Politics of Work and Occupations,* edited by G. Esland, pp. 213–250. University of Toronto Press, Toronto, 1980.

76. Crichton, A. The shift from entrepreneurial to political power in the Canadian health system. *Soc. Sci. Med.* 10: 59–66, 1976.

77. Riska, E. *Power, Politics and Health: Forces Changing American Medicine.* Societas Scientiarum Fennica, Commentationes Scientiarum Socidium 27, Helsinki, Finland, 1985.

78. Roemer, M. I. Proletarianization of physicians or organization of health services? *Int. J. Health Serv.* 16(3): 469–471, 1986.

79. McKinlay, J. B., and Arches, J. Historical changes in doctoring: A reply to Milton Roemer. *Int. J. Health Serv.* 16(3): 473–477, 1986.

Countervailing Power:
The Changing Character of the
Medical Profession in the United States

• • • • • •

Donald W. Light

The medical profession appears to be losing its autonomy even as its sovereignty expands. With the more frequent use of physician profiling and other comparative measures of performance, together with the ability of sophisticated programmers to capture the decision-making trees of differential diagnosis on computers so well that they can check out and improve the performance of practitioners, theories of professionalism that rest on autonomy as their cornerstone need to be reconstructed from the ground up (Light 1988).

Although physicians play a central role in developing tools for scrutinizing the core of professional work, they work for purchasers who use them for the external measure of quality and cost-effectiveness. Thus, not only autonomy but also the monopoly over knowledge as the foundation of professionalism is thrown into question. The computerized analysis of practice patterns and decision making, together with the growth of active consumerism, constitute deprofessionalization as a trend (Haug 1973; Haug and Lavin 1983). Patients, governments, and corporate purchasers are taking back the cultural, economic, and even technical authority long granted to the medical profession.

The sovereignty of the profession nevertheless is growing. Evan Willis (1988) was the first to distinguish between autonomy over one's work and sovereignty over matters of illness. The sovereignty of medicine expands with advances in pharmacology, molecular biology, genetics, and diagnostic tools that uncover more and more pathology not known before. Although chronicity is the residue of cure and the growing proportion of insoluble problems is providing a new legitimacy to nonmedical forms of healing, care, and therapy, no other member of the illness trade has a knowledge and skill base that is expanding so rapidly as is the physician's.

This chapter describes the changes in the American medical profession over the past two decades and outlines the concept of countervailing power as a useful way to understand the profession's relations with the economy and the state.

Some Limitations of Current Concepts

In the special issue of the *Milbank Quarterly* . . . Sol Levine and I reviewed the concepts of professional dominance, deprofessionalization, proletarianization, and corporatization (Light and Levine 1988). Each has its truth and limitations. Each captures in its word one characteristic and trend, but this means that each mistakes the part for the whole and for the future. One set predicts the opposite of the other, yet neither can account for reversals. This is best illustrated by the oldest concept among them, professional dominance.

Professional dominance captured in rich complexity the clinical and institutional grip that the profession had over society in the 1960s, a formulation that supplanted Parsons' benign and admiring theoretical reflections of the 1940s and 1950s (Freidson 1970a, 1970b; Light 1989). But the concept of professional dominance cannot account for decline; dominance over institutions and resources leads only to still more dominance. As the very fruits of dominance itself weakened the profession from within and prompted powerful changes from without, the concept has become less useful. In its defense, Freidson (1984, 1985, 1986e, 1989) has been forced to retreat from his original concept of dominance, by which he meant control over the cultural, organizational, economic, and political dimensions of health care, to a much reduced concept that means control over one's work and those involved in it. Even that diminution to the pre-Freidson concept of professionalism may not stand, given the fundamental challenges to autonomy.

Space precludes reiterating the limitations of the other concepts, but it is worth noting the danger of conflating many by-products of professional dominance after World War II (such as increasing complexity, bureaucratization, and rationalization) with recent efforts by investors to corporatize medicine and by institutional payers such as governments and employers to get more effective health care for less money. The concept of corporatization in particular includes five dimensions that characterize medical work today as segmented and directed by the administrators of for-profit organizations that control the facilities, the technology used, and the remuneration of the physician-workers (McKinlay 1988). As the empirical part of this chapter shows, this characterization is not typical and does not capture the complex relations between doctors and corporations.

The Concept of Countervailing Powers

Sociology needs a concept or framework that provides a way of thinking about the changing relations over time between the profession and the major institutions with which it interacts. The concept of countervailing powers builds on the work of Johnson (1972) and Larson (1977), who analyzed such relations with a dynamic subtlety not found elsewhere. Montesquieu (de Secondat

Montesquieu 1748) first developed the idea in his treatise about the abuses of absolute power by the state and the need for counterbalancing centers of power. Sir James Steuart (1767) developed it further in his ironic observations of how the monarchy's promotion of commerce to enhance its domain and wealth produced a countervailing power that tempered the absolute power of the monarchy and produced a set of interdependent relationships. One might discern a certain analogy to the way in which the American medical profession encouraged the development of pharmaceutical and medical supply companies within the monopoly markets it created to protect its own autonomy. They enriched the profession and extended its power, but increasingly on their terms.

The concept of countervailing powers focuses attention on the interactions of a few powerful actors in a field in which they are inherently interdependent yet distinct. If one party is dominant, as the American medical profession has been, its dominance is contextual and likely to elicit countermoves eventually by other powerful actors in an effort not to destroy it but to redress an imbalance of power. "Power on one side of a market," wrote John Kenneth Galbraith (1956: 113) in his original treatise on the dynamics of countervailing power in oligopolistic markets, "creates both the need for, and the prospect of reward to the exercise of countervailing power from the other side." In states where the government has played a central role in nurturing professions within the state structure but has allowed the professions to establish their own institutions and power base, the professions and the state go through phases of harmony and discord in which countervailing actions emerge. In states where the medical profession has been largely suppressed, we now see their rapid reconstitution once governmental oppression is lifted.

Countervailing moves are more difficult to accomplish and may take much longer when political and institutional powers are involved than in an economic market. Nevertheless, dominance tends to produce imbalances, excesses, and neglects that anger other countervailing (latent) powers and alienate the larger public. These imbalances include internal elaboration and expansion that weaken the dominant institution from within, a subsequent tendency to consume more and more of the nation's wealth, a self-regarding importance that ignores the concerns of its clients or subjects and institutional partners, and an expansion of control that exacerbates the impact of the other three. Other characteristics of a profession that affect its relations with countervailing powers are the degree and nature of competition with adjacent professions, about which Andrew Abbott (1988) has written with such richness, the changing technological base of its expertise, and the demographic composition of its membership.

As a sociological concept, countervailing powers is not confined to buyers and sellers; it includes a handful of major political, social, and other economic groups that contend with each other for legitimacy, prestige, and power, as well as for markets and money. Deborah Stone (1988) and Theodore Marmor with Jonathan Christianson (1982) have written insightfully about the ways in which countervailing powers attempt to portray benefits to themselves as benefits for everyone or to portray themselves as the unfair and damaged victims of other powers (particularly the state), or to keep issues out of public view. Here, the degree of power consists of the ability to override, suppress, or render as irrelevant the challenges by others, either behind closed doors or in public.

Because the sociological concept of countervailing powers recognizes several parties, not just buyers and sellers, it opens the door to alliances between two or more parties. These alliances, however, are often characterized by structural ambiguities, a term based on Merton and Barber's (1976) concept of sociological ambivalence that refers to the cross-cutting pressures and expectations experienced by an institution in its relations with other institutions (Light 1983:345–46). For example, a profession's relationships to the corporations that supply it with equipment, materials, and information technology both benefit the profession and make it dependent in uneasy ways. The corporations can even come to control professional practices in the name of quality. Alliances with dominant political parties (Krause 1988b; Jones 1991) or with governments are even more fraught with danger. The alliance of the German medical profession

with the National Socialist party, for example, so important to establishing the party's legitimacy, led to a high degree of governmental control over work and even the professional knowledge base (Jarausch 1990; Light, Liebfried, and Tennstedt 1986).

Countervailing Powers in American Medicine

In the case of the American medical profession, concern over costs, unnecessary and expensive procedures, and overspecialization grew during the 1960s to the "crisis" announced by President Richard Nixon, Senator Edward Kennedy, and many other leaders in the early 1970s. President Nixon attempted to establish a national network of health maintenance organizations (HMOs) bent on efficiency and cost-effectiveness. He and the Congress created new agencies to regulate the spending of capital, the production of new doctors, and even the practice of medicine through institutionalized peer review. All of these were done gingerly at first, in a provider-friendly way. When, at the end of the 1970s, little seemed to have changed, the government and corporations launched a much more adversarial set of changes, depicted in Table 17–1. The large number of unnecessary procedures, the unexplained variations in practice patterns, the unclear answers to rudimentary questions about which treatments were most cost-effective, and the burgeoning bills despite calls for self-restraint had eroded the sacred trust enjoyed by the profession during the golden era of medicine after World War II. To some degree, the dominance of the medical profession had been allowed on the assumption that physicians knew what they were doing and acted in the best interests of society. Unlike the guilds of earlier times, however, the medical profession had failed to exercise controls over products, practices, and prices to ensure uniformly good products at fair prices.

The reassertion of the payers' latent countervailing powers called for a concentration of will and buying power that was only partially achieved. Larger corporations, some states, and particularly the federal government changed from passively paying bills submitted by providers to scrutinizing bills and organizing markets for competitive contracts that covered a range of services for a large pool of people. The health insurance industry, originally designed to reimburse hospitals and doctors, was forcefully notified that it must serve those who pay the premiums or lose business. Today, thousands of insurance sales representatives are now agents of institutional buyers, and insurance companies have developed a complex array of managed care products. Hundreds of utilization management companies and entire divisions of insurance companies devoted to designing these products have arisen (Gray and Field 1989: Ch. 3).

These changes have produced analogous changes among providers: more large groups, vertically integrated clinics, preferred provider organizations (PPOs), health maintenance organizations (HMOs), and hospital-doctor joint ventures. When the federal government created and implemented a national schedule of prospective payments for hospital expenses, termed diagnosis related groups (DRGs), doctors and health care managers countered by doing so much more business outside the DRG system that they consumed nearly all the billions saved on inpatient care. Congress more than ever now regards doctors as the culprits, and it has countered by instituting a fee schedule based on costs. In response, the specialties affected have joined hands in a powerful political countermove designed to water down the sharp reductions in the fee schedule for surgeons and technology-based specialists (like radiologists).

Thus, although the buyers' revolt depicted in Table 17-1 spells the end of dominance, it by no means spells the end to professional power. Closely monitored contracts or payments, corporate amalgamation, and significant legal changes to foster competition are being met by responses that the advocates of markets, as the way to make medicine efficient, did not consider. Working together (or, as the other side terms it, collusion), appropriate referrals (known as cost shifting to somebody else's budget), market segmentation, market expansion, and service substitution are all easier and often more profitable than trying to become more efficient, particularly when the work is complex, contingent, and uncertain (Light 1990). Moreover, most ineffi-

ciencies in medicine are embedded in organizational structures, professional habits, and power relations so that competitive contracting is unlikely to get at them (Light 1991).

On the buyers' side, the majority of employers and many states have still not been able to take concerted action, much less combine their powers. The utilization management industry has produced a bewildering array of systems and criteria, which are adjusted to suit the preferences of each employer-client. The Institute of Medicine (IOM) study on the subject states that the Mayo Clinic deals with a thousand utilization review (UR) plans (Gray and Field 1989: 59), and large hospitals deal with one hundred to two hundred of them. Who knows which are more "rational" or effective? Moreover, the countervailing efforts of institutional buyers rest on a marshland of data. "Studies continue to document," states the IOM report, "imprecise or inaccurate diagnosis and procedure coding, lack of diagnostic codes on most claim forms, only scattered documentation about entire episodes of treatment or illness, errors and ambiguities in preparation and processing of claims data, and limited information on patient and population characteristics" (Gray and Field 1989:48).

In spite of this morass, a profound restructuring of incentives, payments, and practice environments is beginning to take place, and more solid, coordinated data are rapidly being accumulated. The threat of denial, or of being dropped as a high-cost provider in a market, has probably reduced treatments but in the process increased diagnostic services and documentation, a major vehicle for the expansion of medical sovereignty. Accountability, then, may be the profession's ace card as governments and institutional buyers mobilize to make the profession accountable to their concerns.

Changing Practice Patterns

Cost and Income

If the first round in the struggle to control rising medical expenditures consisted of tepid and unsuccessful efforts to regulate capital and ser-

Table 17-1. Axes of Change in the American Health Care System

Dimensions	Provider Driven	Buyer Driven
Ideological	Sacred trust in doctors	Distrust of doctors' values, decisions, even competence
Economic	Carte blanche to do what seems best; power to set fees; incentives to specialize, develop techniques	Fixed prepayment or contract with accountability for decisions and their efficacy
	Informal array of cross-subsidizations for teaching, research, charity care, community services	Elimination of "cost shifting"; pay only for services contracted
Political	Extensive legal and administrative power to define and carry out professional work without competition and to shape the organization and economics of medicine	Minimal legal and administrative power to do professional work but not shape the organization and economics of services
Clinical	Exclusive control of clinical decision making	Close monitoring of clinical decisions—their cost and their efficacy
	Emphasis on state-of-the-art specialized interventions; disinterest in prevention, primary care, and chronic care	Emphasis on prevention, primary care, and functioning; minimize high-tech and specialized interventions
Technical	Political and economic incentives to develop new technologies in protected markets	Political and economic disincentives to develop new technologies
Organizational	Cottage industry	Corporate industry
Potential disruptions and dislocations	Overtreatment; iatrogenesis; high cost; unnecessary treatment; fragmentation; depersonalization	Undertreatment; cuts in services; obstructed access; reduced quality; swamped in paperwork

vices in the 1970s, then providers again emerged as the winners of the second round in the 1980s. They expanded services, took market share away from hospitals, packaged services to the most attractive market niches, featured numerous products developed by the highly profitable companies specializing in new medical technology, and advertised vigorously. Eye centers, women's centers, occupational medicine clinics, ambulatory surgical centers, imaging centers, detoxification programs: these and other enterprises caused medical expenditures to rise from $250 billion in 1980 to about $650 billion in 1990. This equals 12 percent of the nation's entire gross national product (GNP), one-third higher than the average for Western Europe. There seems to be no way to avoid health expenditures' rising to 16 percent of GNP by 1995.

At the level of personal income, many physicians tell anyone who will listen that one can no longer make "good money" in medicine, but the facts are otherwise. From 1970 to about 1986, their average income stayed flat after inflation, but since then it has been rising. The era of cost containment and dehospitalization has actually been an opportunity for market expansion. Although physicians' market share of national health expenditures declined from 20 to 17 percent as hospitals' share rose between 1965 and 1984, it has climbed back up to 19 percent since then (Roback, Randolph, and Seidman 1990:Table 105). The profession appears thoroughly commercialized (Potter, McKinlay, and D'Agostino 1991), doing more of what pays more and less of what pays less. Although the profession likes to think it was more altruistic in the golden era of medicine after World War II, this was a time when physicians' incomes rose most rapidly and when it controlled insurance payment committees.

In addition, the range of physicians' incomes has spread. For example, surgeons earned 40 percent more than general practitioners in 1965 but 57 percent more in 1985 (Statistical Abstract 1989). As of 1989, surgeons earned on average $200,500 after expenses but before taxes, while family or general practitioners earned $95,000. All specialties averaged a sixty-hour week. Beleaguered obstetricians, even after their immense malpractice premiums, are doing well. They netted $194,300, up $14,000 from 1988, which was up $17,500 from 1987.

Despite the success so far of the profession in generating more demand, services, and income, the tidal force of population growth is against them. The number of physicians increased from 334,000 in 1970 to 468,000 in 1980 to 601,000 in 1990. By the year 2000, there will be about 722,000 physicians (Roback, Randolph, and Seidman 1990:Table 88). Although about 8.5 percent are inactive or have unknown addresses, the number of physicians in America is growing rapidly nevertheless, as it is in many European countries. There is no slowdown in sight, given the number of doctors graduating from medical schools and the nation's ambivalence about reducing the influx of foreign-trained doctors, many of whom are American born. In fact, between 1970 and 1989, foreign-trained doctors increased 126 percent compared to a 72 percent increase in American-trained doctors, and they constituted 130,000 of the 601,000 doctors in 1990 (Roback, Randolph, and Seidman 1990). As a result, the number of persons per physician is steadily dropping, from around 714 people per doctor thirty years ago to about 417 today and 370 in the year 2000. Will 370 men, women, and children be enough to maintain the average doctor in the style to which he or she is accustomed—about five and a half times the average income—in the face of countervailing forces? And how will the gross imbalance between the number of specialists and the need for their services play itself out? Today we have what could be called the 80-20 inversion: 80 percent of the doctors are specialists, but only about 20 percent or fewer of the nation's patients have problems warranting the attention of a specialist. Nearly all growth depends on an increasing number of subspecialties in medicine and surgery, and there are now about two hundred specialty societies, many not officially recognized but vying for legitimacy and a market niche (Abbott 1988). Thus, the rapid growth of physicians and their specialty training has set the stage for sharp clashes between countervailing powers.

Trends in the Organization of Practice

The post-Freidson era, from 1970 to the late 1980s, saw a steady trend of dehospitalization and a long-term shift back to office-based care. Most doctors (82%) are involved in patient care, and despite all the talk today about physician-executives, the data show no notable uptrend in numbers (Roback, Randolph, and Seidman 1990: Table A-2). Office-based practice has been rising slowly since 1975 (from 55% to 58.5%), and full-time hospital staff has declined from 10.4 to 8.5 percent in the same period. Hospital-based practice still makes up 23.6 percent of all practice sites because of all the residents and fellows in training. These data underscore the immense role that medical education, practically an industry in itself, plays in staffing and supporting hospital-based practice. The total number of residents has grown since 1970 by 60 percent, and they are a major source of cheap labor. They grew in use during the golden age of reimbursement, and curtailment of the workweek from 100 hours to 80 or fewer is already raising costs.

An increasing number of the 58 percent of doctors practicing in offices (that is, not a hospital or institution) do so in groups. Since the mid-1960s, when private and public insurance became fully established and funded expansion with few restraints, more and more doctors have combined into groups and formed professional corporations. The motives appear largely to have been income and market share. There were 4,300 groups in 1965 (11% of all nonfederal physicians), 8,500 in 1975, and 16,600 in 1988 (30%, or 156,000) (Havlicek 1990:Ch. 8). Supporting this emphasis on economic rather than service motives, an increasing percentage have been single specialty groups, up from 54 percent in 1975 to 71 percent in 1988. They tend to be small, from an average of 5 in 1975 to 6.2 in 1988, and their purpose seems largely to share the financing of space, staff, and equipment and to position themselves for handling larger specialty contracts from institutional buyers.

The future of groups will be affected by demands of the buyers' market. For example, almost all fee-for-service care now is managed by having an array of monitoring activities and cost-containment programs. These complex and expensive controls favor larger groups, and Havlicek (1990:8–38) believes we will see more mergers than new groups in the 1990s. He also suspects there will be more cooperative efforts with hospitals, which have more capital and staff but are subject to more cost controls.

Capitalist Professionals

An important, perhaps even integral, part of the rapid expansion of groups since the mid-1970s has involved doctors' investing in their own clinical laboratories (28% of all groups), radiology laboratories (32%), electrocardiological laboratories (28%), and audiology laboratories (16%). (Additionally, 40 percent of all office-based physicians have their own laboratories.) The larger the group is, the more likely it owns one or more of these facilities. For example, 23 percent of three-person groups own clinical laboratories and 78 percent of all groups with seventy-six to ninety-nine doctors. Large groups also own their own surgical suites: from 15 percent of groups with sixteen to twenty-five people to 41 percent of groups ranging from seventy-six to ninety-nine physicians. The hourly charges are very attractive (Havlicek 1990).

Growth of HMOs, PPOs, and Managed Care

The countervailing power of institutional buyers has forced practitioners to reorganize into larger units of health care that can manage the costs and quality of the services rendered. Health mainte-nance organizations, first developed in the 1920s, became the centerpiece of President Nixon's 1971 reforms to make American health care efficient and affordable. Medical lobbies fought the reform; when they saw it would pass, they weighed it down with requirements and restrictions. By 1976, there were 175 HMOs with 6 million members, half of them in just six HMOs that had built a solid reputation for good, coordinated care (Gruber, Shadle, and Polich 1988). Among them, PruCare and U.S. Health Care represented the new wave of expansion: national systems of HMOs run by insurers as a key "product" to sell to employers for cost containment or run by investors for the same purpose. Moreover, most of the new HMOs consisted of networks of private practitioners linked by part-time contracts rather than a core dedicated staff.

By December 1987, there were 650 HMOs with about 29 million members. Both Medicare and Medicaid revised terms to favor these groups as a way to moderate costs, as did many revised benefit plans by corporations. HMOs keep annual visits per person down to 3.8 and hospital inpatient bed-days down to 438 per thousand enrollees, well below the figures for autonomous, traditional care (Hodges, Camerlo, and Gold 1990). There were now forty-two national firms, and they enrolled half the total. The proportion of these firms that use networks of independent practitioners rose from 40 percent in 1980 to 62 percent in 1987. To increase their attractiveness, new hybrid HMOs were beginning to form that allowed members to get services outside the HMO's list of physicians if they paid a portion of the bill.

Preferred provider organizations come in many varieties, but all essentially consist of groups of providers who agree to give services at a discount. Employers then structure benefits to encourage employers to use them. For example, they offer to pay all of the fees for PPO providers but only 80 percent of fees from other doctors.

PPOs became significant by the mid-1980s, and by 1988 they had 20 million enrollees (Rice, Gabel, and Mick 1989). This figure is only approximate because patterns of enrollment are constantly changing. Perhaps more reliable are data from employers, who say that 13 to 15 percent of all employees and half their dependents are covered by PPOs (Sullivan and Rice 1991). Increasingly insurers are using PPOs as a managed care product, and they are forming very large PPOs—in the range of 200,000 enrollees each with 100 to 200 hospitals and 5,000 to 15,000 physicians involved in their systems. From the other side, physician group practices derive from 13 to 30 percent of their income from PPOs as group size increases. Besides volume discounts on fees, half to three-quarters of the PPOs use physician profiling (to compare the cost-effectiveness of different doctors), utilization review, and preselection of cost-effective providers.

In response to the "buyers' revolt" and the growth of HMOs and PPOs, a growing number of traditional, autonomous, fee-for-service practices have taken on the same techniques of managed care: preadmission review, daily concurrent review to see if inpatients need to stay another day, retrospective review of hospitalized cases, physician profiling to identify high users of costly services, and case management of costly, complex cases. By 1990, the most thorough study of all small, medium, and large employers, including state and local governments, found that only 5 percent of all employees and their families now have traditional fee-for-service physicians without utilization management (Sullivan and Rice 1991).

Conclusion

The countervailing power of institutional buyers certainly ends the kind of dominance the medical profession had in 1970, but by no means does it turn doctors into mere corporatized workers. The medical profession's relations with capital are now quite complex. Physicians are investing heavily in their own buildings and equipment, spurred by a refocus of the medical technology industry on office or clinic-based equipment that will either reduce costs or generate more income. Employers and their agents (insurance companies, management companies) are using their oligopolistic market power to restructure medical practice into managed care systems, but physicians have many ways to make those systems work for them. Hospitals are using their considerable capital to build facilities and buy equipment that will attract patients and their physicians, whom they woo intensively.

The state is by far the largest buyer and has shown the greatest resolve to bring costs under control. The federal government has pushed through fundamental changes to limit how much it pays hospitals and doctors. Each year brings more stringent or extensive measures. At the same time, the state faces a societal duty to broaden benefits to those not insured and to deepen them to cover new technologies or areas of treatment. And the state is itself a troubled provider through its Veterans Administration health care system and its services to special populations.

Both buyers and providers constantly attempt to use the legal powers of the state to advance their interests. Thus, regulation is best analyzed from this perspective as a weapon in the competition between countervailing powers rather than as an alternative to it. At the same time, competition itself is a powerful form of regulation (Leone 1986). However, Galbraith warned that the self-regulating counterbalance of contending power-blocs works poorly if demand is not limited, because it undermines the bargaining power of the buyers of the agents. This is another basic reason why institutional buyers are, so far, losing.

In response, buyers and the state are using other means besides price and contracts to strengthen their hand. Even as providers keep frustrating the efforts of institutional buyers through "visit enrichment," more bills, and higher incomes, a fundamental change has taken place. The game they are winning (at least so far) has ceased to be their game. Most of the terms are being set by the buyers.

The paradox of declining autonomy and growing sovereignty indicates a larger, more fundamental set of countervailing powers at work than simply the profession and its purchasers. As the dynamic unfolds, capitalism comes face to face with itself, for driving the growing sovereignty or domain of medicine is the medical-industrial complex, perhaps the most successful and largest sector of the entire economy. It is Baxter-Travenol or Humana versus General Motors or Allied Signal, with each side trying to harness the profession to its purposes. Different parts of the profession participate in larger institutional complexes to legitimate their respective goals of "the best medicine for every sick patient" and "a healthy, productive work force at the least cost." The final configuration is unclear, but the concept of professionalism as a countervailing power seems most clearly to frame the interactions.

REFERENCES

Abbott, A. 1988. *The System of Professions: An Essay on the Division of Expert Labor*. Chicago: University of Chicago Press.

de Secondat Montesquieu, C. L. 1748. *De l'Esprit des Loix*. Geneva: Barillot & Sons.

Freidson, E. 1970a. *Professional Dominance: The Social Structure of Medical Care*. Chicago: Aldine.

Freidson, E. 1970b. *Profession of Medicine: A Study of the Sociology of Applied Knowledge*. New York: Dodd, Mead.

Freidson, E. 1984. The Changing Nature of Professional Control. *Annual Review of Sociology* 10:1–20.

Freidson, E. 1985. The Reorganization of the Medical Profession. *Medical Care Review* 42:11–35.

Freidson, E. 1986a. *Professional Powers: A Study of the Institutionalization of Formal Knowledge*. Chicago: University of Chicago Press.

Freidson, E. 1989a. Industrialization or Humanization? In *Medical Work in America*. New Haven: Yale University Press.

Galbraith, J. K. 1956. *American Capitalism: The Concept of Countervailing Power*. Boston: Houghton Mifflin.

Gray, B. H., and M. J. Field., eds. 1989. *Controlling Costs and Changing Patient Care: The Role of Utilization Management*. Washington, D.C.: Institute of Medicine, National Academy Press.

Gruber, L. R., M. Shadle, and C. L. Politch. 1988. From Movement to Industry: The Growth of HMOs. *Health Affairs* 7(3):197–298.

Haug, M. R. 1973. Deprofessionalization. *An Sociological Review Monograph* 20:195–211.

Haug, M. R., and B. Lavin. 1983. *Consumerism in Medicine: Challenging Physician Authority*. Beverly Hills: Sage.

Havlicek, P. L. 1990. *Medical Groups in the U.S.: A Survey of Practice Characteristics*. Chicago: American Medical Association.

Hodges, D., K. Camerlo, and M. Gold. 1990. *HMO Industry Profile*. Vol. 2: *Utilization Patterns, 1988*. Washington, D.C.: Group Health Association of America.

Jarausch, K. H. 1990. *The Unfree Professions: German Lawyers, Teachers, and Engineers, 1900–1950*. New York: Oxford University Press.

Johnson, T. J. 1972. *Professions and Power*. London: Macmillan.

Jones, A., ed. 1991. *Professions and the State: Expertise and Autonomy in the Soviet Union and Eastern Europe*. Philadelphia: Temple University Press.

Krause, E. A. 1988b. Doctors, Partitocrazia, and the Italian State. *Milbank Quarterly* 66(Suppl. 2): 148–66.

Larson, M. S. 1977. *The Rise of Professionalism: A Sociological Analysis*. Berkeley: University of California Press.

Light, D. W. 1983. The Development of Professional Schools in America. In *The Transformation of Higher Learning, 1860–1930*, ed. K. H. Jarausch, 345–66. Chicago: University of Chicago Press.

Light, D. W. 1988. Turf Battles and the Theory of Professional Dominance. *Research in the Sociology of Health Care* 7:203–25.

Light, D. W. 1989. Social Control and the American Health Care System. In *Handbook of Medical Sociology*, ed. H. E. Freeman and S. Levine, 456–74. Englewood Cliffs, N.J.: Prentice-Hall.

Light, D. W. 1990. Bending the Rules. *Health Services Journal* 100(5222):1513–15.

Light, D. W. 1991. Professionalism as a Countervailing Power. *Journal of Health Politics, Policy and Law* 16:499–506.

Light, D. W., and S. Levine, 1988. The Changing Character of the Medical Profession: A Theoretical Overview. *Milbank Quarterly* 66(Suppl. 2):10–32.

Light, D. W., S. Liebfried, and F. Tennstedt. 1986. Social Medicine vs. Professional Dominance: the German Experience. *American Journal of Public Health* 76(1):78–83.

Marmor, T. R., and J. B. Christianson. 1982. *Health Care Policy: A Political Economy Approach*. Beverly Hills: Sage.

Merton, R. K. and B. Barbar, eds. 1976. Sociological Ambivalence. In *Sociological Ambivalence and Other Essays*. New York: Free Press.

Potter, D. A., J. B. McKinlay, and R. B. D'Agostino. 1991. *Understanding How Social Factors Affect Medical Decision Making: Application of a Factorial Experiment*. Watertown, Mass.: New England Research Institute.

Rice, T., J. Gabel, and S. Mick. 1989. *PPOS: Bigger, Not Better*. Washington, D.C.: HIAA Research Bulletin.

Roback, G., L. Randolph, and S. Seidman. 1990. *Physician Characteristics and Distribution in the U.S.* Chicago: American Medical Association.

Starr, P. 1982. *The Social Transformation of American Medicine: The Rise of a Sovereign Profession and the Making of a Vast Industry*. New York: Basic Books.

Statistical Abstract of the United States. 1989. Washington, D.C.: Department of Commerce.

Steuart, J. 1767. *Inquiry into the Principles of Political Economy*, vol. 1. London: A. Miller and T. Cadwell.

Stone, D. A. 1988. *Policy Paradox and Political Reason*. Glenview, Ill.: Scott, Foresman.

Sullivan, C., and T. Rice. 1991. The Health Insurance Picture in 1990. *Health Affairs* 10(2):104–15.

Willis, E. 1988. Doctoring in Australia: A View at the Bicentenary. *Milbank Quarterly* 66 (Suppl 2): 167–81.

The Social Organization
of Medical Workers

. . . . . .

Medical care in the United States is an enormous and complex industry involving thousands of organizations, the expenditure of billions of dollars each year, and the employment of millions of workers. There are discernible patterns in the types and distribution of medical services available in any society. These patterns reflect and reinforce the sociocultural context in which they are found, including the political, economic, and cultural priorities of a society. The composition of the labor force in most sectors of society reflects that society's distribution of power and privilege. This section examines the organization and distribution of medical care services and the nature of the medical care labor force in this country.

Our medical care system has been described as "acute, curative, [and] hospital-based" (Knowles, 1977: 2). That is, we have a *medical* care system (as distinguished from a *health* care system) organized around the cure and/or control of serious diseases and the repairing of physical injuries rather than the "caring" for the sick or the prevention of disease. The American medical care system is highly technological, specialized, and increasingly centralized. More and more medical care is delivered in large bureaucratic institutions. For decades, hospitals dominated medical organizations, employing at one time 75 percent of all medical care workers. With the emergence of managed care, especially of health maintenance organizations (HMOs), the number of hospital workers has declined to 64 percent of the medical work force (DHHS, 1994: 197).

From 1900 to 1975 the number of hospitals in the United States gradually increased, reaching a total of over 6300. Since then there has been a slight decline in the number of hospitals (DHHS, 1994). The seeming trend toward fewer yet larger hospitals threatens the existence of some community hospitals. Approximately 56 percent of all hospitals in 1992 were owned by non-profit organizations, with another 30 percent owned by federal, state, or local governments. The remaining 13 percent were owned by profit-making organizations; in addition, 81 percent of all nursing homes were profit-making institutions (DHHS, 1994). The number of for-profit hospitals, especially in the form of hospital chains, has increased dramatically in the past decade (see selection 21 by Arnold S. Relman in this volume and Light, 1986).

The medical care system has changed enormously in the past three decades. In 1960 U.S. national health expenditures were 5.2 percent of the gross national product (GNP); in 1994 totaling nearly $940 billion, they made up nearly 14 percent of the GNP. While most of the health policy analysts have focused on the spiraling cost of U.S. medical care, changes in the social organization of the medical system have been equally dramatic. Perhaps no institution in American society is changing as rapidly as the medical system. In 1960 the solo practitioner in private practice was the norm of medical service; by the late 1980s medical care was typically delivered through an organization, be it an HMO, PPO, ambulatory care center, or hospital emergency department. It is also more likely that the physician is a salaried employee rather than an independent professional, and that payment is made by a third party rather than directly by the patient (see also McKinlay and Stoeckle in the previous section).

The first selection, "The US Health Care System," by John Fry and his associates, presents on overview of a changing medical care system, emphasizing its impact on physicians. The authors show the historic impact of the increas ing specialization of physicians, including increasing medical costs and physician incomes. They document the shift back from hospital to office-based care, noting how with the rise of "managed care" the demand for primary care physicians is increasing. As we approach the twenty-first century, there will be an increasing demand for primary care physicians, and most of these will be employed by large bureaucratic organizations, especially HMOs and hospitals.

The growth and expansion of medical care institutions has engendered a rapid expansion of the medical labor force. From 1970 to 1986, the number of people employed in the medical care industry in the United States almost doubled—from 4.2 million to 8.1 million. Medical care workers constitute about 8 percent of the total American labor force. Some of these workers are physicians, but the vast majority are not. In fact, physicians make up only 6 percent of the entire medical work force (DHHS, 1994). Nurses make up the largest group of health workers, with over a million registered nurses (RNs) and half a million more licensed practical nurses (LPNs).

Medical care workers include some of the highest paid employees in our nation (physicians) and some of the lowest paid (until the early 1970s, many hospital workers were not even covered by minimum wage laws). More than 75 percent of all medical workers are women, although more than 85 percent of all physicians are men. Many of these women are members of Third World and minority groups, and most come from working-class and lower-middle-class backgrounds. Almost all physicians are white and upper-middle-class. Blacks, for example, account for only 5 percent of medical school graduates (Lloyd and Miller, 1989). In short, the structure of the medical work force reflects the inequalities of American society in general.

This medical care work-force structure can be pictured as a broad-based triangle, with a small number of highly paid physicians and administrators at the very top. These men—and they are mostly men—by and large control the administration of medical care services *within* institutions. As one moves toward the bottom of the triangle there are increasing numbers of significantly lower-paid female workers with little or no authority in the medical delivery organization. This triangle is layered with a growing number of licensed occupational categories of workers, a number close to 300 different medical occupations (Caress, 1976: 168). There is practically no movement of workers from one category to another, since each requires its own specialized training and qualifications, requirements that are largely controlled through licensing procedures authorized by the AMA Committee on Education. Professional dominance, as discussed in the previous section, is highly evident throughout the division and organization of medical labor.

The development of a rigidly stratified medical labor force is the result of a complex historical process as deeply connected to the gender and class of those providing services as to the development of organizations themselves. In

"A Caring Dilemma: Womanhood and Nursing in Historical Perspective," Susan Reverby traces the emergence of nursing, focusing in particular on how "caring as a duty" was connected to the fact that it was women who were doing the caring. In women, medical administrators could find a caring, disciplined, and cheap labor force. Reverby shows how the dilemmas nurses faced and the struggles they engaged in to improve the image, stature, and authority of nursing were shaped by the gender stratification of society. She argues that this historical past is reflected in nursing's current position in the health care hierarchy and its continuing dilemmas.

In the final selection, "AIDS and Its Impact on Medical Work," Charles L. Bosk and Joel E. Frader present a doctor's view of the medical culture surrounding AIDS in an academic urban hospital. Bosk and Frader see doctors as workers on the "shop floor" of the hospital and examine how AIDS affected the medical work culture of the medical house officers (i.e., residents). The young physicians now perceive themselves at greater risk and their sense of lost invulnerability has engendered rather negative views about treating AIDS patients. While the pressures of work in medical residency often create negative views toward patients (e.g., Mizrahi, 1986), such views are transformed and amplified by the existence of AIDS. As Bosk and Frader note, not all physicians share this view of AIDS patients; the negative attitudes of some physicians are in part a product of their current work situation. It is interesting to note, however, that a recent study found that the "culture of caring" that permeates nursing socialization and work engenders a much more positive view of AIDS patients (Fox, Aiken, and Messikomer, 1991). Nurses see caring for AIDS patients as part of their mission, and many even volunteer to work in AIDS treatment settings. It is thus clear that the cultures of medical workers vary and that the culture of one's work can affect the care that one provides.

REFERENCES

Caress, Barbara. 1976. "The health workforce: Bigger pie, smaller pieces." Pp. 163–170 in David Kotelchuck, Prognosis Negative. New York: Vintage Books. [Reprinted from Health/PAC Bulletin, January/February, 1975.]

Department of Health and Human Services. 1994. Health, United States 1994. Washington, D.C.: U.S. Government Printing Office.

Fox, Reneé C., Linda H. Aiken, and Carlo M. Messikomer. 1991. "The culture of caring: AIDS and the nursing profession." In Dorothy Nelkin, David P. Willis, and Scott V. Parris (eds.), A Disease of Society. New York: Cambridge University Press.

Knowles, John. 1977. "Introduction." John Knowles (ed.), Doing better and feeling worse: Health in the United States. Daedalus. 106, 1: Winter.

Light, Donald W. 1986. "Corporate medicine for profit." Scientific American. 255 (December): 38–45.

Lloyd, Sterling M. Jr., and Russell L. Miller. 1989. "Black student enrollment in U.S. medical schools." Journal of the American Medical Association. 261: 272–4.

Mizrahi, Terry. 1986. Getting Rid of Patients. New Brunswick: Rutgers University Press.

18

The US Health Care System

. . . . . .

John Fry, Donald Light, Jonathan Rodnick, and Peter Orton

Introduction

The US is a young nation born out of pioneers and with philosophies of equality of opportunities, freedom and democracy, self-reliance and entrepreneurship—all of which have been transmitted into the health care system.

There is no single system; health care is provided through a multi-mix of private and public schemes. Private insurance through employment covers most of the population, but it is not full and comprehensive. Publicly funded programs like Medicare (for the elderly), Medicaid (for the poor) and state schemes have slowly filled the gaps over the decades and now generate over 40% of health costs. Personal out-of-pocket payments are the highest of developed countries and make up almost one third of patient expenses, although there are some special, voluntary and charitable programs to help the poor or those without insurance through work, but a sizeable proportion of the population (17%) has no medical insurance.

The US health system is the most expensive at over 14% of GDP, or $3,600 per head in 1993, and may reach 15% of GDP or $5,000 per head, by the year 2000. There is no shortage of physicians and the rate per population is higher than in many other countries. Nor does there appear to be a dearth of primary physicians, but they are distributed unevenly and have poorly defined roles.

While there are recognizable levels of professional care the lines are blurred because of the patient's free choice and access to any physician, the lack of gatekeeping roles for primary physicians, and the mixture of generalists and special-ists. Primary care is in crisis with falling recruitment, uncertainty of roles, and low status. The fragmentation of primary care physicians, with family physicians, general internists and general pediatricians having varying responsibilities, leads to unnecessary competition and a waste of resources.

A priority for the future must be to achieve a national health system more appropriate to the needs of the US people and with primary care playing its part to the full.

The Nation

American policies still reflect the nation's original emphasis on personal freedom and minimal government interference. Such historical factors have been translated into features of its health system and services, largely through the efforts of the medical profession. Thus professional autonomy, free choice and treating citizens as self-reliant individuals until they come in for help, have characterized the US health care system. Private individual charges, voluntary insurance and public support only for the needy and elderly, have been the financial principles underlying the system. Although it is the funding mechanisms and levels that have impeded equal access to services, most Americans believe that governmental programs are inefficient and unresponsive. It has often been noted that the US and South Africa are the only industrialized countries without universal health insurance or a national heath system.

The US is a vast, diverse and changing society. About one million new immigrants enter each year, half of them illegally. Its multi-ethnic groups are growing more numerous and more distinct. At present, caucasians of many origins make up 75%, African-Americans 12%, and Hispanics, Asians and others 13% of the population. It is these last groups that are the majority of the new immigrants. More than one in five of the population is under 15 years, but the society is aging fast (13% over 65) because of falling birth rates and longer life (Table 18-1).

Health indices overall are among the lowest of industrialized nations and vary dramatically by educational, income and ethnic group. Paradoxically, this affluent and successful nation is afflicted with many modern social pathologies in its rates of crime, homicide, drug abuse, AIDS and poverty, which are substantially higher than in other nations.

With varied health needs, mainly not addressed by the existing health care system, and spiraling medical expenses that exceed 14% of GDP, the nation seeks a new delivery system that can guarantee access for all yet hold costs down.

Origins of the Health Care System

The modern American health care system arose from a wide range of therapies practices by large numbers of healers in the late 19th century. This frustrated the American Medical Association (AMA) and its leaders trained in the new scientific medicine. Through a series of remarkably successful campaigns, the AMA and state medical societies gained control of medical education and licensure on behalf of scientific medicine. The systematic improvement in medical education at the beginning of the century was followed by the increasing importance of the hospital, the specialization of most physicians and the rise of the research oriented academic medical center in the mid-century.

The shift in the locus of care and a mounting pile of unpaid bills caused by the Depression led hospitals and then doctors to create provider-run, non-profit health insurance on a voluntary basis. Commercial insurers joined in, and coverage rapidly expanded, providing pass-through reimbursement for hospital and specialty care. The proportion of physicians who were general

Table 18-1. Demography (US:UK) (*The Economist*, 1992; Health US, 1990; National Center for Health Statistics, 1991; OHE, 1992)

	UK	US
Population (millions)	57.5	250
(annual growth)	(0.3%)	(1%)
Population		
Under 15	18.9%	21.4%
Over 65	15.5%	12.6%
Birth rate		
Annual per 1,000 population	13.4	14.1
Cesarean section rate per births	10%	25%
Infant mortality per 1,000 births	8.4	9.0
Legal abortions		
per 1,000 women	11.7	28.0
per 100 births	18.0	29.7
Fertility rate		
(children per woman 15–45)	1.8	1.9
Life expectancy (at birth)	M 72 F 78	M 73 F 80
Deaths		
Annual per 1,000	11.4	8.3
Place of death (hospital)	65%	75%
Social		
Unemployed workers	9%	8%
Marriage (annual per 1,000 population)	6.7	9.7
Divorce (annual per 1,000 population)	2.9	4.8
Number persons per household	2.6	2.8
Wealth		
Annual GDP per capita ($)	16,000	21,700
Health expenditure		
% GDP	6.3	12 +
(Public)	(5.3)	(4.8)
(Private)	(1.0)	(7.2)

practitioners (GPs) fell from 75% in 1935, to 45% in 1957, to 34% in 1990.

Between the 1930s and the 1980s the AMA, along with other provider groups, successfully opposed national health insurance and emphasized employer-based insurance that paid for care only when billed by physicians and hospitals (Starr, 1982). Thus most medicine was done by private practitioners, clinics and hospitals who charged fees.

When Congress finally legislated in 1965 coverage for the elderly (Medicare) and the poor (Medicaid), it reinforced the fee for service payments. Direct federal funds were confined largely to capital for building more hospital beds and for research. Thus by the late 1960s, the majority of doctors were specialists, there developed a crisis in primary care, and costs began to rise rapidly. People could see any specialists they wished—and did. Few physicians chose to go into general practice and those few were isolated from the mainstream medical community. Hospitals expanded rapidly and competed to offer the latest in technical services, which were generously reimbursed. The term "medical-industrial complex" appeared, and the protected markets of medical services flourished at high profits.

The Structure

From this brief history one can see that the organization of the American system is a loose one, emphasizing the hospital and technical services. There is a blurring between all four levels of care, because there is no clear division of labor between generalists and specialists. An arrangement to this end was discussed earlier this century but rejected because GPs wanted to retain hospital privileges (Stevens, 1971).

General Practice among Specialists

Since the 1960s, the primary care vacuum has meant in effect that much "primary care" is done by specialists, what Fry (1960) calls "specialoids." To fill the vacuum, internal medicine, pediatrics, obstetrics, and psychiatry each declared themselves to be a "primary care specialty," and all but psychiatry have succeeded. In fact, about 80% of internists and 50% of pediatricians end up in subspecialties, but all American statistics count them as primary care doctors.

Most important, after years of campaigning, general practice attained specialty status by requiring residency training and board certification centered on its new focus, family practice. The Millis Report of 1966 proposed that primary care be recognized as a specialty and receive federal funding and that community health centers be established in poor areas. Both of these changes were made, and the American Board of Family Practice was established in 1969. This change partially stopped the loss of physicians in primary care by encouraging thousands of new doctors to become residency trained. However, as older GPs retire, there has continued to be a significant decrease in the percentage of American physicians in general and family practice.

Family physicians (FPs) and general internists represent the largest groups to whom people turn for primary care. They provide a wide range of services, but a different blend from the British GPs who have access to a broader range of resources through the NHS. Patients go to a wide variety of generalists and specialists for first-contact care, as illustrated in Figure 18-1. With some exceptions, there is no counterpart to community nursing, primary medical teams, and the wide array of services for the disabled, the chronically ill, and the feeble. Home health care is expanding in the US, but largely as a set of high-tech services (such as home intravenous therapy or home physical therapy) provided by for-profit teams. US FPS and internists take care of hospitalized patients and do more procedures (such as sigmoidoscopy) than British GPs.

About 39% of all expenditures go on hospital services, and this percentage has been dropping slightly as insurers and government programs have become much more strict about hospital admissions and length of stay. American hospital lengths of stay are the shortest in the world, but also the most expensive, because those few days are packed with sophisticated procedures, advanced equipment, and highly trained staff working in expensively built facilities. As more and more complex procedures are done on an outpatient basis, doctors and hospitals have been competing for market share. Many have joined forces to establish surgi-centers, women's centers, imaging centers etc., so that the term "hospital" now includes many facilities and side

Figure 18-1. *Percent Distribution of US Generalist and Specialty Physicians*

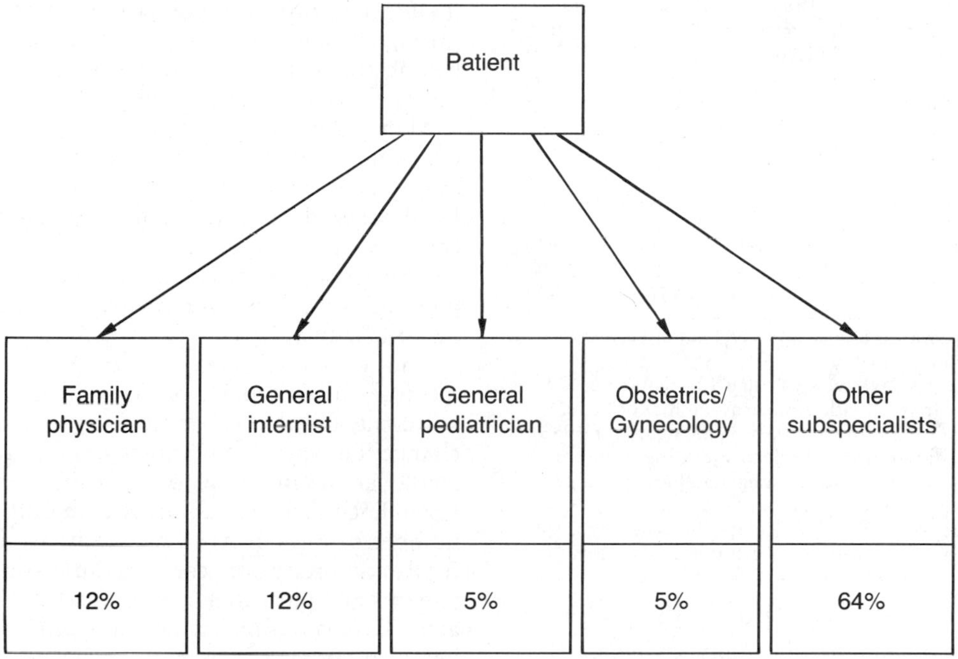

Family physician	General internist	General pediatrician	Obstetrics/ Gynecology	Other subspecialists
12%	12%	5%	5%	64%

corporations besides the central building with inpatient beds. Recently there has also been a strong trend to "vertical integration," with hospitals setting up organizations to be involved in and potentially control all aspects of patient care from primary-care practice to nursing homes.

Medical Manpower

Surprisingly, the manpower crisis of the late 1960s precipitated a major federal program to expand medical schools. In fact, much of the "crisis" stemmed from there being too few generalists and too many specialists. The number of graduates doubled, and the number of doctors has been expanding rapidly ever since. However, in the absence of an overall manpower plan, most graduates have chosen specialty training. By the mid-1970s, a surplus was predicted in all but a few of the specialties.

From 1965 to 1990, the numbers of family practitioners in the US declined slowly (0.1% per annum), while general internists and general practitioners rose by 6% annually. Specialists rose much faster so that the percentage of primary care doctors fell from 43 in 1965 to 34 in 1990 (Table 18-2).

Many of the new physicians are women, and they now make up 40–60% of medical school classes. Intensive recruitment of minorities has generated only a slowly increasing number of candidates against the many other careers open to the talented. What used to be called "foreign medical graduates" (FMGs) became a significant factor in the 1960s, when rapidly expanding hospital and specialty programs searched for young doctors, who had graduated from non-US medical schools, to fill the more unpopular (inner-city) residencies. After medical schools doubled the national class size, there was increasing pressure to cut back on FMGs. An increasing number of them, however, were Americans who went abroad to obtain a medical degree, and their families mounted a powerful lobby. Subsequent actions have neutralized the term to "international medical graduates" (IMGs) and tightened standards, slowly reducing their pro-

Table 18-2. Proliferation of Provider

Practitioners	1960	1980	2000
Physicians (MDs, DOs)	251,200	457,500	704,700
Persons per active physician	735	508	369
Chiropractors	unknown	24,400	88,100
Registered nurses[a]	592,000	1,272,900	1,900,000
Licensed practical nurses[a]	217,000	549,300	724,500
Nurse-midwives[b]	500(?)	2,000	4,800
Physician assistants[c]	0	11,000	32,800
Nurse-practitioners[d]	0	14,700	36,400

[a] The figure for 2000 was an interpolation between high and low estimates.
[b] The figure for 2000 was calculated by assuming 200 graduates per year, with gross attrition rate of 20%.
[c] The figure for 1980 was based on the figure for 1983 minus attrition projected back to 1980; the figure for 2000 was calculated by assuming 1,500 graduates per year, with gross attrition rate of 20%.
[d] The figure for 2000 was calculated by assuming 2,100 graduates per year, with gross attrition rate of 20%.

portion from 32% of residents in 1970 to 23% in 1990. IMGs tend to fill empty residency slots, many of them now in internal medicine.

Financing Medical Care

The voluntary health insurance system works best in mid-size and large companies, which provide coverage for employees and their dependents as a benefit. Employers typically pay a "middle-man" insurance company, who then administers the benefits and pays the doctors and hospitals. Some employers offer employees a range of insurance policies to choose from, each administered by a different company. Each policy may cover different services, have different charges and co-payments to the employee and involve different doctors and hospitals. Some companies are "self-insured" and administer the plan themselves or contract with only one insurance company to do so. These policies are "experience-rated," which means that the premiums reflect the health status and illnesses of each employee group. As firm size falls below 50 employees, so the percentage of companies providing health insurance drops rapidly, and

staff in these companies must buy insurance on an individual basis (which is very expensive—often double or triple the cost to the employer) or through volunteer associations to which they belong (these plans are uncommon and usually involve very large deductibles and co-insurance).

Many large companies also cover employees' dependents, often for an additional charge. Because of the wide variability of medical coverage by employers and the universal exclusion of coverage for pre-existing conditions in new employees, many people are reluctant to change jobs and run the risk of receiving markedly fewer, or no benefits.

Another complicating factor in the American medical care system is that companies are usually searching for a cheaper health plan; they may change the types and numbers of plans offered to employees annually (who may shift plans once a year). Each plan may contract with only a certain number of physicians or hospitals, so that long-term continuity of care is impossible. Both patients and physicians are confused as to what is actually covered and what has been carried out before by other clinicians or facilities. Insurance plans adopt a one-year mentality, in part because employees are likely to change plans, and in part to make a profit by minimizing the amount of medical or hospital bills paid for that year. Thus they are unlikely to invest in preventive care, and they put as many administrative hurdles as possible in the way of getting care (Light, 1993).

Medicare was provided for the elderly, when a plan focused on hospital and specialty care; ironically it covers few home or long-term services for the chronically ill. In addition, Medicare often covers only a portion of physician bills, no drug costs, no other health professions (such as dentists or psychologists), and has significant deductibles before any charges are paid. Because of these gaps in coverage, over 80% of the elderly purchase a supplementary insurance policy for relatively high premiums to help with the uncovered expenses.

Under federal law, the states also provide Medicaid for the poor, with the Federal Government paying about half the costs, more for poorer states and less for affluent ones. The 50 states, however, have made very different decisions about how many services they will cover and about who is eligible. On the whole, they use strict eligibility rules that allow only half or less of those with survival incomes (the poverty line) to be covered—primarily poor women with children and poor elderly with chronic disorders who have used up all their life savings paying for what Medicare does not cover. Once their savings are below about $2,000, they become eligible for Medicaid, which does pay for long-term care and a broad range of home services as well as all acute services. In some states, only a third of those on survival incomes are eligible.

Another difficulty is that payment levels for most Medicaid services are set so low that only a few providers will treat Medicaid patients. These providers may "compensate" by treating a high volume of poor patients.

For many years, about 35 million Americans have had no health insurance. Three quarters of these uninsured are in working families. Latinos and African-Americans are twice as likely to be uninsured. When they need care, these citizens (one in every six) use the relatively small and underfunded system of public hospital emergency rooms and clinics, as well as non-physician providers and healers.

An unknown but estimated 40 to 70 million Americans have "Swiss cheese policies" with substantial holes of medical insurance coverage in the middle (exclusion clauses for not covering existing illnesses or high risks, ranging from mental illness to pregnancy, to diabetes), on the front edge (increased deductibles), the sides (co-payments), or the back edge (payment caps). No systematic records are kept of these internal policy features, but they have perpetrated a crisis for both physicians and their patients (Light, 1992a). There are over 1200 insurance companies selling medical insurance. Because they compete on price, and because there is no definition of what must be covered by insurance, almost every conceivable and confusing exclusion is used to reduce claims paid. . . .

The US health care financing system is now like a giant shell game, every payer trying to shift costs to other payers, especially back to the patient or to the doctor in the form of unpaid or partially paid bills. In addition, patients pay 30% of all medical costs out of their own pockets. When insurance companies or patients do not pay part or all of a claim, the providers often come after patients through collection agencies, which have the power of ruining their credit for all other financing in their lives.

These problems have led to widespread dissatisfaction of both patients and physicians. The US spends the most money on health care yet registers the highest consumer dissatisfaction with their medical care of any industrialized nation (Blendon and Edwards, 1991).

Physician Income

Although physician costs are about 20% of total medical costs and half of that goes to overhead expenses, only 10% of all health care dollars go to physicians' "take-home" pay. However, this still amounts to very high incomes; among the highest in the world. Most doctors still bill privately and are paid on a fee-for-service basis. But a growing number work for a salary plus bonuses, for a contract, or on the basis of capitation fees in various managed care organizations. This situation is complex and changing rapidly.

Primary care doctors and a few specialties that involve considerable listening or counselling (such as psychiatry and geriatrics) average about $100,000 per year. Many of the medical subspecialties, such as cardiology, gastroenterology, general surgery and obstetrics and gynecology, average about $200,000, while subspecialty surgeons, such as orthopedics, cardiothoracic and neurosurgery, average over $300,000 (AAFP, 1992 and Light, 1993). These are 1990 figures, and although the mean is about $150,000, there is a long right-handed tail to the distribution stretching out to $800,000 or more. These payment patterns date back to the payments committees of Blue Cross and other insurance plans, which were dominated by hospital-based specialties. They reflect higher charges allowed for new "experimental" procedures, the use of which soon becomes widespread (such as laparoscopy), and also reflect critical moments when, for example, radiologists and pathologists refused to be billed as part of hospital services and set up independent businesses that contract with several hospitals. The so-called competition of the last 15 years has generally not brought down the earnings of these high-end specialties. Indeed, this disparity has been exaggerated. In the 1960s, specialists typically earned 50% more than primary care physicians; now, it is two to three times as much. These drastic inequities in earnings, without any difference in hours worked (about 55 per week) are one of the key reasons for students deciding to pursue subspecialty careers.

Organization of Services

From 1970 to the late 1980s, there was a steady trend of less hospitalization and a shift back to office-based care for patients. Most doctors (82%) are principally involved in patient care (the remainder in teaching, research or administration), and despite all the talk today about physician-executives, the data show no notable increase (Roback, Randolph and Seidman, 1990: Table A-2). The number of physicians in office-based practice (not associated with a hospital) has been rising slowly since 1970 (from 55% to 58.5%), and the percentage of physicians practicing full-time in hospitals has declined from 10.4 to 8.5. However, hospital-based practice makes up 23.6% of all practice sites because of all the residents and fellows in training. This underscores the immense role that medical education, as practically an industry in itself, plays in manning and supporting hospital-based practice. The total number of residents has grown since 1970 by 60%, and they are a major source of "cheap" labor.

An increasing number of the 58% of doctors practicing in "offices" (i.e., not a hospital or institution) do so in groups. Since the mid-1960s, when private and public insurance became fully established and funded expansion with few restraints, more and more doctors have combined into groups to form professional corporations.

While there were 4,300 groups in 1965, this figure rose to 8,500 in 1975 and 16,600 in 1988 (Havlicek, 1990: Chapter 8). This means that while 11% of all non-federal physicians worked in group practice in 1965, 30% did so by 1988. Supporting this emphasis on economic rather than service motives, an increasing percentage

practise in single specialty groups, up from 54% in 1975 to 71% in 1988. These groups tend to be small, with an average of 6.2 physicians in 1988, and their purpose is largely to share the financing of space, staff and equipment, and to position themselves for handling larger contracts from institutional payers.

An important, perhaps even integral part of the rapid expansion of groups since the mid-1970s has involved doctors investing in their own clinical laboratories, radiology labs, electro-cardiological labs and audiology labs. (In addition, 40% of all office-based physicians have their own labs for blood tests or sample cultures.) The larger the group, the more likely it will own one or more of these facilities.

For example, while 23% of three-person groups own clinical labs, this rises steadily to 78% for groups with more than 75 doctors. Large groups also own their own surgical duties, from 15% of groups size 16–25, to 41% of groups size 76–99. The reason is primarily economic, as current reimbursement levels allow large profits to be made in lab, X-ray and surgical areas. Because the purchase of equipment and staff is so expensive, larger groups are more easily able to afford the initial costs and refer enough patients to keep the facilities busy.

Reorganization Towards Managed Care

In 1970–71, President Richard Nixon, Senator Edward Kennedy (who chaired the Senate Labor and Human Resources Committee), and the business community (which paid and pays most premiums as an employee benefit) all declared that the health care system was in crisis. Problems included:

> weak and dwindling primary care
> too much surgery, hospital care, tests, and specialty visits
> escalating costs that would soon bankrupt the nation
> fragmented, impersonal care
> millions of uninsured citizens, including half the poor who should have been covered by Medicaid.

Each group proposed its own version of national health insurance and met with opposition by

Table 18-3. Definitions of Managed Care

Managed care	Any system of health service payment or delivery arrangements where the health plan attempts to control or coordinate use of health services by its enrolled members in order to contain health expenditures, by either improving quality or lowering it
Managed competition	An approach to health system reform in which health plans compete to provide health insurance coverage and services for enrollees. Typically, enrollees sign up with a health plan purchasing entity and choose a service plan during an open enrolment period
Managed indemnity	This is traditional private fee for service care with utilization controls and reimbursement of fees by the insurance company

doctors, insurance companies and medical supply companies. However, Nixon's proposal for managed competition between hundreds of health maintenance organizations (HMOs) passed into legislation. HMOs provide nearly all medical services for a fixed subscription per annum. One of the key components of the HMO legislation was that all employers with over 25 employees, who offered medical insurance as a benefit (many do not), must offer an HMO as an option if one exists in the nearby region. Overnight, HMOs had a built-in market.

Currently, managed care in the US means essentially that someone in addition to the physician is trying to decrease medical costs by "managing" the patient's care through aggressive contracting or utilization controls (Table 18-3). Typically the primary care physician is the key player and could be rewarded by ordering fewer tests or procedures, i.e., rewarded for more "appropriate" utilization.

Managed care now comes in many variants, but a useful framework is provided by the four basic types of HMOs and PPOs.

1. *Staff or group model HMOs*—center around a full-time staff who take care of a defined number of patients (or enrollees). They look like more traditional medical multispecialty groups but with greater numbers of primary care physicians. The groups must figure out how to best serve their subscribers on a fixed budget. These groups are better at holding costs down, primarily by reducing hospital admissions. In staff model HMOs, the plan employs the physicians, while in group models, the plan contracts with medical groups who only take care of that plan's patients.
2. *IPA (Independent Practice Association) HMOs*—contract with hundreds of private physicians, each of whom takes on varying numbers of their subscribers in return for a capitation or fee-for-service contract, plus incentives for holding down hospital and specialty costs. Hundreds of new for-profit HMOs have chosen the IPA approach to increase subscribers' choices and therefore market appeal. Typically, lower start-up costs are needed as physicians still have their own offices and staff. But IPA controls over actual practice patterns are tenuous, which often leads to micromanagement by the IPA central staff or the insurance company to control patient utilization.
3. *Network HMOs*—lie in between, contracting with many group practices. This means that some of the clinical management can be done within the groups of colleagues, rather than externally by monitors from the central office. Network HMOs try to combine the best of both worlds—colleague self-management and wide choice for market appeal.
4. *Preferred Provider Organizations (PPOs)*—groups of doctors who offer volume discounts to insurers or employers in return for preferred status (usually by having their reduced fees covered by the subscriber's insurance policy instead of a patient's co-payment). They can be narrow (an obstetrical PPO) or broad (a primary care PPO). Initially hailed as a panacea, they are not proving to save money, and the decrease in fees has been accompanied by an increase in patient volume. PPOs typically do not have a central office to do utilization review; it is more frequently done by the insurance company.

New hybrids have been created to attract more subscribers, such as the Point of Service HMO that allows subscribers to go outside the HMO when they want to see another physician who is not a member of the plan. In that case, the patient ends up paying much more (but not all) of that physician's bill.

Currently, over 50 million Americans get their care from HMOs. This is growing steadily, though much more slowly than envisioned originally. Details of enrollment and disenrollment led some to believe this shows that most Americans have "rejected" the restrictions of HMOs and lead others to believe that Americans are being converted. Managed care in less rigorous forms is part of most health insurance plans. Indeed, in many states Medicaid and Medicare are turning to HMOs to enroll their patients. True endemnity medical insurance, where a portion or all of the physician's fee for each service is paid without a contract or review, is getting rare and very expensive. In some areas of the US, only 5% of medical insurance is the old-style indemnity insurance. . . .

Conclusion

The US medical system is in the midst of rapid change. Whether or not the Congress passes sweeping legislation to correct the lack of universal coverage, changes will continue. These changes include:

- increasing control by employers of how their medical care dollars are spent
- a weakening of hospitals' control over the organization and financing of medical care
- increasing formation and growth of physician group practices
- increasing managed care (by insurance companies and physicians), with increasing numbers of people taken care of by HMOs and few people insured through plans offering indemnity coverage or contracting with PPOs
- less choice (for patients) of doctors and hospitals.

However, without additional national congressional action, these financing and power changes may slow the acceleration in medical costs, but are unlikely to curtail the growth entirely. They fail to address many issues which are a necessary part of reform, including: malpractice and tort reform, simplification of the administration/financing of the medical system, and an over-reliance on technology to diagnose and treat illness.

Only through addressing the basic building block of any medical system—medical care—can the US make the kind of organizational and philosophical changes that will help the system evolve into one which is more efficient and effective. Primary care physicians are the key to appropriate triage and referrals, to co-ordinated and comprehensive care, and to patient education and community orientation.

REFERENCES

American Academy of Family Physicians. 1992. *Hospital practice characteristics survey.* Kansas City: AAFP.

Blendon, R. J. and Edwards, J. N. 1991. "Utilization of hospital services: A comparison of internal medicine and family practice. *J Fam Prac.* 28: 91–96.

Fry, J. 1969. *Medicine in three societies.* New York: American Elsevier.

Havlicek, P. L. 1990. *Prepaid groups in the U.S.: A survey of practice characteristics.* Chicago: AMA.

Light, D. W. 1992. "The practice and ethics of risk-rated health insurance." *JAMA* 267: 2503–08.

Light, D. W. 1993. "Countervailing power: The changing character of the medical profession in the United States." In Hafferty, F. and McKinlay, J. (eds.) *The changing character of the medical profession: An international perspective.* New York: Oxford University Press.

National Center for Health Statistics. 1991. *Health, United States, 1990.* Hyattsville, Maryland: U.S. Department of Health and Human Resources.

Robeck, G., Randolph, L., and Seidman, B. 1990. *Physician characteristics and distribution in the US.* Chicago: AMA.

Starr, P. 1982. *The social transformation of American medicine.* New York: Basic.

Stevens, R. *American medicine and the public interest.* New Haven: Yale University Press.

19

A Caring Dilemma: Womanhood and Nursing in Historical Perspective

· · · · · ·

Susan Reverby

"Do not undervalue [your] particular ability to care," students were reminded at a recent nursing school graduation.[1] Rather than merely bemoaning yet another form of late twentieth-century heartlessness, this admonition underscores the central dilemma of American nursing: The order to care in a society that refuses to value caring. This article is an analysis of the historical creation of that dilemma and its consequences for nursing. To explore the meaning of caring for nursing, it is necessary to unravel the terms of the relationship between nursing and womanhood as these bonds have been formed over the last century.

The Meaning of Caring

Many different disciplines have explored the various meanings of caring.[2] Much of this literature, however, runs the danger of universalizing caring as an element in female identity, or as a human quality, separate from the cultural and structural circumstances that create it. But as policy analyst Hilary Graham has argued, caring is not merely an identity; it is also work. As she notes, "Caring touches simultaneously on who you are and what you do."[3] Because of this duality, caring can be difficult to define and even harder to control. Graham's analysis moves beyond seeing caring as a psychological trait; but her focus is primarily on women's unpaid labor in the home. She does not fully discuss how the forms of caring are shaped by the context under which they are practiced. Caring is not just a

subjective and material experience; it is a historically created one. Particular circumstances, ideologies, and power relations thus create the conditions under which caring can occur, the forms it will take, the consequences it will have for those who do it.

The basis for caring also shapes its effect. Nursing was organized under the expectation that its practitioners would accept a duty to care rather than demand a right to determine how they would satisfy this duty. Nurses were expected to act out of an obligation to care, taking on caring more as an identity than as work, and expressing altruism without thought of autonomy either at the bedside or in their profession. Thus, nurses, like others who perform what is defined as "women's work" in our society, have had to contend with what appears as a dichotomy between the duty to care for others and the right to control their own activities in the name of caring. Nursing is still searching for what philosopher Joel Feinberg argued comes prior to rights, that is, being "recognized as having a claim on rights."[4] The duty to care, organized within the political and economic context of nursing's development, has made it difficult for nurses to obtain this moral and, ultimately, political standing.

Because nurses have been given the duty to care, they are caught in a secondary dilemma: forced to act as if altruism (assumed to be the basis for caring) and autonomy (assumed to be the basis for rights) are separate ways of being. Nurses are still searching for a way to forge a link between altruism and autonomy that will allow them to have what philosopher Larry Blum and others have called "caring-with-autonomy," or what psychiatrist Jean Baker Miller labeled "a way of life that includes serving others without being subservient."[5] Nursing's historical circumstances and ideological underpinnings have made creating this way of life difficult, but not impossible, to achieve.

Caring as Duty

A historical analysis of nursing's development makes this theoretical formulation clearer. Most of the writing about American nursing's history begins in the 1870s when formal training for nursing was introduced in the United States. But nursing did not appear de novo at the end of the nineteenth century. As with most medical and health care, nursing throughout the colonial era and most of the nineteenth century took place within the family and the home. In the domestic pantheon that surrounded "middling" and upper-class American womanhood in the nineteenth century, a woman's caring for friends and relatives was an important pillar. Nursing was often taught by mother to daughter as part of female apprenticeship, or learned by a domestic servant as an additional task on her job. Embedded in the seemingly natural or ordained character of women, it became an important manifestation of women's expression of love of others, and was thus integral to the female sense of self.[6] In a society where deeply felt religious tenets were translated into gendered virtues, domesticity advocate Catharine Beecher declared that the sick were to be "commended" to a "woman's benevolent ministries."[7]

The responsibility for nursing went beyond a mother's duty for her children, a wife's for her husband, or a daughter's for her aging parents. It attached to all the available female family members. The family's "long arm" might reach out at any time to a woman working in a distant city, in a mill, or as a maid, pulling her home to care for the sick, infirm, or newborn. No form of women's labor, paid or unpaid, protected her from this demand. "You may be called upon at any moment," Eliza W. Farrar warned in the *The Young Lady's Friend* in 1837, "to attend upon your parents, your brothers, your sisters, or your companions."[8] Nursing was to be, therefore, a woman's duty, not her job. Obligation and love, not the need of work, were to bind the nurse to her patient. Caring was to be an unpaid labor of love.

The Professed Nurse

Even as Eliza Farrar was proffering her advice, pressures both inward and outward were beginning to reshape the domestic sphere for women of the then-called "middling classes." Women's obligations and work were transformed by the expanding industrial economy and changing cultural assumptions. Parenting took on increasing importance as notions of "moral mothering" filled the domestic arena and other productive labor entered the cash nexus. Female benevolence similarly moved outward as women's charitable efforts took increasingly institutional forms. Duty began to take on new meaning as such women were advised they could fulfill their nursing responsibilities by managing competently those they hired to assist them. Bourgeois female virtue could still be demonstrated as the balance of labor, love, and supervision shifted.[9]

An expanding economy thus had differing effects on women of various classes. For those in the growing urban middle classes, excess cash made it possible to consider hiring a nurse when circumstances, desire, or exhaustion meant a female relative was no longer available for the task. Caring as labor, for these women, could be separated from love.

For older widows or spinsters from the working classes, nursing became a trade they could "profess" relatively easily in the marketplace. A widow who had nursed her husband till his demise, or a domestic servant who had cared for an employer in time of illness, entered casually into the nursing trade, hired by families or individuals unwilling, or unable, to care for their sick alone. The permeable boundaries for women between unpaid and paid labor allowed nursing to pass back and forth when necessary. For many women, nursing thus beckoned as respectable community work.

These "professed" or "natural-born" nurses,

as they were known, usually came to their work, as one Boston nurse put it, "laterly" when other forms of employment were closed to them or the lack of any kind of work experience left nursing as an obvious choice. Mehitable Pond Garside, for example, was in her fifties and had outlived two husbands—and her children could not, or would not, support her—when she came to Boston in the 1840s to nurse. Similarly Alma Frost Merrill, the daughter of a Maine wheelwright, came to Boston in 1818 at nineteen to become a domestic servant. After years as a domestic and seamstress, she declared herself a nurse.[10]

Women like Mehitable Pond Garside and Alma Frost Merrill differed markedly from the Sairy Gamp character of Dickens' novel, *Martin Chuzzlewit*. Gamp was portrayed as a merely besotted representative of lumpen-proletarian womanhood, who asserted her autonomy by daring to question medical diagnosis, to venture her own opinions (usually outrageous and wrong) at every turn, and to spread disease and superstition in the name of self-knowledge. If they were not Gamps, nurses like Garside and Merrill also were not the healers of some more recent feminist mythology that confounds nursing with midwifery, praising the caring and autonomy these women exerted, but refusing to consider their ignorance.[11] Some professed nurses learned their skills from years of experience, demonstrating the truth of the dictum that "to make a kind and sympathizing nurse, one must have waited, in sickness, upon those she loved dearly."[12] Others, however, blundered badly beyond their capabilities or knowledge. They brought to the bedside only the authority that their personalities and community stature could command: Neither credentials nor a professional identity gave weight to their efforts. Their womanhood, and the experience it gave them, defined their authority and taught them to nurse.

The Hospital Nurse

Nursing was not limited, however, to the bedside in a home. Although the United States had only 178 hospitals at the first national census in 1873, it was workers labeled "nurses" who provided the caring. As in home-based nursing, the route to hospital nursing was paved more with necessity than with intentionality. In 1875, Eliza Higgins, the matron of Boston's Lying-In Hospital, could not find an extra nurse to cover all the deliveries. In desperation, she moved the hospital laundress up to the nursing position, while a recovering patient took over the wash. Higgins' diaries of her trying years at the Lying-In suggest that such an entry into nursing was not uncommon.[13]

As Higgins' reports and memoirs of other nurses attest, hospital nursing could be the work of devoted women who learned what historian Charles Rosenberg has labeled "ad hoc professionalism," or the temporary and dangerous labor of an ambulatory patient or hospital domestic.[14] As in home-based nursing, both caring and concern were frequently demonstrated. But the nursing work and nurses were mainly characterized by the diversity of their efforts and the unevenness of their skills.

Higgins' memoirs attest to the hospital as a battleground where nurses, physicians, and hospital managers contested the realm of their authority. Nurses continually affirmed their right to control the pace and content of their work, to set their own hours, and to structure their relationships to physicians. Aware that the hospital's paternalistic attitudes and practices toward its "inmates" were attached to the nursing personnel as well, they fought to be treated as workers, "not children," as the Lying-In nurses told Eliza Higgins, and to maintain their autonomous adult status.[15]

Like home-based nursing, hospital nurses had neither formal training nor class status upon which to base their arguments. But their sense of the rights of working-class womanhood gave them authority to press their demands. The necessity to care, and their perception of its importance to patient outcome, also structured their belief that demanding the right to be relatively autonomous was possible. However, their efforts were undermined by the nature of their onerous work, the paternalism of the institutions, class differences between trustees and workers, and ultimately the lack of a defined ideology of caring. Mere resistance to those above them, or contending assertions of rights, could not become the basis for nursing authority.

The Influence of Nightingale

Much of this changed with the introduction of training for nursing in the hospital world. In the aftermath of Nightingale's triumph over the British Army's medical care system in the Crimea, similar attempts by American women during the Civil War, and the need to find respectable work for daughters of the middling classes, a model and support for nursing reform began to grow. By 1873, three nursing schools in hospitals in New York, Boston, and New Haven were opened, patterned after the Nightingale School at St. Thomas' Hospital in London.

Nightingale had envisioned nursing as an art, rather than a science, for which women needed to be trained. Her ideas linked her medical and public health notions to her class and religious beliefs. Accepting the Victorian idea of divided spheres of activity for men and women, she thought women had to be trained to nurse through a disciplined process of honing their womanly virtue. Nightingale stressed character development, the laws of health, and strict adherence to orders passed through a female hierarchy. Nursing was built on a model that relied on the concept of duty to provide its basis for authority. Unlike other feminists of the time, she spoke in the language of duty, not rights.

Furthermore, as a nineteenth-century sanitarian, Nightingale never believed in germ theory, in part because she refused to accept a theory of disease etiology that appeared to be morally neutral. Given her sanitarian beliefs, Nightingale thought medical therapeutics and "curing" were of lesser importance to patient outcome, and she willingly left this realm to the physician. Caring, the arena she did think of great importance, she assigned to the nurse. In order to care, a nurse's character, tempered by the fires of training, was to be her greatest skill. Thus, to "feminize" nursing, Nightingale sought a change in the class-defined behavior, not the gender, of the work force.[16]

To forge a good nurse out of the virtues of a good woman and to provide a political base for nursing, Nightingale sought to organize a female hierarchy in which orders passed down from the nursing superintendent to the lowly probationer. This separate female sphere was to share power in the provision of health care with the male-dominated areas of medicine. For many women in the Victorian era, sisterhood and what Carroll Smith-Rosenberg has called "homosocial networks" served to overcome many of the limits of this separate but supposedly equal system of cultural division.[17] Sisterhood, after all, at least in its fictive forms, underlay much of the female power that grew out of women's culture in the nineteenth century. But in nursing, commonalities of the gendered experience could not become the basis of unity since hierarchial filial relations, not equal sisterhood, lay at the basis of nursing's theoretical formulation.

Service, Not Education

Thus, unwittingly, Nightingale's sanitarian ideas and her beliefs about womanhood provided some of the ideological justification for many of the dilemmas that faced American nursing by 1900. Having fought physician and trustee prejudice against the training of nurses in hospitals in the last quarter of the nineteenth century, American nursing reformers succeeded only too well as the new century began. Between 1890 and 1920, the number of nursing schools jumped from 35 to 1,775, and the number of trained nurses from 16 per 100,000 in the population to 141.[18] Administrators quickly realized that opening a "nursing school" provided their hospitals, in exchange for training, with a young, disciplined, and cheap labor force. There was often no difference between the hospital's nursing school and its nursing service. The service needs of the hospital continually overrode the educational requirements of the schools. A student might, therefore, spend weeks on a medical ward if her labor was so needed, but never see the inside of an operating room before her graduation.

Once the nurse finished her training, however, she was unlikely to be hired by a hospital because it relied on either untrained aides or nursing student labor. The majority of graduate nurses, until the end of the 1930s, had to find work in private duty in a patient's home, as the patient's employee in the hospital, in the branches of public health, or in some hospital staff positions. In the world of nursing beyond the training school, "trained" nurses still had to compete with the thousands of "professed" or "practical" nurses who continued to ply their trade in an overcrowded and unregulated marketplace. The title of nurse took on very ambiguous meanings.[19]

The term, "trained nurse," was far from a uniform designation. As nursing leader Isabel Hampton Robb lamented in 1893, "the title 'trained nurse' may mean then anything, everything, or next to nothing."[20]

The exigencies of nursing acutely ill or surgical patients required the sacrifice of coherent educational programs. Didactic, repetitive, watered-down medical lectures by physicians or older nurses were often provided for the students, usually after they finished ten to twelve hours of ward work. Training emphasized the "one right way" of doing ritualized procedures in hopes the students' adherence to specified rules would be least dangerous to patients.[21] Under these circumstances, the duty to care could be followed with a vengeance and become the martinet adherence to orders.

Furthermore, because nursing emphasized training in discipline, order, and practical skills, the abuse of student labor could be rationalized. And because the work force was almost entirely women, altruism, sacrifice, and submission were expected, encouraged, indeed, demanded. Exploitation was inevitable in a field where, until the early 1900s, there were no accepted standards for how much work an average student should do or how many patients she could successfully care for, no mechanisms through which to enforce such standards. After completing her exhaustive and depressing survey of nursing training in 1912, nursing educator M. Adelaide Nutting bluntly pointed out: "Under the present system the school has no life of its own."[22] In this kind of environment, nurses were trained. But they were not educated.

Virtue and Autonomy

It would be a mistake, however, to see the nursing experience only as one of exploitation and the nursing school as a faintly concealed reformatory for the wayward girl in need of discipline. Many nursing superintendents lived the Nightingale ideals as best they could and infused them into their schools. The authoritarian model could and did retemper many women. It instilled in nurses idealism and pride in their skills, somewhat differentiated the trained nurse from the untrained, and protected and aided the sick and dying. It provided a mechanism for virtuous women to contribute to the improvement of humanity by empowering them to care.

For many of the young women entering training in the nineteenth and early twentieth centuries, nursing thus offered something quite special: both a livelihood and a virtuous state. As one nursing educator noted in 1890: "Young strong country girls are drawn into the work by the glamorer [sic] thrown about hospital work and the halo that sanctifies a Nightingale."[23] Thus, in their letters of application, aspiring nursing students expressed their desire for work, independence, and womanly virtue. As with earlier, nontrained nurses, they did not seem to separate autonomy and altruism, but rather sought its linkage through training. Flora Jones spoke for many such women when she wrote the superintendent of Boston City Hospital in 1880, declaring, "I consider myself fitted for the work by inclination and consider it a womanly occupation. It is also necessary for me to become self-supporting and provide for my future."[24] Thus, one nursing superintendent reminded a graduating class in 1904: "You have become self-controlled, unselfish, gentle, compassionate, brave, capable—in fact, you have risen from the period of irresponsible girlhood to that of womanhood."[25] For women like Flora Jones, and many of nursing's early leaders, nursing was the singular way to grow to maturity in a womanly profession that offered meaningful work, independence, and altruism.[26]

Altruism, Not Independence

For many, however, as nursing historian Dorothy Sheahan has noted, the training school, "was a place where . . . women learned to be girls."[27] The range of permissible behaviors for respectable women was often narrowed further through training. Independence was to be sacrificed on the altar of altruism. Thus, despite hopes of aspiring students and promises of training school superintendents, nursing rarely united altruism and autonomy. Duty remained the basis for caring.

Some nurses were able to create what they called "a little world of our own." But nursing had neither the financial nor the cultural power to create the separate women's institutions that provided so much of the basis for women's reform and rights efforts.[28] Under these conditions, nurses found it difficult to make the collective transition out of a woman's culture of obligation into an activist assault on the structure and beliefs that oppressed them. Nursing remained bounded by its ideology and its material circumstances.

The Contradictions of Reform

In this context, one begins to understand the difficulties faced by the leaders of nursing reform. Believing that educational reform was central to nursing's professionalizing efforts and clinical improvements, a small group of elite reformers attempted to broaden nursing's scientific content and social outlook. In arguing for an increase in the scientific knowledge necessary in nursing, such leaders were fighting against deep-seated cultural assumptions about male and female "natural" characteristics as embodied in the doctor and nurse. Such sentiments were articulated in the routine platitudes that graced what one nursing leader described as the "doctor homilies" that were a regular feature at nursing graduation exercises.[29]

Not surprisingly, such beliefs were professed by physicians and hospital officials whenever nursing shortages appeared, or nursing groups pushed for higher educational standards or defined nursing as more than assisting the physician. As one nursing educator wrote, with some degree of resignation after the influenza pandemic in 1920: "It is perhaps inevitable that the difficulty of securing nurses during the last year or two should have revived again the old agitation about the 'over-training' of nurses and the clamor for a cheap worker of the old servant–nurse type."[30]

First Steps toward Professionalism

The nursing leadership, made up primarily of educators and supervisors with their base within what is now the American Nurses' Association and the National League for Nursing, thus faced a series of dilemmas as they struggled to raise educational standards in the schools and criteria for entry into training, to register nurses once they finished their training, and to gain acceptance for the knowledge base and skills of the nurse. They had to exalt the womanly character, self-abnegation, and service ethic of nursing while insisting on the right of nurses to act in their own self-interest. They had to demand higher wages commensurate with their skills, yet not appear commercial. They had to simultaneously find a way to denounce the exploitation of nursing students, as they made political alliances with hospital physicians and administrators whose support they needed. While they lauded character and sacrifice, they had to find a way to measure it with educational criteria in order to formulate registration laws and set admission standards. They had to make demands and organize, without appearing "unlady-like." In sum, they were forced by the social conditions and ideology surrounding nursing to attempt to professionalize altruism without demanding autonomy.

Undermined by Duty

The image of a higher claim of duty also continually undermined a direct assertion of the right to determine that duty. Whether at a bedside, or at a legislative hearing on practice laws, the duty to care became translated into the demand that nurses merely follow doctors' orders. The tradition of obligation almost made it impossible for nurses to speak about rights at all. By the turn of the century necessity and desire were pulling more young women into the labor force, and the women's movement activists were placing rights at the center of cultural discussion. In this atmosphere, nursing's call to duty was perceived by many as an increasingly antiquated language to shore up a changing economic and cultural landscape. Nursing became a type of collective female grasping for an older form of security and power in the face of rapid change. Women who might have been attracted to nursing in the 1880s as a womanly occupation that provided some form of autonomy, were, by the turn of the century, increasingly looking elsewhere for work and careers.

A Different Vision

In the face of these difficulties, the nursing leadership became increasingly defensive and turned on its own rank and file. The educators and supervisors who comprised leadership lost touch with the pressing concern of their constituencies in the daily work world of nursing and the belief systems such nurses continued to hold. Yet many nurses, well into the twentieth century, shared the nineteenth-century vision of nursing as the embodiment of womanly virtue. A nurse named Annette Fiske, for example, although she authored two science books for nurses and had an M.A. degree in classics from Radcliffe College before she entered training, spent her professional career in the 1920s arguing against increasing educational standards. Rather, she called for a reinfusion into nursing of spirituality and service, assuming that this would result in nursing's receiving greater "love and respect and admiration."[31]

Other nurses, especially those trained in the smaller schools or reared to hold working-class ideals about respectable behavior in women, shared Fiske's views. They saw the leadership's efforts at professionalization as an attempt to push them out of nursing. Their adherence to nursing skill measured in womanly virtue was less a conservative and reactionary stance than a belief that seemed to transcend class and educational backgrounds to place itself in the individual character and work-place skills of the nurse. It grounded altruism in supposedly natural and spiritual, rather than educational and middle-class, soil. For Fiske and many other nurses, nursing was still a womanly art that required inherent character in its practitioners and training in practical skills and spiritual values in its schools. Their beliefs about nursing did not require the professionalization of altruism, nor the demand for autonomy either at the bedside or in control over the professionalization process.

Still other nurses took a more pragmatic viewpoint that built on their pride in their workplace skills and character. These nurses also saw the necessity for concerted action, not unlike that taken by other American workers. Such nurses fought against what one 1888 nurse, who called herself Candor, characterized as the "missionary spirit . . . [of] self-immolation" that denied that nurses worked because they had to make a living.[32] These worker-nurses saw no contradiction between demanding decent wages and conditions for their labors and being of service for those in need. But the efforts of various groups of these kinds of nurses to turn to hours' legislation, trade union activity, or mutual aid associations were criticized and condemned by the nursing leadership. Their letters were often edited out of the nursing journals, and their voices silenced in public meetings as they were denounced as being commercial, or lacking in proper womanly devotion.[33]

In the face of continual criticism from nursing's professional leadership, the worker-nurses took on an increasingly angry and defensive tone. Aware that their sense of the nurse's skills came from the experiences of the work place, not book learning or degrees, they had to assert this position despite continued hostility toward such a basis of nursing authority.[34] Although the position of women like Candor helped articulate a way for nurses to begin to assert the right to care, it did not constitute a full-blown ideological counterpart to the overwhelming power of the belief in duty.

The Persistence of Dilemmas

By midcentury, the disputes between worker-nurses and the professional leadership began to take on new forms, although the persistent divisions continued. Aware that some kind of collective bargaining was necessary to keep nurses out of the unions and in the professional associations, the ANA reluctantly agreed in 1946 to let its state units act as bargaining agents. The nursing leadership has continued to look at educational reform strategies, now primarily taking the form of legislating for the B.S. degree as the credential necessary for entry into nursing practice, and to changes in the practice laws that will allow increasingly skilled nurses the autonomy and status they deserve. Many nurses have continued to be critical of this educational strategy, to ignore the professional associations, or to leave nursing altogether.

In their various practice fields nurses still need a viable ideology and strategy that will help them adjust to the continual demands of patients and an evermore bureaucratized, cost-conscious, and rationalized work setting. For many nurses it is still, in an ideological sense, the nineteenth century. Even for those nurses who work as practitioners in the more autonomous settings of health maintenance organizations or public health offices, the legacy of nursing's heritage is still felt. Within the last two years, for example, the Massachusetts Board of Medicine tried to push through a regulation that health practitioners acknowledge their dependence on physicians by wearing a badge that identified their supervising physician and stated that they were not doctors.

Nurses have tried various ways to articulate a series of rights that allow them to care. The acknowledgment of responsibilities, however, so deeply ingrained in nursing and American womanhood, as nursing school dean Claire Fagin has noted, continually drown out the nurse's assertion of rights.[35]

Nurses are continuing to struggle to obtain the right to claim rights. Nursing's educational philosophy, ideological underpinnings, and structural position have made it difficult to create the circumstances within which to gain such recognition. It is not a lack of vision that thwarts nursing, but the lack of power to give that vision substantive form.[36]

Beyond the Obligation to Care

Much has changed in nursing in the last forty years. The severing of nursing education from the hospital's nursing service has finally taken place, as the majority of nurses are now educated in colleges, not hospital-based diploma schools. Hospitals are experimenting with numerous ways to organize the nursing service to provide the nurse with more responsibility and sense of control over the nursing care process. The increasingly technical and machine-aided nature of hospital-based health care has made nurses feel more skilled.

In many ways, however, little has changed. Nursing is still divided over what counts as a nursing skill, how it is to be learned, and whether a nurse's character can be measured in educational criteria. Technical knowledge and capabilities do not easily translate into power and control. Hospitals, seeking to cut costs, have forced nurses to play "beat the clock" as they run from task to task in an increasingly fragmented setting.[37]

Nursing continues to struggle with the basis for, and the value of, caring. The fact that the first legal case on comparable worth was brought by a group of Denver nurses suggests nursing has an important and ongoing role in the political effort to have caring revalued. As in the Denver case, contemporary feminism has provided some nurses with the grounds on which to claim rights from their caring.[38]

Feminism, in its liberal form, appears to give nursing a political language that argues for equality and rights within the given order of things. It suggests a basis for caring that stresses individual discretion and values, acknowledging that the nurses' right to care should be given equal consideration with the physician's right to cure. Just as liberal political theory undermined more paternalistic formulations of government, classical liberalism's tenets applied to women have much to offer nursing. The demand for the right to care questions deeply held beliefs about gendered relations in the health care hierarchy and the structure of the hierarchy itself.

Many nurses continue to hope that with more education, explicit theories to explain the scientific basis for nursing, new skills, and a lot of assertiveness training, nursing will change. As these nurses try to shed the image of the nurse's being ordered to care, however, the admonition to care at a graduation speech has to be made. Unable to find a way to "care with autonomy" and unable to separate caring from its valuing and basis, many nurses find themselves forced to abandon the effort to care, or nursing altogether.

Altruism with Autonomy

These dilemmas for nurses suggest the constraints that surround the effectiveness of a liberal feminist political strategy to address the problems of caring and, therefore, of nursing. The individualism and autonomy of a rights framework often fail to acknowledge collective social need, to provide a way for adjudicating conflicts over rights, or to address the reasons for the devaluing of female activity.[39] Thus, nurses have often rejected liberal feminism, not just out of their oppression and "false consciousness," but because of some deep understandings of the limited promise of equality and autonomy in a health care system they see as flawed and harmful. In an often inchoate way, such nurses recognize that those who claim the autonomy of rights often run the risk of rejecting altruism and caring itself.

Several feminist psychologists have suggested that what women really want in their lives is autonomy with connectedness. Similarly, many modern moral philosophers are trying to articulate a formal modern theory that values the emotions and the importance of relationships.[40] For nursing, this will require the creation of the conditions under which it is possible to value caring and to understand that the empowerment of others does not have to require self-immolation. To achieve this, nurses will have both to create a new political understanding for the basis of caring and to find ways to gain the power to implement it. Nursing can do much to have this happen through research on the importance of caring on patient outcome, studies of patient improvements in nursing settings where the right to care is created, or implementing nursing control of caring through a bargaining agreement. But nurses cannot do this alone. The dilemma of nursing is too tied to society's broader problems of gender and class to be solved solely by the political or professional efforts of one occupational group.

Nor are nurses alone in benefiting from such an effort. If nursing can achieve the power to practice altruism with autonomy, all of us have much to gain. Nursing has always been a much conflicted metaphor in our culture, reflecting all the ambivalences we give to the meaning of womanhood.[41] Perhaps in the future it can give this metaphor and, ultimately, caring, new value in all our lives.

NOTES

This selection is based on the author's book, *Ordered to Care: The Dilemma of American Nursing*, published in 1987 by Cambridge University Press, New York.

1. Gregory Wticher, "Last Class of Nurses Told: Don't Stop Caring," *Boston Globe*, May 13, 1985, pp. 17–18.
2. See, for examples, Larry Blum et al., "Altruism and Women's Oppression," in *Women and Philosophy*, eds. Carol Gould and Marx Wartofsy (New York: G.P. Putnam's, 1976), pp. 222–247; Nel Noddings, *Caring*. Berkeley: University of California Press, 1984; Nancy Chodorow, *The Reproduction of Mothering*. Berkeley: University of California Press, 1978; Carol Gilligan, *In a Different Voice*. Cambridge: Harvard University Press, 1982; and Janet Finch and Dulcie Groves, eds., *A Labour of Love, Women, Work and Caring*. London and Boston: Routledge, Kegan Paul, 1983.
3. Hilary Graham, "Caring: A Labour of Love," in *A Labour of Love*, eds. Finch and Groves, pp. 13–30.
4. Joel Feinberg, *Rights, Justice and the Bounds of Liberty* (Princeton: Princeton University Press, 1980), p. 141.
5. Blum et al., "Altruism and Women's Oppression," p. 223; Jean Baker Miller, *Toward a New Psychology of Women* (Boston: Beacon Press, 1976), p. 71.
6. Ibid; see also Iris Marion Young, "Is Male Gender Identity the Cause of Male Domination," in *Mothering: Essays in Feminist Theory*, ed. Joyce Trebicott (Totowa, NJ: Rowman and Allanheld, 1983), pp. 129–146.
7. Catherine Beecher, *Domestic Receipt-Book* (New York: Harper and Brothers, 1846) p. 214.
8. Eliza Farrar, *The Young Lady's Friend—By a Lady* (Boston: American Stationer's Co., 1837), p. 57.
9. Catherine Beecher, *Miss Beecher's Housekeeper and Healthkeeper*. New York: Harper and Brothers, 1876; and Sarah Josepha Hale, *The Good Housekeeper*. Boston: Otis Brothers and Co., 7th edition, 1844. See also Susan Strasser, *Never Done: A History of Housework*. New York: Pantheon, 1982.
10. Cases 2 and 18, "Admissions Committee Records," Volume I, Box 11, Home for Aged Women Collection, Schlesinger Library, Radcliffe College, Cambridge, Mass. Data on the nurses admitted to

the home were also found in "Records of Inmates, 1858–1901," "Records of Admission, 1873–1924," and "Records of Inmates, 1901–1916," all in Box 11.

11. Charles Dickens, *Martin Chuzzlewit*. New York: New American Library, 1965, original edition, London: 1865; Barbara Ehrenreich and Deirdre English, *Witches, Nurses, Midwives: A History of Women Healers*. Old Westbury: Glass Mountain Pamphlets, 1972.

12. Virginia Penny, *The Employments of Women: A Cyclopedia of Women's Work* (Boston: Walker, Wise, and Co., 1863), p. 420.

13. Eliza Higgins, Boston Lying-In Hospital, *Matron's Journals*, 1873–1889, Volume I, January 9, 1875, February 22, 1875, Rare Books Room, Countway Medical Library, Harvard Medical School, Boston, Mass.

14. Charles Rosenberg, " 'And Heal the Sick': The Hospital and the Patient in 19th Century America," *Journal of Social History* 10 (June 1977): 445.

15. Higgins, *Matron's Journals*, Volume II, January 11, 1876, and July 1, 1876. See also a parallel discussion of male artisan behavior in front of the boss in David Montgomery, "Workers' Control of Machine Production in the 19th Century," *Labor History* 17 (Winter 1976):485–509.

16. The discussion of Florence Nightingale is based on my analysis in *Ordered to Care*, chapter 3. See also Charles E. Rosenberg, "Florence Nightingale on Contagion: The Hospital as Moral Universe," in *Healing and History*, ed. Charles E. Rosenberg. New York: Science History Publications, 1979.

17. Carroll Smith-Rosenberg, "The Female World of Love and Ritual," *Signs: Journal of Women in Culture and Society* 1 (Autumn 1975):1.

18. May Ayers Burgess, *Nurses, Patients and Pocketbooks*. New York: Committee on the Grading of Nursing, 1926, reprint edition (New York: Garland Publishing Co, 1985), pp. 36–37.

19. For further discussion of the dilemmas of private duty nursing, see Susan Reverby, " 'Neither for the Drawing Room nor for the Kitchen': Private Duty Nursing, 1880–1920," in *Women and Health in America*, ed. Judith Walzer Leavitt. Madison: University of Wisconsin Press, 1984, and Susan Reverby, " 'Something Besides Waiting': The Politics of Private Duty Nursing Reform in the Depression," in *Nursing History: New Perspectives, New Possibilities*, ed. Ellen Condliffe Lagemann. New York: Teachers College Press, 1982.

20. Isabel Hampton Robb, "Educational Standards for Nurses," in *Nursing of the Sick 1893* (New York: McGraw–Hill, 1949), p. 11. See also Janet Wilson James, "Isabel Hampton and the Professionalization of Nursing in the 1890s," in *The Therapeutic Revolution*, eds. Morris Vogel and Charles E. Rosenberg. Philadelphia: University of Pennsylvania Press, 1979.

21. For further discussion of the difficulties in training, see JoAnn Ashley, *Hospitals, Paternalism and the Role of the Nurse*. New York: Teachers College Press, 1976, and Reverby, *Ordered to Care*, chapter 4.

22. *Educational Status of Nursing*, Bureau of Education Bulletin Number 7, Whole Number 475 (Washington, D.C.: Government Printing Office, 1912), p. 49.

23. Julia Wells, "Do Hospitals Fit Nurses for Private Nursing," *Trained Nurse and Hospital Review* 3 (March 1890):98.

24. Boston City Hospital (BCH) Training School Records, Box 4, Folder 4, Student 4, February 14, 1880, BCH Training School Papers, Nursing Archives, Special Collections, Boston University, Mugar Library, Boston, Mass. The student's name has been changed to maintain confidentiality.

25. Mary Agnes Snively, "What Manner of Women Ought Nurses To Be?" *American Journal of Nursing* 4 (August 1904):838.

26. For a discussion of many of the early nursing leaders as "new women," see Susan Armeny, " 'We Were the New Women': A Comparison of Nurses and Women Physicians, 1890–1915." Paper presented at the American Association for the History of Nursing Conference, University of Virginia, Charlottesville, Va., October 1984.

27. Dorothy Sheahan, "Influence of Occupational Sponsorship on the Professional Development of Nursing." Paper presented at the Rockefeller Archives Conference on the History of Nursing, Rockefeller Archives, Tarrytown, NY, May 1981, p. 12.

28. Estelle Freedman, "Separatism as Strategy: Female Institution Building and American Feminism, 1870–1930," *Feminist Studies* 5 (Fall 1979):512–529.

29. Lavinia L. Dock, *A History of Nursing*, volume 3 (New York: G.P. Putnam's, 1912), p. 136.

30. Isabel M. Stewart, "Progress in Nursing Education during 1919," *Modern Hospital* 14 (March 1920):183.

31. Annette Fiske, "How Can We Counteract the Prevailing Tendency to Commercialism in Nursing?" *Proceedings of the 17th Annual Meeting of the Massachusetts State Nurses' Association*, p. 8, Massachusetts Nurses Association Papers, Box 7, Nursing Archives.

32. Candor, "Work and Wages," Letter to the Editor, *Trained Nurse and Hospital Review* 2 (April 1888):167–168.

33. See the discussion in Ashley, *Hospitals, Paternalism and the Role of the Nurse*, pp. 40–43, 46–48, 51, and in Barbara Melosh, *"The Physician's Hand": Work Culture and Conflict in American Nursing* (Philadelphia: Temple University Press, 1982), passim.

34. For further discussion see Susan Armeny, "Resolute Enthusiasts: The Effort to Professionalize American Nursing, 1880–1915." PhD dissertation, University of Missouri, Columbia, Mo., 1984, and Reverby, *Ordered to Care*, chapter 6.

35. Feinberg, *Rights*, pp. 130–142; Claire Fagin, "Nurses' Rights," *American Journal of Nursing* 75 (January 1975):82.

36. For a similar argument for bourgeois women, see Carroll Smith-Rosenberg, "The New Woman as Androgyne: Social Disorder and Gender Crisis," in *Disorderly Conduct* (New York: Alfred Knopf, 1985), p. 296.

37. Boston Nurses' Group, "The False Promise: Professionalism in Nursing," *Science for the People* 10 (May/June 1978):20–34; Jennifer Bingham Hull, "Hospital Nightmare: Cuts in Staff Demoralize Nurses as Care Suffers," *Wall Street Journal*, March 27, 1985.

38. Bonnie Bullough, "The Struggle for Women's Rights in Denver: A Personal Account," *Nursing Outlook* 26 (September 1978):566–567.

39. For critiques of liberal feminism see Allison M. Jagger, *Feminist Politics and Human Nature* (Totowa, NJ: Rowman and Allanheld, 1983), pp. 27–50, 173, 206; Zillah Eisenstein, *The Radical Future of Liberal Feminism*. New York and London: Longman, 1981; and Rosalind Pollack Petchesky, *Abortion and Women's Choice* (Boston: Northeastern University Press, 1984), pp. 1–24.

40. Miller, *Toward A New Psychology;* Jane Flax, "The Conflict Between Nurturance and Autonomy in Mother-Daughter Relationships and within Feminism," *Feminist Studies* 4 (June 1978): 171–191; Blum et al., "Altruism and Women's Oppression."

41. Claire Fagin and Donna Diers, "Nursing as Metaphor," *New England Journal of Medicine* 309 (July 14, 1983):116–117.

20

AIDS and Its Impact on Medical Work:
The Culture and Politics
of the Shop Floor

▪ ▪ ▪ ▪ ▪

Charles L. Bosk and Joel E. Frader

In 1979 when undergraduates applied in record numbers for admission to medical school, AIDS was not a clinical and diagnostic category. In 1990 when the applications to medical schools are plummeting, AIDS is unarguably with us, and not just as a clinical entity. AIDS has become what the French anthropologist Marcel Mauss called a "total social phenomenon—one whose transactions are at once economic, juridical, moral, aesthetic, religious and mythological, and whose meaning cannot, therefore, be adequately described from the point of view of any single discipline" (Hyde 1979). For cultural analysts, present and future, the 1980s and beyond are the AIDS years.

This chapter is about the impact of AIDS on the shop floor of the academic urban hospital, an attempt to understand the impact of AIDS on everyday practices of doctors providing inpatient care. Following Mauss, we wish to view AIDS as a total social phenomenon rather than as a mere disease. Procedurally, we shall concentrate on the house officer (someone who, after graduation from medical school, participates in medical specialty training) and the medical student to see how this new infectious disease changes the content of everyday work and the education of apprentice physicians learning how to doctor and to assume the social responsibilities of the role of the physician. We are going to look at professional and occupational culture as a set of shop-floor practices and beliefs about work.

At the close of this article we will make some generalizations about the impact of AIDS on medical training and reflect on how this affects the professional culture of physicians. This may distort the picture somewhat, as the urban teaching hospital is not representative of the whole world of medical practice. To the degree that AIDS patients are concentrated in them, any inferences drawn from large teaching hospitals overstate or exaggerate the impact of AIDS. At the very least, such sampling fails to catalogue the variety of strategies individual physicians may use to avoid patients with AIDS. It fails, as well, to capture the innovative approaches to AIDS of pioneering health professionals (many of whom also happen to be gay) in nontraditional settings.

This sampling problem notwithstanding, the urban academic teaching hospital is the arena of choice for studying the impact of AIDS on the medical profession. The concentration of cases in urban teaching hospitals means that students and house officers have a high likelihood of treating patients with AIDS. They are the physicians on the clinical front lines, the ones with the heaviest day-to-day operational burdens.

Further, our attention to the house officers and students possesses a secondary benefit for this inquiry into shop-floor or work-place culture: namely, the natural state of the work place in its before-AIDS condition has been extensively documented. We use the terms shop-floor and work-place culture to invoke the sociological tradition for inquiries into work begun by Everett C. Hughes (1971) at the University of Chicago in the post-World War II years. This tradition emphasizes equivalencies between humble and proud occupations, the management of "dirty work," the procedures that surround routines and emergencies, and the handling of mistakes. Above all, the perspective invites us to reverse our "conventional sentimentality" (Becker 1967) about occupations. The idea of the hospital as a shop floor is one rhetorical device for reminding us that house officers and students are workers in a very real and active sense.

Numerous autobiographical accounts beginning with the pseudonymous Dr. X of *Intern*, catalogue the conditions of the shop floor (Dr. X. 1965; a partial list of subsequent narratives includes Nolen 1970; Rubin 1972; Sweeney 1973; Bell 1975; Haseltine and Yaw 1976; Horowitz and Offen 1977; Mullan 1976; Morgan 1980). There have also been similar commentaries on medical schools (Le Baron 1981; Klass 1987; Klein 1981; Konner 1987; Reilly 1987). Novels by former house officers have also described the work-place culture of physicians in training and the tensions inherent in it. (Examples of this genre include Cook 1972; Glasser 1973; and Shem 1978.)

In addition, there is a large literature on the socialization of medical students and house officers; each of these can be viewed as studies of shop-floor culture. (For a critical overview of this literature see Bosk 1985; individual studies of note include Fox 1957; Fox and Lief 1963; Becker et al. 1961; and Coombs 1978.) The literature on house officers is even more extensive. (See Mumford 1970 and Miller 1970 on medical internships; Mizrahi 1986 on internal medicine residencies; Light 1980 and Coser 1979 on psychiatry; Scully 1980 on obstetrics and gynecology; and Bosk 1979 and Millman 1976 on surgery; Burkett and Knafl 1976 on orthopedic surgeons; and Stelling and Bucher 1972 have focused on how house officers either avoid or accept monitoring by superordinates.)

We can construct a before-AIDS shop-floor culture as a first step in assessing what difference AIDS makes in the occupational culture of physicians. Our picture of the after-AIDS shop floor arises from the pictures drawn in the medical literature, our teaching and consulting experience in large university health centers, and 30 interviews with medical personnel caring for AIDS patients in ten teaching hospitals. These interviews were conducted with individuals at all levels of training and provide admittedly impressionistic data, which need more systematic verification. The interviews averaged an hour in length and explored both how workers treated AIDS patients and how they felt about the patients.

Shop-floor Culture before AIDS: Exploitation and Powerlessness

The pre-AIDS shop floor in academic medical centers is not a particularly happy place, as depicted in first-hand accounts of medical education. The dominant tone of many of the volumes is a bitter cynicism, captured in two of the dedications: Glasser's work is "For all the Arrowsmiths"; Cook dedicates his volume "to the ideal of medicine we all held the year we entered medical school." The set of everyday annoyances extends considerably beyond the long hours of work, although these alone are burdensome. Beyond that there is the fact that much of the work is without any profit for the house officer; it is "scut" work, essential drudgery whose completion appears to add little to the worker's overall sense of mastery and competence. (Becker et al. 1961 first commented that medical students, like their more senior trainees, disliked tasks that neither allowed them to exercise medical responsibility nor increased their clinical knowledge.) Consider here a resident's reaction to a day in the operating room, assisting on major surgery:

I urinated, wrote all the preoperative orders, changed my clothes, and had some dinner, in that order. As I walked across to the dining room, I felt as if I'd been run over by a herd of wild elephants in heat. I was exhausted and, much worse, deeply frustrated. I'd been assisting in surgery for nine hours. Eight of them had been the most important in Mrs. Takura's [a patient] life; yet I felt no sense of accomplishment. I had simply endured, and I was probably the one person they could have done without. Sure, they needed retraction, but a catatonic schizophrenic would have sufficed. Interns are eager to work hard, even to

sacrifice—above all, to be useful and to display their special talents—in order to learn. I felt none of these satisfactions, only an empty bitterness and exhaustion (Cook 1972, 74).

The complaint is not atypical.

In all accounts, house officers and students complain about the ways their energies are wasted because they are inundated with scut work of various types. If procedures are to be done on time, house officers have to act as a back-up transport service. If test results are to be interpreted and patients diagnosed, then house officers have to track down the results; they are their own messenger service. In many hospitals house officers and students do the routine venipunctures and are responsible for maintaining the intravenous lines of patients requiring them. Routine bloodwork composes a large amount of the physician-in-training's everyday scut work.

Their inability to control either their own or their patients' lives, their fundamental powerlessness, and the exploitation of their labors by the "greedy" institution (Coser 1979) that is the modern academic hospital are all at the center of physicians' accounts of their training.

Clinical Coups and Defeats

The juxtaposition of labors that are both Herculean and pointless account for the major narrative themes in accounts of patient care. First, there are stories of "clinical coups." These are dramatic instances where the house officer's labors were not pointless, where a tricky diagnostic problem was solved and a timely and decisive intervention to save a life was initiated. Such stories are rare but all the house officer accounts, even the most bitter, tell at least one. These tales reinforce—even in the face of the contradictory details of the rest of the narrative—that the house officer's efforts make a difference, however small; that the pain and suffering of both doctors and patients are not invariably pointless; and that professional heroism may still yield a positive result, even if only rarely.

More numerous by far in the narratives are accounts of "clinical defeats." A few of these tales concern the apprentice physician's inability to come to the right decision quickly enough; these are personal defeats. The bulk of these tales, however, concern defeat (indexed by death) even though all the right things were done medically. Narratives of clinical defeats generally emphasize the tension in the conflict between care and cure, between quantity and quality of life, between acting as a medical scientist and acting as a human being.

The repeated accounts of clinical defeats reinforce at one level the general pointlessness of much of the house officers' effort. They recount situations in which house officers either are too overwhelmed to provide clinical care or in which the best available care does not ensure a favorable outcome. But the stories of defeat tell another tale as well. Here, house officers describe how they learn that despite the failings of their technical interventions they can make a difference, that care is often more important than cure, and that the human rewards of their medical role are great. Each of the first-hand accounts of medical training features a tale of defeat that had a transformative effect on the physician in training. Each tale of defeat encodes a lesson about the psychological growth of the human being shrouded in the white coat of scientific authority. For example, Glasser's *Ward 402* (1973) centers on the unexpected decline and death, following initial successful treatment, of an eleven-year-old girl with acute leukemia. The interaction with her angry, anxious, and oppositional parents and the futile medical struggle to overcome neurologic complications forces the protagonist to see beyond the narrow medical activism that he had been carefully taught. In the end the interim hero literally pulls the plug on the child's respirator and goes off to see the angry, drunken father vowing, this time, to listen.

Psychological Detachment and Adolescent Invulnerability

The shop-floor culture of house officers and students is largely a peer culture. The senior authority of faculty appears absent, at best, or disruptive and intrusive, at worst, in the first-hand narratives of clinical training. That is to say, the clinical wisdom of faculty is unavailable when house officers need it; when clinical faculty are present, they "pimp" (humiliate by questioning) house officers during rounds with questions on obscure details or order them to perform mindless tasks easily performed by those (nurses, technicians) far less educated about the pathophysiology of disease.

As a result, house officers feel isolated and embattled. Patients, other staff, and attending faculty are the enemy; each is the source of a set of never-ending demands and ego-lacerating defeats. Konner (1987, 375), an anthropologist who acquired a medical degree, is quite eloquent on the theme of the patient as enemy:

> It is obvious from what I have written here that the stress of clinical training alienates the doctor from the patient, that in a real sense the patient becomes the enemy. (Goddamit did she blow her I.V. again? Jesus Christ did he spike a temp?) At first I believed that this was an inadvertent and unfortunate concomitant of medical training, but I now think that it is intrinsic. Not only stress and sleeplessness but the sense of the patient as the cause of one's distress contributes to the doctor's detachment. This detachment is not just objective but downright negative. To cut and puncture a person, to take his or her life in your hands, to pound the chest until ribs break, to decide upon drastic action without being able to ask permission, to render a judgment about whether care should continue or stop—these and a thousand other things may require something stronger than objectivity. They may actually require a measure of dislike.

This sentiment is not, of course, unique to Konner. One sociologist, writing about the socialization process in internal medicine, found negative sentiments about patients so rife that she titled her account *Getting Rid of Patients* (Mizrahi 1986).

Feelings about patients are most visibly displayed in the slang that physicians in training use to describe patients. Beyond the well-known "Gomer" (George and Dundes 1978; Leiderman and Grisso 1985), there is a highly articulated language that refers to patients in distress. Along with the slang, there is much black and "gallows" humor. This black humor is a prominent feature of Shem's (1978) *House of God*.

The slang and humor highlight the psychological and social distance between patients and those who care for them medically. This distance is best exemplified in Shem's "Law IV" of the House of God: "The patient is the one with the disease." The reverse, of course, is that the doctor does not have a problem. He or she is invulnerable. In the first-hand accounts of training, physicians' feelings of invulnerability appear and reappear. The doctors treat disease but they are rarely touched by it (save for the occasional exemplary patient with whom physicians make a psychological connection). To these young apprentice physicians, disease is rarely, if ever, personally threatening and rarely, if ever, presented as something that could happen to the physician. (Many doctors reacted with shock to Lear's (1980) account of her urologist-husband's careless and callous treatment. These readers seemed to have assumed their M.D.s protected them somehow.) Moreover, given that hospitals (outside of pediatrics and before AIDS) housed a high proportion of patients substantially older than house officers, patterns of mortality and morbidity themselves reinforced the sense of invulnerability. It is the rare patient close in age to the author who provokes distress and introspection about doctoring on the part of writers of first-hand narratives.

The fantasy of invulnerability takes on an adolescent quality when one notes the cavalier tone used to describe some of life's most awful problems and the oppositional stance taken toward patients and attending faculty. There may be something structural in this; just as adolescence is betwixt and between childhood and adulthood, the physician-in-training is likewise liminal, betwixt studenthood and professional independence.

The Coming of AIDS to the Shop Floor: Risk and the Loss of Invulnerability

Before AIDS entered the shop floor, physicians in training had many objections to work-place conditions. Not only that, AIDS entered a shop floor that was in the process of transformation from major political, social, organizational, and economic policy changes regarding health care.

These changes have been elaborated in detail elsewhere (Light 1980; Starr 1982; Relman 1980; Mechanic 1986) and need only brief mention here. Acute illnesses, especially infectious diseases, have given way to chronic disorders. The patient population has aged greatly. There has been a relatively new public emphasis on individual responsibility for one's medical problems—diet, smoking, nontherapeutic drug use, "excessive" alcohol use, exercise, etc. (Fox 1986).

Of great importance has been the redefinition of medical care as a service *like any other* in the economy with individual medical decisions subject to the kind of fiscal scrutiny applied to the purchase of automobiles or dry cleaning. Achieving reduced costs through shorter hospitalizations and other measures, however, has created more intensive scheduling for those caring for patients on the hospital's wards—even if the hospital's capacity shrinks in the name of efficiency. Fewer patients are admitted to the hospital and they stay for shorter periods of time, yet more things are done to and for them, increasing the house officers' clerical, physical, and intellectual work while decreasing the opportunity for trainees to get to know their patients (Rabkin 1982; Steiner et al. 1987). The beds simply fill up with comparatively sicker, less communicative patients who need more intensive care.

All the shifts in the medical care system have changed the reality of hospital practice in ways that may not conform to the expectations of those entering the medical profession. In addition to the usual disillusionment occurring in training, the contemporary urban teaching hospital brings fewer opportunities for hope (Glick 1988). To the extent that AIDS contributes to the population of more desperately ill hospitalized patients, it exacerbates house officers' feelings of exploitation and, because of its fatal outcome, AIDS adds to their sense of powerlessness. We must assess the impact of AIDS against this background of old resentments and new burdens.

AIDS has certainly not improved the work climate of the medical shop floor. The most apparent phenomenon related to AIDS in the contemporary urban teaching hospital is risk or, more precisely, the *perception* of risk. The orthodox medical literature proclaims, over and over, that the AIDS virus does not pass readily from patient to care giver (Lifson et al. 1986; Gerberding et al. 1987). But some medical writing dwells on risks (Gerbert et al. 1988; Becker, Cone, and Gerberding 1989; O'Connor 1990) and observations of behavior make clear that fear on the wards is rampant. Workers of all types, including doctors, have at times sheathed themselves in inappropriate armor or simply refused to approach the patients at all. Klass (1987, 185) put it quite starkly: "We have to face the fact that we are going through these little rituals of sanitary precaution partly because we are terrified of this disease and are not willing to listen to anything our own dear medical profession may tell us about how it actually is or is not transmitted."

Perceptions of risk can and do change with time and experience. Our interviewees and commentators in the literature indicate that as individuals and institutions have more patients with AIDS they begin to shed some of their protective garb. In one hospital we were told that the practice of donning gown, gloves, and masks became less frequent as doctors, nurses, housekeepers, and dietary workers "saw" that they did not get AIDS from their patients. This, of course, raises another interesting question: In what sense did personnel come to this conclusion? After all, the diseases associated with HIV infection typically have long latencies, up to several years, before symptoms develop. None of the institutions where our informants worked conducted routine surveillance to assess development of HIV antibody among personnel. Thus, staff could not really know if they had "gotten" HIV infection. Moreover, reports of individual physicians anxiously awaiting the results of HIV tests after needle sticks have now become a staple of the oral culture of academic medical centers.

On AIDS wards all personnel are far less likely to place barriers between themselves and patients for activities where blood or other body fluids might be transmitted. Beyond subspecialty units, however, medical, nursing, and support staff are far more fearful and employ many more nonrational techniques to prevent contamination. (We refer to simple touching, as in noninvasive patient examinations, back rubs, etc., as well as activities involving no patient contact at all, such

as the placing of meal trays on overbed tables or sweeping the floor.) One informant told us that HIV-infected hemophilia patients in one hospital often refuse hospitalization if it means getting a room on certain floors or nursing units. The patients prefer to delay needed treatment until a bed becomes available on a unit where they feel more humanely treated.

Several other curious phenomena have emerged regarding risks and AIDS in the medical work place. While in some locations lack of experience has led to classic reactions of fear and avoidance, in other places the paucity of experience permits denial to dominate. The comments of house staff in a hospital with only an occasional AIDS patient indicated that few residents followed Centers for Disease Control or similar guidelines for "universal precautions." Various explanations were offered, including the conviction that starting intravenous infusions, blood drawing, or similar procedures is more difficult when wearing gloves. When asked how surgeons accomplish complex manual tasks while wearing one or two pairs of gloves, residents usually replied that they had not learned to do things "that way." Here, one kind of inexperience (with gloves) reinforces another (with AIDS), bolstering the feeling of invulnerability that was widespread before AIDS.

Some medical students and physicians have dealt with the problem of risk globally. They want to avoid encountering patients with AIDS altogether. In one medical school where we teach, there is a policy prohibiting students from refusing to care for HIV-infection patients. The policy infuriates many students, a fact we learned in medical-ethics discussion groups that met to discuss an AIDS case. They cited several reasons. The rules, some felt, were changed midstream. Had they known about the policy, they might have chosen another school. They felt they had no role in the formation of the policy and that the tremendous economic investment they made in the institution, in the form of tuition, entitles them to some decision-making authority. They objected to the rule's existence. They said such rules have no place in medicine. Doctors, they believe, should have as much freedom as lawyers, accountants, executives, or others to accept or reject "clients" or "customers." When presented with the notion of a professional obligation or duty, based upon generally acknowledged moral precepts, they balked. At other institutions we know there has been more controversy among medical students, with some making impassioned statements about the physician's obligation to treat. In this debate we see AIDS as a total social phenomenon acting as a vehicle for debating and defining standards of professional conduct.

Another aspect of medical risk avoidance may be revealed through the changing patterns of residency selection. For some time there has been a shift away from primary care specialties like internal medicine, family practice, and pediatrics toward specialties such as orthopedics, ophthalmology, otolaryngology, and radiology (McCarty 1987). The reasons for this phenomena are not entirely clear, but include the technical, rather than personal, orientation of the medical training system and the higher compensation available in the latter group of specialties, sought, in part, because of staggering educational debts. In the past few years, the trend may have accelerated, with internal medicine (whose house staff and practitioners provide the bulk of the care for AIDS patients) training programs failing to find sufficient qualified applicants (Graettianger 1989; Davidoff 1989). This crisis has been most marked in the cities with large numbers of HIV-infected patients (Ness et al. 1989). A similar trend toward avoiding residencies in AIDS-endemic areas may be emerging in pediatrics, according to faculty rumors; a substantial proportion of pediatric house officers, like those in internal medicine, would not care for AIDS patients if given the choice, according to one survey (Link et al. 1988). (This does not imply that defenses such as denial and risk avoidance were not part of the medical educational culture prior to AIDS. Indeed, denial is at the center of the syndrome of adolescent invulnerability. Distinctive now is the appearance of such sentiments in professional journals.)

Surgical Risk and Historical Precedent

Even more remarkable in the AIDS-risk reaction has been the appearance in prestigious medical journals of complaints, whines, and pleas for understanding from doctors worried about contamination and ruination (Guy 1987; Ponsford 1987; Dudley and Sim 1988; Carey 1988; Guido 1988). These pieces offer various estimates of risk to person, career, family, future patients deprived of the skills of the author or his or her esteemed colleagues, and other justifications for not treating HIV-infected persons. (At last, the attending authors may have forged an alliance with their house officers by championing the cause of self-protection.) The articles proclaim a kind of anticoup, that is, they are declarations of futility, contrasting sharply with the verbal swaggering of pre-AIDS narratives. It is important to note that the medical literature on AIDS is not entirely negative; complaints can be matched against calls to duty (Gillon 1987; Zuger and Miles 1987; Pellegrino 1987; Kim and Perfect 1988; Friedland 1988; Emanuel 1988; Sharp 1988; Peterson 1989). On the shop floor and in the literature, AIDS as a total social phenomenon has become the lens for focusing on the obligations of members of the medical profession.

Surgeons have been particularly outspoken about the extent to which they are threatened, and there is reason for their special concerns (Hagen, Meyer, and Pauker 1988; Peterson 1989). After all, these doctors have a high likelihood of contact with the blood of patients. This involves not just working in blood-perfused tissues, but also a risk of having gloves and skin punctured by the instruments of their craft or having blood splash onto other vulnerable areas of the body (mucous membranes in professional parlance). Surgeons, by the very nature of their work, do more of this than many other doctors. But other physicians do find themselves in similar circumstances, depending on their activities. Intensive-care specialists, invasive cardiologists, emergency physicians, pulmonary and gastrointestinal specialists, and others have frequent and/or sustained contact with the blood or other body fluids of patients who may be infected with HIV. House staff, as the foot soldiers doing comprehensive examinations, drawers of blood specimens, inserters of intravenous catheters or other tubes in other places, cleaners of wounds, or simply as those first on the scene of bloody disasters, are particularly likely to be splashed, splattered, or otherwise coated with patients' blood, secretions, or excretions.

We do not have data on the extent to which fears have or have not been translated into changes in behavior in operating and/or procedure rooms. In some communities there may now be fewer operations and these procedures may take longer as extra time is taken to reduce bleeding and avoid punctures. This may not turn out to be as good as it might at first seem. To the extent that high-risk patients have operations delayed or denied or must undergo longer anesthetics and have wounds open longer, patient care may be compromised.

It is interesting to compare the current outcry with what happened when medical science discovered the nature of hepatitis and recognized the medical risks to personnel of serum hepatitis, now known as hepatitis B. As long ago as 1949 (Liebowitz et al. 1949), the medical literature acknowledged that medical personnel coming in contact with blood stood at risk from hepatitis. A debate continued through the 1950s, 1960s, and early 1970s about whether surgeons were especially vulnerable because of their use of sharp instruments, the frequency of accidental puncture of the skin during surgical procedures, and the likelihood of inoculation of the virus into the bloodstream of the wounded party. The risks were felt to be clearly documented in an article (Rosenberg et al. 1973) in the *Journal of the American Medical Association* that commented: "This study demonstrates the distinct occupational hazard to surgeons when they operate on patients who are capable of transmitting hepatitis virus. . . . We believe that serious attempts should be made to prevent future epidemics. . . . Education and constant vigilance in surgical technique are central to any preventive program." Nowhere does the article suggest surgeons should consider not operating on patients at risk for hepatitis.

Of course, hepatitis B is not associated with a fatal prognosis in a large proportion of cases and is not entirely comparable to AIDS. Nonetheless, the epidemiologic evidence gathered in the 1970s suggested that hepatitis B was very prevalent among physicians, especially surgeons (Denes et al. 1978), and that medical personnel seemed especially vulnerable to having severe courses of the disease (Garibaldi et al. 1973). A portion become chronic carriers of the virus, with the added risk later of liver cancer and liver failure

from cirrhosis. Moreover, secondary spread from infected medical workers can occur to patients (through small cuts and sores on the workers' skin) and sexual partners (through exchange of bodily fluids). Despite all this, major medical journals did not carry discussions of whether doctors at risk might be excused from professional activities. It may be that our society's general risk aversiveness (Fairlie 1989) and tolerance of self-centeredness have escalated sufficiently to make public renunciation of professional responsibility more acceptable. More likely, the general medical professional ethic has changed to one closer to that of the entrepreneur, as was true for our students. But perhaps something else is going on that, being synergistic with the perceived loss of invulnerability brought on by AIDS, makes the AIDS era distinctive.

AIDS as a Total Social Phenomenon

The reaction to AIDS on the shop floor must be examined in light of the perceptions of risk, the epidemiology of AIDS, and moral judgments some make about activities that lead to acquiring the disease. Most AIDS patients have come from identifiable populations: the gay community, intravenous drug users and their partners, and those who have gotten the disease from medical use of blood and blood products. While hepatitis B infections were prevalent in these populations and also entailed risks to medical personnel, hepatitis in such patients did not cause doctors to deny their professional responsibility to provide treatment. We are arguing that the unique combination of factors associated with AIDS prompts the negative reactions among doctors: changing tolerances of risk, the shift to an occupation bounded by entrepreneurial rules rather than professional duties, a specific fear of the terrible outcome should one acquire AIDS from a patient, objections to some of the specific behaviors that lead to AIDS, and class and racial bias. Below, we discuss some of the social characteristics of AIDS patients that affect the negativity of the professionals.

The demographics of AIDS is striking and flies rudely in the face of the last several decades of medical progress. Most AIDS patients are young adults. This is true of gays, drug users, and even the hemophiliacs, by and large. Most house officers, however naive and unprepared they are to confront devastating illness and death, at least have a general cultural and social expectation of, if not experience with, the death of old people. With AIDS, many of the sickest patients filling teaching hospital wards in high-prevalence cities are in their prime years, similar in age to the house staff providing the front-line care (Glick 1988). People so young are not supposed to die. These deaths challenge the ideology of the coming-if-not-quite-arrived triumph of modern medical science implicitly provided young doctors in medical education. (Two former house officers have written about the effects of AIDS on medical training: Wachter 1986; Zuger 1987.)

We do not want to paint with too broad a brush here. There are some important differences among the groups of AIDS patients, which influence the reactions of resident physicians. Our informants describe three nonexhaustive groups of patients to whom young doctors and students react: hemophiliacs and others who acquired AIDS through transfusion, young gay men, and drug users and their partners. (We have insufficient information to comment on the reaction to the rapidly growing infant AIDS population. Also, we cannot fully assess how attitudes toward any of these groups may have changed from the pre-AIDS era. Clearly, some in the health care system treated gays and IV drug users badly before they perceived a threat from them.)

In many ways, the patients who develop AIDS from blood products constitute a simple set. These patients are clearly seen as innocents, true victims of unfortunate but inevitable delay between recognition of a technical problem—blood-borne transmission of a serious disease—and its reliable and practical prevention—cleaning up of the blood supply. A chief resident commented that her house officers talk differently about patients with AIDS caused by transfusions from the way they speak about other AIDS patients. "The residents see these cases [with blood-product-related disease] as more tragic; their hearts go out to them more." Hemophiliacs have an air of double tragedy about them: an often crippling, always inconvenient genetic disorder made worse as a direct consequence of their medical treatment.

Hemophiliac patients with AIDS in one of the hospitals where we made inquiries went out of their way to make the origins of their disease or other emblems of their identity known. These patients "display" wives and children to differentiate themselves from homosexual patients. One hemophiliac, reflecting on his desire to have others know that his HIV-positive status preceded his drug abuse, commented that this public knowledge was important because there is "always a pecking order" in who gets scarce nursing care. Even though few people hold these patients in any way responsible for their disease, behavior on the wards toward HIV-positive hemophiliacs clearly differs from attention given non-AIDS or non HIV-infected patients. As mentioned earlier, their hospital rooms are not as clean as the rooms of hemophiliac patients not infected with HIV; the staff does not touch them as often as they once did. (Many of these patients were frequently hospitalized before the HIV epidemic; in effect, they have served as their own controls in a cruel experiment of nature.) Their care is compromised in small but painful ways.

Gay patients with AIDS occupy an intermediate position in the hierarchy. The social characteristics of many of these patients, in the eyes of our informants, were positive ones: the patients were well educated, well groomed, took an active interest in their treatments, had supportive family and/or networks that relieved some of the burdens from their care providers, and the like. Of course, not all medical personnel appreciate all of these features. Interest in care has emerged into social activism about treatment, which some physicians resent. For example, one patient who had developed severe difficulty swallowing, and was starving as a consequence, requested insertion of a feeding tube through his abdominal wall into his intestinal tract. His primary physicians tried to put him off, apparently believing he would succumb soon, no matter what was done. When he persisted, a surgical consultant was called. The surgeon initially treated the request as a joke, finally agreed after an attempt to dissuade the patient ("So, you really want to do this?"), and then provided no follow-up care. This is but one case, but our general impression is that the "turfing" (transferring) that Shem (1978) described as a major feature of shop-floor culture before AIDS has intensified. Physicians want to shift the burdens and responsibilities of care to others.

From the resident's point of view, there may also be a down side to the extensive support systems many gay patients enjoy. In the final stages of AIDS, little more can be done for patients beyond providing comfort. For the interested and compassionate resident, titration of pain medication and less technical interaction, that is, talking with the patient, can be therapeutic for both. If the patient has become invested in alternative treatments for discomfort, from herbal medicine to medication to imaging, and if the patient is surrounded by loving family and community, the house officer may feel she or he has nothing whatsoever to contribute. This helplessness amplifies the despair and the pointlessness of whatever scut work must be done. Here, there can be no transforming, heroic intervention, no redemption arising from clinical defeat.

The IV-drug-using HIV-infected patients represent one of the fastest growing and most problematic set of patients. Teaching hospitals have always had more than their share of patients who are "guilty" victims of disease, that is, patients whose medical problems are seen as direct consequences of their behavior. Many of our prestigious teaching hospitals have been municipal or county facilities filled with substance-abusing patients with a wide spectrum of problems from which house staff have learned. Our informants suggested that the coming of AIDS to this population had subtly altered the way these patients are regarded. Now, drug users cannot be regarded with mere contempt or simple disrespect: there is fear among doctors who are afraid of acquiring AIDS from the patients. Whereas frustration and anger in some cases (especially when drug users were manipulative or physically threatening) and indifference in others used to constitute much of the response to drug-using patients, fear of AIDS has added a difficult dimension.

One might argue that before HIV, this underclass population had a set of positive social roles to play. Their very presence reminded doctors and nurses, perhaps even other patients, that things might not be as bad as they seemed. The intern might be miserable after staying up an entire weekend, but she/he could look to a better life ahead and know that she/he did not have to face homelessness and desperate poverty when finally leaving the hospital to rest. Moreover, the underclass patients provided chances to learn and practice that private patients could not offer. (The poor often have more complex or advanced medical problems, compared with wealthier patients, because of limited access to care and delays in diagnosis and treatment. In addition, attendings often permit house staff to exercise greater responsibility with "service" patients.) But AIDS seems to have changed the balance for many who might have tolerated or welcomed the opportunities to care for the underserved. For a medical student contemplating a residency, what was previously a chance to gain relative autonomy quickly in an institution with many substance-abusing patients may have become predominantly unwelcome exposure to a dreadful illness. If this is so, AIDS will trigger, in yet another way, a dreadful decline in the availability and quality of care for America's medical underclass.

Conclusion

The full impact of AIDS on the modern system of medical care will not be clear for many years. Nevertheless, the disease has already affected the culture of American medicine in a pivotal place: the urban teaching center. Already a scene beset with anger, pain, sadness, and high technology employed soullessly against disease, AIDS has added to the troubles. We cannot know for certain whether this new plague has contributed to the decline in interest in medicine as a career or to the flight from primary care. There is certainly no evidence that AIDS has prompted many to seek out a life of selfless dedication to tending the hopelessly ill.

For those who have chosen to train in hospitals with large numbers of AIDS patients, the disease has added to the burdens of the shop floor. The perception of risk of acquiring AIDS has undermined one of the best-established defenses house officers have relied on: the maintenance of an air of invulnerability. Some doctors are so scared they are abandoning their traditional duty and no longer seem able or willing to try to bring off the heroic coup against daunting clinical odds. To be sure, this fear is fed by other factors on the social scene: the economic changes in medicine, transforming the profession into the province of the entrepreneur; the youth and other characteristics of many AIDS patients; and the willingness of the entire society to turn away from the underclass, especially from those who are seen as self-destructive.

Nothing here suggests that AIDS will spark a turn to a kinder, gentler medical care system. Those in the educational system inclined to seek models providing compassionate medical care will likely find few attractive mentors. Instead, they will meet burned-out martyrs, steely-eyed technicians, and teachers filled with fear. Tomorrow's first-hand accounts of medical education and fictionalized autobiographies may, as a result, be even grimmer than yesterday's.

There is the possibility that this conclusion is too stark, too depressing. For those desperate for a more hopeful scenario, at least one other alternative suggests itself. As the numbers of medical students dwindle, perhaps those who enter will be more committed to ideals of professional service and, among those, some will enter with a missionary zeal for caring for AIDS patients. There is little to suggest this other than the portraits of the few heroic physicians one finds in Shilts's (1987) account of the early years of the AIDS epidemic. If these physicians inspire a new generation of medical professionals, then the tone of future first-hand accounts will be more in line with the highest ideals and aspirations of the medical profession.

NOTE

Acknowledgments: The listing of the authors reflects the alphabet rather than the efforts of the contributors. This is in every sense an equal collaboration. The authors gratefully acknowledge the contributions of our informants, who must remain nameless. Helpful comments on earlier drafts were made by Robert Arnold and Harold Bershady.

REFERENCES

Becker, H. 1967. Whose Side Are We On? *Social Problems* 14:239–47.

Becker, C.E., J.E. Cone and J. Gerberding. 1989. Occupational Infection with Human Immunodeficiency Virus (HIV): Risks and Risk Reduction. *Annals of Internal Medicine* 110:653–56.

Becker, H., B. Geer, E.C. Hughes, and A. Strauss. 1961. *Boys in White: Student Culture in Medical School.* Chicago: University of Chicago Press.

Bell, D. 1975. *A Time To Be Born.* New York: Dell.

Bosk, C. 1979. *Forgive and Remember: Managing Medical Failure.* Chicago: University of Chicago Press.

———. 1985. Social Controls and Physicians: The Oscillation of Cynicism and Idealism in Sociological Theory. In *Social Controls and the Medical Profession,* ed. J.P. Swazey and S.R. Scherr, 31–52. Boston: Oelgeschlager, Gunn and Hain.

Burkett, G., and K. Knafl. 1974. Judgment and Decision-making in a Medical Specialty. *Sociology of Work and Occupations* 1:82–109.

Carey, J.S. 1988. Routine Preoperative Screening for HIV (Letter to the Editor). *Journal of the American Medical Association* 260:179.

Cook, R. 1972. *The Year of the Intern.* New York: Harcourt Brace Jovanovich.

Coombs, R.H. 1978. *Mastering Medicine: Professional Socialization of Medical School.* New York: Free Press.

Coser, L. 1974. *Greedy Institutions: Patterns of Undivided Commitment.* New York: Free Press.

Coser, R.L. 1979. *Training in Ambiguity: Learning through Doing in a Mental Hospital.* New York: Free Press.

Davidoff, F. 1989. Medical Residencies: Quantity or Quality? *Annals of Internal Medicine* 110:757–58.

Denes, A.E., J.L. Smith, J.E. Maynard, I.L. Doto, K.R. Berquist, and A.J. Finkel. 1978. Hepatitis B Infection in Physicians: Results of a Nationwide Seroepidemiologic Survey. *Journal of the American Medical Association* 239:210–12.

Dudley, H.A.F., and A. Sim. 1988. AIDS: A Bill of Rights for the Surgical Team? *British Medical Journal* 296:1449–50.

Emanuel, E.J. 1988. Do Physicians Have an Obligation to Treat Patients with AIDS? *New England Journal of Medicine* 318:1686–90.

Fairlie, H. 1989. Fear of Living: America's Morbid Aversion to Risk. *New Republic* January 23:14–19.

Fox, D. 1986. AIDS and the American Health Polity: The History and Prospects of a Crisis of Authority. *Milbank Quarterly* 64 (suppl. 1):7–33.

Fox, R.C. 1957. Training for Uncertainty. In *The Student-Physician: Introductory Studies in the Sociology of Medical Education,* ed. R.K. Merton, G.C. Reader, and P.L. Kendall, 207–41. Cambridge: Harvard University Press.

Fox, R.C., and H. Lief. 1963. Training for "Detached Concern" in Medical Students. In *The Psychological Basis of Medical Practice,* ed. H. Lief, V. Lief, and N. Lief, 12–35. New York: Harper and Row.

Friedland, G. 1988. AIDS and Compassion. *Journal of the American Medical Association* 259:2898–99.

Garibaldi, R.A., J.N. Forrest, J.A. Bryan, B.F. Hanson, and W.E. Dismukes. 1973. Hemodialysis-Associated Hepatitis. *Journal of the American Medical Association* 225:384–89.

George, V., and A. Dundes. 1978. The Gomer: A Figure of American Hospital Folk Speech. *Journal of American Folklore* 91:568–81.

Gerberding, J.L., C.E. Bryant-LeBlanc, K. Nelson, A.R. Moss, D. Osmond, H.F. Chambers, J.R. Carlson, W.L. Drew, J.A. Levy, and M.A. Sande. 1987. Risk of Transmitting the Human Immunodeficiency Virus, Cytomegalovirus, and Hepatitis B Virus to Health Care Workers Exposed to Patients with AIDS and AIDS-related Conditions. *Journal of Infectious Diseases* 156:1–8.

Gerbert, B., B. Maguire, V. Badner, D. Altman, and G. Stone. 1988. Why Fear Persists: Health Care Professionals and AIDS. *Journal of the American Medical Association* 260:3481–83.

Gillon, R. 1987. Refusal to Treat AIDS and HIV Positive Patients. *British Medical Journal* 294:1332–33.

Glasser, R.J. 1973. *Ward 402.* New York: George Braziller.

Glick, S.M. 1988. The Impending Crisis in Internal Medicine Training Programs. *American Journal of Medicine* 84:929–32.

Graettinger, J.S. 1989. Internal Medicine in the National Resident Matching Program 1978–1989. *Annals of Internal Medicine* 110:682.

Guido, L.J. 1988. Routine Preoperative Screening for HIV (Letter to the Editor). *Journal of the American Medical Association* 260:180.

Guy, P.J. 1987. AIDS: A Doctor's Duty. *British Medical Journal* 294–445.

Hagen, M.D., K.B. Meyer, and S.G. Pauker. 1988. Routine Preoperative Screening for HIV: Does the Risk to the Surgeon Outweigh the Risk to the Patient? *Journal of the American Medical Association* 259: 1357–59.

Haseltine, F., and Y. Yaw. 1976. *Woman Doctor: The Internship of a Modern Woman.* Boston: Houghton Mifflin.

Horowitz, S., and N. Offen. 1977. *Calling Dr. Horowitz.* New York: William Morrow.

Hughes, E.C. 1971. *The Sociological Eye: Selected Papers on Work, Self, and Society.* Chicago: Aldine-Atherton.

Hyde, L. 1979. *The Gift: Imagination and the Erotic Life of Property.* New York: Vintage Books.

Kim, J.H., and J.R. Perfect. 1988. To Help the Sick: An Historical and Ethical Essay Concerning the Refusal to Care for Patients with AIDS. *American Journal of Medicine* 84:135–38.

Klass, P. 1987. *A Not Entirely Benign Procedure: Four Years as a Medical Student.* New York: Putnam.

Klein, K. 1981. *Getting Better: A Medical Student's Story.* Boston: Little, Brown.

Konner, M. 1987. *Becoming a Doctor: A Journey of Initiation in Medical School.* New York: Viking.

Lear, M.W. 1980. *Heartsounds.* New York: Pocket Books.

LeBaron, C. 1981. *Gentle Vengeance: An Account of the First Year at Harvard Medical School.* New York: Richard Marek.

Liebowitz, S., L. Greenwald, I. Cohen, and J. Lirwins. 1949. Serum Hepatitis in a Blood Bank Worker. *Journal of the American Medical Association* 140(17):1331–33.

Liederman, D., and J. Grisso. 1985. The Gomer Phenomenon. *Journal of Health and Social Behavior* 26:222–31.

Lifson, A.R., K.G. Castro, E. McCray, and H.W. Jaffe. 1986. National Surveillance of AIDS in Health Care Workers. *Journal of the American Medical Association* 265:3231–34.

Light, D. 1980. *Becoming Psychiatrists: The Professional Transformation of Self.* New York: W.W. Norton.

Link, R.N., A.R. Feingold, M.H. Charap, K. Freeman, and S.P. Shelov, 1988. Concerns of Medical and Pediatric House Officers about Acquiring AIDS from Their Patients. *American Journal of Public Health* 78:455–59.

McCarty, D.J. 1987. Why Are Today's Medical Students Choosing High-technology Specialties over Internal Medicine? *New England Journal of Medicine* 317:567–69.

Mechanic, D. 1986. *From Advocacy to Allocation: The Evolving American Health Care System.* New York: Free Press.

Miller, S.J. 1970. *Prescription for Leadership: Training for the Medical Elite.* Chicago: Aldine.

Millman, M. 1977. *The Unkindest Cut: Life in the Backrooms of Medicine.* New York: William Morrow.

Mizrahi, T. 1986. *Getting Rid of Patients: Contradictions in the Socialization of Physicians.* New Brunswick: Rutgers University Press.

Morgan, E. 1980. *The Making of a Woman Surgeon.* New York: G.P. Putnam.

Mullan, F. 1976. *White Coat, Clenched Fist: The Political Education of an American Physician.* New York: Macmillan.

Mumford, E. 1970. *Interns: From Students to Physicians.* Cambridge: Harvard University Press.

Ness, R., C.D. Killian, D.E. Ness, J.B. Frost, and D. McMahon. 1989. Likelihood of Contact with AIDS Patients as a Factor in Medical Students' Residency Selections. *Academic Medicine* 64:588–94.

Nolen, W. 1970. *The Making of a Surgeon.* New York: Random House.

O'Connor, T.W. 1990. Do Patients Have the Right to Infect Their Doctors? *Australia and New Zealand Journal of Surgery* 60:157–62.

Pellegrino, E.D. 1987. Altruism, Self-interest, and Medical Ethics. *Journal of the American Medical Association* 258:1939–40.

Peterson, L.M. 1989. AIDS: The Ethical Dilemma for Surgeons. *Law, Medicine, and Health Care* 17 (Summer):139–44.

Ponsford, G. 1987. AIDS in the OR: A Surgeon's View. *Canadian Medical Association Journal* 137: 1036–39.

Rabkin, M. 1982. The SAG Index. *New England Journal of Medicine* 307:1350–51.

Reilly, P. 1987. *To Do No Harm: A Journey through Medical School.* Dover, Mass.: Auburn House.

Relman, A.S. 1980. The New Medical-Industrial Complex. *New England Journal of Medicine* 303: 963–70.

Rosenberg, J.L., D.P. Jones, L.R. Lipitz, and J.B. Kirsner. 1973. Viral Hepatitis: An Occupational Hazard to Surgeons. *Journal of the American Medical Association* 223:395–400.

Rubin, T.I. 1972. *Emergency Room Diary.* New York: Grosset and Dunlap.

Scully, D. 1980. *Men Who Control Women's Health.* Boston: Houghton Mifflin.

Sharp, S.C. 1988. The Physician's Obligation to Treat AIDS Patients. *Southern Medical Journal* 81: 1282–85.

Shem, S. 1978. *The House of God.* New York: Richard Marek.

Shilts, R. 1987. *And the Band Played On.* New York: St. Martins.

Starr, P. 1982. *The Social Transformations of American Medicine.* New York: Basic Books.

Steiner, J.F., L.E. Feinberg, A.M. Kramer, and R.L. Byyny. 1987. Changing Patterns of Disease on an Inpatient Medical Service: 1961–62 to 1981–82. *American Journal of Medicine* 83:331–35.

Stelling, J., and R. Bucher. 1972. Autonomy and Monitoring on Hospital Wards. *Sociological Quarterly* 13:431–47.

Sweeney, III. W. 1973. *Woman's Doctor: A Year in the Life of an Obstetrician-Gynecologist.* New York: Morrow.

Wachter, R.M. 1986. The Impact of the Acquired Immunodeficiency Syndrome on Medical Residency Training. *New England Journal of Medicine* 314: 177–80.

X, Dr. 1965. *Intern.* New York: Harper and Row.

Zuger, A. 1987. AIDS on the Wards: A Residency in Medical Ethics. *Hastings Center Report* 17(3):16–20.

Zuger, A., and S.H. Miles. 1987. Physicians, AIDS, and Occupational Risk: Historical Traditions and Ethical Obligations. *Journal of the American Medical Association* 258:1924–28.

Medical Industries

. . . . . .

The medical industries have "commodified" health in a number of ways. They have turned certain goods and services into products or commodities that can be marketed to meet "health needs" created by the industry itself. A recent and commonplace example of "commodification" was the promotion of Listerine as a cure for the "disease" of "halitosis" (bad breath). A wide range of products have been marketed to meet commodified health needs, such as products designed to alleviate feminine hygiene "problems" and instant milk formulas to meet the "problem" of feeding infants.

In the late twentieth century, medical care is a profitable investment, at least for stockholders and corporations. With the increase in medical technology and the growth of for-profit hospitals, medicine itself is becoming a corporate industry. The 1960s saw the rise of a large nursing home industry (Vladeck, 1980); in the 1970s, there were huge increases in investment in for-profit hospital chains; and in the 1980s, new free-standing emergency rooms began to dot the suburban landscape. The nonprofit, and especially the public, sector of medicine has decreased while the for-profit sector continues to increase. The closing of many urban, public hospitals is a piece of this change (Sager, 1983). As Starr (1982) notes, the corporatization of medicine presents a threat to the long-standing physician sovereignty. This is part of a shift of power in medicine from the "professional monopolists" (AMA physicians) to the "corporate rationalizers" (Alford, 1972).

Technology has long been central to medicine. In recent years, medical technology has become a major industry. Innovations such as CT scanners, hemodialysis machines, electronic fetal monitors, and neonatal infant care units have transformed medical care. Those medical technologies contribute significantly to the increasing costs of medical care, although these are usually justified by claims of saving lives or reducing maladies. But medical technologies usually are adopted before they are adequately tested and become "standard procedures" without sufficient evidence of their efficacy (McKinlay, 1981). This proliferation of medical technology is expensive and often unnecessary. It is doubtful that every hospital needs a CT scanner, a cardiac care unit, or an open heart surgery suite, but most states have exerted little control over the spread of such technology. Further, the medical technological imperative of "can do, should do" has frequently bypassed issues of cost-effectiveness or efficacy. For a detailed discussion of these issues, see "Dilemmas of Medical Technology," the final section of Part 2.

The selections in this section examine two predominant examples of change in the medical industries: increasing corporate control of medical care and expanding medical technology. The selections show the importance of the profit motive in the growth of medical industry; the authors see real problems with the increases in profit-making medical care. In a sense, medical care itself is becoming more overtly commodified.

In the first selection, Arnold S. Relman, a physician and former editor of the prestigious *New England Journal of Medicine,* examines the growth of the for-profit health care industry. He reviews the expansion of the commercialization

238

of health care since 1980, when his classic article on "the new medical industrial complex" first focused attention on this development. Relman finds that while the growth of for-profit hospital chains has slowed, many other aspects of the medical–industrial complex are increasing rapidly—with revenues now encompassing over 20 percent of our health care expenditures. Moreover, voluntary ("nonprofit") hospitals now also see themselves as businesses and are becoming more entrepreneurial. The orientation of hospitals and medical care institutions is changing from social service to business and shifting in focus from altruism to the bottom line. Advertising health services and "product" competition are now common. The roots of the commercialization of medical care are in the uncontrolled third-party reimbursement system. Little evidence exists as yet that patients benefit more from "for-profit" care and some evidence indicates that they do not (Gray, 1991). For-profit health care puts the incentives in the wrong place—on profitability instead of on necessary care. Thus it is very doubtful that corporatization and profit-making of health care are in the public interest.

In "A Marxian Interpretation of the Growth and Development of Coronary Care Technology," physician and sociologist Howard Waitzkin examines how coronary care units gained acceptance despite high costs and contradictory evidence of their effectiveness. Waitzkin argues that this apparently "irrational" health policy becomes understandable when viewed in the context of a capitalist society. He shows the complex interactions among medicine, industry, and philanthropy in the development and dissemination of the technology (cf. Bell, 1985) and raises the issue of corporate profit versus the cost-effectiveness of technology.

REFERENCES

Alford, Robert L. 1972. "The political economy of health care: Dynamics without changes." Politics and Society. Winter: 127–64.

Bell, Susan. 1985. "A new model of medical technology development: A case study of DES." In Julius Roth and Sheryl Ruzek (eds.), The Adoption and Social Consequences of Medical Technology (Research in the Sociology of Health Care, Volume 4). Greenwich, CT: JAI Press.

Gray, Bradford H. 1991. The Profit Motive and Patient Care: The Changing Accountability of Doctors and Hospitals. Cambridge, MA: Harvard University Press.

McKinlay, John B. 1981. "From 'promising report' to 'standard procedure': Seven stages in the career of a medical innovation." Milbank Memorial Fund Quarterly/Health and Society. 59: 374–411.

Sager, Alan. 1983. "The reconfiguration of urban hospital care: 1937–1980." In Ann Lennarson Greer and Scott Greer (eds.), Cities and Sickness: Health Care in Urban America. Urban Affairs Annual Review, Volume 26, Chapter 3. Beverly Hills, CA: Sage.

Starr, Paul. 1982. The Social Transformation of American Medicine. New York: Basic Books.

Vladeck, Bruce. 1980. Unloving Care: The Nursing Home Tragedy. New York: Basic Books.

21

The Health Care Industry: Where Is It Taking Us?

■ ■ ■ ■ ■ ■

Arnold S. Relman

Eleven years ago, in the Annual Discourse presented before the Massachusetts Medical Society and later published in the *New England Journal of Medicine*,[1] I first addressed the issue of commercialism in medical care. Referring to what I called "the new medical-industrial complex," I described a huge new industry that was supplying health care services for profit. It included proprietary hospitals and nursing homes, diagnostic laboratories, home care and emergency room services, renal hemodialysis units, and a wide variety of other medical services that had formerly been provided largely by public or private not-for-profit community-based institutions or by private physicians in their offices. The medical-industrial complex had developed mainly as a response to the entrepreneurial opportunities afforded by the expansion of health insurance coverage offering indemnification through Medicare and employment-based plans. Given the open-ended, piece-work basis of third-party payment, business ownership of a medical facility virtually guaranteed a profit, provided that practicing physicians could be persuaded to use the facility and that services were limited to fully insured patients.

At that time, I estimated that the new medical–industrial complex had revenues of perhaps $35 to $40 billion, which would have been about 17 to 19 percent of total health expenditures for the calendar year 1979, and I was concerned about the possible consequences of the continued growth of the complex. I suggested that its marketing and advertising strategies might lead to high costs and widespread overuse of medical resources; that it might overemphasize expensive technology and neglect less profitable personal care, that it might skim off paying patients, leaving the poor and uninsured to an increasingly burdened not-for-profit sector; and that it might come to exercise undue influence on national health policy and the attitude of physicians toward their profession. I suggested that physicians should avoid all financial ties with the medical-industrial complex in order to be free to continue acting as unbiased protectors of their patients' interests and critical evaluators of new products and services. Finally, I recommended that the new health care industry be studied carefully to determine whether it was providing services of acceptable quality at reasonable prices and to ensure that it was not having adverse effects on the rest of the American health care system.

Two years later, in a lecture at the University of North Carolina,[2] I expressed increasing concern about the future of medical practice in the new medical marketplace. I said,

> The key question is: Will medicine now become essentially a business or will it remain a profession? . . . Will we act as businessmen in a system that is becoming increasingly entrepreneurial or will we choose to remain a profession, with all the obligations for self-regulation and protection of the public interest that this commitment implies?

In the decade that has elapsed since then, the problems posed by the commercialization of health care have grown. So have the pressures on the private practice of medicine, and now our profession faces an ethical and economic crisis of unprecedented proportions, as it struggles to find its bearings in a health care system that has become a vast and highly lucrative marketplace.

What I want to do here is, first, describe how the commercialization of health care has progressed since 1980, with a brief summary of the initial studies of the behavior of for-profit hospitals. I shall describe how the investor-owned sector has continued to grow, but in new directions. At the same time, our voluntary not-for-profit hospitals have become much more entrepreneurial and have come to resemble their investor-owned competitors in many ways. I shall then consider how the new market-oriented health system has been influencing practicing physicians and how, in turn, the system has been influenced by them. Medical practice inevitably reflects the incentives and orientation of the health care system, but it also plays a critical part in determining how the system works. Finally, I shall briefly analyze the tensions between medical professionalism and the health care market.

The Medical-Industrial Complex since 1980

Turning first to the recent history of the medical-industrial complex, I am glad to report that my earlier concern about the possible domination of the hospital sector by investor-owned chains was not justified by subsequent events. In 1980 there were approximately 1000 investor-owned hospitals. Ten years later their number had increased to barely 1400 of a total of some 5000 hospitals. In the past few years there has been virtually no growth in the chains. The reason is that hospitals are no longer as profitable as they were in the days before the institution of diagnosis-related groups (DRGs) and all the other cost-control measures now used by third-party payers.

Numerous studies published during the past decade have compared the economic behavior of investor-owned hospitals during the early pre-DRG days with that of similar voluntary hospitals.[3] Most reports (including those of the most carefully conducted studies) have found that the investor-owned hospitals charged approximately 15 to 20 percent more per admission, even when similar cases with similar degrees of severity were compared. This difference was largely attribut-

able to increased use of, and higher charges for, ancillary services such as laboratory tests and radiologic procedures. During that earlier period, investor-owned hospitals were no more efficient, as measured by their operating costs per admission; if anything, their costs were a little higher than those of comparable voluntary hospitals. Furthermore, there was strong evidence that the investor-owned hospitals spent substantially less of their resources for the care of uninsured patients than did the voluntary hospitals.[4] There are few or no published data on whether these differences persisted after all hospitals began to face a more hostile and competitive market, but from what we already know it seems clear that for at least the initial phase of their existence, the investor-owned hospitals did not use their alleged corporate advantages for the public benefit. In fact, by seeking to maximize their revenues and avoiding uninsured patients, they contributed to the problems of cost and access our health care system now faces. A few studies have attempted to compare the quality of care in voluntary and investor-owned hospitals, but quality is much more difficult to measure objectively than economic performance, and there is no convincing evidence on this point.

Although the predicted rapid expansion of for-profit hospital chains did not materialize, investor-owned facilities for other kinds of medical care have been growing rapidly. Most of the recent expansion has been in services provided on an ambulatory basis or at home. This is because there has been much less governmental and third-party regulation of those services, and the opportunities for commercial exploitation are still very attractive. Investor-owned businesses have the largest share of this new sector.

Free-standing centers for ambulatory surgery are a good case in point. Ten or 15 years ago, all but the most minor surgery was performed in hospitals. It has now become apparent that at least half of all procedures, even those involving general anesthesia, can be safely performed on an outpatient basis, and in the past decade there has been a rapid proliferation of ambulatory surgery. Some of it is performed in special units within hospitals, but most of it is done in free-standing centers, of which there are now at least 1200. Most of the free-standing facilities are investor-owned, with the referring surgeons as limited partners, and many of the in-hospital units are joint ventures between hospitals and their staff surgeons.

Sophisticated high-technology radiologic services, formerly found only in hospital radiology units, are now provided at hundreds of free-standing facilities called "imaging centers." Most of them feature magnetic resonance imagers and CT scanners. They usually are investor-owned and have business arrangements with practicing physicians who refer patients to the facilities. Diagnostic laboratory services, formerly provided only in hospitals, are now available in thousands of free-standing laboratories, many of which also have physicians as limited partners. Walk-in clinics, offering services such as those provided in hospital emergency rooms and other services formerly provided in doctors' offices, now flourish on street corners and in shopping centers and are operated by investor-owned businesses that employ salaried physicians. Investor-owned companies now provide all sorts of services to patients in their homes that were formerly available only in hospitals. These include oxygen therapy, respiratory therapy, and intravenous treatments.

Health maintenance organizations (HMOs) are another important part of the ambulatory care sector. Over the past decade they have continued to grow at the rate of 4 or 5 percent per year, and now there are an estimated 40 million patients enrolled in some 570 different plans. Approximately two thirds of these plans are investor-owned.[5] Some investor-owned hospital chains have expanded "vertically"—that is, they offer not only inpatient, outpatient, and home services, but also nursing home and rehabilitation services. One or two of the largest chains have even gone into the health insurance business. The largest now insures more than 1.5 million subscribers, under terms that offer financial incentives to use the corporation's own hospitals.

In short, the investor-owned medical-industrial complex has continued to grow, but in new directions. No one has any clear idea of its present size, but I estimate that its revenues during 1990 were probably more than $150 billion, of a total national expenditure for health care of some $700 billion. This would mean that it represents an even larger fraction of total health care expenditures than it did a decade ago. The absence of reliable data on this point reflects the unfortunate consequence of government indifference and proprietary secrecy. And yet we obviously need such information to make future health policy decisions.

The Commercialization of Voluntary Hospitals

What I had not fully appreciated in 1980 was that the pressures on our voluntary hospitals would lead many of them to behave just like their investor-owned competitors. The growing transfer of diagnostic and therapeutic procedures out of the hospital, the mounting cost-control constraints imposed by third-party payers, which reduced the hospitals' freedom to shift costs, and the general excess of hospital beds resulting from decades of rapid and uncontrolled expansion have all conspired to threaten the economic viability of voluntary hospitals. Philanthropy and community contributions, a mainstay of support when hospital costs were relatively low, are no longer of much help. Hospitals now must pay higher wages and much more money for supplies and equipment, but they cannot count on third-party payers and charitable contributions to cover costs. To compound the problem, those voluntary institutions traditionally committed to caring for large numbers of uninsured patients now find their resources strained to the limit. Private patients covered by the old-fashioned, open-ended kind of indemnity insurance are in ever shorter supply, and the voluntary hospitals now must compete aggressively in an increasingly unfriendly economic climate.

The result of all this has been a gradual shift in the focus of our voluntary hospital system. Altruistic motives that formerly guided the decisions of voluntary hospital management are giving way in many institutions to a primary concern for the bottom line. Hospital administrators have become corporate executives (with business titles such as chairman, chief executive officer, president, and the like) who are required first of all to ensure the economic survival of their institutions. For many hospitals, this means aggressive use of marketing and advertising strategies, ownership of for-profit businesses, and joint ventures with physicians on their staff. Decisions about the allocation of hospital resources, the creation of new facilities, or the elimination of existing ones are now based more on considerations of what is likely to be profitable than on the priorities of community health needs.

Many if not most of our voluntary hospitals now view themselves as businesses competing for paying patients in the health care marketplace. They have, in effect, become part of the medical-industrial complex. Voluntary hospitals have always been tax-exempt because they are not owned by investors and they do not distribute profits to their owners. Because they are tax-exempt, they have been expected to provide necessary community services, profitable or not, and to care for uninsured patients. Many, of course, do exactly that, to the limit of their ability. But, sad to say, many do not, and this has raised questions in some quarters about the justification of their continued tax exemption.[6]

In any case, we are witnessing a pervasive change in the ethos of the voluntary hospital system in America from that of a social service to that of a business. Leaders of hospital associations now commonly refer to themselves as part of an industry, and the management philosophy of private hospitals, investor-owned or not, is increasingly dominated by business thinking. It would be interesting to compare current prices and unreimbursed care in the voluntary and investor-owned hospital sectors. My guess is that much of the earlier difference in price has disappeared, but the voluntary hospitals probably still provide proportionately more uninsured care.

A Market-Oriented Health Care System

What we see now is a market-oriented health care system spinning out of control. Costs are rising relentlessly in a competitive marketplace heavily influenced by private commerce and still largely dominated by more or less open-ended indemnity insurance and payment by piecework. The financial arrangements in such a system inevitably stimulate the provision of service with little or no regard for cost. Unlike the usual kind of market, in which consumer demand and ability to pay largely determine what is produced and sold, the health care market is not controlled by consumers, because most payment comes from third parties and most decisions are made by physicians.

The fraction of the gross national product devoted to health care has been rising steeply ever since the advent of Medicare and Medicaid in the mid-1960s. In 1965 we spent about 6 percent of our gross national product on health care; in 1975, approximately 8 percent; in 1985, about 10.5 percent; and last year, over 12 percent, or approximately $700 billion.[7] Despite the high cost, or maybe because of it, the system is unable to provide adequate care for all citizens. At least 15 percent of Americans have no health insurance, and probably at least an equal number are inadequately or only intermittently insured. After all, a system that functions as a competitive marketplace has no more interest in subsidizing the uninsured poor than in restricting the revenues generated by services to those who are insured.

Evidence of inefficiency, duplication, and excessive overhead is everywhere apparent. Administrative costs have recently been estimated to make up between 19 and 24 percent of total spending on health care, far more than in any other country.[8] Nearly half of all the beds in investor-owned hospitals and from 35 to 40 percent of all the beds in voluntary hospitals are, on the average, unused. On the other hand, expensive high-technology diagnostic and therapeutic procedures are being carried out in hospitals, doctors' offices, and growing numbers of specialized free-standing facilities at a rate that many studies suggest is excessive among insured patients, though probably inadequate among the poor.

Medical Practice as a Competitive Business

Adding to the competition and cost in our health care system is the recent rapid increase in the number of practicing physicians, most of whom are specialists. In 1970 there were 153 active physicians per 100,000 members of the population; in 1980 there were 192; and the number for 1990 was estimated to exceed 220.[9] Among these new practitioners, the number of specialists is increasing more rapidly than that of primary care physicians. When doctors were in relatively short supply two or three decades ago, they worried less about their livelihood. Now, as the economists would say, we are in a buyer's market, in which not only underused hospitals but also specialists—available in increasing, sometimes even excessive, numbers—are forced to compete for the diminishing number of paying patients who are not already part of the managed care network.

How have all these developments affected the practice of medicine? In the first place, they have resulted in more regulation of the private practice of medicine by third-party payers, who are trying to control costs. There is more interference with clinical practice decisions, more second-guessing and paperwork, and more administrative delays in billing and collecting than ever before, as third-party payers attempt to slow down cost increases through micromanagement of the medical care system.

Second, doctors are increasingly threatened by malpractice litigation as a strictly business relationship begins to replace the trust and mutual confidence that traditionally characterized the doctor–patient relationship.

Third, the courts, which formerly kept the practice of medicine out of the reach of antitrust law, now regard the physician as just another person doing business, no longer immune from antitrust regulation. In 1975 the Supreme Court handed down a landmark decision that found that the business activities of professionals were properly subject to antitrust law.[10] As a consequence, physicians can no longer act collectively on matters affecting the economics of practice, whether their intent is to protect the public or simply to defend the interests of the profession. Advertising and marketing by individual physicians, groups of physicians, or medical facilities, which used to be regarded as unethical and were proscribed by organized medicine, are now protected—indeed, encouraged—by the Federal Trade Commission.

Advertisements now commonly extol the services of individual physicians or of hospital and ambulatory facilities staffed by physicians. Most of them go far beyond simply informing the public about the availability of medical services. Using the slick marketing techniques more appropriate for consumer goods, they lure, coax, and sometimes even frighten the public into using the services advertised.

I recently saw a particularly egregious example of this kind of advertising in the *Los Angeles Times*. A free-standing imaging center in southern California was urging the public to come for magnetic resonance imaging (MRI) studies in its new "open air" imager, without even suggesting the need for previous examination or referral by a physician. The advertisement listed a wide variety of common ailments about which the MRI scan might provide useful information—a stratagem calculated to attract large numbers of worried patients whose insurance coverage would pay the substantial fee for a test that was probably not indicated.

Before it was placed under the protection of antitrust law, such advertising would have been discouraged by the American Medical Association (AMA) and viewed with disfavor by the vast majority of physicians. Now it is ubiquitous, on television and radio, on billboards, and in the popular print media. Of course, not all medical advertising is as sleazy. Many respectable institutions and reputable practitioners advertise in order to bring their services to the public's attention. But in medical advertising there is a fine line between informing and promoting; as competition grows, this line blurs. Increasingly, physicians and hospitals are using marketing and public relations techniques that can only be described as crassly commercial in appearance and intent.

Advertising and marketing are just a part of the varied entrepreneurial activities in which practicing physicians are now engaged. Perceiving the trend toward the industrialization of medicine, sensing the threat to their access to paying patients from hospitals, HMOs, and other closed-panel insurance plans, and feeling the pressures of competition from the growing army of medical practitioners, doctors have begun to think of themselves as beleaguered businesspersons, and they act accordingly. I occasionally hear from physicians expressing this view. For example, a doctor from Texas recently sent me a letter saying: "Medicine is a service business, despite the fact that it deals with human beings and their health problems. . . . Physicians are an economic entity, just like the corner service station." Although I suspect many of his colleagues would not appreciate the analogy, I am afraid that too many would agree with the writer's opinion about the primacy of economic considerations in medical practice. In that respect, they would support the oft-expressed views of the leaders of the for-profit hospital industry. For example, the executive director of the Federation of American Hospitals (the trade association of the investor-owned chains) wrote in a letter published in the *New England Journal of Medicine* 10 years ago: "I fail to see a difference between health services and other basic necessities of life—food, housing, and fuel—all of which are more oriented to the profit motive than is health care."[11]

Of course, the private practice of medicine has always had businesslike characteristics, in that practicing physicians earn their livelihood through their professional efforts. For the vast majority of physicians, however, professional commitments have dominated business concerns. There was always more than enough work for any physician to do, and few physicians had to worry about competition or earning a livelihood. Furthermore, it had long been generally accepted that a physician's income should derive exclusively from direct services to patients or the supervision of such services, not from any entrepreneurial activities.

All that seems to be changing now in this new era of medical entrepreneurialism and health care marketing. Increasing numbers of physicians have economic interests in health care that go beyond direct services to patients or the supervision of such services. The AMA, which formerly proscribed entrepreneurialism by physicians, now expressly allows it, with some caveats, apparently recognizing that a very substantial fraction of practitioners supplement their income by financial interests in all sorts of health care goods, services, and facilities.

The arrangements are too numerous and varied to describe in full here, so I shall simply cite some of them, a few of which I have already alluded to: (1) practitioners hold limited partnerships in for-profit diagnostic-laboratory facilities, to which they refer their patients but over which they exercise no professional supervision; (2) surgeons hold limited partnerships in for-profit ambulatory surgery facilities to which they refer their own patients; (3) office-based practitioners make deals with prescription-drug wholesalers, who supply them with drugs that the physicians prescribe for their patients and for which they charge retail prices; (4) physicians purchase prostheses at reduced rates from manufacturers and make a profit in addition to the professional fees they receive for implanting the prostheses; and (5) practitioners own interests in imaging units to which they refer their patients. Most of the free-standing imaging units are owned by investor-owned businesses, but some were originally owned by radiologists in private practice who have told me that they were persuaded to form joint partnerships with their referring physicians because these physicians threatened to refer their patients elsewhere.

Such arrangements create conflicts of interest that undermine the traditional role of the doctor.[12] In the minds of some physicians, the old Samaritan tradition of our profession has now given way to the concept of a strict business contract between doctor and patient. According to this view, good physicians are simply honest and competent vendors of medical services who are free to contract for whatever services they are willing to provide and patients or their insurers are willing to pay for. Society has no more stake in the practice of medicine than in the conduct of any other business activity, and therefore no right to interfere with the terms of the private contract between doctor and patient.[13,14]

The Threat to the Morale of Physicians and Their Social Contract

. . . Today's market-oriented, profit-driven health care industry . . . sends signals to physicians that are frustrating and profoundly disturbing to the majority of us who believe our primary commitment is to patients. Most of us believe we are parties to a social contract, not a business contract. We are not vendors, and we are not merely free economic agents in a free market. Society has given us a licensed monopoly to practice our profession protected in large part against competition from other would-be dispensers of health services. We enjoy independence and the authority to regulate ourselves and set our own standards. Much of our professional training is subsidized, and almost all the information and technology we need to practice our profession have been produced at public expense. Those of us who practice in hospitals are given without charge the essential facilities and instruments we need to take care of our patients. Most of all, we have the priceless privilege of enjoying the trust of our patients and playing a critical part in their lives when they most need help.

All this we are given in exchange for the commitment to serve our patients' interests first of all and to do the very best we can. In my view, that means we should not only be competent and compassionate practitioners but also avoid ties with the health care market, in order to guide our patients through it in the most medically responsible and cost-effective way possible. If the present organization and incentives of our health care system make it difficult or impossible for us to practice in this way (and I believe they do), then we must join with others in examining ways of reforming the system.

What our health care system needs now is not more money, but different incentives and a better organization that will enable us to use available resources in a more equitable and efficient manner to provide necessary services for all who need them. We can afford all the care that is medically appropriate according to the best professional standards. We cannot afford all the care a market-driven system is capable of giving.

REFERENCES

1. Relman AS. The new medical-industrial complex. N Engl J Med 1980; 303:963–70.
2. *Idem*. The future of medical practice. Health Aff (Millwood) 1983; 2(2):5–19.
3. Gray BH, ed. For-profit enterprise in health care. Washington, D.C.: National Academy Press, 1986.
4. Lewin LS, Eckels TJ, Miller LB. Setting the record straight: the provisions of uncompensated care by not-for-profit hospitals. N Engl J Med 1988; 318:1212–5.
5. Langwell KM. Structure and performance of health maintenance organizations: a review. Health Care Financ Rev 1990; 12(1):71–9.
6. General Accounting Office. Report to the Chairman, Select Committee on Aging, House of Representatives. Nonprofit hospitals: better standards needed for tax exemption. Washington, D.C.: Government Printing Office, 1990. (GAO publication no. (HRD) 90–84.)
7. Levit KR, Lazenby HC, Letsch SW, Cowan CA. National health care spending, 1989. Health Aff (Millwood) 1991; 10(1):117–30.
8. Woolhandler S, Himmelstein DU. The deteriorating administrative efficiency of the U.S. health care system. N Engl J Med 1991; 324:1253–8.
9. Kletke PR. The demographics of physician supply: trends and projections. Chicago: American Medical Association, 1987.
10. Goldfarb v. Virginia State Bar, 421 U.S. 773, 1975.
11. Bromberg MD. The new medical-industrial complex. N Engl J Med 1981; 304:233.
12. Relman AS. Dealing with conflicts of interest. N Engl J Med 1984; 313:749–51.
13. Sade RM. Medical care as a right: a refutation. N Engl J Med 1971; 285:1288–92.
14. Engelhardt HT Jr, Rie MA. Morality for the medical-industrial complex: a code of ethics for the mass marketing of health care. N Engl J Med 1988; 319:1086–9.

22

A Marxian Interpretation
of the Growth and Development
# of Coronary Care Technology

■ ■ ■ ■ ■ ■

Howard Waitzkin

The financial burden of health care has emerged as an issue of national policy. Legislative and administrative maneuvers purportedly aim toward the goal of cost containment. New investigative techniques in health services research, based largely on the cost-effectiveness model, are entering into the evaluation of technology and clinical practices. My purposes in this paper are to document the analytic poverty of these approaches to health policy and to offer an alternative interpretation that derives from Marxian analysis.

In the Marxian framework, the problem of costs never can be divorced from the structure of private profit in capitalist society. Most non-Marxian analyses of costs either ignore the profit structure of capitalism or accept it as given. But the crisis of health costs intimately reflects the more general fiscal crisis, including such incessant problems as inflation and stagnation, that advanced capitalism is facing worldwide. Wearing blinders that limit the level of analysis to a specific innovation or practice, while not perceiving the broader political-economic context in which costly and ineffective procedures are introduced and promulgated, will only obscure potential solutions to the enormous difficulties that confront us.

In this paper I focus on coronary care, having selected this topic merely as one example of apparent irrationalities of health policy that make sense when seen from the standpoint of the capitalist profit structure. The overselling of many other technologic advances such as comput-erized axial tomography and fetal monitoring (which have undeniable usefulness for a limited number of patients) reflects very similar structural problems.

One cautionary remark is worthwhile. The Marxian framework is not a conspiratorial model. The very nature of capitalist production necessitates the continuing development of new products and sales in new markets. From the standpoint of potential profit, there is no reason that corporations should view medical products differently from other products. The commodification of health care and its associated technology is a necessary feature of the capitalist political-economic system.[1-3] Without fundamental changes in the organization of private capital, costly innovations of dubious effectiveness will continue to plague the health sector. It is the structure of the system, rather than decision-making by individual entrepreneurs and clinicians, that is the appropriate level of analysis.

Historical Development of Intensive Coronary Care

Early Claims

Intensive care emerged rapidly during the 1960s. The first major reports of coronary care units (CCUs) were written by Day, who developed a so-called "coronary care area" at the Bethany

247

Hospital in Kansas City, with financial help from the John A. Hartford Foundation.[4] From these early articles until the mid-1970s, claims like Day's were very common in the literature. Descriptions of improved mortality and morbidity appeared, based totally on uncontrolled data from patients with myocardial infarction (MI) admitted before and after the introduction of a CCU. Until the 1970s, no major study of CCUs included a randomized control group.

However, Day's enthusiasm spread. In 1967, the classic descriptive study by Lown's group at the Peter Bent Brigham Hospital in Boston appeared.[5] This study was supported by the U.S. Public Health Service, the Hartford Foundation, and the American Optical Company, which manufactured the tape-loop recall memory system that was used in the CCU. The CCU's major objective, as the article pointed out, was to anticipate and to reduce early heart rhythm disturbances, thereby avoiding the need for resuscitation. The paper cited several other articles showing before-after decreases in mortality with a CCU, but never with randomization or other forms of statistical control introduced, and certainly never with a random controlled trial.

This publication led to a conference in 1968, sponsored by the Department of Health, Education, and Welfare (HEW), in which greater development and support of CCUs were advocated, despite clear-cut statements within the conference that the effectiveness of CCUs had not been demonstrated. For example, at the conference the Chief of the Heart Disease Control Program of the Public Health Service claimed: "An attempt was made a few years ago to make some controlled studies of the benefits of CCU efforts, but it was not possible to carry out those investigations for many reasons, some of them fiscal. Therefore, we do not have proper studies for demonstrating the advantages of CCUs. But now that these opportunities and occasions to prevent heart rhythm disturbances have become a great deal more common, we can be assured that our efforts are worthwhile. . . . Upon advice of our colleagues in the profession, we have not considered it ethically acceptable, at this time, to make a controlled study which would necessitate shunting of patients from a facility without a CCU (but with the support that CCUs provide) to one with a CCU."[6]

Table 22-1. Growth of Coronary Care Units in the United States, by Region, 1967–1974

| Regions | Coronary Care Units (% of hospitals) | |
	1967	1974
United States	24.3	33.8
New England	29.0	36.8
Mid-Atlantic	33.8	44.2
East North Central	31.0	38.2
West North Central	17.0	25.3
South Atlantic	23.3	38.2
East South Central	13.4	30.1
West South Central	15.3	24.3
Mountain	21.4	29.3
Pacific	32.7	37.8

SOURCE: Reference 8

So, despite the lack of controlled studies showing effectiveness, there were many calls for the expansion of CCUs to other hospitals and increased support from the federal government and private foundations. In 1968 HEW also issued a set of Guidelines for CCUs.[7] Largely because of these recommendations, CCUs grew rapidly in the following years. Table 22-1 shows the expansion of CCUs in the United States between 1967 and 1974.[8]

Later Studies of Effectiveness*

Serious research on the effectiveness of CCUs did not begin until the 1970s. As several critics have pointed out, the "before-after" studies during the 1960s could not lead to valid conclusions about effectiveness, since none of these studies had adequate control groups or randomization.[9–13]

Several later studies compared treatment of MI patients in hospital wards vs. CCU settings.[14–17] Patients were "randomly" admitted to the CCU or the regular ward, simply based on the availability of CCU beds. Ward patients were the "control" group; CCU patients were the "experimental" group. Table 22-2 reviews the findings of these studies, which are very contradictory. From

---

*A more detailed review of research summarized in this section is available from the author.

Table 22-2. Recent Studies Comparing Coronary Care Unit and Ward Treatment for Myocardial Infarction

Studies	No CCU		CCU	
	N	% Mortality	N	% Mortality
Prospective				
Hofvendahl[14]	139	35	132	17
Christiansen[15]	244	41	171	18
Hill[16]				
<65 yrs	186	18	797	15
≥65 yrs	297	32	200	31
Retrospective				
Astvad[17]	603	39	1108	41

this research it is unclear, at this late date, that CCUs improve in-hospital mortality.

More recent research contrasted home vs. hospital care (Table 22-3). One major study was the prospective, random controlled trial by Mather and his colleagues in Great Britain.[18,19] This was an ambitious and courageous study, of the type that was not considered possible by HEW in the 1960s.[6] Although some methodologic problems arose concerning the randomization of patients to home vs. hospital care, the cumulative 1-year mortality was not different in the home and hospital groups, and there was no evidence that MI patients did better in the hospital. A second random controlled trial of home vs. hospital treatment tried to correct the methodologic difficulties of the Mather study by achieving a higher rate of randomization and strict criteria for the entry and exclusion of patients from the trial. The preliminary findings of this later study, conducted by Hill's group in Great Britain, confirmed the earlier results: the researchers concluded that for the majority of patients with suspected MI, admission to a hospital "confers no clear advantage."[20] A third study of the same problem used an epidemiologic approach in the Teesside area of Great Britain. This investigation was not a random controlled trial but simply a 12-month descriptive epidemiologic study of the incidence of MIs, how they were treated in practice, and the outcomes in terms of mortality. Both the crude and age-standardized mortality rates were better for patients treated at home.[21,22]

In summary, these issues are far from settled even now. The thrust of recent research indicates that home care is a viable treatment alternative to hospital or CCU care for many patients with MI. Early CCU promotion used unsound clinical research. More adequate research has not confirmed CCU effectiveness. One other question is clear—if intensive care is not demonstrably more effective than simple rest at home, how can we explain the tremendous proliferation during the past two decades of this very expensive form of treatment?

Table 22-3. Recent Studies Comparing Hospital and Home Care for Myocardial Infarction

Studies	Hospital		Home	
	N	% Mortality	N	% Mortality
Prospective Randomized				
Mather[18,19]				
<60 yrs	106	18	117	17
≥60 yrs	112	35	103	23
TOTAL	218	27	220	20
Hill[20]	132	11	132	13

Studies	Hospital CCU		Hospital Ward		Home	
	N	% Mortality	N	% Mortality	N	% Mortality
Epidemiologic						
Dellipiani[22]	248	13	296	21	193	9

From a Marxian perspective, these events cannot be chance phenomena. Nor are they simply another expression of the Pollyanna-like acceptance of high technology in industrial society. People are not stupid, even though the enormously costly development of CCUs occurred without any proof of their effectiveness. Therefore, we must search for the social, economic, and political structures that fostered their growth.

The Political Economy of Coronary Care

The Corporate Connection

To survive, capitalist industries must produce and sell new products. Expansion is an absolute necessity for capitalist enterprises. The economic surplus (defined as the excess of total production over "socially essential production") must grow continually larger. Medical production also falls in this category, although it is seldom viewed in this way. The economist Mandel emphasizes the contradictions of the economic surplus: "For capitalist crises are incredible phenomena like nothing ever seen before. They are not crises of scarcity, like all pre-capitalist crises; they are crises of over-production."[23] This scenario also includes the health-care system, where an overproduction of intensive care technology contrasts with the fact that many people have little access to the most simple and rudimentary medical services.

Large profit-making corporations in the United States participated in essentially every phase of CCU research, development, promotion, and proliferation. Many companies involved themselves in the intensive care market. Here I consider the activities of two such firms: Warner-Lambert Pharmaceutical Company and the Hewlett-Packard Company. I selected these corporations because information about their participation in coronary care was relatively accessible and because they have occupied prominent market positions in this clinical area. However, I should emphasize that many other firms, including at least 85 major companies, also have been involved in coronary care.[24]

Warner-Lambert Pharmaceutical Company (W-L) is a large multinational corporation, with $2.1 billion in assets and over $2.5 billion in annual sales during recent years.[25] The corporation comprises a number of interrelated subsidiary companies: Warner-Chilcott Laboratories, the Parke-Davis Company, and Warner-Lambert Consumer Products (Listerine, Smith Brothers [cough drops], Bromo-Seltzer, Chiclets, DuBarry, Richard Hudnut, Rolaids, Dentyne, Certs, Coolray Polaroid [sunglasses], and Oh Henry! [candy]).[26] Warner-Lambert International operates in more than 40 countries. Although several divisions of the W-L conglomerate participated actively in the development and promotion of coronary care, the most prominent division has been the American Optical Company (AO), which W-L acquired during 1967.

By the early 1960s, AO already had a long history of successful sales in such fields as optometry, ophthalmology, and microscopes. The instrumentation required for intensive coronary care led to AO's diversification into this new and growing area. The profitable outcomes of AO's research, development and promotion of coronary care technology are clear from AO's 1966 annual report: "In 1966, the number of American Optical Coronary Care Systems installed in hospitals throughout the United States more than tripled. Competition for this market also continued to increase as new companies, both large and small, entered the field. However, we believe that American Optical Company . . . will continue a leader in this evolving field."[27]

After purchasing AO in 1967, W-L maintained AO's emphasis on CCU technology and sought wider acceptance by health professionals and medical centers. Promotional materials contained the assumption, never proven, that the new technology was effective in reducing morbidity and mortality from heart disease. Early products and systems included the AO Cardiometer, a heart monitoring and resuscitation device; the first direct current defibrillator; the Lown Cardioverter; and an Intensive Cardiac Care System that permitted the simultaneous monitoring of 16 patients by oscilloscopes, recording instruments, heart rate meters, and alarm systems.[28] In 1968, after introducing a new line of monitoring instrumentation and implantable demand pacemakers, the company reported that "acceptance has far exceeded initial estimates" and that the Medical Division was doubling the size of its plant in Bedford, Massachusetts.[29] By 1969, the company introduced another completely new line of Lown Cardioverters and Defibrillators.[30] The company continued to register expanding sales throughout the early 1970s.

Despite this growth, W-L began to face a typical corporate problem: the potential saturation of markets in the United States. Coronary care technology was capital-intensive. The number of hospitals in the United States that could buy coronary care systems, although large, was finite. For this reason, W-L began to make new and predictable initiatives to assure future growth. First, the company expanded coronary care sales into foreign markets, especially the Third World. Subsequently, W-L reported notable gains in sales in such countries as Argentina, Canada, Colombia, France, Germany, Japan, and Mexico, despite the fact that during the 1970s "political difficulties in southern Latin America slowed progress somewhat, particularly in Chile and Peru."[31]

A second method to deal with market saturation was further diversification within the coronary care field with products whose intent was to open new markets or to create obsolescence in existing systems. For example, in 1975 the AO subsidiary introduced two new instruments. The "Pulsar 4," a light-weight portable defibrillator designed for local paramedic and emergency squads, created "an exceptionally strong sales demand." The Computer Assisted Monitoring System used a computer to anticipate and control changes in cardiac patients' conditions and replaced many hospitals' CCU systems that AO had installed but that lacked computer capabilities. According to the company's 1975 annual report, these two instruments "helped contribute to record sales growth in 1975, following an equally successful performance in the previous year."[32]

A third technique to assure growth involved the modification of coronary care technology for new areas gaining public and professional attention. With an emphasis on preventive medicine, AO introduced a new line of electrocardiogram telemetry instruments, designed to provide early warning of MI or rhythm disturbance in ambulatory patients. In addition, AO began to apply similar monitoring technology to the field of

occupational health and safety, after the passage of federal OSHA legislation in 1970.[33]

W-L is only one of many companies cultivating the coronary care market. Another giant is the Hewlett-Packard Company (H-P), a firm that in 1977 held more than $1.1 billion in assets and reported over $1.3 billion in sales. Since its founding in 1939 H-P has grown from a small firm, manufacturing analytical and measuring instruments mainly for industry, to a leader in electronics. Until the early 1960s, H-P's only major product designated for medical markets was a simple electrocardiogram machine. Along with pocket computers, medical electronic equipment has since become the most successful of H-P's product groups. During the 1960s, H-P introduced a series of innovations in coronary care (as well as perinatal monitoring and instrumentation for respiratory disease) that soon reached markets throughout the world.

Initially the company focused on the development of CCU technology. H-P aggressively promoted CCU equipment to hospitals, with the consistent claim that cardiac monitors and related products were definitely effective in reducing mortality from MI and rhythm disturbances. Such claims as the following were unambiguous: "In the cardiac care unit pictured here at a Nevada hospital, for example, the system has alerted the staff to several emergencies that might otherwise have proved fatal, and the cardiac mortality rate has been cut in half."[34] Alternatively, "hundreds of lives are saved each year with the help of Hewlett-Packard patient monitoring systems installed in more than 1,000 hospitals throughout the world. . . . Pictured here is an HP system in the intensive care ward of a hospital in Montevideo, Uruguay."[35]

Very early, H-P emphasized the export of CCU technology to hospitals and practitioners abroad, anticipating the foreign sales that other companies like W-L also later enjoyed. In 1966, the H-P annual report predicted that the effects of a slumping economy would be offset by "the great sales potential for our products, particularly medical instruments, in South American, Canadian and Asian markets. These areas should support substantial gains in sales for a number of years."[36] In materials prepared for potential investors, H-P made explicit statements about the advantages of foreign operations. For example, because H-P subsidiaries received "pioneer status" in Malaysia and Singapore, income generated in these countries remained essentially tax-free during the early 1970s: "Had their income been taxed at the U.S. statutory rate of 48 per cent in 1974, our net earnings would have been reduced by 37 cents a share."[37] By the mid-1970s, H-P's international medical equipment business, as measured by total orders, surpassed its domestic business. More than 100 sales and service offices were operating in 64 countries.

Like W-L, H-P also diversified its products to deal with the potential saturation of the coronary care market. During the late 1960s, the company introduced a series of complex computerized systems that were designed as an interface with electrocardiogram machines, monitoring devices, and other CCU products. For example, a computerized system to analyze and interpret electrocardiograms led to the capability of processing up to 500 electrocardiograms per 8-hour day: "This and other innovative systems recently introduced to the medical profession contributed to the substantial growth of our medical electronics business during the past year. With this growth has come increasing profitability as well."[38] Similar considerations of profitability motivated the development of telemetry systems for ambulatory patients with heart disease and battery-powered electrocardiogram machines designated for regions of foreign countries where electricity was not yet available for traditional machines. In 1973, H-P provided a forthright statement of its philosophy: "Health care expenditures, worldwide, will continue to increase significantly in the years ahead, and a growing portion of these funds will be allocated for medical electronic equipment. Interestingly, this growth trend offers the company . . . the unique opportunity to help shape the future of health care delivery."[39] From the corporate perspective, spiraling health-care expenditures, far from a problem to be solved, are the necessary fuel for desired profit.

The Academic Medical Center Connection

Academic medical centers have played a key role in the development and promotion of costly innovations like those in coronary care. This role

has seldom attracted attention in critiques of technology, yet both corporations considered here obtained important bases at medical centers located in geographic proximity to corporate headquarters.

Before its purchase by W-L, American Optical—with headquarters in Southbridge, Massachusetts—had established ties with the Peter Bent Brigham Hospital in Boston. Specifically, the company worked with Bernard Lown, an eminent cardiologist who served as an AO consultant, on the development of defibrillators and cardioverters. Lown pioneered the theoretical basis and clinical application of these techniques; AO engineers collaborated with Lown in the construction of working models. As previously discussed, AO marketed and promoted several lines of defibrillators and cardioverters that bore Lown's name.

AO's support of technologic innovation at the Peter Bent Brigham Hospital is clear. The CCU developed in the mid-1960s received major grants from AO that Lown and his group acknowledged.[5] AO also used data and pictures from the Brigham CCU in promotional literature distributed to the medical profession and potential investors.[40] Lown and his group continued to influence the medical profession through a large number of publications, appearing in both the general and cardiologic literature, that discussed CCU-linked diagnostic and therapeutic techniques (Table 22-4). In these papers, Lown emphasized the importance of automatic monitoring. He also advocated the widespread use of telemetry for ambulatory patients and computerized data-analysis systems, both areas into which AO diversified during the late 1960s and early 1970s. AO's relationship with Lown and his colleagues apparently proved beneficial for everybody concerned. The dynamics of heightened profits for AO and prestige for Lown were not optimal conditions for a detached, systematic appraisal of CCU effectiveness.

H-P's academic base has been the Stanford University Medical Center, located about one-half mile from corporate headquarters in Palo Alto, California. For many years William Hewlett, H-P's chief executive officer, served as a trustee of Stanford University. In addition, as I will discuss later, a private philanthropy estab-

Table 22-4. Publications Concerning Coronary Care from Peter Bent Brigham Hospital and Stanford University Medical Center Groups, 1965–1975

Year	Peter Bent Brigham Hospital	Stanford University Medical Center
1965	1	1
1966	3	1
1967	3	4
1968	7	4
1969	11	3
1970	6	1
1971	7	2
1972	3	4
1973	4	5
1974	3	5
1975	2	4

SOURCE: *Index Medicus,* citations listing B Lown or DC Harrison as author or co-author and dealing specifically with diagnostic or therapeutic techniques in coronary care units.

lished by Hewlett was prominent among the University's financial benefactors.

Since the late 1960s, Donald Harrison, professor of medicine and chief of the Division of Cardiology, has acted as H-P's primary consultant in the development of coronary care technology. Harrison and his colleagues at Stanford collaborated with H-P engineers in the design of CCU systems intended for marketing to both academic medical centers and community hospitals. H-P helped construct working models of CCU components at Stanford University Hospital, under the direction of Harrison and other faculty members. Stanford physicians introduced these H-P systems into clinical use.

Innovations in the treatment of patients with heart disease had a profound impact on the costs of care at Stanford. As documented in a general study of the costs of treatment for several illnesses at Stanford, Scitovsky and McCall stated: "Of the conditions covered by the 1964–1971 study, the changes in treatment in myocardial infarction had their most dramatic effect on costs. This was due principally to the increased costs of intensive care units. In 1964, the Stanford Hospital had a relatively small Intensive Care Unit (ICU). It was used by only three of the 1964 coronary cases. . . .

By 1971, the hospital had not only an ICU but also a Coronary Care Unit (CCU) and an intermediate CCU. Of the 1971 cases, only one did not receive at least some care in either the CCU or the intermediate CCU."[41]

During the late 1960s and early 1970s, many articles from the Harrison group described new technical developments or discussed clinical issues tied to intensive care techniques (Table 22-4). Several articles directly acknowledged the use of H-P equipment and assistance. These academic clinicians also participated in continuing medical education programs on coronary care, both in the United States and abroad. The Stanford specialists thus played an important role in promoting technology in general and H-P products in particular.

Private Philanthropies

Philanthropic support figured prominently in the growth of CCUs. Humanitarian goals were doubtless present, but profit considerations were not lacking, since philanthropic initiatives often emerged from the actions of corporate executives whose companies produced medical equipment or pharmaceuticals.

Primary among the philanthropic proponents of CCUs was the American Heart Association (AHA). The AHA sponsored research that led to the development of CCU products, especially monitoring systems. In addition, the AHA gave financial support directly to local hospitals establishing CCUs. "The underlying purpose" of these activities, according to the AHA's 1967 annual report, was "to encourage and guide the formation of new [CCU] units in both large and small hospitals."[42] Justifying these expenditures, the AHA cited some familiar "data": "Experience with the approximately 300 such specialized units already established, mostly in large hospitals, indicated that a national network of CCUs might save the lives of more than 45,000 individuals each year."[42] The source for this projected number of rescued people, though uncited, presumably was a "personal communication" from an HEW official to which Day referred in his 1963 article.[4] Later in the 1960s, the AHA's annual number of estimated beneficiaries rose still higher, again with undocumented claims of effectiveness. According to the 1968 annual report, "only about one-third of hospitalized heart attack patients are fortunate enough to be placed in coronary care units. If all of them had the benefits of these monitoring and emergency service facilities, it is estimated that 50,000 more heart patients could be saved yearly."[43] This unsubstantiated estimate, raised from the earlier unsubstantiated figure of 45,000, persisted in AHA literature into the early 1970s. During this same period the AHA co-sponsored, with the U.S. Public Health Service and the American College of Cardiology, a series of national conferences on coronary care whose purpose was "the successful development of the CCU program" in all regions of the United States.[42]

Other smaller foundations also supported CCU proliferation. For example, the John A. Hartford Foundation gave generous support to several hospitals and medical centers during the early 1960s to develop monitoring capabilities. The Hartford Foundation's public view of CCU effectiveness was unequivocal: the Kansas City coronary care program "has demonstrated that a properly equipped and designed physical setting staffed with personnel trained to meet cardiac emergencies will provide prophylactic therapy which will materially enhance the survival of these patients and substantially reduce the mortality rates."[44] Another foundation that supported CCU growth, although somewhat less directly, was the W. R. Hewlett Foundation, founded by H-P's chief executive officer. The Hewlett Foundation earmarked large annual grants to Stanford University which chose H-P equipment for its CCU and other intensive-care facilities.[45]

The commitment of private philanthropy to technologic innovations is a structural problem that transcends the personalities that control philanthropy at any specific time. The bequests that create philanthropies historically come largely from funds generated by North American industrial corporations, that are highly oriented to technologic advances. Moreover, the investment portfolios of philanthropic organizations usually include stocks in a sizable number of industrial companies. These structural conditions encourage financial support for technological advances, like those in coronary care.

In addition, it is useful to ask which people made philanthropic decisions to fund CCU development. During the mid-1960s, the AHA's officers included eight physicians who had primary commitments in cardiology, executives of two pharmaceutical companies (L. F. Johnson of American Home Products Corporation's drug subsidiaries and Ross Reid of Squibb Corporation), a metals company executive (A. M. Baer of Imperial Knife Associated Companies), a prominent banker (W. C. Butcher, president of Chase Manhattan Bank), and several public officials (including Dwight Eisenhower). At the height of CCU promotion in 1968, the chairman of the AHA's annual Heart Fund was a drug company executive (W. F. Laporte, president of American Home Products Corporation, former chief of its phramaceutical subsidiaries, and director of several banks).[43] During the 1960s and early 1970s, bankers and corporate executives also dominated the board at the Hartford Foundation. The Hewlett Foundation remained a family affair until the early 1970s, when R. W. Heyns—former chancellor of the University of California, Berkeley, and also a director of Norton Simon, Inc., Kaiser Industries, and Levi-Strauss—assumed the Foundation's presidency. It is not surprising that philanthropic policies supporting CCU proliferation showed a strong orientation toward corporate industrialism.

The Role of the State

Agencies of government played a key role in CCU growth. Earlier I discussed the financial support that the U.S. Public Health service provided to clinicians in the early 1960s for CCU development. An official of HEW provided an "estimate" of potential lives saved by future CCUs[4]; without apparent basis in data, this figure became a slogan for CCU promotion. Conferences and publications by HEW during the late 1960s specified guidelines for adequate CCU equipment, even though the effectiveness of this approach admittedly remained unproven by random controlled trial.

In these activities, three common functions of the state in capitalist societies were evident.[2] First, in health policy the state generally supports private enterprise by encouraging innovations that enhance profits to major industrial corporations. The state does not enact policies that limit private profit in any serious way. Recognizing the high costs of CCU implementation, state agencies could have placed strict limitations on their number and distribution. For example, HEW could have called for the regionalization of CCU facilities and restrictions on their wider proliferation. Subsequently, studies of CCU mortality rates generally have shown better outcomes in larger, busier centers and have suggested the rationality of regionalized policies.[46] HEW's policies supported just the opposite development. By publishing guidelines that called for advanced CCU technology and by encouraging CCU proliferation to most community hospitals, HEW assured the profitability of corporate ventures in the coronary-care field.

A second major function of the state is its legitimation of the capitalist political-economic system.[2,3] The history of public health and welfare programs shows that state expenditures usually increase during periods of social unrest and decrease as unrest becomes less widespread. The decade of the 1960s was a time of upheaval in the United States. The civil rights movement called into question basic patterns of injustice. Opposition to the war in Indochina mobilized a large part of the population against government and corporate policies. Labor disputes arose frequently. Under such circumstances, when government and corporations face large-scale crises of legitimacy, the state tends to intervene with health and welfare projects. Medical technology is a "social capital expenditure" by which the state tries to counteract the recurrent legitimacy crises of advanced capitalism.[47] Technologic innovations like CCUs are convenient legitimating expenditures, since they convey a message of deep concern for the public health, while they also support new sources of profit for large industrial firms.

Thirdly, government agencies provide market research that guides domestic and foreign sales efforts. The Global Market Survey, published by the U.S. Department of Commerce, gives a detailed analysis of changes in medical facilities, hospital beds, and physicians throughout the world. The Survey specifies those countries that are prime targets for sales of biomedical equipment. For example, the 1973 Survey pointed out that "major foreign markets for biomedical equipment are expected to grow at an average annual rate of 15 per cent in the 1970s, nearly double the growth rate predicted for the U.S. domestic market."[48] The same report predicted that West Germany (which would emphasize CCU construction), Japan, Brazil, Italy, and Israel would be the largest short-term markets for products manufactured in the United States. According to the report "market research studies identified specific equipment that present [sic] good to excellent U.S. sale opportunities in the 20 [foreign] markets"; "cardiological-thoracic equipment" headed the list of products with high sales potential.[48] Market research performed by state agencies has encouraged the proliferation of CCUs and related innovations, whose capacity to generate profits has overshadowed the issue of effectiveness in government planning.

Changes in the Health Care Labor Force

Intensive care involves workers as well as equipment. Throughout the twentieth century, a process of "deskilling" has occurred, by which the skilled trades and professions have become rationalized into simpler tasks that can be handled by less skilled and lower paid workers.[49] In medicine, paraprofessionals take on rationalized tasks that can be specified by algorithms covering nearly all contingencies. This deskilling process applies equally to CCUs and other intensive care facilities, where standard orders—often printed in advance—can deal with almost all situations that might arise.

The deskilling of the intensive care labor force has received support from professional, governmental, and corporate planners. During the late 1960s and early 1970s, the training of allied health personnel to deal with intensive care technology became a priority of educators and administrators. According to this view, it was important to train a "cadre of health workers capable of handling routine and purely functional duties."[50] The linkage between allied health workers and new technology was a clear assumption in this approach. There were limits on "the extent to which a markedly greater delegation of tasks can be achieved without the introduction of new technology" that compensates for aides' lack of "decisional training."[51] The availability of monitoring equipment in CCUs made this setting adaptable to staffing partly by technicians who could receive lower wages than doctors or nurses.[52] Paramedical training programs, focusing on intensive care, became a goal of national policy makers, even though they recognized the "built in obsolescence of monitoring equipment" and the tendency of industrial corporations to "capitalize" in this field.[53,54]

Conclusions

Although not exhaustive, an overview helps clarify the history of CCUs and other technologic "advances" (Figure 22-1). Corporate research and development leads to the production of new technology, pharmaceuticals, and related innovations. The guiding motivation for corporations is profit; in this sense the commodification of health care resembles non-medical goods and services. Closely linked to corporations, philanthropies support research and clinical practices that enhance profits. Agencies of the state encourage innovation by grants for investigation, finan-

Figure 22-1. *Overview of the Development, Promotion, and Proliferation of CCUs and Similar Medical Advances*

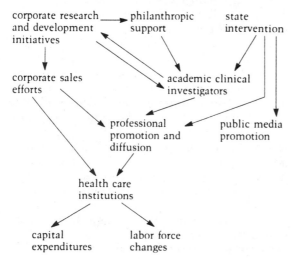

cial assistance to medical centers adopting new technology, and advocacy of new practices. While state intervention benefits private enterprise, it also enhances the faltering legitimacy of the capitalist political-economic system. Academic clinicians and investigators, based in teaching hospitals, help develop technology and foster its diffusion through professional publications and pronouncements in the public media. Corporate sales efforts cultivate markets in health institutions, both domestic and foreign. Technologic change generates the need for allied health workers who are less skilled than professionals. The cyclical acceptance of technologic innovations by medical institutions involves capital expenditures that drive up the overall costs of health care.

Cost containment activities that do not recognize these dynamics of the capitalist system will remain a farce. During the last decade, sophisticated methodologies to analyze costs and effectiveness have emerged in medical care research. These techniques include clinical decision analysis and a variety of related methods.[55–58] Ironically, economists first developed this type of analysis at the Pentagon, to evaluate technologic innovations like new missiles.[59] This methodology led to disastrous policy decisions in Indochina, largely because the cost-effectiveness approach did not take into account the broader, so-called "imponderable" context. This analysis did not predict accurately the political response of the Indochinese people to such technologies as napalm and mechanized warfare. Ironically, many of the same people who developed cost-effectiveness research at the Department of Defense now are moving into the health field, where this approach has become quite fashionable.[60]

In health care as in other areas, cost-effectiveness methodology restricts the level of analysis to the evaluation of specific innovations.[61–65] Studies using this framework generally ignore, or make only passing reference to, the broader structures of capitalism.[66] As a result, this approach obscures one fundamental source of high costs and ineffective practices: the profit motive. Because of this deficiency, cost-effectiveness analysis mystifies the roots of costly, ineffective practices in the very nature of our political-economic system.

Defects of research, however, are less dangerous than defects of policy. Cost containment has become a highly touted national priority. In a climate of fiscal crisis, an ideology of austerity is justifying cutbacks in health and welfare programs. Services whose effectiveness is difficult to demonstrate by the new methodologies are prime candidates for cutbacks and therefore face a bleak future. Poor people and minority groups, historically victimized by the free enterprise system, will be the first to suffer from this purported rationalization of policy. Meanwhile, private profit in health care, a major fuel for high costs, continues unabated. Just as it eludes serious attention in research, the structure of profit evades new initiatives in health policy.

Cost containment will remain little more than rhetoric in the United States unless we begin to address the linkages between cost and profit. It is foolish to presume that major restrictions on profit in the health system can succeed without other basic changes in the political-economic system. On the other hand, working toward progressive alternatives in health care is part of longer-term efforts aimed at social reconstruction.

An initial step involves support for policies that curtail private profit. Unlimited corporate involvement in medicine must end. The corporations that develop and successfully promote ineffective innovations like those in coronary care must cease these activities. Because this will not happen voluntarily, we need compulsory restriction of profit in health care and eventual public ownership of medical industries, especially pharmaceutical and medical equipment manufacturing.[67] A national formulary of permitted drugs and equipment, like that established in several socialist countries, would reduce costs by eliminating the proliferation of unneeded products. Socialization of medical production is no more fanciful than public ownership of utilities, transportation facilities, or schools.

In summary, CCU development and promotion may seem irrational when analyzed in terms of proven medical effectiveness. These trends appear considerably more rational when viewed from the needs of a capitalist system in crisis. By questioning what capitalism does with our hearts, we get closer to the heart of many of our other problems.

REFERENCES

1. Waitzkin H, Waterman B: The Exploitation of Illness in Capitalist Society. Indianapolis, Bobbs-Merrill, 1974.
2. Waitzkin H: A Marxist view of medical care. Ann Intern Med 89:264–278, 1978.
3. Navarro V: Medicine Under Capitalism. New York, Prodist, 1976.
4. Day HW: An intensive coronary care area. Dis Chest 44:423–427, 1963.
5. Lown B, Fakhro AM, Hood WB, et al: The coronary care unit: new perspectives and directions. JAMA 199:188–198, 1967.
6. United States Department of Health, Education, and Welfare: Heart Disease Control Program: Proceedings of the National Conference on Coronary Care Units. DHEW Pub. No. 1764. Washington, DC, Govt Printing Office, 1968.
7. United States Department of Health, Education and Welfare: Heart Disease and Stroke Control Program: Guidelines for Coronary Care Units. DHEW Pub. No. 1824. Washington, DC, Govt Printing Office, 1968.
8. Geographical distribution of coronary care units in the United States. Metropolitan Life Insurance Company Statistical Bulletin 58:7–9, July–August 1977.
9. Peterson OL: Myocardial infarction: unit care or home care? Ann Intern Med 88:259–261, 1978.
10. Martin SP, Donaldson MC, London CD, et al: Inputs into coronary care during 30 years: a cost effectiveness study. Ann Intern Med 81:289–293, 1974.
11. Anti-dysrhythmic treatment in acute myocardial infarction (editorial). Lancet 1:193–194, 1979.
12. Coronary-care units—where now? (editorial). Lancet 1:649–650, 1979.
13. Waitzkin H: How capitalism cares for our coronaries: a preliminary exercise in political economy. In The Doctor-Patient Relationship in the Changing Health Scene, Gallagher EB (ed.) DHEW Pub. No. (NIH) 78-183. Washington, DC, Govt Printing Office, 1978.
14. Hofvendahl S: Influence of treatment in a CCU on prognosis in acute myocardial infarction. Acta Med Scand (Suppl) 519:1–78, 1971.
15. Christiansen I, Iversen K, Skouby AP: Benefits obtained by the introduction of a coronary care unit: a comparative study. Acta Med Scand 189:285–291, 1971.
16. Hill JC, Holdstock G, Hampton JR: Comparison of mortality of patients with heart attacks admitted to a coronary care unit and an

ordinary medical ward. Br Med J 2:81–83, 1977.

17. Astvad K, Fabricius-Bjerre N, Kjaerulff J, et al: Mortality from acute myocardial infarction before and after establishment of a coronary care unit. Br Med J 1:567–569, 1974.

18. Mather HG, Morgan DC, Pearson NG, et al: Myocardial infarction: a comparison between home and hospital care for patients. Br Med J 1:925–929, 1976.

19. Mather HG, Pearson NG, Read KLQ, et al: Acute myocardial infarction: home and hospital treatment. Br Med J 3:334–338, 1971.

20. Hill JC, Hampton JR, Mitchell JRA: A randomized trial of home-versus-hospital management for patients with suspected myocardial infarction. Lancet 1:837–841, 1978.

21. Colling A, Dellipiani AW, Donaldson RJ: Teesside coronary survey: an epidemiological study of acute attacks of myocardial infarction. Br Med J 2:1169–1172, 1976.

22. Dellipiani AW, Colling WA, Donaldson RJ, et al: Teesside coronary survey—fatality and comparative severity of patients treated at home, in the hospital ward, and in the coronary care unit after myocardial infarction. Br Heart J 39:1172–1178, 1977.

23. Mandel E: An Introduction to Marxist Economic Thought. New York, Pathfinder, 1970.

24. DeSalvo RJ: Medical marketing mixture—update. Med Marketing & Media 13:21–35, September, 1978.

25. Warner-Lambert Pharmaceutical Company: Annual Report. Morris Plains, NJ, 1977.

26. Idem: Annual Report. Morris Plains, NJ, 1969, p 8.

27. American Optical Company: Annual Report. Southbridge, MA, 1966, p 9.

28. Warner-Lambert Pharmaceutical Company: Annual Report. Morris Plains, NJ, 1967, p 7.

29. Idem: Annual Report. Morris Plains, NJ, 1968, p 25.

30. Idem: Annual Report. Morris Plains, NJ, 1969, pp 18–19.

31. Idem: Annual Report. Morris Plains, NJ, 1970, p 19.

32. Idem: Annual Report. Morris Plains, NJ, 1975, p 5.

33. Idem: Annual Report. Morris Plains, NJ, 1970, p 16.

34. Hewlett-Packard Company: Annual Report. Palo Alto, CA, 1966, p 11.

35. Idem: Annual Report. Palo Alto, CA, 1969, p 11.

36. Idem: Annual Report. Palo Alto, CA, 1966, p 4.

37. Idem: Annual Report. Palo Alto, CA, 1974, p 2.

38. Idem: Annual Report. Palo Alto, CA, 1971, p 5.

39. Idem: Annual Report. Palo Alto, CA, 1973, pp 18–19.

40. Warner-Lambert Pharmaceutical Company: Annual Report. Morris Plains, NJ, 1967, p 7.

41. Scitovsky AA, McCall N: Changes in the Costs of Treatment of Selected Illnesses, 1951–1964–1971. DHEW Pub. No. (HRA) 77-3161. Washington, DC, Govt Printing Office, 1977.

42. American Heart Association: Annual Report. New York, 1967, p 11.

43. Idem: Annual Report. New York, 1968, pp 2, 13–14.

44. John A. Hartford Foundation: Annual Report. New York, 1963, p 58.

45. W.R. Hewlett Foundation: Annual Report to the Internal Revenue Service. Palo Alto, CA, 1967, 1971.

46. Bloom BS, Peterson OL: End results, cost and productivity of coronary-care units. N Engl J Med 288:72–78, 1974.

47. O'Connor J: The Fiscal Crisis of the State. New York, St. Martin's Press, 1973.

48. United States Department of Commerce, Domestic and Internal Business Administration: Global Market Survey: Biomedical Equipment. USDC Pub., unnumbered. Washington, DC, Govt Printing Office, 1973.

49. Braverman H: Labor and Monopoly Capital. New York, Monthly Review Press, 1974.

50. Rosinski EF: Impact of technology and evolving health care systems on the training of allied health personnel. Milit Med 134:390–393, 1969.

51. Moore FJ: Information technologies and health care: the need for new technologies to offset the shortages of physicians. Arch Intern Med 125:351–355, 1970.

52. Foster FL, Casten GG, Reeves TJ: Nonmedical personnel and continuous ECG monitoring. Arch Intern Med 124:110–112, 1969.

53. Sanazaro PJ: Physician support personnel in the 1970s. JAMA 214:98–100, 1970.

54. Barnett GO, Robbins A: Information technology and manpower productivity. JAMA 209:546–548, 1969.

55. McNeil BJ, Keeler E., Adelstein SJ: Primer on certain elements of medical decision making. N Engl J Med 293:211–215, 1975.

56. Schoenbaum SC, McNeil BJ, Kavet J: The swine-influenza decision. N Engl J Med 295:759–765, 1976.

57. Costs, Risks, and Benefits of Surgery. JP Bunker, BA Barnes, F Mosteller (eds.) New York, Oxford University Press, 1977.

58. Abrahms HL, McNeil BJ: Medical implications of

computed tomography ("CAT scanning"). N Engl J Med 289:255–261, 310–318, 1978.

59. Hitch CJ, McKean RN: The Economics of Defense in the Nuclear Age. New York, Atheneum, 1967.

60. Enthoven AC: Consumer-choice health plan. N Engl J Med 298:650–658, 709–720, 1978.

61. Cochrane AL: Efficiency and Effectiveness: Random Reflections on Health Services. London, Nuffield Hospitals Trust, 1972.

62. Illich I: Medical Nemesis. New York, Pantheon, 1976.

63. Rose G: The contribution of intensive coronary care. Br J Prev Soc Med 29:147–150, 1975.

64. Mechanic D: Approaches to controlling the costs of medical care: short-range and long-range alternatives. N Engl J Med 298:249–254, 1978.

65. United States Congress, Office of Technology Assessment: Development of Medical Technology: Opportunities for Assessment (OTA Pub. unnumbered). Washington, DC, Govt Printing Office, 1976.

66. Stevenson G: Laws of motion in the for-profit health industry: a theory and three examples. Internat J Health Serv 8:235–256, 1978.

67. Dellums RV, et al: Health Service Act (H.R. 11879). Washington, DC, Govt Printing Office, 1978.

Financing Medical Care

· · · · · ·

Medical care is big business in the United States. Billions of dollars are spent each year on medical services, with nearly half of each dollar coming from public funds. Medical costs, a significant factor in the economy's inflationary spiral, were until quite recently practically unregulated. Most of the money spent on medical care in the United States is spent via *third-party payments* on a fee-for-service basis.[1] Unlike *direct* (or *out-of-pocket*) payments, third-party payments are those made through some form of insurance or charitable organization for someone's medical care. Third-party payments have increased steadily over the past forty years. In 1950 a total of 32 percent of personal health care expenditures were made via third-party payments; in 1965 that figure was up to 48 percent; and by 1974 the ratio of third-party payments had increased to 65 percent (*Medical Care Chart Book*, 1976: 117). By 1993 third-party payments represented approximately 82 percent of all medical care expenditures. Almost all third-party payments are made by public or private insurance. The insurance industry is thus central to the financing of medical care services in this country. This section examines the role of insurance in financing medical care and the influence of the insurance industry on the present-day organization of medical services.

The original method of paying for medical services directly or individually, in money or in kind, has today been replaced by payment via insurance. Essentially, insurance is a form of "mass financing" ensuring that medical care providers will be paid and people will be able to obtain and pay for the medical care they need. Insurance involves the regular collection of small amounts of money (premiums) from a large number of people. That money is put into a pool, and when the insured people get sick, that pool (the insurance company) pays for their medical services either directly or indirectly by sending the money to the provider or patient.

Although most Americans are covered by some form of third-party insurance, many millions are not. Approximately 37 million people are without health insurance (Friedman, 1991); these are mostly young and working people whose employers do not provide insurance, who earn too little to afford the premiums, or who earn too much to be eligible for Medicaid. In addition, having an insurance plan does not mean that all of one's medical costs are paid for.

The United States has both private and public insurance programs. Public insurance programs, including Medicare and Medicaid, are funded primarily by monies collected by federal, state, or local governments in the form of taxes. The nation has two types of private insurance organizations: *nonprofit* tax-exempt Blue Cross and Blue Shield plans and for-profit *commercial* insurance companies.

Blue Cross and Blue Shield emerged out of the Great Depression of the 1930s as mechanisms to ensure the payment of medical bills to hospitals (Blue Cross) and physicians (Blue Shield). The Blues (Blue Cross and Blue Shield) were developed as community plans through which people made small "pre-payments" on a regular basis—generally monthly. If they became sick, their hospital bills were paid directly by the insurance plan.

Although commercial insurance companies existed as early as the nineteenth century, only after World War II did they really expand in this country. Blue Cross and Blue Shield originally set the price of insurance premiums by what was called "community rating," giving everybody within a community the chance to purchase insurance at the same price. Commercial insurers, on the other hand, employed "experience rating," which bases the price of insurance premiums on the statistical likelihood of the insured needing medical care. People less likely to need medical care are charged less for premiums than are people more likely to need it. By offering younger, healthier workers lower rates than could the Blues, commercials captured a large segment of the labor union insurance market in the 1950s and 1960s. In order to compete, Blue Cross and Blue Shield eventually abandoned community rating and began using experience rating as well. One unfortunate result of the spread of experience rating has been that those who most need insurance coverage—the elderly and the sick—are least able to afford or obtain it.

Medicare and Medicaid were passed by Congress in 1965 as amendments to the Social Security Act. Medicare pays for the medical care of people over sixty-five years of age and other qualified recipients of Social Security. Medicaid pays for the care of those who qualify as too poor to pay their own medical costs. However, commercial and nonprofit insurance companies act as intermediaries in these government programs. Providers of medical care are not paid directly by public funds; instead, these funds are channeled through the private insurance industry. For example, 93 percent of Medicare payments to hospitals and 53 percent of Medicare payments to nursing homes are administered by Blue Cross. The Blues also act as intermediaries in most Medicaid programs, which are state-controlled. Public funding via private insurance companies has resulted in enormous increases in the costs of both of these public insurance programs, high profits for the insurance intermediaries and their beneficiaries—physicians and hospitals—and near exhaustion of available public funds for the continuation of Medicare and Medicaid. Before 1965, the federal government paid about 10 percent of all medical expenditures. By 1993, it paid for nearly 37 percent of health care costs. The federal contribution to Medicare alone had risen from a couple of billion dollars in 1965 to 150 billion in 1993 and is still rising.

The Medicare-Medicaid response had a number of consequences. Medicare has provided basic medical insurance coverage for 99 percent of Americans over sixty-five. While the elderly still face significant out-of-pocket expenses, this widespread coverage is a stark contrast to their lack of coverage before 1965 (Davis, 1975). Medicaid has been much less comprehensive. Because it is a federal-state matching program, coverage varies from state to state. While many poor people receive greater coverage than they did before Medicaid, severe restrictions in eligibility leave many others with no coverage. Utilization of services has increased under Medicaid so that the poor, who are generally sicker than the nonpoor, visit medical services more frequently. The major impact of Medicaid has been on maternal and child health.

Although federal programs have surely helped some sick people and reduced inequality and inaccessibility of medical services, their effect is limited. The Republican administrations in the 1980s cut back a number of these programs. But even before these cutbacks Medicare covered less than half the elderly's health expenses, and Medicaid covered only a third of those of the poor (Starr, 1982: 374).

The intent of Medicare and Medicaid is certainly worthy, even if the results are limited. But these programs also created new problems. They put billions of new dollars into the health system with no cost controls, so by the 1970s Medicare and Medicaid were clearly fueling escalating health costs, which now comprise nearly 14 percent of the GNP. Some people were reaping enormous profits from the system, especially owners of shoddy nursing homes and so-called Medicaid mills. Tightening restrictions eliminated the worst offenders but medical costs continued to soar.

In the early 1970s the federal government began to mandate a series of programs aimed at reducing spiraling costs, especially with Medicare. In 1972 utilization review boards—hospital-based committees—were instituted to review the appropriateness of medical utilization. These were followed by Professional Standard Review Organizations (PSROs) set up to monitor both quality and cost of care. In the middle 1970s the nation was divided into dozens of Health System Agencies (HSAs), which were to be regionalized health planning agencies. HSAs attempted to regulate uncontrolled hospital and technological growth by requiring a "certificate of need" approval to justify any new investment over $100,000. There were even attempts to put a "cap" (ceiling) on the total amount that could be allocated to a program. Some cost control programs had limited effects in specific situations, but the federal attempt to control costs has so far been generally a failure.

A recent federal attempt to control costs is a complex reimbursement system called "Diagnostically Related Groups" (DRGs). Mandated in 1984 for Medicare, this program replaces the fee-for-service system with a form of "prospective reimbursement" whereby the government will pay only a specific amount for a specified medical problem. The prices of hundreds of diagnoses are established in advance. Medicare will pay no more, no less. If a hospital spends less than the set amount, it gets to pocket the difference. The idea is to give hospitals the incentive to be efficient and save money. The concern is that patients will get poorer treatment. The rise of managed care as a method for delivering health care (see Selection 18 by Fry et al.) is largely a response to rising costs. Managed care requires pre-approvals for many forms of medical treatment and sets limits on some types of care, in an effort to control medical expenditures. This has given third-party payers more leverage and constrained both the care given by doctors (or providers) and the care received by patients (or subscribers).

This section investigates the origins and consequences of financing medical care in the particular way the American medical system has evolved. In the first selection, "A Century of Failure: Health Care Reform in America," David J. Rothman examines why the United States has not developed a national health insurance plan. Tracing the historical development of private health insurance. Rothman suggests that one key is the absence of the middle class from a coalition favoring government health reform. Both Blue Cross, as the leading insurance company, and physicians, as professionals and businesspeople, opposed government intervention. Voluntary, private health insurance for the middle class became seen as the best alternative to government involvement in health care.

Thomas Bodenheimer and Kevin Grumbach discuss the historical process of health care financing in "Paying for Health Care," illustrating the impact of shifts in payment mechanisms. Using vignettes as illustrations, they show how each solution for financing health care created a new set of problems. In particular, they examine the emergence of four modes of payment for patients or consumers: out of pocket, individual private health insurance, employment-based group private insurance, and government financing. While private insurance certainly has helped many sick people, it has not been provided in a fair and equitable manner. The shift from community-rated to experience-rated insurance was a regressive policy change and had a negative effect on those who were old, sick, poor, or at risk. In other words, while experience rating gave the commercial insurers a competitive edge (Starr, 1982), it undermined insurance as a principle of mutual aid and eroded any basis of distributive justice in insurance (Stone, 1993). And, as noted earlier, it left approximately 37 million people without any insurance and another 20 million people with insurance that is generally considered inadequate in the face of serious illness (Bodenheimer, 1992).

The continuing rising costs of health care and the large number of people without adequate health insurance engendered calls for health reform in the early 1990s. In the final article of this section, "Costs and Coverage: Pressures toward Health Care Reform," Philip R. Lee, Denise Soffel, and Harold S. Luft examine the roots of spiraling health costs, especially "market failure," new technologies, excessive administrative costs, unnecessary care, increased patient complexity, and the oversupply and maldistribution of physicians—all of which spurred reform proposals. Although President Clinton's plan for major health reform failed (Starr, 1995), it is important to understand the sources of our "health care crisis" as we assess attempts at implementing partial solutions. The inequities and discontents with our health care system will not disappear and will soon produce new calls for reform. The history and the operation of our health care financing structure will remain the key to meaningful change in the health care system.

NOTE

1. Fee-for-service is a central feature of the economic organization of medicine in our society. Since medical providers are paid a fee for every service they provide, many critics argue that a fee-for-service system creates a financial incentive to deliver unnecessary services, making medical care more profitable and costly.

REFERENCES

Bodenheimer, Thomas. 1992. "Underinsurance in America." New England Journal of Medicine. 327: 274–278.

Davis, Karen. 1975. "Equal treatment and unequal benefits: The Medicare program." Milbank Memorial Fund Quarterly. 53, 4:449–88.

Friedman, Emily. 1991. "The uninsured: From dilemma to crisis." Journal of the American Medical Association. 265: 2491–2495.

Medical Care Chart Book. Sixth Edition. 1976. School of Public Health, Department of Medical Care Organization, University of Michigan. Data on third-party payments computed from Chart D-15: 117.

Starr, Paul. 1982. The Social Transformation of American Medicine. New York: Basic Books.

Starr, Paul. 1995. "What happened to health care reform?" American Prospect. Winter: 20–31.

Stone, Deborah A. 1993. "The struggle for the soul of health insurance." Journal of Health Politics, Policy and Law. 18: 287–317.

23

A Century of Failure:
Health Care Reform in America

. . . . . .

David J. Rothman

There are some questions that historians return to so often that they become classics in the field, to be explored and reexplored, considered and reconsidered. No inquiry better qualifies for this designation than the question of why the United States has never enacted a national health insurance program. Why, with the exception of South Africa, does it remain the only industrialized country that has not implemented so fundamental a social welfare policy?

The roster of answers that have been provided is impressive in its insights. Some outstanding contributions to our understanding of the issues come from James Morone, Paul Starr, Theodore Marmor, and Theda Skocpol. Their explanations complement, rather than counter, each other. In like manner, the elements that this essay will explore are intended to supplement, not dislodge, their work. A failure in policy that is so basic is bound to be overdetermined, and therefore, efforts to fathom it will inevitably proceed in a variety of directions.

The Liberal State

Morone's frame for understanding American health policy in general and the failure of national health insurance in particular centers on the definitions of the proper role of the state, the acceptable limits for all governmental actions. His starting point is with the fact that the medical

The research for this article was conducted under a grant from the Twentieth Century Fund.

profession successfully "appropriated public authority to take charge of the health care field," taking for itself the task of defining the content, organization, and, perhaps most important, the financing of medical practice (Morone 1990: 253–84). This accomplishment points to more than the power of the American Medical Association's lobbying machine; AMA rhetoric, which has seemed to other observers to be bombastic, comical, or even hysterical, in Morone's terms was effective precisely because it drew on popularly shared assumptions about the proper relationship between governmental authority, professional capacity, and professional autonomy. By the terms of this consensus, the government's duty was to build up professional capacity without infringing on professional autonomy— and as long as the medical profession defined national health insurance as an infringement on its autonomy, such a policy would not be enacted. Government was permitted to build hospitals (witness the implementation of the Hill-Burton Act) and to endow the research establishment (witness the extraordinary growth of the National Institutes of Health), but it was not allowed, at least until very recently, to challenge or subvert professional autonomy.

Paul Starr also focuses on conceptions of state authority to explain health policy. Alert to the markedly different course of national health insurance in European countries, he posits that where a spirit of liberalism and a commitment to the inviolability of private property interests in relation to the state were strongest, movements for social insurance made the least headway.

Thus, Bismarck's Germany could accomplish what Theodore Roosevelt's or Franklin Roosevelt's United States could not. Put another way, the fact that socialism never put down strong roots in this country, the absence here of a socialist tradition or threat, obviated the need for more conservative forces to buttress the social order through welfare measures.

Starr is more ready than Morone to credit the raw political power of the AMA, but he also reminds us that the AMA found allies among not only corporations but also labor unions. Union leaders preferred to obtain health care benefits for its members through contract negotiation, not through government largesse—even if that meant, or precisely because that meant, that nonunion members would go without benefits (Starr 1982: part 2).

Paralleling their studies are detailed accounts of the legislative histories of various health insurance proposals, the fate of Progressive, New Deal, and Fair Deal initiatives. The work of Theodore Marmor has clarified the political alliances that came together to enact Medicare and Medicaid (Marmor 1982). So too, the writings of Theda Skocpol place health care legislation more directly in the tradition of American welfare policies (Weir et al. 1988). In all, the existing literature illuminates the effects of both conceptions of governmental authority and the realities of constituent policies to tell us why the United States stands alone in its failure to enact national health insurance.

Co-Opting the Middle Class

Despite the sophisticated and perceptive quality of these arguments, still other considerations underlie the failure to enact national health insurance. An analysis of them does not subvert the basic contours of the other interpretations but provides a deeper social context for the story.

The starting point for such an analysis is a frank recognition of the fact that what is under discussion is essentially a moral failure, a demonstration of a level of indifference to the well-being of others that stands as an indictment of the intrinsic character of American society. This observation, however, is not meant to inspire a jeremiad on American imperfections as much as to open an inquiry into the dynamics of the failure—not only how it occurred but how it was rationalized and tolerated. Americans do not think of themselves as callous and cruel, and yet, in their readiness to forgo and withhold this most elemental social service, they have been so. This question arises: How did the middle class, its elected representatives, and its doctors accommodate themselves to such neglect? To be sure, Morone, Starr, and others have made it clear that ideas on the proper scope of government were powerful determinants of behavior, that leaders like FDR made strategic political calculations that traded off health insurance for other programs, and that the AMA smugly equated physician self-interest with national interest. But given the signal importance of health care—and, a minority of commentators aside, the ongoing recognition that it is more than one more commodity to be left to the vagaries of the marketplace—there is a need for an even broader framework for understanding these events. The chess moves of politicians, and even the rules of the game of politics, seem somewhat too removed and abstract. Put most succinctly: How could Americans ignore the health needs of so many fellow countrymen and still live with themselves? How could a society that prides itself on decency tolerate this degree of unfairness?

For answers, it is appropriate to look first to the 1930s. As a result of the Great Depression, American social welfare legislation was transformed, as exemplified by the passage of the Social Security Act. Moreover, by the 1930s, the popular faith in the efficacy of medical interventions was firmly established and the consequences of a denial of medical care, apparent. Already by the 1910s, some would-be reformers defined the goal of health insurance not merely as compensation to the sick for wages lost during illness but as the opportunity to obtain curative medical care. Twenty years later, this credo was accepted by almost all reformers, although the efficacy of medical interventions was, at least by current standards, far from impressive. Also by the 1930s, the hospital, which had earlier been almost indistinguishable from the almshouse, had become a temple of science and its leaders, Men in White, widely celebrated. In keeping with these changes, physician visits and hospital occupancy now correlated directly, not inversely, with income.

Why then was national health insurance omitted from the roster of legislation enacted in the 1930s? If medicine was so valued and government so receptive to novel (at least for Americans) social insurance programs, why was health insurance kept off the roster? Although such considerations as FDR's reluctance to do battle with the AMA or to fragment his southern alliance were important, perhaps even more determinative were the tactics, thoroughly self-conscious, that were helping to remove the middle classes from the coalition of advocates for change. And eliminating the middle classes from the alignment successfully deflated the political pressure for national health insurance.

One of the pivotal groups in designing and implementing this strategy was a newly founded, private health insurance company, Blue Cross. Against the backdrop of the report of the Committee on the Costs of Medical Care, urging greater federal intervention in health care, Blue Cross presented itself as the best alternative to government involvement. Its organizers and supporters, such as Rufus Rorem and Walter Dannreuther, held out the promise that enrolling the middle class in its plan would blunt the thrust for national health insurance. Blue Cross, declared Dannreuther, would "eliminate the demand for compulsory health insurance and stop the reintroduction of vicious sociological bills into the state legislature year after year." Blue Cross advertisements, pamphlets, radio programs, and publications insisted that neither the rich nor the poor confronted difficulties in obtaining medical services, the rich because they could easily afford it, the poor because they had ready access to public hospitals. Only the middle classes faced a problem, and unless their needs were met, they were bound to agitate for a change in governmental policy. ("It is the people in the middle income group who often find it most difficult to secure adequate medical and hospital care," declared Louis Pink, president of New York Blue Cross. "It is sometimes said that the very poor and the rich—if there are any rich left—get the best medical care.")[1] The idea was not to buy the middle classes off by expanding the services of public hospitals and persuading them to take a place on the wards to meet emergency needs. Such a solution, as Blue Cross proponents explained, would not only strain the public hospital system beyond its capacity, but would not work because the middle classes considered the public hospitals to be charity, with all innuendo intended, and they were not about to accept charity. As one Blue Cross official insisted: "The average man, with the average income, has pride. He is not looking for charity; he is not looking for ward care. He wants the best of attention for himself and his family. . . . Yet out of his savings, he is very seldom prepared to meet unexpected sickness or accident expenses." Thus, to use the public hospital was not only to get second-best care but to be stigmatized as dependent, incapable of standing on one's own two feet. Like the dole, the public hospital violated the American way. Were this the only choice, the middle classes would push for, and obtain, national health insurance.

The alternative that embodied the American way was a private subscription plan, which, for as little as three cents a day (the Blue Cross slogan), protected members from the high cost of hospitalization. "The Blue Cross Plans are a distinctly American institution," declared one of its officials, "a unique combination of individual initiative and social responsibility. They perform a public service without public compulsion." Another executive asserted that Blue Cross exemplified "the American spirit of neighborliness and self-help [which] solves the difficult and important problem of personal and national health." All of which led inexorably to the conclusion: "Private enterprise in voluntarily providing hospital care within the reach of everyone is solving the public health problem in the real democratic way. The continued growth of the Blue Cross Movement might well be considered the best insurance against the need of governmental provision for such protection" (quoted in Rothman 1991).

Blue Cross was notably successful in enrolling middle-class subscribers, serving, as intended, to reduce or eliminate their concern over the payment of hospital bills. To be sure, it took some time to build up a membership, but by 1939 there were thirty-nine Blue Cross plans in operation with more than 6 million subscribers. Indeed, the plans became even more over time, with some 31 million subscribers by 1949 (Starr 1982: 298, 327).[2] In fact, from its inception the impact of Blue Cross was probably greater than even the membership statistics indicate. Its extraordinarily active advertising campaigns made a compelling case that private, as against public, initiatives were more than sufficient to meet the problem, so that even those who did not immediately enroll may have accepted the viability of this alternative. There was no reason to press for political change when the private sector seemed to have resolved the issue. Thus both in rhetoric and in reality, Blue Cross helped to undercut middle-class interest in and concern for national health insurance. The result, fully intended, was that they did not join or lend strength to a coalition for change. Politics could do business as usual, allowing a variety of other considerations to outweigh support for such an innovation.[3]

In fact, the dynamic set off by Blue Cross in the 1930s gained strength in the post-1945 period, not only from its own growth but from the labor movement. Not just private insurance but union benefits served to cushion the middle classes from the impact of health care costs. Over these years, contract provisions negotiated with business corporations provided unionized workers with health care benefits, reducing their felt need for government programs. With that many more middle-class households effectively covered, it would require empathy, not self-interest, to push for national health insurance, and that empathy, for reasons that we will explore further below, was in short supply. As a result, public responsibility for health care became linked to the welfare system, serving only the poor, not the respectable. Coverage was something to be provided for "them," not what "we" needed or were entitled to as citizens.

How this divide between "we" and "they" shaped welfare policy emerges with particular vividness in the history of the almshouse in the 1930s. When the decade began, the institution was still one of the mainstays of public welfare policy, particularly for the elderly and for those considered the "unworthy poor." Although the post–World War II generation associates the almshouse with Dickensian England, it was of

major importance in this country even at the start of the Great Depression. Only in the mid-1930s did the almshouse begin to lose its hold on welfare programs, moved aside by such New Deal relief programs as the Works Project Administration (WPA) and the Social Security Act. In fact, WPA regulations prohibited the expenditure of funds to build or enlarge these institutions; the WPA was ready to build roads but not to build or refurbish almshouses. Why this distinction? Why the abandonment, at long last, of the almshouse? Because for the first time, almshouse relief would have had to include the middle classes. With state and city budgets staggering under the burden of relief and private charities altogether unequal to the task, absent a WPA or Social Security Act, many of the once-employed would have had to enter the almshouse. The prospect of having respectable middle-class citizens in such a facility was so disturbing as to transform government relief policy.

Imagine this same dynamic at work in health care. Picture the middle classes having no alternative but to crowd into the public hospital, to receive medical services in the twelve-bed wards. It is by no means fanciful to suggest that had this been the case, a different kind of pressure would have been exerted on the government to enact health insurance coverage. Blue Cross, however, self-consciously and successfully short-circuited the process and thereby allowed the play of politics to go on uninterrupted.

The Physician as Entrepreneur

A second critical element that underlay the American failure to implement national health insurance was the character of its medical profession. The speeches, letters, and writings of American doctors over the period 1920–1950 indicate broad sympathy for the positions of the AMA, perhaps somewhat less dogmatic but fully sharing of the organization's commitment to a fee-for-service system. Although some historians have found significant diversity of medical opinion on national health insurance earlier in the Progressive Era, by the 1920s most physicians were profoundly uncomfortable with proposed government intrusions into health care.

Narrow financial self-interest, the fear of a loss of income through national health insurance, was a force in shaping some doctors' attitudes, but it was far from the only consideration. For one, physicians' earnings were not so large as to turn them necessarily into dogged defenders of the status quo. Physicians' average income, for example, was below that of lawyers and engineers; in 1929, of the 121,000 physicians in private practice, 53 percent had incomes below $4,000, and 80 percent, less than $8,000. To be sure, some 12 percent of physicians had incomes over $11,500, but the profession was far from a lucrative one (President's Research Committee 1933: 1104). In strictly financial terms, it would not have been illogical for doctors generally to have supported national programs, particularly in the 1930s. They might have accepted government intervention with some enthusiasm, on the grounds that it was better to receive some payment from Washington than no payment from a patient. But this was not the position commonly adopted, and to understand why requires an appreciation of the essentially entrepreneurial character of American medicine. In more precise terms, the mind-set of physicians was that of the independent proprietor. They identified themselves as businessmen and, as such, shared an aversion to government interference.

It may be that the very differentiation in income among physicians at once reflected and reinforced a scramble for income that is not commonly associated with the practice of medicine. This was the conclusion that the Lynds reached in their portrait of "Middletown" in the 1920s. "The profession of medicine," they wrote, "swings around the making of money as one of its chief concerns. As a group, Middletown physicians are devoting their energies to building up and maintaining a practice in a highly competitive field. Competition is so keen that even the best doctors in many cases supplement their incomes by putting up their own prescriptions" (Lynd and Lynd [1929] 1956: 443). It was not unusual for physicians to invest in proprietary hospitals or to accept fee-splitting arrangements. Doctors also purchased common stocks and invested in local businesses—albeit not always very cleverly. By the 1920s, doctors had such a reputation for being suckers that advice

books on business addressed to them devoted large sections to discussions of "Why Do Doctors Fail to Choose the Right Investments?" The answers were generally variations on the theme of "There is a host of people who have found out that the doctor likes to take a chance. . . . He has worked so hard to accumulate his small savings and the possibility of making prodigious returns are presented to him so plausibly by some glib talker that all too frequently this nest egg is frittered away on some unsavory scheme, for he seldom has the time, inclination and facilities to make the essential investigation" (Thomas 1923: 174–75). In effect, the financial dealings that occupy physicians today are far less novel than critics like Arnold Relman might like to imagine.

To account for physicians' entrepreneurial perspective, it is vital to remember that their social world overlapped with that of the local business elite, particularly in smaller towns. When one upper-class resident of "Regionville" was asked by sociologist Earl Koos to list the five most important people in the town, he responded: "I put Doc X on that list because . . . he is one of the best-educated men in town, and makes good money—drives a good car, belongs to Rotary, and so forth. . . . Of course, some doctors aren't as important as others, here or anywhere else, but unless they're drunks or drug addicts, they're just automatically pretty top rank in town" (Koos 1954: 54).

The pattern of recruitment to the profession also encouraged this orientation. Medical school classes in the 1920s and 1930s were the almost exclusive preserve of white, upper-middle-class males. From birth, it would seem, physicians were comfortable, socially and ideologically, in the clubhouse locker room. The image is properly one of Wednesday afternoon off, doctor chatting with town banker, lawyer, and principal store owner about investment opportunities and politics, with a shared antagonism to what all of them considered the evil of Government Control.

Physicians voiced their opposition to national health insurance not only collectively through the AMA but individually as well, in the process helping to mold public attitudes. As Koos aptly observed, in towns like Regionville, especially before 1950 (before the rise of a more national media and greater opportunities for travel), doctors were opinion leaders: "In the small town, the doctor is most often 'a big frog in a little puddle'; what he thinks and does can assume an importance in the community not paralleled in the life of his urban counterpart" (Koos 1954: 150). In brief, the entrepreneurial style of American physicians helps explain much of their own and some of their neighbors' disinclination to support national health insurance.

The Ethos of Voluntarism

But then how did Americans live with the consequences of their decision? How did they justify to themselves and to others their unwillingness to provide so essential a service as medical care to those unable to afford it? The need for pragmatism in politics (we dare do no other) and definitions of the boundaries of state authority (we should do no other) surely mattered. So, too, in health care as in matters of social welfare more generally, they could always fall back on such truisms as "The poor have only themselves to blame for their poverty—they should have saved for the rainy day." And middle-class Americans could also invoke the safety net of the public hospital, noting that its services were available to all comers, regardless of income.

But there were other justifications as well, particularly the celebration of the ethos of voluntarism, the credo that individual and organizational charity obviated the need for government intervention. Individual physicians and community charities ostensibly provided the needy with requisite medical care. This idea was not fabricated from whole cloth, for Americans, and their doctors, had good reason to believe that their own initiatives were sufficient to meet the problem.

Physicians, for their part, insisted that they turned no one away from their offices because of an inability to pay for services. They used a sliding scale for setting fees, charging the "haves" more and the "have-nots" less, so as to promote the social good. The claim was incessantly repeated and undoubtedly had some validity to it. "It was probably true," reported Koos, "that no physician in Regionville would leave a worthy case untreated." The physician, claimed the New

York Medical Society in 1939, "has socialized his own services. Traditionally, he is at the call of the indigent without recompense. . . . For those who are self-supporting, he graduates his fees to meet the ability to pay, and extends time for payment over long periods." As late as 1951, a survey of physicians in Toledo, Ohio, found overwhelming support for a sliding scale of fees and widespread agreement that, to quote one response: "It's fair, the fairest thing we can do. If a man is wealthy, you certainly would charge him more than if he didn't have a dime. It's not uncommon for a doctor to call me and say, 'These people don't have any money,' or can pay only a little, and I say, 'Sure send 'em on in. I'll take care of 'em' " (Schuler et al. 1952: 60, 69, 85). Thus, physicians justified their opposition to national health insurance by citing their own altruism. Their charity rendered government intervention unnecessary.

By the same token, community philanthropy often stepped in where the circumstances went beyond the scope of individual physicians. It was not only a matter of a voluntary society establishing not-for-profit hospitals or organizing outpatient dispensaries. Voluntarism seemed capable of meeting the most exceptional challenge. To choose one of the most noteworthy examples, in the case of polio, private charitable efforts helped to make certain that no child, whatever the family's income, would lack for access to an iron lung or to rehabilitative services. By November 1931, only two years after Philip Drinker perfected the iron lung, there were 150 respirators to be found in hospitals across the country. Foundations, including Milbank and Harkness, underwrote the cost of some of the machines, and their efforts were supplemented by the fund-raising work of local ladies' auxiliaries. As for patient rehabilitation, the National Foundation for Infantile Paralysis, founded in 1938 by FDR and directed by onetime Wall Street attorney Basil O'Connor, supported both research and the delivery of clinical services. Several thousand local chapters and one hundred thousand volunteers made certain that no person with polio was denied medical assistance because of economic hardship. And the foundation defined "hardship" liberally, to cover the case where medical expenditures would force a family to lower its standard of living.

The polio experience was particularly important in confirming a belief in the adequacy of voluntarism. With a world-famous patient, in the person of President Franklin Roosevelt, and an extraordinarily successful foundation, a compelling case could be made for the capacity of voluntary action to meet the most unusual and costly health care needs. Moreover, the lesson was felt particularly strongly by the middle classes, because polio was in many ways their disease, disproportionately striking children raised in hygienic, uncrowded, and (epidemiologically speaking) protected environments. Those from lower-class and urban backgrounds were more likely to be exposed to the virus at a young age and had thereby built up immunities to it. Thus the foundation, like Blue Cross, served the middle classes so well that it insulated them from the predicament of health care costs. No wonder, then, that they, and their political representatives, to the degree that they looked out on the world from their own experience, found little need for government intervention and were able to maintain this position without either embarrassment or guilt.

The Dual Message of Medicare

Surprising as it may seem, the rhetoric that surrounded the enactment of Medicare reinforced many of these constricted views. The most significant government intervention in health care did not, the wishes of many of its proponents notwithstanding, enlarge the vision of the middle classes or make the case for national health insurance. To the contrary. The debate around Medicare in a variety of ways made it seem as though, the elderly aside, all was well with the provision of medical services.

In the extensive hearings and debates that Congress devoted to Medicare between 1963 and 1965, proponents of the bill, undoubtedly for strategic political reasons, repeatedly distinguished Medicare from a national health insurance scheme. So intent were they on securing the passage of this act that they went to great pains to minimize the need for any additional interventions once Medicare was in place. And as they offered these arguments, perhaps unintentionally but nevertheless quite powerfully, they reinforced very traditional perspectives on poverty and welfare and the special character of middle-class needs.

The opening statement given in November 1963 to the House Committee on Ways and Means by then secretary of Health, Education, and Welfare, Anthony Celebrezze, laid out the themes that other advocates consistently followed. His goal was to demonstrate that the elderly presented "a unique problem," and thereby warranted special support. Just when their postretirement incomes were declining, they faced disproportionately higher health care costs: "People over sixty-five," Celebrezze calculated, "use three times as much hospital care, on the average, as people under sixty-five." Moreover, the private health insurance system that worked so well for others did not meet their needs: the premiums were too expensive (one-sixth of their medium income), and the policies often included restrictive clauses (for example, ruling out preexisting conditions). Hence, Celebrezze concluded, "this combination of high health costs, low incomes, and unavailability of group insurance is what clearly distinguishes the situation of the aged as a group from the situation of younger workers as a group" (U.S. Congress 1964: 28).

It was a shrewd argument, but it left open several problems. The first was to justify excluding the young from a federal program. To this end, Celebrezze and the other Medicare proponents frankly and wholeheartedly endorsed the status quo: "The vast majority of young workers can purchase private insurance protection. . . . I think for younger employed people, voluntary private plans can do the job" (U.S. Congress 1964: 36). Those below sixty-five were less likely to require health care interventions, and, should they encounter sudden needs, they could always borrow the sums and pay them back through their future earnings. In effect, the Medicare proponents swept under the table the problems of access to health care for those who were outside the net of employer-provided private insurance.

The second and even tougher issue for the Medicare supporters was to explain why the elderly in need should not be required to rely on the welfare system to meet their health care requirements. After all, as one critic noted, these people had been remiss in not saving for the rainy day, and the government ought not to bail them out. They would not have to forgo health care services. Rather, to the opponents of Medicare, which included to the very end the AMA, the just solution was to aid them through a program like Kerr-Mills. Under its provisions, the needy elderly would demonstrate (to public assistance officials) their lack of resources, take a place on the welfare rolls, and then receive their health care services under a combined federal-state program. The counterargument from the Medicare camp was that to compel the elderly to demonstrate their dependency was too demeaning. "We should take into account the pride and independent spirit of our older people," Celebrezze insisted. "We should do better than say to an aged person that, when he has become poor enough and when he can prove his poverty to the satisfaction of the appropriate public agency, he may be able to get help." But if welfare was so humiliating, why should anyone have to suffer such a process? If welfare demeaned the elderly, why did it not demean the young? To which the tacit answer was that if the young were poor, they had only themselves to blame. Those on welfare, the elderly apart, were so "unworthy" that humiliation was their due, at least until they reached sixty-five (U.S. Congress 1964: 31).

The third and probably most difficult question was whether a federal health insurance program for the elderly ultimately rested, as one opponent put it, on the premise that "the federal government, as a matter of right, owes medical care to elderly people." Again Celebrezze backed off a general principle in order to separate out the case of the elderly. Admittedly, he had opened his testimony with the statement that for the elderly, "the first line of defense is protection furnished as a right." But in response to hostile questions, he retreated, declaring that the federal government did not owe anyone "medical attention as a right." Medicare was to be part of the social security system, which meant that beneficiaries had paid for their benefits. And even if the first recipients would not have done so in strictly actuarial terms, still they had made their contributions "on a total program basis" (U.S. Congress

1964: 158). Although the meaning of that phrase was altogether obscure, the gist of the argument was clear: Medicare would not establish a right to health care. Ostensibly, it was not the opening shot in a larger campaign. In some oblique but still meaningful way, the principle remained that you got what you paid for, more or less.

Clearly, all these maneuvers were part of a strategy to get Medicare enacted, and many proponents insisted after the fact that they had been confident, undoubtedly too confident, that Medicare would be the first step on the road to national health insurance. They were, of course, wrong—for all the reasons we have been exploring, along with one other consideration. These Medicare proponents may have been too successful in marking off the case of the elderly. Having taken the pragmatic route, they reinforced older attitudes, afraid to come out in favor of a right to health care, afraid to break out of the mold of a quid pro quo mentality for benefits, afraid to advocate a program in terms that were more universal than middle-class interests. It was the 1930s almshouse dynamic revisited—because the worthy middle class could not be expected to go on relief to gain medical benefits, the system had to change. True, others would benefit from the program, including non-middle-class elderly. But that seemed almost serendipitous. Medicare was to protect the elderly middle classes from burdensome health care costs, not break new ground more generally by changing demeaning welfare policies or rethinking health care rights or the limits of private insurance for those under sixty-five. Thus, it should be less surprising that for the next several decades, Medicare did not inspire a new venture in government underwriting of health care.

Future Prospects

In light of a tradition of narrow middle-class self-interest, the entrepreneurial quality of American medicine, and the tradition of voluntarism, what are the current prospects for a national health insurance program?

Perhaps the most encouraging point is that each of the elements that have been discussed here are in flux. The middle classes, by all accounts, are feeling the impact of rising health insurance costs and are becoming increasingly vulnerable (through periodic unemployment or narrowing eligibility requirements of insurance companies) to the loss of insurance benefits. The weaknesses of a private system are in this way becoming quite apparent to them. At the same time, there are signs that American medicine is becoming less entrepreneurial, witness the increased numbers of salaried physicians employed by HMOs, corporations, and hospitals. And by now, the limits of voluntarism are glaringly obvious: whether the case is kidney dialysis or the future of the voluntary hospital, it is practically indisputable that the not-for-profit sector is incapable of shouldering the burden of health care.

All this would be grounds for optimism, were it not for one final element: the persistence of a narrowed vision of middle-class politics. With no largesse of spirit, with no sense of mutual responsibility, the middle classes—and their representatives—may advocate only minimal changes designed to provide protection only for them, not those in more desperate straits. In policy terms, it may bring changes that are more exclusive than inclusive, serving the employed as against the unemployed, protecting the benefits of those who have some coverage already as opposed to bringing more people to the benefits table. It may also promote schemes that will serve the lower classes in the most expedient fashion. The Oregon model, through which health insurance expands by restricting the benefits that Medicaid patients can receive, may become the standard response. Our past record suggests all too strongly that politics will find a way to protect those several rungs up the social ladder, while doing as little as possible for those at the bottom. Whether we will break this tradition and finally enact a truly national health insurance program remains an open question.

NOTES

1. Statements from Blue Cross representatives are taken from Rothman 1991.
2. In addition, there were another 28 million people enrolled for health care benefits with commercial insurance companies, so the private system was extensive.
3. It may well be that a felt need for health insurance was an acquired, not innate, characteristic. The first Blue Cross advertisements tried to build up a demand for insurance by emphasizing the unexpected character of illness, the sudden and unanticipated strike of disease. One of its popular advertising images represented Blue Cross as a helmet protecting against the club of the hospital bill that lay hidden, waiting to assail the unaware victim; the accompanying slogan read: "You never know what jolt is around the corner." Blue Cross's strategy, to emphasize the unpredictability of health care needs and that illness could strike anyone at any time, suggests that just when it raised consciousness about the need to carry health insurance, it provided an answer as to how best arrange it.

REFERENCES

Koos, E. L. 1954. *The Health of Regionville.* New York: Columbia University Press.

Lynd, R., and H. M. Lynd. [1929] 1956. *Middletown.* New York: Harcourt, Brace & World, Harvest Books.

Marmor, T. 1982. *The Politics of Medicare.* New York: Aldine.

Morone, J. 1990. *The Democratic Wish.* New York: Basic.

President's Research Committee. 1933. *Recent Social Trends in the United States.* 2 vols. New York: McGraw Hill.

Rothman, D. J. 1991. The Public Presentation of Blue Cross, 1935–1965. *Journal of Health Politics, Policy and Law* 16: 672–93.

Schuler, E. A., R. J. Mowitz, and A. J. Mayer. 1952. *Medical Public Relations: A Study of the Public Relations Program of the Academy of Medicine of Toledo and Lucas County, Ohio, 1951,* Detroit, MI: Academy of Medicine of Toledo.

Starr, P. 1982. *The Social Transformation of American Medicine.* New York: Basic.

Thomas, V. C. 1923. *The Successful Physician.* Philadelphia: W. B. Saunders.

U.S. Congress. 1964. *Medical Care for the Aged.* Hearings before the Committee on Ways and Means, House of Representatives, 88th Cong., 1st Sess. 1.

Weir, M., A. Orloff, and T. Skocpol. 1988. *The Politics of Social Policy in the United States.* Princeton, NJ: Princeton University Press.

24

Paying for Health Care

. . . . . .

Thomas Bodenheimer and Kevin Grumbach

At the center of the debate over health system reform in the United States lies the decision of how to pay for health care. Health care financing in the United States evolved to its current state as a series of social interventions. Each intervention solved a problem but in turn created its own problems requiring further intervention. In this article, we discuss the historical process of health care financing as solution-creating-new-problem-requiring-new-solution. The four basic modes of paying for health care are out-of-pocket payment, individual private insurance, employment-based group private insurance, and government financing. These four modes can be viewed both as an historical progression and as a categorization of current health care financing (Table 24-1).

Out-of-Pocket Payments

Fred Farmer broke his leg in 1892. His son ran 4 miles to get the doctor who came to the farm to splint the leg. Fred gave the doctor a couple of chickens to pay for the visit.

Fred Farmer's great-grandson, who is uninsured, broke his leg in 1992. He was driven to the emergency department where the physician ordered an X ray and called in an orthopedist who placed a cast on the leg. Mr Farmer was charged $580.

In the 19th century, people like Fred Farmer paid physicians and other health care practitioners in cash or through barter. In the first half of the 20th century, out-of-pocket cash payments were the dominant transaction. Out-of-pocket payment represents the simplest mode of financing: direct purchase by the consumer of goods and services (Figure 24-1).

Americans purchase most consumer items, from VCRs to haircuts, through direct out-of-pocket payments. Why has direct out-of-pocket payment been relegated to a lesser role in health care? Economists such as Evans[1] and Arrow[2] have discussed some of the problems with treating health care as a typical consumer item. First, whereas a VCR is a luxury, the great majority of Americans regard health care as a basic human need.[3]

For 2 weeks, Marina Perez has had vaginal bleeding and is feeling dizzy. She has no insurance and is terrified that medical care might eat up her $250 in savings. She scrapes together $30 to see her doctor, who finds a blood pressure that decreases to 90/50 mm Hg on standing and a hematocrit of 0.26. The doctor calls Ms Perez' sister, Juanita, to drive her to the hospital. Getting into the car, Marina tells Juanita to take her home.

If health care is a basic human need, then people who are unable to afford health care must have a payment mechanism available that is not reliant on out-of-pocket payments.

Second, although the purchase and price of VCRs are relatively predictable (i.e., people can choose whether or not to buy them, and the price is known), the need for and cost of health care services is unpredictable. Most people do not know if or when they may become severely ill or injured or what the cost of care will be.

Jake has a headache and visits the doctor, but Jake does not know whether the headache will cost $35

273

Table 24-1. Health Care Financing in 1991[4,5]*

Type of Payment	Personal Health Care Expenditures, %
Out-of-pocket	22
Individual private insurance	5
Employment-based private insurance	27[†]
Government financing	43
Total	97[‡]

Principal Source of Coverage	Population, %
Uninsured	14
Individual private insurance	9
Employment-based private insurance	52[†]
Government	25
Total	100

*For out-of-pocket payments, the percentage of expenditures is greater than the percentage of the uninsured population, because out-of-pocket dollars are paid not only by the uninsured but also by the insured and medicare populations in the form of deductibles, co-payments, and uncovered services. Because private insurance tends to cover healthier people, the percentage of expenditures is far less than the percentage of population covered. Public expenditures are far higher per population, because the elderly and disabled are concentrated in the public Medicare and Medicaid programs.
†This includes private insurance obtained by federal, state, and local government employees, which is in part purchased by tax funds.
‡Total expenditures total only 97%; philanthropy and other private funds account for the other 3%.

for a physician visit plus a bottle of aspirin, $1200 for magnetic resonance imaging, or $70,000 for surgery and radiation for a brain tumor.

The unpredictability of many health care needs makes it difficult to plan for these expenses. The medical costs associated with serious illness or injury usually exceed a middle-class family's savings.

Third, unlike purchasers of VCRs, consumers of health care may have little idea what they are buying at the point of needing care.

Jenny develops acute abdominal pain and goes to the hospital to purchase a remedy for her pain. The

Figure 24-1. *Direct purchase. Individuals pay out-of-pocket for services.*

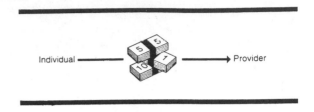

physician tells her that she has acute cholecystitis or a perforated ulcer and recommends hospitalization, abdominal sonogram, and upper endoscopy. Will Jenny, lying on a gurney in the emergency department and clutching her abdomen with one hand, use her other hand to leaf through her *Textbook of Internal Medicine* to determine whether she really needs these services, and should she have brought along a copy of *Consumer Reports* to learn where to purchase them at the cheapest price?

Health care is the foremost example of an asymmetry of information between providers and consumers.[3] Patients in abdominal pain are in a poor position to question the physician's ordering of laboratory tests, X rays, or surgery. In instances of elective care, health care consumers can weigh the pros and cons of different treatment options, but those options may be filtered through the biases of the physician providing the information. Compared with the voluntary demand for VCRs (the influence of advertising notwithstanding), the demand for health care services may be partially involuntary and physician driven rather than consumer driven.

For these reasons, among others, out-of-pocket payments are flawed as a dominant method of paying for health care services. Because direct purchase of health care services became increasingly difficult for consumers and was not meeting the needs of hospitals and physicians for payment, health insurance came into being.

Individual Private Insurance

Bud Carpenter was self-employed. Mr Carpenter recently purchased a health insurance policy from his insurance broker for his family. To pay the $250 monthly premiums required taking on extra jobs on weekends, and the $2000 deductible meant he would still have to pay quite a bit of his family's medical costs out-of-pocket. But Bud preferred to pay these costs rather than to risk spending his savings for his children's college education on a major illness. When his son was diagnosed with leukemia and ran up a $50,000 hospital bill, Mr Carpenter appreciated the value of health insurance. Nonetheless, he had to wonder when he read a newspaper story that listed his insurance company among those that paid out less than 50 cents in benefits on average for every dollar collected in premiums.

Under private health insurance, a third party, the insurer, is added to the patient and health care provider who comprise the basic two parties of the health care transaction. Although the out-of-pocket mode of payment is limited to a single financial transaction, private insurance requires two transactions: a premium payment from individual to insurance plan and a reimbursement payment from insurance plan to provider (Figure 24-2). (Under indemnity insurance, the process requires three transactions: the premium from individual to insurer, the payment from individual to provider, and the reimbursement from insurer to individual. For simplicity, we will treat health insurance as reimbursement from insurance plan to provider.)

In 19th-century Europe, voluntary benefit funds were established by guilds, industries, and mutual societies. In return for paying a monthly sum, people received assistance in case of illness. This early form of private health insurance was slow to develop in the United States. In the early 20th century, European immigrants established some small benevolent societies in US cities to provide sickness benefits for their members. During the same period, two commercial insurance companies, Metropolitan Life and Prudential, collected from 10 to 25 cents per week from workers for life insurance policies that also paid for funerals and the expenses of a final illness. Because the policies were paid by individuals on a weekly basis, large numbers of insurance agents had to visit their clients to collect the premiums as soon after payday as possible. Because of its huge administrative costs, individual health insurance never became a dominant method of paying for health care.[6]

Currently, individual policies provide health insurance for only 9% of the US population (Table 24-1).

Employment-Based Private Insurance

Betty Lerner and her schoolteacher colleagues paid $6 per year to Prepaid Hospital in 1929. Ms Lerner suffered a heart attack and was hospitalized at no cost. The following year Prepaid Hospital built a new wing and raised the teachers' prepayment to $12.

Rose Riveter retired in 1961. Her health insurance premium for hospital and physician care, formerly paid by her employer, had been $25 per month. When she called the insurance company to obtain individual coverage, she was told that premiums at age 65 years cost $70 per month. She could not afford the insurance and wondered what would happen if she became ill.

The development of private health insurance in the United States was impelled by the increasing efficacy and cost of hospital care. Hospitals became places not only in which to die, but also in which to get better. Many patients, however, were unable to pay for hospital care, which meant that hospitals were unable to attract customers.[6]

In 1929, Baylor University Hospital agreed to provide up to 21 days of hospital care to 1500 Dallas, Tex, schoolteachers such as Betty Lerner, if they paid the hospital $6 per person per year.[7] As the depression deepened and private hospital occupancy in 1931 decreased to 62%, similar hospital centered private insurance plans spread.

Figure 24-2. *Individual model of private insurance. A third party—the health insurance plan—is added, dividing payment into a financing transaction and a reimbursement transaction.*

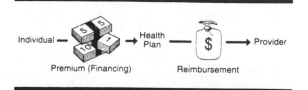

These plans (anticipating more modern health maintenance organizations) restricted care to a particular hospital. The American Hospital Association built on this prepayment movement and established statewide Blue Cross hospital insurance plans allowing free choice of hospital. By 1940, 39 Blue Cross plans, controlled by the private-hospital industry, had a total enrollment of more than 6 million people.[6] The Great Depression of the 1930s cut into the amounts patients could pay physicians out-of-pocket, and in 1939 the California Medical Association established the first Blue Shield plan to cover physician services. These plans, controlled by state medical societies, followed Blue Cross in spreading across the nation.[6]

In contrast to the consumer-driven development of health insurance in European nations, US health care coverage was initiated by health care providers seeking a steady source of income. Hospital and physician control over the "Blues," a major sector of the health insurance industry, guaranteed that reimbursement would be generous and that cost control would remain on the back burner.[6,8]

The rapid growth of private insurance was spurred by an accident of history. During World War II, wage and price controls prevented companies from granting wage increases but allowed the growth of fringe benefits. With a labor shortage, companies competing for workers began to offer health insurance to employees such as Rose Riveter as a fringe benefit. After the war, unions picked up on this trend and negotiated for health benefits. The results were dramatic. Enrollment in group hospital insurance plans increased from 12 million in 1940 to 101 million in 1955.[9]

Under employer-sponsored health insurance, employers usually pay all or part of the premium that purchases health insurance for their employees (Figure 24-3). However, the flow of money is not so simple. The federal government views employer-premium payments as a tax-deductible business expense. Moreover, the government does not treat the health insurance fringe benefit as taxable income to the employee, even though the payment of health insurance premiums for employees could be interpreted as a form of employee income. Because each premium dollar of employer-sponsored health insurance results

Figure 24-3. *Employment-based model of private insurance.*

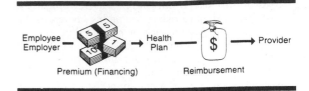

in a reduction in taxes collected, the federal government is in essence subsidizing employer-sponsored health insurance. This subsidy is enormous, estimated at $75 billion in 1991.[10]

The growth of employer-sponsored health insurance attracted commercial insurance companies to the health care field to compete with the Blues for customers. The commercial insurers changed the entire dynamic of health insurance. The new dynamic—which applies to both individual and employment-based health insurance—was called "experience rating."

> Healthy Insurance Company insures three groups of people: (1) a young, healthy group of bank managers; (2) an older, healthy group of truck drivers; and (3) an older group of coal miners with a high rate of chronic illness. Under experience rating, the Healthy Insurance Company sets its premiums according to the experience of each group in using health care services. Since the bank managers rarely use health care, each pays a premium of $100 per month. Because the truck drivers are older, their risk of illness is higher than that of the bankers and their premium is $300. The miners, who have high rates of black lung disease, are charged a premium of $500. The average premium income for the Healthy Insurance Company is $300 per member per month.
>
> Blue Cross insures the same three groups and needs the same $300 per member per month to cover health care plus administrative costs for these groups. Blue Cross sets its premiums by the principle of "community rating." For a given health insurance policy, all subscribers in a community pay the same premium. The bank managers, truck drivers, and mine workers all pay $300 per month.

Health insurance provides a mechanism to distribute health care more in accordance with human need rather than exclusively on the basis of ability to pay. To achieve this goal, health insurance contains a subsidy—a redistribution of funds from the healthy to the sick—that helps pay the health care costs of those unable to purchase services on their own.

Community rating achieves this redistribution in two ways: (1) within each group (bank managers, truck drivers, or mine workers) people who become ill receive health benefits in excess of the premiums they pay, whereas people who remain healthy pay premiums while receiving few or no health benefits; (2) among the three groups, the bank managers, who use a smaller amount of health care than their premiums are worth, help pay for the miners, who use a larger amount of health care than their premiums could buy.

Experience rating is far less redistributive than community rating. Within each group, those who become ill are subsidized by those who remain well. But looking at groups as a whole, healthier groups (bank managers) do not subsidize high-risk groups (mine workers). Thus, the principle of health insurance, to distribute health care more in accordance with human need rather than exclusively on the basis of ability to pay, is diluted by experience rating.[11]

In their early years, Blue Cross plans set insurance premiums by the principle of community rating. Commercial insurers, on the other hand, used experience rating as a weapon to compete with the Blues.[7] Under experience rating, commercials such as the Healthy Insurance Company could offer less expensive premiums to low-risk groups such as bank managers, who would naturally choose a Healthy Insurance Company commercial plan at $100 over the Blue Cross plan at $300. Experience rating helped commercial insurers overtake the Blues in the private-insurance market. In 1945 commercial insurers had only 10 million enrollees compared with 19 million for the Blues; by 1955 the score was commercials, 54 million, vs Blues, 51 million.[9]

Many commercial insurers would not market policies to such high-risk groups as mine workers, who would then be left to Blue Cross. To survive the competition from the commercials, Blue Cross had no choice but to seek younger and healthier groups by abandoning community rating and reducing the premiums for those groups. In this way, most Blue Cross and Blue Shield plans switched to experience rating.[12] Without community rating, older and sicker groups became less and less able to afford health insurance.

From the perspective of the elderly and those with chronic illness, experience rating is discriminatory, but let us view health insurance from the opposite viewpoint. Why would healthy people voluntarily transfer their wealth to sicker people through the insurance subsidy? The answer lies in the unpredictability of health care needs. When purchasing health insurance, individuals do not know if they will suddenly change from their state of good health to one of illness. Thus, within a group, people are willing to risk paying for health insurance even though they may not use the insurance. On the other hand, among different groups, healthy people have no economic incentive to voluntarily pay for community rating and subsidize another group of sicker people. This is why community rating cannot survive in a laissez-faire, competitive, private-insurance environment.[12]

The most positive aspect of health insurance—that it assists people with serious illness to pay for their care—has also become one of its main drawbacks: the difficulty of controlling costs in an insurance environment. Under direct purchase, the "invisible hand" of each individual's ability to pay holds down the price and quantity of health care. Yet a well-insured patient, for whom the cost of care causes no immediate fiscal pain, will use more services than someone who must pay for care out-of-pocket.[7] In addition, health care providers can increase fees far more easily if a third party is available to foot the bill; recall the case of Betty Lerner in which Prepaid Hospital doubled its premium in 1 year.

Health insurance, then, was a social intervention attempting to solve the problem of unaffordable health care under an out-of-pocket payment system; but its capacity to make health care more affordable created a new problem. If people no longer had to pay out-of-pocket for health care, they would use more health care, and if health care providers could charge insurers rather than patients, they could more easily raise prices—especially if the major insurers (the Blues) were controlled by hospitals and physicians. The solution of insurance fueled the problem of rising costs. As private insurance became largely experience rated and employment based, Americans who were low income, chronically ill, or elderly found it increasingly difficult to afford private insurance.

Government Financing

In 1984, Rose Riveter developed colon cancer. Because of the enactment of Medicare in 1965, she was no longer uninsured. However, her Medicare premium, hospital deductible, physician co-payments, short nursing-home stay, and uncovered prescriptions cost her $2700 the year she became ill with cancer.

Employer-sponsored private health insurance grew rapidly in the 1950s, helping working Americans and their families afford health care. However, two groups in the population received little or no benefit: the poor and the elderly. The poor were usually unemployed or employed in jobs without the fringe benefit of health insurance; they could not afford insurance premiums. The elderly, who needed health care the most and whose premiums had been partially subsidized by community rating, were hit hard by the tilt toward experience rating. In the late 1950s, less than 15% of the elderly had any health insurance.[13] Only one thing could provide affordable care for the poor and the elderly: tax-financed government health insurance.

The government entered the health care financing arena long before the 1960s through such public programs as municipal hospitals and dispensaries to care for the poor and state-operated mental hospitals. Only with the 1965 enactment of Medicare (for the elderly) and Medicaid (for the poor) did public insurance paying for privately operated health care services become a major feature of American health care.[6]

Medicare Part A is a hospital insurance plan for the elderly financed largely through Social Security taxes from employers and employees. Medicare Part B insures the elderly for physicians' services and is paid for by federal taxes and monthly premiums from the beneficiaries. Medicaid is a program run by the states and funded from federal and state taxes that pays for the care of a portion of the population be-

Figure 24-4. *Public insurance. In the social insurance model of public insurance, individual eligibility is linked to making tax contributions into the plan (e.g., Medicare Part A). In other models, eligibility is uncoupled from tax contributions (e.g., Medicaid).*

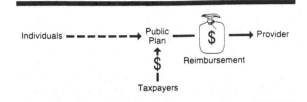

low the poverty line. Because Medicare has large deductibles, co-payments, and gaps in coverage, many Medicare beneficiaries also carry supplemental ("Medigap") private insurance or Medicaid.

Government health insurance for the poor and the elderly added a new factor to the health care financing equation: the taxpayer (Figure 24-4). Under government programs, the taxpayer can interact with the health care consumer in two distinct ways. Under the social insurance model exemplified by Medicare, only those who have paid a certain amount of Social Security taxes are eligible for Part A and only those who pay a monthly premium receive benefits from Part B. As with private insurance, people insured under social insurance must contribute, and those that contribute receive benefits. The contrasting model for government programs is the Medicaid welfare model in which those who contribute (taxpayers) may not be eligible for benefits.[14]

Recall that private insurance contains a subsidy: a redistribution of funds from healthy to sick. Tax-funded insurance has the same subsidy and generally adds another: redistribution of funds from the wealthy to the poor. Under this double subsidy, exemplified by Medicare and Medicaid, healthy middle-income employees generally pay more in Social Security payments and other taxes than they receive in health care services, whereas unemployed, disabled, and lower-income elderly persons tend to receive more in health care services than they contribute in taxes.

The advent of government financing improved financial access to care for some people but in turn aggravated the problem of rising costs. Over time, as costs rose, access declined: Medicaid cutbacks pushed low-income people out of the program, and uncovered services under Medicare left the elderly increasingly unable to pay for prescriptions and long-term care. At the same time, the rising costs of private insurance were placing coverage out of the fiscal reach of more and more employers.

The Burden of Financing Health Care

Different methods of financing health care place differential burdens on the various income levels of society. Payments are classified as progressive if they take an increasing percentage of income as income increases and regressive if they take a decreasing percentage of income as income increases. Payments are proportional when the ratio of the payment to income is the same for all income classes.[15]

Mary Blue earns $10 000 per year for her family of four. She develops pneumonia, and her out-of-pocket health care costs come to $1000, 10% of her family income.

Cathy White earns $100,000 per year for her family of four. She develops pneumonia, and her out-of-pocket health care costs come to $1000, 1% of her family income.

Out-of-pocket payments are a regressive mode of financing. The National Medical Care Expenditure Survey confirms that in 1977, direct payments (mainly out-of-pocket payments) took 14.0% of the income of families in the nation's lowest-income decile compared with 1.9% for families in the highest decile.[16] Many economists and health policy experts would consider this regressive burden of payment unfair. Yet out-of-pocket payments constitute fully 22% of total US personal health care expenditures.[4] Aggravating the regressivity of out-of-pocket payments is the fact that lower-income people tend to be sicker[17]

and thus have more out-of-pocket payments than the wealthier and healthier.

John Hale is a young, healthy, self-employed accountant whose monthly income is $6000 with a health insurance premium of $200, or 3% of his income.

Jack Hurt is a disabled mine worker with black lung disease. His income is $1800 per month of which $400 (22%) goes for his health insurance.

Experience-rated private health insurance is a regressive method of financing health care, because increased risk of illness tends to correlate with reduced income.[17] If Mr Hale and Mr Hurt were enrolled in a community-rated plan, each with a premium of $300, they would pay 5% and 17% of their income for health insurance, respectively. Under community rating, the burden of payment is regressive, but less so.

Most private insurance is not individually purchased but obtained through employment. How is the burden of employer-linked health insurance premiums distributed?

Jill is an assistant hospital administrator. To attract Jill to the job, the hospital offered her a package of salary plus health insurance of $5250 per month. She chose to take $5000 in salary, leaving the hospital to pay $250 for her health insurance.

Bill is a nurse's aide whose union negotiated with the hospital for a total package of $1750 per month; of this, $1500 is salary and $250 pays his health insurance premium.

Do Jill and Bill pay nothing for their health insurance? Not exactly. Employers generally agree on a total package of wages and fringe benefits; if Jill and Bill did not receive health insurance, their pay would probably increase by close to $250 per month. This arrangement is the reason why employer-paid health insurance premiums are generally considered deductions from wages or salary.[16,18] For Jill, health insurance amounts to only 5% of her income. For Bill, the premium is 17% of his income. The National Medical Expenditure Survey corroborates the regressivity of employer-linked health insurance; in 1977, employment-based health insurance premiums took 5.7% of the income of families in the lowest-income decile compared with 1.8% for those in the highest decile.[16]

John Low earns $10,000 and pays $410 in federal and state income taxes, 4.1% of his income.[16]

Harold High earns $100,000 and pays $12,900 in income taxes, 12.9% of his income.[16]

The largest tax supporting government-financed health care is the progressive individual income tax. Because most other taxes are regressive (e.g., sales and Social Security taxes), the combined burden of all taxes that finance health care is roughly proportional.[15]

About 54% of health care is financed through out-of-pocket payments and premiums, which are regressive, whereas 43% is funded through government revenues,[4] which are proportional. The total of health care financing is regressive. Data from 1977 reveal that the poorest decile of households spent 20% of income on health care, the middle deciles spent 12%, and the highest-income decile paid 8%.[16]

Conclusion

Neither Fred Farmer nor his great-grandson had health insurance. Yet the modern-day Mr Farmer's predicament differs drastically from that of his ancestor. Third-party financing of health care has fueled an expansive health care system that offers treatments unimaginable a century ago, but at tremendous expense.

Each of the four modes of financing US health care developed historically as a solution to the inadequacy of the previous modes. Private insurance provided protection to patients against the unpredictable costs of medical care, as well as protection to providers of care against the unpredictable ability of patients to pay. But the private-insurance solution created three new and interrelated problems: (1) the ability of health care providers to increase fees to insurers led to an increasing unaffordability of health care services for those with inadequate insurance or no insurance; (2) the employment-based nature of group insurance placed Americans who were unemployed, retired, or working part-time at a disadvantage for the purchase of insurance and partially masked the true costs of insurance for employees who did receive health benefits at the workplace; and (3) competition inherent in a deregulated private-insurance market encouraged the practice of experience rating, which made insurance premiums unaffordable to many elderly people and other medically needy groups. To solve these problems, government financing was required. In turn, government financing fueled an even greater inflation in health care costs.

As each solution was introduced, health care financing improved for a time. However, by the 1990s, rising costs were jeopardizing private and public coverage for many Americans and making services unaffordable for those without a source of third-party payment. The problems of each financing mode, and the problems created by each successive solution, had accumulated into a complex crisis characterized by inadequate access for some and rising costs for everyone.

The United States is now deliberating on a new solution to these financing problems, a solution that will undoubtedly beget its own problems. Plans for reforming health insurance in the United States may be characterized by how they propose to rearrange the four basic modes of financing. The plan drafted by the Heritage Foundation, Washington, DC, for example, emphasizes individually purchased private insurance and increased reliance on out-of-pocket payments.[19] Other proposals call for expansion of employment-based financing of private insurance.[20] Single-payer plans would make government financing the dominant mode of payment.[21] . . .

REFERENCES

The authors express their appreciation to Robert G. Evans, PhD, for making health economics intelligible.

1. Evans RG. *Strained Mercy.* Stoneham, Mass: Butterworths; 1984.
2. Arrow KJ. Uncertainty and the welfare economics of medical care. *Am Econ Rev.* 1963;53:941–973.
3. Shapiro RY, Young JT. The polls: medical care in the United States. *Public Opinion Q.* 1986; 50:418–428.
4. Levit KR, Lazenby HC, Levit KR, Cowan CA. National health expenditures, 1991. *Health Care Financing Rev.* 1992;14(2):1–30.
5. Levit KR, Olin GL, Letsch SW. American's health insurance coverage, 1980–91. *Health Care Financing Rev.* 1992;14(1):31–57.

6. Starr P. *The Social Transformation of American Medicine*. New York, NY: Basic Books; 1982.

7. Fein R. *Medical Care, Medical Costs*. Cambridge, Mass: Harvard University Press; 1986.

8. Law SA. *Blue Cross: What Went Wrong?* New Haven, Conn: Yale University Press; 1974.

9. *Source Book of Health Insurance Data, 1990*. Washington, DC: Health Insurance Association of America; 1990.

10. Reinhardt UE. Reorganizing the financial flows in US health care. *Health Aff (Millwood)*. 1993; 12(suppl):172–193.

11. Light DW. The practice and ethics of risk-rated health insurance. *JAMA* 1992;267:2503–2508.

12. Aaron HJ. *Serious and Unstable Condition: Financing America's Health Care*. Washington, DC: The Brookings Institution; 1991.

13. Harris R. *A Sacred Trust* New York, NY: The New American Library; 1966.

14. Bodenheimer T, Grumbach K. Financing universal health insurance: taxes, premiums, and the lessons of social insurance. *J Health Polit Policy Law*. 1992;17:439–462.

15. Pechman JA. *Who Paid the Taxes, 1966–85*. Washington, DC: The Brookings Institution; 1985.

16. Cantor JC. Expanding health insurance coverage: who will pay? *J Health Polit Policy Law*. 1990;15:755–778.

17. US Dept of Health and Human Services. *Health: United States, 1992*. Washington, DC: US Government Printing Office; 1993.

18. Reinhardt UE. Are mandated benefits the answer? *Health Manage Q*. 1988;10:10–14.

19. Butler SM. A tax reform strategy to deal with the uninsured. *JAMA*. 1991;265:2541–2544.

20. Todd JS, Seekins SV, Krichbaum JA, Harvey LK. Health Access America: strengthening the US health care system. *JAMA*. 1991;265:2503–2506.

21. Himmelstein DU, Woolhandler S. A national health program for the United States: a physicians' proposal. *N Engl J Med*. 1989;320:102–108.

25

Costs and Coverage:
Pressures toward Health Care Reform

■ ■ ■ ■ ■ ■

Philip R. Lee, Denise Soffel, and Harold S. Luft

Early in the 1990s, as signs of discontent continued to build about the United States health care system, an experienced observer of the health policy process was led to remark, "There will be no more politics as usual" (E. B. Dowell, former Director of Governmental Affairs, Blue Cross of California, oral communication, April 1992). After years of neglecting issues related to health care, except for a limited interest in the acquired immunodeficiency syndrome (AIDS) epidemic, the media have suddenly turned their attention to this subject. In addition to national newspapers, in the past year *Time, Fortune, The National Journal,* and *Business Week* have run cover stories on the health care crisis. Public television produced a special program on health care, and major news programs, "60 Minutes" and the "MacNeil/Lehrer NewsHour," dedicated segments to this dilemma. Media activity increased rapidly throughout 1991, and issues concerning management of the health care system have shown the greatest increase in media activity (*IssueScan*, 4th quarter, 1991).

A survey conducted by Louis Harris and

Associates in 1988 found that 89% of Americans wanted to see a dramatic change in the health care system: 29% thought that the health care system needs to be completely rebuilt, and an additional 60% thought that the system needs fundamental changes.[1] A poll conducted by *Time* and the Cable News Network found that 91% of Americans thought that the health care system needs fundamental change, and 75% of those surveyed said that costs are much higher than they should be (J. Castro, "Condition: Critical," *Time*, November 25, 1991, p 34). A poll in 1990 found only 10% of Americans satisfied with the current health care system, in contrast to 56% in Canada, 41% in West Germany, and 22% in Great Britain.[1]

The results of many of these polls were summarized in 1991 by Blendon and Donehue:

> Opinion polls indicate that support for a national health plan is at a 40-year high point and more than 10 national and statewide surveys conducted since 1989 indicate that between 60 and 72 percent of Americans are in favor of such a plan. . . . By some of these measures, the public's enthusiasm for the concept of a comprehensive program of national health insurance exceeds the level of support for Medicare in the year prior to its enactment. In fact, a recent Roper Organization survey indicates that 69 percent of all Americans surveyed would approve extending Medicare coverage to all citizens.[2(pp 173, 175)]

More recent polls indicate continuing discontent with the present system, particularly the high costs of care. In an exit poll after the Pennsylvania special senatorial election in November 1991, people were asked what they thought was the biggest problem with health care for themselves and their families; 77% of the voters responded that the biggest problem was cost. Voters in the New Hampshire primary cited health care and national health insurance as the second most important factor in deciding their votes—after the recession and concerns for the economy ("Health Reform Number Two Issue in New Hampshire," News Release, Henry J. Kaiser Family Foundation, Menlo Park, Calif, February 1992). The most recent Kaiser/Commonwealth Health Insurance Survey found that Americans are increasingly dissatisfied with their health care and with the health care system ("Survey Shows

Widespread Public Concern about Health Insurance Coverage and Costs," News Release, Henry J. Kaiser Family Foundation, Menlo Park, Calif, April 1992) and that 60% of Americans think it is the responsibility of government to provide health insurance to all, compared with 34% who believe it is the responsibility of the private sector.

Clearly the public perceives a problem that stems from the high cost of health care, and they call for the federal government to engineer major reforms. Research by the Public Agenda Foundation, in association with the Gallup organization and the Employee Benefit Research Institute,[3] suggests that the public is particularly concerned about out-of-pocket costs. According to the Public Agenda Foundation, people attribute high costs to "unnecessary tests, overpaid doctors, wasteful hospitals, profiteering drug companies, and greedy malpractice lawyers."[3(p4)] Surveys have found that the great majority of the public thinks that spending on physician services is too high and that physicians are too interested in financial reward.[4]

The general public concern is that physician fees are too high, and, in fact, physicians' real earnings have increased considerably in the past decade. Average inflation-adjusted physician income grew by 24% from 1982 to 1989.[5] This increase was not spread equally across all specialties, however, with some experiencing only modest gains as others reaped dramatic increases. In areas like family practice and internal medicine, income levels have been relatively flat.

Although Medicare policy changes to control costs have been enacted by Congress since 1983, little interest has been shown for systemic reforms until recently. Only in the past year has the notion of a major federal role in cost containment for the private sector begun to attract serious attention. In recent years, more than 40 bills have been introduced in Congress, ranging from incremental changes in health insurance and malpractice reform to sweeping "top-down" reform. The three basic approaches before Congress are a market approach, a single-payer approach, and a "play or pay" approach.[6,7]

At the state level, discontent is also evident, particularly with reduced state revenues and climbing Medicaid expenditures.[8] Minnesota recently enacted a plan to cover the uninsured,[9] and more than 30 states are considering major health care reforms.

Physicians agree that there is a problem, although they tend to focus on the uninsured rather than on rising costs. Health care reform issues are beginning to attract attention within medicine. The American Medical Association, the American College of Physicians, and the American Academy of Family Practice all supported the Medicare fee schedule included as part of the 1989 Medicare physician payment reforms enacted by Congress. One of the first physician-authored health care reform proposals, set forth by the Physicians for a National Health Program, appeared in an article published in January 1989.[10] The landmark May 15, 1991, issue of the *Journal of the American Medical Association* and now a second special issue dedicated to health care reform proposals illustrate a broad, open approach, in contrast to the past when most proposals suggesting government intervention were rejected out of hand by physician organizations. Indeed, the American Medical Association has endorsed the idea of government-mandated private insurance coverage[11] and has hinted that it might support some form of overall cost containment. The California Medical Association qualified a proposition for the November 1992 ballot called Affordable Basic Care that would require employers to provide health insurance for their employees.[12] In September 1992 the American College of Physicians published their plan for systemwide reform in the organization and financing of health care.[13]

Factors Driving Reform—Rising Costs and the Uninsured

Growing calls for health care reform in the United States are largely the result of two factors: the continued increase in health care costs, which have been well above increases in gross national product (GNP) for most of the past 20 years and the large number of uninsured and underinsured.[14] In addition, as costs increase, employer coverage is deteriorating. Millions of people will not change jobs for fear of losing their employment-based private health insurance. This is due in part to the erosion of risk-pooling and the increasing use of experience rating, the practice of pegging a group's insurance premiums to its historical use patterns. This practice is in contrast to community rating, which charges insurance premiums based on the experience of an entire community rather than a small group. Insecurity about changing health plans is further exacerbated by preexisting condition clauses that exclude or impose restrictions on coverage for health problems documented at the time of enrollment. Finally, it is a matter of increasing concern that the United States does not compare well with other industrial democracies in universal coverage, cost containment, and health status.

Rising Health Care Costs

The most important factor propelling health care reform in the United States is the cost of health care, both in absolute terms and in the rate of cost increases. A few figures tell the story. Measured in current dollars, health care spending of the United States between 1970 and 1990 rose at an annual rate of 11.6% whereas national income, as measured by the GNP, increased at an average annual rate of 8.8%.[5] As a result, the share of the GNP devoted to health care grew by more than half in 20 years: from 7.3% to 12.3%. The Commerce Department predicts that the share of the GNP devoted to health care will rise to 14% in 1992. The Health Care Financing Administration (HCFA) projects that health care will absorb more than 16% of the GNP by the year 2000.

The pluralistic nature of health care financing means that persons, families, insurers, employers, and government at all levels (federal, state, and local) are affected by high costs. Steuerle estimated that total US health care expenditures in fiscal year 1992 will be $768 billion, drawn from the following sources of financing: individuals (out of pocket), private health insurance (employer's share), Medicare, Medicaid, other public programs, federal tax subsidies, private health insurance (employee's share), other private sources, and state tax subsidies (Figure 25-1)[16]

In the end, it is families and individuals who bear the financial burden. In his report, Steuerle

Figure 25-1. *The graph shows the estimated sources of financing for United States health care expenditures, fiscal year 1992 (adapted from Steuerle[16]).*

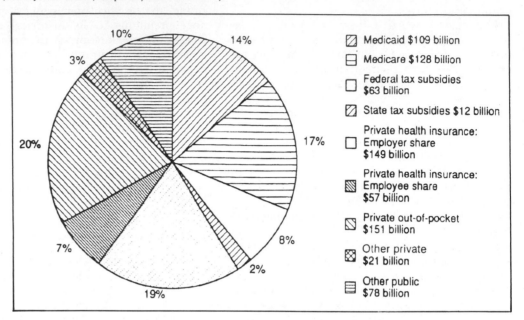

Legend:
- Medicaid $109 billion
- Medicare $128 billion
- Federal tax subsidies $63 billion
- State tax subsidies $12 billion
- Private health insurance: Employer share $149 billion
- Private health insurance: Employee share $57 billion
- Private out-of-pocket $151 billion
- Other private $21 billion
- Other public $78 billion

analyzes the cost to families in a manner that reveals the true cost of health care.[16] He estimates that the average expenditure per household is $8,000 per year. Of this, only about a third is paid directly by household members. The largest costs are indirect, particularly through taxes that finance public programs and reduced wages that are siphoned into insurance premiums paid by employers (Table 25-1).[16]

Spiraling costs are also endured by Medicare beneficiaries. Although Medicare is a major source of financial security for older Americans, the proportion of their income spent on health care is increasing. In 1972 they spent 10.6% of their income on health care. This rose to 16.2% in 1984 and 17.1% in 1991.[17] The bulk of the increase has been in Medi-Gap premiums and direct out-of-pocket costs—deductibles and coinsurance for private health insurance and Medicare Part A and Part B; balance bills and uncovered services, such as prescription drugs; and nursing home costs.

Health care is also taking a growing portion of federal funds. In 1970, spending on health constituted 7.1% of the federal budget, a share that rose to 13.4% in 1990. The Congressional Budget Office projects that health care will account for more than 20% of the federal budget by 1996.[18] Although federal health expenditures are projected to rise by 7.0% annually, Social Security expenditures are expected to rise by 2.2%, net interest on the debt 1.4%, and the percentages devoted to all other federal expenditures are expected to decline.[19]

Uninsured Americans

The second major factor stimulating a host of health care reform proposals is the growing population of uninsured persons. Most estimates place the number of Americans without public or private health insurance between 31 and 36 million.[20] The 1987 National Medical Care Expenditure Survey found that 18.5% of the population (47.8 million Americans) lacked health insurance for all or part of 1987. On any given day, between 34 and 36 million were uninsured, and 24.5 million were uninsured throughout the year.[14] Analysis of the March 1990 Current Population Survey found that 33.4 million people

Table 25-1. How US Households Pay for Health Care*

Estimated Costs, 1992	Average per Household, $	Percent of GNP	Percent of Personal Income
Paid indirectly			
Taxes			
Federal hospital insurance payroll tax	860	1.4	1.6
Other federal, state, and local†	3,070	4.9	5.8
Reduced wages (paid by employers)‡	1,580	2.5	3.0
Other§	190	0.3	0.4
Paid directly			
Personal contributions to private health insurance‖	590	0.9	1.1
Out-of-pocket payments	1,580	2.5	3.0
Premiums			
Federal supplemental medical insurance	130	0.2	0.2
Total	8,000	12.9	15.1

GNP = gross national product.

*Adapted from Steuerle.[16]
†Includes taxes needed to finance direct government health spending out of general revenues, plus the amount of general taxes that must be raised to compensate for revenue lost due to special tax treatment of certain health-related income (about 26% of total).
‡Employer contributions for health insurance, less government tax subsidies.
§Nonpatient revenue for the health care industry, such as charitable donations, interest income, hospital parking, and gift shops.
‖ Includes employee contributions to private group health insurance plans and individual policy premiums.

(13.6% of the population) had no health insurance (public or private) throughout 1989.[21] Thus, millions of people in this country lack access to even the most basic health services.

The 1987 survey found that of the uninsured population, 70% were employed or dependents of employed persons. Approximately 10% are unemployed persons and their dependents, and the remainder are nonworkers, such as students.[14]

The number of uninsured increased rapidly between 1979 and 1984, from 28.8 million in 1979 to 37.3 million in 1984.[14] The most notable factor in the rising number of uninsured Americans was the recession of the early 1980s. From 1984 through 1989 the number of uninsured seems to have stabilized. It is not yet clear what effect the current recession has had on the number of uninsured persons. Unemployment is currently more than 7% nationwide (B. Holey, Bureau of Labor Statistics, US Department of Labor, oral communication, September 1992), and it is even higher in some regions, such as California, where it is 9.5%. Signs of an economic recovery are still faint.

The continuing realignment of the economy, with changes in the mix of industries and occupations, is also contributing to the rise in the number of uninsured. The volume of jobs in the manufacturing sector is declining as the service sector is growing. The manufacturing sector has a strong union tradition with generous employee benefits. Whereas 90% of persons working in manufacturing had health insurance in 1990,[21] employees in most other sectors of the economy did not receive health benefits at this level. Of those employed in agriculture 30% did not have health insurance, and of those in service sector jobs 25% did not.[21] Also, the erosion of Medicaid in many states has resulted in a growing number of poor without Medicaid eligibility. Where 65% of the poor were once eligible for Medicaid, the program now covers less than 40% of the population below poverty.[22]

Lack of public or private insurance coverage

ranges from less than 10% in 13 states, including Hawaii, Massachusetts, Connecticut, Michigan, Wisconsin, and Iowa, to more than 20% in Texas, Louisiana, and New Mexico.[21] California has the largest number of uninsured, a figure that has climbed to 6 million.[23] Uninsured persons are found in disproportionate numbers among those 18 to 28 years of age, Hispanics and African Americans, those with low incomes, and those living in rural areas.[14]

A lack of insurance has several important consequences. It places a substantial financial burden on persons and families with relatively low incomes. High costs reduce access to care for appropriate services. Poor access to primary care is associated with increased health care costs and decreased health status.[24]

Factors Contributing to Rising Health Care Costs

As problems related to costs and the uninsured motivate policymakers to explore ways to improve or revamp the medical care system, assessments of various proposals must consider how they address these twin issues. . . . To assess the plausibility of various approaches, it is helpful to examine first the causes of spiraling health care costs.

The rise in personal health care expenditures can be broken into four components: general inflation, as measured by the consumer price index; population growth; medical care price inflation above general inflation; and all other factors, including increases in volume and intensity of services. Whereas the components that are not controllable within the health care system— general inflation and population growth— accounted for about 55% of the increase in the past 20 years, medical care price inflation has accounted for 17% of the increase and the volume and intensity of services for approximately 28%.[25]

It is difficult to differentiate the effects of medical care inflation, quality improvements, and increased volume and intensity. This collection of components, however, is affected by a variety of factors, including,

Market failure
Technology
Administrative costs
Unnecessary care and defensive medicine
Patient complexity
Excess capacity
Productivity[26]

Market Failure

Market failure is an economic term describing a situation in which normal marketplace behavior cannot be assumed to lead automatically to an efficient allocation of resources. In this context "failure" is a technical explanation of the common observation that medical care is different from other goods and services. Five factors contribute to market failure in the United States: Suppliers may influence demand, consumers are usually cost "unconscious" when using medical care, workers are shielded from the true costs of insurance, uncertainty in the services needed for treating individual patients leads to the predominance of fee-for-service reimbursement, and information is lacking on what works.

An inherent aspect of medical care, regardless of the organizational and economic system, is uncertainty at the outset concerning the need for and efficacy of specific treatments. Arrow's classic article on this issue laid the groundwork for the field of health economics.[27]

In the United States, the consumers' desire to insure against the risk of costly medical care led to the growth of private health insurance, both employment-based and self-purchased. The number of companies providing group health insurance has grown from only 37 such companies in 1942 to more than 1,500 companies today. Although about 100 companies provide coverage to 90% of the covered population and an additional 250 companies provide most of the rest, hundreds of other companies provide some type of health coverage (H. Raymond, Health Insurance Association of America, oral communication, May 1992).

Fragmentation of the insurance market has several deleterious effects. First, because providers are reimbursed by many insurers, each company represents a small fraction of a physician's caseload. Thus, it is impossible for an individual carrier to collect valid information about a provider's quality and practice style. It also becomes infeasible to negotiate average payment rates for episodes of care as an alternative to fee-for-service reimbursement while protecting physicians from costs associated with treating patients with unusually complicated conditions. Second, competition among insurers for enrollees leads to fragmentation of the risk pool (those being insured) because of the voluntary nature of health insurance and the fact that more and more insurers use experience rating. Voluntary enrollment means that a given premium will be most attractive to those most in need of treatment. Because of this, insurers will seek to avoid high-risk enrollees.

Technology

Developments in technology—new drugs, devices, and procedures—play an important role in improving the quality and effectiveness of health care and in escalating costs. After pharmaceuticals are developed and approved as safe and effective for specific indications, their application may be broadened, and they may be used when they are only marginally effective or even ineffective. Diagnostic technologies such as endoscopy, computed tomographic scan, and magnetic resonance imaging may also be used initially for a limited number of indications, but gradually the application is broadened, and there may be misuse, overuse, and underuse.

During the past 30 years, faculty at the Institute for Health Policy Studies at the University of California, San Francisco,[28–30] and the Palo Alto (California) Medical Foundation,[31,32] as well as other investigators[33] have studied the effects of medical technology on costs. Studies in the 1960s strongly suggested that for most conditions it was "little ticket" items that contributed most to expenditure increases, and technology was not driving up costs. By the mid-1970s this began to shift, and studies in the 1980s and 1990s clearly indicate that "big ticket," high-technology items, such as coronary artery bypass grafting, are of growing importance.

The complex factors related to the development and diffusion of medical devices have recently been carefully analyzed by Foote,[14] who notes the federal policies, such as funding for research through the National Institutes of Health, that promoted their development, as well as those that may retard them, such as Food and Drug Administration regulation. The same is true for health care financing policies that may either promote (Medicare, Medicaid) or retard (HCFA hospital prospective payment) the diffusion of technology. In contrast to Canada and many European countries, which place far more restrictions on the deployment of new technologies, particularly big ticket items, there is little connection in the United States between policies that promote and those that retard this development and diffusion, and no overall policy is in place related to medical technology. Furthermore, in the United States there are few constraints on the ability of providers to offer new technologies, so it is commonly the case that excess capacity develops with attendant incentives to increase use.

Administrative Costs

Administrative costs have been the focus of considerable interest and complaint but not a large amount of careful research. These include the costs of claims processing to pay physician and hospital bills, marketing, enrollment, and eligibility determination, including risk profiling. A particularly difficult problem is posed for small businesses: health insurance premiums are higher because of administrative costs that can be as much as 35% greater than those for large employers with the same coverage.[14] In addition, in their effort to contain costs through constraining use, payers have developed extensive review and authorization programs, further adding to administrative costs. Not only are administrative costs high for third-party payers, but costs of administration must be borne by hospitals, nursing homes, physicians, and consumers.

It has been estimated that administrative costs account for about 25% of the $738 billion health care expenditures in 1990.[35] Estimated savings in administrative costs for various health care reform proposals range from $31 billion[36] to $67 billion[37] or even $100 billion for single-payer systems.[35]

Unnecessary Care and Defensive Medicine

Growing attention in recent years has been focused on the potential importance of unnecessary care, including defensive medicine, in rising health care costs.[3] Whereas some care may be deemed unnecessary or inappropriate on retrospective review, it is difficult to make such a judgment at the time the care is provided. The existence of uncertainty in clinical decision making has always been recognized, but it has long been thought to be a random occurrence with few economic or policy implications. Studies in the early 1970s, however, showed wide variation among adjacent communities in Vermont and other New England states in the population-based admission rates for such elective procedures as tonsillectomy and hysterectomy.[38,39] Later studies showed marked differences in patterns of use and the costs of care in Boston, Massachusetts, and New Haven, Connecticut,[40] with no apparent differences in mortality between the two cities. A major factor, in Wennberg's view, has been uncertainty about outcomes of care and the fact that practice styles and patterns of practice vary idiosyncratically from one community to another.[41] Additional evidence regarding inappropriate or unnecessary care has come from the work of Chassin and associates.[42,43] Their studies suggest that for some procedures the application to specific clinical situations may be inappropriate as much as a third of the time.

It is difficult to estimate the effect of malpractice on defensive medicine and the cost of health care. In a study reported in 1987, Reynolds and co-workers estimated that the costs of defensive medicine were more than 3.5 times the cost of malpractice insurance premium increases.[44] They estimated the component of physician cost related to professional liability, including defensive medicine, using two different methods and found these costs were about 15% of the total cost of physicians' services in 1984. Of these professional liability costs, $3 billion was spent on insurance premiums and $100 million on settling claims not covered by insurance. Practice changes prompted by the risk of claims account for the rest. A 1991 study estimated that between 1982 and 1989, about 1% per year has been added to expenditures for physician services as a result of the professional liability system. The authors concluded that 30% of professional liability costs went to the direct payment of malpractice premiums, whereas 70% was attributable to practicing defensive medicine.[45]

Patient Complexity

Patient complexity is recognized as a factor of importance in the cost of care, particularly for low-birth-weight infants; older persons with multiple chronic diseases and disabilities; patients infected with the human immunodeficiency virus or AIDS, particularly those with numerous infections, including drug-resistant tuberculosis; trauma patients with multiple injuries associated with the growing wave of violence; and patients requiring such major procedures as heart, lung, and liver transplants. It is evident to most clinicians that because of the rapid increase in ambulatory and hospital outpatient services,[46] patients are coming to the hospital with more complex and difficult problems. Although these factors are important clinically and affect increases in hospital costs, they are not a major factor in overall cost increases because the less complicated segment of patients is being treated in less costly settings.

Excess Capacity

The issue of excess capacity is yet to be seriously addressed by policymakers, but it is likely to become more and more important. Excess capacity is evident in some areas, such as in the number of hospital beds and the availability of medical technologies. Statewide hospital occupancy rates in 1988 were as low as 49% in Alaska, 52% in Wyoming, and 55% in Louisiana, Nebraska, and Texas.[47] Nationwide, one in three hospital beds has been empty since 1985, as hospital occupancy rates have dropped below 65%. Recent work by Fisher and associates, using the techniques of small area analysis, estimated savings in Oregon of as much as $50 million if the hospital bed supply were reduced.[48]

The current supply of physicians is also in excess of what is needed, and there is certainly a maldistribution by specialty and geographic area. Most of the imbalance by medical speciality has resulted from a rapid growth in surgical specialties and medical subspecialties. A projection of the supply of physicians by specialty for 1990 showed shortages in the 5 specialties of child psychiatry, physical medicine, emergency medicine, preventive medicine, and psychiatry and an oversupply in 16, with cardiology, endocrinology, neurosurgery, and pulmonary showing the greatest surpluses.[49] More recently, both the Council of Graduate Medical Education[50] and the Bureau of Health Professions[51] reported a physician surplus, although persistent problems of maldistribution, both by specialty and by geography, continue to leave some areas underserved. Data on the distribution of physicians show extreme variations by geographic area. The federal government designates 2,143 areas as health professional shortage areas,[52] the major criterion being defined by physician-to-population ratios. Not everyone agrees with this assessment of the physician supply problem, however. Schwartz and colleagues, for example, suggest that the increasing supply of physicians is leading to an outward movement by specialists to smaller communities, narrowing the maldistribution problem.[53]

Physician supply has increased rapidly since the mid-1960s when federal and state policies were implemented to increase medical student enrollments and expand physician supply. Total, nonfederal patient care physicians per 100,000 population increased from 125 in 1965 to 193 in 1989. The United States now has more physicians per capita than almost all other nations. Exceptions include Israel, Belgium, West Germany, and the former Soviet Union.[54] It is expected that this number will continue to increase. This oversupply has important implications for health care costs. A study by Grumbach and Lee suggests that projected costs for physician services in the year 2000, given projections about physician supply, could be as much as $40 billion in additional costs.[55]

Schwartz and co-workers, however, argue that the demand for physician services will continue to expand rapidly because of the aging of the population, the development of new diseases, and the increasing array of technically sophisticated medical services. These trends, they argue, will lead to a shortage of physicians, not a surplus.[56]

Productivity

Assessing productivity in medical care is important, but conventional measures of productivity are inherently limited. Productivity is usually defined in terms of output per labor hour, and industry typically attempts to increase productivity by substituting new machinery for workers. The service and cognitive aspects of medical care make it difficult to achieve productivity increases in this manner, although some opportunities do exist. Changes ranging from lapardscopic surgical procedures to computerized billing systems can reduce labor input. In some instances, productivity increases are not well measured in conventional statistics. For example, as hospital lengths of stay have fallen, nursing hours per patient-day have increased (suggesting falling productivity) and nursing hours per admission have fallen (suggesting rising productivity).

Health care professionals increasingly look to broader measures of productivity by redefining the unit of output. Based on the concept that avoiding errors is less expensive than fixing them, the "total quality management" and "continuous quality improvement" movements are focused on enhancing both quality and productivity. From a population perspective, the greatest productivity improvements are likely to come from two areas: increased prevention of illness and reduced use of marginally effective interventions.

Health Care Reforms—Setting the Stage

During the past 20 years, and particularly in the past decade, actions have been taken by the private and public sectors to slow the rate of increase in health care costs. Considerably less has been done to expand health insurance coverage to uninsured persons. Beginning in 1984, however, Congress has mandated incremental changes in Medicaid eligibility. This legislation, culminating with the Omnibus Budget Reconciliation acts of 1989 and 1990, required all states to establish minimum Medicaid income eligibility thresholds at 133% of the poverty level for children younger than 6 and then to phase in coverage, one year at a time, for children ages 18 and younger.[57] Several states have taken limited additional actions in an attempt to increase access for the uninsured.[58] Minnesota recently enacted a major reform proposal to cover uninsured persons,[9] and Vermont passed legislation to set in motion a plan for statewide health care coverage by 1995 (F. Butterfield, "Universal Health Care Plan Is Goal of Law in Vermont," *The New York Times*, May 12, 1992, p A12). . . .

The first major federal attempt to contain Medicare costs was the "prospective payment system" for hospitals, passed in 1983 and implemented in the mid-1980s. It had two important effects, one intended and one unintended. As intended, expenditures for Part A (hospital services) slowed notably relative to previous trends.[59] An unintended consequence of the fixed payments, however, was that hospitals were no longer able to cross-subsidize uninsured patients through cost reimbursement with paying patients. This difficulty was exacerbated by the growth of contracting with hospitals by Medicaid programs, particularly Medi-Cal in California,[60] and preferred provider organizations and insurers. The spread of fixed-payment arrangements and contracts by payers unwilling to cross-subsidize led to rapid increases in charges (list prices) paid by the shrinking pool of conventionally insured. This, in turn, has forced up the premiums for small group enrollees—large groups typically have the power to negotiate discounts—and often to a loss of coverage. It has also deprived hospitals of implicit subsidies, which had been used for uncompensated care, adding to hospitals' financial stress and an increasing reliance on public facilities to provide care for uninsured persons.

The second major step by the federal government to curtail Medicare expenditures began in 1984, when Congress froze physician payments in the Medicare program. Congress followed by reducing payments for overvalued procedures, including many surgical and imaging procedures, limiting charges by physicians above the Medicare allowed charge—the Maximum Actual Allowable Charge program—and establishing the participating physician and provider program. These efforts culminated in 1989 with the enactment of the comprehensive Medicare physician payment reforms, including establishment of the Medicare fee schedule, limits on balance billing, and volume performance standards.[61–63]

Following implementation of the Medicare fee schedule on January 1, 1992, many private payers began to consider applying a fee schedule based on the Medicare relative value scale but with a different conversion factor. How widespread this will become remains to be seen.

In the private sector, actions have been taken by self-insured employers and by commercial and nonprofit insurance companies. In their attempt to control costs, employers have emphasized competitive market-based strategies. These include shifting costs to employees through co-payments, deductibles, and increased premium costs; reducing benefits, sometimes eliminating coverage for dependents; cost management, including utilization review, concurrent review, preadmission or preprocedure certification, and case management; managed competition; and selective contracting.[64] Many of these approaches have affected practicing physicians, adding to what has been called the "hassle factor."[65]

In response, physician groups, including the California Medical Association, have proposed major initiatives to extend health insurance coverage universally. Many of these proposals have called for employer-mandated health insurance and an expansion of Medicaid to cover the unemployed and unemployable younger than 65.[11] The Physicians for a National Health Program proposal suggests a more basic restructuring of the way health care is financed, proposing a single, comprehensive public insurance program.[66] . . .

As this and other articles in the series will show, the problems of the health care system arise from a combination of social, legal, historical, political, and technologic factors. Simple solutions are unlikely to work, but the prospect of important changes has energized the policy debate.

REFERENCES

1. Blendon RJ, Leitman R, Morrison I, Donelan K: Satisfaction with health systems in ten nations. Health Aff (Millwood) 1990; 9:185–192
2. Blendon RJ, Donelan K: The public and the future of US health care system reform, *In* Blendon RJ, Edwards JN (Eds): System in Crisis: The Case for Health Care Reform. Chicago, Ill, Faulkner & Gray, 1991, pp 173–194

3. Faulty Diagnosis: Public Misconception About Health Care Reform. New York, NY, Public Agenda Foundation, April 1992

4. Taylor H, Leitman R: Consumers' satisfaction with their health care, In Blendon RJ, Edwards JN (Eds): System in Crisis: The Case for Health Care Reform. Chicago, Ill, Faulkner & Gray, 1991, pp 75–102

5. Pope GC, Schneider JE: Trends in physician income. Health Aff (Millwood) 1992; 11:181–193

6. Kosterlitz J: A sick system. National Journal 1992 Feb 15; 24:376–388

7. Caring for the Uninsured and Underinsured. JAMA 1991; 265:2491–2596

8. Battle of the (Medicaid) Bulge: States Gird for Sizeable Cutbacks, In State Health Notes 122. Washington, DC, The George Washington University, Intergovernmental Health Policy Project, Dec 16, 1991

9. Minnesota Health Care Reform Act of 1992, 549 HF §2800

10. Himmelstein DU, Woolhandler S: A national health program for the United States—A physician's proposal. N Engl J Med 1989; 320:102–108

11. Todd JS, Seekins SV, Krichbaum JA, Harvey LK: Health access America—Strengthening the US health care system. JAMA 1991; 265:2503–2506

12. Lee S: Affordable Basic Care: The California Medical Association Plan. Presented at the Institute for Health Policy Studies, University of California, San Francisco, May 1992

13. Scott HD, Shapiro HB: Universal insurance for American health care—A proposal of the American College of Physicians. Ann Intern Med 1992; 117:511–519

14. Critical Issues in American Health Care Delivery and Financing Policy, Advisory Council on Social Security, Washington, DC, December 1991

15. Health Care Spending Control: The Experience of France, Germany, and Japan. US General Accounting Office HRD-92-9, November 1991

16. Steuerle CE: The search for adaptable health policy through finance-based reforms, In Helms RB (Ed): American Health Policy: Critical Issues for Reform. Washington, DC, DAEI Press, in press

17. Health Spending: The Growing Threat to the Family Budget. Washington, DC, Families USA Foundation, December 1991

18. Reischauer RD: Congressional Budget Office Testimony before the Committee on Ways and Means. US House of Representatives, October 9, 1991

19. Annual Report to Congress. Washington, DC, Physician Payment Review Commission, 1992

20. Friedman E: The uninsured—From dilemma to crisis. JAMA 1991; 265:2491–2495

21. Himmelstein D, Woolhandler S, Wolfe S: The Vanishing Health Care Safety Net: New Data on Uninsured Americans. Cambridge, Mass, Center for National Health Program Studies, Dec 1991

22. Jones JM: Director's note, In Demkovich L (Ed): The States and the Uninsured: Slowly But Surely, Filling the Gaps. Washington, DC, National Health Policy Forum, Washington, DC, October 1990

23. Brown ER, Valdez RB, Morgenstern H, Cumberland W, Wang C, Mann J: Health Insurance Coverage of Californians in 1989. Los Angeles, California Policy Seminar, 1991

24. Weissman JS, Stern R, Fielding SL, Epstein AM: Delayed access to health care: Risk factors, reasons, and consequences. Ann Intern Med 1991; 114:325–331

25. Levit KR, Lazenby HC, Cowan CA, Letsch SW: National health expenditures, 1990. Health Care Financ Rev 1991; 13:29–54

26. Who Will Cure America's Health Care Crisis? Harvard Community Health Plan Annual Report 1991. Brookline, Mass, Harvard Community Health Plan, 1991

27. Arrow KJ: Uncertainty and welfare economics of medical care. Am Econ Rev 1963; 53:941–973

28. Showstack JA, Schroeder SA, Steinberg HR: Evaluating the costs and benefits of a diagnostic technology—The case of upper gastrointestinal endoscopy. Med Care 1981; 19:498–509

29. Showstack JA, Schroeder SA, Matsumoto MF: Changes in the use of medical technologies, 1972–1977—A study of 10 inpatient diagnoses. N Engl J Med 1982; 306:706–712

30. Showstack JA, Stone MH, Schroeder SA: The role of changing clinical practices in the rising costs of hospital care. N Engl J Med 1985; 313:1201–1207

31. Scitovsky AA: The high cost of dying: What do the data show? Milbank Q 1984; 62:591–608

32. Scitovsky AA: Changes in the costs of treatment of selected illnesses, 1971–1981. Med Care 1985; 23:1345–1356

33. Altman SH, Blendon R (Eds): Medical Technology: The Culprit Behind Health Care Costs? Proceedings of the 1977 Sun Valley Forum on National Health. Washington, DC, US Dept of Health, Education and Welfare publication No. (PHS) 79-3216, 1979

34. Foote SB: Managing the Medical Arms Race: Public Policy and Medical Device Innovation. Berkeley, Calif, University of California Press, 1992

35. Woolhandler S, Himmelstein DU: The deteriorat-

ing administrative efficiency of the US health care system. N Engl J Med 1991; 324:1253–1258

36. Darman R: Comprehensive Health Reform: Observations About the Problem and Alternative Approaches to Solutions. Office of Management and Budget Testimony before the Committee on Ways and Means, US House of Representatives, October 10, 1991

37. Canadian Health Insurance: Lessons for the United States. US General Accounting Office, HRD-91-90, June 1991

38. Wennberg JE, Gittelsohn AM: Small area variations in health care delivery. Science 1973; 183: 1102–1108

39. Wennberg JE, Gittelsohn AM: Variations in medical care among small areas. Sci Am 1982; 246: 120–134

40. Wennberg JE, Freeman JL, Shelton RM, Bubolz TA: Hospital use and mortality among Medicare beneficiaries in Boston and New Haven. N Engl J Med 1989; 321:1168–1173

41. Wennberg J: Dealing with medical practice variations: A proposal for action. Health Aff (Millwood) 1984; 3:6–32

42. Chassin MR, Kosecoff J, Park RE, et al: Does inappropriate use explain geographic variations in the use of health care services? A study of three procedures. JAMA 1987; 258:2533–2537

43. Chassin MR, Kosecoff J, Solomon DH, Brook RH: How coronary angiography is used—Clinical determinants of appropriateness. JAMA 1987; 258:2543–2547

44. Reynolds RA, Rizzo JA, Gonzales ML: The cost of medical professional liability. JAMA 1987; 257:2776–2781

45. Moser J, Musacchio R: The cost of medical professional liability in the 1980's. J Med Pract Manage 1991; 7:6–9

46. Sulvetta MB: Achieving cost control in the hospital outpatient department—1991 Annual Supplement. Health Care Financ Rev 1992 Mar, pp 95–106

47. AHA Hospital Statistics, 1989–1990 ed. Chicago, Ill, American Hospital Association, 1989

48. Fisher ES, Welch HG, Wennberg JE: Prioritizing Oregon's hospital resources. JAMA 1992;267: 1925–1931

49. Bowman MA, Katzoff JM, Garrison LP, Wills J: Estimates of physician requirements for 1990 for the specialties of neurology, anesthesiology, nuclear medicine, pathology, physical medicine and rehabilitation, and radiology—A further application of the GMENAC methodology. JAMA 1983; 250:2623–2627

50. The First Report of the Council, Vol 1. Rockville,

Md, Council on Graduate Medical Education, 1988

51. Sixth Report to the President and Congress on the State of Health Personnel in the US. Washington, DC, Bureau of Health Professions, US Dept of Health and Human Services (DHHS) publication No. HRS-P-OD-88-1, 1988

52. Selected Statistics on Health Professional Shortage Areas (as of December 31, 1991): Office of Shortage Designation, Bureau of Health Care Delivery and Assistance, Health Resources and Services Administration, US DHHS, 1992

53. Schwartz WB, Newhouse JP, Bennett BW, Williams AP: The changing geographic distribution of board-certified physicians. N Engl J Med 1980; 303:1032–1038

54. Geyman JP: Family Practice: Foundation of Changing Health Care. Norwalk, Conn, Appleton-Century-Crofts, 1985

55. Grumbach K, Lee PR: How many physicians can we afford? JAMA 1991; 265:2369–2372

56. Schwartz WB, Sloan FA, Mendelson DN: Why there will be little or no physician surplus between now and the year 2000. N Engl J Med 1988; 318:892–897

57. Lee PR, Newacheck PW: Physician reimbursement under Medicaid. Pediatrics 1992; 89:778–780

58. Access to Health Care: State Strategies and Legislation (1991). Washington, DC, Intergovernmental Health Policy Project, George Washington University, 1992

59. Russell LB, Manning CL: The effect of prospective payment on Medicine expenditures. N Engl J Med 1989; 320:439–444

60. Johns L: Selective contracting in California: An update. Inquiry 1989; 26:345–353

61. Annual Report to Congress. Washington, DC, Physician Payment Review Commission, 1989

62. Lee PR, Ginsburg PB: Physician payment reform: An idea whose time has come. JAMA 1988; 260:2441–2443

63. Lee PR, Ginsburg PB: The trials of Medicare physician payment reform JAMA 1991; 266:1562–1565

64. Anderson R: Employer Initiatives to Better Manage Their Health Benefit Programs. Presented at the Institute for Health Policy Studies, University of California San Francisco, March 1992

65. The Hassle Factor: America's Health Care System Strangling in Red Tape Washington, DC, American Society of Internal Medicine, 1990

66. Grumbach K, Bodenheimer T, Himmelstein DU, Woolhandler S: Liberal benefits, conservative spending—The Physicians for a National Health Program proposal JAMA 1991; 265:2549–2554

Medicine in Practice

. . . . . .

The social organization of medicine is manifested on the interactional as well as the structural levels of society. There is an established and rich tradition of studying medical work "firsthand" in medical settings, through participant-observation, interviewing, or both. Researchers go "where the action is"—in this case among doctors and patients—to see just how social life (i.e., medical care) happens. Such studies are time-consuming and difficult (see Danziger, 1979), but they are the only way to penetrate the structure of medical care and reveal the sociological texture of medical practice. For it is here that the structure of medicine shapes the type of care that is delivered.

There are at least three general foci for these qualitative studies. Some studies focus on the organization of the institution itself, such as a mental hospital (Goffman, 1961), a nursing home (Gubrium, 1975), or an intensive care unit (Zussman, 1992). Others examine the delivery of services or practitioner-patient interaction ranging from childbirth (Shaw, 1974) to dying (Sudnow, 1967). A third general focus is on collegial relations among professionals (e.g., Freidson, 1975; Bosk, 1979; Guillemin and Holmstrom, 1986). All of these studies give us a window on the backstage world of medical organization. No matter what the focus, they bring to life the processes through which organizations operate and how participants manage in their situations. It is worth noting also that most of these close-up studies end up with the researchers taking a critical stance toward the organization and practice of medicine.

The four selections in this section reveal different aspects of medicine in practice. The readings represent a range of medical settings and situations: outpatient encounters, an emergency room, an intensive-care nursery, and nurse-midwives' experience of home births. As well as illuminating the texture of medical practice, the selections individually and together raise a number of significant sociological issues.

In "The Struggle between the Voice of Medicine and the Voice of the Lifeworld," Elliot G. Mishler offers a detailed analysis of the structure of doctor-patient interviews. His analysis allows us to see two distinct "voices" in the interview discourse. In this framework, the "voice of medicine" dominates the interviews and allows physicians to control the interview. When "the voice of the lifeworld"—patients talking "about problems in their lives that were related to or resulted from their symptoms or illness" (Mishler, 1984: 91)—disrupts the voice of medicine, it is often interrupted, silenced, or ignored. This perspective shows how physician dominance is re-created in doctor-patient encounters, and it gives some clues to why patients may say their doctors don't understand them.

In the second selection, "Some Contingencies of the Moral Evaluation and Control of Clientele: The Case of the Hospital Emergency Service," Julius A. Roth demonstrates how everyday "prejudices" and evaluations by the staff of a patient's social worth affect the type of treatment people receive. (For another example of this process, see Sudnow, 1967.) Emergency room staff make moral judgments of patients' worthiness based on their evaluations of the patients' social attributes and the "appropriateness" of their demands on the staff. This not only reinforces and amplifies existing inequalities in medical care and services, but it creates new ones as well.

Renée R. Anspach, in "The Language of Case Presentation," analyzes the way doctors talk to each other, especially about patients. Based on data collected in a study of neonatal infant-care nurseries, Anspach shows how the language used by medical housestaff in presenting "cases" to their superiors reveals important aspects of physicians' socialization; she also provides insights into assumptions of the medical world view and how physicians mitigate responsibility for errors. She contends that language used in medical work not only communicates information and organizes the task, but reflects underlying attitudes and affects the delivery of patient care (see also Anspach, 1993).

The final selection, "Midwives in Transition: The Structure of a Clinical Revolution" by Barbara Katz Rothman, gives us a look at an alternative conception to the dominant model of childbirth. Nurse-midwives attending home births are presented with anomalies to what they expected given the medical conceptions of birth. They found the "timetables" for normal labor and birth in the home situation to differ from that in the hospital. Rothman argues that the hospital context shaped medical understandings of timetables for birthing. She shows how practice in a nonmedical setting can influence the construction and reconstruction of medical knowledge—in this case, timetables for birth—and create an alternative knowledge for health care.

All four selections highlight the structure of medical practice. Each illustrates how the social organization of medicine constrains and shapes the physician's work. Aside from delivering services, it appears that a very important element of the physician's task is sustaining the medical order in which services are delivered, although there can be meaningful challenges.

REFERENCES

Anspach, Renée. 1993. Deciding Who Lives. Berkeley: University of California Press.
Bosk, Charles. 1979. Forgive and Remember. Chicago: University of Chicago.
Danziger, Sandra Klein. 1979. "On doctor watching: Fieldwork in medical settings." Urban Life. 7 (January): 513–31.
Freidson, Eliot. 1975. Doctoring Together: A Study of Professional Social Control. New York: Elsevier.
Goffman, Erving. 1961. Asylums. New York: Doubleday.
Gubrium, Jabar. 1975. Living and Dying at Murray Manor. New York: St. Martin's Press.
Guillemin, Jeanne Harley and Linda Lytle Holmstrom. 1986. Mixed Blessings: Intensive Care for Newborns. New York: Oxford.
Mishler, Eliot G. 1984. The Discourse of Medicine: Dialectics of Medical Interviews. Norwood, NJ: Ablex.
Shaw, Nancy Stoller. 1974. Forced Labor: Maternity Care in the United States. New York: Pergamon.
Sudnow, David. 1967. Passing On: The Social Organization of Dying. Englewood Cliffs, NJ: Prentice-Hall.
Zussman, Robert. 1992. Intensive Care. Chicago: University of Chicago Press.

26

The Struggle between
the Voice of Medicine and
the Voice of the Lifeworld

• • • • • •

Elliot G. Mishler

Introduction
....

The work reported here assumes that the discourse of patients with physicians is central to clinical practice and, therefore, warrants systematic study. . . . Principal features of the approach and the general plan of the study will be outlined briefly in this introductory section.

The inquiry begins with a description and analysis of "unremarkable interviews." This term is applied to stretches of talk between patients and physicians that appear intuitively to be normal and nonproblematic. The interviews are drawn from the large sample collected by Waitzkin and Stoeckle[1] in their study of the informative process in medical care (Waitzkin & Stoeckle, 1976; Waitzkin et al. 1978). In these interviews patients and physicians talk to each other in ways that we, as members of the same culture, recognize as contextually appropriate. Our sense of appropriateness depends on shared and tacit understandings; on commonly held and often implicit assumptions of how to talk and of what to talk about in this situation.

Our intuitive sense of the unremarkable nature of these interviews merely locates the phenomenon for study. The central task of this chapter is to develop and apply concepts and methods that allow us to go through and beyond our ordinary, implicit, and shared understanding of the "normality" and "unremarkableness" of these interviews. The aim is to make explicit features of the talk that produce and warrant our sense as investigators and, by implication, the sense made by physicians and patients that the talk is unremarkable, and that the interview is going as it "should" go. The investigation proceeds through four analytically distinct but intertwined phases discussed in the review of alternative approaches to the study of discourse: description, analysis, interpretation, and interruption.

An adequate description is a prerequisite to further study. As noted earlier, a transcription of speech is neither a neutral or "objective" description. Transcription rules incorporate models of language in that they specify which features of speech are to be recorded and which are to go unremarked. Thus, they define what is relevant and significant. The typescript notation system used here is a modification and simplification of one developed by Gail Jefferson (1978) and used by many conversation analysts; . . . The general aim is to retain details of the talk believed to be significant for clarifying and understanding the structure and meaning of patient-physician discourse. The relevance of particular details will be demonstrated in the analyses.

In reviewing various approaches to the analysis of discourse, I noted a number of problems in the use of standardized coding systems. A particularly serious limitation is its neglect of the structure and organization of naturally occurring talk between speakers. For this reason alone, this method would be inappropriate to the study of medical interviews which, like other forms of human discourse, is both structured and meaningful. Speaking turns are connected both through the forms of utterances, as in question and answer pairs, and by content. The analyses undertaken here are directed to determining the organization of medical interviews with respect to both form and content.

A structural unit of discourse is proposed that appears to be typical and pervasive in such interviews. It consists of a sequential set of three utterances: Physician Question-Patient Response-Physician Assessment/Next Question. The specific features and functions of this unit will be examined. Problems that arise during the interview are discussed in terms of the disruption and repair of this unit. Finally, the ways in which meaning is developed and organized over the course of the interview are documented and shown to be related to this basic structure.

The effort to make theoretical sense of analytical findings is the work of interpretation, referred to here as the third stage of an investigation. This is usually considered the last stage, but I have adopted a distinction made by Silverman and Torode (1980) between interpretation and interruption. The latter will be discussed below. Intepretations, as would be expected, may take many forms, reflecting different theories of language and of social action. All of them, nonetheless, focus primarily on the questions of "what" is done in and through the talk, and "how" it is done. Thus, in their sociolinguistic analysis of a therapeutic interview, Labov and Fanshel (1977) state their interest as the discovery of "what is being done." They conclude that much of the talk of therapy consists of "requests" and "responses to requests." The framework for the analysis of discourse that they develop and apply is, in large part, a set of definitions, rules, and methods for describing, locating, and interpreting the interactional functions of different types of requests and responses.

The analytic question for ethnomethodologists and conversation analysts shifts toward the "how." For any particular instance of a "request," for example, conversation analysts wish to determine how speakers "do the work" of requesting. That is, how do speakers convey to each other their mutual recognition that what their talk is about is "requesting." But more is involved than a shift from "what" to "how." For conversation analysts, forms of requests and general rules of use cannot be specified and listed in a coding manual, as Labov and Fanshel attempt. The contextual embeddedness of speech would make any such manual a poor guide for conversationalists, and for investigators as well. The "how" of discourse for ethnomethodologists concerns the speaker practices through which "requesting" is routinely done, or "accomplished," to use the ethnomethodologists' term, in any context, despite the problem that a formal rule cannot take into account the specific features of particular contexts.[2]

Much of the work of conversation analysts, like that of sociolinguists, is directed to the study of how general tasks of conversation are accomplished, how conversations are initiated and terminated, how turns are taken, how topics are switched, and how mistakes are repaired. All these conversational tasks are "done" in medical interviews, as in all other types of discourse. One aim of the present study is to determine if there are systematic and typical ways in which patients and physicians accomplish these general tasks of a conversation. For example, there are a number of ways in which speakers may ask and answer questions. How is questioning and answering done by patients and physicians?

Linked to this approach is another level of interpretation that represents a more central topic in our inquiry, namely, the nature of clinical work. Our speakers are physicians and patients, and in how they begin their discourse, take their turns, and take leave of each other they are also doing the work of doctoring and patienting. Interpretation of findings on conversational practices is directed to an understanding of how the work of doctoring and patienting is done. For example, the strong tendency for physicians to ask closed- rather than open-ended questions is interpreted as serving the function of maintaining control over the content of the interview. In turn, this assures the dominance of the biomedical model as the perspective within which patients' statements are interpreted and allows doctors to accomplish the "medical" tasks of diagnosis and prescription. At the same time, the fact that their utterances are almost exclusively in the form of questions gives doctors control of the turn-taking system and, consequently, of the structure and organization of the interview. The interpretation of particular discourse practices developed here will refer to both form and content.

Finally, borrowing from Silverman and Torode, I have referred to a second mode, or line of theorizing, as interruption. Of particular relevance to our purpose is Silverman and Torode's notion of "voices." As I understand it, a voice represents a particular assumption about the relationship between appearance, reality, and language, or, more generally, a "voice" represents a specific normative order. Some discourses are closed and continually reaffirm a single normative order; others are open and include different voices, one of which may interrupt another, thus leading to the possibility of a new "order." There are occasions in medical interviews where the normal and routine practice of clinical work appears to be disrupted. In order to understand both the routine, fluent course of the interview as well as its occasional disruption, a distinction will be introduced between the "voices" representing two different normative orders: the "voice of medicine" and the "voice of the lifeworld." Disruptions of the discourse during interviews appear to mark instances where the "voice of the lifeworld" interrupts the dominant "voice of medicine." How this happens, and whether the discourse is then "opened" or remains "closed" will be of major interest in succeeding analyses.

In sum, the principal aim of this chapter is to develop methods for the study of discourse that are informed by considerations of the research tasks of description, analysis, interpretation, and interruption. The methods are applied to a set of unremarkable interviews to bring out more clearly those features that are associated with our intuitive recognition of the interviews as instances of routine, normal, and ordinary clinical practice. After a close look at how these interviews work to produce a sense of normality and appropriateness, stretches of talk between patients and physicians that depart in some way from the normal and typical pattern will be examined. The departures suggest that something has become problematic. The analysis of problem-

atic interviews is undertaken in the context of the findings from analyses of nonproblematic or unremarkable interviews. This will provide an initial set of contrasting features and their functions for use in further analyses that compare the "voice of medicine" with the "voice of the lifeworld."

Unremarkable Medical Interviews

Diagnostic Examination (W:02.014)[3]

The excerpt presented as Transcript 26-1 is taken from the beginning of an interview. Through this opening series of exchanges the patient (P) responds to the physician's (D) questions with a report of her symptoms. After each response, the physician asks for further details or other symptoms with the apparent aim of determining the specific nature of the problem and arriving at a diagnosis. On its surface, their talk proceeds as we would expect in a routine medical interview; it is unremarkable.

The physician initiates the interview with a question that Labov and Fanshel (1977, pp. 88–91) would code as a request for information: "What's the problem." Although its syntactic form is that of an open-ended Wh-question, the physician's voice does not carry question intonation. For that reason, the transcript does not show a question mark. The utterance is a request in the imperative mode, a paraphrase of a statement such as, "Tell me what the problem is." The phrasing of a request for action or information as an imperative is not unusual, and Labov and Fanshel argue that "the imperative is the unmarked form of a request for action" and "the central element in the construction of requests" (pp. 77–78).

In his first turn, the physician has set the general topic of discussion, namely, the patient's "problem." Or, more precisely, the physician's request is mutually understood to be germane and to express their joint recognition of the reason for the patient's presence in this setting: she is here because she has, or believes she has, a medically relevant problem. We, as investigators, knowing that this is a medical interview, are able to "read" the physician's utterance in the same

Transcript 26-1

W:02.014

```
        001 D  What's the problem.
   I                              (Chair noise)
                                        [
        002 P                                (...) had since . last
        003    Monday evening so it's a week of sore throat
        004 D                                      hm hm
        005 P  which turned into a cold .......... uh:m ........
        006    and then a cough.
        007 D              A cold you mean what? Stuffy nose?
        008 P  uh Stuffy nose yeah not a chest ...... cold. ........
                                        [
        009 D                          hm hm
        010 P  uhm
               [
        011 D  And a cough.
        012 P            And a cough .. which is the most irritating
        013    aspect.
               [
   II   014 D  Okay. (hh) uh Any fever?
        015 P                      ...... Not that I know of.
        016    .... I took it a couple of times in the beginning
        017    but . haven't felt like-
                 [
   III  018 D    hm              How bout your ears?
        019 P                                        ........
        020 P  (hh) uhm .... Before anything happened .... I thought
        021    that my ears ...... might have felt a little bit
        022    funny but (....) I haven't got any problem(s).
   IV   023 D                                      Okay.
   IV'  024    ........ (hh) Now this uh cough what are you producing
        025    anything or is it a dry cough?
        026 P                        Mostly dry although
        027    ...... a few days . ago it was more mucusy ....
```

way as the patient does. More than simply expressing a mutual understanding of the situation, his request confirms it and by confirming it contributes to the definition of the situation as a medical interview. It is in this sense that the "fact" that a medical interview is taking place is constructed through discourse. Such a definition of the situation excludes others. It is not a social occasion, a casual conversation, or an exchange of gossip, and we do not find initial greetings, an exchange of names, or other courtesies with which such conversations commonly begin.

```
IV"    028        cause there was more (cold). Now (there's) mostly cough.
                         [                                              [
  V   ┌029  D          hm hm                              What
      │ 030        about the nasal discharge? Any?
      │ 031  P                            ....A little.
      │ 032  D                                    What
      │ 033        color is it?
      │ 034  P              ...... uh:m ........ I don't really know
      │ 035        .... uhm I suppose a whitish- (....)
      │                                    [
      │ 036  D                          hm hm What?
      │ 037  P                                    There's been
      │ 038        nothing on the hankerchief.
      │                       [
 VI   ┌039  D                   hm hm     Okay. .... (hh) Do you have
      │ 040        any pressure around your eyes?
      │ 041  P                            No.
VII   ┌042  D                            Okay. How do you feel?
      │ 043  P  .......... uh:m ........ Tired. heh I couldn-(h)
      │ 044        I couldn't(h) sleep last night(h) uhm
      │                               [
      │ 045  D                            Because of the . cough.
      │                                       [
      │ 046  P                                    Otherwise-
      │ 047        Yup. Otherwise I feel fine.
VIII  ┌048  D                            Alright. Now . have you .
      │ 049        had good health before (generally).
      └050  P                              Yeah . fine.
```

(1'25")

(Their absence must be treated with caution since it may reflect when the tape recorder was turned on).

The patient responds to the physician's request for information; she begins to report her symptoms, when they began, and the change from a sore throat that began a week ago, "which turned into a cold," "and then a cough." As she gives her account, the physician indicates that he is attending to her, understands, and wants her to continue by a go-ahead signal, "hm hm."

As the patient responds to his opening question, the physician requests further clarification and specification: "A cold you mean what? Stuffy nose?" A little later he asks for confirmation of what he heard her say earlier, "And a cough." Through his questions the physician indicates that although he has asked her to talk about the nature of her "problem," the topic remains under his control. That is, his questions define the relevance of particular features in her account. Further, when the patient mentions a cold, sore throat, and cough as her symptoms, the physician suggests additional dimensions and distinctions that may be of medical relevance that the patient has neglected to report. Thus, a "cold" is not a sufficient description for his purpose; he must know what is "meant" by a cold and what kind of cold it is, "Stuffy nose?" The patient recognizes that there are at least two kinds, nose colds and chest colds, and introduces this contrast pair in order to specify her own: "uh stuffy nose yeah not a chest . . . cold."

The physician acknowledges her distinction, "hm hm," and adds to it the other symptom she has mentioned, "And a cough." The patient reconfirms his addition and goes on to give this symptom particular emphasis: "And a cough . . . which is the most irritating aspect." The physician's "Okay," inserted to overlap with the end of the patient's utterance, terminates the first cycle of the interview. He acknowledges the adequacy of the patient's response to his opening question, "What's the problem," and his "Okay" serves to close this section of the interview; no more is to be said about the problem in general and he will now proceed with more specific questions.

The first cycle is marked on the transcript by a bracket enclosing utterances 001–014 under Roman Numeral I. Its basic structure may be outlined as consisting of: a request/question from the physician, a response from the patient, and a post-response assessment/acknowledgment by the physician, to which is added a new request/question to begin the next cycle. The remainder of the excerpt is made up of seven additional cycles with structures identical to the first one. The first six cycles focus on the "cold" symptoms, the last two open with more general questions.

There are two variants within the basic structure. In the first type, the basic structure is expanded internally by requests from the physician for clarification or elaboration of the patient's response; this occurs in the first, fifth, and seventh cycles. In the second variant, the physician's assessments are implicit. Although his post-response assessments are usually explicit (an "Okay" or "Alright" comment), there are occasions when they are implicitly conveyed by the physician proceeding immediately to a next question. Alternatively, his assessment may occur before the patient's completion of her utterance through an overlapping "hm hm"; this occurs in the linkage between cycles IV and V.

This three-part utterance sequence is a regular and routine occurrence in the talk between pa-

tients and physicians. For that reason, I will refer to it as the basic structural unit of discourse in medical interviews. We recognize and accept interviews with these structures as normal, standard, and appropriate—as unremarkable. The medical interview tends to be constituted, overwhelmingly, by a connected series of such structural units. They are linked together through the physician's post-response assessment utterance that serves the dual function of closing the previous cycle and initiating a new one through his next question.

I do not mean to imply that this structure is unique to medical interviews, although it is one of their distinctive features. The same general type of structure appears in other settings of interaction where the aim is assessment, diagnosis, or selection, that is, when one person has the task of eliciting information from another. Thus, the same three-utterance sequence initiated by questions is found in classroom exchanges between teachers and pupils, although these are not interviews and teachers may direct successive questions to different pupils.[4] We might also expect to find it in psychological test situations and personnel interviews. Further work would be needed to determine how these discourses with similar general structures differed in their particular features.

Since I am proposing that this discourse structure is the basic unit of the medical interview and that its pervasive presence in a linked series is what makes this interview unremarkable, it is important to look more closely at how it is constructed and how it functions. The first and most obvious impression is of the physician's strong and consistent control over the content and development of the interview. . . . Here, I am trying to show how physicians exercise control through the structure of their exchanges with patients in the course of an interview.

There are a number of ways in which the physician uses his position as a speaker in this structure to control the interview: he opens each cycle of discourse with his response/question; he assesses the adequacy of the patient's response; he closes each cycle by using his assessment as a terminating marker; he opens the next cycle by another request/question. Through this pattern of opening and terminating cycles the physician controls the turn-taking process; he decides when the patient should take her turn. He also controls the content of what is to be discussed by selectively attending and responding to certain parts of the patient's statements and by initiating each new topic.

The physician's control of content through the initiation of new topics is particularly evident. After the first cycle in which the patient introduces her problem, there are seven new topics, each introduced by the physician through a question that opens a new cycle. In sequence, the physician asks the patient about: presence of fever, ear problems, type of cough, presence and type of nasal discharge, pressure around her eyes, how she feels, and her general state of health. The list is hardly worth noticing; these are the questions we might expect a physician to ask if a patient reports having a sore throat and a cold. The fit between our expectations and the interview is very close, which is why I have referred to it as an unremarkable interview.

We may learn more, however, about the significance and functions of the physician's control if we examine how his questions not only focus on certain topics, but are selectively inattentive to others. Through the questions he asks the physician constructs and specifies a domain of relevance; in Paolo Freire's phrase, he is "naming the world," the world of relevant matters for him and the patient (Freire, 1968).[5] The topics that the patient introduces, all of which are explicit, but not attended to by the physician, are: the history and course of her symptoms, and the effects they have had on her life—that the cough is the most irritating aspect, that she's tired and has had a sleepless night. Both of these latter topics, opened up by the patient but not pursued by the physician, bear on a question that remains unasked but whose potential "relevance" is close to the surface: why she has come to see the physician at this point even though the problem began a week before.

In summary, this analysis shows that the physician controls the content of the interview, both through his initiation of new topics and through what he attends to and ignores in the patient's reports. Further, there is a systematic bias to his focus of attention; the patient's reports of how the problem developed and how it affects her—the "life contexts" of her symptoms—are systematically ignored. The physician directs his attention solely to physical-medical signs that might be associated with her primary symptoms, such as ear or eye problems, or to the further physical specification of a symptom, such as type of cough or color of nasal discharge. . . .

. . . We may now move beyond this level of interpretation to the stage referred to earlier as "interruption." The particular patterning of form and content shown in the analysis documents and defines the interview as "unremarkable," a characterization that was made on intuitive grounds. The clear pattern suggests that the discourse expresses a particular "voice," to use Silverman and Torode's (1980) term. Since the interview is dominated by the physician, I will refer to this as the "voice of medicine."

The topic introduced by the patient in VII, her tiredness and difficulty sleeping, is in another voice; I will call it the "voice of the lifeworld." It is an interruption, or an attempted interruption, of the ongoing discourse being carried on in the "voice of medicine." It is of some interest that the patient's introduction of another voice occurs in response to the open-ended question: "How do you feel?" Except for his initial question, this is the only open-ended question asked by the physician in this excerpt. In this instance, the second voice is suppressed; it does not lead to an opening of the discourse into a fuller and more mutual dialogue between the two voices. Rather, the physician reasserts the dominance of the voice of medicine through his response: "Because of the cough." Interruptions of the discourse and their effects will receive further attention in the following analyses.

It is instructive to examine in some detail the patterns of pauses and hesitations in the respective utterances of physician and patient. The findings of this analysis that pauses are not randomly distributed, but located systematically at certain points, particularly in the transitions between speakers, reinforces the argument made earlier about the importance of including such details of speech in transcripts. If we look at the cycle transition points (that is, from I–II, II–III, etc., that the physician controls through his utterance with a dual function—terminating the previous cycle with a post-response assessment and initiating the new cycle with a question), we find a relatively consistent pattern. The physician either breaks into the patient's statement before she has completed it, thus terminating her statement with his own comment—an "Okay" or "hm hm"—as in I–II, II–III, IV–V, and V–VI, or he takes his next turn without pause as soon as the patient finishes, as in III–IV, VI–VII, and VII–VIII. Often, the assessment-terminating part of his utterance is followed by a pause, filled or unfilled, before the question that begins the next cycle, as in the utterances marking the beginnings of cycles II, III, IV, and VI.

. . . Findings from this analysis of one "unremarkable" interview will be summarized at this point. They provide a characterization, albeit tentative and preliminary, of normal and routine clinical practice, and can be used as a framework for comparing and contrasting analyses of other interviews.

First, the basic structural unit of a medical interview is a linked set of three utterances: a physician's opening question, a patient's response, and the physician's response to the patient which usually, but not always, begins with an assessment followed by a second question. The second utterance of the physician serves the dual function of terminating the first unit, or cycle, and initiating the next. In this way, the separate units are connected together to form the continuous discourse of the interview.

The primary discourse function of the basic structure is that it permits the physician to control the development of the interview. His control is assured by his position as both first and last speaker in each cycle, which allows him to control the turn-taking system and the sequential organization of the interview. This structure of dominance is reinforced by the content of the physician's assessments and questions that he asks, which selectively attend to or ignore particulars of the patient's responses. The physician's dominance is expressed at still another level through the syntactic structure of his questions. These tend to be restrictive closed-end questions, which limit the range of relevance for patient responses. At all these levels, the focus of relevance, that is, of appropriate meaning, is on medically relevant material, as is defined by the physician.

Within utterances, two patterns of pauses were identified that are consistent with the overall structure and its functions. Typically, in physician utterances there is a pause between the assessment and the next question. This serves to mark the termination of the prior unit and the initiation of the next one. The length of initial pauses in patient responses appears to depend on the location of a cycle within a sequence of cycles. Patient utterances in the first cycle of a series are preceded by a short pause, in the second cycle by a long pause, and in the third cycle by no pause. This seems to be related to the degree of disjunction between successive physician questions and whether or not he "helps" the patient prepare for a response by making his next question relevant to her prior response.

Finally, all the features and functions of this unit of discourse have been brought together under a general analytic category referred to as the "voice of medicine." The physician's control of the interview through the structure of turn-taking and through the form and content of his questions expresses the normative order of medicine. The dominance of this voice produces our intuitive impression of the interview as an instance of normal clinical practice, that is, as unremarkable. Patients may attempt to interrupt the dominant voice by speaking in the "voice of the lifeworld." This alternative voice may be suppressed, as it was in this interview, or may open up the interview to a fuller dialogue between voices. Relationships between the two voices will be explored further. . . .

. . . .

The Interruption of Clinical Discourse
. . . .

The structure of clinical discourse has been explicated through analyses of two unremarkable interviews. The basic three-part unit of such discourse and the ways in which these units are linked together has been described, as well as the functions served by this structure—the physician's control of organization and meaning. I referred to this patterned relationship between structure and function as the "voice of medicine," and suggested that it expressed the normative order of medicine and clinical practice. This voice provides a baseline against which to compare other medical interviews that depart in some way from normal and routine practice.

Some preliminary comparisons have already been made. In each of these unremarkable interviews the patient interrupted the flow of the discourse by introducing the "voice of the lifeworld." In both instances, the new voice was quickly silenced and the physician reasserted his dominance and the singularity of the clinical perspective. In the following interview, the patient makes more of an effort to sustain an alternative voice. Examining how the patient does this and how the physician responds will extend our understanding of the specific features and functions of medical interviews and will also alert us to problems that develop when there are departures from normal and routine clinical work. This discussion will also bring forward an issue that will be central to later analyses; the struggle between the voices of medicine and of the lifeworld.

Symptom and Lifeworld Context: Negotiation of Meaning (W: 13.121/01)

The patient is a 26-year-old woman with stomach pains, which she describes as a sour stomach beginning several weeks prior to this medical visit. The excerpt (Transcript 26-2) begins about 3½ minutes into the interview, preceded by a review of her history of peptic ulcers in childhood and the time and circumstances of the present complaint.

In the excerpt, the first four cycles and the beginning of the fifth are similar in structure to the interviews analyzed earlier. Each one begins with the physician's question about the symptom. This is followed by a response from the patient, sometimes preceded by a pause, and is terminated by the physician's next question. His question is sometimes preceded by an assessment, which then initiates the next cycle.

Two other features of the first four cycles may be noted. Although there are occasional pauses prior to the patient's responses and some false starts as she appears to search for an appropriate answer, there are few within-utterance pauses and those that occur are of short duration. For the physician, the pattern found earlier of a pause between assessment and question is occasionally present, but there are no false starts or pauses between the patient's responses and the physician's next questions. Again, there is a high degree of fluency in his speech.

The routine breaks down in cycle V. The patient's response to the physician's question with its false start includes a signal of trouble: "How- How soon after you eat it?" The patient's response is preceded by her longest pre-utterance pause (one of 2.5″), and contains two relatively long intra-utterance pauses. A major change comes in her next response, after restating her previous answer, "Maybe less," in response to his clarification question: "About an hour?" This physician question is treated as an internal expansion within V, although it might also be considered as beginning a new cycle, V′. Her answer, "Maybe less," is followed by a moderately long intra-utterance pause of 1.2″, after which she introduces a new topic, her drinking.

This new topic comes in the form of a "tag" comment added to her answer to the physician's question and it has some features that mark it as different from what has previously been said. ". . . I've cheated and I've been drinking which I shouldn't have done," has a quality of intonation that is unusual when compared with her earlier responses. Those who have heard the tape recording easily recognize the difference and describe her speech as "teasing," "flirtatious," or "childish."

The physician's next question, which terminates V and initiates VI, is preceded by his first long pre-question hesitation: ". . . Does drinking make it worse?" This is the first break in the fluency of his pattern of questioning. Further, he talks over the patient's attempt to say something more. His uncertainty, indicated by his pause, reflects two changes in the nature of the interview. The patient's comment introduces her drinking and, since this new topic is not in response to a direct question from the physician, it also shifts the control of the interview from physician to patient. I pointed out in earlier analyses that the basic structure of the medical interview, physician question-patient response-physician (assessment) question, permits the physician to control the form and content of the

Transcript 26-2

W:13.121/01

```
    ┌001 D  Hm hm .... Now what do you mean by a sour stomach?
I   │002 P  ................. What's a sour stomach? A heartburn
    │003    like a heartburn or something.
    └                                  [
    ┌004 D                             Does it burn over here?
II  │005 P                                                   Yea:h.
    │006    It li- I think- I think it like- If you take a needle
    │007    and stick ya right .... there's a pain right here ..
    │                 [          [                      [
    │008 D           Hm hm Hm hm              Hm hm
    └009 P  and and then it goes from here on this side to this side.
    ┌010 D  Hm hm Does it go into the back?
III │                         [
    │011 P          It's a:ll up here. No. It's all right
    │012    up here in the front.
    └               [
    ┌013 D  Yeah          And when do you get that?
IV  │014 P                                         .......
    │015    .......... Wel:l when I eat something wrong.
    ┌016 D                                    How- How
V   │017    soon after you eat it?
V'  │018 P            ....................... Wel:l
    │019    ...... probably an hour .... maybe less.
    │                                [
    ┌020 D                           About an hour?
V"  │021 P  Maybe less ............ I've cheated and I've been
    │022    drinking which I shouldn't have done.
    └023 D                                          ..........
    ┌024    Does drinking making it worse?
VI  │                [
    │025 P  (...)                         Ho ho uh ooh Yes. ....
    │026    ...... Especially the carbonation and the alcohol.
    ┌027 D  ........ Hm hm ........ How much do you drink?
VII │028 P                                               ......
VII'│029    ............... I don't know. .. Enough to make me
```

```
        ┌ 030      go to sleep at night ........ and that's quite a bit.
        │ 031 D    One or two drinks a day?
  VII"  │ 032 P                        O:h no no no humph it's (more
        │ 033      like) ten. ...... at night.
        │                    [
        │ 034 D            How many drinks- a night.
        │ 035 P                                At night.
        └ 036 D                                          .....
          037      ..... Whaddya ta- What type of drinks? .... I (...)-
 VIII  ┌                                                    [
       │  038 P                                          Oh vodka
       │  039      .. yeah vodka and ginger ale.
       └  040 D                        ........................
  IX    ┌ 041      ...... How long have you been drinking that heavily?
  IX'   ┌ 042 P    ................... Since I've been married.
        │ 043 D                                    ......
  IX"   └ 044      .. How long is that?
        ┌ 045 P                    (giggle..) Four years. (giggle)
        │ 046      huh Well I started out with before then I was drinkin
        │ 047      beer but u:m I had a job and I was .... ya know ......
        │ 048      had more things on my mind and ya know I like- but
        │ 049      since I got married I been in and out of jobs and
        │ 050      everything so ........ I- I have ta have something to
        │ 051      go to sleep.
        │ 052 D           ...... Hm:m.
        │ 053 P                          ............ I mean I'm not
        │ 054      gonna- ...... It's either gonna be pills or it's
        │ 055      gonna be .. alcohol ............ and uh alcohol seems
        │ 056      to satisfy me moren than pills do .... They don't
        │ 057      seem to get strong enough ........ pills that I have
        │ 058      got I had- I do have Valium .... but they're two
        │ 059      milligrams ................. and that's supposed to
        │ 060      quiet me down during the day but it doesn't.
        └ 061 D                                          ......
   X    ┌ 062      How often do you take them?
        ┌              (1'47")
```

interview. As the "questioner," the physician controls the turn-taking structure and through the focus of his assessments and questions controls the development of meaning; he defines what is and what is not relevant. By her tag comment, the patient has taken control both of form and meaning; she has introduced another voice.

With this tentative hypothesis that the normal structure of the medical interview has been interrupted and that as a result, the normal pattern of control has also been disrupted, we might expect to find evidence of: (a) other indicators of disruption and breakdown in the continuing exchange, and (b) efforts on the part of the physician to repair the disruption, to restore the normal structure, and to reassert the dominant voice of medicine.

The physician's pre-question hesitation after the patient introduces the new topic has already been noted as a sign of disruption, a change from his usual response timing: ". . . Does drinking make it worse?" Similar and frequently longer pauses appear before all of his succeeding questions initiating new cycles at VII, VIII, IX, and X. The regularity of these pauses is quite striking, particularly when it is contrasted with the equally striking occurrence of no pauses preceding questions in cycles with a normal structure (I–IV).

Throughout the second half of this excerpt, from cycles VI–X, there is a continuing struggle between physician and patient to take control of the interview. The patient tries to maintain her control by restatements of the problem of drinking in her life situation exemplifying the voice of the lifeworld. The physician, on the other, persistently tries to reformulate the problem in narrower, more medically-relevant terms. For example, to his question, "How much do you drink?" (the transition between cycles VI and VII), she replies, after a long pause of 2.2″, "I don't know . . . Enough to make me go to sleep at night . . . and that's quite a bit." He persists with two further questions, within cycle VII, requesting the specific number of drinks. In this manner, the physician attempts to recapture control of the meaning of her account; he is excluding her meaning of the function of drinking in her life and focusing on "objective" measures of quantity.

The physician persists in this effort. To his question about how long she has been drinking heavily (IX), she responds, "Since I've been married," again preceding her response with a long pause. But this is not considered an adequate or relevant answer from the physician's point of view and he asks for an actual, objective time, "How long is that?" Finally, in a relatively extended account in cycle IX, the patient talks about her drinking, of problems since her marriage, and her preference for alcohol over pills. There is much surplus information in her story to which the physician might respond. He chooses to attend selectively to that part of her account which is of clear medical relevance, the taking of pills, and asks again for a precise, objective, and quantitative answer. "How often do you take them?"

Another way to indicate that a significant change has taken place in the structure of the interview during the fifth cycle is to take note of the difficulty encountered in attempting to describe this interview in terms of the structural units found in the analyses of the first two interviews. Although I have marked the cycles of the interview in the same way, distinguishing such successive series of physician question-patient response-physician (assessment) question exchanges, there are problems in using this unit here. This structural unit assumes that an exchange is initiated by the physician's question and that the three-part exchange cycle is then terminated by the physician as he initiates the next cycle.

The problem may be seen in cycle V, at the point of the patient's comment about her drinking. This statement is not in response to a direct question; rather it is a statement introducing a new topic. The physician's next question refers to this new topic and he thus remains "in role." The reader will note that all of the physician's statements, except for his "Hm" assessments, are questions. The implicit function of questions remains which is to control the form and content of the interview, however in this instance there is a break in the continuity of the physician's control. As an alternative structure to the one presented, we could ask whether a new cycle should begin with the patient's tag comment. If that were done, the physician's next question would be treated as a "response" to her statement, even though it is framed as a question. I'm not proposing an answer to the problem of structural analysis at this preliminary stage. However, I am suggesting that the change in the interview resulting from the patient's comment introduces problems for analysis. These problems provide another line of evidence for the assertion that there has been a breakdown in the normal structure of the clinical interview. . . .

. . . In this discussion, I have been using the occurrence of a noticeable change in the structure and flow of an interview to raise questions about how to analyze and understand the workings of medical interviews. The introduction of a new topic by the patient altered the routine pattern of the interview found in earlier "unremarkable" interviews. The features of physician and patient utterances varied in specific ways from those found earlier. These changes raised questions about which speaker was controlling the development of the interview, and hence controlling the development of meaning. The idea of "voices," and the distinction between the "voice of medicine" and the "voice of the lifeworld," was introduced to characterize alternative orders of meaning and the struggle between them. . . .

NOTES

1. Waitzkin and Stoeckle's original corpus of nearly 500 interviews included a stratified random sample of physicians in private and clinic sessions in Boston and Oakland. For the present study, a small series of about twenty-five tapes was selected initially from the larger sample. Male and female patients were equally represented in the series, and both single and multiple interviews of a patient with the same physician were included. The original tapes were sequentially ordered by code numbers assigned to physicians and each of their successive patients. The selection procedure was to choose the "next" code number in the sequence where the interview met the criteria noted above until the cells were filled. Although this was not a random sampling procedure it ensured heterogeneity among the interviews and there was no reason to believe that the series was biased in a systematic way with reference to the original sample. The analyses presented here are based on a small number of interviews drawn from this series. Further, analyses are restricted to brief excerpts from the full interviews which exemplify issues of primary theoretical interest. This description of the procedure is intended to clarify the grounds on which the claim is made that the interviews examined in this study are "typical" medical interviews. This claim does not rely on statistical criteria or rules for selecting a "representative" sample. Rather, it rests on a shared understanding and recognition of these interviews as "representative," that is, as displays of normatively appropriate talk between patients and physicians.

2. Examples of these studies may be found in Schenkein (1978); and in Psathas (1979). A perceptive discussion of the way that ethnomethodology approaches the study of talk, and some of its unresolved problems, is found in Wooton (1975).

3. The typescript numbers used here are the codes on the tapes assigned by Waitzkin and Stoekle; the number is preceded by a "W" to indicate the source.

4. In earlier studies of classroom interaction, I referred to the set of three utterances initiated by a question as an Interrogative Unit. Connections between units through the dual function of the second question were called Chaining (see Mishler 1975a, 1975b, 1978).

5. Another example of the ways in which a physician's selectivity of attention and inattention, through his pattern of questioning, shapes the development of meaning in a medical interview may be found in Paget (1983).

27

Some Contingencies of the
Moral Evaluation and Control of Clientele:
The Case of the Hospital Emergency Service

■ ■ ■ ■ ■ ■

Julius A. Roth

The moral evaluation of patients by staff members has been explored in detail in the case of "mental illness" (Scheff 1966, chap. 5; Strauss et al. 1964, chaps. 8 and 12; Belknap 1956; Scheff 1964; Goffman 1961, pp. 125–70, 321–86; Hollingshead and Redlich 1958; Szasz 1960). The assumption is made by some (especially Thomas Szasz) that mental illness is a special case which readily allows moral judgments to be made because there are no technical criteria to be applied and because psychiatric concepts in their historical development have been a pseudoscientific replacement of moral judgments. Charles Perrow (1965) stresses lack of technology as a factor which forces psychiatric practitioners to fall back on commonsense concepts of humanitarianism which open the way to moral evaluations of the clientele.

I contend that the diagnosis and treatment of mental illness and the "care" of mental patients are not unique in incorporating moral judgments of the clientele, but are only obvious examples of a more general phenomenon which exists no matter what the historical development or the present state of the technology. Glaser and Strauss (1964) put forward such a notion when they demonstrated how the "social worth" of a dying patient affects the nursing care he will receive. I would add that moral evaluation also has a direct effect on a physician's diagnosis and treatment recommendations. This is obvious in extreme cases, such as when a monarch or the

president of the United States is attended by teams of highly qualified diagnosticians to insure a detailed and accurate diagnosis and has outstanding specialists flown to his bedside to carry out the treatment. I will discuss some aspects of this same process as it applies on a day-to-day basis in a routine hospital operation involving more "ordinary" patients.

The data are taken from observations of six hospital emergency services in two parts of the country—one northeastern location and one West Coast location. My co-workers and I spent several periods of time (spread over two or three months in each case) in the emergency department of each of the hospitals. In one hospital we worked as intake clerks over a period of three months. At other times we observed areas in the emergency unit without initiating any interaction with patients, visitors, or personnel. At other points we followed patients through the emergency service from their first appearance to discharge or inpatient admission, interviewing patient and staff during the process. During these periods of observation, notes were also kept on relevant conversations with staff members.

The hospital emergency service is a setting where a minimum of information is available about the character of each patient and a long-term relationship with the patient is usually not contemplated. Even under these conditions, judgments about a patient's moral fitness and the appropriateness of his visit to an emergency service are constantly made, and staff action concerning the patient—including diagnosis, treatment, and disposition of the case—are, in part, affected by these judgments.

The Deserving and the Undeserving

The evaluation of patients and visitors by emergency-ward staff may be conveniently thought of in two categories: (1) The application by the staff of concepts of social worth common in the larger society. (2) Staff members' concepts of their appropriate work role. In this section I will take up the first of these.

There is a popular myth (generated in part by some sociological writing) that persons engaged in providing professional services, especially medical care, do not permit the commonly accepted concepts of social worth in our culture to affect their relationship to the clientele. An on-the-spot description of *any* service profession—medicine, education, law, social welfare, etc.—should disabuse us of this notion. There is no evidence that professional training succeeds in creating a universalistic moral neutrality (Becker et al. 1961, pp. 323–27). On the contrary, we are on much safer ground to assume that those engaged in dispensing professional services (or any other services) will apply the evaluations of social worth common to their culture and will modify their services with respect to those evaluations *unless discouraged from doing so by the organizational arrangements under which they work*. Some such organizational arrangements do exist on emergency wards. The rapid turnover and impersonality of the operation is in itself a protection for many patients who might be devalued if more were known about them. In public hospitals, at least, there is a rule that *all* patients presenting themselves at the registration desk must be seen by a doctor, and clerks and nurses know that violation of this rule, if discovered, can get them into serious trouble. (Despite this, patients are occasionally refused registration, usually because they are morally repugnant to the clerk.) Such arrangements restrict the behavior of the staff only to a limited extent, however. There remains a great deal of

room for expressing one's valuation of the patient in the details of processing and treatment.

One common concept of social worth held by emergency-ward personnel is that the young are more valuable than the old. This is exemplified most dramatically in the marked differences in efforts to resuscitate young and old patients (Glaser and Strauss 1964; Sudnow 1967, pp. 100–109). "Welfare cases" who are sponging off the taxpayer—especially if they represent the product of an immoral life (such as a woman with illegitimate children to support)—do not deserve the best care. Persons of higher status in the larger society are likely to be accorded more respectful treatment in the emergency ward just as they often are in other service or customer relationships, and conversely those of lower status are treated with less consideration. (The fact that higher-status persons are more likely to make an effective complaint or even file lawsuits may be an additional reason for such differential treatment.)

Of course, staff members vary in the manner and degree to which they apply these cultural concepts of social worth in determining the quality of their service to the clientele. The point is that they are in a position to alter the nature of their service in terms of such differentiation, and all of them—porters, clerks, nursing personnel, physicians—do so to some extent. Despite some variations, we did in fact find widespread agreement on the negative evaluation of some categories of patients—evaluations which directly affected the treatment provided. Those who are the first to process a patient play a crucial role in moral categorization because staff members at later stages of the processing are inclined to accept earlier categories without question unless they detect clear-cut evidence to the contrary. Thus, registration clerks can often determine how long a person will have to wait and what kind of treatment area he is sent to, and, occasionally, can even prevent a person from seeing a doctor at all. Some patients have been morally categorized by policemen or ambulance crewmen before they even arrive at the hospital—categorization which affects the priority and kind of service given.

In the public urban hospital emergency service, the clientele is heavily skewed toward the lower end of the socioeconomic scale, and nonwhite and non-Anglo ethnic groups are greatly overrepresented. Also, many patients are in the position of supplicating the staff for help, sometimes for a condition for which the patient can be held responsible. With such a population, the staff can readily maintain a stance of moral superiority. They see the bulk of the patients as people undeserving of the services available to them. Staff members maintain that they need not tolerate any abuse or disobedience from patients or visitors. Patients and visitors may be issued orders which they are expected to obey. The staff can, and sometimes does, shout down patients and visitors and threaten them with ejection from the premises. The staff demands protection against possible attack and also against the possibility of lawsuits, which are invariably classified as unjustified. There is no need to be polite to the clientele and, in fact, some clerks frequently engage patients and visitors in arguments. The staff also feels justified in refusing service to those who complain or resist treatment or refuse to follow procedures or make trouble in any other way. From time to time the clients are referred to as "garbage," "scum," "liars," "deadbeats," people who "come out from under the rocks," by doctors, nurses, aides, clerks, and even housekeepers who sweep the floor. When we spent the first several days of a new medical year with a new group of interns on one emergency service, we found that an important part of the orientation was directed toward telling the interns that the patients were not to be trusted and did not have to be treated politely. At another public hospital, new registration clerks were told during their first few days of work that they would have to learn not to accept the word of patients but to treat everything they say with suspicion.

Despite the general negative conception of the clientele, differentiations are made between patients on the basis of clues which they present. Since this is typically a fleeting relationship where the staff member has little or no background information about the patient, evaluations must usually be made quickly on the basis of readily perceivable clues. Race, age, mode of dress, language and accents and word usage, and the manner in which the client addresses and responds to staff members are all immediate clues on which staff base their initial evaluations. A little questioning brings out other information which may be used for or against a patient: financial status, type of employment, insurance protection, use of private-practice doctors, nature of medical complaint, legitimacy of children, marital status, previous use of hospital services. In the case of unconscious or seriously ill or injured patients, a search of the wallet or handbag often provides informative clues about social worth.

Some characteristics consistently turn staff against patients and affect the quality of care given. Dirty, smelly patients cause considerable comment among the staff, and efforts are made to isolate them or get rid of them. Those dresssed as hippies or women with scanty clothing (unless there is a "good excuse," e.g., a woman drowned while swimming) are frowned upon and are more likely to be kept waiting and to be rushed through when they *are* attended to. We observed hints that certain ethnic groups are discriminated against, but this is difficult to detect nowadays because everyone is extremely sensitive to the possibility of accusations of racial discrimination. If a woman with a child is tabbed a "welfare case" (from her dress, speech, and manner, or in the explicit form of a welfare card which she presents), the clerk is likely to ask, "Is there a father in the house?" while better-dressed, better-spoken women with children are questioned more discreetly.

Attributes and Categories: A Reciprocal Relationship

On one level, it is true to say that the staff's moral evaluation of a patient influences the kind of treatment he gets in the emergency room. But this kind of causal explanation obscures important aspects of the network of interrelationships involved. On another, the definition of devalued or favored categories and the attributes of the patient reinforce each other in a reciprocal manner.

Take, for example, patients who are labeled as drunks. They are more consistently treated as undeserving than any other category of patient. They are frequently handled as if they were baggage when they are brought in by police; those with lacerations are often roughly treated by physicians; they are usually treated only for drunkenness and obvious surgical repair without being examined for other pathology; no one believes their stories; their statements are ridiculed; they are treated in an abusive or jocular manner; they are ignored for long periods of time; in one hospital they are placed in a room separate from most other patients. Emergency-ward personnel frequently comment on how they hate to take care of drunks.

Thus, it might seem that the staff is applying a simple moral syllogism: drunks do not deserve to be cared for, this patient is drunk, therefore, he does not deserve good treatment. *But* how do we know that he is a drunk? By the way he is treated. Police take him directly to the drunk room. If we ask why the police define him as drunk, they may answer that they smell alcohol on his breath. But not all people with alcohol on their breath are picked up by the police and taken to a hospital emergency room. The explanation must come in terms of some part of the patient's background— he was in a lower-class neighborhood, his style of dress was dirty and sloppy, he was unattended by any friend or family member, and so on. When he comes to the emergency room *he has already been defined as a drunk.* There is no reason for the emergency-room personnel to challenge this definition—it is routine procedure and it usually proves correct insofar as they know. There is nothing to do for drunks except to give them routine medications and let them sleep it off. To avoid upsetting the rest of the emergency room, there is a room set aside for them. The police have a standard procedure of taking drunks to that room, and the clerks place them there if they come in on their own and are defined as drunk on the basis, not only of their breath odor (and occasionally there is no breath odor in someone defined as drunk), but in terms of their dress, manner, and absence of protectors. The physicians, having more pressing matters, tend to leave the drunks until last. Of course, they may miss some pathology which could cause unconsciousness or confusion because they believe the standard proves correct in the great majority of cases. They really do not know *how* often it does not prove correct since they do not check up closely

enough to uncover other forms of pathology in most cases, and the low social status of the patients and the fact that they are seldom accompanied by anyone who will protect them means that complaints about inadequate examination will be rare. There *are* occasional challenges by doctors—"How do you know he's drunk?"—but in most cases the busy schedule of the house officer leaves little time for such luxuries as a careful examination of patients who have already been defined as drunks by others. Once the drunk label has been accepted by the emergency-room staff, a more careful examination is not likely to be made unless some particularly arresting new information appears (for example, the patient has convulsions, a relative appears to tell them that he has diabetes, an examination of his wallet shows him to be a solid citizen), and the more subtle pathologies are not likely to be discovered.

Thus, it is just as true to say that the *label* of "drunk" is accepted by hospital personnel because of the way the patient is treated as it is to say that he is treated in a certain way because he is drunk. Occasional cases show how persons with alcohol on their breath will not be treated as drunks. When an obviously middle-class man (obvious in terms of his dress, speech, and demands for service) was brought in after an automobile accident, he was not put in the drunk room, although he had a definite alcohol odor, but was given relatively quick treatment in one of the other examining rooms and addressed throughout in a polite manner.

Most drunks are men. A common negative evaluation for women is PID (pelvic inflammatory disease). This is not just a medical diagnostic category, but, by implication, a moral judgment. There are many women with difficult-to-diagnose abdominal pains and fever. If they are Negro, young, unmarried, lower class in appearance and speech, and have no one along to champion their cause, doctors frequently make the assumption that they have before them the end results of a dissolute sex life, unwanted pregnancy and perhaps venereal disease, illegal abortion, and consequent infection of the reproductive organs. The label PID is then attached and the patient relegated to a group less deserving of prompt and considerate treatment. This is *not* the same thing as saying a diagnosis of PID leads to rejection by medical personnel.

We observed one patient who had been defined as a troublemaker because of his abusive language and his insistence that he be released immediately. When he began to behave in a strange manner (random thrashing about), the police were promptly called to control him and they threatened him with arrest. A patient who was not defined as a troublemaker and exhibited like behavior prompted an effort on the part of the staff to provide a medical explanation for his actions. Here again, we see that the category into which the patient has been placed may have more effect on determining the decisions of medical personnel than does his immediate behavior.

Thus, it is not simply a matter of finding which "objective" pathological states medical personnel like or dislike dealing with. The very definition of these pathological states depends in part on how the patient is categorized in moral terms by the screening and treatment personnel.

The Legitimate and the Illegitimate

The second type of evaluation is that related to the staff members' concept of their appropriate work roles (Strauss et al. 1964, chap. 13). Every worker has a notion of what demands are appropriate to his position. When demands fall outside that boundary, he feels that the claim is illegitimate. What he does about it depends on a number of factors, including his alternatives, his power to control the behavior of others, and his power to select his clientele (more on this later).

Interns and residents who usually man the larger urban emergency services like to think of this assignment as a part of their training which will give them a kind of experience different from the outpatient department or inpatient wards. Here they hope to get some practice in resuscitation, in treating traumatic injuries, in diagnosing and treating medical emergencies. When patients who are no different from those they have seen *ad nauseam* in the outpatient department present themselves at the emergency ward, the doctors in training believe that their services are being misused. Also, once on the emergency ward, the patient is expected to be "cooperative" so that the doctor is not blocked in his effort to carry out his tasks. Nurses, clerks, and others play "little doctor" and to this extent share the concepts of the boundaries of legitimacy of the doctors. But, in addition to the broadly shared perspective, each work specialty has its own notions of appropriate patient attributes and behavior based on their own work demands. Thus, clerks expect patients to cooperate in getting forms filled out. Patients with a "good reason," unconsciousness, for example, are excused from cooperating with clerical procedures, but other patients who are unable to give requested information or who protest against certain questions bring upon themselves condemnation by the clerks who believe that a person who subverts their efforts to complete their tasks has no business on the emergency ward.

A universal complaint among those who operate emergency services is that hospital emergency rooms are "abused" by the public—or rather by a portion of the public. This is particularly the case in the city and county hospitals and voluntary hospitals with training programs subsidized by public funds which handle the bulk of emergency cases in urban areas. The great majority of cases are thought of as too minor or lacking in urgency to warrant a visit to the emergency room. They are "outpatient cases" (OPD cases), that is, patients who could wait until the outpatient department is open, or if they can afford private care, they could wait until a physician is holding his regular office hours. Patients should not use the emergency room just because it gives quicker service than the outpatient department or because the hours are more convenient (since it is open all the time). Pediatricians complain about their day filled with "sore throats and snotty noses." Medical interns and residents complain about all the people presenting longstanding or chronic diseases which, though sometimes serious, do not belong in the emergency room. In every hospital—both public and private—where we made observations or conducted interviews, we repeatedly heard the same kinds of "atrocity stories": a patient with a sore throat of two-weeks' duration comes in at 3:00 A.M. on Sunday and expects immediate treatment from an intern whom he has got out of bed (or such variations as an itch of 75-days' duration, a congenital defect in a one-year-old child—always coming in at an extremely inconvenient hour).

Directors of emergency services recognize that some of their preoccupation with cases which are not "true emergencies" is not simply a matter of "abuse" by patients, but the result of tasks imposed upon them by other agencies—for example, giving routine antibiotic injections on weekends, caring for abandoned children, giving routine blood transfusions, receiving inpatient admissions, giving gamma globulin, providing venereal disease follow-up, examining jail prisoners, arranging nursing-home dispositions for the aged. But the blame for most of their difficulty is placed upon the self-referred patient who, according to the emergency-room staff, does not make appropriate use of their service.

The OPD case typically gets hurried, routine processing with little effort at a careful diagnostic work-up or sophisticated treatment unless he happens to strike the doctor as an interesting case (in which case he is no longer classified as an OPD case). Thus, pediatric residents move rapidly through their mass of sore throats and snotty noses with a quick look in ears and throat with the otolaryngoscope, a swab wiped in the throat to be sent to the laboratory, and if the child does not have a high fever (the nurse has already taken his temperature), the parent is told to check on the laboratory results the next day, the emergency-ward form is marked "URI" (upper respiratory infection), and the next child moves up on the treadmill. If a patient or a visitor had given anyone trouble, his care is likely to deteriorate below the routine level. Often, doctors define their task in OPD cases as simply a stopgap until the patient gets to OPD on a subsequent day, and therefore a careful work-up is not considered necessary.

Medical cases are more often considered illegitimate than surgical cases. In our public hospital tabulations, the diagnostic categories highest in the illegitimate category were gynecology, genitourinary, dental, and "other medical." The lowest in proportion of illegitimate cases were pediatrics (another bit of evidence that children are more acceptable patients than adults), beatings and

stabbings, industrial injuries, auto accidents, other accidents, and "other surgical." Much of the surgical work is suturing lacerations and making other repairs. Although these are not necessarily serious in terms of danger to life (very few were), such injuries were seen by the staff as needing prompt attention (certainly within 24 hours) to reduce the risk of infection and to avoid scarring or other deformity.

It is not surprising that in surgical cases the attributes and behavior of the patients are of lesser consequence than in medical cases. The ease with which the condition can be defined and the routine nature of the treatment (treating minor lacerations becomes so routine that anyone thinks he can do it—medical students, aides, volunteers) means that the characteristics and behavior of the patient can be largely ignored unless he becomes extremely disruptive. (Even violence can be restrained and the treatment continued without much trouble.) Certain other things are handled with routine efficiency—high fevers in children, asthma, overdose, maternity cases. It is significant that standard rules can be and have been laid down in such cases so that everyone—clerks, nurses, doctors (and patients once they have gone through the experience)— knows just how to proceed. In such cases, the issue of legitimacy seldom arises.

We find no similar routines with set rules in the case of complaints of abdominal pains, delusions, muscle spasms, depression, or digestive upset. Here the process of diagnosis is much more subtle and complex, the question of urgency much more debatable and uncertain. The way is left open for all emergency-ward staff members involved to make a judgment about whether the case is appropriate to and deserving of their service. Unless the patient is a "regular," no one on the emergency service is likely to have background information on the patient, and the staff will have to rely entirely on clues garnered from his mode of arrival, his appearance, his behavior, the kind of people who accompany him, and so on. The interpretation of these clues then becomes crucial to further treatment and, to the casual observer, may appear to be the *cause* of such treatment.

It is also not surprising that "psychiatric cases" are usually considered illegitimate. Interns and residents do not (unless they are planning to go into psychiatry) find such cases useful for practicing their diagnostic and treatment skills,[1] and therefore regard such patients as an unwelcome intrusion. But what constitutes a psychiatric case is not based on unvarying criteria. An effort is usually made to place a patient in a more explicit medical category. For example, a wrist slashing is a surgical case requiring suturing. An adult who takes an overdose of sleeping pills is a medical case requiring lavage and perhaps antidotes. Only when a patient is troublesome—violent, threatening suicide, disturbing other patients—is the doctor forced to define him as a psychiatric case about whom a further decision must be made. (In some clinics, psychiatrists are attempting to broaden the definition by making interns and residents aware of more subtle cues for justifying a psychiatric referral and providing them with a consulting service to deal with such cases. However, they must provide a prompt response when called upon, or their service will soon go unused.)

It is no accident either that in the private hospitals (especially those without medical school or public clinic affiliation) the legitimacy of a patient depends largely on his relationship to the private medical system. A standard opening question to the incoming patient in such hospitals is, "Who is your doctor?" A patient is automatically legitimate if referred by a physician on the hospital staff (or the physician's nurse, receptionist, or answering service). If he has not been referred, but gives the name of a staff doctor whom the nurse can reach and who agrees to handle the case, the patient is also legitimate. However, if he does not give a staff doctor's name, he falls under suspicion. The hospital services, including the emergency room, are designed primarily to serve the private physicians on the staff. A patient who does not fit into this scheme threatens to upset the works. It is the receptionist's or receiving nurse's job to try to establish the proper relationship by determining whether the case warrants the service of the contract physician or the doctor on emergency call, and if so, to see to it that the patient gets into the hands of an attending staff doctor for follow-up treatment if necessary. Any patient whose circumstances make this process difficult or impossible becomes illegitimate. This accounts for the bitter denunciation of the "welfare cases"[2] and the effort to deny admission to people without medical insurance or other readily tappable funds. (Most physicians on the hospital staff do not want such people as patients, and feel they have been tricked if a colleague talks them into accepting them as patients; neither does the hospital administration want them as inpatients.) Also, such hospitals have no routine mechanism for dealing with welfare cases, as have the public hospitals which can either give free treatment or refer the patient to a social worker on the premises. Such patients are commonly dealt with by transferring them to a public clinic or hospital if their condition permits.

The negative evaluation of patients is strongest when they combine an undeserving character with illegitimate demands. Thus, a patient presenting a minor medical complaint at an inconvenient hour is more vigorously condemned if he is a welfare case than if he is a "respectable citizen." On the other hand, a "real emergency" can overcome moral repugnance. Thus, when a presumed criminal suffering a severe abdominal bullet wound inflicted by police was brought into one emergency ward, the staff quickly mobilized in a vigorous effort to prevent death because this is the kind of case the staff sees as justifying the existence of their unit. The same patient brought in with a minor injury would almost certainly have been treated as a moral outcast. Even in the case of "real emergencies," however, moral evaluation is not absent. Although the police prisoner with the bullet wound received prompt, expert attention, the effort was treated simply as a technical matter—an opportunity to display one's skill in keeping a severely traumatized person alive. When the same emergency ward received a prominent local citizen who had been stabbed by thugs while he was trying to protect his wife, the staff again provided a crash effort to save his life, but in this case they were obviously greatly upset by their failure, not simply a failure of technical skills but the loss of a worthy person who was the victim of a vicious act. One may speculate whether this difference in staff evaluations of the two victims may have resulted in an extra effort in the case of the respected citizen despite the appearance of a similar effort in the two cases.

Staff Estimates of "Legitimate" Demands

As is common in relationships between a work group and its clientele, the members of the work group tend to exaggerate their difficulties with the clients when they generalize about them. In conversations, we would typically hear estimates of 70 percent–90 percent as the proportion of patients who were using the emergency service inappropriately. Yet, when we actually followed cases through the clinic, we found the majority were being treated as if they were legitimate. In one voluntary hospital with an intern and residency training program, we classified all cases we followed during our time on the emergency room as legitimate or illegitimate whenever we had any evidence of subjective definition by staff members, either by what they said about the patient or the manner in which they treated the patient. Among those cases suitable for classification, 42 were treated as legitimate, 15 as illegitimate, and in 24 cases there was insufficient evidence to make a classification. Thus, the illegitimate proportion was about 20 percent–25 percent depending on whether one used as a base the total definite legitimate and illegitimate cases or also included the unknowns. In a very active public hospital emergency room we did not use direct observation of each case, but rather developed a conception of what kind of diagnostic categories were usually considered legitimate or illegitimate by the clinic staff and then classified the total consensus for two days according to diagnostic categories. By this method, 23 percent of 938 patients were classified as illegitimate. This constitutes a minimum figure because diagnostic category was not the only basis for an evaluation, and some other patients were almost certainly regarded as illegitimate by the staff. But it *does* suggest that only a minority were regarded as illegitimate.

The number of specific undesirable or inappropriate categories of patients were also consistently exaggerated. Thus, while in the public hospital the interns complained about all the drunks among the men and all the reproductive organ infections among the women ("The choice between the male and the female service is really a choice between alcoholics and PIDs," according to one intern), drunks made up only 6 percent of the total emergency-room population and the gynecology patients 2 percent. Venereal disease was also considered a common type of case by clerks, nurses, and doctors, but in fact made up only about 1 percent of the total E.R. census. Psychiatric cases were referred to as a constant trouble, but, in fact, made up only a little over 2 percent of the total. Some doctors believed infections and long-standing illnesses were common among the E.R. population and used this as evidence of neglect of health by the lower classes. Here again, however, the actual numbers were low—these two categories made up a little more than 3 percent of the total census. In two small private hospitals, the staffs were particularly bitter toward "welfare cases" whom they regarded as a constant nuisance. However, we often spent an entire shift (eight hours) in the emergency rooms of these hospitals without seeing a single patient so classified.

Workers justify the rewards received for their labors in part by the burdens which they must endure on the job. One of the burdens of service occupations is a clientele which makes life hard for the workers. Thus, the workers tend to select for public presentation those aspects of the clientele which cause them difficulty. Teachers' talk deals disproportionately with disruptive and incompetent students, policemen's talk with dangerous criminals and difficult civilians, janitors' talk with inconsiderate tenants. A case-by-case analysis of contacts is likely to demonstrate in each instance that the examples discussed by the staff are not representative of their total clientele.

Control of Inappropriate Demands for Service

When members of a service occupation or service organization are faced with undesirable or illegitimate clients, what can they do? One possible procedure is to select clients they like and avoid those they do not like. The selecting may be done in categorical terms, as when universities admit undergraduate students who meet given grade and test standards. Or it may be done on the basis of detailed information about specific individuals, as when a graduate department selects particular students on the basis of academic record, recommendations from colleagues, and personal information about the student. Of course, such selection is not made on a unidimensional basis and the selecting agent must often decide what weight to give conflicting factors. (Thus, a medical specialist may be willing to take on a patient who is morally repugnant because the patient has a medical condition the specialist is anxious to observe, study, or experiment with.) But there is an assumption that the more highly individualized the selection and the more detailed the information on which it is based, the more likely one is to obtain a desirable clientele. Along with this process goes the notion of "selection errors." Thus, when a patient is classed as a good risk for a physical rehabilitation program, he may later be classed as a selection error if doctors uncover some pathology which contraindicates exercise, or if the patient proves so uncooperative that physical therapists are unable to conduct any training, or if he requires so much nursing care that ward personnel claim that he "doesn't belong" on a rehabilitation unit (Roth and Eddy 1967, pp. 57–61).

Selectivity is a relative matter. A well-known law firm specializing in a given field can accept only those clients whose demands fit readily into the firm's desired scheme of work organization and who are able to pay well for the service given. The solo criminal lawyer in a marginal practice may, for financial reasons, take on almost every case he can get, even though he may despise the majority of his clients and wish he did not have to deal with them (Smigel 1964; Wood 1967). A common occupational or organizational aspiration is to reach a position where one can be highly selective of one's clientele. In fact, such power of selection is a common basis for rating schools, law firms, hospitals, and practitioners of all sorts.[3]

If one cannot be selective in a positive sense, one may still be selective in a negative sense by avoiding some potentially undesirable clients. Hotels, restaurants, and places of entertainment may specifically exclude certain categories of persons as guests, or more generally reserve the right to refuse service to anyone they choose. Cab drivers will sometimes avoid a presumed "bad fare" by pretending another engagement or just not seeing him. Cab driving, incidentally, is a

good example of a line of work where judgments about clients must often be made in a split second on the basis of immediate superficial clues—clues based not only on the behavior and appearance of the client himself, but also on such surrounding factors as the area, destination, and time of day (Davis 1959: Henslin 1968, pp. 138–58). Ambulance crewmen sometimes manage to avoid a "bad load," perhaps making a decision before going to the scene on the basis of the call source or neighborhood, or perhaps refusing to carry an undesirable patient if they can find a "good excuse" (Douglas 1969, pp. 234–78).

Medical personnel and organizations vary greatly in their capacity to select clients. Special units in teaching hospitals and specialized outpatient clinics often are able to restrict their patients to those they have individually screened and selected. The more run-of-the-mill hospital ward or clinic is less selective, but still has a screening process to keep out certain categories of patients. Of all medical care units, public hospital emergency wards probably exercise the least selectivity of all. Not only are they open to the public at all times with signs pointing the way, but the rule that everyone demanding care must be seen provides no legal "out" for the staff when faced with inappropriate or repugnant patients (although persons accompanying patients can be, and often are, prevented from entering the treatment areas and are isolated or ejected if troublesome). In addition, the emergency ward serves a residual function for the rest of the hospital and often for other parts of the medical-care system. Any case which does not fit into some other program is sent to the emergency ward. When other clinics and offices close for the day or the weekend, their patients who cannot wait for the next open hours are directed to the emergency service. It is precisely this unselective influx of anyone and everyone bringing a wide spectrum of medical and social defects that elicits the bitter complaints of emergency-service personnel. Of course, they are not completely without selective power. They occasionally violate the rules and refuse to accept a patient. And even after registration, some patients can be so discouraged in the early stages of processing that they leave. Proprietary hospitals transfer some patients to public hospitals. But compared with other parts of the medical-care system, the emergency-service personnel, especially in public hospitals, have very limited power of selection and must resign themselves to dealings with many people that they believe should not be there and that in many cases they have a strong aversion to.

What recourse does a service occupation or organization have when its members have little or no control over the selection of its clients? If you cannot pick the clients you like, perhaps you can transform those you *do* get somewhere closer to the image of desirable client. This is particularly likely to occur if it is a long-term or repeated relationship so that the worker can reap the benefit of the "training" he gives the client. We tentatively put forth this proposition: *The amount of trouble one is willing to go to to train his clientele depends on how much power of selection he has. The easier it is for one to avoid or get rid of poor clients (that is, those clients whose behavior or attributes conflict with one's conception of his proper work role), the less interested one is in putting time and energy into training clients to conform more closely to one's ideal. And, of course, the converse.*

Janitors have to endure a clientele (that is, tenants) they have no hand in selecting. Nor can a janitor get rid of bad tenants (unless he buys the building and evicts them, as happens on rare occasions). Ray Gold (1964, pp. 1–50) describes how janitors try to turn "bad tenants" into more tolerable ones by teaching them not to make inappropriate demands. Tenants must be taught not to call at certain hours, not to expect the janitor to make certain repairs, not to expect him to remove certain kinds of garbage, to expect cleaning services only on given days and in given areas, to expect heat only at certain times, and so on. Each occasion on which the janitor is able to make his point that a given demand is inappropriate contributes to making those demands from the same tenant less likely in the future and increases the janitor's control over his work load and work pacing. One finds much the same long-term effort on the part of mental hospital staffs who indoctrinate inmates on the behavior and demands associated with "good patients"—who will be rewarded with privileges and discharge— and behavior associated with "bad patients"—

who will be denied these rewards (Stanton and Schwartz 1954, pp. 280–89; Belknap 1956, chaps. 9 and 10). Prisons and schools are other examples of such long-term teaching of clients.[4]

The form that "client-training" takes depends in part on the time perspective of the trainers. Emergency-ward personnel do not have the longtime perspective of the mental hospital staff, teachers, or janitors. Despite the fact that the majority of patients have been to the same emergency ward previously and will probably be back again at some future time, the staff, with rare exceptions, treats each case as an episode which will be completed when the patient is discharged. Therefore, they seldom make a direct effort to affect the patient's future use of their services. They are, however, interested in directing the immediate behavior of clients so that it will fit into their concept of proper priorities (in terms of their evaluation of the clients) and the proper conduct of an emergency service, including the work demands made upon them. Since they do not conceive of having time for gradual socialization of the clients, they rely heavily on demands for immediate compliance. Thus, patients demanding attention, if not deemed by staff to be urgent cases or particularly deserving, will be told to wait their turn and may even be threatened with refusal of treatment if they are persistent. Visitors are promptly ordered to a waiting room and are reminded of where they belong if they wander into a restricted area. Patients are expected to respond promptly when called, answer questions put to them by the staff, prepare for examination when asked, and cooperate with the examination as directed without wasting the staff's time. Failure to comply promptly may bring a warning that they will be left waiting or even refused further care if they do not cooperate, and the more negative the staff evaluation of the patient, the more likely he is to be threatened.[5]

Nursing staff in proprietary hospitals dealing with the private patients of attending physicians do not have as authoritative a position vis-à-vis their clients as public hospital staff have: therefore, the demands for prompt compliance with staff directions must be used sparingly. In such a case more surreptitious forms of control are used. The most common device is keeping the patient waiting at some step or steps in his processing or treatment. Since the patient usually has no way of checking the validity of the reason given for the wait, this is a relatively safe way that a nurse can control the demands made on her and also serves as a way of "getting even" with those who make inappropriate demands or whom she regards as undeserving for some other reason.

In general, we might expect that: *The longer the time perspective of the trainers, the more the training will take the form of efforts toward progressive socialization in the desired direction; the shorter the time perspective of the trainers, the more the training wil take the form of overt coercion ("giving orders") if the trainers have sufficient power over the clients, and efforts at surreptitious but immediate control if they lack such power.*

Conclusion

When a person presents himself at an emergency department (or is brought there by others), he inevitably sets off a process by which his worthiness and legitimacy are weighed and become a factor in his treatment. It is doubtful that one can obtain any service of consequence anywhere without going through this process. The evidence from widely varying services indicates that the servers do not dispense their service in a uniform manner to everyone who presents himself, but make judgments about the worthiness of the person and the appropriateness of his demands and take these judgments into account when performing the service. In large and complex service organizations, the judgments made at one point in the system often shape the judgments at another.

The structure of a service organization will affect the manner and degree to which the servers can vary their service in terms of their moral evaluation of the client. This study has not explored this issue in detail. A useful future research direction would be the investigation of how a system of service may be structured to control the discretion of the servers as to whom they must serve and how they must serve them. This paper offered some suggestions concerning the means of controlling the inappropriate de-

mands of a clientele. The examples I used to illustrate the relationships of power of selection and the nature of training of clients are few and limited in scope. An effort should be made to determine whether these formulations (or modifications thereof) apply in a wider variety of occupational settings.

NOTES

The study on which this paper is based was supported by National Institutes of Health grants HM 00437 and HM 00517, Division of Hospital and Medical Facilities. Dorothy J. Douglas, currently at the University of Connecticut Health Center, worked with me and made major contributions to this study.

1. The authors of *Boys in White* (Becker et al. 1961, pp. 327–38) make the same point. A "crock" is a patient from whom the students cannot learn anything because there is no definable physical pathology which can be tracked down and treated.
2. "Welfare cases" include not only those who present welfare cards, but all who are suspected of trying to work the system to get free or low-priced care.
3. I am glossing over some of the intraorganizational complexities of the process. Often different categories of organizational personnel vary greatly in their participation in the selection of the clientele. Thus, on a hospital rehabilitation unit, the doctors may select the patients, but the nurses must take care of patients they have no direct part in selecting. Nurses can influence future selection only by complaining to the doctors that they have "too many" of certain kinds of difficult patients or by trying to convince doctors to transfer inappropriate patients. These attempts at influencing choice often fail because doctors and nurses have somewhat different criteria about what an appropriate patient is (Roth and Eddy 1967, pp. 57–61).
4. Of course, my brief presentation greatly oversimplifies the process. For example, much of the teaching is done by the clients rather than directly by the staff. But, ultimately, the sanctions are derived from staff efforts to control work demands and to express their moral evaluation of the clients.
5. Readers who are mainly interested in what happens on an emergency ward should not be misled into thinking that it is a scene of continuous orders and threats being shouted at patients and visitors. Most directives are matter-of-fact, and most

clients comply promptly with directions most of the time. But when the staff's directive power is challenged, even inadvertently, the common response is a demand for immediate compliance. This situation arises frequently enough so that on a busy unit an observer can see instances almost every hour.

REFERENCES

Becker, Howard S., Blanche Geer, Everett C. Hughes, and Anselm Strauss. 1961. *Boys in White*. Chicago: University of Chicago Press.

Belknap, Ivan. 1956. *Human Problems of a State Mental Hospital*. New York: McGraw-Hill.

Davis, Fred. 1959. "The Cab Driver and His Fare." *American Journal of Sociology* 65 (September): 158–65.

Douglas, Dorothy J. 1969. "Occupational and Therapeutic Contingencies of Ambulance Services in Metropolitan Areas." Ph.D. dissertation, University of California.

Glaser, Barney, and Anselm Strauss. 1964. "The Social Loss of Dying Patients." *American Journal of Nursing* 64 (June): 119–21.

Goffman, Erving. 1961. *Asylums*. New York: Doubleday.

Gold, Raymond L. 1964. "In the Basement—the Apartment-Building Janitor." In *The Human Shape of Work*, edited by Peter L. Berger. New York: Macmillan.

Henslin, James. 1968. "Trust and the Cab Driver." In *Sociology and Everyday Life*, edited by Marcello Truzzi. Englewood Cliffs, N.J.: Prentice-Hall.

Hollingshead, August B., and Frederick C. Redlich. 1958. *Social Class and Mental Illness*. New York: Wiley.

Perrow, Charles. 1965. "Hospitals, Technology, Structure, and Goals." In *Handbook of Organizations*, edited by James G. March. Chicago: Rand McNally.

Roth, Julius A., and Elizabeth M. Eddy. 1967. *Rehabilitation for the Unwanted*. New York: Atherton.

Scheff, Thomas J. 1964. "The Societal Reaction to Deviance: Ascriptive Elements in the Psychiatric Screening of Mental Patients in a Midwestern State." *Social Problems* 11 (Spring): 401–13.

———. 1966. *Being Mentally Ill*. Chicago: Aldine.

Smigel, Erwin. 1964. *Wall Street Lawyer*. New York: Free Press.

Stanton, Alfred, and Morris Schwartz. 1954. *The Mental Hospital*. New York: Basic.

Strauss, Anselm, Leonard Schatzman, Rue Bucher, Danuta Ehrlich, and Melvin Sabshin. 1964. *Psychiatric Ideologies and Institutions*. New York: Free Press.

Sudnow, David. 1967. *Passing On*. Englewood Cliffs, N.J.: Prentice-Hall.

Szasz, Thomas. 1960. "The Myth of Mental Illness." *American Psychologist* 15 (February): 113–18.

Wood, Arthur Lewis. 1967. *Criminal Lawyer*. New Haven, Conn.: College and Universities Press.

28

The Language of Case Presentation

· · · · · ·

Renée R. Anspach

This paper examines a significant segment of medical social life: formal presentations of case histories by medical students, interns, and residents. Although physicians in training spend much of their time presenting cases to their superiors (Mizrahi, 1984), little is known about the social and cultural significance of the case presentation.[1] The ostensible purpose of the case history is quite simple: imparting information about patients to peers, superiors, and consultants. However, basing my analysis on case presentations collected in two intensive care nurseries and an obstetrics and gynecology service, I argue that the case presentation does much more than that. It is an arena in which claims to knowledge are made and epistemological assumptions are displayed, a linguistic ritual in which physicians learn and enact fundamental beliefs and values of the medical world. By analyzing the language of this deceptively simple speech event, much can be learned about contemporary medical culture.

Approaches to Medical Language

This analysis of case presentations combines the concerns of two traditions in medical sociology: the study of medical discourse and the study of professional socialization. I will summarize briefly the major findings of each approach, in order to discuss how this analysis is informed by their concerns.

Over the past 10 years an extensive literature on doctor-patient interaction has emerged. This literature builds upon the findings of studies which suggest that practitioners restrict the flow of information to patients, often withholding critical facts about their diagnosis and treatment (Davis, 1963; Glaser and Strauss, 1965; Korsch, Gozzi, and Francis, 1968; Korsch and Negrete, 1972; Lipton and Svarstad, 1977; Waitzkin, 1985). Recently, more systematic and detailed studies, often informed by conversation analysis and discourse analysis, have emphasized the following issues. First, the medical interview is a socially structured speech exchange system, organized hierarchically into phases (Drass, 1981) and sequentially into provider-initiated questions, patient responses, and an optional comment by the physician (Fisher, 1979; Mishler, 1985; West, 1983). Second, the interaction between patients and providers is *asymmetrical* (see Fisher and Groce, 1985). Doctors control the medical interview tightly by initiating the topics of conversation (Fisher, 1979), asking the questions (West, 1983), limiting patients' questions, and often deflecting patients' concerns (Beckman and Frankel, 1984; Frankel, forthcoming; West, 1983). Third, medical interaction is shaped by the context in which it takes place: cultural assumptions of providers and patients, the logic of differential diagnosis, and the demands of bureaucratic organizations combine to constrain doctor-patient communications (Cicourel, 1981; Drass, 1981; Fisher and Groce, 1985). Finally, by subordinating the patient's concerns, beliefs, and life world to the demands of medical discourse (Beckman and Frankel, 1984; Cicourel, 1983; Mishler, 1985), the medical interview may become a form of repressive communication which seriously compromises the quality of patient care.

This very extensive literature on medical discourse contains a significant omission. Although much has been written about how doctors talk *to* patients, very little has been written about how doctors talk *about* patients. (Notable exceptions are studies of the written case record by Cicourel [1983] and Beckman and Frankel [1984]). This analytic focus on the medical interview occurs even though the way in which physicians talk about patients is a potentially valuable source of information about medical culture. Rarely do doctors directly reveal their assumptions about patients when talking to them; it is in talking and writing to other doctors about patients that cultural assumptions, beliefs, and values are displayed more directly. A consequence of this omission is that with few exceptions, much information about medical culture is inferred directly or introduced ad hoc into discussions of medical discourse.

By contrast, the way in which doctors talk to each other, particularly about patients, is an analytic focus of the second medical sociological tradition: studies of professional socialization. This largely ethnographic literature uses medical language, particularly slang, as a key to understanding the subculture that develops among medical students and residents as a response to problems created by their work environment (Becker, Geer, Hughes, and Strauss, 1961; Coombs and Goldman, 1973; Mizrahi, 1987). This unofficial, subterranean culture that flourishes among physicians in training includes a rich and graphic slang which contains reference to uninteresting work as "scut" (Becker et al., 1961); "gallows humor" in the face of tragedy (Coombs and Goldman, 1973); and the use of strongly pejorative terms to characterize those patients having low social worth (Sudnow, 1967), those with chronic or supposedly self-inflicted illness, those presenting complaints with a suspected psychogenic etiology, or those with diminished mental capacity; such patients are termed respectively "gomers," "turkeys," "crocks," "gorks," or "brain stem preparations" (Becker et al., 1961; Leiderman and Grisso, 1985; Mizrahi, 1984).

Ethnographers of medical socialization have been fascinated by this typing of patients because it flies in the face of the ostensible aim of medical training: to impart humanitarian values or a service orientation (Parsons, 1951). How sociologists assess the ultimate significance of this slang depends partly on their theoretical orientation; that is, whether medical training is seen as partly successful in instilling a collectivity orientation, as it is by functionalists (e.g., Bosk, 1979; Fox, 1957); or whether (alternatively) medical training entails a suspension or relinquishment of idealism, as conflict theorists contend (see, for example, Becker et al., 1961; Light, 1980; Mizrahi, 1984). A more sanguine view holds that these terms are healthy psychosocial mechanisms designed to cope with the limits of medical knowledge or incurable illness which frustrate the active meliorism of the physician (e.g., Leiderman and Grisso, 1985). According to this view, medical slang need not represent a loss of humanitarian values, but may even be beneficial in developing "detached concern" (Fox, 1979; Fox and Lief, 1963). From a more critical perspective, medical slang displays a blunted capacity to care and a deeply dehumanizing orientation to patients which blames them for their illness, views them as potential learning material, and jeopardizes their care (Millman, 1977; Mizrahi, 1984; Schwartz, 1987; Scully, 1980). These ethnographics of socialization, despite their sometimes differing conclusions, treat medical slang as a cultural artifact and analyze its deeper social and cultural significance.

While addressing the cultural meaning of medical language, studies of professional socialization are limited by their exclusive reliance upon ethnographic methods. Medical slang is often presented out of context and is divorced from the actual occasions in which it is used. Moreover, these studies have been confined to slang words and humor, often glaring violations of the service ethic which are readily apparent to the field worker. Rarely do ethnographers address the more subtle assumptions embedded in physicians' routine talk. For these reasons, the ethnography of professional socialization would be enhanced by the more detailed approach of discourse analysis.

The present analysis of case presentations is informed by both approaches to medical language. As a study of medical discourse, it attempts a detailed analysis of language as it is actually used. Like ethnographers of professional socialization, I emphasize the cultural significance of this language. The approach used here might be termed "symbolic sociolinguistics"; the emphasis is less on the social structure of the case presentation (the hierarchical and sequential organization of speech exchange) and more on the symbolic content of language. I attempt an interpretive analysis of the connotative, cultural meanings of the language of case presentation—meanings which are taken for granted and may not always be readily apparent to those who use it.

Learning to present a case history is an important part of the training of medical students, interns, and residents. Because case histories are presented by subordinates before their superiors, sometimes in front of large audiences, presenting a case skillfully assumes considerable importance in the eyes of physicians in training. The case presentation, then, is a speech event which serves both to impart information and as a vehicle for professional socialization, and herein lies its sociological import. As I will suggest, case presentations, as highly conventionalized linguistic rituals, employ a stylized vocabulary and syntax which reveal tacit and subtle assumptions, beliefs, and values concerning patients, medical knowledge, and medical practice to which physicians in training are covertly socialized. The case presentation, then, provides an opportunity to study an important aspect of professional socialization and is a window to the medical world view.

Methods

This analysis of case presentations is based on data collected in three settings. I first observed case presentations as part of a 16-month field study of life-and-death decisions in two newborn intensive care units. I spent 12 months in the 20-bed intensive care nursery of Randolph Hospital (a pseudonym), which serves as a referral center for a region that spans fully half the state. Because of the diverse nature of this region, the clientele was heterogeneous from a demographic and socioeconomic standpoint. Because Randolph Hospital is an elite institution and part of a major medical school, competition for its pediatric residency program is rather

intense. I also undertook four months of field work in the 40- to 50-bed nursery I will call General, an acute care hospital for the indigent having a largely Hispanic clientele. Although both Randolph and General are teaching hospitals, closely affiliated with major medical schools, the settings contrast sharply with respect to size, prestige, and the demographic composition of their patient populations. In both settings, my observations focused on the pediatric interns and residents and the neonatology fellows who rotated through the nursery and presented cases to attending neonatologists.

In order to compare case presentations in neonatal intensive care to presentations concerning adult patients, I then conducted three months of field work in the obstetrics and gynecology department of the hospital I will call Bennett, a teaching hospital having a demographically and socioeconomically heterogeneous clientele. About 300 infants are delivered each month in the inpatient obstetrics and gynecology ward, which accommodates about 90 obstetrics and 20 gynecology patients. Interns and residents complete rotations in labor and delivery, the gynecology clinic, gynecological oncology, and an affiliated hospital. I observed cases presented by the eight residents and three interns to full-time attending physicians, perinatologists, and part-time clinical faculty members.

In all three settings, participant observation and interviews provided information about the daily life and organizational context of case presentations. I also conducted interviews with residents of Bennett Hospital concerning strategies of presenting cases. The major method of data collection, however, was nonparticipant observation of a total of 50 cases presented by interns, residents, and fellows in daily rounds, consultations, formal conferences, and morbidity and mortality conferences. In Bennett Hospital, my observations focused primarily on formal presentations in weekly "statistical conferences" and on the very formal didactic presentations at breakfast conferences. A total of 15 case presentations were tape recorded, nine from obstetrics and six from neonatology; I transcribed the others in shorthand and attempted to approximate a verbatim transcript.

In addition, I examined nine written histories in

handouts and patients' case records. I also obtained and examined 200 admitting, operative, and discharge summaries from Bennett Hospital, and subjected a random sample of 100 summaries to detailed analyis. I coded and content analyzed these field notes, transcripts, and written summaries to reveal the features of case presentations that will be discussed. In order to provide a comparative framework, I analyzed a total of 14 journalistic medical articles from *Time* and *Newsweek* from September 1987 through February 1988. These journalistic accounts, which I selected because they were comparable in content to case presentations, made it possible to determine whether the features of case presentations that will be discussed here are also used in other occupations.

The Case Presentation as a Speech Event

Occasions

Over the course of his or her career, virtually every resident must present a formal case history. In fact, case presentation is so important to the work routine of the housestaff that, as one researcher notes, "interns spend most of their time keeping charts and presenting cases to senior staff" (Mizrahi, 1984, p. 243). Formal case histories are presented on certain occasions, which include (1) formal conferences (e.g., mortality review, chief of services rounds, statistical rounds, and didactic conferences); (2) daily rounds, when a new patient is admitted to the nursery or when a new attending physician takes charge of the nursery; (3) instances when a specialist is consulted; (4) written summaries distributed in conferences; and (5) certain points in the case record (e.g., on-service notes, off-service notes, and in admission, operative, and discharge summaries). Case presentations vary on a continuum of formality, ranging from relatively informal presentations on daily rounds to formal presentations in large conferences, attended by the senior staff of a department. Although fellows, who are between residents and faculty in the medical hierarchy, occasionally present cases, generally cases are presented

by the intern or the resident assigned to the particular case.

Format

Although the specific features of the history vary according to the purpose of the occasion, the case history—whether presented in written or in verbal form—tends to follow an almost ritualized format, characterized by the frequent use of certain words, phrases, and syntactic forms and by a characteristic organization. Histories presented in rounds generally begin with a sentence introducing the patient and the presenting problem. This is followed by a history of the patient's problem and its management and then by a list and summary of the present problems in each organ system, presented in order of importance. Because social aspects of the case are always presented (if at all) only after medical problems have been discussed, the semantic structure of the base presentation attests to the relatively low priority accorded to social issues in the reward structure of residency programs (Frader and Bosk, 1981).

Evaluation

Case presentations provide attendings (faculty) with an opportunity to evaluate house officers' competency—their mastery of the details of the case, clinical judgment, medical management, and conscientiousness. Interns and residents are aware that case presentations are a significant component of the evaluation process; for this reason, presenting skills are part of that elusive quality called "roundsmanship" (for a detailed discussion of roundsmandship see Arluke, 1978). As one resident noted when asked about the importance of presentations:

> Competency or surgical skills carry some weight (in attendings' evaluations); the ability to get along with team members carries even more weight; and the most important is the case presentation.

Although the importance of this evaluative component varies according to the occasion, the evaluative element is a background feature of most case presentations. Even the written case record serves as an informal social control mechanism, which provides physicians with the opportunity to evaluate their colleagues (Mizrahi, 1984)—to say nothing of opening the door to community scrutiny in the case of malpractice suits. At the Bennett obstetrical and gynecology service, the evaluative element looms large, particularly in the weekly statistical conferences, in which residents present cases before 15 or 20 senior staff members.

At any point, attendings can interrupt the resident's presentation to ask questions about the details of the particular case, its clinical management, or general issues of pathophysiology or medical/surgical techniques. Attendings employ a version of the Socratic method, in which the first question invites further questions until a "correct" answer is received and no further questions are deemed necessary. As Bosk notes, this questioning process follows Sacks's chain rule for question-answer sequences in which the floor belongs to the questioner (Bosk, 1979, p. 95); once the process begins, the presenter loses control of the interaction. Any omission of details relevant to the case (e.g., laboratory values), oversights, or displays of ignorance on the part of the resident are occasions for this questioning process to begin.

> During a presentation, a Bennett resident was discussing tocolyzing a preterm labor (administering a drug for the purpose of stopping uterine contractions). An attending asked, "How much ritadine was given?" The resident replied, "Per protocol." The resident, in referring to the nurses' protocol, had displayed his ignorance of the details of the case and implied that he left the details of case management to the nurses. The attending, detecting this thinly disguised ignorance, then asked, "Well, exactly how *many* milliequivalents were given?", forcing the resident to respond that he didn't know, thereby admitting his ignorance.

Attendings' questions, then, are questions in the second sense of the word, designed to call a resident's competency into question rather than to request information. Residents refer to this questioning process as "pimping"; they distinguish between "benign pimping" (helpful and constructive questions, usually by the senior resident) and "malignant pimping" (questioning,

usually in the part of the attending, for the purpose of humiliating a resident). Residents are aware that once a resident falters in rounds, he or she will be suspected of incompetence and will be targeted for future questioning.

> Take Melvin, for instance. He really wasn't so dumb, but he got raked over the coals all the time because he just didn't know how to present cases so well that it really sounded like he really knew what he was talking about. They go for the jugular. They'll pick on someone that they don't think knows what's going on, and they get labeled and then picked on, and, once labeled, that's pretty much it—unless they invent the Salk vaccine or something.

Case Presentation as Self-Presentation

Because of this evaluative element, as Arluke (1978) also notes, case presentations become self-presentations. Beginning in medical school and continuing throughout their training, physicians develop a set of skills and strategies designed to display competence and to avoid questions from the attendings. Among the most basic of these skills are "dressing professionally" and mastering "the correct medical terminology" and the semantic organization of the case presentation. One of the "rules" by which a successful presentation is judged appears to be "be concise and be relevant"; that is, a history should contain all and only those points deemed to be relevant, with a minimum of wasted words. Interns are instructed by senior residents in the nursery to omit a detailed chronology of the history and to move from detailed account of the delivery, resuscitation, and the infant's first few hours of life to an enumeration of the patient's problems in relevant organ systems—that is, to present an analytic summary rather than a chronological account.

More senior residents attend to the issue of a confident style. One resident, when asked about presentation strategies, emphasized the importance of a smooth presentation, avoiding the pauses and hesitations which would display uncertainty and would provide a conversational slot for questions from the attendings.

Roundsmanship is salesmanship. You gotta put on an air so that you will convince the attendings that you know about the case, and that you're smarter than they are. You've gotta display an air of confidence. (How do you do that?) You show confidence by the way you talk. (How do you talk?) You don't stop between sentences, you don't hesitate. They don't want to see you flipping through the chart. If you make a mistake in the hemoglobin value, don't say it was a mistake. . . . If you have to say "I don't know," don't apologize for it or say it unconfidently. You can say, "I don't know," but it has to be done in the right way, like nobody else would know either, not like you should've known. Just keep up the flow so you don't get interrupted.

Errors of all kinds are occasions for intense questions by the attendings; as Arluke (1978) also notes, skillful presenters employ strategies which anticipate and deftly deflect these questions. In the case of minor errors, these include "covering" to avoid displays of ignorance, presenting justifications for choosing a questionable course of action, and excusing or mitigating responsibility by blaming another department or a physician in the community. (In fact, cases involving errors by outside physicians are selected frequently for presentation.)

If the attending asks you, "What is the hemoglobin?" don't say, "I don't remember." That's the worst thing you can say—it's blood in the water. If you know it's normal but you can't remember the value, give a normal value. . . . You have to anticipate the questions. If you are asked, "Why wasn't that done?" you can say, "We considered that, but . . ." For instance, in the case of an elective caesarean hysterectomy (a controversial procedure), where blood was transfused, you can anticipate you'll be asked about the caesarean hysterectomy and about the blood transfusions, and you're likely to get raked over the coals. So you bring it up by deflecting or defusing the attending's questions. You say, "This patient received three units of blood. We felt the hematological indices didn't warrant transfusions, but anesthesiology disagreed." This way the attending will get sidetracked (because a discussion of another department's competency would ensue).

Attempts to cover up a major error in medical management, however, represent instances of what Bosk (1979) calls "normative errors," likely to arouse suspicions about the presenter's moral character. Even in such cases, residents, much like the attendings discussed by Bosk, are able to transform a mistake into a moral virtue by a candid admission.

In the case of the little stuff, you can blame the mistake on someone else, and if not, you can try to cover it up. If you overlook the little details, you can get away with it, as long as it is confidently presented. If it's a major mistake, the worst thing is to cover it up—that's the worst thing you can do. If you're caught trying to cover up, then they'll look upon you as someone who will cover up the next time, and it will follow you around. The way you treat a major mistake can transform you from a villain to a hero by simply stating, "In retrospect, we wish we had done it this way." Then you're a hero—you've showed you've learned from your mistake. They'll admire you and everyone will become your champion. You'll get questioned far less and you won't get pimped by the other attendings. They'll say, "That's OK, it happens to all of us."

This discussion is intended to convey the climate surrounding the case presentation: the importance that case presentations assume in the training of residents; the extent to which case presentations contain an evaluative element; and the fact that case presentations are simultaneously self-presentations. Case presentations, then, are rituals for the display of credibility—a background issue that informs some of the linguistic practices which will be discussed in the following section.

Features of Case Presentations

In the highly interpretive analysis of case presentations that follows, I will focus on epistemological assumptions and rhetorical features by which claims to knowledge are made and conveyed. I will emphasize four aspects of case presentations, which I call (1) the separation of biological processes from the person (de-personalization); (2) omission of the agent (e.g., use of the passive voice); (3) treating medical technology as the agent; and (4) account markers, such as "states," "reports," and "denies," which emphasize the subjectivity of the patient's accounts. Table 28-1 presents the frequencies with which these features were used in the larger corpus of materials. These features of case presentations are variable, but, as the table suggests, some are employed so frequently as to be considered conventions of the language of case presentation. Although it would be useful to compare the frequency with which these features are used in case presentations to the frequency with which they are used in ordinary speech, unfortunately no study of the use of these features in the vernacular exists. As the table shows, however, most of these features are found more frequently in ordinary speech than in a study of the passive voice in English language novels (Estival and Myhill, 1988) and in journalism, in which the author's goal is to create a heightened sense of agency.

At the conclusion of this paper, I present segments of five case histories. These presentations were selected according to two criteria: (1) the frequency with which the features of case presentations are used, and (2) the extent to which they represent oral and written presentations in neonatology and obstetrics. The first is a summary written by a neonatology fellow for the morbidity and mortality conference which followed the death of Robin Simpson, an infant with serious chronic lung disease of unknown etiology, who died rather unexpectedly. The next two are the initial portions of tape-recorded transcripts of histories in two ethics conferences concerning an infant who had a very unusual brain lesion (Roberta Zapata). One was presented by a fellow and the other by a resident approximately six weeks later. The fourth is an excerpt from a presentation in statistical rounds by a resident in obstetrics and gynecology. This case, which concerns a woman with cervical cancer, involved serious medical mismanagement by an outside community physician. The final case is the history portion of the written admission summary presented by a resident concerning a patient admitted for obstetrical care. A detailed analysis of these case presentations provides the basis for the discussion of the four features of medical language that follows.

De-Personalization

The case history presented in the morbidity and mortality conference which followed Robin Simpson's death begins with the statement: "Baby Girl Simpson was the 1044-gram product of a 27 week gestation." Outside observers of medical settings have commented that physicians sometimes employ an impersonal vocabulary when referring to their patients (Emerson 1970, pp. 73–100; Lakoff, 1975, p. 65). A clear example of this phenomenon is reference to patients in case presentations. Robin Simpson is identified as a member of a class of baby girls having a particular weight and gestational age. A typical introduction in obstetrics is presented in Line 66: "The patient is a 21-year-old Gravida III, Para I, AbI black female at 32 weeks gestation." This introduction lists the patient's age, previous pregnancies, live births, abortions, race, and weeks of pregnancy. Throughout the presentations, neonatology patients are identified as "the infant" or "the baby" (Lines 4, 23, 25, 35) or "s/he" (Lines 6–10, 13, 15). (Note that the second presenter is mistaken about Roberta's gender.) Obstetrics and gynecology patients are identified as "the patient" (38, 60, 66, 69, 81) or "she" (45, 46, 47, 67, 69, 71, 72, 74, 77, 79). These references invite the audience to see infants or patients rather than individuals; except in the written summary patients are never referred to by their proper names.[2] I will not comment in detail about this phenomenon of no-naming (for a discussion of this issue, see Frader and Bosk, 1981). Nor will I comment extensively on what may appear, from an outsider's perspective, to be the rather impersonal and mechanistic connotative imagery of "expiration date" and "product."

When I speak of de-personalization, I am referring not merely to the use of an impersonal vocabulary but rather to a more subtle set of assumptions: to refer to a baby as a "product" of a "gestation" seems to emphasize that it is the gestation, a biological process, rather than the parents, who produced the baby. Similar formulations are found in all three histories; for example: "the pregnancy was complicated by . . ." (1) "SROM (spontaneous rupture of membranes) occurred" (2), "the bruit (murmur) has decreased significantly . . ." (16), "the vagina and the cervix were noted to be clear," "the cervix was described . . ." (51). Each of these expressions invites the question "To whom?" or "Whose?" These formulations draw attention to the subject of the sentence: a disease or an organ rather than the patient. Of course the physicians know that parents have babies and that persons become ill, but the use of this language seems to suggest that biological processes can be separated from the persons who experience them. The language I have just described is not confined to physicians; in ordinary conversation we speak of a person "having a disease," thereby separating the disease from the subject. This usage may reflect deeply rooted cultural conceptions of the duality between mind and body. The most egregious examples of de-personalization occur in the everyday talk of physicians (and also nurses) when they refer to patients as "the" + "(disease)" (e.g., "the trisomy in Room 311"). On surgical wards and, less frequently, in the intensive care nursery, practitioners sometimes refer to patients as "the" + "(procedure)" (e.g., "the tonsillectomy in 214"). It is debatable whether or not these forms of de-personalization may impel practitioners to adopt certain attitudes toward their patients. By using these designations, however, practitioners leave themselves open to the criticism made by many consumers: that doctors "treat diseases rather than patients."

Omission of the Agent (e.g., Use of the Passive Voice)

Case presentations not only fail to mention the patient's personal identity; they also omit the physician, nurses, or other medical *agents* who perform procedures or make observations, as Table 28-1 suggests. A common example of a form that omits the agent is the "existential": "There was no mention of bleeding pattern . . ." (41). The canonical form which omits the agent is the "agentless passive." The presenters use the agentless passive voice frequently, and they do so in two contexts. First, they use it when reporting on treatments and procedures; for example: "The infant was transferred . . ." (4) , "She was treated with high FiO2's (respirator settings) . . ." (6), "She was extubated" (taken off the respirator) (7), "He was transferred here" (13) and "was put on phenobarb" (30), "The patient was admitted

to . . . the hospital" (54), and "was referred to the _____ Cancer Center" (61). In this case the presenters are not omitting reference to the patient on whom the procedures were performed, but rather are omitting the persons who performed the procedures. This omission has the effect of emphasizing what was done rather than who did it or why a decision was made to engage in a given course of action.

This usage becomes particularly significant when the decisions are controversial, problematic, or questionable. For example, in two sentences in the summary concerning Robin Simpson, the use of the passive voice obscures the fact that the actions that were performed resulted from rather problematic and highly significant decisions (in venturing this interpretation, I am going outside the text to interviews and discussions that I observed). For example, "She was extubated" (7) refers to a life-and-death decision, discussed later in the same conference, in which Robin Simpson was weaned from the respirator and was expected to die. Consider also the statement "No betamethasone was given" (3). Bethamethasone is a steroid administered in several large university centers to mothers whose membranes are ruptured prematurely for the purpose of maturing the baby's lungs. In a subsequent interview, a resident who had been present when Robin Simpson was admitted to the Randolph nursery suggested that the failure of physicians at St. Mary's, a small community hospital, to administer betamethasone may have contributed to the severity of Robin's illness. Because betamethasone is given commonly in the Randolph nursery, I am assuming that the fellow alludes to the failure to give betamethasone in an effort to make sense of Robin's illness, and that other participants in the conference understand this implication. Of course it is impossible to discern the fellow's intention in using the passive voice. It seems to me, however, that by divorcing the action from the person who performed the action, the passive voice has the effect of muting an allusion to an unfortunate decision about medical management. (Compare this statement with "The doctors at St. Mary's did not give betamethasone.")

Case D concerns a serious error in medical management on the part of a community physician, a type of case frequently chosen for presenta-

Table 28-1. Frequency of Features of Case Presentation

	Depersonalization	Personalization	Depersonalized[1] References	Personalized[2] References	Reports on Treatments, Procedures, and Actions Which Omit Medical Agent	Reports on Treatments, Procedures, and Actions Which Mention Medical Agent	Claims to Knowledge Which Omit Medical Agent	Claims to Knowledge Which Mention Medical Agent
Obstetrics, Written	3271	92	870	2	1687	29	697	10
Obstetrics, Oral	102	4	92	0	58	3	153	5
Neonatology, Written	160	66	135	4	85	16	178	5
Neonatology, Oral	103	58	129	1	30	35	107	36
Total Number of Presenters Using More Than 60% of Forms	3636	220	1226	7	1860[3]	83[4]	1135[5]	56[6]
Comparisons Estival and Myhill (1988)	18	3	16	5	15	6	17	4
Journalism Number of Authors Using 60% of Forms[12]	69	186	78	49	97	101	193	120
	12	5	3	4	0	5	4	0

[1]De-personalized references are those instances in which the patient is not referred to by name, but as the/this patient, woman, gravida, para, infant, twins, parents, child or by pronouns which refer to the above.

[2]Personalized references are those in which the patient or family is referred to by name.

[3]This includes 1757 agencies passive (e.g., an ultrasound was done), 60 actives with a recipient subject (she had/received an ultrasound), 8 ambiguous without agent (attempts to obtain fetal heart tones were unsuccessful), 6 adverbials (the patient was in the lithotomy position), 4 passive actives (she had an ultrasound done), 2 agentive passives with treatment as agent (this was followed by progesterone), 1 active with the procedure as agent (the surgery removed . . . her disease).

[4]This includes 56 actives, 21 agentive passives (an ultrasound was done by Dr. H.), 2 partial agentive passives (she was followed at the Cancer Center), 2 quasi-agentive declaratives (Her prenatal care was by Dr. H.), and 2 agentive actives (This 29-year-old . . . underwent treatment by the emergency room doctor).

[5]This includes 265 agentless, 114 scores, 111 descriptive statements (she was afebrile), 77 existentials (there was . . .), 66 sponge and needle count were correct, 63 estimated blood loss was, 62 actives with a recipient subject, 46 technology as agent (auscultation revealed), 40 quasi-passives (patient is well-known), 42 consistent with, 28 appeared, seemed, felt (patient appears pale), 26 adverbials (she did well), 25 is (patient is), 24 Apgars, 21 scores and descriptive (electrolytes were within normal limits), 21 exam revealed, 14 organ revealed, 9 presented with, 8 palpable, visible, 6 agentive passives with non-human agent, 5 found to have, 4 results in, 4 improved, worsened, 4 developed, 3 it extrapositions (it extrapositions . . .), 3 required, 3 participles, 13 other actives with non-human agent (the surgery removed the disease), and 28 others.

Omission of the Agent: Other Contexts[7]		All Contexts								
Forms Which Omit Medical Agent	Forms Which Mention Medical Agent	Forms Which Omit Medical Agent	Forms Which Mention Medical Agent	(Agentless) Passive Voice	Active Voice	Percent Passive	Technology as Agent	Alternatives	Account Markers Used	Account Markers Not Used
28	229	2412	268	2029	389	83.91	23	105	129	2247
0	4	211	12	64	51	55.65	21	55	11	161
0	10	263	31	101	156	39.30	5	49	N/A	N/A
0	30	137	101	26	161	13.90	9	8	N/A	N/A
28[8]	273[9]	3023	412	2220	757	74.57	58	217[10]	140[11]	2408
1	20	15	2	14 / 206	7 / 1940	— / 9.60%	4	17	0	21
33	56	1	277	116	390	22.92%	4	3	66	291
2	5	1	4	1	6	—	1	1	0	7

[6]This includes 37 actives, 6 agentive passives, 5 partial agentive passives, 3 descriptive statements (they were in agreement), 2 it extrapositions, and 3 other.

[7]"Other contexts" pertain primarily to instances in which the patient or family is the agent.

[8]This includes 12 descriptives, 5 patient presented, 5 equivalences, 3 agentive passives and 3 existentials.

[9]This includes 205 actives, 46 intransitives with agentive subjects (the mother died), 11 prepositional verbs (complained of), 8 other intransitives (the infant died), and 3 agentive passives.

[10]These include, most commonly, scores, estimated blood loss, consistent with, and scores and descriptive statements. "Consistent with" was coded as an alternative to technology as agent, since it can designate uncertainty (Prince, Frader, and Bosk, 1982).

[11]Account markers include states, reports, claims, complains of, no known history of, no history was reported, admits, and denies.

[12]Although a total of 14 articles were examined, they were written by a total of seven authors, and anonymously authored articles were excluded from this calculation.

tion in rounds. A woman had come to her gynecologist complaining of vaginal bleeding. The physician, noting the enlarged uterus, simply assumed that the patient had fibroid tumors and scheduled her for a total hysterectomy. The gynecologist failed to perform a pap smear during the examination, and, therefore, did not know that, in addition to fibroids, the patient also had cervical cancer. Consequently the physician inadvertently cut into the tumor during surgery, an error which may have seriously compromised the patient's prognosis. As the resident confirmed when interviewed after the presentation, the case was chosen to deflect attendings' questions by emphasizing the error of an outside doctor, while at the same time symbolically affirming superior management at the teaching hospital and the resident's ability to learn from the error. The presentation is constructed as a morality play, a drama beginning with allusions to the errors (40, 52), proceeding to the denouement in which revelations from the pathology report are disclosed (58), and ending with a moral lesson (62). Note the resident's language to describe the errors: "No further details were noted in the history" (40); "No pap smear was performed at the time of this initial visit" (52). By placing the negative at the beginning of the sentence, the resident draws the listener's attention to the errors. Although it is understood clearly that the error was committed by an outside doctor, the passive voice softens the accusation by leaving this implicit and deflecting attention from the perpetrator. (Compare this construction to the active voice in ordinary conversation: "The doctor didn't perform a pap smear." Such a formulation, according to the resident in describing the case to me, "would not have been subtle.")

There is yet another context in which the fellow and the residents use the agentless passive voice: when they refer to observations and make claims to knowledge, as in "Both babies were noted to have respiratory problems on examination" (10), "The baby was noted to have congestive heart failure" (23), "She was found on physical exam . . ." (47), and "The vagina and the cervix were noted to be clear" (50). The use of the passive voice is an extremely common, though not invariant, feature of medical discourse. When one compares this use of the passive voice with its

alternative ("They noted that the baby had temporal bruits"), I believe that something can be learned about the epistemological assumptions of the case presentation: to delete mention of the person who made the observation seems to suggest that the observer is irrelevant to what is being observed or "noted," or that anyone would have "noted" the same "thing." In other words, using the passive voice while omitting the observer seems to imbue what is being observed with an unequivocal, authoritative factual status.

Technology as Agent

Physicians occasionally do use the active voice. For example, in Case Histories, B, C, and D, the fellow and the residents make the following statements:

> "Auscultation of the head revealed a very large bruit, and angiography showed a very large arteriovenous malformation in the head . . ." (11, 12)

> "Follow-up CT-scans have showed the amount of blood flow to be very minimal . . ." (18)

> "The arteriogram showed that this AVM was fed . . ." (26, 27)

> "The EEG showed . . . an abnormal . . ." (31–32)

> "The path revealed endometrial curettings . . ." (57)

These formulations seem to carry the process of objectification one step farther than the use of the passive voice: not only do the physicians fail to mention the person or persons who performed the diagnostic procedures, but they also omit mention of the often complex processes by which angiograms and CT scans are interpreted. Moreover, these forms actually treat medical technology as though it were the *agent*. (Again, compare these claims with others which seem somewhat less objectified: "Dr. _____ evaluated . . ." (13), "They . . . did an EMI scan (CT-scan)" (25). Moreover, using the terms "revealed" and "showed" seems to suggest that the information received by using the stethoscope, angiogram, or brain scan was obtained by a process of scientific revelation rather than by equivocal interpretation. Having had the opportunity to observe radiology rounds, I was impressed by the considerable amount of negotiation and debate that takes place as the participants come to "see" evidence of lesions on X-rays. Although physicians undoubtedly would acknowledge that this interpretation takes place, they tend to attribute variations in interpretation to the vagaries of "observer error" or "opinion" rather than viewing the process of interpretation as an intrinsic feature of the way in which data obtained via measurement instruments are produced. The use of such formulations as "Auscultation revealed" or "Angiography showed" supports a view of knowledge in which instruments rather than people create the "data."

Account Markers

If physicians imbue the physical examination and diagnostic technology with unquestioned objectivity, they treat the patient's reports with an ethnomethodological skepticism—that is, as subjective accounts with only tenuous links to reality. When presenting a clinical history obtained from a patient, the physician has two choices. One is to present events and symptoms reported by the patient as facts, just as physical findings and laboratory results are presented. This is done occasionally, as in the last clinical history: "She takes prenatal vitamins daily" (79), "The patient has a male child with sickle cell trait" (81–82), and "She has had no other surgeries (74)." Alternatively and more commonly, the history is treated as a subjective narrative consisting of statements and reports. For example, the patient "reports" that she was seen in the emergency room (70), "states" that she has been having uterine contractions (67), that there is fetal movement (7), and that she has a history of sickle cell trait (72). "States" and "reports" are markers which signal that we have left the realm of fact and have entered the realm of the subjective account. Note that this information is attributed to the patient, which implies that the physician's knowledge was obtained via hearsay (Prince, Frader, and Bosk 1982, p. 91).

Another frequently used account marker, "denies," actually calls the patient's account into question or casts doubt on the validity of the history. Although sometimes it is used simply when the patient gives a negative answer to the physician's question, "denies" is used most frequently in three other contexts. First, it is almost always used in the context of deviant habits likely to compromise the health of the patient or the unborn child, as in "She denies tobacco, alcohol, coffee, or tea" (78–79). (Compare this statement with the alternative: "She does not use tobacco, alcohol, etc. . ."). In this case, "denies" suggests that the patient may not be telling the truth or may be concealing deviant behavior, and it casts doubt upon her credibility as a historian. Second, "denies" is used frequently in connection with allergies, as in Line 75: "She denies any allergies." Another frequently used phrase is "She has no *known* allergies." In this case I suspect that "denies" has a self-protective function, however unintentional. If the patient were to have an allergic reaction to a drug administered during treatment, the responsibility would rest with the patient's faulty account rather than with the physician. Third, "denies" is used when a patient reports a symptom which usually belongs to a larger constellation of symptoms, but does not report the others that he or she would be likely to have, as in "She denies any dysuria, frequency, or urgency" (76–77).

Physicians "note," "observe," or "find"; patients "state," "report," "claim," "complain of," "admit," or "deny." The first verbs connote objective reality (i.e., only concrete entities can be noted or observed); the second verbs connote subjective perceptions. As Table 28-2 suggests,

Table 28-2. Presentation of Information by Source of Information

Presentation of Information	Source of Information		
	Information Obtained from Physician	Information Obtained from Patient	Total
As Fact (No Account Markers Used)	2009	399	2408
As Account (Account Markers Used)	19	131	151
Total	2028	530	2558

$X^2 = 430.451$.
$df = 1$.
$p = .0001$.

physicians are inclined to present information obtained from the physician as though it were factual, while treating information from the patient as accounts.

It is significant that medical training teaches physicians to distinguish between *subjective* symptoms, apparent only to the patient, and *objective* signs, apparent to the expert. Moreover, according to the Weed (SOAP) system for recording progress notes, any medical information provided by the patient should be classified as "subjective," while observations by the physician or laboratory studies should be classified as "objective."

The one exception to this rule is the rare occasion on which the presenter calls another physician's account into question. This is precisely what happens in Case History D, which is structured around mismanagement by the community doctor who failed to perform a pap smear. The resident explicitly emphasizes the rather cursory history taken by the community gynecologist, which does not include several pertinent facts.

> No further details were noted in the history. There was no mention of bleeding pattern, frequency duration, female dyspareunia (pain on intercourse), or dysmenorrhea or coital bleeding.... In the family history *that was obtained*, her mother was deceased of gastric carcinoma at age 64 (Lines 40–45).

Because a major theme of this history is the physician's cursory examination, which did not include a pap smear, it is not surprising that the resident uses an account marker when relating the physician's physical findings: "The vagina and cervix were noted to be clear, and the cervix *was described as* 'closed' " (50–51). The account marker "described" has the effect of casting doubt on the accuracy of the physician's observations or report and is in keeping with the overall emphasis on a lack of thoroughness. It is significant that in the handwritten notes which the resident used in this history and gave to me, the phrase "noted to be" was crossed out and replaced by "described as." As is the case when used with patients, account markers call attention to the subjective nature of the narrative.

"So What?" . . . Social Consequences of the Language of Case Presentation

Before discussing the implications of the language of case presentation, I should mention some caveats. In venturing into the realm of connotative meaning, I am aware that I am treading on perilous ground, for these are *my* interpretations of the language of case presentation. Many other interpretations can be made and I will briefly mention two of them. First, some people might suggest that the features of case histories are "merely" instances of "co-occurrence phenomena." Sociolinguists have observed that certain words and phrases tend to "go together" and to be used in certain social situations. Thus formulations such as "This patient is the product of a gestation" and "Auscultation revealed . . ." are parts of a style within an "occupational register." When presenting a case history, the resident simply may slip into this style rather automatically. To be sure, the practices I have just discussed represent instances of linguistic co-occurrence, and may be used without regard for whatever deeper meanings the observer may attribute to them. Yet I am asking a very different set of questions: What assumptions seem to be embodied in this style? What are the possible sociological consequences of this particular form of co-occurrence? The welfare administrator who writes a memo might automatically slip into "bureaucratese," but what does this occupational register tell us about the assumptive world of the bureaucrat?

Second, my interpretation of the language of case presentation is an outsider's interpretation. When questioned about their use of the formulations I have discussed, some physicians agreed with my interpretations; others responded that this style within what linguists call an "occupational register" exists merely for the purpose of imparting information as briefly and concisely as possible (for a discussion of this issue, see Ervin-Tripp, 1971). The characteristic formulations of case presentations, however, may not always be the most parsimonious. (Compare "The baby was noted to have congestive heart failure," Lines 23–24, with "They noted that the baby had temporal bruits," Line 25—an equally succinct formulation). Although brevity is important in resident culture, the fact that the residents and fellows sometimes use alternative, equally brief, formulations suggests that more may be at issue than the requirement of the brief transmission of information. Moreover, to claim that linguistic forms exist merely for the transmission of information is to subscribe to a rather narrow view of language. Ordinary language philosophers argue that words not only transmit information but accomplish actions and produce certain effects on those who hear them. Although transmitting information is clearly a manifest function of case presentations, the discursive practices I have described may have other consequences which are less obvious, as noted below.

Mitigation of Responsibility

Sociolinguists who have discussed the passive voice note that it is a responsibility-mitigating device. The discursive practices I identified in the previous section minimize responsibility in two ways. First, by suggesting that the observer is irrelevant to what is "observed," "noted," or "found," using the passive voice minimizes the physician's role in producing findings or observations. A similar point can be made about the use of technology as agent ("Auscultation revealed . . ."), which locates responsibility for producing the data in diagnostic technology rather than in the physician's observations and interpretations.

Second, the passive voice minimizes the physician's role in medical decision making. When used in reporting on treatments and procedures, the passive voice calls attention to the action and deflects attention from the actors or the decisions which led to the action. This effect becomes particularly significant when the passive voice is used to report problematic decisions, such as life-and-death decisions, obscuring both the decision makers and the controversy surrounding those decisions. Even on those occasions when physicians call attention to mistakes in medical management or clinical judgment, in using the passive voice they blunt the accusation by emphasizing the error rather than the perpetrator. In short, by eliminating both the actor and the element of judgment from medical decision-making, the passive voice places physicians, their knowledge, and their decisions beyond the pale of linguistic scrutiny.

One might ask whether these practices arise out of a structural imperative in the medical profession to protect itself from scrutiny. This is precisely what the professional dominance perspective would suggest (Friedson, 1970). For example, Millman's (1977) study of mortality review in three community hospitals depicts these conferences as rituals designed to neutralize medical mistakes. Writing from a neofunctionalist perspective, Bosk (1979) takes a different view of mortality review in a university-based teaching hospital. According to Bosk, attendings do acknowledge their mistakes, but turn their contrite admissions into displays of authority. This study provides data from a third context: cases presented by housestaff who are being evaluated by their superiors. Like the physicians described by Millman, housestaff openly admit major errors, if only to escape moral censure and to benefit from their candor, and they openly discuss mistakes of community doctors, if only to deflect criticism and to demonstrate the superior management of teaching hospitals. In each instance the intent is the same: to protect their credibility from challenge by the attendings. Because it mitigates responsibility for clinical decisions, the passive voice, while perhaps not used intentionally and strategically for this purpose, clearly serves this aim.

Oral presentations are private affairs open only to physicians. In the written case record, however, the ambit of evaluation widens. Not only is the case record open to evaluation by other physicians; potentially it can become a public record in malpractice suits. In view of the salience of malpractice in medical culture, the rise of so-called "defensive medicine," and the demand for documentation and the use of diagnostic technology, a language that treats findings as unproblematic and minimizes the responsibility of physicians for decision making has the effect of protecting those who use it from public scrutiny.

Passive Persuasion: The Literary Rhetoric of Medical Discourse

The practices I have just mentioned are by no means the exclusive province of physicians. Quite the contrary; some are found commonly in academic prose. For instance, one need look no farther than the two previous sentences for examples of parallel devices: the presentation of practices apart from the persons who engage in them and the use of passive voice ("found" by whom?). Regardless of my intention in using these devices, they do seem to cloak the claims that are made in the garb of objectivity. In an analysis of the academic prose in a well-known paper on alcoholism, Gusfield (1977) suggests that science has a "literary rhetoric." If one accepts this interpretation of academic prose, it might be possible that medicine, too, has its literary rhetoric. Some of the devices I have just mentioned have the effect of convincing the listener or reader of the unequivocal "truth" of the findings. By suggesting that observers are irrelevant to what is observed and that measurement instruments create the data, the language of case presentation approaches rhetoric or the art of persuasion.

Writing from the perspective of ordinary language philosophy, Austin (1975) suggests that every linguistic utterance has three dimensions: a locutionary or referential dimension (it imparts information), an illocutionary dimension (it accomplishes an action), and a perlocutionary dimension (it produces certain effects on the hearer, including convincing and persuading). Some of the practices I have described as part of the language of case presentation may be used by physicians to convince the audience of the credibility of their claims to knowledge, and hence may belong to the "perlocutionary" realm (which is another way of saying that there may be a literary rhetoric of medical discourse). For two reasons I suspect that at least on certain occasions, the language of case presentation may be used precisely because of its persuasive power. First, case histories are presented by medical students, interns, residents, and fellows to status superiors—attending physicians—who are evaluating them. Case presentations, as physicians acknowledge, are self-presentations, displays of credibility. By adopting a mode of presentation in which observations and diagnostic findings are endowed with unequivocal certainty, these younger physicians may be exploiting the persuasive power of words at the very moments when

they may feel most uncertain. Second, I observed a very interesting instance of "style switching," in which a resident, when criticized by his attending physician for failing to conduct certain diagnostic tests, switched immediately from the active voice into the language of case presentation ("This infant was the . . . product of a . . . gestation . . . was noted", etc.) Case presentations are not only rituals affirming the value of scientific observation and diagnostic technology, but perlocutionary acts, affirming the speaker's credibility as well. For this reason the epistemology of the case presentation serves the social psychology of self-presentation.

The Surrender of Subjectivity

If information produced by means of diagnostic technology is valued in the language of case presentation, information obtained from the patient is devalued. Technology "reveals" and "shows"; the physician "notes" or "observes"; the patient "reports" and "denies." The language of case presentation reflects a clear epistemological hierarchy in which diagnostic technology is valued most highly, followed in descending order by the physician's observations and finally by the patient's account. The case presentation concerning mismanagement is not only a symbolic affirmation of the superior management by the resident in a teaching hospital, but also a ritual affirming the value of diagnostic technology over the physical examination and the patient's history.

This hierarchy reflects an historical transformation that is described by Reiser (1978). In the early nineteenth century, physicians diagnosed and treated patients in their homes or by mail; the major source of data was the patient's subjective narrative, accepted at face value. As the locale of diagnosis moved to the hospital and the laboratory, medical practice turned away from reliance on the patient's account toward reliance on the physician's clinical perceptions (observation, palpation, and percussion), which in turn gave way to reliance on sophisticated diagnostic technology. Reiser suggests that each juncture in this epistemological evolution was accompanied by an increasing alienation in the doctor-patient relationship. The new diagnostic armamentarium entailed changes in the physician's role, wherein history taking assumed less importance in medical practice. Patients in turn were compelled to surrender their subjective experience of illness to the expert's authority.

There is another sense in which the language of case presentation reflects a culture that objectifies patients and devalues their subjective experience. The discursive practices which I call "depersonalization" refer to patients rather than to people. In fact, the subject of sentences—and the real object of medical intervention—is not the patient, but diseases and organs (this phenomenon appears to exist in other settings, described by Donnely, 1986 and by Frader and Bosk, 1981). The ability to "see" diseases, tissues, and organs as entities apart from patients, also a recent historical development, is what Foucault (1975) calls "the clinical mentality."[3] In its most extreme form, the language of case presentation treats the patient as the passive receptacle for the disease rather than as a suffering subject.

Socialization to a World View

Because it is delivered before superordinates, the case presentation serves as an instrument for professional socialization. Because case presentations are self-presentations, interns and residents learn a set of strategies designed to display and protect their own credibility in the eyes of their superiors. Whereas the skills of presentation are conscious and strategic, many of the deeper assumptions of case presentations are tacit and taken for granted; for this reason, much of the learning is unintentional and implicit. In fact,

many of the values and assumptions in the language of case presentation contradict the explicit tenets of medical education. Thus, although medical students are taught to attach more weight to the patient's history than to the physical examination or laboratory findings, the language of case presentation devalues patients' accounts. By using this language, physicians learn a scale of values which emphasizes science, technology, teaching, and learning at the expense of interaction with patients.

Whether used intentionally or unwittingly, the language of case presentation contains certain assumptions about the nature of medical knowledge. The practices I have discussed both reflect and create a world view in which biological processes exist apart from persons, observations can be separated from those who make them, and the knowledge obtained from measurement instruments has a validity independent of the persons who use and interpret this diagnostic technology. Inasmuch as presenting a case history is an important part of medical training, those who use the language of case presentation may be impelled to adopt an unquestioning faith in the superior scientific status of measurable information and to minimize the import of the patient's history and subjective experience. In a restatement of the Whorf hypothesis,[4] one linguist comments that "language uses us as much as we use language" (Lakoff 1975, p. 3). This discussion suggests that the medical students, residents, and fellows who present case histories may come to be used by the very words they choose.

EXAMPLES OF CASE PRESENTATIONS

A. WRITTEN SUMMARY FROM MORBIDITY AND MORTALITY CONFERENCE
Simpson, Baby Girl
Birthdate: 5/13/78
Expiration Date: 12/9/78

1 Baby Girl Simpson was the 1044-gram product of a 27-week gestation. The pregnancy was
2 complicated by the mother falling 2 weeks prior to delivery. SROM occurred on 5/9/78
3 and the infant was delivered by repeat C-section on 5/13/78 at St. Mary's. No betame-
4 ethasone was given before delivery. Apgars were 4 and 8. The infant was transferred to
5 Randolph in room air. The infant developed chronic lung disease after being intubated
6 at about 24 hours of age for increasing respiratory distress. She was treated with high
7 F_1O_2's and a course of steroids as well. She was extubated and at the time she ex-

8 pired, she required an F_1O_2 of 1.0 by hood. She was on chronic diuretics and potassium
9 supplement and had problems with hyperkalemia. She expired on 12/9/78.

10 B. NURSERY ETHICS ROUNDS, Fellow: _____ both babies were noted to have respiratory
11 problems on examination and auscultation of the head revealed a very large
12 bruit and angiography showed a very large arterio-venous malformation in the
13 head . . . ah he was transferred here and Dr. S evaluated and decided to
14 introduce the wires and then within 48 hours there was another baby diagnosed
15 as having the same problem. He was transferred here and his physician had
16 the wires inserted into the malformation. Ah post op, the bruit has decreased
17 significantly in the first baby and follow up CT-scans have showed the
18 amount of blood flow to be very minimal at this time. The second baby is due
19 to go through a CT-scan in the very near future, but has had a lot of other
20 neurological problems, and it has also been much more difficult to control
21 the second one's congestive failure post op.

22 C. NURSERY ETHICS ROUNDS, ROBERTA Z. Res: _____ the mother was 44 years old,
23 gravida 10, para 8. At about 24 hours of age, the baby was noted to have
24 congestive heart failure and was transferred to (hospital). At about 48
25 hours of age they noted that the baby had temporal bruits, did an emi scan
26 and found a very large vein of galen malformation. The arteriogram showed
27 that this AVM was fed by both the anterior cerebral arteries, both posterior
28 arteries and the vertebrals and the (hospital) neurosurgeons thought the
29 baby to be inoperable, so the baby was transferred here. The baby had some
30 right sided seizures as of 24 hours of age, the baby was put on phenobarb.
31 The EEG done at that time—this was still at (hospital)—showed an
32 abnormal—it was abnormal in that this was a space occupying lesion, but
33 there were no other abnormalities. Since then the baby has been on and off
34 phenobarb, but has still been on maintenance phenobarb most of the time. The
35 baby was transferred here and on the fourth of December had wires placed in
36 the malformation in hopes of inducing a thrombosis and closing off the
37 malformation.

38 D. OB-GYN ROUNDS The patient is a 43-year-old Taiwanese female Gravida-
39 6, Para-3, Ab-3 initially seen by her gynecologist for about a six-week history
40 of vaginal bleeding. No futher details were noted in the history. There
41 was no mention of bleeding pattern, frequency, duration, female dyspareunia,
42 discharge, or dysmenorrhea or coital bleeding. Her past medical history
43 included no hypertension, diabetes mellitus, and blood dyscrasias. In the
44 family history that was obtained, her mother was deceased of gastric car-
45 cinoma at age 64, but it was otherwise non-contributory. She had no previous
46 surgeries. She had been in the U.S. for about five years from Taiwan, and
47 had no pelvic exam during this time. She was found on physical exam to be a
48 well developed, well-nourished, slender Asian female with no acute distress;
49 5'0" 113 pounds; the blood pressure was 130/70; pulse 80, respirations, 18.
50 The physical exam was unremarkable. The vagina and cervix were noted to be
51 clear, and the cervix was described as "closed." The uterus was a 10 to 12-
52 week size and the adenexa were clear. No pap smear was performed at the time
53 of this initial visit. The hematocrit was 12.9 and the hemoglobin was 36.9.
54 The patient was immediately admitted to the hospital and underwent a D and C,
55 total hysterectomy-left salpingo-oophorectomy with a pre-operative diagnosis
56 of fibroid uterus. The path report of the specimen revealed
57 endometrial curettings-secretory endometrium, the uterus was 180 grams with
58 andenomyosis and a left corpus luteum cyst. Of particular note was the
59 incidental finding of infiltrating squamous cell carcinoma involving the
60 surgical margins that had been cut through. Two weeks later, the patient was
61 referred to the _____ Cancer Center for further evaluation and treat-

62 ment. . . . This case was presented to demonstrate the need for systematic
63 evaluation of vaginal bleeding. This patient's prognosis may have been
64 compromised by cutting through the cervical tumor.

65 E. HISTORY (OB)   DATE OF ADMISSION: 11/07/84
66 The patient is a 21-year-old Gravida III, Para I, Ab I black female at 32
67 weeks gestation, by her dates. She states that she has been having uterine
68 contractions every thirty minutes, beginning two days prior to admission.
69 The patient has a history of vaginal bleeding on 10/23, at which time she
70 reports she was seen in the _____ Emergency Room and sent home. Additionally,
71 she does state that there is fetal movement. She denies any rupture of
72 membranes. She states that she has a known history of sickle cell trait.
73 PAST MEDICAL HISTORY: Positive only for spontaneous abortion in 1980, at 12
74 weeks gestation. She has had no other surgeries. She denies any trauma.
75 She denies any allergies.

76 REVIEW OF SYSTEMS: Remarkable only for headaches in the morning. She denies
77 any dysuria, frequency, or urgency. She denies any vaginal discharge or
78 significant breast tenderness. HABITS: She denies tobacco, alcohol,
79 coffee, or tea. MEDICATIONS: She takes pre-natal vitamins daily.

80 FAMILY HISTORY: Positive for a mother with sickle cell anemia. It is
81 unknown whether she is still living. The patient also has a male child with
82 sickle cell trait. Family history, is otherwise, non-contributory.

NOTES

I would like to thank Jeanne Efferding, Kirsten Holm, Duane Alwin, Charles Bosk, James S. House, Deborah Keller-Cohen, John Myhill, Polly Phipps, Emmanuel Schegloff, and Howard Schuman for assistance with data analysis. Most significantly, I wish to thank Jane Sparer and Candace West for giving their time, their encouragement, and their ideas, and in so doing, making this paper possible.

1. A notable exception is Arluke's (1980) discussion of the social control functions of roundsmanship.
2. In contrast to the practice in psychiatry, this omission of names is not intended to protect the confidentiality of the patient, whose name is noted in the written summary.
3. Foucault's use of the term "clinical mentality" differs from Friedson's (1970) use of the term to describe an insular, defensive posture on the part of the physician.
4. According to the Whorf hypothesis, language structures, rather than merely reflects, perceptions of reality.

REFERENCES

Arluke, Arnold. 1978. "Roundsmanship: Inherent Control on a Medical Teaching Ward." *Social Science and Medicine* 14A:297–302.

Austin, J.L. *How to Do Things with Words*. Cambridge: Harvard University Press.

Becker, Howard S., Blanche Geer, Everett C. Hughes, and Anselm S. Strauss. 1961. *Boys in White*. Chicago: University of Chicago Press.

Beckman, Howard B. and Richard M. Frankel. 1984. "Effect of Patient Behavior on Collection of Data." *Annals of Internal Medicine* 102:520–28.

Bosk, Charles. 1979. *Forgive and Remember*. Chicago: University of Chicago Press.

Cicourel, Aaron V. 1981. "Notes on the Integration of Micro and Macro Levels of Analysis." Pp. 1–40 in *Advances in Social Theory and Methodology: Toward an Integration of Macro- and Micro-Sociologies,* edited by Karin Knorr-Cetina and Aaron Cicourel. London: Routledge and Kegan Paul.

———. 1983. "Language and the Structure of Belief in Medical Communication." Pp. 221–40 in *The Social Organization of Doctor-Patient Communication,* edited by Sue Fisher and Alexandra Dundas Todd. Washington, DC: Center for Applied Linguistics.

Coombs, Robert H. and Lawrence J. Goldman. 1973. "Maintenance and Discontinuity of Coping Mechanisms in an Intensive Care Unit." *Social Problems* 20:342–55.

Davis, Fred. 1963. *Passage through Crisis*. Indianapolis: Bobbs-Merrill.

Donnely, William J. 1986. "Medical Language as Symptom: Doctor Talk in Teaching Hospitals." *Perspectives in Biology and Medicine* 30.

Drass, Kris A. 1981. "The Social Organization of

Mid-Level Provider-Patient Encounters." Ph.D. dissertation, Indiana University.

Emerson, Joan. 1970. "Behavior in Private Places: Sustaining Definitions of Reality in The Gynecological Exam." Pp. 74–97 in *Recent Sociology,* Vol. 2, edited by Hans Peter Dreitzel. New York: Macmillan.

Ervin-Tripp, Susan. 1971. "Sociolinguistics." Pp. 15–91 in *Advances in the Sociology of Language,* Vol. I, edited by Joshua Fishman. The Hague: Mouton.

Estival, Dominique and John Myhill. 1988. "Formal and Functional Aspects of the Development from Passive to Ergative Systems. Typological Studies in Language." Chapter in *Passive and Voice,* edited by Masayoshi Shibatani. Amsterdam/Philadelphia: John Benjamins.

Fisher, Sue. 1979. "The Negotiation of Treatment Decisions in Doctor/Patient Communication and Their Impact on Identity of Women Patients." Ph.D. dissertation, University of California, San Diego.

Fisher, Sue and Stephen B. Groce. 1985. "Doctor-Patient Negotiation of Cultural Assumptions." *Sociology of Health and Illness* 7:72–85.

Foucault, Michel. 1975. *The Birth of the Clinic.* New York: Vintage.

Fox, Renée C. 1957. "Training for Uncertainty." Pp. 207–41 in *The Student Physician,* edited by Robert K. Merton, George G. Reader, and Patricia L. Kendall. Cambridge: Harvard University Press.

———. 1979. "The Human Condition of Health Professionals." Lecture, University of New Hampshire.

Fox, Renée C. and Harold I. Lief. 1963. "Training for Detached Concern in Medical Students." pp. 12–35 in *The Psychological Basis of Medical Practice,* edited by Harold Lief, Victor F. Lief, and Nina R. Lief. New York: Harper and Row.

Frader, Joel E. and Charles L. Bosk. 1981. "Parent Talk at Intensive Care Rounds." *Social Science and Medicine* 15E:267–74.

Frankel, Richard M. Forthcoming. "Talking in Interviews: A Dispreference for Patient-Initiated Questions in Physician-Patient Encounters." in *Interactional Competence,* edited by Richard Frankel. New York: Irvington.

Friedson, Eliot. 1970. *Profession of Medicine.* Chicago: Aldine.

Glaser, Barney and Anselm Strauss. 1965. *Awareness of Dying.* Chicago: Aldine.

Gusfield, Joseph. 1977. "The Literary Rhetoric of Science: Comedy and Pathos in Drinking Driver Research." *American Sociological Review* 41:16–34.

Korsch, B.M., E.K. Gozzi, and V. Francis. 1968. "Gaps in Doctor-Patient Communication: Doctor-Patient Interaction and Patient Satisfaction." *Pediatrics* 42:855–71.

Korsch, B.M. and V.F. Negrete. 1972. "Doctor-Patient Communication." *Scientific American* 227:66–74.

Lakoff, Robin. 1975. *Language and Woman's Place.* New York: Harper.

Leiderman, Deborah B. and Jean-Anne Grisso. 1985. "The Gomer Phenomenon." *Journal of Health and Social Behavior* 26:222–31.

Light, Donald. 1980. *Becoming Psychiatrists: The Professional Transformation of Self.* New York: Norton.

Lipton, Helene L. and Bonnie Svarstad. 1977. "Sources of Variation in Clinicians' Communication to Parents about Mental Retardation." *American Journal of Mental Deficiency* 82:155–61.

Millman, Marcia. 1977. *The Unkindest Cut.* New York: Morrow.

Mishler, Eliot. 1985. *The Discourse of Medicine* New York: Ablex.

Mizrahi, Terry. 1984. "Coping with Patients: Subcultural Adjustments to the Conditions of Work among Internists-in-Training." *Social Problems* 32:156–65.

———. 1987. "Getting Rid of Patients: Contradictions in the Socialization of Internists to the Doctor-Patient Relationship." *Sociology of Health and Illness* 7:214–35.

Parsons, Talcott. 1951. *The Social System.* New York: Free Press.

Prince, Ellen F., Joel Frader, and Charles Bosk. "On Hedging in Physician-Physician Discourse." Pp. 83–96 in *Linguistics and the Professions; Proceedings of the Second Annual Delaware Symposium on Language Studies,* edited by Robert J. Di Pietro. Norwood, Nj: Ablex.

Reiser, Stanley. 1978. *Medicine and the Reign of Technology.* Cambridge: Cambridge University Press.

Schwartz, Howard D. 1987. *Dominant Issues in Medical Sociology,* 2nd ed. New York: Random House.

Scully, Diana. 1980. *Men Who Control Women's Health: The Miseducation of Obstetrician-Gynecologists.* Boston: Houghton Mifflin.

Sudnow, David. 1967. *Passing On.* Englewood Cliffs, NJ: Prentice-Hall.

Waitzkin, Howard. 1985. "Information Giving in Medical Care." *Journal of Health and Social Behavior* 26:81–101.

West, Candace. 1983. "Ask Me No Questions . . . An Analysis of Queries and Replies in Physician-Patient Dialogues." Pp. 75–106 in *The Social Organization of Doctor-Patient Communication,* edited by Sue Fisher and Alexandra Dundas Todd. Washington, DC: Center for Applied Linguistics.

29

Midwives in Transition:
The Structure of a Clinical Revolution

· · · · · ·

Barbara Katz Rothman

There has been considerable interest in the United States in recent years in the medical management of the reproductive processes in healthy women. Much of this interest represents a growing recognition by many mothers that hospital births impose structures upon the birth process unrelated to and in many cases disruptive of the process itself.

This paper contends that changing the setting of birth from hospital to home alters the timing of the birth process, a result of the social redefinition of birth. Through an analysis of the medical literature on birth, I compare the social construction of timetables for childbirth—how long normal labor and birth takes—by hospital and home-birth practitioners. I argue that, like all knowledge, this knowledge is socially determined and socially constructed, influenced both by ideology and social setting.

This paper is based on interviews I conducted in 1978 with one subgroup of the home-birth movement: nurse-midwives certified by the State of New York to attend births. I located 12 nurse-midwives in the New York metropolitan area who were attending births in homes and at an out-of-hospital birth center. Nurse-midwives in the United States are trained in medical institutions one to two years beyond nursing training and obtain their formative experience in hospitals. They differ from lay midwives, who receive their training outside of medical institutions and hospitals. Once nurse-midwives are qualified, most of them continue to practice in hospitals. I use the term *nurse-midwives* throughout this paper to distinguish them from lay midwives. I discuss those parts of the interviews with these nurse-midwives which focus on their reconceptualization of birth timetables as they moved from hospital to home settings.

This sample was selected for two reasons: first, because of the position that nurse-midwives hold in relation to mothers compared with that held by physicians; while physicians in hospital settings control the birth process, nurse-midwives in home settings permit the birth process to transpire under the mother's control. Second, because nurse-midwives have been both formally trained within the medical model and extensively exposed to the home-birth model, data gathered in monitoring their adjustment to and reaction to the home-birth model provide a cross-contextual source for comparing the two birth settings.

Observation of the reactions of nurse-midwives to the home-birth setting demonstrates the degree to which their medical training was based on social convention rather than biological constants. The nurse-midwives did not embrace their non-medical childbirth work as ideological enthusiasts; rather, they were drawn into it, often against what they perceived as their better medical judgment. The nurse-midwives were firmly grounded in the medical model. Their ideas of what a home birth should and would be like, when they first began doing them, were based on their extensive experience with hospital births. While they believed that home birth would provide a more pleasant, caring, and warm environment than that ordinarily found in hospital birth, they did not expect it to challenge medical knowledge. And at first, home births did not. What the nurse-midwives saw in the home setting was screened through their expectations based on the hospital setting. The medical model was only challenged with repeated exposures to the anomalies of the home-birth experience.

The nurse-midwives' transition from one model to another is comparable to scientists' switch from one paradigm to another—a "scientific revolution," in Kuhn's (1970) words. Clinical models, like paradigms, are not discarded lightly by those who have invested time in learning and following them. The nurse-midwives were frequently not prepared for the anomalies in the timetable that they encountered at home. These involved unexpected divergences from times for birthing stages as "scheduled" by hospitals. Breaking these timetable norms without the expected ensuing "complications" provided the nurse-midwives attending home births with anomalies in the medical model. With repeated exposure to such anomalies, the nurse-midwives began to challenge the basis of medical knowledge regarding childbirth.

The medical approach divides the birth process into socially structured stages. Each of these stages is supposed to last a specific period of time. Roth (1963) notes that medical timetables structure physical processes and events, creating sanctioned definitions and medical controls. Miller (1977) has shown how medicine uses timetables to construct its own version of pregnancy. Similarly, medical timetables construct medical births: challenging those timetables challenges the medical model itself.

There are four parts of the birth process subject to medical timetables: (1) term (the end of pregnancy); (2) the first stage of labor; (3) delivery; and (4) expulsion of the placenta. I describe the hospital and home-birth approaches to these four parts and how each part's timetable issues arise. Then I consider the function of these timetables for doctors, hospitals, and the medical model.

1. Term: The End of Pregnancy

The Hospital Approach

In the medical model, a full-term pregnancy is 40 weeks long, though there is a two-week allowance made on either side for "normal" births. Any baby born earlier than 38 weeks is "premature;" after 42 weeks, "postmature." Prematurity does not produce any major conceptual anomalies between the two models. If a woman attempting home birth goes into labor much before the beginning of the 38th week, the nurse-midwives send her to a hospital because they, like physicians, perceive prematurity as abnormal, although they may not agree with the subsequent medical management of prematurity. In fact, few of the nurse-midwives' clients enter labor prematurely.

Post-maturity however, has become an issue for the nurse-midwives. The medical treatment for postmaturity is to induce labor, either by rupturing the membranes which contain the fetus, or by administering hormones to start labor contraction, or both. Rindfuss (1977) has shown that physicians often induce labor without any "medical" justification for mothers' and doctors' convenience.

Induced labor is more difficult for the mother and the baby. Contractions are longer, more frequent, and more intense. The more intense contractions reduce the baby's oxygen supply. The mother may require medication to cope with the more difficult labor, thus further increasing the risk of injury to the baby. In addition, once the induced labor (induction) is attempted, doctors will go on to delivery shortly thereafter, by Cesarian section if necessary.

The Home-Birth Approach

These techniques for inducing labor are conceptualized as "interventionist" and "risky" within the home-birth movement. The home-birth clients of the nurse-midwives do not want to face hospitalization and inductions, and are therefore motivated to ask for more time and, if that is not an option, to seek "safe" and "natural" techniques for starting labor. Some nurse-midwives suggest nipple stimulation, sexual relations, or even castor oil and enemas as means of stimulating uterine contractions. As I interviewed the 12 nurse-midwives about their techniques it was unclear whether their concern was avoiding postmaturity *per se* or avoiding medical treatment for postmaturity.

The nurse-midwives said that the recurring problem of postmaturity has led some home-birth practitioners to re-evaluate the length of pregnancy. Home-birth advocates point out that the medical determination of the length of pregnancy is based on observations of women in medical care. These home-birth advocates argue that women have been systematically malnourished by medically ordered weight-gain limitations. They attribute the high level of premature births experienced by teenage women to malnourishment resulting from overtaxing of their energy reserves by growth, as well as fetal, needs. The advocates believe that very well nourished women are capable of maintaining a pregnancy longer than are poorly nourished or borderline women. Thus, the phenomenon of so many healthy women going past term is reconceptualized in this developing model as an indication of even greater health, rather than a pathological condition of "postmaturity."

The first few times a nurse-midwife sees a woman going past term she accepts the medical definition of the situation as pathological. As the problem is seen repeatedly in women who manifest no signs of pathology, and who go on to have babies, the conceptualization of the situation as pathological is shaken. Nurse-midwives who have completed the transition from the medical to home-birth model, reject the medical definition and reconceptualize what they see from "postmature" to "fully mature."

2. The First Stage of Labor

The Hospital Approach

Childbirth, in the medical model, consists of three "stages" that occur after term. (In this paper I consider term as the first part of the birth process, occurring at the end of pregnancy.) In the first stage of childbirth, the cervix (the opening of the uterus into the vagina) dilates to its fullest to allow for the passage of the baby. In the second stage, the baby moves out of the open cervix, through the vagina, and is born. The third stage is the expulsion of the placenta. The second example of a point at which anomalies arise is in "going into labor," or entering the first stage.

The medical model of labor is best represented by "Friedman's Curve" (Friedman, 1959). To develop this curve, Friedman observed labors and computed averages for each "phase" of labor. He defined a *latent phase* as beginning with the onset of labor, taken as the onset of regular uterine contractions, to the beginnings of an *active phase,* when cervical dilation is most rapid. The onset of regular contractions can only be determined retroactively. *Williams Obstetrics* (Hellman and Pritchard, 1971), the classic obstetric text, says that the first stage of labor (which contains the two "phases") "begins with the first true labor pains and ends with the complete dilation of the cervix" (1971:351). "True labor pains" are distinguished from "false labor pains" by what happens next:

> The only way to distinguish between false and true labor pains, however, is to ascertain their effect on the cervix. The labor pains in the course of a few hours produce a demonstrable degree of effacement (thinning of the cervix) and some dilation of the cervix, whereas the effect of false labor pains on the cervix is minimal (1971:387).

The concept of "false" labor serves as a buffer for the medical model of "true" labor. Labors which display an unusually long "latent phase," or labors which simply stop, can be diagnosed as "false labors" and thus not affect the conceptualization of true labor. Friedman (1959:97) says:

> The latent phase may occasionally be found to be greater than the limit noted, and yet the remaining portion of the labor, the active phase of dilatation, may evolve completely normally. These unusual cases may be explained on the basis of the difficulty of determining the onset of labor. The transition from some forms of false labor into the latent phase of true labor may be completely undetectable and unnoticed. This may indeed be an explanation for the quite wide variation seen among patients of the actual duration of the latent phase.

In creating his model, Friedman obtained average values for each phase of labor, both for women with first pregnancies and for women with previous births. Then he computed the statistical limits and equated statistical normality with physiological normality:

> It is clear that cases where the phase-duration falls outside of these (statistical) limits are probably abnormal in some way.... We can see now how, with very little effort, we have been able to define average labor and to describe, with proper degree of certainty, the limits of normal (1959:97).

Once the equation is made between statistical abnormality and physiological abnormality, the door is opened for medical intervention. Thus, statistically abnormal labors are medically treated. The medical treatments are the same as those for induction of labor: rupture of membranes, hormones, and Cesarian section.

"Doing something" is the cornerstone of medical management. Every labor which takes "too long" and which cannot be stimulated by hormones or by breaking the membranes will go on to the next level of medical management, the Cesarian section. Breaking the membranes is an interesting induction technique in this regard: physicians believe that if too many hours pass after the membranes have been ruptured, naturally or artificially, a Cesarian section is necessary in order to prevent infection. Since physicians within the hospital always go on from one intervention to the next, there is no place for feedback; that is, one does not get to see what happens when a woman stays in first stage for a long time without her membranes being ruptured.

Hospital labors are shorter than home-birth labors. A study by Mehl (1977) of 1,046 matched, planned home and hospital births found that the average length of first-stage labor for first births was 14.5 hours in the home and 10.4 hours in the hospital. *Williams Obstetrics* reports the average length of labor for first births was 12.5 hours in 1948 (Hellman and Pritchard, 1971:396). For subsequent births, Mehl found first-stage labor took an average of 7.7 hours in the home and 6.6 hours in the hospital. Hellman and Pritchard reported 7.3 hours for the same

stage. Because 1948 hospital births are comparable to contemporary home births, and because contemporary hospital births are shorter, it is probable that there has been an increase in "interventionist obstetrics," as home-birth advocates claim. These data are summarized in Table 29-1.

The Home-Birth Approach

Home-birth advocates see each labor as unique. While statistical norms may be interesting, they are of no value in managing a particular labor. When the nurse-midwives have a woman at home, or in the out-of-hospital birth-center, both the nurse-midwife and the woman giving birth want to complete birth without disruption. Rather than using arbitrary time limits, nurse-midwives look for progress, defined as continual change in the direction of birthing. A more medically-oriented nurse-midwife expressed her ambivalence this way:

> They don't have to look like a Friedman graph walking around, but I think they sould make some kind of reasonable progress (Personal interview).

Unable to specify times for "reasonable" progress, she nonetheless emphasized the word "reasonable," distinguishing it from "unreasonable" waiting.

A nurse-midwife with more home-birth experience expressed more concern for the laboring woman's subjective experience:

> There is no absolute limit—it would depend on what part of the labor was the longest and how she was handling that. Was she tired? Could she handle that? (Personal interview).

A labor at home can be long but "light," uncomfortable but not painful. A woman at home may spend those long hours going for a walk, napping, listening to music, even gardening or going to a movie. This light labor can go for quite some time. Another nurse-midwife described how she dealt with a long labor:

> Even though she was slow, she kept moving. I have learned to discriminate now, and if it's long I let them do it at home on their own and I try and listen care-

Table 29-1. Labor Timetables for the First and Second Stages of Birth, for First and Subsequent Births

Birth	Length of First Stage of Labor (hours)		
	Home 1970s	*Hospital 1948*	*Hospital 1970s*
First	14.5	12.5	10.4
Subsequent	7.7/8.5[a]	7.3[b]	6.6/5.9[a]
	Length of Second Stage of Labor (minutes)		
First	94.7	80	63.9
Subsequent	48.7/21.7[a]	30[b]	19/15.9[a]

Note: a. Second births and third births; b. second and all subsequent births.

fully and when I get there it's toward the end of labor. This girl was going all Saturday and all Sunday, so that's 48 hours worth of labor. It wasn't forceful labor, but she was uncomfortable for two days. So if I'd have gone and stayed there the first time, I'd have been there a whole long time, then when you get there you have to do something. (Personal interview).

3. Delivery: Pushing Time Limits

The Hospital Approach

The medical literature defines the second stage of labor, the delivery, as the period from the complete dilatation of the cervix to the birth of the fetus. Hellman and Pritchard (1971) found this second stage took an average of 80 minutes for first births and 30 minutes for all subsequent births in 1948. Mehl (1977) found home births took an average of 94.7 minutes for first births and, for second and third births, 48.7 to 21.7 minutes. Contemporary medical procedures shorten the second stage in the hospital to 63.9 minutes for first births and 19 to 15.9 minutes for second and third births (Mehl, 1977).

The modern medical management of labor and delivery hastens the delivery process, primarily by the use of forceps and fundal pressure (pressing on the top of the uterus through the abdomen) to pull or push a fetus out. Friedman (1959) found the second stage of birth took an average of 54 minutes for first births and 18

minutes for all subsequent births. He defined the "limits of normal" as 2.5 hours for first births and 48 minutes for subsequent births. Contemporary hospitals usually apply even stricter limits, and allow a maximum of two hours for first births and one hour for second births. Time limits vary somewhat within U.S. hospitals, but physicians and nurse-midwives in training usually do not get to see a three-hour second stage, much less anything longer. "Prolonged" second stages are medically managed to effect immediate delivery.

Mehl (1977) found low forceps were 54 times more common and mid-forceps 21 times more common for prolonged second-stage and/or protracted descent in the hospital than in planned home births. This does not include the elective use of forceps (without "medical" indication), a procedure which was used in none of the home births and 10 percent of the hospital births (four percent low forceps and six percent mid-forceps). Any birth which began at home but was hospitalized for any reason, including protracted descent or prolonged second stage (10 percent of the sample), was included in Mehl's home-birth statistics.

The Home-Birth Approach

Nurse-midwives and their out-of-hospital clients were even more highly motivated to avoid hospitalization for prolonged delivery than for prolonged labor. There is a sense of having come so far, through the most difficult and trying part. Once a mother is fully dilated she may be so close to birth that moving her could result in giving birth on the way to the hospital. Contrary to the popular image, the mother is usually working hard but not in pain during the delivery, and as tired as she may be, is quite reluctant to leave home.

Compare the situation at home with what the nurse-midwives saw in their training. In a hospital birth the mother is moved to a delivery table at or near the end of cervical dilation. She is usually strapped into leg stirrups and heavily draped. The physician is scrubbed and gowned. The anesthetist is at the ready. The pediatric staff is in the room. It is difficult to imagine that situation continuing for three, four, or more hours. The position of the mother alone makes that impossible. In the medical model, second stage begins with complete cervical dilation. Cervical dilation is an "objective" measure, determined by the birth attendant. By defining the end of the first stage, the birth attendant controls the time of formal entry into second stage. One of the ways nurse-midwives quickly learn to "buy time" for their clients is in measuring cervical dilation:

> If she's honestly fully dilated I do count it as second stage. If she has a rim of cervix left, I don't count it because I don't think it's fair. A lot of what I do is to look good on paper (Personal interview).

Looking good on paper is a serious concern. Nurse-midwives expressed their concern about legal liability if they allow the second stage to go on for more than the one- or two-hour hospital limit, and then want to hospitalize the woman. One told of allowing a woman to stay at home in second stage for three hours and then hospitalizing her for lack of progress. The mother, in her confusion and exhaustion, told the hospital staff that she had been in second stage for five hours. The nurse-midwife risked losing the support of the physician who had agreed to provide emergency and other medical services at that hospital. Even when a nurse-midwife's experiences cause her to question the medical model, the constraints under which she works may thus prevent her from acting on new knowledge. Nurse-midwives talked about the problems of charting second stage:

If I'm doing it for my own use I start counting when the woman begins to push, and push in a directed manner, really bearing down. I have to lie sometimes. I mean I'm prepared to lie if we ever have to go to the hospital because there might be an hour or so between full dilation and when she begins pushing and I don't see—as long as the heart tones are fine and there is some progress being made—but like I don't think—you'd be very careful to take them to the hospital after five hours of pushing— they [hospital staff] would go crazy (Personal interview).

All my second stages, I write them down under two hours: by hospital standards two hours is the upper limit of normal, but I don't have two-hour second stages except that one girl that I happened to examine her. If I had not examined her, I probably would not have had more than an hour and a half written down because it was only an hour and a half that she was voluntarily pushing herself (Personal interview).

Not looking for what you do not want to find is a technique used by many of the nurse-midwives early in their transition away from the medical model. They are careful about examining a woman who might be fully dilated for fear of starting up the clock they work under:

> I try to hold off on checking if she doesn't have the urge to push, but if she has the urge to push, then I have to go in and check (Personal interview).

With more home-birth experience, the nurse-midwives reconceptualized the second stage itself. Rather than starting with full dilatation, the "objective" measure, they measured the second stage by the subjective measure of the woman's urge to push. Most women begin to feel a definite urge to push, and begin bearing down, at just about the time of full dilatation. But not all women have this experience. For some, labor contractions ease after they are fully dilated. These are the "second-stage arrests" which medicine treats by the use of forceps or Cesarian section. Some nurse-midwives reconceptualized this from "second-stage arrest" to a naturally occurring rest period at the end of labor, after becoming fully dilated, but before second stage. In the medical model, once labor starts it cannot stop and start again and still be "normal." If it stops, that calls for medical intervention. But a nurse-midwife can reconceptualize "the hour or so between full dilation and when she starts pushing" as other than second stage. This is more than just buying time for clients: this is developing an alternative set of definitions, reconceptualizing the birth process.

Nurse-midwives who did not know each other and who did not work together came to the same conclusions about the inaccuracy of the medical model:

My second stage measurement is when they show signs of being in second stage. That'd be the pushing or the rectum bulging or stuff like that. . . . I usually have short second stages [laughter]. Y'know, if you let nature do it, there's not a hassle (Personal interview).

I would not, and this is really a fine point, encourage a mother to start pushing just because she felt fully dilated to me. I think I tend to wait till the mother gets a natural urge to push. . . . the baby's been in there for nine months (Personal interview).

It may be that buying time is the first concern. In looking for ways to avoid starting the clock, nurse-midwives first realize that they can simply not examine the mother. They then have the experience of "not looking" for an hour, and seeing the mother stir herself out of a rest and begin to have a strong urge to push. The first few times that hour provokes anxiety in the nurse-midwives. Most of the nurse-midwives told of their nervousness in breaking timetable norms. The experience of breaking timetable norms and having a successful outcome challenges the medical model; it is a radicalizing experience. This opportunity for feedback does not often exist in the hospital setting, where medicine's stringent control minimizes anomalies. A woman who has an "arrested" second stage will usually not be permitted to sleep, and therefore the diagnosis remains unchallenged. Forceps and/or hormonal stimulants are introduced. The resulting birth injuries are seen as inevitable, as if without the forceps the baby would never have gotten out alive.

4. Expulsion of the Placenta

The Hospital Approach

Third stage is the period between the delivery of the baby and the expulsion of the placenta. In hospitals, third stage takes five minutes or less (Hellman and Pritchard, 1971; Mehl, 1977). A combination of massage and pressure on the uterus and gentle pulling on the cord are used routinely. Hellman and Pritchard (1971:417) instruct that if the placenta has not separated within about five minutes after birth it should be removed manually. In Mehl's (1977) data, the average length of the third stage for home births was 20 minutes.

The Home-Birth Approach

For the nurse-midwives, the third stage timetable was occasionally a source of problems. Sometimes the placenta does not slip out, even in the somewhat longer time period that many nurse-midwives have learned to accept. Their usual techniques—the mother putting the baby to suckle, squatting, walking—may not have shown immediate results:

I don't feel so bad if there's no bleeding. Difficult if it doesn't come, and it's even trickier when there's no hemmorhage because if there's a hemmorhage then there's a definite action you can take; but when it's retained and it isn't coming it's a real question— is it just a bell-shaped curve and that kind of thing— in the hospital if it isn't coming right away you just go in and pull it out (Personal interview).

I talked with my grandmother—she's still alive, she's 90, she did plenty of deliveries—and she says that if the placenta doesn't come out you just let the mother walk around for a day and have her breastfeed and it'll fall out. And I believe her. Here I would have an hour because I am concerned about what appears on the chart (Personal interview).

If there was no bleeding, and she was doing fine, I think several hours, you know, or more could elapse, no problem (Personal interview).

Why the Rush? The Functions of Timetables
....

The Hospital Approach

There are both medical and institutional reasons for speeding up the birth. The medical reasons are: (1) A prolonged third stage is believed to cause excessive bleeding. (2) The second stage is kept short in order to spare the mother and the baby, because birth is conceptualized as traumatic for both. (3) The anesthetics which are routinely used create conditions encouraging, if not requiring, the use of forceps. The position of the woman also contributes to the use of forceps because the baby must be pushed upwards.

There are several institutional reasons for speeding up birth. Rosengren and DeVault (1963) discussed the importance of timing and tempo in the hospital management of birth. Tempo relates to the number of deliveries in a given period of time. The tempo of individual births are matched to the space and staffing limitations of the institution. If there are too many births, the anesthetist will slow them down. An unusually prolonged delivery will upset the hospital's tempo, and there is even competition to maintain optimal tempo. One resident said, "Our [the residents'] average length of delivery is about 50 minutes, and the pros' [the private doctors'] is about 40 minutes" (1963: 282). That presumably includes delivery of baby and placenta, and probably any surgical repair as well. Rosengren and DeVault further note:

> This "correct tempo" becomes a matter of status competition, and a measure of professional adeptness. The use of forceps is also a means by which the tempo is maintained in the delivery room, and they are so often used that the procedure is regarded as normal (1963:282).

Rosengren and DeVault, with no out-of-hospital births as a basis for comparison, apparently did not perceive the management of the third stage as serving institutional needs. Once the baby is quickly and efficiently removed, one certainly does not wait 20 minutes or more for the spontaneous expulsion of the placenta. Hospitals so routinize the various obstetrical interventions that alternative conceptualizations

are unthinkable. A woman attached to an intravenous or a machine used to monitor the condition of the fetus cannot very well be told to go out for a walk or to a movie if her contractions are slow and not forceful. A woman strapped to a delivery table cannot take a nap if she does not feel ready to push. She cannot even get up and move around to find a better position for pushing. Once the institutional forces begin, the process is constructed in a manner appropriate to the institutional model. Once a laboring woman is hospitalized, she will have a medically constructed birth.

Therefore, not only the specific rules, but also the overall perspective of the hospital as an institution, operate to proscribe hospital-birth attendants' reconceptualization of birth. Practitioners may "lose even the ability to think of alternatives or to take known alternatives seriously because the routine is so solidly established and embedded in perceived consensus" (Holtzner, 1968:96).

The Home-Birth Approach

In home births the institutional supports and the motivations for maintaining hospital tempo are not present; birth attendants do not move from one laboring woman to the next. Births do not have to be meshed to form an overriding institutional tempo. Functioning without institutional demands or institutional supports, nurse-midwives are presented with situations which are anomalies in the medical model, such as labors stopping and starting, the second stage not following immediately after the first, and a woman taking four hours to push out a baby without any problems—and feeling good about it. Without obstetrical interventions, medically defined "pathologies" may be seen to right themselves, and so the very conceptualization of pathology and normality is challenged.

In home or out-of-hospital births, the routine and perceived consensus is taken away. Each of the nurse-midwives I interviewed stressed the individuality of each out-of-hospital birth, saying that each birth was so much "a part of each mother and family." They described tightly-knit extended-kin situations, devoutly religious births, party-like births, intimate and sexual births—an infinite variety. The variety of social contexts seemed to overshadow the physiological constants. That is not to say that constraints are absent, but that at home the constraints are very different than they are within hospitals. At home, the mother as patient must coexist or take second place to the mother, wife, daughter, sister, friend, or lover.

Summary and Conclusions

The hospital setting structures the ideology and the practice of hospital-trained nurse-midwives. Home birth, by contrast, provides an ultimately radicalizing experience, in that it challenges the taken-for-granted assumptions of the hospital experience. Timetables provide structure for the hospital experience: structures—statistical constructions, models, or attempts at routinization or standardization—are not necessarily bad in and of themselves. Medical timetables, however, have termed pathological whatever does not conform to statistical norms, which are themselves based on biased samples and distorted by structural restraints imposed in the interests of efficiency. Thus, the range of normal variation does not permeate the model.

One final conclusion to be drawn from this research is a reaffirmation that knowledge, including medical knowledge, is socially situated. Medical reality is a socially constructed reality, and the content of medical knowledge is as legitimate an area of research for medical sociology as are doctor-patient relations, illness behavior, and the other more generally studied areas.

NOTE

The author thanks Maren Lockwood Carden, Leon Chazanow, Sue Fisher, Betty Leyerle, Judith Lorber, Eileen Moran, and the anonymous *Social Problems* reviewers.

REFERENCES

Friedman, Emmanuel
1959 "Graphic analysis of labor." Bulletin of the American College of Nurse-Midwifery 4(3): 94–105.
Hellman, Louis, and Jack Pritchard (eds.)
1971 Williams Obstetrics. 14th edition. New York: Appleton-Century-Croft.
Holtzner, Bukart
1968 Reality Construction in Society. Cambridge, MA: Schenkmann.
Kuhn, Thomas S.
1970 The Structure of Scientific Revolutions. Chicago: University of Chicago Press.
Mehl, Lewis
1977 "Research on childbirth alternatives: What can it tell us about hospital practices?" Pp. 171–208 in David Stewart and Lee Stewart (eds.), Twenty-First Century Obstetrics Now. Chapel Hill, N.C.: National Association of Parents and Professionals for Safe Alternatives in Childbirth.
Miller, Rita Seiden
1977 "The social construction and reconstruction of physiological events: Acquiring the pregnant identity." Pp. 87–145 in Norman K. Denzin (ed.), Studies in Symbolic Interaction. Greenwich, CT: JAI Press.
Rindfuss, Ronald R.
1977 "Convenience and the occurrence of births: Induction of labor in the United States and Canada." Paper presented at the 72nd annual meeting of the American Sociological Association, Chicago, August.
Rosengren, William R., and Spencer DeVault
1963 "The sociology of time and space in an obstetric hospital." Pp. 284–285 in Eliot Friedson (ed.), The Hospital in Modern Society. New York: Free Press.
Roth, Julius
1963 Timetables: Structuring the Passage of Time in Hospital Treatment and Other Careers. Indianapolis: Bobbs Merrill.
Rothman, Barbara Katz
1982 In Labor: Women and Power in the Birthplace. New York: Norton.

Dilemmas of Medical Technology

......

Medical technology exemplifies both the promise and the pitfalls of modern medicine. Medical history is replete with technological interventions that have reduced suffering or delayed death. Much of the success of modern medicine, from diagnostic tests to heroic life-saving individual interventions, has its basis in medical technology. For example, new imaging techniques, including CT scans, MRI (magnetic resonance imaging) machines, and ultrasound devices allow physicians to "see" body interiors without piercing the skin; powerful antibiotics and protective vaccinations have reduced the devastation of formerly dreaded diseases; and developments in modern anesthesia, lasers, and technical life-support have made previously unthinkable innovations in surgery possible. Technology has been one of the foundations of the advancement of medicine and the improvement of health and medical care.

But along with therapeutic and preventive successes, various medical technologies have created new problems and dilemmas. There are numerous recent examples. Respirators are integral to the modern medical armamentarium. They have aided medical treatment of respiratory, cardiac, and neurological conditions and extended anesthetic capabilities, which in turn have promoted more sophisticated surgical interventions. Yet, they have also created a new situation where critically injured or terminally ill persons are "maintained" on machines long after the brain-controlled spontaneous ability to breathe has ceased. These "extraordinary" life-support measures have produced ethical, legal, political, and medical dilemmas that have only been partially resolved by new definitions of death (Zussman, 1992). The technology around neonatal infant care has allowed premature babies less than 500 grams to survive, but has created new problems: great financial burdens (often over $250,000) and the babies' ultimate outcome. While some such babies go on to live a normal life, many die, and others survive with significant and costly disabilities (Guillemin and Holmstrom, 1986). Parental and staff decisions regarding these tiny neonates are often difficult and painful (Anspach, 1987). One tragic example of medical technology is DES (diethylstilbestrol), a synthetic estrogen prescribed to millions of pregnant women up until the 1970s to prevent miscarriages. DES turned out not only to be ineffective but years later to cause cancer and other reproductive disorders in the daughters of the women who took the drug (Bell, 1986; Dutton, 1988).

Perhaps the most interesting example of a recent technological intervention is the case of end-stage renal disease (ESRD), or chronic kidney failure. Before the development of dialysis (an artificial kidney machine) and kidney transplantation, kidney failure was a death warrant. For sufferers of renal failure, these medical technologies are life-saving or at least life-extending. The dialysis machine, for all of its limitations, was probably the most successful of the first generation of artificial organs. Dialysis was expensive, and the choice of who would receive this life-saving intervention was so difficult that the federal government passed a special law in 1972 to include dialysis coverage under Medicare. The number of patients involved and the costs of dialysis have far exceeded what legislators expected: Today, over $2 billion a year is spent on treating a disease that affects 70,000 people (Plough, 1986). Given the cost containment initiatives that dominate health policy, it is unlikely that any other disease will be specifically funded in the same way.

The issues raised by dialysis treatment are profound. Before federal funding was available, the issue of who should receive treatment was critical and difficult. How should limited resources be allocated? Who would decide and on what grounds (social worth, ability to pay)? Despite the greater availability of funds, important questions remain. Is it economically reasonable to spend billions of dollars on such a relatively small number of patients? Is this an effective way to spend our health dollars? Can we, as a society with spiraling health costs, make this type of investment in every new medical technology? For example, if an artificial heart were ever perfected, would we make it available to all 700,000 people who suffer from severe coronary disease? With the heart perhaps costing (at $50,000 each) up to $35 billion, who would pay for it? Beyond the economic issues is the quality of extended life. Dialysis patients must go three times a week for six- to eight-hour treatments, which means relatively few patients can work a conventional schedule (Kutner, 1987). Quality-of-life issues are paramount, with many patients suffering social and psychological problems; their suicide rate is six times the normal rate. Finally, a large percentage of the dialysis treatment facilities in the United States are owned by profit-making businesses, thus raising the question of how much commercialization should exist in medical care and whether companies should make large profits from medical treatment (Relman and Rennie, 1980; Plough, 1986).

While many social issues surround medical technology, two are particularly important. The first concerns our great faith in technological expertise and the general medical belief in "doing whatever can be done" for the sick and dying, which has created a "can do, should do" ethic. That is, if we can provide some type of medical intervention—something that would keep an individual alive—we ought to do it no matter what the person's circumstances are or how old or infirm he or she may be. This results in increasing the amount of marginal or questionable care, inflating medical expenses, and creating dilemmas for patients and their kin. The second issue is cost. Medical technology is often expensive and is one of the main factors in our rising health-care costs. We may reach a point soon, if we have not already, that as a society we will not be able to afford all of the medical care we are capable of providing. Thus, we need to seriously consider what we can afford to do and what the most effective ways to spend our health care dollars are. This raises the issue of "rationing" (or apportioning) medical care. Do we ration explicitly, on the basis of need or potential effectiveness, or implicitly, as we often already do, by the ability to pay? In Great Britain, with more limited resources devoted to medical care, rationing is built into the expectations of health policy (since it is virtually completely government-funded). For example, no one over fifty-five is begun on dialysis; it is simply not considered a suitable treatment for kidney disorders after that age (patients under fifty-five receive treatment comparable to American patients) (Aaron and Schwartz, 1984). (See also the debate on "Rationing Medical Care" in Part Three of this book.)

The two selections in this section highlight some of the dilemmas of medical technology. Barton J. Bernstein tells the story of "The Misguided Quest for the Artificial Heart." He shows how the faith in medical technology spawned overly optimistic predictions in the 1960s that largely overlooked the questions of who would benefit and who would pay (see also Dutton, 1988). While Bernstein depicts a failure of medical technology, the second selection examines dilemmas of success. In this reading, "Issues in the Application of High Cost Medical Technology: The Case of Organ Transplantation," Nancy G. Kutner examines the complex social issues that surround the transplantation of organs. She discusses cost effectiveness, the limited supply of organs, the donors, the selection criteria, and the quality of life for recipients. These issues illustrate how the dilemmas of medical technology extend far beyond the challenges of developing the technology and medical expertise needed to deliver satisfactory treatments.

Genetics is the rising paradigm in medicine. The Human Genome Project commenced in 1990 to map the entire human genetic structure in fifteen years. The prime goal is to locate the causes of the thousands of genetically related diseases and ultimately to develop new treatments and interventions. Research has already discovered genes for cystic fibrosis, Huntington's disease, types of breast and colon cancer, and other disorders, although we are clearly in the early stages of genetic research. Beyond diseases, some scientists have applied the genetic paradigm to behavioral traits, presenting claims for genetic predisposition's to alcoholism, homosexuality, obesity, and intelligence. Although genetic discoveries may eventually yield treatments and preventions of diseases, genetic testing as a medical technology raises serious social and ethical issues. In the final article in this section, "Genetics and Social Policy," Dorothy Nelkin warns of the dangers of biological reductionism, especially in terms of "genetic essentialism" (Nelkin and Lindee, 1995), as an increasingly pervasive explanation for human problems. New technologies like genetic tests will allow medical and nonmedical organizations to detect small deviations from the normal, which may have serious consequences for individuals. In particular, the availability of the genetic testing may engender new forms of genetic discrimination (Geller et al., 1996), especially for health insurance and in the workplace. Genetic technologies may well bring on a new age in medicine, but their social implications need to be monitored carefully (Duster, 1990).

Medical technology continues to expand, bringing new "miracles" and new dilemmas. Most poignantly reflected in the issues of quality of life and costs, the social and economic consequences of medical technology will need to be addressed in the next decade.

REFERENCES

Aaron, Henry J., and William B. Schwartz. 1984. The Painful Prescription: Rationing Hospital Care. Washington, D.C.: Brookings Institution.

Anspach, Renée. 1987. "Prognostic conflict in life and death decisions: The organization as an ecology of knowledge." Journal of Health and Social Behavior. 28: 215–31.

Bell, Susan. 1986. "A new model of medical technology development: A case study of DES." Pp. 1–32 in Julius A. Roth and Sheryl Burt Ruzek (eds.), The Adoption and Social Consequences of Medical Technology (Research in the Sociology of Health Care, Volume 4). Greenwich, CT: JAI Press.

Duster, Troy. 1990. Backdoor to Eugenics. New York: Routledge.

Dutton, Diana B. 1988. Worse than the Disease: Pitfalls of Medical Progress. New York: Cambridge University Press.

Geller, Lisa N., Joseph S. Alper, Paul R. Billings, Carol I. Barash, Jonathan Beckwith, and Marvin R. Natowicz. 1996. "Individual, family, and societal dimensions of genetic discrimination: A case study analysis." Science and Engineering Ethics. 2: 71–88.

Guillemin, Jeanne Harley, and Lynda Lytle Holmstrom. 1986. Mixed Blessings: Intensive Care for Newborns. New York: Oxford University Press.

Kutner, Nancy G. 1987. "Social worlds and identity in end-stage renal disease (ESRD)." Pp. 107–146 in Julius A. Roth and Peter Conrad (eds.), The Experience and Control of Chronic Illness (Research in the Sociology of Health Care, Volume 6). Greenwich, CT: JAI Press.

Nelkin, Dorothy, and M. Susan Lindee. 1995. The DNA Mystique: The Gene as a Cultural Icon. New York: Freeman.

Plough, Alonzo L. 1986. Borrowed Time: Artificial Organs and the Politics of Extending Lives. Philadelphia: Temple University Press.

Relman, Arnold S., and Drummond Rennie. 1980. "Treatment of end-stage renal disease: Free but not equal." New England Journal of Medicine. 303: 996–98.

Zussman, Robert. 1992. Intensive Care. Chicago: University of Chicago Press.

30

The Misguided Quest
for the Artificial Heart

■ ■ ■ ■ ■ ■

Barton J. Bernstein

The early 1960s constituted an era of euphoria in which federal funds seemed plentiful, social problems soluble, and scientific triumphs imminent. Money, technology, and prowess, it appeared, would speedily produce any number of medical miracles. Prominent among the expected achievements of medical science was the totally implantable artificial heart (TIAH). The device would fit neatly inside the chest cavity of human patients with major heart problems, giving them much, if not all, of the freedom and flexibility that they possessed when equipped with their own natural, healthy heart.

Biomedical scientists, heart surgeons, and bureaucrats viewed the TIAH as a partial response to the scourge of heart disease, which at that time killed about 700,000 Americans each year. "The artificial heart is feasible now and ripe for development, and it can be effectively achieved," declared a statement by the National Heart Institute (NHI), a federal agency that embarked on the quest to develop a TIAH in 1964.

Today, two decades later, scientists have failed to achieve the lofty goal of a working TIAH. The best the researchers have to show for more than $200 million expenditure is the so-called totally artificial heart implanted just two years ago [1982—eds.] in retired Seattle dentist Barney Clark. Clark's device gave him minimal freedom; he was tethered by six-foot lines to a 350-pound console that supplied power for the heart. He struggled through 112 painful days linked up to the console before he died—hardly a testament to technology triumphant.

The pursuit of the artificial heart provides an opportunity to examine important themes about biomedicine in particular, and about technology in modern industrial society in general. The quest reflects modern industrial society's great optimism about technology, its emphasis on high-technology solutions in medicine, and its neglect of the so-called "soft" (social, psychological, economic, and ethical) issues. The quest also emphasizes America's great reliance upon technical expertise, its patterns of closed decision making in biomedicine, a lack of congressional scrutiny of ongoing research, and the absence of a public dialogue about a device that raises profound social questions and could add billions of dollars to this country's strained medical budget. On the positive side, it may teach us how to deal better with similar issues in the future.

The Early Enthusiasm

Twenty years ago, technological optimism reigned—along with social naivete. Consider, for example, the reports prepared in 1965–66 by six firms hired by NHI to analyze the need for and feasibility of developing the artificial heart, and particularly the concluding study by a seventh firm. The results, published in 1966, included the following:

> How many people would annually need an artificial heart? The consultants reached the specific number of 132,500 by ignoring the incredible estimate

of 500,000 to 600,000 by one unusually exuberant contractor (General Dynamics) and roughly averaging the others. One contractor had forecast an annual need of about 257,000 hearts and another about 10,000—a range of about 2,500 percent.

How much would an artificial heart cost? A few thousand dollars, based on very optimistic estimates. Since the operation to implant the heart and the ensuing medical care would cost a few thousand more, the total would reach about $10,000 per patient. The consultants did not anticipate that, like Barney Clark, patients might linger in intensive care for months.

How many artificial heart recipients would live and lead normal lives? In the official set of assumptions, nobody died on the operating table. Rather, all recipients of the TIAH would return to normal life and, on the average, live longer and more healthy lives than other people because their mechanical hearts would not fail. How was that startling set of conclusions reached? Preparers of the report simply *assumed* that all the operations would succeed and that the artificial heart would work perfectly. Furthermore, the report forecast that by returning 132,500 people annually to normal life, the artificial heart would add $19 billion to the GNP during the first decade of its use and another $41 billion during the second decade. The program, in short, would improve life, improve its quality for both the patients and their families, and make a "profit" for America.

Most of the studies did not adequately explore four serious technological problems: those of developing appropriate biomaterials, a pump, and a power source, and of simulating the autonomic nervous system. At the time, experts did not know of any material that could safely interact with the blood over a prolonged period without destroying it and producing clots, thereby killing the patient. Nor did they know how to design a pump with a material that could flex—like a natural heart—about 40 million times a year without beating up the blood and impairing its capacity to serve the body. Furthermore, experts knew of no power source small enough, reliable enough, and safe enough to be implanted permanently. Nor did they know how to simulate the autonomic nervous system, which, among other functions, regulates the heart so that it can shift its rate of pumping blood from the require-

ment for, say, sitting down to that necessary for climbing stairs.

The studies did not dwell upon the possible psychological and social effects of the artificial heart on the recipient, the family, and the community. The use of a mechanical device to pluck an individual from the brink of death might create great anxieties for the recipient concerning worthiness and dependence upon the device, and would also require major adjustments by family members. For example, if the device left the recipient largely disabled and dependent on others, the individual might feel guilty and angry and the family resentful. Such problems could increase the need for psychological counseling for many people.

Additionally, a greatly successful TIAH would extend the life of millions, swell the older population, create a need for more care of the chronically ill, and strain the Social Security and welfare systems. And in the short run, if artificial hearts were scarce, questions would arise concerning who should receive them, what criteria should be used, and who should decide. For example, should the government pay for the whole research and development program and for the devices and other medical expenses or should the poor do without and the wealthy buy their own?

There was no open dispute about the quest for the TIAH. National Heart Institute officials forecast that it could be devised in about five years, at a cost of $40 million to $100 million, and that the first implant, according to their master plan, would occur on February 14, 1970—Valentine's Day. Capturing this enthusiasm, Rep. John Fogarty (D-R.I.), chairman of the House Subcommittee on Health Appropriations, declared that any delay would condemn Americans to needless death. The appropriations subcommittees, key allies of the federal health agencies, welcomed the opportunity to fund the program, and Congress comfortably endorsed it in 1964. Thus, the program has ambled along ever since at annual funding levels, discounting inflation, of about $9 million to $12 million.

From the beginning, medical experts—heart surgeons and bioengineers—and their allies in federal health agencies have shaped the issues surrounding development of the artificial heart, defined the agenda, determined how to evaluate progress, implemented the program, and spent the money. A cozy alliance with congressional appropriations and health subcommittees, which often pushed for even greater expenditures in the early years, blocked any larger scrutiny.

Even members of Congress outside this "iron triangle" relationship have shown great respect for the program. Though many enlightened representatives have learned not to trust Department of Defense estimates, they still largely believe the promises of medical experts. These specialists seem nonpartisan, objective, and dedicated to doing good. Indeed, most people trust physicians when they pronounce on the need for technology, its cost and feasibility, and its benefits.

Although no probing public dialogue about the artificial heart occurred in the mid-sixties, there was at least one powerful dissenter—Dr. James Shannon. He was the director of the National Institutes of Health (NIH), the umbrella organization that oversees NHI and other federal institutes doing medical research. Shannon, a cardiologist, distrusted the contractors' reports and deemed the NHI schedule wildly optimistic. He believed that the science needed to develop the biomaterials, the pump, an internal power source, and the autonomic nervous system were inadequate to achieve the quest within a handful of years, or even a decade. He decided that NHI should instead concentrate on partial heart-assist devices, especially the left-ventricular assist device (LVAD). The LVAD raised fewer scientific problems than the TIAH, could be a way-station to the artificial heart, and might meet the needs of many heart patients since left ventricular failure is a common problem.

When Skepticism Surfaced

Shannon maneuvered effectively within the executive branch to undercut the NHI program and reduce its funding. Testifying on the hill, he indicated that the project could be completed even more cheaply than NHI had proposed. Thus, he persuaded the appropriations subcommittees to deflect to other research activities some of the money originally targeted for the artificial heart. However, this undercover strategy helped

block a public dialogue, a result Shannon self-righteously celebrated in 1980, decrying what he sneeringly called "the age of populism."

As Shannon had foreseen, the effort to develop an artificial heart made little progress in the first few years. The dramatic heart transplant carried out in 1967 by South African surgeon Dr. Christiaan Barnard, as well as concern about mechanical heart devices, propelled NHI to establish a task force in 1968 to analyze the issues of cardiac replacement. This group consisted almost entirely of medical people; their focus was narrow and their optimism about technology strong. Basically, their report, published in 1969, was optimistic about the costs of the program, hopeful about scientific problems, and skimpy on social issues.

The report estimated that the total cost of a TIAH (including surgical and hospital expenses) would be $10,000 to $20,000 per recipient, that the number of candidates would not exceed 32,000 yearly and thus that the total annual cost would reach the range of $320 million to $640 million. The group did not confront problems about who should pay for the artificial heart and whether it would be fair to spend federal funds to develop the device and then allow only those who could afford the expense to buy it.

In 1972, the federal government appointed a second committee to look at many of the same questions that the 1968 group had considered. This committee, composed of people in fields such as law, sociology, ethics, and political science, proved more realistic, more probing, and less optimistic about the artificial heart; it defined many profound ethical, economic, personal, and social problems.

For example, members gently raised questions about whether the artificial heart should be pursued, whether other opportunities (especially in preventive medicine) were being sacrificed, whether the quality of life with an artificial heart would be decent, what would happen if it was not, and even whether the public might wish the project to be terminated.

The committee concluded that the cost of the device and medical and surgical expenses could easily exceed $25,000 per recipient, and that 50,000 patients might receive implants annually, leading to a total yearly cost exceeding $1.25

billion. Unless the federal government paid all the expenses for most citizens, the report stressed, only the rich might be able to buy a device developed largely on federal funds, and concepts of justice would be violated.

What would happen, the committee shrewdly asked, if artificial-heart recipients faced roughly the same problems as kidney-dialysis patients? Many of those patients did not live normal lives, and their suicide rate was 600 percent above the normal rate. They sometimes became preoccupied with their dependence upon a machine, worried excessively about costs, developed guilt feelings, and emotionally burdened their families.

"Perhaps the worst outcome," the committee warned, "would be for the device to work just well enough to induce patients to want it . . . but not well enough to prevent typical recipients from burdening others." Once the device was developed, the committee members feared, society would probably "balk at any explicit decisions which would deny life for those for whom it could be technologically preserved." But if the quality of life was expected to be poor, "society might well elect to restrict development" before the device was created. The committee wisely understood that terminating a life-saving technology, even on grounds of inadequacy, would be much easier—morally and politically—if done before the technology was developed.

Not only was this second committee, not wedded to biomedicine, more critical than the 1968 task force; it gave better advice, even on technology. For example, members warned that a nuclear-powered heart might irradiate the recipient and people nearby, noted that adequate lead shielding would probably make it too heavy for the chest, and suggested that the recipient would be a target for kidnapping because of the $25,000–$53,000 value of plutonium. These criticisms persuaded the government to phase out funding of the nuclear-powered heart.

It is significant that the two committees, which came to rather different conclusions, were strikingly different in composition. The contrast suggests the danger of allowing medical experts almost exclusively to shape and define medical policy. The greater success of the 1972 panel in foreseeing the problem involved in developing the artificial heart suggests that experts outside medicine, and possibly the general public, should have a role in policy decisions in medicine.

The Saga of Barney Clark

By the late seventies, bioengineers had devised better pumps for the heart and had found a material (polyurethane) that they believed could safely interact with the blood. However, they had made little progress in simulating the autonomic nervous system and had failed to build a compact, safe, and reliable power source for implantation. At the University of Utah, a group led by Dr. Willem Kolff, inventor of the artificial kidney, and Dr. Robert Jarvik, a young protege, had put together a partly implantable artificial heart that was being tested on calves. Known as the Jarvik 5, it and its successor, the Jarvik 7, tethered the calves to a large external power console; to test the hearts, the animals walked on a treadmill.

The Utah group was optimistic that it had solved the biomaterials problem, but two others remained. A number of animals died of infection because the tubes into the body broke the skin and created a ripe area for sepsis. And calcium deposits built up in the mechanical heart. Two possible explanations emerged for the deposits: either the biomaterial was not fully blood-compatible, or the calves, because they were still growing and had considerable calcium in their blood, were producing deposits that adults would not. The ambiguity would not be resolved until the mechanical heart was tested in older animals or an adult human. Ultimately the test occurred in 61-year-old Barney Clark, who suffered from cardiomyopathy, an irreversible degenerative disease of the heart muscles.

When the Utah group delivered its test information to the Food and Drug Administration (FDA) to gain approval for experimental use in humans, it provided results from tests on both the Jarvik 5 and 7, probably because it did not have adequate information on the 7 alone. The group had also been careless in keeping records on use of the heart's valves. Because of their $500 cost, valves were transferred to new artificial hearts when calves died, so the reliability of individual valves was unclear. Occasionally they had broken—perhaps as many as twenty times. At least five animals had died as a result.

Nevertheless, the FDA granted approval, and on December 2, 1982—the fifteenth anniversary of Dr. Christiaan Barnard's first heart transplant—Dr. William DeVries and his Utah team inserted a Jarvik 7 in Barney Clark amid the strains of Ravel's *Bolero,* chosen by Jarvik.

Dr. Chase Peterson, then vice-president for health sciences at Utah, likened Barney Clark to Columbus: "He is striking out for new territory." The Utah doctors stressed that they had rescued Clark from the brink of death; because his cardiomyopathy had suddenly become more serious, they had moved up the scheduled operation by about half a day to save his life. In their interpretation, therapeutic intervention and human experimentation were comfortable allies.

Reporters camped out at Utah, as the events were front-page news. Jarvik and DeVries became medical heroes. And the world watched as serious problems developed—a broken ventricle in the mechanical heart on the operating table, bubbles in the lungs and a second major operation, seizures, a broken valve and a third major operation, serious nosebleeds and thus another operation, mental disorientation, pneumonia, failure of Clark's kidneys and other natural organs, and then death after the 112 days.

The carefully managed publicity from Utah stressed the pathbreaking nature of the experiment, emphasized Clark's courage, sometimes predicted that he would recover, tended to minimize and even conceal many of his difficulties on the artificial heart, and belatedly disclosed some problems. Only after the patient died did DeVries admit that Clark (earlier likened by Peterson to a rugged old sagebrush) had asked a few times, "Why don't you let me die?"

Clark's own hopes and expectations remain unclear. After seeing the calves tethered to a power console about two months before the December operation, he had rejected the artificial heart because of the poor quality of life it allowed. As his condition deteriorated, he changed his mind. "I don't think he really thought it would succeed," his son, a surgeon, recalled. After his father's death, the son stressed: "His interest in going ahead, he told this to me, was to

make this contribution [to research], whereas the only other way was to die of the disease."

Before and after the operation, various experts gave their opinions. Jarvik had earlier forecast that "it's likely a patient could live a year if he lives a day." Dr. Yukihiko Nosé, an artificial-heart researcher at the Cleveland Clinic predicted that Clark would live at least six or seven months, since a few animals had lived nine months. Afterward, Peterson admitted that "we felt . . . that Dr. Clark would die in the first day or two or that he'd leave the hospital in about ten days."

Dr. Denton Cooley of Houston's Texas Heart Institute, the world-famous heart surgeon who had twice used artificial hearts temporarily before transplants, derisively likened the Utah action to putting "John Glenn in a rocket in 1950 and aiming him at the moon." Though Cooley soon softened his harsh judgment, the fact remained, as he had emphasized, that the quality of life on an artificial heart would be poor—constantly noisy thudding in the chest and the immobility of being tied to external power. Dr. Norman Shumway of Stanford, another prominent heart surgeon who preferred transplants, described the artificial heart as "crude" and inappropriate. Even Kolff, given to wild predictions that artificial-heart recipients would be barred from marathons within fifteen years because they would be too strong, had stipulated that the device would be a success only if Clark was happy. "That has always been our criterion," he explained, "to restore happiness."

Shortly after the operation, Kolff Medical, Inc., the company that made Jarvik 7 and was now headed by Jarvik, announced that it had raised $20 million dollars from investors. Because the firm had previously issued stock and options to employees, Jarvik and Kolff were suddenly worth over $6 million each on paper, and DeVries about $350,000.

Officials at the National Heart, Lung, and Blood Institute (NHLBI), the successor to NHI that had provided much of the financial support for the Utah research, were privately annoyed by the implant. But because the Utah group did not have any NHLBI funding for the Jarvik 7 at the time, the agency—which had never formulated standards for experimental use of the heart—had no authority over the decision.

Troubling Issues

The operation on Barney Clark raises troubling questions about the ethics and politics of this experiment. Was Clark's death possibly hastened—rather than delayed—by implantation of the artificial heart? Were the FDA standards that allowed the use of questionable valves sufficiently demanding, considering that about twenty had proved defective and some had killed animals? Was the experiment premature, and did Clark have any chance for the "happy life" that Kolff had stipulated, or even the six or seven months of extended life that Nosé had forecast?

Early death is likely for anyone suffering from cardiomyopathy, as Clark was. But the prediction of imminent death is not reliable during the illness, and thus experiments may be conducted on individuals who might live longer without the device. As Peterson himself admitted earlier, "However ill a person may be, no one can predict the exact longevity of a living heart or the implications of replacing it with an artificial one." This problem is underscored by the case of a Florida firefighter, suffering from cardiomyopathy and judged near death, who had sought an artificial heart from the Utah group in April 1982, eight months before Clark's operation. Although he was turned down, he actually went on to outlive Barney Clark by about a year.

Clark's operation was basically an experiment. There was no realistic basis for concluding that he was going to live a comfortable life. His new heart made him susceptible to infection, and largely immobile. At best, if Nosé's optimistic prediction had been correct, Clark might have lived only a few more months.

Nor was Barney Clark, when judged by medical standards, a good choice for this experiment. After his death, several members of the Utah hospital review board complained that the doctors had overlooked problems with his other organs, particularly his lungs. In their concentration upon Clark's poor heart, DeVries and his associates had reportedly not recognized his severe emphysema, perhaps the result of his twenty-five years of smoking two packs of cigarettes a day. The condition of his lungs may have been worsened by anesthesia and the major operations.

Should not the NHLBI have drawn up clear, well-publicized guidelines on what kind of artificial heart was acceptable in an experiment on humans? For years, the agency had avoided raising—much less resolving—the basic questions.

The Lingering Problems

Other problems—of cost, justice, and control—continue to hang over the artificial heart program. The earlier estimates that implanting a heart would cost $25,000 to $60,000 proved wildly optimistic. Barney Clark's expenses exceeded $275,000. As a retired dentist he might have been able to pay the bill, even if medical insurance and donations had not covered it. But unless America is going to restrict artificial hearts to the wealthy, the government that contributed over $200 million in development costs would have to pay for most other operations of this type. With a likely average cost of $125,000 to $250,000 for possibly 50,000 patients, that would mean $6.25 to $12.5 billion per year. That's roughly 2 to 4 percent of the nation's medical budget for .02 percent of the population. The benefits for individuals with heart disease would not be great—between, on the average, eight months ("best case") and eleven weeks ("worst case") for a twenty-five-year-old, and between two months ("best case") and two days ("worst case") for a fifty-five-year-old.

The possibility of meaningful political control over the development and distribution of the artificial heart may slip away. Business firms, less susceptible to effective control than medical schools such as Utah's, may soon dominate the artificial-heart business. Indeed DeVries, complaining of delays by the University of Utah's Institutional Review Board (IRB), recently moved to Louisville, Ky., to join the Humana Heart Institute owned by Humana, Inc. It is America's third largest for-profit hospital company and a major stockholder of Symbion, the successor firm to Kolff Medical. Humana has promised to subsidize up to 100 implants. DeVries believes that Humana's ethics panel, the counterpart to Utah's IRB, will create fewer problems for him. Since the committee is apparently dominated by the firm's employees, DeVries is probably correct. Put another way, independent judgment may yield to Humana's quest for prestige and profits.

DeVries' move to Humana is a dramatic reminder that biomedicine is big business, that the artificial-heart business is attractive to venture capitalists, and that researchers who earlier benefited from federal funding can build upon that work, keep many of their discoveries secret, and even slide away from federal oversight. Their own conception of "doing good"—whether pushing for FDA approval, pressing the IRB, or selecting another heart recipient—may be influenced, often subtly, by their own quest for fortune and fame.

Unless Congress decides to exercise more scrutiny and control, investors and researchers—not the polity—are likely to determine the development of the artificial heart. Congress has not yet focused on the possibility that its present $10 million annual program might leap to yearly costs of $6.25 to $12.5 billion. Legislators will eventually have to face the issue they have avoided—whether to pay for artificial hearts or allow only the wealthy to have them. In the process, America will either strain its medical budget or move further away from the standard of providing health care as a right.

Prescriptions for Decisions

Why should money be spent on the artificial heart rather than on finding ways to help people prevent heart disease? Perhaps an ideal society with unlimited resources could do both, but this is not such a society. The sense of abundance of the mid-sixties has faded. Social programs are being cut back. Medical care for the poor—whether young or old—is often unavailable. The emphasis on a glamorous technology may mean the sacrifice of other medical programs that benefit more people for a longer period. The issue is not the $9 million to $12 million annual expenditures for development, but the huge cost of an artificial-heart project serving possibly 50,000 patients annually.

Why are technological "fixes" more attractive than preventive measures? Part of the answer is that prevention, by its nature, seldom involves a dramatic intervention, a glamorous struggle against death. The required activities are systematic and even repetitive. In prenatal care, for example, diet and medical checkups are the keys to healthier mothers and babies, and lower mortality. Preventing heart disease seems to involve daily do's and don'ts—among them, eating a well-balanced, moderate diet, not overeating, getting exercise, and not smoking. Research that would easily double NHLBI's skimpy budget for prevention remains to be done on weighing the factors that contribute to heart disease and defining precise standards for avoiding it.

Research in preventive medicine seldom captures headlines or creates heroes. Even when it does, it is usually for some dramatic chemical intervention—for example, the polio vaccines of Jonas Salk and Albert Sabin. We admire the success of scientists in controlling nature by some dramatic device or chemical. Intervention —beating nature—helps make high-technology medicine glamorous.

Heart surgeons and bioengineers are, accordingly, grand candidates for "heroes." Because the heart, like the brain, is defined as the seat of life, the surgery has glamor. The artificial heart represents the defiance of death.

There is a need to reevaluate how we spend our money on health—to reconsider purposes, means, and emphases. There is no easy route to redefining priorities, for the present ways often have the support of established institutions and cozy alliances. They also fulfill some of the larger values in the society while clashing with others.

But one way to change priorities, suggested by the artificial heart and other forms of biotechnology, is to broaden decision making, to acknowledge uncertainty, and to challenge accepted expertise. Such involvement, possibly including citizen participation at various levels, may allow us to have greater control of our world. At a minimum, biomedical experts would be compelled to defend their predictions and analyses. For what experts propose, and ultimately what they create, especially in technology, shapes society in subtle but powerful ways. Issues involving technology in general, and biomedicine in particular, are not value-free but value-laden. The quest to "do good" is profoundly ideological.

31

Issues in the Application of
High Cost Medical Technology:
The Case of Organ Transplantation

• • • • • •

Nancy G. Kutner

Sophisticated medical technologies save lives that would otherwise be lost, but they also generate complex economic, social, legal and/or ethical problems. Human organ transplantation, for example, is a high cost technology, not only in the conventional economic sense, but also because it involves a scarce resource donated in life or in death by other human beings and because it can compromise quality of life as well as patient survival. Advances in transplant technology generate a particularly diverse set of questions and issues.

Appropriate resource allocation among alternative health-care needs is an ongoing debate (e.g., Beierle 1985; Fuchs 1984). Is it appropriate for a relatively small number of people to benefit from public financing of an expensive technology when a larger number of people could benefit from expenditures on a broader range of less expensive health problems? Related issues include the extent of the total health-care commitment that society is willing to make and whether a formal rationing policy would be normatively acceptable. Regardless of total cost and cost-effectiveness concerns, when a potentially life-saving technology becomes available it will certainly be used: "there can be no decision not to transplant" (Nightingale 1985, p. 142).

Organ-transplant technology depends on more than sophisticated equipment and the skills of medical personnel; an adequate supply of viable human organs must be available. A critical question is how the public can be encouraged to supply organs to meet the needs of waiting recipients. In order for organ transplantation to fulfill its potential, the cooperation of the general public is essential, which lends a quasi-public health dimension to the establishment of a wide-scale organ-transplant program.

A third set of questions concerns the criteria for allocating a technology to those who could potentially benefit from it. Since an inadequate supply of donor organs limits the availability of the technology, what criteria should be used to select organ transplant recipients, and are these criteria consistent with the values of a democratic society?

Finally, what are the medical and quality-of-life outcomes associated with organ transplantation? It is too soon to know what the long-term health outcomes will be for persons treated with powerful new immunosuppressive drugs or what outcomes are associated with transplanting at different stages in the course of a disease process. Transplant technology is now labeled therapeutic in the case of kidneys, hearts, and livers but the technology remains "experimental" even in these areas. Lives are saved—but for how long, and with what outcomes?

Before examining these issues related to use of organ-transplant technology, I provide a brief overview of the emergence and current status of this technology in the United States.

Background: Organ Transplantation in the United States
....

This paper focuses on issues surrounding solid organ transplants (kidney, heart, liver, pancreas, lung, heart-lung). Corneal and bone marrow transplants are also important components of transplant technology, however. Medical prerequisites for successful organ transplantation include perfected surgical techniques, adequate organ procurement and preservation systems, methods to prevent rejection of the transplanted organ, and understanding of the role of tissue matching.

Growth and Current Status of Solid Organ Transplant Programs

Organ transplantation was initiated in the United States when the first kidney transplant was performed in 1954. In 1960 a permanent shunt was developed for use in chronic kidney dialysis treatments; this was a significant event for kidney transplantation because it provided a backup procedure to keep patients alive if a transplant failed, and it allowed patients to be kept alive while they waited for a suitable donor kidney to become available. The so-called modern era of solid organ transplants did not begin, however, until the identification in the early 1960s of an effective combination of drugs (azathioprine and steroids) to prevent rejection of the foreign organ. Kidney transplantation and kidney dialysis developed as complementary treatment procedures for persons whose own kidneys no longer fulfill the essential function of removing toxic wastes from the body.[1] By 1971, 150–175 kidney transplants were being performed per year by Veterans Administration medical centers (Rettig 1980). When Medicare funding for kidney transplants and kidney dialysis became available in 1973, the annual number of kidney transplants began to increase dramatically (Figure 31-1). Patient survival at one year following a first kidney transplant is at least 90 percent, and 55 percent or more of patients who undergo kidney transplantation still have the new kidney one year later (Banowsky 1983).[2]

Heart transplantation was initiated in the United States as early as 1968, but early survival rates were poor. For many years, Dr. Norman Shumway's program at Stanford University was virtually alone in the field. In the early 1980s, the introduction of cyclosporine, a new immunosuppressive drug capable of significantly reducing organ rejection, stimulated a dramatic increase in heart transplantation. With cyclosporine, a two-year patient survival of 75 percent became possible, compared to 58 percent with conventional types of immunosuppression (Austen and Cosimi 1984).[3] Five-year survival rates climbed to between 50 and 60 percent (Casscells 1986). By 1985 the total number of heart transplants performed in the United States had risen to almost 1,200 (Seabrook 1985) and more than 80 centers were participating in heart transplantation.

Liver transplantation in the United States is closely associated with the work of one individual, Dr. Thomas Starzl. His teams at the University of Colorado (Denver) and the University of Pittsburgh have performed some 900 transplants since 1963, and he has personally trained most of the other liver-transplant surgeons. Cyclosporine's introduction significantly improved survival rates in liver transplant recipients. With conventional immunosuppression, a patient's chances for living one year after liver transplantation were about one in three, but with cyclosporine therapy, survival chances more than doubled (Starzl, Iwatsuki, Shaw, Gordon, Esquivel, Todo, Kam, and Lynch 1985). An important factor contributing to this improved survival was the aggressive use of retransplantation that cyclosporine made possible.

Pancreas transplantation, the only example of widespread endocrine organ transplantation, was initiated in 1966 at the University of Minnesota. The goal of pancreas transplantation is to provide a self-regulating source of insulin for patients who are insulin-dependent diabetics. Diabetics are overrepresented among kidney failure patients, and for these patients it appears that pancreas transplantation performed in conjunction with kidney transplantation may produce better results than pancreas transplantation by itself (Elick and Sutherland, forthcoming). Although cyclosporine has contributed to improved patient and graft survival rates, results achieved with pancreas transplantation are inferior to those achieved with kidney, heart, or

Figure 31-1. *Number of Kidney Transplants (Medicare and Non-Medicare)*

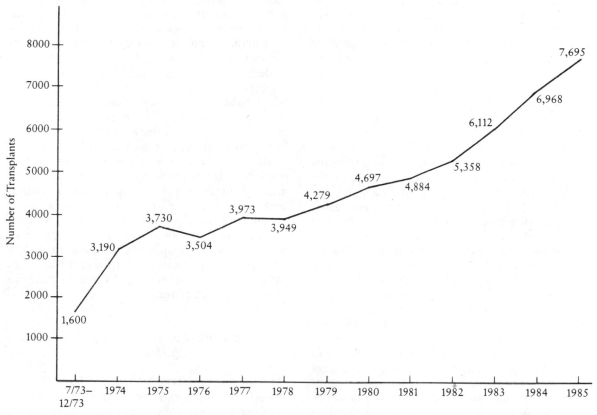

Source: *Dateline 1986*, p. 545.

liver transplantation (Pisano 1985; Toledo-Pereyra 1986).

Lung transplants and heart-lung transplants are the least attempted solid organ transplants. Heart-lung transplants, first performed at Stanford University in 1981, are more successful than lung transplants. Again cyclosporine drug therapy appears to promote the success of these procedures. As of 1985, about 140 heart-lung transplants had been performed in the United States.

Legislative Support for Organ Transplantation in the U.S.

In the early 1970s, despite the availability of kidney transplant technology, a number of treatment barriers prevented suitable patients from receiving a new kidney. Only a limited number of medical centers, located in large cities or university areas often geographically distant from where patients lived, were equipped to perform transplants. Moreover, the cost was prohibitive for many patients. Only about eight to ten percent of the American population had adequate insurance coverage for transplantation, and Medicaid coverage was only available to low-income patients. Federal research grants only covered the surgery as long as it was classified "experimental." As legislators were made aware that a shortage of facilities and money was preventing patients from utilizing transplant and dialysis technologies, pressure was generated to attack the problem at the federal level. The result was passage in Fall, 1972, of PL 92–603, an amendment to the Social

Security Bill that established the End-Stage Renal Disease (ESRD) Program of Medicare.

Under the amendment Medicare paid 80 percent of the cost of kidney treatment. As a result the number of transplant procedures, transplant centers, and dialysis treatment centers began to increase. The number of transplant candidates maintained by dialysis therapy also increased dramatically. An ironic consequence of PL 92–603 was a growing discrepancy between the number of cadaver kidneys available and the number of potential recipients.

By the early 1980s, advances in immunosuppressive therapy improved the success rates for all types of transplants, and the demand for hearts and livers, as well as kidneys, increased. Equitable distribution of scarce organs became increasingly problematic. Desperate parents of sick children needing liver transplants pleaded with the White House for help, and prominent media coverage increased the pressure on Congress to act. The Organ Procurement and Transplantation Act, PL 98–507, was ready for the president's signature on October 19, 1984. This legislation (1) established a Task Force to examine the medical, legal, ethical, economic and social issues presented by human organ procurement and transplantation (Title I) and to formulate recommendations, (2) authorized assistance for organ procurement agencies in the form of grants (Title II), (3) mandated establishment of an organ procurement and transplantation network and a scientific registry (Title II), and (4) prohibited organ purchases (Title III).

Under PL 98–507, the federal government was authorized to spend up to $25 million during fiscal years 1985–87 to facilitate the planning, establishment, initial operation, or expansion of organ procurement organizations, with special consideration to grant applications from organizations in underserved geographical areas. A national listing of patients in need of organs and a computerized system to match organs and patients, especially patients for whom obtaining a close tissue match is difficult, was to be developed through an organ procurement and transplantation network. This network was directed to maintain a 24-hour telephone service, assist organ procurement organizations in distributing organs that could not be placed within their immediate service areas, and coordinate the actual transporting of organs to transplant centers. These activities would centralize organ procurement and distribution in a manner analogous to the system used in European countries but without actual government involvement. Because of federal cost-cutting policies, funds for the network had not been allocated by mid-1986, and the distribution of scarce organs continued to be influenced by the high visibility of individual cases selected for publicity by the media (Mayfield 1986; Reiner, Eagles, and Watson 1986).

Although the Organ Procurement and Transplantation Act of 1984 signalled federal endorsement of human organ transplants as a component of medical care in the United States, it did not include such definitive steps as establishing the optimal location, number, and program components of transplant centers, or providing for the public funding of expensive medications patients need to take on a long-term basis in order to prevent rejection.

Organ Transplantation in the Context of Rising Health Costs

Health expenditures in 1986 in the United States represented almost 11 percent of the Gross National Product (GNP). Even if it were agreed that a greater share of the GNP should go to health care, American society increasingly faces difficult decisions about how health care dollars should be allocated (Annas 1985a; Culyer and Horisberger 1983; Evans 1983a, b).

Advances in medical technology contribute to rising total health care costs. The cost of a heart transplant and postsurgery care is easily $100,000 or more (Roughton 1986), and the average cost of a liver transplant can be even higher (Table 31-1). The immunosuppressive drugs that patients must take after receiving a transplant are expensive, and there is support at the Congressional level for Medicare to assume this cost (Gore 1986). Finally, transplant rejection episodes are not uncommon—acute rejection episodes were experienced by about 60 percent of the patients who received kidney transplants in 1984—and those episodes involved hospitalization costs.

Table 31-1. Estimated Costs Associated with Various Solid Organ Transplant Procedures

Organ	Estimated Cost[a]		
	Low	High	Average
Kidney	$25,000	$45,000	$35,000
Heart	$57,000	$110,000	$95,000
Liver	$68,000	$238,000	$130,000
Pancreas	$18,000	$50,000	$35,000

[a]Total first-year costs including immunosuppressive drugs (Evans, 1985:131). It should be noted that some sources provide even higher estimates, e.g., $170–200,000 for heart transplants and $230–340,000 for liver transplants when "fully-allocated average-one-year-cost" is considered (Massachusetts Task Force on Organ Transplantation, 1985:9).

Cost-effectiveness of a medical therapy is compromised when medical professionals "unconsciously extend the application of care beyond that which is prudent" (Roberts 1980, p. 500). Defining what is "prudent" is very difficult, however. Cost-effectiveness discussions tend to become clouded by the inclusion of different parameters and the application of different data sets (cf. Annas 1985a; Evans 1985; Overcast and Evans 1985). For example, Health Care Financing Administration (HCFA) determined that after four years, a group of kidney transplant patients cost the Medicare Program less than a group of kidney dialysis patients "when considering aggregate costs across the four-year period for the respective groups" (Davis 1983, p. 9). This conclusion, however, did not take into consideration the comparability of these hypothetical groups; regardless of type of therapy, coincident disease (e.g., diabetes) and frequency of hospitalization significantly influence the total costs incurred. Significant costs of failure must also be counted in analyzing the cost-effectiveness of transplantation. The cost of a transplant procedure can also be "one component in the overall cost of treating an end-stage disease. In the absence of a transplant, many end-stage patients incur considerable costs for medical treatment (i.e., the cost of dying)" (Overcast and Evans 1985, p. 107).

There is public support for transplantation regardless of its economic cost, demonstrated, for example, by votes obtained from insurance sub-

scribers. Although there is some public awareness of an increasing strain on Medicare resources, transplantation coverage is not viewed as a major "culprit."

Supply and Demand in Organ Transplantation: Legal and Ethical Issues

The U.S. Centers for Disease Control have reported the nationwide retrieval rate for cadaver organs as 16.5 percent effective, at maximum (Rapaport and Cortesini 1985). Each year, as many as 75,000 people have conditions that require heart transplantation, but as few as 2,000 donor hearts may be available (Merrikin and Overcast 1985). At least twice as many kidney transplants could be performed annually if organs were available.

Voluntary Organ Donation: A Quasi-Public Health Problem

National survey data indicate that the degree of public support for organ transplantation exceeds the degree of public support for organ donation (Blendon and Altman 1984; Manninen and Evans 1985). Although about 90 percent of Americans express support for continued development of transplantation programs, a smaller percentage (50%–60%) indicate willingness to donate their own organs or those of a relative, and only 19 percent of those who know something about organ transplantation report carrying donor cards (U.S. News 1986).

In a majority of states, surgeons require family approval for removal of organs even when a signed donor card is available and despite the fact that such approval is not required by the Uniform Anatomical Gift Act. It has been argued that "while donor cards are an excellent educational medium and certainly facilitate the activities of transplant coordination, they are not an effective means of substantially increasing the supply of organs for transplantation" (Overcast, Evans, Bowen, Hoe, and Livak 1984, p. 1559). What is needed, according to some observers, is a policy of "presumed consent" under which organs can be legally removed from a brain-dead individual unless the individual carries a refusal card or an objection is raised by a family member (Dukeminier and Sanders 1968; Kaplan 1983). This solution has also been called the "opting out" system; consent for organ retrieval is presumed unless the patient or family explicitly opt out (Strong and Strong 1985). When a presumed consent law allowing removal of eye tissue from autopsy subjects without prior permission from next of kin took effect in Georgia, the number of people receiving corneal transplants increased from 25 in 1983 to more than 1,000 in 1984 (Palmer 1985). As of 1985, thirteen countries in the world had presumed consent laws, and their ability to supply cadaver organs needed for transplants was significantly greater than that of the United States. Less than 10 percent of Americans questioned in a national poll supported the concept of presumed consent, however (Manninen and Evans 1985).

As of 1986, polls indicated that more than 50 percent of Americans supported a policy termed "required [professional] request" (Caplan 1984) or "routine inquiry" (Peele and Salvatierra 1986), requiring hospital personnel to ask next of kin about organ donation when the treating physician determines that brain death has occurred and that medical interventions should cease. This policy can be mandated through legislation or can be made part of a hospital's accreditation criteria (Caplan 1985a). By mid-1986, required request laws had been passed in 25 states. Supporters of the required request policy believe that grieving families can derive significant psychological reward by exercising the organ donation option and that the required request policy can therefore simultaneously serve dual functions. Medical professionals' behavioral and emotional reactions to required request policies represent an unknown variable, however. Physicians and nurses may fear upsetting family members, and they know that organ retrieval will involve them in aggressive procedures that seem inherently disrespectful to the deceased patient. Medical professionals need clear norms about procedures to be followed when organs are retrieved; and they themselves may need emotional support (Corlett 1985; Youngner, Allen, Bartlett, Cascorbi, Hau, Jackson, Mahowald, and Martin 1985). Without a well-developed system of insti-

tutional supports, efforts to initiate organ donation may be avoided.

Persistent Ethical Questions Affecting Cadaver and Live-Organ Donation

As Simmons and Simmons (1971) observed, deep-seated ethical questions surround organ donation, e. g. when can a potential donor be defined as dead? What protections are there for the powerless? What are the physician's ethical responsibilities? Questions such as these were widely debated during the early years of kidney- and heart-transplantation (Brewer 1970; Hamburger and Crosnier 1968; Kass 1968; McGeown 1968; Stickel 1966; Wolstenholme and O'Connor 1966).

Transplants from live donors raise a special set of ethical questions. Interestingly, European countries avoid these questions by depending almost totally on cadaver donors in their transplant programs.[4] Approximately 30 percent of all kidneys transplanted annually in the United States are obtained from living-related donors. The likelihood of a close tissue match between donor and recipient is increased when the donor is a relative, thereby increasing the graft survival rate. A small statistical risk to the health of the donor does exist, however, and significant interpersonal strain can arise within a family when relatives who are potentially kidney donors are reluctant to donate (Simmons, Hickey, Kjellstrand, and Simmons, 1971).

Because the rejection rate for organs taken from live donors is less than for organs taken from cadaver donors and because organ shortage has been persistent, attention in recent years has increasingly been given to the use of kidneys from nonrelated living donors (Burley and Stiller 1985; Levey, Hou, and Bush 1986). So-called "emotionally-related" donors (spouses, friends, etc.) may derive psychological benefit from donating to a significant other, but without this emotional link, nonrelated living donation becomes more problematic. An international living-related donor and recipient "exchange" has been proposed, using families who have been tissue-typed but who cannot donate to their own family member because the tissue match is not immunologically acceptable. However, it is difficult to imagine that individuals would donate organs within such a system unless they were assured that their family member would benefit within the exchange system or that they themselves might be financially rewarded. The latter possibility, financial compensation for human organs, has been the focus of considerable discussion.

The Market Model and Organ Donation

It is conceivable that a healthy individual, fully informed about the consequences of his/her action, might feel that the financial reward for selling a kidney was worth the personal cost involved. National Kidney Foundation (NKF) chapters have received numerous inquiries from individuals offering to sell a kidney. The possibility of donors selling organs for large fees received media attention during the Congressional hearings that preceded passage of PL 98–507 (Adams 1983), and the resulting legislation specifically stated that organs cannot be transferred for "valuable consideration."

Theoretically, a market system of organ procurement could operate simultaneously with an altruistic system of organ donation, but it is difficult to imagine that individuals or families would not want to receive compensation for organs if others were benefitting financially. An alternative would be to give tax credits to individuals who donate, or to families whose relatives are postmortem donors (Bassett 1985; Sharpe 1985), or to offer "a savings in health care costs for healthy adults who make premortem commitments to cadaveric organ donations" (Surman 1985, p. 318), but even these policies could raise legal, administrative, and social questions that would be difficult to resolve. The market model does not seem to offer a workable solution to the problem of organ shortage in the United States.

Cui Bono? Transplant Recipient Selection

Two important sets of criteria can be identified that shape decisions about which patients are selected to receive scarce organs. One set of criteria is related to the developmental status of the particular transplantation program, i.e. its location on a continuum from experimental to therapeutic. The other set of criteria is related to the individual patient's social background and social characteristics.

Variation in Patient Selection Models

The lower the success rate associated with particular transplant procedures, the more likely it is that patients referred for these procedures have distinctive medical needs (e.g., severe diabetes) or are considered "gravely and irreversibly ill" (Fox and Swazey 1978, p. 308). Pancreas, lung, and heart-lung transplants, therefore, tend to be performed with limited, well-defined categories of patients.

According to the paradigm of therapeutic innovation set forth by Fox and Swazey (1978), as a transplant comes to be regarded as therapeutic in nature, as opposed to an experimental and/ or last-chance effort, patient selection criteria begin to enlarge. Liver and heart transplantation moved from an experimental to a therapeutic status in the mid-1980s, and liver transplants were no longer reserved for patients under the age of 18. Both liver and heart transplant programs remained characterized for the most part by well-defined patient selection criteria, however, favoring selection of "best risk" patients in order to maximize use of scarce organs in procedures that remain very expensive.

Patient and graft survival rates characterizing kidney transplantation in the 1980s began to stimulate selection of not only "good risk" patients but also of patients characterized by significant medical risk factors, especially patients with diabetes mellitus, who were virtually excluded from consideration during the early years of kidney transplantation. Because a cadaver donor can provide two kidneys but only one heart or liver, and because living-related donors can provide a kidney, the supply of kidneys is larger than it is for other organs. Despite this, many potential transplant candidates are not able to obtain a transplant because of a shortage of *usable* kidneys. It appears that two factors influencing the receipt of a kidney transplant are patients' socioeconomic status (Kutner, Brogan, and Kutner, forthcoming) and patients' race (Evans, Manninen, Maier, Garrison, and Hart 1985; Hoe, Evans, and Elworth 1984; Kutner 1985).

Social Equity Issues in Transplantation

According to guidelines of the American Medical Association, human organs should be allocated to patients purely on a medical basis; social worth is not an appropriate criterion for organ allocation. The basic prerequisites for transplantation are supposed to be patients' need for the procedure and their ability to "do well" with the particular organ that is available. The latter consideration creates a difficult issue, however. Patients with a history of prior mental, emotional, or family problems are less likely to be selected to receive transplants. It is argued that a stable personal and family life are essential to patient/family compliance with therapeutic regimens and that, without such compliance, transplant success is seriously jeopardized (therefore wasting the organ). This argument received extensive media attention in 1986 when a heart transplant was needed by an infant born to young, unmarried parents. The legality of applying such stringent selection criteria can be questioned:

> Is it a legitimate goal to select those candidates judged to have not merely a fair, but the *greatest* probability of surviving transplantation? To what extent should patient-selection decisions be based on general evaluations of emotional stability, as a factor in survivability, or upon specific criteria (such as the presence of a stable home life, or absence of past psychological treatment) that may well exclude some of the handicapped? (Merrikin and Overcast 1985, p. 8).

These are difficult questions which may stimulate legal battles in coming years. In the context of severe organ shortages, however, the transplant gatekeepers are likely to remain committed to reserving this treatment option for patients who do not have characteristics that might prevent them from "doing well."

Differential financial resources at patients' disposal are another source of disparity in access to organ transplants. Although Medicare funding for kidney transplants has existed since 1973, it did not become available for heart transplants until 1986. Medicaid coverage of transplants varies across states. Although the Task Force on Organ Transplantation established by PL 98–507 strongly advocated that transplant centers not give favored access on the basis of a patient's wealth, it has been charged that "flagrant abuse" of this principle occurs, with medical institutions that obtain organs for well-to-do recipients benefitting by receiving large contributions (Johnson 1986; Manne 1985). It is also important to note that, regardless of the availability of Medicare/ Medicaid funding for transplants, a patient's financial status can affect transplant success, because financial resources influence a person's ability to travel to, and spend time at, a distant center that is skilled in treating particular types of patients.

Social equity questions also exist in regard to transplant recipients' nationality and race. Making transplants available to nonimmigrant aliens has generated much debate (Anast 1984). Those who argue that scarce organs should be reserved for U. S. citizens feel that this policy is justified because the donors are Americans and because federal tax dollars are used in organ procurement. Those who oppose an exclusionary transplant policy against non-U.S. citizens argue that persons from other countries are willing to spend large sums to receive transplants and thereby benefit the U.S. economy. Furnishing a specialized medical service to patients from countries that lack these services is also viewed as humanitarian and beneficial to the U.S. image abroad. The Task Force on Organ Transplantation finally concluded that 10 percent of the kidneys harvested in the United States should be reserved for nonresident immigrant recipients, but the hearts and livers should be given to foreigners only as a "last resort." The rationale for this decision was that Americans denied access to a heart or liver would die (whereas kidney patients can be maintained on dialysis), that close proximity to the transplant hospital is necessary for follow-up after heart or liver transplant surgery, and that the short period of viability for hearts and livers precludes their exportation to other countries.

Among American transplant candidates, patients' race appears to act as a screening variable. Kidney transplant data indicate that blacks are less likely than whites to be transplant recipients.

Approximately 35 percent of the kidney dialysis population in the United States is black (Forum of ESRD Networks 1984), but the percentage of kidney transplant recipients who are black appears to be much lower, perhaps 12 percent (Hoe et al. 1984). It is true that blacks are less likely than whites to donate kidneys, but both black recipients and white recipients fare better when the kidney is from a white donor (Terasaki 1985). In an effort to explore factors that might contribute to the racial differential in kidney transplant rates, the author examined transplant attitudes and experiences in a stratified random sample of 224 never-transplanted chronic kidney dialysis patients in the Atlanta metropolitan area (Kutner 1985). Blacks and whites in the sample were similar in age, total months of dialysis treatment, and perception of overall health status (Garrity, Somes, and Marx 1978), but black patients were significantly less likely to have completed 12 or more years of school and more likely to be unemployed. Black patients (49%) were significantly more likely than whites (36%) to say that no one had mentioned the possibility of their having a transplant. The reasons given by black respondents for not having raised the question themselves suggested that communication barriers, real or perceived, existed, e.g., "I didn't know who to talk to." Similarly, communication barriers regarding kidney donation seemed to exist within black families; black patients (62%) were much more likely than whites (38%) to say that they had never discussed kidney donation with their relatives.

Although the claim has been made that blacks do not get equal access to the kidney transplant system and that "de facto discrimination" exists (Newsclips 1985, p. 9), a variety of factors undoubtedly contribute to a lower kidney transplantation rate in the black population. It would be difficult to establish that discriminatory policies are involved. In the Atlanta sample of dialysis patients, whites (29%) were more likely than blacks (23%) to say that they would like to have a transplant. White patients (14%) were also less likely than blacks (20%) to state that they definitely did not want a transplant. Thus, the attitudes of white patients toward receiving a transplant were more positive than the attitudes of black patients, although they were not significantly different. As noted, black patients were less likely to indicate that they had received sufficient information about transplantation as a treatment option. If blacks tend to be excluded from consideration for kidney and other types of transplantation, socioeconomic factors may be an important reason. Medical professionals may expect higher posttransplant compliance from better educated patients and from patients with strong, intact family support systems. As long as organs remain in scarce supply, patients expected to "do well" are likely to receive preference, but it would be unfortunate if nonmedical criteria were unfairly emphasized in the development of transplant recommendations.

Outcome Assessment: Quality-of-Life Issues

Although transplantation provides a miraculous "second chance" for patients with end-stage diseases, the long-term immunosuppressive therapy that is required to prevent rejection is associated with physical and psychological problems that can seriously compromise quality of life. For example, it is not uncommon for kidney transplant recipients to experience complications such as cataracts, asepptic necrosis (necessitating hip replacement), and gastrointestinal disorders (peptic ulcer, pancreatitis, liver dysfunction) which may require hospitalization. Severe hypertension is a problem for a subset of kidney transplant recipients (Curtis 1985). If transplant recipients are overwhelmed by their gift of life, wondering how to be "worthy" of their gift or how to ever "pay back" the donor, the new organ can become a psychological burden (Simmons, Klein, and Simmons 1977; Simmons 1985). Fear that the organ will be rejected is another psychological burden.

> . . . The majority of these people usually do not break down, but they do manifest definite psychological needs that must be addressed by the transplant team. . . . Depression, organic brain syndromes, anxiety, compliance problems, and an occasional stress psychosis will surface despite skilled intervention. These will usually respond to a variety of supportive psychotherapies, judicious use of medication, and enlistment of all members of the transplant team in a sensitive, consistent, and caring manner.

Awareness of psychological implications is not a luxury, but is essential if the benefits of transplantation are to be maximized to enhance subsequent life contentment for the patient. . . (Gulledge, Buszta, and Montaque 1983, p. 333).

A number of potential complications can limit heart transplant recipients' long-term survival (Schroeder and Hunt 1986), and these patients seem to have a lower overall quality of life than kidney transplant recipients (Evans et al. 1985). Questions have also been raised about quality of life following liver transplantation:

. . . a number of problems remain, and new problems are encountered as more patients undergo this procedure at more centers. . . the potential for these patients to have satisfactory quality of life is not clear. . . (Najarian and Ascher 1984, pp. 1180–81).

Assessment of quality-of-life outcomes associated with transplantation is an important area for continuing study. Being given a second chance to live may require much reorganization of individual priorities, styles of relating to others, and own self-image; the availability of psychological support services is obviously very important. An organ transplant does not represent an immediate cure-all for the recipient, either physically or psychologically. Comprehensive (and successful) transplant programs are those that (1) educate patients fully in advance about transplant surgery and its ramifications, especially the risks associated with immunosuppression, and (2) maintain close patient follow-up that deals both with medical and psychological problems posttransplant. Unfortunately, not all transplant centers are willing or able to commit the resources that are required to establish a comprehensive program.

Conclusion

Viewed within the broad spectrum of modern medicine, it is probably fair to say that organ transplantation has received an undue amount of attention. Individuals whose survival depends on the timely receipt of a suitable organ quickly become the focus of human-interest media ac-

counts. Physicians remain intrigued by the challenge of trying to outsmart the human body's natural response of rejecting a foreign organ, and successful transplantation represents a "quick fix" (the most satisfying aspect of medical practice to many medical students and physicians). Medical institutions know that transplant center status brings prestige, financial rewards, and the ability to expand related institutional programs such as immunology research.

The issues surrounding application of transplant technology remain complex, despite passage of a national organ transplant act and the deliberations of a national task force. Although the affordability of organ transplant technology can be questioned, we continue to expand entitlement programs, and once established, it is very difficult to consider retreating from these programs because the expected outcome is that people will die. It can also be rationalized that, as Rushing (1985) points out, advances in medical technology represent only one of the factors that contribute to rising total health care costs; other factors include an aging population, inflated prices for health services, health insurance, cultural values associated with industrialization ("the medicalization of society"), and an increase in the supply of physicians.

States that have enacted required request laws have reported an average increase of 100 percent in organ and tissue donations (U.S. News 1986). Whether we will ever reach a point where the supply of organs is reasonably adequate to fill transplant needs is unknown. Because progress toward the goal of preventing traffic accidents and other causes of untimely death would simultaneously decrease the supply of cadaver organs, it is difficult to avoid experiencing mixed feelings about the goal of increasing the supply of cadaver organs suitable for transplantation.

Determining which patients should be recommended for a life-saving therapy, when the therapy cannot be made available to all who might benefit from it, is clearly a "painful prescription." Entitlement programs represent a partial answer to this dilemma. Although criteria for selection of individual recipients still must be employed, in theory the U.S. government made it financially possible in 1972 for any patient to obtain a kidney transplant—an option not available anywhere else in the world. A similar program of support for heart and liver transplants is emerging (Casscells 1986).

Quality-of-life outcomes can be maximized for transplant recipients within a comprehensive transplant program that takes into consideration psychosocial as well as medical needs of patients and anticipates potential transplant-related problems. It is difficult, however, for smaller medical centers to support a comprehensive program that provides continuity of care from the transplant work-up stage through ongoing management of outpatient care. The probability of complications is increased if these centers lack expertise in services such as immunology and infectious disease control. Finally, the greater the competition with other centers for scarce organs, the fewer the number of transplant procedures that are likely to be performed at a particular center, which may in turn make it more difficult for the transplant team to maintain a high skill level. All of these factors suggest a need to limit the number of transplant centers and to specify the essential components of transplant programs. More than 80 centers were performing heart transplants in the United States in 1985, but fewer than 40 centers could have handled the available donor supply and performed an optimal number of transplants (Overcast and Evans 1985).

The legislation establishing the ESRD program of Medicare (PL 92–603) and the legislation designed to facilitate organ transplants (PL 98–507) represent unprecedented efforts to structure health care delivery for a particular disease category and a particular medical technology. In the characteristic American pattern, however, both pieces of legislation allowed for operational details to be worked out in a competitive, political context. The proliferation since 1973 of proprietary dialysis centers has been a very important determinant of the nature of dialysis services in this country (cf. Kutner 1982; Plough 1986). Shaped to an important degree by the philosophies of the medical directors who head these centers, the comprehensiveness of the supportive services available to patients varies. An "ESRD network" system was established by HCFA to monitor the quality of kidney dialysis services, but this monitoring process has been carried out with limited and nonuniform success across the 32 HCFA-designated networks, largely because physicians resist monitoring their peers.

The issues reviewed in this paper indicate the need for carefully designed and implemented transplant programs, in order to maximize the efficiency and fairness of organ procurement and distribution systems and the quality of patient outcomes. Reaching decisions about such programs, in the absence of a regulatory system such as is used by Great Britain (Simmons and Marine 1984), is not easy, as illustrated by the lengthy deliberations of a Task Force on Transplantation in Massachusetts and the responses elicited by that Task Force Report (Massachusetts Task Force on Organ Transplantation 1985; Annas 1985a, b; Caplan 1985b; Casscells 1985; Jonsen 1985; Kissick 1985; Miller 1985; Overcast and Evans 1985; Pauly 1985; Skelley 1985). Experience has shown that making kidney dialysis widely available without at the same time taking steps to encourage maximum rehabilitation of patients has resulted in a patient population that is significantly less likely than the pre-Medicare-supported dialysis population to return to productive, gainful activity (Evans, Blagg, and Bryan 1981). When a technology becomes so available that it is no longer necessary to offer it only to those patients most likely to return to active lives (the "best-risk" patients), the patient population becomes a more challenging one to treat and rehabilitate, and the system must include more patient service and dedicated medical personnel in order to further patients' total rehabilitation.

Understandably, we are reluctant to retreat from using technologies that save lives.

> If there is a tenet that forms the bedrock of clinical theory in ESRD (or biomedical science in general), it is the value of increased survival. The ability of a treatment to significantly extend a patient's life where no treatment would surely result in immediate death is almost in itself an operational standard for clinical effectiveness.... If a technology extends life, use it! (Plough 1986, p. 39)

We are making a concerted effort to "use" organ transplantation more widely, by expanding entitlement programs and organ procurement programs, and by adopting required request laws to increase organ donation. Greater availability of donated organs may ease the stringent criteria that are currently used in the transplant candidate selection process. If we are also committed to using transplant technology, and the valued resources that are involved, as effectively as possible, we will need to more honestly confront the issues that affect quality-of-life outcomes among organ transplant recipients.

NOTES

Supported in part by the National Institute of Handicapped Research, Grant No. G008006809. An earlier version of this paper was presented at the 1983 Annual Meeting of the Society for the Study of Social Problems in Washington, D.C. I would like to thank J. Michael Henderson and three anonymous reviewers for their valuable comments.

1. Because of the availability of validated back-up procedure, dialysis *via* an artificial kidney, the development of renal transplantation included a dimension of safety not shared by other types of transplantation. The only other types of artificial organs besides the artificial kidney now in routine medical practice are prosthetic heart valves, prosthetic arteries, and the heart-lung machine. However, versions of an artificial liver and an artificial pancreas, in addition to the permanent implantable heart pump (artificial heart), are being tested at several medical centers.
2. Both patient and graft survival rates in kidney transplantation are better when a living-related donor is used instead of a cadaver donor. Transplantation success rates also vary across transplant centers.
3. Unlike other immunosuppressive drugs, cyclosporine appears to inhibit the hormone that controls cells specifically involved in tissue rejection without at the same time destroying the body's immune defenses against infection. However, cyclosporine has also been shown to have undesirable side-effects, especially lymphoma, high blood pressure, and kidney damage, and the dosages given to transplant recipients are tapered off as soon as possible after surgery.
4. In Japan, however, the opposite is true; use of cadaver organs is viewed as a violation of the integrity of the soul.

REFERENCES

Adams, Timothy. 1983. "Debate Over Sale of Transplant Organs." *Atlanta Journal and Constitution,* November 13:sec. C, p. 17.

Anast, David. 1984. "Congressional Hearing on 'Transplantation into Nonimmigrant Aliens.' " *Contemporary Dialysis* 5:18, 20–21, 24.

Annas, George J. 1985a. "Regulating Heart and Liver Transplants in Massachusetts: An Overview of the Report of the Task Force on Organ Transplantation." *Law, Medicine & Health Care* 13:4–7.

———. 1985b. "The Dog and His Shadow: A Response to Overcast and Evans." *Law, Medicine & Health Care* 13:112–29.

Austen, W. Gerald, and A. Benedict Cosimi. 1984. "Heart Transplantation After 16 Years." *New England Journal of Medicine* 311:1436–38.

Banowsky, Lynn H.W. 1983. "Current Results and Future Expectations in Renal Transplantation." *Urologic Clinics of North America* 10:337–46.

Bassett, Beth Dawkins. 1985. "Hearts for Sale?" *Emory Magazine* 61:31.

Beierle, Andrew W.M. 1985. "A Conversation with Harrison Rogers; The President of the AMA Talks About the Problems and Priorities of Organized Medicine." *Emory Magazine* 61:19–23.

Blendon, Robert J., and Drew E. Altman. 1984. "Public Attitudes About Health-Care Costs: A Lesson in National Schizophrenia." *New England Journal of Medicine* 311:613–16.

Brewer, S.P. 1970. "Donors of Organs Seen as Victims." *New York Times,* April 19:36.

Burley, June A., and Calvin R. Stiller. 1985. "Emotionally Related Donors and Renal Transplantation." *Transplantation Proceedings* 17:123–27.

Caplan, Arthur L. 1984. "Ethical and Policy Issues in the Procurement of Cadaver Organs for Transplantation." *New England Journal of Medicine* 311:981–83.

———. 1985a. "Toward Greater Donor Organ Availability for Transplantation." *New England Journal of Medicine* 312:319.

———. 1985b. "If There's a Will, Is There a Way?" *Law, Medicine & Health Care* 13:32–34.

Casscells, Ward. 1985. "A Clinician's View of the Massachusetts Task Force on Organ Transplantation." *Law, Medicine & Health Care* 13:27–28.

———. 1986. "Heart Transplantation: Recent Policy Developments." *New England Journal of Medicine* 315:1365–68.

Corlett, Sue. 1985. "Professional and System Barriers to Organ Donation." *Transplantation Proceedings* 17:111–19.

Culyer, Anthony J., and Bruno Horisberger (eds.). 1983. *Economic and Medical Evaluation of Health Care Technologies.* New York: Springer-Verlag.

Curtis, John J. 1985. "Hypertension: A Common Problem for Kidney Transplant Recipients." *The Kidney* 18:2–8.

Dateline. 1986. "Latest HCFA Statistics Released." *Dialysis & Transplantation* 15:544–45.

Davis, Carolyne K. 1983. *Statement Before the Subcommittee on Investigations and Oversight, House Committee on Science and Technology.* Washington, D.C.: U.S. Department of Health & Human Services.

Dukeminier, Jesse, Jr., and David Sanders. 1968. "Organ Transplantation: A Proposal for Routine Salvaging of Cadaver Organs." *New England Journal of Medicine* 279:413–19.

Elick, Barbara A., and David E.R. Sutherland. Forthcoming. "Renal Transplantation Within A Multi-Organ Transplant System: One Institution's Experience." In *Maximizing Rehabilitation in Chronic Renal Disease,* edited by N.G. Kutner, D.D. Cardenas, and J.D. Bower. New York: SP Medical.

Evans, Roger W. 1983a. "Health Care Technology and the Inevitability of Resource Allocation and Rationing Decisions: Part I." *Journal of the American Medical Association* 249:2047–53.

———. 1983b. "Health Care Technology and the Inevitability of Resource Allocation and Rationing Decisions: Part II." *Journal of the American Medical Association* 249:2208–19.

———. 1985. "The Socioeconomics of Organ Transplantation." *Transplantation Proceedings* 17:129–36.

Evans, Roger W., Christopher R. Blagg, and Fred A. Bryan, Jr. 1981. "Implications for Health Care Policy: A Social and Demographic Profile of Hemodialysis Patients in the United States." *Journal of the American Medical Association* 245:487–91.

Evans, Roger W., Diane L. Manninen, Anthony Maier, Louis P. Garrison, Jr., and L. Gary Hart. 1985. "The Quality of Life of Kidney and Heart Transplant Recipients." *Transplantation Proceedings* 17:1579–82.

Forum of ESRD Networks. 1984. "1983 Program Report." *Contemporary Dialysis & Nephrology* 5(12): 56–58.

Fox, Renée C., and Judith P. Swazey. 1978. *The Courage to Fail: A Social View of Organ Transplants and Dialysis.* Chicago: University of Chicago Press.

Fuchs, Victor R. 1984. "The 'Rationing' of Medical Care." *New England Journal of Medicine* 311: 1572–73.

Garrity, Thomas F., Grant W. Sommes, and Martin B. Marx. 1978. "Factors Influencing Self-Assessment of Health." *Social Science & Medicine* 12:77–81.

Gore, Albert, Jr. 1986. "Ignoring the National Organ Transplant Act 'Appears More and More to Be the Administration's Transplant Policy.' " *Contemporary Dialysis & Nephrology* 7:40–41.

Gulledge, A. Dale, Caroline Buszta, and Drogo K. Montague. 1983. "Psychosocial Aspects of Renal Transplantation." *Urologic Clinics of North America* 10:327–35.

Hamburger, Jean, and Jean Crosnier. 1968. "Moral and Ethical Problems in Transplantation." Pp. 37–44 in *Human Transplantation,* edited by F.T. Rapaport and J. Dausset. New York: Grune & Stratton.

Hoe, Marilyn M., Roger W. Evans, and Julie T. Elworth. 1984. *National Kidney Dialysis and Kidney Transplantation Study: A Summary of Results.* Baltimore: Health Care Financing Administration.

Johnson, Roger S. 1986. "Restrictive Policies Voted on by U.S. Task Force on Organ Transplantation." *Contemporary Dialysis & Nephrology* 7:18,20.

Jonsen, Albert R. 1985. "Organ Transplants and the Principle of Fairness." *Law, Medicine & Health Care* 13:37–39+.

Kaplan, Arthur. 1983. "Organ Transplants Must Not Be Put on Highest Bidder Basis." *Atlanta Journal and Constitution,* October 2:sec. C, p. 16.

Kass, L.R. 1968. "A Caveat on Transplants." *Washington Post,* January 14:sec. B, p. 1.

Kissick, William L. 1985. "Organ Transplantation and the Art of the Possible." *Law, Medicine & Health Care* 13:34–35.

Kutner, Nancy G. 1982. "Cost-Benefit Issues in U.S. National Health Legislation: The Case of the End-Stage Renal Disease Program." *Social Problems* 30: 51–64.

———. 1985. "Racial Differences in the Transplant Attitudes and Experiences of Chronic Dialysis Patients." Paper presented at annual meeting of National Kidney Foundation, Inc., New Orleans, December 14.

Kutner, Nancy G., Donna Brogan, and Michael H. Kutner. Forthcoming. "ESRD Treatment Modality and Patients' Quality of Life: Longitudinal Assessment." *American Journal of Nephrology.*

Levey, Andrew S., Susan Hou, and Harry L. Bush, Jr. 1986. "Kidney Transplantation from Unrelated Living Donors: Time to Reclaim a Discarded Opportunity." *New England Journal of Medicine* 314: 914–16.

Manne, Henry G. 1985. "U.S. Should Allow Sale of Organs for Transplants." *Atlanta Journal and Constitution,* October 20:sec. B, pp.1,7.

Manninen, Diane L., and Roger W. Evans. 1985. "Public Attitudes and Behavior Regarding Organ Donation." *Journal of the American Medical Association* 253:3111–15.

Massachusetts Task Force on Organ Transplantation. 1985. "Report." *Law, Medicine & Health Care* 13:8–26.

Mayfield, Mark. 1986. "Transplants: Needs Many, Donors Few." *USA Today*, July 24:sec. A, pp. 1–2.

McGeown, Mary G. 1968. "Ethics for the Use of Live Donors in Kidney Transplantation." *American Heart Journal* 75:711–14.

Merriken, Karen J., and Thomas D. Overcast. 1985. "Patient Selection for Heart Transplantation: When Is a Discriminating Choice Discrimination?" *Journal of Health Politics, Policy and Law* 10:7–32.

Miller, Frances H. 1985. "Reflections on Organ Transplantation in the United Kingdom." *Law, Medicine & Health Care* 13:31–32.

Najarian, John S., and Nancy L. Asher. 1984. "Liver Transplantation." *New England Journal of Medicine* 311:1179–81.

Newsclips. 1985. "Blacks Not Getting Fair Share of Transplants." *Renalife* 2:9–10.

Nightingale, Joan E. 1985. "New Organ Transplantation Program: The Decision Tree." *Transplantation Proceedings* 17:137–42.

Overcast, Thomas D., and Roger W. Evans. 1985. "Technology Assessment, Public Policy and Transplantation: A Restrained Appraisal of the Massachusetts Task Force Approach." *Law Medicine & Health Care* 13:106–11.

Overcast, Thomas D., Roger W. Evans, Lisa E. Bowen, Marilyn M. Hoe, and Cynthia L. Livak. 1984. "Problems in the Identification of Potential Organ Donors." *Journal of the American Medical Association* 251:1559–62.

Palmer, Prentice. 1985. "High Court Upholds Law on Corneal Transplants." *Atlanta Constitution*, October 10:sec. B, p. 9.

Pauly, Mark V. 1985. "Equity and Costs." *Law Medicine & Health Care* 13:28–31.

Peele, Amy S., and Oscar Salvatierra, Jr. 1986. "Is Routine Inquiry the Answer to Solving the Organ Donor Shortage?" *Contemporary Dialysis & Nephrology* 7:5,43–44.

Pisano, L. 1985. "Critical Comments on Present and Future Possibilities and Advantages of Pancreas Transplantation in Insulin-Dependent Diabetes Mellitus." *Transplantation Proceedings* 17:135.

Plough, Alonzo L. 1986. *Borrowed Time: Artificial Organs and the Politics of Extending Lives*. Philadelphia: Temple University.

Rapaport, Felix T., and Raffaello Cortesini. 1985. "The Past, Present, and Future of Organ Transplantation, with Special Reference to Current Needs in Kidney Procurement and Donation." *Transplantation Proceedings* 17:3–10.

Reiner, Mark, William Eagles, and Ken Watson. 1986. "Organ Bingo: Choice or Chance?" *Dialysis & Transplantation* 15:441–42.

Rettig, Richard A. 1980. *Implementing the End-Stage Renal Disease Program of Medicare*. Santa Monica: Rand Corporation.

Roberts, Stephen D. 1980. "Cost-Effective Oxygen Therapy." *Annals of Internal Medicine* 93:499–500.

Roughton, Bert. 1986. "More than $50,000 Is Pledged to Help 5-Year-Old Heart Patient." *Atlanta Constitution*, March 18:sec. C, p. 7.

Rushing, William A. 1985. "The Supply of Physicians and Expenditures for Health Services with Implications for the Coming Physician Surplus." *Journal of Health and Social Behavior* 26:297–311.

Schroeder, John Speer, and Sharon A. Hunt. 1986. "Cardiac Transplantation: Where Are We?" *New England Journal of Medicine* 315:961–63.

Seabrook, Charles. 1985. "Augusta's Transplant Rate Poor: Survival Record of Heart Recipients Falling Short." *Atlanta Journal and Constitution*, June 9:sec. A, pp.1,14.

Sharpe, Gilbert. 1985. "Commerce in Tissue and Organs." *Transplantation Proceedings* 17:33–39.

Simmons, Roberta G. 1985. "Social and Psychological Posttransplant Adjustment." Pp. 85–97 in *Rehabilitation and the Chronic Renal Disease Patient,* edited by N.G. Kutner, D.D. Cardenas, and J.D. Bower. New York: SP Medical.

Simmons, Roberta G., Kathy Hickey, Carl M. Kjellstrand, and Richard L. Simmons. 1971. "Family Tension in the Search for a Kidney Donor." *Journal of the American Medical Association* 215:909–12.

Simmons, Roberta G., Susan D. Klein, and Richard L. Simmons. 1977. *Gift of Life: The Social and Psychological Impact of Organ Transplantation.* New York: Wiley.

Simmons, Roberta G., and Susan Klein Marine. 1984. "The Regulation of High Cost Technology Medicine: The Case of Dialysis and Transplantation in the United Kingdom." *Journal of Health and Social Behavior* 25:320–34.

Simmons, Roberta G., and Richard L. Simmons. 1971. "Organ Transplantation: A Societal Problem." *Social Problems* 19:36–57.

Skelley, Luke. 1985. "Practical Issues in Obtaining Organs for Transplantation." *Law, Medicine & Health Care* 13:35–37.

Starzl, Thomas E., S. Iwatsuki, B.W. Shaw, Jr., R.D. Gordon, C. Esquivel, S. Todo, I. Kam, and S. Lynch. 1985. "Factors in the Development of Liver Transplantation." *Transplantation Proceedings* 17:107–18.

Stickel, D.L. 1966. "Ethical and Moral Aspects of Transplantation." *Monographs of Surgical Science* 3:267–301.

Strong, Margaret, and Carson Strong. 1985. "The Shortage of Organs for Transplantation." *ANNA Journal* 12:239–42.

Surman, Owen S. 1985. "Toward Greater Donor Organ Availability for Transplantation." *New England Journal of Medicine* 312:318.

Terasaki, Paul. 1985. "Renal Transplantation in Blacks: Special Issues and Challenges." Paper presented at First International Symposium on Renal Failure in Blacks, Washington, D.C., April 29.

Toledo-Pereyra, Luis H. 1986. "Practical Immunologic Aspects of Clinical Pancreas and Islet Cell Transplantation." *Dialysis & Transplantation* 15(a): pp. 514–16, 520, 522.

U.S. News. 1986. "Gallup Organ Survey Results Reported." *Contemporary Dialysis & Nephrology* 7:15–16.

Wolstenholme, Gordon Ethelbert Ward, & Maeve O'Connor (eds.). 1966. *Ethics in Medical Progress: With Special Reference to Transplantation.* Boston: Little, Brown.

Youngner, Stuart J., Martha Allen, Edward T. Bartlett, Helmut F. Cascorbi, Toni Hau, David L. Jackson, Mary B. Mahowald, and Barbara J. Martin. 1985. "Psychosocial and Ethical Implications of Organ Retrieval." *New England Journal of Medicine* 313:321–24.

32

Genetics and Social Policy

▪ ▪ ▪ ▪ ▪ ▪

Dorothy Nelkin

For several years, philosophers, sociologists, and policy analysts have been trying to explore the social, legal, and ethical implications of the tests that will emerge from the Human Genome Project. Except for prenatal screening, genetic tests are not yet very widely employed. What can one actually study that would allow some fairly concrete prediction of how these technologies—as they become available—will actually be used? In writing our book, *Dangerous Diagnostics: The Social Power of Biological Information,*[1] Laurence Tancredi and I struggled over this question. Two approaches seemed reasonable. First, new technologies need to be socially acceptable. What cultural predispositions might suggest how predictive testing will be used in acceptable ways? This is, I believe, a critical question and is the topic of my current research. Second, technologies are mediated through social institutions. On the basis of existing institutional practices and needs, how can we expect predictive genetic tests to be employed? Third, in light of considerable past experience with other kinds of tests, what can we anticipate will be the implications of the growing use of genetic tests?

Cultural Predispositions

The preoccupation with testing in American society reflects two cultural tendencies: an actuarial mind-set evident in our prevailing approach to problems of potential risk and a related tendency to reduce problems to biological or medical terms. Actuarial thinking is designed to limit liability. It places value on weighing costs and benefits and developing quantitative means of planning and prediction so as to minimize risk. Controlling risk requires calculating the cost of future contingencies, taking into account expected losses and selecting good risks while excluding bad ones. To do so it is necessary to understand the individual actuarially, that is, as part of a statistical aggregate.

The actuarial mentality thrives on information about the health, habits, and behavior of individuals. Accumulation of data is thus an important feature of every organization, and testing is part of this trend. Nothing indicates popular support more clearly than a market. There is demand for testing, so much so that in anticipation of a market for testing, several biotech firms are in the business of collecting blood samples for future genetic tests as they become available. Faith in facts and in numbers derived from tests has frequently obscured the uncertainties intrinsic to most tests—for drugs, for IQ—and tests are widely viewed as neutral, necessary, and benign.

If faith in facts is part of the actuarial mentality, so too is the tendency to reduce social problems to measurable biological or medical dimensions. We routinely use medical judgments to define the boundaries of "normal" behavior and thereby to identify competence, deviance, or capacity to work. Biological reductionism has evolved from the tendency to medicalize social problems. In its contemporary manifestation, medicalization has incorporated notions of biological fitness or perfectibility, and the idea that these are matters of personal choice. It is assumed that there exists an ideal of normality or perfection against which individuals can be measured, that complex human behavior can be reduced to biological or genetic explanations, and that behavioral problems can be attributed to biological determinants with minimal reference to social or environmental influences.

The media have been quick to respond to these ideas. Covering the Baby M case, a story in *U.S. News and World Report*[2] proclaimed that "solid evidence demonstrates that our very character is molded by heredity." The article, therefore, questioned whether Baby M's future really hinged on which family would bring her up. In tracing the genetic themes in popular culture, I am finding these themes expressed in several ways—a pervasive emphasis on the critical importance of preserving genetic relationships; a persistent notion that biology is destiny, that all traits, behavioral as well as physical, are genetically predetermined; a growing preoccupation with identifying the genetic characteristics of specific groups (mainly women and blacks); and even a fear that the human species is threatened with evolutionary decline. The media coverage of sociobiology, the appeal of the Bouchard twin studies, the popularity of genealogies and the search for roots, the remarkable media interest in studies of the genetic basis of alcoholism and crime, all suggest a culture predisposed to accept genetic explanations.

A great deal has been written about the social policy implications of biological determinism in the late 19th and early 20th centuries. Less has been said about the reemergence of genetic explanations in more recent cultural discourse. Scientists themselves, encouraged by recent advances, have expounded on the social meanings inherent in their work, and on applications of genetic understanding to social policy. Geneticist Marjorie Shaw has asserted that "the law must control the spread of genes causing severe deleterious effects, just as disabling pathogenic bacteria and viruses are controlled."[3] Dan Koshland, editor of *Science,* writes that "In the warfare between nature and nurture, nature has clearly won."[4] Others refer to "pollution of the human gene pool," "genetically healthy societies," or "optimal genetic strategies" to predict and therefore control genetic health.

Both the scientific and popular discourse focuses increasingly on the importance of genetics in predicting behavior and health. This discourse, in effect, reduces the body to a machine-like system permeable to visualization and understandable by deciphering a code. It provides a theoretical structure to explain human behavior and a justification for a growing use of genetic tests in a range of social institutions, including schools, workplaces, and the courts.

Institutional Use of Tests

Diagnostic tools obviously serve many useful and humane purposes: they identify potential health problems for therapeutic or preventive action. In nonclinical contexts, tests are used to channel learning disabled children into appropriate educational channels, to protect vulnerable workers from exposure to toxic substances, to provide solid evidence for legal decisions. We also know, however, that diagnostic tools can be abused; that testing has frequently served to justify racial or gender biases, to legitimate exclusionary practices, or to enhance institutional power and control with little regard for the rights of individuals.

The prerogative to test has long been recognized as a source of institutional power. Foucault saw the examination as a strategy of political domination, a means of "normalization." In *Discipline and Punish* he described the examination as "a normalizing gaze, that introduces the constraints of conformity . . . that compares, differentiates, hierarchizes, excludes." Foucault also observed the extension of testing throughout the society. "The judges of normality are present everywhere. We are a society of the teacher-judge, the educator-judge, the social worker-judge . . . we are entering the age of the infinite examination and of compulsory objectification."

Foucault wrote of pedagogical tests.[5] Others, such as Walter Reich,[6] have developed a similar analysis of the role of psychiatric tests to reinforce political hierarchies and social values. Similarly, anthropologists have long described the way cultures employ nature to support the ongoing social system. As Mary Douglas put it:[7] "Institutions bestow sameness. . . . They trim the body's shape to their conventions." In our society as well, we call upon nature by using biological tests to assure that individuals conform to institutional values. In some cases, institutions exercise control through force, but most often they control their constituents by symbolic manipulation. Sanctioned by scientific authority and implemented by medical professionals, tests are an effective means of manipulation; for they imply that decisions are implemented for the good of the individual. They are, therefore, a powerful tool in shaping individual choices in ways that conform to institutional values.

Schools, employers, insurers, the courts all stand to gain from better understanding of the present and future health status and behavioral syndromes of their clients. In these settings economic constraints and administrative pressures for accountability enhance the appeal of tests that can uncover latent conditions and predict the future health or behavior of their client populations. Let me briefly explore how tests are used by such institutions to meet their economic and political needs.

First of all, with their aura of scientific objectivity, biology-based tests are a means to redefine problematic behavior in individuals in ways that protect routine practices. Public schools, for example, have faced consistent criticism from government and advocacy groups because of educational failures. In particular, they must explain the large number of middle class children who have academic difficulties but normal IQs and no obvious hearing or visual loss. In the late 1960s the category of "learning disabled" came into common use, replacing such labels as "emotionally disturbed," "culturally deprived," or "nutritionally deficient," even as "working mother's syndrome." With the help of diagnostic tests, several million school children have since been diagnosed as learning disabled. Some suggest that one in 10 children are undiscovered victims of "minimal neural dysfunctions" or "minimal brain disorders" that affect their performance in school.

Behavioral problems, once explained in terms of environmental or social influences, are also attributed to the biology of the child. Hyperactivity, at one time a problem in classroom dynamics, has been redefined as "attention deficit disorder," a problem located in the students' brain. The behavioral or learning difficulties of such children are, of course, real. But the new labels are also an institutional convenience, removing blame from schools, families, or other social influences.

These biological explanations of learning difficulties have both reflected and encouraged the use of diagnostic tests that can identify small differences in brain activity among children. These include electroencephalograms, neuropsychological tests, genetic analyses, and left-right brain lateralization tests. Some are expected to predict at an early age children likely to be slow learners, dyslexic, or disruptive during their school years. With refinement in testing, the numbers of children classified as disabled has more than doubled during the past decade.

Second, the predictive capacity of biological tests is also useful to organizations as a means to facilitate long-term planning in a context of growing cost containment pressures. Prediction and planning are, of course, important to all organizations but let us focus on the health care system. The economics and efficiency of treatment decisions is increasingly urgent in light of the growing number of prepaid medical plans and the financial dilemmas of insurance companies. Pressure for efficiency also comes from government policies linking Medicaid reimbursement to diagnostic categories. These pressures, along with the ubiquitous threat of litigation, create powerful incentives to back up health care decisions with objective and predictive evidence. They encourage competition for "profitable" patients, people who carry no dangerous genetic characteristics and who have predictable and reimbursable illnesses. Diagnostic tests facilitate the process of categorizing patients; they provide technical evidence to support complicated or controversial decisions, and they provide the patient profiles necessary to control access to health care facilities or to plan for future institutional demands.

Genetic disorders are believed to account for 20 to 30% of all live births and 12% of all hospital admissions in the United States. At present about 31 to 37 million people in the United States have no health insurance. About 15% of those insured are individually covered and must meet underwriting standards by providing their health histories, information on their family illnesses, and evidence of their current state of health to obtain insurance. Sometimes tests are required. According to a survey by the Office of Technology Assessment, in 1987 20% of these individual applicants were issued policies that excluded pre-existing conditions or paid higher premiums; 8% were denied coverage for diseases including obesity, alcoholism, cancer, schizophrenia, and AIDS. Health Maintenance Organizations denied membership to 24% of individual applicants. Those with "bad" genetic markers may simply be added to the growing number of people without access to medical coverage.

A third source of the appeal of genetic testing follows from its promise of enhancing institutional efficiency. As employers increasingly assume responsibility as insurers or health care providers, biological tests have become a means to justify the exclusion of high risk individuals from work. The predisposition to use testing as a means of exclusion from work is well established.

In 1985 49% of American employers required pre-employment medical examinations, a 10% increase since the early 1970s. Pre-employment examinations include various predictive tests ranging from psychological tests for future executives to lower back roentgenograms for construction workers. Even dubious diagnostic procedures persist. About one million pre-employment roentgenograms are taken on asymptomatic individuals despite evidence that only 2% of those screened out ever develop serious back trouble. Faced by regulatory pressures and litigation and concerned about absenteeism and illness, chemical companies have used genetic screening techniques to predict and exclude employees susceptible of being genetically predisposed to illness from exposure to chemicals. Justified in the first instance as a way to protect worker health, genetic tests can be used to avoid making costly changes in the workplace environment. But they have also operated to exclude not only specific individuals, but certain groups.

Recent debates over fetal protection policies have highlighted problems involved in such practices. Yet, in the context of growing economic competition, employers view screening techniques that will identify those predisposed to genetic disease as a cost-effective way to control absenteeism, reduce compensation claims and debilitating lawsuits, and avoid future medical costs. While politically charged, the use of tests that facilitate the selection and maintenance of a productive low risk work force is simply rational economic policy. Greater certainty in testing is expected to mute political opposition.

Finally, organizations use tests to provide hard evidence that can justify or guide ambiguous decisions about those who will not or cannot conform. In hospital, tests can define an uncooperative patient as biologically incompetent, unable to make autonomous decisions, and in need of paternalistic control. And in face of disaffection with psychiatric evidence underlying the insanity defense, the courts are predisposed to adopt biological tests that can provide "hard" facts—that is, a more objective scientific basis—on which to make decisions about the responsibility and disposition of defendants.

Grounded in science, genetic tests will be compelling; and their limits are likely to be ignored. The tendency, certainly in the popular press, is to talk about all genetic tests as if they were predicting rather simple single gene disorders, ignoring that in most diseases the manifestation of symptoms, their severity, and when they will appear rest on the interaction of multiple genes and on intervening factors—diet, lifestyle, or the influence of environmental or social interactions.

Implications

Let me conclude by anticipating some consequences of the growing availability of genetic tests. The refinement of tests, the ability to detect small deviations from the normal, expands the number of disease categories and the number of people judged deviant or abnormal. Those identified as disabled and excluded from insurance and prepaid health plans are growing. Genetic testing, in the context of the expectations of insurers for full information, will add to those uninsurable.

Furthermore, expansion of testing and concomitant belief in the biological causes of disease is likely to enhance the role of medical experts in nonclinical settings. Physicians have long interacted with other institutions to assist in and legitimize social policy. They interact with the law by reporting venereal disease or gunshot wounds, with schools by evaluating absenteeism or learning disabilities, with industry by judging responsibility for accidents or illness, or the ability to perform certain jobs, with the military by authorizing deferments, with the courts by determining the mental status and moral responsibility of criminals and their competency to stand trial. Ability to provide more reliable characterizations of physical and psychological disorders gives greater power to medical professionals—the company doctor, the school psychologist, the forensic psychiatrist. Because of their conflicting interests these professionals welcome testing as a neutral data base to justify controversial decisions. But such tests may further complicate their already ambiguous roles.

Expansion of genetic testing also implies certain therapeutic options. On the one hand this can be useful to patients; tests can help to assess the effectiveness of specific therapies. On the other hand, the use of tests to evaluate behavioral problems has already encouraged extensive use of drugs such as Ritalin® for school children, and shifted the focus from social influences on their behavior. Moreover, as tests become more refined, professionals may rely more on test results than on symptoms of individuals. In the context of malpractice litigation, credibility—provided by tests—may prevail over validity, especially in cases of potential conflict.

Finally, predictive screening opens possibilities for biological discrimination and state control. At present, prenatal genetic screening is used to expand the reproductive options of the family. Choices are theoretically left to the discretion of individuals. This, however, does not rule out professional or state control over reproductive decisions. State chromosomal registries are demanding more information on birth defects from genetic laboratories. There are precedents for state intervention. It was not so long ago that some states provided for the sterilization of the mentally retarded and seriously psychotically ill. In 1976 the Supreme Court of North Carolina ruled that the State had a right to "prevent the procreation of children who will become a burden on the state."

The possibilities for discrimination are evident. Tarasoff-like arguments about compelling social interest have been used to support compulsory genetic testing of high risk people and informing family members. Data banks are proliferating—some for crime detection, but others for screening disease. Vivigen, a biotech lab, has a genetic repository for people who want to bank their DNA so it will be available when there are linkage tests. The caveats in their contracts suggest that questions of medical confidentiality are not resolved.

Cases of genetic discrimination are proliferating; people who are asymptomatic but suspected of having a genetic disease have been barred from insurance, drivers' licenses, or employment because of their genetic labels. In one publicized case, an insurer warned a women whose fetus tested positive for cystic fibrosis that she would not receive medical coverage for the child if it were born with the disease. One can imagine families demanding information about their genetic roots or commercial firms selling genetic information to such interested agencies as insurers.

Questions of access to test results will juxtapose the privacy of individuals against the interests of relations and employers. Do members of a family have a right to information about the biological status of their relations? Should a physician have the right or obligation to communicate information abut genetic disease to family members who may be similarly afflicted? Should people seeking to adopt a child be able to probe the genetic history of those children available to shop for an appropriate match? Can the right to be employed depend on having the right genes?

The significance of biological information rests, of course, on just how it will be used. But it is clear that many groups have strong interests in the biological condition of those in their domain, including Departments of Motor Vehicles, immigration authorities, creditors, professional sports teams, the military, and even university tenure committees.

As Foucault observed,[8] tests that establish statistical standards of normal behavior against which to measure individuals have long been used to measure competence, to define deviance, to exclude, to define those who are more or less worthy or desirable. Technologies that tap into biological understanding about how the body functions and how it can be expected to function during the course of an individual's life are but an extension of earlier pedagogical and psychiatric tests. But they have greater credibility as assumptions of neutrality conceal the values embedded in technological findings and the specificity of tests mute moral reservations about privacy, personhood, or individual rights. Considering the rapid development of diagnostic technologies, there has been little discussion about the employment of tests in such nonmedical contexts, about the critical questions of access to biological information, and the need to avoid abuse.

Diagnosis remains an uncertain art. But even as tests increase in accuracy and expand the range of what they can predict, key questions of interpretation will remain. What degree of correlation between existing markers and subsequent physical or behavioral manifestations is necessary before taking social action such as exclusion from work, tracking in special educational programs, establishing competency to stand trial? How do we balance an organization's need for stability and the rights of individuals? What is to be defined as normal or abnormal and whose yardstick should prevail? Perhaps most important, even if there were to be perfect predictive information, can we afford policies that further expand the number of people who are unemployable and uninsurable? Can we afford a genetic underclass?

REFERENCES

1. Nelkin, D. and Tancredi, L.: *Dangerous Diagnostics: The Social Power of Biological Information.* New York, Basic Books, 1989 (paperback 1990).
2. How genes shape personality. *U.S. News and World Report:* p. 58, April 13, 1987.
3. Shaw, M. W.: Conditional prospective rights of the fetus. *J. Legal Med.* 63:63–116, 1984.
4. Koshland, D., Jr.: Editorial. *Science* 235:1445, 1987.
5. Foucault, M.: *Discipline and Punish.* New York, Vintage, 1979, pp. 183–84, 304.
6. Reich, W.: Diagnostic Ethics. In: *Ethical Issues in Epidemiological Research,* Tancredi, L., editor. New Brunswick NJ, Rutgers University Press, 1986, pp. 37–69.
7. Douglas, M.: *How Institutions Think.* Syracuse NY, Syracuse University Press, 1976, pp. 63, 92.
8. Foucault, op. cit.

Presented as part of a *Conference on The Human Genome Project: An Agenda for Science and Society* held by the New York Academy of Medicine April 1, 1991.

Material from this lecture is from Dorothy Nelkin and Laurence Tancredi: *Dangerous Diagnostics: The Social Power of Biological Information.* New York, Basic Books, 1989 and Dorothy Nelkin: The Social Power of Genetics. In: *The Code of Codes,* Kevies, D. and Hood, L., editors. Cambridge, MA, Harvard University Press, 1992.

Contemporary Critical Debates

· · · · · ·

Up until this point, we have presented our analysis of health and medical care as if all critical analysts were more or less in agreement. But in health care, as in any social and intellectual enterprise, controversies rage over the source of problems and over appropriate solutions. In Part Three we present selections illustrative of contemporary debates on three different but related critical issues in the sociology of health and illness.

Individual Responsibility and Health

· · · · · ·

With growing recognition of the limitations of medical care and the environmental and behavioral components of much of modern disease, a debate has emerged as to who is responsible for individual health. For many years the medical model conceptualized disease as one of those things, like earthquakes or tornados, over which humans simply had no control. When critics began to articulate the relationships among society, behavior, and sickness, however, it became clear that disease is socially patterned, that it is connected with the values of society, and importantly, that it can often be prevented.

One example of this connection is between working conditions and worker health. Companies in the petrochemical industry are testing workers to see if they have "defective" genes that may make them particularly vulnerable to chemicals to which they are exposed in the workplace (Draper, 1991). This type of genetic testing raises a number of questions. If a worker is likely to get sick, who is to blame: the susceptible worker for his or her faulty genes or the company for its dangerous workplace? Should prevention consist of screening individuals or cleaning up the workplace? Companies would rather focus on moving or removing susceptible individuals because they find it cheaper and more efficient. Unions and workers resist attempts to blame the individual and insist that the work environment must be clean to protect everybody (Nelkin and Tancredi, 1989).

Central to the controversy surrounding genetic screening (and the topic of the selections in this section) is the issue of who is responsible for an individual's health. Specifically, to what extent are we as individuals responsible for preventing disease and maintaining our own health? One of the most articulate spokespersons for the argument that individuals are ultimately responsible for their own health was John Knowles, former Director of Massachusetts General Hospital and past President of the Rockefeller Foundation. In "The Responsibility of the Individual," Knowles argues that people are born healthy and made sick by personal "misbehavior" and environmental conditions. While acknowledging the role of the environment in creating disease, he emphasizes the "bad habits" of individuals, which he sees as the cause of much of our current state of unhealthiness. These bad habits include "overeating, too much drinking, taking pills, staying up at night, engaging in promiscuous sex, driving too fast, and smoking cigarettes." According to this view, our society has encouraged these behaviors by subordinating individual responsibility to "individual rights." Solutions to health problems should by and large focus on education, rewards, and punishments to change the behaviors of people who are themselves simultaneously victims and victimizers, thus allowing them to improve their health through their own efforts. Preservation of health should be a public duty. Knowles rejects what he terms the "liberal" ideology that stresses societal responsibility for the ills of humanity, and in fact he blames this ideology for eroding individual responsibility in the first place.

Knowles makes a good case for the importance of individual change and self-improvement. There is little doubt that better health could be promoted and much disease prevented if only we could adopt healthier lifestyles and relinquish some of our "bad habits." There are, however, several problems with his argument. Knowles condemns "sloth, gluttony, alcoholic intemperance, reckless driving, sexual frenzy, and smoking" in essentially moralistic terms. He does not address the problem of pain and suffering, which has its roots in flawed institutions and environments over which, at least as individuals, people have little or no control. He ignores the obvious efforts—the huge sums of money expended for medical help, the hours spent waiting to see physicians—that people *do* make in an attempt to make or keep themselves healthy. If these efforts are misdirected, then we must ask why people believe in them. Nor does Knowles address the problem of the very limited power people have to effect changes over those social organizations and institutions that produce the toxic chemicals, the noise, and the stress that lead so many to seek relief through such unhealthy means as alcohol, cigarettes, and licit or illicit mood-altering drugs.

Robert Crawford's selection "Individual Responsibility and Health Politics" explores the problems of seeing individual responsibility for health in the context of what he sees as a "victim-blaming" ideology. As Crawford notes, focusing attention on the victims of such problems as environmental pollution or stress-induced alcohol or cigarette addiction ignores—and thereby masks—the role of the particular social arrangements that may be disease-producing as well as the inability of individuals to prevent or cure those diseases themselves. He also argues that the ideology of individual responsibility helps "justify shifting the burden of costs back to users" and legitimate a retrenchment from social responsibility. The moralism of much of the writing of those advocating individual responsibility for health, as Crawford observes, is a moralism that ultimately blames ill health on those with the least power and resources to effect change for the better.

The social scientist must ask who gains and who "pays" in these differing views of the relative responsibility of individuals for their own health—that is, what are the social consequences of each perspective? For those who advocate individual responsibility, existing broad social arrangements (the status quo) are not to be challenged. Rather, strategies of *adaptation* should be developed for individuals who, from the "liberal" perspective, are the victims of those very social arrangements to which they're being encouraged to adapt.

No one, of course, claims that the individual has absolutely no power to effect changes in lifestyle that will promote health and well-being. It can be argued, however, that these efforts need not be limited to individual adjustment, but can involve collective efforts at community change and social reform in addition to individual self-help. The balance ultimately struck between the opposing views expressed by Knowles and Crawford is likely to be a crucial determinant of the future course of medical care in the United States.

REFERENCES

Draper, Elaine. 1991. Risky Business: Genetic Testing and Exclusionary Practices in the Hazardous Workplace. New York: Cambridge University Press.
Nelkin, Dorothy, and Laurence Tancredi. 1989. Dangerous Diagnostics: The Social Power of Biological Information. New York: Basic Books.

33

The Responsibility of the Individual

■ ■ ■ ■ ■ ■

John H. Knowles

More than half the reduction in mortality rates over the past three centuries occurred before 1900 and was due in nearly equal measure to improved nutrition and reduced exposure to air- and water-borne infection. The provision of safe water and milk supplies, the improvement in both personal and food hygiene, and the efficient disposal of sewage all helped to reduce the incidence of infectious disease. Vaccination further reduced mortality rates from smallpox in the nineteenth century and from diphtheria, pertussis, tetanus, poliomyelitis, measles, and tuberculosis in the twentieth century, although the contribution of vaccinations to the overall reduction in mortality rates over the past hundred years is small (perhaps as small as 10 percent) as contrasted with that due to improved nutrition and reduction in the transmission of infectious disease.[1] An even smaller contribution has been made by the introduction of medical and surgical therapy, namely antibiotics and the excision of tumors, in the twentieth century.

Over the past 100 years, infanticide has declined in the developed countries as changes in reproductive practice, such as the use of contraceptives, have been introduced to contain family size and reduce national growth rates of population, thus sustaining the improvement in health and standards of living. The population of England and Wales trebled between 1700 and 1850 without any significant importation of food. If the birth rate had been maintained, the population by now would be some 140 million instead of the 46 million it actually is. Changes in reproductive behavior maintained a rough balance between food production and population growth and allowed standards of living to rise. A similarly remarkable change in reproductive behavior occured in Ireland following the potato famines of the eighteen-forties, and birth rates have been sustained voluntarily at a low level to this day in that largely Catholic country.

Improvement in health resulted from changes in personal behavior (hygiene, reproductive practices) and in environmental conditions (food supplies, provision of safe milk and water, and sewage disposal). Cartesian rationalism, Baconian empiricism, and the results of the Industrial Revolution led the medical profession into scientific and technical approaches to disease. The engineering approach to the human machine was strengthened by the germ theory of disease which followed the work of Pasteur and Koch in the late nineteenth century. The idea was simple, unitary, and compelling: one germ—one disease—one therapy. Population factors, personal behavior, and environmental conditions were neglected in such a pure model or paradigm of approach and were picked up by elements less powerful and perceived increasingly as marginal to health, i.e., politicians, state departments, and schools of public health. The medical profession hitched its wagon to the rising stars of science and technology. The results have been spectacular for some individuals in terms of cure, containment of disease, and alleviation of suffering; as spectacular in terms of the horrendous costs compounding now at a rate of 15 percent annually; and even more spectacular to some because allocation of more and more men and women, money, and machines has affected mortality and morbidity rates only marginally. The problem of diminishing returns, if current trends continue, will loom as large and pregnant to the American people in the future as the mushrooming atomic cloud does today.

I will not berate the medical profession, its practitioners and its professors—they reflect our culture, its values, beliefs, rites, and symbols. Central to the culture is faith in progress through science, technology, and industrial growth; increasingly peripheral to it is the idea, vis-à-vis health, that over 99 percent of us are born healthy and made sick as a result of personal misbehavior and environmental conditions. The solution to the problems of ill health in modern American society involves individual responsibility, in the first instance, and social responsibility through public legislative and private voluntary efforts, in the second instance. Alas, the medical profession isn't interested, because the intellectual, emotional, and financial rewards of the present system are too great and because there is no incentive and very little demand to change. But the problems of rising costs; the allocation of scarce national resources among competing claims for improving life; diminishing returns on health from the system of acute, curative, high-cost, hospital-based medicine; and increasing evidence that personal behavior, food, and the nature of the environment around us are the prime determinants of health and disease will present us with critical choices and will inevitably force change.

Most individuals do not worry about their health until they lose it. Uncertain attempts at healthy living may be thwarted by the temptations of a culture whose economy depends on high production and high consumption. Asceticism is reserved for hair-shirted clerics and constipated cranks, and everytime one of them dies at the age of 50, the hedonist smiles, inhales deeply, and takes another drink. Everyone is a gambler and knows someone who has lived it up and hit 90 years, so bad nurture doesn't necessarily spell doom. For others, a genetic fatalism takes hold: Nature—your parents' genes—will decide your fate no matter what you do. For those who remain undecided, there is always the reassuring story—and we all know it—of someone with living parents who has led a temperate, viceless life and died of a heart attack at the age

of 45. As for stress, how about Winston Churchill at the age of 90! And he drank brandy, smoked cigars, never exercised, and was grossly overweight! Facing the insufferable insult of extinction with the years, and knowing how we might improve our health, we still don't do much about it. The reasons for this peculiar behavior may include: (1) a denial of death and disease coupled with the demand for instant gratification and the orientation of most people in most cultures to living day by day; (2) the feeling that nature, including death and disease, can be conquered through scientific and technologic advance or overcome by personal will; (3) the dispiriting conditions of old people lead to a decision by some that they don't want infirmities and unhappiness and would just as soon die early; (4) chronic depression in some individuals to the extent that they wish consciously or unconsciously for death and have no desire to take care of themselves; and (5) the disinterest of the one person to whom we ascribe the ultimate wisdom about health—the physician.

Prevention of disease means forsaking the bad habits which many people enjoy—overeating, too much drinking, taking pills, staying up at night, engaging in promiscuous sex, driving too fast, and smoking cigarettes—or, put another way, it means doing things which require special effort—exercising regularly, going to the dentist, practicing contraception, ensuring harmonious family life, submitting to screening examinations. The idea of individual responsibility flies in the face of American history which has seen a people steadfastly sanctifying individual freedom while progressively narrowing it though the development of the beneficent state. On the one hand, Social Darwinism maintains its hold on the American mind despite the best intentions of the neo-liberals. Those who aren't supine before the Federal Leviathan proclaim the survival of the fittest. On the other, the idea of individual responsibility has been submerged to individual rights—rights, or demands, to be guaranteed by government and delivered by public and private institutions. The cost of sloth, gluttony, alcoholic intemperance, reckless driving, sexual frenzy, and smoking is now a national, and not an individual, responsibility. This is justified as individual freedom—but one man's freedom in health is another man's shackle in taxes and insurance premiums. I believe the idea of a "right" to health should be replaced by the idea of an individual moral obligation to preserve one's own health—a public duty if you will. The individual then has the "right" to expect help with information, accessible services of good quality, and minimal financial barriers. Meanwhile, the people have been led to believe that national health insurance, more doctors, and greater use of high-cost, hospital-based technologies will improve health. Unfortunately none of them will.

More and more the artificer of the possible is "society"—not the individual; he thereby becomes more dependent on things external and less on his own inner resources. The paranoid style of consumer groups demands a fight against something, usually a Big Bureaucracy. In the case of health, it is the hospitals, the doctors, the medical schools, the Medicaid-Medicare combine, the government. Nader's Raiders have yet to allow that the next major advances in the health of the American people will come from the assumption of individual responsibility for one's own health and a necessary change in habits for the majority of Americans. We do spend over $30 billion annually for cigarettes and whiskey.

The behavior of Americans might be changed if there were adequate programs of health education in primary and secondary schools and even colleges—but there aren't. School health programs are abysmal at best, confining themselves to preemptory sick calls and posters on brushing teeth and eating three meals a day; there are no examinations to determine if anything's been learned. Awareness of danger to body and mind isn't acquired until the mid-twenties in our culture, and by then patterns of behavior are set which are hard to change. Children tire of "scrub your teeth," "don't eat that junk," "leave your dingy alone," "go to bed," and "get some exercise." By the time they are sixteen, society says they shall have cars, drink beer, smoke, eat junk at drive-ins, and have a go at fornication. If they demur, they are sissies or queer or both. The pressure of the peer group to do wrong is hardly balanced by the limp protestations of permissive parents, nervously keeping up with the Joneses in suburban ranch houses crammed with snacks and mobile bars.

The barriers to the assumption of individual responsibility for one's own health are lack of knowledge (implicating the inadequacies of formal education, the all-too-powerful force of advertising, and of the informal systems of continuing education), lack of sufficient interest in, and knowledge about, what is preventable and the "cost-to-benefit" ratios of nationwide health programs (thereby implicating all the powerful interests in the heath establishment, which couldn't be less interested, and calling for a much larger investment in fundamental and applied research), and a culture which has progressively eroded the idea of individual responsibility while stressing individual rights, the responsibility of society-at-large, and the steady growth of production and consumption ("We have met the enemy and it is us!"). Changing human behvior involves sustaining and repeating an intelligible message, reinforcing it through peer pressure and approval, and establishing clearly perceived rewards which materialize in as short a time as possible. Advertising agencies know this, but it is easier to sell deodorants, pantyhose, and automobiles than it is health.

What is the problem? During the nineteenth and early twentieth centuries, communicable disease was the major health problem in the United States. In 1900, the average life expectancy at birth was 49.2 years. By 1966, it had increased to 70.1 years, due mainly to marked reduction in infant and child mortality (between birth and age 15). By mid-century, accidents were by far the leading cause of death in youngsters, and the majority of accidents were related to excessive use of alcohol by their parents, by adults generally, and even occasionally by themselves. While 21 years were added to life expectancy at birth, only 2.7 years were added to it at age 65—the remaining life expectancy at age 65 being 11.9 years in 1900 and 14.6 in 1966. The marked increase in life expectancy at birth was due to the control and eradication of infectious disease, directly through improved nutrition and personal hygiene, and environmental changes, namely, the provision for safe water and milk supplies and for sewage disposal.

Today, the major health problems in the United States are the chronic diseases of middle and later age, mainly heart disease, cancer, and strokes. Death and disability in middle age is premature and potentially preventable. For those under 44 years, the leading causes of death are accidents, heart disease, cancer, homicide, and suicide. For those under 25 years, accidents are by far the most common cause of death, with homicide and suicide the next leading causes. Of the roughly 2 million deaths in the United States in 1969, 50 percent were due to heart disease (40%) and strokes (10%); 16 percent to cancer; and 8 percent to accidents (6%), homicide (1%), and suicide (1%). But death statistics tell only a small part of the story. For every successful suicide, an estimated ten others, or 200,000 people, have made the attempt. For every death due to accidents, hundreds of others are injured, and many of those are permanently disabled. Over 17 percent, or 36 million people, have serious disabilities limiting their activities.

Premature death and disability are far too common. For the 178,000 people between the ages of 45 and 64 years who died of heart disease in 1969, 1.2 million (or 3 percent of the 40.5 million people in this age group) were chronically disabled because of heart disease.[2] For the over 30,000 people who died of cirrhosis of the liver in 1969—a disease related directly to excessive ingestion of alcohol together with poor nutrition—as many as 10 million people suffer from alcoholism and varying degrees of malnutrition. Twenty-six million Americans, 11 million of whom receive no federal food assistance, live below the federally defined poverty level, a level which does not support an adequate diet.

The control of communicable disease depended as much (or even more) on broad changes in the environment attendant upon economic development (improved housing and nutrition, sanitary engineering for safe water supplies, and sewage disposal) as it did on the individual's knowledge and behavior (need for immunization, personal hygiene, and cooperation with case finding). However, control of the present major health problems in the United States depends directly on modification of the individual's behavior and habit of living. The need for improved nutrition remains unchanged. The knowledge required to persuade the individual to change his habits is far more complex, far

less dramatic in its results, far more difficult to organize and convey—in short, far less appealing and compelling than the need for immunization, getting rid of sewage, and drinking safe water. Even the problems of immunizing the population in contemporary America are difficult, however—witness the failure to eradicate measles ten years after the technical means became available.

Studies by Breslow and Belloc[3] of nearly 7,000 adults followed for five and one-half years showed that life expectancy and health are significantly related to the following basic health habits:

1) three meals a day at regular times and no snacking;
2) breakfast every day;
3) moderate exercise two or three times a week;
4) adequate sleep (7 or 8 hours a night);
5) no smoking;
6) moderate weight;
7) no alcohol or only in moderation.

A 45-year-old man who practiced 0–3 of these habits has a remaining life expectancy of 21.6 years (to age 67), while one with 6–7 of these habits has a life expectancy of 33.1 years (to age 78). In other words, 11 years could be added to life expectancy by relatively simple changes in habits of living, recalling that only 2.7 years were added to life expectancy at age 65 between 1900 and 1966. Breslow also found that the health status of those who practiced all seven habits was similar to those 30 years younger who observed none.

A large percentage of deaths (estimates up to 80 percent) due to cardiovascular disease and cancer are "premature," that is, occur in relatively young individuals and are related to the individual's bad habits. Heart disease and strokes are related to dietary factors, cigarette smoking, potentially treatable but undetected hypertension, and lack of exercise. Cancer is related to smoking (oral, buccal, lung, and bladder cancer) and probably to diets rich in fat and refined foodstuffs and low in residue (gastrointestinal and perhaps breast and prostatic cancer) and to the ingestion of food additives and certain drugs, or the inhalation of a wide variety of noxious agents. Certain occupational exposures and personal hygienic factors account for a small but important fraction of the total deaths due to cancer. Theoretically, all deaths due to accidents, homicide, and suicide are preventable.

Stress appears to play a critical role in disease. The stress of adjusting to change may generate a wide variety of diseases, and change is the hallmark of modern society. It is known that the death rate for widows and widowers is 10 times higher in the first year of bereavement than it is for others of comparable age; in the year following divorce the divorced persons have 12 times the incidence of disease that married persons have. People living in primitive societies insulated from change have low blood pressures and blood cholesterol levels which do not vary from youth to old age. Blood pressure and cholesterol tend to rise with age in our culture and are thought to be a prime cause of heart attacks and strokes. Studies indicate that up to 80 percent of serious physical illnesses seem to develop at a time when the individual feels helpless or hopeless. Studies on cancer patients have revealed lives marked by chronic anxiety, depression, or hostility and a lack of close emotional ties with parents—significantly greater than in a control group.

Despite the well-known hazards of smoking, per-capita consumption of cigarettes is expected to increase in 1975–76 after having been relatively stable between 1963—when the Surgeon General sounded the warning against smoking—and 1973, at 211 packs annually per person over 18 years. Some 15 percent of boys and girls under 18 years smoke cigarettes. Cigarette production is increasing at about 3.5 percent per year due to population growth and to a marked increase in smoking in teenage girls, which has risen from 8 to 15 percent in the past several years. If cigarette smoking were to be eliminated entirely, a 20 percent reduction in deaths due to cancer would result (based on the assumption that 85 percent of lung cancer is causally related to cigarette smoking). If all contributing environmental factors and personal bad health habits were eliminated, it is possible that cancer could be virtually eliminated as a cause of death. This would increase the average life expectancy at birth by 6 to 7 years, and at age 65 by 1.4 years for men and 2.1 years for women. The use of averages gives an erroneous impression, however, for one out of six people die of cancer. The elimination of cancer would mean that one out of six people would live 10.8 years longer.

Bad nutritional status (of the too-much-fat-intake-resulting-in-obesity type) can predispose the individual to heart attacks, strokes, cancer of the gastrointestinal tract, diabetes, liver and gallbladder disease, degenerative arthritis of the hips, knees, and ankles, and injuries. It is estimated that 16 percent of Americans under the age of 30 years are obese, while 40 percent of the total population, or 80 million Americans, are 20 or more pounds above the ideal weight for their height, sex, and age. Over 30 percent of all men between 50 and 59 years are 20 percent overweight and 60 percent are at least 10 percent overweight.

Excessive use of alcohol is directly related to accidents and to liver disease (cirrhosis) as well as to a wide variety of other disorders, including vitamin deficiencies, inflammation of the pancreas, esophagus, and stomach, and muscular and neurologic diseases. Alcohol is a strong "risk factor" in cancer of the mouth, pharynx, larynx, and esophagus. More than 50 percent and probably nearer to 75 percent of all deaths and injuries due to automobile accidents are associated with the excessive use of alcohol. Alcoholism in one or both parents is significantly associated with home injuries to children (more than 50 percent in some studies). The prevalence of "heavy-escape" drinkers in the United States has been estimated at 6.5 million people (5.4 percent of total adult population), and the figures for those who use alcohol chronically and excessively range up to 10 million adults. Teenage drinking is now nearly universal. A study of high school students revealed that 36 percent reported getting drunk at least four times a year (remember, 15 percent smoke!). An increased frequency of cancer of the mouth, pharynx, larynx, and esophagus is seen in those who both smoke and drink and is less frequent, but still significantly higher than normal, in those who only smoke or only drink.

Dietary factors play a major role in cardiovascular disease and cancer. The major variable, as deduced from studies of migrant populations, seems to be fat content. For example, cancer of the large bowel as well as that of the breast and prostate is much more common in the United States than in Japan, and seems to be related to the difference in fat intake. The American derives 40 to 45 percent of his calories from fat, whereas the Japanese obtains only 15 to 20 percent of his calories from that source. Japanese descendants living in the United States have an incidence of bowel cancer similar to that seen in native Americans. Although the mechanism has not been established, it would appear that high fat intake (usually with resultant obesity) predisposes the American to both cancer and cardiovascular disease. Data from a long-term study of cardiovascular disease in Framingham, Massachusetts, indicate that each 10 percent reduction in weight in men 35–55 years old would result in a 20 percent decrease in the incidence of coronary disease. A 10 percent increase in weight would result in a 30 percent increase in coronary disease.[4]

The incidence of cancer of the colon and rectum in Americans both white and black is 10 times the incidence estimated for rural Africans. The removal of dietary fiber and a high intake of refined carbohydrates typical of diets in developed countries such as the United States result in a slowed transit time of food through the intestines. This is thought to facilitate the development of cancer, along with such diseases as diverticulitis, appendicitis, and even hemorrhoids. Prudence would dictate a reduction in fat and refined carbohydrates (and therefore increased fiber content) in the American diet. High-carbohydrate diets typical in the American culture also lead to dental caries, and may, over time, increase the risk of acquiring diabetes.

Knowledge of cancer and evidence for its multiple causes have increased to the point where the statement can be made with confidence that over 80 percent of human neoplasms depend either directly or indirectly on environmental factors. The term "environmental factors" includes cancer-provoking substances or carcinogens in the food and the drugs we ingest, the air we breathe, the water we drink, the occupations we pursue, and the habits we indulge. There are three major groups at high risk of cancer: (1) those with known host factors such as genetic and other congenital defects and immunologic-deficiency disease; (2) those with exposure to environmental contaminants known to produce cancer; and (3) those with certain demographic characteristics which reflect as yet unknown carcinogenic factors such as place of residence or migration.[5]

The familial occurrence of cancer is a well-known phenomenon. A significant two to four times excess occurrence in relatives of patients has been noted in cancer of the stomach, breast, large intestine, uterus, and lung. Increased familial incidence has also been noted in leukemia, brain tumors in children, and sarcomas. Individuals with hereditary deficiencies of the immune system of the body develop malignant diseases of the blood vessels and lymphatic system. Acquired immunodeficiency also leads to the development of cancer. When patients with kidney transplants are given drugs over a long time to suppress the immune system in order to prevent rejection of the grafted kidney, cancer of the lymphatic system (lymphoma of the reticulum-cell-sarcoma type), frequently confined to the brain, and cancer of the skin develop in a significant proportion of the patients. Women who have had genital herpes (herpes simplex virus 2) have an increased incidence of cancer of the cervix of the uterus and constitute a high-risk population. People with pernicious anemia with associated gastritis develop cancer of the stomach at five times the rate of the normal population. Cirrhosis is associated with an increased incidence of cancer of the liver. Patients with diabetes have two times the incidence of cancer of the pancreas as normal individuals. The presence of gallstones and kidney stones increases the risk of developing cancer in the respective organs. Single episodes of trauma have been implicated in cancer of the bone, breast, and testicles. Chronic irritation of a skin mole may lead to cancerous degeneration, called malignant melanoma.

Environmental factors include tobacco, alcohol, radiation, occupation, drugs, air pollutants, diet, viruses, and other organisms, and sexual factors. The evidence on cigarette smoking is incontrovertible. It greatly increases the risk of lung cancer as well as cancer of the mouth, pharynx, larynx, esophagus, and urinary bladder. The incidence of cancer in cigarette smokers is higher in urban than rural dwellers, suggesting that air pollutants are additional major causative factors. Occupational exposure to asbestos fibers results in lung cancer, but here again the incidence is higher in those who smoke. Alcohol as a carcinogenic agent in malignancy of the mouth, larynx, esophagus, and liver (in association with cirrhosis) has been noted. A major long-term effect of radiation is cancer. Radiologists are ten times more likely to die of leukemia than are physicians not exposed to x-rays.

The list of drugs known or thought to be carcinogenic also continues to expand. Studies have shown that post-menopausal women given estrogens (so-called "replacement therapy" to diminish menopausal complaints and advertised to "keep women feminine") are five to fourteen times more likely to develop cancer of the uterus (endometrial cancer) than post-menopausal women not given the drug. (Other factors known to be associated with uterine cancer such as obesity, high blood pressure, never having borne a child, and age were not significant variables in these studies.) The risk increased with dosage size and duration of estrogen therapy. Other studies have shown beyond a doubt that the daughters of women given diethylstilbestrol (DES) during pregnancy are at higher risk of developing a rare form of cancer of the vagina. Despite this knowledge, DES is still being given to pregnant women to prevent spontaneous abortion. Most astounding has been the discovery of over 100 cases of liver tumors in women taking oral contraceptive pills. Most of the tumors were benign, but some showed cancerous degeneration and others ruptured with hemorrhage into the abdomen. Many carcinogenic agents incite the disease only many years after the initial exposure (e.g., atomic-bomb radiation) or after prolonged use, so it is not known whether an epidemic of liver tumors will ultimately develop in oral-contraceptive users. (The "pill" also causes a small but significant risk for heart attacks in users.) Long-term epidemiologic research is needed to establish knowledge necessary for control programs, but there is sufficient knowledge now to suggest that we should sharply restrict use of many drugs.

Sexual factors (both hormonal and behavioral) play a role in the causation of cancer of the breast and uterus (cervix and body of the uterus), penis, prostate, and testis. Cancer of the cervix occurs much more frequently in women who have had many sexual partners beginning at an early age, who come from a lower socioeconomic status, and who have had infection with Herpes simplex virus type 2, which is transmitted venereally. Celibate women are at very low risk, although they are at high risk for cancer of the breast. Cancer of the penis occurs in those who have poor penile hygiene and are uncircumcised in infancy (circumcision after the age of two years does not protect against the disease).

Attempts to prevent disease and improve and maintain health involve multifaceted strategies and expertise from many disciplines. Fundamental to any and all such attempts is sufficient empirical knowledge, i.e., knowledge gained through observation and trial-and-error experimentation that allows the advocate to convey his information with sufficient conviction to change the behavior of his audience. Although a great deal of information is available, the whole field of preventive medicine and health education needs far more fundamental research and long-term field experimentation. The biological and epidemiological effects of a wide variety of pollutants, the cost-benefit ratios of many available screening services, the influence of financial sanctions on changing health behavior, the use of the mass media and their effect on cognition and behavior, the long-term effects of various therapeutic regimens on the morbidity and mortality of individuals with asymptomatic high blood pressure, the long-term effects of marked reduction of fat in the diet on the incidence of cancer and heart disease, the influence of personal income on the development of cancer and coronary disease (the death rate from both lung cancer and coronary disease is significantly lower for the affluent than for the poor) are all examples of problems that need study. These problems demand for their solution the participation and integration of the disciplines of the biological sciences, the behavioral and social sciences (psychology, economics, cultural anthropology, political science), and public health (epidemiology and biostatistics).

It is a sad fact that of a total annual national expenditure on health of $120 billion, only 2 to

2.5 percent is spent on disease prevention and control measures, and only 0.5 percent each for health education and for improving the organization and delivery of health services. The national (federal) outlay for environmental-health research is around 0.25 percent of total health expenditures. These relatively meager expenditures speak for the lack of interest in fields that rationally demand a much heavier commitment. The support of fundamental biomedical research has also flagged alarmingly in the past several years. The basic biological mechanisms of most of the common diseases are still not well enough known to give clear direction to preventive measures.

Strategies for improving health must include the incorporation of preventive measures into personal health services and into the environment, and individual and mass educational efforts.[6] For example, in dealing with the health problem of heart attacks, preventive measures would include screening for high-risk factors (high blood pressure, elevated blood cholesterol and fat levels, overweight, cigarette smoking, stress, and family history) and making available emergency services and measures for rapid transit to hospital-based coronary-care units; environmental measures would include altering food supply to reduce the intake of fat (i.e., those substances that raise blood cholesterol) and encouraging experiments in reducing work-related stress; and individual and mass educational efforts would include encouraging the use of screening examinations, the cessation of smoking, the maintenance of optimal weight with a balanced, low-fat diet, and obtaining regular exercise. Carrying out such a strategy involves many variables—convincing the doctor to play his pivotal role (and most medical educators and physicians are singularly uninterested in prevention), altering financing mechanisms to provide incentives to use preventive services (and most health insurance is, in fact, "disease insurance" which does not cover health education and preventive measures), and stimulating public as well as private efforts to exercise restraint on advertising and to exert positive sanctions for dissemination of health information through the mass media.

The health catastrophe related to automobile accidents presents a different type of problem. Here, personal-health services include availability of rapid transportation and first aid, emergency medical services, and definitive acute-care services in regional general hospitals; environmental measures would relate to road and highway construction (including lighting, warning signs, speed limits, safety rails), and the design and construction of automobiles for safety; and educational measures would include driver training, relicensing with eye examination, avoidance of alcohol and other drugs before driving, and reduction of speed. Which of these efforts will produce the most benefit at least cost? An interesting answer was provided during the oil-embargo energy crisis which necessitated reductions in speed limits and in the use of vehicles. The result in California was a 40 percent reduction in death rates from automobile accidents during the month of February, 1974, as contrasted with the previous February. Accidents on the New Jersey Turnpike dropped by one-fifth from 1973 to 1974, and fatalities were down by almost one-half, the lowest figure since 1966. Meanwhile, many people won't change their habits and wear seat belts, stop drinking, or reduce speed—and are annoyed with the restrictions on their freedom when someone tries to make them.

Dental health involves the personal services of the dentist and dental hygienist, the environmental measures of fluoridation of water supplies and the dietary restriction of refined carbohydrates, and the educational measures of prudent dietary habits, brushing the teeth, and visiting the dentist regularly. Where is the greatest benefit-cost ratio to be found? There is unequivocal evidence that fluoridation of water supplies will reduce dental caries by as much as 60 percent. It is safe and inexpensive, costing only 20 cents a year per person to prevent dental decay in children. Fluoridation of water supplies began about 1950. By 1967 over 3,000 communities with some 60 million people had adopted fluoridation. But the pace of change has slowed considerably, and the majority of people still lack fluoridated water due to fears of poisoning and resistance to what is perceived as an encroachment on their freedom. This highest benefit-cost dental-health program is still unavailable to the majority of Americans. Personal dental services are unavailable to large segments of our population and qualify as a luxury item.

· ·

But what is the responsibility of the individual in matters pertaining to health? The United States now spends more on health in absolute terms and as a percentage of the gross national product than any other nation in the world—from $39 billion or 5.9 percent of the GNP in 1965 to $120 billion or 8.3 percent of the GNP in 1975 (over $550 per person per year). No one—but no one—can deny the fact that billions of dollars could be saved directly—and billions more indirectly (in terms of family suffering, time lost, and the erosion of human capital)—if our present knowledge of health and disease could be utilized in programs of primary, secondary, and tertiary prevention. The greatest portion of our national expenditure goes for the caring of the major causes of premature, and therefore preventable, death and/or disability in the United States, i.e., heart disease, cancer, strokes, accidents, bronchitis and emphysema, cirrhosis of the liver, mental illness and retardation, dental caries, suicide and homicide, venereal disease, and other infections. If no one smoked cigarettes or consumed alcohol and everyone exercised regularly, maintained optimal weight on a low fat, low refined-carbohydrate, high fiber-content diet, reduced stress by simplifying their lives, obtained adequate rest and recreation, understood the needs of infants and children for the proper nutrition and nurturing of their intellectual and affective development, had available to them, and would use, genetic counseling and selective abortion, drank fluoridated water, followed the doctor's orders for medications and self-care once disease was detected, used available health services at the appropriate time for screening examinations and health education-preventive medicine programs, the savings to the country would be mammoth in terms of billions of dollars, a vast reduction in human misery, and an attendant marked improvement in the quality of life. Our country would be strengthened immeasurably, and we could divert our energies—human and financial—to other pressing issues of national and international concern.

But so much conspires against this rational

ideal: our historic emphasis on rugged individualism, social Darwinism, and unrestricted freedom together with our recent emphasis on individual rights as contrasted with responsibilities; a neoliberal ideology which has stressed societal responsibility and the obligations of the beneficent state, resulting in an erosion of individual responsibility and initiative; a credit-minded culture which does it now and pays for it later, whether in drinking and eating or in buying cars and houses; an economy which depends on profligate production and consumption regardless of the results to individual health, or to the public health in terms of a wide variety of environmental pollutants; ignorance (and therefore a lack of conviction and commitment) on the part of both producers and consumers as to exact costs and benefits of many preventive and health-education measures, a reflection of the sparse national commitment to research in these areas: the failure, conceptually, to view health holistically, i.e., its interdependence with educational attainment, poverty, the availability of work, housing and the density of populations, degree of environmental pollution (air, water, noise, mass-media offerings), and levels of stress in work, play, and love; and finally, the values and habits of the health establishment itself. One cannot hope to develop a rational health system if the parts of the whole that bear on health are moving in irrational ways.

Within the health system, medical educators and the teaching hospitals display only acute curative, after-the-fact medicine. The rewards—intellectually, financially, and emotionally—for specialist care far outweigh those for the low-status generalist (primary-care physican) or public health worker. The specialty organizations (surgeons, internists, radiologists, for example), the American Medical Association, the Association of American Medical Colleges, the American Hospital Association, the "disease-insurance" companies, as well as governmental insurance programs (Medicare-Medicaid), pay lip service or no service to reordering priorities and sanctions to the needs of the people for prevention and health education. Present plans for national health insurance do not contend with the issues of preventive medicine and health education. Over 65 percent of the 4.5 million workers in the health system are employed in hospitals, and their interests demand more expenditures and an even higher priority for acute, curative, after-the-fact medicine and the care of those with chronic disease. There is one health educator for every 17,000 people, while there is one physician for every 650 and one nurse for every 280 people.

Research priorities stress biological and not epidemiological, social, and environmental research. Even here, we should be willing to take decisive action when inferential evidence, e.g., the production of cancer in animals by drugs, is available, unacceptable as this may be to scientists. I cannot believe that man was meant to ingest drugs and artificial-food substances, breathe polluted air, or have his ears banged mercilessly by the uproar of industrial society. Those who do work in the field of prevention and health education have too often stressed social control (some have called them "health fascists") rather than social change and have become curiously indifferent to the needs and aspirations of families, communities, and particularly minority groups. Those places where benefit-cost ratios are potentially most favorable for programs of health education and prevention—and where long-range research could be conducted—have been neglected: the schools and universities, places of work, hospitals and clinics, and obviously, doctors' offices. Very little is known about how television functions as a cognitive medium; little sophistication is shown by interested experts in developing sanctions, i.e., financial or other incentives, to modify bad habits of living. Those in the health professions play a minimal role in supporting the needs of minority groups for better housing and jobs, higher income, and improved transportation—not realizing that the fulfillment of these needs will reduce stress and anxiety and therefore improve health by reducing susceptibility to disease or to the disease-provoking habits of smoking and drinking.

If the health establishment isn't interested and the consumers don't want or demand health education and preventive medicine, what is to be done? First of all we should look at a few concrete changes in behavior which, through a variety of mechanisms, have improved health:

1) When the Surgeon General issued his report on the hazards of smoking in 1964, 52 percent of the male population smoked cigarettes. Through massive public educational programs and restrictions on advertising, the percentage was reduced over a 10-year period to roughly 42 percent. (This desirable change has been accompanied, however, by an equally undesirable increase in teen-age smoking, particularly among females, and no change in the 41 percent of 17-to-25-year-olds who smoke.)

2) During World War I, the United Kingdom increased taxes on alcohol, reduced the amount of alcohol available for consumption, and restricted the hours of sale. Consumption of alcohol fell and, with it, deaths from cirrhosis of the liver—from 10.3 per 100,000 people in 1914 to 4.5 in 1920. Following the war, the regulations governing the amount of alcohol allowed for consumption and the hours of its sale were relaxed, but taxes on alcoholic beverages were continually increased. By 1936, the death rate due to cirrhosis was down to 3.1 per 100,000, and it has remained at this level in that country. In the United States, wartime prohibition also reduced the cirrhosis death rate, from 11.8 per 100,000 in 1916 to 7.1 per 100,000 in 1920; it was still 7.2 in 1932, the year before prohibition was ended. But following the repeal of prohibition, the death rate from cirrhosis climbed steadily to an all-time high of 16.0 deaths per 100,000 in 1973, five times the rate in Great Britain. These results suggest a national strategy for the United States of (a) steadily increasing taxes on alcoholic beverages, (b) a massive public education program on the hazards of alcohol plus restrictions on all advertising, (c) aid to farmers and companies to help them shift to other crops and products. Increased tax income should temporarily help to defray the costs of public health education. The same strategy should be applied to cigarettes.

3) The marked reduction in auto fatalities and injuries during the oil crisis suggests that a permanent reduction of speed limits combined with sanctions to limit the use of automobiles would more than justify the cost of enforcing such a program.

4) A program to improve the self-care of patients with diabetes (tertiary prevention) at the University of Southern California resulted in a 50 percent reduction in emergency-ward visits, a decrease in the number of patients with diabetic coma from 300 to 100 over a two-year period, and

the avoidance of 2,300 visits for medications. The theme was, "You must take responsibility for your own health." Savings were estimated at $1.7 million. In other studies involving the care and education of diabetics, hemophiliacs, and others, hospital readmissions decreased by over 50 percent. These efforts resulted in tremendous savings of time and money and reflected vastly improved self-care in cases of chronic disease.

5) A heart-disease-prevention program run by Stanford University similarly demonstrated that an intensive program of health education and preventive medicine—utilizing personal instructions, television spots, and printed material—resulted in a markedly higher level of information about the disease by the community and a marked improvement in dietary habits and in the reduction of smoking among those at high risk.

. . . .

I began by saying that the health of human beings is determined by their behavior, their food, and the nature of their environment. Over 99 percent of us are born healthy and suffer premature death and disability only as a result of personal misbehavior and environmental conditions. The sociocultural effects of urban industrial life are profound in terms of stress, and unnatural sedentary existence, bad habits, and unhealthy environmental influences.[7] The individual has the power—indeed, the moral responsibility—to maintain his own health by the observance of simple, prudent rules of behavior relating to sleep, exercise, diet and weight, alcohol, and smoking. In addition, he should avoid where possible the long-term use of drugs. He should be aware of the dangers of stress and the need for precautionary measures during periods of sudden change, such as bereavement, divorce, or new employment. He should submit to selective medical examination and screening procedures.

These simple rules can be understood and observed by the majority of Americans, namely the white, well-educated, and affluent middle class. But how do individuals in minority groups follow these rules, when their members include disproportionately large numbers of the impoverished and the illiterate, among whom fear, ignorance, desperation, and superstition conspire

against even the desire to remain healthy? Here we must rely on social policies *first,* in order to improve education, employment, civil rights, and economic levels, along with efforts to develop accessible health services.

Beyond these measures, the individual is powerless to control disease-provoking environmental contaminants, be they drugs, air and water pollutants, or food additives, except as he becomes knowledgeable enough to participate in public debate and in support of governmental controls. Here, we must depend on the wisdom of experts, the results of research, and the national will to legislate controls for our protection, as damaging as they may be, in the short run, to our national economy.

When all is said and done, let us not forget that he who hates sin, hates humanity. Life is meant to be enjoyed, and each one of us in the end is still able in our own country to steer his vessel to his own port of desire. But the costs of individual irresponsibility in health have now become prohibitive. The choice is individual responsibility or social failure. Responsibility and duty must gain some degree of parity with right and freedom.

REFERENCES

1. T. McKeown, *The Modern Rise of Population* (London, 1976), pp. 152–63.
2. M. Susser, ed., *Prevention and Health Maintenance Revisited (Bulletin of the New York Academy of Medicine.* 51[January, 1975], pp. 5–243), p. 96.
3. N. B. Belloc and L. Breslow, "The Relation of Physical Health Status and Health Practices," *Preventive Medicine,* 1(August, 1972), pp. 409–21; see also "Relationship of Health Practices and Mortality." *Preventive Medicine,* 2(1973), pp. 67–81.
4. F. W. Ashley, Jr., and W. B. Kannel, "Relation of Weight Change to Changes in Atherogenic Traits: The Framingham Study," *Journal of Chronic Diseases,* 27(March, 1974), pp. 103–14.
5. J. F. Fraumeni, ed., *Persons at High Risk of Cancer: An Approach to Cancer Etiology and Control* (New York, 1975), p. 526.
6. L. Breslow, "Research in Strategy for Health Improvement," *International Journal of Health Services.* 3(1973), pp. 7–16.
7. J. H. Knowles, *Health in America. Health Service Prospects: An International Survey* (London, 1973), pp. 307–34.

34

Individual Responsibility and Health Politics

· · · · · · ·

Robert Crawford

... The contention ... is ... that although health is a complex matter and therefore requires several kinds of efforts, individual responsibility is the key ingredient. In place of admittedly expensive and ineffective medical services, it is said, individual change must be the focus of the nation's efforts to promote and maintain health. People should use the medical system less and instead adopt healthy lifestyles: or, as it was declared by one pundit, "living a long life is essentially a do-it-yourself proposition." These assertions perform the function of *blaming the victim*. They avert any serious discussion of social or environmental factors and instead locate the problem of poor health and its solution in the individual. Further, they imply, sometimes explicitly, that since people's own misbehavior is the heart of the problem of health and illness, people should *demand less* medical care. Rights and entitlements for access to medical services are almost by definition now considered inappropriate. Thus, in becoming a premise for public policy, these pronouncements are providing the material for a new public philosophy by which problems are defined and answers proposed.

Similar ideologies of individual responsibility have always been popular among providers and academics trying to justify inequality in the utilization of medical services. During the period of rapid expansion in the health sector, higher morbidity and mortality rates for the poor and minorities were explained by emphasizing their lifestyle habits, especially their health and utilization behavior. These "culture of poverty" explanations emphasized delay in seeking medical help, resistance to medical authority, and reliance on unprofessional folk healers or advisors. As Catherine Riessman summarizes:

> According to these researchers, the poor have undergone multiple negative experiences with organizational systems, leading to avoidance behavior, lack of trust, and hence a disinclination to seek care and follow medical regimens except in dire need.[1]

Now, in a period of fiscal crisis and cost control, the same higher morbidity rates and demands for more access through comprehensive national health insurance are met with a barrage of statements about the limits of medicine and the lack of appropriate health behavior. Several commentators now link overuse by the poor with their faulty health habits. Again, education is seen as the solution. Previously the poor were blamed for not using medical services enough, for relying too much on their own resources, for undue suspicion of modern medicine. Now they are blamed for relying too much on medical services and not enough on their own resources. In both cases, of course, structural factors are rarely mentioned; but structural factors are behind this ideological shift.

The Crisis of Costs
·················

The cost crisis is transforming the entire political landscape in the health sector. What makes inflation in the health sector so critical in the 1970s is not only its spectacular rate but also its concurrence with wider economic and fiscal crises. We now face a situation in which inflation and expenditures for human services have become the primary targets of a strategy aimed at restoring "optimal conditions" for investment and growth in the corporate sector. The costs of medical services to government have aggravated a fiscal crisis in which the direction of public spending is the issue and raising taxes is considered inimical to corporate priorities. Further, high medical costs have become a direct threat to the corporate sector in two important ways: first, by adding significantly to the costs of production through increases in health benefit settlements with labor; and, second, by diverting consumer expenditures from other corporate products. The fact that large corporations have extensively invested in medical and health-related products does not significantly alter this picture.

The costs of production for corporations are being dramatically affected by increases in benefit settlements. General Motors claims it spent more money with Blue Cross and Blue Shield in 1975 than it did with U.S. Steel, its principal supplier of metal. Standard Oil of Indiana announced that employee health costs for the corporation had tripled over the past seven years.[2] Chrysler estimates that in 1976 it paid $1,500 per employee for medical benefits or a total of $205 million in the United States. "Unlike most other labor costs that can and do vary with the level of production," the corporation complains, "medical costs continue to rise in good times as well as bad."[3] The implications for consumer costs are obvious. General Motors added $175 to the price of every car and truck by passing on its employee medical benefit costs. In a period in which consumption and investment are stalled, while foreign competition adds an additional barrier to raising prices, such figures are startling. Corporate and union leaders are expressing in every possible forum their concern over the impact of rising medical costs upon prices, wages, and profits.

Thus, substantial political pressures are being mobilized to cut the direct costs to corporations and to cut the indirect costs of social programs generally. The politics of growth that dominated the previous period are giving way to the politics of curbing the growth in the present period. Just a few years ago the political emphasis was on increasing utilization. Now it is on reducing utilization. Besides regulatory measures, the strategies being adopted include cutbacks in public programs, especially Medicaid, and public hospitals and a shifting of the burden of costs back to employees, old people, and consumers in general.[4] In addition, corporations, often with the participation of unions, are adopting new internal strategies aimed at curbing costs.[5]

Most important is the growing consensus among corporate and governmental leaders that comprehensive national health insurance is unacceptable at current cost levels. In his campaign for the presidency, Jimmy Carter, aware of its popular appeal and importance to organized labor, committed himself to a comprehensive insurance program; but, in reminding the nation in April 1977 that balancing the budget by 1981 is his paramount domestic goal, Carter warned that the costs of such a program would be prohibitive. Secretary of Health, Education, and Welfare, Joseph Califano, more explicitly argued that cost control is a necessary precondition for national health insurance or "some other system."[6] These and numerous other signs indicate that the prospects for comprehensive insurance are receding behind a shield of rhetoric and a language of gradualism.

Popular Demand for the Extension of Rights and Entitlements
·················

In order to understand the importance of a new ideology that tells people they must rely less on the medical system and more on themselves, the cost crisis must be viewed in the context of the legacy of the preceding period, a time in which popular expectations of medicine and political demands for unhindered access to medical services reached their highest levels. Growth reinforced those expectations, as did years of propaganda by a medical and research establishment strengthened by occasional but spectacular medical successes. Medicine was promoted in almost religious terms, a promise of deliverance from pain and illness even a "death of death."

For years people were conditioned to believe in the value of consuming high levels of medical services and products. At a time when these beliefs became celebrated cultural values, large numbers of people continued to experience difficulty in obtaining regular access to primary care services and faced financial disaster for unusual medical expenses. Access came to be considered an essential component of family and personal security and an integral part of the wage bargain for organized labor. The idea of medical care as a right became widely accepted in a period in which rights were forced onto the political agenda of the nation. By the early 1970s popular pressures for national health insurance began to swell. As benefits shrink in the face of uncontrollable inflation, the sentiment for a comprehensive program continues to build.

Now, however, just at the point when medical care had become broadly viewed as a right and there is a growing demand for the extension of entitlements, people are suddenly being pressured to use the system less. If people are to modify their expectations, if their demands for guaranteed access are to be sidetracked, and if legislators and other policymakers are to be convinced of the necessity for retrenchment, a new ideology must be developed to replace the unquestioned power of medicine and to break the link between the provision of services and popular political demands. People will not relinquish their expectations unless their belief in medicine as a panacea is broken and the value of access is replaced with a new preoccupation with boot-strapping activities aimed at controlling at-risk behaviors. In a political climate of fiscal, energy, and cost crises, self-sacrifice and self-discipline emerge as popular themes. In lieu of rights and entitlements, individual responsibility, self-help and holistic health move to the center of discussion.[7]

The Politics of Retrenchment

The flavor of the ideology is evident in the comments of some of its more explicit propo-

nents. Both direct policy proposals and indirect policy implications are abundant. With an implied attack on social programs, for example, Victor Fuchs, a noted health economist, writes: "Some future historian, in reviewing mid-twentieth century social reform literature may note . . . a 'resolute refusal' to admit that individuals have any responsibility for their own stress."[8] Robert Whalen, Commissioner of the New York Department of Health, more explicitly makes the tie with high medical costs: "Unless we assume such individual and moral responsibility for our own health, we will soon learn what a cruel and expensive hoax we have worked upon ourselves through our belief that more money spent on health care is the way to better health."[9]

As do many advocates of individual responsibility, Walter McNerney, president of the Blue Cross Association, incorporates elements of both the Illichian and radical critiques of technology-heavy, distorted, and iatrogenic medicine: "We must stop throwing an array of technological processes and systems at lifestyle problems and stop equating more health services with better health. . . . People must have the capability and the will to take greater responsibility for their own health."[10] John Knowles, the late president of the Rockefeller Foundation, spoke more directly to the problem of expectations: "The only thing we've heard about national health insurance from everybody is that it won't solve the problems."[11] Knowles argued that the "primary critical choice" facing the individual is "to change his personal bad habits or stop complaining. He can either remain the problem or become the solution to it: Beneficent Government cannot—indeed, should not—do it for him or to him."[12]

The attack on rights is explicit. Leon Kass, writing in *The Public Interest,* states that "it no more makes sense to claim a right to health than a right to health care.[13] "How can we go talking about a right to health," Robert Morrison asks, "without some balancing talk about an individual's responsibility to keep healthy."[14] Again, Knowles offers a clear articulation:

The idea of individual responsibility has been submerged in individual rights—rights or demands to be guaranteed by Big Brother and delivered by public and private institutions. The cost of sloth, gluttony, alcoholic intemperance, reckless driving, sexual frenzy and smoking have now become a national, not an individual, responsibility, and all justified as individual freedom. But one man's or woman's freedom in health is now another man's shackle in taxes and insurance premiums.[15]

What Knowles is suggesting by national responsibility is public policy aimed at changing individual behavior—and using economic or other sanctions to do it. Economic sanctions on individuals, such as higher taxation on the consumption of cigarettes and alcohol, or higher insurance premiums to those engaging in at-risk behaviors are becoming a popular theme. A guest editorial appeared last year in *The New York Times,* for example, introducing the idea of "Your Fault Insurance."[16] More extreme sanctions are proposed by Leon Kass:

> All the proposals for National Health Insurance embrace, without qualification, the no-fault principle. They therefore choose to ignore, or to treat as irrelevant, the importance of personal responsibility for the state of one's own health. As a result, they pass up an opportunity to build both positive and negative inducements into the insurance payment plan, by measures such as *refusing or reducing benefits for chronic respiratory disease care to persons who continue to smoke* (emphasis added).[17]

These sanctions may be justified under the rubric of "lack of motivation," "unsuitability for treatment," or "inability to profit from therapy."[18] Why waste money, after all, on people whose lifestyle contravenes good therapeutic results, or, as Morrison put it, on a "system which taxes the virtuous to send the improvident to the hospital."[19] In the new system the pariahs of the medical world and larger numbers of people in general could be diagnosed as lifestyle problems, referred to a health counselor, and sent home. At the very least, the victim-blaming ideology will help justify shifting the burden of costs back to users. A person who is responsible for his or her illness should be responsible for the bill as well.[20]

The Social Causation of Disease

If the victim-blaming ideology serves as a legitimization for the retrenchment from rights and entitlements, in relation to the social causation of disease it functions as a colossal masquerade. The complexities of social causation are only beginning to be explored. The ideology of individual responsibility, however, inhibits that understanding and substitutes instead an unrealistic behavioral model. It both ignores what is known about human behavior and minimizes the importance of evidence about the environmental assault on health. It instructs people to be individually responsible at a time when they are becoming less capable as individuals of controlling their total health environment.[21] Although environmental factors are often recognized as "also relevant," the implication is that little can be done about an ineluctable, technological, and industrial society.

A certain portion of illness is, at some level, undoubtedly associated with individual behavior, and if that behavior were altered, it could lead to improved health. Health education efforts aimed at changing individual behavior should be an important part of any health strategy. Offered in a vacuum, however, such efforts will achieve only marginal results. Sociologist John McKinlay has argued convincingly that the frequent failure of health education programs is attributable to the failure to address the social context. He concludes that:

> Certain at-risk behaviors have become so inextricably intertwined with our dominant cultural system (perhaps even symbolic of it) that the routine display of such behavior almost signified membership in this society.... To request people to change or alter these behaviors is more or less to request the abandonment of dominant culture.[22]

What must be questioned is both the effectiveness and the political uses of a focus on lifestyles and on changing individual behavior without changing social structure and processes. Just as the Horatio Alger myth was based on the fact that just enough individuals achieve mobility to make the possibility believable, so too significant health gains might be realized by some of those able to resist the incredible array of social forces aligned against healthy behavior. The vast majority, however, will remain unaffected.

The crisis of social causation is characterized by a growing awareness and politicization of environmental and occupational sources of disease in the face of the failure of medicine to have a significant impact on the modern epidemics, especially cancer. In just the last few years the American people have been inundated with scientific and popular critiques of the environmental and occupational sources of cancer. These revelations have been accompanied by a constant flow of warnings about environmental dangers: air pollution, contamination of drinking supplies, food additive carcinogens, PCB, asbestos, kepone, vinyl chlorides, pesticides, nuclear power plants, saccharine, and even more. The Environmental Protection Agency, the Occupational Safety and Health Administration, and the Food and Drug Administration have been among the most embattled government agencies in recent years.

While there is considerable debate over threshold-limit values, the validity of animal research applications to humans, and specific policy decisions by the above agencies, awareness is growing that the public is being exposed to a multitude of environmental and work place carcinogens. Although many people still cling to the "it won't happen to me" response, the fear of cancer is becoming more widespread. A recent Gallup Poll found that cancer is by far the disease most feared by Americans, almost three times its nearest competitor.[23] The fear is not unwarranted. Cancer is a disease of epidemic proportions. Samuel Epstein, a noted cancer expert, claims that "more than 53 million people in the U.S. (over a quarter of the population) will develop some form of cancer in their lifetimes, and approximately 20 percent will die of it."[24]

Pressure on industrial corporations has been building for years. An occupational health and safety movement from within industry is gaining momentum. Many unions are developing programs and confronting corporate management on health and safety issues. Although suffering from severe setbacks, the environmental movement still poses a serious challenge as environmental consciousness is reinforced by the politicization of public health issues. Government agencies and the courts have never been so assertive, despite the repeated attempts by industry to undermine these efforts. The political constraints on the growth of the nuclear power industry and governmental pressures on steel are not lost on other industries.

The threat to corporate autonomy is clear. One reads almost daily of the economic blackmail threatened by corporations if regulations are imposed, whether production shutdowns, plant closings, or investment strikes. Corporations move their plants to more tractable communities or countries. Advertising campaigns promoting the image of public-spirited corporate activities attempt to counter the threat that the decision to subordinate people's health to profits will become yet more apparent. In short, the "manufacturers of illness" are on the defensive. They must seek new ways to blunt the efforts of the new health activists and to shift the burden of responsibility for health away from their doorstep.

The Politics of Diversion

Victim-blaming ideology offers a perfect opportunity. "For once we cannot blame the environment as much as we have to blame ourselves," says Ernst Wynder, president of the American Health Foundation. "The problem is now the inability of man to take care of himself."[25] Or as New York Health Commissioner Whalen writes: "Many of our most difficult contemporary health problems, such as cancer, heart disease and accidental injury, have a built-in behavioral component. . . . *If they are to be solved at all*, we must change our style of living" (emphasis added).[26] Alternatively, Leon Kass, fearing the consequences of a focus on social causation, warns of "excessive preoccupations, as when cancer phobia leads to government regulations that unreasonably restrict industrial activity."[27]

One after another, the lifestyle proponents admit to the environmental and occupational factors that affect health, but then go on to assert their pragmatism. Victor Fuchs, for example, while recognizing environmental factors as "also relevant," asserts that "the greatest potential for reducing coronary disease, cancer, and other major killers still lies in altering personal behavior." He philosophizes that "emphasizing social responsibility can increase security, but it may be the security of the 'zoo'—purchased at the expense of freedom."[28] Carlson recognizes that social causation "raises some difficult political problems, because if we find the carcinogens in certain places in our environment, we run into institutional forces which will oppose dealing with them." Thus, "we may have to intervene at other levels here."[29] The practical focus of health efforts, in other words, should not be on the massive, expensive, politically difficult, or even politically dangerous task of overhauling our work and community environments. Instead, the focus must be on changing individuals who live and work within those settings. In the name of pragmatism, efficacy is thus ignored.

There are several other expressions of the ideology that should be noted. The diffusion of a psychological world view often reinforces the masking of social causation. Even though the psychiatric model substitutes social for natural explanations, problems still tend to be seen as amenable to change through personal transformation, with or without therapy. And, with or without therapy, individuals are ultimately held responsible for their own psychological well-being. Usually no one has to blame us for some psychological failure; we blame ourselves. Thus, psychological impairment can be just as effective as moral failing or genetic inferiority in blaming the victims and reinforcing dominant social relations.[30] People are alienated, unhappy, dropouts, criminals, angry, and activists, after all, because of maladjustment to one or another psychological norm.

The ideology of individual responsibility for health lends itself to this form of psychological obfuscation. Susceptibility to at-risk behaviors, if not a moral failing, is at least a psychological failing. New evidence relating psychological state to resistance or susceptibility to disease and accidents can and will be used to shift more responsibility to the individual. Industrial psychologists have long been employed with the intention that intervention at the individual level is the best way to reduce plant accidents in lieu of costly production changes. The implication is that people make themselves sick, not only mentally but physically. If job satisfaction is important to health, people should seek more rewarding employment. Cancer is a state of mind.

In another vein, many accounts of the current disease structure in the United States link disease with affluence. The affluent society and the lifestyles it has wrought, it is suggested, are the sources of the individual's degeneration and adoption of at-risk behaviors. Michael Halberstam, for example, writes that "most Americans die of excess rather than neglect or poverty."[31] Knowles's warnings about "sloth, gluttony, alcoholic intemperance, reckless driving, sexual frenzy and smoking," and later about "social failure," are reminiscent of a popularized conception of decaying Rome.[32] Thus, even though some may complain about environmental hazards, people are really suffering from overindulgence of the good society; it is overindulgence that must be checked. Further, by pointing to lifestyles, which are usually presented as if they reflect the problems of homogenized, affluent society, this aspect of the ideology tends to obscure the reality of class and the impact of social inequality of health. It is compatible with the conception that people are free agents. Social structure and constraints recede amid the abundance.

Of course, several diseases do stem from the lifestyles of the more affluent. Discretionary income usually allows for excessive consumption of unhealthy products; and, as Joseph Eyer argues, everyone suffers in variable and specific ways from the nature of work and the conditioning of lifestyles in advanced capitalist society.[33] But are the well-established relationships between low income and high infant mortality, diseases related to poor diet and malnutrition, stress, cancer, mental illness, traumas of various kinds, and other pathologies now to be ignored or relegated to a residual factor?[34] While long-term inequality in morbidity and mortality is declining, for almost every disease and for every indicator of morbidity, incidence increases as income falls.[35] In some specific cases the health gap appears to be widening.[36] Nonetheless, health economist Anne Somers reassures that contemporary society is tending in the direction of homogeneity:

If poverty seems so widespread, it is at least partly because our definition of poverty is so much more generous than in the past—a generosity made possible only by the pervasive affluence and the impressive technological base upon which it rests. . . . This point—that the current crisis is the result of progress rather than retrogression or decay—is vitally important not only as a historical fact but as a guide to problem solving in the health field as elsewhere.[37]

Finally, by focusing on the individual, the ideology performs the classical role of individualist ideologies in obscuring the class structure of work and the worker's lack of control over working conditions. The failure to maintain health in the work place is attributed to some personal flaw. The more than 2.5 million people disabled by occupational accidents and diseases each year and the 114,000 killed are not explained by the hazards or pace of work as much as by the lack of sufficient caution by workers, laziness about wearing respirators or other protective equipment, psychological maladjustment, including an inability to minimize stress, and even by the worker's genetic susceptibility. Correspondingly, the overworked, overstressed worker is offered transcendental meditation, biofeedback, psychological counseling, or some other holistic approach to healthy behavior change, leaving intact the structure of employer incentives and sanctions that reward the retention of work place hazards and health-denying behavior.

Moreover, corporate management appears to be integrating victim-blaming themes into personnel policies as health becomes an important rubric for traditional managerial strategies aimed at controlling the work force. Holding individual workers responsible for their susceptibility to illness or for their psychological state is not only a response to growing pressures over occupational hazards but it also complements management attempts to control absenteeism and enhance productivity. Job dissatisfaction and job-induced stress (in both their psychological and physical manifestations), principal sources of absenteeism and low productivity, will more and more become identified as lifestyle problems of the worker. Workers found to be "irresponsible" in maintaining their health or psychological stability, as

manifest in attendance and productivity records, will face sanctions, dismissals or early retirement, rationalized as stemming from employee health problems. Already the attack on sick-day benefits is well underway. The push toward corporate health maintenance organizations will further reinforce managerial use of health criteria for control purposes.

One such control mechanism is pre-employment and periodic health screening, which is now in regular use in large industry. New businesses are selling employee risk evaluations, called by one firm "health hazard appraisals." Among the specific advantages cited for health screening by the Conference Board, a business research organization, is the selection "of those judged to present the least risk of unstable attendance, costly illness, poor productivity, or short tenure."[38] Screening also holds out the possibility of cost savings from reduced insurance rates and compensation claims. It also raises, however, the possibility of a large and growing category of "high-risk" workers who become permanently unemployable—not only because of existing, incapacitating illnesses but because of their *potential* for becoming ill.

In a period in which we have become accustomed to ozone watches in which "vulnerable" people are warned to reduce activity, workers are being screened for susceptibility to job hazards. Even though they alert individuals to their higher risks, these programs do not address the hazardous conditions that to some degree affect all workers. Thus, all workers may be penalized *to the extent* that such programs function to divert attention from causative conditions. To the degree that the causative agent remains, the more susceptible workers are also penalized in that they must shoulder the burden of the hazardous conditions either by looking for another, perhaps nonexistent, job; or, if it is permitted, by taking a risk in remaining. At a United Auto Workers conference on lead, the union's president summed up industry's tactics as "fix the worker, not the workplace." He further criticized the "exclusion of so-called 'sensitive' groups of workers, the use of dangerous chemical agents to artificially lower workers' blood lead levels, the transfer of workers in and out of high lead areas, and the forced use of personal respirators instead of engineering controls to clean the air in the workplace."[39] These struggles to place responsibility are bound to intensify.

. . . .

NOTE

For helpful comments and editorial suggestions, mostly on an earlier draft, thanks to Evan Stark, Susan Reverby, John McKnight, Nancy Hartsock, Sol Levine, Cathy Stepanek, Isaac Balbus, and participants in the East Coast Health Discussion Group. I am especially indebted to Lauren Crawford who provided many hours in discussion and in preparation of this manuscript.

REFERENCES

1. "The Use of Health Services by the Poor," *Social Policy 5*, 1 (1974): 42.
2. *Chicago Sun-Times,* 16 March 1976.
3. "Inflation of Health Care Costs, 1976," hearings before the Sub-Committee on Health of the Committee on Labor and Public Welfare, United States Senate, 94th Congress (Washington, D.C.: U.S. Government Printing Office, 1976), pp. 656–60.
4. Daniel Fox and Robert Crawford, "Health Politics in the United States," in *Handbook of Medical Sociology,* edited by H. E. Freeman, S. Levine, and L. Reeder, (Englewood Cliffs, N.J.: Prentice-Hall 3rd ed., 1979); Ronda Kotelchuck, "Government Cost Control Strategies," *Health-PAC Bulletin,* no. 75, March–April 1977, pp. 1–6.
5. *The Complex Puzzle of Rising Health Costs: Can the Private Sector Fit it Together?* (Washington, D.C.: Council on Wage and Price Stability, December 1976).
6. *New York Times,* 26 April 1977.
7. The ideology of individual responsibility threatens to incorporate and use the self-help movement for its own purposes. Self-help initially developed as a political response to the oppressive character of professional and male domination in medicine. As such, the self-help movement embodies some of the best strands of grassroots, autonomous action, of people attempting at some level to regain control over their lives, and a response to the overmedicalization of American life. However, because the movement has focused on individual behavior and only rarely addressed the social and physical environment, and because it has not built a movement that goes beyond self-care to demanding the medical and environmental prerequisites for maintaining health, it lends itself to the purposes of victim-blaming. Just as the language of helping obscured the unequal power relationships of a growing therapeutic state (in other words, masking political behavior by calling it therapeutic) the language of self-help obscures the power relations underlying the social causation of disease and the dominant interests that now seek to reorder popular expectations of rights and entitlements for access to medical services.
8. Fuchs, *Who Shall Live?* (New York: Basic Books, 1974), p. 27.
9. *New York Times,* 17 April 1977.
10. *Conference on Future Directions in Health Care,* pp. 4–5.
11. Ibid., pp. 28–29.
12. "The Responsibility of the Individual," in *Doing Better and Feeling Worse: Health in the United States,* ed. by John Knowles (New York: Norton and Co., 1977), p. 78.
13. L. Kass, "Regarding the End of Medicine and the Pursuit of Health," *Public Interest* 40 (Summer 1975): 38–39.
14. Quoted in ibid., p. 42.
15. *Conference in Future Directions in Health Care,* pp. 2–3.
16. 14 October 1976.
17. Kass, p. 71.
18. William Ryan, *Blaming the Victim* (New York: Vintage Books, 1971).
19. Quoted in Kass, p. 42.
20. These remarks are in no way intended to imply that access to more services, regardless of their utility for improved health status, is a progressive position. Medical services as a means to maintain health have been grossly oversold. As Paul Starr comments "a critic like Illich argues that because medical care has made no difference in health, we should not be particularly concerned about access. He has turned the point around. We will have to be especially concerned about inequalities if we are to make future investments in medical care effective" (p. 52). The argument here is that medical expenditures are presently distorted toward unnecessary and ineffective activities that serve to maximize income for providers and suppliers. Political conditions favoring an effective and just reallocation of expenditures are more likely to develop in the context of a publicly accountable system that must allocate services within statutory contraints and a politically determined budget. In such a system political struggles against special interests, misallocation,

or underfunding will obviously continue, as will efforts to achieve effectiveness and responsiveness. The concept and definition of need will move to the center of policy discussions. With all the perils and ideological manipulations that process will entail, it is better that such a debate take place in public than be determined by the private market.

Further, viable programs of cost control must be formulated, first as an alternative to the cutback strategy and, second, as the necessary adjunct to establishing effective and relevant services. Technology-intensive and overuse-related sources of inflationary costs are directly related to the problem of ineffectiveness as well as to iatrogenesis.

21. "Special Issue on the Economy, Medicine and Health," ed. by Joseph Eyer, *International Journal of Health Services 7*, 1 (January 1977); "The Social Etiology of Disease, Part I," *HMO-Network for Marxist Studies in Health*, no. 2, January 1977.
22. "A Case for Refocussing Upstream: The Political Economy of Illness" (Boston University, unpublished paper, 1974). Reprinted in this book.
23. *Chicago Sun-Times*, 6 February 1977.
24. "The Political and Economic Basis of Cancer," *Technology Review 78*, 8(1976): 1.
25. *Conference on Future Directions in Health Care*, p. 52.
26. *New York Times*, 17 April 1977.
27. Kass, p. 42
28. Fuchs, pp. 26, 46.
29. *Conference on Future Directions in Health Care*, p. 116.
30. Thomas Szasz, *Ideology and Insanity: Essays on the Psychiatric Dehumanization of Man* (Garden City, N.Y.: Doubleday-Anchor Press, 1970).
31. Quoted in Anne Somers, *Health Care in Transition: Directions for the Future* (Chicago: Hospital Research and Educational Trust, 1971), p. 32.
32. See note 15, above.
33. "Prosperity as a Cause of Disease," *International Journal of Health Services 7*, 9(January 1977) 125–50.
34. R. Hurley, "The Health Crisis of the Poor," in *The Social Organization of Health*, ed. by H. P. Dreitzel (New York: Macmillan, 1971), pp. 83–122; *Infant Mortality Rates: Socioeconomic Factors*, Washington, D.C.: U.S. Public Health Service, series 22, no. 14, 1972; *Selected Vital and Health Statistics in Poverty and Nonpoverty Areas of 19 Large Cities, U.S., 1969–71*, Washington, D.C.: U.S. Public Health Service, series 21, no. 26, 1975; E. Kitagaw and P. Hauser, *Differential Mortality in the U.S.: A Study of Socioeconomic Epidemiology* (Cambridge: Harvard University Press, 1973); Hila Sherer, "Hypertension," *HMO* no. 2, January 1977.
35. *Preventive Medicine USA* (New York: Prodist Press, 1976), pp. 620–21; A. Antonovsky, "Social Class, Life Expectancy and Overall Mortality," *Milbank Memorial Fund Quarterly 5*, 45, no. 2-part 1(1967): 31–73.
36. C. D. Jenkins, "Recent Evidence Supporting Psychologic and Social Risk Factors for Coronary Heart Diseases," *New England Journal of Medicine* 294, 18(1976). 987–94; and 294, 19(1976): 1,003–38, J. Eyer and P. Sterling, "Stress Related Mortality and Social Organization," *Review of Radical Political Economy*, Summer 1977.
37. Somers, p. 77.
38. S. Lusterman, *Industry Roles in Health Care* (New York: National Industrial Conference Board, 1974) p. 31.
39. *Dollars and Sense*, April 1977, p. 15.

The Medicalization of American Society

. . . . . .

Only in the twentieth century did medicine become the dominant and prestigious profession we know today. The germ theory of disease, which achieved dominance after about 1870, provided medicine with a powerful explanatory tool and some of its greatest clinical achievements. It proved to be the key that unlocked the mystery of infectious disease and it came to provide the major paradigm by which physicians viewed sickness. The claimed success of medicine in controlling infectious disease, coupled with consolidation and monopolization of medical practice, enabled medicine to achieve a position of social and professional dominance. Medicine, both in direct and indirect ways, was called upon to repeat its "miracles" with other human problems. At the same time, certain segments of the medical profession were intent on expanding medicine's jurisdiction over societal problems.

By mid-century the domain of medicine had enlarged considerably: childbirth, sexuality, death as well as old age, anxiety, obesity, child development, alcoholism, addiction, homosexuality, amongst other human experiences, were being defined and treated as medical problems. Sociologists began to examine the process and consequences of this *medicalization of society* (e.g., Freidson, 1970; Zola, 1972) and most especially the medicalization of deviance (Conrad and Schneider, 1980a; Conrad, 1992). It was clear that the medical model—focusing on individual organic pathology and positing physiological etiologies and biomedical interventions—was being applied to a wide range of human phenomena. Human life, some critics observed, was increasingly seen as a sickness-wellness continuum, with significant (if not obvious) social consequences (Zola, 1972; Conrad, 1975).

Other sociologists, however, argue that although some expansion of medical jurisdiction has occurred, the medicalization problem is overstated. They contend that we recently have witnessed a considerable *de*medicalization. Strong (1979), for instance, points out that there are numerous factors constraining and limiting medicalization, including restrictions on the number of physicians, the cost of medical care, doctor's primary interests in manifestly organic problems, and the bourgeois value of individual liberty.

Conrad and Schneider (1980b) attempted to clarify the debate by suggesting that medicalization occurs on three levels: (1) the conceptual level, at which a medical vocabulary is used to define a problem; (2) the institutional level, at which medical personnel (usually physicians) are supervisors of treatment organizations or gatekeepers to state benefits; and (3) the interactional level, at which physicians actually treat patients' difficulties as medical problems. While there has been considerable discussion about the types and consequences of medicalization, there has thus far been little research on the actual extent of medicalization and its effects on patients' and other peoples' lives.

In "Medicine as an Institution of Social Control," Irving Kenneth Zola presents the medicalization thesis in terms of the expansion of medicine's social control functions. Renée Fox, in "The Medicalization and Demedicalization of American Society," contends that a substantial demedicalization has occurred in American society and that the concerns of critics of medicalization are overdrawn.

REFERENCES

Conrad, Peter. 1975. "The discovery of hyperkinesis: Notes on the medicalization of deviant behavior." Social Problems 23 (1): 12–21.

Conrad, Peter. 1992. "Medicalization and Social Control." Annual Review of Sociology 18: 209–32.

Conrad, Peter, and Joseph W. Schneider. 1980a. Deviance and Medicalization: From Badness to Sickness. St. Louis: C.V. Mosby.

———. 1980b. "Looking at levels of medicalization: A comment on Strong's critique of the thesis of medical imperialism." Social Science and Medicine 14A (1): 75–9.

Freidson, Eliot. 1970. Profession of Medicine. New York: Dodd, Mead.

Strong, P. M. 1979. "Sociological imperialism and the profession of medicine: A critical examination of the thesis of medical imperialism." Social Science and Medicine 13A (2): 199–215.

Zola, Irving Kenneth. 1972. "Medicine as an institution of social control." Sociological Review 20 (November): 487–504.

35

Medicine as an Institution of Social Control

. . . . . .

Irving Kenneth Zola

The theme of this essay is that medicine is becoming a major institution of social control, nudging aside, if not incorporating, the more traditional institutions of religion and law. It is becoming the new repository of truth, the place where absolute and often final judgments are made by supposedly morally neutral and objective experts. And these judgments are made, not in the name of virtue or legitimacy, but in the name of health. Moreover, this is not occurring through the political power physicians hold or can influence, but is largely an insidious and often undramatic phenomenon accomplished by "medicalizing" much of daily living, by making medicine and the labels "healthy" and "ill" *relevant* to an ever increasing part of human existence.

Although many have noted aspects of this process, by confining their concern to the field of psychiatry, these criticisms have been misplaced.[1] For psychiatry has by no means distorted the mandate of medicine, but indeed, though perhaps at a pace faster than other medical specialties, is following instead some of the basic claims and directions of that profession. Nor is this extension into society the result of any professional "imperialism," for this leads us to think of the issue in terms of misguided human efforts or motives. If we search for the "why" of this phenomenon, we will see instead that it is rooted in our increasingly complex technological and bureaucratic system— a system which has led us down the path of the reluctant reliance on the expert.[2]

Quite frankly, what is presented in the following pages is not a definitive argument but rather a case in progress. As such it draws heavily on observations made in the United States, though similar murmurings have long been echoed elsewhere.[3]

An Historical Perspective

The involvement of medicine in the management of society is not new. It did not appear full-blown one day in the mid-twentieth century. As Sigerist[4] has aptly claimed, medicine at base was always not only a social science but an occupation whose very practice was inextricably interwoven into society. This interdependence is perhaps best seen in two branches of medicine which have had a built-in social emphasis from the very start— psychiatry[5] and public health/preventive medicine.[6] Public health was always committed to changing social aspects of life—from sanitary to housing to working conditions—and often used the arm of the state (i.e. through laws and legal power) to gain its ends (e.g. quarantines, vaccinations). Psychiatry's involvement in society is a bit more difficult to trace, but taking the histories of psychiatry as data, then one notes the almost universal reference to one of the early pioneers, a physician named Johan Weyer. His, and thus psychiatry's involvement in social problems lay in the objection that witches ought not to be burned; for they were not possessed by the devil, but rather bedeviled by their problems—namely they were insane. From its early concern with the issue of insanity as a defense in criminal proceedings, psychiatry has grown to become the most dominant rehabilitative perspective in dealing with society's "legal" deviants. Psychiatry, like public health, has also used the legal powers of the state in the accomplishment of its goals (i.e. the cure of the patient through the legal proceedings of involuntary commitment and its concomitant removal of certain rights and privileges).

This is not to say, however, that the rest of medicine has been "socially" uninvolved. For a rereading of history makes it seem a matter of degree. Medicine has long had both a *de jure* and a *de facto* relation to institutions of social control. The *de jure* relationship is seen in the idea of reportable diseases, wherein, if certain phenomena occur in his practice, the physician is required to report them to the appropriate authorities. While this seems somewhat straightforward and even functional where certain highly contagious diseases are concerned, it is less clear where the possible spread of infection is not the primary issue (e.g. with gunshot wounds, attempted suicide, drug use and what is now called child abuse). The *de facto* relation to social control can be argued through a brief look at the disruptions of the last two or three American Medical Association Conventions. For there the American Medical Association members—and really all ancillary health professions—were accused of practicing social control (the term used by the accusers was genocide) in first, *whom* they have traditionally treated with *what*—giving *better* treatment to more favored clientele; and secondly, *what* they have treated—a more subtle form of discrimination in that, with limited resources, by focusing on some diseases others are neglected. Here the accusation was that medicine has focused on the diseases of the rich and the established—cancer, heart disease, stroke—and ignored the diseases of the poor, such as malnutrition and still high infant mortality.

The Myth of Accountability

Even if we acknowledge such a growing medical involvement, it is easy to regard it as primarily a "good" one—which involves the steady destigmatization of many human and social problems. Thus Barbara Wootton was able to conclude:

> Without question . . . in the contemporary attitude toward antisocial behaviour, psychiatry and humanitarianism have marched hand in hand. Just because it is so much in keeping with the mental atmosphere of a scientifically-minded age, the medical treatment of social deviants has been a most powerful, perhaps even the most powerful, reinforcement of humanitarian impulses; for today the prestige of humane proposals is immensely enhanced if these are expressed in the idiom of medical science.[7]

The assumption is thus readily made that such medical involvement in social problems leads to their removal from religious and legal scrutiny and thus from moral and punitive consequences. In turn the problems are placed under medical scientific scrutiny and thus in objective and therapeutic circumstances.

The fact that we cling to such a hope is at least partly due to two cultural-historical blindspots— one regarding our notion of punishment and the other our notion of moral responsibility. Regarding the first, if there is one insight into human behavior that the twentieth century should have firmly implanted, it is that punishment cannot be seen in merely physical terms, nor only from the perspective of the giver. Granted that capital offenses are on the decrease, that whipping and torture seem to be disappearing, as is the use of chains and other physical restraints, yet our ability if not willingness to inflict human anguish on one another does not seem similarly on the wane. The most effective forms of brain-washing deny any physical contact and the concept of relativism tells much about the psychological costs of even relative deprivation of tangible and intangible wants. Thus, when an individual because of his "disease" and its treatment is forbidden to have intercourse with fellow human beings, is confined until cured, is forced to undergo certain medical procedures for his own good, perhaps deprived forever of the right to have sexual relations and/or produce children, *then* it is difficult for the patient *not* to view what is happening to him as punishment. This does not mean that medicine is the latest form of twentieth century torture, but merely that pain and suffering take many forms, and that the removal of a despicable inhumane procedure by current standards does not necessarily mean that its replacement will be all that beneficial. In part, the satisfaction in seeing the chains cast off by Pinel may have allowed us for far too long to neglect examining with what they had been replaced.

It is the second issue, that of responsibility, which requires more elaboration, for it is argued here that the medical model has had its greatest impact in the lifting of moral condemnation from the individual. While some sceptics note that while the individual is no longer condemned his disease still *is*, they do not go far enough. Most analysts have tried to make a distinction between illness and crime on the issue of personal responsibility.[8] The criminal is thought to be responsible and therefore accountable (or punishable) for his act, while the sick person is not. While the distinction does exist, it seems to be more a quantitative one rather than a qualitative one, with moral judgments but a pinprick below the surface. For instance, while it is probably true that individuals are no longer directly condemned for being sick, it does seem that much of this condemnation is merely displaced. Though his immoral character is not demonstrated in his having a disease, it becomes evident in what he does about it. Without seeming ludicrous, if one listed the traits of people who break appointments, fail to follow treatment regimen, or even delay in seeking medical aid, one finds a long list of "personal flaws." Such people seem to be ever ignorant of the consequences of certain diseases, inaccurate as to symptomatology, unable to plan ahead or find time, burdened with shame, guilt, neurotic tendencies, haunted with traumatic medical experiences or members of some lower status minority group—religious, ethnic, racial or socio-economic. In short, they appear to be a sorely troubled if not disreputable group of people.

The argument need not rest at this level of analysis, for it is not clear that the issues of morality and individual responsibility have been fully banished from the etiological scene itself. At the same time as the label "illness" is being used to attribute "diminished responsibility" to a whole host of phenomena, the issue of "personal responsibility" seems to be re-emerging within medicine itself. Regardless of the truth and insights of the concepts of stress and the perspective of psychosomatics, whatever else they do, they bring man, *not* bacteria to the center of the stage and lead thereby to a re-examination of the individual's role in his own demise, disability and even recovery.

The case, however, need not be confined to professional concepts and their degree of acceptance, for we can look at the beliefs of the man in the street. As most surveys have reported, when an individual is asked what caused his diabetes, heart disease, upper respiratory infection, etc., we may be comforted by the scientific terminology if not the accuracy of his answers. Yet if we follow this questioning with the probe: "Why did you get X now?", or "Of all the people in your community, family, etc. who were exposed to X, why did you get . . . ?", then the rational scientific veneer is pierced and the concern with personal and moral responsibility emerges quite strikingly. Indeed the issue "why me?" becomes of great concern and is generally expressed in quite moral terms of what they did wrong. It is possible to argue that here we are seeing a residue and that it will surely be different in the new generation. A recent experiment I conducted should cast some doubt on this. I asked a class of forty undergraduates, mostly aged seventeen, eighteen and nineteen, to recall the last time they were sick, disabled, or hurt and then to record how they did or would have communicated this experience to a child under the age of five. The purpose of the assignment had nothing to do with the issue of responsibility and it is worth noting that there was no difference in the nature of the response between those who had or had not actually encountered children during their "illness." The responses speak for themselves.

The opening words of the sick, injured person to the query of the child were:
"I feel bad"
"I feel bad all over"
"I have a bad leg"
"I have a bad eye"
"I have a bad stomach ache"
"I have a bad pain"
"I have a bad cold"
The reply of the child was inevitable:

"What did you do wrong?"
The "ill person" in no case corrected the child's perspective but rather joined it at that level.
On bacteria
"There are good germs and bad germs and sometimes the bad germs . . ."
On catching a cold
"Well you know sometimes when your mother says, 'Wrap up or be careful or you'll catch a cold,' well I . . ."
On an eye sore
"When you use certain kinds of things (mascara) near your eye you must be very careful and I was not . . ."
On a leg injury
"You've always got to watch where your're going and I . . ."

Finally to the treatment phase:
On how drugs work
"You take this medicine and it attacks the bad parts . . ."
On how wounds are healed
"Within our body there are good forces and bad ones and when there is an injury, all the good ones . . ."
On pus
"That's the way the body gets rid of all its bad things . . ."
On general recovery
"If you are good and do all the things the doctor and your mother tell you, you will get better."

In short, on nearly every level, from getting sick to recovering, a moral battle raged. This seems more than the mere anthropomorphising of a phenomenon to communicate it more simply to children. Frankly it seems hard to believe that the English language is so poor that a *moral* rhetoric is needed to describe a supposedly amoral phenomenon—illness.

In short, despite hopes to the contrary, the rhetoric of illness by itself seems to provide no absolution from individual responsibility, accountability and moral judgment.

The Medicalizing of Society

Perhaps it is possible that medicine is not devoid of potential for moralizing and social control. The first question becomes: "what means are

available to exercise it?" Freidson has stated a major aspect of the process most succinctly:

> The medical profession has first claim to jurisdiction over the label of illness and *anything* to which it may be attached, irrespective of its capacity to deal with it effectively.[9]

For illustrative purposes this "attaching" process may be categorized in four concrete ways: first, through the expansion of what in life is deemed relevant to the good practice of medicine; secondly, through the retention of absolute control over certain technical procedures; thirdly, through the retention of near absolute access to certain "taboo" areas; and finally, through the expansion of what in medicine is deemed relevant to the good practice of life.

1. The Expansion of What in Life Is Deemed Relevant to the Good Practice of Medicine

The change of medicine's commitment from a specific etiological model of disease to a multicausal one and the greater acceptance of the concepts of comprehensive medicine, psychosomatics, etc., have enormously expanded that which is or can be relevant to the understanding, treatment and even prevention of disease. Thus it is no longer necessary for the patient merely to divulge the symptoms of his body, but also the symptoms of daily living, his habits and his worries. Part of this is greatly facilitated in the "age of the computer," for what might be too embarrassing, or take too long, or be inefficient in a face-to-face encounter can now be asked and analyzed impersonally by the machine, and moreover be done before the patient ever sees the physician. With the advent of the computer a certain guarantee of privacy is necessarily lost, for while many physicians might have probed similar issues, the only place where the data were stored was in the mind of the doctor, and only rarely in the medical record. The computer, on the other hand, has a retrievable, transmittable and almost inexhaustible memory.

It is not merely, however, the nature of the data needed to make more accurate diagnoses and treatments, but the perspective which accompanies it—a perspective which pushes the physician far beyond his office and the exercise of technical skills. To rehabilitate or at least alleviate many of the ravages of chronic disease, it has become increasingly necessary to intervene to change permanently the habits of a patient's lifetime—be it of working, sleeping, playing or eating. In prevention the "extension into life" becomes even deeper, since the very idea of primary prevention means getting there *before* the disease process starts. The physician must not only seek out his clientele but once found must often convince them that they must do something *now* and perhaps at a time when the potential patient feels well or not especially troubled. If this in itself does not get the prevention-oriented physician involved in the workings of society, then the nature of "effective" mechanisms for intervention surely does, as illustrated by the statement of a physician trying to deal with health problems in the ghetto.

> Any effort to improve the health of ghetto residents cannot be separated from equal and simultaneous efforts to remove the multiple social, political and economic restraints currently imposed on inner city residents.[10]

Certain forms of social intervention and control emerge even when medicine comes to grips with some of its more traditional problems like heart disease and cancer. An increasing number of physicians feel that a change in diet may be the most effective deterrent to a number of cardiovascular complications. They are, however, so perplexed as to how to get the general population to follow their recommendations that a leading article in a national magazine was entitled "To Save the Heart: Diet by Decree?"[11] It is obvious that there is an increasing pressure for more explicit sanctions against the tobacco companies and against high users to force both to desist. And what will be the implications of even stronger evidence which links age at parity, frequency of sexual intercourse, or the lack of male circumcision to the incidence of cervical cancer, can be left to our imagination!

2. Through the Retention of Absolute Control over Certain Technical Procedures

In particular this refers to skills which in certain jurisdictions are the very operational and legal definition of the practice of medicine—the right to do surgery and prescribe drugs. Both of these take medicine far beyond concern with ordinary organic disease.

In surgery this is seen in several different subspecialties. The plastic surgeon has at least participated in, if not helped perpetuate, certain aesthetic standards. What once was a practice confined to restoration has now expanded beyond the correction of certain traumatic or even congenital deformities to the creation of new physical properties, from size of nose to size of breast, as well as dealing with certain phenomena—wrinkles, sagging, etc.—formerly associated with the "natural" process of aging. Alterations in sexual and reproductive functioning have long been a medical concern. Yet today the frequency of hysterectomies seems not so highly correlated as one might think with the presence of organic disease. (What avenues the very possibility of sex change will open is anyone's guess.) Transplantations, despite their still relative infrequency, have had a tremendous effect on our very notions of death and dying. And at the other end of life's continuum, since abortion is still essentially a surgical procedure, it is to the physician-surgeon that society is turning (and the physician-surgeon accepting) for criteria and guidelines.

In the exclusive right to prescribe and thus pronounce on and regulate drugs, the power of the physician is even more awesome. Forgetting for the moment our obsession with youth's "illegal" use of drugs, any observer can see, judging by sales alone, that the greatest increase in drug use over the last ten years has not been in the realm of treating any organic disease but in treating a large number of psychosocial states. Thus we have drugs for nearly every mood:

> to help us sleep or keep us awake
> to enhance our appetite or decrease it
> to tone down our energy level or to increase it
> to relieve our depression or stimulate our interest.

Recently the newspapers and more popular magazines, including some medical and scientific ones, have carried articles about drugs which may be effective peace pills or anti-aggression tablets, enhance our memory, our perception, our intelligence and our vision (spiritually or otherwise). This led to the easy prediction:

> We will see new drugs, more targeted, more specific and more potent than anything we have. . . . And many of these would be for people we would call healthy.[12]

This statement incidentally was made not by a visionary science fiction writer but by a former commissioner of the United States Food and Drug Administration.

3. Through the Retention of Near Absolute Access to Certain "Taboo" Areas

These "taboo" areas refer to medicine's almost exclusive license to examine and treat that most personal of individual possessions—the inner workings of our bodies and minds. My contention is that if anything can be shown in some way to affect the workings of the body and to a lesser extent the mind, then it can be labelled an "illness" itself or jurisdictionally "a medical problem." In a sheer statistical sense the import of this is especially great if we look at only four such problems—aging, drug addiction, alcoholism and pregnancy. The first and last were once regarded as normal natural processes and the middle two as human foibles and weaknesses. Now this has changed and to some extent medical specialties have emerged to meet these new needs. Numerically this expands medicine's involvement not only in a longer span of human existence, but it opens the possibility of medicine's services to millions if not billions of people. In the United States at least, the implication of declaring alcoholism a disease (the possible import of a pending Supreme Court decision as well as laws currently being introduced into several state legislatures) would reduce arrests in many jurisdictions by 10 to 50 percent and transfer such "offenders" when "discovered" directly to a medical facility. It is pregnancy,

however, which produces the most illuminating illustration. For, again in the United States, it was barely seventy years ago that virtually all births and the concomitants of birth occurred outside the hospital as well as outside medical supervision. I do not frankly have a documentary history, but as this medical claim was solidified, so too was medicine's claim to a whole host of related processes: not only to birth but to prenatal, postnatal, and pediatric care; not only to conception but to infertility; not only to the process of reproduction but to the process and problems of sexual activity itself; not only when life begins (in the issue of abortion) but whether it should be allowed to begin at all (e.g. in genetic counselling).

Partly through this foothold in the "taboo" areas and partly through the simple reduction of other resources, the physician is increasingly becoming the choice for help for many with personal and social problems. Thus a recent British study reported that within a five year period there had been a notable increase (from 25 to 41 percent) in the proportion of the population willing to consult the physician with a personal problem.[13]

4. Through the Expansion of What in Medicine Is Deemed Relevant to the Good Practice of Life

Though in some ways this is the most powerful of all "the medicalizing of society" processes, the point can be made simply. Here we refer to the use of medical rhetoric and evidence in the arguments to advance any cause. For what Wootton attributed to psychiatry is no less true of medicine. To paraphrase her, today the prestige of *any* proposal is immensely enhanced, if not justified, when it is expressed in the idiom of medical science. To say that many who use such labels are not professionals only begs the issue, for the public is only taking its cues from professionals who increasingly have been extending their expertise into the social sphere or have called for such an extension.[14] In politics one hears of the healthy or unhealthy economy or state. More concretely, the physical and mental health of American presidential candidates has been an issue in the last four elections and a recent book claimed to link faulty political decisions with faulty health.[15] For years we knew that the environment was unattractive, polluted, noisy and in certain ways dying, but now we learn that its death may not be unrelated to our own demise. To end with a rather mundane if depressing example, there has always been a constant battle between school authorities and their charges on the basis of dress and such habits as smoking, but recently the issue was happily resolved for a local school administration when they declared that such restrictions were necessary for reasons of health.

The Potential and Consequences of Medical Control

The list of daily activities to which health can be related is ever growing and with the current operating perspective of medicine it seems infinitely expandable. The reasons are manifold. It is not merely that medicine has extended its jurisdiction to cover new problems,[16] or that doctors are professionally committed to finding disease,[17] nor even that society keeps creating disease.[18] For if none of these obtained today we would still find medicine exerting an enormous influence on society. The most powerful empirical stimulus for this is the realization of how much everyone has or believes he has something organically wrong with him, or put more positively, how much can be done to make one feel, look or function better.

The rates of "clinical entities" found on surveys or by periodic health examinations range upwards from 50 to 80 percent of the population studied.[19] The Peckham study found that only 9 percent of their study group were free from clinical disorder. Moreover, they were even wary of this figure and noted in a footnote that, first, some of these 9 percent had subsequently died of a heart attack, and, secondly, that the majority of those without disorder were under the age of five.[20] We used to rationalize that this high level of prevalence did not, however, translate itself into action since not only are rates of medical utilization not astonishingly high but they also have not gone up appreciably. Some recent studies, however, indicate that we may have been

looking in the wrong place for this medical action. It has been noted in the United States and the United Kingdom that within a given twenty-four to thirty-six hour period, from 50 to 80 percent of the adult population have taken one or more "medical" drugs.[21]

The belief in the omnipresence of disorder is further enhanced by a reading of the scientific, pharmacological and medical literature, for there one finds a growing litany of indictments of "unhealthy" life activities. From sex to food, from aspirins to clothes, from driving your car to riding the surf, it seems that under certain conditions, or in combination with certain other substances or activities or if done too much or too little, virtually anything can lead to certain medical problems. In short, I at least have finally been convinced that living is injurious to health. This remark is not meant as facetiously as it may sound. But rather every aspect of our daily life has in it elements of risk to health.

These facts take on particular importance not only when health becomes a paramount value in society, but also a phenomenon whose diagnosis and treatment has been restricted to a certain group. For this means that that group, perhaps unwittingly, is in a position to exercise great control and influence about what we should and should not do to attain that "paramount value."

Freidson in his recent book *Profession of Medicine* has very cogently analyzed why the expert in general and the medical expert in particular should be granted a certain autonomy in his researches, his diagnosis and his recommended treatments.[22] On the other hand, when it comes to constraining or directing human behavior *because* of the data of his researches, diagnosis and treatment, a different situation obtains. For in these kinds of decisions it seems that too often the physician is guided not by his technical knowledge but by his values, or values latent in his very techniques.

Perhaps this issue of values can be clarified by reference to some not so randomly chosen medical problems: drug safety, genetic counselling and automated multiphasic testing.

The issue of drug safety should seem straightforward, but both words in that phrase apparently can have some interesting flexibility—namely what is a drug and what is safe. During Prohibition in the United States alcohol was medically regarded as a drug and was often prescribed as a medicine. Yet in recent years, when the issue of dangerous substances and drugs has come up for discussion in medical circles, alcohol has been officially excluded from the debate. As for safety, many have applauded the A.M.A.'s judicious position in declaring the need for much more extensive, longitudinal research on marihuana and their unwillingness to back leglization until much more data are in. This applause might be muted if the public read the 1970 Food and Drug Administration's "Blue Ribbon" Committee Report on the safety, quality and efficacy of *all* medical drugs commercially and legally on the market since 1938.[23] Though appalled at the lack and quality of evidence of any sort, few recommendations were made for the withdrawal of drugs from the market. Moreover there are no recorded cases of anyone dying from an overdose or of extensive adverse side effects from marihuana use, but the literature on the adverse effects of a whole host of "medical drugs" on the market today is legion.

It would seem that the value positions of those on both sides of the abortion issue needs little documenting, but let us pause briefly at a field where "harder" scientists are at work— genetics. The issue of genetic counselling, or whether life should be allowed to begin at all, can only be an ever increasing one. As we learn more and more about congenital, inherited disorders or predispositions, and as the population size for whatever reason becomes more limited, then, inevitably, there will follow an attempt to improve the quality of the population which shall be produced. At a conference on the more limited concern of what to do when there is a documented probability of the offspring of certain unions being damaged, a position was taken that it was not necessary to pass laws or bar marriages that might produce such offspring. Recognizing the power and influence of medicine and the doctor, one of those present argued:

> There is no reason why sensible people could not be dissuaded from marrying if they know that one out of four of their children is likely to inherit a disease.[24]

There are in this statement certain values on marriage and what it is or could be that, while they may be popular, are not necessarily shared by all. Thus, in addition to presenting the argument against marriage, it would seem that the doctor should—if he were to engage in the issue at all—present at the same time some of the other alternatives:

> Some "parents" could be willing to live with the risk that out of four children, three may turn out fine.
>
> Depending on the diagnostic procedures available they could take the risk and if indications were negative abort.
>
> If this risk were too great but the desire to bear children was there, and depending on the type of problem, artificial insemination might be a possibility.
>
> Barring all these and not wanting to take any risk, they could adopt children.
>
> Finally, there is the option of being married without having any children.

It is perhaps appropriate to end with a seemingly innocuous and technical advance in medicine, automatic multiphasic testing. It has been a procedure hailed as a boon to aid the doctor if not replace him. While some have questioned the validity of all those test-results and still others fear that it will lead to second class medicine for already underprivileged populations, it is apparent that its major use to date and in the future may not be in promoting health or detecting disease but to prevent it. Thus three large institutions are now or are planning to make use of this method, not to treat people, but to "deselect" them. The armed services use it to weed out the physically and mentally unfit, insurance companies to reject "uninsurables" and large industrial firms to point out "high risks." At a recent conference representatives of these same institutions were asked what responsibility they did or would recognize to those whom they have just informed that they have been "rejected" because of some physical or mental anomaly. They calmly and universally stated: none—neither to provide them with any appropriate aid nor even to ensure that they get or be put in touch with any help.

Conclusion

C. S. Lewis warned us more than a quarter of a century ago that "man's power over Nature is really the power of some men over other men, with Nature as their instrument." The same could be said regarding man's power over health and illness, for the labels health and illness are remarkable "depoliticizers" of an issue. By locating the source and the treatment of problems in an individual, other levels of intervention are effectively closed. By the very acceptance of a specific behavior as an "illness" and the definition of illness as an undesirable state, the issue becomes not whether to deal with a particular problem, but *how* and *when*.[25] Thus the debate over homosexuality, drugs or abortion becomes focused on the degree of sickness attached to the phenomenon in question or the extent of the health risk involved. And the more principled, more perplexing, or even moral issue, of *what* freedom should an individual have over his or her own body is shunted aside.

As stated in the very beginning this "medicalizing of society" is as much a result of medicine's potential as it is of society's wish for medicine to use that potential. Why then has the focus been more on the medical potential than on the social desire? In part it is a function of space, but also of political expediency. For the time rapidly may be approaching when recourse to the populace's wishes may be impossible. Let me illustrate this with the statements of two medical scientists who, if they read this essay, would probably dismiss all my fears as groundless. The first was commenting on the ethical, moral, and legal procedures of the sex change operation:

> Physicians generally consider it unethical to destroy or alter tissue except in the presence of disease or deformity. The interference with a person's natural pro-creative function entails definite moral tenets, by which not only physicians but also the general public are influenced. The administration of physical harm as treatment for mental or behavioral problems—as corporal punishment, lobotomy for unmanageable psychotics and sterilization of criminals—is abhorrent in our society.[26]

Here he states, as almost an absolute condition of human nature, something which is at best a recent phenomenon. He seems to forget that there were laws promulgating just such procedures through much of the twentieth century, that within the past few years at least one Californian jurist ordered the sterilization of an unwed mother as a condition of probation, and that such procedures were done by Nazi scientists and physicians as part of a series of medical experiments. More recently, there is the misguided patriotism of the cancer researchers under contract to the United States Department of Defense who allowed their dying patients to be exposed to massive doses of radiation to analyze the psychological and physical results of simulated nuclear fall-out. True, the experiments were stopped, but not until they had been going on for *eleven* years.

The second statement is by Francis Crick at a conference on the implications of certain genetic findings:

> Some of the wild genetic proposals will never be adopted because the people will simply not stand for them.[27]

Note where his emphasis is: on the people, not the scientist. In order, however, for the people to be concerned, to act and to protest, they must first be aware of what is going on. Yet in the very privatized nature of medical practice, plus the continued emphasis that certain expert judgments must be free from public scrutiny, there are certain processes which will prevent the public from ever knowing what has taken place and thus from doing something about it. Let me cite two examples.

> Recently, in a European country, I overheard the following conversation in a kidney dialysis unit. The chief was being questioned about whether or not there were self-help groups among his patients. "No" he almost shouted "that is the last thing we want. Already the patients are sharing too much knowledge while they sit in the waiting room, thus making our task increasingly difficult. We are working now on a procedure to prevent them from even meeting with one another."

The second example removes certain information even further from public view.

The issue of fluoridation in the U.S. has been for many years a hot political one. It was in the political arena because, in order to fluoridate local water supplies, the decision in many jurisdictions had to be put to a popular referendum. And when it was, it was often defeated. A solution was found and a series of state laws were passed to make fluoridation a public health decision and to be treated, as all other public health decisions, by the medical officers best qualified to decide questions of such a technical, scientific and medical nature.

Thus the issue at base here is the question of what factors are actually of a solely technical, scientific and medical nature.

To return to our opening caution, this paper is not an attack on medicine so much as on a situation in which we find ourselves in the latter part of the twentieth century; for the medical area is the arena or the example *par excellence* of today's identity crisis—what is or will become of man. It is the battleground, not because there are visible threats and oppressors, but because they are almost invisible; not because the perspective, tools and practitioners of medicine and the other helping professions are evil, but because they are not. It is so frightening because there are elements here of the banality of evil so uncomfortably written about by Hannah Arendt.[28] But here the danger is greater, for not only is the process masked as a technical, scientific, objective one, but one done for our own good. A few years ago a physician speculated on what, based on current knowledge, would be the composite picture of an individual with a low risk of developing atherosclerosis or coronary-artery disease. He would be:

> ... an effeminate municipal worker or embalmer completely lacking in physical or mental alertness and without drive, ambition, or competitive spirit; who has never attempted to meet a deadline of any kind; a man with poor appetite, subsisting on fruits and vegetables laced with corn and whale oil, detesting tobacco, spurning ownership of radio, television, or motorcar, with full head of hair but scrawny and unathletic appearance, yet constantly straining his puny muscles by exercise. Low in income, blood pressure, blood sugar, uric acid and cholesterol, he has been taking nicotinic acid, pyridoxine, and long term antocoagulant therapy ever since his prophylactic castration.[29]

Thus I fear with Freidson:

> A profession and a society which are so concerned with physical and functional wellbeing as to sacrifice civil liberty and moral integrity must inevitably press for a "scientific" environment similar to that provided laying hens on progressive chicken farms—hens who produce eggs industriously and have no disease or other cares.[30]

Nor does it really matter that if, instead of the above depressing picture, we were guaranteed six more inches in height, thirty more years of life, or drugs to expand our potentialities and potencies; we should still be able to ask: what do six more inches matter, in what kind of environment will the thirty additional years be spent, or who will decide what potentialities and potencies will be expanded and what curbed.

I must confess that given the road down which so much expertise has taken us, I am willing to live with some of the frustrations and even mistakes that will follow when the authority for many decisions becomes shared with those whose lives and activities are involved. For I am convinced that patients have so much to teach to their doctors as do students their professors and children their parents.

NOTE

This paper was written while the author was a consultant in residence at the Netherlands Institute for Preventive Medicine, Leiden. For their general encouragement and the opportunity to pursue this topic I will always be grateful.

It was presented at the Medical Sociology Conference of the British Sociological Association at Weston-Super-Mare in November 1971. My special thanks for their extensive editorial and substantive comments go to Egon Bittner, Mara Sanadi, Alwyn Smith, and Bruce Wheaton.

REFERENCES

1. T. Szasz: *The Myth of Mental Illness*, Harper and Row, New York, 1961; and R. Leifer: *In the Name of Mental Health*, Science House, New York, 1969.
2. E.g. A. Toffler: *Future Shock*, Random House, New York, 1970; and P. E. Slater: *The Pursuit of Loneliness*, Beacon Press, Boston, 1970.

3. Such as B. Wootton: *Social Science and Social Pathology*, Allen and Unwin, London, 1959.

4. H. Sigerist: *Civilization and Disease*, Cornell University Press, New York, 1943.

5. M. Foucault: *Madness and Civilization*, Pantheon, New York, 1965; and Szasz: *op. cit.*

6. G. Rosen: *A History of Public Health*, MD Publications, New York, 1955; and G. Rosen: "The Evolution of Social Medicine", in H. E. Freeman, S. Levine and L. G. Reeder (eds): *Handbook of Medical Sociology*, Prentice-Hall, Englewood Cliffs, N.J., 1963, pp. 17–61.

7. Wootton: *op. cit.*, p. 206.

8. Two excellent discussions are found in V. Aubert and S. Messinger: "The Criminal and the Sick", *Inquiry*, Vol. 1, 1958, pp. 137–160; and E. Freidson: *Profession of Medicine*, Dodd-Mead, New York, 1970, pp. 205–277.

9. Freidson: *op. cit.*, p. 251.

10. J. C. Norman: "Medicine in the Ghetto", *New Engl. J. Med.*, Vol. 281, 1969, p. 1271.

11. "To Save the Heart; Diet by Decree?" *Time Magazine*, 10th January, 1968, p. 42.

12. J. L. Goddard quoted in the *Boston Globe*, August 7th, 1966.

13. K. Dunnell and A. Cartwright: *Medicine Takers, Prescribers and Hoarders*, in press.

14. E.g. S. Alinsky: "The Poor and the Powerful", in *Poverty and Mental Health*, Psychiat. Res. Rep. No. 21 of the Amer. Psychiat. Ass., January 1967; and B. Wedge: "Psychiatry and International Affairs", *Science*, Vol. 157, 1961, pp. 281–285.

15. H. L'Etang: *The Pathology of Leadership*, Hawthorne Books, New York, 1970.

16. Szasz: *op. cit.*, and Leifer: *op. cit.*

17. Freidson: *op. cit.*; and T. Scheff: "Preferred Errors in Diagnoses", *Medical Care*, Vol. 2, 1964, pp. 166–172.

18. R. Dubos: *The Mirage of Health*, Doubleday, Garden City, N.Y., 1959; and R. Dubos: *Man Adapting*, Yale University Press, 1965.

19. E.g. the general summaries of J. W. Meigs: "Occupational Medicine", *New Eng. J. Med.*, Vol. 264, 1961, pp. 861–867; and G. S. Siegel: *Periodic Health Examinations—Abstracts from the Literature*, Publ. Hlth. Serv. Publ. No. 1010, U.S. Government Printing Office, Washington, D.C., 1963.

20. I. H. Pearse and L. H. Crocker: *Biologists in Search of Material*, Faber and Faber, London, 1938; and I. H. Pearse and L. H Crocker: *The Peckham Experiment*, Allen and Unwin, London, 1949.

21. Dunnell and Cartwright: *op. cit.*; and K. White, A. Andjelkovic, R. J. C. Pearson, J. H. Mabry, A. Ross and O. K. Sagan: "International Comparisons of Medical Care Utilization", *New Engl. J. of Med.*, Vol. 277, 167, pp. 516–522.

22. Freidson: *op. cit.*

23. *Drug Efficiency Study—Final Report to the Commissioner of Food and Drugs*, Food and Drug Adm. Med. Nat. Res. Council, Nat. Acad. Sci., Washington, D.C., 1969.

24. Reported in L. Eisenberg: "Genetics and the Survival of the Unfit", *Harper's Magazine*, Vol. 232, 1966, p. 57.

25. This general case is argued more specifically in I. K. Zola: *Medicine, Morality, and Social Problems—Some Implications of the Label Mental Illness*, Paper presented at the Amer. Ortho-Psychiat. Ass., March 20–23, 1968.

26. D. H. Russell: "The Sex Conversion Controversy", *New Engl. J. Med.*, Vol. 279, 1968, p. 536.

27. F. Crick reported in *Time Magazine*, April 19th, 1971.

28. H. Arendt: *Eichmann in Jerusalem—A Report on the Banality of Evil*, Viking Press, New York, 1963.

29. G. S. Myers quoted in L. Losagna: *Life, Death and the Doctor*, Alfred Knopf, New York, 1968, pp. 215–216.

30. Freidson: *op. cit.*, p. 354.

36

The Medicalization and Demedicalization of American Society

■ ■ ■ ■ ■ ■

Renée C. Fox

Along with progressive medicalization, a process of demedicalization seems also to be taking place in the society. To some extent the signs of demedicalization are reactions to what is felt by various individuals and groups to be a state of "*over*-medicalization." One of the most significant manifestations of this counter-trend is the mounting concern over implications that have arisen from the continuously expanding conception of "sickness" in the society. Commentators on this process would not necessarily agree with Peter Sedgwick that it will continue to "the point where everybody has become so luxuriantly ill" that perhaps sickness will no longer be "in" and a "blacklash" will be set in motion;[1] they may not envision such an engulfing state of societally defined illness. But many observers from diverse professional backgrounds have published works in which they express concern about the "coercive" aspects of the "label" illness and the treatment of illness by medical professionals in medical institutions.[2] The admonitory perspectives on the enlarged domain of illness and medicine that these works of social science and social criticism represent appear to have gained the attention of young physicians- and nurses-in-training interested in change, and various consumer and civil-rights groups interested in health care.

This emerging view emphasizes the degree to which what is defined as health and illness, normality and abnormality, sanity and insanity varies from one society, culture, and historical period to another. Thus, it is contended, medical diagnostic categories such as "sick," "abnormal," and "insane" are not universal, objective, or necessarily reliable. Rather, they are culture-, class-, and time-bound, often ethnocentric, and as much artifacts of the preconceptions of socially biased observers as they are valid summaries of the characteristics of the observed. In this view, illness (especially mental illness) is largely a mythical construct, created and enforced by the society. The hospitals to which seriously ill persons are confined are portrayed as "total institutions": segregated, encompassing, depersonalizing organizations, "dominated" by physicians who are disinclined to convey information to patients about their conditions, or to encourage paramedical personnel to do so. These "oppressive" and "counter-therapeutic" attributes of the hospital environment are seen as emanating from the professional ideology of physicians and the kind of hierarchial relationships that they establish with patients and other medical professionals partly as a consequence of this ideology, as well as from the bureaucratic and technological features of the hospital itself. Whatever their source, the argument continues, the characteristics of the hospital and of the doctor-patient relationship increase the "powerlessness" of the sick person, "maintain his uncertainty," and systematically "mortify" and "curtail" the "self" with which he enters the sick role and arrives at the hospital door.

This critical perspective links the labeling of illness, the "imperialist" outlook and capitalist behavior of physicians, the "stigmatizing" and "dehumanizing" experiences of patients, and the problems of the health-care system more generally to imperfections and injustices in the society as a whole. Thus, for example, the various forms of social inequality, prejudice, discrimination, and acquisitive self-interest that persist in capitalistic American society are held responsible for causing illness, as well as for contributing to the undesirable attitudes and actions of physicians and other medical professionals. Casting persons in the sick role is regarded as a powerful, latent way for the society to exact conformity and maintain the status quo. For it allows a semi-approved form of deviance to occur which siphons off potential for insurgent protest and which can be controlled through the supervision or, in some cases, the "enforced therapy" of the medical profession. Thus, however permissive and merciful it may be to expand the category of illness, these observers point out, there is always the danger that the society will become a "therapeutic state" that excessively restricts the "right to be different" and the right to dissent. They feel that this danger may already have reached serious proportions in this society through its progressive medicalization.

The criticism of medicalization and the advocacy of demedicalization have not been confined to rhetoric. Concrete steps have been taken to declassify certain conditions as illness. Most notable among these is the American Psychiatric Association's decision to remove homosexuality from its official catalogue ("Nomenclature") of mental disorders. In addition, serious efforts have been made to heighten physicians' awareness of the fact because they share certain prejudiced, often unconscious assumptions about women, they tend to over-attribute psychological conditions to their female patients. Thus, for example, distinguished medical publications such as the *New England Journal of Medicine* have featured articles and editorials on the excessive readiness with which medical specialists and textbook authors accept the undocumented belief that dysmenorrhea, nausea of pregnancy, pain in labor, and infantile colic are all psychogenic disorders, caused or aggravated by women's emotional problems. Another related development is feminist protest against what is felt to be a too great tendency to define pregnancy as an illness, and childbirth as a "technologized" medical-surgical event, prevailed over by the obstetrician-gynecologist. These sentiments have contributed to the preference that many middle-class couples have shown for natural childbirth in recent years, and to the revival of midwifery. The last example also illustrates an allied movement, namely a growing tendency to shift some responsibility for medical care and authority over it from the physician, the medical team, and hospital to the patient, the family, and the home.

A number of attempts to "destratify" the doctor's relationships with patients and with other medical professionals and to make them more open and egalitarian have developed. "Patients' rights" are being asserted and codified, and, in some states, drafted into law. Greater emphasis is being placed, for example, on the patient's "right to treatment," right to information (relevant to diagnosis, therapy, prognosis, or to the giving of knowledgeable consent for any procedure), right to privacy and confidentiality, and right to be "allowed to die," rather than being "kept alive by artificial means or heroic measures . . . if the situation should arise in which there is no reasonable expectation of . . . recovery from physical or mental disability."[3]

In some medical milieux (for example, community health centers and health maintenance organizations), and in critical and self-consciously progressive writings about medicine, the term "client" or "consumer" is being substituted for "patient." This change in terminology is intended to underline the importance of preventing illness while stressing the desirability of a non-supine, non-subordinate relationship for those who seek care to those who provide it. The emergence of nurse-practitioners and physician's assistants on the American scene is perhaps the most significant sign that some blurring of the physician's supremacy vis-à-vis other medical professionals may also be taking place. For some of the responsibilities for diagnosis, treatment, and patient management that were formerly prerogatives of physicians have been incorporated into these new, essentially marginal roles.[4]

Enjoinders to patients to care for themselves rather than to rely so heavily on the services of medical professionals and institutions are more frequently heard. Much attention is being given to studies such as the one conducted by Lester Breslow and his colleagues at the University of California at Los Angeles which suggest that good health and longevity are as much related to a self-enforced regimen of sufficient sleep, regular, well-balanced meals, moderate exercise and weight, no smoking, and little or no drinking, as they are to professionally administered medical care. Groups such as those involved in the Women's Liberation Movement are advocating the social and psychic as well as the medical value of knowing, examining, and caring for one's own body. Self-therapy techniques and programs have been developed for conditions as complicated and grave as terminal renal disease and hemophilia A and B. Proponents of such regimens affirm that many aspects of managing even serious chronic illnesses can be handled safely at home by the patient and his family, who will, in turn, benefit both financially and emotionally. In addition, they claim that in many cases the biomedical results obtained seem superior to those of the traditional physician-administered, health-care-delivery system.

The underlying assumption in these instances is that, if self-care is collectivized and reinforced by mutual aid, not only will persons with a medical problem be freed from some of the exigencies of the sick role, but both personal and public health will thereby improve, all with considerable savings in cost. This point of view is based on the moral supposition that greater autonomy from the medical profession coupled with greater responsibility for self and others in the realm of health and illness is an ethically and societally superior state.

We have the medicine we deserve. We freely choose to live the way we do. We choose to live recklessly, to abuse our bodies with what we consume, to expose ourselves to environmental insults, to rush frantically from place to place, and to sit on our spreading bottoms and watch paid professionals exercise for us. . . . Today few patients have the confidence to care for themselves. The inexorable professionalization of medicine, together with reverence for the scientific method, have invested practi-

tioners with sacrosanct powers, and correspondingly vitiated the responsibility of the rest of us for health. . . . What is tragic is not what has happened to the revered professions, but what has happened to us as a result of professional dominance. In times of inordinate complexity and stress we have been made a profoundly dependent people. Most of us have lost the ability to care for ourselves. . . . I have tried to demonstrate three propositions. First, medical care has less impact on health than is generally assumed. Second, medical care has less impact on health than have social and environmental factors. And third, given the way in which society is evolving and the evolutionary imperatives of the medical care system, medical care in the future will have even less impact on health than it has now. . . . We have not understood what health is. . . . But in the next few decades our understanding will deepen. The pursuit of health and of well-being will then be possible, but only if our environment is made safe for us to live in and our social order is transformed to foster health, rather than suppress joy. If not, we shall remain a sick and dependent people. . . . The end of medicine is not the end of health but the beginning. . . .[5]

The foregoing passage (excerpted from Rick Carlson's book, *The End of Medicine*) touches upon many of the demedicalization themes that have been discussed. It proclaims the desirability of demedicalizing American society, predicting that, if we do so, we can overcome the "harm" that excessive medicalization has brought in its wake and progress beyond the "limits" that it has set. Like most critics of medicalization on the American scene, Carlson inveighs against the way that medical care is currently organized and implemented, but he attaches exceptional importance to the health-illness-medical sector of the society. In common with other commentators, he views health, illness, and medicine as inextricably associated with values and beliefs of American tradition that are both critical and desirable. It is primarily for this reason that in spite of the numerous signs that certain *structural* changes in the delivery of care will have occurred by the time we reach the year 2000, American society is not likely to undergo a significant process of *cultural* demedicalization.

Dissatisfaction with the distribution of professional medical care in the United States, its costs, and its accessibility has become sufficiently acute and generalized to make the enactment of a national health-insurance system in the foreseeable future likely. Exactly what form that system should take still evokes heated debate about free enterprise and socialism, public and private regulation, national and local government, tax rates, deductibles and co-insurance, the right to health care, the equality principle, and the principle of distributive justice. But the institutionalization of a national system that will provide more extensive and equitable health-insurance protection now seems necessary as well as inevitable even to those who do not approve of it.

There is still another change in the health-illness-medicine area of the society that seems to be forthcoming and that, like national health insurance, would alter the structure within which care is delivered. This is the movement toward effecting greater equality, collegiality, and accountability in the relationship of physicians to patients and their families, to other medical professionals, and to the lay public. Attempts to reduce the hierarchical dimension in the physician's role, as well as the increased insistence on patient's rights, self-therapy, mutual medical aid, community medical services and care by non-physician health professionals, and the growth of legislative and judicial participation in health and medicine by both federal and local government are all part of this movement. There is reason to believe that, as a consequence of pressure from both outside and inside the medical profession, the doctor will become less "dominant" and "autonomous," and will be subject to more controls.

This evolution in the direction of greater egalitarianism and regulation notwithstanding, it seems unlikely that all elements of hierarchy and autonomy will, or even can, be eliminated from the physician's role. For that to occur, the medical knowledge, skill, experience, and responsibility of patients and paramedical professionals would have to equal, if not replicate, the physician's. In addition, the social and psychic meaning of health and illness would have to become trivial in order to remove all vestiges of institutionalized charisma from the physician's role. Health, illness, and medicine have never been viewed casually in any society and, as indicated, they seem to be gaining rather than losing importance in American society.

It is significant that often the discussions and developments relevant to the destratification and control of the physician's role and to the enactment of national health insurance are accompanied by reaffirmations of traditional American values: equality, independence, self-reliance, universalism, distributive justice, solidarity, reciprocity, and individual and community responsibility. What seems to be involved here is not so much a change in values as the initiation of action intended to modify certain structural features of American medicine, so that it will more fully realize long-standing societal values.

In contrast, the new emphasis on health as a right, along with the emerging perspective on illness as medically and socially engendered, seems to entail major conceptual rather than structural shifts in the health-illness-medical matrix of the society. These shifts are indicative of a less fatalistic and individualistic attitude toward illness, increased personal and communal espousal of health, and a spreading conviction that health is as much a consequence of the good life and the good society as it is of professional medical care. The strongest impetus for demedicalization comes from this altered point of view. It will probably contribute to the decategorization of certain conditions as illness, greater appreciation and utilization of non-physician medical professionals, the institutionalization of more preventive medicine and personal and public health measures, and, perhaps, to the undertaking of non-medical reforms (such as full employment, improved transportation, or adequate recreation) in the name of the ultimate goal of health.

However, none of these trends implies that what we have called *cultural* demedicalization will take place. The shifts in emphasis from illness to health, from therapeutic to preventive medicine, and from the dominance and autonomy of the doctor to patient's rights and greater control of the medical profession do not alter the fact that health, illness, and medicine are central preoccupations in the society which have diffuse symbolic as well as practical meaning. All signs suggest that they will maintain the social, ethical, and existential significance they have acquired, even though by the year 2000 some structural aspects of the way that medicine and care are organized and delivered may have changed. In fact, if the issues now being considered under the rubric of bioethics are predictive of what lies ahead, we can expect that in the future, health, illness, and medicine will acquire even greater importance as one of the primary symbolic media through which American society will grapple with fundamental questions of value and belief. What social mechanisms we will develop to come to terms with these "collective conscience" issues, and exactly what role physicians, health professionals, biologists, jurists, politicians, philosophers, theologians, social scientists, and the public at large will play in their resolution remains to be seen. But it is a distinctive characteristic of an advanced modern society like our own that scientific, technical, clinical, social, ethical, and religious concerns should be joined in this way.

REFERENCES

1. Sedgwick, "Illness—Mental and Otherwise," *The Hastings Center Studies*, 1:3(1973), p. 37.

2. In addition to Illich, *Medical Nemesis,* and Kittrie, *The Right To Be Different,* see, for example, Rick J. Carlson, *The End of Medicine* (New York, 1975); Michael Foucault, *Madness and Civilization* (New York, 1967); Eliot Freidson, *Professional Dominance* (Chicago, 1970); Erving Goffman, *Asylums* (New York, 1961); R. D. Laing, *The Politics of Experience* (New York, 1967); Thomas J. Scheff, *Being Mentally Ill* (Chicago, 1966); Thomas S. Szasz, *The Myth of Mental Illness* (New York, 1961); and Howard D. Waitzkin and Barbara Waterman, *The Exploitation of Illness in Capitalist Society* (Indianapolis, 1974).

3. This particular way of requesting that one be allowed to die is excerpted from the "Living Will" (revised April, 1974 version), prepared and promoted by the Euthanasia Educational Council.

4. See the article by David Rogers, "The Challenge of Primary Care," in *Daedalus*, 106, Winter, 1977:81–103.

5. Carlson, *The End of Medicine*, pp. 44, 141, and 203–31.

Rationing Medical Care

. . . . . .

Rising health care costs have dominated health policy discussions for two decades. Although numerous attempts have been made to control health costs with some minor successes, overall such measures have not managed to slow rising health care costs. From 1975 to 1980 the percentage of GNP spent on health care rose from 8.3 to 9.1 percent, while from 1980 to 1985 it rose from 9.1 to 10.6 percent. Thus there was a 9.6 percent rise from 1975–80 compared to a 16.5 percent rise in the next five years (Reinhardt, 1987). The subsequent years have been no better. It is hard to draw any conclusion other than that the overall result of cost containment efforts in the last decade has been failure.

In this context numerous policy analysts have suggested "rationing" medical care as a way to control rapidly rising costs. In the United Kingdom rationing specific medical services and technology has been for many years an accepted feature of the national health care system (Aaron and Schwartz, 1984). The issue of rationing or "limiting the use of potentially beneficial [medical] resources" has come to the forefront and may well become the preeminent health policy issue of the 1990s. The introduction to the "Dilemmas of Medical Technology" section in Part Two briefly discussed this issue from the perspective of ethical and economic considerations for limiting medicine's technological arsenal under certain conditions. Here we focus more directly on the concept of rationing as part of the ongoing debate concerning the future of our nation's health policy.

Numerous health policy analysts argue that resources for medical care are not unlimited and that inevitably medical practitioners will soon be able to provide more medical care than society can afford. Some analysts believe we have reached that point already. While they do not necessarily agree with one another, health economists (e.g., Aaron and Schwartz, 1990), bioethicists (e.g. Callahan, 1987), and physicians (Relman, 1990) have all contributed to the discourse on rationing.

The focus of most of the discussion is whether we ought to consider implementing some type of program to ration or limit access to expensive medical services. Sociologists (Mechanic, 1979; Conrad and Brown, 1993) and others (e.g., Blank, 1988) have pointed out that the real question is not *whether* but *how* we should ration. These analysts contend that we already do ration medical services in the United States on the basis of the ability to pay. Those with access to medical services and insurance or some other means of paying for them receive appropriate care, while others, particularly the uninsured, do not. Perhaps because this form of rationing is not the result of specific policies limiting health care, it is often ignored in discussions on rationing. But in our view it is important not to exclude from such discussions the fact that rationing already occurs in outcome, if not in name. Sociologists have called this phenomenon *implicit rationing* to differentiate it from the proposed more explicit rationing policies that dominate current debate.

A few years ago the state of Oregon developed an explicit rationing plan for its Medicaid program. Recognizing that the state could not fund limitless health care and that many people were not covered by Medicaid or private insurance, Oregon passed a law that sought to ensure health coverage for everyone in the state. To achieve this aim, the "Oregon Health Decisions" project was devised to decide with public input what should be the health priorities for the 1990s. Based on the responses thus obtained and cost-benefit analysis, a state health commission developed an extensive, specific, prioritized list of services. Any services that fell below a certain point on this list would not be paid for by Medicaid (for details, see Crawshaw et al., 1990). In short, the plan allowed for extending Medicaid to all people, including the currently uninsured, in exchange for limitations on the types of services to be made available. Analysts who disapproved of rationing in principle of course opposed the proposed program; others criticized the proposal for targeting only the poor, i.e. Medicaid recipients, and not those with private insurance; and many physicians contended that the list of covered services was too narrow and that the cut-off points would not work. Under the Bush administration, the federal government, which oversees Medicaid programs, did not approve the Oregon proposal; the Clinton administration reversed this decision and will allow Oregon to implement the program. Though Americans are obviously very uncomfortable with explicit rationing of medical care, it seems clear that in the next few years we must confront the rationing issue directly as we reform our health care system.

In this section's first selection, "Rationing Medical Progress," bioethicist Daniel Callahan argues that we can only meet basic health needs while living within our societal means. To achieve an equitable base level of health care for all, we must limit ineffective, marginal or overly expensive procedures. While acknowledging medical progress as a great human achievement, Callahan argues that the costs of unlimited progress in medical technology are too high, and that for the sake of justice and equity, we must ration technology's use. In the second selection, "The Trouble with Rationing," physician and health analyst Arnold S. Relman contends that rationing is not necessary if we eliminate "overuse of services, inefficient use of facilities and excessive overhead and administrative expenses." In short, reform the medical system, change the incentives, and cut out unnecessary or inefficient care and we won't need to ration health care. Relman believes physicians can and do ethically allocate services to patients, but opposes explicit rationing policies.

Short of some yet unconsidered resolution of the complex issues involved in health care reform, the debate over rationing is certain to continue throughout the next decade.

REFERENCES

Aaron, Henry, and William B. Schwartz. 1984. The Painful Prescription: Rationing Hospital Care. Washington, D.C.: Brookings Institution.

Aaron, Henry, and William B. Schwartz. 1990. "Rationing health care: The choice before us." Science 247:418–22.

Blank, Robert H. 1988. Rationing Medicine. New York: Columbia University Press.

Callahan, Daniel. 1987. Setting Limits: Medical Goals in an Aging Society. New York: Simon and Schuster.

Conrad, Peter, and Phil Brown. 1993. "Rationing medical care: A sociological reflection." Research in the Sociology of Health Care, Volume 12:3–32.

Crawshaw, Ralph, Michael Garland, Brian Hines, and Betty Anderson. 1990. "Developing principles for prudent health care allocation: The continuing Oregon experiment." Western Journal of Medicine 152:441–6.

Mechanic, David. 1979. Future Issues in Health Care: Policy and the Rationing of Medical Services. New York: Free Press.

Reinhardt, Uwe. E. 1987. Medical Economics. August 24.

Relman, Arnold S. 1990. "Is rationing inevitable?" New England Journal of Medicine 322:1809–10.

37

Rationing Medical Progress:
The Way to Affordable Health Care

． ． ． ． ． ．

Daniel Callahan

We are engaged in a great struggle to reform the American health care system, a system addicted to increasing costs and decreasing equity. The first tactic of someone suffering from addictive behavior is twofold: to try to remove the bad habit with the least possible disruption to the ordinary way of life, and to try to change the undesirable behavior in a painless, incremental way.

This tactic rarely works, as any reformed smoker or alcoholic can testify. The price of real change is harsher self-examination and the revision of basic values and habits. With the health care crisis, we have not quite reached that point. As a society we are still playing out the incrementalist tactic, hoping against hope that it will work. But I doubt that it will, and I want to argue that it is time to move on toward deeper change, however uncomfortable the next step may be.

There is considerable agreement on the outline of the problem: we spend an increasingly insupportable amount of money on health care but get neither good value for our money nor better equity in terms of access to health care. Greater efficiency and greater equity are widely accepted as goals in response to our troubles. They are being pursued through cost-containment efforts on the one hand, and proposals for universal health care on the other.

Yet for all the vigor behind these efforts, there seems to be an enormous reluctance to engage in the kind of self-examination that will quickly make these goals realities. There is similar resistance to the even more intimidating task of finding the ingredients needed to sustain a health care system—one that can provide decent care in the face of increased demand even when all the necessary efficiencies have been achieved. Such a quest leads to a relatively simple insight, that an economically sound health care system must combine three elements: access for all to a base level of health care (equity), a means of limiting the use of procedures that are ineffective or marginally effective as well as some of the procedures that are effective but too expensive (efficiency), and some consensus on health care priorities, both social and individual (so that we can live within our means while meeting our basic health needs).

Working against those goals are several deeply ingrained values that have come to characterize our system. First, we prize autonomy and freedom of choice and want everyone to have them: patients, physicians and other health care workers, and hospital and health administrators. In the name of freedom we indulge our hostility to governmental control and planning, thus setting ourselves apart from every other developed country. Second, we cherish the idea of limitless medical progress, which has come to mean that every disease should be cured, every disability rehabilitated, every health need met, and every evidence of mortality, especially aging, vigorously challenged. Moreover, we embrace the good living that can be made in the effort to combat mortality. Doing good and doing well have found their perfect meeting place in American health care. Finally, we long for quality in medicine and health care, which in practice we define as the presence of high-class amenities (no gross queuing or open wards for us) and a level of technology that is constantly improving and welcoming innovations. High-quality medicine is understood, in effect, as a kind of medicine that is better today than yesterday and will be even better tomorrow.

I have stressed values that are admirable and progressive on the whole—values, in fact, that have given the American health care system many of its characteristic strengths. Choice is better than constraint, individual freedom better than government regulation, progress better than stagnation, capitalism better than socialism, and quality better than mediocrity. Yet one can say all this while noting something else: that the unrestrained embodiment of these values in the system is precisely what creates contradictions and renders meaningful reform so hard.

Cost containment is a striking case in point. Beginning with the efforts of President Nixon in 1970 and continuing in every subsequent administration, one obvious and laudable intention has been to control the constant and unremitting escalation of health care costs, rising well beyond the level of overall inflation. Yet not a single serious observer that I know of has shown that cost containment has come anywhere near reaching its goal, although there have been modest successes here and there. Despite this notable failure, it still is commonly believed that serious cost containment is compatible with our cherished values. If we could only eliminate unnecessary, untested, or wasteful diagnostic devices and medical treatments, do away with excessive malpractice claims, pare away expensive bureaucracy, and so forth, we could avoid rationing (the deliberate withholding of beneficial medical care) and provide efficient, equitable care. Indeed, some believe it would be both a mistake and morally objectionable to ration health care before we have exhausted all means of achieving cost containment and making medical care more efficient.

There is much truth in that contention, and I do not want to deny that there is ample room for efficiency in our present system, much less suggest that we should not pursue a wide range of cost-containment efforts. There is much that can and should be done, and the possibilities of savings are enormous and well documented. Will this be enough, however? I doubt it. There is a double error in looking to cost containment to save us from rationing and limit setting. Even if it did not constitute rationing as strictly defined, effective cost containment entails an austerity that would itself have much of the weight and effect of rationing. By that I mean that serious cost containment must compel some degree of externally regulated treatment standards, often called protocol treatment. To control overspending, it must invoke tight regulation, full of sanctions and penalties for failure to conform. It must force unpleasant choices, the kind that compel priority setting. Most of all, it must force us to reconsider our values, so that we either give them up or scale them down when necessary.

If 20 years of failed efforts at cost containment have not convinced us of these realities, we might consider some other troubling thoughts. The most important is this: even if we had the most efficient system of health care in the world, the fact of an aging population and the intensification of services that medical progress ordinarily engenders would still tend to expand costs. This is coming to be the experience of Canada and the European countries, which already have in place many of the very reforms we believe will be our economic salvation; even so, strain is beginning to appear in those systems. They find it increasingly difficult to live within budgets that are fixed or growing only slowly, and even if they can achieve greater efficiency, they are cautiously beginning to talk the language of rationing also. As Dr. Adam L. Linton of the Ontario Medical Association put it recently in these pages, "Perhaps all structural tinkering is doomed to fail. The root causes of the problem are the increase in demand and the explosion of new forms of technology. These make the rationing of health care inevitable and the chief issue we should be addressing publicly."[1]

Why is this so? One aspect of our American effort to contain costs is illuminating in this regard. As fast as we try to remove high costs, we are adding a steady stream of new, usually expensive forms of technology. If one takes 1970 as the base-line year, the number of new forms of technology introduced since then is astonishing;

there are so many that I, at least, have not even been able to list them fully. Our commitment to unlimited medical innovation has not been seriously hampered by cost-containment efforts. How, then, are we supposed to hold down costs while constantly adding new forms of technology? What known types of efficiency are designed to take such inherent economic pressure into account?

Assessment of our technology can get us out of such problems, of course, at least insofar as it allows us to discover and eliminate useless or only marginally useful forms of technology. It will do little, however, to solve the most troubling problem of technological medicine—that of tests and procedures that are effective, that really work, and yet are costly, either in individual cases or in the aggregate. The great but rarely confronted failing of much of the faith in technology assessment might be called the efficacy fallacy—that if it works and is beneficial, it must be affordable, or at least ought to be. That, of course, does not follow at all. Unless we are prepared to spend an unconscionable proportion of our resources on health care—letting schools, roads, housing, and manufacturing investments suffer in comparison—we cannot possibly afford every medical advance that might be of benefit. Nor is there any reason to think we would automatically and proportionately increase our happiness and improve our general welfare by even trying to do so.

The trouble with medical progress, one of our great human glories, is that it is intrinsically limitless in its economic possibilities, and no less so in its capacity for puzzlement and contrariness. For one thing, it is impossible to meet every human need merely by pursuing further progress. In this pursuit, we redefine "need" constantly, escalating and expanding it. For example, we do not think of people 100 years of age as needing artificial hearts. But we should know that if an effective heart is eventually developed and someone will die without it, then there will be a need for it. A medical need is usually understood as a need that if fulfilled, would bring life and health, and there is no end to what we can want for that purpose. The contrariness of the pursuit of progress too often shows itself, however. With the steady decline in death rates for all age groups

has come an increase in the incidence of disability and chronic illness, as if the body itself will only stand so much progress.

The quest for greater efficiency, as embodied in successful cost containment, does not in itself provide a sufficient long-term alternative to the limitation of some forms of efficacious health care. Nor is it a good substitute for change in our deepest values and aspirations. We need both an effective, potent, and stringent cost-containment movement and a shift in fundamental values. It is not a matter of "either/or," but of "both/and." By continuing to hope that cost containment alone will do the job, we put off the other task that should be taking place—that of changing our values. By thinking that this task should await the outcome of further efforts at cost containment, we underestimate the short-term pressure that serious cost containment places on our values. Such a tactic also distracts us from the most urgent long-term task—best begun at once—of devising and learning to live with a less expansive health care system and a less expansive idea of health.

How can we start thinking differently about our values? We might first distinguish between bringing to everyone the medical knowledge and skills that are already available and pressing forward on the frontiers of medicine to find new ways to save and improve life. If we could make all our present knowledge available to everyone right now, we could achieve substantial improvement in the health of people whose poverty and lack of knowledge put them particularly at risk of avoidable illness. Substantial progress in health could be achieved by increasing equity in the access to care. After that, spending more money on schools and housing would make as good a contribution to improved health, in an indirect fashion, as medical expenditures would directly.

Second, we might remind ourselves that we are the healthiest, longest-living human beings in the history of the human race, healthy enough to run a well-educated, economically prosperous, and culturally vital society. Further progress would help some of us, perhaps many, but we have already come a long way and have sufficient general health for most important human purposes. We can always improve our health and extend our life, but that will be true no matter how much progress we make. This is not to deny the obvious and extraordinary benefits of medical progress or to suggest a return to a pretechnological past. It is only to put the idea of unlimited progress in a more modest, perhaps more affordable, light: we want more progress, but we will not necessarily be in terrible shape as a society if we do not get it.

In any case, we must be prepared to ration medical progress and in particular to forgo potentially beneficial advances in the application and development of new techniques. I am not proposing a diminution of efforts to extend our store of theoretical biologic and medical knowledge. A strong commitment to basic biomedical research remains an attractive and desirable goal. That commitment is not incompatible, however, with several insistent requirements: (1) that clinical applications be subjected to stringent technological assessments before dissemination; (2) that the social and economic standards for the assessment be biased toward restrictiveness ("strait is the gate and narrow the way" might be a pertinent maxim here); and (3) that it is understood and accepted that some, perhaps many, beneficial applications will have to be passed over on grounds of cost and other, more pressing social priorities.

Third, we might come to understand that the demand for autonomy and choice, as well as for high-quality care, represents values that can be scaled back considerably without a serious loss in actual health. The great hazard of American individualism is that if we are patients, we sometimes confuse what we want with what is good for us; and if we are physicians, we confuse the way we would prefer to treat patients with what is actually beneficial to them. This is a delicate point, because there is a profound sense in which the gratification we get from making our own choices or practicing medicine according to our own lights makes our life or profession satisfying. Nonetheless, in the face of economic restraints, it is important to decide what we are after most: better health, greater choice, or some wonderful combination of both. We probably cannot have both in equal degrees, and if we had more health than choice, we would still be reasonably well off.

Finally, we might come to understand that there is a diminishing social return from attempts to make health care a source of expanding profit and personal enrichment. If we make medicine so expensive that we can ill afford even adequate emergency rooms, we have gone backward in providing decent care. If we make the provision of adequate health care to working people too expensive, employees will have to provide inadequate coverage or reduce the workers' pay. If we spend too much on health care in relation to everything else (for instance, spending 11.4 percent of our gross national product on health care but only 6.8 percent on education), we risk becoming a hypochondriacal society, one that has sacrificed much that is good and necessary for a rounded life out of an obsession with health.

Is there a politically acceptable and feasible way to restrain the market forces in our health care system without jeopardizing the centrality of a free market in our political economy? One way is already being tried: government uses its buying power under entitlement programs to control fees and costs and uses its regulatory power to promote competitiveness among providers. But that may not be sufficient. My own guess is that unless we can come to see health care as being like fire, police, and defense protection—a necessity for the public interest rather than a market commodity—we will not be able to resolve that problem. We must be willing to exempt some health care policies and decisions from the market ideology and to do so in the name of the common good.

Whether we like modifying our basic values or not, it seems impossible to achieve equity and efficiency without doing so. Having a minimal level of adequate care available to all means that if such care is to be affordable, it must be combined with limits on choices, progress, and profit. Setting limits means we cannot have everything we want or dream of. The demand for priorities arises when we try to live with both decent minimal care and limits to care. At that point we must decide what it is about health care that advances us most as a society and as individuals. We have bet that we could have it all. That bet is not paying off. There remains no reason, however, that we cannot have a great deal.

We do not necessarily have to limit decent health care in any serious, drastic fashion.

What we do need to do is to restrain our demands for unlimited medical progress, maximal choice, perfect health, and profits and income. This is not the same as rationing good health care.

Note

1. Linton AL. The Canadian health care system: a Canadian physician's perspective. N Engl J Med 1990; 322:197–9.

38

The Trouble with Rationing

■ ■ ■ ■ ■ ■

Arnold S. Relman

Suddenly everyone is talking about rationing. First brought to public attention in this country by Schwartz and Aaron's study of the allocation of hospital services in the United Kingdom,[1,2] rationing is now widely advocated as the only effective way to control health care costs.

The argument goes like this: An aging and growing population, rising public expectations, and the continual introduction of new and expensive forms of technology generate a virtually unlimited demand for medical services, which inevitably exhausts the resources we are willing and able to devote to health care. Sooner or later we will be forced to limit expenditures by restricting services, even those that are beneficial. Of course, we are already restricting services through our failure to provide health insurance to many who cannot afford it, but we now must confront the necessity of explicitly denying certain services to insured patients—at least to those whose insurance is subsidized by government or business.

On the surface it is a persuasive argument. Many observers now seem convinced that the question is not whether but how we will ration health services.[3] A closer examination of the problem suggests, however, that rationing is not necessary, nor would it be likely to work without major changes in our health care system. Furthermore, as even some of its strongest advocates admit, a fair and workable rationing plan would be, to say the least, difficult to design.

The supposed necessity of rationing rests on the assumption that no other expedient can prevent for long the continued escalation of health costs. Advocates of rationing usually acknowledge the growing evidence of overuse of services, inefficient use of facilities, and excessive overhead and administrative expenses. They may even accept the proposition that substantial elimination of such defects might reduce the cost of health care by as much as 20 or 30 percent. But they maintain that any reforms of this kind would produce only a one-time savings that would soon be nullified by a resumption of the inexorable rise in costs.

This argument, it seems to me, fails to recognize the crux of the problem. New forms of technology and insatiable demand are not the fundamental causes of cost inflation, nor are overuse, inefficiency, duplication, or excessive overhead expenses. They are simply the manifestations of a system that has built-in incentives for waste and inflation. It is the way we organize and fund the delivery of health care that rewards the profligate use of technology and stimulates demand for nonessential services; it is the system that allows duplication and waste of resources and produces excessive overhead costs. Change certain features of the system, and you will not only reduce costs in the short run, but moderate the inherent forces causing inflation. As a result, future costs will rise at a slower, more affordable rate without the need to restrict essential services and without loss of quality. To avoid rationing, what we require most is not more money but the will to change those aspects of the present system that are responsible for the present cost crisis. In a subsequent editorial I will discuss what might be done to control costs and avoid rationing. My purpose here is to explain why, even if there were no alternatives, rationing would probably not be acceptable or workable. I will also suggest that unless the funding of health care were to become far more centralized and prospectively budgeted than at present, rationing would not control costs.

To be seen as fair and therefore have a chance of acceptance by the public and the medical profession, a rationing plan needs to have medical and ethical, not simply economic, justification. To be medically justified, rationing decisions have to be personalized, because no two patients are exactly the same and the anticipated benefits of a given procedure vary from patient to patient. As Schwartz and Aaron[4] have recently pointed out in a convincing critique of the method of rationing initially proposed by the state of Oregon,[5] any plan to assign priorities to specific medical interventions on the basis of cost-benefit considerations must take into account individual circumstances, balancing costs against potential benefits in each patient. Thus, for example, it would make no sense simply to approve or disapprove all kidney transplantations, or to assign the procedure a single overall priority rating. In some patients a kidney transplant might have an excellent chance of substantially extending life and improving its quality while saving money as well, but in others a transplant would be worse than useless. Setting out formal guidelines to cover all the clinical circumstances under which kidney transplantation might or might not be worthwhile would be a complex task. The same would be true of bone marrow transplantations, coronary bypass operations, total parenteral nutrition, mag-

netic resonance imaging, or any other procedure that might become the object of rationing. With each procedure, the cost-benefit assessment depends so heavily on individual circumstances that it is almost impossible to devise medically sound rules applicable to all patients. In fact, the task is so formidable that no one has yet offered a practical suggestion about how personalized rationing might be carried out systematically and on a wide scale. In a recent interview reported in the *Boston Globe*,[6] Dr. Schwartz said, "I don't know that any scheme [of rationing] will be satisfactory." With that candid opinion by one of the most thoughtful students of the subject I emphatically concur.

Beyond these practical difficulties, attempts to ration medical services in our present health care system would create serious ethical and political problems. Doctors would find themselves in the uncomfortable position of having to deny services to some insured patients they would ordinarily have treated in accordance with accepted medical practice. In a system with a fixed global health care budget established by national policy, as in the United Kingdom, physicians forced to withhold potentially useful services from their patients because of costs at least can be assured that the money saved will be appropriately spent to help other patients and that all publicly financed patients will be treated more or less alike. But this is not so in a disorganized and fragmented health care system like ours, which has multiple programs for the care of publicly subsidized patients and no fixed budget. When medical resources are uniformly limited for all, physicians can ethically and in good conscience allocate services to the patients most likely to benefit, but in the absence of clearly defined limits they feel morally bound to do whatever might be of benefit.[7] For rationing to be perceived as equitable, public insurance programs like Medicare and Medicaid would need to have fixed budgets committed to health care, and a method of allocation that was uniformly applied. Present political realities make these conditions unlikely, and therefore I believe that a public rationing plan would not be ethically or politically acceptable at this time.

Even if a workable, medically sensible, ethically and politically acceptable rationing plan could be devised, it would not save money in the long run. The present health care environment generally encourages—virtually requires—physicians and hospitals to be expansive rather than conservative in providing medical services. Aggressive marketing, not the prudent use of resources, is the prevailing imperative. Any limitation of a medical service by rationing would place economic pressures on health care providers to protect their revenues by expanding the delivery of other services that are not rationed. In an open-ended, competitive system with more and more new physicians, new forms of technology, and new health care facilities entering the market, it is inevitable that costs will continue to escalate despite targeted restrictions on the delivery of certain services. Each decision to restrict services might temporarily reduce costs in one part of the system, but no single decision or group of decisions could stop for long the relentless progress of inflation in the rest of the system. With no overall cap on expenditures there would be no way to keep costs under control except by an endless series of rationing decisions that would cut ever more deeply into the body of accepted medical practice. The gap between optimal care and what the regulations allowed would widen. Sooner or later strong general opposition to further cuts would arise, and it would become apparent that rationing is not the solution to the U.S. health care crisis—at least not without more fundamental reforms in the system.

Our cost crisis, and the limitations on access that result from high costs, stem from an inherently inflationary and wasteful health care system. Rationing is not likely to be successful in controlling costs unless we deal with that basic problem. Given the huge sums we are now committing to medical care as compared with other developed countries, we should be able to afford all the services we really need, provided we use our resources wisely. Concerted attempts to improve the system rather than ration its services are the next sensible step. Even if reform of the system should prove to be an insufficient remedy, it would still be necessary for the ultimate acceptance and success of any rationing plan.

REFERENCES

1. Schwartz WB, Aaron HJ. Rationing hospital care: lessons from Britain. N Engl J Med 1984; 310:52–6.
2. Aaron HJ, Schwartz WB. The painful prescription: rationing hospital care. Washington, D.C.: Brookings Institution, 1984.
3. Rochrig CB. Rationing: not "if" but "how?" The Internist. July–August 1990:5.
4. Schwartz WB, Aaron HJ. The Achilles heel of health care rationing. New York Times. July 9, 1990.
5. Relman AS. Is rationing inevitable? N Engl J Med 1990; 332:1809–10.
6. Stein C. Strong medicine for health care costs. Boston Globe. July 24, 1990:21, 23.
7. Daniels N. Why saying no to patients in the United States is so hard: cost containment, justice, and provider autonomy. N Engl J Med 1986; 314:1380–3.

Toward Alternatives in Health Care

. . . . . .

As part of a critical sociological examination of American health and medical care, it is important that we explore what can be done to create alternatives to improve health in our society. In so doing, we look beyond the "medical model" and the current organization and delivery of medical services. We can conceptualize these alternatives as Community Initiatives, Comparative Health Policies, and Prevention and Society. In the first section of Part Four, we examine several community-based alternatives to existing medical services and discuss their problems and limitations, as well as their potential for improving health care. In the second section, we examine alternatives on the broader, societal level by looking at the health care systems of three other countries. In the final section, we consider the potential of prevention as an alternative way of reorienting our approach to health problems. We cannot claim to provide *the* answer to our "health crisis" here. However, we believe the answers to our health care problems will ultimately be found by searching in the directions pointed out in this part of the book.

....

Community Initiatives

. . . . . .

Several issues emerge when we examine and evaluate community-level efforts to improve medical care. The first such issue pertains to the inherent limitations of such efforts. It is widely argued that the possibilities for change within the existing societal and medical care system are inherently limited. Although some of the most exciting and interesting health innovations have occurred through local efforts on the community level—e.g., women's self-help clinics, neighborhood health centers—these efforts are constantly being shaped and limited by the societal context in which they emerge and in which, often, they must struggle to survive. The realities of the present system (e.g., the professional dominance of physicians, the control of medical payments by the insurance industry and medical care providers, and the limitations imposed by existing medical organizations on access to their services) constitute systemic boundaries to the power of community alternative health-care organizations to effect real change. Some critics even contend that these societal-level constraints will, in the very nature of things, always undermine the progressive potential of alternative services: the medical establishment will either coopt their successes or use their unavoidable difficulties as evidence of their failure (Taylor, 1979; Kronenfeld, 1979).

A central issue related to this entire discussion of community alternatives is the idea of medical "self-help." The 1970s saw a widespread and increasing interest in self-help, or self-care. Self-help groups and other indigenous initiatives in health care emerged as adjuncts and alternatives to medical care. Self-help and mutual aid have a long history in Western society (Katz and Bender, 1976). While critics like Ivan Illich (1976) see self-help as a panacea for our medical ills, most view it as having a more limited role. Self-help groups can provide assistance, encouragement, and needed services to people with chronic and disabling conditions that involve emotional and social problems not provided for by traditional medical care (Gussow and Tracy, 1976). They can also create alternative services, as in the women's health movement. Equally important, self-help groups can aid in demystifying medicine, build a sense of community among people with similar problems, and provide low-cost services and consumer control of services.

While the idea of self-help is not new, it appears on today's medical scene as a somewhat radical departure from the traditional medical notion of a compliant patient and an expert physician. Self-help organizations such as Alcoholics Anonymous (AA) predate the current self-help wave and have apparently successfully demonstrated the possibility of people helping themselves and one another to better health. Often taken as a model for other groups, AA focuses upon behavior, symptoms, and a perception of alcoholism as a chronic and individual problem. It also insists that alcoholics need the continuous social support of other nondrinking alcoholics to maintain their sobriety. A number of analysts (e.g., Kronenfeld, 1979: 263) have noted that AA and other self-help programs modeled on it are somewhat authoritarian in their structure. For example, AA does not question existing societal and cultural arrangements that may have contributed to the drinking problems of its members.

Partly in response to the recognition of the limitations of modern medicine and in reaction to frustrations with existing medical care options, self-help groups and the ideology of self-help have become increasingly popular, not only among former patients of the existing system, but also among professional critics of American medical care (see for example, Illich, 1976; Levin, Katz and Holst, 1976; Carlson, 1975). However, these approaches often focus on individual responsibility for change without stressing simultaneously the difficulties of individual change within existing social arrangements. This has led several critics to note the potential for victim-blaming in recommendations for self-help (Kronenfeld, 1979; Ehrenreich, 1978) and the limitations of self-help for many of the health problems of various, especially non–middle-class, populations in the United States.

It is nonetheless clear that the idea of self-help is an exciting prospect, and one would certainly not want to see the energy and excitement contained within it diminished. The self-help movement has given rise to a range of important criticisms of existing medical care and to a number of significant discoveries for improved health. Self-help approaches envision the possibility of people taking control over their own lives as well as of demystifying traditional medical care. However, unless self-help incorporates a strategy for community *and* societal change, it is likely to reduce this potential vision to the simplistic contention that people are responsible for their own stresses and diseases. Although providing mutual support and encouraging individuals to alter their "unhealthy" behaviors, self-help programs only rarely confront the real options of what people can do as individuals. What is needed, then, is a linking together of self-help movements with struggles for community and social change—in essence, a politicization of self-help.

Among the most interesting community health initiatives in the 1980s and 1990s are a number of unconnected social movements that have attempted to change the way we address health issues. Mothers Against Drunk Driving (MADD) has focused on alcohol-related traffic accident injuries. The MADD approach centers on injury prevention, relying on punitive and educational action and depicting drunk drivers as "violent criminals" while still accepting the medicalized disease concept of alcoholism (see Reinarman, 1988). ACT-UP (AIDS Coalition to Unleash Power) has become a major force in shaping the response to AIDS. This organization has publicly and often emphatically demanded greater government and institutional support for confronting AIDS and committing more of society's substantial resources towards AIDS prevention and treatment (Gamson, 1989; Crimp, 1990). The Independent Living Movement has attempted to reframe living with disabilities as a personal and political rather than a medical matter (DeJong, 1983). This group seeks to demedicalize disabilities and to create situations and work environments where people with disabilities can live independently and reduce their dependence on medical care. Social movements such as these and community responses to problems like toxic wastes (see Article 7 by Phil Brown) are changing the way our society thinks about and responds to health problems.

The promise and reality of community initiatives are evident in each selection in this section. In the first, "Improving the Health Experiences of Low Income Patients," Catherine Kohler Riessman discusses how innovations in medical care for the poor usually locate the target problem either in the "culture of poverty" or, more rarely, in the "culture of medicine." After noting some of the inherent biases and difficulties of the culture-of-poverty approach, she examines two community-based alternatives—birthing centers and pediatric home care—that attempt to change the organization and culture of medical care. These alternatives are largely initiated by professionals, although not necessarily doctors, and are not self-help projects in any major sense. Yet programs like these and hospices for the terminally ill are significant innovations in medical care. While they leave services in professional control, they create a more cooperative situation between patient and provider, support more social and family involvement, encourage noninstitutional care, are less expensive, and in the cases presented here, are real alternatives available for poor patients.

The other two selections focus more directly on self-help, providing quite different examples of people reassessing their own health needs and developing alternative health services through collective, community efforts.

The second reading, "Politicizing Health Care" by John McKnight, describes a fascinating and innovative community effort to assess health needs and design local medical-care alternatives aimed at improving health in the community. In this project, people discovered a number of important things, including: (1) many "medical" problems had little to do with disease, and could more accurately be termed "social problems"; (2) they could, as a community, take collective action to make real changes in their own health; (3) they could build alternative organizations for meeting their health and social needs and in the process include heretofore ignored groups (e.g., the elderly) as productive contributors to the community's health; and (4) they could develop new "tools" of production that would remain under their own control and serve their own particular needs. Despite these marvelous lessons, McKnight acknowledges the limitations of local efforts to change the basic maldistribution of resources and services and notes the need for self-help efforts to come to grips with "external" authorities and structures.

In the last selection, Ann Withorn, in "Helping Ourselves," discusses the limits and potentials of self-help. Focusing her discussion in part on two of the most influential health-related self-help movements—the women's health movement and Alcoholics Anonymous—Withorn evaluates the place of self-help in progressive change. For over two decades, the womens' health movement has been the most important self-help movement in the health field. It emerged as part of the Women's Movement and in the context of a growing recognition of the role of medicine in the oppression of women. The women's health movement has established gynecological self-help clinics, educated women about their health and bodies (e.g., books like *Our Bodies, Our Selves*), challenged the use of dangerous medicines and procedures (e.g., DES, the Dalkon Shield, Caesarean rates), organized politically to protect the choice of abortion and reproductive rights, and empowered women to question their medical care. As with other community initiatives, there have been struggles. The women's self-help movement has been faced with conflicts arising from its challenge of medical prerogative and has been continually faced with problems in financing its alternative services, particularly for poor women who must rely on public funds and other third-party payments for their medical services. The women's health movement has sometimes imposed limitations on itself by rejecting much of what traditional medicine has to offer.

But even with these difficulties, the women's health movement manages to connect supportive mutual aid with a struggle for political change and is our best exemplar for seeing the potential of self-help in the larger context of progressive reform.

REFERENCES

Carlson, R. J. 1975. The End of Medicine. New York: John Wiley.

Crimp, Douglas. 1990. AIDS/DEMOGRAPHICS. San Francisco: Bay Press.

DeJong, Gerben. 1983. "Defining and implementing the Independent Living concept." Pp. 4–27 in Nancy M. Crewe and Irving Kenneth Zola, Independent Living for Physically Disabled People. San Francisco: Jossey-Bass.

Ehrenreich, John. 1978. "Introduction: The cultural crisis of modern medicine." Pp. 1–35 in John Ehrenreich [ed.], The Cultural Crisis of Modern Medicine. New York: Monthly Review Press.

Gamson, Josh. 1989. "Silence, death and the invisible enemy: AIDS, activism and social movement "newness." Social Problems 36: 351–67.

Gussow, Zachary, and George Z. Tracy. 1976. "The role of self-help clubs in the adaptation to chronic illness and disability." Social Science and Medicine 10 (7/8): 407–14.

Illich, Ivan. 1976. Medical Nemesis: The Expropriation of Health. New York: Pantheon Books.

Katz, A. H., and E. I. Bender. 1976. "Self-help groups in Western society." Journal of Applied Behavioral Science 12: 265–82.

Kronenfeld, Jennie J. 1979. "Self care as a panacea for the ills of the health care system: An assessment." Social Science and Medicine 13A: 263–7.

Levin, L., A. Katz, and E. Holst. 1976. Self-Care: Lay Initiatives in Health. New York: Prodist.

Reinarman, Craig. 1988. "The social construction of an alcohol problem: The case of Mothers Against Drunken Driving and social control in the 1980s." Theory and Society 17: 91–120.

Taylor, Rosemary C. R. 1979. "Alternative services: The case of free clinics." International Journal of Health Services 9, 2: 227–53.

39

Improving the Health Experiences of
Low Income Patients

■ ■ ■ ■ ■ ■

Catherine Kohler Riessman

Over the last several decades there has been a debate about the relationship between social class and the use of medical care. Historically, the poor used fewer health services than the middle class. More recently, however, low income groups have come to exceed the middle class in service use,[1] leading some to conclude that equality of access has been achieved.

However, analyses based on rates of use are severely misleading, since they fail to take into account the poor health of the economically disadvantaged. In studies which compare individuals with the same level of illness, low income groups have the lowest use of services.[2] In addition, crude comparisons of physician visits obscure important regional, racial, and age differences. For although income differentials in total use have narrowed considerably since the early 1960s, sizable gaps remain for particular groups and for particular health problems.

Children's health visits reveal particularly marked class and racial differentials. Young children from families with incomes less than $5,000 a year are almost twice as likely as children from families with incomes $25,000 or more not to have had a physician visit in the last year. Despite higher rates of disability, poor and minority children have fewer total visits than affluent and white children. The difference in the average number of physician visits by race is especially striking, with white children under seventeen having 4.3 visits per year compared to 2.9 for black children. Class and racial differ-

ences in immunization rates are also striking. A recent national survey found that 45 percent of children ages 1–4 who lived in urban poverty areas were immunized against polio, compared to 54 percent of equivalent non-poverty area children. In comparing racial groups the findings were even more marked: 40 percent of non-white children compared to 64 percent of whites.[3]

Cumulatively, these findings suggest that despite improvements since the 1960s, social class and race continue to limit access to medical care. This article will focus primarily on class. As a theoretical context for the later discussion, I will identify the two perspectives which have shaped the analysis of class differences in health behavior, briefly evaluating the evidence for each perspective. Following this, I will describe two programs which represent structural innovations in the delivery of medical care to low income women and children: birth centers and pediatric home care. These programs provide the beginnings of an alternative vision of care, for they depart from customary structures and medical practices in certain key ways.

Two major explanations have been suggested for the relationship between social class and the use of health services. The first argues that the poor are less likely than the middle class to use health services—and particularly preventive services—because of a "culture of poverty." Others argue that the explanation lies in social structural arrangements.

The Culture of Poverty View

The culture of poverty explanation argues that the lack of attention to health is part of a "way of life"—an entrenched culture of values and attitudes which encourages dependency and discourages self reliance.[4] According to this view, the poor are less likely to use medical care because of a constellation of culturally transmitted health beliefs and predispositions.[5] Important among these is a crisis-oriented approach to life which leads the poor to accord greater priority to immediate rewards than to long-term goals. As a consequence, medical care is sought only in emergency situations or in times of severe illness, and often after considerable delay. Poor groups seek immunizations, prenatal care, and asymptomatic checkups less frequently because they lack a "psychological readiness" and future orientation. Low income people use preventive services less and are less knowledgeable about appropriate health behavior because their culture does not place a high value on health. They have negative attitudes toward medical care and do not believe in its efficacy. Experiencing a sense of helplessness and resignation in coping with their environment, the poor do not exhibit the active, individually responsible, and disciplined behavior necessary in seeking appropriate medical care. As Rosenblatt and Suchman state:

> The body can be seen as simply another class of object to be worn out but not repaired. Thus teeth are left without dental care. . . . Corrective eye examinations, even for those who wear glasses, are often neglected. . . . It is as though . . . blue collar groups think of the body as having a limited span of utility, to be enjoyed in youth and then to suffer with and to endure stoically with age and decrepitude.[6]

This culture is passed from generation to generation, creating a self-propelling cycle of poverty and poor health. Efforts to intervene and change patterns of behavior will be largely fruitless given the values and traditions deeply embedded in the culture. Rosenstock summarizes this perspective:

> The culture of poverty may originally have been based on a history of economic deprivation, but it seems to be a culture exhibiting its own rationale, and structure, and reflecting a way of life that is transmitted to new generations. It is therefore suggested that while financial costs may serve as barriers to obtaining health services, their removal would probably not have the effect of creating widespread changes in health behavior of the poor, at least not in the foreseeable future.[7]

While the culture of poverty concept has been widely criticized,[8] it remains an influential paradigm within the social sciences. Many health investigators rely implicitly on aspects of this theory when they use personal and cultural deficits to explain class differences in health behavior (e.g. particular health attitudes, individual and subcultural belief systems, and psychological predispositions such as external locus of control).[9] These individual and social characteristics are often examined without taking into account the context of care—the characteristics of the medical systems to which different classes have access. The paradigm is also influential in current national health policy, which emphasizes improving health by changing individual values and behaviors.

The Structural View

The alternative perspective emphasizes the structural constraints which prevent low income people from having genuine access to quality medical care.[10] There are, according to this view, two types of constraint. The first is material. Poor people, by definition, have fewer financial resources with which to purchase care in the medical marketplace, particularly services of a preventive nature. Even with health insurance programs, such as Medicaid, there is evidence that equal access does not exist for all groups. Many low income people are not eligible for these governmental programs and many states provide inadequate coverage because benefits are limited.[11] Thus low utilization may be seen as a realistic adaptation to economic circumstances.

The second set of structural constraints stems from the very organization of medical care services. In our two-class system of care, middle-class people are likely to receive care in private offices whereas poor people are likely to receive care in public clinics, or in out-patient departments and emergency rooms of general hospitals.[12] In these settings, care can often be impersonal and dehumanized. Further compounding the problem is inadequate transportation in poor neighborhoods, as well as inconvenient clinic hours and long waits in the hospitals themselves. Providers in these settings have little control over the nature of their work, for they are responsible typically for seeing large numbers of patients in block appointment systems. Under these conditions, there is little chance for providers to have on-going relationships with particular patients. In addition, the patients in these settings often have to maneuver between many specialty clinics to obtain the services they need, and the services themselves are likely to be disease-oriented (or curative) rather than preventive. Cumulatively, these characteristics of the system have a deterrent effect, discouraging people from seeking care, particularly preventive care.

According to the structural argument, it is this "culture of medicine,"[13] rather than deficits in the culture of the patient, that is responsible for the low utilization rates among some segments of the poor. This medical culture is comprised of the particular habits, customs, and expectations of health professionals as well as the needs of the bureaucratic organizations in which they work. An important part of the medical culture is the emphasis on high technology and sub-specialty care. To low income patients, this culture and its attendant institutions may seem, in Anselm Strauss's words:

> ... terribly massive and complex, crowded and busy; while the personnel seem often impersonal, brusque, or even insulting ... physicians go from patient to patient, spending brief moments with most ... patients may sit for long periods of time waiting to be called. ... Patients see all of this and may simply respond fatalistically to the rush and bustle.[14]

In sum, the structural view assigns primary responsibility for the alienation of low income patients to their material disadvantage and to the systems barriers they face when seeking care. According to this perspective, the poor have had multiple negative experiences with organizational systems, leading to avoidance behavior, lack of trust, and hence a disinclination to seek care and follow medical regimens except in dire need. The assumption is that "good" experiences will result in behavior change. The lack of appropriate utilization of health care by lower socioeconomic groups is not deeply culture bound, according to this view. It can be modified if there are changes in professionals and the organization of medical care.

The Evidence

Ten years ago I reviewed the evidence on the relationship between social class and the use of medical services in an attempt to test the power of the culture of poverty explanation compared to the structural view.[15] I critically examined evaluative research from a series of demonstration programs which were initiated in the 1960s, including neighborhood health centers, family planning and comprehensive care programs. Cumulatively, the data revealed that the health behavior of the poor could be radically altered, and within a relatively short period of time, by introducing structural changes in the way services were offered.

More recent research provides further support for these findings. Although methodological problems remain,[16] the findings confirm the primary importance of characteristics of the medical care system in suppressing or enhancing use among low income groups.[17,18]

Interestingly, there is some recent evidence that attitudes themselves may no longer be a factor at all in determining utilization among the poor. In a study in the Chicago area, blacks and persons with low education, compared to whites and the well-educated, had more symptoms and were *more* likely to endorse the idea of visiting a doctor for symptoms. However, these same groups used public services as their source of care and, consistent with previous research, this type of medical care was associated with fewer visits.[19]

In sum, the evidence reveals that deficits in the system of care rather than individual characteristics of patients are primarily responsible for unequal use. Moreover, it appears that the problem is not economic, at least in a narrow sense. When a variety of factors are examined simultaneously, different levels of financial coverage do not explain why those with lower incomes use medical care less frequently.[20] Rather, the evidence strongly suggests that the problem lies in broader economic arrangements which insure a two-class system of care. Diana Dutton underscores the implications of the results:

> neither improved financial access nor health education efforts alone will eliminate current income differentials in use, unless accompanied by structural improvements in existing delivery systems. Fundamental changes in the organization and distribution of care must occur, if equitable patterns of use are to be more than health policy rhetoric.[21]

The Current Crisis

Increasingly conservative national health care policy has dramatically changed the availability of medical services in the United States. Federal budget cuts have eliminated many medical organizations, most notably neighborhood health centers, that were developed in the 1960s as structural alternatives to traditional medical services. Despite the indisputable evidence of the efficacy of these programs in reducing or eliminating class differences in access and use of preventive medical services, national health policy seems to have rejected a structural approach in favor of a policy of changing individuals.

Paralleling the increasingly conservative changes in national health policy, the past decade has seen a growing scholarship that has reexamined many of the assumptions and claims of medical practice, concluding that much of the "health crisis" is a consequence of medicine itself. These writings locate the cause of a range of problems in the "culture" of medicine, including the beliefs, customs, and behaviors of physicians, as well as the political and economic relationship of medicine to other institutions, including the state. Some have used their critiques to challenge the medical paradigm itself, including its reliance on technology, professional expertise, and curative treatments that result in, among other things, the separation of the sick from potentially supportive networks of friends and family. These critiques are perhaps best exemplified in the statements of the women's health movement.[22]

In light of government retrenchment from structural solutions, as well as the simultaneous recognition of the questionable value of those services that do exist, an analysis of utilization needs to be reconceptualized. The issue is not simply the availability and access of medical services to the poor, but also an assessment of the services themselves.

Are there models in the current period which offer any promise? More specifically, do programs exist which improve the health experiences of low income patients by changing the structure of medical care, so as to provide easier access, greater equality between provider and consumer, and more humane care?

I will describe two programs which are currently operating and which can be evaluated on the basis of these criteria. The two models are birth centers and home care for chronically ill children. These programs represent alternative approaches to meeting the health care needs of women and children. In addition, each program provides a model of care which is potentially corrective of key aspects of the culture of medicine.

Perhaps most interesting, these programs represent innovations which emerged from challenges from within the professional community. The first set of programs—birth centers—is an innovation from nurse-midwifery. This service arose at the same time feminists were challenging traditional medical approaches to women's problems, including birth. The second program—home care for chronically ill children—is an innovation from medicine. It was developed by a Department of Pediatrics of an urban teaching hospital.

Birth Centers

The management of childbirth has undergone dramatic changes in this century. Whereas in 1900 only 5 percent of babies were born in hospitals, by 1979 97.4 percent of all births occurred in hospitals—the vast majority of these attended by physicians. More recently, there is evidence of a trend away from hospital and physician-centered birth. In particular, there has been an increase in planned home births as well as in free standing birth centers. Although precise data are not available on the proportion of total births occurring in these alternative sites,[23] it is suggestive that the number of free standing birth centers increased from three in 1975 to over one hundred in 1982.[24] Primary care in these centers is generally provided by certified nurse-midwives rather than by obstetricians.

The growth of free standing birth centers has been spurred by a number of factors. Most important, the childbirth education movement of the 1960s leveled a pointed critique at childbirth practices, drawing attention to the "cultural warping of childbirth"[25] by American medicine. Birth is defined as a pathological event and treated in ways which remove the woman's control over the experience. As part of this medicalization of birth, drugs and technology are routinely used—to induce labor, to speed it up, to dull the pain, to monitor the fetus, to remove it surgically. The high rate of Caesarian sections is of particular concern—now estimated to be 25 percent of all births. Critics argue that all these procedures carry risks for both mother and infant. In addition, the critique of childbirth challenges the medical practice of separating the woman from family during labor and from the infant after delivery. Although an alienating experience for women in general, research has shown that hosptial based birth is particularly dehumanized for low income women.[26]

Out of this critique, an alternative childbirth movement began, as women—particularly middle-class women—began to question their doctors' advice. Frustrated by traditional obstetrical practice, child bearing families searched for alternative ways to handle birth. This social movement occurred simultaneously with the emergence of a general increase in the valuing of the "natural." Some women chose to bypass the medical care system entirely, having their babies at home attended by lay midwives, family, and friends. Others turned to the new specialists within nursing—certified nurse-midwifes— who had been trained in the 1960s and 1970s to provide maternity care to poor women in medically underserved areas.

One response of medicine to these challenges was to try to make the hospital a more humane

place for childbirth. Hospitals made efforts to modify birth, rather than run the risk of losing it. "Birthing rooms" were established where "low risk"* women could deliver in a home-like atmosphere, accompanied by family. Although preferable to the delivery room atmosphere, some argue that these changes involve primarily cosmetic improvements and do not fundamentally alter medical control over the birth process.[27] Moreover, few women (less than 10 percent) ever enter and give birth in these hospital birthing rooms.

In this context, nurse-midwives established free standing birth centers, aided by a small group of progressive obstetricians. The centers are facilities separate from hospitals and provide prenatal, peripartum, and neonatal care for low risk pregnancies. It is estimated that in 45 percent of the centers, the primary care provider is a certified nurse-midwife, who refers to consulting physicians those clients needing medical supervision, hospitalization for pregnancy, labor or delivery. In an additional 29 percent of the centers, both physicians and certified nurse-midwives provide care within the Center.[28] Structured typically as nonprofit corporations, most centers are licensed and meet local health and safety codes. They generally have cooperative agreements with a laboratory, an ambulance service, and a tertiary care hospital in case these are needed. The recognized prototype for birth centers is the Maternity Center Association in New York City, which developed and evaluated risk criteria, staffing patterns, and programs of care.

Su Clinica Familiar is one of the oldest birth centers.[29] Unlike others, this birth center is part of a family oriented rural health clinic. Located in the Rio Grande valley of Southern Texas, it services a predominantly Mexican-American population of agricultural workers and their families. Almost half of the families are below the poverty level in the two counties served by the program, and the birth rate is high. One-third of the patients are teenage mothers. As a consequence of economic disadvantage and age, these women are at high risk for delivering low birth weight infants and for other complications. Before the center opened, women did not have easy access to prenatal care. These women delivered either at home, frequently in the temporary shelters erected for migrant farm workers, or in hospitals which were geographically remote. The local hospital refused to admit them because they were uninsured. Maternity services began in 1972, initially provided only by nurse-midwives. These were joined in practice in 1978 by several obstetrician-gynecologists who were funded by the National Health Service Corps. This added staff made care accessible for those patients who previously were referred to hospitals because of high risk, and also allowed for consultation by the midwives regarding complications of labor and delivery. Between 1972 and 1979, over 1,400 babies were born in *Su Clinica Familiar*—93 percent attended by nurse-midwives.

Maternity care in a birth center is distinctive. Typically, a woman is seen for all phases of the birth process in the center—for childbirth education, prenatal care, and for labor and delivery. In order to insure a healthy mother and baby, nutritional counseling is a major emphasis of the prenatal period. Because many of the women at *Su Clinica Familiar* are poor, supplementary foods are provided, if possible, through the Women and Infant Care (WIC) program. Through a sanitary program staff members stress the improvement of environmental conditions and identify deficient conditions such as impure water and housing code violations. These are brought to the attention of local authorities for correction.

The management of the labor and delivery in a birth center is in sharp contrast to customary hospital practice. Family members are encouraged to take turns staying with the woman during labor. Every member of the family is encouraged to visit, including children. A nurse-midwife is also in constant attendance. The woman is encouraged not to lie on her back, but otherwise any position for labor and delivery is acceptable. There are no routine pubic hair shaves or enemas. Nor are fetal monitors and IVs typically used. Women are allowed oral intake of fluids or food. During labor and delivery, pain medication is used minimally. Instead, women are carefully prepared for the birth experience and supported emotionally through it by family and staff. Women are encouraged to deliver in a variety of positions, because it is believed that the customary lithotomy position (on the back) is responsible for a large proportion of episiotomies and other complications, as well as failure to progress in labor.

Immediately upon delivery, the infant is placed on the mother's abdomen. The mother is encouraged to touch the baby while the cord is being clamped and cut. The mother's gown is removed and the nude baby is placed between the mother's breasts. A warmed pad is placed over both. It is routine practice to keep the infant skin to skin with the mother for an extended period after the delivery. For those mothers wishing to breastfeed, the initial feeding occurs shortly after birth.

After the birth, the woman spends twenty-four hours at the center and then returns home. At *Su Clinica,* she is visited by a nurse-midwife on the third and tenth days after delivery.

Although evaluative data are limited, there are several indicators which suggest the maternity program at *Su Clinica Familiar* is effective in improving the health of the infants born there. The first is the prematurity rate. As stated earlier, these women are at greater risk than middle-class women for delivering low birth weight babies. In 1974 the prematurity rate (babies weighing less than 5½ pounds) was 3.5 percent at *Su Clinica,* compared to 7.4 percent for the nation as a whole, 7.6 percent for Texas. Second, evidence is provided by the favorable birth weight distribution for the 760 babies born at the center between 1972 and 1976. Also, Apgar scores for these babies suggest excellent fetal outcome.[30]

Although these descriptive data are impressive, they still leave a number of questions unanswered. The 760 consecutive births on which the evaluation was based represent a selected sample of women who gave birth in the center during the first four years of the program's operation. Not all applicants, however, were accepted to the program and also information is lacking on patients transferred to hospitals because of complications during labor and delivery. Studies in other birth centers have shown that a proportion of cases are found ineligible for service initially, and a significant number are transferred later. For example, at the Childbearing Center of the Maternity Center Association in New York City (which serves a middle-class population and as a prototype has the most restrictive criteria in the U.S.), almost 9 percent were considered ineligible at application, 16 percent were transferred during pregnancy, and an additional 19 percent during labor.[31]

Birth centers offer an alternative for women who want active, involved births, as free as possible from technological intervention and attended by providers who are also women. As such, they can be seen as a response to the critique of the culture of medicine. They also can be evaluated in relation to the structural critique for, as the case of *Su Clinica* shows, this center provides greater access to prenatal care and a safe birth environment for low income migrant women.

Yet there may be a paradox here. While clearly a more humane approach to childbirth for all women, the birth center approach may have particular problems for low income women. These women are more likely than middle-class women to have complicating conditions of pregnancy such as hypertension and diabetes, suggesting greater need for physician input. Birth centers usually refer these patients who need more intensive care. In addition, research suggests that low income women are less overtly critical of technology-intensive, hospital-based childbirth practice. Margaret Nelson found strong class differences in women's attitudes and expectations about the birth experience. Working-class women wanted their births to be fast and easy, whereas middle-class women wanted a pleasurable, natural experience.[32] Further, working-class women do not expect their mates to be involved in the pregnancy and birth, whereas the norms among middle-class couples are for a high degree of involvement by men.

These findings suggest that the expectations and realities of poor women's lives may not be entirely congruent with the birth center approach to childbirth. Of course, poor women might prefer alternative approaches to managing birth once they had experience with them.

In this regard, it is interesting to note that *Su Clinica* has made greater use of forceps and antepartum oxytocin than centers serving more middle-class populations.[33] While strict comparisons are impossible, *Su Clinica* also appears to use medication with greater frequency than the national average in birth centers, although still less than the hospital average. It is not clear whether this is due to a higher rate of complications at *Su Clinica* (as the women are in poorer health) or to the interventions of physicians in the early years of the Center (rather than transferring complicated cases to the hospital physicians came to *Su Clinica* to deal with problems). It is also possible that the women themselves have a difficult orientation to childbirth and the nurse-midwives are responding to that orientation by greater use of medication.

Besides the social class issue, there are a series of other issues confronting birth centers. There has been considerable political controversy, particularly among professional organizations representing different medical interests. On the one hand, the American Public Health Association has endorsed the birth center concept, stating that birth to healthy mothers can occur safely in birth centers outside of acute care hospitals and that these centers have a potential for reducing health costs. This organization developed guidelines for licensing and regulating birth centers.[34] On the other hand, the American College of Obstetrics and Gynecology (A.C.O.G.) remains opposed to birth outside of hospitals. In a position paper, this group stated that "the potential hazards to both mother and fetus . . . required standards of safety which are provided in the hospital setting."[35]

Another wing of the attack by organized medicine has been against the professional autonomy of certified nurse-midwives—a central feature of the birth center. The A.C.O.G. insists on physician direction of the health care team. At Congressional hearings the organization submitted written testimony which stated that it was:

unalterably opposed to independent practice (i.e. practice without physician direction) by nurse midwives. . . . The health care team must be responsible for maternal health services, and that team must function *with the direction of a physician*. . . . The A.C.O.G. approves of reimbursement to the health care team for midwifery services *if those services are rendered by a member of a health care team directed by a qualified obstetrician-gynecologist* (emphasis in original).[36]

These Congressional hearings documented that in many parts of the country nurse-midwives are facing stiff resistance from physicians, medical societies, hospital departments of obstetrics and pediatrics, companies which provide malpractice insurance, state boards of health, and not infrequently, resistance by nurses as well. Forms of harassment have included placement of unjustifiable restrictions on practice, difficulty in obtaining a Medicaid provider number, and reimbursement and licensure refusal.[37] A widespread form of harassment by obstetricians has been the refusal to provide the usual medical consultation and referral services available to other health care providers in any given community, such as family practitioners. After hearing extensive testimony on these issues, the committee concluded that certified nurse-midwives are facing restraint of trade and unfair intimidation, which is preventing them from responding to consumer demand for their services.[38]

It is significant that physicians are less concerned about the practice of nurse-midwifery in medically underserved areas, such as the Frontier Nursing Services in Kentucky. Opposition may be related to the middle-class composition of women who are now opting for nurse-midwifery services. Opposition may also be related to the tightening market conditions facing obstetricians nationally. According to a government report, there is a surplus of obstetrics professionals, due to a declining birth rate and the consolidation of underutilized obstetric services. The ideal solution might be a complementary relationship between physicians and nurse-midwives, with obstetricians and neonatologists managing only the high risk cases. Yet this sort of rational allocation of obstetric resources has not occurred, perhaps because the management of only 10 percent of cases would not insure high incomes. According to one government study, obstetricians may be unwilling to relinquish the low risk mother because she represents the obstetrician's "bread and butter."[39]

Maternity center births managed by nurse-midwives in consultation with obstetrical specialists are clearly more cost effective than traditional hospital and physician centered births. This is due to lower overhead, the absence of expensive technology, and the lower salaries of the professionals providing care (nurse-midwives' incomes on average are one-fifth of the incomes of obstetrician-gynecologists).[40] In a recent survey,

the average reported charge for birth center services was $801 with a range of $200 to $1,700. The average comparable hospital care was $1,713, with a range from $550 to $3,750. Thus birth center charges are roughly 48 percent of the hospital charges.[41] Many birth centers have also become eligible for third-party reimbursement.

In light of these economic facts, it is not surprising that the birth industry is looking increasingly attractive to the corporate sector, as well as to physician investors. A recent article in the *Wall Street Journal* described plans for expansion by several proprietary chains into the delivery business.[42] In addition, physicians increasingly have been employing certified nurse-midwives in their private practices. The hope is that women may be more attracted to these practices and less to birth centers. Cumulatively, these trends suggest that physician opposition lessens only when physicians can gain control over nurse-midwives.

In spite of the promise of alternative birth centers, good evaluation research is lacking on these programs. A recent report by the Institute of Medicine of the National Academy of Sciences underscored the need for more rigorous research on all birth settings.[43] Most studies of birth centers have been observational, frequently based on samples from single centers. Only a few studies have compared centers.[44] Although results are encouraging and suggest many beneficial effects, descriptive data need to be augmented by more rigorous evidence if public policy is to be changed. For example, although it is clearly beneficial for children's health that roughly 95 percent of infants born in birth centers are being breastfed upon discharge (compared to 45 percent nationally) and that 60 percent of these births on average were unmedicated,[45] it is not clear to what extent these effects are attributable to the birth setting itself. Selection factors may be responsible, for women who are desirous of a "natural" birth experience may be more likely to select birth centers. A prospective study currently in process is examining a wide array of variables and promises to shed some light on the selection issue. Preliminary findings suggest no difference in pregnancy outcome between births in a birth center and a carefully matched group of women delivering in a hospital.[46]

Pediatric Home Care

Another alternative to traditional medical practice for low income patients is home care for chronically ill children. The program that I will describe serves a predominantly poor and largely black and Hispanic population in New York City. It represents a structural innovation, for it provides access to care for a population of children who have many unmet health care needs.[47] The program also alters the culture of medicine in certain key respects.

During the recent decades, home care programs have developed for the elderly and for home bound adults, but rarely for other groups. In particular, it is assumed that children are portable and therefore can be brought to the doctor for care. Especially if they have major illnesses, it is thought that care should be provided in the hospital or its clinics, where special facilities and technologies are available. There is some research evidence that home care can be as effective as traditional hospital care for children with specific medical problems, but until recently there was little evidence that home care was a viable model for children with a variety of illness conditions.

A movement to establish a home care program for children began among physicians in a hospital in the Bronx in the early 1970s.[48] The impetus for the program was the presence of a number of seriously ill children who spent extended periods of time living in the wards of a large municipal hospital. Many factors had led to the hospital's becoming a "home" for these children. They had serious on-going medical problems, resulting in frequent life-threatening situations and crises. They were on many medications and received complex treatments in an effort to control their symptoms. These realities may have frightened their families and, as a result, some appeared to have virtually turned over the ill child to the hospital. At the same time, there was a lack of alternative facilities for these children, as well as a lack of community supports to assist their families—many of whom were poor. Finally, the bureaucratic institution created its own form of dependency in both the parents and children. Children were less active because the hospital treated them as if they were sick. Families

relinquished control because hospital routines allowed for only limited parental participation.

The movement to establish the program also received impetus from the particular intellectual and political climate of the late 1960s. Programs to provide primary care for poor children in the community had been established with seed money from the Office of Economic Opportunity and the Child and Youth Programs. The success of these programs influenced the perceptions of some of the physicians about what might be possible with more seriously ill children. Other physicians—particularly the subspecialists—continued to believe that hospital care was preferable medically for these children. It was only with a promise of a rigorous evaluation that the program gained administrative approval.

In this context, Pediatric Home Care was established at Bronx Municipal Hospital Center, a 950 bed general hospital which is a major clinical affiliate of the Albert Einstein College of Medicine.[49] The program is physically located in an out-patient wing of the hospital. Services are provided to patients throughout the Bronx by a team composed of a pediatrician, a pediatric nurse practitioner, a social worker, a case aide, a technician, a part-time physical therapist, and a consulting psychiatrist. Other specialists from the Department of Pediatrics are available for specific cases.

Care is provided in the home whenever possible. The pediatric nurse practitioner makes frequent home visits, handling much of the routine care in this setting. Because the patient's family is considered a critical part of the health care team, family members are encouraged in these home visits to ask questions and to become involved in understanding the child's illness. Also, family members are taught how to perform essential medical procedures to keep the child out of crisis. For example, parents of children with tracheostomies are trained to do suctioning and provided with the necessary equipment. In order to encourage this self care, the family's problem solving methods and coping patterns are reinforced and supported. By integrating medical and social services in this way, the staff expects that families can assume greater care for their children and children can remain in their homes. If hospitalization is needed, the pediatric home care staff admits the child and continues its involvement throughout the hospitalization, thus ensuring continuity of care.

In 1978, the program was evaluated, using a pre-test–post-test experimental design.[50] A sample of 219 children with a variety of chronic physical conditions was randomly assigned either to the pediatric home care program or to the sources of care traditionally available in the hospital complex (standard care). The children had a wide variety of chronic conditions, with most having multiple conditions.[51] Regarding their social characteristics, the children were predominantly poor and largely black or Hispanic. Thirty-three percent of the families had annual income of less than $5,000, and 55 percent were receiving public assistance. Fifty-six percent of the mothers had less than a high school education. The study compared home care with standard care on a broad spectrum of outcome indicators which might be sensitive to the kinds of interventions described earlier. In particular, the evaluation assessed whether the program affected both the child's and the mother's psychological adjustment, as well as whether there were differences in levels of satisfaction between the programs. Data on these indicators were obtained by bilingual interviewers in structured household interviews with mothers in both groups at three points in time. A statistical analysis compared home care and standard care at the various follow up points.

After six months in the home care program, children had significantly fewer psychological problems. Their mothers also tended to fare better emotionally. In fact, women whose children did not receive the home care program became more symptomatic over the first six month period. Not surprisingly, mothers who received home care were significantly more satisfied with their children's medical care. There were no significant differences between home care and standard care on the impact of the illness on the family or the functional status of the child.

These findings suggest some of the beneficial effects that can occur when the structure of care is altered. More specifically, the results show that many of the secondary sequelae of chronic illness in children—behavioral problems, for example— can be reversed by a program of medical care which integrates a psychosocial perspective. In addition, the program has positive effects on the mothers. It is well known that the presence of a severely ill child is a major stressor which creates psychological distress for parents in general and for mothers in particular. Symptomatology in mothers can be ameliorated, the results suggest, by a program of care which emphasizes home visiting and emotional support.

In contrast to the concerns of some of the hospital physicians, the home care program did not lead to a deterioration in the child's health, as measured by functional status. Nor did it lead to a greater burden for the family. In fact, the impact of the child's illness on the family was considerable for both groups but declined in a similar fashion over time.

Unfortunately, data are not available on some other indicators which should be assessed—such as the health status of the child, number of days of hospitalization, frequency of immunizations and other preventive care, as well as cost of service. Admittedly, some of these factors are very difficult to measure, especially with a diagnostically mixed group of children of varying ages. Yet, it is important to state that while satisfaction with care is important and the reduction of secondary sequelae in both mother and child is impressive, these may not be sufficient indicators of a successful health strategy, even for a population as severely ill as this. Nor do the data tell us what particular ingredients in the program of home care were associated with the beneficial effects. Was it the home visiting and support provided by pediatric nurse practitioners? Was it the environmental interventions made by social service staff? Was it the continuity of care assured by a stable group of permanent staff, in contrast to the staff of trainees rotating through various clinics in the standard care model? Future research is needed to answer these questions.

Conclusion

This paper described two medical care programs which can improve the health experiences of low income people by making structural changes in the medical care system, as opposed to changing individual behavior of patients. Birth centers represent an alternative approach for women. Pediatric home care represents an alternative approach for children which, in turn, also benefits women.

The two programs represent strategies for correcting the structural barriers to care for low income people. Both programs are alternatives to traditional hospital or clinic-based care. The birth center I described made care available to a population that previously lacked maternity services. Although systematic data are lacking on various indicators of access, on the face of it the evidence points to an increase in availability of community based services for pregnant women. The pediatric home care program I described also removed structural barriers to care in a most graphic way—by home visits. Using rigorous research methods the program demonstrated its effectiveness.

In addition to structural change, each program can be evaluated in light of a broader critique of medicine. The two programs altered the traditional "culture of medicine" in certain key ways. First, professional roles were modified. In particular, nurses expanded their functions in both programs. Moreover, in the case of certified nurse-midwives, they altered the care giving role, rather than merely assuming the physician's role in birth. These changes in professional roles were not without conflict, as the birth center example particularly shows. Second, the patient-provider relationship was modified. There was greater emphasis on mutual participation and self care in both programs rather than the more usual model of active physician and passive patient.[52] Third, medical knowledge was shared and thus, perhaps, demystified. Information about the birth process and about specific childhood illnesses was communicated and, it appears, in ways that enhanced patients' sense of control over these experiences. Finally, patients in both programs were treated within a kinship context. Both programs encouraged social network members to assist in care, rather than stripping the patient from potentially supportive relationships. In sum, there were improvements in the *terms of care*, as well as in the *availability of care*.

At the same time, however, neither program addresses certain other aspects of the critique of medicine. Neither birth centers nor home care fundamentally challenge the biomedical model. Rather, the human experiences of birth and childhood illness are still seen as medical events— albeit family centered medical events. Care is still entrusted primarily to health professionals— albeit nurses with extended training. There is little overt criticism of medicine's notions of risk, and thus physican control over care in "high risk" situations is often unquestioned. In other words, disease is still understood as residing with the individual body, with treatment entrusted to a hierarchically ordered system of medical practitioners. A broader vision would place illness in a broader ecological context and see its occurrence and treatment as inextricably linked to broader social arrangements.

As a consequence of the more limited vision of the two programs, it is unlikely that either program by itself would improve the unfavorable health status of low income populations. In spite of model services, the poor are likely to continue to have more disease, disability, and distress than their middle class counterparts. Neither of the medical care programs I described fundamentally addressed the social determinants of disease. Both programs were, in McKinlay's words, "downstream efforts."[53] Neither altered the pathogenic conditions of life which poor people face in this capitalist society: inadequate food and housing, exploitation and occupational hazards at the workplace, and the other constraints imposed by the absence of power. Yet the programs do demonstrate the limited benefits that can be achieved when we simultaneously alter both structures of care and aspects of the culture of medicine.

This analysis suggests a number of broader implications for progressive health policy. First, we now have ample evidence that by removing structural barriers to care and increasing access, we can eradicate class differences in the use of both preventive and curative services. Research findings overwhelmingly support the significance of structural change, as opposed to changing individual attitudes and behaviors—the strategy suggested by the culture of poverty position. At the same time, the argument suggests that increasing access by itself is not enough. In addition, it is necessary to alter the nature of the service itself— or the culture of medicine. More specifically, we need to change how medical care is experienced by low income patients. Both programs I described represent beginning steps in this direction. Finally, if the ultimate goal is to improve health itself, the provision of medical care alone is insufficient, no matter how accessible and humanely offered it may be. Simply put, poor health is the outcome of the circumstances of poor people's lives. Thus if we are to improve health, and not merely access, potent social medicines will be necessary.

NOTE

*The concept of risk appears to be somewhat elastic and therefore subject to considerable ideological use. First, although it has been estimated that roughly 90 percent of births are uncomplicated, estimates appear to be expanding in the medical literature. Now included are social criteria, such as age, marital status, and poverty, as well as more traditional medical criteria, such as diabetes, previous birth history, etc. This may provide further evidence of medicalization. Second, prediction of complications appears to be limited. In the Institute of Medicine review, approximately 20 percent of women evaluated as low risk experienced complications necessitating transfer during labor or delivery. Alternatively, approximately 14 percent of women assessed ineligible for delivery in a low risk setting experienced no complications. Thus "risk" appears to be, in some respects, a retrospective diagnosis; all women are assumed to be "at risk" for complications, thereby legitimating routine hospitalization. Thirdly, in medical discourse, the notion of risk is always considered in the context of alternative birth practices, and never with respect to hospital based birth, the interventions of physicians, or medical technology. These aspects are assumed to be benign, or risk free.

REFERENCES

1. National Center for Health Statistics, *Health, United States, 1982.* DHHS Pub. No. (PHS) 83-1232. Public Health Service. Washington: U.S. Government Printing Office, 1982, Table 90.
2. J. Kleinman, M. Gold, and D. Makuc, "Use of Ambulatory Care by the Poor: Another Look at Equity." *Medical Care* 19 (1981): 1011–1029; M. P. LaPlante, "Have the Disadvantaged Really Achieved Equal Access to Medical Care? A Reconsideration." Paper read at Annual Meeting, American Public Health Association, Montreal, 1982.
3. D.B. Dutton, "Children's Health Care: The Myth of Equal Access," in *Better Health for Our Children: A National Strategy,* Volume 4. DHHS (PHS) Pub. No 79-55071. Public Health Service. Washington: U.S. Government Printing Office, 1981. National Center for Health Statistics, *Health, United States 1982,* Table 25.
4. O. Lewis, "The Culture of Poverty," *Scientific American* 215, 4 (1966): 19–25.
5. Classic works in sociology which employ this perspective include E. Suchman, "Social Patterns of Illness and Medical Care," in *Patients, Physicians and Illness,* E.G. Jaco (ed.) (New York: Free Press, 1972), pp. 262–279; S.S. Kegeles et al., "Surveys of Beliefs about Cancer Detection and Taking Papanicolauo Tests, *Public Health Reports* 80 (September 1965): 815–824; E.L. Koos, *The Health of Regionville* (New York: Columbia University Press, 1954).
6. D. Rosenblatt and E. Suchman, "Blue Collar Attitudes and Information Toward Health and Illness, in *Blue Collar World,* Shostak and Gomberg (eds.) (Englewood Cliffs, N.J: Prentice Hall, 1964), pp. 341–349.
7. I.M. Rosenstock, "Prevention of Illness and Maintenance of Health" in *Poverty in Health: A Sociological Analysis,* Kosa, Antonovsky, and Zola (eds.) (Cambridge, Ma.: Harvard Univ. Press, 1975), p. 188.
8. E.B. Leacock (ed.), *The Culture of Poverty: A Critique* (New York: Simon and Schuster, 1971); W. Ryan, *Blaming the Victim* (New York: Pantheon, 1971); C.A. Valentine, *Culture and Poverty: Critique and Counterproposals* (Chicago: Univ. of Chicago Press, 1968); B. Valentine, *Hustling and Other Hard Work* (New York: Free Press, 1978).
9. M.H. Becker, C.A. Nathanson, R.H. Drachman, and J.P. Kirscht, "Mothers' Health Beliefs and Children's Clinic Visits: A Prospective Study," *Journal of Community Health* 3 (1977): 125–35; L.A. Crandall and R. P. Duncan, "Attitudinal and Situational Factors in the Use of Physicians Services by Low Income Persons," *Journal of Health and Social Behavior* 22 (1981): 64–77; M. Seeman and T.E. Seeman, "Health Behavior and Personal Autonomy: A Longitudinal Study of the Sense of Control in Illness," *Journal of Health and Social Behavior* 24 (1983): 144–160.
10. Classic works which employ this perspective include R.S. Duff and A.B. Hollingshead, *Sickness and Society* (New York: Harper and Row, 1968); A. Strauss, "Medical Ghettos" in *Patients, Physicians and Illness,* pp. 381–388.
11. E. Blake, "Medicaid: The Fading of a Dream."

Health PAC Bulletin 51 (1973): 13–19; K. Davis, "Equal Treatment and Unequal Benefits: The Medicare Program" in *Health, Illness and Medical Care*, G.L. Albrecht and P.C. Higgins (eds.) (Chicago: Rand McNally, 1979), pp. 384–415.

12. National Center for Health Statistics. *Health, United States 1982*, Table 35.

13. S. Levine, N. Scotch, and G. Vlasak, "Unraveling Technology—Culture and Public Health," *American Journal of Public Health* 59 (1969): 237–244.

14. A. Strauss, "Medical Ghettos," p. 152.

15. C.K. Riessman, "The Use of Health Services by the Poor," *Social Policy* 5 (1974): 41–49.

16. D. Mechanic, "Correlates of Physician Utilization: Why Do Major Multivariate Studies of Physician Utilization Find Trivial Psychosocial and Organizational Effects?" *Journal of Health and Social Behavior* 20 (1979): 387–396.

17. D.B. Dutton, "Explaining the Low Use of Health Services by the Poor: Costs, Attitudes, or Delivery Systems," *American Sociological Review* 43 (1978): 348–368; D.B. Dutton, "Patterns of Ambulatory Health Care in Five Different Delivery Systems," *Medical Care* 17 (1979): 221–243.

18. T.G. Rundall and J.R.C. Wheeler, "The Effect of Income on Use of Preventive Care: An Evaluation of Alternative Explanations," *Journal of Health and Social Behavior* 20 (1979): 397–406.

19. K. Sharp, C.E. Ross, and W.C. Cockerham, "Symptoms, Beliefs and the Use of Physicians Services Among the Disadvantaged." *Journal of Health and Social Behavior* 24 (1983): 255–263.

20. D.B. Dutton, "Explaining the Use of Health Services by the Poor . . ."; T.G. Rundall and J.R.C. Wheeler, "The Effect of Income on Use of Preventive Care. . . ."

21. D.B. Dutton, "Explaining the Use of Health Services by the Poor . . . ," p. 363.

22. See S. Bell, "Political Gynecology," *Science for the People* 11 (Sept./Oct. 1979): 8–29; Boston Women's Health Book Collective, *Our Bodies, Our Selves*, 2nd ed. rev. (New York: Simon and Schuster, 1979); S.B. Ruzek, *The Women's Health Movement* (New York: Praeger, 1979).

23. Current recording methods classify births that take place in free standing birth centers as hospital births. The precise type of provider is also not reliably entered on birth certificates.

24. A.B. Bennetts and E.K.M. Ernest, "Free Standing Birth Centers," in *Research Issues in the Assessment of Birth Settings*. Institute of Medicine Pub. No. IOM-82-04. Washington, D.C.: National Academy Press, 1982.

25. D. Haire, *The Cultural Warping of Childbirth*.

(Hillside, N.J.: International Childbirth Education Association, 1972).

26. S. Arms, *Immaculate Deception* (New York: Bantam, 1975); C.K. Riessman "Women and Medicalization: A New Perspective." *Social Policy* 14 (Summer, 1983): 3–18; N.S. Shaw, *Forced Labor* (New York, Pergamon, 1974).

27. B.K. Rothman, *In Labor* (New York: Norton, 1982); R.G. DeVries "The Alternative Birth Center: Option or Cooptation?" *Women and Health* 5 (1980): 47–60.

28. Cooperative Birth Center Network News 1 (Summer, 1983).

29. The material on *Su Clinica* is drawn from A. Murdaugh, "Experiences of a New Migrant Health Clinic," *Women and Health* 1 (1976): 25–29; Annual Report of Su Clinica, 1979; Ten Years of Health Care at Su Clinica Familiar, 1982.

30. A. Murdaugh, "Experiences of a New Migrant Health Clinic."

31. R.W. Lubic, "Evaluation of an Out of Hospital Maternity Center for Low Risk Patients," in *Health Policy and Nursing Practice*, L. Aikin (ed.) (New York: McGraw Hill, 1981), pp. 90–116.

32. M.K. Nelson, "Working Class Women, Middle Class Women, and Models Childbirth," *Social Problems* 30 (1983): 284–297; M.K. Nelson, "The Effect of Childbirth Preparation on Women of Different Social Classes," *Journal of Health and Social Behavior* 23 (1982): 339–352.

33. A.B. Bennetts and E.K.M. Ernst, "Free Standing Birth Centers."

34. American Public Health Association, Guidelines for Licensing and Regulating Birth Centers: Policy Statement 8209 (PP). *American Journal of Public Health* 73 (1983): 331–334.

35. American College of Obstetrics and Gynecology, District II, Position Paper on Out of Hospital Maternity Care, 1976.

36. Letter from E.E. Nichols, M.D., Director of Practice Activities, A.C.O.G. Subcommittee on Oversight and Investigations of the Committee on Interstate and Foreign Commerce, House of Representatives, 96th Congress, December, 1980. (Washington, D.C.: U.S. Government Printing Office, 1981), p. 176.

37. U.S. Federal Trade Commission, "Competition Among Health Practitioners—The Influence of the Medical Profession on the Health Manpower Market; Case Study: The Childbearing Center." Unpublished report, February, 1981.

38. Senator Albert Gore, Subcommittee on Oversight and Investigations . . . ,1981.

39. U.S. Federal Trade Commission, 1981.

40. Cooperative Birth Center Network News, 1983.

41. Cooperative Birth Center Network News, 1983. Caution is indicated in interpreting these cost data, as the charges for "comparable care" in a hospital are difficult to quantify and likely to be unreliable.
42. *Wall Street Journal* "Special Deliveries." November 29, 1983, p. 60.
43. *Research Issues in the Assessment of Birth Settings, 1982.*
44. A.B. Bennetts and R.W. Lubic, "The Free Standing Birth Center," *The Lancet* (1982): 378–380; Cooperative Birth Center Network News, 1983.
45. A.B. Bennetts and R.W. Lubic, "The Free Standing Birth Center."
46. G.E. Baraffi and W.S. Dellinger, "Alternative Birthing: An Evaluation of Quality of Care." Paper presented at Annual Meeting of the American Public Health Association, Los Angeles, Ca., 1981.
47. R.E.K. Stein, D.J. Jessop, C.K. Riessman, "Health Care Services Received by Children with Chronic Illness," *American Journal of Disabled Children* 137 (1983): 225–230.
48. For a full description of how the Pediatric Home Care Program came about see D.J. Jessop and R.E.K. Stein, "A Service Delivery Program and its Evaluation: A Case Study in the Sociology of Applied Research," *Evaluation and the Health Professions,* Vol. 6, No. 1 (Sage, 1983), pp. 99–114.
49. For a full description of the program see R.E.K. Stein, "Pediatric Home Care: An Ambulatory Special Care Unit," *Journal of Pediatrics* 92 (1978) 495–499.
50. For a full description of the evaluation see R.E.K. Stein and D.J. Jessop, "The Effects of Pediatric Home Care: Findings from the Pediatric Ambulatory Care Treatment Study," *Pediatrics,* forthcoming.
51. These included asthma, seizure disorders, hemoglobinopathy, congenital heart disease, malignancies, diabetes mellitus, and congenital anomalies such as meninglomyocele/hydrocephaleus and biliary atresia.
52. T. Szasz and M. Hollender, "A Contribution to the Philosophy of Medicine: The Basic Models of the Doctor-Patient Relationship," *Journal of the American Medical Association* 97 (1956): 585–88.
53. John B. McKinlay, "A Case for Refocussing Upstream: The Political Economy of Illness" in this volume, pp. 519–533.

40

Politicizing Health Care

▪ ▪ ▪ ▪ ▪ ▪

John McKnight

Is it possible that out of the contradictions of medicine one can develop the possibilities of politics? The example I want to describe is not going to create a new social order. It is, however, the beginning of an effort to free people from medical clienthood, so that they can perceive the possibility of being citizens engaged in political action.

The example involves a community of about 60,000 people on the west side of Chicago. The people are poor and Black, and the majority are dependent on welfare payments. They have a voluntary community organization which encompasses an area in which there are two hospitals.

The neighborhood was originally all white. During the 1960s it went through a racial transition and over a period of a few years, it became largely populated with Black people.

The two hospitals continued to serve the white people who had lived in the neighborhood before transition, leaving the Black people struggling to gain access to the hospitals' services.

This became a political struggle and the community organization finally "captured" the two hospitals. The boards of directors of the hospitals then accepted people from the neighborhood, employed Black people on their staffs, and treated members of the neighborhood rather than the previous white clients.

After several years, the community organization felt that it was time to stand back and look at the health status of their community. As a result of their analysis, they found that, although they had "captured" the hospitals, there was no significant evidence that the health of the people had changed since they had gained control of the medical services.

The organization then contacted the Center for Urban Affairs where I work. They asked us to assist in finding out why, if the people controlled the two hospitals, their health was not any better.

It was agreed that the Center would do a study of the hospitals' medical records to see why people were receiving medical care. We took a sample of the emergency room medical records to determine the frequency of the various problems that brought the people into the hospitals.

We found that the seven most common reasons for hospitalization, in order of frequency, were:

1. Automobile accidents.
2. Interpersonal attacks.
3. Accidents (non-auto).
4. Bronchial ailments.
5. Alcoholism.
6. Drug-related problems (medically administered and nonmedically administered).
7. Dog bites.

The people from the organization were startled by these findings. The language of medicine is focused upon disease—yet the problems we identified have very little to do with disease. The medicalization of health had led them to believe that "disease" was the problem which hospitals were addressing, but they discovered instead that the hospitals were dealing with many problems which were not disease. It was an important step in increasing consciousness to recognize that modern medical systems are usually dealing with maladies—social problems—rather than disease.

Maladies and social problems are the domain of citizens and their community organizations.

A Strategy for Health

Having seen the list of maladies, the people from the organization considered what they ought to do, or could do, about them. First of all, as good political strategists, they decided to tackle a problem which they felt they could win. They didn't want to start out and immediately lose. So they went down the list and picked dog bites, which caused about four percent of the emergency room visits at an average hospital cost of $185.

How could this problem best be approached? It interested me to see the people in the organization thinking about that problem. The city government has employees who are paid to be "dog-catchers," but the organization did not choose to contact the city. Instead, they said: "Let us see what we can do ourselves." They decided to take a small part of their money and use it for "dog bounties." Through their block clubs they let it be known that for a period of one month, in an area of about a square mile, they would pay a bounty of five dollars for every stray dog that was brought in to the organization or had its location identified so that they could go and capture it.

There were packs of wild dogs in the neighborhood that had frightened many people. The children of the neighborhood, on the other hand, thought that catching dogs was a wonderful idea—so they helped to identify them. In one month, 160 of these dogs were captured and cases of dog bites brought to the hospitals decreased.

Two things happened as a result of this success. The people began to learn that their action, rather than the hospital, determines their health. They were also building their organization by involving the children as community activists.

The second course of action was to deal with something more difficult—automobile accidents. "How can we do anything if we don't understand where these accidents are taking place?" the people said. They asked us to try to get information which would help to deal with the accident problem, but we found it extremely difficult to find information regarding when, where, and how an accident took place.

We considered going back to the hospitals and looking at the medical records to determine the nature of the accident that brought each injured person to the hospital. If medicine was thought of as a system that was related to the possibilities of community action, it should have been possible. It was not. The medical record did not say, "This person has a malady because she was hit by an automobile at six o'clock in the evening on January 3rd at the corner of Madison and Kedzie." Sometimes the record did not even say that the cause was an automobile accident. Instead, the record simply tells you that the person has a "broken tibia." It is a record system that obscures the community nature of the problem, by focusing on the therapeutic to the exclusion of the primary cause.

We began, therefore, a search of the data systems of macroplanners. Finally we found one macroplanning group that had data regarding the nature of auto accidents in the city. It was data on a complex, computerized system, to be used in macroplanning to facilitate automobile traffic! We persuaded the planners to do a printout that could be used by the neighborhood people for their own action purposes. This had never occurred to them as a use for their information.

The printouts were so complex, however, that the organization could not comprehend them. So we took the numbers and transposed them onto a neighborhood map showing where the accidents took place. Where people were injured, we put a blue X. Where people were killed, we put a red X.

We did this for all accidents for a period of three months. There are 60,000 residents living in the neighborhood. In that area, in three months, there were more than 1,000 accidents. From the map the people could see, for example, that within three months six people had been injured, and one person killed, in an area 60 feet wide. They immediately identified this place as the entrance to a parking lot for a department store. They were then ready to act, rather than be treated, by dealing with the store owner because information had been "liberated" from its medical and macroplanning captivity.

The experience with the map had two consequences. One, it was an opportunity to invent several different ways to deal with a health problem that the community could understand. The community organization could negotiate with the department store owner and force a change in its entrance.

Two, it became very clear that there were accident problems that the community organization could not handle directly. For example, one of the main reasons for many of the accidents was the fact that higher authorities had decided to make several of the streets through the neighborhood major throughways for automobiles going from the heart of the city out to the affluent suburbs. Those who made this trip were a primary cause of injury to the local people. Dealing with this problem is not within the control of people at the neighborhood level—but they understood the necessity of getting other community organizations involved in a similar process, so that together they could assemble enough power to force the authorities to change the policies that serve the interests of those who use the neighborhoods as their freeway.

The third community action activity developed when the people focused on "bronchial problems." They learned that good nutrition was a factor in these problems, and concluded that they did not have enough fresh fruit and vegetables for good nutrition. In the city, particularly in the winter, these foods were too expensive. So could they grow fresh fruit and vegetables themselves? They looked around, but it seemed difficult in the heart of the city. Then several people pointed out that most of their houses were two story apartments with flat roofs. "Supposing we could build a greenhouse on the roof, couldn't we grow our own fruit and vegetables?" So they built a greenhouse on one of the roofs as an experiment. Then, a fascinating thing began to happen.

Originally, the greenhouse was built to deal with a health problem—inadequate nutrition. The greenhouse was a tool, appropriate to the environment, that people could make and use to improve health. Quickly, however, people began to see that the greenhouse was also an economic development tool. It increased their income because they now produced a commodity to use and also to sell.

Then, another use for the greenhouse appeared. In the United States, energy costs are extremely high and a great burden for poor people. One of the main places where people lose (waste) energy is from the rooftops of their houses—so the greenhouse on top of the roof converted the energy loss into an asset. The energy that did escape from the house went into the greenhouse where heat was needed. The greenhouse, therefore, was an energy conservation tool.

Another use for the greenhouse developed by chance. The community organization owned a retirement home for elderly people, and one day one of the elderly people discovered the greenhouse. She went to work there, and told the other old people and they started coming to the greenhouse every day to help care for the plants. The administrator of the old people's home noticed that the attitude of the older people changed. They were excited. They had found a function. The greenhouse became a tool to empower older people—to allow discarded people to be productive.

Multility vs. Unitility

The people began to see something about technology that they had not realized before. Here was a simple tool—a greenhouse. It could be built locally, used locally and among its "outputs" were health, economic development, energy conservation and enabling older people to be productive. A simple tool requiring a minimum "inputs" produced multiple "outputs" with few negative side effects. We called the greenhouse a "multility."

Most tools in a modernized consumer-oriented society are the reverse of the greenhouse. They are systems requiring a complex organization with multiple inputs that produce only a single output. Let me give you an example. If you get bauxite from Jamaica, copper from Chile, rubber from Indonesia, oil from Saudi Arabia, lumber from Canada, and labor from all these countries, and process these resources in an American corporation that uses American labor and professional skills to manufacture a commodity, you can produce an electric toothbrush. This tool is what we call a "unitility." It has multiple inputs

and one output. However, if a tool is basically a labor-saving device, then the electric toothbrush is an anti-tool. If you added up all the labor put into producing it, its sum is infinitely more than the labor saved by its use.

The electric toothbrush and the systems for its production are the essence of the technological mistake. The greenhouse is the essence of the technological possibility. The toothbrush (unitility) is a tool that disables capacity and maximizes exploitation. The greenhouse (multility) is a tool that minimizes exploitation and enables community action.

Similarly, the greenhouse is a health tool that creates citizen action and improves health. The hospitalized focus on health disables community capacity by concentrating on therapeutic tools and techniques requiring tremendous inputs, with limited output in terms of standard health measures.

Conclusions

Let me draw several conclusions from the health work of the community organization.

First, out of all this activity, it is most important that the health action process has strengthened a community organization. Health is a political issue. To convert a medical problem into a political issue is central to health improvement. Therefore, as our action has developed the organization's vitality and power, we have begun the critical health development. Health action must lead away from dependence on professional tools and techniques, towards community building and citizen action. Effective health action must convert a professional-technical problem into a political, communal issue.

Second, effective health action identifies what you can do at the local level with local resources. It must also identify those external authorities and structures that control the limits of the community to act in the interest of its health.

Third, health action develops tools for the people's use, under their own control. To develop these tools may require us to diminish the resources consumed by the medical system. As the community organization's health activity becomes more effective, the swollen balloon of medicine should shrink. For example, after the dogs were captured, the hospital lost clients. Nonetheless, we cannot expect that this action will stop the medical balloon from growing. The medical system will make new claims for resources and power, but our action will intensify the contradictions of medicalized definitions of health. We can now see people saying: "Look, we may have saved $185 in hospital care for many of the 160 dogs that will not now bite people. That's a lot of money! But it still stays with that hospital. We want our $185! We want to begin to trade in an economy in which you don't exchange our action for more medical service. We need income, not therapy. If we are to act in our health interest, we will need the resources

medicine claims for its therapeutic purposes in order to diminish our therapeutic need."

These three principles of community health action suggest that improved health is basically about moving away from being "medical consumers."

The experience I have described suggests that the sickness which we face is the captivity of tools, resources, power, and consciousness by medical "unitilities" that create consumers.

Health is a political question. It requires citizens and communities. The health action process can enable "another health development" by translating medically defined problems and resources into politically actionable community problems.

41

Helping Ourselves

▪ ▪ ▪ ▪ ▪

Ann Withorn

Self help has emerged as a widely acclaimed "major thrust" of the eighties. Popular magazines, *The New York Times* and the federal government have all recognized the potential of the "self help movement" to influence human service policies and programs. Hundreds of thousands of self help groups now exist across the country. Some are affiliated with nation-wide organizations while others are more isolated local efforts where people join together to help themselves cope with and cure a wide range of human problems. Ideologically they range from the conservative piety of an Alcoholics Anonymous to the radical feminism of feminist "self health" activities.[1]

Is this activity simply an extension of the self-absorption of the seventies? Is it a retreat into

individual solutions and a ploy to keep people from demanding what they need from the state? Or does it reflect a growing, healthy skepticism of professionals and the welfare state bureaucracy? Could it be a sign of a potentially important rise in commitment to popular democracy?

These questions are of some importance in the United States. The simple magnitude of current self help activity, especially among working class people, calls upon us to have, at least, an analysis of its political implications and an understanding of its appeal. Further, the experience of feminist self help suggests that there may be ways to combine selected self help activity with a broader socialist and feminist strategy. At its best, self help may even serve as one way to formulate a progressive politics which is more grounded in the daily experience of working class life and which thereby helps define socialism more broadly than the economistic formulations which so often characterize it. In addition, an understanding of the power of self help as a means for individual change may also go farther in comprehending the fundamental inadequacies of the social service provided by the modern welfare state.

What Is Self Help?

The nature of self help itself gives rise to the contradictory questions raised above. Self help is the effort of people to come together in groups in order to resolve mutual individual needs. Today this activity consists of individuals sharing concerns about personal, emotional, health or family problems. Sometimes community or ethnic groups which organize to improve their neighborhoods or social situations also call themselves self-help groups. The major reasons for defining an activity as self help are that it involves group activity and meetings of the people with the problem, not outside experts or professionals, and that the main means by which difficulties are addressed are mutual sharing, support, advice-giving and the pooling of group resources and information. Members benefit as much from the sharing of their problems and the process of helping others as they do from the advice and resources provided by others. In most cases there is a strong ethic of group solidarity, so that individual members become concerned about the progress of other group members as well as in their own "cure."

Within this broad common definition, however, there is wide variety in focus and emphasis for self help groups. At one end of the spectrum are the politically aware feminist self-help efforts, in health care, rape crisis, battered women shelters and other service areas. Here self help is self-conscious, empowering democratic effort where women help each other and often provide an analysis and an example from which to criticize and make feminist demands on the system. At the other end are groups which focus on the specific problem only, like AA, other "anonymous" groups or disease victim groups, with self help used only as a means for coping with a problem, not an alternative model for society or even

service delivery. In between are groups which have selected self help as a means to help themselves but which also come to draw from the process ways to suggest broader changes, often in the social services system and sometimes in the whole social system. While all share key aspects of self help and all may teach certain critical lessons about the importance of social networks and group solidarity, their differences are crucial and need to be understood and evaluated as a part of any critique of self help.

Historical Roots of Self Help

Some of the comforts and supports now provided by self-conscious self help groups have always been available. Prior to industrial development village and family networks were the primary means by which people helped each other survive the economic, health and other social difficulties associated with a hard life. As industrial disruption made such supports less accessible early nineteenth century workers began to band together in new forms of "mutual aid" organizations composed of individual craft workers or, in America especially, of groups of ethnically homogeneous workers. These early groups formed to provide for the basic economic and social needs not available from employers, the state, the church or geographic community. Meager resources were pooled to provide burial and family insurance, limited food, clothing and economic support in times of ill health, disability and family crisis. In Britain and the U.S., the emergence of these "burial societies," "workingmen's aid" associations, "friendly societies" and immigrant aid associations reflected constant efforts by workers to help each other and help themselves to cope with the health and social problems associated with capitalist development. The remaining records of such groups show a growing sense of collective responsibility within the groups and the gradual creation of social networks which performed wider social functions than only the insurance of economic survival.[2]

It is easy to admire these self-consious workers' efforts, like that of Workmen's Circle, to form "an organization that could come to their assistance in terms of need, and especially in case of sickness, that would provide them and their families with plots and decent burials in case of death and extend some measure of help to their surviving dependents, that would, finally, afford them congenial fellowships and thereby lessen the loneliness of their lives in a strange land."[3] It is important, however, to avoid romanticizing this early self help activity. Some groups were controlled by the more conservative and established elements in the craft or community who kept the groups from gaining a more broad "class" identification. Others served as a base from which to distrust or ignore, rather than identify with, the needs of other workers not in the same craft or ethnic group. And, at best, these early groups could only provide the most minimal assistance to their members, still leaving them with major social disadvantages. All these problems were pointed out at the time by radicals in the labor and black movements, especially. But, in times when public aid was extremely punitive and largely non-existent even such limited efforts were recognized as crucial to the survival and strength of workers and their families. But they were also, perhaps, the only means of survival. Self help was the only help available. It was not developed as a better, more humane, alternative means of support; originally it was the only means of support. This is a crucial difference between early self help and current efforts.

. . . .

Self Help as a Service Activity

There is an interesting parallel to these tensions in the professional developments of the period. Just as the more conservative trade unionists and black leadership supported self help as a means for worker and community independence, so did the more conservative doctors, lawyers and social workers who worked in the private sector. The private health and welfare establishment saw individual and group change coming out of self help activities. More liberal professionals argued that this strategy abandoned the poor and they, therefore, allied with progressive people in demanding more public programs. They argued that it was unrealistic to expect the victims of society to

help themselves and that outside intervention—from expert professionals funded by the government—was the only reasonable hope for change. These liberal social workers and medical experts gained power in federal and state programs throughout the 1930s and 40s, so that by the 1950s the public health and welfare establishment had become as critical of self help as a service strategy as leftists were of it as a political tactic.

Yet self help came into its own as a service activity during the 1930s and 40s, in spite (or perhaps because) of increasing professional hostility. As the private and public insurance and welfare establishments grew, self help changed form, moving from group provision of welfare insurance and burial services to a process of social supports for dealing with a range of personal, family and emotional problems. The process of self help became important not for itself, as a model and base for democratic self-support, but as a means to achieve personal goals for change or to come to terms with unavoidable difficulties.

The poverty of the Depression gave rise to many self help service projects. Food, clothing and housing exchanges developed, European refugees and internal immigrants organized mutual aid groups. Most important, however, was the birth of Alcoholics Anonymous (AA) in 1935; it has served as a primary model for self help service activities since its inception. It was founded by a pair of mid-western professionals who found little help in the medical, social work or psychiatric professionals and who began to develop a behavior oriented, religiously imbued, program of group support and pressure for alcoholics. The model consisted of admitting the power of one's problem and drawing help from fellow alcoholics, as well as from a "higher power," in order to learn to stop drinking. This was to be done by developing a network of fellow alcoholics, by attending frequent—even daily—meetings where discussions take place about personal experiences with alcohol and where the goal of sobriety is to be achieved "one day at a time." Drawing upon such basic, simple principles AA grew rapidly, reaching 400,000 by 1947 and currently involving more than 700,000 alcoholics a year.

It is easy for socialists and professionals to criticize Alcoholics Anonymous. Its religious pietism is fundamentalist and limiting. Despite its proclaimed organizational refusal to take federal money or political positions, its veterans have increasingly designed and defined alcholism services across the country in harmony with AA principles. These programs often exclude women and those who have not "hit bottom" with their drinking, as well as a range of people less comfortable with the somewhat simplistic "Twelve Steps." Its appeal has been largely limited to whites. Yet AA does appear to have a higher success rate than other forms of professional help with the complex problems associated with alcoholism. It does attract a largely working-class population who have little recourse to private services. It also offers alcoholics the experience of a non-drinking community where they can learn to like themselves better, admit to their problems, trust others and begin to rebuild their lives.

. . . .

Other self help services have formed using the Anonymous model, where the focus is on the problem faced and the process of mutual help and support is valued as an effective means to the end, not as a goal in itself. Gamblers Anonymous, Overeaters Anonymous, Parents Anonymous (for people who have abused their children) are only three of the dozens of groups which are modelled closely on AA and attempt to help people admit that they have a problem and get help from others in the same situation to overcome it. All groups rely on "recovering" victims to help others, a helping role which is often a major form of continuing improvement for the old time members. Although some groups make greater use of professionals than others, in all peers assume primary roles and outside social networks often grow out of such groups which provide people with a wide range of supports. While there is no hard data, such anonymous groups (most of which, except AA, have been founded since the mid-fifties) seem to attract a largely white working- and middle-class population and create strong loyalities among those helped.

Since the 1940s other services which use self as a major means of helping people cope with solve personal difficulties have emerged.

Many drug programs have used self help activities to create "alternative communities" characterized by mutual disclosure, support and pressure. Since the 1940s (and mushrooming in the 1970s) there has been a steady increase in health-oriented self help programs for the families of victims of cancer and other diseases, and for the victims themselves. Stroke victims, cancer victims, heart disease patients, parents of children with Down's Syndrome (to name only a few of thousands) have come together to discuss their feelings, reactions and symptoms and to help each other emotionally. While these programs are often supported by the medical system they frequently come to share vocal and strong criticisms of professionalism and professional care.

The social welfare and medical establishments have reacted to all this increasing self help activity with different types of responses. Sometimes groups have been criticized (often during the initial phases) for "resisting professional treatment" or for avoiding reality. The more critical the groups become of the quality of professional care (a component of almost all self help groups, no matter what their origins) the more they are resisted by doctors and social workers. However, until this happens they are often supported by professionals as another form of service, especially for people with "difficult" problems, i.e. those problems like alcoholism, drug abuse, "incurable" cancer, senility and other afflictions not amenable to conventional intervention. Indeed, the federal government has become enamoured with self help approaches, providing funds for certain efforts and even identifying the existence of a "continuum of care" including self help at one end and full institutional care at the other, all of which will require some form of public support and monitoring.

As with AA, it is easy to criticize. Most of these self help service efforts can be legitimately viewed as methods by which the established medical, mental health and social work professions get people to provide services to themselves which the professionals won't or can't provide. Cheap care and an avoidance of public responsibility may be obvious. Yet progressives working in these fields also have supported self help services, in recognition of the limits of professional care and in order to support the creation of a stronger, less fearful consumer consciousness, among clients or victims of problems as varied as alcoholism, drug abuse, cancer and chronic disease. In addition, many members of such self help service groups find them much more helpful and acceptable forms of care than other, more professional, services. Such groups may provide release and support which come from sharing and comraderie. These results cannot be disregarded, especially for people who felt desperately alone before the experience. A working class veteran of AA, Overeaters Anonomyous and Smoke Enders reflected similarly on what self help meant to her:

> Self help groups really help. They make you feel like you are not alone with yourself or your problem. You share with others and find out you are not the only one who smokes in the shower or bakes two pies for your family and eats one before anyone comes home. I'm not sure how it works, but somehow you feel like trying again.
>
> My sister had, in fact, a daughter that died. She had always laughed at me for my "groups," but after that happened she joined one herself. She just couldn't handle it alone, feeling so guilty and not knowing anyone with the same problem. That's what self help means to me.

Particularly important to many people in self help groups is the opportunity to help others with similar problems. The experience of doing this can be powerful and strengthening, especially for people who have only felt like victims before.

In short, as a form of social service, self help groups have proven themselves to be helpful and empowering to many, despite their potential use as a vehicle for providing cheaper services to unwanted clients. As one aspect of the general social services system, self help services seem a secure and welcome addition. The question remains, however, whether this increased self help activity has any underlying impact for progressive change. For such discussions we must look to recent efforts of the women's movement.

The Importance of Feminist Self Help

If it weren't for the development of feminist self help, especially in health, we might be less interested in the whole question of whether self

help can be a serious part of a socialist strategy. Self help would be seen as merely a social service with little broader political impact. But the impressive efforts of women around the country to take self help seriously as a healthy form of relationship between women and to wed this with feminist analysis may suggest a more general model for reuniting self help with political practice.

Self help has been a central part of most feminist service work, which has, in turn, been a major area of the feminist movement. Since the late sixties, when women's liberation groups developed "consciousness-raising," the model of women sharing and helping other women has been a basic feminist strategy. Feminist historians looked back and found self help equivalents throughout the history of women—who have formed strong self helping women's networks within the family, neighborhoods and community as a means for basic survival and emotional support.

Out of this history, and an emerging understanding that "the personal is political," feminists were able to take the process of self help more seriously, to value the experience of working and sharing together in itself, as well as to appreciate the quality of the product of such work. Women were compelled, then, to be more self-conscious in their self help approaches and to proclaim them as central to feminist goals. In "Jane," an early underground Chicago-based abortion clinic, for example, women developed models of abortion care which included sharing all processes and procedures, discussion of feelings and the trading of mutual experiences among the women abortion-workers and the women seeking abortions. Their approach became standard in many feminist services. *Our Bodies, Our Selves,* the classic women's self health care book offered professional information mixed with personal experiences and has been used as a basis for women's health groups across the country. It too has helped to establish the notion of self help—mutual sharing of feelings, information and skills—as a basic tenet of feminist activity.[4]

As feminist services became a major approach of the women's movement—including everything from women's multi-purpose centers, to day care, health and nutrition services, rape and battered women's programs—self help came along as standard feminist practice. The meaning varied, however. In some places it simply meant collective decision-making by staff and a sharing of feelings and information with women who came for service. It was seen as a natural outgrowth of ideas of sisterhood and feminist theory. In the feminist health clinics, however, feminist self help has been most fully defined, has become in Elizabeth Somer's words "both a philosophy and a practice through which we become active creators of our destinies."[5]

Feminist clinics insisted on education and group involvement of all who came to the clinics. This was viewed as an important antidote to the standard medical model of doctor as god and patient as grateful recipient of his care. Health care workers forged different relationships with women who came for care and also began to explore and share a growing criticism of the medical "knowledge" about women's bodies. The most self-conscious programs, the Femininst Women's Health Centers, led in developing clear guidelines for self help in health care which included pelvic self examinations, group examinations and discussions. They shared an explicit philosophy that self help is more than, and different from, the traditional "delivery" of service:

> Self help is not being simply service oriented . . . we do not want to be middle women between the MD's and the patients. We want to show women how to do it themselves. . . . We do not examine women. We show women how to examine themselves. . . . We neither sell nor give away self help . . . we share it. (Detroit Women's Clinic, 1974)

Feminist self help in health care and other service areas developed in conjunction with the broader feminist movement. Knowledge of the inadequacies and brutality of male dominated medicine came along with a heightened awareness of the prevalence of rape and women-battering. The system-supporting aspects of all medical and welfare care forced women into developing new models and into looking to each other for information and support. The early successes of many groups in raising the conscious-

ness of women who came for "service" was heartening and sustaining. Sustained practice meant that feminists have been able to put the principles of self help to the test, to explore the need for structure and specialization within a self help framework, to discover the complexities of many health and emotional problems and to determine when professional help may, indeed, be necessary.

All this learning and growth has not been without costs, however. Health centers, particularly, have suffered intense bureaucratic harassment from the medical profession which has been anxious to protect its right to control who practices medicine. Most self help programs have suffered from funding problems of a similar sort. The medical and social welfare establishments demand "legitimacy" before they provide money—through third party payments (Medicaid, private insurance) or direct service contracts. They require, at the very least, a professional "cover" for most alternative services and often refuse funding until bureaucratic, hierarchical structures are actually in place. Some battered women's shelters originally received money, in light of favorable publicity, with minimal hassles, but as time passed welfare agencies pressed to fund a "range" of services (i.e., non-feminist programs), with more familiar, professional approaches. In addition, inflation and cut backs have also limited the amount of money available.

The problems have not been all external either. The time and emotional demands of most self help services have made it hard for most groups to sustain staff, much less to do the continual political education neccessary to make the self help offered truly feminist in content. Women with professional aspirations and a lack of feminist values have been drawn to self help efforts. Their pressure can push already overextended feminists to leave rather than fight creeping bureaucracy, "efficiency" and professionalization in their midst. When this happens the mutual aid, democratic and sharing aspects of the service fade as surely as they do when public bureaucracies directly take over.

When such problems are coupled with current general decline in a broad-based feminist movement, they become even more difficult to endure and struggle with. Even in well-functioning self help projects women feel more isolated and less sure of what it all means, as expressed by a women's health worker in 1979:

> After we finally got our license then we had all this paperwork to do all the time. The women's community seemed less interested because we weren't in crisis anymore. The women who wanted to work in the center are more interested in health care than feminism. It just seems to take more effort to be feminist these days, to raise political issues in the groups or work meetings. We're still trying and do OK but I guess it's a lot harder than it used to be.

Feminist services, then, have not totally solved old problems with self help. They have shown that it is possible for participation in self help to be an effective means for political growth and development. Especially the health services have shown us that self help may often be an intrinsically better model of care and may, thereby, offer an immediate and personal way for people to understand what is wrong with public and private health and welfare services. All have shown the natural links between a democratic feminist movement and the process of self help. Women who have participated in such programs talk about themselves as "permanently changed. I don't think I can ever accept without criticism the old authoritarian models again." But over time the pressures to provide services on a large scale, with adequate funding, work against the ability to work in a self help manner. Is it reasonable to assume that we could really provide feminist self help services to all the battered women who need them, for example? And if it is not, we are always stuck with the limits of even the most effective self help efforts—that the harder we work and the better we function, the greater the demand and the more impossible it is to meet.

Problems and Potential of Self Help

Given all this, how should progressive people respond to the likelihood that self help services are likely to continue to grow and re-form in the future? The current momentum and recognition of existing programs seems unstoppable and will probably be even more appealing to administrators wishing to support an image of continued service provision in times of real cut backs. An increasingly popular answer to anyone with a problem will predictably be: "Join, or form, a self help group."

. . . .

As advanced capitalism lurches along, services and the service economy will become more important. Self help services may play an increasingly important role in this. On the hopeful side, self help activity has the potential to become a base from which people can criticize, demand and affect the nature of the service system in a positive way and out of which progressive workers and clients can form meaningful alliances. On the negative side, self help services may help to provide an opportunity for another professional cover-up. See, we have a humane system. We even let people take care of each other, after they are near death or incapacitated by emotional and personal problems.

The problem, assuming these options, becomes one of how to assist self help efforts in achieving their potential as a base for criticism and change rather than providing tacit reaffirmation of professional hegemony and the capitalist welfare state.

In promoting the potential of self help we cannot, however, ignore certain limits which may be built into the activity. First, we cannot deny that the nature of self help, and the enormity of the difficulties which bring people to it, often emphasize only the personal dimensions of people's problems. Even if the social components of problems are admitted, as they are in feminist and some other self help efforts, the stress remains on how the victim can change, rather than on the implications for broader social action. There can even be a new form of victim blaming which takes place in self help: "We are so fucked up only we can help each other." Admittedly this is an aspect of all psychological services, but the self help model, with emphasis on social support and reciprocity, may serve to mask the individualistic approach more. It also may make it harder for people to move on to other activities because the self help group may form the only support system people know (AA has a strong history of this: people become professional alcoholics, still centered in the group and their problem, long after drinking has ceased to define their lives). For self help activity to lead to broader criticism of the social service system or the whole of society, these tendencies must be recognized and alternatives made available, at least to those who can make use of them.

Second, even with self help set in a broader context, the questions of scope and relationship to the state will still affect us. Self help activity is probably only a limited service tactic which, while it can form a base for criticizing and pressuring the larger system, can never fully replace the professional, bureaucratized services, at least under capitalism. This is a more difficult proposition to accept in practice than it sounds in theory. We get sucked in, we want to "save the world" and it is difficult to remember the political analysis which tells us that the problems we face are generated by social forces beyond our immediate control. It is hard, as those involved in self help often admit, to have to push the state to provide services which we know will be inferior to what we can do through self help (but on a limited scale). All this leads to burnout and frustration, especially when broader movements are not active enough to help us keep our activity in perspective.

Finally, there are some philosophical problems associated with self help, which are similar to those surrounding many populist efforts. Many self help groups, especially including feminist activities, become so skeptical of organization and expertise that they become almost mystical and anti-intellectual. While the social origins of current organizations and expertise may lead to this, as an overall approach it becomes self-defeating. In the process of self help, some people become "experts" in the problem: must they then leave the group? Or groups tend to "reinvent the wheel," perpetually relearning everything about problems from a feminist, working class, consumer or black perspective. While Barbara Ehrenreich's and Deidre English's suggestion that we "take what we want of the technology without buying the ideology" sounds good, the full criticism of all professionalism which is inherent in healthy self help may make this difficult.[6]

Furthermore, we still have to fight rampant specialization in self help groups. Granted, DES daughters have different needs from mastectomy patients and from ex-mental patients, but to be effective, self help concerns will need to be linked together in broader analysis of processes and problems. All this must be accomplished while recognizing that people in immediate pain may resent any deviation from their immediate problems.

These are serious drawbacks, not to be ignored. Yet current circumstances suggest that progressive people should, still, become involved in many facets of self help. We have the accumulated experience of feminist self help to guide us away from some of the worst pitfalls. We have the undeniable broad public interest in self help to provide a responsive climate for our efforts. Finally, and most importantly, we have a national social and economic situation which may make self help once again a necessity for survival. Inflation and creeping recession have already made daily living more tenuous and pressured. The cut backs in social services make professional supports less available, subject to more competition among those deserving service and more bureaucratization and formalities before services can be delivered. Given such a set of factors, it is not unreasonable to support and initiate self help efforts as both a broad base for criticism and change in the social service system as well as favorable settings for people to become exposed to socialist and feminist ideas and practice.

The primary base for our involvement in self help groups can even be personal. Most of us experience problems in our lives as women, men, parents, children, lovers, survivors, drinkers, procrastinators, shy people, fat people, lonely people. Joining or starting a self help group can help us as people, not just as activists with an agenda. This has been a major source of strength within the women's movement. Women have helped each other and been helped themselves with some real personal and political issues in their lives. The sharing and loss of isolation which comes from self help activity are real and can provide us with tangible energy and strength.

. . . .

Finally, then, the impulse which brings people, including ourselves, to seek mutual aid instead of professional care is a healthy one. It embodies the faith in oneself and others that is essential if we are ever to achieve a more equal society. We cannot allow the all-too-real limitations of the current practice of self help to obscure the equally real opportunity.

NOTES

1. There is a very large current literature on self help. The leading figures in this area are Frank Riessmann and Alan Gartner, who have written *Self Help in the Human Services* (Jossey-Bass, 1977) and sponsor the National Self Help Clearinghouse (CUNY, 33 West 42nd St., Room 1227, New York, NY 10036).

2. For a useful review of this history see Alfred H. Katz and Eugene I. Bender, "Self Help Groups in Western Society: History and Prospects," in *The Journal of Applied Behavioral Science,* XII, no. 3 (1976).

3. Maximillian C. Hurwitz, *The Workers Circle* (New York, 1936).

4. Pauline B. Bart, "Seizing the Means of Reproduction: An Illegal Feminist Abortion Collective—How and Why It Worked," Abraham Lincoln School of Medicine, University of Illinois, Chicago.

5. *Ibid.*

6. Helin I. Marieskind and Barbara Ehrenreich, "Towards Socialist Medicine: The Women's Health Movement," *Social Policy,* September–October, 1975.

Comparative Health Policies

. . . . . .

When we seek alternatives to our own medical care organization, we do well to look at other societies for comparison and guidance, especially societies that have similar health problems or have developed innovative organizational solutions. While no medical system is without problems and none is completely transferable to the United States, there are lessons to be learned in considering alternative models to our own.

In this section, we briefly examine the health policies of Germany, Canada, and Great Britain. These countries are western, industrialized democracies with powerful and advanced medical professions, which makes them generally comparable to the United States. It should be noted that there are, of course, specific ways in which they are not comparable. Nevertheless, by comparing health systems, we are better able to see the consequences and potentials of different national policies on the provision of medical services.

The United States remains the only industrialized nation without a national health program. Many such proposals have been introduced in Congress in the past seventy-five years only to be ultimately defeated. After the passage of Medicare and Medicaid in 1965, many policymakers felt that national health insurance was an idea whose time had come (Margolis, 1981). Dozens of different proposals were introduced during the 1960s and 1970s, and many analysts believed that we would have a national health insurance program by 1980. With the advent of the Reagan administration and a general orientation toward reductions in government spending on social programs, there was little discussion among American policymakers about national health insurance. It appears that national health insurance is again on the political agenda; President Clinton made health care reform one of his top priorities, but unfortunately this attempt at reform failed to pass Congress (Starr, 1995). While proposals of universal health care are again dormant, the continuing problems with costs and access will not disappear. So the struggle for health care reform will continue.

It is problematic to reform health policies piecemeal as has occurred in the United States. Fixing one problem creates another; for example, Medicare and Medicaid paid for medical services for the elderly and poor but, lacking cost controls, fueled inflationary medical costs. Some type of comprehensive and universal national health system is necessary in the United States to increase equity, improve access to services, and control costs. Hence, we look to other societies for models and guidance. Before proceeding, it is important to make one distinction clear. When we discuss national health policies, we can differentiate between national health *insurance* (NHI) and a national health *service* (NHS). Both assume that adequate health care is a basic right of the population. NHI essentially puts the financing of a medical system under government control, typically by providing some type of health insurance where the premiums are paid by taxes. NHI also pays for medical services, so there is no or minimal direct cost to the patient. Canada and Germany are examples of such policies. An NHS, on the other hand, reorganizes medical services in addition to having the government pay directly for those services. It "socializes" medicine in that it treats medical care as a public utility and places much more control of the medical system in the hands of the government. Great Britain is an example of such a policy.

Donald W. Light, in "Comparative Models of 'Health Care' Systems," presents us with four contrasting models of health care systems. By examining these "ideal-typical" models we can see how different underlying *values* affect the politics, social goals, control, costs, and types of administration and shape the organization and delivery of medical services. Using the case of Germany, Light shows how these models vied with one another, leading to the current strains between the corporatist and professional model. When looking at other health care systems, especially in the context of health care reform, we would do well to consider such a schema for comparison. Light's perspective highlights how the values underlying the different models will be manifested in different types of health care systems, with certain consequences for control, cost, and medical care.

Canada is a country rather similar to the United States, although it has a a much smaller population (27 million). Between 1947 and 1971, Canada gradually introduced a national health policy that guaranteed medical care as a right for everyone (as opposed to the fragmented American system, which excludes over 8 percent of the population—about 37 million people). The form of NHI that Canada adopted is financed out of a progressive income tax and results in increased equity of health services and substantial control of health costs.

The NHI policy implemented by the Canadian provinces has largely been able to control health expenditures; while the U.S. currently spends over 14 percent of its GNP on health care, Canada spends less than 10 percent. Canada's cost for a health system that covers everyone is actually over $100 per capita *less* than that of the United States (Fuchs, 1990). This saving results from lowering administrative costs, removing the profitability of selling health insurance, limiting the use of some high-technology diagnostic and surgical procedures, and setting a national policy for cost controls. Although Canada has implemented a progressive financing system, it has maintained a fee-for-service, private enterprise orientation in the delivery of health services. Recent research suggests that physicians are increasingly accommodating to the new system and wouldn't want to return to the older commercially controlled health system (Williams et al., 1995). From all indications, the health status of Canadians is equal to or better than that of Americans.

Numerous health policy analysts have suggested that the U.S. should look to its northern neighbor as a model of health reform. One of the most compelling favorable reports on the Canadian system came from the United States General Accounting Office (GAO), suggesting that if the U.S. adopted a Canadian-style system, it could extend health insurance to all without any new costs.

If the universal coverage and single-payer features of the Canadian system were applied to the United States, the savings in administrative costs alone would be more than enough to finance insurance coverage for the millions of Americans who are currently uninsured. There would be enough left over to permit a reduction, or possibly even the elimination, of copayments and deductibles, if that were deemed appropriate.

If the single payer also had the authority and responsibility to oversee the system as a whole, as in Canada, it could potentially constrain growth in long-run health care costs. (U.S. General Accounting Office, 1991: 3)

In "Canada's Health Insurance and Ours: The Real Lessons, the Big Choices," Theodore R. Marmor and Jerry L. Mashaw describe the Canadian health care system and compare its operation to the U.S. system. They specifically dispel a number of myths that are often presented as reasons why we should not adopt a Canadian-style system. Marmor and Mashaw view such a government-based health insurance as both feasible and the preferable mode of health care reform. While the obstacles to reform remain real, the principles of universal coverage, a single payer, and global budgeting must be critical pieces of any plan.

Another model for health service delivery is Great Britain's National Health Service (NHS). In 1948, Britain reorganized its medical system to create a national health service. (See Stevens, 1966, for an account of NHS's formation and early development.) The NHS is a public system of medicine: hospitals, clinics, physicians, and other medical personnel work under the auspices and control of the Ministry of Health of the British government. The fee-for-service system has all but been eliminated: the NHS is financed by tax revenues (through "progressive taxation"), with essentially no cost to the patient at the time of services and with physicians paid stipulated yearly salaries. This system has reduced the "profit motive" in medicine. For example, it is well known that Great Britain has about half the amount of surgery per capita as does the United States. The incomes of physicians are relatively low by American standards (or, perhaps more correctly, American physicians' incomes are astronomical by international standards). Two levels of physicians exist in the NHS, the community-based GP and the hospital-based consultant. Until recently the higher status and incomes of the hospital consultants were a source of dissatisfaction to GPs. While the rigid two-tier system still exists, some of the inequities have been reduced.

During its thirty-year development, the NHS has managed admirable accomplishments, including: (1) eliminating financial barriers to access; (2) making the system more rational and equitable; (3) providing care on a community level with community-based primary physicians; (4) maintaining a high level of medical-care quality; and (5) controlling costs. This final point deserves elaboration.

The NHS seems to be a more cost efficient method of delivering health care than the largely private American system. Great Britain spends about 6 percent of its gross national product on health. Specifically, the British government spent only about $581 per citizen per year in 1986 for health care, compared to $1837 per person for all public and private health care in the United States that same year (McIlrath, 1988: 16). And by most measures, the health status of the populations are roughly equal. Furthermore, there is evidence that the NHS delivers medical care more equitably (Stevens, 1983). The British have controlled costs by "rationing" medical services (Aaron and

Schwartz, 1984). While all necessary medical services are more or less readily available, patients who wish elective services must "queue up" for them. There are, in fact, two- and three-year waiting lists for some elective medical care. There is little doubt that we as a nation cannot afford all the medical services we are scientifically capable of providing (Fuchs, 1975), so it is likely we too will have to adopt some type of rationing. It is undoubtedly more humane and just when medical services are rationed on the basis of need rather than on the ability to pay. (See also the critical debate on "Rationing Medical Care" in Part Three.)

The NHS is by no means a medical utopia. As a public service, it must compete for funding with other services (e.g., education) and thus by some accounts is perpetually underfinanced. In the past two decades under conservative governments, the NHS has been literally starved for funds. While inequities have lessened, they have not disappeared. The high status of the hospital consultant is a continuing problem and reinforces NHS emphasis on "sick care" rather than prevention. The NHS has recently engaged in a sweeping set of reforms, largely in an attempt to increase efficiency and reduce costs (Holland and Graham, 1994). In the final analysis, however, the NHS delivers better care to more parts of the population at less cost (and with no discernible difference in "health" status) than is accomplished in the United States, and so it needs to be considered in discussions of health reform.

In "Continuity and Change in the British National Health Service," Jonathan Gabe examines some of the achievements and dilemmas of the NHS. He traces the origins of the NHS and points to some of the continuing problems with persistent inequities. He details some of the major reforms of the past decade, including shifts in management organization, creation of internal markets and competition, empowering the consumer, and the perils of privatization that changed the way the NHS operates. Throughout these changes, however, the NHS remains a socialized system of health care that is "reasonably successful in providing cost-effective and equitable health care in the face of an aging population, increasingly expensive medical technology and heightened patient expectations." While there are clearly some limits on what medical care is available, it seems clear that the NHS as a health policy results in the provision of more-equitable care at a far lower cost than is currently delivered in the United States.

A fundamental emphasis of all three health policies is that they view health care as a right and develop a universal and comprehensive orientation toward the delivery of medical services. As we struggle to achieve a more equitable and reasonable American health system, we will want to look closely at these other systems for ways of reforming our own. David Himmelstein and his associates (1989) proposed an NHI program, largely based on the Canadian model, that represents the type of restructuring that our own medical system requires. These analyses should be benchmarks against which we can measure progressive reform.

REFERENCES

Aaron, J. Henry, and William B. Schwartz. 1984. The Painful Prescription: Rationing Hospital Care. Washington, D.C.: The Brookings Institution.

Fuchs, Victor. 1975. Who Shall Live? New York: Basic Books.

Fuchs, Victor. 1990. "How does Canada do it? A comparison of expenditures for physician services in the United States and Canada." New England Journal of Medicine 323:884–90.

Himmelstein, David U., Steffie Woolhandler, and the Writing Committee of the Working Group on Program Design. 1989. "A national health program for the United States: A physician's proposal." New England Journal of Medicine 320: 102–8.

Holland, Walter W., and Clifford Graham. 1994. "Recent reforms in the British National Health Service: Lessons for the United States." American Journal of Public Health 84: 186–9.

McIlrath, Sharon. 1988. "NHS concept of equality has undergone change." American Medical News. August 26, 1988: 16.

Margolis, Richard J. 1981. "National Health Insurance—A Dream Whose Time Has Come?" Pp. 486–501 in Peter Conrad and Rochelle Kern (eds.), The Sociology of Health and Illness: Critical Perspectives. New York: St. Martin's.

Stevens, Rosemary. 1966. Medical Practice in Modern England. New Haven: Yale University Press.

Stevens, Rosemary. 1983. "Comparisons in Health Care: Britain as a Contrast to the United States." Pp. 281–304 in David Mechanic (ed.), Handbook of Health, Health Care and the Health Professions. New York: Free Press.

United States General Accounting Office. 1991. Canadian Health Insurance: Lessons for the United States. Washington, D.C.: U.S. Government Printing Office.

Williams, A. Paul, Eugene Vayda, May L. Cohen, Christel A. Woodward, and Barbara Ferrier. 1995. "Medicine and the Canadian state: From the politics of conflict to the politics of accommodation." Journal of Health and Social Behavior 36: 303–21.

42

Comparative Models of "Health Care" Systems

■ ■ ■ ■ ■ ■

Donald W. Light

The leaders of virtually every industralized nation think that the cost of medical care is spiraling out of control, and they look abroad for solutions and fresh ideas. In the states of the former Soviet Union and Eastern Europe, the crisis centers on legitimacy: given the rejection and overthrow of centrally planned services, what kind of a system should replace the old one, especially when per capita income is only a fraction of the income available in Western models? In the United States and Western Europe, the crisis centers on money, despite their spending more (often much more) than systems anywhere else in the world. This is somewhat akin to a millionaire on his yacht declaring a crisis in his household budget. It implies that something more profound is at issue, namely the high living of systems centered on high-tech medical repairs that endlessly drive up costs rather than focusing on keeping people healthier in the first place. Moreover, these systems encourage societies to medicalize a wide array of social problems that—as non-diseases—are difficult to "treat" and run up costs even more.[1] The exceptions, perhaps, are delivery systems that center on each person having one primary-care physician who looks after his or her health. Even these have begun to devote modest resources to prevention only in the past decade.

Many policy makers and students today compare the ways in which different nations (or sub-systems with nations, like their military) deliver medical services. Milton Roemer[2] suggests several reasons why. First, comparative studies are interesting in their own right, like comparing how different people raise children or design their homes. They are also "at the heart of the scientific enterprise," as a veteran of the comparative analysis, Mark Field, points out.[3] Comparative studies can also help give us perspective on our own system. They may even turn up lessons we can apply to our problems. In particular, the basic problems of inequity, inefficiency, ineffectiveness, and cost overruns may be illuminated by comparative studies. These problems, however, involve the whole society more than the nature of medical services. Roemer and many others are quick to point out that medical care has far less impact on health itself than the culture (or the cult) of medicine has led people to believe. Medicine is largely a repair service that patches up or rescues people *after* they get in trouble. Their relative poverty or affluence; their nutrition and housing; the health hazards of their work, home and community environment; their age, sex, and genetic make-up; and their cultural beliefs and habits are the basic determinants of health. Likewise, inequalities in medical care largely reflect class relations, the structure of the economy, and the degree of political oppression or participation. Thus, comparative studies need to take into account these more basic aspects of the societies in which they operate.

To analyze simultaneously all aspects of medical delivery systems and their societies is such a daunting task that most authorities limit themselves largely to just the systems. Some authors provide no comparative framework and

Table 42-1. Basic Issues in Comparing Health Care Systems

1. Legitimation and Regulation
2. Services and Benefits
3. Finances
4. Rules of Eligibility
5. Organization and Administration
6. Benefits and Liabilities for different parties

describe each country as they see fit or around a few basic questions.[4,5] Some use a list of factors and choose from them the factors that suit each country.[6] While this is not a comparative framework, it does provide a useful checklist of things to take into consideration. A third approach culls critical questions from a review of the literature. One such effort came up with the six listed in Table 42-1.[7] First, in what ways are services and policies legitimated and regulated? Second, what are the services and benefits? Third, how are they financed? Fourth, what are the rules of eligibility that determine who is covered for what? Fifth, how are services and benefits organized and administered? Finally, what are the benefits and liabilities, for patients, for providers, for suppliers, for the government, and for the public? Some systems, like the American one, seem designed to benefit the army of providers, insurers, administrators, monitors, regulators, and corporations that supply it more than the patients treated.

A few authors have provided real comparative

frameworks.[3] Roemer,[2] for example, in his massive new study of health care systems around the world, discusses all the socio-political dimensions that affect health and medicine and then presents a framework (Table 42-2) focused on how affluent or poor a nation is and how decentralized or centralized the health care system is. Within this frame one looks at the ways in which different systems organize resources and delivery services. Roemer attempts to capture all of these in five components: resources, economic supports, organization, management, and delivery of services. Their relationships to each other are illustrated in Figure 42-1. This is a useful scheme until one gets into the details of what goes into the five components. There, one finds hospitals and clinics under "resources," but curative services under "organization," and hospital care under "delivery of services." The ministries of health are part of "organization," but regulation is part of "management." Social security is part of "economic supports" but social security programs like disability insurance are part of "organization." When one of the world's most distinguished and experienced scholars of comparative health care systems runs into such problems, it shows how difficult it is to formulate good comparative schemes. Moreover, a scheme like Figure 42-1 is not really comparative as is Table 42-2. Rather, like Table 42-1 it serves as a template to apply to different systems.

One other template that can provide valuable

Table 42-2. Health Care Systems by Wealth and Control*

Affluence (GNP/capita)	The Degree of Governmental Control			
	Decentralized .... *Centralized*			
	Private Insurance, Private, Entrepreneurial Services	National Insurance, Private, Regulated Services	National Insurance, Public, Regulated Services	National Insurance State-run System
Affluent	United States	Germany Canada	Great Britain Norway	former East Germany former Soviet Union
Wealthy but Developing	—	Libya	Kuwait	—
Modest and Developing	Thailand	Brazil	Israel	Cuba
Poor	Ghana	India	Tanzania	China

*Modified from Roemer (1991) Fig. 4.1 and Anderson (1989) Fig. 1, to make the dimensions more internally consistent.

Figure 42-1. *National Health System: Components, Functions, and Their Interdependence*

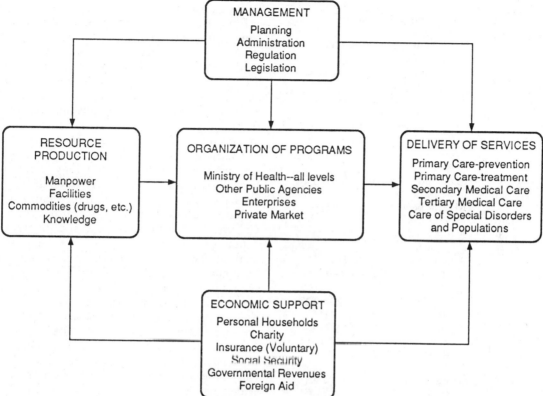

insights lists the various targets and modalities at issue.[3] To what extent are different systems focused on death vs disease vs discomfort, and so forth, as illustrated in Table 42-3? How does the balance of focus change over time? Likewise, how heavily do different systems focus on diagnosis to the finest point, versus prevention, versus rehabilitation, and the like? It would be useful to develop zero-sum weights to these different foci. Finally, how does the proportion of resources vary between systems for different sectors listed in Figure 42-1?

Comparative Models Based on Values

Ideally, comparative models would take one through a common set of characteristics in parallel. Moreover, the characteristics would be connected somehow, so that each model would have a unifying or master characteristic at the same time that it had a comparative parallel structure. Unfortunately, virtually no such models exist, but let us try by identifying what the master characteristic might be. A popular and obvious one is modes of financing, such as general taxes vs employment-based insurance vs earmarked taxes vs out-of-pocket or cash payments, or ways to pay for them such as salary vs contracts vs fee for service. Field,[3] for example, developed such a typology of models along an axis from privately paid services to socialized medicine. More fundamental, we would contend, are values; for values shape financing.[8] They have to change before financing can change.

Political and social values shape not only finances but also the institutional structure of medical services and health care more broadly.

Table 42-3. The Mutual-Aid or Community Model of a Health Care System

Key Values and Goals	*To support fellow members and their families when ill.* To minimize accidents, illness, and unhealthy conditions. To promote ties and mutual support among members. To minimize the financial impact of illness.
Image of the Individual	An active, self-responsible, informed member of the group.
Power	Local control. Mutual decision making. State and profession relatively weak.
Key Institutions	Mutual benefit associations.
Organization	A loose federation of member groups. Administratively collegial. Organized around work or communities. Emphasis on low-tech, primary care and prevention. Strong ties to community programs (educational, occupational, social service).
Division of Labor	Egalitarian. More health care teams. Fewer doctors and specialists.
Finance and Costs	Members contribute to an insurance fund which contracts with doctors and facilities for service. Costs low compared to the Professional model.
Medical Education	Generally not an issue. Logically would favor training health care teams in community-based health care.

They influence how power is exercised. Medicalization itself is an important value. Seemingly neutral acts such as seeking a cure for cancer, treating hypertension with drugs, or dressing rat-bite wounds on patients who return to the same rat-infested apartment building are acts freighted with value judgments about the scope of medicine, the cause of health problems, and the distribution of responsibility. Is the medical issue just the infection of the rat bite, or the infestation of rats in the building, or the neglect of the building by an absentee landlord, or the abject level of poverty allowed in the United States?

From this starting point of values, a set of comparative models have been constructed that show the differences and similarities of the models across several dimensions. These models are *ideal types,* which means they attempt to characterize, not actual delivery systems, but essential and coherent relationships that inform them. Most systems are a mixture of these models, often in tension with one another.

The term *values* means more than "ideology" yet less than "culture." Ideology connotes a logically consistent and coherent set of beliefs. Yet often it cannot fully account for the shape of social welfare institutions such as the health care system. Culture, on the other hand, has such breadth and contains so many elements that it is not useful for analysis. Thus the four models that follow show how values shape the organization, financing, and power of different health care systems.

In order to show the relationship between these comparative models and a real system, we will use Germany as an illustration. We choose Germany not only because all four models clarify the dynamics of its development, but also because the German system has been the most widely emulated in the history of modern health care systems. It may still be. A number of the Eastern bloc countries that have liberated themselves from their Communist past look to "the German model" in designing their medical delivery system for the 21st century. As we shall see, however, what is often called today "the German model" is a post-Nazi model quite different from the original German model, and not well suited to the health needs of industrialized societies in the 21st century.

The Mutual-Aid Model

Long before the world's first national health insurance law was passed in Germany in 1883, groups of people banded together to cope with the impact of accidents, illness, and death on their families' lives. Friendly societies, or fraternal organizations, or mutual-aid societies appear to have started up as early as the 16th century among miners in the Ruhr valley. They pooled small, regular contributions in order to provide funds to members who fell ill or to their families if they died. As early as 1784, sickness funds were protected under Prussian law. By 1854, Prussian law required the workers in all mines and foundries to join either a *freie Hilfskasse* (free help fund) or a *Fabrikkrankenkasse* (factory sickness fund).[9] The main expense and principal benefit was sick pay to compensate for lost wages. Some funds also provided medical services and medications. This movement of workers forming what we shall call generically mutual aid societies became international during the 19th century, spreading to parts of Europe, the United States, and Latin America.[10,11] Employers resisted efforts to make them have such funds, but when they existed, in Germany employees customarily paid two-thirds of the premiums and "managed the sickness funds with the assistance of a master tradesman representing the employer."[12]

Table 42-3 presents the ideal typical model of such mutual-aid health care "systems," centrally driven by the commitment to support fellow members when ill and to minimize illness. Historically, this latter phrase refers to efforts by unions and their sickness funds to advocate for safer working conditions; and by the early 20th century we shall see that some of the most advanced sickness funds also developed programs in disease prevention and health promotion. A corollary goal was to minimize the financial impact of illness. As medical services gained importance in the 20th century, alongside lost wages, mutual aid societies became actively involved in providing or purchasing inexpensive medical services.

The implications of this model for power are local control and mutual decision-making. Perhaps the key word in this model's anchor goal is "*fellow* members." Authority rests in the group as a whole. Social relations are informal and collegial. Social control comes from peer pressure and commitment to the organization's goals. However, as early as 1876 the Prussian state began to lay down regulations concerning contributions and the management of the moneys in order to prevent irregularities and abuses. Otherwise, both the state and the profession take a back seat in this model. The image of the individual implicit in this model is an active, self-responsible, and informed member of the group. Medical services emphasize primary care, and the model implies health care teams that are also egalitarian. Organizationally, the mutual aid features local, small work- and community-based organizations of services and benefits, loosely tied to other similar societies or funds. The society or fund is itself the key institution. As this model began to mature into local health care systems, it tended to emphasize primary care and the use of nonphysicians as well. The mutual aid perspective leads to planning and coordination of services within a consumer-controlled health care system. "Thus," concludes Brian Abel-Smith, "in these countries the consumers of medical care came to be organized before the doctors were effectively organized, and they were in a position to dictate the terms of service of doctors whom they engaged to provide services."[11]

The State Model

States develop national health insurance and/or services for a variety of reasons that center on strengthening the state. In Bismarck's case, he wanted to head off the growing popularity of labor parties by convincing laborers that they could look to the state for social benefits rather than unions or socialist parties. In other cases, political leaders push for health benefits or a health care program to strengthen the workforce and/or the army. In still other cases, national health insurance or services are realized through popular demand, to eliminate the swift impoverishment that illness can bring even to successful families. As Table 42-4 indicates, states exhibit growing interest in minimizing the costs of medical services and likewise minimizing illness in the first place through prevention and health promotion. As an ideal type, the state model reflects the desire of the state to control the health care system, and indeed one is struck by the ways in which different states have taken over and recast the activities of mutual aid groups. Finally, states divide into democratic and autocratic or dictatorial types. The latter often regard health care as a vital political tool for indoctrinating the population. They also use medical services to control dissidents and eliminate "undesirables." Torture and "psychiatric treatment" are

Table 42-4. The Societal or State Model of a Health Care System

Key Values and Goals	*To strengthen the state via a healthy, vigorous population.* To minimize illness and maximize self-care. To minimize the cost of medical services to the state. To provide good, accessible care to all sectors of the population.
	*To indoctrinate or control, through health care. To enhance loyalty to the state.
Image of the Individual	A member of society. Thus responsibility of the state, but also responsible to stay healthy.
Power	Centered on the governance structure of the society, either democratic or autocratic or a cross-mixture. Secondary power to medical associations.
Key Institutions	The ministry of health and its delegated system of authorities.
Organization	A national, integrated system, administratively centralized and decentralized. Organized around the epidemiological patterns of illness. Organized around primary care. Relatively egalitarian services and recruitment patterns. Strong ties with health programs in other social institutions.
Division of Labor	Proportionately fewer doctors and more nurses, etc. Proportionately fewer specialists, reflecting epidemiology. More teamwork, more delegation.
Finance and Cost	All care free or nearly free. Taxes, premiums, or a mix. Costs relatively low. Doctor's share relatively low.
Medical Education	A state system, free, with extensive continuing education.

*Goals of the autocratic state variation.

examples of the former; the role of medicine in concentration camps, medical "experiments," and genocide are examples of the latter.[13,14]

Power in this model lies with the state and not much with the people, a critical difference between it and the mutual aid model. Even democratic state systems like Britain's National Health Service (NHS) involve little decision-making by the citizens affected. Ironically, their market reforms to make services more "consumer oriented" only do so to the extent that providers and managers act on consumers' behalf. Still, democratic states delegate more and have various systems of councils down to the district or local level. Autocratic states may have such structures but appoint the members and retire them if they do not toe the line. This, for example, is a major concern in Great Britain, where the elimination of civil service protections and the appointment from the center of people who chair regional and local boards mean that the current "decentralization" of the National Health Service (NHS) actually involves more central control than ever before.[15] As these observations imply, a democratically constituted government can be more or less autocratic when it comes to medical services.

The extent of organizational consequences for this model depend on whether the system involves just insurance as a financial mechanism to pay for services that lie outside the state system, or includes medical services as well. It also depends on how autocratic the state is. The key institutions are the ministry of health and the hierarchy of policy-making bodies. The power of the medical and nursing professions seems inversely related to that of the state: the more democratic the state, the more power and influence the professions have. State systems tend to cost less than other systems, and services center around primary care. The NHS, with every citizen having a broadly trained anchor physician, exemplifies this model.

Financially, the ideal typical system would raise funds through general taxes, although often in reality insurance premiums are used or a combination of both. In either case, the state model provides good to excellent overall budgetary control, and it keeps costs within politically acceptable bounds. Granted that six percent of GNP seems high to British politicians, while half again as much defines Germany's sense of an upper limit; when expenditures reach that level, governments take strong measures to cap costs. The United States, by contrast, has neither a budget nor a consensus about the upper bounds of expenditures. It has been declaring a health cost crisis nearly every year since at least 1971, when President Richard Nixon delivered his famous speech to Congress; yet expenditures have kept rising, from six, to nine, to twelve, and now to fifteen percent of GNP. Medical costs now are cutting into such fundamentals as funds for education and into wages.

The world's first national health insurance plan was created by Germany's iron-fisted ruler, Otto von Bismarck, in 1883.[16] In order to quell the Social Democratic Party, which was gaining popularity among dispossessed factory workers who had uprooted themselves from the security of their villages, Bismarck had the police smash 45 of the 47 party newspapers and forbid unions or parties from assembling. Berlin, the seat of both socialism and the largest concentration of Jews in Europe, was put into a minor state of siege. Hatred of socialism and Jews fused in the minds of many, as they would again fifty years later under Hitler. At the same time, Bismarck realized that this suppression did not solve the underlying problems, and therefore he proposed a series of social insurance schemes. He understood the limitations of sickness funds on a voluntary basis and realized that every person at risk must be compelled to join. He seems to have realized the benefits of having employees make premium contributions so that they would share the burden at the same time that official taxes would not have to be increased. Bismarck seems to have favored a state-run system, so workers would realize it was he as the embodiment of the state, and not the unions, to whom they could look for support in times of need.[9,10,17]

Opposing Bismarck were some 20,000 local company, miner, and guild sickness funds averaging 215 members. They appealed to employers and legislators who did not want to see Bismarck and the state gain still more power and patronage. This coalition succeeded in modifying the legislation so that the national health insurance operated through the sickness funds instead of being run by the state. Thus, the final law was a melding of the mutual-aid and the state models, a national set of rules to establish a largely self-funding health insurance scheme to which workers and their employers contributed, but run locally by the sickness funds. Thus, the German system is not "socialist" in the American sense of being state-run or state-financed. Bismarck used the new law "to preserve the existing social order, to minimize social conflicts, and to preserve the state from radical overthrow."[12] Ironically, the operation of the law through the sickness funds enabled workers and union members to retain a good deal of control nevertheless. Bismarck tied the workers more closely to the state but did not alienate them from the unions and the Social Democrats.

Workers in the sickness funds agreed to pay two thirds of the premiums so that they could have two thirds of the seats on the funds' governing boards and thus retain control as they had in the past. Now, however, the workers' mutual-aid funds had a stable, much-expanded financial footing, and as the years passed, the legislature steadily widened the circle of workers covered.

The Professional Model

It may seem odd that a study of medical services should only come to a professional model of those services so late, but in fact the medical profession's collective identity and concept of medical services coalesced under the adversity of the other two models.[11] Both the state and mutual aid models tend to draw on doctors when their services are needed and at prices they can afford in their drive to minimize costs. Under German law, doctors were a trade, not a profession, and they were not well organized as national health insurance was being formed. This left sickness funds free to contract with any kind of providers they wished, and they did use a variety of nonphysician providers. Moreover, doctors had to compete for block or volume discount contracts on a *per capita* basis to treat sick fund members, and given the intense competition, the winning bids were low. The impact on local doctors' practices intensified with each round: as more people were covered at less cost per person, it took more business away from private practices at far lower rates.

Perhaps most deeply offensive to gentlemen physicians was being controlled by and answerable to committees of workers with only an elementary school education and from unrecognizable social origins. The committees that reviewed contracts, that investigated patient complaints, and that monitored services were run by workers.

Private practitioners found sickness fund contracts and their clinics politically offensive as well. They stood for a socialist or Marxist concept of health care. Their programs to educate workers about how to manage health problems, their consumer health pamphlets, their programs for off-hours and weekend coverage, their use of nonphysician providers, and their systems for reducing the number of referrals and hospitalizations stuck in their craw. It did not help that the number of physicians more than doubled from 1880 to 1910, putting sickness funds in a buyers' market. Moreover, many of the doctors who helped develop these programs had socialist leanings and were disproportionately Jewish. Their early commitment to developing programs in public health and social medicine is not well known,[18,19,20] though it would become the object of spite by the private practitioners in the years to come.

Little by little, the unsympathetic majority of physicians organized themselves to protect themselves. Only gradually, and after many failed attempts, did physicians succeed in getting one German state after another to change their status from that of a business to a profession. Local medical societies formed committees that insisted on reviewing doctors' contracts with the sickness funds as a condition of membership. These committees focused on strengthening the professional status of the doctors by restricting the criteria for termination, by rejecting a salary if fees had been paid before, and by refusing to work in facilities where unlicensed practitioners were employed. By shaming and/or expelling uncooperative members, medical societies began to bring contract doctors into line.[9,11,17,21]

Then in 1898, a physician, Dr. Landmann, developed a system for reducing medical costs by making drugs available to members directly through the funds at reduced cost, by limiting the number of referrals and admissions to the average rates over the previous three years, and by establishing a system of rotation to expand coverage to nights and weekends. When the doctors under contract with the local sickness fund in Barmen refused to cooperate, they were fired. The doctors protested and went on strike,

and eight days later the government intervened on behalf of the doctors. Other strikes followed in towns where the Landmann system was being introduced. In 1900 Dr. Herman Hartmann, concluding that the medical societies were too polite and spineless, formed a militant physicians' union. It launched an all-out attack on the worker-run sickness funds, their contracts, and their clinics. It organized over 200 strikes and boycotts against sickness fund contracts per year. It developed strike funds to provide income to striking doctors. It boycotted employers who tried to bring in "scab" physicians. It set up a job placement service, a credit union, a pension fund, and a burial fund. By 1904, half the private practitioners in German belonged to the new union. By 1913, the government stepped in and negotiated equal representation of physicians on all key sickness fund committees. The medical profession, barely visible in the negotiations for national health insurance in 1883, was now a fully equal partner in the sickness funds. It went on to bend them to their interests.

The ideal typical model of a health care system which underlies these and a wide array of other activities by doctors centers, as Table 42-5 illustrates, on providing the best possible clinical care to every sick patient. This means that medicine must be developed to its highest level. This central mission requires professional autonomy and respect. At the collective or organizational level, as Table 42-5 indicates, a central goal is to increase the power, prestige and wealth of the profession.

To achieve these goals, the profession must predominate, and financing must be private or passive so that it interferes as little as possible into clinical judgment and the doctor-patient relationship. Medical services, then, are loosely organized around physicians' practices, hospitals, and other facilities run locally for the benefit of the medical profession. Medical schools play a particularly central role in this model, because they concentrate the effort to improve on the best clinical medicine for every sick patient. The professional model results in an increasingly elaborate division of labor and technical arsenal.

The ideal professional health care system has as few entanglements with other social institutions and community health as is gracefully possible, except to mobilize their enthusiasm and

Table 42-5. The Professional Model of a Health Care System

Key Values and Goals	*To provide the best possible clinical care to every sick patient* (who can pay and who lives near where a doctor has chosen to practice). To develop scientific medicine to its highest level. To protect the autonomy of physicians and services. To increase the power and wealth of the profession. To increase the prestige of the profession.
Image of the Individual	A private person who chooses how to live and when to use the medical system.
Power	Centers on the medical profession, and uses state powers to enhance its own.
Key Institutions	Professional associations. Autonomous physicians and hospitals.
Organization	Centered on doctors' preferences of specialty, location, and clinical cases. Emphasizes acute, hi-tech interventions. A loose federation of private practices and hospitals. Weak ties with other social institutions as peripheral to medicine.
Division of Labor	Proportionately more doctors, more specialists. Proportionately more individual clinical work by physicians; less delegation.
Finance and Costs	Private payments by individual or through passive reimbursement by insurance plans. Costs about twice the % GNP of the Societal model. Doctors' share greater than Societal model.
Medical Education	Private, autonomous school with tuition. Disparate, voluntary continuing education.

support for professional medical work. It regards the individual as a private person who chooses how to live and then comes in when the need arises. To do this, doctors must be free to proceed as they best see fit with as little concern with costs as possible. The nearly exclusive focus on the individual patient contrasts with the state and mutual aid models.

The United States is the purest example of the professional ideal type of a health care system, with all its strengths and weaknesses played out over the past several decades. Its clinical care has risen from the bottom of Western systems to the top. It dominates the world in technical advances, diagnostic sophistication, and esoteric interventions. On the other hand, specialization together with professional autonomy results in fragmented services and spiraling costs. The freedom to practice elaborate medicine and charge fees for it actually weakens the quality of professional work. For fees reward easily countable, technical work over time with the patient and exercising clinical judgment, and they result in many specialists having to take on cases too simple for their training or outside their area of expertise. Besides the maldistribution of specialists and procedures, fees tend to exacerbate geographical and class maldistribution. On another level, the core values of the professional model pay little attention to public health, community medicine, health education, or social inequities. In fact, since the professional model allows doctors to practice what they wish and where and charge whatever fees they can, significant inequities arise between specialties, geographical areas, and particularly social classes.

The pitched battle between the mutual aid and the professional model continued well after the years of physicians' strikes won major concessions in 1913. On one hand, a National Association of German Sick Funds was chartered in 1914 and founded its own publishing company which issued *The Panel Doctor (Der Kassenarzt)* a periodical focusing on health reforms and monopolistic actions of medical societies. Based on an analysis of archives in Potsdam, the National Association also published literature on innovative practices in social medicine, sources of cheaper medical equipment and drugs, and lists of generic drugs with sources "to oppose the plethora of drugs and special remedies which had been produced after the war by the chemical industries."[22] Some of the larger sickness funds set up screening clinics, and many were actively involved in public programs of health promotion and prevention. Some established ambulatory clinics, the forerunners of polyclinics. The largest local fund, in Berlin, created an integrated system of health care for over 400,000 members which included two hospitals, 38 clinics, X-ray institutes, dental clinics, pharmaceutical dispensaries, and health baths. Like other larger funds, it offered courses in social hygiene, public lectures, and outreach services. An indication of efficiency comes from records of the sickness fund in the Lehe Quarters of Bremerhaven. Its four physicians treated about one-fourth of all patients in the lower Weser region, while forty-five private physicians treated the other three-quarters. Fund members could choose either the clinic doctors or a private physician.

On the other hand, continued protests and pressure by the militant physicians' union (Hartmannbund) resulted in its becoming in effect the statutory body representing insurance physicians, and the sickness funds had to give them a lump sum for each subscriber for all services, known as a "capitation payment." This effectively eliminated competitive contracting and converted the funds from being *providers* of services to being *payers* of services. Medical societies or physicians' association also took the sickness funds to court many times for practicing medicine in illegal ways or breaching their contracts. The courts generally upheld the funds over the protesting physicians.

Thus, when the National Socialist (Nazi) Party wooed professionals with its anti-union, anti-socialist and anti-Semitic platform, private physicians joined the Party early and in greater numbers than any other profession.[23] The percent of doctors in the Party was almost three times greater than in the population as a whole. This is rarely discussed and not commonly known in Germany, despite all the attention today to the dark history of the Nazi period. Physicians' early support was richly rewarded. Soon after Hitler assumed power in April 1933, he issued two regulations which allowed all "non-Aryan," socialist or communist physicians to be prohibited from practicing in national health insurance panels. The central archives show that physicians' associations did not protect their members from prosecution but instead

took up the cause with such zeal that Hitler's Minister of Labor actually threw out a good number of them for lack of sufficient evidence, commenting on the "wantonness" and "enormous sum of injustice and material damage" on excluded doctors.[22,24] Since "non-Aryans" constituted 14 percent of the medical profession, 25–30 percent of the panel doctors in large cities who worked for the sickness fund clinics, and nearly 60 percent of the panel doctors in Berlin, Aryan physicians in private practice stood to benefit from their elimination. Of the 9000 Jewish physicians, only 135 still treated patients (on a private basis) by the end of 1938. How many thousands of other panel doctors deemed "socialist" or "communist" lost their right to practice cannot be easily estimated.

Besides giving private practitioners the "final solution" to their thirty-year-old problem of removing those doctors who supported the mutual-aid model of health care, Hitler also took over control of the sickness funds from their lay boards so they would no longer be "missionary agencies in the area of public health."[22] Ambulatory care centers were closed, because in being more cost-effective, they were "uneconomical." The explanation of this paradox was "that proportional to their expansion, the economic space [in this case of physicians in private practice] is being destroyed. . . ."[25] One physician in an ambulatory clinic cuts into the income of four in private practice. "[These clinics] violate sound economic principles according to which the free enterprise spirit, creativity, individual endeavors and personal responsibility should find roots with a maximum number of citizens."[22] What court battles through the twenties had failed to do was finally accomplished, to shut down what today would be called ambulatory HMOs as the enemy of professionalism and free choice. And finally, Hitler granted doctors the legal status of a profession that they had spent decades pursuing.

The Corporatist Model

This rise to power by the medical profession through the first four decades of the 20th century took place in the context of a fourth model of health care, shown in Table 42-6. This model is a

Table 42-6. The Corporatist Model of a Health Care System

Key Values and Goals	*To join together buyers and sellers, providers and patients in deciding the range and costs of services.* To minimize conflict through mandatory negotiation and consensus. To balance costs against provider interests.
Image of the Individual	Implied in resulting negotiations. Image has been that of a private citizen who comes in when ill.
Power	Countervailing power structure. Subject to imbalance by one party or another. Statutory powers to determine range and costs in the corporatist body itself. State as ultimate setter of rules and referee.
Key Institutions	The corporatist body. Insurers, payers, providers. State as ultimate setter of rules and referee.
Organization	Depends on the organization of the underlying health care system and resulting terms of countervailing negotiations.
Division of Labor	Depends on the organization of the underlying health care system and resulting terms of countervailing negotiations.
Finance and Costs	Depends. . .etc. In German model, employers and employees contribute premiums. Costs depend on results of negotiations and on society's sense of limits. Doctors' share has tended to be high because they run services and dominate negotiations, but not inherent in the model.
Medical Education	Has not been a focus of concern, though model allows for it.

synthesis of the other three, a structured counterbalancing of the conflicting priorities and values of citizen/consumers (mutual-aid), providers (profession), and payers (the state and employers). This model is called "corporatist," a European term connoting an independent but publicly constituted body which is not common in the United States.[17] The government sets the rules and acts as umpire; so the corporatist structure is not a welfare body in the American sense of the term. If one party begins to dominate the others, or if the counterbalancing does not work properly, the government may step in and alter the rules. The corporatist model in Table 42-6 centers around the goal of joining together employers, employees, physicians, hospitals, and other providers so that they must negotiate a budget for the medical costs of next year's illnesses. Thus a cardinal goal of the corporatist model is to channel and structure conflict between payers, providers, and patients as they address the problems of meeting demands with limited funds.

In order for the corporatist model to work, each of the major parties must be organized, and as we have seen this happened during the first two decades. An American analogy might be if the medical society, the hospital association, the Chamber of Commerce, a union council, and an insurance council in each state were required by statute to hammer out a total annual budget for all the citizens in that state. Most of the money would come from the premiums of employers and employees (but note that employees pay half the premiums), while the government would cover the unemployed, part-time workers, students, and other individuals who did not fit into the basic employment-based system. This might not be unlike President Clinton's health care purchasing cooperatives.

As one can see, a good deal is subject to negotiation and depends on the balance of power. In the German case, the medical profession institutionalized the goals of the professional model of autonomy, fees, and an emphasis on acute clinical intervention. But this is not inherent in the model itself, and as we shall see, the relentless pressure of costs generated by the professional model eventually has led to some basic restructuring. It is this point which outside admirers of the [postwar] German system have not appreciated.

Roots: The Postwar East German System

After 1945 in the Soviet occupied zone, both East German Communists and Russian advisors were eager to correct what they regarded as the abandonment by the German health care system of its original design. It was the concept of social medicine, developed by German pioneers such as Johann Peter Frank, Alfred Grotjahn, Beno Chages, Frank-Karl Meyer-Brodnitz, and others both before Bismarck and in the early days of the sickness fund clinics, that Lenin had emulated to refocus the centralized system he had inherited from the Tsars towards public and occupational health.[26] Faced with mass starvation and epidemics, Lenin established a national system of local health stations.

The East German zone also faced great public health problems from the mass bombings, dismantled economy, and immigrants pouring in from the east. It is notable that one of the first actions by the transition government was to disband organized medical associations. They then set about to establish a network of local clinics and larger polyclinics [multi-specialty group practices] in the cities. They integrated hospital and ambulatory care and hired doctors as civil servants under a central ministry. In short, they created an autocratic state model. As that model indicates, the East German system linked up with other sectors. It established an extensive occupational medicine program, with medical stations at places of work and what we call day care centers for the infants and children of working mothers. A particularly generous system of payments and services was developed for pregnant women and babies, as the single best investment a system can make in preventive medicine.[27,28] The East Germans also recognized women's right to abortion, even though they desparately wanted to replenish the labor force lost to the war's toll through large families and population growth. In general, the public health program was extensive. The East German system also developed an extensive health education program in the public schools, and it made concerted efforts (partially successful) to recruit medical students from working-class backgrounds.

This system manifested several marked differences from the system that continued on its trajectory in the West. First, following the state vs professional models, the East German system regarded individuals as citizens whose health was the responsibility of the state and who had a responsibility to minimize illness, while the West German system tended to regard individuals as private citizens who come in when they want medical services. This led to a second difference, a much greater emphasis on prevention in East Germany. Third, for the East Germans the concept of health was more functional—whether you could carry out your domestic duties and work—while the West Germans increasingly reflected a concept of health as feeling good. A fourth difference is between physicians as agents of a state ministry versus as autonomous professionals. A resulting fifth difference reflected in the models is that in East Germany more work was done by health care teams and by nonphysician providers. The results were impressive. Starting with significantly worse health statistics after the war, the East German system attained nearly the same level of health status as the West German system for half the money by 1970.

After that, the East German system became more run-down and rigid. Morale dropped, coordination declined, and bureaucratic sclerosis set in. When unification occurred in 1989–90, no one had a kind thing to say about any part of the East German system. As the international analyst, Jeremy Hurst concluded, the system "could also lay some claims to past successes. . . . However, physical standards were low, high technology was lacking, doctors had little autonomy, and such patient choice as existed was not translated into financial incentives for providers. The whole system is discredited by its association with the former GDR."[29] Since similar state models have achieved impressive gains in other nations, one should not let the faulty execution of the system blind one from its merits.

West Germany: Postwar Professional Capture

When the Allied forces took over after 1945, their policy of self-determination contradicted their policy of de-Nazification; for self-determination meant in effect that the advocates professionalizing the delivery system were the only ones left after the panel doctors had been expatriated or killed.[23] They locked in a professional model of health care with measures that prohibited sickness funds from delivering services or running clinics, effectively prohibited group practice, curtailed competition from public health or industrial programs by prohibiting them from treating patients, eliminated the direct election of board members, and required all participating physicians to be members in good standing so that dissidents could be kept from earning a living. As Deborah Stone concluded, "it seems clear from this history that the idea that the medical profession's political strength derives entirely from its special status as a profession or from its monopoly of technical expertise must be dismissed."[17]

There are many parallels in other countries to this striking example of professional dominance from 1900 to the 1960s. In the United States, medical societies mounted fierce campaigns against competitive contracting near the turn of the century and then used a combination of professional pressure, state regulations, and court rulings to oppose any form of prepaid group practice from the end of World War I to the 1960s.[30] The only major difference was that American medicine successfully opposed national health insurance as well.

During the 1960s, the West German system's expenditures rose from 4.7 to 5.5 percent of gross domestic product (GDP), an increase of 17 percent and in line with other countries, but still of some concern.[31] (By comparison, the U.S. system increased by 42 percent, from 5.2 to 7.4.) Then, in just five years, the share of GDP in Germany grew by 42 percent, largely in the hospital sector and through expanded coverage of orthodontic work.[32] The corporatist model engenders consensus and a sense of global responsibility, but here was a case where the government stepped in and changed the rules. The cost containment act of 1977 created a National Health Conference (Konzertierte Aktion) consisting of all stakeholders, state and federal. It mandated that the Conference develop annually a consensus on expenditure caps, by type of service, which would then be monitored by Monitoring Committees in each state. The Committees had to profile the charges of each doctor, and if they were excessive and not warranted, reimbursements could be cut. In the second half of the 1970s, expenditures as a percentage of GDP rose only 1.3 percent.

The government was equally successful in holding down increases during the 1980s, with only a 2.5 percent increase in the percent of GDP from 1980 to 1990.[33] This contrasts with a 31 percent increase for the U.S., from 9.2 to 12.1% GDP. Yet underlying this success was a constant need for the government to intervene because the profession was dominating the corporatist model and creating costly imbalances. The government, as the British so gracefully put it, clawed back many of the profession's postwar prerogatives and attempted through financial reforms to make the German health care system behave less like the hi-tech, highly professionalized system that it is. This was done largely through financial measures that ration providers and suppliers rather than benefits or patients. The Germans seem to understand the basic point that what something costs, or how much providers get paid, is separable from the product or service rendered. Doctors' incomes, or pharmaceutical profits, do not *have* to be at the level they are. The Germans have kept doctors' incomes from rising as fast as average wages for two decades. They also realize that a government does not have to bail out sickness funds when they have cost overruns. Rather, the government's role in a corporatist model is to restructure things so that the funds can control the providers more effectively.

Other reforms suggest the corporatist structure is being shifted towards a state-model system which aims to keep people healthy or get them better by thinking epidemiologically rather than clinically. For example, besides adding co-payments for drugs and services as patient disincentives against overuse, the first wave of reforms reintroduced global prospective budgets and set up tougher, more detailed utilization review by payers. Forms of capitation, which the medical profession had beaten back for decades, are back. These changes in effect redefine doctors, from autonomous professionals devoted to providing each patient with the best clinical medicine, to experts on a large team devoted to keeping people well at reasonable cost. In the mid 1980s, a second wave of laws brought hospitals under prospective global budgets and detailed treatment profiles. Even this was not enough, as the professionally driven system kept increasing and elaborating services, and in 1989 the most important law since 1911 was passed. From an historical and systemic point of view, its most important features included (1) breaking down the time-honored separation of hospital from office care in terms of waste and duplication in service and equipment; (2) adding a number of new preventive benefits, and (3) providing people who take care of the long-term sick with both monthly pay and four weeks of paid holiday.

To some with an historical perspective, these echoed some of the changes the East Germans made when they restructured their half of the system after the war. Such an analogy, however, is unthinkable in German policy circles today. Other state-model changes included (4) measures to restrict the number of doctors being admitted to practice with the sickness funds, to force older doctors to retire, and to restrict the number of students trained; (5) moving the service that reviews doctors' practice patterns to an independent, arms-length status and adding more measures of quality/cost review; (6) setting prices for and monitoring drugs; and (7) facilitating the closing of beds and hospitals, including permission for a fund to cancel a contract with an uneconomical hospital.[31,34] There is every sign that the legislative and executive branches, even after these fundamental changes, will intervene again as rule setter and referee, to restructure the German system even more toward the goals and structure of a state rather than a professional model.

Reforms at this basic level indicate that the corporatist model is barely working. Yet under intense pressure from the West German medical profession to bring its professionalized model of health care to the East, together with a general conviction that the West German way is the best way, unification has meant a grand dismantling of the East German system. As of fall 1992, observers reported that about 10,000 of the 14,000 doctors in East Germany were now in solo practice, a decision which almost no independent health care analyst would support given that the German medical profession and training system is not devoted to a sophisticated general practice model like the British. This transformation is heavily subsidized to look successful. Doctors are borrowing heavily to upgrade their facilities through government-sponsored loans with no payback for the first several years. At the same time, they are steadily moving up from receiving 60 percent of West German fees to 80 percent, a major jump in revenues for them.[35] These rates of pay far exceed what East Germans, with up to 30 percent unemployment, can pay in premiums; so operating costs too are heavily supported from the West.

The deeper point here is that the (West) German medical lobby and government are extending to their Eastern half the professionally oriented system which is breaking down in their own backyard and which is ill-suited either to the health needs of East German communities or to the 21st century. Realization is growing in some quarters that the old, quaint mutual-aid or community model may be the one that works best. For example, German citizens have created thousands of community-based, voluntary organizations to provide kinds of care that even their comprehensive medical delivery system does not offer. These center around coping with chronic problems as well as promoting healthier life styles. This is the ingredient which only the mutual-aid model has that fits the needs of future populations, with so many long-term disabilities, problems, and risks through a very long life span: *local involvement.* At its heart are people talking, listening, helping, advocating, and working together so that the culture and way of life changes as well as medical services. This idea is informing the most advanced parts of the NHS reforms in Great Britain, where the purchasing of primary, secondary, and community health care are being combined with a national prevention program around the health needs of communities.[36] In the United States, a similar animus informs such groups as The Healthcare Forum and the communitarian movement.[37,38] Yet professionalized medical care will not yield easily; for it is one of the major growth industries of the 21st century, with heavy commitments from governments and universities. For the long-term success of health care reform, one needs to go beyond financial solutions to the cost containment issues and incorporate the values of the mutual-aid or community model, with a focus on prevention, illness management, and community change.

REFERENCES

1. Conrad P. and Schneider J.W. *Deviance and Medicalization: From Badness to Sickness.* (ex-

panded edition.) Philadelphia: Temple University Press. 1992.

2. Roemer M.I. Introduction, in *National Health Systems of the World* Vol. 1:3–10. Oxford University Press. New York. 1991.

3. Pg. 5 in Field M.G. *Success and Crisis in National Health Systems: A Comparative Approach*. New York: Routledge. 1989.

4. Saltman R.B., ed., *The International Handbook of Health-Care Systems*. Westport, Conn.: Greenwood Press. 1988.

5. Raffel M.W. *Comparative Health Systems*. University Park, Penn.: Pennsylvania State University Press. 1984.

6. Leichter H.M. *A Comparative Approach to Policy Analysis*. New York: Cambridge University Press. 1979.

7. Widman M. and D. W. Light. On Methods: The Paradox of Comparative Policy Research. Pp. 587–595 in Light D.W. and Schuller A.S. eds. *Political Values and Health Care: The German Experience*. Boston: The M.I.T. Press. 1986.

8. Zelizer V. The Social Meaning of Money: 'Special Monies'. *American Journal of Sociology* 95:614 634. 1989.

9. Peters H. *Geschichte der Sozialversicherung*. Bad Godesberg. 1959.

10. Rimlinger G.V, *Welfare Policy and Industrialization in Europe, America, and Russia*. New York: John Wiley & Sons. 1971.

11. Pg. 9 in Abel-Smith B. *Value for Money in Health Services: A Comparative Study*. New York: St. Martin's Press. 1976.

12. Pg. 110 in Rosenberg P. The origin and the development of compulsory health insurance in Germany. Pp. 105–126 in Light D.W. and Schuller A. eds. *Political Values and Health Care: The German Experience*. Boston: The M.I.T. Press. 1986.

13. Pg. 114 in Jones A. ed. *Professions and the State*. Philadelphia: Temple University Press. 1991.

14. Lifton R.A. *Nazi Doctors: Medical Killing and the Psychology of Genocide*. New York: Basic. 1988.

15. Light D. Learning from their mistakes? *Health Service Journal* 100 (5221), 1740–1472, 1990.

16. Craig G. *Germany: 1860–1945*, Ch. V. New York: Oxford. 1978.

17. See ref. 8, 11, 13, and pg. 53 in Stone D. A. *The Limits of Professional Power: National Health Care and the Federal Republic of Germany*. Chicago: University of Chicago Press. 1980.

18. Plaut T. *Der Gwerkschaftskampf der Deutschen Artze*. Karlsruhe: G. Braunsche. 1913.

19. Kaznelson S. ed. *Juden im deutschen Kultur-berich: Ein Sammelwerk*. Berlin: Juedischer verlag. 1962.

20. Acherknecht E.H. German Jews, English dissenters and French protestants as pioneers of modern medicine and science during the 19th century. In Rosenberg C. ed. *Health and Healing: Essays for George Rosen*. New York: Neale Watson. 1979.

21. Naschold F. *Kassenarzte und Krankenversicherungsreform: Zu einer Theorie der Statuspolitik*. Freiberg im Breisgau: Rombach. 1967.

22. *Zentrales Staatsarchiv* RAM. 5361, pp. 317–318. Quoted from archival work done by Leibfried S. and Tennstedt F. See, for example, their essay, "Health-Insurance Policy and Berufsverbote in the Nazi Takeover." Pp. 127–184 in Light D.W. and Schuller A.S. eds. *Political Values and Health Care: The German Experience*. Boston: The M.I.T. Press. 1986.

23. Pg. 157 in Kater M.H. *The Nazi Party: A Social Profile of Members and Leaders 1919–1945*. Cambridge, Mass.: Harvard University Press. 1983.

24. Leibfried S. and Tennstadt F. See ref. in 21 above.

25. Stadtarchiv Bremerhaven: F 288.

26. Rosen G. "The evolution of social medicine." Pp. 23–50 in Freeman H.E., Levine S., Reeder L.G. eds. *Handbook of Medical Sociology*. Englewood Cliffs, NJ: Prentice-Hall. 1979.

27. Henning A. Mother and child care. Pp. 443–468 in Light D. and Schuller A. eds. *Political Values and Health Care: The German Experience*. Boston: M.I.T. Press. 1986.

28. Pg. 84 in Keiner G. The question of induced abortion. Pp. 425–468 in Light and Schuller.

29. Hurst J. Reform of health care in Germany. *Health Care Financing Review* 12 (3):84.

30. Starr P. *The Social Transformation of American Medicine*. New York: Basic. 1982.

31. Scheiber G.J., Poullier J-P. International health care expenditures trends: 1987. *Health Affairs* 8(3) 1989: 169–177.

32. Reinhardt U.E. Health insurance and health policy in the federal republic of Germany. *Health Care Financing Review* 3(2) 1981: 1–14.

33. This is based on Scheiber and Poullier's 1989 figure for 1980 (7.9% GDP) and their 1992 figure for 1990 (8.1% GDP). See Scheiber G.J., Poullier J-P, and Greenwald L.M. U.S. health expenditure performance: an international comparison and data update. *Health Care Financing Review* 13(3) 1992: 1–88. However, in the latter article, they put the 1980 figure at 8.4%.

34. Schneider M. Health care cost containment in the Federal Republic of Germany. *Health Care Financing Review* 12(3) 1991: 87–101.

35. Based on interviews with medical sociologists and research physicians who made extensive visits to the Eastern parts of Germany in 1992.
36. North West Thames Regional Health Authority. *Strategic Framework 1993/4-196/7.* London. 1992.
37. Etzioni A., ed. *The Responsive Community* (a quarterly journal).
38. Shortell S.M. A model for state health care reform. *Health Affairs* 11(1) 1992: 108–127.

43

Canada's Health Insurance and Ours: The Real Lessons, the Big Choices

▪ ▪ ▪ ▪ ▪ ▪

Theodore R. Marmor and Jerry L. Mashaw

As medical costs continue to escalate and more Americans find themselves without insurance, Canada's approach to financing health care has taken center stage in the debate in the United States. Congressional committees have invited Canadian experts to testify, and political organizations have sent parades of representatives on crash study tours to Canada. Leaders of the Chrysler Corporation—particularly its flamboyant chairman, Lee Iacocca, and Joseph A. Califano, Jr., a board member and former Secretary of Health and Human Services—have lauded Canada's success. All three television networks, National Public Radio, the major national newspapers, and *Consumer Reports* have recently done stories on Canadian national health insurance.

. . . .

Canada's national health system has managed to insure all citizens for a comprehensive range of medical and hospital services, all the while containing medical costs. Contrary to reports, serious limitations on medically necessary services are not common. Moreover, the system is vastly more popular among Canadians than America's health system is among our citizens. Universal access, controlled costs, good care, a satisfied public—when taken together, no fair-minded American can help but be impressed, particularly because so many experts have been telling us that we could not possibly achieve all these goals together.

. . . Canada is not the only country that has provided universal health care at a lower proportionate cost than the United States spends for more restricted coverage. France and West Germany have universal health insurance at a cost of between 8 and 9.5 percent of gross national product (GNP). Britain, Japan, and Australia do it for between 6 and 8 percent of GNP. The United States, by comparison, spends 11.5 percent of GNP on health—more than any other nation—and yet ranks below all of the advanced nations except Spain on measures of infant mortality and life expectancy. For all the money spent, we have approximately 35 million people totally without health insurance and other undetermined millions whose health insurance is inadequate. Surely we are doing something wrong.

When other countries are doing things we would like to do, it makes good sense to set aside national pride and learn from abroad. But we need to be careful in drawing lessons, particularly because the pressure groups in the United States with the largest stake in the status quo have powerful incentives to distort other nations' experience and slant information to their own purposes. With admirable frankness, Carl Schramm, president of the Health Insurance Association of America (HIAA), the trade association for private health insurance companies, told *Consumer Reports* that under a Canadian approach to health-care financing "we'd be out of business. It's a life-and-death struggle." Conceding it cannot make a credible case that Canadian health insurance is a failure, HIAA claims instead that American politics would never permit us to enact and carry out a Canadian-style program. Of course, the insurance industry would do its best to make sure that was true.

But if ever there were an opportunity for cross-national learning by American policy makers, it is Canada's path to national health insurance (NHI). We share with Canadians a diverse population with a similar distribution of living standards, increasingly integrated economies, and a tradition of fractious, constitutional federalism. Until Canada consolidated its national insurance in 1971, our patterns and styles of medical care closely resembled each other. Canadian regulators even used our Joint Commission on Hospital Accreditation to judge their own hospitals until well after World War II. If public financing of medical care has come to work well in Canada, it is reasonable to think it would work well in the United States, too.

In fact, Canada's health system raises three separable issues for the United States. The first is whether Canada really has an exemplary medical care system, well worth importing if only we could.

A second question is whether Canada's program, no matter how desirable, is politically feasible in the United States. Are the two nations just too different? Is it too late to do what the Canadians did more than twenty years ago?

And, third, even if the Canadian model is desirable and politically acceptable, can the United States successfully adapt it to American circumstances?

Canada's Exemplary Performance

Health insurance in Canada is actually provided not by the national government but by Canada's ten provinces. The Canadian federal government conditionally promises to repay each province a substantial portion of the costs of all necessary medical care, now roughly 40 percent. The federal grant is available as long as the province's health insurance program is *universal* (covering all citizens), *comprehensive* (covering all conventional hospital and medical care), *accessible* (no limits on services or extra charges to patients), *portable* (each province must recognize the others' coverage), and *publicly administered* (under control of a public, nonprofit organization).

Annual negotiations between provincial governments and the providers of care determine the total budgets of hospitals and the level of physicians fees. As in the United States, most hospitals are nonprofit community institutions. Unlike U.S. hospitals, they never worry about itemized billings. Instead, they receive their annual budget in monthly installments. Their budgets are adjusted each year, taking into account inflation, new programs, and changes in their volume of services.

As in the United States, physicians practice in diverse individual and group settings and most are paid on a fee-for-service basis rather than by salary. The provincial medical associations determine the structure of a binding fee schedule and negotiate with their governments, usually on an annual basis, a percentage increase in the total pool of money budgeted for paying physicians. In most provinces, if the fees billed to the provincial insurance fund exceed the budget ceiling, the government grants less than it otherwise would at the next round of negotiations. Escalating physician costs—largely because of increases in procedures per patient—have led most Canadian provinces to explore more explicit limits on total payments to physicians. Quebec and British Columbia have already set global budget caps—which, if exceeded, result in reduced physician

Figure 43-1. *Health Expenditures in the United States and Canada as Percent of Gross National Product*

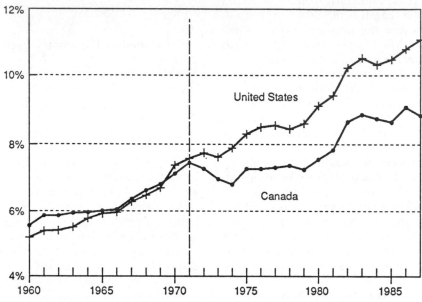

1971: Enactment of Canadian National Health Insurance

fees—and other provinces, despite predictable physician outrage, are likely to follow suit.

As Figure 43-1 shows, the growth patterns of Canadian and American health care expenditures were nearly identical until 1971, when Canada fully implemented its national insurance plan. From then on, American health expenditures have continued to rise at a considerably faster rate than in Canada (or, for that matter, any other developed democracy). The gap now amounts to nearly three percentage points of GNP. It appears that America's higher payments to doctors, increased administrative expenses, and larger hospital outlays account for about equal shares of this large difference in spending. Few Americans would regard Canada's lower physician payments as harmful; fewer still would regret cutting administrative costs. Some, however, might wonder whether the Canadians spend too much. Hospital technology is where the biggest questions about the Canadian system arise. Nonetheless, compared with other countries in the world, the oddity is America's lavish spending on technology, not Canada's more limited expenditures.

Cost control is not the only test of a good health care system. Neither is universal access. A good system should provide high quality care, timely treatment, good working conditions for health care professionals and other workers, and ultimately a satisfied and healthy citizenry. On these questions, it is time to separate myth from fact.

Myth 1: NHI Leads to Bureaucratic Red-Tape and High Administrative Costs

Doctors and hospitals in Canada receive all their payments from one source, a provincial ministry. They do not have to keep track of the eligibility requirements or complicated definitions of insured services in hundreds of insurance plans. Canadian patients never have to file claims, much less deal with incomprehensible forms. Americans, by contrast, have to file multiple, complicated claims, as do most physicians. One reason both patients and doctors in America fear any further government role in health insurance is their frustrating experience with Medicare and

Figure 43-2. *Costs of Health Insurance and Administration as Percent of Gross National Product*

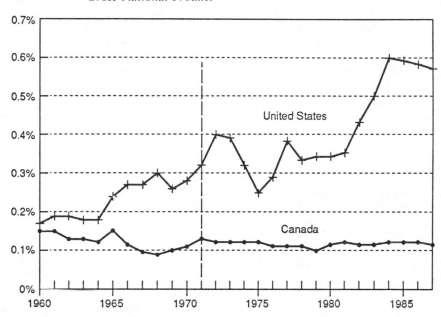

Medicaid. A federal agency recently estimated that about one million Medicare enrollees a year find filing claims so complicated or time-consuming that they do not seek reimbursement, losing about $100 million in benefits to which they are entitled. In some states many physicians say they will not treat Medicaid patients, or do not bother to seek reimbursement for treating them, because the meager payments do not even cover the administrative overhead. American providers typically wait 60 to 120 days and often longer for reimbursement from public programs. Canadian providers, in contrast, receive payment in about 30 days.

Because of the simplicity of the Canadian system, administrative costs are negligible by American standards. Moreover, the gap between U.S. and Canadian administrative costs has been widening steadily since Canada completed its program. (See Figure 43-2.) This six-to-one ratio clearly understates the real difference in cost. It does not count the paper-shuffling burden borne by American patients. Nor does it include the large proportion of recorded payments to doctors and hospitals that are really administrative over-

head required by our complex financing arrangements. "An increasing share of the sums Americans *think* they are spending on hospital and medical care," the Canadian economist Robert Evans notes, "are going in fact to pay for administrators, accountants, lawyers, public relations specialists, and other forms of personnel whose services are not usually considered as contributing to the health of patients."

Myth 2: NHI Interferes with the Doctor-Patient Relationship

One ad in the AMA series asks, "Elective surgery—should it be up to you?" The ad implies that Canada reduces the ordinary citizen's freedom of choice in medical care. It is a thinly veiled message to those Americans with either broad insurance coverage or ample funds to buy whatever care they desire. Seeking allies, the AMA represents Canadian-style reform as a threat to America's affluent and insured.

That same message, of course, will hold little appeal to the millions of Americans without the money or coverage to get elective surgery. Nor is it likely to appeal to Americans whose choice of doctor is limited by their health maintenance organization (HMO) or by lower reimbursement for visits to out-of-plan doctors (under so-called "preferred provider organizations," or PPOs). An increasing number of companies are trimming their health care costs by adopting these alternatives. Under the rubric of "managed care," many such plans limit elective surgery, require second opinions, or require approval by an insurance company administrator.

In Canada, by contrast, citizens have no restrictions on their choice of physicians, and their physicians do not have to obtain approval from administrators for treatment they recommend. If freedom of choice is the deciding criterion for many people, it actually works in favor of the Canadian model, not the forms of health care that are now growing most rapidly under the aegis of market-oriented reform in the United States.

Myth 3: NHI Leads to Long Queues for Treatment

Another advertisement in the AMA series pictures a worried woman and warns, "In some countries she could wait months for her surgery." Every country, including the United States, has waiting lists for elective procedures and sometimes even essential ones. The important question is the impact on the patients' well-being. Americans being treated in hospital emergency rooms, particularly in big cities, often wait for hours for critical care. Private hospitals routinely turn away uninsured patients, dumping them on the public sector. These "economic transfers," estimated at 250,000 annually in the United States, often result in serious delays in treatment, cause long-term harm, and have cost some patients their lives, though federal law now requires hospitals to assure that patients are in stable condition before transfer.

When most Canadians are sick or injured, they are cared for in a timely manner. Indeed, the overall rates of hospital use per capita are considerably higher in Canada than in the United States. Nonetheless, there have developed long waiting lists for some services, particularly for open-heart surgery and magnetic resonance imag-

ing, the newest radiological procedure for diagnosis. These delays typically reflect managerial problems and labor bottlenecks more than chronic shortages of facilities. If they involve patients in urgent, life-threatening condition, there is political outrage. Open-heart surgery is currently the most controversial example. Government officials in British Columbia watched their waiting list for cardiac surgery grow to more than 500 during 1990 and, in response, purchased surgery from Seattle hospitals with excess beds and heart surgeons. This incident is the sort that opponents of the Canadian system cite as illustrating its failure. But such cases reveal as much about American slack as Canadian restrictiveness—and they bring us to the next myth.

Myth 4: National Health Insurance Lowers the Quality of Medical Care

As Table 43-1 shows, some expensive, high-technology items are less available in Canada than in the United States. It is unclear, however, whether the rates of investment in such technologies in the United States represent a standard for judging other countries. Many analysts believe the United States has overinvested and overused some technologies. Hospitals competing for market share have installed equipment that stands idle much of the time or, even worse, is being used without good medical justification to generate reimbursement from insured patients. The fundamental patterns of investment in the United States have been distorted by differences in insurance coverage. There is no incentive to invest in preventive care if the health benefits are high but reimbursement is uncertain. There is every incentive to invest in high technology if health benefits are uncertain but reimbursement is assured.

Canada has a full range of high technology facilities, but there is considerably less abundance and little competition for market share. Expensive capital equipment is first approved only for specialized medical centers, and subsequent diffusion is closely controlled by provincial ministries of health. This control results in lower rates of cardiac surgery, magnetic resonance imaging, lithotripsy, and some other complex services. In

Table 43-1. Comparative Availability of Selected Medical Technologies: Units per Million Persons

	U.S.	Canada	Ratio :U.S/Canada
Open-heart surgery	3.26	1.23	2.7:1
Cardiac catheterization	5.06	1.50	3.4:1
Organ transplantation	1.31	1.08	1.2:1
Radiation therapy	3.97	0.54	7.4:1
Extracorporeal shock wave lithotripsy	0.94	0.16*	5.9:1
Magnetic-resonance imaging	3.69	0.46*	8.0:1

Notes: U.S. data from 1987, Canada for 1989 except where indicated *1988.
SOURCE: D.A. Rublee, "Medical Technology in Canada, Germany, and the U.S." *Health Affairs* (Fall 1989), 180.

some cases, these lower rates are probably appropriate: The additional use in the United States reflects incentives for overtreatment. In other cases, Canadians are not receiving services that would have some health benefit at a high cost (instead choosing to provide other forms of care and reserving more national income for other purposes). Of course, no nation can provide early service that would conceivably give someone benefit. The question is whether the Canadians are making a reasonable choice and providing medical care of high quality.

The quality of a nation's health care is never simple to measure. The United States certainly offers medical care of higher quality than does Canada if quality is defined as easier access to complex technologies regardless of their effectiveness. And American medical care may be the best in the world if quality is defined by the technologies and facilities available to the most privileged members of a population. But if we define quality by some measure that reflects both the effectiveness of treatment and the respect and consideration shown to patients—all patients, not just the affluent and insured—America ranks lower than other countries in the West, including Canada, that have national health insurance.

There is certainly no evidence of any Canadian disadvantage if our standard is the actual health of the public, though medical care is only one of the many factors affecting health and by no means the most important. (Canada actually has a clear advantage in life expectancy and infant mortality, but probably for reasons unrelated to

its system of health care finance.) And if consumer satisfaction is our basis for judgment, both polls and political behavior give a big edge to Canada.

According to a ten-nation survey published in *Health Affairs,* Canadians are the most satisfied and Americans the least satisfied with their country's health care system. While only 10 percent of Americans surveyed say their health system functions "pretty well," 56 percent of Canadians thought their health care system works well. Eighty-nine percent of Americans say their system needs "fundamental changes" or "complete rebuilding."

The higher levels of satisfaction in Canada suggest the importance of the distributive dimension of health care quality. Major aspects of American medical care—the widespread inability to obtain health insurance, the limited extent of immunization, the large number of pregnant women without regular medical attention, and the risk of bankruptcy from illness—would be considered intolerable in other comparably wealthy nations. Canada has fewer centers of technological excellence, but the average level of care is, by any definition, at least the equal of that in the United States.

Myth 5: NHI Leads to Rationing

Critics warn that Canada "rations" medical care. If by rationing they simply mean limiting services, every country in the world rations health care. The question is how and how much. The

United States limits services by ability to pay and, accordingly, shows significant differences in access to health care by race, class, and employment cirumstances. By contrast, Canada and most other developed countries attempt to provide more uniform access to the entire population. Medical care then depends more on a professional assessment of medical need than on insurance status.

Rationing, in this context, is another name for allocation. Whether it is objectionable depends also on the extent of free choice and the distribution of control. Americans in HMOs and other systems of "managed care" face systems of corporate rationing; the rules for rationing are matters of business strategy. To be sure, some employees in the United States are offered a choice among such plans, but they are hardly in a position to know much about how the HMOs control their spending. They have no way of knowing, for example, whether an HMO might deny them referral to a specialist in the event of a rare disease or difficult procedure. Because Canadians have free choice of physician, they do not have to worry about that kind of rationing. And while the rationing choices of an American HMO are private, Canada's choices about spending on hospitals and other health services are publicly debated and democratically decided. If Canadians come to feel that they should spend more on high technology services, their system allows them to do so more efficiently and equitably than does ours.

Myth 6: NHI Causes an Exodus of Physicians

Some Canadian physicians were coming to the United States long before Canada introduced national health insurance. Emigration did not increase significantly afterwards. The numbers of emigrants to the U.S. has always been small, never enough to offset a steady increase in the number of Canadian physicians. The ratio of physicians to population has steadily increased and actually grown closer to the U.S. level. In 1987 we had 234 doctors per 100,000 people, while Canada had 216.

Stories about deep discontent among Canadian physicians are much exaggerated. Physicians were the highest-paid professionals in Canada

prior to the introduction of universal medical insurance; they still are. When national health insurance began, the provincial governments accepted the existing fee schedules of provincial medical associations, although in most provinces payments were initially set somewhat below 100 percent to reflect the elimination of doctors' risks of unpaid debts. Since that time, provincial medical associations and ministries of health have negotiated changes. Since much of the bargaining for resources and control gets carried out in the public arena, these negotiations are contentious. Provincial ministers of finance typically forecast imminent bankruptcy; medical associations threaten dire service cutbacks if they don't get more money; and the media, always hungry for conflict, seize on the extremes of these positions. These controversies sell newspapers; they do not mean the system is about to collapse.

Is It Politically Feasible Here?

Skeptics claim that the United States and Canada are too different to borrow from each other. Americans are allegedly too individualistic to accept a government program. Skeptics also argue that the United States, with its elaborate checks and balances, cannot adapt programs from a parliamentary system.

But the same arguments could as easily have been offered in 1935 against Social Security or at other times against other national programs. In fact, Canadian doctors remain in individual practice, and Canadians choose freely what practitioners to consult. It is unclear that America's current system represents any higher level of individualism.

Moreover, just as the Canadians have set up their program on a federal basis, so might we. The impediments to borrowing the Canadian model do not lie much in the structure of government. They lie in the power of the opposition. America's political leaders have traditionally allowed the providers and insurers of health care to control the substance of policy and boundaries of debate. Is it true, as Stanford economist Alain Enthoven argues, that borrowing from Canada is "off the radar screen of American possibility"? A good many people have an interest in maintaining that assumption and thereby contribute to keeping fundamental changes off the radar screen and off the agenda.

We are hardly sanguine that Canadian-style reform is likely in the near term. Nevertheless, the Canadian approach has growing support from unlikely quarters. Like Chrysler's Lee Iacocca, many large employers see themselves threatened in international and domestic markets by the high costs of insuring their employees. The small business community is pleading for government help because their health insurance costs are even more onerous. In 1989 the American Chamber of Commerce, eschewing free market ideology and its usual preference for state and local authority, called for federal legislation guaranteeing small employers health insurance options at reasonable rates. Employers large and small see a clear likelihood that they will soon be required to pay for health insurance for both their own employees and others currently uninsured. All around the country, state governments are seeking the equivalent of universal health insurance.

The opposition of private insurance companies to health insurance reform is changing, too. Making money on health insurance is not easy these days. Relentless medical inflation, costly technology, a growing number of doctors, and an aging population have put the insurance industry repeatedly on the wrong side of the cost curve. More important, consumer hostility to insurers is fueling demands for legislative action. The insurers are seeking a solution that will bring insurance to the uninsured, make less visible the industry's practice of "skimming" (competing for the healthiest customers and ignoring or pricing out the less healthy), and yet leave the future administration of health insurance to them rather than to the state. They fear a political choice between a universal, mandated private insurance program, with substantial regulation of terms and rates, and a state-run insurance scheme that eliminates their role entirely.

Of course, no one should be misled about the recent, death-bed conversion of the health insurers to industry reform. They are as resistant as ever to a Canadian-style plan and have fully participated in the mythmaking about Canada's supposed unsuitability to American circum-

stances. After all, administrative costs to citizens and policy-holders are income to the industry. But this truism should not obscure the defensiveness of the health insurers, their inclination to discuss reform, and the greater likelihood in the present climate that they might be forced to accept terms they publicly say are unacceptable.

Finally, U.S. physicians are increasingly aware that they cannot avoid regulation. Their actions and decisions are already being scrutinized and limited by hospitals, insurance companies, and governmental agencies, all seeking to control costs. Looking at Canada's Medicare, they should be struck by the independence of Canadian physicians, the preservation of fee-for-service practice, and the reduction of bureaucracy, particularly as it affects physicians' everyday practice. If they can overcome their reflexive rejection of government, American physicians will find that a Canadian-style alternative has considerable advantages for their profession—and their patients.

The obstacles to reform of American medical care, nonetheless, are enormous. Medical expenditures now divided among the government, employers, private insurance companies, and consumers would have to be converted or channeled into publicly controllable funds. American politicians would have to be willing to put aside their fixation with where costs are counted and deal with real issues of public economics—how much is spent overall, for what, and on whose behalf. The complaints of pro-market commentators would have to be answered, a task that is much harder now than during the fight over Medicare because free-market ideology has gained influence in economics and policy analysis. Ideology would have to be countered with pragmatic argument, illusion with fact; and all this would have to be done by politicians who were elected by running against government.

Yet there are the makings of a political compromise here. The public wants broadened, simplified, and stable coverage at reasonable out-of-pocket cost. Firms want to reduce their costs of insuring employees and, at the very least, to avoid paying for the health insurance of the unemployed and uninsured. Insurers fear that they may be in a new ball game in which at best they will be the unwelcome administrators of so-called managed care and at worst they may be excluded from the market. Perhaps they could manage everyone's care on behalf of state insurance schemes. Or, at least, some insurers might play this reduced administrative role, as was the case in Ontario during the mid-1960s. In short, although movement toward something like Canadian national health insurance may appear ideologically a large step, most of the pieces needed for a state insurance program are already in place, and interest-group politics might join with popular sentiment to permit such a move.

What would it take to make the Canadian model work in the United States? Part of the answer lies in distinguishing the necessary from the incidental elements of the Canadian success story. We see two essential elements:

- ▪ Near universality of coverage: Canadians in each province are in the same boat, all insured on the "same terms and conditions." Universality has made it politically impossible to deal with cost pressures by cutting the benefits or eligibility of some people.
- ▪ Clear concentration of responsibility: Canadians lodge financing responsibility in a ministry of health or its equivalent. Financing medical care under concentrated rather than fragmented auspices eliminates the administrative costs of multiple payers. Furthermore, it creates more leverage in bargaining with providers. Concentrating responsibility also means leaders cannot disguise costs by shifting them to other groups of patients. All this adds up to clear political accountability: Canadians know whom to hold accountable for the cost and quality of their health care.

What sorts of changes could be made in these elements without losing what has been necessary for Canada's relatively successful experience?

Modified Universalism

Canada's universalism is strong in two ways. Every Canadian belongs to the same provincial health insurance plan as his neighbor and enjoys the same coverage under the plan. Private insurers are legally forbidden to sell coverage duplicating publicly insured services, though they may provide supplementary coverage for such things

as private rooms in hospitals or outpatient prescription drugs.

To maintain the "equal terms" of access, Canadian doctors have been barred since 1984 from charging patients anything above the government's fee schedule (a practice known as "balance billing" or "extra billing"). In these respects, Canada is probably more egalitarian than any other comparable industrial democracy.

Perhaps not all of these features of Canadian universalism are necessary to an acceptable and workable form of health insurance. Canada itself did not start with such a firmly egalitarian version. The Hall Commission of 1964–66, a governmental commission that helped lay the foundations of Canada's current program, defined universal as no less than 95 percent of the citizens within each province. The political force of universality arises not from complete inclusiveness but from the breadth of the constituency affected. (Our public water supply is closely monitored even if a few people drink bottled water exclusively.)

There is consequently no reason for American reformers to insist on Canada's very strong contemporary form of universal enrollment. Universal health insurance means providing insurance to all, not necessarily requiring that everyone share exactly the same system. About a tenth of the West German population opts for more expensive commercial insurance without impairing the rest of the system. There is a zone of adaptation and compromise between identical treatment and unacceptably different treatment. What is essential is that the health insurance boat include most Americans on roughly comparable terms, not that all the boat's cabins be the same size or have the same view.

American public schools are a good analogy. Where state and local arrangements keep public schools strong, the competition of private alternatives does not undermine public support and school quality. But the balance is delicate and easily upset. We cannot force Americans to use public health insurance any more than public schools. But we should worry a lot if many citizens take up the private option. The public program must be sufficiently attractive that most citizens will want to be included.

Would it be acceptable to permit physicians or

other medical professionals to be paid on a fee-for-service basis to bill for more than the insurance program provided? The answer here is clear. The capacity to contain medical costs depends on establishing firm limits. Balance billing allows providers to escape those limits; it reintroduces barriers to access that universal health insurance is meant to lower. No successful national health insurance program has permitted this practice for long. Canada found over time that balance billing became a serious problem in many communities, threatening both the uniformity of citizen treatment and access to treatment itself.

Concentrating Financial Control

Cross-national evidence suggests that it is the *concentration* of financial responsibility, not its precise location, that is crucial to countervailing inflationary health pressures. It so happens that Canada, by constitutional requirement, had no choice but to use provincial governments to administer health insurance. Great Britain, by contrast, concentrates financial responsibility in the national ministry of health, and Sweden does so in each of its county councils. The lesson for the United States is that there are options here.

The more difficult question is whether Canada's public financing and direct governmental administration are required for political accountability. Public financing—through earmarked provincial premiums and various federal and provincial taxes—makes Canadian outlays for health care highly visible. At the same time, Canadian provinces could, and some did, use existing health insurance companies as political buffers between physicians and government. In Ontario in the mid-1960s, private companies served as "post office" intermediaries for the flow of funds and the processing of claims. Such a buffer seemed terribly important then, a concession to the deeply felt hostility of many Canadian doctors to government medical insurance. In fact, the provinces that used financial intermediaries at the outset gave them up within a few years. They made administration complicated and expensive and, once their role in moderating conflict was no longer necessary, they seemed useless (except to the insurance companies).

One can certainly imagine the use of such intermediaries in the United States. This, after all, has been the pattern with our own Medicare since 1965—an arrangement that draws upon private expertise and "economizes" on the number of public employees. The Canadians, we should clearly note, found such indirect management cumbersome and more expensive than direct administration. But contracting out of financial tasks is certainly, on the Canadian evidence, compatible with political accountability. Were this a vital element in an American compromise, giving some limited role to the health insurance industry would not be devastating.

In the United States of the 1990s, the crucial political problem facing national health insurance advocates may not be the clout of the health insurance industry, but the public's hostility toward increased taxes. It is worth pondering whether it is possible to have the right level of countervailing power without the fusion of taxing power and negotiating responsibility in a single public agency. What would be lost if, for example, state regulatory authorities set the terms of medical care finance, negotiated with hospitals and physicians, and required that employers finance health insurance directly or pay into a state fund a fixed amount per employee?

In West Germany, national and state governments constrain the negotiations among physicians, hospitals, and the thousands of sickness funds without channeling social insurance financing through the public budget. But the U.S. lacks the German history of lifelong membership with one health insurance institution and the tradition of "corporatist" bargaining between payers and providers.

Financing medical care out of general tax revenues, as in Great Britain and in Canada, does seem to reinforce constraints on medical inflation. Other government departments are dependent on the same tax revenues and are, in effect, organized constituencies for controlling health costs. Although contrary to the "privatization" mythology of recent years, there is a strong positive relationship between public finance of health care and cost control.

Important as it is to concentrate taxing, negotiating, and budgeting power, concentration alone will not constrain health costs. The political will to restrain health care costs is itself a necessary ingredient for success. In the early years of Canadian hospital insurance, budget overruns were very common, and the provincial governments typically covered the deficit. In later years, deficits were much less generously treated and hospital administrators who did not play by those rules often lost their positions. Some version of a spending target—with serious consequences for missing the mark—is crucial for the containment of health care costs. That is not a matter of administrative architecture or policy technique.

American health economists have persistently advised that making patients pay a portion of their hospital and doctor bills is essential to cost containment. Cost-sharing by patients is said to make them cost-conscious and more restrained in their use of medical care. Cost-sharing, of course, adds millions of additional payers to the system

of financing, with all the extra administrative costs that entails. Moreover, cost-sharing threatens equity of access by raising the price of medical care to patients who may not be able to afford it. But the real lesson from abroad is that significant patient cost-sharing is unnecessary to control medical inflation. With negligible cost-sharing, Canada and Western Europe all achieve greater cost-control than we do.

The message conveyed to the American public since 1975—that less reliance on government is the key to controlling medical costs—needs to be challenged. That is partly why the Canadian example has become so important. Canada's experience shows that the choice Americans have given themselves—increasing access or controlling costs—is false. We have another alternative. The reality, bluntly put, is that as a nation we cannot afford to do without sensibly structured national health insurance. That is what the public says it wants. And it is what the country genuinely needs.

44

Continuity and Change in the British National Health Service

▪ ▪ ▪ ▪ ▪ ▪

Jonathan Gabe

Introduction

The British National Health Service (NHS), since its inception nearly half a century ago, has frequently been recognized as providing an alternative model to the predominantly private health insurance based system found in the United States. For some American commentators the NHS appears to be the answer to escalating

health care costs, spiralling medical negligence cases and gross inequalities in access to health care. For others it represents the worst aspects of centralized planning and collectivism, restricted by underfunding, an inability to keep pace with the latest medical advances and a lack of responsiveness to consumer demand.

This chapter will attempt to provide an account of the British model of health care organization and in so doing offer a basis for assessing these competing versions of reality. It will start by briefly documenting the origins of the NHS and the way in which its structure derived from attempts to resolve the competing claims of different interest groups. Consideration will then be given to the achievements and failures of the health service, especially prior to its reorganization in the late 1980s. The consequences of this reorganization for the social relations of health care within the NHS and for the boundary between public and private health care provision will then be assessed.

The Origins of the NHS

The National Health Service became a reality in July 1948, two years after it was established under the NHS Act. It represented a radical departure from the previous system of health care organization in Britain, with health care being provided free to all at the point of delivery and funded mainly by direct taxation, with limited finance from social insurance contributions.

The new service rested on four principles—collectivism, comprehensiveness, equality and universalism.[1] It was accepted that the state should take responsibility for the health of all its citizens and that the service provided should be comprehensive. The new service was also expected to be of a uniformly high standard throughout the country and to be available to everyone, free at the point of use.

Under the new arrangements hospitals were to be nationalized and organized on a regional basis, with consultants and their juniors being paid a salary for the hours worked. Community based General Practitioners (GPs) (and other professionals such as dentists), on the other hand, remained independent entrepreneurs who determined how and where they worked and were to be paid by a capitation fee for each NHS patient on their list. Both consultants and GPs could still undertake private practice but the conditions under which they did so were somewhat different. A patient consulting a GP privately would have to pay both a fee and the full cost of any prescription. The hospital consultant, on the other hand, having seen a patient privately, could admit them as an NHS patient to be treated at the

public's expense.[2] The third element of the system, alongside hospitals and general practice, was the local authorities. They were to provide domiciliary care such as health visiting and environmental and preventive services.

These reforms had not been achieved without a struggle. The post-war Labour government and in particular its Minister of Health, Aneurin Bevan, had had to work hard to persuade the different sections of the medical profession to join the service and the resulting arrangements reflected the compromises he had had to make. For instance he won over the influential hospital consultants by giving up plans for local authority control of hospital services and agreeing to their nationalization. This shift to national state ownership was seen by the consultants as the best way of generating the resources needed for the development of scientific medicine.[3] At the same time the teaching hospitals, in which many of the more influential consultants worked, were advantaged by an agreement to finance them directly from the Ministry of Health. These doctors were also persuaded by plans to allow them to maintain a high degree of control over their conditions of employment (e.g., deciding promotions and additional payments through merit awards) and clinical decision making (almost regardless of explicit resource implications) and to continue to undertake private work. As Bevan subsequently put it, he had won the support of the consultants by "stuffing their mouths with gold."[4]

General Practitioners, represented by the British Medical Association, were for the most part also persuaded at the eleventh hour by the offer of continuing independent status, free from the constraints of the local authorities. In addition, they retained clinical autonomy to prescribe and refer patients to hospital specialists at their own discretion. This countered the trend to increasing specialization found in the US and elsewhere and made sure that general practice survived in Britain.[1]

In addition to winning the support of most of the medical profession Bevan was also able to count on the backing of the civil servants and administrators, or "rational paternalists,"[5] who were responsible for negotiating the future form of the health service. Apparently they favored a move to a National Health Service less on grounds of righting social injustice than because of what they perceived as organizational incompetence and inefficiency.

Moreover, the time was ripe for change. Over the previous two decades dissatisfaction about the funding and organization of the existing National Health Insurance (NHI) based system had grown. In the 1930s the NHI scheme was facing increasing financial difficulties as those covered found themselves unable to pay their premiums, and influential voices criticized the service's organizational arrangements for being fragmentary and muddled.[6] In addition, there appeared to be widespread public support for change, especially amongst the labour movement whose support for the war effort between 1939 and 1945 had arguably been underpinned by the promise of a health service (in the Beveridge Report of 1942) that would meet the needs of the people.[7] And the war had already resulted in the government creating a temporary administrative framework for co-ordinating both public and private hospitals on a regional basis. Such an experience was said to have "brought home to all concerned the failings of Britain's hospital system."[8]

These circumstances thus provided a favorable context for the radical changes which the Labour government had proposed. As we have seen, however, they were won at the price of the medical profession's continuing autonomy.

The Strengths and Weaknesses of the NHS

When the NHS was first established it was naively assumed that it would lead to a reduction in health care costs as avoidable problems of ill health were cleared up and demand declined.[9] In practice, along with other industrialized countries, the NHS soon found that demand continued to outstrip supply, partly as a result of an ageing population and heightened patient and doctor expectations following medical advances in diagnosis and treatment.

Against this background, how successful has the NHS been in providing an economical and equitable health service that meets patients' needs? In financial terms the NHS has had some success, although supporters have long argued that it has suffered from underfunding. From the start there was a lack of political will to commit the resources necessary to meet Bevan's remit for the service.[9] With the government determining and controlling the level of overall spending to meet health needs, costs were, for the most part, rigidly contained. By 1960, however, shortcomings in the service such as long waiting lists and dilapidated hospital buildings were so apparent that the Conservative government was forced to increase expenditure and subsequent governments have followed suit. Between 1960 and 1975 the NHS's share of the Gross National Product (GNP) rose from 3.8% to 5.7%. During the 1980s expenditure stayed at 6.1% but increased to 6.6% in 1991.[10] Despite this increase the UK still spends significantly less of its GNP on health compared with other OECD countries, and in particular Canada and the US (see Table 44-1). Moreover, its administrative costs are said to be substantially less than other countries, amounting to less than 5%, compared with 10% in France and 20% in the US.[11]

The desire to control NHS costs has also resulted in the introduction of direct charges for some services, thereby breaking with the principle of free treatment. In 1951 the Labour government imposed charges for spectacles and dentures and the Conservatives followed suit later in the year by introducing prescription charges.[9] Thereafter both Labour and Conservative governments gradually increased charges,

Table 44-1. Health Expenditure as a Proportion of Gross Domestic Product

Country	% of GDP on Public and Private Health Care (1991)
Canada	10.0
France	9.1
Germany	8.5
Greece	5.2
Netherlands	8.3
Sweden	8.6
UK	6.6
US	13.4

SOURCE: OECD/CREDES databank (cited in Abel-Smith 1994).

although with varying degrees of enthusiasm. For instance, in the mid 1970s the Labour government held down health charges so that they constituted only 2% of NHS expenditure. Since 1979, however, Conservative administrations have increased income derived from charges to approximately 4% of NHS expenditure, with prescription charges increasing by 2300% between 1979 and 1994.[12] These increases have been offset to some extent by exemptions but it is generally accepted that it has had the effect of reducing service demand, especially by the poor and the elderly.[9]

At the same time budgetary constraints have helped to explain why the UK has adopted new medical technologies more slowly and in smaller quantities than other countries. Despite being at the forefront of many technological advances from artificial hips to CT scanners, their uptake in the UK has often been relatively slow when compared with, say, other European countries. For instance, in 1986 there were 2.7 CT scanners per million inhabitants in the UK compared with 6.9 in Germany and 4.6 in Denmark.[13] A similar variability, with the UK low down the league, is found in data for the number of patients receiving kidney dialysis or with functioning kidney transplants. In 1986 242 patients per million were treated for irreversible kidney failure in the UK compared with 333 per million in West Germany and 392 per million in Belgium.[14] Likewise, the volume of medicines consumed in the UK is well below the European Community average[15] (see Table 44-2).

It would thus seem that the NHS has been reasonably economical but what has been the cost in terms of health care provision? How equitable a service has the NHS provided? And has it provided equal access to all citizens regardless of where they live, their class, gender or race? In terms of equitable spatial distribution the NHS seems to have had some success. In 1948 one of the most glaring inequalities was in the unequal distribution of GPs, with inner cities and socially isolated rural areas being particularly poorly served. The NHS attempted to tackle the situation by requiring GPs who wanted to set up practice to apply for permission to do so, with those wanting to practice in "over-doctored" areas being turned down. As a result the propor-

Table 44-2. Consumption of Pharmaceuticals in the European Community, 1987

Country	Volume of Drugs Consumed per Person*
Belgium	210
France	292
Greece	74
Netherlands	75
Italy	174
Spain	105
UK	100
West Germany	168
European Community average	149

*The volume data are scaled so that the UK consumption is defined as 100.
SOURCE: Burstall 1990.

tion of the population in "under-doctored" areas fell sharply from around 50% in 1952 to less than 2% in 1982.[16] Within Inner London, however, access to GPs has remained relatively poor.[17]

Attempts to reduce regional inequalities in access to hospital facilities took rather longer to develop and, as a result, inherited spatial inequalities became "entrenched."[12] It was not until 1975 that the Labour government established the Resource Allocation Working Party (RAWP) to calculate the needs of each region by size of population (controlling for age and gender) and standardized mortality ratios. The resources required to meet the regions' needs in terms of these criteria were then compared with actual revenue and distributed accordingly.

In addition to spatial inequality there is also the question of inequality of access and use by class, gender and race. Studies concerned with class differences in access and use have presented a rather mixed picture. It seems that working class people use NHS general practitioners and hospital out patient services more than those from other social classes, but they also have greater need as a larger proportion of them are ill at any one time.[18] When it comes to illness prevention and health promotion, however, those in lower occupational groups who are in greatest need make the least use of the services provided. Class differences have been found in the use of family planning clinics, ante-natal classes, immunization, well men clinics and screening for cervical cancer.[18,19]

There is also some evidence that the quality of care provided varies by class. Studies of general practice consultations indicate that better-off patients have longer consultations and ask for and are given more explanations.[20] Such preferential treatment however does not necessarily lead to a better understanding of the information provided by the doctors. One study which observed GP consultations and then interviewed the patients found that while better-off patients were slightly less likely to misunderstand what they had been told, their commitment to treatment was similar to that of other social classes.[21]

These class variations are in turn reinforced by gender and racial inequalities. For example, while women have benefitted from much greater access to medical care under the NHS, their needs have only been partially met.[22] While they are more likely than men to suffer from chronic, degenerative illnesses treatment for these illnesses on the NHS has been underresourced compared with treatments for acute illnesses.[23] At the same time women tend to find that their experiences continue to be devalued in comparison with the "expert" knowledge of their doctors and consequently end up as the passive victims of these doctors' ministrations.[24] This experience is most commonly reported by women in pregnancy and childbirth, although some NHS maternity units have recently developed strategies to enable women to be more active participants in their own labor.[24]

Similarly, class differences in access and use of services are exacerbated by racial factors. While black people use the NHS less than white people because of their younger demographic profile— relatively few are over 65 years of age—the services that they do use tend to be of poorer quality. This is because black people are concentrated in inner city areas where services tend to be more poorly resourced.[25] For example, it is in the inner city that one finds most single-handed GPs, often working from inadequate premises and lacking support from a primary health care team.[26] Indeed it is the recognition of these inferior services which has lead some black people to seek a second opinion from a private medical practitioner, despite the cost which they can often ill afford.[27] At the same time insufficient concern has been shown by the health service for their specific health needs. For instance, the level of service for sickle cell sufferers amongst Afro-Caribbeans remains poor despite persistent lobbying and local activism.[3] In addition to this institutional racism, there is evidence that black people experience personal racism at the hands of NHS health care workers. For example, hospital midwives and GPs have been shown to hold negative stereotypes of South Asian patients as attention seeking and non-compliant which has affected the quality of care provided.[28]

Despite these inequalities in access and use of the service the NHS as an institution still remains remarkably popular across all social groups. According to the results of the British Attitude Survey collective support for the NHS, as for other welfare services, remained high and even increased during the 1980s. At a time when the dominant theme in welfare policy was to constrain public spending the proportion of people who said that they would be prepared to pay more in taxes to support the welfare state rose form 32% in 1983 to 56% in 1989.[29] The NHS was a particular beneficiary with 84% stating that they saw it as a priority for extra spending in 1989 compared with 63% in 1983. Despite its high level of popularity, however, there also appears to have been an increased concern about the quality of NHS provision. The proportion who said that they were satisfied with the service fell from 56% to 36% between 1983 and 1989 while the proportion who claimed they were dissatisfied rose from a quarter to a half.[29] The response of the Conservative government has been to blame poor management and organization and embark on a major process of restructuring. This has involved the application of business ethics to management, the introduction of an "internal market" for the selling and purchasing of health care, the advocacy of a consumer oriented system based on the principles of empowerment and self-help and the promotion of welfare pluralism involving cooperation between the NHS and the private health care sector. It is to these developments that we now turn.

The Restructuring of the National Health Service
....

1. The New Managerialism

Poor NHS management, in one form or another, has long been blamed by governments of all political persuasions for short comings in the service. The Conservative administrations of the 1980s, however, attached particular weight to this assessment as it coincided with their ideological attachment to the New Right with its emphasis on monetarism, political liberalism, professional deregulation and the application of private sector business principles to the public sector as a way to control expenditure. Moreover, as noted above, it also served the political function of distancing the Conservatives from the impact which the application of monetarist principles to public spending would have on the level of service. As Klein put it, "to decentralize responsibility is also to disclaim blame."[30]

In 1983 the Conservatives decided to institute change by appointing a businessman, Roy Griffiths—then the managing director of Sainsbury's supermarket chain—to review the management of the NHS. His proposed solution was to alter the organizational culture of the service by introducing features of business management, along the lines suggested particularly by US management theorists.[31] Previously management had been based on consensus teams involving representatives from medicine, nursing and administration each of whom had the power of veto. Griffiths recommended the creation of general managers at each level of the service, in place of consensus teams, who would take responsibility for developing management plans, ensuring quality of care, achieving cost improvements and monitoring and rewarding staff.[1] At the same time the managers were to be appointed on short term contracts and to be paid by performance as a spur to good management, as happened in the private sector.[32]

The proposals, which were accepted wholesale by the Government, were designed to alter the balance of power in favor of managers, at the expense of other professionals, especially doctors, whose clinical freedom to make decisions about individual patients regardless of cost had previously been a major determinant of the level of expenditure. In the new system doctors were to be more accountable to managers who had stricter control over professional and labor costs through a system of management budgets which related workload objectives to the resources available.[33]

Doctors were encouraged to participate in this micromanagement system and help secure and oversee the most effective use of resources. While some doctors applied for and were appointed as general managers and a few experiments were set up involving the delegation of budgetary responsibility to doctors, many were reluctant to give their unequivocal support to these developments.[34] As a result doctors continued to exercise considerable autonomy and managers continued to lack real control over medical work.

Not to be put off, in 1989 the government published a White Paper, Working for Patients, subsequently enacted through the 1990 NHS and Community Care Act, which attempted, amongst other things, to shift the balance of power more forcefully in the direction of managers. The White Paper recommended that managers should have greater involvement in the specification and policing of consultants' contracts.

At the same time a plethora of new techniques of managerial evaluation were developed. Quality assurance and performance indicators, made possible by advances in information technology, increased opportunities for the managerial determination of work content, productivity, resource use and quality standards.[35] In addition, managers now had available a growing body of evidence from the NHS Research and Development program regarding clinical effectiveness and health outcomes which could be used to challenge clinical autonomy.[36]

Such developments would seem to have given managers the opportunity to constrain British doctors as never before, along the lines identified in the proletarianization thesis. Advocates of this position argue that doctors are being deskilled, are losing their economic independence and are being required to work in bureaucratically organized institutions under the instruction of managers, in accordance with the requirements of advanced capitalism.[37] However, as Freidson[38] indicates, the widespread adoption of new techniques for monitoring the efficiency of performance and resource allocation does not on its own illustrate reduced professional autonomy. What really matters is whose criteria for evaluation and appraisal are adopted and who controls any actions which are taken.[39] Moreover, doctors are perfectly capable of transforming themselves into managers while exerting themselves in such a way that no fundamental challenge is mounted to their view of the health service.[36] It is quite conceivable that the increasing devolution of budgets to clinicians will provide the opportunity for new forms of autonomy for consultants.[34]

In sum, while doctors in the NHS now have to account for their actions in ways which were unthinkable a decade ago it is far from certain that the new managerialism in the NHS will result in a victory for the "corporate rationalizers" over the "professional monopolists."[40] What is certain, however, is that the policy changes outlined above have been good for the managers themselves. Their number increased by 53% between 1975 and 1991 while their total salaries have risen by £380 million over the decade since the Griffiths reforms were introduced.[12] This is somewhat ironic given that Conservative governments responsible for this new managerialism have consistently maintained that reducing bureaucracy was an important policy objective.

2. The Internal Market in Health Care

In addition to enhancing the role of management, Working for Patients and the 1990 NHS and Community Care Act also introduced a market system to the NHS, while reaffirming the principle of providing health care free at the point of use. Premised on the assumption that competition enhances efficiency, it was proposed that the NHS should be divided into providers and purchasers of services; purchasers, it was assumed, would shop around for the cheapest health care while providers would minimize their price in order to remain competitive in the market.

The idea for an internal market apparently originated with the US economist, Alain Enthoven, who, on a visit to Britain in 1985, declared that the NHS was in a state of "gridlock" or general rigidity and inflexibility and that this could only be broken if the most efficient providers were rewarded with economic incentives.[41] Enthoven's solution, based on experience with US Health Maintenance Organizations,[42,43] proved to be attractive to New Right "think tanks" such as the Centre for Policy Studies, but the government did not take up the idea until the winter of 1987/8 when it faced a political crisis as a result of mounting public and professional concern about the financial problems facing the health service.[44] It was this set of circumstances which triggered Prime Minister Margaret Thatcher's decision to review the NHS, the outcome of which was Working for Patients.

The White Paper and the subsequent Act turned District Health Authorities (DHAs) into purchasers (or commissioning agencies), with capitation budgets, who were responsible for assessing local needs, determining priorities and buying community services. These services could be bought from either the public or private sector. Larger general practices could also opt to become purchasers, known as fundholders.

Providers of care such as large hospitals and community units were given the opportunity to become self governing Trusts with the promise of increased financial freedom and greater autonomy. They were to be allowed to set the rate of pay for their staff, invest in capital projects and alter their service according to the needs of the market. The idea was that self government would encourage a greater sense of ownership and pride, or corporatism, on the part of those providing services, as well as encouraging local initiative and greater competition.

The reforms were implemented within two years of the publication of Working for Patients. Purchasers found some opportunities for cost savings but were constrained by the lack of choice between service providers (e.g., only one district general hospital in the area) and the need to provide services locally, whatever the savings to be achieved by contracting further afield.[31]

On the supply side, the formation of hospitals and community units into Trusts seems to have provided certain benefits for the service and for patients. Costs seem to have been kept down and the number of patients waiting over a year for hospital treatment has been reduced. At the same time the Trusts' attempts to create a corporate spirit have not been entirely successful and there is a danger that they will respond to purchasing power at the expense of social need and concentrate on more profitable areas of work to the detriment of certain categories of patient.[31]

Overall, the internal market would seem to have produced a decentralized and fragmented system with numerous buyers and sellers, in place of a centrally planned, uniform, top down approach. There have been certain benefits for patients from this most radical of recent reforms but these appear to have been offset by a series of problems stemming from a system which puts efficiency before equity. It seems likely that these will be dealt with by regulating rather than replacing the market. The new commercial culture and the vested interests of those who have benefitted from the reforms will make it extremely difficult for any government to put this "genie back in the bottle."[45]

3. Empowering the Consumer

Another strand of the health service reforms has involved greater emphasis on consumer choice and redress. The application of consumerist principles to the NHS was given a major impetus with the publication of the 1983 Griffiths Report on management.[46] In line with New Right thinking with its emphasis on individuals exercising choice through the market, Griffiths stated that managers should give pride of place to "patient," or as they were renamed "consumer," preferences when making health care decisions. He argued that they should try and establish how well the service for which they were responsible was being delivered by employing market research techniques and other methods to find out the views of their customers. They were then to act on this information by amending policy and monitoring subsequent performance against it. Thereafter, this management-led consumerist approach was promoted vigorously, with Directors of Quality Assurance appointed to Health Authorities to establish users' views, and staff sent on customer relations courses and encouraged to follow newly established "mission statements" outlining their organizations' common goals. However, the benefits to patients seems to have been limited, with managers being mainly concerned with hotel aspects of care such as cleanliness and food rather than with patients' views of clinical effectiveness.[46]

Further policy initiatives to enhance consumer choice followed in the 1990s. The 1990 NHS and Community Care Act required Health Authorities, as purchasers, to discuss services with community groups, amongst others, before drawing up contracts. This policy was reinforced in Listening to Local Voices, published by the NHS Management Executive in 1992, which stressed that purchasing authorities should listen to the views of local people about their priorities for health care before making rationing decisions.[1]

The 1990 Act also required GP fundholders to purchase services on their patients' behalf. As Paton states, however, "the fact that the individual was not the purchaser meant that any new consumerism in the NHS was not to be based on the individual's purchasing rights."[47] Rather, GP fundholders, along with Health Authorities, were to be proxy consumers. It was assumed that these fundholders had the incentive to fulfil this role effectively as otherwise their patients would simply switch to a competing practice.[5] However, as patients lack the necessary knowledge or inclination to shop around in the medical market place and often do not have a great choice of alternative GPs with which to register, there is little evidence that this aspect of the reforms has markedly increased consumer choice.[5] Moreover, for those patients who remain with non-fundholding GPs the 1990 reforms may have had the perverse effect of actually restricting choice. These patients' GPs are no longer free to refer their patients to a consultant of their choice but instead must refer them to providers with whom the District has a contract (unless they can obtain special permission to do otherwise from their local DHA manager).

In addition, consumerism has been promoted by the introduction in 1992 of a Patient's Charter, one of a number intended to transform the management of the public services. Taking its lead from the first of the charters, The Citizen's

Charter, introduced by Prime Minister Margaret Thatcher's successor, John Major, the Patient's Charter was intended to make the health service more responsive to consumers by setting the rights and service standards which they could expect. These standards were to provide the basis for targets against which the performance of managers could be measured. In addition to seven existing rights, for example the right to change doctor, three new rights were established. These were the right to: detailed information on local health services, including quality standards and waiting lists; guaranteed admission to hospital within two years of being put on the waiting list; and having any complaint about the service fully investigated and promptly dealt with. Subsequently, doubt has been expressed about whether these rights will be realized in practice as they are not legally binding.

Despite the rhetoric of consumerism over the last decade there is some doubt as to whether the quality of the service provided to NHS patients has greatly increased. Certainly the number of people complaining has increased substantially since the early 1980s. For example, while 3.1 written complaints per 100,000 of the population were made about community services in England in 1981, there were 9.9 per 100,000 in 1989–90, an increase of almost 220%.[48]

As these developments reveal, the model of consumerism employed in the reform of the NHS is concerned with promoting the self-interest of individual users of the service rather than with enhancing patients' collective representation or involvement in service planning.[49] Given the attachment of the Conservatives to the business ethic and individual choice this is not surprising and reflects a belief in a supermarket approach to consumerism. In this approach the consumer is confined to purchasing what is on the shelf or complaining when a product is faulty, and has no direct voice in determining what appears on the shelf in the first place.[46] As Nettleton and Harding[48] recognize, this supermarket model presupposes a certain type of citizenship in which citizen rights are reduced to consumer rights and the social right to representation and participation in decision making is downplayed.

The Conservative government's emphasis on empowering the individual consumer also reflects a distrust of professionals, another tenet of New Right ideology.[39] The restrictive practices and collegiate control of the medical profession were seen to have resulted in an unresponsive service which could only be improved if power was shifted to users of the service by giving them sufficient information to participate in the market. But to what extent have users been empowered at the expense of the medical profession? Have the reforms contributed to the deprofessionalization of medicine?[50-1] As noted above no attempt was made in the reforms explicitly to empower individual patients by giving them direct purchasing power. Nor was consideration given to the differences in ability of particular social groups to use the information newly available to shop around for medical services. Consequently, much will depend on where people live as this will determine the choice of doctor or hospital available to them.[52] It would thus seem that the power of the individual patient has changed relatively little as a result of these reforms, leaving doctors with their specialized knowledge and skills still largely in control.

Finally, it should be noted that some commentators[48,53] have argued that the emphasis on consumerism in the health service reforms parallels more general socio-economic changes from a society based on Fordist principles (mass production, universalization of welfare, mass consumption) to one based on post-Fordism (flexible production techniques designed to take account of rapid changes in consumer demand and fragmented market tastes). In a post-Fordist society it is the consumers rather than the producers who call the tune. While this approach has some value in placing the health policy changes under consideration in a broader context, it fails to distinguish between surface changes in appearance and underlying social relations. As we have seen, while the rhetoric has been about enhanced consumer power, producers in the form of the medical profession continue to dominate the users of the service.

4. Promoting Welfare Pluralism

A further principle underpinning the NHS reforms is welfare pluralism. While the health services in Britain, like all others in the developed world,[54] have long been pluralist in the sense of having both public and private funding, planning and provision, the reforms of the 1980s and 1990s have attempted to shift the balance profoundly in favour of greater private sector involvement.[55-6] Again this is in line with New Right thinking which abhors monopoly and lack of choice. Changing the balance of provision has the attraction of providing the desired levels of services without the need for extra government spending. The latter would be anathema for a government wedded to cutting or at least controlling public expenditure in order to reduce the tax burden on individuals.[56]

One strategy for shifting the balance between the public and private sector has involved the development of policies to encourage the growth of private medicine. Planning controls have been relaxed on private hospital development,[57] NHS consultants' contracts have been revised so that they have greater scope to undertake private practice in addition to their NHS commitments,[58] and tax changes have been introduced to encourage higher levels of private health cover.[59] These changes have created the climate for private hospital development and provided opportunities which have been fully exploited by the private sector. Between 1979 and 1989 the number of private hospitals increased by 30% and the number of private beds by 58%.[59] Many of these hospitals were located in the prosperous South East of England, compounding rather than eliminating the geographical inequalities in the distribution of resources noted earlier.

Shifting the balance between the public and private sector has also been enhanced by those reforms which have encouraged greater collaboration between the two sectors. An early attempt was the government's policy of requiring NHS District Health Authorities to introduce competitive tendering for domestic, catering and laundry services in 1983. The intention was to challenge the monopoly of the in-house providers of services in the expectation that costs would be reduced and greater "value for money" would be achieved. In practice the financial benefits proved relatively modest, at least initially, and the savings that have been achieved seem to have been at the expense of quality of service.[12] More recently, the NHS has been encouraged to con-

tract out patient care to the private sector. Such cooperative arrangements were initially undertaken on a voluntary basis by individual Health Authorities faced with no in-house alternatives, for example as a result of capacity constraints.[58] Subsequently, HAs were directed by the government to use private hospitals as a way of reducing NHS waiting lists for non-urgent cases and those waiting more than one year.

While the reforms introduced by the Conservatives have generally been advantageous to the private sector they have not all been beneficial. In particular, the government's willingness to encourage the NHS to expand their pay-bed provision has served to sharpen competition for private patients and threaten the private providers' profit margins.

Originally introduced in 1948 as a concession to hospital consultants, as noted earlier, pay-beds were in decline when the Conservatives came to power in 1979 and their number continued to fall subsequently. In the late 1980s, however, the government decided to revitalize this provision in the face of increasingly severe financial constraints. It was also in line with its belief in generating competition between providers so as to enhance consumer choice and maximize efficiency. In 1988 it therefore used the Health and Medicines Act to relax the rules governing pay-bed charges so that hospitals could make a profit rather than simply cover costs. As a result pay-bed income increased dramatically between 1991–2 and 1993–4 from just over £32 million to nearly £116 million.[60] The NHS now has 16% of the private market and is set to become the biggest provider of private health care in the UK by 1997.

These three examples illustrate the shift to a new public/private mix of services, a mixed economy of health care. The policy has been driven by ideological considerations and by economic and political calculations. The goal seems to have been to increase the role of the private sector and limit that of the public sector while improving its performance. As such it arguably represents an attempt to "privatize from within."[61]

It has also been suggested that these policies illustrate a shift towards post-Fordism in the sense that Health Authorities have become "flexible firms," concentrating on core functions and buying in peripheral services from outside.[62] While this argument is superficially attractive, it ignores the extent to which the reforms have been the result of deliberate political decisions in the face of external economic considerations and ideological preferences.[12] Rather than simply mirroring structural developments in the economy, the policy of welfare pluralism is best seen as an attempt to erode services that people experience collectively and persuade them to act instead in terms of their own immediate self interest.

Conclusion

This chapter has provided an account of the development of the British National Health Service from its inception in the late 1940s until the present. It has shown that the newly nationalized health service represented a significant departure from the previous system in offering health care free at the point of use, but that the new structure was agreed to at the cost of the medical profession's continuing autonomy.

As we have seen, subsequent events proved this socialized system of health care to be reasonably successful in providing cost-effective and equitable health care in face of an ageing population, increasingly expensive medical technology and heightened patient and doctor expectations. Costs have been held in check and the spatial distribution of services has become more equitable. However, while greater equality of access and use has been achieved in terms of class, gender and race significant disparities continue to exist.

Despite this picture of relative success the Conservatives have embarked on a series of policy changes in recent years which have had the effect of radically restructuring the NHS while keeping the service free at the point of use. Driven by a deep ideological attachment to the New Right and faced with a financial crisis and public disquiet they have introduced managerialism and an internal market into the health service, along with a Patient's Charter and policies to encourage welfare pluralism. While these changes have seen certain benefits such as

increasing the accountability of the medical profession, reducing hospital waiting times for patients, making rationing decisions explicit and creating a more responsive service, there have also been serious disadvantages. Of these perhaps the most significant is the possibility that a two tier system will develop with the wealthy paying for private care and the NHS providing a safety net for those who can not afford it. The growth of the private health care sector, the regeneration of NHS pay beds, and the development of GP fundholding along the lines of HMOs all make this a realistic prospect. Indeed they could be seen to reflect a policy of Americanizing health care in the UK[59,63–4] at a time when the US has been looking at the old style NHS as one possible alternative model of health care. This reference to convergence illustrates the extent to which the NHS has changed in recent times and makes it unlikely that the clock will ever be turned back.

Acknowledgments
I should like to thank Mike Bury and Mary Ann Elston for their comments on an earlier draft of this chapter.

REFERENCES

1. Allsop, J. *Health Policy and the NHS*. Second Edition. London: Longman, 1995.
2. Stacey, M. *The Sociology of Health and Healing*. London: Unwin Hyman, 1988.
3. Ginsburg, N. *Divisions of Welfare*. London: Sage, 1992.
4. Campbell, J. *Nye Bevan and the Mirage of British Socialism*. London: Weidenfeld and Nicholson, 1987: 168.
5. Klein, R. *The Politics of the NHS*. Third edition. London: Longman, 1995.
6. Berridge, V., Harrison, M., and Weindling, P. The impact of war and depression, 1918 to 1948. In *Caring for Health: History and Diversity*. Ed., Webster, C. Buckingham: Open University Press, 1993.
7. Doyal, L., with Pennell, I. *The Political Economy of Health*. London: Pluto Press, 1979.
8. Abel-Smith, B. *The Hospitals 1800–1948*. London: Heinemann, 1964: 440.
9. Berridge, V., Webster, C., and Walt, G. Mobilisation for total welfare, 1948 to 1974. In *Caring for Health: History and Diversity*. Ed., Webster, C. Buckingham: Open University Press, 1993.

10. Abel-Smith, B. *Introduction to Health: Policy, Planning and Financing*. London: Longman, 1994.

11. Levitt, R., and Wall, A. *The Reorganized National Health Service*. Fourth edition. London: Chapman and Hall, 1992.

12. Mohan, J. *A National Health Service? The Restructuring of Health Care in Britain since 1979*. Basingstoke: Macmillan, 1995.

13. Stocking, B. The introduction and costs of new technologies. In *In the Best of Health*. Eds., Beck, E., et al. London: Chapman and Hall, 1992.

14. Mays, N. Innovations in health care. In *Dilemmas in Health Care*. Eds. Davey, B., and Popay, J. Buckingham: Open University Press, 1993.

15. Burstall, M. *1992 and the Regulation of the Pharmaceutical Industry*. IEA Health Series No 9. London: Institute of Economic Affairs, 1990.

16. Gray, A. Rationing and choice. In *Dilemmas in Health Care*. Eds. Davey, B., and Popay, J. Buckingham: Open University Press. 1993.

17. Jarman, B., and Bosanquet, N. Primary health care in London: Changes since the Acheson Report. *British Medical Journal*. 305, 1130–6, 1992.

18. Townsend, P., and Davidson, N. *Inequalities in Health: The Black Report*. Harmondsworth: Penguin, 1982.

19. Whitehead, M. *The Health Divide*. London: Health Education Council, 1987.

20. Pendleton, D., and Bochner, S. The communication of medical information in GP consultations as a function of social class. *Social Science and Medicine* 14a, 669–73, 1980.

21. Boulton, M., Tuckett, D., Olson, C., and Williams, A. Social class and the general practice consultation. *Sociology of Health and Illness* 8, 325–50, 1986.

22. Doyal, L. Women and the National Health Service. In *Women, Health and Healing: Toward a New Perspective*. Eds. Lewin, E., and Olesen, V. New York: Tavistock Publications, 1985.

23. Pascall, G. *Social Policy: A Feminist Analysis*. London: Tavistock, 1986.

24. Doyal, L. Changing medicine? Gender and the politics of health care. In *Challenging Medicine*. Eds. Gabe, J., Kelleher, D., and Williams, G. London: Routledge, 1994.

25. Leese, B., and Bosanquet, N. High and low incomes in general practice. *British Medical Journal*, 298, 932–4, 1989.

26. GLC Health Panel. *Ethnic Minorities and the National Health Service in London*. London: Greater London Council, 1985.

27. Thorogood, N. Private medicine: "You pay your money and you gets your treatment." *Sociology of Health and Illness* 14, 1, 23–38, 1992.

28. Smaje, C. *Health, "Race" and Ethnicity: Making Sense of the Evidence*. London: King's Fund Institute, 1995.

29. Taylor-Gooby, P. *Social Change, Social Welfare and Social Science*. London: Harvester Wheatsheaf, 1991.

30. Klein, R. *The Politics of the NHS*. Harlow: Longman, 1983, 141.

31. Ranade, W. *A Future for the NHS?* Harlow: Longman, 1994.

32. Cox, D. Crisis and opportunity in health service management. In *Continuity and Crisis in the NHS*. Eds. Loveridge, R., and Starkey, K. Buckingham: Open University Press, 1992.

33. Hunter, D. Managing medicine: A response to the crisis. *Social Science and Medicine* 32, 4, 441–9, 1991.

34. Cox, D. Health service management—a sociological view: Griffiths and the non-negotiated order of the hospital. In *The Sociology of the Health Service*. Eds. Gabe, J., Calnan, M., and Bury, M. London: Routledge, 1991.

35. Flynn, R. *Structures of Control in Health Management*. London: Routledge, 1992.

36. Hunter, D. From tribalism to corporatism: The managerial challenge to medical dominance. In *Challenging Medicine*. Eds. Gabe, J., Kelleher, D., and Williams, G. London: Routledge, 1994.

37. McKinlay, J., and Arches, J. Towards the proletarianization of physicians. *International Journal of Health Services* 15, 161–95, 1985.

38. Freidson, E. *Medical Work in America: Essays in Health Care*. New Haven: Yale University Press, 1989.

39. Elston, M. A. The politics of professional power: Medicine in a changing health service. In *The Sociology of the Health Service*. Eds. Gabe, J., Bury, M., and Calnan, M. London: Routledge, 1991.

40. Alford, R. *Health Care Politics*. Chicago: University of Chicago Press, 1975.

41. Enthoven, A. *Reflections on the Management of the NHS*. London: Nuffield Provincial Hospitals Trust, 1985.

42. Allsop, J., and May. A. Between the devil and the deep blue sea: Managing the NHS in the wake of the 1990 Act. *Critical Social Policy* 38, 5–22, 1993.

43. The British reforms however parted company with the HMOs by splitting purchasers/insurers and providers. See Paton, C. *Competition and Planning in the NHS: The Danger of Unplanned Markets*. London: Chapman and Hall, 1992.

44. Baggott, R. *Health and Health Care in Britain*. Basingstoke, Macmillan, 1994.

45. Baggott, R. op. cit., p. 200.
46. Seale, C. The consumer voice. In *Dilemmas in Health Care*. Eds. Davey, B., and Popay, J. Buckingham: Open University Press, 1993.
47. Paton, C. op. cit.
48. Nettleton, S., and Harding, G. Protesting patients: A study of complaints submitted to a Family Health Service Authority. *Sociology of Health and Illness* 16, 38–61, 1994.
49. Hughes, D. The reorganization of the National Health Service: The rhetoric and reality of the internal market. *The Modern Law Review* 54, 88–103, 1991.
50. Haug, M. Deprofessionalisation: An alternative hypothesis for the future. *Sociological Review Monograph*, 20, 195–211, 1973.
51. Haug, M. A re-examination of the hypothesis of deprofessionalisation. *Milbank Quarterly*, 66 (Suppl. 2), 48–56, 1988.
52. Walsh, K. Citizens, charters and contracts. In *The Authority of the Consumer*. Eds. Keat, R., Whiteley, N., and Abercrombie, N. London: Routledge, 1994.
53. Nettleton, S. *The Sociology of Health and Illness*. Cambridge/Oxford: Polity in association with Blackwell Publishers, 1995.
54. Klein, R. Private practice and public policy: Regulating the frontiers. In *The Private/Public Mix for Health*. Eds. McLachlan, G., and Maynard, A. London: Nuffield Provincial Hospitals Trust, 1982.
55. Davies, C. Things to come: The NHS in the next decade. *Sociology of Health and Illness* 9, 302–17, 1987.
56. Harrison, S., Hunter, D., and Pollitt, C. *The Dynamics of British Health Policy*. London: Unwin Hyman, 1990.
57. Mohan, J., and Woods, K. Restructuring health care: The social geography of public and private health care under the British Conservative government. *International Journal of Health Services* 15, 197–215, 1985.
58. Rayner, G. Lessons from America? Commercialization and growth of private medicine in Britain. *International Journal of Health Services* 17, 197–216, 1987.
59. Calnan, M., Cant, S., and Gabe, J. *Going Private: Why People Pay for Their Health Care*. Buckingham: Open University Press, 1993.
60. Higgins, J. Goldrush. *Health Service Journal* 23 November 24–6, 1995.
61. Ranade, W., and Haywood, S. Privatizing from within: The National Health Service under Thatcher. *Local Government Studies* 15, 19–34, 1989.
62. Kelly, A. The enterprise culture and the welfare state: Restructuring the management of health and personal social services. In *Deciphering the Enterprise Culture*. Ed. Burrows, R. London: Routledge, 1991.
63. Navarro, V. The relevance of the US experience to the reforms in the British National Health Service: The case of general practitioner fund holding. *International Journal of Health Services* 21, 381–7, 1991.
64. Hudson, D. Quasi-markets in health and social care in Britain: Can the public sector respond? *Policy and Politics* 20, 131–42, 1992.

Prevention and Society

■　■　■　■　■　■

Prevention became a watchword for health in the 1980s. A number of factors contributed to the renewed interest in prevention. While a few fresh concepts emerged (e.g., focus on lifestyle's effect on health) and a few new discoveries were made (e.g., relating hypertension to heart disease), the current attention paid to prevention has not been spurred by scientific breakthroughs. Rather, it is primarily a response to the situations described in this book: the dominant sick-care orientation of the medical profession; the increase in chronic illness; the continuing uncontrolled escalation of costs; and the influence of third-party payers. And prevention efforts are going beyond the medical profession. Insurance companies give rate reductions to individuals with healthy lifestyles (e.g., nonsmokers) and numerous major corporations are introducing worksite "wellness" and health promotion programs. This new prevention orientation is occurring in a cultural environment that has become sensitized to various forms of health promotion including health foods, health clubs, jogging, and exercise.

If we are serious about reorienting our approach to health from "cure" to prevention of illness, medicine must become more of a "social science." Illness and disease are socially as well as biophysiologically produced. For over a century, under the reign of the germ-theory "medical model," medical research searched for specific etiologies (e.g., germs or viruses) of specific diseases. With the present predominance of chronic disease in American society, the limitations of this viewpoint are becoming apparent. If we push our etiological analysis far enough, as often as not we come to sociological factors as primary causes. We must investigate environments, lifestyles, and social structures in our search for etiological factors of disease with the same commitment and zeal with which we investigate bodily systems, and we must begin to conceptualize preventive measures on the societal level as well as the biophysical. This is not to say that we should ignore or jettison established biomedical knowledge; rather, we need to focus on the production of disease in the interaction of social environments and human physiology.

The Surgeon General's report on disease prevention and health promotion titled *Healthy People* (1979) took steps in this direction. The report recognized the "limitations of modern medicine" and highlighted the importance of behavioral and social factors for health. It deemphasized the role of physicians in controlling health activities and argued persuasively for the need to turn from "sick care" to prevention. Most significantly, the report officially legitimatized the centrality of social and behavioral factors in caring for our health. It argued that people must both take responsibility for changing disease-producing conditions and take positive steps toward good health. In some circles, *Healthy People* was deemed a revolutionary report, more significant even than the 1964 Surgeon General's report on smoking. The fact, however, that many people have not yet heard about this 1979 report, much less are familiar with what it says, raises some questions about its potential impact on health behavior.

Yet from a sociological perspective, the 1991 revision, *Healthy People*

Table 1. Conceptualization of Prevention

Level of Prevention	Type of Intervention	Place of Intervention	Examples of Intervention
Medical	Biophysiological	Individual's body	Vaccinations; early diagnosis; medical intervention.
Behavioral	Psychological (and Social Psychological)	Individual's behavior and lifestyle	Change habits or behavior (e.g., eat better, stop smoking, exercise, wear seat belts); learn appropriate coping mechanisms (e.g., meditation).
Structural	Sociological (Social and Political)	Social structure, systems, environments	Legislate controls on nutritional values of food; change work environment; reduce pollution; fluoridate water supplies.

2000 (U.S. Department of Health and Human Services, 1991), is also something of a disappointment. While social and behavioral factors are depicted as central in causation and prevention of ill health, a close reading shows that most of these factors are little more than "healthy habits." The report exhorts people to adopt better diets, with more whole grains and less red meat, sugar, and salt; to stop smoking; to exercise regularly; to keep weight down; to seek proper prenatal and postnatal care; and so forth. While these things are surely important to prevention of illness, we must today conceptualize prevention more broadly and as involving at least three levels; medical, behavioral, and structural (see Table 1). Simply put, medical prevention is directed at the individual's body; behavioral prevention is directed at changing people's behavior; and structural prevention is directed at changing the society or environments in which people work and live.

Healthy People mostly urges us to prevent disease on a behavioral level. While this is undoubtedly a useful level of prevention, some problems remain. For example, social scientists have very little knowledge about *how* to change people's (healthy or unhealthy) habits. The report encourages patient and health education as a solution, but clearly this is not sufficient. Most people are aware of the health risks of smoking or not wearing seat belts, yet more than 25 percent of Americans smoke and 60 percent don't regularly use the seat belts. Sometimes, individual habits are responses to complex social situations, such as smoking as a coping response to stressful and alienating work environments. Behavioral approaches focus on the individual and place the entire burden of change on the individual. Individuals who do not or cannot change their unhealthy habits are often seen merely as "at risk" or noncompliant patients, another form of the blame-the-victim response to health problems. *Healthy People* rarely discusses the structural level of causation and intervention. It hardly touches on significant social structural variables such as gender, race, and class and is strangely silent about the corporate aspects of prevention (Conrad and Schlesinger, 1980).

In "Wellness in the Work Place: Potentials and Pitfalls of Worksite Health Promotion," Peter Conrad examines a popular corporate strategy for health promotion and disease prevention. This fundamentally behavioral-level intervention grew significantly in the 1980s, largely in response to rising health-care costs and increasing corporate concerns about competitiveness and worker productivity (Conrad and Walsh, 1992). Throughout American industry, many major corporations have introduced health promotion or "wellness" programs at the workplace (Hollander and Lengerman, 1988). While there are broad claims made for these programs and while they are very popular with employees (Sloan, Gruman, and Allegrante, 1987), Conrad argues it is not yet clear whether they are effective in improving health, containing costs, or influencing productivity. When examined in their sociopolitical context, worksite wellness programs have several subtler and potentially disturbing unintended consequences.

In the final selection, "A Case for Refocussing Upstream: The Political Economy of Illness," John McKinlay argues that we need to change the way we think about prevention and start to "refocus upstream," beyond healthy habits to the structure of society. He suggests we should concentrate on and investigate political-economic aspects of disease causation and prevention, paying particular attention to "the manufacturers of illness." McKinlay singles out the food industry as a major manufacturer of illness. However, the major contribution of his selection is to go beyond the conventional view of prevention as a biomedical or lifestyle problem to a conceptualization of prevention as a socioeconomic issue.

Prevention can be a key alternative to our health care dilemma when it focuses at least as directly on the structural as on the behavioral level of intervention.

REFERENCES

Conrad, Peter, and Lynn Schlesinger. 1980. "Beyond healthy habits: Society and the pursuit of health." Unpublished manuscript.

Conrad, Peter, and Diana Chapman Walsh. 1992. "The New Corporate Health Ethic: Lifestyle and the Social Control of Work." International Journal of Health Services 22: 89–111.

Hollander, Roberta B., and Joseph J. Lengermann. 1988. "Corporate characteristics and worksite health promotion programs: Survey findings from Fortune 500 companies." Social Science and Medicine 26: 491–502.

Sloan, Richard P., Jessie C. Gruman, and John P. Allegrante. 1987. Investing in Employee Health. San Francisco: Jossey-Bass.

U.S. Department of Health, Education and Welfare. 1979. Healthy People: The Surgeon General's Report on Health Promotion and Disease Prevention. Washington D.C.: U.S. Government Printing Office.

45

Wellness in the Work Place:
Potentials and Pitfalls of
Work-Site Health Promotion

■ ■ ■ ■ ■ ■

Peter Conrad

In the past decade work-site health promotion or "wellness" emerged as a manifestation of the growing national interest in disease prevention and health promotion. For many companies it has become an active part of their corporate health care policies. This article examines the potentials and pitfalls of work-site health promotion.

Work-site health promotion is "a combination of educational, organizational and environmental activities designed to support behavior conducive to the health of employees and their families" (Parkinson et al. 1982, 13). In effect, work-site health promotion consists of health education, screening, and/or intervention designed to change employees' behavior in order to achieve better health and reduce the associated health risks.

These programs range from single interventions (such as hypertension screening) to comprehensive health and fitness programs. An increasing number of companies are introducing more comprehensive work-site wellness programs that may include hypertension screening, aerobic exercise and fitness, nutrition and weight control, stress management, smoking cessation, healthy back care, cancer-risk screening and reduction, drug and alcohol abuse prevention, accident prevention, and self-care and health information. Many programs use some type of health-risk appraisal (HRA) to determine employees' health risks and to help them develop a regimen to reduce their risks and improve their health.

Work-site health promotion has captured the imagination of many health educators and corporate policy makers. Workers spend more than 30 percent of their waking hours at the work site, making it an attractive place of health education and promotion. Corporate people are attracted by the broad claims made for work-site health promotion (see O'Donnell 1984). For example:

> Benefits of worksite health promotion have included improvements in productivity, such as decreased absenteeism, increase employee morale, improved ability to perform and the development of high quality staff; reduction in benefit costs, such as decreases in health, life and workers compensation insurance; reduction in human resource development costs, such as decreased turnover and greater employee satisfaction; and improved image for the corporation (Rosen 1984, 1).

If these benefits are valid, probably no company would want to be without a wellness program.

Many major corporations have already developed work-site health promotion programs, including Lockheed, Johnson and Johnson, Campbell Soup, Kimberly-Clark, Blue Cross-Blue Shield of Indiana, Tenneco, AT&T, IBM, Metropolitan Life, CIGNA Insurance, Control Data, Pepsico, and the Ford Motor Company. Nearly all the programs have upbeat names like "Live for Life," "Healthsteps," "Lifestyle," "Total Life Concept," and "Staywell."

The programs' specific characteristics vary in terms of whether they are on- or off-site, company or vendor run, on or off company time, inclusive (all employees eligible) or exclusive, at some or no cost to employees, emphasize health or fitness, year-round classes or periodic modules, have special facilities, and are available to employees only or families as well. All programs are voluntary, although some companies use incentives (from T-shirts to cash) to encourage participation. In general, employees participate on their own time (before and after work or during lunchtime). The typical program is on site, with modest facilities (e.g., shower and exercise room), operating off company time, at a minimal cost to participants and managed by a part-time or full-time health and fitness director.

The number of work-site wellness programs is growing; studies report 21.1 percent (Fielding and Breslow 1983), 23 percent (Davis et al. 1984), 29 percent (Reza-Forouzesh and Ratzker 1984–1985), and 37.6 percent (Business Roundtable Task Force on Health 1985) of surveyed companies had some type of health-promotion program. It is difficult to interpret these figures. Not only are there serious definitional problems as to what counts as a program, but many may yet be only pilot programs and not available to all employees and at all corporate sites. Estimated employee participation rates range from 20 to 40 percent for on-site to 10 to 20 percent for off-site programs (Fielding 1984), but accurate data are very scarce (Conrad 1987a).

Work-site health promotion as a widespread corporate phenomenon only began to emerge in the 1970s and has developed largely outside of the medical care system with little participation by physicians. The dominant stated rationale for work-site health promotion has been containing health care costs by improving employee health. Business and industry pays a large portion (estimated at over 30 percent) of the American national health care bill, and its health insurance costs have been increasing rapidly. By the late 1970s corporate health costs were rising as much as 20 to 30 percent a year (Stein 1985, 14). This has become a corporate concern. In an effort to reduce these costs, corporations have redesigned benefit plans to include more employee "cost-sharing," less coverage of ambulatory surgery, mandated second opinions, increased health care options and alternative delivery plans (e.g., health

maintenance organizations and preferred provider organizations), as well as work-site health promotion programs. Although wellness programs are only a piece of a multipronged cost-containment strategy, they may be especially important as a symbolic exchange for employer cost shifting and reductions in other health benefits. They are moderate in cost and very popular with employees.

Corporations are restructuring their benefit packages to shift more cost responsibility to employees in the form of deductibles, cost sharing, and the like. A national survey of over a thousand businesses found that 52 percent of companies provided free coverage to their employees in 1980; by 1984 only 39 percent did so. In 1980 only 5 percent had deductibles over $100; four years later 40 percent had such deductibles (Allegrante and Sloan 1986).

Cost containment may be the most commonly stated goal of wellness programs, but it is not the only one. Reducing absenteeism, improving employee morale, and increasing productivity are also important corporate rationales for work-site health promotion (Hertzlinger and Calkins 1986, 74; Davis et al. 1984, 542). "Hidden" absenteeism can be very costly, especially when skilled labor is involved (Clement and Gibbs 1983). Improved morale is expected to reduce turnover, increase company loyalty, and improve workforce productivity (Bellingham, Johnson, and McCauley 1985). The morale-loyalty-absenteeism-productivity issue may be as important as health costs in the development of work-site wellness. The competitive international economic situation in the 1980s makes the productivity of American workers a critical issue for corporations.

Despite the broad claims for work-site health promotion, the scientific data available to evaluate them are very limited. While more scientific data could better enable us to assess the claims of the promoters of work-site wellness, it is not necessarily helpful for addressing some of the difficult social and health policy issues raised by work-site health promotion. To examine these more policy-oriented dimensions, it is useful to distinguish between potentials and pitfalls—potentials roughly aligning with the claims made for work-site programs, the pitfalls with less-discussed sociopolitical implications. These distinctions are for analytic purposes and are somewhat arbitrary; there may be downsides to potentials as well as upsides to pitfalls. This framework, however, provides us with a vehicle for examining work-site health promotion that includes yet goes beyond the dominant corporate/medical concerns of reducing individual health risks and containing costs.

Potentials
....

The Work-Site Locale

More people are in the "public" (i.e., nonhome or farm) work force today than ever before—estimated to be 85 million in the United States. Roughly one-third of workers' waking hours are spent in the work place. Work sites are potentially the single most accessible and efficient site for reaching adults for health education. From an employee's perspective, on-site wellness programs may be convenient and inexpensive, thus increasing the opportunities for participation in health promotion. The work site has potentially indigenous social support for difficult undertakings such as quitting smoking, exercising regularly, or losing weight. Work-site programs may raise the level of discourse and concern about health matters, when employees begin to "talk health" with each other. And since corporations pay such a large share of health costs, there is a built-in incentive for corporations to promote health and healthier workers.

One of the most underdeveloped potentials of the work site is possible modification of the "corporate culture." When the term "corporate culture" is used by the health promotion advocates, they generally mean improved health changes in the organizational culture and physical environment. Some also include changing company norms or the creation of the healthy organization (Bellingham 1985), often meaning making healthy behavior a desirable value among employees and management. Such goals, however noble, are vague and difficult to assess. In practice, changing the corporate culture has meant introducing more concrete interventions like company smoking policies (Walsh 1984),

"healthy" choices and caloric labeling in cafeterias and vending machines, fruit instead of donuts in meetings, and developing on-site fitness facilities. Very rarely, however, have proposed wellness interventions in the corporate culture included alterations in work organization, such as stressful management styles or the content of boring work, or even shop floor noise.

Health Enhancement

Screening and intervention for risk factors are the most common vehicles for enhancing employee health. Medical screening includes tests for potential physiological problems; interventions are preventive or treatment measures for the putative problem. Medical screening at the work site, including chest X-rays, sophisticated serological (blood) testing, blood pressure and health risk appraisals (HRAs), can identify latent health problems at a presymptomatic stage. To achieve an improvement in health, however, work-site screening must also include appropriate behavioral intervention, medical referral, and back-up when necessary. Thus far, hypertension screening has produced scientific evidence supporting positive work-site results (Foote and Erfurt 1983).

The scientific evidence available to support specific work-site interventions is also, as yet, limited. Examining the extant literature on specific interventions, Fielding (1982) found good evidence for the health effectiveness of work-site hypertension control and smoke-cessation programs. He concluded that the data on physical fitness and weight-reduction were not yet available. Hallet (1986), on the other hand, argued that well-controlled studies of work-place smoking intervention are not yet available. The evidence for physical fitness is still contentious (e.g., Paffenbarger et al. 1984; Solomon 1984) although the health effects of thirty minutes of vigorous exercise three times a week are probably positive, at least for cardiovascular health. There are reports of using work-place competitions (Brownell et al. 1984) or incentives (Forster et al. 1985) for increasing weight reduction, but the studies are short term and lack follow-up.

In the past few years large research projects to study the effects of work-site health promotion were initiated at AT&T (Spilman et al. 1986),

Johnson and Johnson (Blair et al. 1986a) and Blue Cross-Blue Shield of Indiana (Reed et al. 1985). Most of the results currently available are from pilot programs or one or two years of work-site health promotion activity (except the Blue Cross-Blue Shield of Indiana study, which is a five year evaluation). In general, these studies show health improvements in terms of exercise (Blair et al. 1986a), reduced blood pressure and cholesterol (Spilman et al. 1986), although the findings are not entirely consistent. The five-year Blue Cross-Blue Shield of Indiana study also found that interventions led to a significant reduction in serum cholesterol and high blood pressure and a lesser reduction in cigarette smoking (Reed et al. 1985). These reductions in risk factors are positive signs of health enhancement, but the studies are too short term to measure actual effect on disease. Limited scientific evidence aside, the interventions are at worst benign, since few appear harmful (save infrequent exercise-related injuries) and likely health effects seem between mildly and moderately positive.

Cost Containment

The effect of work-site health promotion on health costs, while highly touted, is difficult to measure and has engendered little rigorous research. Most companies do not keep records of their health claims in a fashion that is easy for researchers to assess. Since most research in this area tends to be short-term, and cost-containment benefits may be long-term (say five to ten years), the long time frame makes rigorous research on this topic unattractive to corporations and expensive for investigators. Finally, it is difficult to ascertain which, if any, work-site wellness interventions effected any changes in corporate health costs. Many studies of health promotion "project" potential cost savings from reductions in risk, which while unsatisfactory for scientific evaluation often satisfy the corporate sponsors.

There are a few studies of cost benefits that report promising findings. A national survey of 1,500 of the largest United States employers conducted by Health Research Institute found that health care costs for employers with wellness programs in place for four years was $1,311 per employee compared to $1,868 for companies without such programs (*Blue Cross-Blue Shield Consumer Exchange* 1986, 3). Such cross-sectional surveys, however, do not adequately control for confounding variables (e.g., different employee populations or benefit plans) that certainly affect health costs. Blue Cross-Blue Shield of California initiated a single intervention—a self-care program—through twenty-two California employers, that reduced outpatient visits, especially among households with first dollar coverage (Lorig et al. 1985, 1044). The authors don't calculate the estimated cost savings, but since the cost of the intervention was small, the cost-savings potential is high.

The most compelling cost-containment data to date come from the Blue Cross-Blue Shield of Indiana (Reed et al. 1985; Gibbs et al. 1985) and Johnson and Johnson (Bly, Jones, and Richardson 1986) studies. The Blue Cross-Blue Shield study tracked and compared claims data for participants and nonparticipants (N = 2,400) in a comprehensive wellness program for five years. They found that although participants submitted more claims than nonparticipants (i.e., had a higher utilization), the average payment per participant was *lower* throughout the course of the study. When payments were adjusted in 1982 dollars, the mean annual health cost of participants was $227.38 compared to $286.73 for nonparticipants. For five years, the average "savings" per employee was $143.60 compared to the program cost of $98.60 per person, giving a savings to cost ratio of 1.45. A possible selection bias in terms of who is attracted to the program could have affected the results. Overall, the five-year cost of the program was $867,000, with a saving of $1,450,000 in paid claims and an additional $180,000 saved in absence due to illness. The savings is estimated to be 8 to 10 percent of total claims (Mulvaney et al. 1985).

The Johnson and Johnson study compares health care costs and utilization of employees over a five-year period at work sites with or without a health-promotion program (Bly, Jones, and Richardson 1986). Adjusting for differences among the sites, the investigators found that the mean annual per capita inpatient cost increased $42 and $43 at the two sites with the wellness program as opposed to $76 at the sites without one. Health-promotion sites also had lower increases in hospital days and admissions, although there were no significant differences in outpatient or other health costs. The investigators calculate a cost savings of $980,316 for the study period. What is interesting is that this study was based on *all* employees at a work site. The suggestion here is that a work-site wellness program may produce a cost-containing effect on the entire cohort, not just on participants. The "Live for Life" program is an exemplary and unique program in terms of Johnson and Johnson's corporate investment in wellness; the effect of health promotion on an entire employee cohort needs to be replicated in other work-site settings.

Without further prospective studies, cost containment remains a promising but unproven benefit of work-site health promotion. Changes in health status—which are more easily measurable—do not automatically translate into health cost savings. It is often difficult to quantify health effect and subsequent cost savings. High employee turnover, discovery of new conditions, and other factors may affect actual cost benefits. On the other hand, the usual calculations do not take into account the cost of replacing key employees due to sickness or death. As Clement and Gibbs (1983, 51–52) note, the cost savings may be affected by characteristics of the company:

> For example, more benefits would be achieved by firms with highly compensated, high-risk employees, where turnover is low, recruitment and training costs are high, benefit provisions are generous and employees are likely to participate.

If corporations are serious about using health promotion to contain health costs, programs may need to be reconceptualized and expanded beyond their current scope. An important reality is that roughly *two-thirds* of corporate health costs are paid for spouses and dependents, who are not part of most work-site wellness programs, and that a large portion of health costs is expended for psychiatric care, which may only most indirectly be affected by wellness programs.

Cost containment is an overriding concern for some managers and program evaluators, especially in terms of "cost-benefit ratios." It may be that the current corporate political climate demands such bottom-line rhetoric for the implementation of work-site health promotion, but very few programs have been closed down due to lack of cost effectiveness.

Improving Morale and Productivity

The effects of work-site health promotion on morale and productivity are more difficult to measure than health effects. Participating in wellness activities, especially exercise classes, has several potentially morale-enhancing by-products. Current evidence is only anecdotal, but is generally in a consistent direction. First, there is the "fun" element. In the course of a year's observations at one corporate wellness program, I regularly observed banter, joking, and camaraderie among participants during program activities. There is a sense of people working together to improve their health. Programs that are open to all employees may create a leveling effect; often employees from varying company levels participate in the same classes and corporate hierarchical distinctions make little difference in sweatsuits and gym shorts. As one participant told me, "We all sweat together, including some of the higher ups." But rigorous studies on the effect of the programs on job satisfaction are not yet available.

Despite a legion of claims, virtually no one has even attempted to measure increased productivity as a result of work-site health promotion. Although changes in productivity are difficult to assess, there are two productivity-related effects about which we have some information. Several studies have found a reduction in absenteeism among wellness-program participants (Reed et al. 1985; Baun, Bernacki, and Tsai 1986; Blair et al. 1986b). It is generally believed that a reduction in absenteeism can lead to an increase in overall productivity. Second, several observers have noted that particpants often say they "feel" more energetic and productive from participating regularly in the program, especially in terms of exercising (Spilman et al. 1986, 289; Conrad 1987b). This kind of "subjective positivity" that results from wellness participation may be related to improved morale and productivity, although we are not likely to obtain "hard" measures.

The symbolic effects of offering a work-site wellness program should not be underestimated. Work-site health-promotion programs are often among the most visible and popular employee benefits. The mere existence of a program may be interpreted by employees as tangible evidence that the company cares about the health of its workers, and as contributing to company loyalty and morale. Programs are also a plus in recruiting new employees in a competitive marketplace.

Individual Empowerment

Work-site promotion presents a positive orientation toward health. Its orientation is promotive and preventative rather than restorative and rehabilitative and provides a general strategy aimed at *all* potential beneficiaries, not only those with problems ("deviants," or troubled or sick employees). This makes participation in wellness nonstigmatizing; in fact, the opposite is possible—participants may be seen as self-actualizing and exemplary.

The ideology of health promotion suggests that people are responsible for their health, that they are or ought to be able to do something about it. This may convey a sense of agency to people's relation with health, by seeing it as something over which individuals can have some personal control. Positive experience with these kinds of activities can be empowering and imbue employees with a sense that they are able to effect changes in their lives.

Pitfalls

In their enthusiasm for the positive potentials of work-site health promotion, the promoters and purveyors of wellness programs usually neglect to consider the subtler, more problematic issues surrounding work-site health promotion. In this section I want to examine some of the limitations and potential unintended consequences of promoting health in the work place.

The Limitations of Prevention

Many wellness activities, such as smoking cessation, hypertension control, and cholesterol reduction, are more accurately seen as prevention of disease than promotion of health. Disease prevention may be useful, but these interventions are not specific to the mission of health promotion (i.e., enhancing positive health).

Research within the lifestyle or "risk factor" paradigm has unearthed convincing evidence that a variety of life "habits" are detrimental to our health (e.g., Breslow 1978; U.S. Department of Health, Education, and Welfare 1979), but it is not always clear that this translates directly to health enhancement. Promoters of health promotion have frequently oversold the benefits of intervention (Goodman and Goodman 1986), which are not always well established (Morris 1982), and have ignored such equivocal evidence as the MRFIT study (Multiple Risk Factor Intervention Trial Group 1982). Moreover, just because a behavior or condition is a "risk factor" does not mean automatically that a change (e.g., a reduction) will lead to a corresponding change in health. In addition, clinicians and social scientists do not yet know very well how to change people's habits—witness the mixed results of various smoking-cessation programs or the high failure rate in diet and weight reduction.

In terms of modifying health risks, over what do people actually have control? Surely, there are some behavioral risk factors, but what about the effects of social structure, the environment, heredity, or simple chance? Clearly, the individual is not solely responsible for the development of disease, yet this is precisely what many work-site health-promotion efforts assume (Allegrante and Sloan 1986).

The overwhelming focus of work-site health promotion on individual lifestyle as the unit of intervention muddles the reality of social behavior. The social reality, including class, gender, and race—all known to affect health as well as lifestyle—is collapsed into handy individual risk factors that can be remedied by changing personal habits. This approach takes behavior out of its context and assumes "that personal habits are discrete and independently modifiable, and that individuals can voluntarily choose to alter such behaviors" (Coriel, Levin, and Jaco 1986, 428). At best this is deceptive; at worst it is misguided and useless.

It is often assumed that prevention is more cost effective than treatment and "cure." As Louise Russell (1986) has persuasively shown, for some diseases prevention may actually add to medical costs, especially when interventions are directed to large numbers of people, only a few of whom would have gotten sick without them. She concludes that prevention and health promotion may be beneficial in their own right, but in general should not be seen as a solution for medical expenditures. Ironically, for corporations for whom cost containment is a major goal, there is an additional problem in that if employees are healthier and live longer (by no means yet proven), corporations will have to pay higher retirement benefits. In any case, prevention seems a limited vehicle for medical cost containment. To the extent that controlling health costs is a major rationale, work-site wellness may seem peripheral when the results are limited.

Blurring the Occupational Health Focus

Work-site health promotion's target for intervention is the individual rather than the organization or environment. While the history of the occupational health and safety movement is replete with examples of corporate denial of responsibility for workers' health and individual interpretations of fault (e.g., "accident prone worker") (Bale 1986), by the 1970s a strong measure was established to change the work environment to protect individual workers from disease and disability. This was both symbolized and in part realized by the existence of the Occupational Safety and Health Administration (OSHA). But the promulgators of wellness are uninterested in the traditional concerns of occupational health and safety and turn attention from the environment to the individual. One virtually never hears wellness people discussing occupational disease or hazardous working conditions. Whether they view it as someone else's domain or as simply too downbeat for upbeat wellness programs is difficult to know. But this may in part explain why work-site health

promotion has been greeted with skepticism by occupational health veterans.

The ideology of work-site wellness includes a limited definition of what constitutes health promotion. For example, it does not include improvement of working conditions. As noted earlier, wellness advocates neglect evaluating the work environment and conceptualize "corporate cultures" in a limited way. In fact, the individual lifestyle focus deflects attention away from seriously examining the effects of corporate cultures or the work environment. Little attention is given to how the work-place organization itself might be made more health enhancing. Perhaps it is feared that organizational changes to improve health may conflict with certain corporate priorities. For example, by focusing on individual stress reduction rather than altering a stressful working environment, work-site health promotion may be helping people "adapt" to unhealthy environments.

Moralizing Health Concerns

The ideology of health promotion is creating a "new health morality," based on individual responsibility for health, by which character and moral worth are judged (Becker 1986, 19). This responsibility inevitably creates new "health deviants" and stigmatizes individuals for certain unhealthy lifestyles. While this process is similar to medicalization (Conrad and Schneider 1980) in that it focuses on definitions and interventions on the individual level and fuses medical and moral concerns, it is better thought of as a type of "healthicization." With medicalization we see medical definitions and treatments for previously social problems (e.g., alcoholism, drug addition) or natural events (e.g., menopause); with healthicization, behavioral and social definitions and treatments are offered for previously biomedically defined events (e.g., heart disease). Medicalization proposes biomedical causes and interventions; healthicization proposes lifestyle and behavioral causes and interventions. One turns the moral into the medical; the other turns health into the moral.

The work-site wellness focus on individual responsibility can be overstated and leads to a certain kind of moralizing. For example, although personal responsibility is undeniably an issue with cigarette smoking, social factors like class, stress, and advertising also must be implicated. With other cases like high blood pressure, cholesterol, and stress, attribution of responsibility is even more murky. But when individuals are deemed causally responsible for their health, it facilitates their easily slipping into victim-blaming responses (Crawford 1979). Employees who smoke, are overweight, exhibit "Type A" behaviors, have high blood pressure, and so forth are blamed, usually implicitly, for their condition. Not only does this absolve the organization, society, and even medical care from responsibility for the problem, it creates a moral dilemma for the individual. With the existence of a corporate wellness program, employees may be blamed both for the condition and for not doing something about it. This may be especially true for "high risk" individuals who choose not to participate. And even relatively healthy people may feel uneasy for not working harder to raise their health behavior to the new standards. Thus, work-site health promotion may unwittingly contribute to stigmatizing certain lifestyles and creating new forms of personal guilt.

In a sense, health promotion is engendering a shift in morality in the work place and elsewhere; we need to, at least, raise questions about what value structure is being promoted in the name of health and what consequences might obtain from taking the position that one lifestyle is preferable to another. While it is assumed that work-site wellness is in everyone's interest—I've heard it termed a "win-win" situation—it is important to examine what we are jeopardizing as well as what is gained (cf. Gillick 1984).

Enhancing the Relatively Healthy

In several ways work-site wellness focuses its attention on relatively healthy individuals. Were we to consider the major global or national health problems from a public health perspective, workers would not be listed among the most needy of intervention. Research for decades has pointed out that lower social class (Syme and Berkman 1976) and social deprivation (Morris 1982), in general, are among the most important contributors to poor health. Workers in spite of

having real health problems are a relatively healthy population. Occupational groups have generally lower rates of morbidity and mortality than the rest of the population. This so-called "healthy worker effect" implies that the labor force selects for healthier individuals who are sufficiently healthy to obtain and hold employment (Sterling and Weinkam 1986). There is, furthermore, some evidence suggesting that unemployment may have a detrimental effect on individual health (Liem 1981). The main target of work-site health promotion is a relatively healthy one.

Even within the work-site context, who is it that comes to wellness programs? Although data are limited, a recent review suggests some self-selection occurs:

> Overall, it appears participants are likely to be nonsmokers, more concerned with health matters, perceive themselves in better health, and be more interested in physical activities, especially aerobic exercise, than nonparticipants. There is also some evidence that participants may use less health services and be somewhat younger than nonparticipants (Conrad 1987a, 319).

In general, the data suggest that participants coming to work-site wellness programs may be healthier than nonparticipants (see also Baun, Bernacki, and Tsai 1986).

Finally, the whole health-promotion concept has a middle-class bias (Minkler 1985). Wellness advocates ignore issues like social deprivation and social class, which may have health effects independent of individual behavior (Slater and Carlton 1985), when advocating stress reduction or health enhancement. The health-promotion message itself may have a differential effect on different social classes. As Morris (1982) points out, in 1960 there was little class difference between smokers; by 1980 there were only 21 percent smokers in class I while there were 57 percent smokers in class V. And what little evidence we have suggests that overwhelmingly the participants in work-site wellness programs are management and white-collar workers (Conrad 1987a). For a variety of reasons—including scheduling, time off, and priority setting, blue-collar workers have been less likely to participate (see Pechter 1986). Thus, work-site health-promotion programs may generally be serving the already converted.

Expanding the Boundaries of Corporate Jurisdiction

The boundaries of private and work life are shifting, particularly as to what can legitimately be encompassed under corporate jurisdiction. Work-site programs that screen for drugs, AIDS, or genetic make-up are more obvious manifestations of this, but work-site wellness programs also represent a shift in private corporate boundaries.

Work-site health-promotion programs, with their focus on smoking, exercise, diet, blood pressure, and the like, are entering the domain of what has long been considered private life. Corporations are now increasingly concerned with what employees are doing in off-company time. We have not yet reached a point where corporate paternalism has launched off-site surveillance programs (and this is, of course, highly unlikely), but employers are more concerned about private "habits," even if they do not occur in the work place. These behaviors can be deemd to affect work performance indirectly through a lack of wellness. This raises the question of how far corporations may go when a behavior (e.g., off-hours drug use) or condition (e.g., overweight) does not *directly* affect others or employee job performance. Yet, screening and intervention programs are bringing such concerns into the corporate realm.

With the advent of health insurance, especially when paid for by employers, the boundaries between public and private become less distinct. That is, health-risk behavior potentially becomes a financial burden to others. The interesting question is, however, why are we seeing an increased blurring of boundaries and corporate expansion in the 1980s? The danger of this boundary shift is that it increases the potential for coercion. The current ideology of work-site wellness is one of voluntarism; programs are open to employees who want to participate. But voluntarism needs to be seen in context.

Bureaucracies are not democracies, and any so-called "voluntary" behavior in organizational settings is likely to be open to challenge. Unlike the community setting, the employer has a fairly long-term contractual relationship with most employees, which in many cases is dynamic with the possibility of raises, promotions, as well as overt and covert demotions. This may result in deliberate or inadvertent impressions that participation in a particular active preventive program is normative and expected (Roman 1981, 40).

Employers and their representatives may now coax employees into participation or lifestyle change, but it is also likely that employers will begin to use incentives (such as higher insurance premiums for employees who smoke or are overweight) to increase health promotion. At some point companies could make wellness a condition of employment or promotion. This raises the specter of new types of job discrimination based on lifestyle and attributed wellness.

In a sense, what we are discussing here is the other side of the "responsible corporation" that cares about the health and well-being of its employees. The crucial question is, are corporations able to represent the individual's authentic interests in work and private life?

Conclusion

Work-site health promotion is largely an American phenomenon. Few similar programs exist in Europe or other advanced industrial nations. Work-site wellness is a response to a particular set of circumstances found in the United States: the American cultural preoccupation with health and wellness; the corporate incentive due to the employer-paid health insurance; and the policy concern with spiraling health costs. Its growth is related to a disenchantment with government as a source of health improvement and a retrenchment in the financing of medical services. Its expansion is fueled by the commercialization of health and fitness and the marketing of health-promotion and cost-management strategies (cf. Evans 1982). Moreover, work-site wellness aligns well with the fashion in the 1980s for private-sector "corporate" approaches to health policy.

In their enthusiasm, the promoters of work-site

health promotion make excessive claims for its efficacy. The work-site wellness movement has gained momentum, although it may still turn out to be a passing fad rather than a lasting innovation. It seems clear that work-site wellness programs have some potential for improving individual employees' health and will perhaps contribute to reduce the rate of rise in corporate health costs. The scientific data on program effects, however, are by no means in and to a large extent corporations are operating on faith. The actual results are likely to be more modest than the current claims. How much data are necessary for policy implementation is an open question. For despite the rhetoric of cost containment, corporate concern over health costs may be more of a trigger than a drive toward wellness programs. Concern about morale, loyalty, and productivity—corporate competitiveness in the marketplace—may be of greater import than health.

Rigorous scientific evaluation will enable better evaluation of the potentials of work-site health promotion for improving employee health, reducing costs, and improving morale and productivity. But such data remain largely irrelevant for assessing the more sociopolitical pitfalls of work-site wellness. These can be only adequately evaluated in the context of the social organization of the work place, the relation between employers and employees, and as part of an overall health policy strategy. They cannot be simply counted in terms of reduced employee risk factors or saved corporate health dollars.

Work-site health promotion has the appearance of corporate benevolence. Health is a value like motherhood and apple pie. In modern society, health is deemed a gateway to progress, salvation, and productivity. Despite the pitfalls discussed in this article, work-site health promotion does not appear to be an overt extension of corporate control, at least not in terms of so-called technical or bureaucratic control (Edwards 1979). In fact, on the surface work-site wellness appears as more of a throwback to the largely abandoned policies of "welfare capitalism" (Edwards 1979). Whether work-site health promotion is a valuable health innovation, the harbinger of a new type of worker control, or an insignificant footnote in the history of workers' health remains to be seen.

Acknowledgments
This article was written while the author was a visiting fellow in the Department of Social Medicine and Health Policy at Harvard Medical School, and was partly supported by an NIMH National Research Service Award (1F32MHO333-01). My thanks to Leon Eisenberg, Irving K. Zola, and Diana Chapman Walsh for comments on an earlier draft of this article.

REFERENCES

Allegrante, J.P., and R.P. Sloan. 1986. Ethical Dilemmas in Worksite Health Promotion. *Preventive Medicine* 15:313–20.

Bale, A. 1986. *Compensation Crisis*. Ph.D. diss., Brandeis University. (Unpublished).

Baun, W.B., E.J. Bernacki, and Shan P. Tsai. 1986. A Preliminary Investigation: Effect of a Corporate Fitness Program on Absenteeism and Health Care Cost. *Journal of Occupational Medicine* 28:18–22.

Becker, M.H. 1986. The Tyranny of Health Promotion. *Public Health Reviews* 14:15–25.

Bellingham, R. 1985. Keynote address delivered at the 1985 "Wellness in the Workplace" conference, Norfolk, Va., May.

Bellingham, R., D. Johnson, and M. McCauley. 1985. The AT&T Communications Total Life Concept. *Corporate Commentary* 5(4):1–13.

Blair, S.N., P.V. Piserchia, C.S. Wilbur, and J.H. Crowder. 1986a. A Public Health Intervention Model for Work-site Health Promotion: Impact on Exercise and Physical Fitness in a Health Promotion Plan after 24 Months. *Journal of the American Medical Association* 255:921–26.

Blair, S.N., M. Smith, T.R. Collingwood, R. Reynolds, M. Prentice, and C.L. Sterling. 1986b. Health Promotion for Educators: The Impact on Absenteeism. *Preventive Medicine* 16:166–75.

Blue Cross-Blue Shield Consumer Exchange. 1986. Plan Hopes to Spur Worksite Health Promotion and Wellness Programs. May, p. 3.

Bly, J.L., R.C. Jones, and J.E. Richardson. 1986. Impact of Worksite Health Promotion on Health Care Costs and Utilization: Evaluation of Johnson and Johnson's Live for Life Program. *Journal of the American Medical Association* 256:3235–40.

Breslow, L. 1978. Risk Factor Intervention in Health Maintenance. *Science* 200:908–12.

Brownell, K.B., R.Y. Cohen, A.J. Stunkard, and M.R.J. Felix. 1984. Weight Loss Competitions at the Work Site: Impact on Weight, Morale and Cost-Effectiveness. *American Journal of Public Health* 74:1283–85.

Business Roundtable Task Force on Health. 1985.

Corporate Health Care Cost Management and Private-sector Initiatives. Indianapolis: Lilly Corporate Center.

Castillo-Salgado, C. 1984. Assessing Recent Developments and Opportunities in the Promotion of Health in the American Workplace. *Social Science and Medicine* 19:349–58.

Clement, J., and D.A. Gibbs. 1983. Employer Consideration of Health Promotion Programs: Financial Variables. *Journal of Public Health Policy* 4:45–55.

Conrad, P. 1987a. Who Comes to Worksite Wellness Programs? *Journal of Occupational Medicine* 29:317–20.

———. 1987b. Health and Fitness at Work: A Participant's Perspective. *Social Science and Medicine* 26:545–50.

Conrad, P., and J.W. Schneider. 1980. *Deviance and Medicalization: From Badness to Sickness.* St. Louis: Mosby.

Coriel, J., J.S. Levin, and E.G. Jaco. 1986. Lifestyle: An Emergent Concept in the Social Sciences. *Culture, Medicine and Psychiatry* 9:423–37.

Crawford, R. 1979. Individual Responsibility and Health Politics in the 1970s. In *Health Care in America,* ed. S. Reverby and D. Rosner, 247–68. Philadelphia: Temple University Press.

Cunningham, R.M. 1982. *Wellness at Work.* Chicago: Blue Cross Association.

Davis, M.K., K. Rosenberg, D.C. Iverson, T.M. Vernon, and J. Bauer. 1984. Worksite Health Promotion in Colorado. *Public Health Reports* 99:538–43.

Edwards, R. 1979. *Contested Terrain: The Transformation of the Workplace in the 20th Century.* New York: Basic Books.

Evans, R. 1982. A Retrospective on the "New Perspective." *Journal of Health Politics, Policy and Law* 7:325–44.

Fielding, J.E. 1982. Effectiveness of Employee Health Programs. *Journal of Occupational Medicine* 24:907–15.

———. 1984. Health Promotion and Disease Prevention at the Worksite. *Annual Review of Public Health* 5:237–65.

Fielding, J.E., and L. Breslow. 1983. Health Promotion Programs Sponsored by California Employers. *American Journal of Public Health* 73:533–42.

Foote, A., and J.C. Erfrut. 1983. Hypertension Control at the Worksite. *New England Journal of Medicine* 308:809–13.

Forster, J.L, R.W. Jeffrey, S. Sullivan, and M.K. Snell. 1985. A Work-site Weight Control Program Using Financial Incentives Collected through Payroll Deductions. *Journal of Occupational Medicine* 27: 804–8.

Gibbs, J.O., D. Mulvaney, C. Hanes, and R.W. Reed. 1985. Work-site Health Promotion: Five-year Trend in Employee Health Care Costs. *Journal of Occupational Medicine* 27:826–30.

Gillick, M.R. 1984. Health Promotion, Jogging and the Pursuit of Moral Life. *Journal of Health Politics, Policy and Law* 9:369–87.

Goodman, L.E., and M.J. Goodman. 1986. Prevention: How Misuse of a Concept Undercuts Its Worth. *Hastings Center Report* 16:26–38.

Hallet, R. 1986. Smoking Intervention in the Workplace: Review and Recommendations. *Preventive Medicine* 15:213–31.

Health Research Institute. 1986. *1985 Health Care Cost Containment Survey: Participant Report* (Summary). Walnut Creek, Calif.

Herzlinger, R.E., and D. Calkins. 1986. How Companies Tackle Health Costs: Part 3. *Harvard Business Review* 63(6):70–80.

Liem, R. 1981. Economic Change and Unemployment Contexts of Illness. In *Social Contexts of Health, Illness and Patient Care,* ed. G. Mishler, 55–78. New York: Cambridge University Press.

Levenstein, C., and M. Moret. 1985. Health Promotion in the Workplace. *Journal of Public Health Policy* 6:149–51.

Lorig, K., R.G. Kraines, B.W. Brown, and N. Richardson. 1985. A Workplace Health Education Program that Reduces Outpatient Visits. *Medical Care* 23:1044–54.

Minkler, M. 1985. Health Promotion Research: Are We Asking the Right Questions? Paper presented at the annual meeting of the American Public Health Association, Washington, November 18.

Morris, J.N. 1982. Epidemiology and Prevention. *Milbank Memorial Fund Quarterly/Health and Society* 60(1):1–16.

Multiple Risk Factor Intervention Trial Group. 1982. Multiple Risk Factor Intervention Trial: Risk Factor Changes and Mortality Results. *Journal of the American Medical Association* 248:1465–77.

Mulvaney, D., R. Reed, J. Gibbs, and C. Henes, 1985. Blue Cross and Blue Shield of Indiana: Five Year Payoff in Health Promotion. *Corporate Commentary* 5(1):1–6.

Neubauer, D., and R. Pratt. 1981. The Second Public Health Revolution: A Critical Appraisal. *Journal of Health Politics, Policy and Law* 6:205–28.

O'Donnell, M.P. 1984. The Corporate Perspective. In *Health Promotion in the Work Place,* ed. M.P. O'Donnell and T.H. Ainsworth, 10–36, New York: Wiley.

Paffenbarger, R.S., R.J. Hyde, A.L. Wing, and C.H. Steinmetz. 1984. A Natural History of Athleticism and Cardiovascular Health. *Journal of the American Medical Association* 252:491–95.

Parkinson, R.S., and Associates (eds.). 1982. *Managing Health Promotion in the Workplace*. Palo Alto: Mayfield.

Pechter, K. 1986. Corporate Fitness and Blue-Collar Fears. *Across the Board* 23(10):14–21.

Reed, R. W., D. Mulvaney, R. Bellingham, and K.C. Huber. 1985. *Health Promotion Service: Evaluation Study*. Indianapolis: Blue Cross-Blue Shield of Indiana.

Reza-Forouzesh, M., and L.E. Ratzker. 1984–1985. Health Promotion and Wellness Programs: An Insight into the Fortune 500. *Health Education* 15(7):18–22.

Roman, P. 1981. *Prevention and Health Promotion Programming in Work Organizations*. DeKalb: Northern Illinois University, Office for Health Promotion.

Rosen, R.H. 1984. Worksite Health Promotion: Fact or Fantasy. *Corporate Commentary* 5(1):1–8.

Russell, L.B. *Is Prevention Better Than Cure?* 1986. Washington: Brookings Institute.

Slater, C., and B. Carlton. 1985. Behavior, Lifestyle and Socioeconomic Variables as Determinants of Health Status: Implications for Health Policy Development. *American Journal of Preventive Medicine* 1(5):25–33.

Solomon, H.A. 1984. *The Exercise Myth*. New York: Harcourt Brace Jovanovich.

Spilman, M.A., A. Goetz, J. Schultz, R. Bellingham, and D. Johnson. 1986. Effects of a Health Promotion Program. *Journal of Occupational Medicine* 28:285–89.

Stein, J. 1985. Industry's New Bottom Line on Health Care Costs: Is Less Better? *Hastings Center Report* 15(5):14–18.

Sterling, T.D., and J.J. Weinkam. 1986. Extent, Persistence and Constancy of the Healthy Worker or Healthy Person Effect by All and Selected Causes of Death. *Journal of Occupational Medicine* 28: 348–53.

Syme, L.S., and L.F. Berkman. 1976. Social Class, Susceptibility and Illness. *American Journal of Epidemiology* 104:1–8.

U.S. Department of Health, Education, and Welfare. 1979. *Healthy People: The Surgeon General's Report on Health Promotion and Disease Prevention*. Washington.

Walsh, D.C. 1984. Corporate Smoking Policies: A Review and an Analysis. *Journal of Occupational Medicine* 26:17–22.

46

A Case for Refocussing Upstream: The Political Economy of Illness

▪ ▪ ▪ ▪ ▪ ▪

John B. McKinlay

My friend, Irving Zola, relates the story of a physician trying to explain the dilemmas of the modern practice of medicine:

"You know," he said, "sometimes it feels like this. There I am standing by the shore of a swiftly flowing river and I hear the cry of a drowning man. So I jump into the river, put my arms around him, pull him to shore and apply artificial respiration. Just when he begins to breathe, there is another cry for help. So I jump into the river, reach him, pull him to shore, apply artificial respiration, and then just as he begins to breathe, another cry for help. So back in the river again, reaching, pulling, applying, breathing and then another yell. Again and again, without end, goes the sequence. You know, I am so busy jumping in, pulling them to shore, applying artificial respiration, that I have *no* time to see who the hell is upstream pushing them all in."[1]

I believe this simple story illustrates two important points. *First,* it highlights the fact that a clear majority of our resources and activities in the health field are devoted to what I term "downstream endeavors" in the form of superficial, categorical tinkering in response to almost perennial shifts from one health issue to the next, without really solving anything. I am, of course, not suggesting that such efforts are entirely futile, or that a considerable amount of short-term good is not being accomplished. Clearly, people and groups have important immediate needs which must be recognized and attended to. Nevertheless, one must be wary of the *short-term nature* and *ultimate futility* of such downstream endeavors.

Second, the story indicates that we should somehow cease our preoccupation with this short-term, problem-specific tinkering and begin focussing our attention upstream, where the real problems lie. Such a reorientation would minimally involve an analysis of the means by which various individuals, interest groups, and large-scale, profit-oriented corporations are "pushing people in," and how they subsequently erect, at some point downstream, a health care structure to service the needs which they have had a hand in creating, and for which moral responsibility ought to be assumed.

In this paper two related themes will be developed. *First,* I wish to highlight the activities of the "manufacturers of illness"—those individuals, interest groups, and organizations which, in addition to producing material goods and services, also produce, as an inevitable by-product, widespread morbidity and mortality. Arising out of this, and *second,* I will develop a case for refocussing our attention away from those individuals and groups who are mistakenly held to be responsible for their condition, toward a range of broader upstream political and economic forces.

The task assigned to me for this conference was to review some of the broad social structural factors influencing the onset of heart disease and/or at-risk behavior. Since the issues covered by this request are so varied, I have, of necessity, had to make some decisions concerning both emphasis and scope. These decisions and the reasoning behind them should perhaps be explained at this point. With regard to what can be covered by the

term "social structure," it is possible to isolate at least three separate levels of abstraction. One could, for example, focus on such subsystems as the family, and its associated social networks, and how these may be importantly linked to different levels of health status and the utilization of services.[2] On a second level, one could consider how particular organizations and broader social institutions, such as neighborhood and community structures, also affect the social distribution of pathology and at-risk behavior.[3] Third, attention could center on the broader political-economic spectrum, and how these admittedly more remote forces may be etiologically involved in the onset of disease. . . .

. . . [In this paper] I will argue, for example, that the frequent failure of many health intervention programs can be largely attributed to the inadequate recognition we give to aspects of social context. . . . The most important factor in deciding on the subject area of this paper, however, is the fact that, while there appears to be a newly emerging interest in the political economy of health care, social scientists have, as yet, paid little attention to the *political economy of illness.*[4] It is my intention in this paper to begin to develop a case for the serious consideration of this particular area.

A political-economic analysis of health care suggests that the entire structure of institutions in the United States is such as to preclude the adequate provision of services.[5] Increasingly, it seems, the provision of care is being tied to the priorities of profit-making institutions. For a long time, criticism of U.S. health care focussed on the activities of the American Medical Association and the fee for service system of physician payment.[6] Lately, however, attention appears to be refocussing on the relationship between health care arrangements and the structure of big business.[7] It has, for example, been suggested that:

. . . with the new and apparently permanent involvement of major corporations in health, it is becoming increasingly improbable that the United States can redirect its health priorities without, at the same time, changing the ways in which American industry is organized and the ways in which monopoly capitalism works.[8]

It is my impression that many of the political-economic arguments concerning developments in the organization of health care also have considerable relevance for a holistic understanding of the etiology and distribution of morbidity, mortality, and at-risk behavior. In the following sections I will present some important aspects of these arguments in the hope of contributing to a better understanding of aspects of the political economy of illness.

An Unequal Battle

The downstream efforts of health researchers and practitioners against the upstream efforts of the manufacturers of illness have the appearance of an unequal war, *with a resounding victory assured for those on the side of illness* and the creation of disease-inducing behaviors. The battle between health workers and the manufacturers of illness is unequal on at least two grounds. In the *first* place, we always seem to arrive on the scene and begin to work after the real damage has already been done. By the time health workers intervene, people have already filled the artificial needs created for them by the manufacturers of illness and are habituated to various at-risk behaviors. In the area of smoking behavior, for example, we have an illustration not only of the lateness of health workers' arrival on the scene, and the enormity of the task confronting them, but also, judging by recent evidence, of the resounding defeat being sustained in this area.[9] To push the river analogy even further, the task becomes one of furiously swimming against the flow and finally being swept away when exhausted by the effort or through disillusionment with a lack of progress. So long as we continue to fight the battle downstream, and in such an ineffective manner, we are doomed to frustration, repeated failure, and perhaps ultimately to a sicker society.

Second, the promoters of disease-inducing behavior are manifestly more effective in their use of behavioral science knowledge than are those of us who are concerned with the eradication of such behavior. Indeed, it is somewhat paradoxical that we should be meeting here to consider how behavioral science knowledge and techniques can be effectively employed to reduce or prevent at-risk behavior, when that same body of knowledge *has already* been used to create the at-risk behavior we seek to eliminate. How embarrassingly ineffective are our mass media efforts in the health field (e.g., alcoholism, obesity, drug abuse, safe driving, pollution, etc.) when compared with many of the tax exempt promotional efforts on behalf of the illness generating activities of large-scale corporations.[10] It is a fact that we are demonstrably more effective in persuading people to purchase items they never dreamt they would need, or to pursue at-risk courses of action, than we are in preventing or halting such behavior. Many advertisements are so ingenious in their appeal that they have entertainment value in their own right and become embodied in our national folk humor. By way of contrast, many health advertisements lack any comparable widespread appeal, often appear boring, avuncular, and largely misdirected.

I would argue that one major problem lies in the fact that we are overly concerned with the war itself, and with how we can more effectively participate in it. In the health field we have unquestioningly accepted the assumptions presented by the manufacturers of illness and, as a consequence, have confined our efforts to only downstream offensives. A little reflection would, I believe, convince anyone that those on the side of health are in fact losing. . . . But rather than merely trying to win the war, we need to step back and question the premises, legitimacy and utility of the war itself.

The Binding of At-Riskness to Culture

It seems that the appeals to at-risk behavior that are engineered by the manufacturers of illness are particularly successful because they are constructed in such a way as to be inextricably bound with essential elements of our existing dominant culture. This is accomplished in a number of ways: (a) Exhortations to at-risk behavior are often piggybacked on those legitimized values, beliefs, and norms which are widely recognized and adhered to in the dominant culture. The idea here is that if a person *would only do X,* then they would also be doing Y and Z. (b) Appeals are also advanced which claim or imply that certain courses of at-risk action are subscribed to or endorsed by most of the culture heroes in society (e.g., people in the entertainment industry), or by those with technical competence in that particular field (e.g., "doctors" recommend it). The idea here is that if a person *would only do X,* then he/she would be doing pretty much the same as is done or recommended by such prestigious people as A and B. (c) Artificial needs are manufactured, the fulfilling of which becomes absolutely essential if one is to be a meaningful and useful member of society. The idea here is that if a person *does not do X, or will not do X,* then they are either deficient in some important respect, or they are some kind of liability for the social system.

Variations on these and other kinds of appeal strategies have, of course, been employed for a long time now by the promoters of at-risk behavior. The manufacturers of illness are, for example, fostering the belief that if you want to be an attractive, masculine man, or a "cool," "natural" woman, you will smoke cigarettes; that you can only be a "good parent" if you habituate your children to candy, cookies, etc.; and that if you are a truly loving wife, you will feed your husband foods that are high in cholesterol. All of these appeals have isolated some basic goals to which most people subscribe (e.g., people want to be masculine or feminine, good parents, loving spouses, etc.) and make claim, or imply, that their realization is only possible through the exclusive use of their product or the regular display of a specific type of at-risk behavior. Indeed, one can argue that certain at-risk behaviors have become so inextricably intertwined with our dominant cultural system (perhaps even symbolic of it) that the routine public display of such behavior almost signifies membership in this society.

Such tactics for the habituation of people to at-risk behavior are, perhaps paradoxically, also employed to elicit what I term "*quasi-health behavior.*" Here again, an artificially constructed conception of a person in some fanciful state of physiological and emotional equilibrium is presented as the ideal state to strive for, if one is to meaningfully participate in the wider social system. To assist in the attainment of such a state, we are advised to consume a range of quite worthless vitamin pills, mineral supplements, mouthwashes, hair shampoos, laxatives, pain killers, etc. Clearly, one cannot exude radiance and success if one is not taking this vitamin, or that mineral. The achievement of daily regularity is a prerequisite for an effective social existence. One can only compete and win after a good night's sleep, and this can only be ensured by taking such and such. An entrepreneurial pharmaceutical industry appears devoted to the task of making people overly conscious of these quasi-health concerns, and to engendering a dependency on products which have been repeatedly found to be ineffective, and even potentially harmful.[11]

There are no clear signs that such activity is being or will be regulated in any effective way, and the promoters of this quasi-health behavior appear free to range over the entire body in their never-ending search for new areas and issues to be linked to the fanciful equilibrium that they have already engineered in the mind of the consumer. By binding the display of at-risk and quasi-health behavior so inextricably to elements of our dominant culture, a situation is even created whereby to request people to change or alter these behaviors is more or less to request abandonment of dominant culture.

The term "culture" is employed here to denote that integrated system of values, norms, beliefs and patterns of behavior which, for groups and social categories in specific situations, facilitate the solution of social structural problems.[12] This definition lays stress on two features commonly associated with the concept of culture. The *first* is the interrelatedness and interdependence of the various elements (values, norms, beliefs, overt life-styles) that apparently comprise culture. The *second* is the view that a cultural system is, in some part, a response to social structural problems, and that it can be regarded as some kind of resolution of them. Of course, these social structural problems, in partial response to which a cultural pattern emerges, may themselves have been engineered in the interests of creating certain beliefs, norms, life styles, etc. If one assumes that culture can be regarded as some kind of reaction formation, then one must be mindful of the unanticipated social consequences of inviting some alteration in behavior which is a part of a dominant cultural pattern. The request from health workers for alterations in certain at-risk behaviors may result in either awkward dislocations of the interrelated elements of the cultural pattern, or the destruction of a system of values and norms, etc., which have emerged over time in response to situational problems. From this perspective, and with regard to the utilization of medical care, I have already argued elsewhere that, for certain groups of the population, underutilization may be "healthy" behavior, and the advocacy of increased utilization an "unhealthy" request for the abandonment of essential features of culture.[13]

The Case of Food

Perhaps it would be useful at this point to illustrate in some detail, from one pertinent area, the style and magnitude of operation engaged in by the manufacturers of illness. Illustrations are, of course, readily available from a variety of different areas, such as: the requirements of existing occupational structure, emerging leisure patterns, smoking and drinking behavior, and automobile usage.[14] Because of current interest, I have decided to consider only one area which is importantly related to a range of largely chronic diseases—namely, the 161 billion dollar industry involved in the production and distribution of food and beverages.[15] The present situation, with regard to food, was recently described as follows:

> The sad history of our food supply resembles the energy crisis, and not just because food nourishes our bodies while petroleum fuels the society. We long ago surrendered control of food, a vital resource, to private corporations, just as we surrendered control of energy. The food corporations have shaped the kinds of food we eat for their greater profits, just as the energy companies have dictated the kinds of fuel we use.[16]

From all the independent evidence available, and despite claims to the contrary by the food industry, a widespread decline has occurred during the past three decades in American dietary standards. Some forty percent of U.S. adults are overweight or downright fat.[17] The prevalence of excess weight in the American population as a whole is high—so high, in fact, that in some segments it has reached epidemic proportions.[18] There is evidence that the food industry is manipulating our image of "food" away from basic staples toward synthetic and highly processed items. It has been estimated that we eat between 21 and 25 percent fewer dairy products, vegetables, and fruits than we did twenty years ago, and from 70 to 80 percent more sugary snacks and soft drinks. Apparently, most people now eat more processed and synthetic foods than the real thing. There are even suggestions that a federal, nationwide survey would have revealed how serious our dietary situation really is, if the Nixon Administration had not cancelled it after reviewing some embarrassing preliminary results.[19] The survey apparently confirmed the trend toward deteriorating diets first detected in an earlier household food consumption survey in the years 1955–1965, undertaken by the Department of Agriculture.[20]

Of course, for the food industry, this trend toward deficient synthetics and highly processed items makes good economic sense. Generally speaking, it is much cheaper to make things look and taste like the real thing, than to actually provide the real thing. But the kind of foods that result from the predominance of economic interests clearly do not contain adequate nutrition. It is common knowledge that food manufacturers destroy important nutrients which foods naturally contain, when they transform them into "convenience" high profit items. To give one simple example: a wheat grain's outer layers are apparently very nutritious, but they are also an obstacle to making tasteless, bleached, white flour. Consequently, baking corporations "refine" fourteen nutrients out of the natural flour and then, when it is financially convenient, replace some of them with a synthetic substitute. In the jargon of the food industry, this flour is now "enriched." Clearly, the food industry employs this term in much the same way that coal corporations ravage mountainsides into mud flats, replant them with some soil and seedlings, and then proclaim their moral accomplishment in "rehabilitating" the land. While certain types of food processing may make good economic sense, it may also result in a deficient end product, and perhaps even promote certain diseases. The bleaching and refining of wheat products, for example, largely eliminates fiber or roughage from our diets, and some authorities have suggested that fiber-poor diets can be blamed for some of our major intestinal diseases.[21]

A vast chemical additive technology has enabled manufacturers to accquire enormous control over the food and beverage market and to foster phenomenal profitability. It is estimated that drug companies alone make something like $500 million a year through chemical additives for food. I have already suggested that what is done to food, in the way of processing and artificial additives, may actually be injurious to health. Yet, it is clear that, despite such well-known risks, profitability makes such activity well worthwhile. For example, additives, like preservatives, enable food that might perish in a short period of time to endure unchanged for months or even years. Food manufacturers and distributors can saturate supermarket shelves across the country with their products because there is little chance that they will spoil. Moreover, manufacturers can purchase vast quantities of raw ingredients when they are cheap, produce and stockpile the processed result, and then withhold the product from the market for long periods, hoping for the inevitable rise in prices and the consequent windfall.

The most widely used food additive (although it is seldom described as an additive) is "refined" sugar. Food manufacturers saturate our diets with the substance from the day we are born until the day we die. Children are fed breakfast cereals which consist of 50 percent sugar.[22] The average American adult consumes 126 pounds of sugar each year—and children, of course, eat much more. For the candy industry alone, this amounts to around $3 billion each year. The American sugar mania, which appears to have been deliberately engineered, is a major contributor to such "diseases of civilization" as diabetes, coronary heart disease, gall bladder illness, and cancer—all the insidious, degenerative conditions which most often afflict people in advanced capitalist societies, but which "underdeveloped," nonsugar

eaters never get. One witness at a recent meeting of a U.S. Senate Committee, said that if the food industry were proposing sugar today as a new food additive, its "metabolic behavior would undoubtedly lead to its being banned."[23]

In sum, therefore, it seems that the American food industry is mobilizing phenomenal resources to advance and bind us to its own conception of food. We are bombarded from childhood with $2 billion worth of deliberately manipulative advertisements each year, most of them urging us to consume, among other things, as much sugar as possible. To highlight the magnitude of the resources involved, one can point to the activity of one well-known beverage company, Coca-Cola, which alone spent $71 million in 1971 to advertise its artificially flavored, sugar-saturated product. Fully recognizing the enormity of the problem regarding food in the United States, Zwerdling offers the following advice:

> Breaking through the food industry will require government action—banning or sharply limiting use of dangerous additives like artificial colors and flavors, and sugar, and requiring wheat products to contain fiber-rich wheat germ, to give just two examples. Food, if it is to become safe, will have to become part of politics.[24]

The Ascription of Responsibility and Moral Entrepreneurship

So far, I have considered, in some detail, the ways in which industry, through its manufacture and distribution of a variety of products, generates at-risk behavior and disease. Let us now focus on the activities of health workers further down the river and consider their efforts in a social context, which has already been largely shaped by the manufacturers upstream.

Not only should we be mindful of the culturally disruptive and largely unanticipated consequences of health intervention efforts mentioned earlier, but also of the underlying ideology on which so much of this activity rests. Such intervention appears based on an assumption of the *culpability of individuals* or groups who either manifest illness, or display various at-risk behaviors.

From the assumption that individuals and groups with certain illnesses or displaying at-risk behavior are responsible for their state, it is a relatively easy step to advocating some changes in behavior on the part of those involved. By ascribing culpability to some group or social category (usually ethnic minorities and those in lower socio-economic categories) and having this ascription legitimated by health professionals and accepted by other segments of society, it is possible to mobilize resources to change the offending behavior. Certain people are responsible for not approximating, through their activities, some conception of what *ought* to be appropriate behavior on their part. When measured against the artificial conception of what ought to be, certain individuals and groups are found to be deficient in several important respects. They are *either* doing something that they ought not to be doing, *or* they are not doing something that they ought to be doing. If only they would recognize their individual culpability and alter their behavior in some appropriate fashion, they would improve their health status or the likelihood of not developing certain pathologies. On the basis of this line of reasoning, resources are being mobilized to bring those who depart from the desired conception into conformity with what is thought to be appropriate behavior. To use the upstream-downstream analogy, one could argue that people are blamed (and, in a sense, even punished) for not being able to swim after they, perhaps even against their own volition, have been pushed into the river by the manufacturers of illness.

Clearly, this ascription of culpability is not limited only to the area of health. According to popular conception, people in poverty are largely to blame for their social situation, although recent evidence suggests that a social welfare system which prevents them from avoiding this state is at least partly responsible.[25] Again, in the field of education, we often hold "dropouts" responsible for their behavior, when evidence suggests that the school system itself is rigged for failure.[26] Similar examples are readily available from the fields of penology, psychiatry, and race relations.[27]

Perhaps it would be useful to briefly outline, at this point, what I regard as a bizarre relationship between the activities of the manufacturers of illness, the ascription of culpability, and health intervention endeavors. *First*, important segments of our social system appear to be controlled and operated in such a way that people must inevitably fail. The fact is that there is often no choice over whether one can find employment, whether or not to drop out of college, involve oneself in untoward behavior, or become sick. *Second*, even though individuals and groups lack such choice, they are still blamed for not approximating the artificially contrived norm and are treated as if responsibility for their state lay entirely with them. For example, some illness conditions may be the result of particular behavior and/or involvement in certain occupational role relationships over which those affected have little or no control.[28] *Third*, after recognizing that certain individuals and groups have "failed," we establish, at a point downstream, a substructure of services which are regarded as evidence of progressive beneficence on the part of the system. Yet, it is this very system which had a primary role in manufacturing the problems and need for these services in the first place.

It is around certain aspects of life style that most health intervention endeavors appear to revolve and this probably results from the observability of most at-risk behavior. The modification of at-risk behavior can take several different forms, and the intervention appeals that are employed probably vary as a function of which type of change is desired. People can *either* be encouraged to stop doing what they are doing which appears to be endangering their survival (e.g., smoking, drinking, eating certain types of food, working in particular ways); *or* they can be encouraged to adopt certain new patterns of behavior which seemingly enhance their health status (e.g., diet, exercise, rest, eat certain foods, etc.). I have already discussed how the presence or absence of certain life styles in some groups may be a part of some wider cultural pattern which emerges as a response to social structural problems. I have also noted the potentially disruptive consequences to these cultural patterns of intervention programs. Underlying all these aspects is the issue of behavior control and the attempt to enforce a particular type of behavioral conformity. It is more than coincidental that the at-risk life styles, which we are all admonished to avoid, are frequently the type of behaviors which depart from and, in a sense, jeopardize the prevailing puritanical, middle-class ethic of what ought to be. According to this ethic, activities as pleasurable as drinking, smoking, overeating, and sexual intercourse must be harmful and ought to be eradicated.

The important point here is which segments of society and whose interests are health workers serving, and what are the ideological consequences of their actions.[29] Are we advocating the modification of behavior for the *exclusive* purpose of improving health status, or are we using the question of health as a means of obtaining some kind of moral uniformity through the abolition of disapproved behaviors? To what extent, if at all, are health workers actively involved in some wider pattern of social regulation?[30]

Such questions also arise in relation to the burgeoning literature that links more covert personality characteristics to certain illnesses and at-risk behaviors. Capturing a great deal of attention in this regard are the recent studies which associate heart disease with what is termed a Type A personality. The Type A personality consists of a complex of traits which produces: excessive competitive drive, aggressiveness, impatience, and a harrying sense of time urgency. Individuals displaying this pattern seem to be engaged in a chronic, ceaseless and often fruitless struggle with themselves, with others, with circumstances, with time, sometimes with life itself. They also frequently exhibit a free-floating, but well-rationalized form of hostility, and almost always a deep-seated insecurity.[31]

Efforts to change Type A traits appear to be based on some ideal conception of a relaxed, non-competitive, phlegmatic individual to which people are encouraged to conform.[32] Again, one can question how realistic such a conception is in a system which daily rewards behavior resulting from Type A traits. One can clearly question the ascription of near exclusive culpability to those displaying Type A behavior when the context within which such behavior is manifest is structured in such a way as to guarantee its production. From a cursory reading of job advertisements in any newspaper, we can see that employers actively seek to recruit individuals manifesting Type A characteristics, extolling them as positive virtues.[33]

My earlier point concerning the potentially disruptive consequences of requiring alterations in life style applies equally well in this area of personality and disease. If health workers manage to effect some changes away from Type A behavior in a system which requires and rewards it, then we must be aware of the possible consequences of such change in terms of future failure. Even though the evidence linking Type A traits to heart disease appears quite conclusive, how can health workers ever hope to combat and alter it when such characteristics are so positively and regularly reinforced in this society?

The various points raised in this section have some important moral and practical implications for those involved in health related endeavors. *First,* I have argued that our prevailing ideology involves the ascription of culpability to particular individuals and groups for the manifestation of either disease or at-risk behavior. *Second,* it can be argued that so-called "health professionals" have acquired a mandate to determine the morality of different types of behavior and have access to a body of knowledge and resources which they can "legitimately" deploy for its removal or alteration. (A detailed discussion of the means by which this mandate has been acquired is expanded in a separate paper.) *Third,* [it] is possible to argue that a great deal of health intervention is, perhaps unwittingly, part of a wide pattern of social regulation. We must be clear both as to whose interests we are serving, and the wider implications and consequences of the activities we support through the application of our expertise. *Finally,* it is evident from arguments I have presented that much of our health intervention fails to take adequate account of the social contexts which foster and reinforce the behaviors we seek to alter. The literature of preventive medicine is replete with illustrations of the failure of contextless health intervention programs.

The Notion of a Need Hierarchy

At this point in the discussion I shall digress slightly to consider the relationship between the utilization of preventive health services and the concept of need as manifest in this society. We know from available evidence that upper socio-economic groups are generally more responsive to health intervention activities than are those of lower socio-economic status. To partially account for this phenomenon, I have found it useful to introduce the notion of a *need hierarchy*. By this I refer to the fact that some needs (e.g., food, clothing, shelter) are probably universally recognized as related to sheer survival and take precedence, while other needs, for particular social groups, may be perceived as less immediately important (e.g., dental care, exercise, balanced diet). In other words, I conceive of a *hierarchy of needs*, ranging from what could be termed "primary needs" (which relate more or less to the universally recognized immediate needs for survival) through to "secondary needs" (which are not always recognized as important and which may be artificially engineered by the manufacturers of illness). Somewhere between the high priority, primary needs and the less important, secondary needs are likely to fall the kinds of need invoked by preventive health workers. Where one is located at any point in time on the need hierarchy (i.e., which particular needs are engaging one's attention and resources) is largely a function of the shape of the existing social structure and aspects of socio-economic status.

This notion of a hierarchy of needs enables us to distinguish between the health and illness behavior of the affluent and the poor. Much of the social life of the wealthy clearly concerns secondary needs, which are generally perceived as lower than most health related needs on the need hierarchy. If some pathology presents itself, or some at-risk behavior is recognized, then they naturally assume a priority position, which eclipses most other needs for action. In contrast, much of the social life of the poor centers on needs which are understandably regarded as being of greater priority than most health concerns on the need hierarchy (e.g., homelessness, unemployment). Should some illness event present itself, or should health workers alert people and groups in poverty to possible further health needs, then these needs inevitably assume a position of relative low priority and are eclipsed, perhaps indefinitely, by more pressing primary needs for sheer existence.

From such a perspective, I think it is possible to understand why so much of our health intervention fails in those very groups, at highest risk to morbidity, whom we hope to reach and influence. The appeals that we make in alerting them to possible future needs simply miss the mark by giving inadequate recognition to those primary needs which daily preoccupy their attention. Not only does the notion of a need hierarchy emphasize the difficulty of contextless intervention programs, but it also enables us to view the rejection as a non-compliance with health programs, as, in a sense, rational behavior.

How Preventive Is Prevention?

With regard to some of the arguments I have presented, concerning the ultimate futility of downstream endeavors, one may respond that effective preventive medicine does, in fact, take account of this problem. Indeed, many preventive health workers are openly skeptical of a predominantly curative perspective in health care. I have argued, however, that even our best preventive endeavors are misplaced in their almost total ascription of responsibility for illness to the afflicted individuals and groups, and through the types of programs which result. While useful in a limited way, the preventive orientation is itself largely a downstream endeavor through its preoccupation with the avoidance of at-risk behavior in the individual and with its general neglect of the activities of the manufacturers of illness which foster such behavior.

Figure 46-1 is a crude diagrammatic representa-

Figure 46-1.

1	2	3
The activities of the manufacturers of illness →	Various at-risk behaviors →	Observable morbidity and mortality
↑ Intervention with a political economic focus	↑ Intervention with a preventive focus	↑ Intervention with a curative focus

tion of an overall process starting with (1) the activities of the manufacturers of illness, which (2) foster and habituate people to certain at-risk behaviors, which (3) ultimately result in the onset of certain types of morbidity and mortality.[34] The predominant curative orientation in modern medicine deals almost exclusively with the observable patterns of morbidity and mortality, which are the *end points* in the process. The much heralded preventive orientation focuses on those behaviors which are known to be associated with particular illnesses and which can be viewed as the *midpoint* in the overall process. Still left largely untouched are the entrepreneurial activities of the manufacturers of illness, who, through largely unregulated activities, foster the at-risk behavior we aim to prevent. This *beginning point* in the process remains unaffected by most preventive endeavors, even though it is at this point that the greatest potential for change, and perhaps even ultimate victory, lies.

It is clear that this paper raises many questions and issues at a general level—more in fact than it is possible to resolve. Since most of the discussion has been at such an abstract level and concerned with broad political and economic forces, any ensuing recommendations for change must be broad enough to cover the various topics discussed. Hopefully, the preceding argument will also stimulate discussion toward additional recommendations and possible solutions. Given the scope and direction of this paper and the analogy I have employed to convey its content, the task becomes of the order of constructing fences upstream *and* restraining those who, in the interest of corporate profitability, continue to push people in. In this concluding section I will confine my remarks to three selected areas of recommendations.

Recommended Action

a. Legislative Intervention. It is probably true that one stroke of effective health legislation is equal to many separate health intervention endeavors and the cumulative efforts of innumerable health workers over long periods of time. In terms of winning the war which was described earlier, greater changes will result from the continued politicization of illness than from the modification of specific individual behaviors. There are many opportunities for a legislative reduction of at-riskness, and we ought to seize them. Let me give one suggestion which relates to earlier points in this paper. Widespread public advertising is importantly related to the growth and survival of large corporations. If it were not so demonstrably effective, then such vast sums of money and resources would not be devoted to this activity. Moreover, as things stand at present, a great deal of advertising is encouraged through granting it tax exempt status on some vague grounds of public education.[35] To place more stringent, enforceable restrictions on advertising would be to severely curtail the morally abhorrent pushing in activities of the manufacturers of illness. It is true that large corporations are ingenious in their efforts to avoid the consequences of most of the current legislative restrictions on advertising which only prohibit certain kinds of appeals.

As a possible solution to this and in recognition of the moral culpability of those who are actively manufacturing disease, I conceive of a ratio of advertising to health tax or a ratio of risk to benefit tax (RRBT). The idea here is to, in some way, match advertising expenditures to health expenditures. The precise weighting of the ratio could be determined by independently ascertaining the severity of the health effects produced by the manufacture and distribution of the product by the corporation. For example, it is clear that smoking is injurious to health and has no redeeming benefit. Therefore, for this product, the ratio could be determined as say, 3 to 1, where, for example, a company which spends a non-tax deductible $1 million to advertise its cigarettes would be required to devote a non-tax deductible $3 million to the area of health. In the area of quasi-health activities, where the product, although largely useless, may not be so injurious (e.g., nasals sprays, pain killers, mineral supplements, etc.), the ratio could be on, say, a 1 to 1 basis.

Of course, the manufacturers of illness, at the present time, do "donate" large sums of money for the purpose of research, with an obvious understanding that their gift should be reciprocated. In a recent article, Nuehring and Markle touch on the nature of this reciprocity:

One of the most ironic pro-cigarette forces has been the American Medical Association. This powerful health organization took a position in 1965 clearly favorable to the tobacco interests. . . . In addition, the A.M.A. was, until 1971, conspicuously absent from the membership of the National Interagency Council on Smoking and Health, a coalition of government agencies and virtually all the national health organizations, formed in 1964. The A.M.A.'s largely pro-tobacco behavior has been linked with the acceptance of large research subsidies from the tobacco industy—amounting, according to the industry, to some 18 million dollars.[36]

Given such reciprocity, it would be necessary for this health money from the RRBT to be handled by a supposedly independent government agency, like the FDA or the FTC, for distribution to regular research institutions as well as to consumer organizations in the health field, which are currently so unequally pitted against the upstream manufacturers of illness. Such legislation would, I believe, severely curtail corporate "pushing in" activity and publicly demonstrate our commitment to effectively regulating the source of many health problems.

b. *The Question of Lobbying* Unfortunately, due to present arrangements, it is difficult to discern the nature and scope of health lobbying activities. If only we could locate (a) who is lobbying for what, (b) who they are lobbying with, (c) what tactics are being employed, and (d) with what consequences for health legislation. Because these activities are likely to jeopardize the myths that have been so carefully engineered and fed to a gullible public by both the manufacturers of illness *and* various health organizations, they are clothed in secrecy.[37] Judging from recent newspaper reports, concerning multimillion dollar gift-giving by the pharmaceutical industry to physicians, the occasional revelation of lobbying and political exchange remains largely unknown and highly newsworthy. It is frequently argued that lobbying on behalf of specific legislation is an essential avenue for public input in the process of enacting laws. Nevertheless, the evidence suggests that it is often, by being closely linked to the distribution of wealth, a very one-sided process. As it presently occurs, many legitimate interests on a range of health related issues do not have lobbying input in proportion to their numerical

strength and may actually be structurally precluded from effective participation. While recognizing the importance of lobbying activity and yet feeling that for certain interests its scope ought to be severely curtailed (perhaps in the same way as the proposed regulation and publication of political campaign contributions), I am, to be honest, at a loss as to what should be specifically recommended. . . . The question is: quite apart from the specific issue of changing individual behavior, *in what ways could we possibly regulate the disproportionately influential lobbying activities of certain interest groups in the health field?*

c. *Public Education.* In the past, it has been common to advocate the education of the public as a means of achieving an alteration in the behavior of groups at risk to illness. Such downstream educational efforts rest on "blaming the victim" assumptions and seek to *either* stop people doing what we feel they "ought not" to be doing, *or* encourage them to do things they "ought" to be doing, but are not. Seldom do we educate people (especially schoolchildren) about the activities of the manufacturers of illness and about how they are involved in many activities unrelated to their professed area of concern. How many of us know, for example, that for any "average" Thanksgiving dinner, the turkey may be produced by the Greyhound Corporation, the Smithfield Ham by ITT, the lettuce by Dow Chemical, the potatoes by Boeing, the fruits and vegetables by Tenneco or the Bank of America?[38] I would reiterate that I am not opposed to the education of people who are at risk to illness, with a view to altering their behavior to enhance life chances (if this can be done successfully). However, I would add the proviso that if we remain committed to the education of people, we must ensure that they are being told the whole story. And, in my view, immediate priority ought to be given to the sensitization of vast numbers of people to the upstream activities of the manufacturers of illness, some of which have been outlined in this paper. Such a program, actively supported by the federal government (perhaps through revenue derived from the RRBT), may foster a groundswell of consumer interest which, in turn, may go some way toward checking the disproportionately influential lobbying of the large corporations and interest groups.

NOTES AND REFERENCES

1. I.K. Zola, "Helping—Does It Matter: The Problems and Prospects of Mutual Aid Groups." Addressed to the United Ostomy Association, 1970.

2. See, for example, M.W. Susser and W. Watson, *Sociology in Medicine*, New York: Oxford University Press, 1971. Edith Chen, et al., "Family Structure in Relation to Health and Disease." *Journal of Chronic Diseases*, Vol. 12 (1960), p. 554–567; and R. Keelner, *Family III Health: An Investigation in General Practice*, Charles C. Thomas, 1963. There is, of course, voluminous literature which relates family structure to mental illness. Few studies move to the level of considering the broader social forces which promote the family structures which are conducive to the onset of particular illnesses. With regard to utilization behavior, see J.B. McKinlay, "Social Networks, Lay Consultation and Help-Seeking Behavior," *Social Forces*, Vol. 51, No. 3 (March, 1973), pp. 275–292.

3. A rich source for a variety of materials included in this second level is H.E. Freeman, S. Levine, and L.G. Reeder (Eds.), *Handbook of Medical Sociology*, New Jersey: Prentice-Hall, 1972. I would also include here studies of the health implications of different housing patterns. Recent evidence suggests that housing—even when highly dense—may not be directly related to illness.

4. There have, of course, been many studies, mainly by epidemiologists, relating disease patterns to certain occupations and industries. Seldom, however, have social scientists pursued the consequences of these findings in terms of a broader political economy of illness. One exception to this statement can be found in studies and writings on the social causes and consequences of environmental pollution. For a recent elementary treatment of some important issues in this general area, see H. Waitzkin and B. Waterman, *The Exploitation of Illness in Capitalist Society*, New York: Bobbs-Merrill Co., 1974.

5. Some useful introductory readings appear in D.M. Gordon (Ed.), *Problems in Political Economy: An Urban Perspective*, Lexington: D.C. Heath & Co., 1971, and R. C. Edwards, M. Reich and T. E. Weisskopf (Eds.), *The Capitalist System*, New Jersey: Prentice-Hall, 1972. Also, T. Christoffel, D. Finkelhor and D. Gilbarg (Eds.), *Up Against the American Myth*, New York: Holt, Rinehart and Winston. 1970. M. Mankoff (Ed.), *The Poverty of Progress: The Political Economy of American Social Problems*, New York: Holt, Rinehart and Winston, 1972. For more sophisticated treatment see the collection edited by D. Mermelstein, *Economics: Mainstream Readings and Radical Critiques*, New York: Random House, 1970. Additionally useful papers appear in J. B. McKinlay (Ed.), *Politics and Law in Health Care Policy*. New York: Prodist, 1973, and J. B. McKinlay (Ed.), *Economic Aspects of Health Care*, New York: Prodist, 1973. For a highly readable and influential treatment of what is termed "the medical industrial complex," see B. and J. Ehrenreich, *The American Health Empire: Power, Profits and Politics*, New York: Vintage Books, 1971. Also relevant are T. R. Marmor, *The Politics of Medicare*, Chicago: Aldine Publishing Co., 1973, and R. Alford, "The Political Economy of Health Care: Dynamics Without Change," *Politics and Society*, 2 (1972), pp. 127–164.

6. E. Cray, *In Failing Health: The Medical Crisis and the AMA*, Indianapolis: Bobbs-Merrill, 1970. J.S. Burrow, *AMA—Voice of American Medicine*, Baltimore: Johns Hopkins Press, 1963. R. Harris, *A Sacred Trust*, New York: New American Library, 1966. R. Carter, *The Doctor Business*, Garden City, New York: Dolphin Books, 1961. "The American Medical Association: Power, Purpose and Politics in Organized Medicine," *Yale Law Journal*, Vol. 63, No. 7 (May, 1954), pp. 938–1021.

7. See references under footnote 5, especially B. and J. Ehrenreich's *The American Health Empire*, Chapter VII, pp. 95–123.

8. D.M. Gordon (Ed.), *Problems in Political Economy: An Urban Perspective*, Lexington: D.C. Heath & Co., 1971, p. 318.

9. See, for example, D. A. Bernstein, "The Modification of Smoking Behavior: An Evaluative Review," *Psychological Bulletin*, Vol. 71 (June, 1969), pp. 418–440; S. Ford and F. Ederer, "Breaking the Cigarette Habit," *Journal of American Medical Association*, 194 (October, 1965), pp. 139–142; C. S. Keutzer, et al., "Modification of Smoking Behavior: A Review," *Psychological Bulletin*, Vol. 70 (December, 1968), pp. 520–533. Mettlin considers evidence concerning the following techniques for modifying smoking behavior: (1) behavioral conditioning, (2) group discussion, (3) counselling, (4) hypnosis, (5) interpersonal communication, (6) self-analysis. He concludes that:

> Each of these approaches suggests that smoking behavior is the result of some finite set of social and psychological variables, yet none has either demonstrated any significant powers in predicting the

smoking behaviors of an individual or led to techniques of smoking control that considered alone, have significant long-term effects.

In C. Mettlin, "Smoking as Behavior: Applying a Social Psychological Theory," *Journal of Health and Social Behavior,* 14 (June, 1973), p. 144.

10. It appears that a considerable proportion of advertising by large corporations is tax exempt through being granted the status of "public education." In particular, the enormous media campaign, which was recently waged by major oil companies in an attempt to preserve the public myths they had so carefully constructed concerning their activities, was almost entirely non-taxable.

11. Reports of the harmfulness and ineffectiveness of certain products appear almost weekly in the press. As I have been writing this paper, I have come across reports of the low quality of milk, the uselessness of cold remedies, the health dangers in frankfurters, the linking of the use of the aerosol propellant, vinyl chloride, to liver cancer. That the Food and Drug Administration (F.D.A.) is unable to effectively regulate the manufacturers of illness is evident and illustrated in their inept handling of the withdrawal of the drug, betahistine hydrochloride, which supposedly offered symptomatic relief of Meniere's Syndrome (an affliction of the inner ear). There is every reason to think that this case is not atypical. For additionally disquieting evidence of how the Cigarette Labeling and Advertising Act of 1965 actually curtailed the power of the F.T.C. and other federal agencies from regulating cigarette advertising and nullified all such state and local regulatory efforts, see L. Fritschier, *Smoking and Politics: Policymaking and the Federal Bureaucracy,* New York: Meredith, 1969, and T. Whiteside, *Selling Death: Cigarette Advertising and Public Health,* New York: Liveright, 1970. Also relevant are Congressional Quarterly, 27 (1969) 666, 1026; and U.S. Department of Agriculture, Economic Research Service, *Tobacco Situation,* Washington: Government Printing Office, 1969.

12. The term "culture" is used to refer to a number of other characteristics as well. However, these two appear to be commonly associated with the concept. See J. B. McKinlay, "Some Observations on the Concept of a Subculture." (1970).

13. This has been argued in J. B. McKinlay, "Some Approaches and Problems in the Study of the Use of Services," *Journal of Health and Social Behavior,* Vol. 13 (July, 1972), pp. 115–152; and J. B. McKinlay and D. Dutton, "Social Psychological Factors Affecting Health Service Utilization,"

chapter in *Consumer Incentives for Health Care,* New York: Prodist Press, 1974.

14. Reliable sources covering these areas are available in many professional journals in the fields of epidemiology, medical sociology, preventive medicine, industrial and occupational medicine and public health. Useful references covering these and related areas appear in J. N. Morris, *Uses of Epidemiology,* London: E. and S. Livingstone Ltd., 1967; and M. W. Susser and W. Watson, *Sociology in Medicine,* New York: Oxford University Press, 1971.

15. D. Zwerling, "Death for Dinner," *The New York Review of Books,* Vol. 21, No. 2 (February 21, 1974), p. 22.

16. D. Zwerling, "Death for Dinner." See footnote 15 above.

17. This figure was quoted by several witnesses at the *Hearings Before the Select Committee on Nutrition and Human Needs,* U.S. Government Printing Office, 1973.

18. The magnitude of this problem is discussed in P. Wyden, *The Overweight: Causes, Costs and Control,* Englewood Cliffs: Prentice-Hall, 1968; National Center for Health Statistics, *Weight by Age and Height of Adults: 1960–62.* Washington: *Vital and Health Statistics,* Public Health Service Publication #1000, Series 11, #14, Government Printing Office, 1966; U.S. Public Health Service, Center for Chronic Disease Control, *Obesity and Health,* Washington: Government Printing Office, 1966.

19. This aborted study is discussed in M. Jacobson, *Nutrition Scoreboard: Your Guide to Better Eating,* Center for Science in the Public Interest.

20. M.S. Hathaway and E. D. Foard, *Heights and Weights for Adults in the United States,* Washington: Home Economics Research Report 10, Agricultural Research Service, U.S. Department of Agriculture, Government Printing Office, 1960.

21. This is discussed by D. Zwerling. See footnote 16.

22. See *Hearings Before the Select Committee on Nutrition and Human Needs,* Parts 3 and 4, "T.V. Advertising of Food to Children," March 5, 1973 and March 6, 1973.

23. Dr. John Udkin, Department of Nutrition, Queen Elizabeth College, London University. See p. 225, *Senate Hearings,* footnote 22 above.

24. D. Zwerling, "Death for Dinner." See footnote 16 above, page 24.

25. This is well argued in F. Piven and R. A. Cloward, *Regulating the Poor: The Functions of Social Welfare,* New York: Vintage, 1971; L. Goodwin, *Do the Poor Want to Work?,* Washington: Brookings, 1972; H. J. Gans, "The Positive

Functions of Poverty," *American Journal of Sociology,* Vol. 78, No. 2 (September, 1972), pp. 275–289; R. P. Roby (Ed.), *The Poverty Establishment,* New Jersey: Prentice-Hall, 1974.

26. See, for example, Jules Henry, "American Schoolrooms: Learning the Nightmare," *Columbia University Forum,* (Spring, 1963), pp. 24–30. See also the paper by F. Howe and P. Lanter, "How the School System is Rigged for Failure," *New York Review of Books,* (June 18, 1970).

27. With regard to penology, for example, see the critical work of R. Quinney in *Criminal Justice in America,* Boston: Little Brown, 1974, and *Critique of Legal Order,* Boston: Little Brown, 1974.

28. See, for example, S. M. Sales, "Organizational Role as a Risk Factor in Coronary Disease," *Administrative Science Quarterly,* Vol. 14, No. 3 (September, 1969), pp. 325–336. The literature in this particular area is enormous. For several good reviews, see L.E. Hinkle, "Some Social and Biological Correlates of Coronary Heart Disease," *Social Science and Medicine,* Vol. 1 (1967), pp. 129–139; F. H. Epstein, "The Epidemiology of Coronary Heart Disease: A Review," *Journal of Chronic Diseases,* 18 (August, 1965), pp. 735–774.

29. Some interesting ideas in this regard are in E. Nuehring and G. E. Markle, "Nicotine and Norms: The Reemergence of a Deviant Behavior" *Social Problems,* Vol. 21, No. 4 (April, 1974), pp. 513–526. Also, J.R. Gusfield, *Symbolic Crusade: Status Politics and the American Temperance Movement,* Urbana, Illinois: University of Illinois Press, 1963.

30. For a study of the ways in which physicians, clergymen, the police, welfare officers, psychiatrists and social workers act as agents of social control, see E. Cumming, *Systems of Social Regulation,* New York: Atherton Press, 1968.

31. R. H. Rosenman and M. Friedman, "The Role of a Specific Overt Behavior Pattern in the Occurrence of Ischemic Heart Disease," *Cardiologia Practica,* 13 (1962), pp. 42–53; M. Friedman and R. H. Rosenman, *Type A Behavior and Your Heart,* Knopf, 1973. Also, S. J. Zyzanski and C. D. Jenkins, "Basic Dimensions Within the Coronary-Prone Behavior Pattern," *Journal of Chronic Diseases,* 22 (1970), pp. 781–795. There are, of course, many other illnesses which have also been related in one way or another to certain personality characteristics. Having found this new turf, behavioral scientists will most likely continue to play it for everything it is worth and then, in the interests of their own survival, will "discover" that something else indeed accounts for what they were trying to explain and will eventually move off there to find renewed fame and fortune. Furthermore, serious methodological doubts have been raised concerning the studies of the relationship between personality and at-risk behavior. See, in this regard, G. M. Hochbaum, "A Critique of Psychological Research on Smoking," paper presented to the American Psychological Association, Los Angeles, 1964. Also B. Lebovits and A. Ostfeld, "Smoking and Personality: A Methodologic Analysis," *Journal of Chronic Diseases (1971).*

32. M. Friedman and R.H. Rosenman. See footnote 31.

33. In the *New York Times* of Sunday, May 26, 1974, there were job advertisements seeking "aggressive self-starters," "people who stand real challenges," "those who like to compete," "career oriented specialists," "those with a spark of determination to someday run their own show," "people with the success drive," and "take charge individuals."

34. Aspects of this process are discussed in J. B. McKinlay, "On the Professional Regulation of Change," in *The Professions and Social Change,* P. Halmos (Ed.), Keele: Sociological Review Monograph, No. 20, 1973, and in "Clients and Organizations," chapter in J.B. McKinlay (Ed.), *Processing People—Studies in Organizational Behavior,* London: Holt, Rinehart, and Winston, 1974.

35. There have been a number of reports recently concerning this activity. Questions have arisen about the conduct of major oil corporations during the so-called "energy crisis." See footnote 10. Equally questionable may be the public spirited advertisements sponsored by various professional organizations which, while claiming to be solely in the interests of the public, actually serve to enhance business in various ways. Furthermore, by granting special status to activities of professional groups, government agencies and large corporations may effectively gag them through some expectation of reciprocity. For example, most health groups, notably the American Cancer Society, did not support the F.C.C.'s action against smoking commercials because they were fearful of alienating the networks from whom they receive free announcements for their fund drives. Both the American Cancer Society and the American Heart Association have been criticized for their reluctance to engage in direct organizational conflict with pro-cigarette forces, particularly before the alliance between the television broadcasters and the tobacco industry broke down. Rather, they have directed their efforts to the downstream reform of

the smoker. See E. Nuehring and G. E. Markle, cited in footnote 29.

36. E. Nuehring and G. E. Markle, cited in footnote 29.

37. The ways in which large-scale organizations engineer and disseminate these myths concerning their manifest activities, while avoiding any mention of their underlying latent activities, are discussed in more detail in the two references cited in footnote 34 above.

38. For a popularly written and effective treatment of the relationship between giant corporations and food production and consumption, see W. Robbins, *The American Food Scandal,* New York: William Morrow and Co., 1974.

(Acknowledgments continued from page iv)

Victor R. Fuchs, "A Tale of Two States." From WHO SHALL LIVE? Health Economics and Social Change. BasicBooks, a division of HarperCollins. © 1974. Reprinted with permission of the author.

Barbara Ellen Smith, "Black Lung: The Social Production of Disease." Reprinted with permission of the author and Baywood Publishing Company, Inc. from the *International Journal of Health Services*, vol. 11:3, 1981, pp. 343–59.

Phil Brown, "Popular Epidemiology: Community Response to Toxic Waste-Induced Disease." Reprinted with permission from *Science, Technology & Human Values*, vol. 12, 3–4 (Summer/Fall): 78–85. Copyright © 1987. Reprinted by permission of Sage Publications, Inc.

James S. House, Karl R. Landis, and Debra Umberson, "Social Relationships and Health." Reprinted and excerpted with permission of the *American Association for the Advancement of Science* from *Science*, vol. 214, July 1981, pp. 540–45. Copyright © 1981 by the AAAS.

Michael Marmot and Tores Theorell, "Social Class and Cardiovascular Disease: The Contribution of Work." Reprinted with permission of the author and Baywood Publishing Company, Inc. from the *International Journal of Health Services*, vol. 18, no. 4, 1988.

Joan Jacobs Brumberg, "Anorexia Nervosa in Context." Excerpts from FASTING GIRLS by Joan Jacobs Brumberg, pp. 8–18, 31–40, 268–271. Reprinted with permission of the publishers: Harvard University Press, Cambridge, Mass. Copyright © by the President and Fellows of Harvard College.

Gregory M. Herek and Eric K. Glunt, "An Epidemic of Stigma: Public Reaction to AIDS." Reprinted from *American Psychologist* 43 (11) pp. 886–891. Copyright © 1988 by the American Psychological Association. Reprinted (or adapted) with permission.

Rose Weitz, "Uncertainty and the Lives of Persons with AIDS." Reprinted and excerpted with permission of the *American Sociological Association* from *Journal of Health and Social Behavior*, vol. 30, no. 2, June 1989.

Peter Conrad, "The Meaning of Medications: Another Look at Compliance." Reprinted from *Social Science and Medicine* 20, 1: pp. 29–37. Copyright © 1985, with permission from Pergamon Press Ltd., Headington Hill Hall, Oxford OX3 0BW, UK.

Peter Conrad and Joseph W. Schneider, "Professionalization, Monopoly, and the Structure of Medical Practice." From *Deviance and Medicalization*, © 1992 Temple University. Reprinted by permission of Temple University Press.

Richard W. and Dorothy C. Wertz, "Notes on the Decline of Midwives and the Rise of Medical Obstetricians," from *Lying In: A History of Childbirth in America* by Richard W. and Dorothy C. Wertz. Copyright © 1977 by Richard W. and Dorothy C. Wertz. Used by permission of the authors and Yale University Press.

John B. McKinlay and John D. Stoeckle, "Corporatization and the Social Transformation of Doctoring." Reprinted with permission from the *International Journal of Health Services*, vol. 18 (2), pp. 191–205, 1988, Baywood Publishing Company, Inc.

Donald W. Light, "Countervailing Power." Reprinted from THE CHANGING CHARACTER OF THE MEDICAL PROFESSION: An International Perspective edited by Frederic W. Hafferty and John B. McKinlay (pp. 69–79). Copyright © 1993 by Oxford University Press, Inc. Reprinted by permission.

John Fry, Donald Light, Jonathan Rodnick and Peter Orton, "The US Health Care System." Reprinted with permission from REVIVING PRIMARY CARE: A U.S.-U.K. Comparison (1995) pp. 38–53. Radcliffe Medical Press, Oxford.

Susan Reverby, "A Caring Dilemma: Womanhood and Nursing in Historical Perspective." Copyright 1987 The American Journal of Nursing Company. Reprinted from *Nursing Research,* Jan/Feb, 1987, vol. 36, no. 1. Used with permission. All rights reserved.

Charles L. Bosk and Joel E. Frader, "AIDS and Its Impact on Medical Work: The Culture and Politics of the Shop Floor." Reprinted from *Milbank Quarterly* 68, 2: 257–79, 1990. Reprinted with permission of the Milbank Memorial Fund.

Arnold S. Relman, "The Health Care Industry: Where Is It Taking Us?" *New England Journal of Medicine* 325, 12: 854–59, 1991. Used by permission.

Howard Waitzkin, "A Marxian Interpretation of the Growth and Development of Coronary Care Technology." Reprinted by permission of American Public Health Association from *American Journal of Public Health* 69, 12: 1260–68; December 1979.

David J. Rothman, "A Century of Failure: Health Care Reform in America." *Journal of Health, Politics, Policy and Law* 18:2 (Summer 1993), pp. 271–286. Copyright © Duke University Press, 1993. Reprinted by permission.

Thomas Bodenheimer and Kevin Grumbach, "Paying for Health Care." *Journal of the American Medical Association,* vol. 272: 634–39. © 1994, American Medical Association. Reprinted by permission.

Philip R. Lee, Denise Soffel, and Harold S. Luft, "Costs and Coverage: Pressures toward Health Reform." *Western Journal of Medicine* 157 (November 1992): 576–583. Reprinted by permission.

Elliot G. Mishler, "The Struggle between the Voice of Medicine and the Voice of the Lifeworld." Excerpted and reprinted with permission from *Discourse of Medicine,* Chapter 3. Copyright © 1984 by Albex Publishing Co.: Norwood, New Jersey.

Julius A. Roth, "Some Contingencies of the Moral Evaluation and Control of Clientele: The Case of the Hospital Emergency Service." Reprinted from the *American Journal of Sociology* 77 (1972): 839–56 by permission of the University of Chicago Press. © 1977, the University of Chicago.

Renée R. Anspach, "The Language of Case Presentation." Reprinted and excerpted with permission of the American Sociological Association from the *American Journal of Health and Social Behavior,* vol. 29, no. 4, December 1988.

Barbara Katz Rothman, "Midwives in Transition: The Structure of a Clinical Revolution." Reprinted from *Social Problems,* vol. 30, no. 3, pp. 262–71 by permission. © 1983 by the Society for the Study of Social Problems.

Barton J. Bernstein, "The Misguided Quest for the Artificial Heart." Reprinted with permission from *Technology Review,* 87, 8 (Nov/Dec), copyright 1984.

Nancy G. Kutner, "Issues in the Application of High Cost Medical Technology: The Case of Organ Transplantation." Reprinted and excerpted with permission of the American Sociological Association from *Journal of Health and Social Behavior,* vol. 28 (March 1987); pp. 23–36.

Dorothy Nelkin, "Genetics and Social Policy." Reprinted from *Bulletin of the New York Academy of Medicine* 68 (1): 135–143. Reprinted by permission of the author.

John H. Knowles, "The Responsibility of the Individual." Reprinted by permission of *Daedalus,* Journal of the American Academy of Arts and Sciences, Cambridge, MA. From the issue entitled, "Doing Better and Feeling Worse: Health in the United States." Winter 1977, vol. 106, no. 1.

Robert Crawford, "Individual Responsibility and Health Politics." Reprinted from S. Reverby and D. Rosner (Eds.), *Health Care in America: Essays in Social History* (Philadelphia: Temple University Press, 1979) with the permission of Temple University and the author.

Irving Kenneth Zola, "Medicine as an Institution of Social Control." Reprinted with permission from *Sociological Review*, vol. 20, (1972): 487–504. Copyright © 1972 by The Editorial Board of The Sociological Review.

Renée C. Fox, "The Medicalization and Demedicalization of American Society." Reprinted with permission of *Daedalus*, Journal of the American Academy of Arts and Sciences, Cambridge, MA. From the issue entitled, "Doing Better and Feeling Worse: Health in the United States," Winter 1977, vol. 106, no. 1.

Daniel Callahan, "Rationing Medical Progress: The Way to Affordable Health Care." Reprinted with permission from the *New England Journal of Medicine*, Vol. 322, pp. 810–13, 1990. Copyright © 1990. Massachusetts Medical Society. All rights reserved.

Arnold S. Relman, "The Trouble with Rationing." Reprinted with permission from the *New England Journal of Medicine*, Vol. 323, 13: 911–913, 1990. Copyright © 1990. Massachusetts Medical Society. All rights reserved.

Catherine Kohler Riessman, "Improving the Health Experiences of Low Income Patients." Reprinted by permission of the author.

John McKnight, "Politicizing Health Care." From *Developing Dialogue*, 1978:1. Reprinted with permission of the Dag Hammarskjold Foundation, Uppsala, Sweden and the author.

Ann Withorn, "Helping Ourselves: The Limits and Potential of Self-Help." Reprinted by permission of the author and *Radical America* from *Radical America*, Vol. 14, May/June 1980: pp. 25–59, as edited by the author. *Radical America* is available from the Alternative Education Project, Inc., 1 Summer Street, Somerville, MA 02143.

Donald W. Light, "Comparative Models of 'Health Care' Systems." Reprinted by permission of the author.

Theodore R. Marmor and Jerry L. Mashaw, "Canada's Health Insurance and Ours: The Real Lessons, the Big Choices." From *The American Prospect*, Fall 1990, 3: 18–29. Copyright © New Prospect, Inc. Reprinted with permission of the publisher.

Jonathan Gabe, "Continuity and Change in the British National Health Service." Reprinted by permission of the author.

Peter Conrad, "Wellness in the Workplace: Potentials and Pitfalls of Work-Site Health Promotion." Reprinted from *Milbank Quarterly* 65, 2: 255–275, 1987. Reprinted with permission of the Milbank Memorial Fund.

John B. McKinlay, "A Case for Refocussing Upstream: The Political Economy of Illness," from *Applying Behavioral Science to Cardiovascular Risk*. Copyright © 1974 by the American Heart Association. Reprinted with permission.

Contributing Author Index

Subject Index